Brief Contents

Preface .... SCP-i
Getting to Know Microsoft Office Versions OFF-1
Using SAM Projects and Textbook Projects SAM-1

PowerPoint

Module 1: Creating and Editing Presentations with Pictures.......... PPT 1-1

Module 2: Enhancing Presentations with Shapes and SmartArt.......... PPT 2-1

Module 3: Inserting WordArt, Charts, and Tables.......... PPT 3-1

Module 4: Customizing Slide Masters and Presentations.......... PPT 4-1

Module 5: Collaborating and Adding Animation .... PPT 5-1

Module 6: Formatting Tables and Charts.......... PPT 6-1

Module 7: Adding Media and Enhancing SmartArt.......... PPT 7-1

Module 8: Creating Photo Albums and Delivering Presentations .... PPT 8-1

Index Index-1

Contents

Preface ... SCP-i

Getting to Know Microsoft Office Versions ... OFF-1

Using SAM Projects and Textbook Projects ... SAM-1

PowerPoint

Module 1: Creating and Editing Presentations with Pictures ... PPT 1-1

Objectives ... PPT 1-1
What Is PowerPoint? ... PPT 1-1
Project: Presentation with a Bulleted List and Pictures ... PPT 1-2
Starting and Using PowerPoint ... PPT 1-3
- To Start PowerPoint and Create a Blank Presentation ... PPT 1-4
- The PowerPoint Window ... PPT 1-5
- To Display a Different Tab on the Ribbon ... PPT 1-11

Creating a Title Slide ... PPT 1-11
- To Choose a Presentation Theme ... PPT 1-12
- To Enter the Presentation Title ... PPT 1-14
- Paragraphs ... PPT 1-14
- To Enter the Presentation Subtitle Paragraph ... PPT 1-15
- To Zoom a Slide ... PPT 1-15

Formatting Characters ... PPT 1-16
- Fonts and Font Styles ... PPT 1-16
- To Select a Paragraph ... PPT 1-16
- To Italicize Text ... PPT 1-17
- To Increase Font Size ... PPT 1-17
- To Select a Word ... PPT 1-18
- To Change the Text Color ... PPT 1-18
- To Zoom a Slide ... PPT 1-19
- To Save a Presentation for the First Time ... PPT 1-20

Adding a Slide with a Bulleted List ... PPT 1-22
- To Add a New Title and Content Slide ... PPT 1-22
- Correcting a Mistake When Typing ... PPT 1-23
- Creating a Multilevel Bulleted List ... PPT 1-23
- To Enter a Slide Title ... PPT 1-24
- To Select a Text Placeholder ... PPT 1-24
- To Type a Multilevel Bulleted List ... PPT 1-24
- To Type the Remaining Text ... PPT 1-26
- To Select a Group of Words ... PPT 1-26
- To Bold Text ... PPT 1-27
- To Increase Font Size ... PPT 1-27
- To Underline Text ... PPT 1-27

Adding Slides, Changing Slide Layouts, and Changing the Theme ... PPT 1-28
- To Add a New Slide and Enter a Slide Title and Headings ... PPT 1-28
- To Change the Font ... PPT 1-29
- To Add a Slide with the Title Only Layout ... PPT 1-31
- To Enter a Slide Title ... PPT 1-31
- To Change the Theme ... PPT 1-32
- PowerPoint Views ... PPT 1-33
- To Move to Another Slide in Normal View ... PPT 1-33

Inserting, Resizing, and Moving Pictures ... PPT 1-34
- To Insert a Picture into a Slide without a Content Placeholder ... PPT 1-35
- To Insert another Picture into a Slide without a Content Placeholder ... PPT 1-36
- To Insert Another Picture into a Slide without a Content Placeholder ... PPT 1-37
- To Insert a Picture into a Content Placeholder ... PPT 1-37

Resizing Photos and Illustrations ... PPT 1-38
- To Proportionally Resize Pictures ... PPT 1-39
- To Resize the Pictures on Slides 4 and 2 ... PPT 1-40
- To Move Pictures ... PPT 1-40
- To Insert Another Picture into a Slide without a Content Placeholder ... PPT 1-42
- To Rotate a Picture ... PPT 1-42
- To Nonproportionally Resize the Picture on Slide 2 ... PPT 1-43
- To Move a Slide in Normal View ... PPT 1-44
- To Save a Presentation with the Same File Name ... PPT 1-44
- To Close a File Using Backstage View ... PPT 1-45
- To Open a Recent File Using Backstage View ... PPT 1-45

Making Changes to Slide Text Content ... PPT 1-46
- Replacing Text in an Existing Slide ... PPT 1-46
- Deleting Text ... PPT 1-46
- To Delete Text in a Placeholder ... PPT 1-47
- To Change the Theme Colors ... PPT 1-47
- To Add Notes ... PPT 1-48
- Checking Spelling ... PPT 1-49
- To Check Spelling ... PPT 1-50
- Document Properties ... PPT 1-51
- Changing Views ... PPT 1-52
- To Change Views ... PPT 1-52
- Viewing the Presentation in Slide Show View ... PPT 1-54

The **Shelly Cashman** Series®

Microsoft® 365®
PowerPoint®

First Edition

Comprehensive

Susan L. Sebok

Cengage

Australia • Brazil • Canada • Mexico • Singapore • United Kingdom • United States

Cengage

***The Shelly Cashman Series® Microsoft® 365® PowerPoint® Comprehensive*, First Edition**
Susan L. Sebok

SVP, Product Management: Cheryl Costantini

VP, Product Management & Marketing: Thais Alencar

Senior Product Director, Portfolio Product Management: Mark Santee

Portfolio Product Director: Rita Lombard

Senior Portfolio Product Manager: Amy Savino

Senior Product Assistant: Ciara Boynton

Learning Designer: Zenya Molnar

Senior Content Manager: Anne Orgren

Digital Project Manager: Jim Vaughey

Developmental Editor: Deb Kaufmann

Senior Director, Product Marketing: Danae April

Senior Marketing Manager: Mackenzie Paine

Portfolio Specialist: Matt Schiesl

Content Acquisition Analyst: Nichole Nalenz

Production Service: Lumina Datamatics Ltd.

Senior Designer: Erin Griffin

Cover Image Source: VTT Studio/Shutterstock.com

Mac Users: If you're working through this product using a Mac, some of the steps may vary. Additional information for Mac users is included with the Data files for this product.

Disclaimer: This text is intended for instructional purposes only; data is fictional and does not belong to any real persons or companies.

Disclaimer: The material in this text was written using Microsoft Windows 11 and Office 365 Professional Plus and was Quality Assurance tested before the publication date. As Microsoft continually updates the Windows operating system and Office 365, your software experience may vary slightly from what is presented in the printed text.

Previous edition(s): © 2023, © 2020, © 2017

For product information and technology assistance, contact us at
Cengage Customer & Sales Support, 1-800-354-9706 or support.cengage.com.

For permission to use material from this text or product, submit all requests online at **www.copyright.com.**

Library of Congress Control Number: 2024943231

Student Edition ISBN: 978-0-357-88169-9

Loose-Leaf ISBN: 978-0-357-88170-5

Cengage
5191 Natorp Boulevard
Mason, OH 45040
USA

Cengage is a leading provider of customized learning solutions. Our employees reside in nearly 40 different countries and serve digital learners in 165 countries around the world. Find your local representative at **www.cengage.com.**

To learn more about Cengage platforms and services, register or access your online learning solution, or purchase materials for your course, visit **www.cengage.com.**

Notice to the Reader

Printed at CLDPC, USA, 09-24

To Start Slide Show View....PPT 1-54
To Move Manually through Slides in a Slide Show....PPT 1-55
Saving and Printing Files....PPT 1-57
To Save a File with a Different File Name....PPT 1-57
To Print Full Page Slides....PPT 1-57
To Preview and Print a Handout....PPT 1-59
To Print Speaker Notes....PPT 1-60
To Change the Print Color....PPT 1-61
Using PowerPoint Help....PPT 1-62
To Obtain Help Using the Help Pane....PPT 1-62
Obtaining Help while Working in PowerPoint....PPT 1-64
To Obtain Help Using the Search Box....PPT 1-65
To Sign Out of a Microsoft Account....PPT 1-65
Summary....PPT 1-66
Apply Your Knowledge....PPT 1-67
Extend Your Knowledge....PPT 1-68
Expand Your World....PPT 1-70
In the Lab....PPT 1-71

Module 2: Enhancing Presentations with Shapes and SmartArt....PPT 2-1

Objectives....PPT 2-1
Introduction....PPT 2-1
Project—Presentation with SmartArt and Shapes....PPT 2-1
Downloading a Theme and Editing Slides....PPT 2-3
To Search for and Download an Online Theme....PPT 2-3
To Save the Presentation....PPT 2-4
To Delete a Slide....PPT 2-5
To Create a Title Slide....PPT 2-7
To Align a Paragraph....PPT 2-7
To Create the First Text Slide....PPT 2-9
To Insert a Symbol....PPT 2-9
To Copy a Symbol....PPT 2-11
Creating and Formatting a SmartArt Graphic....PPT 2-11
To Convert Text to a SmartArt Graphic....PPT 2-12
To Edit SmartArt Shape Text....PPT 2-13
Text Pane....PPT 2-14
To Edit SmartArt Text....PPT 2-15
To Format Text Pane Characters....PPT 2-15
To Change the SmartArt Layout....PPT 2-16
To Edit the Title Text....PPT 2-17
To Duplicate a Slide....PPT 2-18
To Insert a SmartArt Graphic....PPT 2-18
To Add Text to the SmartArt Graphic....PPT 2-19
To Apply a SmartArt Style....PPT 2-20
To Add a Hyperlink to a Paragraph....PPT 2-21
Inserting and Formatting a Shape....PPT 2-22
To Insert a Shape....PPT 2-22
Resizing Shapes....PPT 2-24
To Resize a Shape Proportionally....PPT 2-24
To Resize a Shape Nonproportionally by Entering an Exact Measurement....PPT 2-25
To Select Shapes....PPT 2-27
To Apply a Shape Style....PPT 2-27
To Copy and Paste a Shape....PPT 2-28
To Add Text to a Shape....PPT 2-29
To Format Shape Text....PPT 2-29
To Change a Shape Fill Color....PPT 2-30
Positioning Slide Elements....PPT 2-31
Aligning and Distributing Objects....PPT 2-32
To Display the Drawing Guides....PPT 2-32
To Display the Ruler....PPT 2-33
To Display the Gridlines....PPT 2-34
To Position a Shape Using Guides, Gridlines, and the Ruler....PPT 2-34
To Position the Remaining Shapes....PPT 2-35
To Distribute Shapes....PPT 2-35
To Align a Shape....PPT 2-37
To Position the Lightning Bolt Shape....PPT 2-37
To Flip a Shape....PPT 2-38
To Change the Stacking Order....PPT 2-38
To Group Objects....PPT 2-39
To Add a Slide Title....PPT 2-40
To Insert Additional Shapes....PPT 2-40
To Merge Shapes....PPT 2-41
To Apply a Picture Fill to a Shape....PPT 2-43
To Change a Shape Outline Weight....PPT 2-44
To Change a Shape Outline Color....PPT 2-45
To Change a Shape Outline Style....PPT 2-45
To Apply an Effect to a Shape....PPT 2-46
To Rotate a Shape to an Exact Value....PPT 2-46
To Enter the Title Text....PPT 2-47
To Hide the Grid and Guides....PPT 2-47
To Hide Rulers....PPT 2-48
Adding and Modifying a Footer....PPT 2-48
To Add a Footer with Fixed Information....PPT 2-49
Adding a Transition....PPT 2-50
To Add a Transition between Slides....PPT 2-50
To Save and Print the Presentation....PPT 2-52
Summary....PPT 2-53
Apply Your Knowledge....PPT 2-54
Extend Your Knowledge....PPT 2-56
Expand Your World....PPT 2-58
In the Lab....PPT 2-60

Module 3: Inserting WordArt, Charts, and Tables ... PPT 3-1

Objectives ... PPT 3-1
Introduction ... PPT 3-1
Project—Presentation with WordArt, a Chart, and a Table ... PPT 3-1
Adding a Chart to a Slide and Formatting ... PPT 3-3
To Run PowerPoint, Apply a Theme, and Save the Presentation ... PPT 3-3
To Delete a Placeholder ... PPT 3-4
To Insert a Chart ... PPT 3-5
To Replace Sample Data ... PPT 3-6
To Resize a Chart ... PPT 3-8
To Align a Chart ... PPT 3-9
To Change a Chart Style ... PPT 3-11
To Change the Shape Outline Color ... PPT 3-11
To Change the Shape Outline Weight ... PPT 3-13
To Change the Title and Legend Font and Font Size ... PPT 3-13
Adding a Table to a Slide and Formatting ... PPT 3-14
Tables ... PPT 3-14
To Insert an Empty Table ... PPT 3-15
To Enter Data in a Table ... PPT 3-16
To Apply a Table Style ... PPT 3-16
To Add Borders to a Table ... PPT 3-18
To Add an Effect to a Table ... PPT 3-18
To Insert a Table Row ... PPT 3-20
To Insert a Table Column ... PPT 3-21
To Resize a Table ... PPT 3-22
To Align a Table ... PPT 3-23
To Add a Slide Title ... PPT 3-24
Inserting and Formatting a Text Box ... PPT 3-24
To Insert a Text Box and Format Text ... PPT 3-24
To Format Text Box Characters ... PPT 3-25
Inserting and Moving Slides ... PPT 3-26
To Reuse Slides from an Existing Presentation ... PPT 3-27
To Move a Slide in Slide Sorter View ... PPT 3-28
Inserting Pictures and Adding Effects ... PPT 3-30
To Delete a Picture ... PPT 3-30
To Insert and Resize a Picture into a Slide without Content Placeholders ... PPT 3-31
To Crop a Picture ... PPT 3-32
Adjusting Picture Colors ... PPT 3-33
To Recolor a Picture ... PPT 3-34
To Add an Artistic Effect to a Picture ... PPT 3-35
To Change the Picture Softness ... PPT 3-36
To Apply a Picture Style ... PPT 3-37
To Size a Picture ... PPT 3-37
To Move a Picture ... PPT 3-38
To Align Pictures ... PPT 3-39
Creating and Formatting WordArt ... PPT 3-39
To Insert WordArt ... PPT 3-40
To Change the WordArt Shape ... PPT 3-41
To Change the WordArt 3-D Rotation Effect ... PPT 3-43
To Change the WordArt Text Fill Color ... PPT 3-43
To Change the WordArt Text Outline Color ... PPT 3-44
To Convert Text to WordArt ... PPT 3-45
To Resize WordArt Proportionally ... PPT 3-45
Animating Slide Content ... PPT 3-46
Custom Animations ... PPT 3-46
To Animate an Object Using an Entrance Effect ... PPT 3-46
To Change Animation Direction ... PPT 3-47
To Change the Animation Start Option ... PPT 3-48
To Preview an Animation Sequence ... PPT 3-48
To Change the Animation Duration ... PPT 3-49
To Animate Text ... PPT 3-49
To Change the Animation Sequence Effect Option ... PPT 3-50
Adding Media to Slides ... PPT 3-51
To Insert a Video File ... PPT 3-51
To Resize a Video Clip ... PPT 3-52
To Move a Video Clip ... PPT 3-52
To Change Video Contrast ... PPT 3-53
To Play a Video File Automatically ... PPT 3-54
To Add a Transition between Slides ... PPT 3-55
To Run a Slide Show with Animations and Video ... PPT 3-55
To Save and Print the Presentation ... PPT 3-56
Summary ... PPT 3-56
Apply Your Knowledge ... PPT 3-57
Extend Your Knowledge ... PPT 3-60
Expand Your World ... PPT 3-62
In the Lab ... PPT 3-62

Module 4: Customizing Slide Masters and Presentations ... PPT 4-1

Objectives ... PPT 4-1
Introduction ... PPT 4-1
Project: Presentation with Customized Slides ... PPT 4-2
To Run PowerPoint, Apply a Theme, and Save the Presentation ... PPT 4-6
Customizing Presentation Slide Master Backgrounds and Fonts ... PPT 4-6
Slide Master ... PPT 4-6
To Switch to Slide Master View ... PPT 4-6
To Apply a Theme to a Slide Master ... PPT 4-8
To Change the Theme Colors ... PPT 4-8
To Create Custom Theme Colors ... PPT 4-9
To Edit Master Text Styles ... PPT 4-11
To Change the Theme Fonts ... PPT 4-11
To Customize Theme Fonts ... PPT 4-12
To Delete a Content Placeholder ... PPT 4-13
To Change the Theme Effects ... PPT 4-14
Adding and Formatting Placeholders ... PPT 4-15
To Insert a Placeholder into a Blank Layout ... PPT 4-15

To Add and Format Placeholder Text ..... PPT 4-16
To Cut a Placeholder and Paste It into a Slide Master ..... PPT 4-18
To Insert a Picture Placeholder ..... PPT 4-19
To Size and Format the Picture Content Layout ..... PPT 4-20
To Format a Slide Master Background, Apply a Quick Style, and Format Text ..... PPT 4-21
To Crop a Picture to a Shape ..... PPT 4-22
To Rename a Slide Master and a Slide Layout ..... PPT 4-24
To Delete a Slide Layout ..... PPT 4-25
To Close Master View ..... PPT 4-27
To Save a Presentation as a Template ..... PPT 4-28
To Open a Template and Save a Presentation ..... PPT 4-29
To Add Text to the Title Slide Layout ..... PPT 4-30
To Insert Slide 2 and Add Text ..... PPT 4-30
To Insert Slide 3 and Add Text ..... PPT 4-31
To Insert Slide 4 and Add Text ..... PPT 4-31
To Insert Slide 5 and Add Text ..... PPT 4-32
To Use the Thesaurus ..... PPT 4-33
Customizing Slide Elements ..... PPT 4-34
To Change the Theme of a Single Slide ..... PPT 4-34
To Change the Theme Variant ..... PPT 4-36
Formatting Slide Backgrounds ..... PPT 4-37
To Change the Slide Background to a Gradient Fill ..... PPT 4-38
To Change the Slide Background to a Picture ..... PPT 4-39
To Change the Transparency of a Slide Background ..... PPT 4-40
To Change the Slide Background to a Pattern ..... PPT 4-41
To Change the Slide Background to a Texture ..... PPT 4-42
Hiding a Slide ..... PPT 4-44
To Hide a Slide ..... PPT 4-44
To Add a Slide Transition ..... PPT 4-45
Protecting and Securing a Presentation ..... PPT 4-46
To Inspect a Presentation ..... PPT 4-46
Navigating to a Slide During a Slide Show ..... PPT 4-47
Navigating to a Slide Using the Control Bar ..... PPT 4-48
To Highlight Text ..... PPT 4-49
To Use Pen and Pointer Options During a Slide Show ..... PPT 4-49
Rehearsing Slide Timings ..... PPT 4-51
To Rehearse Slide Timings ..... PPT 4-52
To Advance a Slide After a Specified Number of Seconds ..... PPT 4-53
To Run a Slide Show with Timings ..... PPT 4-54
To Save and Print the Presentation ..... PPT 4-54
Summary ..... PPT 4-54
Apply Your Knowledge ..... PPT 4-55
Extend Your Knowledge ..... PPT 4-58
Expand Your World ..... PPT 4-61
In the Lab ..... PPT 4-62

Module 5: Collaborating and Adding Animation ..... PPT 5-1

Objectives ..... PPT 5-1
Introduction ..... PPT 5-1
Project: Presentation with Comments and Animation ..... PPT 5-1
Collaborating on a Presentation ..... PPT 5-2
To Merge a Presentation ..... PPT 5-5
To Preview the Presentation Changes ..... PPT 5-6
To Review, Accept, and Reject Presentation Changes ..... PPT 5-7
To Review, Accept, and Reject Slide Changes ..... PPT 5-11
To Review and Accept Slide Changes on the Remaining Slides ..... PPT 5-12
To Review Comments ..... PPT 5-13
To Reply to a Comment ..... PPT 5-14
To Insert a Comment ..... PPT 5-15
To Edit a Comment ..... PPT 5-16
To Delete a Comment ..... PPT 5-17
To Run the Revised Presentation in Reading View ..... PPT 5-19
To End the Review and Hide Markup ..... PPT 5-19
To Resize Slides ..... PPT 5-20
To Align Pictures ..... PPT 5-21
Formatting and Managing Text ..... PPT 5-22
To Change Line Spacing ..... PPT 5-22
To Change Paragraph Spacing ..... PPT 5-22
To Change Column Spacing ..... PPT 5-23
To Format Text in Columns ..... PPT 5-24
To Find Text ..... PPT 5-25
To Find and Replace Text ..... PPT 5-25
Formatting Pictures ..... PPT 5-26
To Add an Artistic Effect to a Picture ..... PPT 5-27
To Recolor a Picture ..... PPT 5-27
To Add a Picture Border ..... PPT 5-28
To Change a Picture Border Color ..... PPT 5-29
To Apply a Picture Effect ..... PPT 5-29
To Add Alt Text ..... PPT 5-31
Modifying Bullets and Adding Effects ..... PPT 5-31
To Change a Bullet Character to a Picture ..... PPT 5-31
To Change Bullet Size ..... PPT 5-33
To Change a Bullet to a Symbol ..... PPT 5-34
To Format Bullet Color ..... PPT 5-36
To Change a Bullet Character to a Number ..... PPT 5-36
To Change the List Numbering Style ..... PPT 5-37
To Change the Margins for Text in a Shape ..... PPT 5-38
To Format Shape Text ..... PPT 5-39
To Apply a Glow Text Effect ..... PPT 5-40
To Apply a Glow Shape Effect ..... PPT 5-40
Format Painter ..... PPT 5-41
To Use the Format Painter with Text ..... PPT 5-41
To Use the Format Painter with Objects ..... PPT 5-42
Animating Slide Content ..... PPT 5-43
To Animate a Picture Using an Entrance Effect ..... PPT 5-43

To Add an Emphasis Effect Animation ... PPT 5-44
To Add a Delay to an Animation ... PPT 5-44
To Animate Text ... PPT 5-45
To Dim Text after Animation ... PPT 5-45
To Reorder Animations on a Slide ... PPT 5-47
To Use the Animation Painter ... PPT 5-47
To Animate an Object Using a Preset Motion Path ... PPT 5-49
To Animate an Object Using a Custom Motion Path ... PPT 5-50
To Trigger an Animation Effect ... PPT 5-53
To Insert a Connector ... PPT 5-54
To Align Content Placeholders ... PPT 5-55
Creating and Managing Sections ... PPT 5-56
To Add a Section to a Presentation ... PPT 5-56
To Rename a Section ... PPT 5-57
To Collapse Sections ... PPT 5-59
To Reorder Sections ... PPT 5-60
Zoom Links ... PPT 5-61
To Insert Section Zoom Links and Slide Zoom Links ... PPT 5-61
To Change the Zoom Icon Image ... PPT 5-64
To Run a Presentation with Section Zoom Links and Slide Zoom Links ... PPT 5-65
To Save and Print the Presentation ... PPT 5-65
Summary ... PPT 5-66
Apply Your Knowledge ... PPT 5-67
Extend Your Knowledge ... PPT 5-68
Expand Your World ... PPT 5-70
In the Lab ... PPT 5-71

Module 6: Formatting Tables and Charts ... PPT 6-1

Objectives ... PPT 6-1
Introduction ... PPT 6-1
Project: Presentation with Embedded and Linked Files and Formatted Table and Chart ... PPT 6-1
Creating a Presentation from a Word Outline ... PPT 6-4
Converting Documents for Use in PowerPoint ... PPT 6-4
To Insert Slides from an Outline ... PPT 6-5
Inserting Graphics or Other Objects from a File ... PPT 6-6
To Delete a Placeholder ... PPT 6-7
To Embed an Object from Another App ... PPT 6-8
To Edit an Embedded File ... PPT 6-9
Drawing and Formatting a Table ... PPT 6-10
To Draw a Table ... PPT 6-11
To Draw Table Rows ... PPT 6-12
To Draw Table Columns ... PPT 6-13
To Erase a Table Border ... PPT 6-15
To Enter Text in a Table ... PPT 6-16
To Split Table Cells ... PPT 6-17
To Enter Additional Text in a Table ... PPT 6-19
To Select a Table and Apply Shading to Table Cells ... PPT 6-20
To Apply a Bevel Effect to Table Cells ... PPT 6-21
To Apply a Shadow Effect to Table Cells ... PPT 6-22
To Apply a Reflection Effect to Table Cells ... PPT 6-22
To Add an Image to a Table Cell ... PPT 6-23
To Distribute Table Rows ... PPT 6-24
To Resize a Table Column and Row ... PPT 6-25
To Align Data in a Table Cell ... PPT 6-26
To Format Table Data ... PPT 6-28
To Align a Table ... PPT 6-28
Inserting a Linked Excel Worksheet ... PPT 6-29
To Link an Excel Worksheet ... PPT 6-30
To Align a Worksheet ... PPT 6-32
To Update a Linked Worksheet ... PPT 6-33
Copying and Modifying a Linked Excel Chart ... PPT 6-34
To Copy an Excel Chart ... PPT 6-35
To Resize a Chart Proportionally ... PPT 6-36
To Align a Chart ... PPT 6-37
To Switch Chart Rows and Columns ... PPT 6-38
To Change the Chart Type ... PPT 6-39
To Change the Chart Layout ... PPT 6-40
To Apply a Style to a Chart ... PPT 6-41
To Change Chart Colors ... PPT 6-41
To Add an Axis to a Chart ... PPT 6-42
To Add a Title at a Specified Position in a Chart ... PPT 6-44
To Add a Border to a Chart Element ... PPT 6-45
To Edit the Source File of a Linked Chart ... PPT 6-46
To Add a Link to Text ... PPT 6-48
Changing Views ... PPT 6-49
To Navigate between Slides in Reading View ... PPT 6-49
To Switch to Outline View ... PPT 6-50
To Navigate between Slides in Outline View ... PPT 6-50
To Move a Slide in Outline View ... PPT 6-51
To Enter Text in Outline View ... PPT 6-51
To Add a Transition between Slides ... PPT 6-51
To Run, Print, Save, and Exit PowerPoint ... PPT 6-52
Summary ... PPT 6-52
Apply Your Knowledge ... PPT 6-53
Extend Your Knowledge ... PPT 6-55
Expand Your World ... PPT 6-58
In the Lab ... PPT 6-59

Module 7: Adding Media and Enhancing SmartArt ... PPT 7-1

Objectives ... PPT 7-1
Introduction ... PPT 7-1
Project: Presentation with Audio and Video Clips, SmartArt, and Hyperlinks ... PPT 7-1
Modifying a Slide by Changing a Picture and Inserting a Screen Clipping ... PPT 7-5
To Open and Save a Presentation ... PPT 7-5
To Change a Picture ... PPT 7-5

To Resize a Picture to Exact Dimensions .... PPT 7-6
To Insert a Screen Clipping .... PPT 7-7
Creating and Formatting a SmartArt Graphic .... PPT 7-9
To Insert SmartArt Using a Content Placeholder .... PPT 7-9
To Show or Hide the SmartArt Text Pane .... PPT 7-10
To Enter Text in SmartArt .... PPT 7-11
To Format Text Pane Characters .... PPT 7-12
To Add a Picture to SmartArt .... PPT 7-12
To Insert a Picture into a SmartArt Shape .... PPT 7-13
To Add a SmartArt Shape .... PPT 7-13
To Apply 3-D Effects to SmartArt .... PPT 7-14
To Increase the Size of a SmartArt Shape .... PPT 7-15
To Resize SmartArt to Exact Dimensions .... PPT 7-16
To Move a SmartArt Shape Up .... PPT 7-17
To Move a SmartArt Shape Down .... PPT 7-18
To Promote SmartArt Text .... PPT 7-19
To Demote SmartArt Text .... PPT 7-20
To Change the Color of SmartArt .... PPT 7-20
Formatting Pictures .... PPT 7-22
To Remove a Picture Background .... PPT 7-22
To Refine Background Removal .... PPT 7-24
To Flip a Picture .... PPT 7-25
To Change the Brightness and Contrast of a Picture .... PPT 7-25
To Change the Color Saturation of a Picture .... PPT 7-26
To Compress a Picture .... PPT 7-27
Inserting a Video and an Audio Clip .... PPT 7-28
To Insert a Video File without Using a Content Placeholder .... PPT 7-28
To Trim a Video File .... PPT 7-30
To Change the Video Start Option .... PPT 7-31
To Play a Video Full Screen .... PPT 7-32
To Resize a Video Proportionally .... PPT 7-32
To Apply a Video Style .... PPT 7-33
To Add a Video Poster Frame .... PPT 7-34
To Insert an Audio Clip from a File .... PPT 7-35
To Change the Audio Clip Start Option .... PPT 7-37
To Loop an Audio Clip .... PPT 7-37
To Hide an Audio Clip Object during a Slide Show .... PPT 7-38
To Change the Volume of an Audio Clip .... PPT 7-38
To Trim an Audio Clip .... PPT 7-39
To Compress a Video and an Audio File .... PPT 7-40
Adding Hyperlinks and Action Buttons .... PPT 7-41
To Insert a Hyperlink to a Place in the Current Presentation .... PPT 7-41
To Edit a Hyperlink .... PPT 7-42
To Add a ScreenTip to a Hyperlink .... PPT 7-42
To Add a Hyperlink Action Setting to a Picture .... PPT 7-43
To Add a Hyperlink Action Setting to a Shape .... PPT 7-44
To Insert a Hyperlink to a Slide in Another Presentation .... PPT 7-45
Action Buttons .... PPT 7-47
To Insert an Action Button .... PPT 7-48
To Size an Action Button .... PPT 7-49
To Change an Action Button Fill Color .... PPT 7-49
To Add Sound to an Action .... PPT 7-50
To Save the Presentation as a PDF .... PPT 7-51
To Run, Save, and Exit PowerPoint .... PPT 7-53
Summary .... PPT 7-53
Apply Your Knowledge .... PPT 7-54
Extend Your Knowledge .... PPT 7-56
Expand Your World .... PPT 7-58
In the Lab .... PPT 7-59

Module 8: Creating Photo Albums and Delivering Presentations .... PPT 8-1

Objectives .... PPT 8-1
Introduction .... PPT 8-1
Project: Presentation with a Custom Slide Show and Photo Album .... PPT 8-2
To Start PowerPoint and Save a File .... PPT 8-4
Creating a Custom Slide Show .... PPT 8-4
To Select Slides for a Slide Show .... PPT 8-4
To Create a Custom Slide Show .... PPT 8-6
To Open and Edit a Custom Slide Show .... PPT 8-7
To Run a Custom Slide Show .... PPT 8-8
3D Models .... PPT 8-9
Saving and Sharing a Presentation .... PPT 8-10
To Save a Slide as a Picture .... PPT 8-10
To Create Handouts by Exporting to Word .... PPT 8-11
To Save a Presentation as a PowerPoint Show .... PPT 8-13
To Close a Presentation .... PPT 8-14
Checking and Securing a Presentation .... PPT 8-14
To Check Presentation Compatibility .... PPT 8-15
To Check Presentation Accessibility .... PPT 8-16
To Encrypt a Presentation with a Password .... PPT 8-18
To Change or Remove Password Protection .... PPT 8-19
Customizing Handout and Notes Masters .... PPT 8-20
To Switch to Handout Master View .... PPT 8-20
To Customize the Handout Master .... PPT 8-21
To Insert a Header for Handouts .... PPT 8-22
To Switch to Notes Page View .... PPT 8-23
To Switch to Notes Master View .... PPT 8-23
To Insert a Header for Notes .... PPT 8-24
To Customize the Notes Master .... PPT 8-24
To Close Master View .... PPT 8-26
To Print Handouts .... PPT 8-26
Creating a Photo Album .... PPT 8-30
To Start a Photo Album and Add Pictures .... PPT 8-30
To Reorder Pictures in a Photo Album .... PPT 8-32
To Format Photos in an Album .... PPT 8-33
To Change a Photo Album Layout .... PPT 8-34

To Add a Photo Album Theme .... PPT 8-35
To Create a Photo Album .... PPT 8-35
To Edit a Photo Album .... PPT 8-36
Modifying and Presenting Slides .... PPT 8-37
To Change the Slide Orientation .... PPT 8-38
To Change the Slide Show Resolution .... PPT 8-39
To Insert a Summary Zoom Slide .... PPT 8-40
To Run a Presentation with Slide Zoom Links.... PPT 8-43
To Save the Presentation.................................... PPT 8-43
Summary .... PPT 8-43
Apply Your Knowledge .... PPT 8-44
Extend Your Knowledge .... PPT 8-46
Expand Your World .... PPT 8-48
In the Lab .... PPT 8-48

Index Index-1

Preface: The Shelly Cashman Series®: Microsoft® 365® & Office®

The Shelly Cashman Series® offers application-specific comprehensive print titles for Word®, Excel®, PowerPoint®, Access®, Publisher®, Outlook®, and Windows®. The modules (chapters) of the four main Microsoft® applications (Word®, Excel®, PowerPoint®, and Access®) are also offered together in each of three print titles organized by level: introductory, intermediate, and advanced. The MindTap Collection includes all of the preceding content, plus additional digital-only content for Teams®, the Mac operating system, and more.

About the Authors

Word: Misty E. Vermaat has more than 30 years of experience in the field of computer and information technology. In addition to consulting in the field, she was an Associate Professor at Purdue University Calumet, teaching or developing courses in Microsoft® Office, computer concepts, database management, systems analysis and design, and programming. Since 1990, she has led the development of the Shelly Cashman Series and has authored and co-authored numerous series textbooks, including many editions of Discovering Computers, Discovering Computers Fundamentals, Microsoft® Publisher®, and Microsoft® Word® books.

PowerPoint: Susan L. Sebok is a retired professor at South Suburban College in South Holland, Illinois, and is also a licensed attorney. Working with the leading Shelly Cashman Series® since 1993, she has co-authored several successful textbooks, including multiple versions of Discovering Computers and Microsoft® PowerPoint®. She holds both Master of Arts and Juris Doctor degrees.

Excel: Victoria Kaye brings her industry knowledge and instructor experience to Cengage Group for the Shelly Cashman Series. As an avid Excel user with Microsoft teaching experience ranging from secondary to undergraduate levels, she is thrilled to be part of the esteemed Shelly Cashman Excel Series legacy.

Dr. Mark Shellman is an instructor and Chair of the Information Technology Department at Gaston College in Dallas, North Carolina. Dr. Mark, as his students call him, prides himself on being student-centered and loves learning himself. His favorite subjects in the information technology realm include databases and programming languages. Dr. Mark has been teaching for more than 30 years and has co-authored several texts in the New Perspective series on Microsoft® Office 365 & Access®, along with a textbook on Structured Query Language.

Access: Jill West authors Cengage courses for CompTIA Cloud+, CompTIA Network+, Data Communications, Technology for Success, and the popular Shelly Cashman Series. She has taught kindergarten through college and currently teaches computer technology courses at Georgia Northwestern Technical College. Jill specializes in designing innovative, critical-thinking activities and building courses that teach popular IT certifications. She regularly presents at conferences and webinars on preparing for CompTIA certifications, teaching cloud computing and computer networking, and mentoring lifelong student learners in IT. She's a member of the 2019 inaugural cohort of Faculty Ambassadors for AWS Educate and is currently an AWS Academy Accredited Educator. Jill and her husband, Mike, live in northwest Georgia with two children at home and two off to college.

Windows 11: Steven M. Freund serves as a lead instructor of various Microsoft® Office, computer concepts, programming, and Internet technology courses throughout central Florida. An integral author for the successful Shelly Cashman Series since 2001, he has presented at the annual customer conference, the Shelly Cashman Series Institute, and other customer events. Freund has co-authored multiple editions of Discovering Computers, Mozilla Firefox, Windows® Internet Explorer, Windows® Office, and Dreamweaver books. In addition, he has written numerous successful instructor supplements. He attended the University of Central Florida.

Preface for the Instructor

Shelly Cashman's trademark step-by-step, screen-by-screen, project-based approach encourages students to expand their understanding of Office applications through hands-on experimentation and critical thinking. Module learning objectives are mapped to Microsoft Office Specialist certification objectives, reinforcing the critical skills needed for success in college and career. Other Ways boxes help users identify alternate click paths to achieve a step, while BTW sidebars offer helpful hints as readers work through projects, enabling them to make the most of Microsoft Office tools. MindTap and updated SAM (Skills Assessment Manager) online resources are also available to guide additional study to maximize results.

Shelly Cashman prepares students for success in the real world by using current and relevant scenarios that apply to everyday life and careers. It also prepares students to take the Microsoft Office Specialist (MOS) exam, which they can leverage in their careers.

Shelly Cashman is designed for students at two- and four-year schools as well as in continuing education programs. Skill levels can range from experienced — for those with a foundational understanding from prior exposure to technology — to introductory — for those using a computer or technology device for the first time.

The Shelly Cashman Series® offers application-specific comprehensive print titles for Word®, Excel®, PowerPoint®, Access®, Publisher®, Outlook®, and Windows®. The modules (chapters) of the four main Microsoft® applications (Word®, Excel®, PowerPoint®, and Access®) are also offered together in each of three print titles organized by level: introductory, intermediate, and advanced. The MindTap Collection includes all of the preceding content, plus additional digital-only content for Teams®, the Mac operating system, and more.

Market research is conducted semi-annually with both current Cengage users and those who use other learning materials. The focus of the market research is to gain insights into the user experience and overall learner needs so we can continuously evolve our content to exceed user expectations. We survey hundreds of instructors to ensure we gather information from a large and varied demographic.

New to This Edition

Shelly Cashman provides thoroughly updated coverage that reflects current Microsoft® 365® features. Narrative content has been authored using Microsoft® 365 Business Standard. Module projects incorporate career topics that apply diversity, equity, and inclusion principles and ensure accessibility. All projects, assignments, and lessons have been refreshed with authentic case scenarios that focus on practical skills and employability.

Word: New features in the Word content include the enhanced Accessibility Checker, which identifies potential accessibility issues and presents suggestions to make documents more inclusive. The Word coverage also introduces Focus mode, the updated collaboration experience, Microsoft's expanded search tool, and voice options. The Immersive Reader is covered, as is the ability to create a private document copy and use Word's screen reader.

PowerPoint: The PowerPoint content introduces the new commenting experience, which lets users display comments in contextual view or the Comments pane. The comment anchor helps reviewers identify specific slide elements with comments and place the comment bubble anywhere on the slide. With the revised search feature, users can enter a word or phrase in the Search box to find the definition. Microsoft Search also provides support articles to help perform tasks. Users can record and save a presentation that includes digital inking to capture text, drawings, and annotations, and then play back animated drawings. The Speaker Coach uses artificial intelligence (AI) to improve presentation skills by giving feedback on body language, the use of sensitive and filler words, and perceived mispronounced words.

Excel: With the Excel modules, students learn both long-standing Excel functions and tools as well as the most recent innovations. Updates to the Excel content include the new XLOOKUP and LET functions, dynamic arrays, and the Analyze Data feature. Also covered is the Accessibility Checker, which identifies issues and offers solutions to produce an accessible workbook.

Access: New features in the Access coverage include updated, real-world scenarios from a variety of industries that illustrate the relevance of Access databases in today's businesses. Completely updated projects use gapped Start and Solution files to ensure students use new, authentic files for each project from one module to the next. Module projects alternate between two sets of scenarios for expanded relevance and practicality. Further, an off-module scenario database receives updates comparable to the on-module scenario so students see similar progression in all databases. A Solutions to Critical Thinking Questions document for each module guides instructors on what to look for in student work. Critical Thinking Questions invite students to engage with the module's skills and information at a conceptual level, and to reflect on their learning, thinking processes, and the relevance of learned skills to their chosen careers.

Windows: The updates to the Windows modules reflect the changes from Windows 10 to Windows 11. New end-of-module exercises incorporate current terminology and features. Module projects have been updated with the latest Windows 11 features, including widgets, the revised Start and Search menus, and the Immersive Reader.

Organization of the Text

The *Shelly Cashman Series: Microsoft 365 & Office, First Edition* is a comprehensive introduction to Microsoft applications and is intended for students in introductory computing courses. Each application is divided into modules within the three levels — introductory, intermediate, and advanced. Each module introduces a topic through a real-world project and presents content that aligns directly with the learning objectives listed at the beginning of the module. To enable students to practice and apply skills learned, each module ends with a summary and a Consider This: Plan Ahead master planning guide that students use as they complete assignments and create projects on their own. Lastly, the end-of-module assignments are related to the top 25 industries for each application and include critical thinking questions. To increase students' confidence in their abilities, the assignments build from applying skills to experimenting beyond the module content to implementing a solution using creative thinking and problem-solving approaches.

Features of the Text

The features of the text, which are found consistently throughout all modules, are designed to aid the student in a specific way.

The projects are focused on employability based on current research and data. They use authentic case scenarios and a step-by-step approach to be as engaging, comprehensive, and easy to use as possible.

Heading levels organize topics within a module. Unique to the Shelly Cashman Series are "To-Do" heading levels for step-by-step task sequences. A To-Do head lead-in paragraph may include a **Why?** element to clarify why students are performing the steps.

To Display a Different Tab on the Ribbon

When you start Word, the ribbon displays 11 main tabs: File, Home, Insert, Draw, Design, Layout, References, Mailings, Review, View, and Help. (Note that depending on the type of computer or device you are using, the Draw tab may not appear.) The tab currently displayed is called the active tab. To display a different tab on the ribbon, you click the tab. The following step displays the View tab, that is, makes it the active tab. **Why?** When working with Word, you may need to switch tabs to access other options for working with a document or to verify settings.

Step-by-step sequences include the following features:

Q&A boxes provide troubleshooting information, equivalent touch instructions, or an additional explanation for a step.

Experiment steps encourage students to explore a feature such as the Themes gallery.

2

- If necessary, scroll to and then point to Facet in the Themes gallery to display a Live Preview of that theme applied to the document (Figure 1–37).
- **Experiment:** Point to various themes in the Themes gallery to display a Live Preview of the various themes applied to the document in the document window.

Q&A What is Live Preview?
Recall from the discussion earlier in this module that Live Preview is a feature that allows you to point to a gallery choice and see its effect in the document — without actually selecting the choice.

Can I use Live Preview on a touch screen?
Live Preview may not be available on all touch screens.

Other Ways provide additional methods to accomplish the tasks covered in specific To-Do steps.

Other Ways

1. Right-click paragraph (or if using touch, tap 'Show Context Menu' button on Mini toolbar), click Paragraph on shortcut menu, click Indents and Spacing tab (Paragraph dialog box), click Alignment arrow, click Centered, click OK
2. Click Paragraph Dialog Box Launcher (Home tab or Layout tab | Paragraph group), click Indents and Spacing tab (Paragraph dialog box), click Alignment arrow, click Centered, click OK
3. Press CTRL+E

By the Way (BTW) boxes are short marginal elements that add value for students by expanding on information in the module.

BTW
Printing Document Properties
To print document properties, click File on the ribbon to open Backstage view, click Print in Backstage view to display the Print screen, click the first button in the Settings area to display a list of options specifying what you can print, click Document Info in the list to specify you want to print the document properties instead of the actual document, and then click the Print button in the Print screen to print the document properties on the currently selected printer.

Other in-text pedagogical elements include the following:

Key terms are bold and blue in the running text. In the MindTap, each bolded key term is linked to its definition in the Master Glossary.

> Calibri and Calibri Light are **sans serif fonts**, which are fonts that do not
> ends of their characters. Other fonts such as Calisto MT are **serif fonts**,

Consider This is a pedagogical sidebar in the form of a question and answer that appears within the module and in the end-of-module student assignments. The question addresses conceptual or critical thinking topics, general information about the app, or other important information students should know.

> **Consider This**
>
> **How do you use the touch keyboard with a touch screen?**
> To display the on-screen touch keyboard, tap the Touch Keyboard button on the Windows taskbar. When finished using the touch keyboard, tap the X button on the touch keyboard to close the keyboard.

Break Point is a note to students that indicates a good place to take a break. Every module includes at least one break point.

> **Break Point:** If you want to take a break, this is a good place to do so. You can exit Word now. To resume later, start Word and continue following the steps from this location forward.

SAM Upload and Download icons are for SAM users. A SAM download icon appears next to any step where students download a data file to begin a SAM Project.

> 1
> - sam ↓ Click the Start button on the Windows taskbar to display the Start

A SAM upload icon appears next to any step where students submit a file to SAM for a completed SAM Project.

> 3
> - Click the 'Clear Search String' button to remove the search string and redisplay all objects.
>
> Q&A Did I have to click the button to redisplay all objects? Could I simply have erased the current string to achieve the same result?
> You did not have to click the button. You could have used DEL or BACKSPACE to erase the current search string.
>
> - If desired, sign out of your Microsoft account.
> - sam ↑ Exit Access.

Figure callouts point to important parts of a screen and include two types:

Action/navigation callouts point to commands or buttons used in the step. Action/navigation callout boxes are a different color from explanatory callouts to help students easily locate screen elements referenced in step instructions.

Explanatory callouts direct students to other significant screen elements in the figure.

1. With the text selected (shown in Figure 1–55), click the Font Size arrow (Home tab | Font group) to display the Font Size gallery.
2. Click 20 in the Font Size gallery to increase the font size of the selected text.
3. Click anywhere in the document window to remove the selection from the text (Figure 1–56).

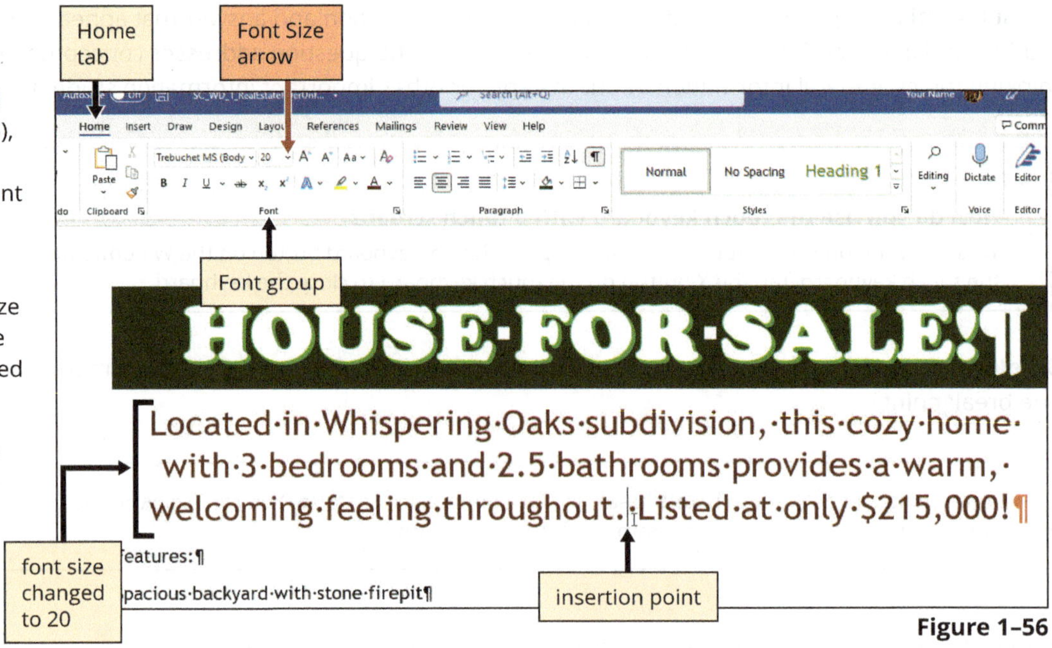

Figure 1–56

Course Solutions

Online Learning Platform: MindTap with SAM

The Shelly Cashman Series MindTap Collection, powered by SAM (Skills Assessment Manager), enables proficiency in Microsoft Office and computing concepts for your Introductory Computing courses. With a library of renowned course materials, including ready-to-assign, auto-graded learning modules, you can easily adapt your course to best prepare students for the evolving job market. In addition to an eReader that includes the full content of the printed book, The Shelly Cashman Series, First Edition MindTap course includes the following:

- SAM Textbook Projects: Follow the steps and scenarios outlined in the textbook readings; enable students to complete projects based on a real-world scenario live in Microsoft Office applications and submit them in SAM for automatic grading and feedback.
- SAM Training and Exam: Trainings teach students to complete specific skills in a simulated Microsoft application environment while exams allow students to demonstrate their proficiency (also in a simulated environment).
- SAM Projects: Students complete projects based on real-world scenarios live in Microsoft applications and submit the projects in SAM for automatic grading and feedback. SAM offers several types of projects, each with a unique purpose: 1A and 1B, critical thinking, end of module, capstone, and integration.

- Microsoft Office Specialist (MOS) resources: Training and exams are based on the Microsoft Office 365 Objective Domains for the MOS Exam and exam simulation that replicates the test-taking environment of the MOS exam for Word, Excel, Access, PowerPoint, and Outlook.

To learn more, go to: https://www.cengage.com/mindtap-collections/

Ancillary Package

Additional instructor and student resources for this product are available online. Instructor assets include an Instructor Manual, an Educator Guide, PowerPoint® slides, a Guide to Teaching Online, Solution Files, a test bank powered by Cognero®, and a Transition Guide. Student assets include data files and a glossary. Sign up or sign in at www.cengage.com to search for and access this product and its online resources. The instructor and student companion sites contain ancillary material for the full Shelly Cashman Series Collection, along with instructions on how to find specific content within the companion site.

- Instructor Manual: This guide provides additional instructional material to assist in class preparation, including module objectives, module outlines, discussion questions, and additional activities and assignments. Each outline corresponds directly with the content in the module, and additional discussion questions and activities are aligned to headings in the book.
- Educator Guide: The MindTap Educator Guide contains a detailed outline of the corresponding MindTap course, including activity types and time on task. The SAM Educator Guide explains how to use SAM functionality to maximize your course.
- PowerPoint slides: The slides may be used to guide classroom presentations, to provide to students for module review, or to print as classroom handouts. The slides align closely with the book while activities and the self-assessment align with module learning objectives and supplement the content in the book.
- Guide to Teaching Online: This guide presents technological and pedagogical considerations and suggestions for teaching the Introductory Computing course when you can't be in the same room with students.
- Solution and Answer Guide: The answers to the critical thinking questions are written by the author and correspond to critical thinking questions in the end-of-module activities.
- Solution files: These files provide solutions to all textbook projects for instructors to use to grade student work.
    - Instructors using SAM do not need solution files since projects are auto-graded within SAM.
    - Solution files are provided on the instructor companion site for instructors *not* using SAM.
- Data files: These files are provided for students to complete the projects in each module.
    - Students using SAM to complete the projects download the required data files directly from SAM.
    - Students who are *not* using SAM to complete the projects can find data files on the student companion site and within MindTap.
- Test banks: A comprehensive test bank, offered in Cognero, Word, Blackboard, Moodle, Desire2Learn, Canvas, and SAM formats, contains questions aligned with each module's learning objectives and is written by subject matter experts. Powered by Cognero, Cengage Testing is a flexible, online system that allows you to author, edit, and manage test bank content from multiple Cengage solutions and to create multiple test versions that you can deliver from your LMS, your classroom, or wherever you want.
- Transition Guide: This guide highlights all of the changes in the text and in the digital offerings from the previous edition to the current one so that instructors know what to expect.

Acknowledgments

Jill West: It's always a privilege to work with the incredible teams Cengage puts together, and this course is no exception. I've worked on many projects under the energetic and resourceful leadership of Amy Savino, whom I greatly admire and will forever be thankful for her vote of confidence in me when I needed it most. I've thoroughly enjoyed getting to know Anne Orgren, who has been our attentive and supportive content manager, providing just enough guidance exactly when needed. I can't say enough good things about MT Cozzola, developmental editor for this project. With her diversity of talents and skills, she has been a learner advocate, bringing the student's perspective to every conversation and providing synergistic insight. And I'm grateful for another opportunity to work with learning designer Zenya Molnar, who brings creative solutions to design challenges. Many other folks worked diligently behind the scenes to ensure consistency of quality, design, and innovation — their efforts are enthusiastically noted and greatly appreciated.

I owe a special thanks to my husband, Mike, for his tireless support and encouragement. And thanks to my kiddos: Winn, Sarah, Daniel, and Zack.

Victoria Kaye: Thank you for the many individuals who have made this edition possible. A text like this is not done without great effort, teamwork, and planning. Thank you to those individuals who contributed their expertise to this text, and an extra special thank you to developmental editors Barbara Clemens and MT Cozzola. Without your vast knowledge and careful consideration, this edition would not be possible. Thank you to the editorial team and their staff: Amy Savino, Senior Portfolio Product Manager; Anne Orgren, Senior Content Manager; and Zenya Molnar, Learning Designer. It is simply not possible to sum up the value of your contributions.

Getting to Know Microsoft Office Versions

Cengage is proud to bring you the next edition of Microsoft Office. This edition was designed to provide a robust learning experience that is not dependent upon a specific version of Office.

Microsoft supports several versions and editions of Office: (Refer to Table 1 below for more information)

- **Microsoft 365 (formerly known as Office 365):** A service that delivers the most up-to-date, feature-rich, modern Microsoft productivity applications direct to your device. There are several combinations of Microsoft 365 programs for business, educational, and personal use. Microsoft 365 is cloud-based, meaning it is stored, managed, and processed on a network of remote servers hosted on the Internet, rather than on local servers or personal computers. Microsoft 365 offers extra online storage and cloud-connected features, as well as updates with the latest features, fixes, and security updates. Microsoft 365 is purchased for a monthly subscription fee that keeps your software up to date with the latest features.
- **Office 2021:** The Microsoft "on-premises" version of the Office apps, available for both PCs and Macintosh computers, offered as a static, one-time purchase and outside of the subscription model. Unlike Microsoft 365, Office 2021 does not include online product updates with new features.
- **Microsoft 365 Online (formerly known as Office Online):** A free, simplified version of Microsoft web applications (Teams, Access, Word, Excel, PowerPoint, and OneNote) that lets users create and edit files collaboratively.
- **Office 365 Education:** A free subscription including Word, Excel, PowerPoint, OneNote, and now Microsoft Teams, plus additional classroom tools. Only available for students and educators at select institutions.

Table 1 Microsoft Office applications — uses and availability

Application	Use	Availability/Editions
Word	Create documents and improve your writing with intelligent assistance features.	Microsoft 365 Family, Home, Business, Office 2021, Office 365 Education
Excel	Simplify complex data into easy-to-read spreadsheets.	Microsoft 365 Personal, Home, Business, Office 2021, Office 365 Education
PowerPoint	Create presentations that stand out.	Home, Business, Office 2021, Office 365 Education
OneNote	A digital notebook for all your note-taking needs.	Home, Office 365 Education
OneDrive	Save and share your files and photos wherever you are.	Home, Business
Outlook	Manage your email, calendar, tasks, and contacts all in one place.	Home, Business
SharePoint	Create team sites to share information, files, and resources.	Business
Publisher	Create polished, professional layouts without the hassle.	Home, Business, Office 2021 (PC only)
Access	Create your own database apps easily in formats that serve your business best.	Home, Business, Office 2021 (PC only)
Teams	Bring everyone together in one place to meet, chat, call, and collaborate.	Business, Office 365 Education
Exchange	Business-class email and calendaring.	Business

Over time, the Microsoft 365 cloud interface will continuously update using its web connection, offering new application features and functions, while Office 2021 will remain static.

Because Microsoft 365 releases updates continuously, your onscreen experience may differ from what you see in this product. For example, the more advanced features and functionalities covered in this product may not be available in Microsoft 365 Online, may have updated from what you see in Office 2021, or may be from a post-publication update of Microsoft 365.

For up-to-date information on the differences between Microsoft 365, Office 2021, and Microsoft 365 Online, please visit the Microsoft Support website.

Cengage is committed to providing high-quality learning solutions for you to gain the knowledge and skills that will empower you throughout your educational and professional careers.

Thank you for using our product, and we look forward to exploring the future of Microsoft Office with you!

Using SAM Projects and Textbook Projects

SAM (Skills Assessment Manager) **Projects** allow you to actively apply the skills you learned in Microsoft Word, Excel, PowerPoint, or Access. You can also submit your work to SAM for online grading. You can use SAM Projects to become a more productive student and use these skills throughout your career.

To complete SAM Textbook Projects, please follow these steps:

SAM Textbook Projects allow you to complete a project as you follow along with the steps in the textbook. As you read the module, look for icons that indicate when you should download **sam** ↓ your SAM Start file(s) and when to upload **sam** ↑ your solution file to SAM for grading.

Everything you need to complete this project is provided within SAM. You can launch the eBook directly from SAM, which will allow you to take notes, highlight, and create a custom study guide, or you can use a print textbook or your mobile app. Download IOS or Download Android.

To get started, launch your SAM Project assignment from SAM, MindTap, or a link within your learning management system.

1. Step 1:
   Download Files
   - Click the "Download All" button or the individual links to download your **Start File** and **Support File(s)** (when available). You must use the SAM Start file.
   - Click the Instructions link to launch the eBook (or use the print textbook or mobile app).
   - Disregard any steps in the textbook that ask you to create a new file or to use a file from a location outside of SAM.
   - Look for the SAM Download icon **sam** ↓ to begin working with your start file.
   - Follow the module's step-by-step instructions until you reach the SAM Upload icon **sam** ↑.
   - Save and close the file.

2. Step 2:
   Save Work to SAM
   - Ensure you rename your project file to match the Expected File Name.
   - Upload your in-progress or completed file to SAM. You can download the file to continue working or submit it for grading in the next step.
3. Step 3:
   Submit for Grading
   - Upload your completed solution file to SAM for immediate feedback and to view the available Reports.
     - The **Graded Summary Report** provides a detailed list of project steps, your score, and feedback to aid you in revising and resubmitting the project.
     - The **Study Guide** provides your score for each project step and links to the associated training and textbook pages.
   - If additional attempts are allowed, use your reports to assist with revising and resubmitting your project.
   - To re-submit your project, download the file you saved in step 2.
   - Edit, save, and close the file, then re-upload and submit it again.

For all other SAM Projects, please follow these steps:

To get started, launch your SAM Project assignment from SAM, MindTap, or a link within your learning management system.

1. Step 1:
   Download Files
   - Click the "Download All" button or the individual links to download your **Instruction File**, **Start File**, and **Support File(s)** (when available). You must use the SAM Start file.
   - Open the Instruction file and follow the step-by-step instructions. Ensure you rename your project file to match the Expected File Name (change _1 to _2 at the end of the file name).

2. Step 2:
   Save Work to SAM
   - Upload your in-progress or completed file to SAM. You can download the file to continue working or submit it for grading in the next step.
3. Step 3:
   Submit for Grading
   - Upload the completed file to SAM for immediate feedback and to view available Reports.
     - The **Graded Summary Report** provides a detailed list of project steps, your score, and feedback to aid you in revising and resubmitting the project.
     - The **Study Guide** provides your score for each project step and links to the associated training and textbook pages.
   - If additional attempts are allowed, use your reports to assist with revising and resubmitting your project.
   - To re-submit the project, download the file saved in step 2.
   - Edit, save, and close the file, then re-upload and submit it again.

For additional tips to successfully complete your SAM Projects, please view our SAM Video Tutorials.

Creating and Editing Presentations with Pictures

Objectives

After completing this module, you will be able to:

- Create a blank presentation
- Select and change a document theme
- Create a title slide and a text slide with a multilevel bulleted list
- Add new slides and change slide layouts
- Change font size and color
- Bold, italicize, and underline text
- Insert pictures into slides with and without content placeholders
- Move and resize pictures
- Arrange slides
- Change theme colors
- Check spelling
- Review a presentation in different views
- Enter slide notes
- Save a presentation
- Print a presentation

What Is PowerPoint?

Microsoft PowerPoint, or PowerPoint, is a full-featured presentation app that allows you to produce compelling presentations to deliver and share with an audience. A PowerPoint **presentation** also is called a **slide show**. The collection of slides in a presentation is called a **deck**, resembling a deck of cards that are stacked on top of each other. A common use of slide decks is to enhance an oral presentation. A speaker might desire to convey information, such as urging students to volunteer at a fund-raising event, explaining changes in employee compensation packages, or describing a new laboratory procedure. The PowerPoint slides should reinforce the speaker's message and help the audience retain the information presented. PowerPoint contains many features to plan, develop, and organize slides, including providing design ideas, formatting text, adding and editing video and audio clips, creating tables and charts, applying artistic effects to pictures, animating graphics, and collaborating with friends and colleagues. An accompanying handout gives audience members reference notes and review material for your presentation.

A PowerPoint presentation can help you deliver a dynamic, professional-looking message to an audience. PowerPoint allows you to produce slides to use in academic, business, or other environments. Custom slides can fit your specific needs and contain diagrams, charts, tables, pictures, shapes, video, sound, and animation effects to make your presentation more effective. You then can print a handout, turn your presentation into a video, broadcast your slide show on the web, or create a photo album.

BTW

Microsoft 365 Suite

PowerPoint is part of the Microsoft 365 suite; other apps in the suite include Word, Excel, Outlook, OneNote, and OneDrive, and on your PC, Access and Publisher. Apps in a suite, such as Microsoft 365, typically use a similar interface and share features.

BTW
The PowerPoint Window
The modules in this book begin with the PowerPoint window appearing as it did at the initial installation of the software. Your PowerPoint window may look different depending on your screen resolution and other PowerPoint settings.

To illustrate the features of PowerPoint, this book presents a series of projects that use PowerPoint to create presentations like those you will encounter in business environments.

Project: Presentation with a Bulleted List and Pictures

In this module's project, you will follow proper design guidelines and learn to use PowerPoint to create, save, and view the slides shown in Figures 1–1a through 1–1d. The objective is to produce a presentation, titled Security, that discusses managing passwords to help prevent online thieves from accessing private information. This slide show has a variety of pictures and visual elements to add interest and give facts about password creation and security threats. Some of the text has formatting and color enhancements, and the slides have a variety of layouts.

Figure 1–1(a): Slide 1 (Title Slide with Picture)

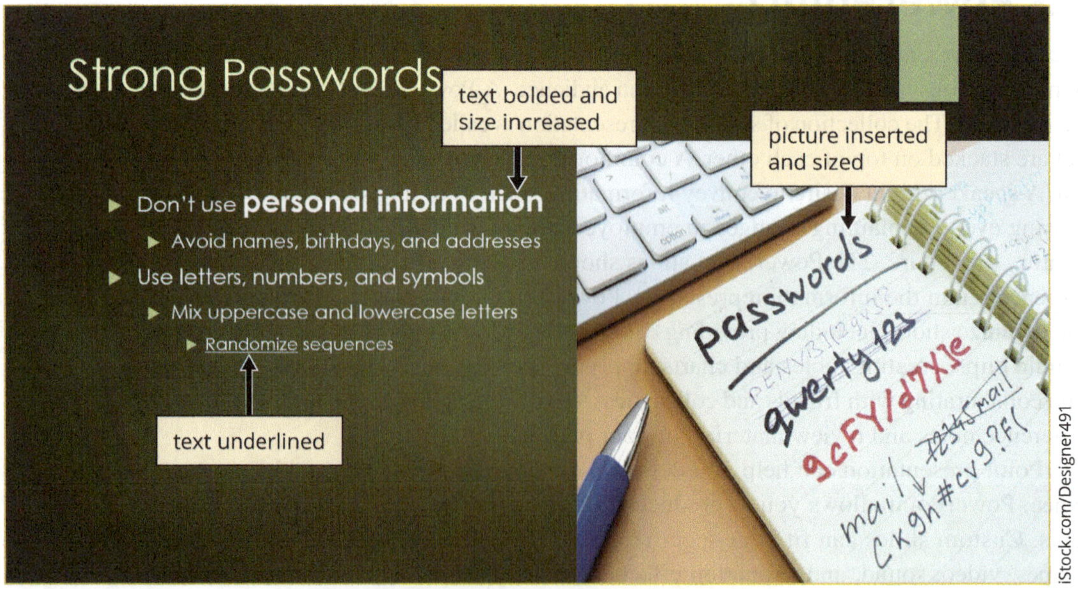

Figure 1–1(b): Slide 2 (Multilevel Bulleted List with Picture)

Figure 1–1(c): Slide 3 (Title and Picture)

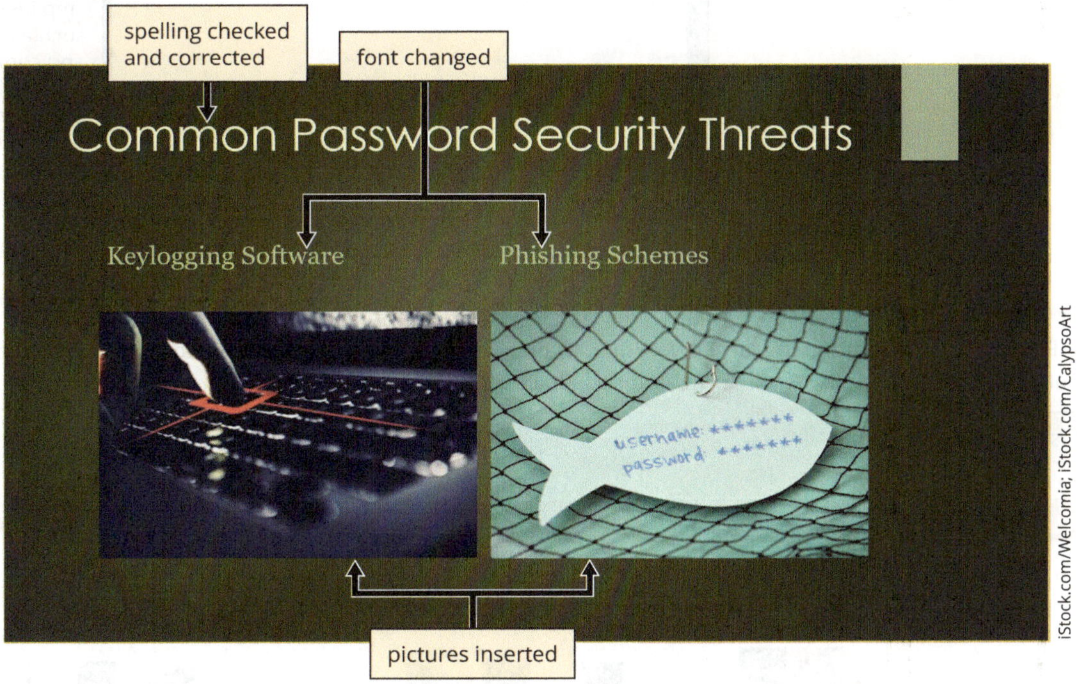

Figure 1–1(d): Slide 4 (Comparison Layout and Pictures)

In this module, you will learn how to perform basic tasks using PowerPoint. You will perform the following general tasks as you progress through this module:

1. Start and use PowerPoint.
2. Insert four presentation slides, using various layouts.
3. Enter and format the text on each slide.
4. Insert, size, and position pictures.
5. Display the slides.
6. Correct errors and print the slides.

BTW
Ribbon and Screen Resolution
PowerPoint may change how the groups and buttons within the groups appear on the ribbon, depending on the screen resolution of your computer. Thus, your ribbon may look different from the ones in this book if you are using a screen resolution other than 1920 × 1080.

Starting and Using PowerPoint

To use PowerPoint, you must instruct the operating system (such as Windows or Mac) to start the app. The following sections start PowerPoint and discuss some elements of PowerPoint.

To Start PowerPoint and Create a Blank Presentation

The following steps, which assume Windows is running, start PowerPoint and create a blank presentation based on a typical installation. You may need to ask your instructor how to start PowerPoint on your computer or device.

1

- sam Click Start on the Windows taskbar to display the Start menu.
- If necessary, scroll through the list of apps on the Start menu until the PowerPoint app name appears (Figure 1–2).

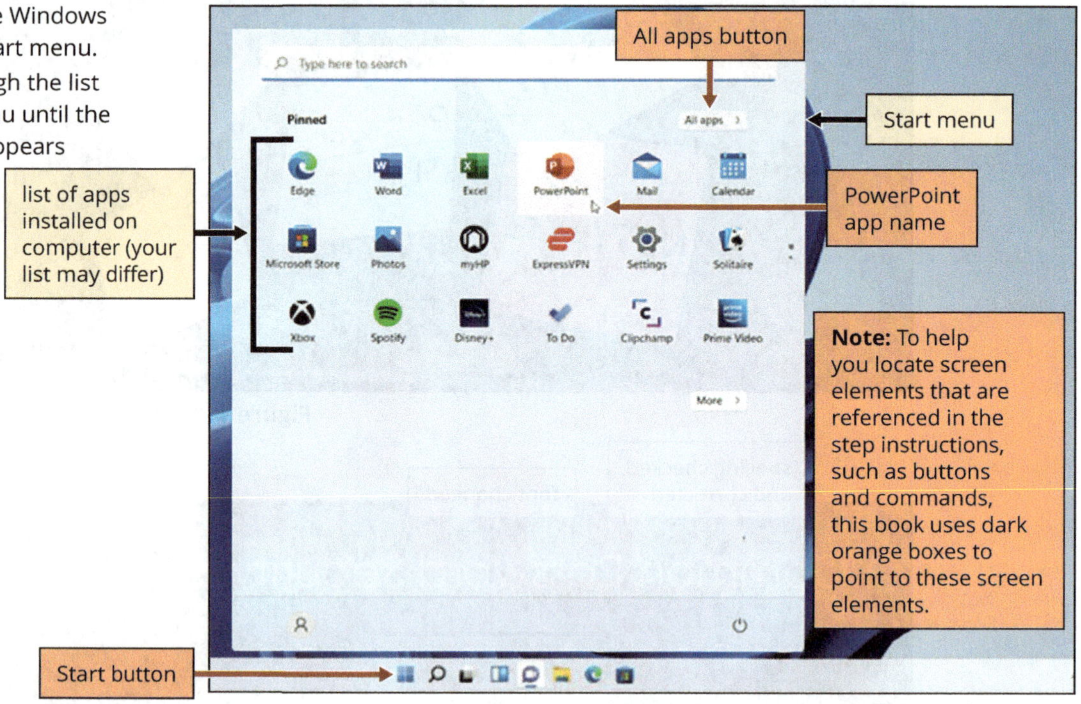

Figure 1–2

2

- Click PowerPoint on the Start menu to start PowerPoint. If the PowerPoint app is not displayed, click the All apps button to display an alphabetical list of apps, scroll down, and click PowerPoint (Figure 1–3).

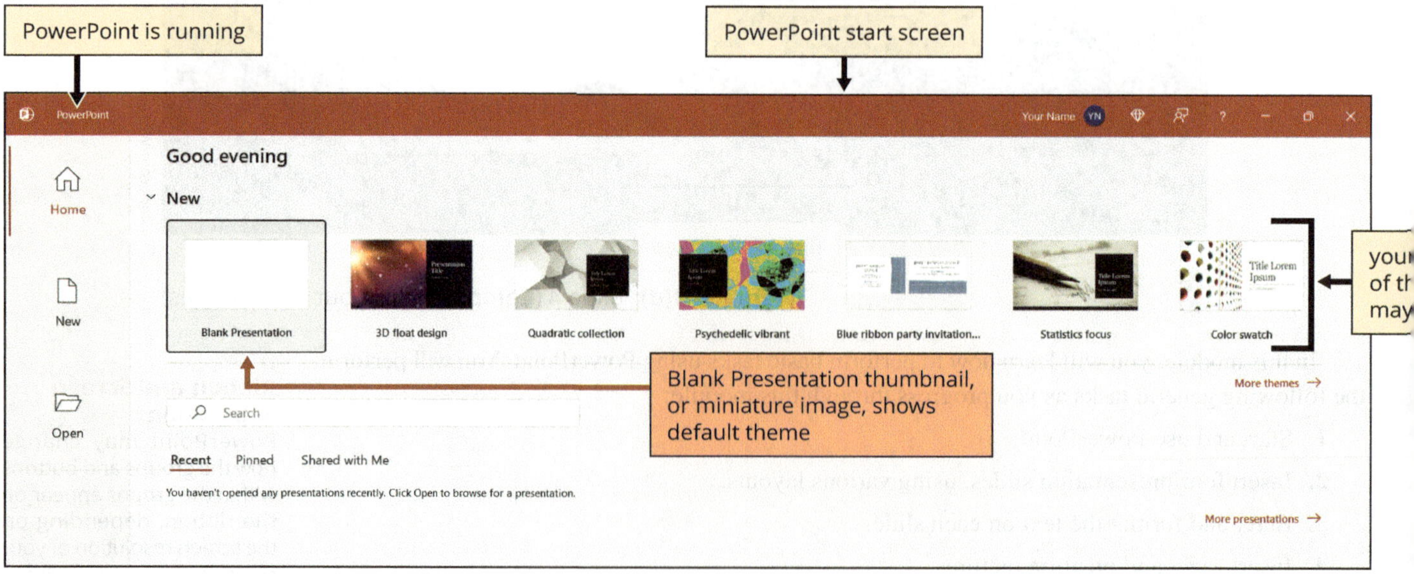

Figure 1–3

BTW
Resolution
For information about how to change a computer's resolution, search for 'change resolution' in your operating system's help files.

Other Ways

1. Click Windows search tool in taskbar, type app name in search box, click app name in results list
2. Double-click PowerPoint icon on desktop or in taskbar, if one is present

3

- Click the Blank Presentation thumbnail on the PowerPoint start screen to create a blank PowerPoint presentation in the PowerPoint window (Figure 1–4).
- If the Design Ideas pane is open, click Stop showing ideas for new presentations or click its Close button to close it.

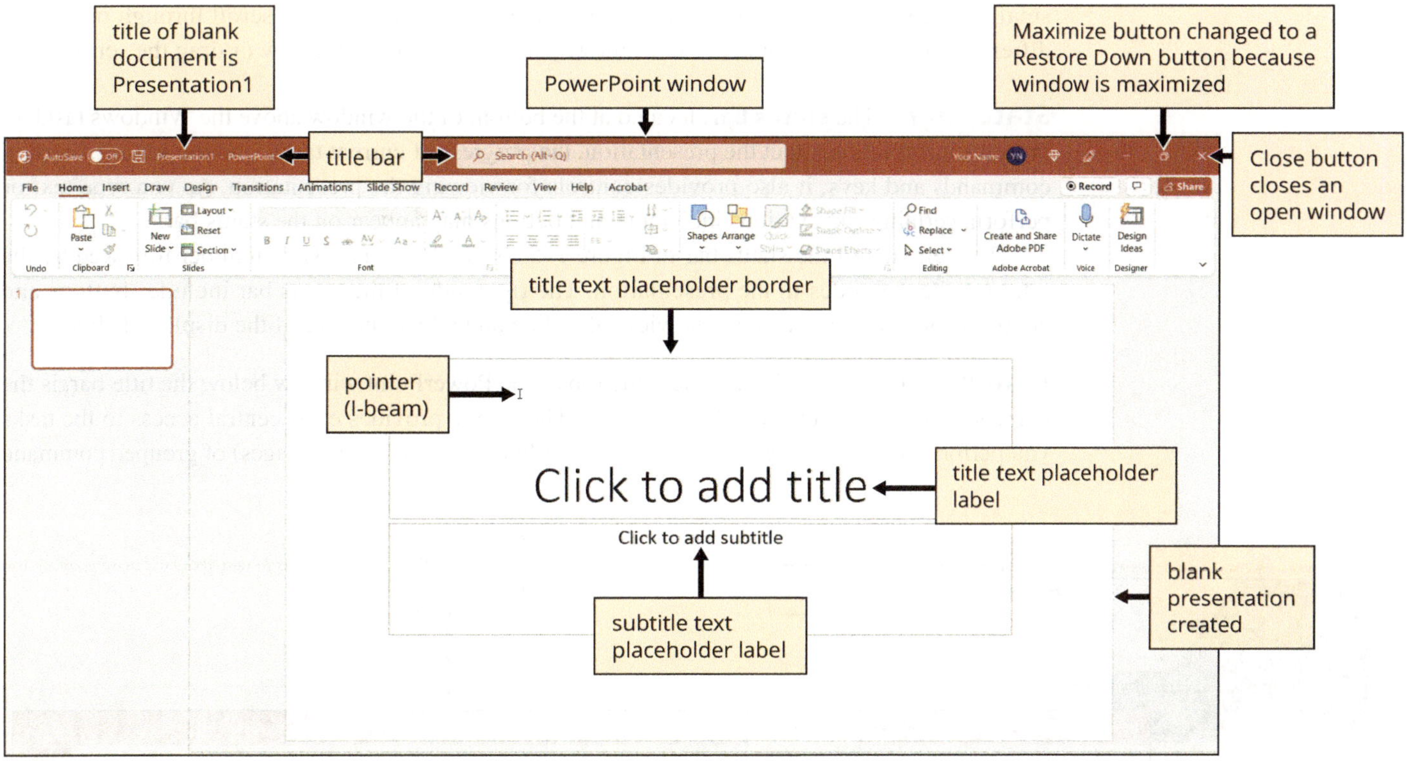

Figure 1–4

4

- If the PowerPoint window is not maximized, click the Maximize button next to the Close button on the title bar to maximize the window.

Q&A How do I know whether a window is maximized?
A window is maximized if it fills the entire display area and the Restore Down button is displayed on the title bar.

The PowerPoint Window

The PowerPoint window consists of a variety of components to make your work more efficient and presentations more professional: the window, ribbon, AutoSave button, Search box, Mini toolbar, shortcut menus, Quick Access Toolbar, and Microsoft Account area. Most of these elements are common to other Microsoft 365 apps; others are unique to PowerPoint.

The basic unit of a PowerPoint presentation is a **slide**. A slide may contain text and objects, such as graphics, tables, charts, and drawings. When you create a new presentation, the default **Title Slide** layout appears (shown in Figure 1–4). PowerPoint includes several other built-in standard layouts. All layouts except the Blank slide layout contain placeholders for text or other content such as pictures, charts, or videos. The title slide in Figure 1–4 has two text placeholders for the main heading (title) and the subtitle.

In the slide, the **insertion point** is a blinking vertical line that indicates where text, pictures, and other objects will be inserted. When you type, the insertion point moves to the right, and when you reach the end of a placeholder, it moves down to the beginning of the next line. The **pointer** is a small screen icon that moves as you move a mouse or pointing device on a surface and becomes different shapes depending on the task you are performing in PowerPoint. You move the pointer with a pointing device, such as a mouse or touchpad. The pointer in Figure 1–4 is the shape of an I-beam.

Scroll Bar You use a **scroll bar** to display different portions of a presentation in the window. At the right edge of the window is a vertical scroll bar. If a slide is too wide to fit in the window, a horizontal scroll bar also appears at the bottom of the window. On a scroll bar, the position of the **scroll box** reflects the location of the portion of the slide that is displayed in the window. A small triangular **scroll arrow** is located at each end of a scroll bar. To scroll through or display different portions of the slide in the window, you can click a scroll arrow or drag the scroll box.

Status Bar The **status bar**, located at the bottom of the window above the Windows taskbar, presents information about the presentation, the progress of current tasks, and the status of certain commands and keys; it also provides controls for viewing the presentation. As you type text or perform certain tasks, various indicators and buttons may appear on the status bar.

The left side of the status bar in Figure 1–5 shows the current slide number followed by the total number of slides in the presentation. The right side of the status bar includes buttons and controls you can use to change the view of a slide and adjust the size of the displayed slide.

Ribbon The **ribbon**, located near the top of the PowerPoint window below the title bar, is the control center in PowerPoint (Figure 1–6a). The ribbon provides easy, central access to the tasks you perform while creating a presentation. The ribbon consists of tabs (pages) of grouped command

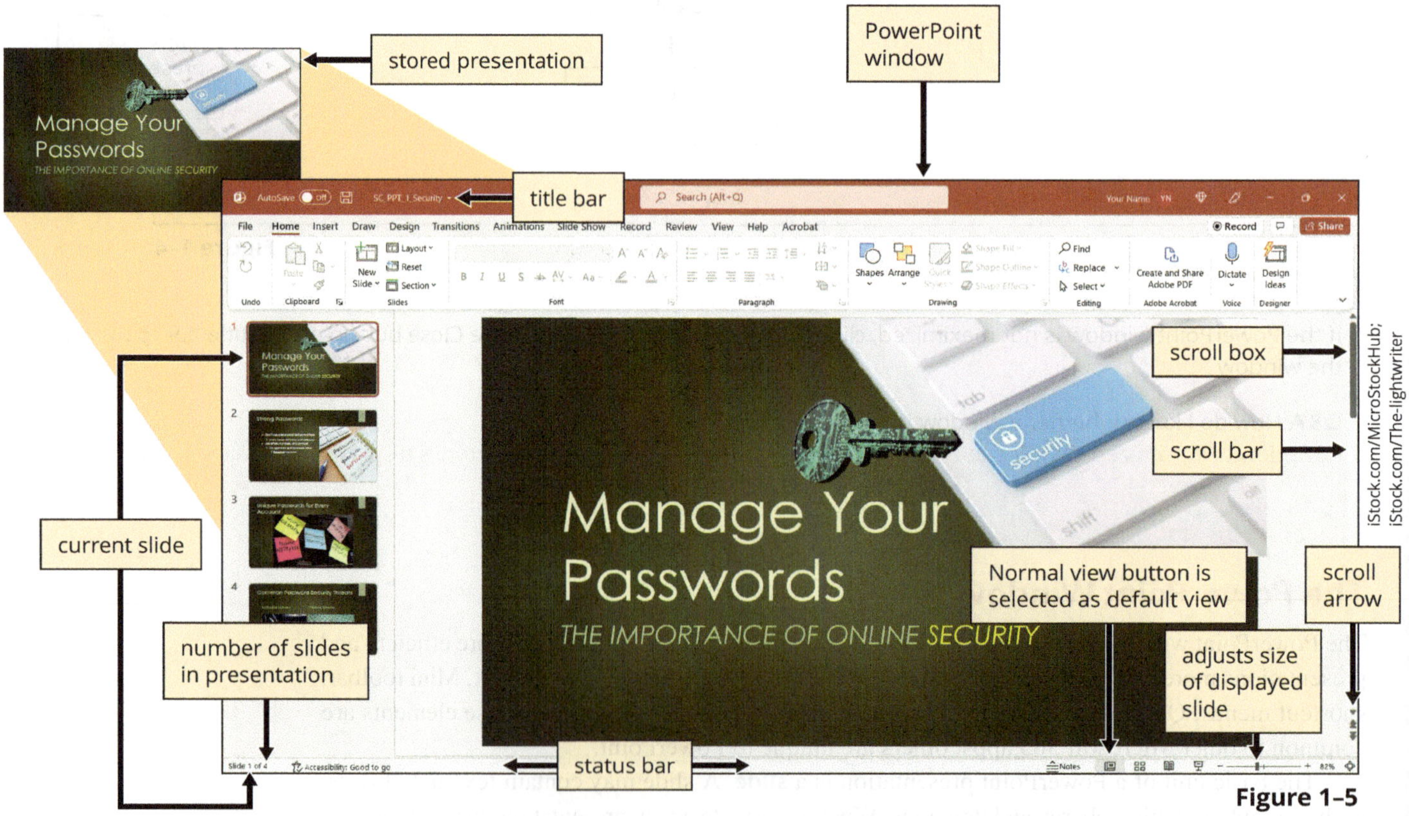

Figure 1–5

buttons that you click to interact with PowerPoint. Each **tab** contains a collection of groups, and each **group** contains related command buttons and boxes.

When you start PowerPoint, the ribbon initially displays several main tabs, also called default or top-level tabs. The **Home tab**, also called the primary tab, contains the more frequently used commands. The ribbon tab currently displayed is called the **active tab**.

To display more of the slide in the window, some users prefer to collapse the ribbon, which hides the groups on the ribbon and displays only the main tabs (Figure 1–6b). To collapse the ribbon when it is visible, double-click any ribbon tab, right-click any ribbon tab, and then click 'Collapse the Ribbon' on the menu, right-click the 'Ribbon Display Options' icon and then click 'Collapse the Ribbon' on the menu, or press CTRL+F1. To use commands on a collapsed ribbon, click the tab that you wish to expand. To expand the ribbon when it is collapsed, double-click any tab, right-click any tab, and then click to uncheck 'Collapse the Ribbon' on the menu or press CTRL+F1. To always display the ribbon, click the 'Ribbon Display Options' button when the ribbon is visible and then click 'Always show Ribbon' on the menu.

BTW
Ribbon Icons
Three icons are displayed on the right side of the ribbon: Record, Comment, and Share. These PowerPoint features allow you to rehearse and save a presentation, view and respond to comments other people have made about your slides, and distribute your presentation with others.

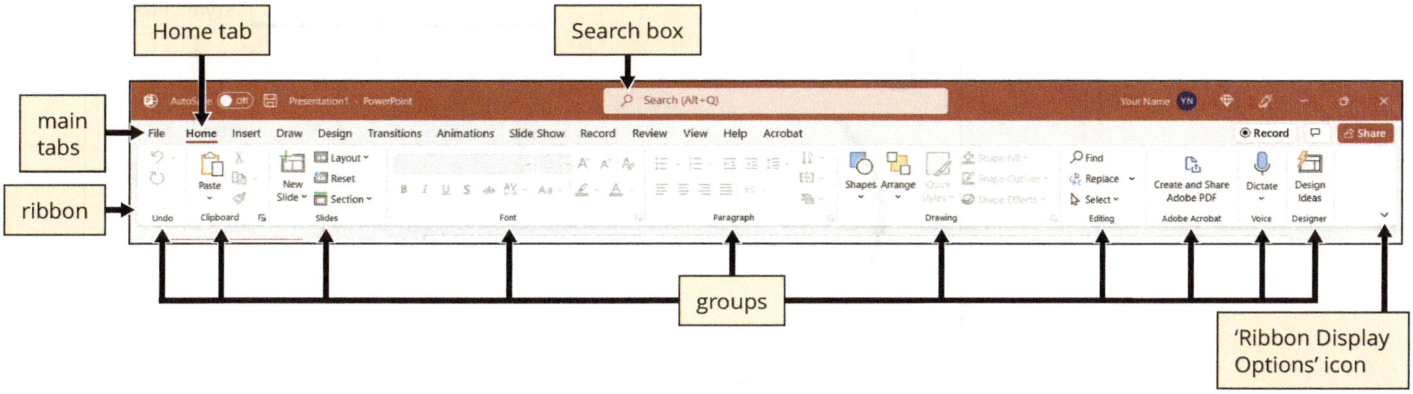

Figure 1–6a

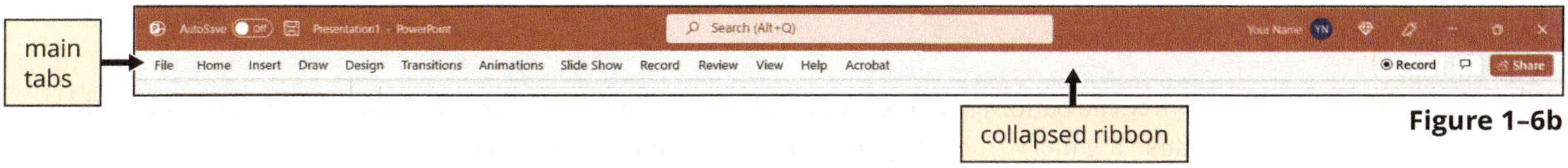

Figure 1–6b

Each time you start PowerPoint, the ribbon appears the same way it did the last time you used PowerPoint. The modules in this book begin with the ribbon always displayed.

In addition to the main tabs, PowerPoint displays **contextual tabs** when you perform certain tasks or work with objects such as pictures or tables. If you insert a picture in a PowerPoint presentation, for example, the Picture Format tab appears (Figure 1–7). When you are finished working with the picture, the Picture Format tab disappears from the ribbon. PowerPoint determines when contextual tabs should appear and disappear based on tasks you perform. Some tasks involve more than one contextual tab. For example, when you work with tables, the Table Design tab and the Layout tab appear.

BTW
Adobe Acrobat
If Adobe Acrobat is installed on your system, you might have a 'Create and Share Adobe PDF' button on the Home tab and an Acrobat tab on the ribbon, as shown in Figure 1-6a and throughout this project.

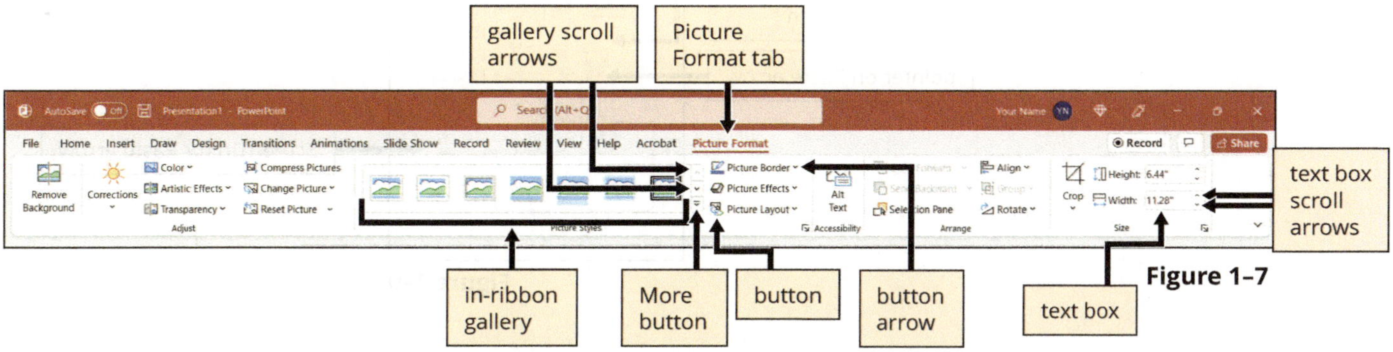

Figure 1–7

Groups on the ribbon include buttons, boxes (text boxes, check boxes, etc.), and galleries (Figure 1–8). A **gallery** is a collection of choices, often graphical, arranged in a grid or in a list that you can browse through before making a selection. You can scroll through choices in an in-ribbon gallery by clicking the gallery's scroll arrows. Or, you can click a gallery's More button to view more gallery options on the screen at a time.

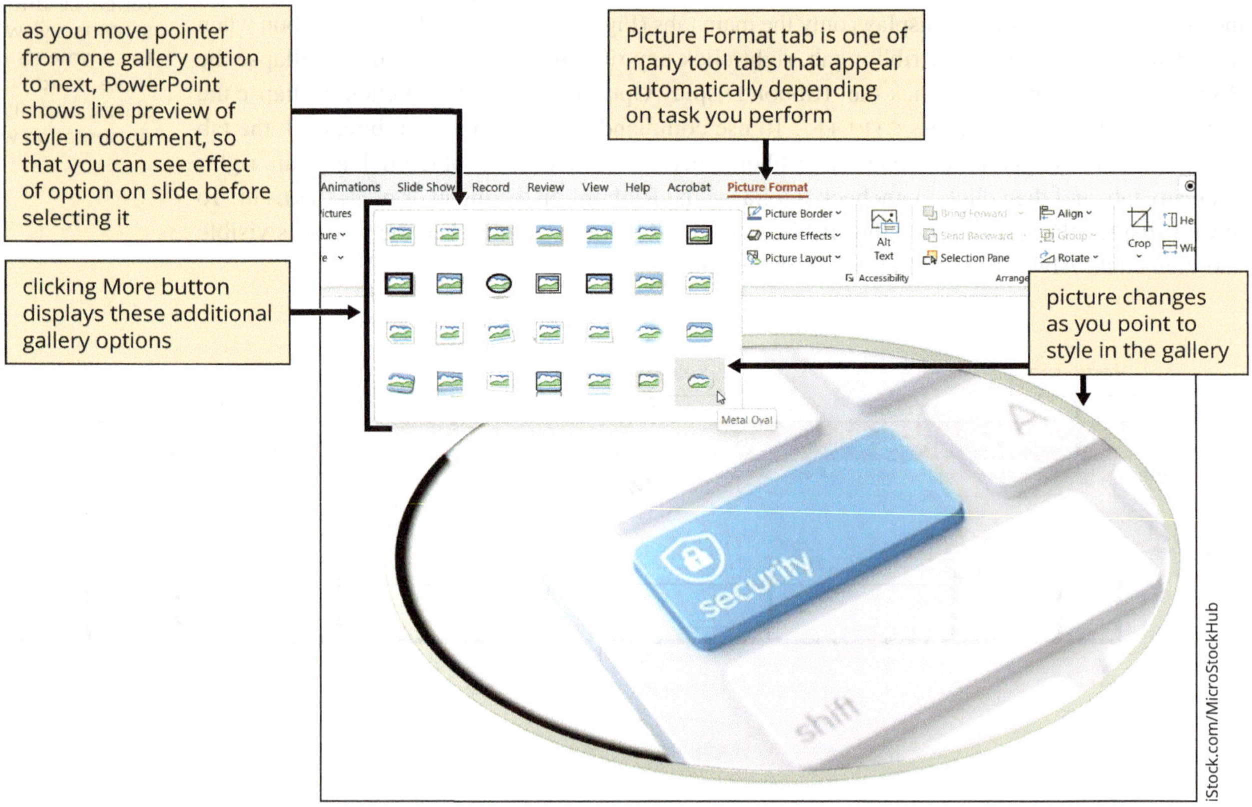

Figure 1–8

Some buttons and boxes have arrows that, when clicked, also display a gallery; others always cause a gallery to be displayed when clicked. Most galleries support **Live Preview**, a feature that allows you to point to a gallery choice and see its effect in the presentation without actually selecting the choice.

Some commands on the ribbon display an image to help you remember their function. When you point to a command on the ribbon, all or part of the command glows in a shade of gray, and a ScreenTip appears on the screen. A **ScreenTip** is a label that appears when you point to a button or object that provides the name of the command, its purpose, available keyboard shortcut(s), and sometimes instructions for how to obtain help about the command (Figure 1–9).

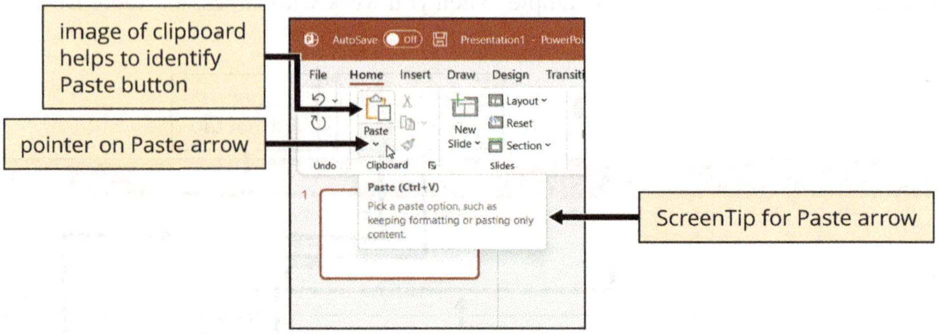

Figure 1–9

Some groups on the ribbon have a small arrow in the lower-right corner, called a **Dialog Box Launcher**, that when clicked, displays a dialog box or a pane with additional options for the group (Figure 1–10). When presented with a dialog box, you make selections and must close the dialog box before returning to the presentation. A **pane**, in contrast to a dialog box, is a window that can remain open and visible while you work in the presentation and provides additional options.

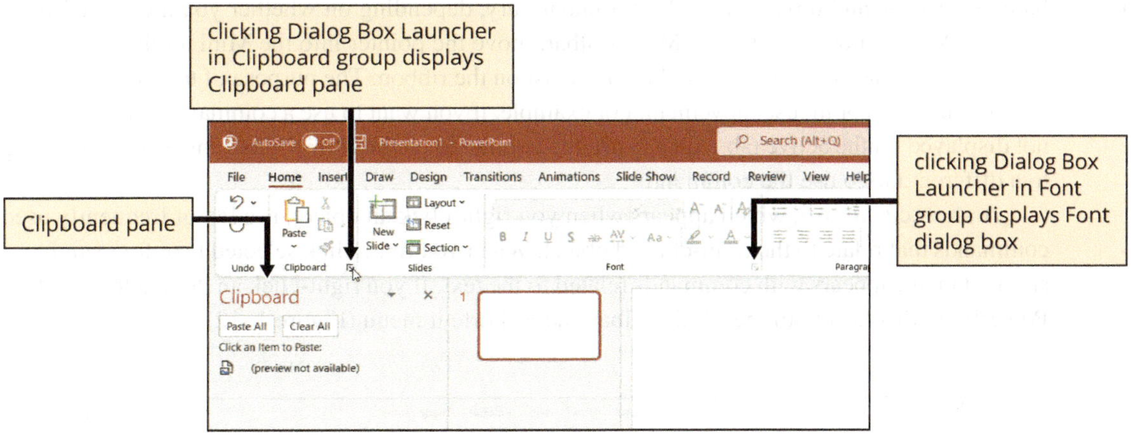

Figure 1–10

Search Box The **Search box**, which appears on the title bar, is used to find a command, perform specific tasks in PowerPoint, or access the PowerPoint Help system (Figure 1–11). As you type in the Search box, the word-wheeling feature displays search results that are refined as you type. For example, if you want to align objects on a slide, you can type "align" in the Search box and then select the appropriate command.

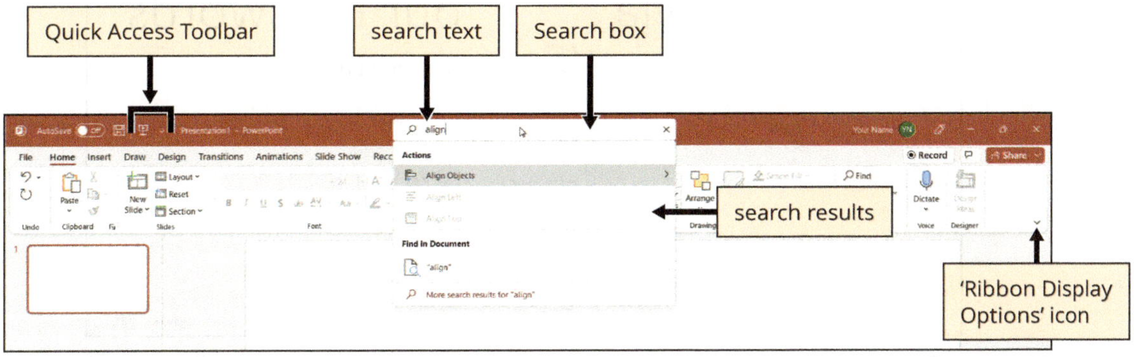

Figure 1–11

Quick Access Toolbar The **Quick Access Toolbar**, located initially (by default) above the ribbon at the left edge of the title bar, provides convenient one-click access to frequently used commands (shown in Figure 1–11). If the Quick Access Toolbar is not displayed, click the 'Ribbon Display Options' icon and then click 'Show Quick Access Toolbar' in the menu. The commands on the Quick Access Toolbar always are available, regardless of the task you are performing.

You can add commands to or delete commands from the Quick Access Toolbar so that it contains the commands you use most often. To do this, click the 'Customize Quick Access Toolbar' button on the Quick Access Toolbar and then select the commands you want to add or remove. As you add commands to the Quick Access Toolbar, its length may interfere with the document title on the title bar. For this reason, PowerPoint provides an option of displaying the Quick Access Toolbar below the ribbon on the Customize Quick Access Toolbar menu.

BTW

Turning Off the Mini Toolbar

If you do not want the Mini toolbar to appear, click File on the ribbon to open Backstage view, click Options in Backstage view, if necessary click General (Options dialog box), remove the check mark from the 'Show Mini Toolbar on selection' check box, and then click OK.

Each time you start PowerPoint, the Quick Access Toolbar appears the same way it did the last time you used PowerPoint. The modules in this book show the Quick Access Toolbar displayed.

Mini Toolbar and Shortcut Menus The **Mini toolbar** is a small toolbar that appears next to selected text and contains the most frequently used text formatting commands such as bold, italic, font color, and font size. If you do not use the Mini toolbar, it disappears from the screen. The buttons, arrows, and boxes on the Mini toolbar vary, depending on whether you are using Touch mode or Mouse mode. To use the Mini toolbar, move the pointer into the Mini toolbar.

All commands on the Mini toolbar also exist on the ribbon. The purpose of the Mini toolbar is to minimize hand or mouse movement. For example, if you want to use a command that currently is not displayed on the active tab, you can use the command on the Mini toolbar instead of switching to a different tab to use the command.

A **shortcut menu**, which appears when you right-click an object, is a list of frequently used commands that relate to the right-clicked object. When you right-click selected text, for example, a shortcut menu appears with commands related to the text. If you right-click an item in the window, PowerPoint displays both the Mini toolbar and a shortcut menu (Figure 1–12).

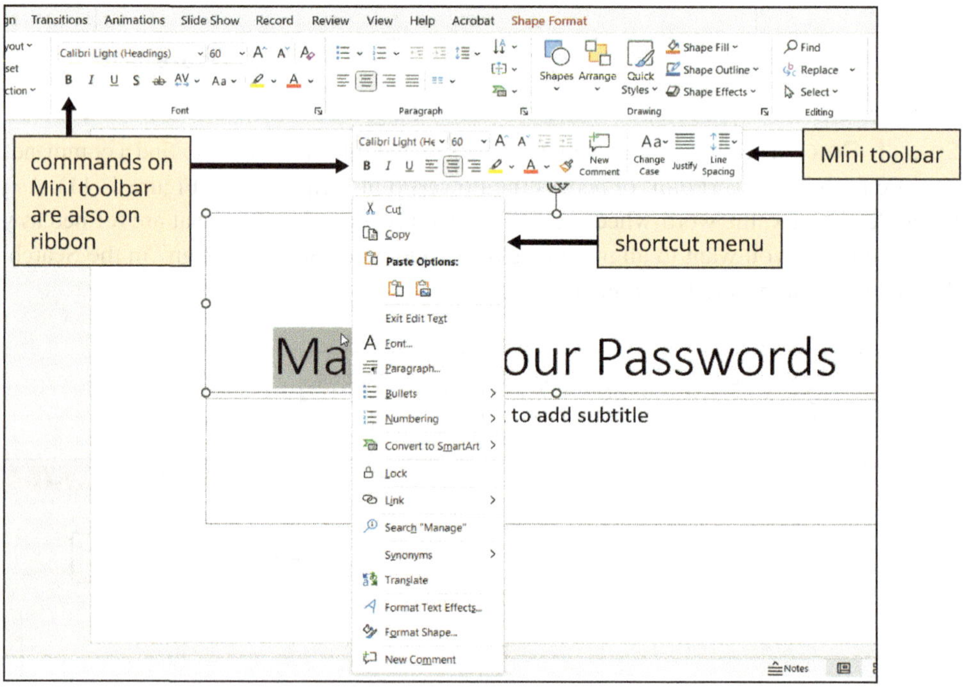

Figure 1–12

KeyTips If you prefer using the keyboard instead of the mouse, you can press ALT on the keyboard to display **KeyTips**, or keyboard code labels, for certain commands (Figure 1–13). To select a command using the keyboard, press the letter or number displayed in the KeyTip, which may cause additional KeyTips related to the selected command to appear. For example, to select the Bold button on the Home tab, press ALT, then press H, and then press 1. To remove KeyTips from the screen, press ALT or ESC until all KeyTips disappear, or click anywhere in the PowerPoint window.

Microsoft Account Area In the **Microsoft account area** (shown in Figure 1–13), you can use the Sign in link to sign in to your Microsoft account. Once signed in, you will see your account information.

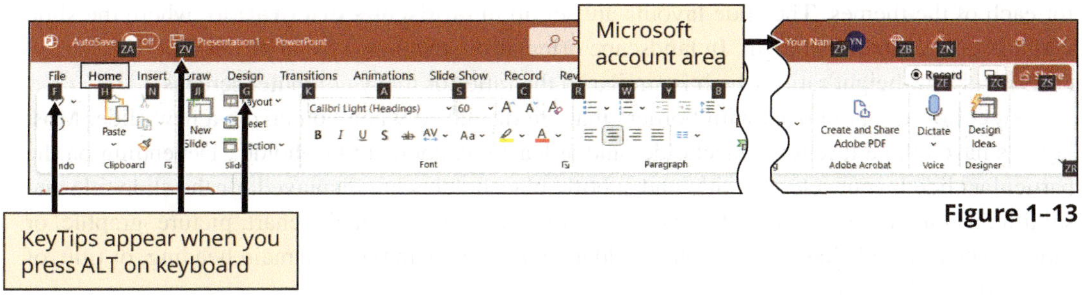

Figure 1–13

To Display a Different Tab on the Ribbon

When you start PowerPoint, the ribbon displays 12 main tabs: File, Home, Insert, Draw, Design, Transitions, Animations, Slide Show, Record, Review, View, and Help. You might have additional tabs, such as Acrobat, depending on the software installed on your system. The tab currently displayed is the active tab. To display a different tab on the ribbon, you click the tab. The following step displays the Design tab, that is, makes it the active tab. **Why?** You are going to change the slide design, so you need to switch tabs to access options for completing this task.

1

- Click Design on the ribbon to display the Design tab (Figure 1–14).
- **Experiment:** Click the other tabs on the ribbon to view their contents. When you are finished, click Design on the ribbon to redisplay the Design tab.

Figure 1–14

Other Ways

1. Press ALT, press letter corresponding to tab to display
2. Press ALT, press LEFT ARROW or RIGHT ARROW until desired tab is displayed

Creating a Title Slide

You easily can give the slides in a presentation a professional and integrated appearance by using a theme. A **theme** is a predefined design with coordinating colors, fonts, and graphical effects such as shadows and reflections that can be applied to presentations to give them a consistent, professional look. Themes are also sometimes called **templates**. Several themes are available when you start PowerPoint, each with a specific name. You also can add or change a theme while you are creating slides. Using one of the formatted themes makes creating a professional-looking presentation easier and quicker than using the Blank Presentation template, where you would need to make all design decisions.

When you open a new presentation, the default Title Slide layout appears. The purpose of this layout is to introduce the presentation to the audience. PowerPoint includes other standard layouts

BTW
Customizing a Slide Layout
PowerPoint provides a wide variety of slide layouts for each theme, but you can customize the layouts to make your deck unique. Display the View tab, click Slide Master (View tab | Master Views group), select the thumbnail below the slide master in the left pane that you would like to customize, and then make the desired modifications.

for each of the themes. The slide layouts are set up in **landscape orientation**, where the slide width is greater than its height. In landscape orientation, the slide size is preset to a Widescreen (16:9) width-to-height ratio, which is similar to the ratio for many computer screens.

Placeholders are boxes with borders that are displayed when you create a new slide. Most layouts have both a title text placeholder and at least one content placeholder. Depending on the particular slide layout selected, title and subtitle placeholders are displayed for the slide title and subtitle; a content text placeholder is displayed for text, art, or a table, chart, picture, graphic, or movie. The title slide has two text placeholders where you can type the main heading, or title, of a new slide and the subtitle.

With the exception of the Blank slide layout, PowerPoint assumes every new slide has a title. Any text you type after a new slide appears becomes title text in the title text placeholder. The following steps change the theme and then create the title slide for this presentation.

Consider This

How do I choose the words for the slide?

All presentations should follow the 7 × 7 rule, which states that each slide should have a maximum of seven paragraphs, and each paragraph should have a maximum of seven words. In most cases, you should use the fewest words possible. PowerPoint designers choose their words carefully and, in turn, help viewers read the slides easily.

In most cases, avoid line wraps. Your audience's eyes want to stop at the end of a line. Thus, plan your words carefully or adjust the font size so that each point displays on only one line.

To Choose a Presentation Theme

As you begin creating a new PowerPoint presentation, you can either start with no design elements by choosing Blank Presentation or you can select one of the available professionally designed themes. A theme provides consistency in design and color throughout the entire presentation by setting the color scheme, font set, and layout of a presentation. This collection of formatting choices includes a set of colors (the Theme Colors group), a set of heading and content text fonts (the Theme Fonts group), and a set of lines and fill effects (the Theme Effects group). These groups allow you to choose and change the appearance of all the slides or individual slides in your presentation. At any time while creating the slide deck, you may decide to switch the theme so that the slides have a totally different appearance. The following steps change the theme for this presentation from the Office Theme to the Berlin theme. **Why?** The title slide will have text and a picture, so you want to select a theme, like Berlin, with a background that attracts attention but does not distract from the picture.

1

- With the Design tab displayed and the slide selected, point to the More button (Design tab | Themes group) (Figure 1–15).

Q&A Why does a gray border display around the first theme thumbnail?
The gray border indicates the current theme. PowerPoint applied the default Office Theme when you chose the Blank Presentation theme.

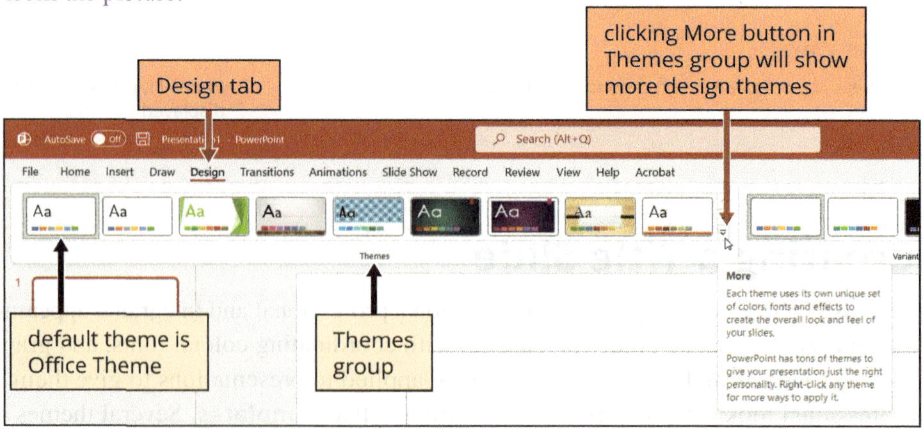

Figure 1–15

2

- Click the More button (Design tab | Themes group) to expand the gallery, which shows more theme gallery options. If necessary, scroll down and then point to the Berlin thumbnail to see a preview of that theme on Slide 1 (Figure 1–16).
- **Experiment:** Point to various themes in the Themes gallery and watch the designs change on Slide 1.

Q&A Are the themes displayed in a specific order?
No. Your themes might be in a different order than shown here.

How can I determine the theme names?
If you point to a theme, a ScreenTip with the theme's name appears on the screen.

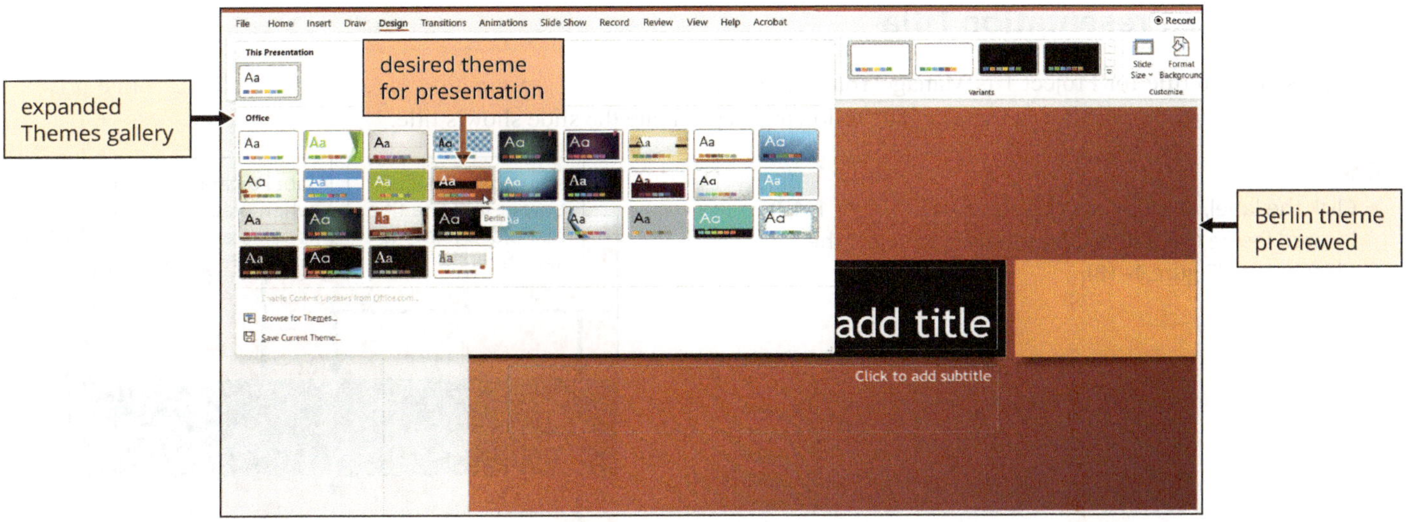

Figure 1–16

3

- Click the Berlin theme to apply this theme to the presentation (Figure 1–17).

Q&A If I decide at some future time that this design does not fit the theme of my presentation, can I apply a different design?
Yes. You can repeat these steps at any time while creating your presentation.

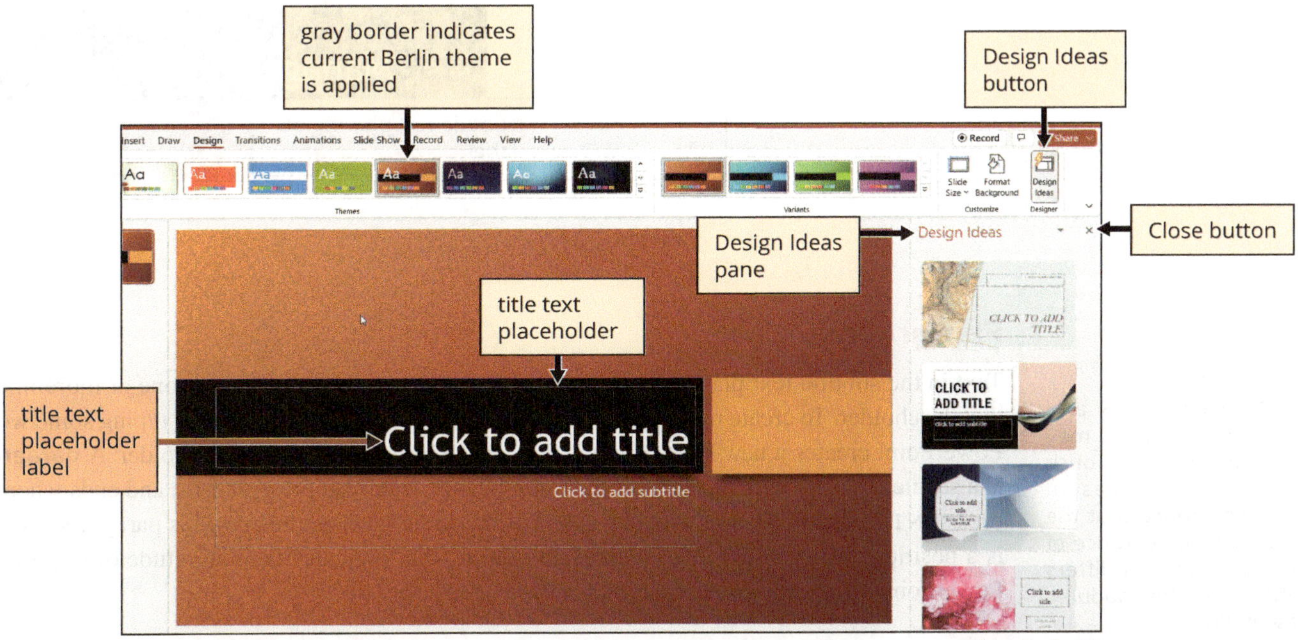

Figure 1–17

4

- If the Design Ideas pane is displayed, click the Close button to close this pane.

Q&A What is the Design Ideas pane?
PowerPoint generates suggestions automatically for arranging pictures, charts, tables, and other content on slides. You can scroll through these ideas and click one that meets your needs. PowerPoint then will arrange your slide content.

How can I view the Design Ideas pane if it is not displayed?
Click the Design Ideas button (Design tab | Designer group) to open the pane.

To Enter the Presentation Title

The presentation title for Project 1 is Manage Your Passwords. **Why?** The presentation focuses on protecting online private information by creating quality passwords. The following steps create the slide show's title.

1

- Click the label, 'Click to add title', (shown in Figure 1-17) located inside the title text placeholder to select the placeholder (Figure 1-18).

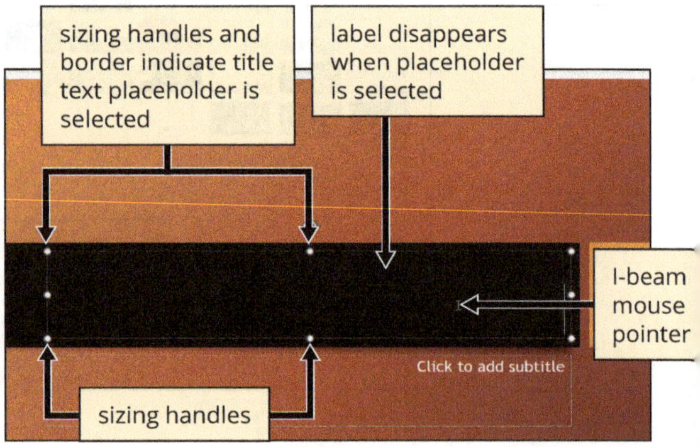

Figure 1-18

2

- Type **Manage Your Passwords** in the title text placeholder. Do not press ENTER (Figure 1-19).

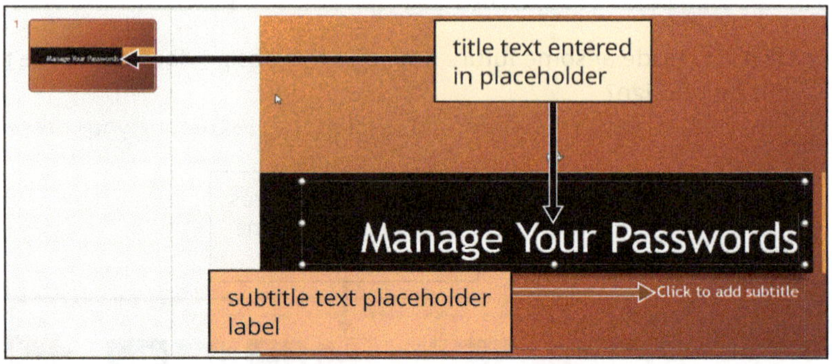

Figure 1-19

BTW
Touch Mode Differences
The Microsoft 365 and Windows interfaces may vary if you are using Touch mode. For this reason, you might notice that the function or appearance of your touch screen differs slightly from this module's presentation.

Paragraphs

Text in the subtitle text placeholder supports the title text. It can appear on one or more lines in the placeholder. To create more than one subtitle line, you press ENTER after typing some words. PowerPoint creates a new line, which is the second paragraph in the placeholder. A **paragraph** is a segment of text with the same format that begins when you press ENTER and ends when you press ENTER again. This new paragraph is at the same level as the previous paragraph. A **level** is a position within a structure, such as an outline, that indicates the magnitude of importance. PowerPoint allows for five paragraph levels.

To Enter the Presentation Subtitle Paragraph

The first subtitle paragraph is related to the title. **Why?** The subtitle emphasizes that strong passwords can offer security when working online. The following steps enter the presentation subtitle.

1

- Click the label, 'Click to add subtitle', located inside the subtitle text placeholder to select the placeholder (Figure 1–20).

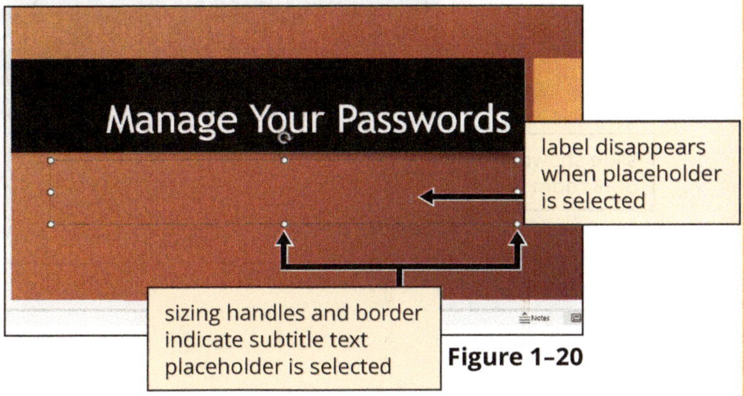

Figure 1–20

2

- Type **The Importance of Online Security** but do not press ENTER (Figure 1–21).

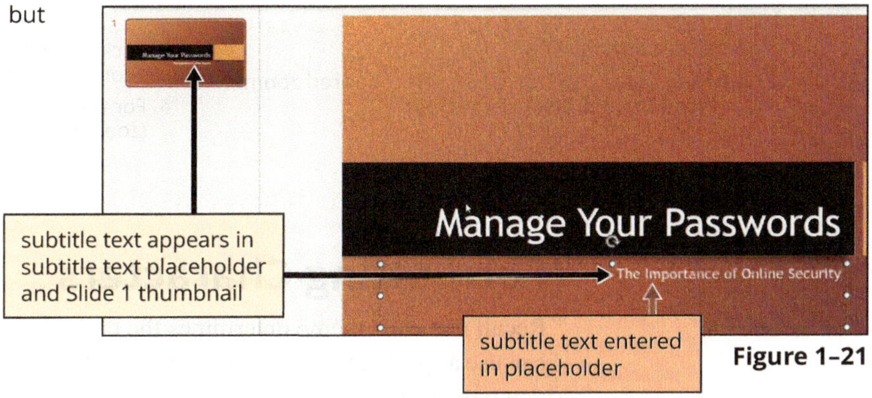

Figure 1–21

To Zoom a Slide

You can **zoom** the view of the slide on the screen so that the text or other content is enlarged or shrunk. When you zoom in, you get a close-up view of your slide; when you zoom out, you see more of the slide at a reduced size. You will be modifying the text and other slide components as you create the presentation, so you can enlarge the slide on the screen. **Why?** Zooming the slide can help you see slide elements more clearly so that you can position them precisely where desired. The following step changes the zoom to 90 percent.

1

- Click the Zoom In or Zoom Out button as many times as necessary until the Zoom button on the status bar displays 90% on its face (Figure 1–22).
- **Experiment:** Repeatedly click the Zoom In and Zoom Out buttons on the status bar and watch the size of the slide change in the Slide pane.

Q&A If I change the zoom percentage, will the slide display differently when I run the presentation?
No. Changing the zoom helps you develop the slide content and does not affect the slide show.

Figure 1–22

Other Ways

1. Drag Zoom slider on status bar
2. Click Zoom level button on status bar, select desired zoom percent or type (Zoom dialog box), click OK
3. Click Zoom button (View tab | Zoom group), select desired zoom percent or type (Zoom dialog box), click OK
4. For touch screens: Pinch two fingers together in Slide pane (zoom out) or stretch two fingers apart (zoom in)

Formatting Characters

Recall that each theme determines the color scheme, font set, and layout of a presentation. You can use a specific theme and then change the characters' formats any time before, during, or after you type the text.

Fonts and Font Styles

Characters that appear on the screen are a specific shape and size. Examples of how you can modify the appearance, or **formatting**, of these typed characters on the screen and in print include changing the font, style, size, color, and alignment. The **font**, or typeface, defines the appearance and shape of the letters, numbers, and special characters. A **font style** indicates how the characters are formatted. PowerPoint's text font styles include regular, italic, bold, and bold italic. **Font size** specifies the height of the characters measured in units called points. A **point** is 1/72 of an inch in height. Thus, a character with a font size of 36 is 36/72 (or 1/2) of an inch in height. **Font color** defines the hue of the characters.

This presentation uses the Berlin document theme, which has particular font styles and font sizes. The Berlin document theme default title text font is named Trebuchet MS. It has no special effects, and its size is 54 point. The Berlin default subtitle text font also is Trebuchet MS with a font size of 20 point.

To Select a Paragraph

You can use many techniques to format characters. When you want to apply the same formats to multiple words or paragraphs, it is helpful to select these words. **Why?** It is efficient to select the desired text and then make the desired changes to all the characters simultaneously. The first formatting change you will make will apply to the title slide subtitle. The following step selects this paragraph.

1

- Triple-click the paragraph, The Importance of Online Security, in the subtitle text placeholder to select the paragraph (Figure 1–23).

Figure 1–23

Other Ways

1. Position pointer to left of first paragraph and drag to end of line

To Italicize Text

Different font styles often are used on slides. **Why?** These style changes make the words more appealing to the reader and emphasize particular text. **Italic** text has a slanted appearance. Used sparingly, it draws the readers' eyes to these characters. The following step adds emphasis to the line of the subtitle text by changing regular text to italic text.

1

- With the subtitle text still selected, click the Italic button on the Mini toolbar to italicize that text on the slide (Figure 1–24).

Q&A If I change my mind and decide not to italicize the text, how can I remove this style?
Immediately click the Undo button on the Home tab in the Undo group, click the Italic button a second time, or press CTRL+Z. Your Quick Access Toolbar also may include the Undo button.

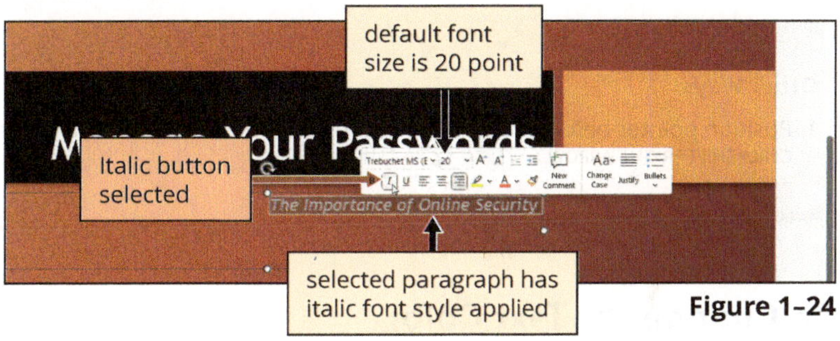

Figure 1–24

Other Ways

1. Right-click selected text, click Italic button in Mini toolbar near shortcut menu
2. Select text, click Italic button (Home tab | Font group)
3. Click Font dialog box launcher (Home tab | Font group), click Font tab (Font dialog box), click Italic in Font style list, click OK
4. Select text, press CTRL+I

To Increase Font Size

Why? To add emphasis, you increase the font size for the subtitle text. The 'Increase Font Size' button on the Mini toolbar increases the font size in preset increments. The following step uses this button to increase the font size.

1

- With the text, The Importance of Online Security, selected, click the 'Increase Font Size' button on the Mini toolbar three times to increase the font size of the selected text from 20 to 32 point (Figure 1–25).

Q&A If the Mini toolbar disappears from the screen, how can I display it again?
Right-click the selected text, and the Mini toolbar should appear below a shortcut menu.

Figure 1–25

Other Ways

1. Click Font Size arrow on Mini toolbar, click desired font size in Font Size gallery
2. Click 'Increase Font Size' button (Home tab | Font group)
3. Click Font Size arrow (Home tab | Font group), click desired font size in Font size gallery
4. Press CTRL+SHIFT+>

To Select a Word

PowerPoint designers use many techniques to emphasize words and characters on a slide. To accentuate the word, Security, on your slide, you want to increase the font size and change the font color to yellow for this word in the title text. To make these changes, you should begin by selecting the word, Security. **Why?** You could perform these actions separately, but it is more efficient to select the word and then change the font attributes. The following step selects a word.

1

- Position the pointer somewhere in the word to be selected (in this case, in the word, Security).
- Double-click the word to select it (Figure 1–26).

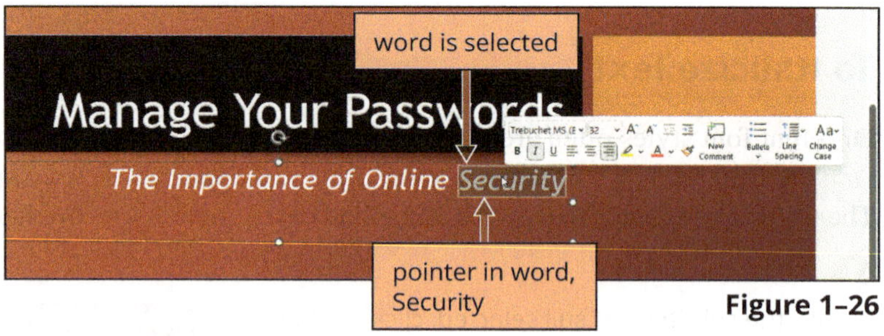

Figure 1–26

Other Ways

1. Position pointer before first character, press CTRL+SHIFT+RIGHT ARROW
2. Position pointer before first character, drag right to select word

To Change the Text Color

PowerPoint allows you to use one or more text colors in a presentation. You decide to change the color of the word you selected, Security. **Why?** The color, yellow, adds subtle emphasis to this word in your subtitle slide text. The following steps change the font color from white to yellow.

1

- With the word, Security, selected, click the Font Color arrow on the Mini toolbar to display the Font Color gallery, which includes Theme Colors and Standard Colors (Figure 1–27).
- **Experiment:** Point to various colors in the gallery and watch the word's font color change.

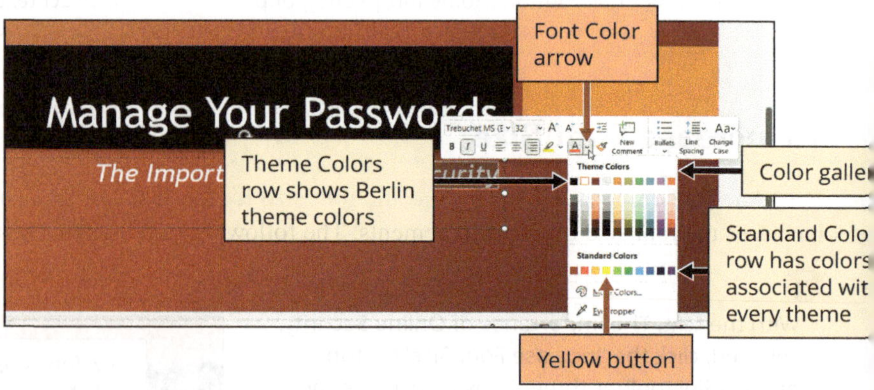

Figure 1–27

2

- Click Yellow in the Standard Colors row on the Mini toolbar (fourth color from left) to change the font color to Yellow (Figure 1–28).

Q&A What is the difference between the colors shown in the Theme Colors area and the Standard Colors?
The 10 colors in the top row of the Theme Colors area are two text, two background, and six accent colors in the Berlin theme; the five colors in each column under the top row display different transparencies. The Standard Colors are available in every document theme.

Figure 1–28

3

- Click outside the selected area to deselect the word.

Other Ways

1. Right-click selected text, click Font on shortcut menu, click Font Color button, click desired color
2. Click Font Color arrow (Home tab | Font group), click desired color

To Zoom a Slide

You have modified the subtitle text on Slide 1, so you now can zoom out to see more of the slide. The following step changes the zoom to 70 percent.

1 Click the Zoom Out button as many times as necessary until the Zoom button on the status bar displays 70% on its face (Figure 1–29).

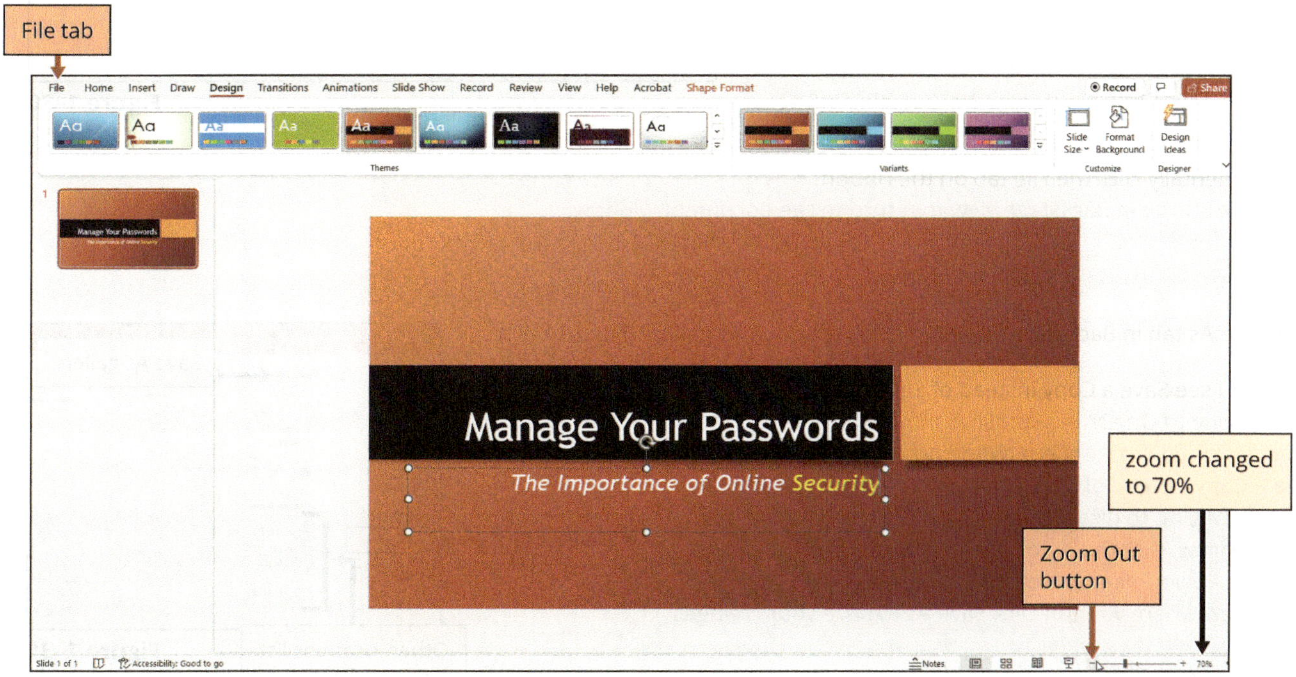

Figure 1–29

To Save a Presentation for the First Time

While you are building slides in a presentation, the computer or device stores it in memory. When you **save** a presentation, it is stored permanently on a storage medium such as a hard disk, USB flash drive, or online using a cloud storage service such as OneDrive so that you can retrieve it later. Once information is saved, it is referred to as a **file**. A **file name** is a unique, descriptive name assigned to a file when it is saved.

When saving a presentation, you must decide which storage medium to use:

- If you always work on the same computer and have no need to transport your projects to a different location, then your computer's hard drive will suffice as a storage location. It is a good idea, however, to save a backup copy of your projects on a separate medium in case the file becomes corrupted or the computer's hard drive fails. The documents created in this book are saved to the computer's hard drive.
- If you plan to work on your documents in various locations or on multiple computers or mobile devices, then you should save your documents on a portable medium, such as a USB flash drive. Alternatively, you can save your documents to an online cloud storage service such as OneDrive.

BTW
Organizing Files and Folders
You should organize and store files in folders so that you easily can find the files later. For example, if you are taking an introductory technology class called CIS 101, a good practice would be to save all PowerPoint files in a PowerPoint folder in a CIS 101 folder.

The following steps save a presentation in the Documents library on your computer's hard drive using the file name, Passwords. **Why?** You have performed many tasks while creating this project and do not want to risk losing the work completed thus far. Accordingly, you should save the presentation.

1

- Click File on the ribbon (shown in Figure 1–29) to display Backstage view (Figure 1–30).

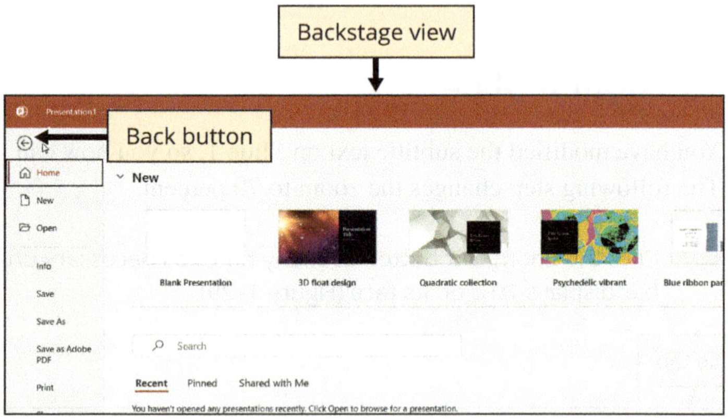

Figure 1–30

Q&A What is the purpose of the File tab on the ribbon, and what is Backstage view?
The File tab opens Backstage view in PowerPoint. **Backstage view** contains commands that allow you to manage files and options for PowerPoint. As you click different tabs along the left side of Backstage view, the associated gallery displays on the right side of Backstage view.

What if I accidentally click the File tab on the ribbon?
Click the Back button in Backstage view to return to the document window.

2

- Click the Save As tab in Backstage view to display the Save As gallery (Figure 1–31).

Q&A What if I see Save a Copy instead of Save As?
If you are saving to OneDrive, AutoSave may be enabled to save your changes as you make them. When AutoSave is enabled, you see Save a Copy instead of Save As. You can use Save a Copy in place of Save As, or, to disable AutoSave, click the Back button in Backstage view, click the AutoSave On button in the upper-left corner of the PowerPoint window to turn it to Off, and return to Backstage view where you can click Save As to save your changes manually.

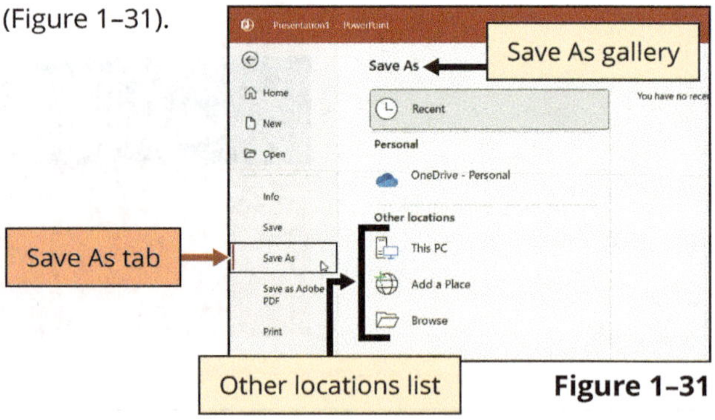

Figure 1–31

3

- If you are saving to OneDrive, click OneDrive in the Save As gallery, or if AutoSave is enabled, click Save a Copy to save to OneDrive. Otherwise, click This PC in the Other locations list to display the default save location on the computer or mobile device (Figure 1–32).

Q&A Can I type the file name below the default save location that displays in the Save As gallery?
If you want to save the file in the default location, you can type the file name in the text box below the default save location and then click the Save button to the right of the default save location. These steps show how to change to a different location on This PC.

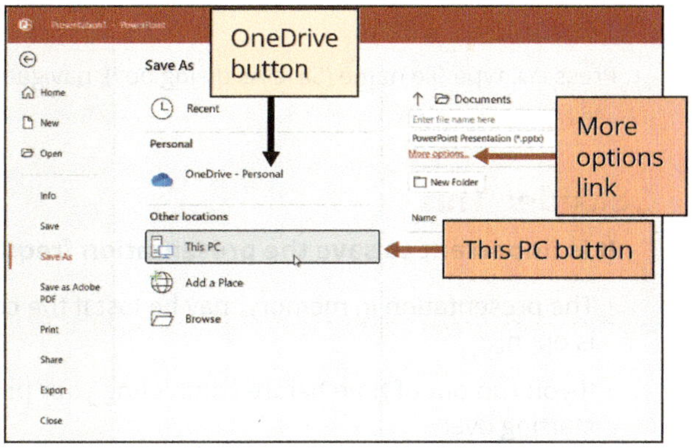

Figure 1–32

4

- Click the More options link to display the Save As dialog box.
- If necessary, click Documents in the Navigation pane to select the Documents library as the save location or navigate to the location specified by your instructor to save your presentation.
- Type **Passwords** in the File name box to specify the file name for the presentation (Figure 1–33).

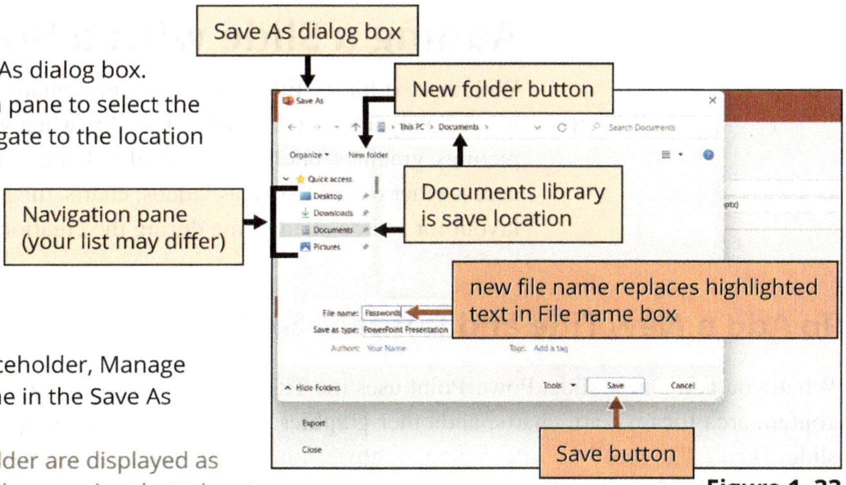

Figure 1–33

Q&A Why did the words from the title text placeholder, Manage Your Passwords, display as the default file name in the Save As dialog box?
Words from the presentation title text placeholder are displayed as the default file name. Because the suggested file name is selected in the File Name box, you do not need to delete it; as soon as you begin typing, the new file name replaces the selected text.

Do I have to save to the Documents library?
No. You can save to any device, default folder, or a different folder. You also can create your own folders by clicking the New folder button shown in Figure 1–33. To save to a different location, navigate to that location in the Navigation pane instead of clicking Documents.

What characters can I use in a file name?
The only invalid characters are the backslash (\), slash (/), colon (:), asterisk (*), question mark (?), quotation mark ("), less than symbol (<), greater than symbol (>), and vertical bar (|).

Why is my list of files, folders, and drives arranged and named differently from those shown in the figure?
Your computer or mobile device's configuration determines how the list of files and folders is displayed and how drives are named. You can change the save location by clicking links in the Navigation pane.

5

- Click the Save button to save the presentation with the file name, Passwords, to the save location (Figure 1–34).

Q&A How do I know that PowerPoint saved the presentation?
While PowerPoint is saving your file, it briefly displays a message on the status bar indicating the amount of the file saved. When the presentation appears after saving, the new file name will be displayed in the title bar.

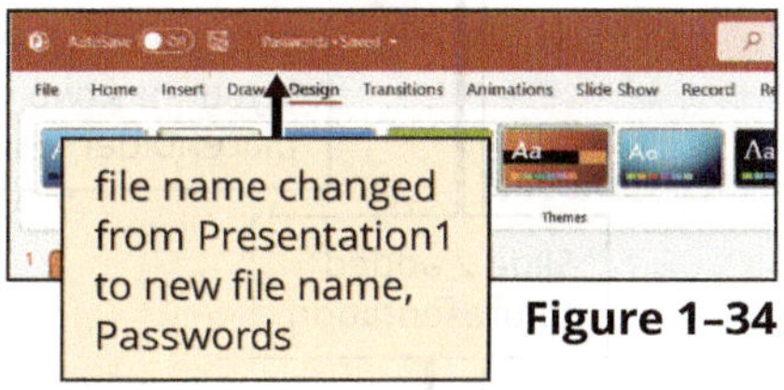

Figure 1–34

BTW
File Type
Depending on your Windows settings, the file type .pptx may be displayed on the title bar immediately to the right of the file name after you save the file. The file type .pptx identifies a PowerPoint presentation.

Other Ways

1. Press F12, type file name (Save As dialog box), navigate to desired save location, click Save

Consider This

It is important to save the presentation frequently for the following reasons:

- The presentation in memory may be lost if the computer is turned off or you lose electrical power while PowerPoint is open.
- If you run out of time before completing your presentation, you may finish your project at a future time without starting over.

Adding a Slide with a Bulleted List

With the text for the title slide for the presentation created, the next step is to add the first text slide immediately after the title slide. Usually, when you create a presentation, you add slides with text, pictures, graphics, or charts. Some placeholders allow you to double-click the placeholder and then access other objects, such as videos, charts, diagrams, and organization charts. You can change the layout for a slide at any time during the creation of a presentation.

To Add a New Title and Content Slide

When you add a new slide, PowerPoint uses the Title and Content slide layout. This layout provides a title placeholder and a content area for text, art, charts, and other graphics. A vertical scroll bar appears in the Slide pane when you add the second slide. **Why?** The scroll bar allows you to move from slide to slide easily. A small thumbnail image of this slide also appears in the Slides tab. The following step adds a new slide with the Title and Content slide layout.

1

- Click Home on the ribbon to display the Home tab.
- Click the New Slide button (Home tab | Slides group) to insert a new slide with the Title and Content layout (Figure 1–35).

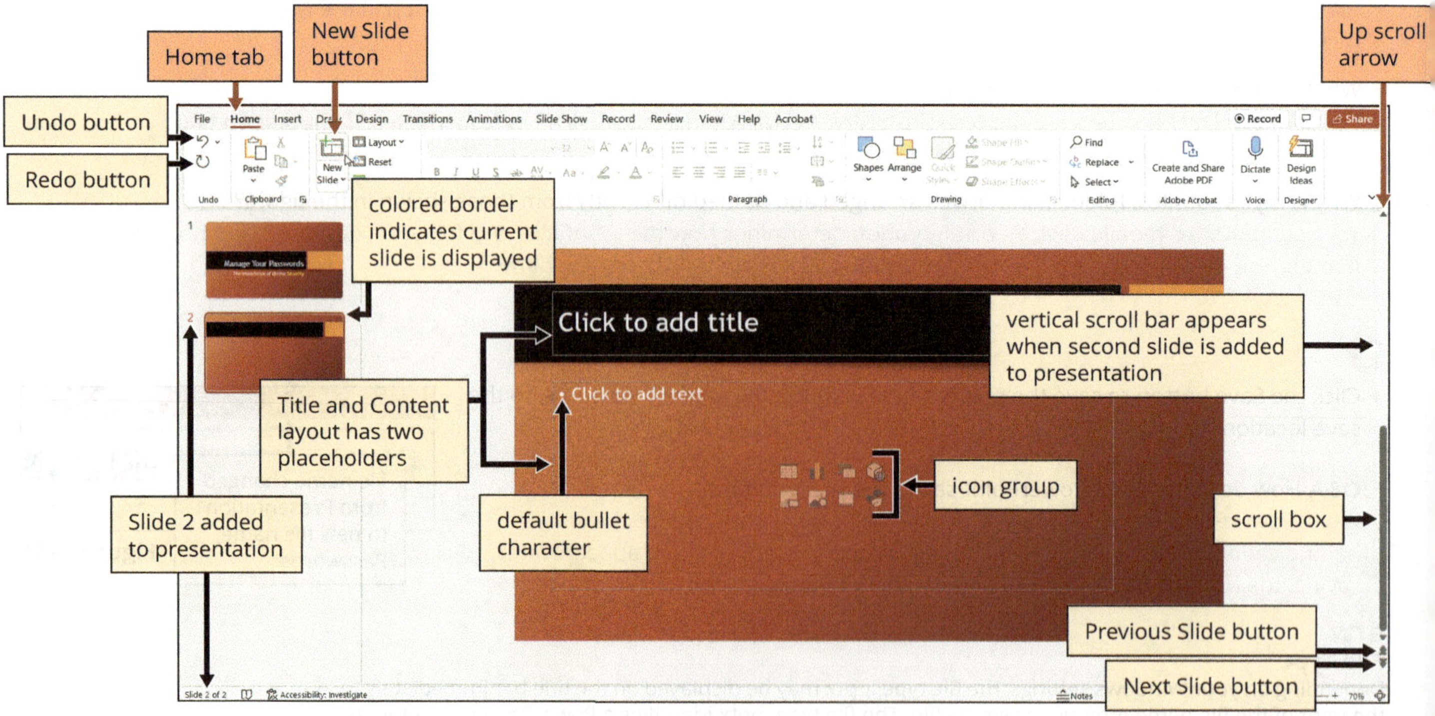

Figure 1–35

Q&A Why does the bullet character display a white dot?
The Berlin document theme determines the bullet characters. Each paragraph level has an associated bullet character.

I clicked the New Slide arrow instead of the New Slide button. What should I do?
Click the Title and Content slide thumbnail in the Berlin layout gallery.

How do I know which slide number I am viewing?
The left edge of the status bar shows the current slide number followed by the total number of slides in the document. In addition, the slide number is displayed to the left of the slide thumbnail.

What are the icons grouped in the middle of the Slide pane?
You can click one of the icons to insert a specific type of content: table, chart, SmartArt graphic, 3D model, picture, online picture, video, or icon.

Other Ways

1. Click New Slide button (Insert tab | Slides group)
2. Press CTRL+M

Correcting a Mistake When Typing

If you type the wrong letter, press BACKSPACE to erase all the characters back to and including the one that is incorrect. If you mistakenly press ENTER after typing the title and the insertion point is on the new line, simply press BACKSPACE to return the insertion point to the right of the last letter in the previous line.

By default, PowerPoint allows you to reverse up to the last 20 changes by clicking the Undo button (Home tab | Undo group), shown in Figure 1–35. The ScreenTip that appears when you point to the Undo button changes to indicate the type of change just made. For example, if you type text in the title text placeholder and then point to the Undo button, the ScreenTip that appears is Undo Typing. For clarity, when referencing the Undo button in this project, the name displaying in the ScreenTip is used. You can reapply a change that you reversed with the Undo button by clicking the Redo button (Home tab | Undo group). Clicking the Redo button reverses the last undo action. The ScreenTip name reflects the type of reversal last performed.

Creating a Multilevel Bulleted List

The information in the Slide 2 text placeholder is presented in a bulleted list with three levels. A **bulleted list** is a series of paragraphs, each of which may be preceded by a bullet character, such as a dot, arrow, or checkmark. Most themes display a bullet character at the start of a paragraph by default. Some slides show more than one level of bulleted text, called a **multilevel bulleted list**. In a multilevel bulleted list, a lower-level paragraph is a subset of a higher-level paragraph. It usually contains information that supports the topic in the paragraph immediately above it.

Looking back at Figure 1–1b, you can see that two of the Slide 2 paragraphs appear at the same level, called the first level: Don't use personal information, and Use letters, numbers, and symbols. Beginning with the second level, each paragraph indents to the right of the preceding level and is pushed down to a lower level. For example, if you increase the indent of a first-level paragraph, it becomes a second-level paragraph. The second and fourth paragraphs on Slide 2 are second-level paragraphs. The last paragraph, Randomize sequences, is a third-level paragraph.

Creating a text slide with a multilevel bulleted list requires several steps. Initially, you enter a slide title in the title text placeholder. Next, you select the content text placeholder. Then, you type the text for the multilevel bulleted list, increasing and decreasing the indents as needed. The next several sections enter the slide title and slide text with a multilevel bulleted list.

To Enter a Slide Title

PowerPoint assumes every new slide has a title. **Why?** The audience members read the title and then can begin to focus their attention on the information being presented on that slide. The title for Slide 2 is Strong Passwords. The following step enters this title.

1

- Click the label, 'Click to add title', to select it and then type **Strong Passwords** in the title text placeholder. Do not press ENTER (Figure 1–36).

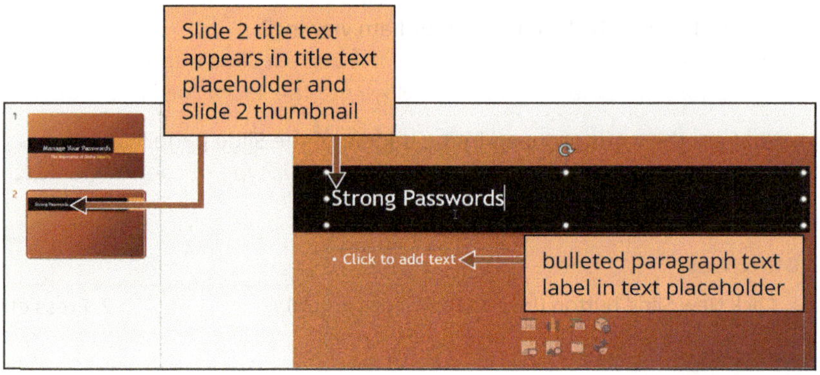

Figure 1–36

To Select a Text Placeholder

Why? Before you can type text into a content placeholder, you first must select it. The following step selects the text placeholder on Slide 2.

1

- Click the label, 'Click to add text', to select the content placeholder (Figure 1–37).

Q&A Why does my pointer have a different shape?
If you move the pointer away from the bullet, it will change shape.

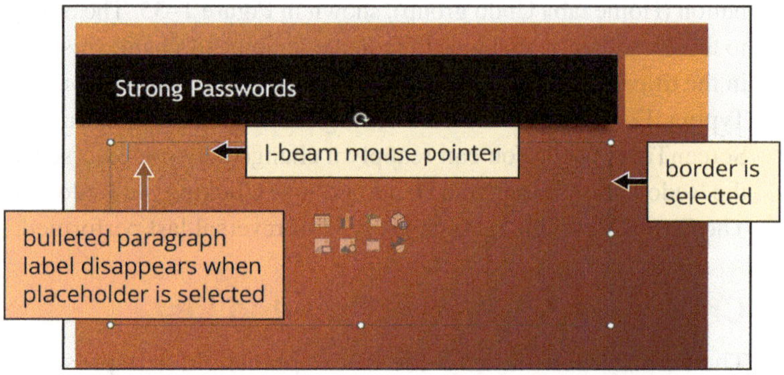

Figure 1–37

Other Ways

1. Press CTRL+ENTER

To Type a Multilevel Bulleted List

The content placeholder provides an area for the text characters. When you click inside a placeholder, you then can type or paste text. As discussed previously, a bulleted list is a list of paragraphs, each of which is preceded by a bullet. A paragraph is a segment of text ended by pressing ENTER. The theme determines the bullets for each level. **Why?** The bullet variations are determined by the specific paragraph levels, and they generally vary in size, shape, and color.

The content text placeholder is selected, so the next step is to type the multilevel bulleted list that consists of six paragraphs, as shown in Figure 1–1b. When you create a lower-level paragraph, you **demote** text (increase the list level); when you create a higher-level paragraph you **promote** text (decrease the list level). The following steps create a multilevel bulleted list consisting of three levels.

1

- Type **Don't use personal information** and then press ENTER (Figure 1–38).

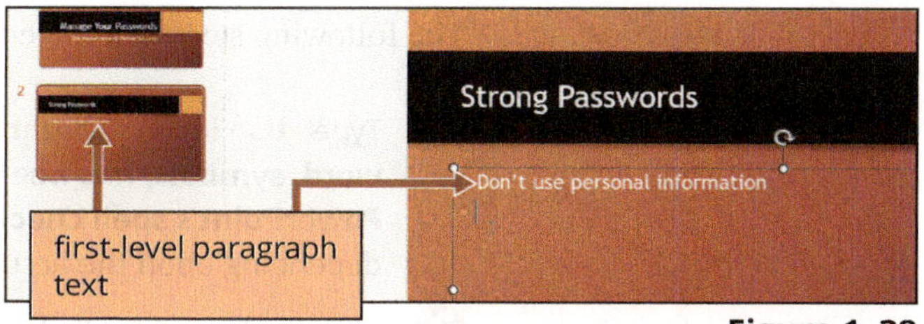

Figure 1–38

2

- Click the 'Increase List Level' button (Home tab | Paragraph group) to indent the second paragraph below the first and create a second-level paragraph (Figure 1–39).

Q&A Why does the bullet for this paragraph have a different size?
A different bullet is assigned to each paragraph level.

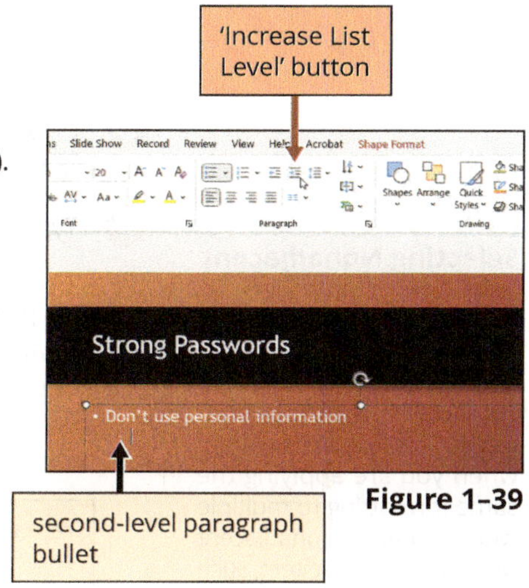

Figure 1–39

3

- Type **Avoid names, birthdays, and addresses** and then press ENTER (Figure 1–40).

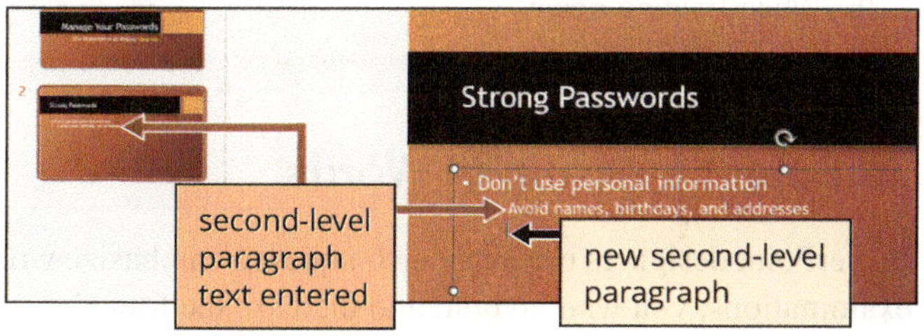

Figure 1–40

4

- Click the 'Decrease List Level' button (Home tab | Paragraph group) so that the second-level paragraph becomes a first-level paragraph (Figure 1–41).

Q&A Can I delete bullets on a slide?
Yes. If you do not want bullets to display in a particular paragraph, click the Bullets button (Home tab | Paragraph group) to toggle them off, or right-click the paragraph and then click the Bullets button on the shortcut menu. You can also position the insertion point at the beginning of the line and press BACKSPACE.

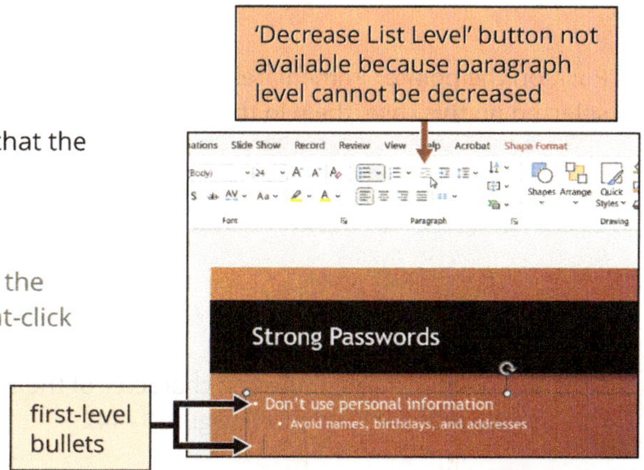

Figure 1–41

Other Ways

1. Press TAB to increase list level; press SHIFT+TAB to decrease list level

To Type the Remaining Text

The following steps complete the text for Slide 2.

1. Type **Use letters, numbers, and simbols** and then press ENTER. **Note: In this step, the word, symbols, has been misspelled intentionally as simbols to illustrate the use of PowerPoint's spell check feature.** Your slides may contain different misspelled words, depending upon the accuracy of your typing.
2. Click the 'Increase List Level' button (Home tab | Paragraph group) to demote the paragraph to the second level.
3. Type **Mix uppercase and lowercase letters** and then press ENTER to add a new paragraph at the same level as the previous paragraph.
4. Click the 'Increase List Level' button (Home tab | Paragraph group) to demote the paragraph to the third level.
5. Type **Randomize sequences** but do not press ENTER (Figure 1–42).

Q&A I pressed ENTER in error, and now a new bullet appears after the last entry on this slide. How can I remove this extra bullet?
Press BACKSPACE twice.

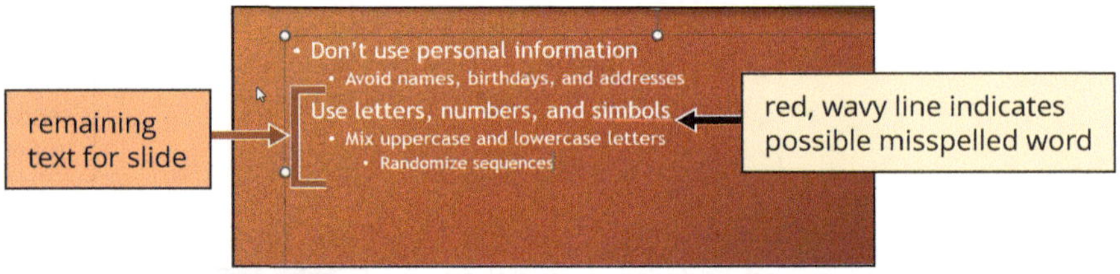

Figure 1–42

BTW
Selecting Nonadjacent Text
In PowerPoint, you can use keyboard keys to select letters, numbers, or special characters not next to each other. This feature is helpful when you are applying the same formatting to multiple words. To select nonadjacent text, select the first item, such as a word or paragraph, and then press and hold down CTRL. While holding down CTRL, select additional items.

To Select a Group of Words

PowerPoint designers use many techniques to emphasize words and characters on a slide. To highlight the availability of regular examinations, you want to bold and increase the font size of the words, personal information, in the body text. The following steps select two words. **Why?** *You could perform these actions separately, but it is more efficient to select the words and then change the font attributes.*

1

- Position the pointer immediately to the left of the first character of the text to be selected (in this case, the p in the word, personal) (Figure 1–43).

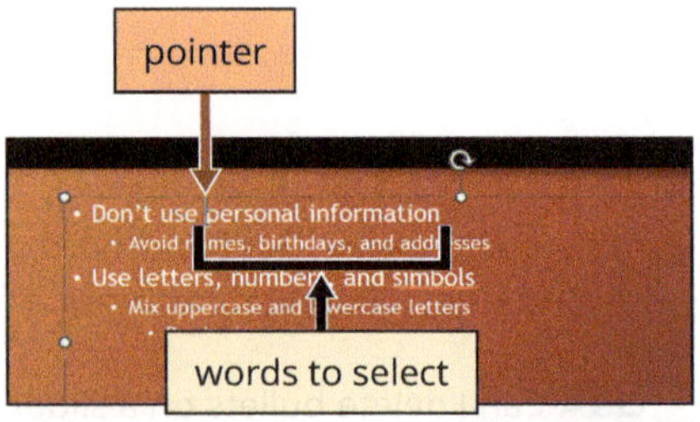

Figure 1–43

2

- Drag the pointer through the last character of the text to be selected (in this case, the n in the word, information) (Figure 1–44).

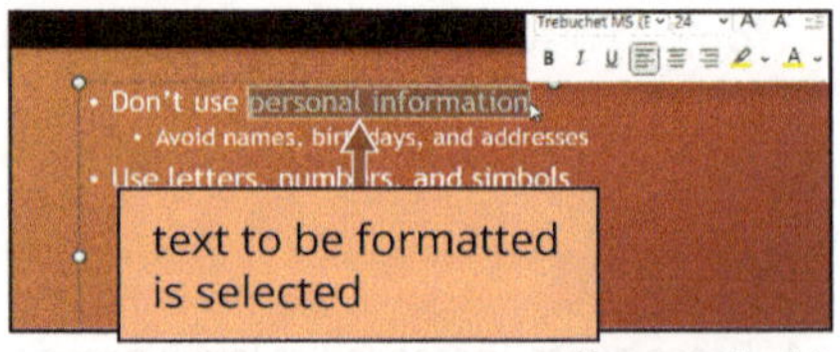

Figure 1–44

Other Ways

1. Press CTRL+SHIFT+RIGHT ARROW repeatedly until desired words are selected

To Bold Text

Why? To add more emphasis to the fact that a person's private details should be avoided, you want to bold the words, personal information. **Bold** characters display somewhat thicker and darker than those that display in a regular font style. Clicking the Bold button on the Mini toolbar is an efficient method of bolding text. The following step bolds this text.

1

- With the words, personal information, selected, click the Bold button on the Mini toolbar to bold the two words (Figure 1–45).

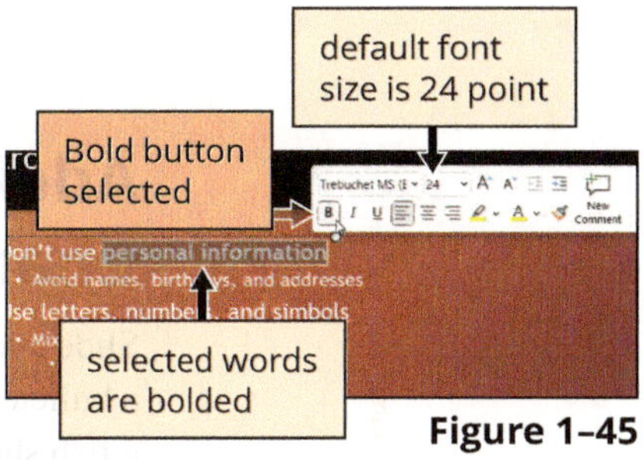

Figure 1–45

Other Ways

1. Right-click selected text, click Font on shortcut menu, click Font tab (Font dialog box), click Bold in Font style list, click OK
2. Select text, click Bold button (Home tab | Font group)
3. Click Font dialog box launcher (Home tab | Font group), click Font tab (Font dialog box), click Bold in Font style list, click OK
4. Select text, press CTRL+B

To Increase Font Size

The following steps increase the font size from 24 to 28 point. **Why?** To add emphasis, you increase the font size for the words, personal information.

1 With the words, personal information, still selected, click the 'Increase Font Size' button on the Mini toolbar once (Figure 1–46).

2 Click outside the selected area to deselect the two words.

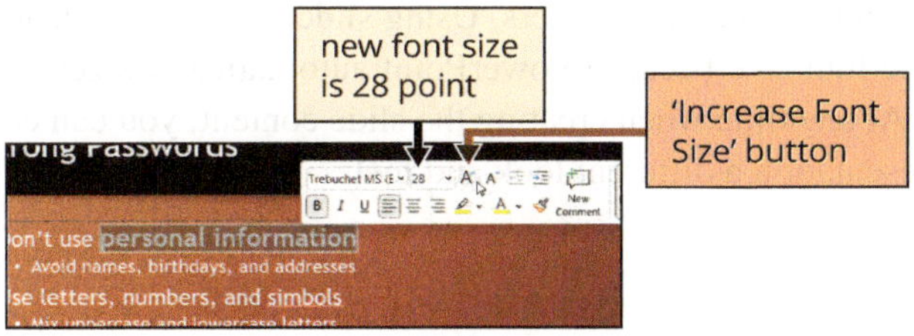

Figure 1–46

To Underline Text

Why? Underlined characters draw the audience's attention to that area of the slide and emphasize important information. Clicking the Underline button on the Mini toolbar is an efficient method of underlining text. To add more emphasis to the fact that the password characters should be arbitrary, you want to underline the word, Randomize. The following steps underline this text.

1

- Select the word, Randomize, on the slide.
- Click the Underline button on the Mini toolbar to underline the word (Figure 1–47).

2

- Click outside the selected area to deselect the word.

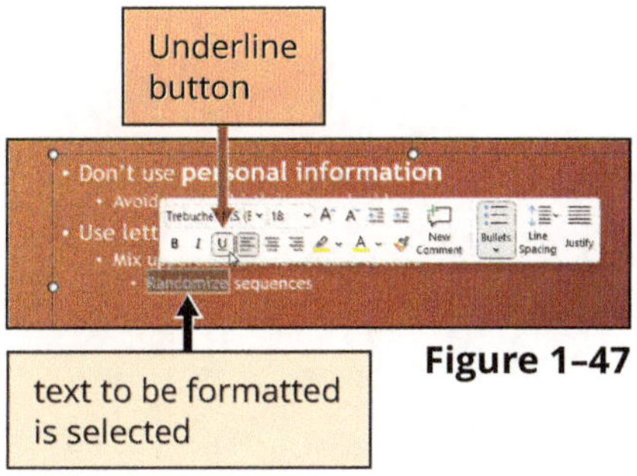

Figure 1–47

Other Ways

1. Right-click selected text, click Font on shortcut menu, click Font tab (Font dialog box), click Underline style arrow, click Single line in Underline style list, click OK
2. Select text, click Underline button (Home tab | Font group)
3. Click Font dialog box launcher (Home tab | Font group), click Font tab (Font dialog box), click Underline style arrow, click Single line in Underline style list, click OK
4. Select text, press CTRL+U

Adding Slides, Changing Slide Layouts, and Changing the Theme

Slide 3 in Figure 1–1c contains a picture of a monitor with several sticky notes and does not contain a bulleted list. Slide 4 in Figure 1–1d contains two pictures: a keyboard with one key selected and a fish shape caught in a net. When you add a new slide, PowerPoint applies the Title and Content layout. This layout and the Title Slide layout for Slide 1 are the default styles. A **layout** specifies the arrangement of placeholders on a slide. These placeholders are arranged in various configurations and can contain text, such as the slide title or a bulleted list, or they can contain content, such as SmartArt graphics, pictures, charts, tables, and shapes. The placement of the text in relationship to the content depends on the slide layout. You can specify a particular slide layout when you add a new slide to a presentation or after you have created the slide.

Using the **layout gallery**, you can choose a slide layout. The nine layouts in this gallery have a variety of placeholders to define text and content positioning and formatting. Three layouts are for text: Title Slide, Section Header, and Title Only. Five are for text and content: Title and Content, Two Content, Comparison, Content with Caption, and Picture with Caption. The Blank layout has no placeholders. If none of these standard layouts meets your design needs, you can create a **custom layout**. A custom layout specifies the number, size, and location of placeholders, background content, and optional slide and placeholder-level properties.

When you change the layout of a slide, PowerPoint retains the text and objects and repositions them into the appropriate placeholders. Using slide layouts eliminates the need to resize objects and change the font size because PowerPoint automatically sizes the objects and text to fit the placeholders. At any time when creating the slide content, you can change the theme and variant to give the presentation a different look and feel.

To Add a New Slide and Enter a Slide Title and Headings

The text on Slide 3 in Figure 1–1c consists of a title and two headings. The appropriate layout for this slide is named Comparison. **Why?** The Comparison layout has two headings and two text placeholders adjacent to each other, so an audience member easily can compare and contrast the items shown side by side. The following steps add Slide 3 to the presentation with the Comparison layout and then enter the title and heading text for this slide.

1

- Click the New Slide arrow in the Slides group to display the Berlin layout gallery (Figure 1–48).

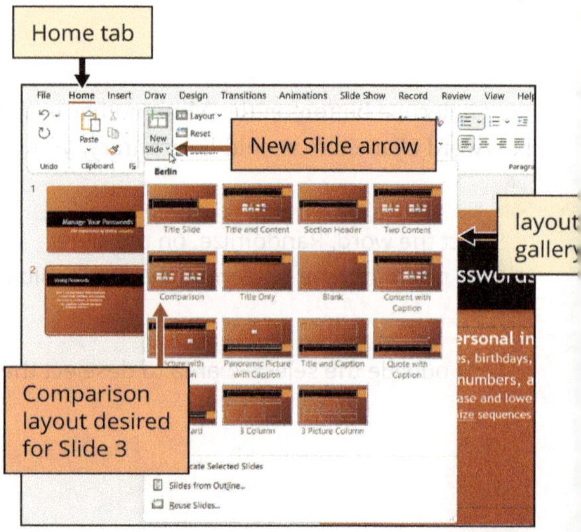

Figure 1–48

2

- Click Comparison to add Slide 3 and apply that layout (Figure 1–49).

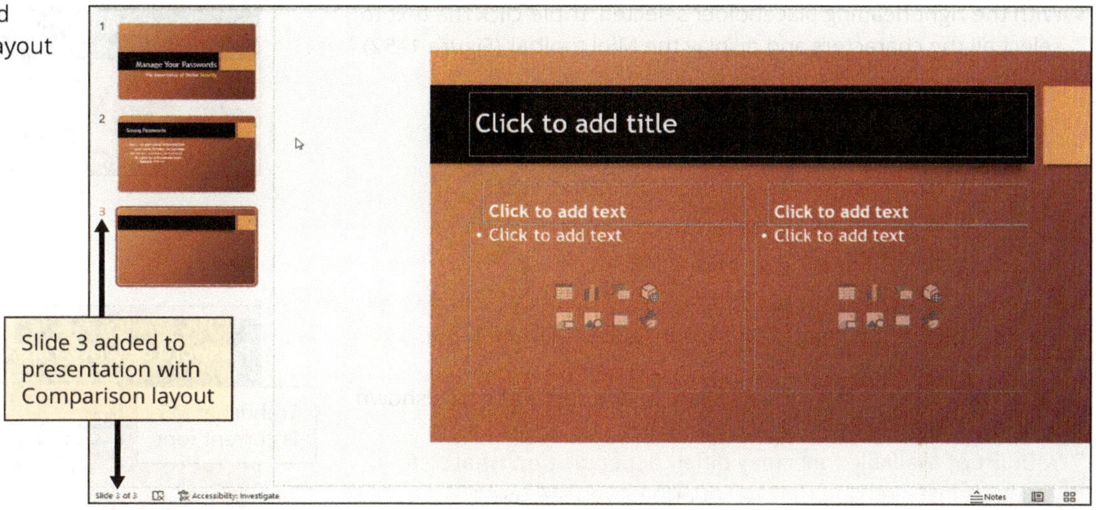

Figure 1–49

3

- Type **Comon Password Security Threats** in the title text placeholder. **Note: In this step, the word, Common, has been misspelled intentionally as Comon to illustrate the use of PowerPoint's spell check feature.** Your slides may contain different misspelled words, depending upon the accuracy of your typing.

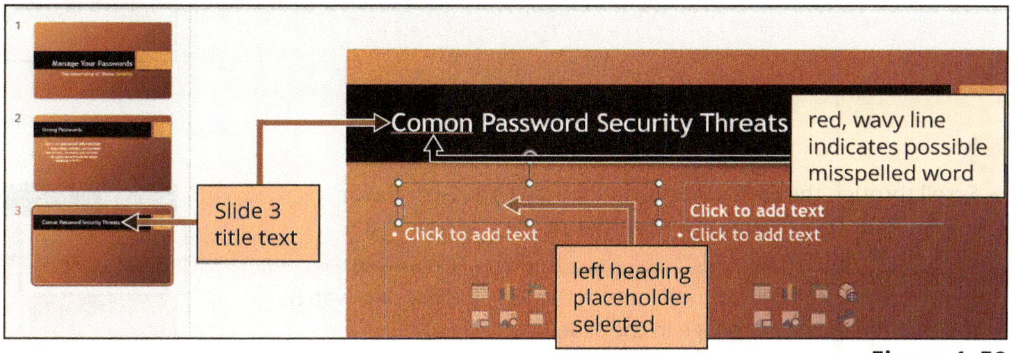

Figure 1–50

- Click the left heading placeholder with the label, 'Click to add text', to select this placeholder (Figure 1–50).

4

- Type **Keylogging Software** in the placeholder.
- Select the right heading placeholder and then type **Phishing Schemes** but do not press ENTER (Figure 1–51).

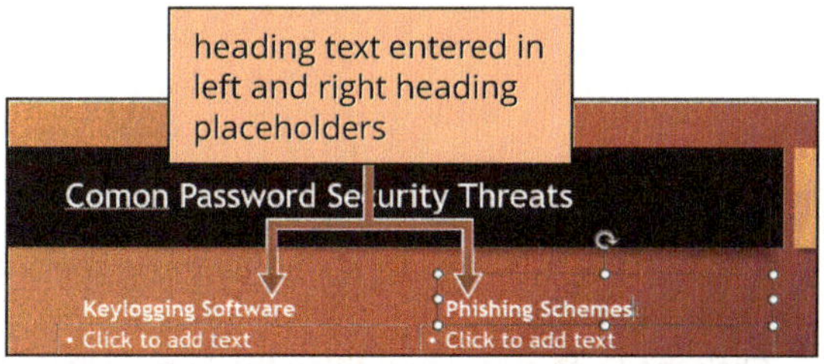

Figure 1–51

To Change the Font

The default theme font is Trebuchet MS, which is shown in the Font box. To draw more attention to two common cybercriminal activities, you want to change the font to Georgia. **Why?** Georgia is a serif typeface, meaning the ends of some of the letters are adorned with small decorations, called serifs. These adornments slow down the viewer's reading speed, which might help them retain the information they saw. To change the font, you must select the text you want to format. Earlier in this module you selected a paragraph and then formatted the characters, and you follow the same procedure to change the font. The following steps change the text font in the two Slide 3 heading placeholders.

1

- With the right heading placeholder selected, triple-click the text to select all the characters and display the Mini toolbar (Figure 1–52).

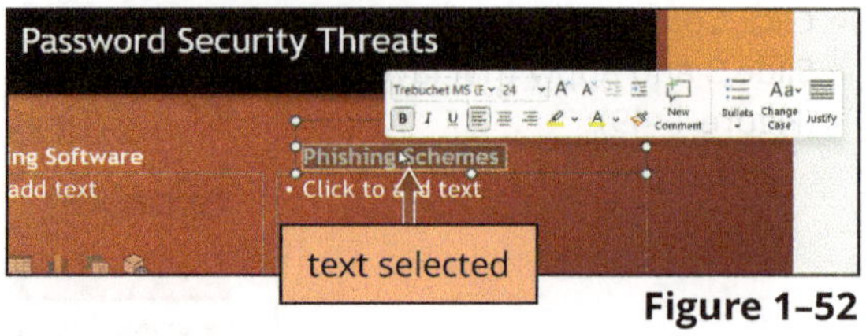

Figure 1–52

2

- Click the Font arrow to display the Font gallery (Figure 1–53).

Q&A Will the fonts in my Font gallery be the same as those shown in Figure 1–53?
Your list of available fonts may differ, depending on what fonts you have installed and the type of printer you are using.

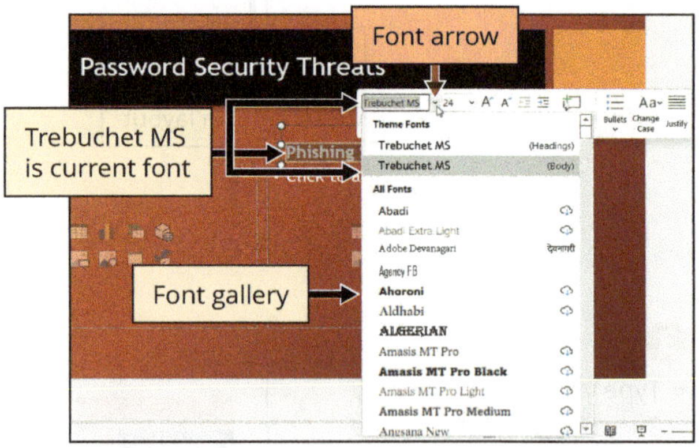

Figure 1–53

3

- Scroll through the Font gallery and then point to Georgia (or a similar font) to display a live preview of the title text in the Georgia font (Figure 1–54).
- **Experiment:** Point to various fonts in the Font gallery and watch the subtitle text font change in the slide.
- Click Georgia (or a similar font) to change the font of the selected text to Georgia.

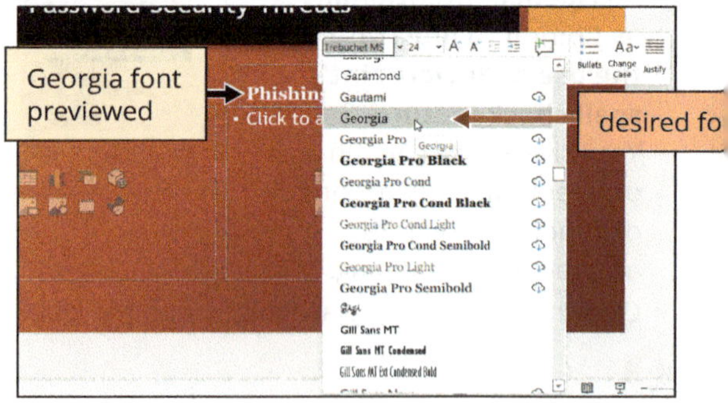

Figure 1–54

4

- Select the words, Keylogging Software, in the left placeholder to display the Mini toolbar.
- Click the Font arrow to display the Font gallery. Note that Georgia is now displayed under Recently Used Fonts.
- Click Georgia (or a similar font) to change the font of the selected text to Georgia (Figure 1–55).

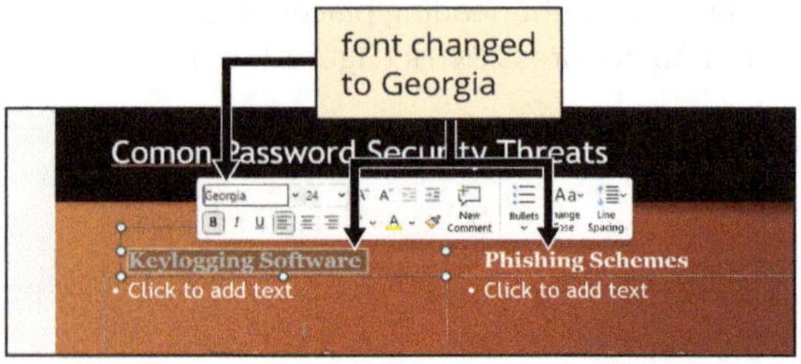

Figure 1–55

Other Ways

1. Click Font arrow (Home tab | Font group), click desired font in Font gallery
2. Right-click selected text, click Font on shortcut menu (Font dialog box), click Font tab, select desired font in Font list, click OK
3. Click Font dialog box launcher (Home tab | Font group), click Font tab (Font dialog box), select desired font in Font list, click OK
4. Press CTRL+SHIFT+F, click Font tab (Font dialog box), select desired font in the Font list, click OK
5. Right-click selected text, click Font arrow on Mini toolbar, select desired font

To Add a Slide with the Title Only Layout

The following steps add Slide 4 to the presentation with the Title Only slide layout style. **Why?** The only text on the slide is the title, and the majority of the slide content is the picture.

1

- If necessary, click Home on the ribbon to display the Home tab.
- Click the New Slide arrow (Home tab | Slides group) to display the Berlin layout gallery (Figure 1–56).

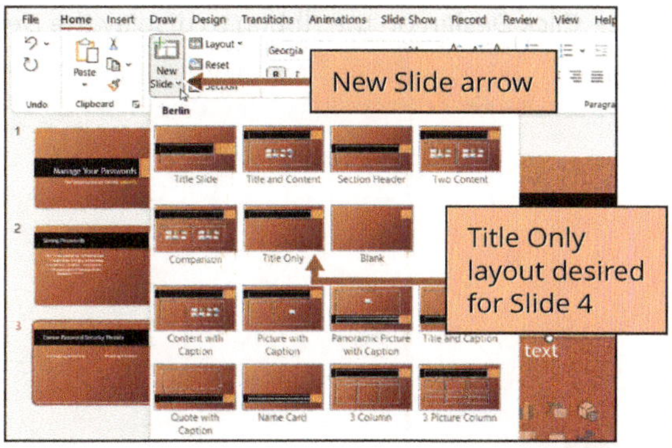

Figure 1–56

2

- Click Title Only to add a new slide and apply that layout to Slide 4 (Figure 1–57).

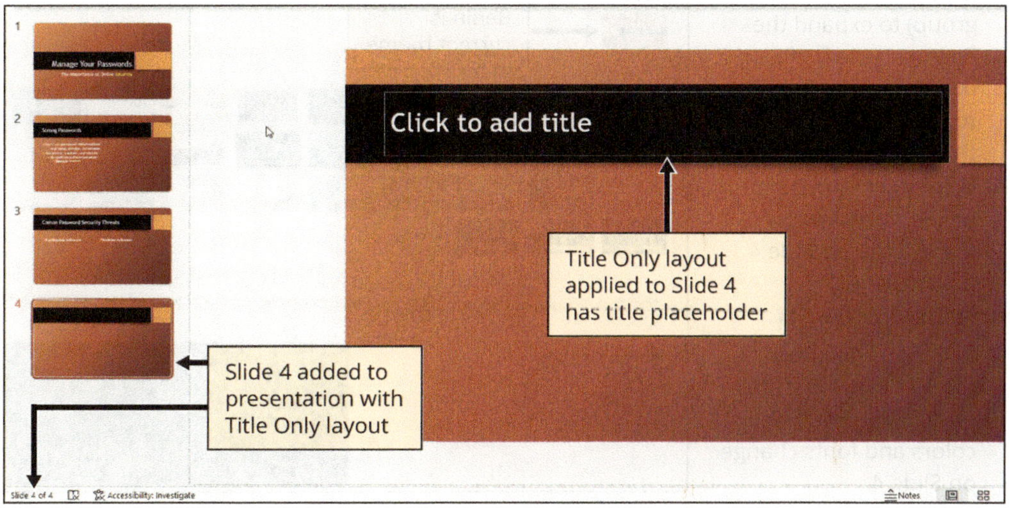

Figure 1–57

To Enter a Slide Title

The only text on Slide 4 is the title. The following step enters the title text for this slide. **Why?** Most slides include a title to identify the main topic of the slide.

1 Type **Different Passwords for Every Account** as the title text but do not press ENTER (Figure 1–58).

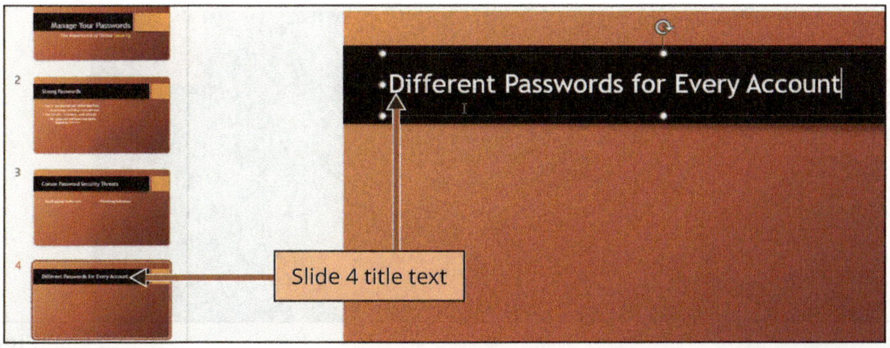

Figure 1–58

To Change the Theme

The Berlin theme applied to the presentation is simple and does not have many design elements. The following steps change the theme for the presentation. **Why?** You want a subtle design that calls attention to the important guidelines provided on the slides.

1

- Click Design on the ribbon to display the Design tab (Figure 1–59).

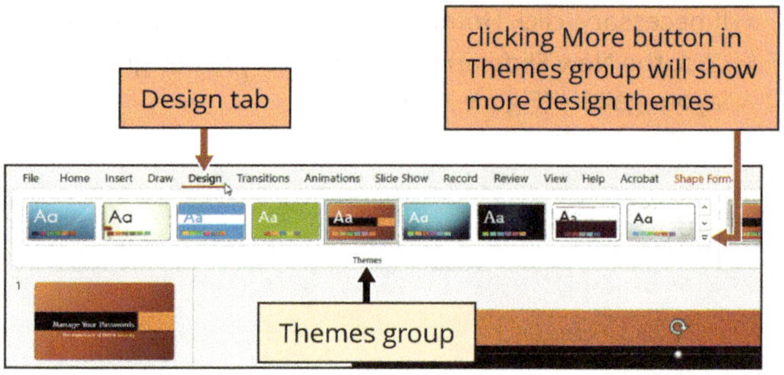

Figure 1–59

2

- Click the More button (Design tab | Themes group) to expand the Themes gallery. If necessary, scroll down to view the Ion theme thumbnail.
- Point to the Ion theme to see a preview of that theme on Slide 4 (Figure 1–60).
- **Experiment:** Point to various document themes in the Themes gallery and watch the colors and fonts change on Slide 4.

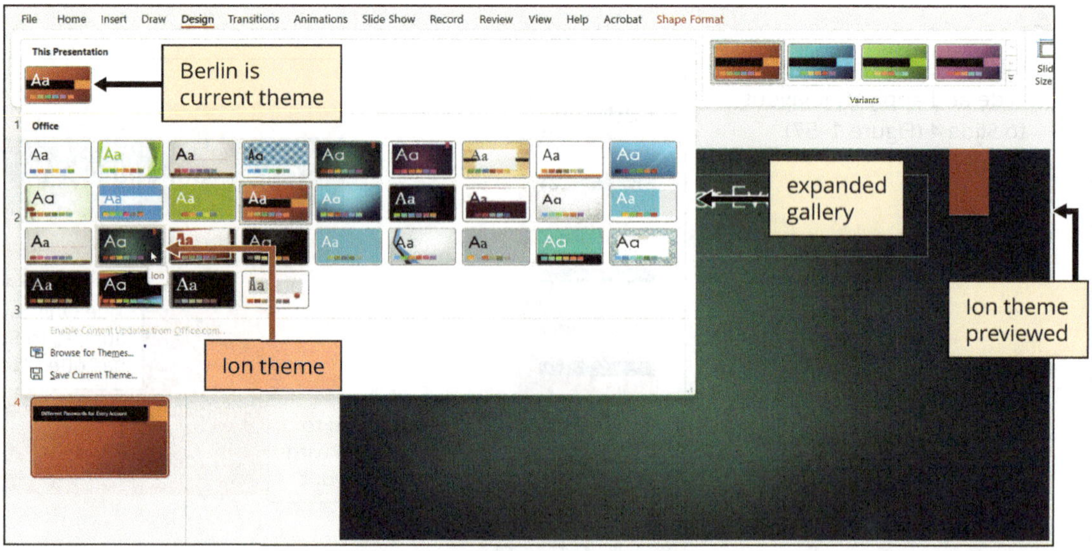

Figure 1–60

3

- Click the Ion theme to apply this theme to all four slides (Figure 1–61).
- If the Design Ideas pane is displayed, close it.

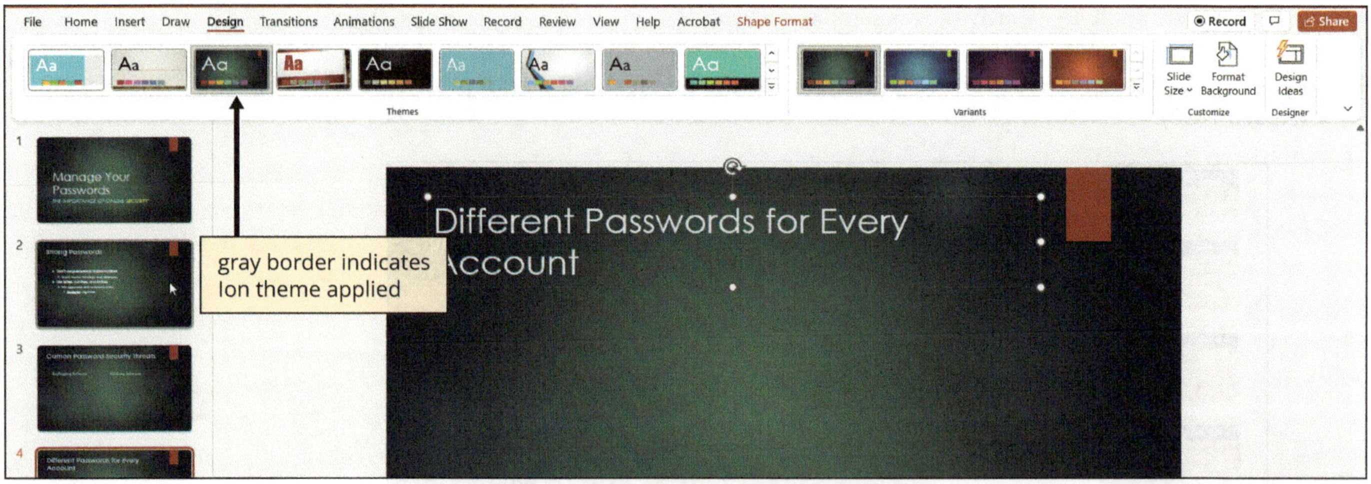

Figure 1–61

PowerPoint Views

The PowerPoint window display varies depending on the view. A **view** is the mode in which the presentation appears on the screen. You will use some views when you are developing slides and others when you are delivering your presentation. When creating a presentation, you most likely will use Normal, Slide Sorter, Notes Pane, and Outline views. When presenting your slides to an audience, you most likely will use Slide Sorter, Presenter, and Reading views.

The default view is **Normal view**, which is composed of three areas that allow you to work on various aspects of a presentation simultaneously. The large area in the middle, called the **Slide pane**, displays the slide you currently are developing and allows you to enter text, tables, charts, graphics, pictures, video, and other elements. As you create the slides, miniature views of the individual slides, called thumbnails, are displayed in the **Slides tab** on the left of the screen. You can rearrange the thumbnails in this pane. The **Notes pane**, by default, is hidden at the bottom of the window. If you want to type notes to yourself or remarks to share with your audience, you can click the **Notes button** in the status bar to open the Notes pane. After you have created at least two slides, a scroll bar containing scroll arrows and scroll boxes will appear on the right edge of the window.

BTW
Pointer
If you are using a touch screen, the pointer may not appear on the screen as you perform touch gestures. The pointer will reappear when you begin using the mouse.

BTW
Touch Screen
If you are using your finger on a touch screen and are having difficulty completing the steps in this module, consider using a stylus. Many people find it easier to be precise with a stylus than with a finger. In addition, with a stylus you see the pointer. If you still are having trouble completing the steps with a stylus, try using a mouse.

To Move to Another Slide in Normal View

Why? When creating or editing a presentation in Normal view (the view you are currently using), you often want to display a slide other than the current one. Before continuing with developing this project, you want to display the title slide. You can click the desired slide in the Slides tab or drag the scroll box on the vertical scroll bar; if you are using a touch screen, you can tap the desired slide in the Slides tab. When you drag the scroll box, the **slide indicator** shows the number and title of the slide you are about to display. Releasing shows the slide. The following steps move from Slide 4 to Slide 1 using the scroll box in the Slide pane.

1

- With Slide 4 displayed, position the pointer on the scroll box.
- Press and hold down the mouse button so that Slide: 4 of 4 Different Passwords for Each Acc... appears in the slide indicator (Figure 1-62).

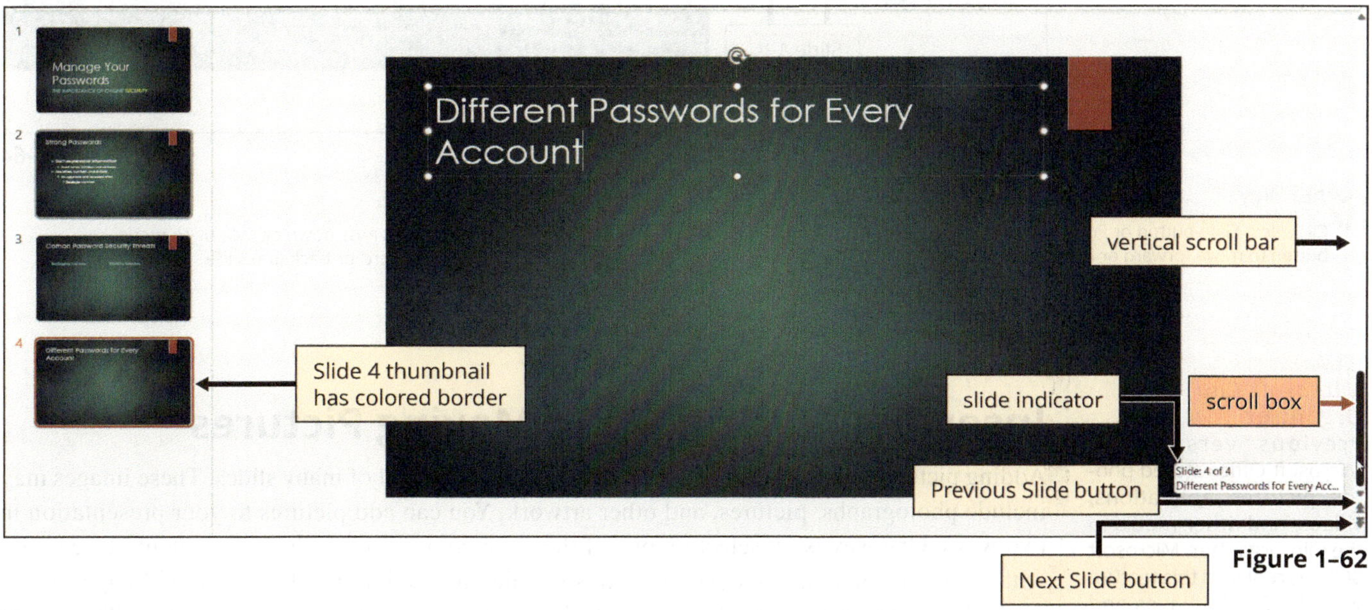

Figure 1-62

2

- Drag the scroll box up the vertical scroll bar until Slide: 1 of 4 Manage Your Passwords appears in the slide indicator (Figure 1–63).

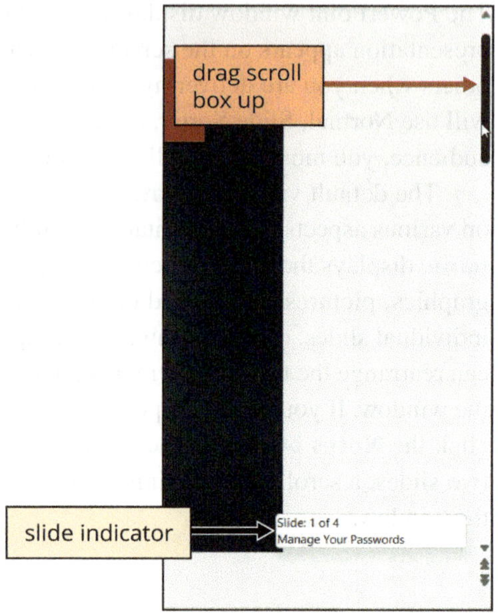

Figure 1–63

3

- Release so that Slide 1 appears in the Slide pane and the Slide 1 thumbnail has a colored border in the Slides tab (Figure 1–64).

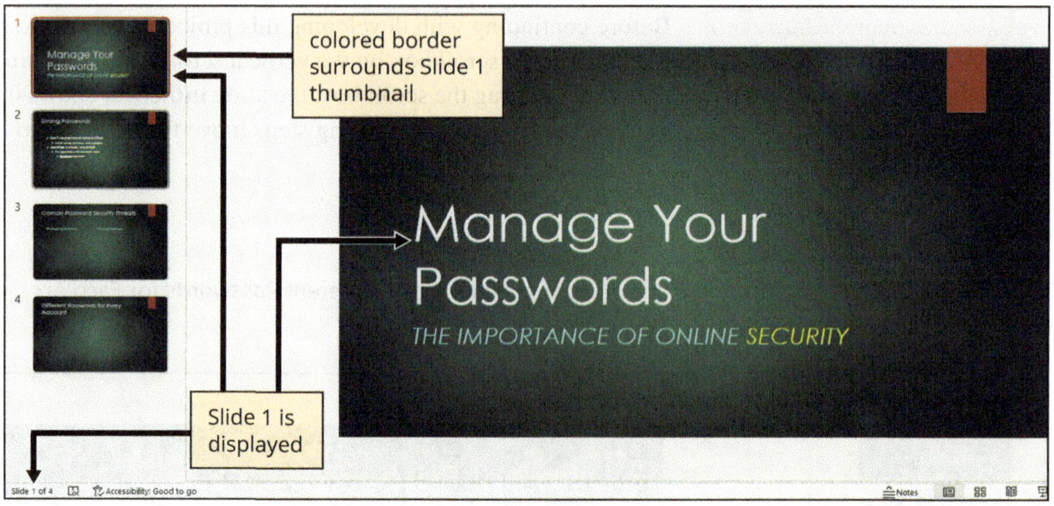

Figure 1–64

Other Ways

1. Click Next Slide button or Previous Slide button to move forward or back one slide
2. Click slide in Slides tab
3. Press PAGE DOWN or PAGE UP to move forward or back one slide

BTW
Microsoft Clip Organizer
Previous versions of Microsoft Office stored photos, pictures, animations, videos, and other media in the Clip Organizer. Microsoft 365 has replaced this feature with the Stock Images and Online Pictures options in the Insert Picture From gallery. Both options provide windows where you can search for and insert files.

Inserting, Resizing, and Moving Pictures

Adding pictures can help increase the visual and audio appeal of many slides. These images may include photographs, pictures, and other artwork. You can add pictures to your presentation in two ways. One way is by selecting one of the slide layouts that includes a content placeholder with a Pictures button. A second method is by clicking the Pictures button in the Images group on the Insert tab and then clicking This Device to open the Insert Picture dialog box. The **Insert Picture dialog box** allows you to search for picture files that are stored on your computer or a storage device. Contact your instructor if you need the pictures used in the following steps.

Consider This

How can you design a title slide that holds your audience's attention?

Develop a slide that reflects the content of your presentation but does so in a thought-provoking way. A title, at the very least, should prepare your audience for the material they are about to see and hear. Look for ways to focus attention on your theme and the method in which you plan to present this theme. A unique photograph or graphic can help generate interest. You may decide to introduce your topic with a startling fact, a rhetorical question, or a quotation. The device you choose depends upon your audience, the occasion, and the presentation's purpose.

To Insert a Picture into a Slide without a Content Placeholder

Slide 1 uses the Title Slide layout, which has two placeholders for text but none for graphical content. If the layout does not have a content placeholder, an inserted image generally displays in the center of the slide. You want to place a graphic on Slide 1. **Why?** *It is likely that your viewers will see an image on this slide before they read any text, so you want to include a picture to create interest in the presentation and introduce your audience to the topic.* For this presentation, you will insert a partial keyboard with the word, security, printed on one key. Later in this module, you will resize and position the picture in an appropriate location. The following steps add a picture to Slide 1.

Note: To complete this assignment, you will be required to use the Data Files. Please contact your instructor for information about accessing the Data Files.

1

- With Slide 1 displayed, click Insert on the ribbon to display the Insert tab (Figure 1–65).

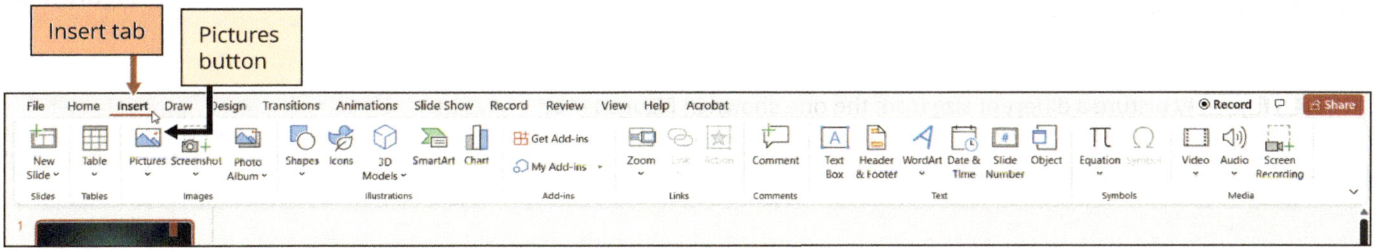

Figure 1–65

2

- Click the Pictures button (Insert tab | Images group) to display the Insert Picture From gallery.
- Click This Device in the Insert Picture From gallery to display the Insert Picture dialog box.

Q&A What should I do if no pictures are displayed when I click the Pictures button?

You may need to click the Online Pictures button instead of the Pictures button.

- Navigate to the PowerPoint1 folder. If necessary, scroll down and then click the picture called Support_PPT_1_Security.png, which is located in the Data Files (Figure 1–66).

Q&A Why do I see only a list of file names and not thumbnails of the pictures in my folder?

Your view is different from the view shown in Figure 1–66.

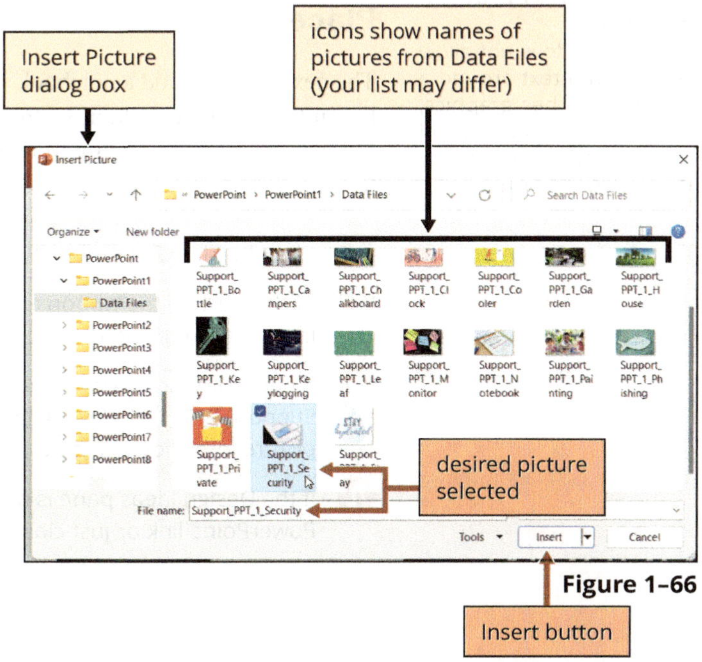

Figure 1–66

3

- Click the Insert button (Insert Picture dialog box) to insert the picture into Slide 1 (Figure 1–67).

Q&A Can I double-click the picture or file name instead of selecting it and clicking the Insert button?
Yes. Either method inserts the picture.

Why is this picture displayed in this location on the slide?
The slide layout does not have a content placeholder, so PowerPoint inserts the file in an area of the slide. You will move and resize the picture later in this module.

What is the Alt Text shown at the bottom of the picture?
Alternative text (Alt text) descriptions help visually impaired people who use screen readers understand the content of pictures.

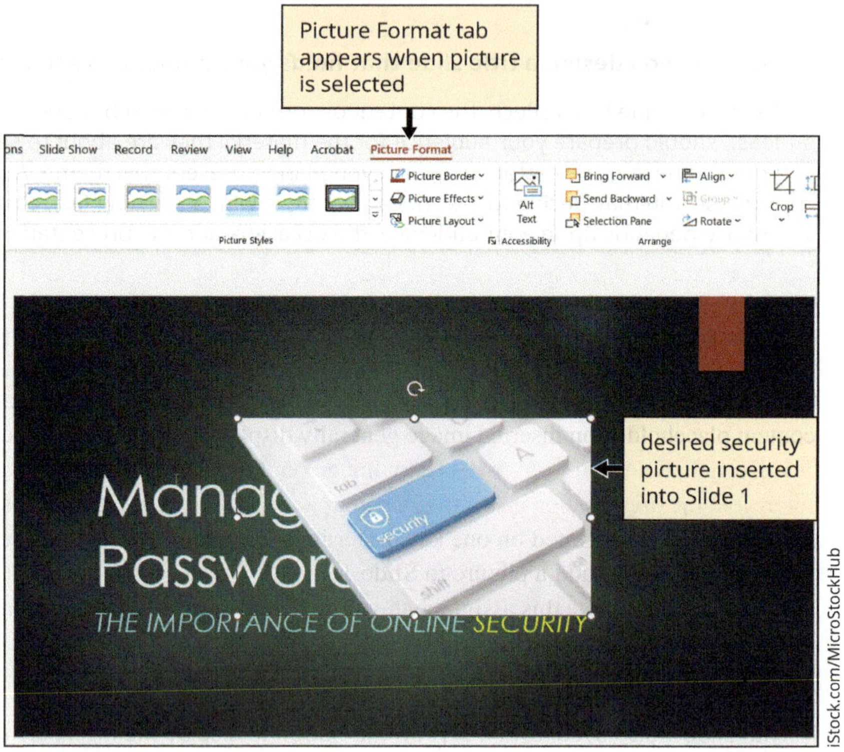

Figure 1–67

4

- If the Design Ideas pane is displayed, click the 'Stop suggesting ideas until I restart PowerPoint' link or just close the pane.

Q&A Why is my picture a different size from the one shown in Figure 1–1b?
The clip was inserted into the slide and not into a content placeholder. You will resize the picture later in this module.

BTW
Wrapping Text around a Photo
PowerPoint does not allow you to wrap text around a picture or other graphics, such as tables, shapes, and charts. This feature, however, is available in Word.

To Insert another Picture into a Slide without a Content Placeholder

The next step is to add a notebook with hand-written passwords to Slide 2. This slide has a bulleted list in the text placeholder, so the icon group does not display in the center of the placeholder. Later in this module, you will resize this inserted picture. The following steps add one picture to Slide 2.

1. Click the Slide 2 thumbnail in the Slides tab to display Slide 2.
2. Click Insert on the ribbon to display the Insert tab, click the Pictures button (Insert tab | Images group), and then click This Device to display the Insert Picture dialog box.
3. If necessary, scroll down the list of files and then open the picture called Support_PPT_1_Notebook.jpg, which is located in the Data Files, to insert the picture into Slide 2 (Figure 1–68).
4. If the Design Ideas pane is displayed, click the 'Stop suggesting ideas until I restart PowerPoint' link or just close the pane.

Figure 1–68

To Insert Another Picture into a Slide without a Content Placeholder

Next, you will add a picture to Slide 4. Later in this module, you will resize this picture. The following steps add a picture to Slide 4.

1. Click the Slide 4 thumbnail in the Slides tab.
2. Display the Insert tab, click the Pictures button, click This Device, and then insert the Support_PPT_1_Monitor.jpg file into Slide 4 (Figure 1–69).
3. If the Design Ideas pane is displayed, click the 'Stop suggesting ideas until I restart PowerPoint' link or just close the pane.

Figure 1–69

To Insert a Picture into a Content Placeholder

Slide 3 uses the Comparison layout, which has a content placeholder below each of the two headings. You desire to insert pictures into both content placeholders. **Why?** You want to display two images depicting two common cybercriminal activities: keylogging and phishing. The following steps insert a keyboard with one key selected into the left content placeholder and a fish shape caught in a net into the right content placeholder on Slide 3.

1

- Click the Slide 3 thumbnail in the Slides tab to display Slide 3 (Figure 1–70).

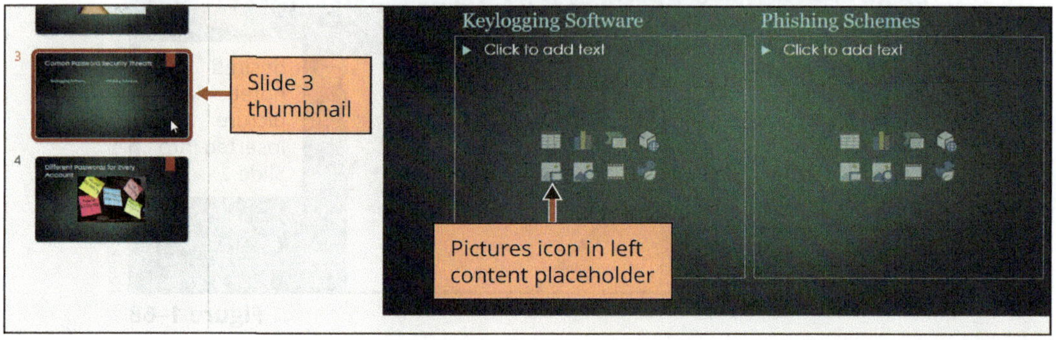

Figure 1–70

2

- Click the Pictures icon in the left content placeholder to select that placeholder and to open the Insert Picture dialog box.
- If necessary, scroll down the list of files, click Support_PPT_1_Keylogging.jpg to select the file, and then double-click to insert the picture into the left content placeholder (Figure 1–71).

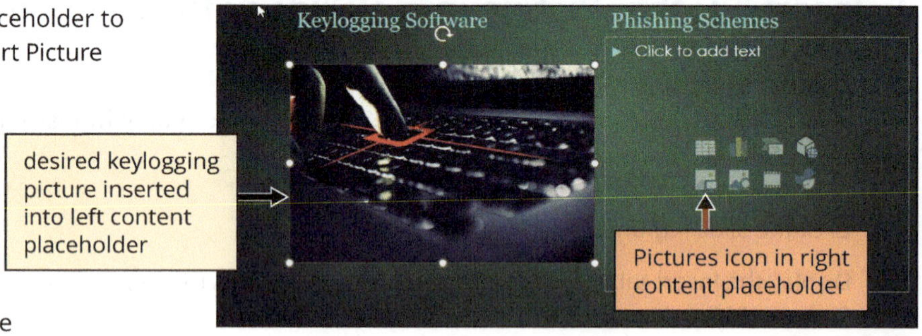

iStock.com/Welcomia

Figure 1–71

Q&A Do I need to select the file name before double-clicking to insert the picture?
No. You just can double-click the file name.

3

- Click the Pictures icon in the right content placeholder to select that placeholder and to open the Insert Picture dialog box.
- If necessary, scroll down the list to display the Support_PPT_1_Phishing.jpg file name and then insert this picture into the right content placeholder (Figure 1–72).

iStock.com/CalypsoArt

Figure 1–72

Resizing Photos and Illustrations

Sometimes it is necessary to change the size of pictures. **Resizing** includes enlarging or reducing the size of a graphic. You can resize these images using a variety of techniques. One method involves changing the size of a picture by specifying exact dimensions in a dialog box or in the Height and Width boxes in the Size group on the Picture Format tab. Another method involves sliding or dragging one of the graphic's sizing handles to the desired location. A selected graphic appears surrounded by a **selection rectangle** which has small circles, called **sizing handles** or move handles, at each corner and middle location.

To Proportionally Resize Pictures

Why? On Slides 1, 2, and 4, the picture sizes are too small to display aesthetically on the slides. At times it is important to maintain the proportions of a picture, such as when a person is featured prominently. To change the size of a picture and keep the width and height in proportion to each other, drag the corner sizing handles to view how the image will look on the slide. Using these corner handles maintains the graphic's original proportions. If, however, the proportions do not need to be maintained precisely, as with the passwords picture you inserted in Slide 2, you can drag the side sizing handles to alter the proportions so that the graphic's height and width become larger or smaller. The following steps proportionally increase the size of the Slide 1 picture using a corner sizing handle.

1

- Click the Slide 1 thumbnail in the Slides tab to display Slide 1.
- Click the security picture to select it and display the selection rectangle.
- Point to the upper-right corner sizing handle on the picture so that the pointer changes to a two-headed arrow (Figure 1–73).

Q&A I am using a touch screen and do not see a two-headed arrow when I press and hold the lower-right sizing handle. Why?
Touch screens may not display pointers; you can just press and slide sizing handles to resize.

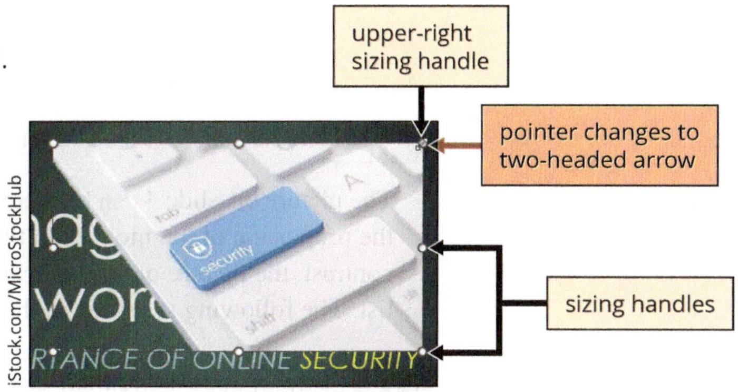

Figure 1–73

2

- Drag the upper-right sizing handle diagonally toward the upper-right corner of the slide until it is positioned approximately as shown in Figure 1–74.

Q&A What if the picture is not the same size as the one shown in Figure 1–74?
Repeat Steps 1 and 2.

Can I drag any corner sizing handle diagonally outward toward the opposite corner to resize the picture?
Yes.

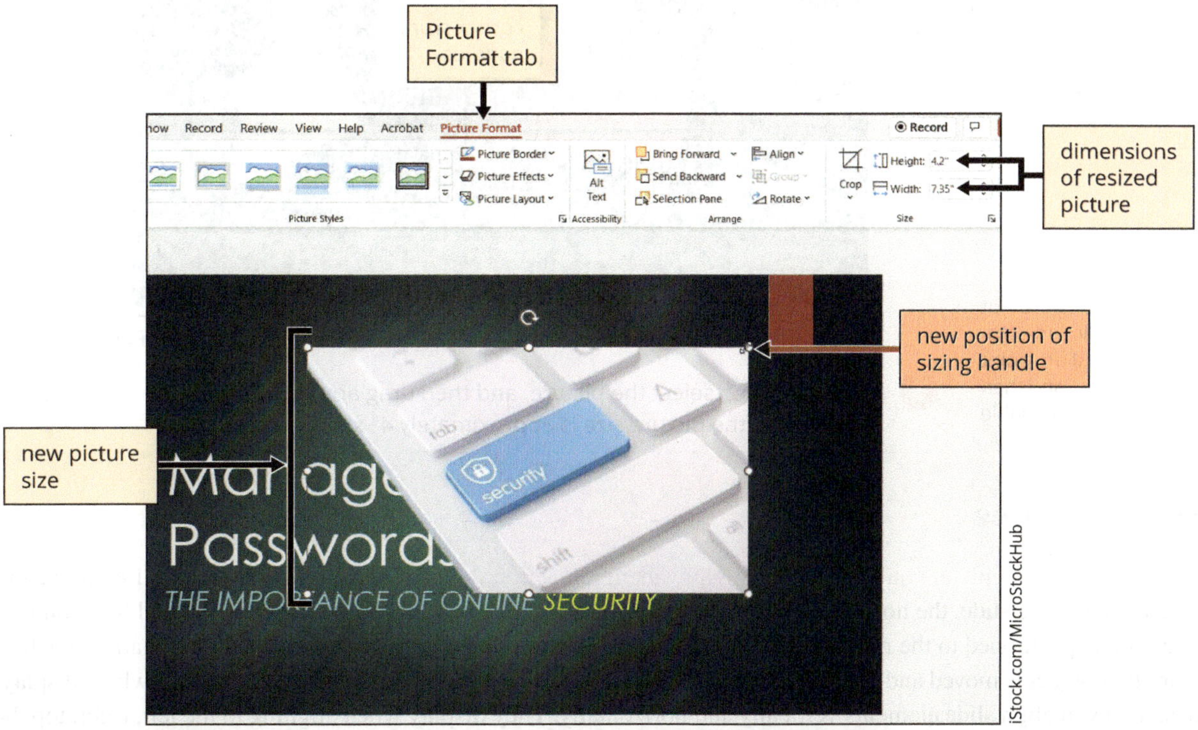

Figure 1–74

3

- Release to resize the picture.
- View the Height and Width boxes (Picture Format tab | Size group) to verify that the picture size is approximately 4.2" x 7.35".

Q&A What if I want to return the picture to its original size and start again?
With the picture selected, click the Reset Picture arrow (Picture Format tab | Adjust group) and then click Reset Picture & Size in the Reset Picture gallery.

Can I resize the picture to exact measurements?
Yes. Click the Height and Width arrows (Picture Format tab | Size group) or manually enter the dimensions to adjust the picture size.

To Resize the Pictures on Slides 4 and 2

The picture on Slide 4 can be increased to fit much of the space on the slide. You want to maintain the proportion of the monitor in this picture, so you will drag one of the corner sizing handles. In contrast, the picture on Slide 2 can be decreased to fill the space on the right side of the bulleted list. The following steps resize these pictures using a corner sizing handle.

1. Display Slide 4 and then click the picture to select it.
2. Drag any corner sizing handle on the picture diagonally outward until the picture is resized approximately as shown in Figure 1–75. The picture size should be approximately 5.6" x 8.4".

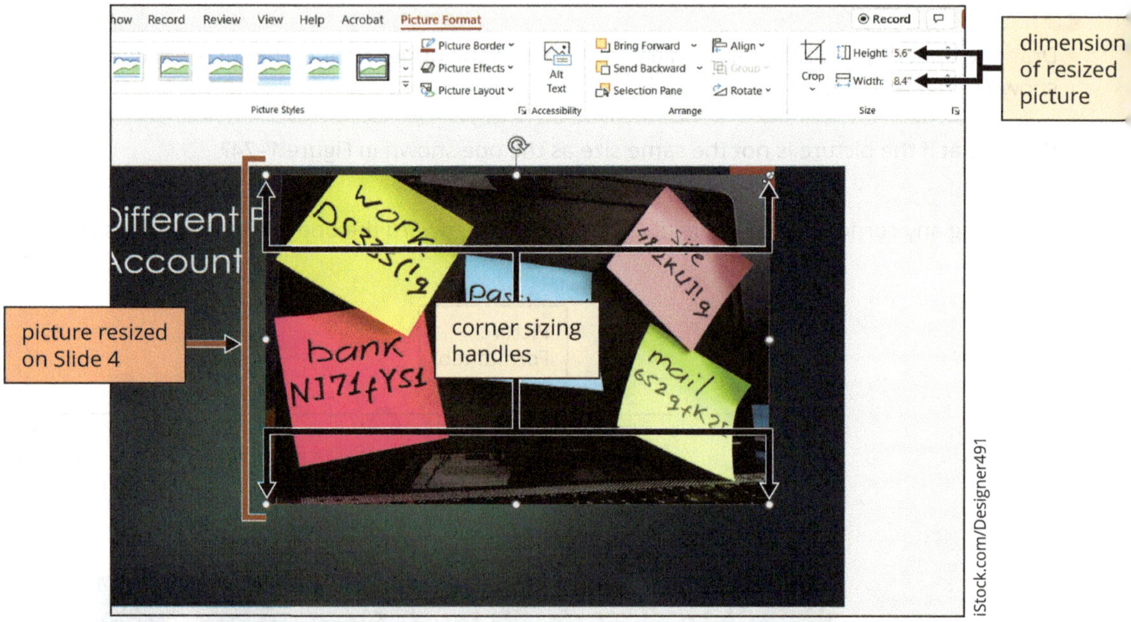

Figure 1–75

3. Display Slide 2, select the picture, and then drag any sizing handle on the picture diagonally inward until the picture size is approximately 4" x 6".

BTW
Displaying Smart Guides
If your smart guides are not displaying, right-click an empty space on your slide, point to 'Grid and Guides', and then click Smart Guides to enable this option.

To Move Pictures

Why? After you insert a picture on a slide, you might want to reposition it. The security picture on Slide 1 could be moved to the upper-right area of the slide, the notebook picture on Slide 2 could be moved beside the bulleted list, and the monitor picture on Slide 4 could be positioned to the right of the word, Account. PowerPoint displays **smart guides** automatically when a picture, shape, or other object is moved and is close to lining up with another slide element. These layout guides, which display as dashed red lines, help you align slide elements vertically and horizontally. They display when aligning to the left, right, top, bottom, and middle of placeholders and other objects on a slide. For example, a smart guide will display to help you align the right or left edge of a picture in relation to a text placeholder or to another picture. The following steps move the pictures on Slides 4, 2, and 1.

1

- If necessary, click the picture on Slide 4 to select it.
- With the four-headed arrow displayed, drag the picture downward until the vertical smart guide is displayed through the center of the picture and the horizontal smart guide is displayed along the bottom of the slide, as shown in Figure 1–76, and then release.
- If necessary, select the picture and then use the ARROW keys to position it precisely as shown in Figure 1–76.

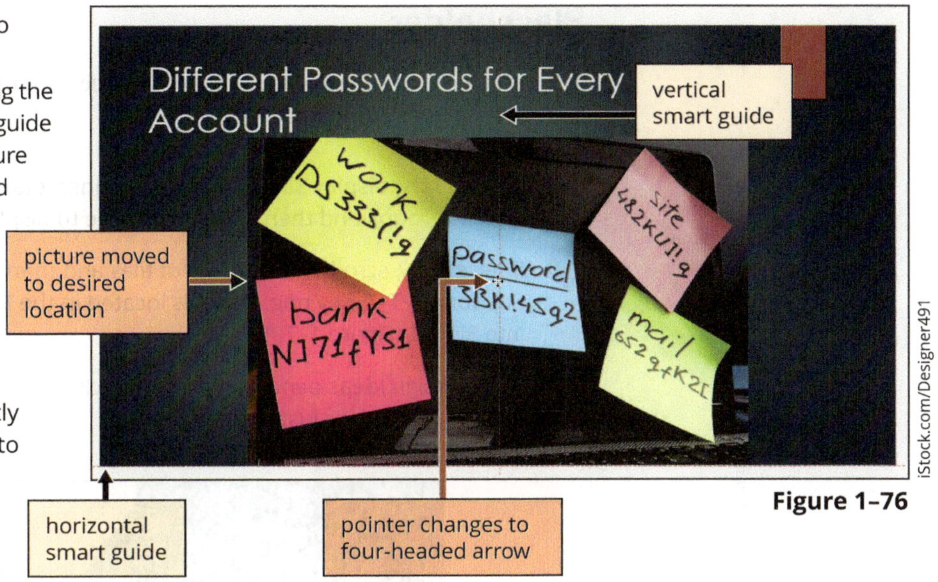

Figure 1–76

Q&A The picture still is not located exactly where I want it to display. What can I do to align the image?
Press CTRL while you press the ARROW keys. This key combination moves the picture in smaller increments than when you press only an ARROW key.

I cannot see the vertical smart guide. What should I do?
Decrease the zoom to less than 100 percent.

2

- Display Slide 2 and then click the picture to select it.
- Drag the picture until the vertical smart guide is displayed on the right side of the picture and the horizontal smart guide is displayed through the center of the picture (Figure 1–77).

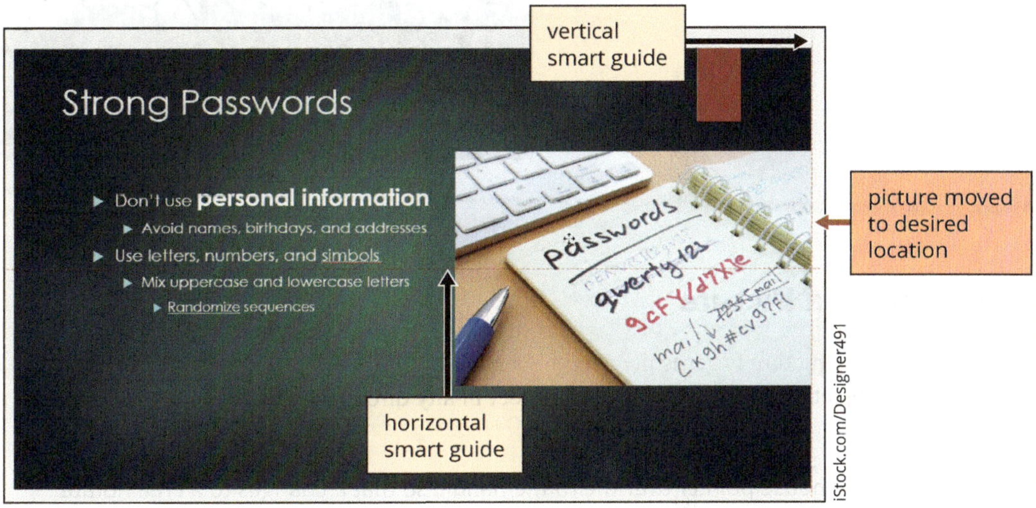

Figure 1–77

3

- Display Slide 1 and then click the picture to select it.
- Drag the picture upward and to the right corner of the slide. The vertical smart guide is displayed along the right edge of the picture and the horizontal smart guide is displayed along the top side of the slide (Figure 1–78).

Figure 1–78

To Insert Another Picture into a Slide without a Content Placeholder

The next step is to add a picture of a key to Slide 1 to fill the space above the title text. The following steps add another picture to Slide 1.

1. If necessary, display Slide 1, display the Insert tab, click the Pictures button (Insert tab | Images group), and then click This Device to display the Insert Picture dialog box.
2. If necessary, scroll down the list of files and then open the picture called Support_PPT_1_Key.png, which is located in the Data Files, to insert the picture into Slide 1 (Figure 1–79).
3. If the Design Ideas pane is displayed, click the 'Stop suggesting ideas until I restart PowerPoint' link or just close the pane.

iStock.com/MicroStockHub; iStock.com/The-lightwriter

Figure 1–79

To Rotate a Picture

Why? The key picture is vertical, and you want to turn it so that it is parallel to the title text. Dragging the **rotate handle** above a selected object allows you to rotate an object in any direction. The following steps rotate the picture.

1
- Position the mouse pointer over the rotate handle so that it changes to a Free Rotate pointer (Figure 1–80).

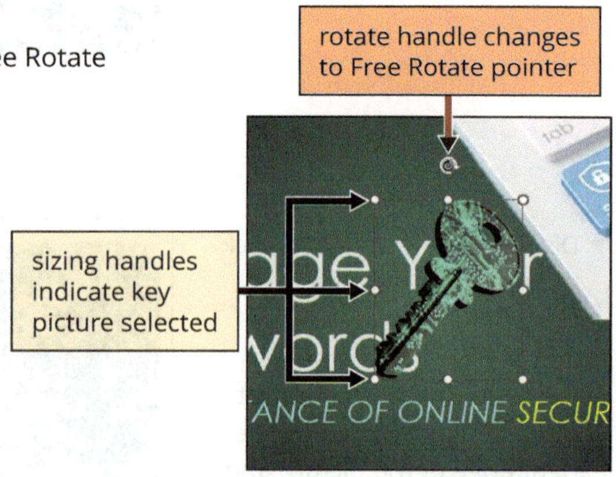

iStock.com/MicroStockHub; iStock.com/The-lightwriter

Figure 1–80

2

- Drag the rotate handle counterclockwise approximately 90 degrees so that it is parallel to the title text.
- Move the picture so that the vertical smart guide is displayed through the center of the picture and the horizontal smart guide is displayed in the center of the slide, as shown in Figure 1-81.

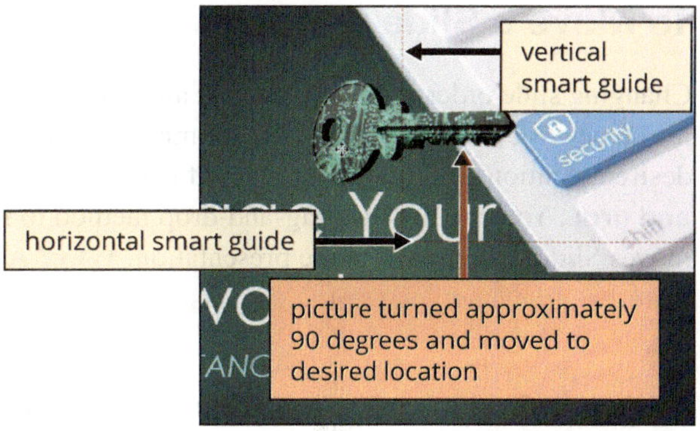

iStock.com/MicroStockHub; iStock.com/The-lightwriter

Figure 1-81

To Nonproportionally Resize the Picture on Slide 2

Why? The height of the notebook picture in Slide 2 can be increased to add to the viewers' interest and fill the space at the bottom of the slide. The height can be increased without negatively distorting the original image. You can change the height and width of a picture by dragging the sizing handles on the sides of the image. The following steps resize the height but not the width of the notebook picture using sizing handles along the sides of the image.

1

- Display Slide 2 and then select the notebook picture.
- With the selection rectangle displayed, point to the middle sizing handle on the bottom edge of the picture so that the pointer changes to a two-headed arrow (Figure 1-82).

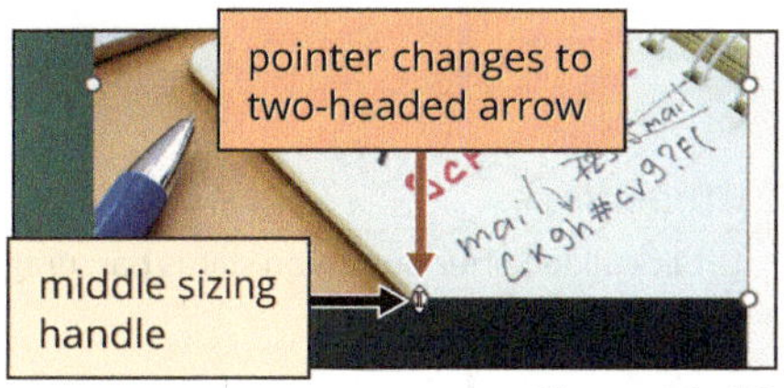

iStock.com/Designer491

Figure 1-82

2

- Drag the sizing handle downward to the bottom edge of the slide until the horizontal smart guide is displayed and the sizing handle or crosshair is positioned as shown in Figure 1-83. The approximate picture size should be 5.75" x 6".

Q&A What if the picture is not the same size as the one shown in Figure 1-83?
Repeat Steps 1 and 2.

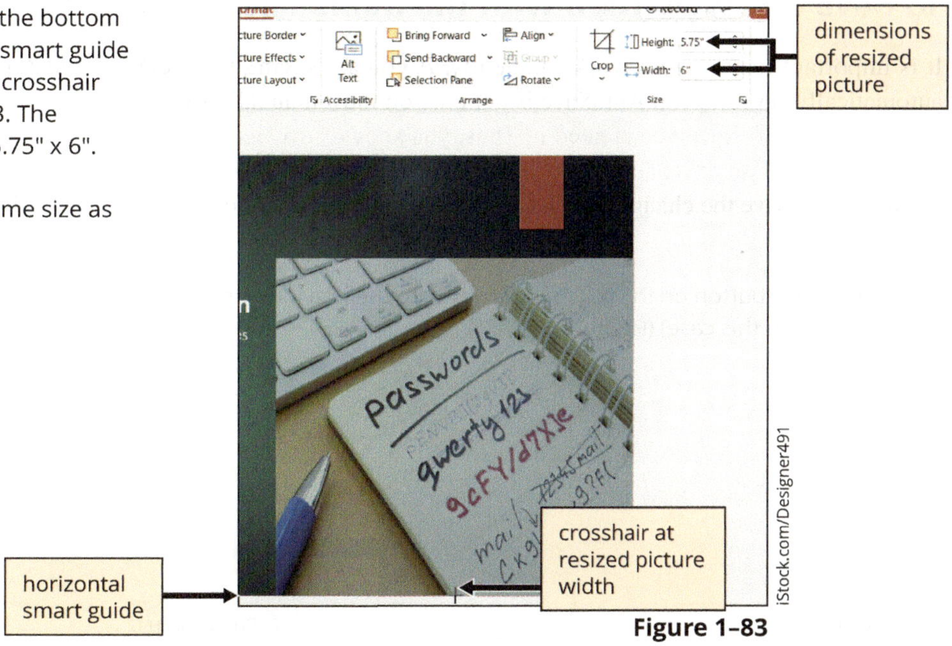

iStock.com/Designer491

Figure 1-83

3

- Release to resize the picture.
- Click outside the picture to deselect it.

Q&A Can I move the picture in small increments?
Yes. To move or nudge the picture in very small increments, hold down CTRL with the picture selected while pressing the ARROW keys. You cannot perform this action using a touch screen.

To Move a Slide in Normal View

Changing slide order is an easy process and is best performed in the Slides tab. When you click the thumbnail and begin to drag it to a new location, the remaining thumbnails realign to show the new sequence. When you release, the slide drops into the desired location. Hence, this process of sliding or dragging and then dropping the thumbnail in a new location is called **drag and drop**. You can use the drag-and-drop method to move any selected item, including text and graphics. The following step moves Slide 3 to the end of the presentation. **Why?** Audience members often remember the final material they see and hear in a presentation, and you want to emphasize two of the cybersecurity threats that are prone to occur with weak passwords.

1

- Select the Slide 3 thumbnail and then drag it below the last slide in the Slides tab so that it becomes the new Slide 4 (Figure 1–84).

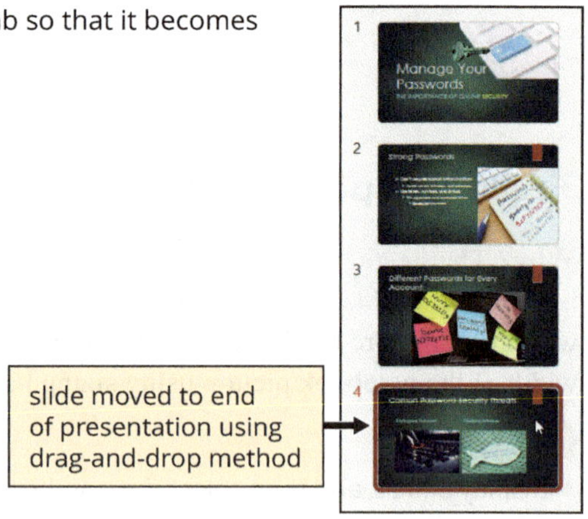

iStock.com/Welcomia; iStock.com/CalypsoArt

Figure 1–84

Other Ways

1. Click Slide Sorter button on status bar, drag thumbnail to new location
2. Click Slide Sorter button (View tab | Presentation Views group), click slide thumbnail, drag thumbnail to new location

To Save a Presentation with the Same File Name

It is important to save your work frequently. If you are saving to OneDrive and AutoSave is On, changes to your file are automatically saved. But if AutoSave is not on, you must manually save your file. **Why?** You have made modifications to the file (presentation) since you created it. Thus, you should save again. Similarly, you should continue saving files frequently so that you do not lose the changes you have made since the time you last saved the file. You can use the same file name, such as Passwords, to save the changes made to the presentation. The following step saves a file again with the same file name.

1

- Click the Save button on the title bar to overwrite the previously saved file (Passwords, in this case) (Figure 1–85).

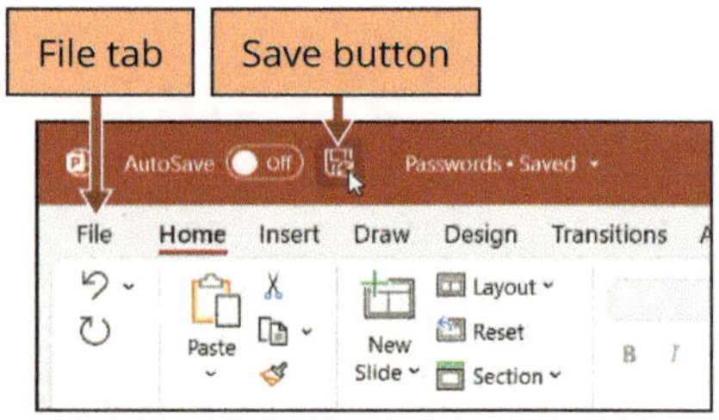

Figure 1–85

Other Ways

1. Press CTRL+S
2. Press SHIFT+F12

To Close a File Using Backstage View

Sometimes, you may want to close a Microsoft 365 file, such as a PowerPoint presentation, entirely and start over with a new file. You also may want to close a file when you are done working with it. **Why?** You should close a file when you are done working with it so that you do not make inadvertent changes to it. The following steps close the current active PowerPoint file, that is, the Passwords presentation, without exiting PowerPoint.

1

- Click File on the ribbon to open Backstage view (Figure 1–86).

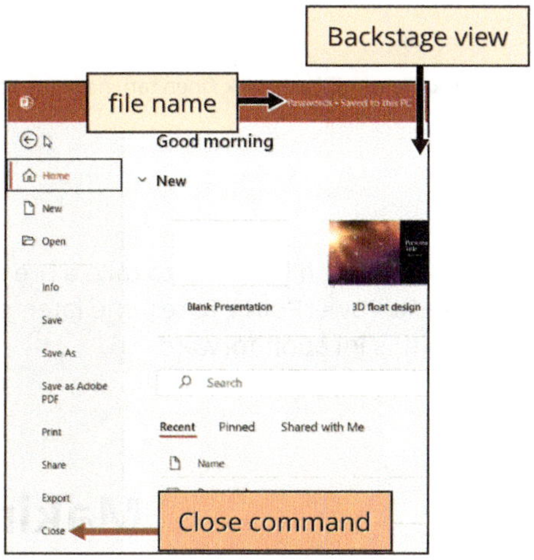

Figure 1–86

2

- Click Close in Backstage view to close the open file (Passwords, in this case) without closing PowerPoint.

Q&A What if PowerPoint displays a dialog box about saving?
Click the Save button if you want to save the changes, click the Don't Save button if you want to ignore the changes since the last time you saved, and click Cancel if you do not want to close the presentation.

Other Ways

1. Press CTRL+F4

To Open a Recent File Using Backstage View

You sometimes need to open a file that you recently modified. **Why?** You may have more changes to make, such as adding more content or correcting errors. Backstage view allows you to access recent files easily. The following steps reopen the Passwords file just closed.

BTW
Welcome Back!
If you are designing a slide in your deck other than Slide 1 and then save and close the document, PowerPoint's Welcome back! feature allows you to continue where you left off at the last save when you open the document. You may need to adjust the zoom if you are working at a different level than the default setting.

1

- Click File on the ribbon to open Backstage view.
- If necessary, click the Open tab in Backstage view to display the Open screen (Figure 1–87).

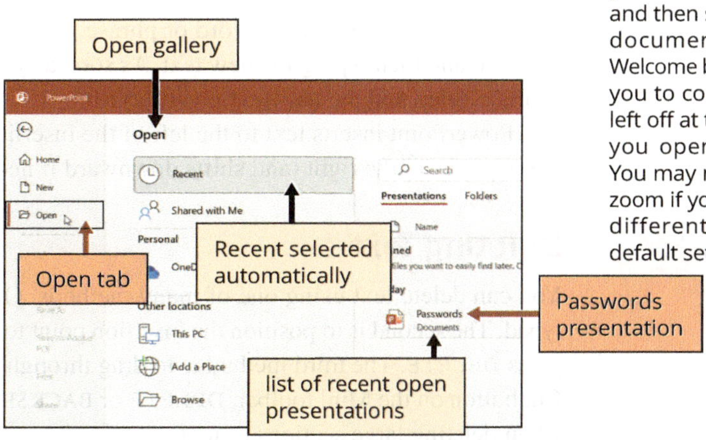

Figure 1–87

2

- Click the desired file name in the Recent list, Passwords in this case, to open the file.

Q&A Can I use Backstage view to open a recent file in other Microsoft 365 apps, such as Word and Excel?
Yes, as long as the file name appears in the list of recent files.

Other Ways

1. Click File on ribbon, click Open tab, navigate to file (Open dialog box), click Open button

Break Point: If you wish to take a break, this is a good place to do so. Be sure the file Passwords file is saved and then you can exit PowerPoint. To resume later, start PowerPoint, open the file called Passwords, and continue following the steps from this location forward.

Making Changes to Slide Text Content

After creating slides in a presentation, you may find that you want to make changes to the text. Changes may be required because a slide contains an error, the scope of the presentation shifts, or the style is inconsistent. This section explains the types of changes that commonly occur when creating a presentation.

You generally make three types of changes to text in a presentation: additions, replacements, and deletions.

- Additions are necessary when you omit text from a slide and need to add it later. You may need to insert text in the form of a sentence, word, or single character. For example, you may want to add the presenter's middle name on the title slide.
- Replacements are needed when you want to revise the text in a presentation. For example, you may want to substitute the word, their, for the word, there.
- Deletions are required when text on a slide is incorrect or no longer is relevant to the presentation. For example, a slide may look cluttered. Therefore, you may want to remove one of the bulleted paragraphs to add more space.

Editing text in PowerPoint basically is the same as editing text in a word processing program. The following sections illustrate the most common changes made to text in a presentation.

Replacing Text in an Existing Slide

When you need to correct a word or phrase, you can replace the text by selecting the text to be replaced and then typing the new text. As soon as you press any key on the keyboard, the selected text is deleted and the new text is displayed.

PowerPoint inserts text to the left of the insertion point. The text to the right of the insertion point moves to the right (and shifts downward if necessary) to accommodate the added text.

Deleting Text

You can delete text using one of many methods. One is to use BACKSPACE to remove text just typed. The second is to position the insertion point to the left of the text you want to delete and then press DELETE. The third method is to drag through the text you want to delete and then click the Cut button on the Mini toolbar, DELETE or BACKSPACE, or press CTRL+X. Use the third method when deleting large sections of text.

To Delete Text in a Placeholder

Why? You want to emphasize that passwords never should be repeated to avoid becoming at risk for cyberattacks. The following steps change Different to Unique in the Slide 3 title.

1

- Select Slide 3 and then position the pointer immediately to the left of the first character of the text to be selected in the title text placeholder (in this case, the D in the word, Different).
- Drag the pointer through the last character of the text to be selected (in this case, the t in the word, Different) (Figure 1–88).

Q&A Can I drag from left to right or right to left?
Yes. Either direction will select the letters.

Could I also have selected the word, Different, by double-clicking it?
Yes. Either method works to select a word.

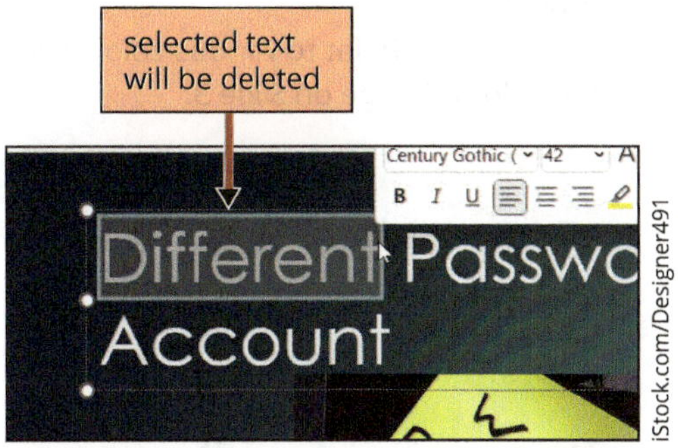

Figure 1–88

2

- Press DELETE to delete the selected text.
- Type **Unique** as the first word in the title text placeholder and then press SPACEBAR (Figure 1–89).

Q&A Could I have typed the word, Unique, while the word, Different, was selected without deleting the text first?
Yes. Either method works to replace words.

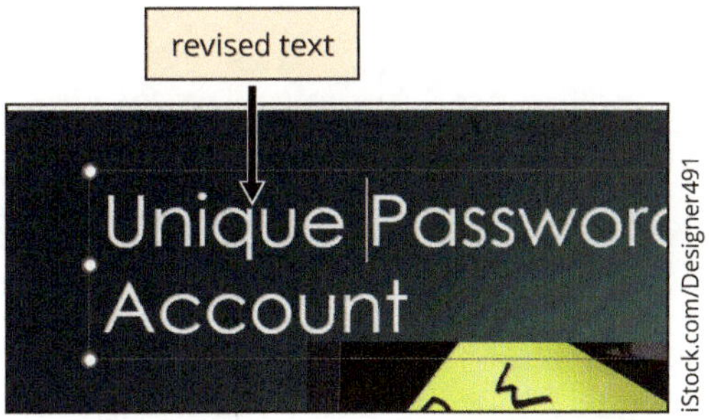

Figure 1–89

Other Ways

1. Right-click selected text, click Cut on shortcut menu
2. Select text, press DELETE or BACKSPACE
3. Select text, press CTRL+X

To Change the Theme Colors

Every theme has 10 standard colors: two for text, two for backgrounds, and six for accents. The following steps change the theme colors for the Passwords slides. **Why?** You can change the look of your presentation and add variety by applying the colors from one theme to another theme.

1

- Display the Design tab and then point to the More button in the Variants group (Design tab | Variants group) (Figure 1–90).

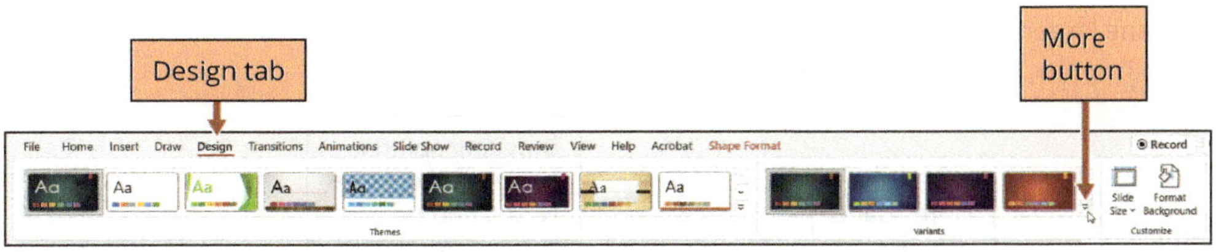

Figure 1–90

2

- Click the More button to expand the gallery.
- Point to Colors in the menu to display the Colors gallery (Figure 1–91).
- **Experiment:** Point to various color rows in the gallery and watch the colors change on Slide 3.

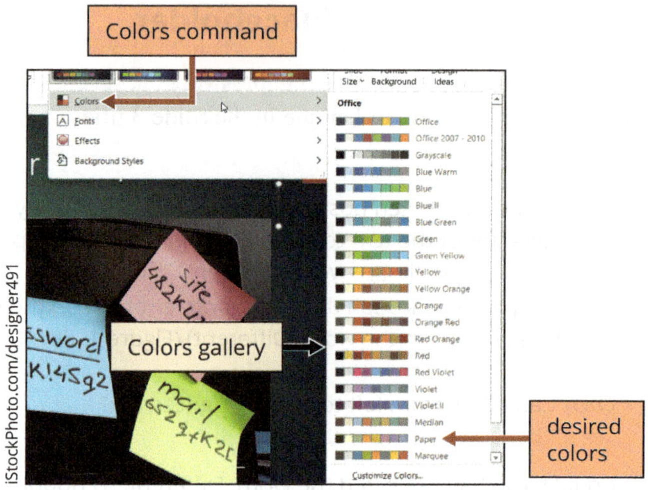

Figure 1–91

3

- Click Paper in the gallery to change the slides' theme colors (Figure 1–92).

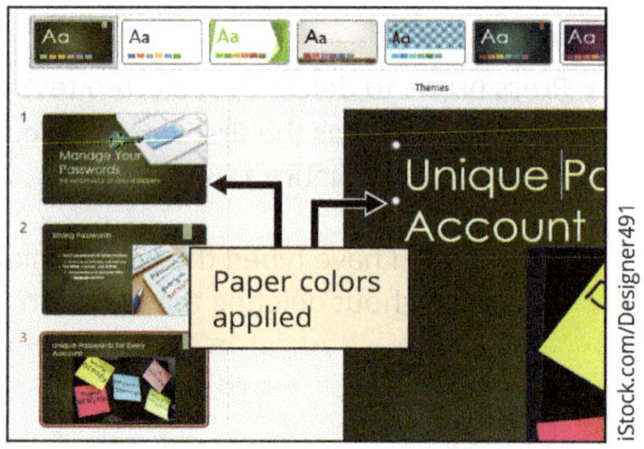

Figure 1–92

To Add Notes

Why? As you create slides, you may find material you want to state verbally and do not want to include on the slide. After adding these comments, you can print a set of speaker notes that will print below a small image of the slide. You can type and format comments in the Notes pane as you work in Normal view and then print this information as **notes pages**. Charts, tables, and pictures added to the Notes pane also print on these pages. The Notes pane is hidden until you click the Notes button on the status bar to open the pane. If you want to close the Notes pane, click the Notes button again. The following steps add text to the Notes pane on Slides 3 and 4.

1

- If necessary, click the Notes button on the status bar to display the Notes pane for Slide 3 (Figure 1–93).

Q&A Why might I need to click the Notes button?
By default, the Notes pane is closed when you begin a new presentation. Once you display the Notes pane for any slide, the Notes pane will remain open unless you click the Notes button to close it.

Can I make the Notes pane larger?
Yes. You can drag the splitter bar up to enlarge the Notes pane.

BTW
Formatting Notes Pane Text
You can format text in the Notes pane in the same manner you format text on a slide. To add emphasis, for example, you can italicize key words or change the font color and size.

Figure 1–93

2

- Click the Notes pane and then type **Common passwords are 12345, qwerty, and password.** (Figure 1–94).

Figure 1–94

3

- Display Slide 4, click the Notes pane, and then type **Keylogging software stores every keystroke in a hidden file for later retrieval. Phishing is a scam in which a perpetrator tricks you into supplying your personal or financial information.** (Figure 1–95).

Q&A What if I cannot see all the lines I typed?
Clicking the Notes pane scroll arrows allows you to view the entire text.

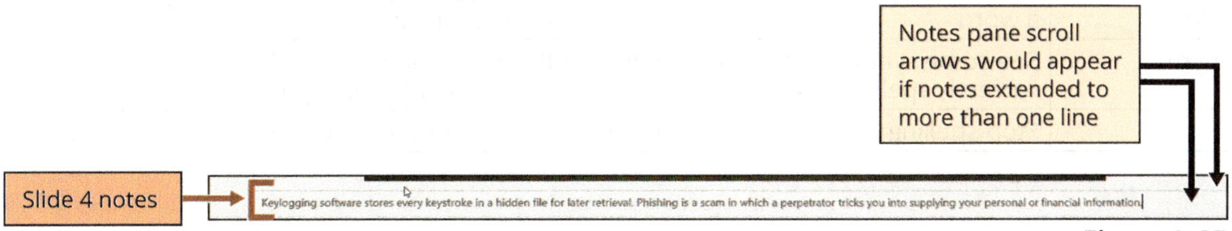

Figure 1–95

Checking Spelling

After you create a presentation, you should check it visually for spelling errors and style consistency. In addition, you can use PowerPoint's Spelling tool to identify possible misspellings on the slides and in the notes. You should proofread your presentation carefully by pointing to each word and saying it aloud as you point to it. Be mindful of commonly misused words such as its and it's, through and though, and to and too.

PowerPoint checks the entire presentation for spelling mistakes using a standard dictionary contained in the Microsoft 365 group. This dictionary is shared with the other Microsoft 365 applications such as Word and Excel. A custom dictionary is available if you want to add special words such as proper nouns, cities, and acronyms. When checking a presentation for spelling errors, PowerPoint opens the standard dictionary and the custom dictionary file, if one exists. When a word appears in the Spelling pane, you can perform one of several actions, as described in Table 1–1.

The standard dictionary contains commonly used English words. It does not, however, contain many proper nouns, abbreviations, technical terms, poetic contractions, or antiquated terms. PowerPoint treats words not found in the dictionaries as misspellings.

BTW
Automatic Spelling Correction
As you type, PowerPoint automatically corrects some misspelled words. For example, if you type overwieght, PowerPoint automatically corrects the misspelling and displays the word, overweight, when you press SPACEBAR or type a punctuation mark. To see a complete list of automatically corrected words, click File on the ribbon to open Backstage view, click the Options tab, click Proofing in the left pane (PowerPoint Options dialog box), click AutoCorrect Options, and then scroll through the list near the bottom of the dialog box.

BTW
Detecting Spelling Errors
The x in the Spell Check icon indicates PowerPoint detected a possible spelling error. A check mark in the icon indicates the entered text contains no spelling errors.

Table 1–1: Spelling Pane Buttons and Actions

Button Name/Action	When to Use	Action
Ignore Once	Word is spelled correctly but not found in dictionaries	Continues checking rest of the presentation but will flag word again if it appears later in document
Ignore All	Word is spelled correctly but not found in dictionaries	Ignores all occurrences of word and continues checking rest of presentation
Add	Add word to custom dictionary	Opens custom dictionary, adds word, and continues checking rest of presentation
Change	Word is misspelled	Click proper spelling of the word in Suggestions list; PowerPoint corrects word, continues checking rest of presentation, but will flag that word again if it appears later in document
Change All	Word is misspelled	Click proper spelling of word in Suggestions list; PowerPoint changes all occurrences of misspelled word and continues checking rest of presentation
Listen to the pronunciation	To hear the pronunciation of a word	Click audio speaker icon next to the properly spelled word near bottom of Spelling pane
View synonyms	See some synonyms for the correctly spelled word	View bullet list of synonyms below correctly spelled word near the bottom of Spelling pane
Close	Stop spelling checker	Closes spelling checker and returns to PowerPoint window

To Check Spelling

Why? Although PowerPoint's spelling checker is a valuable tool, it is not infallible. You should not rely on the spelling checker to catch all your mistakes. The following steps check the spelling on all slides in the Passwords presentation.

1

- Click Review on the ribbon to display the Review tab.
- Click the Spelling button (Review tab | Proofing group) to start the spelling checker and display the Spelling pane (Figure 1–96).

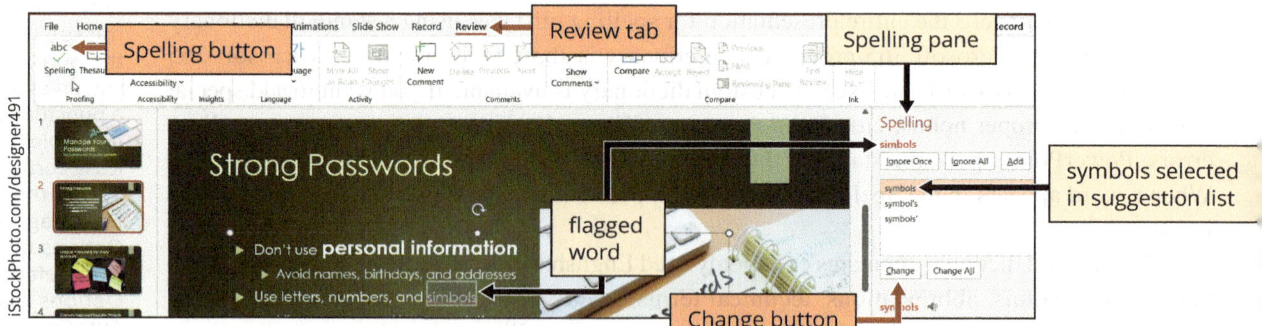

Figure 1–96

2

- With the word, simbols, selected in the slide and in the Spelling pane, click the Change button (Spelling pane) to replace the misspelled flagged word, simbols, with the selected correctly spelled word, symbols.

Q&A Could I have clicked the Change All button instead of the Change button?
Yes. When you click the Change All button, you change the current and future occurrences of the misspelled word. The misspelled word, simbols, appears only once in the presentation, so clicking the Change or the Change All button in this instance produces identical results.

Occasionally a correctly spelled word is flagged as a possible misspelled word. Why?
Your custom dictionary does not contain the word, so it is seen as spelled incorrectly. You can add this word to a custom dictionary to prevent the spelling checker from flagging it as a mistake.

3

- When Slide 4 is displayed, replace the misspelled word, Comon, with the word, Common (Figure 1-97).

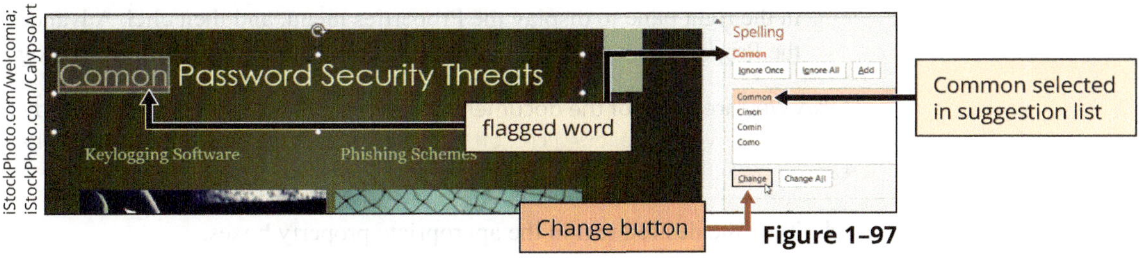

Figure 1-97

4

- Continue the spell check.
- When the Microsoft PowerPoint dialog box appears, click OK (Microsoft PowerPoint dialog box) to close the spelling checker and return to the slide where a possible misspelled word appeared (Figure 1-98).
- If necessary, close the Spelling pane.

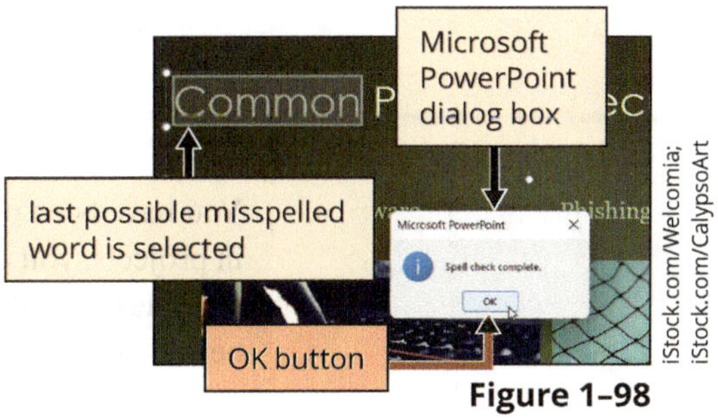

Figure 1-98

Other Ways

1. Click Spell Check icon on status bar
2. Right-click flagged word, click desired correct word
3. Press F7

Document Properties

PowerPoint helps you organize and identify your files by using **document properties**, which are the details about a file such as the project author, title, and subject. For example, a class name or presentation topic can describe the file's purpose or content.

Consider This

Why would you want to assign document properties to a presentation?

Document properties are valuable for a variety of reasons:

- Users can save time locating a particular file because they can view a file's document properties without opening the presentation.
- By creating consistent properties for files having similar content, users can better organize their presentations.
- Some organizations require PowerPoint users to add document properties so that other employees can view details about these files.

The more common document properties are standard and automatically updated properties. **Standard properties** are associated with all Microsoft 365 files and include author, title, and subject. **Automatically updated properties** include file system properties, such as the date you create or change a file, and statistics, such as the file size.

BTW
Printing Document Properties
PowerPoint does not allow you to print document properties. This feature, however, is available in Word.

To Change Document Properties

To change document properties, you would follow these steps.

1. Click File on the ribbon to open Backstage view and then, if necessary, click the Info tab in Backstage view to display the Info screen.
2. If the property you wish to change is displayed in the Properties list in the right pane of the Info screen, try to click that property. If a box with that property is displayed, type the text for the property in the box, and then click the Back button in the upper-left corner of Backstage view to return to the PowerPoint window. Skip the remaining steps.
3. If the property you wish to change is not displayed in the Properties list in the right pane of the Info screen or you cannot change it in the Info screen, click the Properties button in the right pane to display the Properties menu, and then click Advanced Properties on the Properties menu to display the Summary tab in the Properties dialog box.

Q&A Why are some of the document properties in my Properties List already filled in?
The person who installed Microsoft 365 on your computer or network may have set or customized the properties.

4. Type the desired text in the appropriate property boxes.
5. Click OK (Properties dialog box) to close the dialog box.
6. Click the Back button in the upper-left corner of Backstage view to return to the PowerPoint presentation window.

Changing Views

You have been using Normal view to create and edit your slides. Once you complete your slides in projects, you can review the final products by displaying each slide in **Slide Show view**, which occupies the full computer screen, to view how the slides will display in an actual presentation before an audience.

PowerPoint has other views to help review a presentation for content, organization, and overall appearance. **Slide Sorter view** allows you to look at several slides at one time. **Reading view** is similar to Slide Show view because each slide displays individually, but the slides do not fill the entire screen. Using this view, you easily can progress through the slides forward or backward with simple controls at the bottom of the window. Switching between Slide Sorter, Reading, and Normal views helps you review your presentation, assess whether the slides have an attractive design and adequate content, and make sure they are organized for the most impact. After reviewing the slides, you can change the view to Normal so that you may continue working on the presentation.

To Change Views

Why? You have made several modifications to the slides, so you should check for balance and consistency. The following steps change the view from Normal view to Slide Sorter view, then Reading view, and back to Normal view.

1

- Display Slide 1 and then click the Slide Sorter view button on the right side of the status bar to display the presentation in Slide Sorter view (Figure 1–99).

Q&A Why does a colored border display around Slide 1?
It is the current slide in the Slides tab.

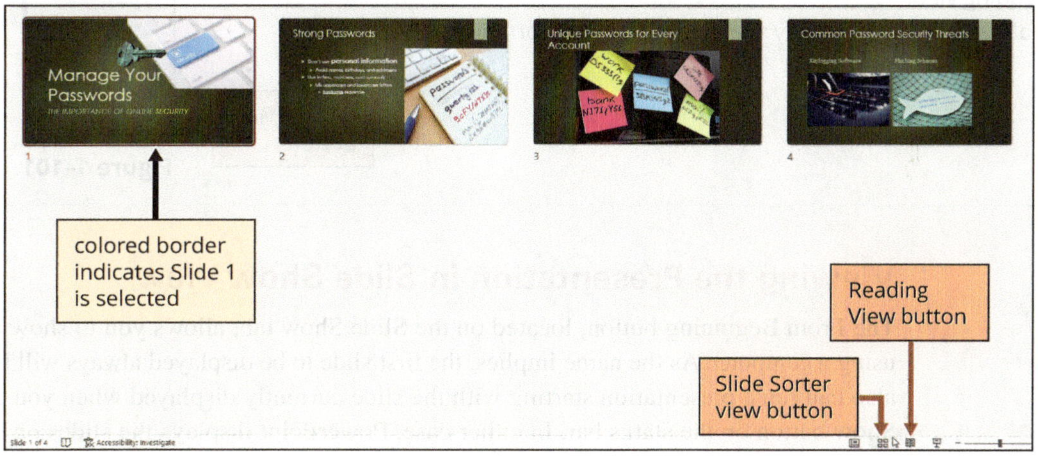

Figure 1–99

iStock.com/MicroStockHub; iStock.com/the-lightwriter; iStock.com/designer491; iStock.com/designer491; iStock.com/welcomia; iStock.com/CalypsoArt

2

- Click the Reading View button on the right side of the status bar to display Slide 1 of the presentation in Reading view (Figure 1–100).

Figure 1–100

iStock.com/MicroStockHub; iStock.com/the-lightwriter

3

- Click the Next button three times to advance through the presentation.
- Click the Previous button two times to display Slide 2.
- Click the Menu button to display commonly used commands (Figure 1–101).

4

- Click End Show to return to Slide Sorter view, which is the view you were using before Reading view.
- Click the Normal view button to display the presentation in Normal view.

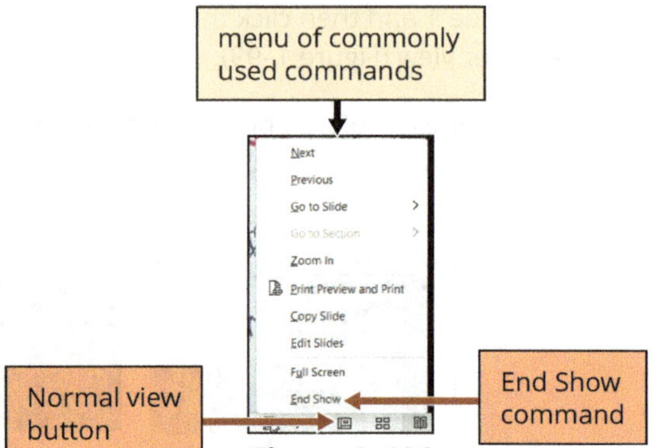

Figure 1–101

Viewing the Presentation in Slide Show View

The From Beginning button, located on the Slide Show tab, allows you to show a presentation using a computer. As the name implies, the first slide to be displayed always will be Slide 1. You also can run a presentation starting with the slide currently displayed when you click the Slide Show button on the status bar. In either case, PowerPoint displays the slides on the full screen without any of the PowerPoint window objects, such as the ribbon. The full-screen slide hides the toolbars, menus, and other PowerPoint window elements.

To Start Slide Show View

Why? You want to see your presentation as your audience would so you can see the slides in their entirety and view any transitions or other effects added to the slides. When making a presentation, you use Slide Show view to display slides so that they fill the entire screen. This is the view you use to show your presentation to an audience. You can start Slide Show view from Normal view or Slide Sorter view. Slide Show view begins when you click the From Beginning button or the Slide Show button. The following steps start Slide Show view starting with Slide 1.

1

- Click Slide Show on the ribbon to display the Slide Show tab.
- Point to the From Beginning button (Slide Show tab | Start Slide Show group) (Figure 1–102).

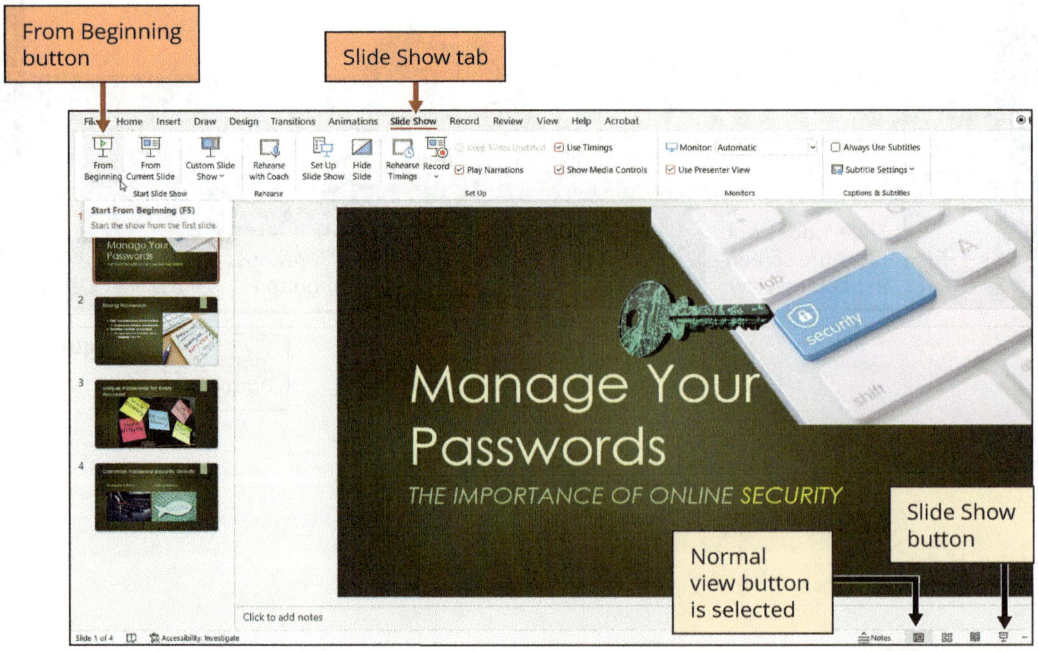

iStock.com/MicroStockHub; iStock.com/the-lightwriter

Figure 1–102

Q&A What would have displayed if I had clicked the Slide Show button on the status bar instead of the From Beginning button?
When you click the Slide Show button to start the presentation, PowerPoint begins the show with the currently displayed slide, which in this case is Slide 1. If, however, a different slide had been displayed, the slide show would have begun with that slide.

2

- Click the From Beginning button to display the title slide (Figure 1–103). The screen goes dark and then Slide 1 displays in the entire window.

Q&A Where is the PowerPoint window?
When you run a slide show, the PowerPoint window is hidden. It will reappear once you end your slide show.

I see a small toolbar in the lower-left corner of my slide. What is this toolbar?
You may see the Slide Show toolbar when you begin running a slide show and then move the pointer or click. The buttons on this toolbar allow you to navigate to the next slide or the previous slide, to mark up the current slide, or to change the current display. If you do not see the toolbar, hover the mouse near the lower-left corner of the screen.

iStock.com/MicroStockHub; iStock.com/the-lightwriter

Figure 1–103

Other Ways

1. Display Slide 1, click Slide Show button on status bar
2. Press F5
3. Click From Beginning button on Quick Access Toolbar, if available

To Move Manually through Slides in a Slide Show

After you begin Slide Show view, you can move forward or backward through the slides. PowerPoint allows you to advance through the slides manually or automatically. During a slide show, each slide in the presentation shows on the screen, one slide at a time. Each time you click the mouse, the next slide appears. The following steps move manually through the slides. **Why?** You can control the length of time each slide is displayed and change the preset order if you need to review a slide already shown or jump ahead to another slide designed to display later in the presentation.

1

- Click each slide until Slide 4 (Common Password Security Threats) is displayed (Figure 1–104).

iStock.com/welcomia; iStock.com/CalypsoArt

Figure 1–104

2

- Click Slide 4 so that the black slide appears with a message announcing the end of the slide show (Figure 1–105).

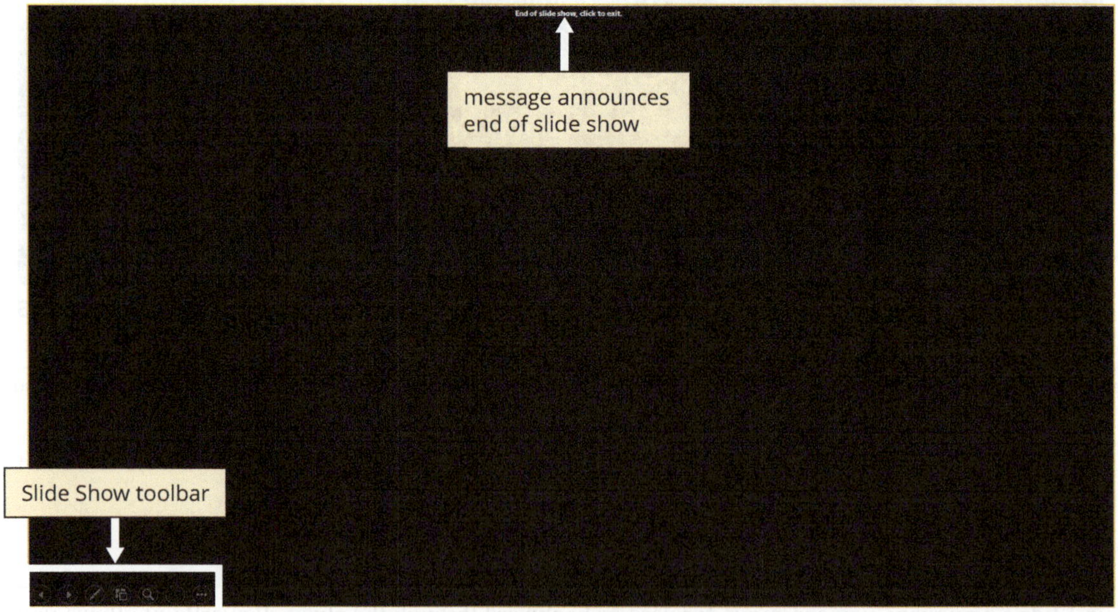

Figure 1–105

3

- Click the black slide to return to Normal view in the PowerPoint window.

Other Ways

1. Press PAGE DOWN to advance one slide at a time, or press PAGE UP to go back one slide at a time
2. Press RIGHT ARROW or DOWN ARROW to advance one slide at a time, or press LEFT ARROW or UP ARROW to go back one slide at a time
3. If Slide Show toolbar is displayed, click Next Slide or Previous Slide button on toolbar

Saving and Printing Files

While you are creating a presentation, the computer or mobile device stores it in memory. When you save a presentation, the computer or mobile device places it on a storage medium, such as a hard drive, solid state drive (SSD), USB flash drive, or cloud storage. The storage medium can be permanent in your computer, may be portable where you remove it from your computer, or may be on a web server you access through a network or the Internet.

To Save a File with a Different File Name

You might want to save a file with a different file name or to a different location. **Why?** You might start a homework assignment with a data file and then save it with a final file name for submission to your instructor, saving it to a different location designated by your instructor.

The following steps save the Passwords file with a different file name.

1. Click File on the ribbon to open Backstage view.
2. Click Save As (or Save a Copy if AutoSave is on) in Backstage view to display the Save As or Save a Copy screen.
3. Type **SC_PPT_1_Security** in the File name box, replacing the existing file name.

Q&A What are all those characters in the file name in this project?
Some companies require certain rules be followed when creating file names; others allow you to choose your own. The file names in this book do not use spaces and all begin with SC (for Shelly Cashman) and PPT (for PowerPoint) followed by the module number and then a descriptor of the file contents, and use underscores instead of spaces so that they work with SAM, if you are using that platform as well.

4. Click the Save button to save the presentation with the new name.

To Print Full Page Slides

With the presentation open, you may want to print it. **Why?** Because you want to see how the slides will appear on paper, you want to print a hard copy on a printer. The following steps print a hard copy of the contents of the presentation.

1.
- Display Slide 1 and then click File on the ribbon to open Backstage view.
- Click the Print tab in Backstage view to display the Print screen and a preview of Slide 1 (Figure 1–106).

Q&A What if I decide not to print the presentation at this time?
Click the Back button in the upper-left corner of Backstage view to return to the document window.

Why does the preview of my slide appear in black and white?
Your printer determines how the preview appears. If your printer is not capable of printing color images, the preview may appear in black and white.

BTW
Conserving Ink and Toner
If you want to conserve ink or toner, you can instruct PowerPoint to print draft quality documents by clicking File on the ribbon to open Backstage view, clicking Options in Backstage view to display the PowerPoint Options dialog box, clicking Advanced in the left pane (PowerPoint Options dialog box), scrolling to the Print area in the right pane, verifying there is no check mark in the High quality check box, and then clicking OK. Then, use Backstage view to print the document as usual.

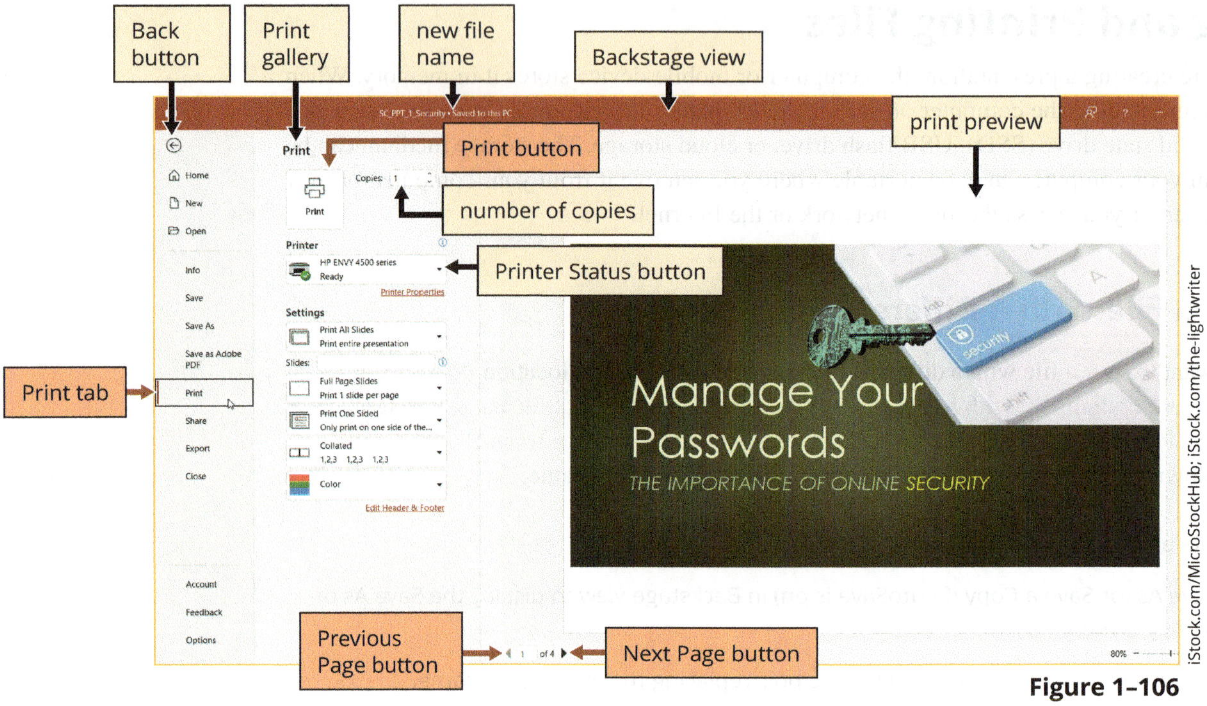

Figure 1–106

2

- Click the Next Page button to display Slide 2.

Q&A Do I need to change the display before I print?
No. You can print all the slides with any slide displaying in the preview window.

- Verify that the selected printer will print a hard copy of the presentation. If necessary, click the Printer Status button to display a list of available printer options and then click the desired printer to change the currently selected printer.

Q&A How can I print multiple copies of my presentation?
Increase the number in the Copies box in the Print screen.

3

- Click the Print button in the Print screen to print the presentation on the currently selected printer.
- When the printer stops, retrieve the hard copies (Figure 1–107).

Q&A What if I want to create a PDF of my presentation instead of printing a hard copy?
You would click the Printer Status button in the Print screen and then select Microsoft Print to PDF, Adobe PDF, or a similar option, which would create a PDF file.

Do I have to wait until my presentation is complete to print it?
No, you can print a presentation at any time while you are creating it.

BTW
Printing Background Images
If you do not use a color printer, background images display on the screen but may not display in the printouts. Graphics are displayed depending upon the settings in the Print gallery. For example, the background will print if Color is specified whereas it will not with a Grayscale or Pure Black and White setting.

iStock.com/MicroStockHub; iStock.com/the-lightwriter; iStock.com/welcomia; iStock.com/CalypsoArt

Figure 1–107

Other Ways

1. Press CTRL+P

To Preview and Print a Handout

Printing handouts is useful for reviewing a presentation. You can analyze several slides displayed simultaneously on one page. Additionally, many businesses distribute handouts of the slide show before or after a presentation so attendees can refer to a copy. Each page of the handout can contain reduced images of one, two, three, four, six, or nine slides. The three-slides-per-page handout includes lines beside each slide so that your audience can write notes conveniently. The following steps preview and print a presentation handout with two slides per page. **Why?** Two of the slides are predominantly pictures, so your audience does not need full pages of those images. The five bulleted paragraphs on Slide 2 can be read easily on one-half of a sheet of paper.

1

- If necessary, click File on the ribbon to open Backstage view and then click the Print tab.
- Click 'Full Page Slides' in the Settings area to display the Full Page Slides gallery (Figure 1–108).

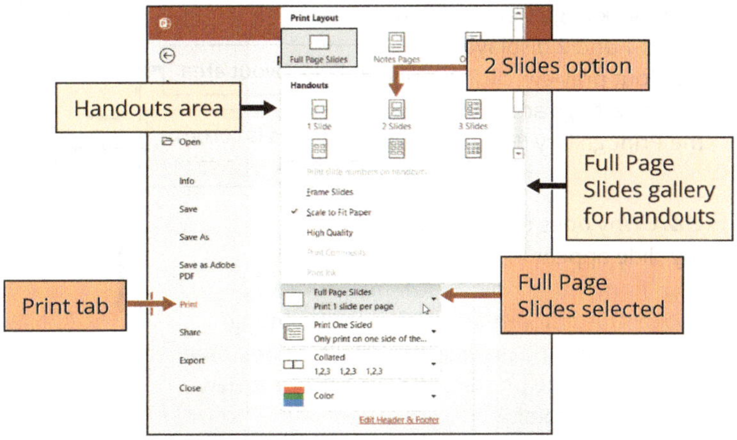

Figure 1–108

BTW

Distributing a Document

Instead of printing and distributing a hard copy of PowerPoint slides, you can distribute the slides electronically. Options include sending the slides via email; posting it on cloud storage (such as OneDrive) and sharing the link with others; posting it on social media, a blog, or other website; and sharing a link associated with an online location of the slides. You also can create and share a PDF or XPS image of the slides, so that users can view the file in Acrobat Reader or XPS Viewer instead of in PowerPoint.

2

- Click 2 Slides in the Handouts area to select this option and display a preview of the handout (Figure 1–109).

Q&A The current date displays in the upper-right corner of the handout, and the page number displays in the lower-right corner of the footer. Can I change their locations or add other information to the header and footer?

Yes. Click the 'Edit Header & Footer' link at the bottom of the Print screen, click the Notes and Handouts tab (Header and Footer dialog box), and then decide what content to include on the handout page.

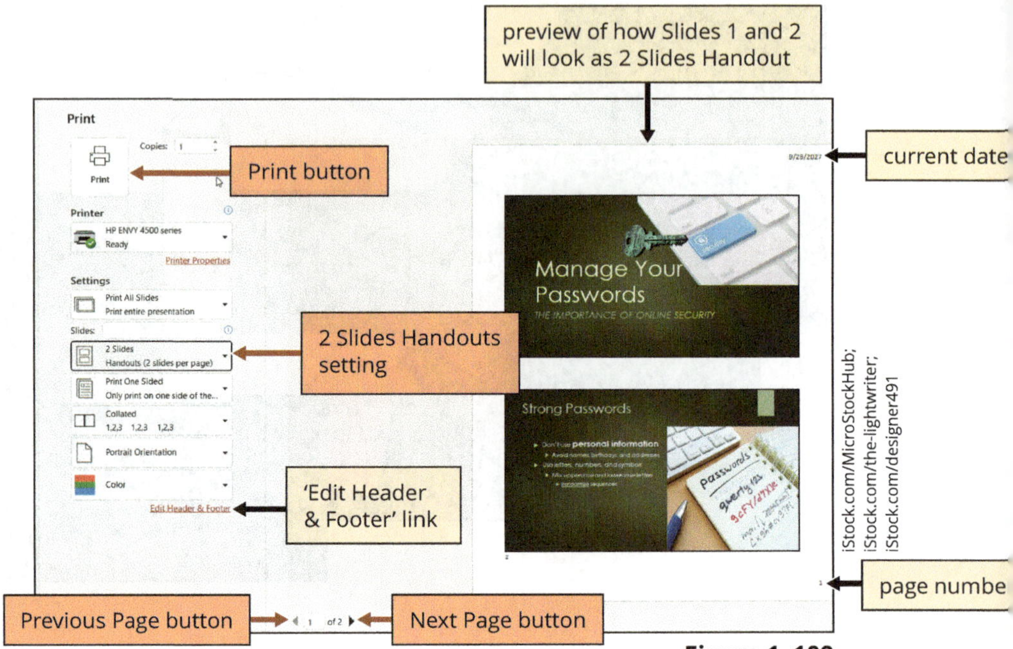

iStock.com/MicroStockHub; iStock.com/the-lightwriter; iStock.com/designer491

Figure 1–109

3

- Click the Next Page and Previous Page buttons to display previews of the two pages in the handout.
- Click the Print button in the Print screen to print the handout.
- When the printer stops, retrieve the printed handout.

To Print Speaker Notes

Why? Comments added to slides in the Notes pane give the speaker information that supplements the text on the slide. Notes will print with a small image of the slide at the top and the comments below the slide. The following steps print the speaker notes.

1

- With Backstage view open and Slides 1 and 2 displayed in the handout preview, click 2 Slides in the Settings area to display the Print gallery (Figure 1–110).

Q&A Why does the preview of my slide appear in color?

Your printer determines how the preview appears. If your printer is capable of printing color images, the preview appears in color. Some black-and-white printers also cause the preview to display in color.

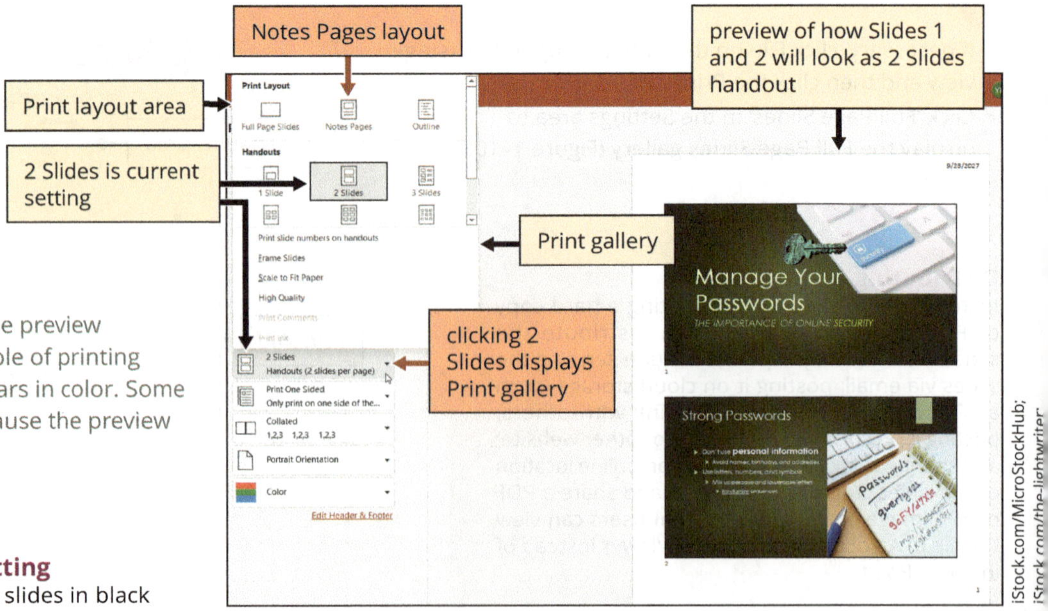

iStock.com/MicroStockHub; iStock.com/the-lightwriter

Figure 1–110

BTW
Using the Black and White Setting
The Black and White option prints slides in black and white. As a result, some objects in the design theme of the slide, such as embossing and drop shadows, will not print. Text will print as black even if you chose gray as the original color of the text.

2

- Click Notes Pages in the Print Layout area to select this option and then click the Next Page button two times to display a preview of Slide 3 and notes in a handout (Figure 1–111).

Q&A Can I preview other slides now?
Yes. Click the Next Page button or the Previous Page button to preview the other slides.

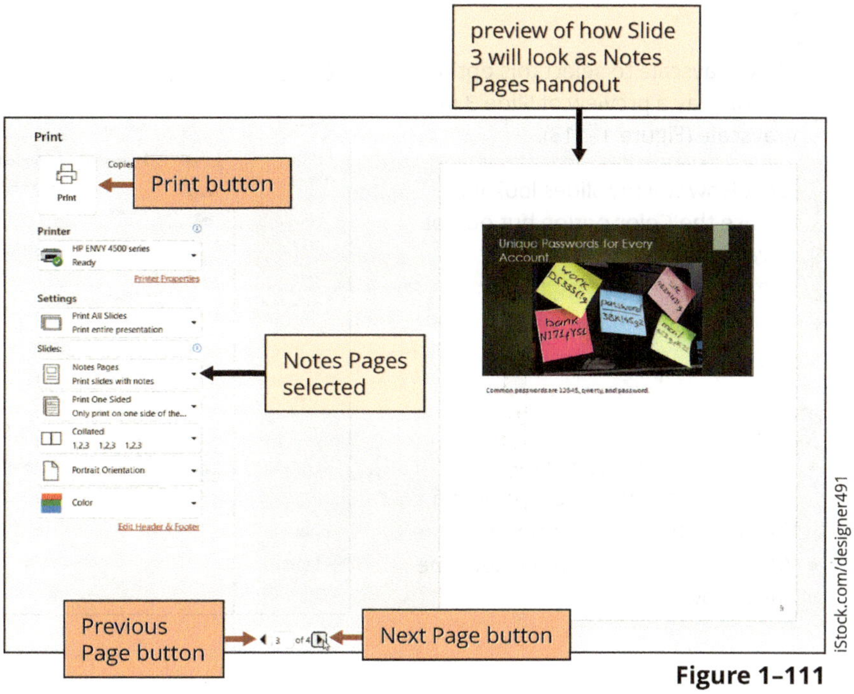

Figure 1–111

3

- Click the Print button in the Print gallery to print the notes pages on the currently selected printer.
- When the printer stops, retrieve the hard copy.

To Change the Print Color

Some printers are capable of printing in color, black and white, or grayscale. **Grayscale**, as the name implies, prints all objects on the page in black, white, and shades of gray. You can specify the print color by changing the setting in Backstage view. The following steps print the speaker notes in grayscale. **Why?** You are going to use a printer that does not have color printing capabilities.

1

- With Backstage view open and Slide 3 displayed in the handout preview, click Color in the Settings area to display the Color gallery (Figure 1–112).

Q&A How does the handout appear in Pure Black and White?
No shades of gray will print when the Pure Black and White setting is selected.

BTW
Using the Grayscale Setting
If you do not have a color printer or do not require a color printout, choosing Grayscale will print all pages in shades of gray. In grayscale, objects such as charts and tables will appear crisper and cleaner than if you chose the Color option on a non-color printer.

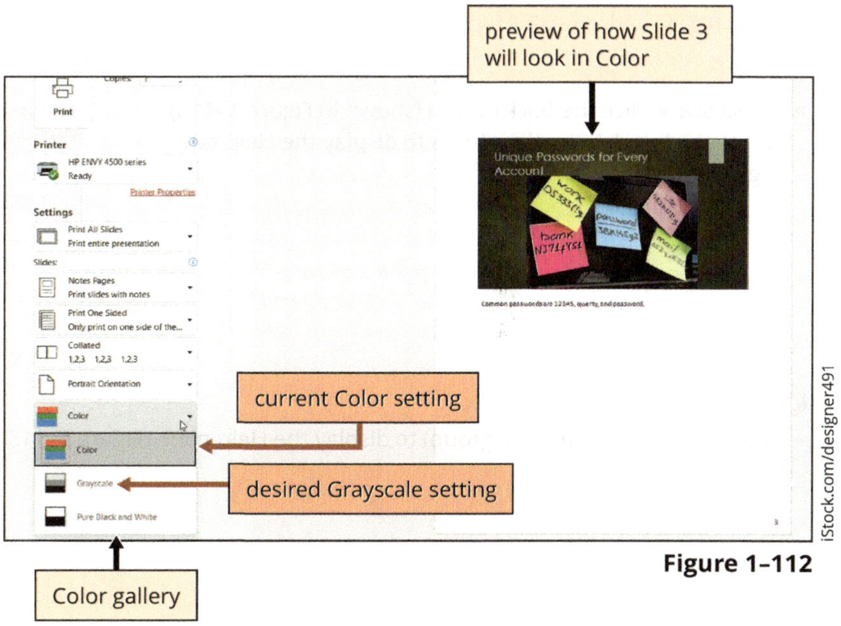

Figure 1–112

2

- Click Grayscale to select this option and display a preview of Slide 3 in grayscale (Figure 1–113).

Q&A How will my slides look if I choose the Color option but do not have a color printer?
The printout will be similar to printing in grayscale, but not of the same quality.

3

- Click the Print button in the Print gallery to print the notes pages on the currently selected printer.
- When the printer stops, retrieve the hard copy.

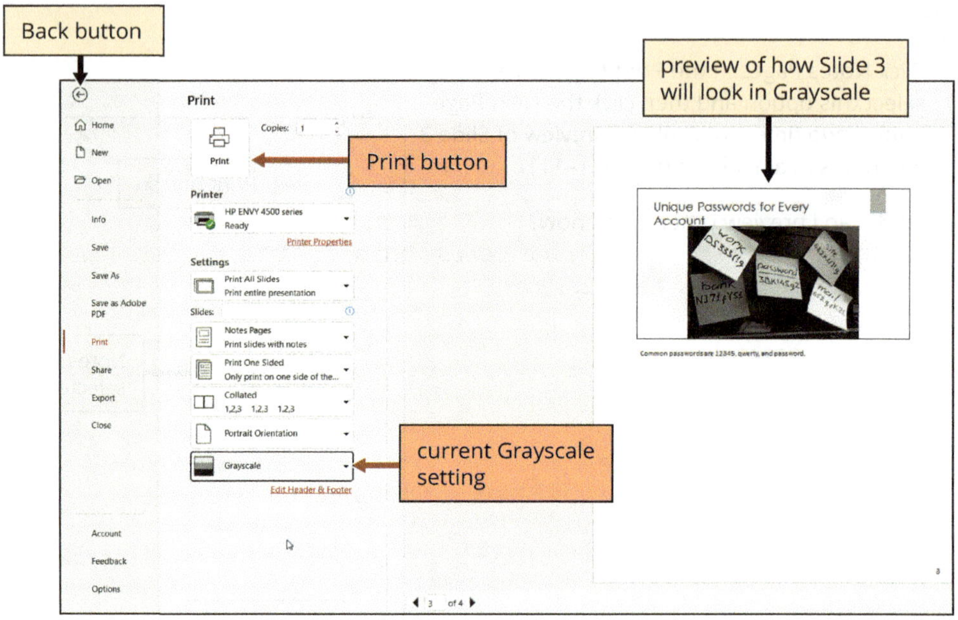

Figure 1–113

Using PowerPoint Help

At any time while you are using PowerPoint, you can use Help to display information about all topics associated with this app. Help is presented in a window that has browser-style navigation buttons. Once a Microsoft 365 app's Help window is open, several methods exist for navigating Help. You can search for help by using the Help pane or the Search box.

To Obtain Help Using the Help Pane

Assume for the following example that you want to know more about fonts. The following steps use the Help pane to obtain useful information about fonts by entering the word, fonts, as search text. **Why?** You may not know the exact help topic you are looking to find, so using keywords can help narrow your search.

1

- If necessary, click the Back button (shown in Figure 1–113) and then click Help on the ribbon to display the Help tab (Figure 1–114).

Figure 1–114

2

- Click the Help button (Help group) to display the Help pane (Figure 1–115).

iStock.com/MicroStockHub; iStock.com/the-lightwriter

Figure 1–115

3

- Type **fonts** in the Search help box at the top of the Help pane to enter the search text and display search suggestions.
- Point to change font in the search suggestions list (Figure 1–116).

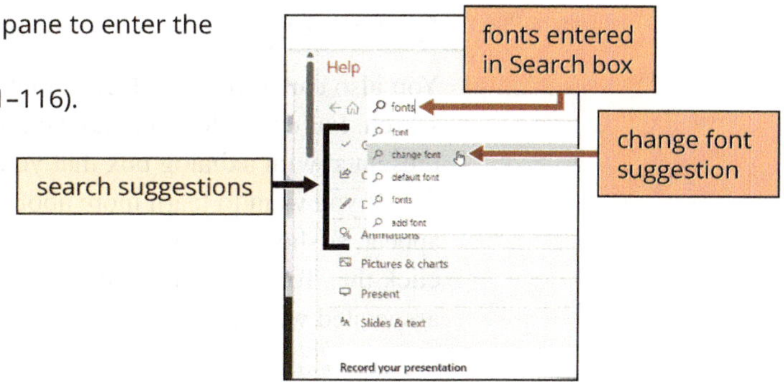

Figure 1–116

4

- Click change font and then scroll down and point to 'Change the fonts in a presentation' or a similar link (Figure 1–117).

Q&A Why do my search results differ?
If you do not have an Internet connection, your results will reflect only the content of the Help files on your computer. When searching for help online, results also can change as content is added, deleted, and updated on the online Help webpages maintained by Microsoft.

Why were my search results not very helpful?
When initiating a search, be sure to check the spelling of the search text; also, keep your search specific to return the most accurate results.

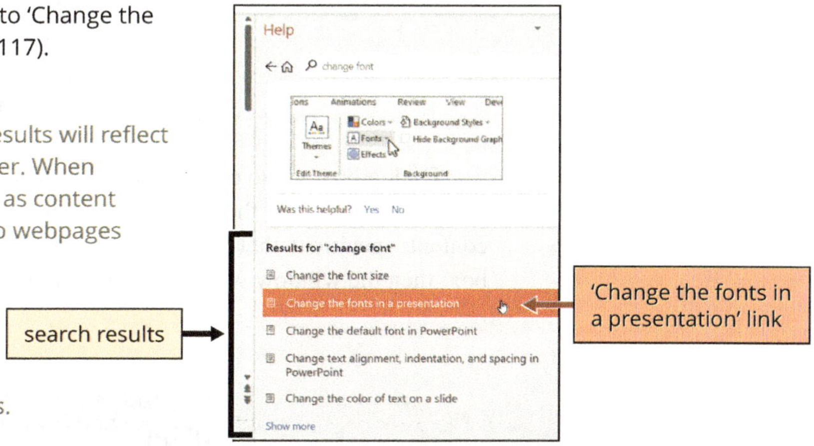

Figure 1–117

5

- Click 'Change the fonts in a presentation' or a similar link to display the Help information associated with the selected topic (Figure 1–118).

6

- Click the Close button in the Help pane to close the pane.
- Click Home on the ribbon to display the Home tab.

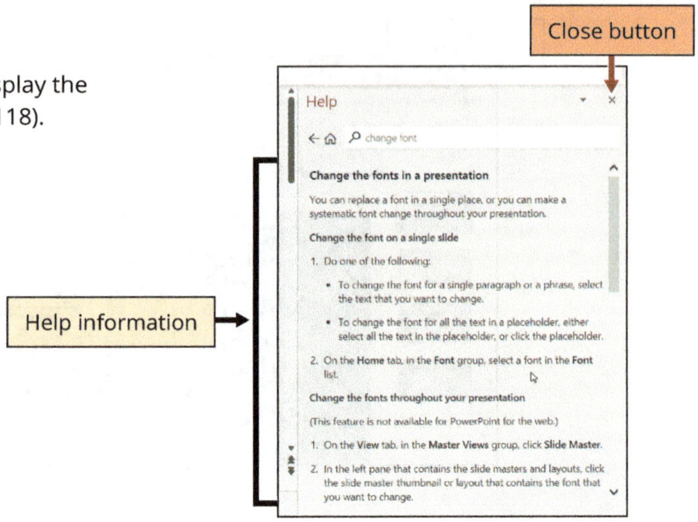

Figure 1–118

Obtaining Help while Working in PowerPoint

You also can access the Help functionality without first opening the Help pane and initiating a search. For example, you may be unsure about how a particular command works, or you may be presented with a dialog box that you are not sure how to use.

If you want to learn more about a command, point to its button and wait for the ScreenTip to appear, as shown in Figure 1–119. If the Help icon and 'Tell me more' link appear in the ScreenTip, click the 'Tell me more' link (or press F1 while pointing to the button) to open the Help window associated with that command.

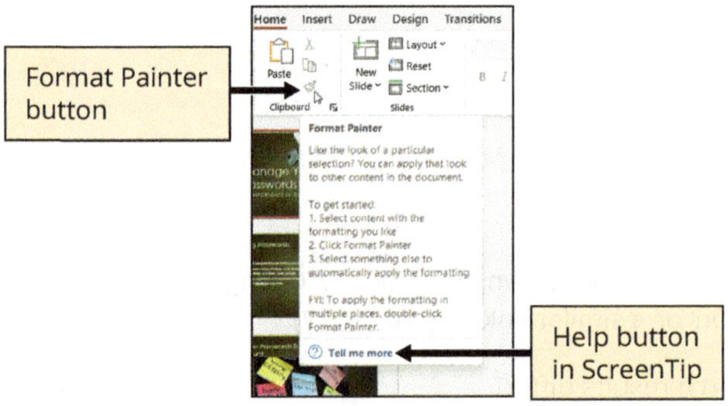

Figure 1–119

Dialog boxes also contain Help buttons, as shown in Figure 1–120. Clicking the Help button or pressing F1 while the dialog box is displayed opens a Help window, which will display help contents specific to that dialog box, if available. If no help file is available for that particular dialog box, then the window will display the Help home page.

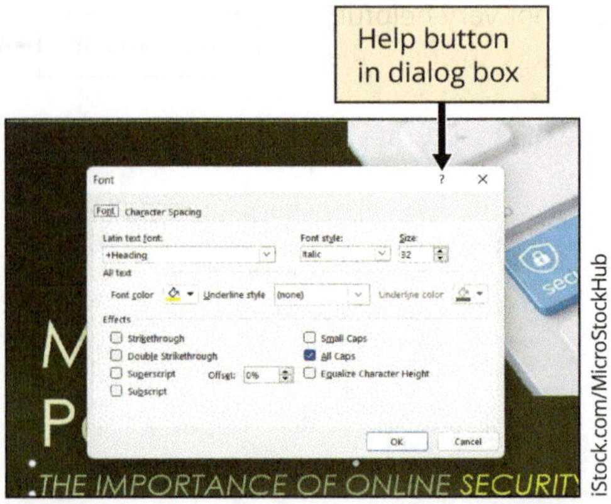

Figure 1–120

As mentioned previously, the Search box is integrated into the title bar in PowerPoint and most other Microsoft 365 apps and can perform a variety of functions. One of these functions is to provide easy access to commands and help content as you type.

To Obtain Help Using the Search Box

If you are having trouble finding a command in PowerPoint, you can use the Search box to search for the function you are trying to perform. As you type, the Search box will suggest commands that match the search text you are entering. **Why?** You can use the Search box to access commands quickly that you otherwise may be unable to find on the ribbon. The following steps find information about borders.

1

- Type **border** in the Search box and watch the search results appear.
- Point to Border Style to display a submenu showing the various border designs (Figure 1–121).

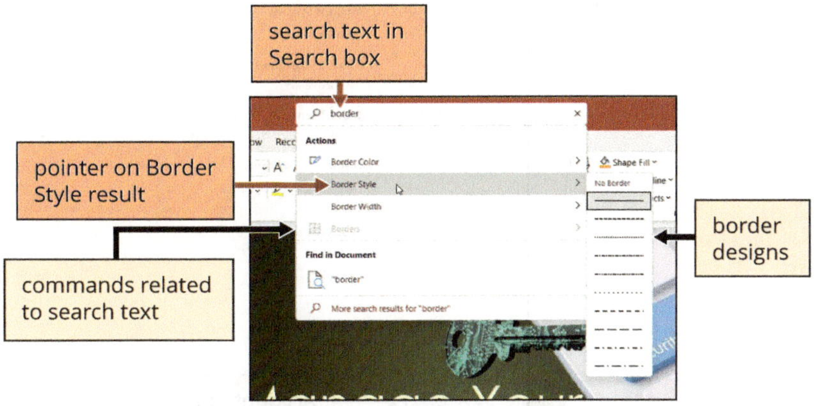

Figure 1–121

iStock.com/MicroStockHub; iStock.com/the-lightwriter

To Sign Out of a Microsoft Account

If you are using a public computer or otherwise wish to sign out of your Microsoft account, you should sign out of the account from the Accounts screen in Backstage view. Signing out of the account is the safest way to make sure that nobody else can access online files or settings stored in your Microsoft account. **Why?** For security reasons, you should sign out of your Microsoft account when you are finished using a public or shared computer. Staying signed in to your Microsoft account might enable others to access your files.

The following steps sign out of a Microsoft account from PowerPoint. If you do not wish to sign out of your Microsoft account, read these steps without performing them.

1. Click File on the ribbon to open Backstage view.
2. Click the Account tab to display the Account screen (Figure 1–122).
3. Click the Sign out link, which displays the Remove Account dialog box. If a Can't remove Windows accounts dialog box appears instead of the Remove Account dialog box, click OK and skip the remaining steps.

Q&A Why does a Can't remove Windows accounts dialog box appear?
If you signed in to Windows using your Microsoft account, then you also must sign out from Windows, rather than signing out from within PowerPoint. When you are finished using Windows, be sure to sign out at that time.

4. Click the Yes button (Remove Account dialog box) to sign out of your Microsoft account on this computer.

Q&A Should I sign out of Windows after removing my Microsoft account?
When you are finished using the computer, you should sign out of Windows for maximum security.

5. Click the Back button in the upper-left corner of Backstage view to return to the presentation.

6 Click the Close button to close the presentation and PowerPoint. If you are prompted to save changes, click Yes to save any changes made to the file since the last save.

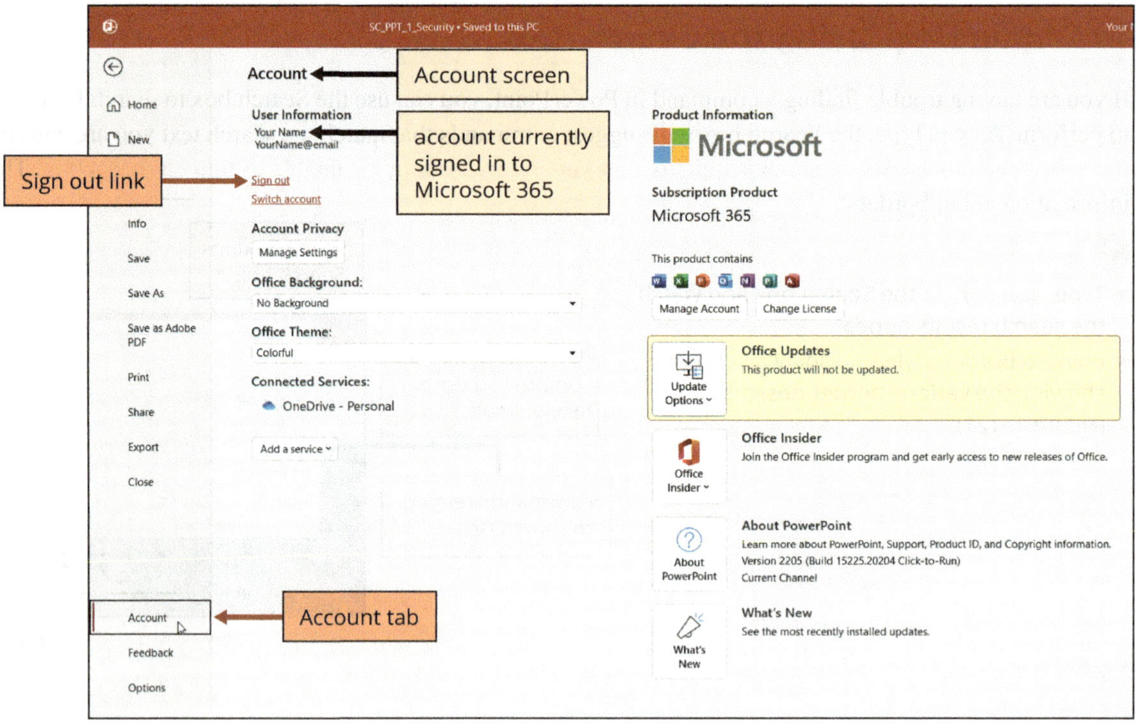

Figure 1–122

Summary

In this module, you learned how to use PowerPoint to create and enhance a presentation. Topics covered included starting PowerPoint, applying and changing a presentation theme and theme colors, creating a title slide and text slides with a multilevel bulleted list, inserting pictures and then resizing and moving them on a slide, formatting and editing text, adding notes, printing the presentation, and reviewing the presentation in several views.

Consider This: Plan Ahead

What decisions do you need to make when creating your next presentation?

Use these guidelines as you complete the assignments in this module and create your own slide show decks outside of this class.

1. Determine the content you want to include on your slides.
2. Determine which theme is appropriate.
3. Identify the slide layouts that best communicate your message.
4. Format various text elements to emphasize important points.
   a) Select appropriate font sizes.
   b) Emphasize important words with bold, italic, or underlined type and color.
5. Locate graphical elements, such as pictures, that reinforce your message.
   a) Size and position them aesthetically on slides.
6. Determine a storage location for the presentation.
7. Determine the best method for distributing the presentation.

Student Assignments

Apply Your Knowledge

Reinforce the skills and apply the concepts you learned in this module.

Modifying Character Formats and Paragraph Levels and Inserting and Moving a Picture

Note: To complete this assignment, you will be required to use the Data Files. Please contact your instructor for information about accessing the Data Files.

Instructions: Start PowerPoint. Open the presentation called SC_PPT_1-1.pptx, which is located in the Data Files. The marketing manager at your local bank has asked you to help develop a presentation for customers on the topic of avoiding identity theft. The manager has started by creating two unformatted slides. You open the presentation and then modify the theme and colors, indent the paragraphs, insert, resize and move a picture, and format the text so the slides look like Figure 1–123.

Perform the following tasks:

1. Change the document theme to Quotable. Change the theme colors to Blue.
2. On the title slide, use your name in place of Student Name and then italicize and underline your name.

   If requested by your instructor, change your first name to your childhood best friend's first name on the title slide.
3. Increase the title text font size to 72 point, change the font to Bookman Old Style, and then italicize this text.
4. Increase the subtitle text font size for both paragraphs to 36 point. Underline the word, Target, and change the color of this word to Red.
5. Insert the picture named Support_PPT_1_Private.jpg. Resize the picture to 4" × 4" and then position the picture using the smart guides to display the vertical guide along the right edge of the image and the horizontal smart guide in the center of the picture (Figure 1–123a).
6. On Slide 2, combine paragraphs two and three (Credit reports available and Three national credit bureaus) to read, **Reports available from three national credit bureaus**, as shown in Figure 1–123b. Increase the indent of this paragraph to second level. Then, increase the indent of the fourth and fifth paragraphs to second-level paragraphs and the sixth paragraph to a third-level paragraph.
7. On Slide 2 in the Notes pane, type **New account fraud is an extremely common form of identity theft. Thieves use personal information to open bank and credit card accounts.**
8. Click the 'Start From Beginning' button to start the show from the first slide. Then click to display the second slide and again to end the presentation.
9. Save the file with the file name, **SC_PPT_1_Identity**, and submit the revised presentation (shown in Figure 1–123) in the format specified by your instructor.
10. **Consider This:** In Step 6, you combined two paragraphs and indented paragraphs. How did these actions improve the slide content?

Continued on next page

Figure 1–123(a): Slide 1 (Title Slide with a Picture)

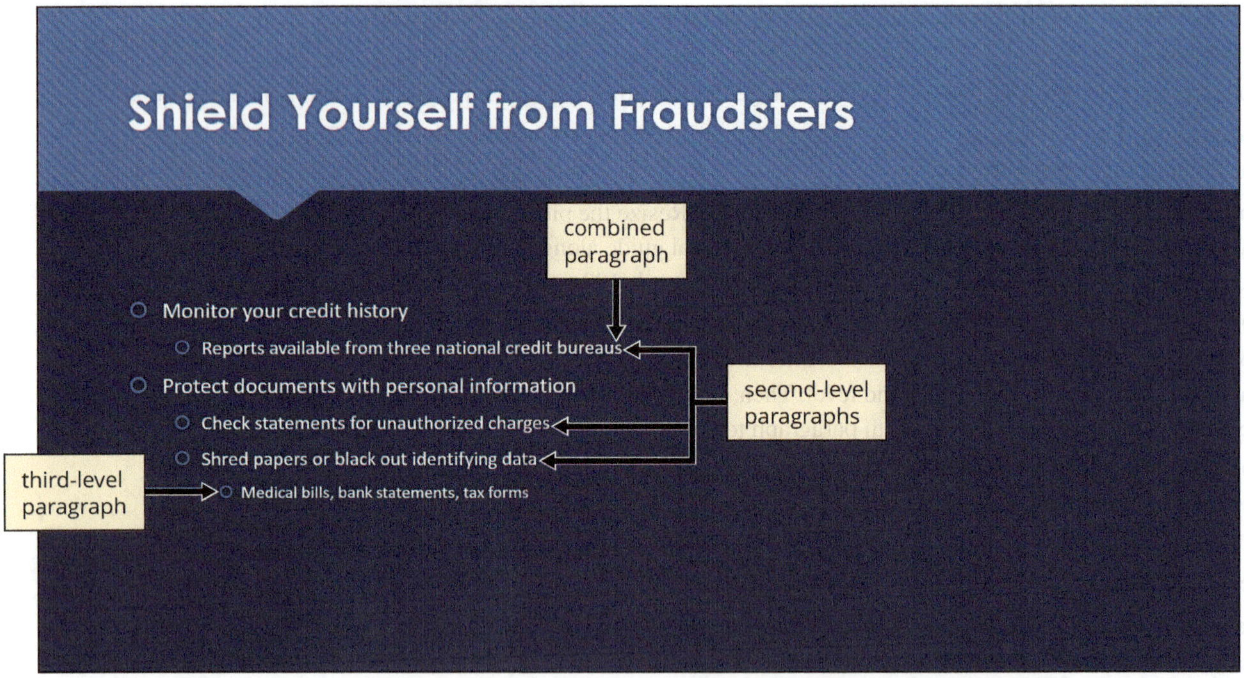

Figure 1–123(b): Slide 2 (Multilevel Bulleted List)

Extend Your Knowledge

Extend the skills you learned in this module and experiment with new skills. You may need to use Help to complete the assignment.

Changing the Slide Theme, Layout, and Text

Note: To complete this assignment, you will be required to use the Data Files. Please contact your instructor for information about accessing the Data Files.

Instructions: Start PowerPoint. Open the presentation called SC_PPT_1-2.pptx, which is located in the Data Files. Slide 1 is shown in Figure 1–124. The adult education instructors at your school offer a free program to educate community residents on how they can beautify their yards with environmentally friendly plants. They have developed three slides to accompany a speech they will be giving at your local garden center, and they have asked you to insert appropriate pictures, choose a theme, and format these slides.

Perform the following tasks:

1. Change the document theme to Organic and the theme colors to Green.
2. On Slide 1, format the title text using techniques you learned in this module, such as changing the font size and color and bolding, italicizing, and underlining words.
3. Replace the text, Student Name, with your name.

   If requested by your instructor, replace your last name on Slide 1 with the name of your hometown.
4. Delete the bullet preceding your name because, in most cases, a bullet is displayed as the first character in a list consisting of several paragraphs, not just one line of text.
5. Resize the picture and move it to an appropriate area on the slide.
6. On Slide 2, add bullets to the six paragraphs in the left content placeholder. To add bullets, select the paragraphs and then click the Bullets button (Home tab | Paragraph group). Insert the picture called Support_PPT_1_Garden.jpg, which is located in the Data Files, in the right content placeholder. Resize this picture and then move it to an appropriate area on the slide.
7. On Slide 3, add bullets to the three paragraphs in the left heading placeholder. Insert the picture called Support_PPT_1_Leaf.jpg, which is located in the Data Files. Resize this picture to approximately 2.5" × 4.0", rotate it 90 degrees, and then move it to the right side of the slide.
8. Duplicate the title slide. To duplicate this slide, select it, click the New Slide arrow (Home tab | Slides group) to display the layout gallery, and then click 'Duplicate Selected Slides' in the layout gallery.
9. Move the new slide to the end of the presentation. Change the title text to **Improve Your Environment** and then underline this text. Delete your name. Insert the two pictures, Support_PPT_1_Leaf.jpg and Support_PPT_1_Garden.jpg, and then size and move all three pictures to appropriate places on the slide.
10. Display Slide 1 and then click the Slide Show button to start the show from the first slide. Then click to display each slide and again to end the presentation.
11. Save the file with the file name, **SC_PPT_1_Yard**, and submit the revised presentation in the format specified by your instructor.
12. **Consider This:** How did you determine the appropriate size and location of the three pictures on the duplicated slide?

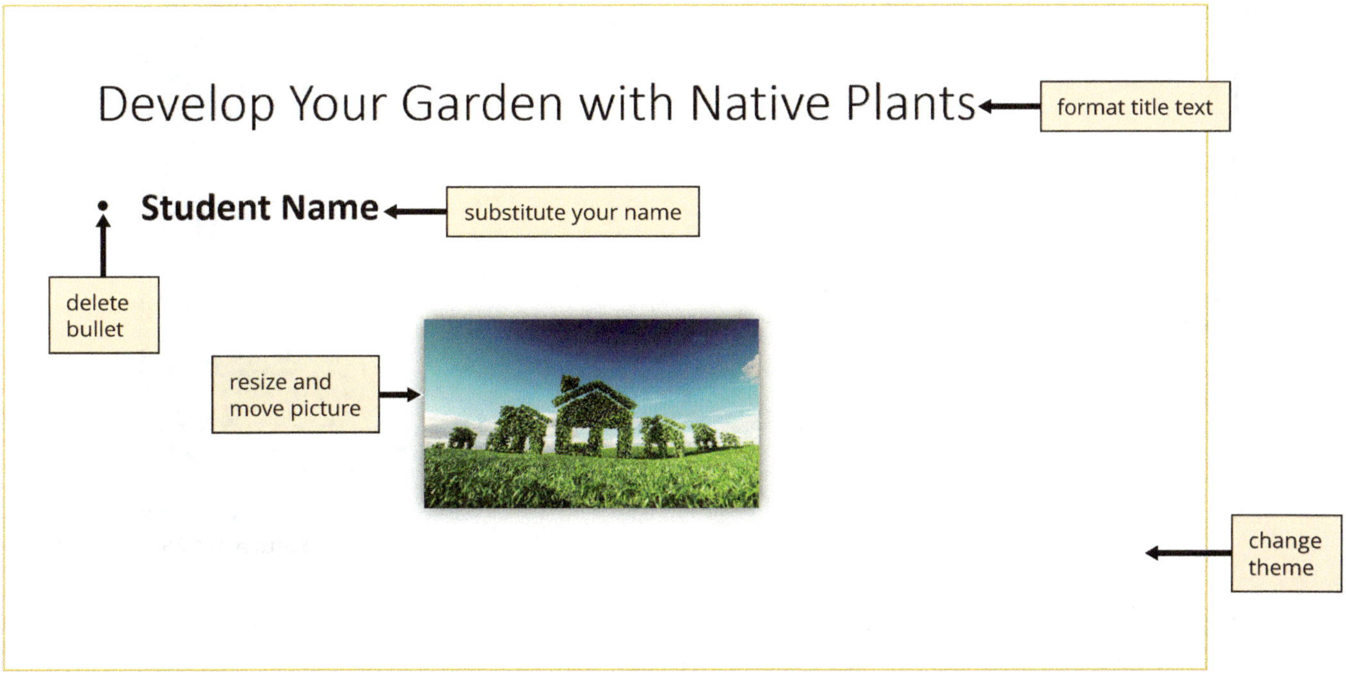

iStock.com/Petmal

Figure 1–124

Expand Your World

Create a solution that uses cloud and web technologies by learning and investigating on your own from general guidance.

Modifying and Exporting a Presentation

Note: To complete this assignment, you will be required to use the Data Files. Please contact your instructor for information about accessing the Data Files.

Instructions: Start PowerPoint. Open the presentation called SC_PPT_1-3.pptx, which is located in the Data Files. The presentation you open contains one title slide promoting drinking water regularly every day. The nutritionists at your community's fitness center want to emphasize the many benefits of drinking water, and they are planning to present a seminar on the topic of reasons to stay hydrated. You are part of a committee to publicize the event and want to share the title slide you developed. You have decided to store the file on OneDrive. You are going to modify the slide you have created, shown in Figure 1–125, and save it to OneDrive.

Perform the following tasks:

1. Insert the pictures called Support_PPT_1_Bottle.jpg and Support_PPT_1_Stay.jpg, which are located in the Data Files. Size and then move them to the areas indicated in Figure 1–125. Use the smart guides to help you position the pictures.

   If requested to do so by your instructor, change the words, Chicago, IL, to the town and state where you were born.
2. Save the file to your OneDrive account.
3. Save the file with the file name, **SC_PPT_1_Water**, and submit the presentation in the format specified by your instructor.
4. **Consider This:** When would you save one of your files for school or your job to OneDrive? Do you think using OneDrive enhances collaboration efforts? Why?

Figure 1–125

In the Lab

Apply your creative thinking and problem-solving skills to design and implement a solution.

Design and Create a Presentation about Summer Camp

Part 1: Your local park district is preparing to advertise its Kids Camp, and the public relations department employees have asked you to develop a PowerPoint presentation as part of your internship responsibilities. They inform you that this year's Camp will begin on July 1 and will run for 4 weeks. Popular activities include artistic workshops and field trips. Registration is being held now at the park district office, which is open from noon to 4 pm daily. The non-refundable Camp fee is $245, which includes lunch, and early registrants will receive a free t-shirt. Use the concepts and techniques presented in this module to prepare a presentation with a minimum of four slides that showcase the Kids Camp program. Research summer day camp programs held in previous years and in other communities for ideas about promoting the various activities. Select a suitable theme and include a title slide and bulleted lists. Use the pictures Support_PPT_1_Chalkboard.jpg, Support_PPT_1_Campers.jpg, Support_PPT_1_Painting.jpg, and Support_PPT_1_Clock.jpg, which are located in the Data Files. When finished, save your presentation with the file name, **SC_PPT_1_Camp**. Review and revise your presentation as needed. Submit your assignment in the format specified by your instructor.

Part 2: **Consider This:** You made several decisions while creating the presentation in this assignment: what theme to use, where to place text, how to format the text (font, font size, paragraph alignment, bulleted paragraphs, italics, bold, underline, color). What was the rationale behind each of these decisions? When you reviewed the slides, what further revisions did you make and why? Where would you recommend showing this slide show?

Enhancing Presentations with Shapes and SmartArt

Objectives

After completing this module, you will be able to:

- Search for and download an online theme
- Insert a symbol
- Convert text to SmartArt
- Edit and format SmartArt text
- Insert a hyperlink to a webpage
- Resize an inserted shape
- Apply effects to a shape
- Add text to a shape
- Apply a shape style
- Move an object smart guides
- Merge shapes
- Insert a picture as a shape fill
- Add a footer
- Add a slide transition and effect options

Introduction

In our visually oriented culture, audience members enjoy viewing effective graphics. Whether reading a document or viewing a PowerPoint presentation, people increasingly want to see photos, artwork, graphics, and a variety of typefaces. Researchers have known for decades that documents with visual elements are more effective than those that consist of only text because the illustrations motivate audiences to study the material. People remember at least one-third more information when the document they are seeing or reading contains visual elements. These graphics help clarify and emphasize details, so they appeal to audience members with differing backgrounds, reading levels, attention spans, and motivations.

BTW
Building Speaker Confidence
As you rehearse your speech, keep in mind that your audience will by studying the visual elements during your actual presentation and will not be focusing on you. Using graphics in a presentation should give you confidence as a presenter because they support your verbal message and help reinforce what you are trying to convey.

Project—Presentation with SmartArt and Shapes

In this module's project, you will follow proper design guidelines and learn to use PowerPoint to create the slides shown in Figures 2–1a through 2–1e. The objective is to produce a presentation for the Career Success Center that provides a variety of services to help students identify majors and find jobs that fit their interests, skills, and personality. The Center has an experienced staff with expertise in exploring careers, and they use the *Occupational Outlook Handbook* to provide information about the qualifications, salary, and work environment for hundreds of jobs. The Center's career coaches also give assessment tests and coordinate internships and networking opportunities. Students can begin their job search by using an online tool that allows them to search for and then apply for openings at a variety of organizations. The presentation shown in Figure 2–1 follows graphical guidelines and has a variety of visual elements that are clear and appealing to students exploring career options and searching for jobs. For example, the shapes have specific designs and effects. They are formatted using styles and SmartArt, which give the presentation a professional look. Transitions help one slide flow gracefully into the next during a slide show.

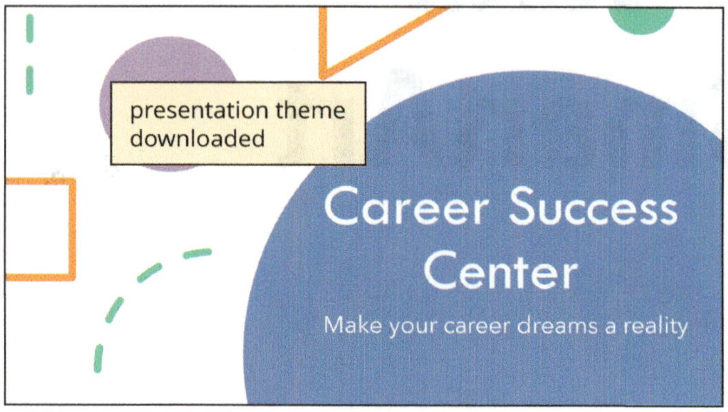

Figure 2–1(a): Slide 1 (Title Slide)

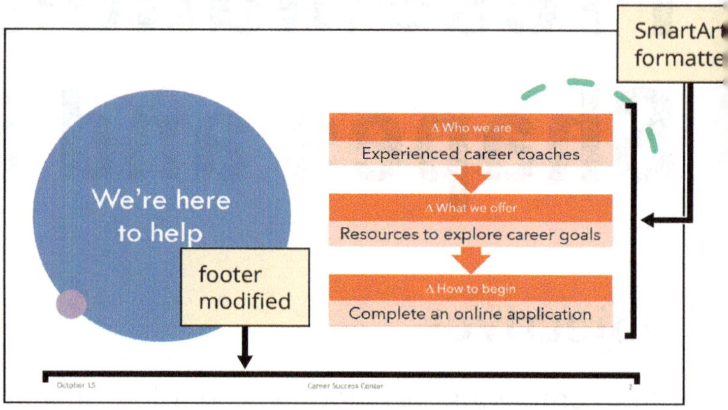

Figure 2–1(b): Slide 2 (Formatted SmartArt)

Figure 2–1(c): Slide 3 (Formatted SmartArt)

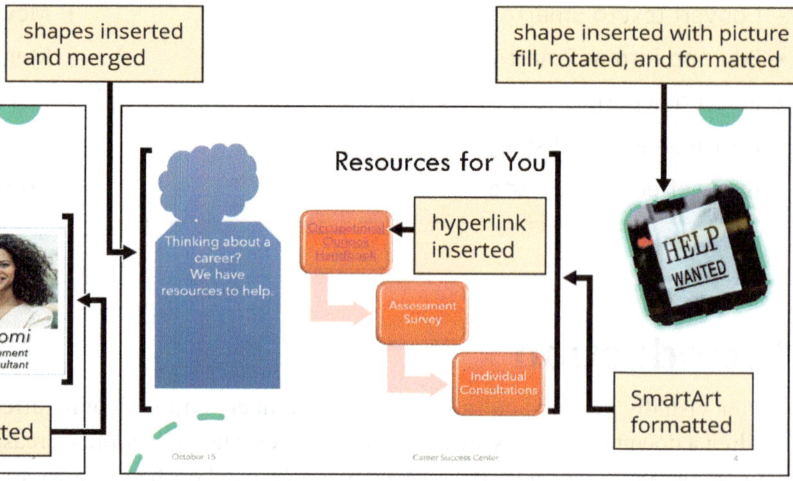

Figure 2–1(d): Slide 4 (Formatted SmartArt and Shape with Picture Fill)

Tim Mossholder/Pexels

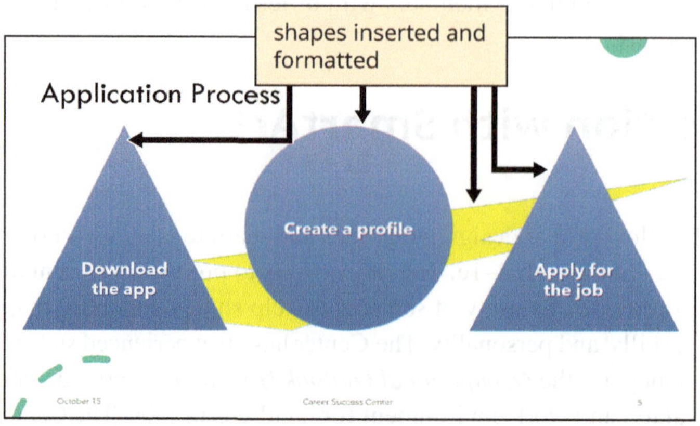

Figure 2–1(e): Slide 5 (Shapes Inserted and Formatted)

In this module, you will learn how to create the slides shown in Figure 2–1. You will perform the following general tasks as you progress through this module:

1. Download a theme and select slides for the presentation.
2. Create, edit, and format SmartArt.
3. Insert and format shapes.
4. Insert a symbol and a hyperlink.
5. Resize and merge shapes.
6. Move shapes using grids, guides, and the ruler.
7. Modify a footer and add a transition.

BTW
Screen Resolution
If you are using a computer to step through the project in this module and you want your screens to match the figures in this book, you should change your screen's resolution to 1920 × 1080.

Downloading a Theme and Editing Slides

In Module 1, you selected a theme and then typed the content for the title and text slides. In this module, you will type the slide content for the title and text slides, insert and format SmartArt, and insert and format shapes. To begin creating the five slides in this presentation, you will download a theme, delete unneeded slides in this downloaded presentation, and then enter content in the slides.

To Search for and Download an Online Theme

PowerPoint displays many themes that are varied and appealing and give you an excellent start at designing a presentation. At times, however, you may have a specific topic and design concept and could use some assistance in starting to develop the presentation. Microsoft offers thousands of predesigned themes and templates that could provide you with an excellent starting point. **Why?** You can search for one of these ready-made presentations, or you can browse one of the predefined categories, such as business or education. The themes and templates can save you time and help you develop content. The following steps search for a theme with a geometric concept.

1

- sam Run PowerPoint and then point to the More themes link (Figure 2–2).

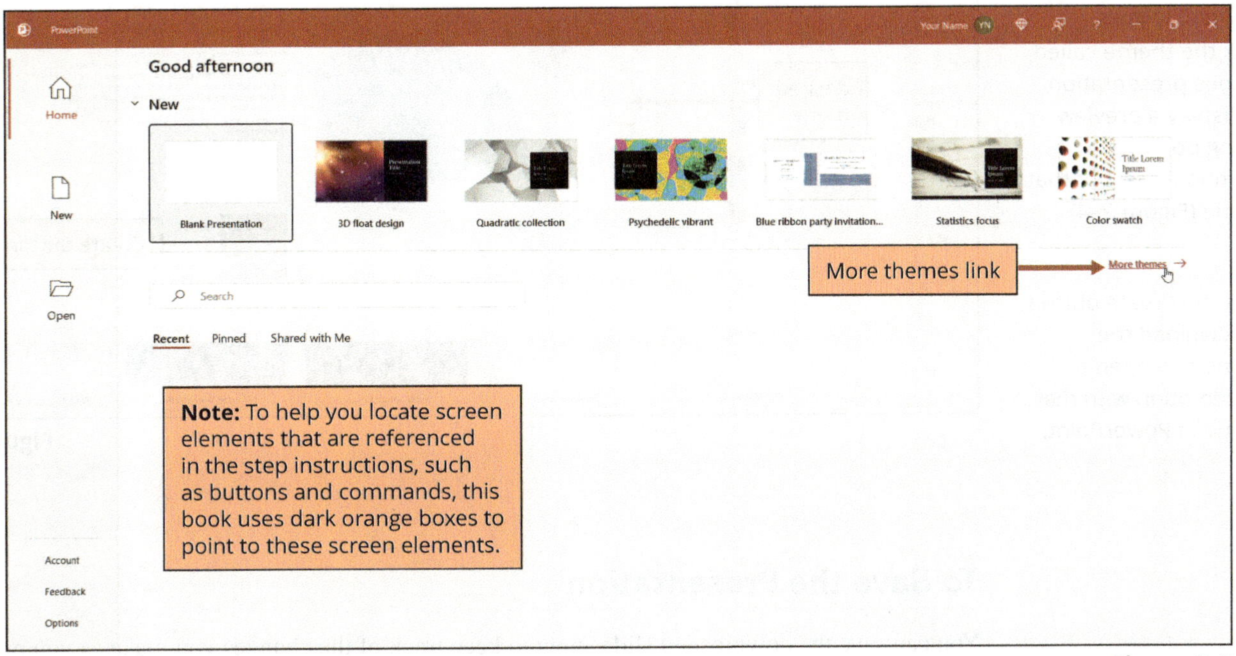

Figure 2–2

2

- Click the More themes link to display the New screen and then type **shapes** in the 'Search for online templates and themes' box (Figure 2–3).

Q&A Why are my theme thumbnails displaying in a different order?
The order changes as you choose themes for presentations. In addition, Microsoft occasionally adds and modifies the themes, so the order may change.

Can I choose one of the keywords listed below the 'Search for online templates and themes' box?
Yes. Click one of the terms in the Suggested searches list to display a variety of templates and themes relating to those topics.

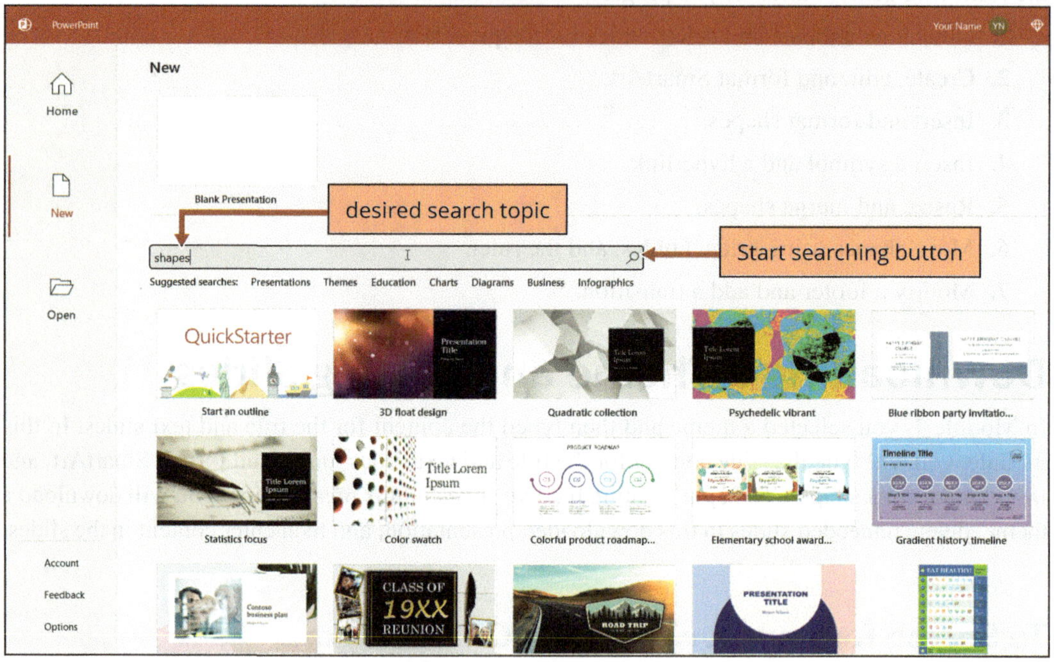

Figure 2–3

3

- Click the Start searching button (the magnifying glass) or press ENTER to search for and display all themes with the keyword, shapes.
- Click the theme called Shapes presentation to display a preview dialog box with a thumbnail view of that theme (Figure 2–4).

4

- Click the Create button to download the theme and open a presentation with that theme in PowerPoint.

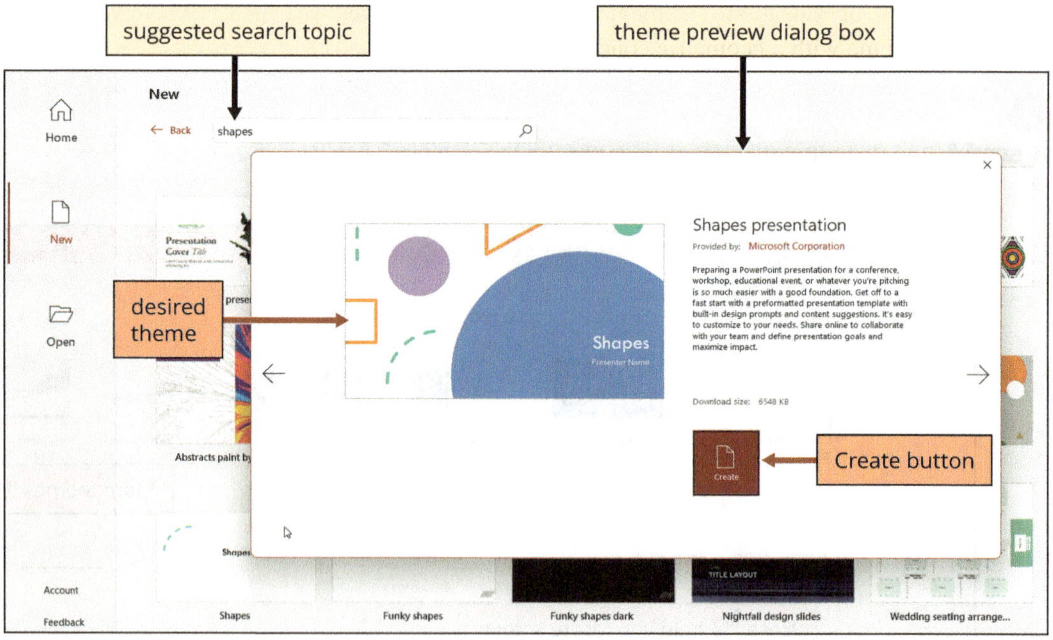

Figure 2–4

To Save the Presentation

You can save the downloaded slides now to keep track of the changes you make as you progress through this module. The following steps save the file as a PowerPoint presentation.

1. Click the File tab to display the Backstage view, click the Save As tab to display the Save As gallery, and then click the default save location or the save location specified by your instructor to display the Save As dialog box.

2. Type **SC_PPT_2_Career** as the file name.

3. Click Save to save the presentation.

BTW
Organizing Files and Folders
You should organize and store files in folders so that you easily can find the files later. For example, if you are taking an introductory technology class called CIS 101, a good practice would be to save all PowerPoint files in a PowerPoint folder in a CIS 101 folder.

To Delete a Slide

The downloaded theme has 13 slides with a variety of layouts. You will use three of these different layouts in your Career presentation, so you can delete the slides you downloaded that you will not need. **Why?** Deleting the extra slides now helps reduce clutter and helps you focus on the layouts you will use. The following steps delete the extra slides.

1

- Click the Slide 3 thumbnail in the Slides tab to select this slide.
- Press and hold SHIFT, scroll down, and then click the thumbnail for Slide 7 to select slides 3 through 7 (Figure 2–5).

Q&A Do I need to select consecutive slides?
No. You can select an individual slide to delete. You also can select nonconsecutive slides by pressing and holding CTRL and then clicking the thumbnails of the slides you want to delete.

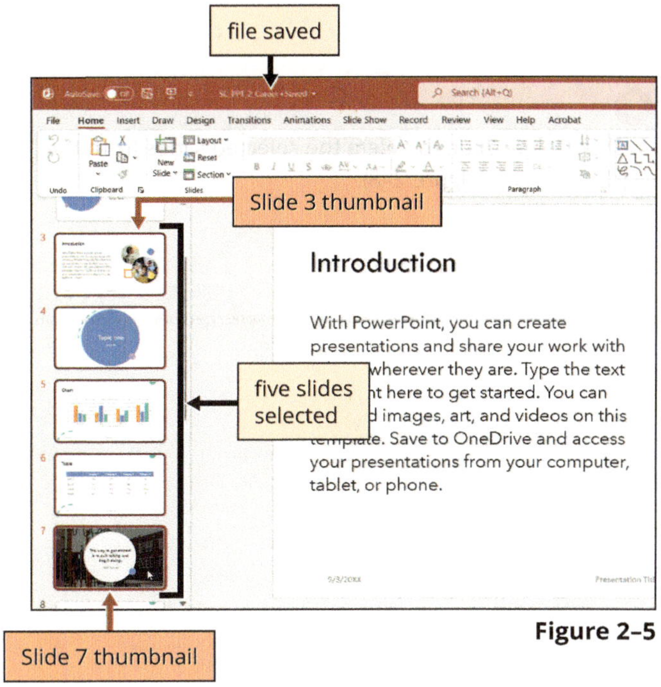

Figure 2–5

2

- Right-click any selected slide to display the shortcut menu (Figure 2–6).

3

- Click Delete Slide to delete the selected slides from the presentation.

4

- Click the Slide 4 thumbnail in the Slides tab to select this slide.
- Press and hold SHIFT, scroll down, and then click the thumbnail for Slide 8 to select slides 4 through 8.

Q&A How can I select nonconsecutive slides?
Hold CTRL and then click only the slides you want to select. In contrast, when you hold down SHIFT, you select consecutive slides between the first and last selected slides.

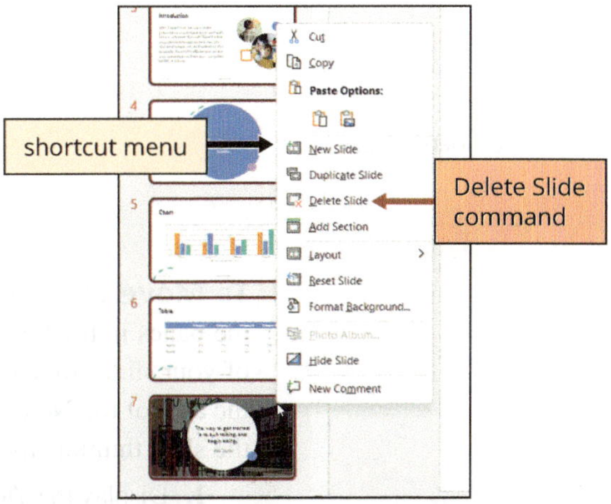

Figure 2–6

5

- Right-click any selected slide to display the shortcut menu (Figure 2–7).

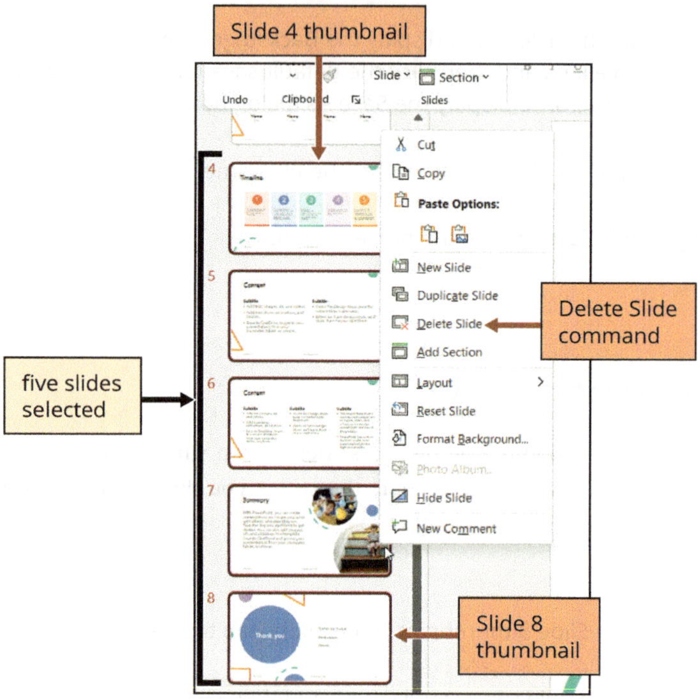

Figure 2–7

6

- Click Delete Slide to delete the selected slides from the presentation (Figure 2–8).

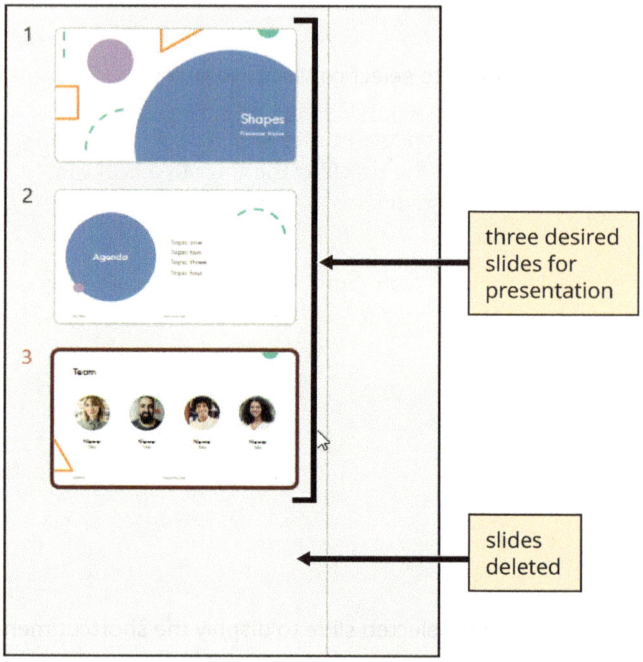

Figure 2–8

Other Ways

1. Select slide(s), press DELETE
2. Select slide(s), press BACKSPACE

To Move the Splitters in a Window You can maximize the working space of each of the panes in the PowerPoint window. You can, for example, hide or narrow the thumbnail views of your slides to maximize the editing space in the Slide pane. You also can increase or decrease the area of the Notes pane by dragging the splitter bar up or down. To hide or decrease the size of the slide thumbnails, you would perform the following steps.

1. Display the View tab and then click the Normal button (View tab | Presentation Views group).
2. Drag the splitter bar to the left until the slide thumbnails are the desired size or they are completely hidden.

To show or increase the size of the slide thumbnails, you would perform the following steps.

1. Display the View tab and then click the Normal button (View tab | Presentation Views group).
2. Point to the splitter bar between the Slide pane and the thumbnails, and then drag the splitter bar to the right.

If the thumbnails are hidden, you will see a collapsed Thumbnails menu. To show the thumbnails, you would perform the following step.

1. Click the collapsed menu button (a downward arrow) located to the right of the word, Thumbnails.

BTW
PowerPoint Help
At any time while using PowerPoint, you can find answers to questions and display information about various topics through PowerPoint Help. Used properly, this form of assistance can increase your productivity and reduce your frustrations by minimizing the time you spend learning how to use PowerPoint.

To Create a Title Slide

Recall from Module 1 that the title slide introduces the presentation to the audience. In addition to introducing the presentation, this project uses the title slide to capture the audience's attention by using title text. The following steps create the slide show's title slide.

1. Display Slide 1, select the title text (Shapes) in the title text placeholder, and then type **Career Success Center** as the title text.

2. Increase the font size of this title text to 80 point.

Q&A Why do I have to select the text in the placeholder before typing?
This downloaded template includes text in some of the placeholders that must be replaced with your own text.

3. Click the subtitle text placeholder, select the text (Presenter Name) in that placeholder, and then type **Make your career dreams a reality** as the subtitle text.

4. Increase the font size of this subtitle text to 32 point (Figure 2–9).

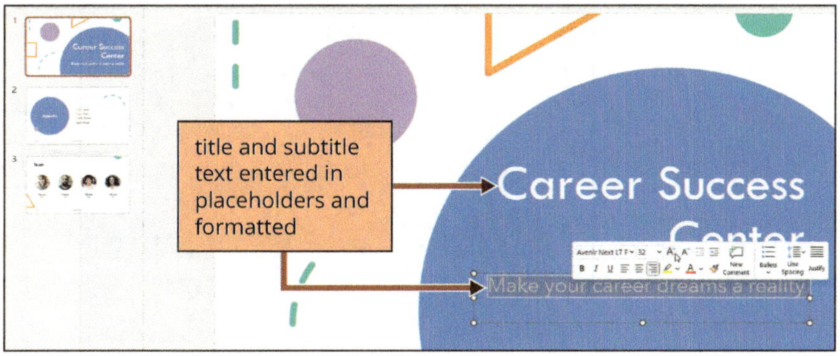

Figure 2–9

To Align a Paragraph

The PowerPoint design themes specify the default alignment of and spacing for text within a placeholder. For example, the text in most paragraphs is **left-aligned**, so the first character of each line is even with the left side of the placeholder. Text alignment also can be horizontally **centered** to position each line evenly between the left and right placeholder edges; **right-aligned**, so that the last character of each line is even with the last character of each line above or below it; and **justified**, where the first and last characters of each line are aligned and extra space is inserted between words to spread the characters evenly across the line.

By default, the title placeholder text in Slide 1 is right-aligned. You want the text to be centered in the blue circle. **Why?** You want the office name, Career Success Center, to display prominently in the center of the blue circle. The following steps center the text in the title placeholder on Slide 1.

1

- Place the insertion point anywhere in the Slide 1 title text (Figure 2–10).

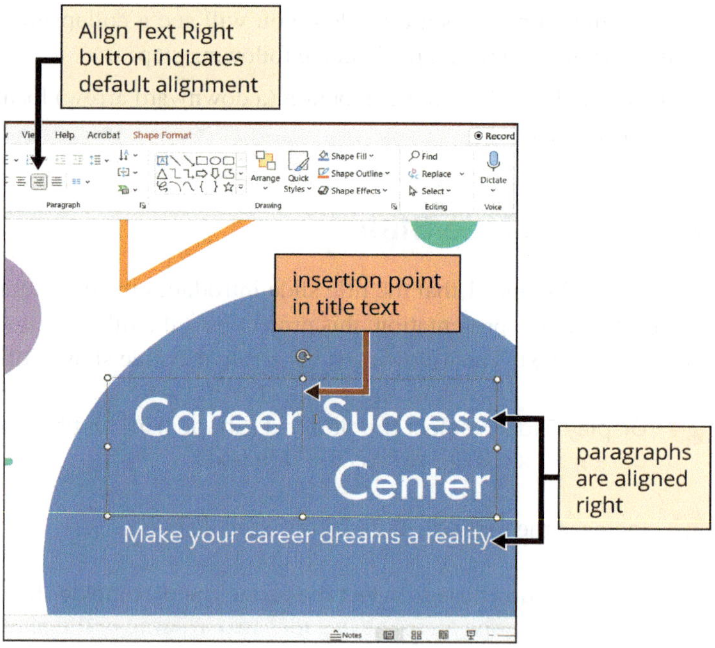

Figure 2–10

2

- Click the Center button (Home tab | Paragraph group) to center this paragraph (Figure 2–11).

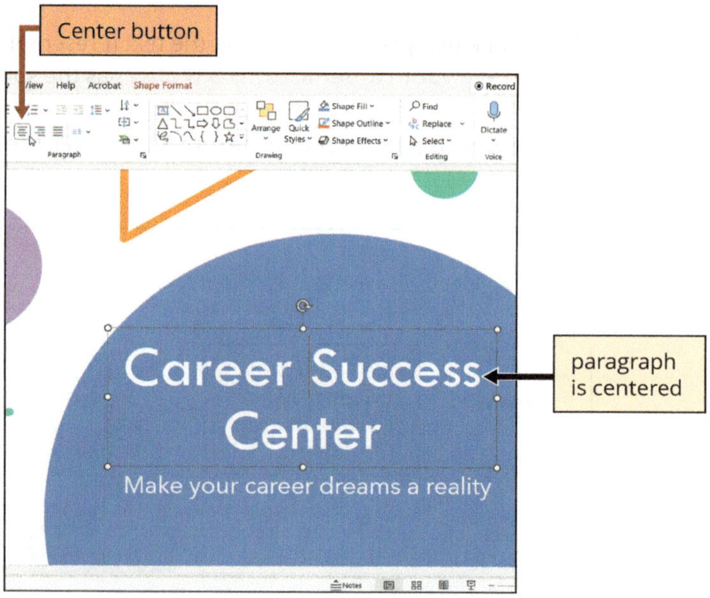

Figure 2–11

Other Ways

1. Click Center button on Mini toolbar
2. Right-click selected text, click Paragraph on shortcut menu, click Alignment arrow (Paragraph dialog box), click Center, click OK
3. Click Paragraph Dialog Box Launcher (Home tab | Paragraph group), click Alignment arrow (Paragraph dialog box), click Center, click OK
4. Press CTRL+E

To Create the First Text Slide

The first text slide you create in Module 2 emphasizes three Center aspects: the career coaches, the available resources, and the process to begin a career search. The following steps create the Slide 2 text slide using the Title and Content layout.

1. Display Slide 2, select the text (Agenda) in the title text placeholder, and then type **We're here to help** in the placeholder.
2. Select the first paragraph text (Topic one) in the content placeholder and then type **Who we are** as the first paragraph.
3. Press ENTER, click the 'Increase List Level' button to indent the second paragraph below the first, and then type **Experienced career coaches** as the first second-level paragraph.
4. Select the text in the next paragraph (Topic two) and then type **What we offer** as the second first-level paragraph.
5. Press ENTER, click the 'Increase List Level' button to indent the next paragraph, and then type **Resources to explore career goals** as the second second-level paragraph.
6. Select the text in the next paragraph (Topic three) and then type **How to begin** as the third first-level paragraph.
7. Press ENTER, click the 'Increase List Level' button, and then type **Complete an online application** as the third second-level paragraph.
8. Select the text in the last paragraph (Topic four) and then press DELETE to delete this paragraph (Figure 2–12).

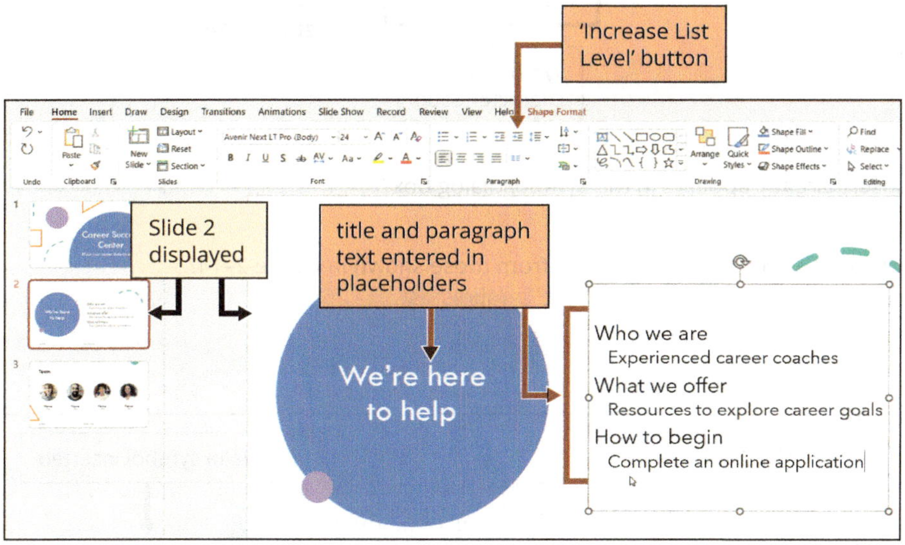

Figure 2–12

BTW
Ribbon and Screen Resolution
PowerPoint may change how the groups and buttons within the groups appear on the ribbon, depending on the screen resolution of your computer. Thus, your ribbon may look different from the ones in this book if you are using a screen resolution other than 1920 × 1080.

To Insert a Symbol

The Shapes presentation template has many geometric shapes on the slides. To add interest and coordinate with these shapes, you want to add a delta symbol (Δ) to the three first-level paragraphs. Many symbols are located in the Symbol, Webdings, and Wingdings fonts. The delta symbol is located in the Symbol font. **Why?** Many mathematical symbols, dots, and geometric shapes are found in this font. You insert symbols by changing the font. The following steps insert a delta symbol before the word, Who, in the first paragraph.

BTW
Delta Symbol
Delta is the fourth letter of the Greek alphabet and also has the value of four in the Greek numeral system. It commonly is used in mathematics, chemistry, and physics to represent change in a variable.

1

- Place the insertion point directly before the word, Who, in the first content paragraph.
- Display the Insert tab and then click the Symbol button (Insert tab | Symbols group) to display the Symbol dialog box (Figure 2–13).

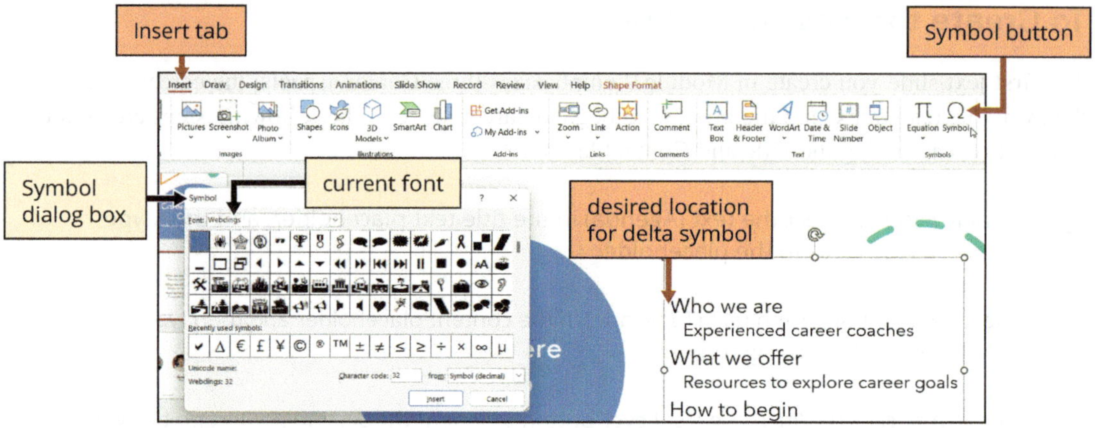

Figure 2–13

Q&A What if the Insert tab includes a Symbols button with an arrow?
Click the Symbols button to display the Symbols menu and then click the Symbol button.

2

- If necessary, click the Symbol dialog box title bar and then drag the dialog box near the left edge of the slide so that the content placeholder paragraphs are visible.

3

- If Symbol is not the font displayed in the Font box, click the Font arrow (Symbol dialog box) and then drag or scroll to Symbol and click this font.
- Click the delta symbol as shown in Figure 2–14. The symbol number and character code (68) appear at the bottom of the dialog box.

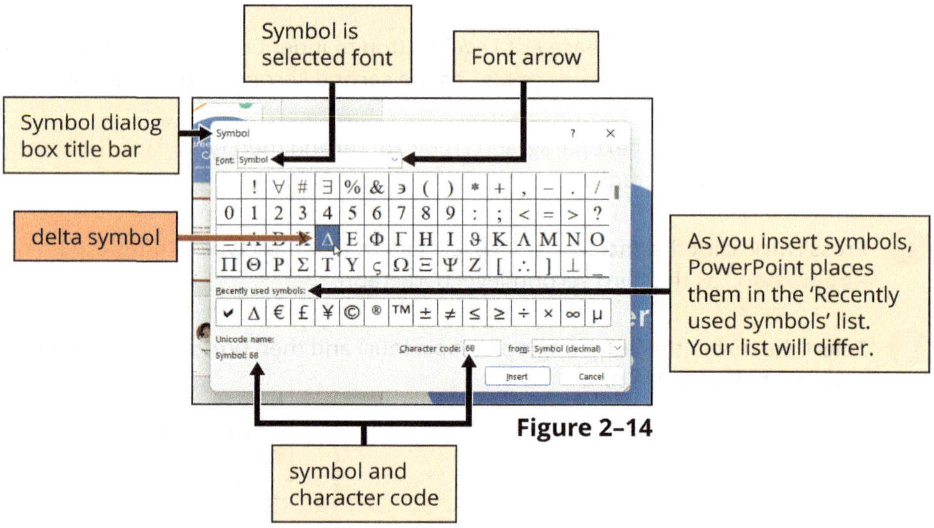

Figure 2–14

Q&A What if the symbol I want to insert already appears in the Symbol dialog box?
You can click any symbol shown in the dialog box to insert it into the slide.

Why does my 'Recently used symbols' list display different symbols from those shown in Figure 2–14?
As you insert symbols, PowerPoint places them in the 'Recently used symbols' list.

4

- Click the Insert button (Symbol dialog box) to place the delta symbol before the word, Who (Figure 2–15).

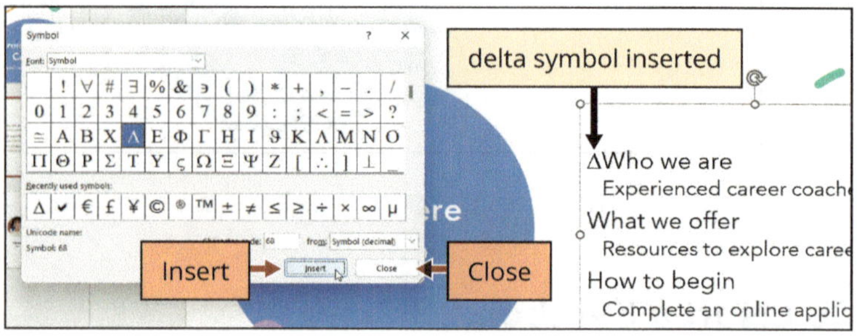

Figure 2–15

Q&A What is the delta symbol?
The uppercase Greek letter delta frequently is used in mathematics to denote "change" or "the change in."

Why is the Symbol dialog box still open?
The Symbol dialog box remains open, allowing you to insert additional symbols.

5

- Click the Close button (Symbol dialog box).

To Copy a Symbol

To add the delta symbol in the second first-level paragraph, you could repeat the process you used to insert the first symbol. Rather than inserting this symbol from the Symbol dialog box, you can copy the symbol and then paste it in the appropriate place. **Why?** This process can be accomplished more quickly with copy and paste when using the same symbol multiple times. The following steps copy the delta symbol before the word, What, in the second paragraph and before the word, How, in the third paragraph.

1

- Select the delta symbol in the first paragraph, display the Home tab, and then click the Copy button (Home tab | Clipboard group) to copy the delta symbol to the Office Clipboard (Figure 2–16).

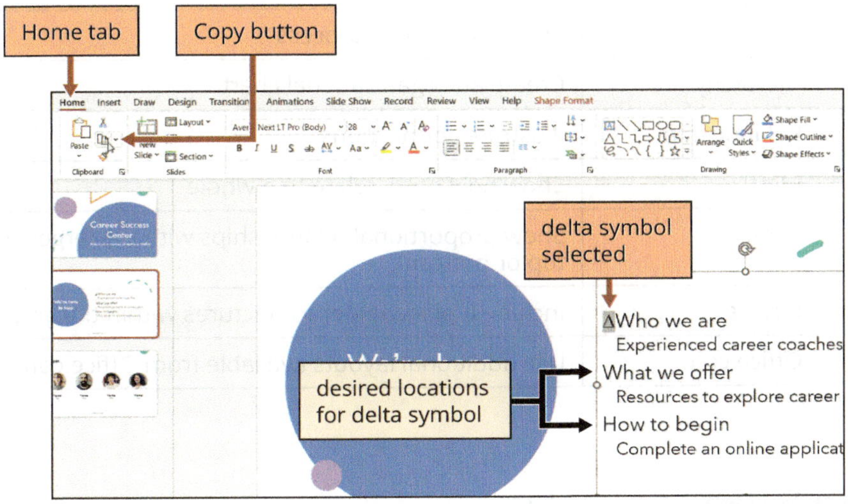

Figure 2–16

2

- Place the insertion point directly before the word, What, in the second first-level paragraph and then click the Paste button (Home tab | Clipboard group) to insert the delta symbol.

Q&A Why did PowerPoint add a space after the symbol when it was pasted?
Some AutoCorrect settings may cause this to occur. If a space is not added, press SPACEBAR to add a space between the symbol and the first word in the paragraph.

- Place the insertion point directly before the word, How, in the third first-level paragraph and then click the Paste button to insert the delta symbol.
- Place the insertion point between the delta symbol and the word, Who, in the first first-level paragraph and then press SPACEBAR to place a space between the symbol and the word (Figure 2–17).

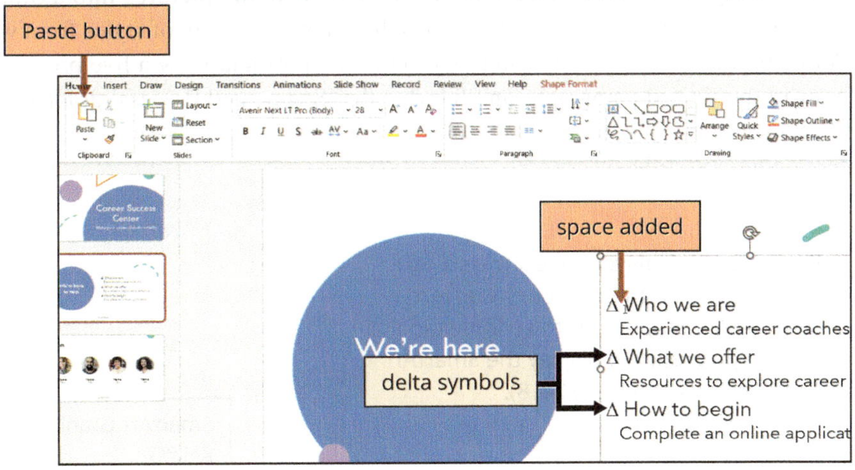

Figure 2–17

Creating and Formatting a SmartArt Graphic

An illustration often can help convey relationships between key points in your presentation. Microsoft 365 includes **SmartArt**, which consists of customizable diagrams that you can use to pictorially present lists, processes, and other relationships. The SmartArt layouts have a variety of shapes, arrows, and lines to correspond to the major points you want your audience to remember.

You can create a SmartArt graphic in two ways: Convert text or pictures already present on a slide to a SmartArt graphic, or select a SmartArt graphic type and then add text and pictures. Once the SmartArt graphic is present, you can customize its look. Table 2–1 lists the SmartArt types and their uses.

BTW
Updated Layouts
Some of the items in the SmartArt Styles gallery may be updates; Microsoft periodically adds layouts to Office.com and corresponding categories.

Table 2–1: SmartArt Graphic Layout Types and Purposes

Type	Purpose
List	Show nonsequential information
Process	Show steps in a process or timeline
Cycle	Show a continual process
Hierarchy	Create an organizational chart
Relationship	Illustrate connections
Matrix	Show how parts relate to a whole
Pyramid	Show proportional relationships with the largest component at the top or bottom
Picture	Include a placeholder for pictures within the graphic
Office.com	Use additional layouts available from Office.com

To Convert Text to a SmartArt Graphic

You quickly can convert small amounts of slide text and pictures into a SmartArt graphic. Once you determine the type of graphic, such as process or cycle, you then have a wide variety of styles from which to choose in the SmartArt Graphics gallery. As with other galleries, you can point to the samples and view a live preview if you are using a mouse. The following steps convert the six text paragraphs on Slide 2 to the 'Segmented Process' graphic, which is part of the Process category. **Why?** This SmartArt style is a good match for the content of Slide 2. It has three large areas for the titles and placeholders for the Level 2 text under each title.

1

- With Slide 2 displayed, select the six text paragraphs and then click the 'Convert to SmartArt Graphic' button (Home tab | Paragraph group) to display the SmartArt Graphics gallery (Figure 2–18).

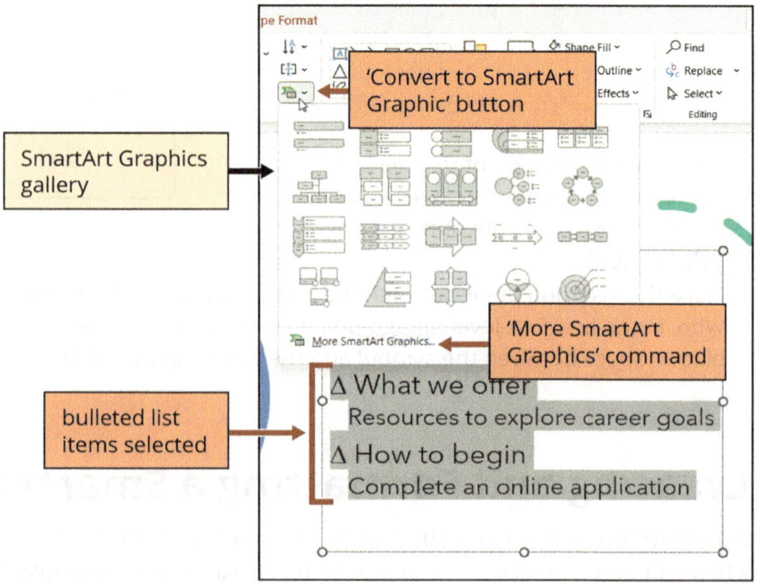

Figure 2–18

2

- Click 'More SmartArt Graphics' in the SmartArt Graphics gallery to display the Choose a SmartArt Graphic dialog box.
- Click Process in the left pane to display the Process gallery.
- Scroll down and then click the Segmented Process graphic (first graphic in the eighth row) to display a preview of this graphic in the right pane (Figure 2–19).
- **Experiment:** Click various categories and graphics in the SmartArt Styles gallery and view the various layouts.

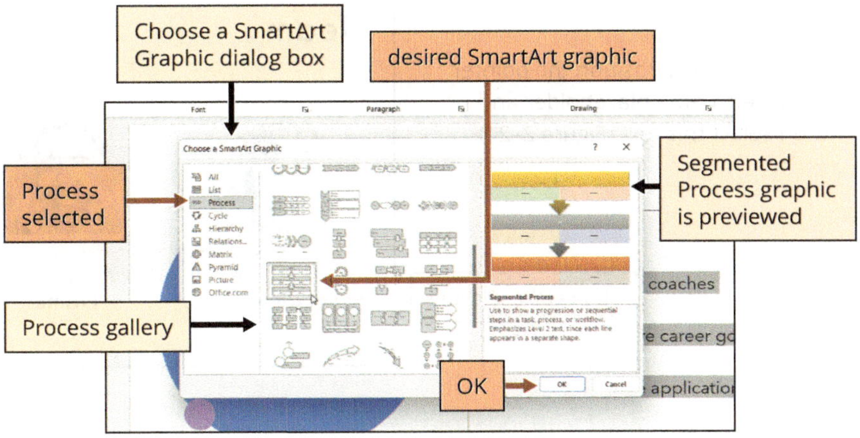

Figure 2–19

3

- Click OK (Choose a SmartArt Graphic dialog box) to apply this shape and convert the text (Figure 2–20).
- If the Text pane is displayed, click its Close button (the X in the upper-right corner) so that it no longer is displayed.

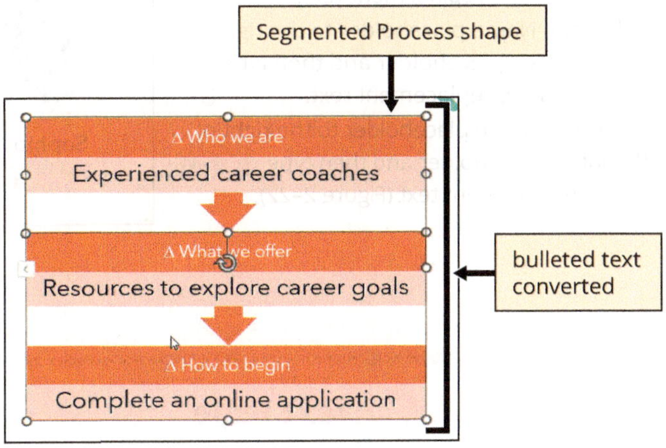

Figure 2–20

Other Ways

1. Select text, click 'Convert to SmartArt' on shortcut menu

To Edit SmartArt Shape Text

You may desire to change the text that appears in a SmartArt graphic. To do so, you can select the text and then make the desired changes. Also, if you display the Text Pane on the left side of the graphic, you can click the text you want to change and make your edits. The Shapes presentation theme included a slide with a People Portrait List SmartArt graphic, which is on Slide 3 of your slide deck. The following steps edit the sample text included in the graphic. First, you will edit the names below the four photos by selecting the text and then typing the replacement name. **Why?** Only first names are used, so it is easy to select the sample text and then type the replacement name.

1

- Display Slide 3. Position the pointer in the left Name placeholder and then select this text (Figure 2–21).

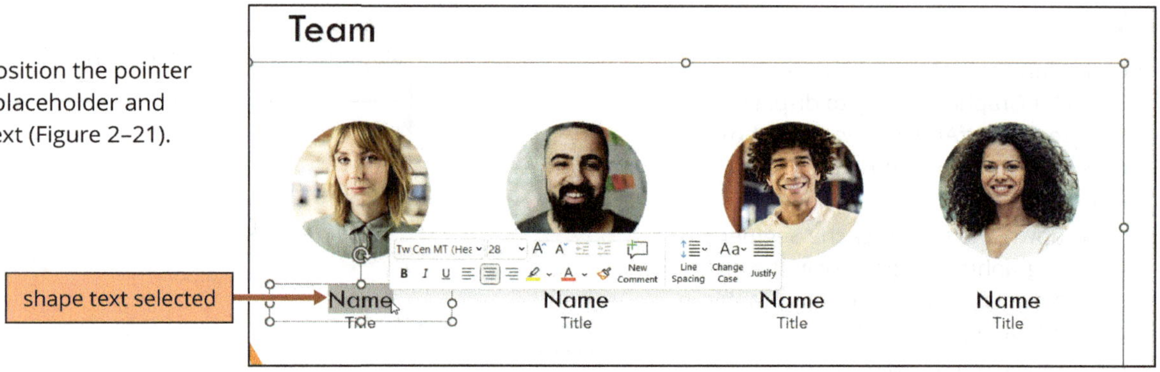

Figure 2–21

2

- Type **Sophia** as the replacement text.
- Select the Name placeholder to the right of the Sophia placeholder and then type **Mateo** as the replacement text.
- Select the Name placeholder to the right of the Mateo placeholder and then type **Julian** as the replacement text.
- Select the Name placeholder to the right of the Julian placeholder and then type **Naomi** as the replacement text (Figure 2–22).

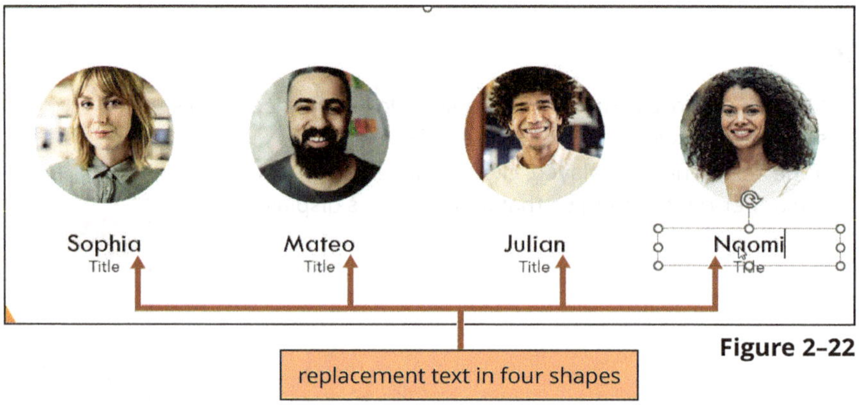

Figure 2–22

Text Pane

The **Text Pane** assists you in creating a graphic because you can direct your attention to developing and editing the message without being concerned with the actual graphic. The Text Pane consists of two areas: The top portion has the text that will appear in the SmartArt layout, and the bottom portion gives the name of the graphic and suggestions of what type of information is best suited for this type of visual. Each SmartArt graphic has an associated Text Pane with bullets that function as an outline and map directly to the image. You can create new lines of bulleted text and then indent and demote these lines. You also can check spelling. Table 2–2 shows the keyboard shortcuts you can use with the Text Pane.

Table 2–2: Text Pane Keyboard Shortcuts

Activity	Keyboard Shortcut
Indent text	TAB or ALT+SHIFT+RIGHT ARROW
Demote text	SHIFT+TAB or ALT+SHIFT+LEFT ARROW
Add a tab character	CTRL+TAB
Create a new line of text	ENTER
Check spelling	F7
Merge two lines of text	DELETE at the end of the first text line
Display the shortcut menu	SHIFT+F10
Switch between the SmartArt drawing canvas and the Text Pane	CTRL+SHIFT+F2
Close the Text Pane	ALT+F4
Switch the focus from the Text Pane to the SmartArt graphic border	ESC

To Edit SmartArt Text

Why? *You want to add the titles of the Center's team.* The graphic has four placeholders with the word, Title, for each of the four people shown. The following steps edit the paragraphs in the Slide 3 Text Pane.

1

- With the Slide 3 SmartArt selected, click the SmartArt Design tab and then click the Text Pane button (SmartArt Design tab | Create Graphic group) or the arrow icon on the left-center edge of the graphic to open the Text Pane.
- Select the text in the first Title second-level paragraph in the Text Pane (Figure 2–23).

2

- Type **Team Leader** as the replacement text for this second-level paragraph.
- Click the second bullet line or press the DOWN ARROW to move the insertion point to the next second-level paragraph. Select the text in this paragraph and then type **Career Specialist** as the replacement text.

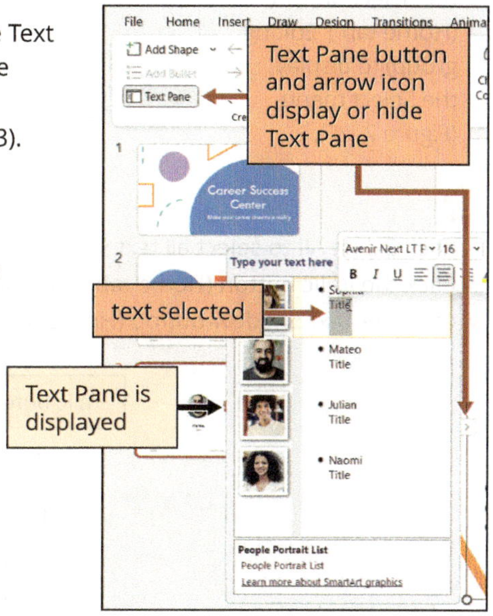

Figure 2–23

3

- Type **Testing Coordinator** as the replacement text for the next second-level paragraph.
- Type **Placement Consultant** as the replacement text for the rightmost second-level paragraph (Figure 2–24).

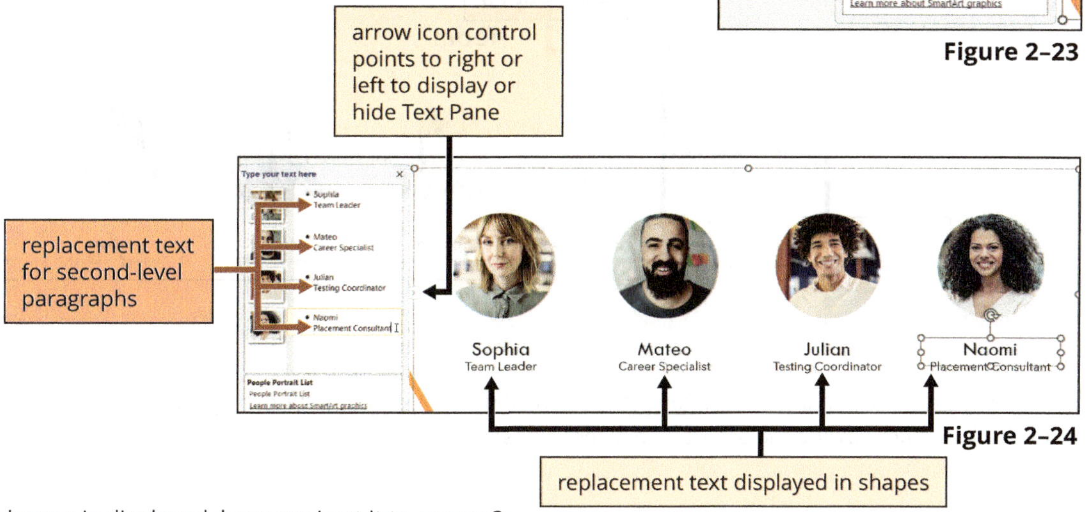

Figure 2–24

Q&A If my Text Pane no longer is displayed, how can I get it to appear?
Click the arrow icon control, which is the tab with a left-pointing arrow, on the left side of the SmartArt graphic.

I mistakenly pressed DOWN ARROW or ENTER. How can I delete the bullet paragraph I just added?
Press BACKSPACE to delete the paragraph.

I mistakenly pressed TAB to move to the next paragraph, and the current paragraph's level was changed. How can I fix it?
Press SHIFT+TAB to return to the previous level.

Other Ways

1. Right-click SmartArt graphic, click Show Text Pane on shortcut menu, enter text in Text Pane

To Format Text Pane Characters

Once the desired characters are entered in the Text Pane, you can change the font size and apply formatting features, such as bold, italic, and underlined text. **Why?** *Changing the font and adding effects can help draw the audience members to the varied slide content and coordinate with the visual content.* The following steps format the text by italicizing the letters and adding a shadow.

1

- With the Text Pane still displayed, display the Home tab and then click the Select button (Home tab | Editing group) to display the Select menu (Figure 2–25).

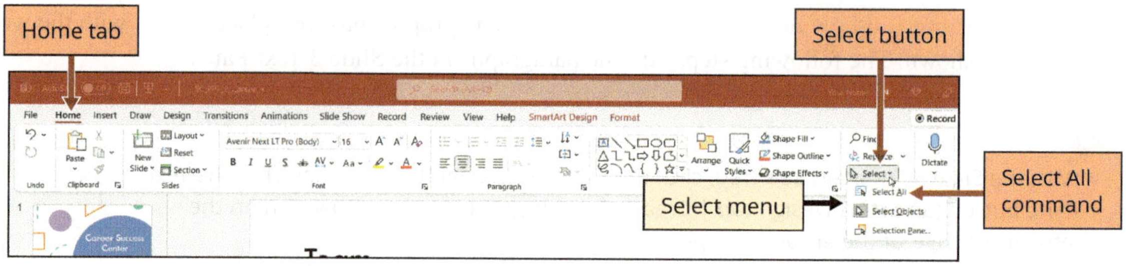

Figure 2–25

2

- Click Select All to select all text shapes in the SmartArt graphic.
- Click the Italic button (Home tab | Font group) to italicize all the text.
- Click the Text Shadow button (Home tab | Font group) to add a shadow to all the SmartArt text (Figure 2–26).

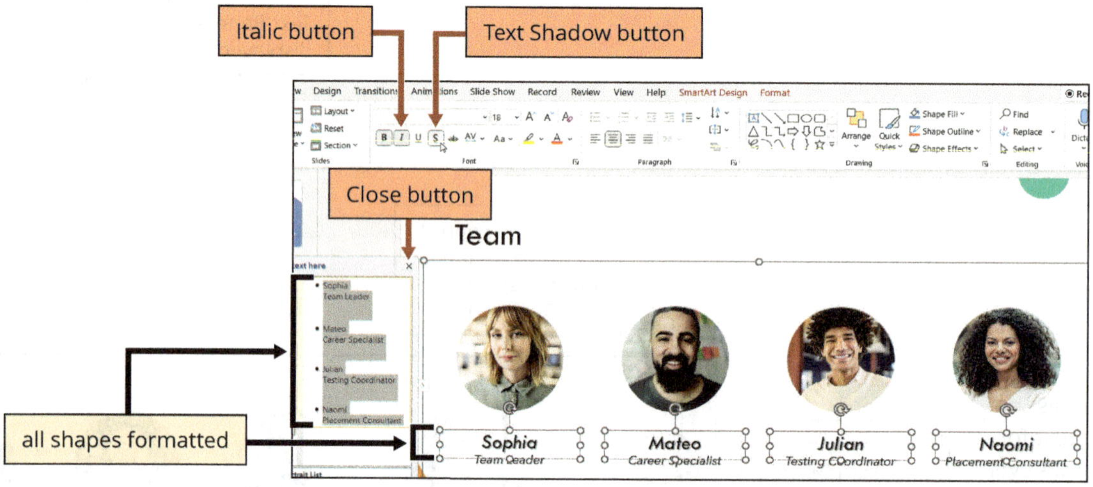

Figure 2–26

3

- Click the Close button in the Text Pane (shown in Figure 2–26) so that it no longer is displayed.
- Click a blank area inside the SmartArt border to deselect the shapes.

Other Ways

1. Drag through all text in Text pane, click Italic button and Text Shadow button on ribbon (Home tab | Font group)

To Change the SmartArt Layout

Once you begin formatting a SmartArt shape, you may decide that another layout better conveys the message you are communicating to an audience. PowerPoint allows you to change the layout easily. Any graphical changes that were made to the original SmartArt, such as changing and formatting text, are applied to the new SmartArt layout. The following steps change the SmartArt layout to Captioned Pictures. **Why?** It works well with the four photos and prominently displays the names and titles.

1

- With the Slide 3 SmartArt graphic still selected, display the SmartArt Design tab (Figure 2–27).

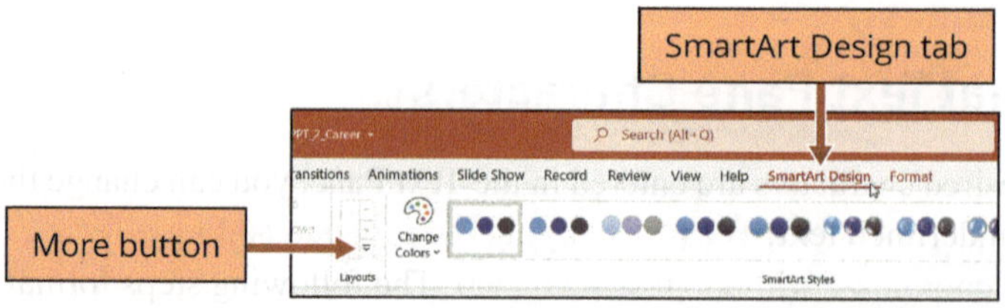

Figure 2–27

2

- Click the More button in the Layouts group (SmartArt Design tab) to display the Layouts menu (Figure 2–28).

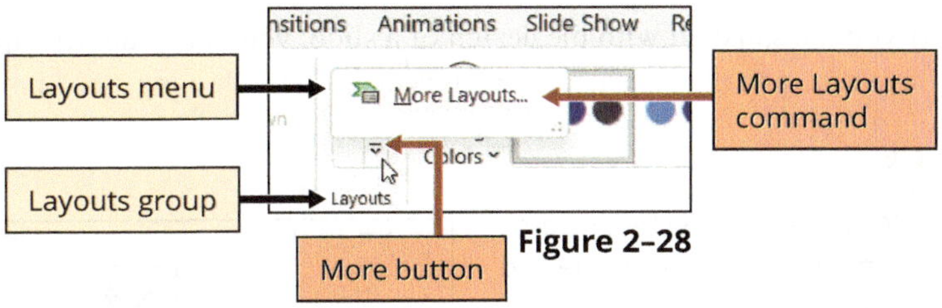

Figure 2–28

3

- Click More Layouts in the Layouts menu to display the Choose a SmartArt Graphic dialog box.
- Click Picture in the list of graphic categories and then click the Captioned Pictures layout (third layout in the second row) to display a picture and a description of this SmartArt layout (Figure 2–29).

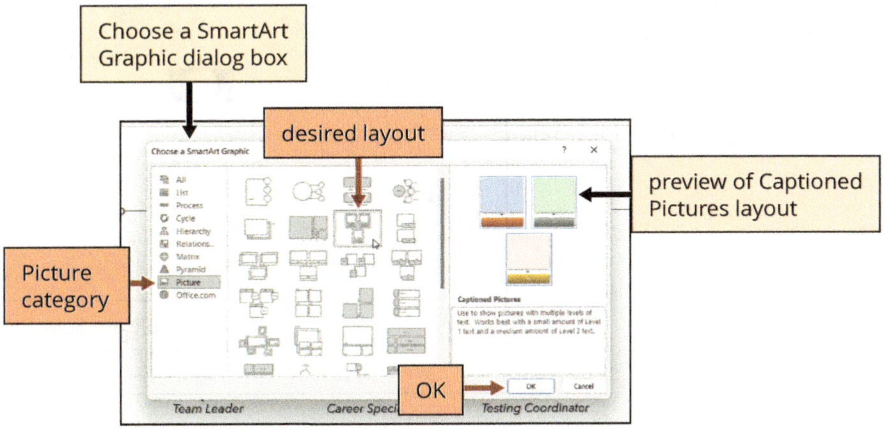

Figure 2–29

4

- Click OK (Choose a SmartArt Graphic dialog box) to change the layout (Figure 2–30).

Figure 2–30

To Edit the Title Text

The Slide 3 title text placeholder has the default wording from the online template. You need to change this text to reflect the current slide content. The following step edits the title text.

1 Select the current title text (Team) and then type **Meet the Career Coaches** as the replacement text (Figure 2–31).

Figure 2–31

To Duplicate a Slide

If you are satisfied with the design of a slide, you may want to duplicate it and then make slight modifications. **Why?** You can save time and provide a consistent design. The following steps insert a new slide and duplicate it.

1

- With Slide 3 selected, insert a new slide with the Title and Content layout.
- With the new Slide 4 selected, click the New Slide arrow (Home tab | Slides group) to display the Shapes presentation layout gallery (Figure 2–32).

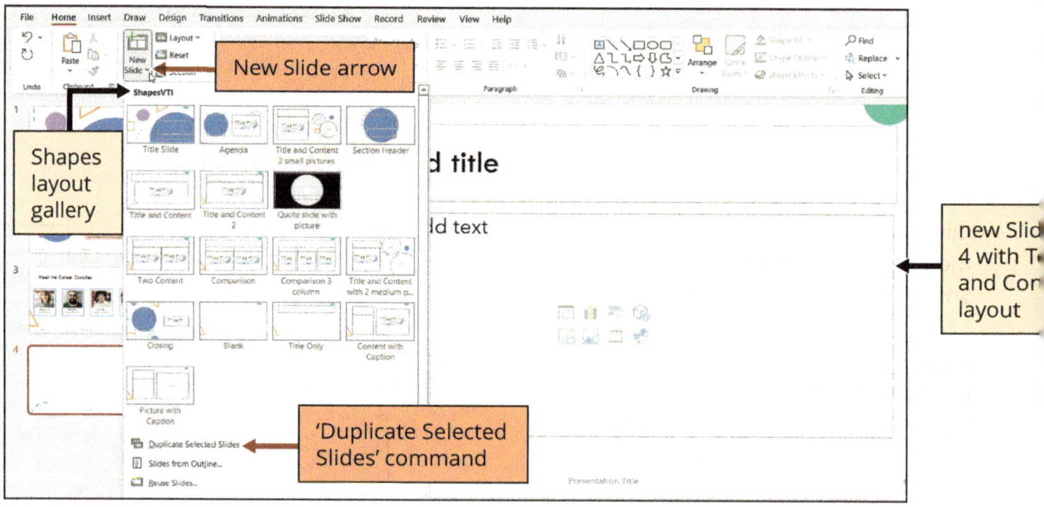

Figure 2–32

2

- Click 'Duplicate Selected Slides' in the Shapes presentation layout gallery to create a new Slide 5, which is a duplicate of Slide 4 (Figure 2–33).

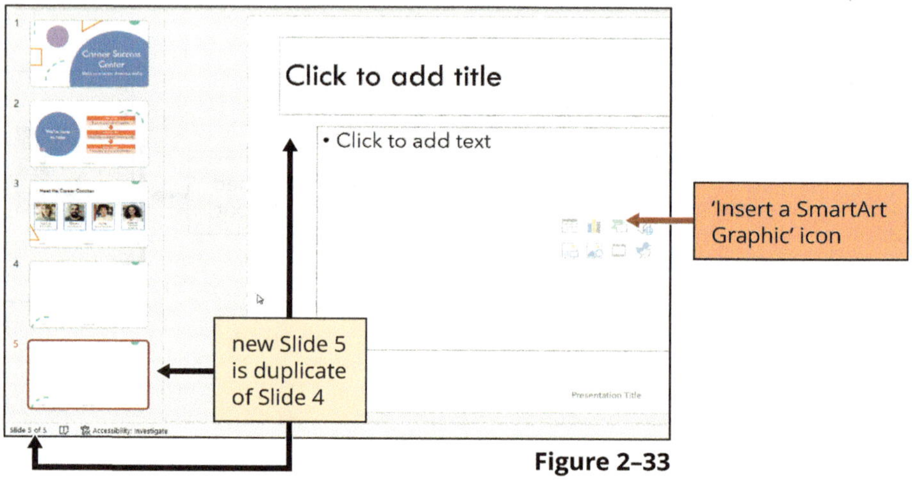

Figure 2–33

Other Ways

1. Right-click slide thumbnail in Slide pane, click Duplicate Slide

To Insert a SmartArt Graphic

Several SmartArt layouts have designs that reinforce concepts presented in a presentation. The Step Down Process graphic is appropriate for this presentation. **Why?** The student can begin by performing some independent research: checking the Occupational Outlook Handbook and then taking a survey to determine possible careers. Afterward, the student can meet with a coach. The following steps insert the Step Down Process SmartArt graphic.

1

- Display Slide 4 and then click the 'Insert a SmartArt Graphic' icon in the content placeholder (shown in Figure 2–33) to display the 'Choose a SmartArt Graphic' dialog box.

- Click Process in the left pane to display the Process gallery.
- Click the 'Step Down Process' graphic (third graphic in the first row) to display a preview of this layout in the right pane (Figure 2-34).
- **Experiment:** Click various categories and graphics in the SmartArt Styles gallery and view the various layouts.

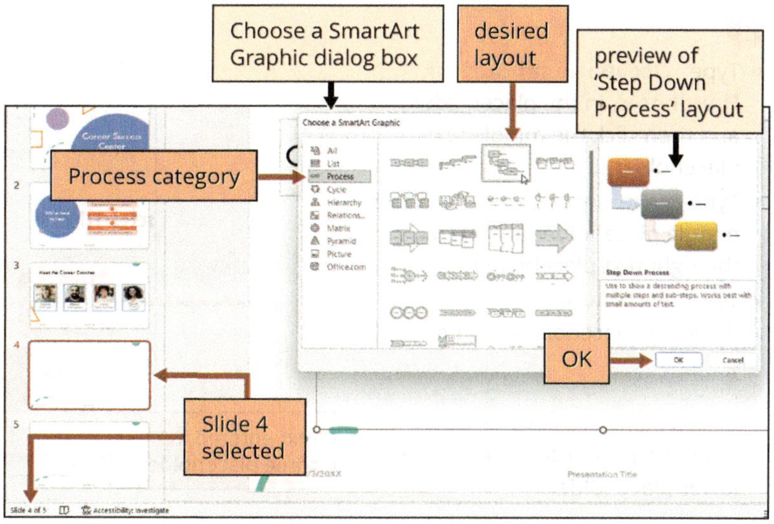

Figure 2-34

2

- Click OK (Choose a SmartArt Graphic dialog box) to insert the 'Step Down Process' SmartArt layout on Slide 4 (Figure 2-35).

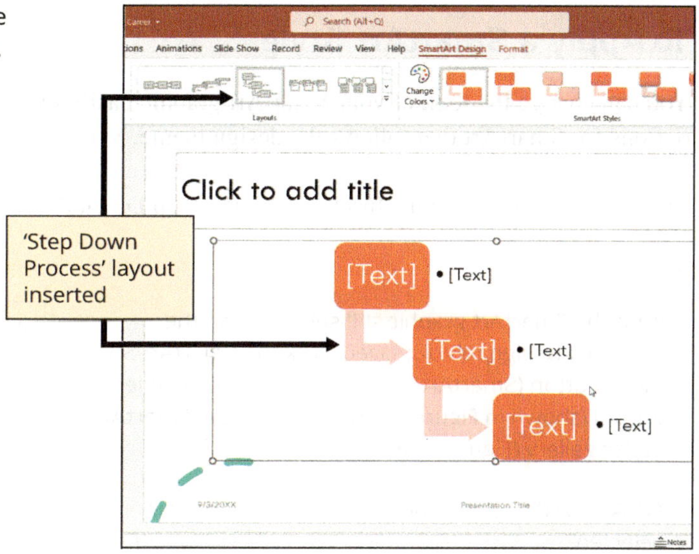

Figure 2-35

Other Ways

1. Click SmartArt button (Insert tab | Illustrations group)

To Add Text to the SmartArt Graphic

The Step Down Process SmartArt layout has three major orange placeholders for text. You can type a small amount of text, and PowerPoint assists with the graphic design. **Why?** PowerPoint automatically adjusts the font size for text in all the placeholders as you type. The following steps insert text into the three major SmartArt placeholders.

1

- Click the upper placeholder labeled [Text] to place the insertion point in that box (Figure 2-36).

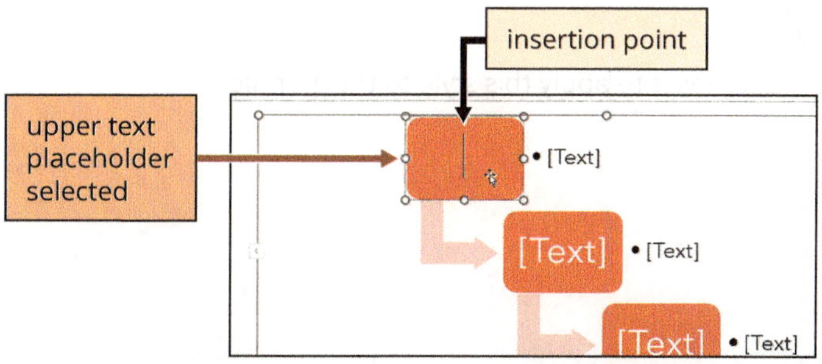

Figure 2-36

2

- Type **Occupational Outlook Handbook** in the placeholder and then click the middle text placeholder.
- Type **Assessment Survey** in the middle placeholder and then click the right text placeholder.
- Type **Individual Consultations** in the lower placeholder (Figure 2–37).

3

- Click a blank area inside the SmartArt border to deselect the lower placeholder.

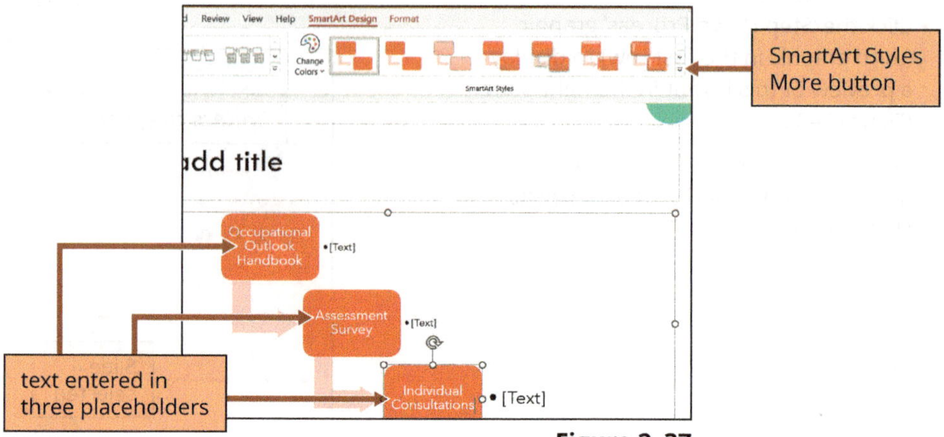

Figure 2–37

To Apply a SmartArt Style

You can change the look of your SmartArt graphic easily by applying a **SmartArt Style**, a pre-set combination of formatting options for SmartArt that follows the design theme. **Why?** You can use these professionally designed effects to customize the appearance of your presentation with a variety of shape fills, edges, shadows, line styles, gradients, and three-dimensional styles. The following steps add the Inset style to the Step Down Process SmartArt graphic.

1

- With the SmartArt graphic still selected and the SmartArt Design tab displayed, click the SmartArt Styles More button (SmartArt Design tab | SmartArt Styles group) (shown in Figure 2–37) to expand the SmartArt Styles gallery (Figure 2–38).

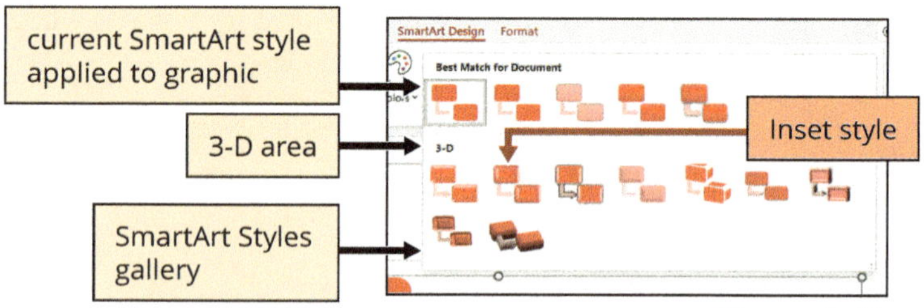

Figure 2–38

Q&A How do I select the graphic if it no longer is selected?
Click anywhere in the graphic.

Can I select one of the styles displayed in the SmartArt Styles group without expanding the SmartArt Styles gallery?
Yes. At times, however, you may want to display the gallery to view and preview the various styles.

2

- Point to the Inset style in the 3-D area (second style in the first 3-D row) in the SmartArt Styles gallery to display a live preview of this style (Figure 2–39).
- **Experiment:** Point to various styles in the SmartArt Styles gallery and watch the Step Down Process graphic change styles.

3

- Click Inset to apply this style to the graphic.

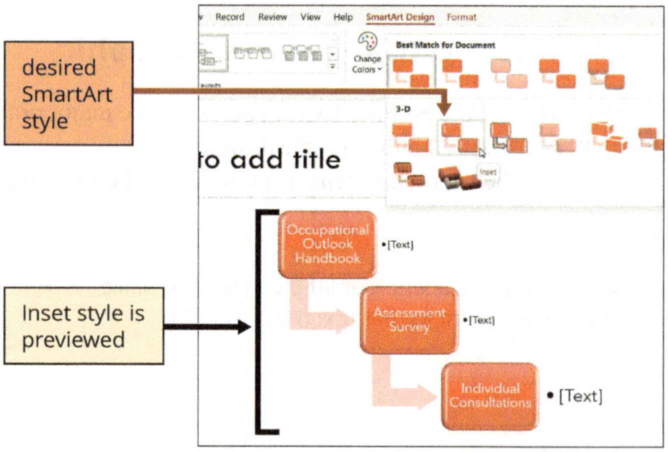

Figure 2–39

Other Ways

1. Right-click SmartArt graphic in an area other than a picture, click Style button

To Add a Hyperlink to a Paragraph

Speakers may desire to display a webpage during a slide show to add depth to the presented material and to enhance the overall message. When displaying Slide 4 of the Career slide show, for example, a speaker could access a website to show a specific resource. One method of accessing a webpage is by clicking a hyperlink on a slide. A **hyperlink**, also called a **link**, connects a slide or slide element to a webpage, another slide, a custom show consisting of specific slides in a presentation, an email address, or a file. A hyperlink can be any element of a slide. This includes a single letter, a word, a paragraph, or any graphical image such as a picture, shape, or graph.

If you are connected to the Internet when you run the presentation, you can click each hyperlinked paragraph, and your browser will open a new window and display the corresponding webpage for each hyperlink. By default, hyperlinked text is displayed with an underline and in a color that is part of the color scheme. The following steps create a hyperlink for the upper SmartArt rectangle on Slide 4. **Why?** The Occupational Outlook Handbook text will be a hyperlink to that website that gives career advice for hundreds of occupations.

1

- Display the Insert tab and then select the upper placeholder text, Occupational Outlook Handbook.
- Click the Link button (Insert tab | Links group) to display the Insert Hyperlink dialog box.
- If necessary, click the 'Existing File or Web Page' button in the Link to area (Figure 2–40).

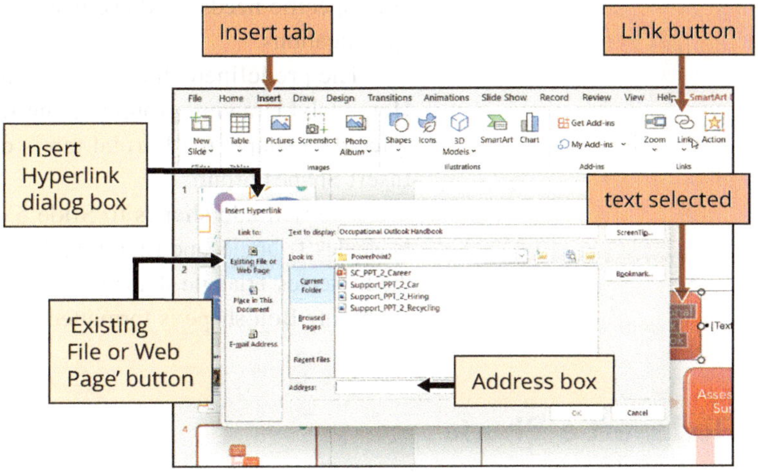

Figure 2–40

2

- If necessary, delete the text in the Address text box and then type **www.bls.gov/ooh** in the Address box (Figure 2–41).

Q&A Why does http:// appear before the address I typed?
PowerPoint automatically adds this protocol identifier before web addresses.

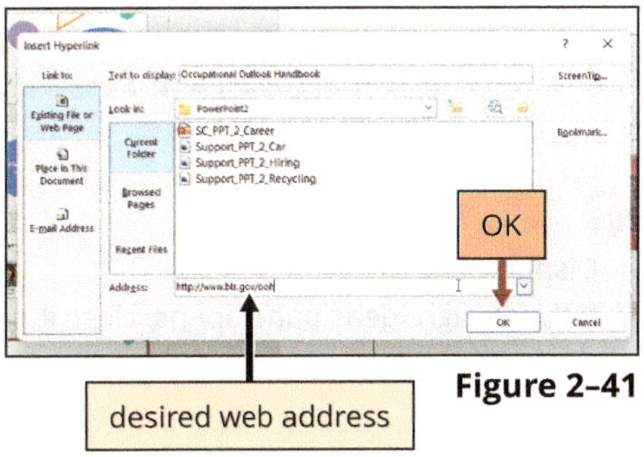

Figure 2–41

3

- Click OK to insert the hyperlink.

Q&A Why is this paragraph now underlined and displaying a new font color?
The default style for hyperlinks is underlined text. The Shapes presentation built-in theme hyperlink color is purple so PowerPoint formatted the paragraph to that color automatically.

- **Experiment:** Click outside the linked text, then press CTRL and click the link to access the website. Then, close the browser to return to PowerPoint.

Other Ways

1. Right-click selected text, click Hyperlink, click 'Existing File or Web Page,' type address, click OK
2. Select text, press CTRL+K, click 'Existing File or Web Page,' type address, press ENTER

Inserting and Formatting a Shape

One method of getting the audience's attention and reinforcing the major concepts being presented is to have graphical elements on the slide. PowerPoint provides a wide variety of predefined shapes that can add visual interest to a slide. Diagrams with labels often help audiences identify the parts of an object. Text boxes with clear, large type and an arrow pointing to a precise area of the object work well in showing relationships between components. You also can use shapes to create your own custom artwork.

Shape elements include lines, basic geometrical shapes, arrows, equation shapes, flowchart symbols, rectangles, banners, and callouts. After adding a shape to a slide, you can change its default characteristics by adding text, bullets, numbers, and styles. You also can combine multiple shapes to create a more complex graphic. At times, you may be unable to find a shape that fits your specific needs. In those instances, you might find a similar shape and then alter it to your specifications.

The predefined shapes are found in the Shapes gallery. This collection is found on the Home tab | Drawing group and the Insert tab | Illustrations group. Once you have inserted and selected a shape, the Format tab is displayed, and the Shapes gallery also is displayed in the Insert Shapes group.

You will add shapes to Slide 5 and then enhance them in a variety of ways. First, Oval, Isosceles Triangle, and Lightning Bolt shapes are inserted on the slide, sized, and formatted. Then, the Isosceles Triangle shape is copied. Then, text is added to the shapes and formatted. Finally, the Lightning Bolt shape is formatted and moved into position.

To Insert a Shape

Many of the shapes included in the Shapes gallery can direct the viewer to important aspects of the presentation. Ovals, squares, arrows, rectangles, and equation shapes are among the items included in the Shapes gallery. These shapes can be combined to show relationships among the elements, and they can help illustrate the basic concepts presented in your slide show. The following steps add Oval, Lightning Bolt, and Isosceles Triangle shapes to Slide 5. **Why?** The Shapes presentation slides have many geometric shapes, so the Oval and triangles complement these slide elements. The Lightning Bolt depicts the positive energy students will experience when they determine their career goals and apply for an appropriate job.

1

- Display Slide 5.
- If the Design Ideas pane opens, close it.

2

- Click the Shapes button (Insert tab | Illustrations group) to display the Shapes gallery (Figure 2–42).

Q&A I do not see a Shapes button shown in Figure 2–42. Instead, I have three rows of shapes and a Shapes More button. Why?
Monitor dimensions and resolution affect how buttons display on the ribbon. Click the Shapes More button to display the entire Shapes gallery.

My shapes are displayed in a different position. Why?
Monitor dimensions and resolution affect how the shapes display in the Shapes gallery.

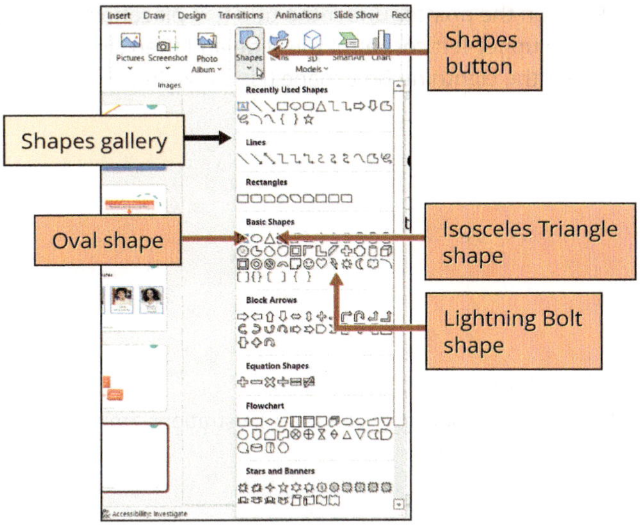

Figure 2–42

3

- Click the Oval shape (second shape in the first row of the Basic Shapes area) in the Shapes gallery.

Q&A Why did my pointer change shape?
The pointer changed to a plus shape to indicate the Oval shape has been added to the Clipboard.

- Position the pointer (a crosshair) near the center of the slide (Figure 2–43).

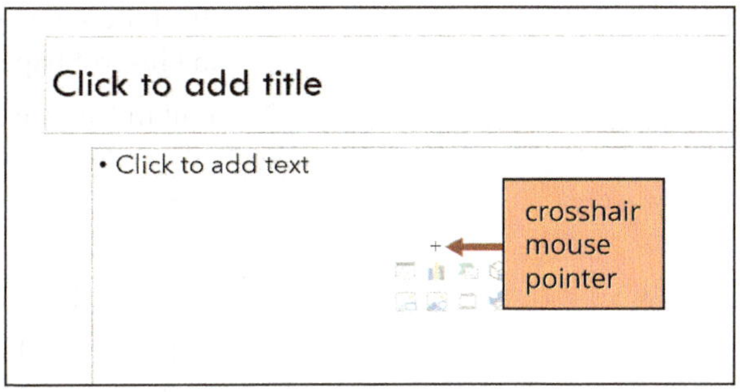

Figure 2–43

4

- Click Slide 5 to insert the Oval shape (Figure 2–44).

Q&A When I inserted the Oval shape, I selected it on the Home tab. Is the same Shapes gallery also displayed on the Shape Format tab?
Yes. The Shapes gallery is displayed on the Shape Format tab once an object is inserted and selected on the slide.

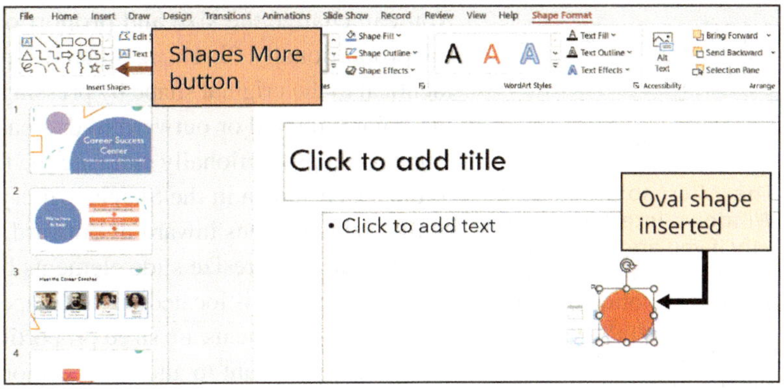

Figure 2–44

5

- Click the Shapes More button (Shape Format tab | Insert Shapes group) to display the Shapes gallery.
- Click the Isosceles Triangle shape (third shape in the first row of the Basic Shapes area) in the gallery (shown in Figure 2–42).
- Position the pointer toward the right side of the Oval and then click to insert the Isosceles Triangle shape.

6

- Display the Shapes gallery again and then click the Lightning Bolt shape (eighth shape in the third Basic Shapes row) in the gallery (shown in Figure 2–42).

- Position the pointer under the title text placeholder in the upper-left corner of the slide and then click to insert the Lightning Bolt shape (Figure 2–45).

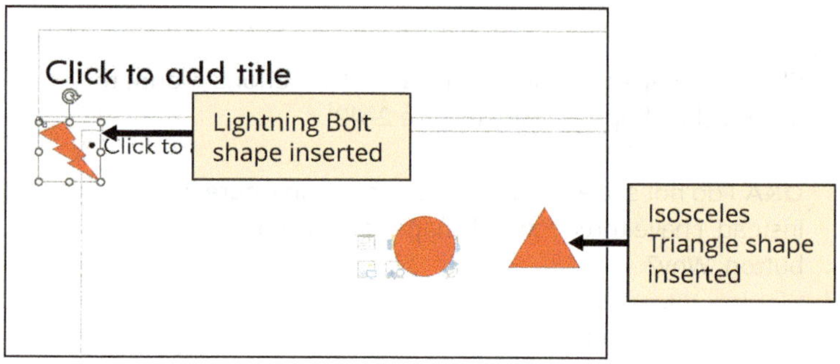

Figure 2–45

Other Ways

1. Click Shapes button (Insert tab | Illustrations group)

To Change a Shape Type Once you insert a shape, you can change it into another shape. To change the shape type, you would do the following.

1. Select the shape you want to change and then click the Edit Shape button (Shape Format tab | Insert Shapes group).
2. Point to Change Shape and then select the desired shape.

To Delete a Shape Once you insert a shape, you can delete it. To delete a shape, you would do the following.

1. Select the shape and then press DELETE.
2. If you want to delete multiple shapes, press CTRL while clicking the undesired shapes and then press DELETE.

Resizing Shapes

You can change the size and proportions of slide elements in two ways: proportionally and nonproportionally. To change them proportionally, you can keep the resized shape proportions identical to the original shape by pressing SHIFT while clicking a sizing handle and then dragging the pointer inward or outward to decrease or increase the size. If you do not hold down SHIFT, you can nonproportionally elongate the height or the width to draw an object that is not identical to the shape shown in the Shapes gallery. If you want to alter the shape's proportions, drag one of the sizing handles inward or outward.

You also can resize slide elements by entering exact height and width measurements in the Size group, which is located on the Shape Format tab and the Format contextual tab for SmartArt. Some graphic elements are sized proportionally, meaning the width changes in proportion to height changes. If you want to alter the slide object nonproportionally, you need to uncheck the 'Lock aspect ratio' check box in the Format Shape pane.

BTW
Touch Mode Differences
The Microsoft 365 and Windows interfaces may vary if you are using Touch mode. For this reason, you might notice that the function or appearance of your touch screen differs slightly from this module's presentation.

To Resize a Shape Proportionally

The three shapes on Slide 5 are the default sizes, and they need to be enlarged to be seen clearly and to allow text to be seen inside of them. The next step is to resize the Isosceles Triangle and Oval shapes. **Why?** The Oval shape should be enlarged so that it is a focal point in the middle area of the slide, and the Isosceles Triangle shape needs to be large enough to contain text. The following steps resize the Slide 5 Isosceles Triangle and Oval shapes.

1

- Select the Isosceles Triangle shape, press and hold down SHIFT, and then drag the lower-right corner sizing handle until the shape is resized approximately as shown in Figure 2–46.

Q&A Why did I need to press SHIFT while enlarging the shape?
Holding down SHIFT while dragging keeps the proportions of the original shape.

What if my shape is not selected?
To select a shape, click it.

If I am using a touch screen, how can I maintain the shape's original proportion?
If you drag one of the corner sizing handles, the object should stay in proportion.

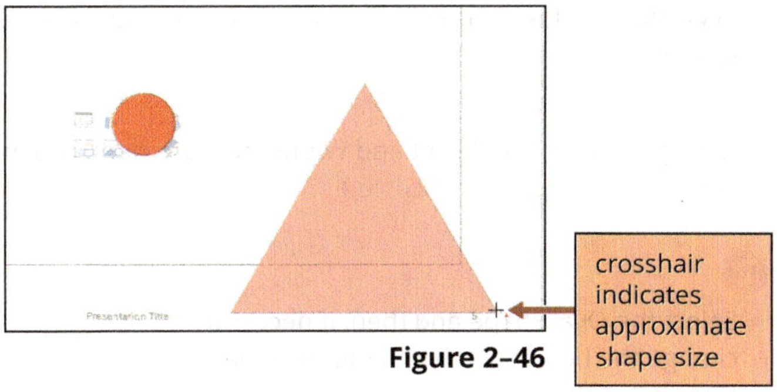

Figure 2-46

2

- Release the mouse button to resize the shape.

3

- Select the Oval shape, press and hold down SHIFT, and then drag the lower-left corner sizing handle until the shape is resized approximately as shown in Figure 2-47.

Q&A What if I want to move the shape to a precise location on the slide?
With the shape selected, press ARROW or CTRL+ARROW to move the shape to the desired location.

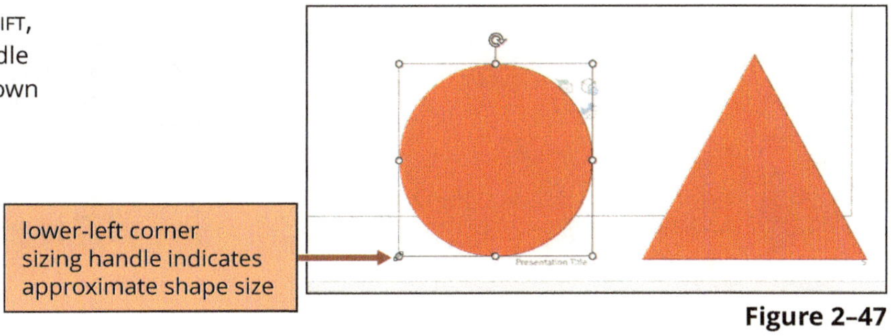

Figure 2-47

To Resize a Shape Nonproportionally by Entering an Exact Measurement

Why? Adequate space exists on the slide to increase all the SmartArt shapes. You can resize a slide element by dragging the sizing handles or by specifying exact measurements for the height and width. The following steps resize the Lightning Bolt shape by entering an exact measurement and then check the dimensions of the resized Oval and Isosceles Triangle.

1

- Select the Lightning Bolt shape and then, if necessary, display the Shape Format tab.

Q&A How will I know the Lightning Bolt shape is selected?
You will see the sizing handles around the outer edge of the shape.

- Click the Shape Height box up arrow (Shape Format tab | Size group) several times until the Height measurement is 3".
- Click the Shape Width box up arrow (Shape Format tab | Size group) several times until the Width measurement is 12.5" (Figure 2-48).

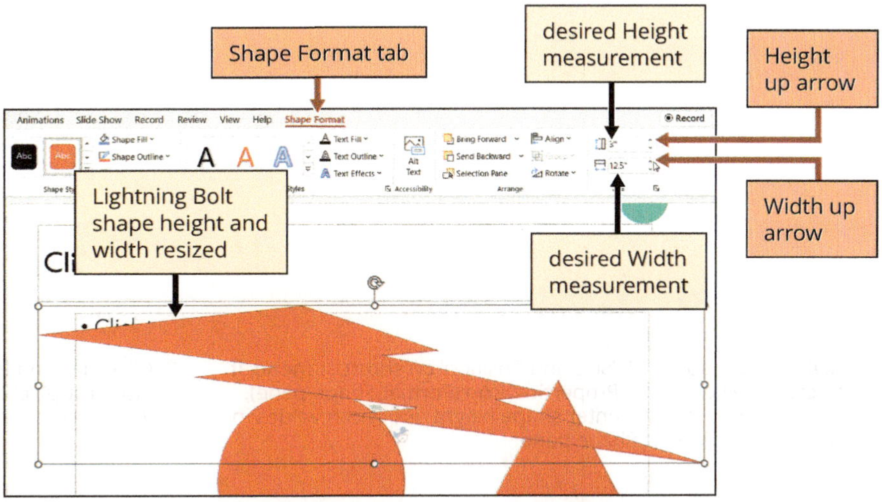

Figure 2-48

Q&A Part of the Lightning Bolt shape is covering the Oval and Isosceles Triangle shapes. Do I need to move it on the slide now?
No. You will position this shape later in this module.

Can I just enter the Height and Width measurements I want in the Height and Width boxes?
Yes. You can replace the existing measurements with your desired sizes.

2

- Select the Oval shape and then, if necessary, change the height and width measurements to 4" (Figure 2–49).

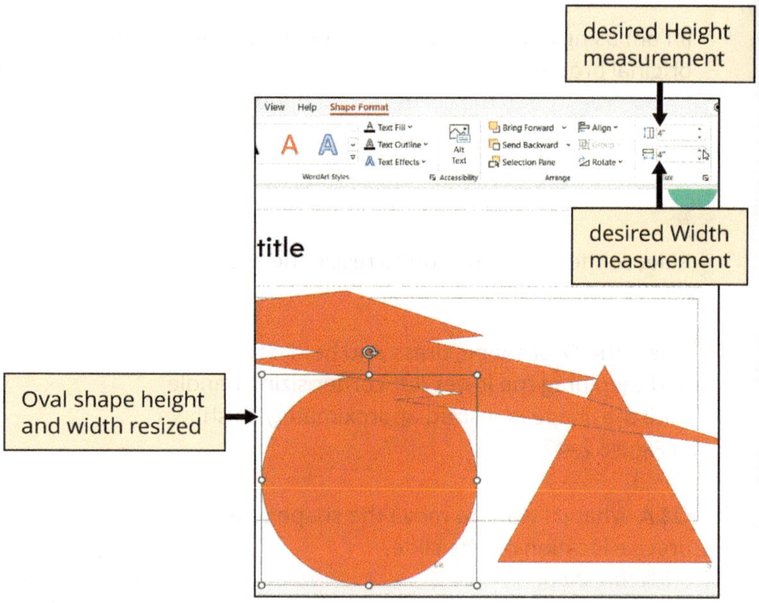

Figure 2–49

3

- Select the Isosceles Triangle shape and then, if necessary, change the height and width measurements to 4" (Figure 2–50).

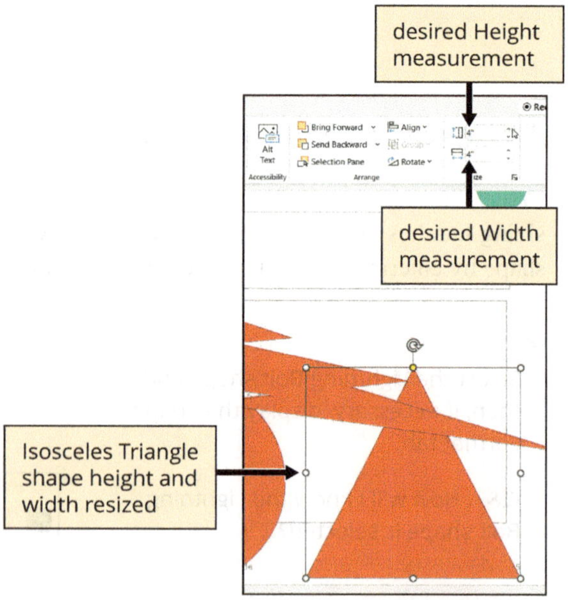

Figure 2–50

Other Ways

1. Right-click shape, click 'Size and Position' on shortcut menu, if necessary click 'Size & Properties' icon (Format Shape pane), if necessary click Size, enter shape height and width values in boxes, close Format Shape pane
2. Click Size and Position pane launcher (Shape Format tab | Size group), click Size tab, enter desired height and width values in boxes, click Close button

To Select Shapes

When you want to format multiple objects on a slide, one efficient method of performing this task is to select all these objects and then apply changes to them simultaneously. **Why?** You want to apply the same changes to all three shapes. Select these objects by selecting one shape, pressing and holding down SHIFT, and then selecting the second and third shapes. The following step selects three shapes on Slide 5.

1

- Select the Isosceles Triangle, if necessary.
- Press and hold down SHIFT and then click the Oval and the Lightning Bolt shapes (Figure 2–51).

Q&A Instead of selecting these three shapes individually, could I have clicked the Select button (Home tab | Editing group) and then chose Select All on the menu?

No. You also would have selected the footer text boxes because they are slide elements.

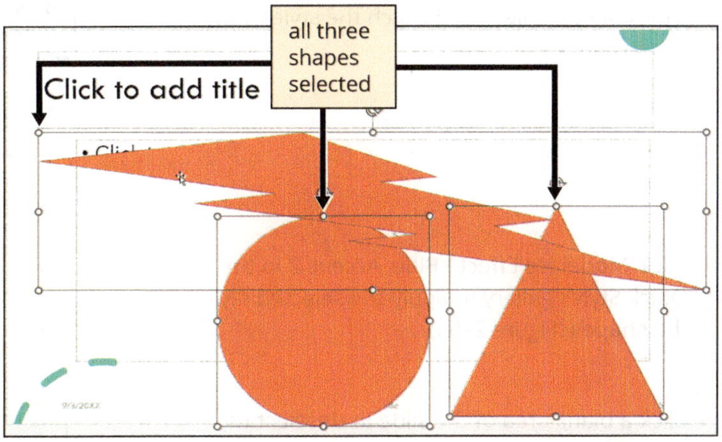

Figure 2–51

To Apply a Shape Style

The Quick Styles gallery has a variety of styles that change depending on the theme applied to the presentation. Formatting text in a shape follows the same techniques as formatting text in a placeholder. You can change the font, font color and size, and alignment. You later will add information to the Oval and Isosceles Triangle shapes, but first you want to apply a shape style. **Why?** The style will give depth and dimension to the object. The following steps apply a style to the three shapes on Slide 5.

1

- Display the Home tab and then click the Quick Styles button (Home tab | Drawing group) to display the Shape Quick Styles gallery (Figure 2–52).

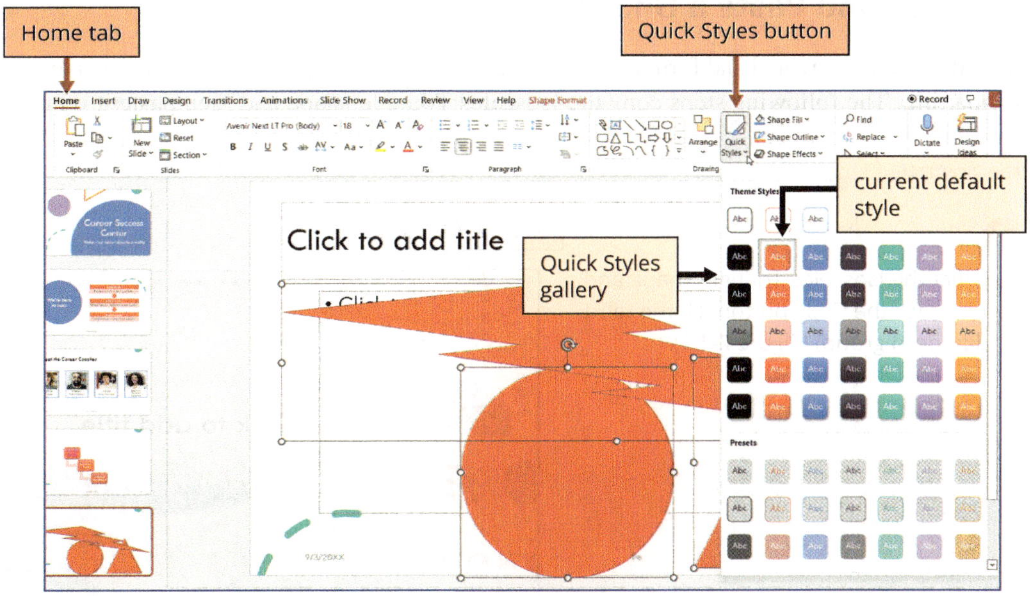

Figure 2–52

2

- Scroll down and then point to 'Moderate Effect - Blue, Accent 2' in the Quick Styles gallery (third shape in the fifth Theme Styles row) to display a live preview of that style applied to the shapes in the slide (Figure 2–53).
  - **Experiment:** Point to various styles in the Quick Styles gallery and watch the style of the shape change.

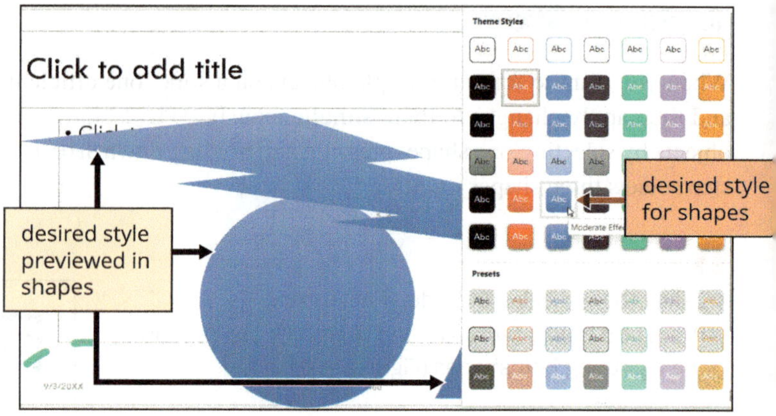

Figure 2–53

3

- Click 'Moderate Effect - Blue, Accent 2' in the Quick Styles gallery to apply the selected style to the shapes (Figure 2–54).

4

- Click a blank area of the slide to deselect the three objects.

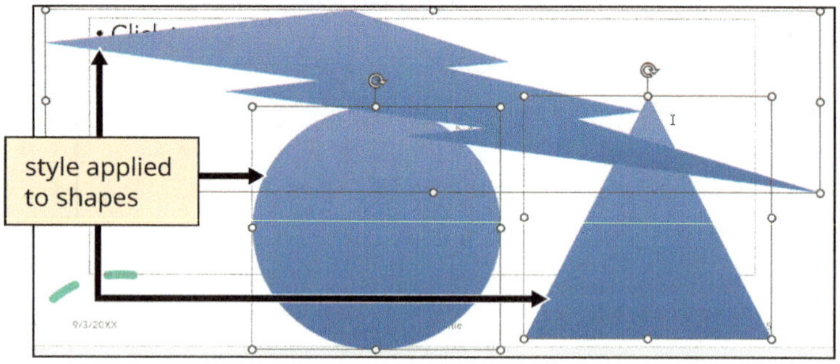

Figure 2–54

Other Ways

1. Click Shape Styles More button (Shape Format tab | Shape Styles group), select style
2. Right-click shape, click Style button on Mini toolbar, select desired style

To Copy and Paste a Shape

You already have created and formatted the Isosceles Triangle shape, and you now need to create a second shape with the same formatting. The following steps copy the Isosceles Triangle shape and then paste it on the left side of the slide. **Why?** You could repeat all the steps you performed to create the first Isosceles Triangle shape, but it is much more efficient to duplicate the formatted shape.

1

- Select the Isosceles Triangle shape and then click the Copy button (Home tab | Clipboard group) (Figure 2–55).

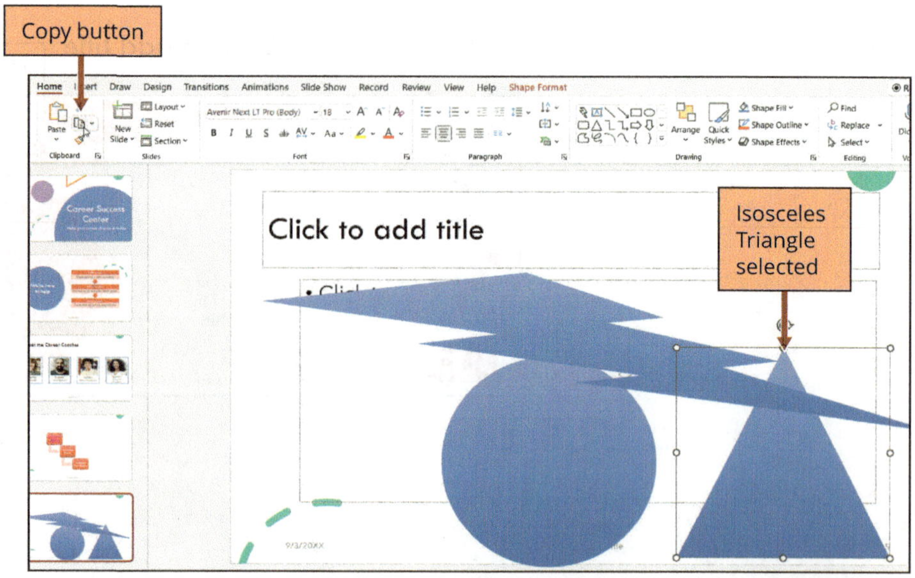

Figure 2–55

2

- Click the Paste button (Home tab | Clipboard group) to insert a duplicate Isosceles Triangle shape on Slide 5.

3

- Drag the new Isosceles Triangle shape to the left side of the slide (Figure 2–56).

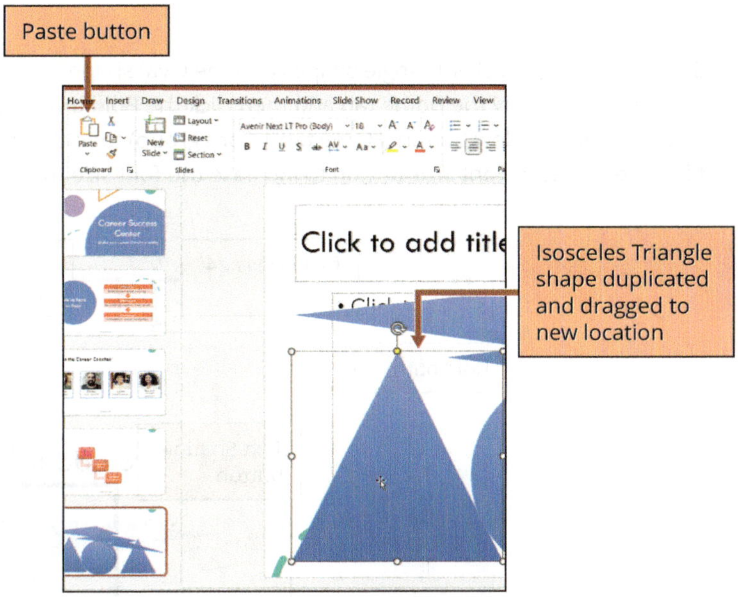

Figure 2–56

Other Ways

1. Right-click selected shape, click Copy on shortcut menu, right-click blank area, click Paste on shortcut menu
2. Select shape, press CTRL+C, press CTRL+V

To Add Text to a Shape

The shapes on Slide 5 help call attention to one of the key aspects of your presentation. **Why?** Your goal is to emphasize the simple process of using the app to create a profile and then apply for a job. The next step is to add this information to Slide 5. The following steps add text to the Isosceles Triangle and Oval shapes.

1

- With the left Isosceles Triangle shape selected, type **Download the app** to add the text in the shape.

2

- Click the Oval shape to select it and then type **Create a profile** to add the text in the shape.

3

- Click the right Isosceles Triangle shape to select it and then type **Apply for the job** to add the text in the shape (Figure 2–57).

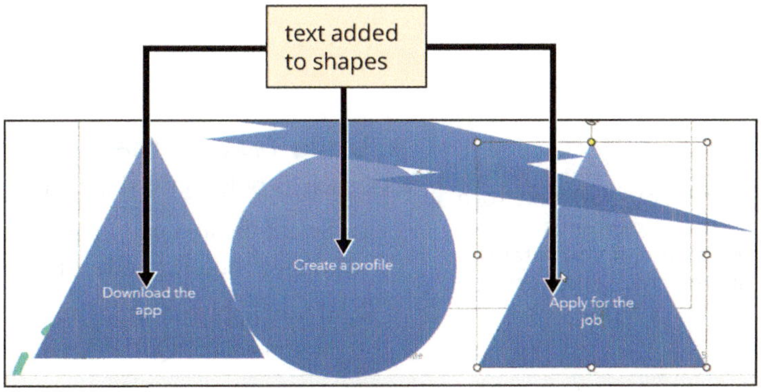

Figure 2–57

To Format Shape Text

The text in the three shapes has the default formatting, but you can enhance these letters. **Why?** The size, color, and other formatting aspects will make the text more readable. You can format shape text with the same features used to format slide placeholder text. The following step bolds the text, adds a shadow, and increases the font size on the text in all three shapes.

1

- Select the two Isosceles Triangle shapes and the Oval shape.
- If necessary, display the Home tab and then click the Bold button (Home tab | Font group).
- Click the Text Shadow button (Home tab | Font group) to add a shadow to the text.
- Click the 'Increase Font Size' button to increase the font size to 24 point (Figure 2–58).

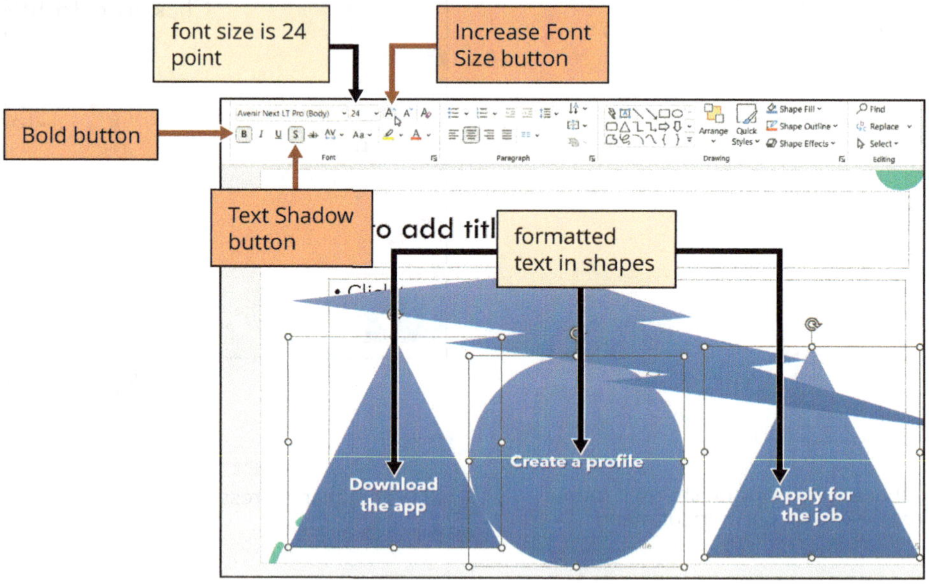

Figure 2–58

Q&A Can I make other formatting changes to the graphics' text?
Yes. You can format the text by making any of the modifications in the Font group.

If I am using a touch screen, can I modify all three rectangles simultaneously?
No. You need to repeat Step 1 for each of the shapes.

Other Ways

1. Right-click selected text, click desired text format button on Mini toolbar

BTW
Using Text in a Shape
When you add text to a shape, it becomes part of the shape. If you rotate or flip the shape, the text also rotates or flips.

To Undo Text Formatting Changes To remove a formatting change you have made to text, such as bolding or shadowing, you would do the following.

1. Select the text and then click the button that originally applied the format. For example, to undo bolding, select the text and then click the Bold button.
2. If you apply a format and then immediately decide to remove this effect, click the Undo button on the Quick Access Toolbar or press CTRL+Z.

To Change a Shape Fill Color

The Lightning Bolt shape has the same blue formatting as the three other slide shapes. You can change the Lightning Bolt shape's fill color to yellow. **Why?** The color yellow is associated with lightning and contrasts with the three blue shapes. The following steps change the fill color of the Lightning Bolt shape.

1

- Click the Lightning Bolt shape to select it and then click the Shape Fill arrow (Home tab | Drawing group) to display the Shape Fill gallery.

- Point to Yellow (fourth color in the Standard Colors row) to display a live preview of this fill color (Figure 2–59).
- **Experiment:** Point to various colors in the gallery and watch the fill color change.

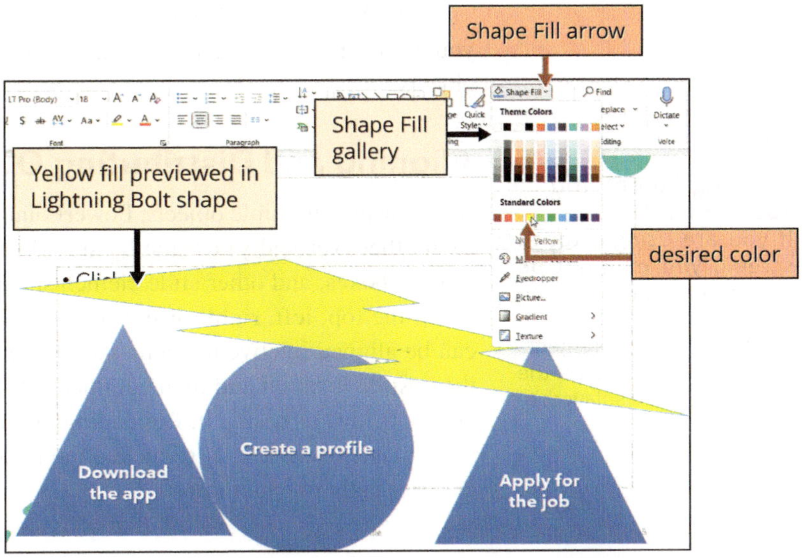

Figure 2–59

2

- Click Yellow to apply this color to the Lightning Bolt shape.
- Click a blank area of the slide outside of the Lightning Bolt shape to deselect this slide element (Figure 2–60).

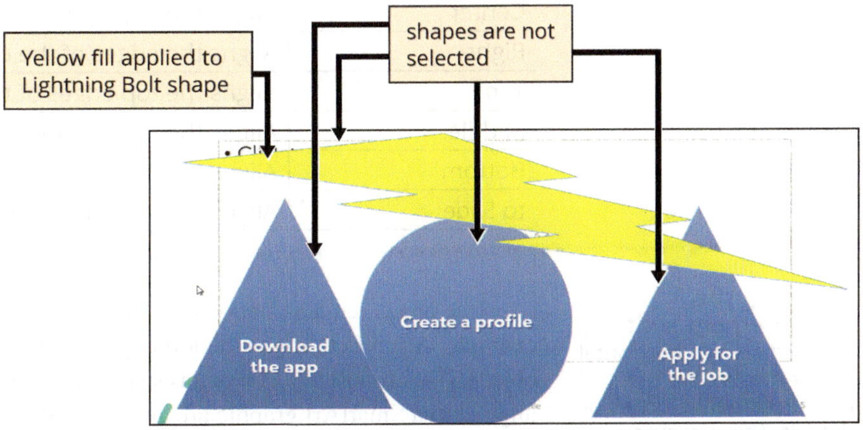

Figure 2–60

Other Ways

1. Click Shape Fill button (Shape Format tab | Shape Styles group)

Break Point: If you wish to take a break, this is a good place to do so. Be sure the Career file is saved and then you can exit PowerPoint. To resume later, start PowerPoint, open the file called SC_PPT_2_Career.pptx, and continue following the steps from this location forward.

Positioning Slide Elements

At times you may desire to arrange slide elements in precise locations. PowerPoint provides useful tools to help you position shapes and objects on slides. **Drawing guides** are two straight dotted lines, one horizontal and one vertical. When an object is close to a guide, its corner or its center (whichever is closer) will **snap**, or align precisely, on top of the guide. You can drag a guide to a new location to meet your alignment requirements. Guides can be added and deleted as you develop slide content. Another tool is the vertical or horizontal **ruler**, which can help you drag an object to a precise location on the slide. The center of a slide is 0.00 on both the vertical and the horizontal rulers.

Gridlines are evenly spaced horizontal and vertical lines that help give you visual cues when you are formatting objects on a slide. You can use gridlines to help you align shapes and other objects.

BTW
Drawing Guides and Touch Screens
If you are using a touch screen, you may not be able to change the position of the drawing guides. In addition, the measurements indicating the position of the guides are not displayed.

Aligning and Distributing Objects

If you display multiple objects, PowerPoint can **align** their center lines or edges above and below each other (vertically) or side by side (horizontally). The objects, such as SmartArt graphics, shapes, boxes, and other slide elements, can be aligned relative to the slide so that they display along the top, left, right, or bottom borders or in the center or middle of the slide. They also can be aligned relative to each other, meaning that you position either the first or last object in the desired location and then command PowerPoint to move the remaining objects in the series above, below, or beside it. Depending on the alignment option that you click, objects will move straight up, down, left, or right, and might cover an object already located on the slide. Table 2–3 describes alignment options.

Table 2-3: Alignment Options

Alignment	Action
Left	Aligns the edges of the objects to the left
Center	Aligns the objects vertically through the centers of the objects
Right	Aligns the edges of the objects to the right
Top	Aligns the top edges of the objects
Middle	Aligns the objects horizontally through the middle of the objects
Bottom	Aligns the bottom edges of the objects
to Slide	Aligns one object to the slide

BTW
Changing the Measurement Unit
The vertical and horizontal rulers display the units of measurement in inches by default. This measurement system is determined by the settings in Microsoft Windows. You can change the measurement unit to centimeters by customizing the numbers format in the 'Clock and Region' area of the Control Panel. Click Region, click Additional Settings, and then choose Metric.

One object remains stationary when you align objects relative to each other by their edges. For example, Align Left aligns the left edges of all selected objects with the left edge of the leftmost object. The leftmost object remains stationary, and the other objects are aligned relative to it. Objects aligned to a SmartArt graphic are aligned to the leftmost edge of the SmartArt graphic, not to the leftmost shape in the SmartArt graphic. Objects aligned relative to each other by their middles or centers are aligned along a horizontal or vertical line that represents the average of their original positions. All of the objects might move.

Smart Guides appear automatically when two or more shapes are in spatial alignment with each other, even if the shapes vary in size. To evenly space multiple objects horizontally or vertically, you **distribute** them. PowerPoint determines the total length between either the outermost edges of the first and last selected object or the edges of the entire slide. It then inserts equal spacing among the items in the series. You also can distribute spacing by using the Size and Position dialog box, but the Distribute command automates this task.

To Display the Drawing Guides

Why? Guides help you align objects on slides. Using a mouse, when you point to a guide and then press and hold the mouse button, PowerPoint displays a box containing the exact position of the guide on the slide in inches. An arrow is displayed below the guide position to indicate the vertical guide either left or right of the center. An arrow also is displayed to the right of the guide position to indicate the horizontal guide either above or below the center. The following step displays the guides.

1

- With Slide 5 displayed, display the View tab and then click the Guides check box (View tab | Show group) to place a checkmark in the box and display the horizontal and vertical guides (Figure 2–61).

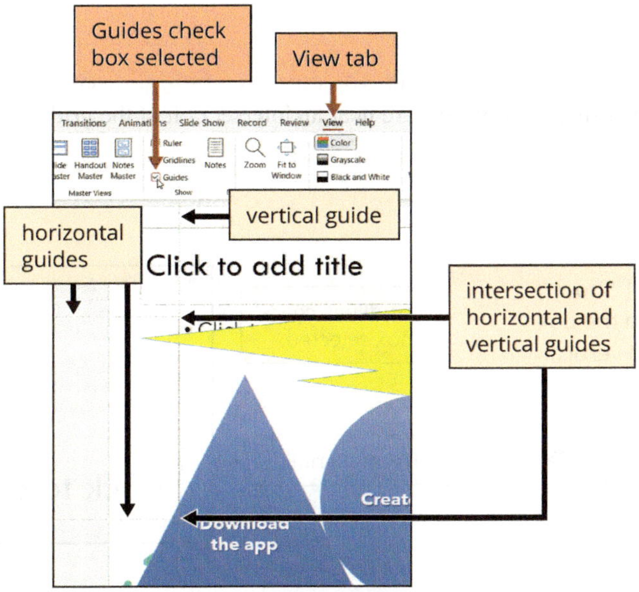

Figure 2–61

Other Ways

1. Right-click area of slide other than a placeholder or object, point to 'Grid and Guides' arrow on shortcut menu, click Guides
2. Press ALT+F9 to toggle guides on/off

To Display the Ruler

The ruler is another feature to use when positioning objects. **Why?** The ruler helps you align slide elements in a precise location on slides. One ruler is displayed horizontally at the top of the slide, and the other is displayed vertically along the left edge of the slide. The following step displays the ruler.

1

- With Slide 5 displayed, click the Ruler check box (View tab | Show group) to place a checkmark in the box and display the horizontal and vertical rulers (Figure 2–62).

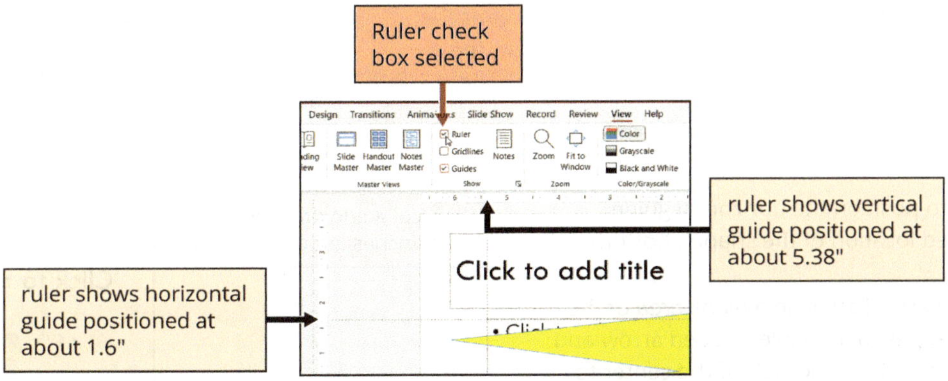

Figure 2–62

BTW
Displaying the Ruler
The ruler is not available in all views, such as Slide Sorter view. If the Ruler box is grayed out, try switching to Normal view.

BTW
Hiding the Vertical Ruler
To permanently hide the vertical ruler, click the File tab, click Options, click Advanced, scroll down to the Display section, and then clear the 'Show vertical ruler' box.

Other Ways

1. Right-click area of slide other than a placeholder or object, point to Ruler on shortcut menu, click Ruler

To Display the Gridlines

Why? The gridlines give you precise visual cues when you are developing slide content. The vertical and horizontal lines are spaced at one-inch intervals. When shapes or objects are near an intersection of the grid, they snap to this location. The following step displays the gridlines.

1

- With Slide 5 displayed, click the Gridlines check box (View tab | Show group) to place a checkmark in the box and display the horizontal and vertical gridlines (Figure 2–63).

Q&A What if I do not see the gridlines after checking the Gridlines box?
If you do not see any gridlines, try a higher zoom level (zoom in).

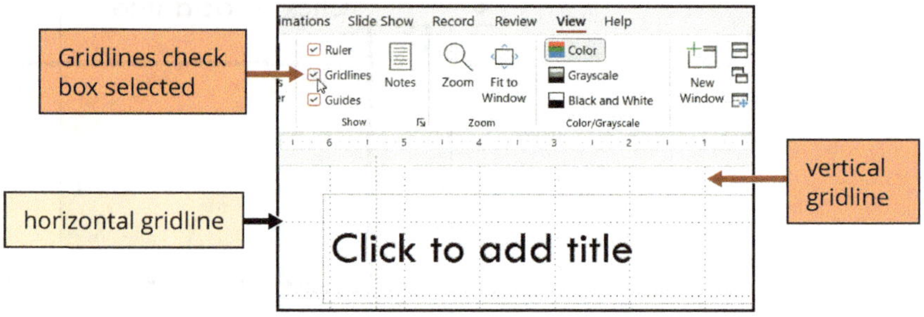

Figure 2–63

Other Ways

1. Right-click area of slide other than a placeholder or object, point to 'Grid and Guides' arrow on shortcut menu, click Gridlines

To Position a Shape Using Guides, Gridlines, and the Ruler

The lower edges of the Isosceles Triangle and the Oval shapes on Slide 5 should be displayed in the same horizontal location. **Why?** The design will look professional if they are aligned precisely near the bottom of the slide. You can use the rulers and gridlines to help you verify the desired guide locations and where to drag an object to an exact location on the slide. The center of a slide is 0.00 on both the vertical and the horizontal rulers. The following steps position the three shapes on Slide 5.

1

- Position the pointer on the lower horizontal guide in a blank area of the slide so that the pointer changes to a double-headed arrow and then drag the horizontal guide to 3.00 inches below the center. Do not release the mouse button (Figure 2–64).

Q&A Why does 3.00 display when I hold down the mouse button?
The ScreenTip displays the horizontal guide's position. A 0.00 setting means that the guide is precisely in the middle of the slide and is not above or below the center, so a 3.00 setting indicates the guide is 3 inches below the center line.

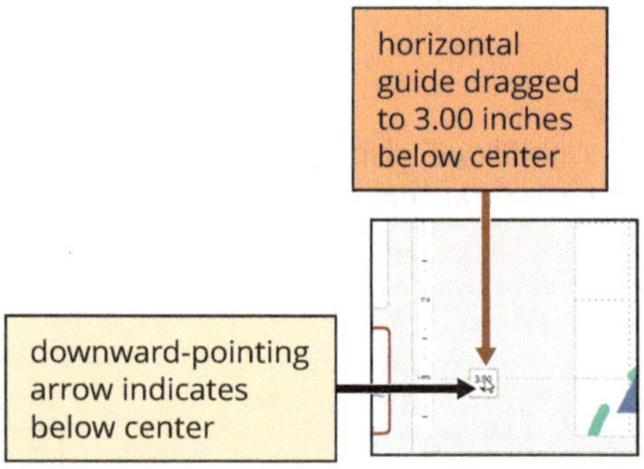

Figure 2–64

2

- Release the mouse button to position the horizontal guide at 3.00, which is the intended location of the shape's bottom border.
- Position the pointer on the vertical guide in a blank area of the slide so that the pointer changes to a double-headed arrow and then drag the vertical guide to 6.00 inches left of the center to position the vertical guide.
- Drag the left Isosceles Triangle shape so its lower-left corner touches the intersection of the vertical and horizontal guides to position the shape in the desired location (Figure 2–65).

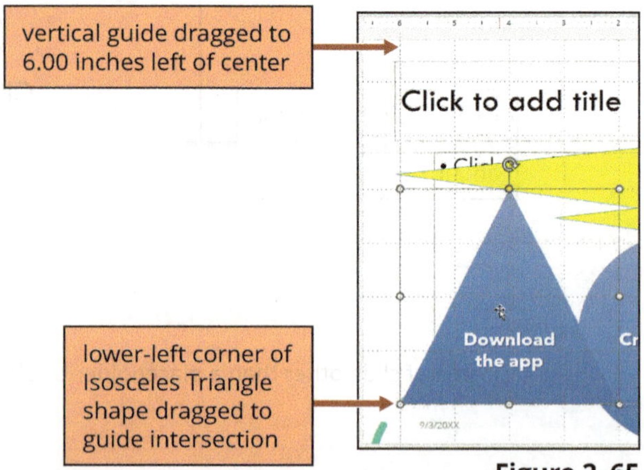

Figure 2–65

Q&A Can I add guides to help me align multiple objects?
Yes. Position the pointer over one guide and then press CTRL. When you drag your pointer, a second guide appears.

To Position the Remaining Shapes

The bottom edges of the Oval and right Isosceles Triangle shapes on Slide 5 should be positioned in the same location as the left Isosceles Triangle. The horizontal guide will display in the same location, but you can move the vertical guide to help you align these objects. The rulers and grid lines will help you verify the desired guide locations. The following steps position the Oval and right Isosceles Triangle shapes.

BTW
Overriding Snap-To Options
To temporarily override the snap-to options, hold down ALT while you drag the object, picture, or chart.

1. Drag the vertical guide to 2.00 left of the center. Select the Oval shape and then position it so its lower-left corner touches the intersection of the vertical and horizontal guides.

2. Drag the vertical guide to 6.00 right of the center. Select the right Isosceles Triangle shape and then position it so its lower-right corner touches the intersection of the vertical and horizontal guides (Figure 2–66).

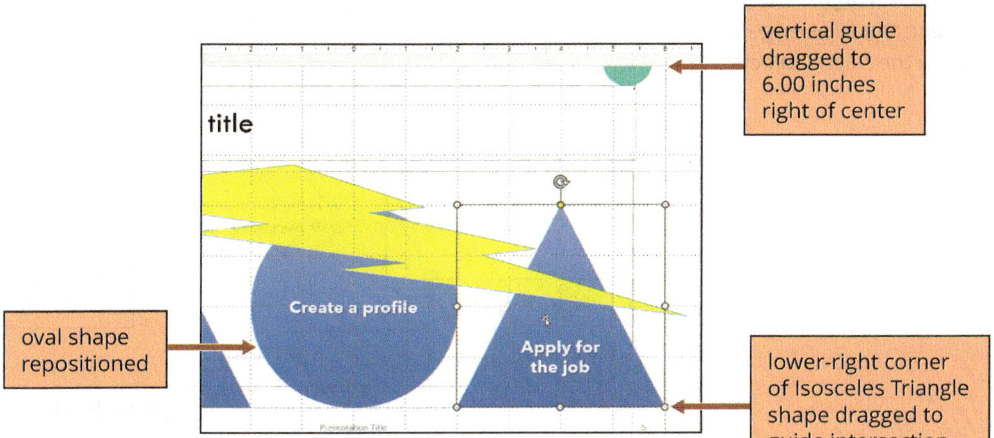

Figure 2–66

To Distribute Shapes

Now that the Isosceles Triangle and Oval shapes are aligned, you can have PowerPoint place the same amount of space between them. You have two distribution options: 'Align to Slide' spaces all the selected objects evenly across the entire width of the slide; 'Align Selected Objects' spaces only the middle objects between the fixed right and left objects. The following steps use the 'Align to Slide' option. **Why?** This option will distribute the three Slide 5 shapes horizontally to fill some of the space along the bottom of the slide.

1

- Select the left Isosceles Triangle, Oval, and right Isosceles Triangle shapes, display the Shape Format tab, and then click the Align button (Shape Format tab | Arrange group) to display the Align Objects menu (Figure 2–67).

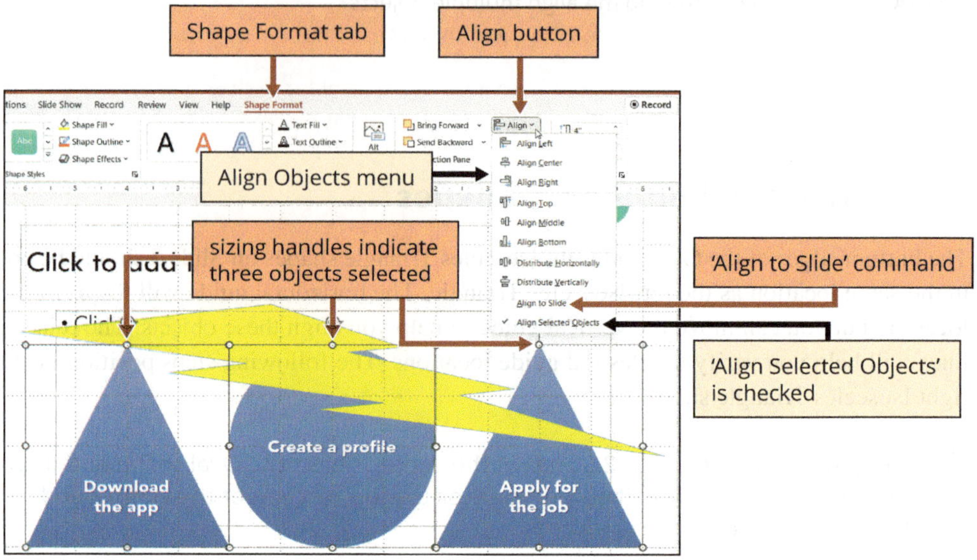

Figure 2–67

2

- Click 'Align to Slide' so that PowerPoint will adjust the spacing of the pictures evenly between the slide edges. Click the Align button again to display the Align Objects menu (Figure 2–68).

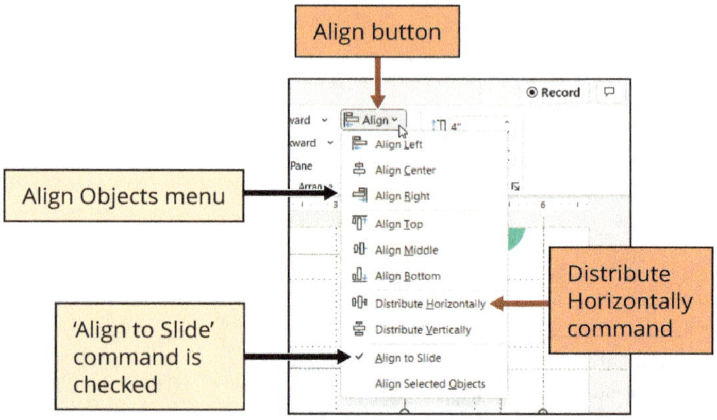

Figure 2–68

3

- Click Distribute Horizontally to adjust the spacing (Figure 2–69).

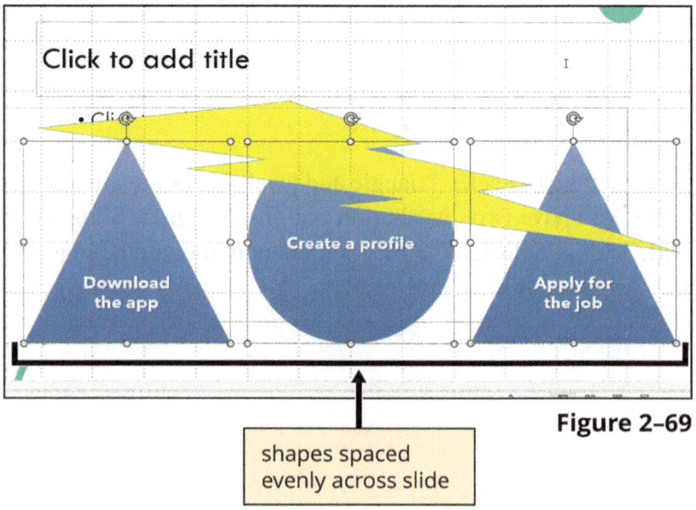

Figure 2–69

BTW

Changing Grid Measurements

You can change the increments of grid measurements, which allows you to adjust the precision of object alignment. In Normal view, right-click an empty area or margin of a slide (not a placeholder) and then click 'Grid and Guides'. Under Grid settings, enter the measurement that you want in the spacing list. If you want these settings to be the default settings for all your presentations, click 'Set as Default'.

To Align a Shape

Now that the Isosceles Triangle and Oval shapes are distributed evenly across the width of the slide, you can have PowerPoint center them vertically in the slide. The following steps use the Align Middle option. **Why?** This option will move the three Slide 5 shapes vertically to fill some of the space in the slide.

1

- With the three shapes still selected and the Shape Format tab displayed, click the Align button to display the Align Objects menu again (Figure 2–70).

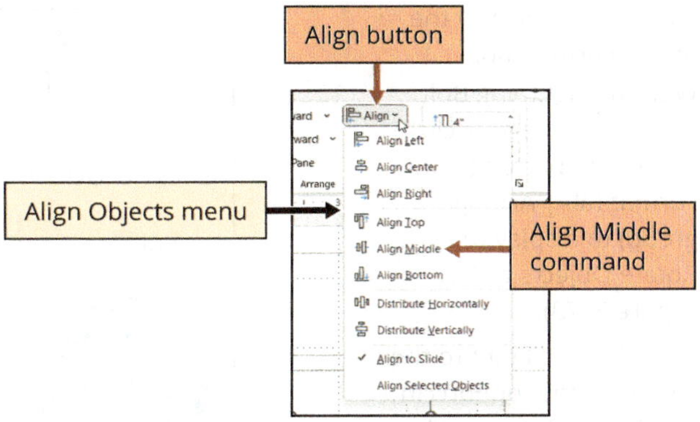

Figure 2–70

2

- Click Align Middle to move the three shapes to the middle of the slide (Figure 2–71).

Q&A What is the difference between the Align Middle and Align Center commands?
Align Middle places the center of each object vertically on the slide; Align Center places all the objects in the center of the slide.

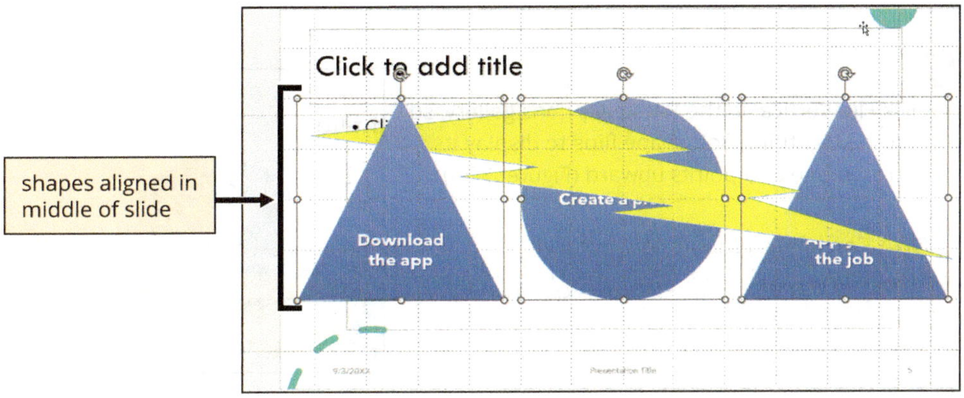

Figure 2–71

To Position the Lightning Bolt Shape

The Lightning Bolt shape represents the energy the students will feel when they pursue the application process, so you want it to display prominently flowing under the shapes and then pointing near the top of the slide. The following step positions the Lightning Bolt shape.

1 Drag the upper horizontal guide to 1.00 inch above the center and the vertical guide 6.00 inches left of the center. Select the Lightning Bolt shape and then drag it downward so the upper-left corner of the selection box touches the intersection of the vertical and horizontal guides (Figure 2–72).

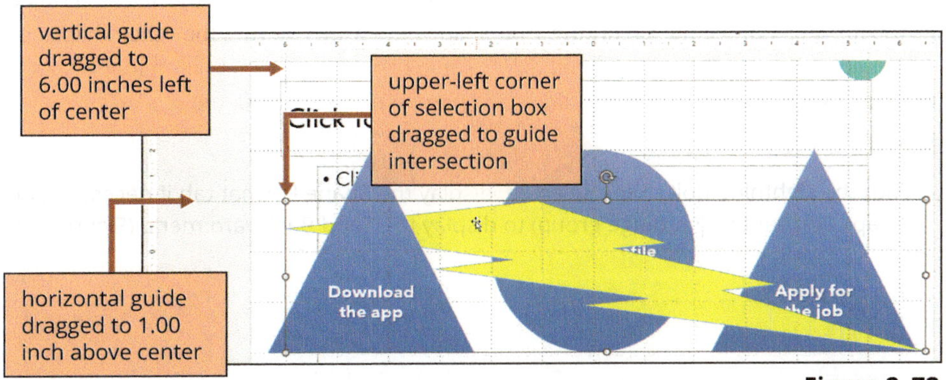

Figure 2–72

To Flip a Shape

The following steps flip the Lightning Bolt shape vertically. **Why?** You want the shape to point upward to indicate positive energy.

1

- If necessary, display the Shape Format tab.
- With the Lightning Bolt shape still selected, click the Rotate button (Shape Format tab | Arrange group) to display the Rotate Objects gallery (Figure 2–73).
- **Experiment:** Point to the various rotate options in the Rotate Options gallery and watch the shape rotate on the slide.

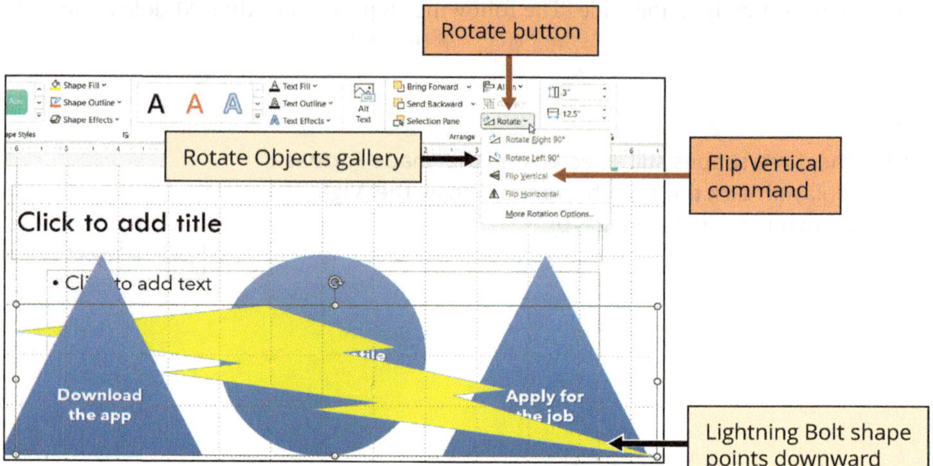

Figure 2–73

2

- Click Flip Vertical in the Rotate Options gallery, so that the Lightning Bolt shape flips to display its mirror image and points upward (Figure 2–74).

Q&A Can I flip a graphic horizontally?
Yes, you would click Flip Horizontal in the Rotate Options gallery. You also can rotate a graphic clockwise or counterclockwise by clicking 'Rotate Right 90°' and 'Rotate Left 90°'.

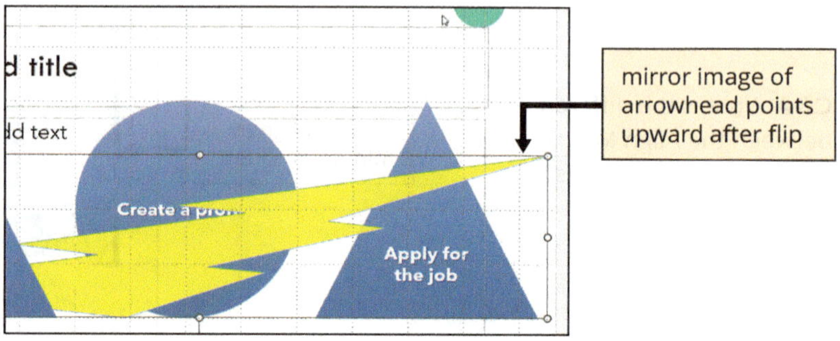

Figure 2–74

To Change the Stacking Order

The objects on a slide stack on top of each other, much like individual cards in a deck. To change the order of these objects, you use the Bring Forward and Send Backward commands. **Bring Forward** moves an object toward the top of the stack, and **Send Backward** moves an object underneath another object. When you click the Bring Forward arrow, PowerPoint displays a menu with an additional command, **Bring to Front**, which moves a selected object to the top of the stack. Likewise, when you click the Send Backward arrow, the **Send to Back** command moves the selected object underneath all objects on the slide. The following steps move the Lightning Bolt shape backwards so that the other shapes on the slide display over it. **Why?** On this slide, the Lightning Bolt shape is on top of some of the shapes, so you no longer can see some of the text. If you send the shape to the bottom of the stack on the slide, the letters will become visible.

1

- With the Lightning Bolt shape selected, display the Shape Format tab if necessary, and then click the Send Backward arrow (Shape Format tab | Arrange group) to display the Send Backward menu (Figure 2–75).

Q&A How can I see objects that are not on the top of the stack?
Press TAB or SHIFT+TAB to display each slide object.

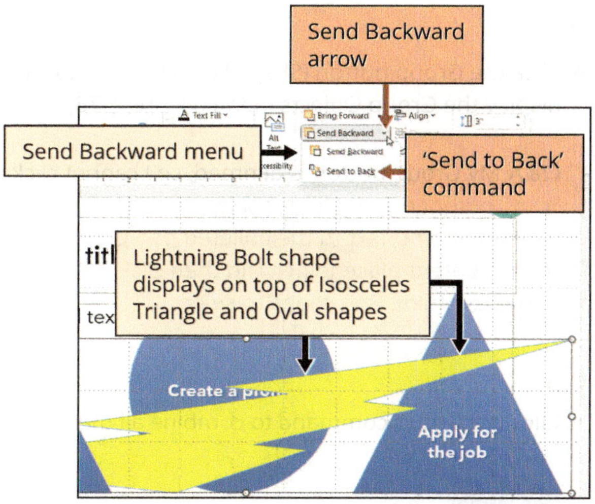

Figure 2–75

2

- Click 'Send to Back' to move the Lightning Bolt shape underneath the Isosceles Triangles and Oval shapes (Figure 2–76).

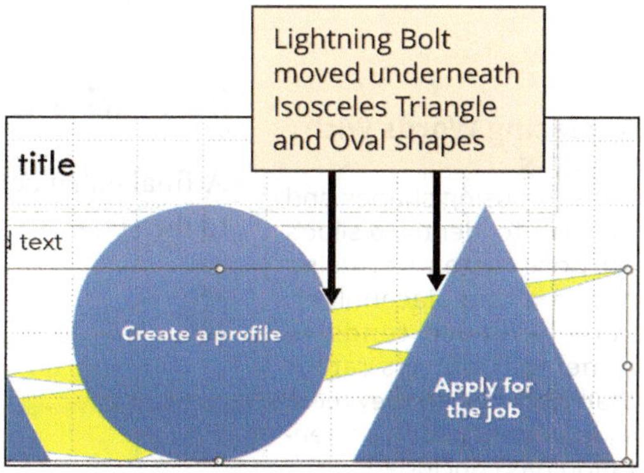

Figure 2–76

Other Ways

1. Click Send Backward arrow (Shape Format tab | Arrange group), press K
2. Right-click shape, point to 'Send to Back' on shortcut menu, click 'Send to Back'

To Group Objects

If you attempt to move or size the four shapes on Slide 5, you might encounter difficulties because the multiple objects are separate objects on the slide. Dragging or sizing affects only a selected object, not the entire collection of objects, so you must use caution when objects are not grouped. You can **group** the objects so they are assembled into a single unit. **Why?** When they are grouped, they cannot be accidentally moved or manipulated. The following steps group these four objects into one object.

1

- Select the two Isosceles Triangle and Oval shapes and then also select the Lightning Bolt shape by clicking the upper-right point that extends past the content placeholder (Figure 2–77).

Q&A Why do I need to click that part of the Lightning Bolt shape to select it?
If you click that shape inside of the content placeholder, the content placeholder also is selected.

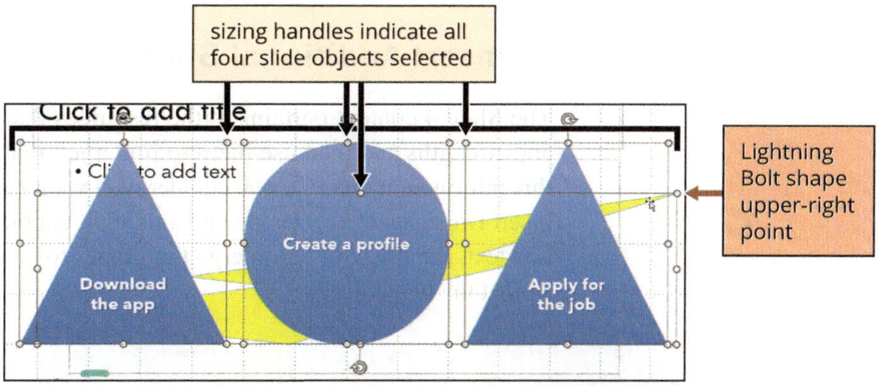

Figure 2–77

2

- Click the Group button (Shape Format tab | Arrange group) to display the Group Objects menu (Figure 2–78).

Q&A My Group button is dimmed, so I cannot click it. Why?
Your content placeholder is selected, as indicated by the insertion point next to the bulleted paragraph. Click outside of the content placeholder and then click the upper-right end of the Lightning Bolt shape to select it.

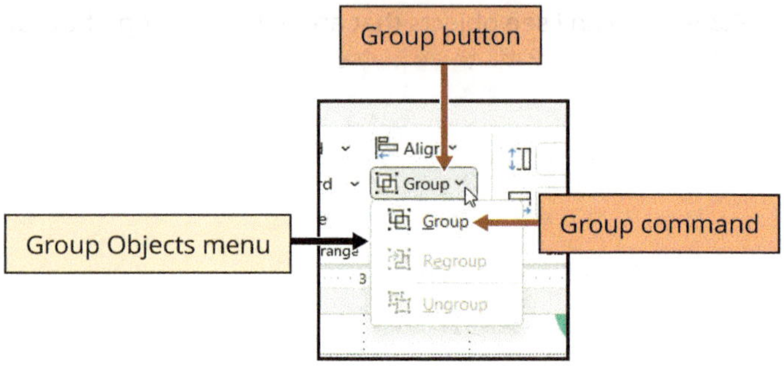

Figure 2–78

3

- Click the Group command to combine all the shapes.

Other Ways

1. Right-click selected shapes, point to Group on shortcut menu, click Group

BTW
Replacing Words with Objects
Consider using shapes and symbols to identify a slide's purpose instead of using text in a title placeholder. Your audience tends to remember objects rather than words when they recall slide content after a presentation has concluded.

To Add a Slide Title

A final enhancement you will make to Slide 5 is to add a title. The following steps add this title to the slide.

1 Type **Application Process** in the title text placeholder (Figure 2–79).

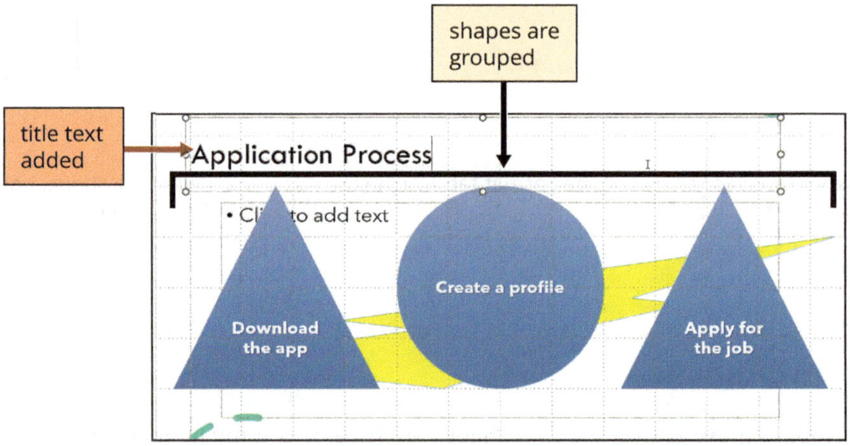

Figure 2–79

To Insert Additional Shapes

The Slide 4 content pertains to the resources that students can use to determine their interests and strengths and then use them to find a job that fits their career goals. Instead of identifying this information in a title placeholder, you want to create a unique shape with text. You first will insert two shapes: a rectangle and a thought bubble. Then, you will arrange and format them and add text. Finally, you will merge the shapes to create one object. The following steps insert and format the two objects.

1. Display Slide 4 and then click the Shapes More button (Home tab | Drawing group) to display the Shapes gallery.

2. Insert the Rectangle: Top Corners Snipped shape (fourth shape in the Rectangles row). Proportionally resize the Rectangle: Top Corners Snipped shape to approximately 3.4" × 2.5".

3. Align the Rectangle: Top Corners Snipped shape so that the left edge is 6 inches left of center (along the first vertical gridline from the left side of the slide) and the lower edge is 2.00 inches below center (along the sixth horizontal gridline).

4. Click the Shapes More button (Shape Format tab | Insert Shapes group) to display the Shapes gallery and then insert the Thought Bubble: Cloud shape (fourth shape in the Callouts row). Proportionally resize the Thought Bubble: Cloud shape to approximately 1.7" × 2".

5. Align the Thought Bubble: Cloud shape so that the left edge is 6 inches left of center (along the first vertical gridline from the left side of the slide) and the upper edge is 3.00 inches above center (along the first horizontal gridline).

6. With the Thought Bubble: Cloud shape selected, click the Shape Styles More button (Shape Format tab | Shape Styles group), and then apply the 'Moderate Effect - Blue, Accent 2' shape style (third style in the fifth Theme Styles row) (Figure 2–80).

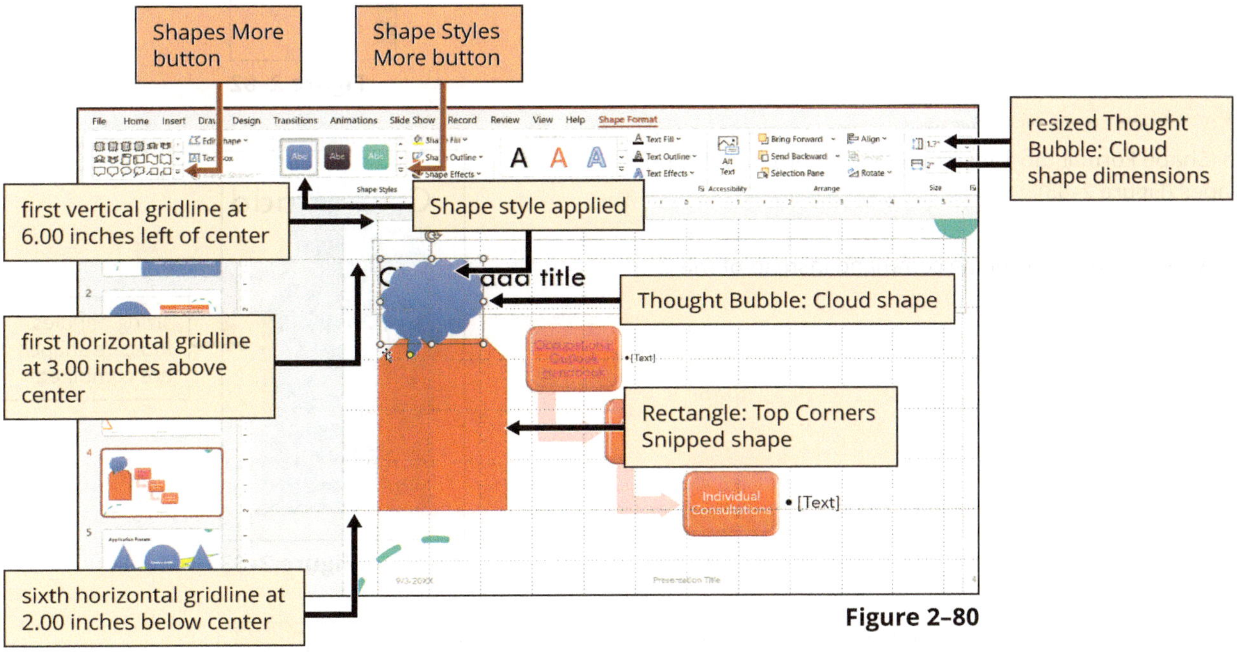

Figure 2–80

To Merge Shapes

The Thought Bubble: Cloud and Rectangle: Top Corners Snipped shapes appear as separate items. You can combine, or merge, them into one object. **Why?** The two elements will appear seamless as a unified graphical element. The following steps merge the two shapes.

1

- Select the Thought Bubble: Cloud and Rectangle: Top Corners Snipped shapes (Figure 2–81).

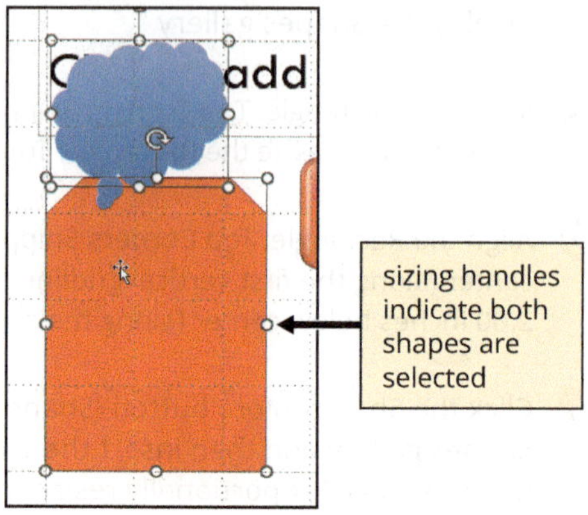

Figure 2–81

2

- With the Shape Format tab displayed, click the Merge Shapes button (Shape Format tab | Insert Shapes group) to display the Merge Shapes menu (Figure 2–82).

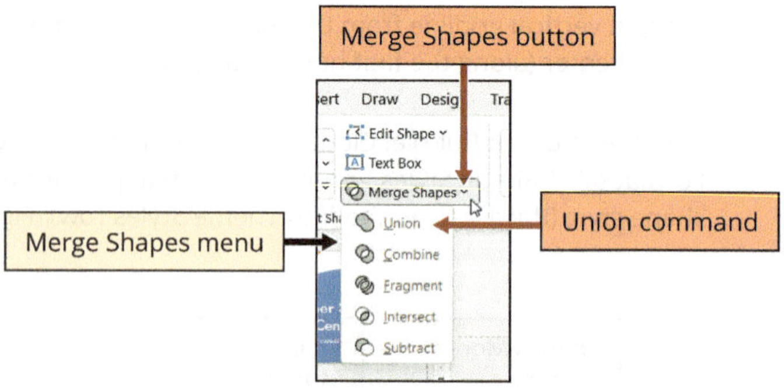

Figure 2–82

3

- Click Union (Shape Format tab | Insert Shapes group) to combine the two shapes (Figure 2–83).

Q&A When would I use the Combine command instead of the Union command?

The Combine command also joins shapes, but it deletes the area where two shapes overlap. The Union command joins the shapes using the formatting of the top shape. Thus, the united shape is now blue.

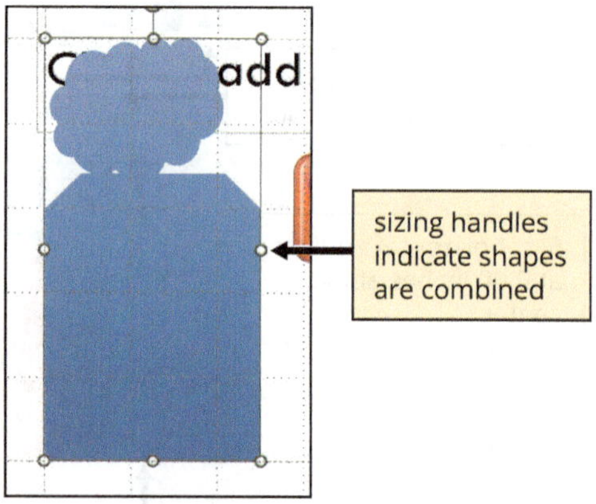

Figure 2–83

4

- Type **Thinking about a career?** and then press ENTER. Type **We have resources to help.** as the next sentence in the shape.
- Increase the font size of the text to 20 point (Figure 2–84).

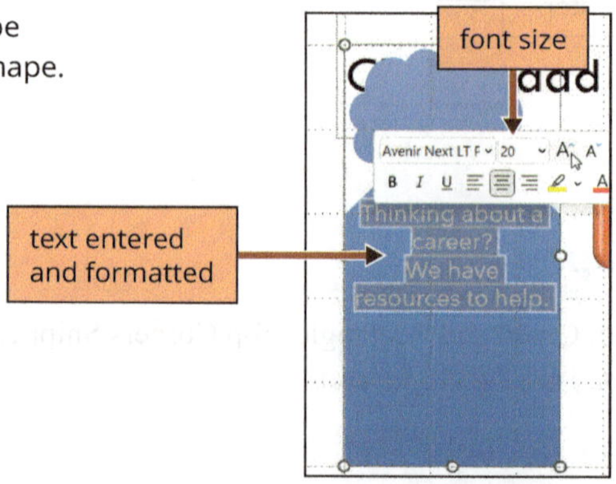

Figure 2–84

To Apply a Picture Fill to a Shape

Sufficient space exists on the right side of Slide 4 to insert a shape filled with a picture. **Why?** A shape and picture help to draw attention to the slide, reinforce the written message, and call attention to the career success theme. A picture with the words, HELP WANTED, coordinates with the resources shapes. You can insert a shape that has the default formatting and then add a picture. The following steps insert a shape and then insert a picture into the shape.

1

- With Slide 4 displayed, insert the Rectangle: Rounded Corners shape (second shape in the Rectangles row).
- Proportionally resize the Rectangle: Rounded Corners shape to 2.5" × 2.5".
- Align the Rectangle: Rounded Corners shape so that the right edge is 6 inches right of center (along the last vertical gridline from the right side of the slide) and the upper edge is 2 inches above center (along the second horizontal gridline) (Figure 2–85).

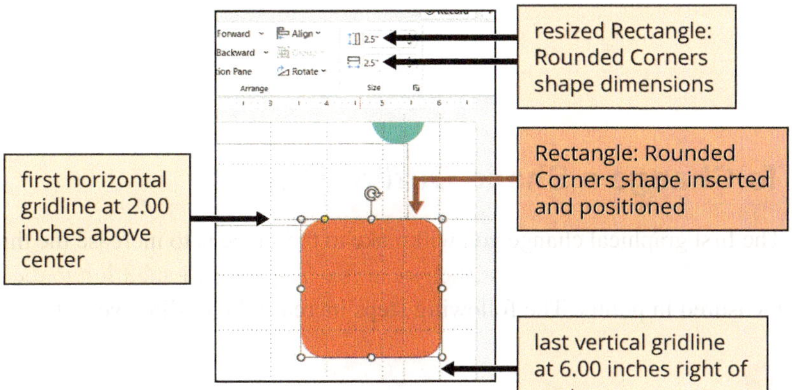

Figure 2–85

2

- With the Shape Format tab displayed, click the Shape Fill arrow (Shape Format tab | Shape Styles group) to display the Shape Fill gallery (Figure 2–86).

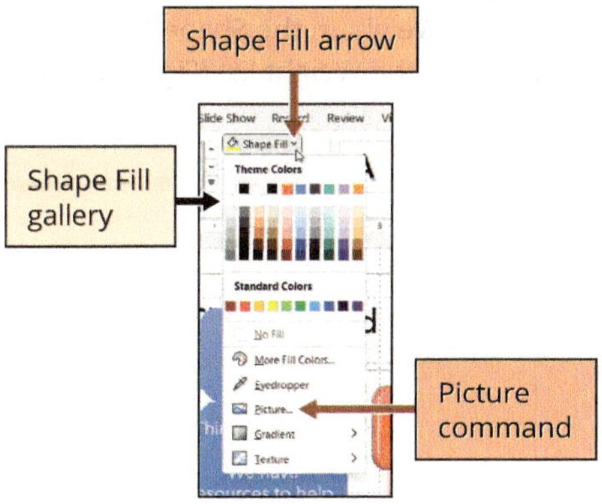

Figure 2–86

3

- Click Picture in the Shape Fill gallery to display the Insert Pictures dialog box, click From a File, and then navigate to the location where your Data Files are stored.
- Click Support_PPT_2_Hiring.jpg to select the file name (Figure 2–87).

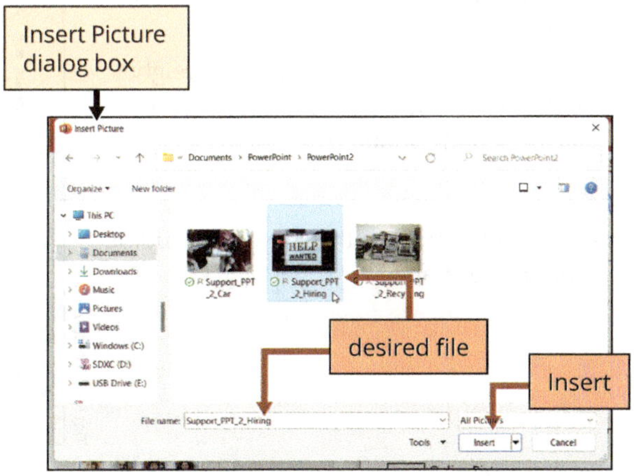

Figure 2–87

4

- Click the Insert button (Insert Picture dialog box) to insert the Hiring picture into the Rectangle: Rounded Corners shape (Figure 2–88).

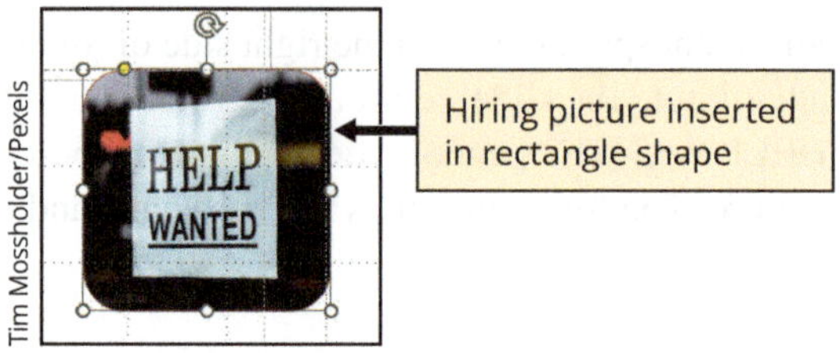

Figure 2–88

To Change a Shape Outline Weight

The first graphical change you will make to the shape is to increase the thickness of the border, which is called the outline. **Why?** This thicker line is a graphical element that helps to call attention to the shape. The weight, or thickness, of the shape border is measured in points. The following steps increase the outline weight.

1

- With the Rectangle: Rounded Corners shape still selected, click the Shape Outline arrow (Shape Format tab | Shapes Styles group) to display the Shape Outline gallery.
- Point to Weight in the Shape Outline gallery to display the Weight list (Figure 2–89).

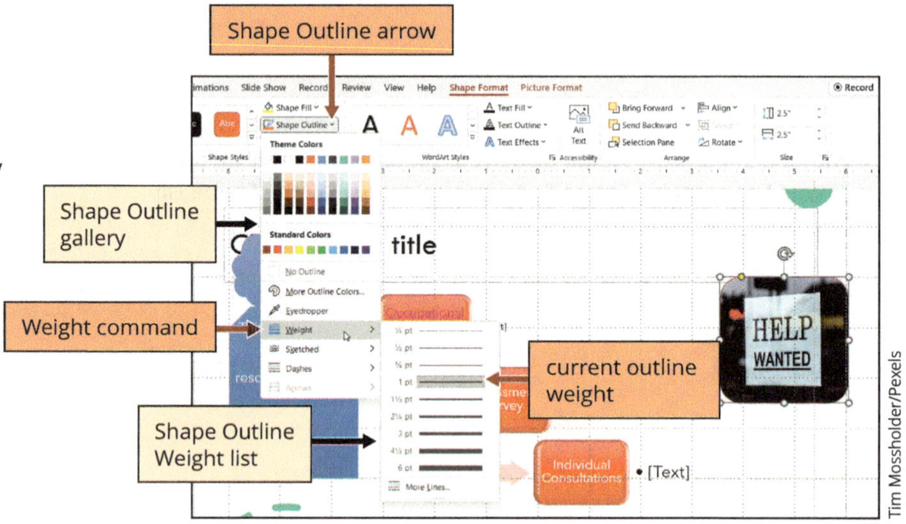

Figure 2–89

2

- Point to 6 pt to display a live preview of this outline line weight (Figure 2–90).
- **Experiment:** Point to various line weights on the Weight list and watch the border weights on the shape change.

3

- Click 6 pt to increase the size of the outline around the shape.

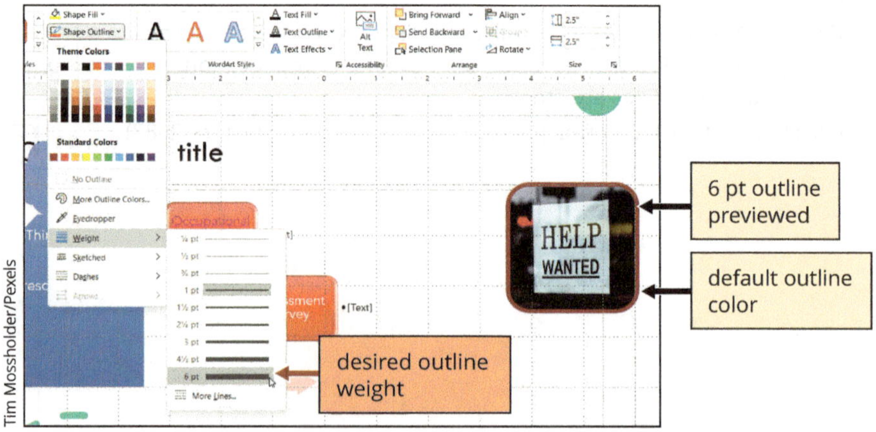

Figure 2–90

Other Ways

1. Click Shape Outline arrow (Home tab | Drawing group), click Weight
2. Right-click shape, click Outline below shortcut menu, click Weight

To Change a Shape Outline Color

The default outline color in the Shapes presentation theme is orange. In this project, you will change the outline color to teal. **Why?** The arc in the lower-left area of the slide and the dot in the upper-right area are teal, so the outline of the rectangle can repeat this color. The following steps change the shape outline color.

1

- With the Rectangle: Rounded Corners shape still selected, click the Shape Outline arrow again to display the Shape Outline gallery.
- Point to Teal, Accent 4 (eighth color in the first Theme Colors row) to display a live preview of that outline color on the shape (Figure 2–91).
- **Experiment:** Point to various colors in the Shape Outline gallery and watch the border colors on the shape change.

2

- Click Teal, Accent 4 to change the shape outline color.

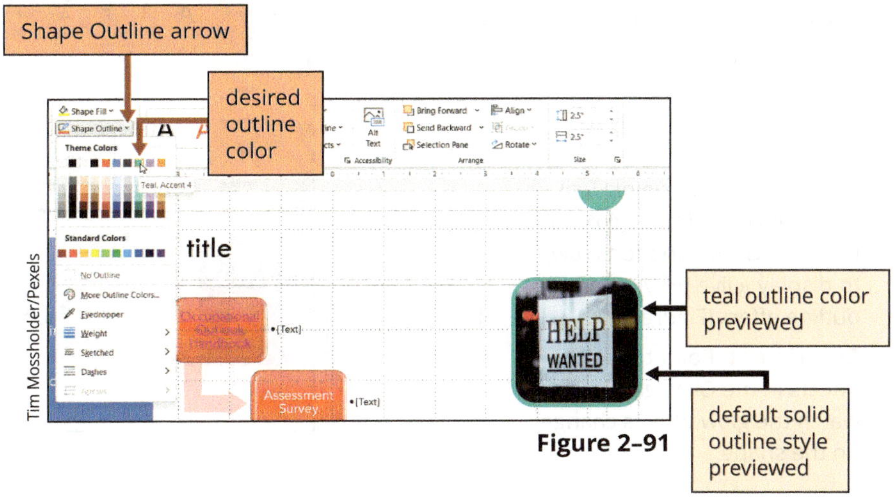

Figure 2–91

To Change a Shape Outline Style

The default outline style is a solid line. You can add interest by changing the style to dashes, dots, or a combination of dashes and dots. The following steps change the shape outline style to Dash. **Why?** The dashes in this pattern coordinate with the arc in the lower-right corner of the slide.

1

- With the Rectangle: Rounded Corners shape still selected, display the Shape Outline gallery again and then point to Dashes to display the Dashes list.
- Point to 'Long Dash Dot' to display a live preview of this outline style (Figure 2–92).
- **Experiment:** Point to various styles in the Shape Outline gallery and watch the outlines on the shape change.

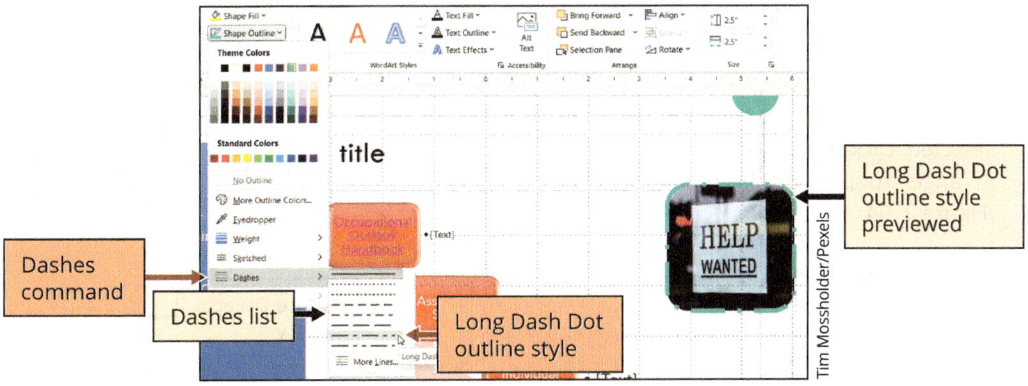

Figure 2–92

2

- Click 'Long Dash Dot' to change the shape outline style.

To Apply an Effect to a Shape

PowerPoint provides a variety of visual effects to add to the shape. They include shadow, glow, reflection, and 3-D rotation. The following steps apply a teal glow effect to the shape. **Why?** The outline color on the slide is teal.

1

- Click the Shape Effects button (Shape Format tab | Shape Objects group) to display the Shape Effects gallery.
- Point to Glow to display the Glow gallery.
- Point to 'Glow: 11 point; Teal, Accent color 4' (fourth color in the third Glow Variations row) to display a live preview of this outline effect (Figure 2–93).

- **Experiment:** Point to various effects in the Glow gallery and watch the glow effects change on the shape.

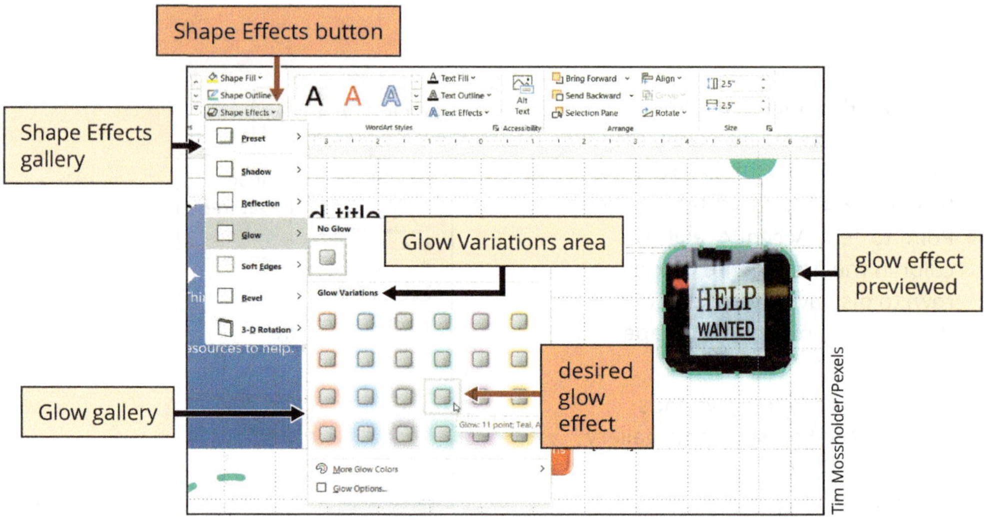

Figure 2–93

2

- Click the 'Glow: 11 point; Teal, Accent color 4' variation to apply the glow effect.

To Rotate a Shape to an Exact Value

In Module 1 you rotated a picture using the rotate handle. Similarly, you can rotate a shape using the rotate handle. You also can rotate a shape clockwise or counterclockwise in two preset values: Right 90° and Left 90°. In addition, you have the option of rotating the shape to any specific degree from 0 to 360. On Slide 4, you will rotate the Rectangle: Rounded Corners shape counterclockwise to the exact value of -15°. **Why?** You want to call attention to this slide element. The following steps rotate the Rectangle: Rounded Corners shape.

1

- With the Rectangle: Rounded Corners shape still selected, click the Rotate button (Shape Format tab | Arrange group) to display the Rotate Objects gallery (Figure 2–94).

Q&A I also see a Picture Format tab. Could I use the Rotate button on this tab?
Yes. The Rectangle: Rounded Corners shape includes a picture, so you see both the Shape Format tab and the Picture Format tab with similar commands in the Arrange group.

- **Experiment:** Point to the various rotate options in the Rotate Objects gallery and watch the shape rotate on the slide.

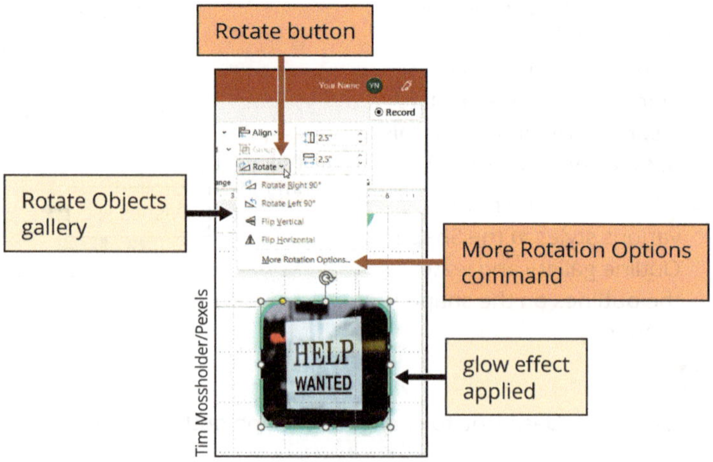

Figure 2–94

2

- Click 'More Rotation Options' in the Rotate Objects gallery to display the Format Picture pane.
- Click the Rotation down arrow several times until −15° is displayed (Figure 2–95).

Q&A Why is the rotation value negative?
When you rotate a shape counterclockwise, the degrees are expressed as a negative number.

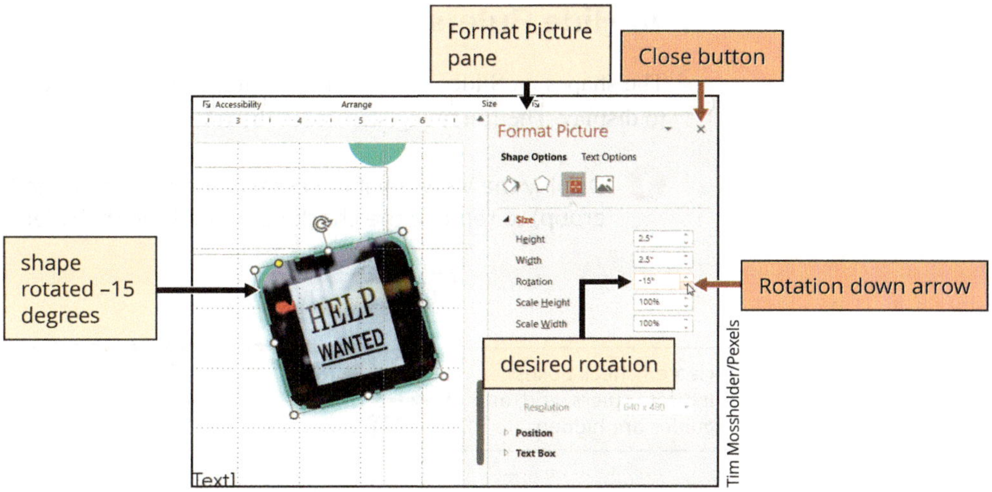

Figure 2–95

3

- Click the Close button (shown in Figure 2–95) to close the Format Picture pane.

To Enter the Title Text

You want to add a title to Slide 4. The following steps add the title text.

1. Type **Resources for You** in the title text placeholder.
2. Center the Slide 4 title text.
3. Click a blank area outside the title text placeholder to deselect this slide element.

To Hide the Grid and Guides

The shapes on Slides 4 and 5 are positioned in the desired locations, so the grid and guides no longer are needed. The following steps hide the grid and the guides.

1. Display the View tab and then click the Gridlines check box (View tab | Show group) to clear the checkmark and hide the grid.
2. Click the Guides check box to clear the checkmark and hide the guides.

Other Ways

1. Right-click area of slide other than a placeholder or object, click Grid and Guides on shortcut menu, click Gridlines to turn off Gridlines or Guides to turn off Guides
2. Press ALT+F9 to toggle guides on/off

To Hide Rulers

The shapes on Slides 4 and 5 are positioned in the desired locations, so the rulers no longer need to display. The following step hides the rulers.

1. Display the View tab if necessary, and then click the Ruler check box (View tab | Show group) to remove the checkmark and hide the rulers (Figure 2–96).

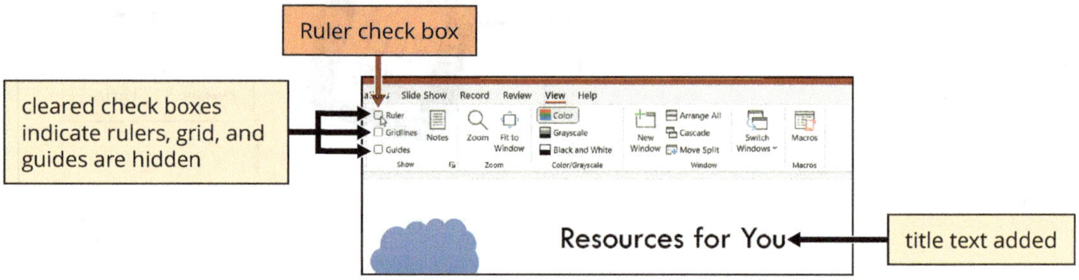

Figure 2–96

Other Ways

1. Right-click area of slide other than a placeholder or object, click Ruler
2. Press SHIFT+ALT+F9 to toggle ruler on/off

Consider This

How can I use handouts to organize my speech?

As you develop a lengthy presentation with many visuals, handouts can help you organize your material. Print handouts with the maximum number of slides per page. Use scissors to cut each thumbnail and then place these miniature slide images adjacent to each other on a flat surface. Any type on the thumbnails will be too small to read, so the images will need to work with only the support of the verbal message you provide. You can rearrange these thumbnails as you organize your speech. When you return to your computer, you can rearrange the slides on your screen to match the order of your thumbnail printouts. Begin speaking the actual words you want to incorporate in the body of the talk. This process of glancing at the thumbnails and hearing yourself say the key ideas of the speech is one of the best methods of organizing and preparing for the actual presentation. Ultimately, when you deliver your speech in front of an audience, the images on the slides or on your note cards should be sufficient to remind you of the accompanying verbal message.

Adding and Modifying a Footer

Slides can contain information at the top or bottom. The area at the top of a slide is called a **header**, and the area at the bottom is called a **footer**. In general, footer content displays along the lower edge of a slide, but the theme determines where these elements are placed. As a default, no information is displayed in the header or footer. You can choose to apply only a header, only a footer, or both a header and footer. In addition, you can elect to have the header or footer display on single slides, all slides, or all slides except the title slide.

Slide numbers are one footer element. They help a presenter organize a talk. While few audience members are cognizant of this aspect of a slide, the presenter can glance at the number and know which slide contains particular information. If an audience member asks a question pertaining to information contained on a slide that had been displayed previously or is on a slide that has not yet been viewed, the presenter can jump to that slide in an effort to answer the question. In addition, the slide number helps pace the slide show. For example, a speaker could have the presentation timed so that Slide 4 is displayed three minutes into the talk.

PowerPoint gives the option of displaying the current date and time obtained from the system or a fixed date and time that you specify. In addition, you can add relevant information, such as your name, your school or business name, or the purpose of your presentation in the Footer area of the Header and Footer dialog box.

BTW
Distributing a Document
Instead of printing and distributing a hard copy of PowerPoint slides, you can distribute the slides electronically. Options include sending the slides via email; posting it on cloud storage (such as OneDrive) and sharing the link with others; posting it on social media, a blog, or other website; and sharing a link associated with an online location of the slides. You also can create and share a PDF or XPS image of the slides, so that users can view the file in Acrobat Reader or XPS Viewer instead of in PowerPoint.

To Add a Footer with Fixed Information

The Shapes presentation theme you downloaded displays three footer placeholders for the date, text, and slide number. To reinforce the fact that the Career Success Center has created this presentation, you can modify this information by adding the Center's name and a date. The following steps add this text to all slides in the presentation except the title slide. **Why?** In general, the footer text should not display on the title slide.

1

- Display the Insert tab.
- Click the 'Header & Footer' button (Insert tab | Text group) to display the Header and Footer dialog box.
- If necessary, click the Slide tab to display the Slide sheet (Figure 2–97).

Q&A Can I use this dialog box to add a header?
The slide theme determines the location of the placeholders at the top or bottom of the slide. The footer elements generally are displayed along the lower edge of the slide. Some themes, however, have the footer elements along the top edge, so they are considered header text.

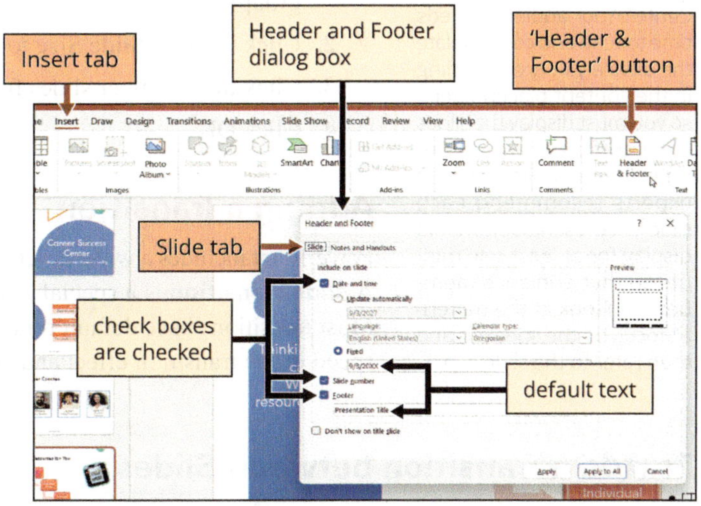

Figure 2–97

2

- With the Fixed option button selected, select the existing date (9/3/20XX) and then type **October 15** in the Fixed box.

Q&A Why is the date on my slide different from today's date?
The Shapes theme you downloaded uses the existing date instead of the current date in the Fixed box.

- Select the existing Footer text (Presentation Title) and then type **Career Success Center** in the Footer box.
- Click the 'Don't show on title slide' check box to place a checkmark in the box (Figure 2–98).

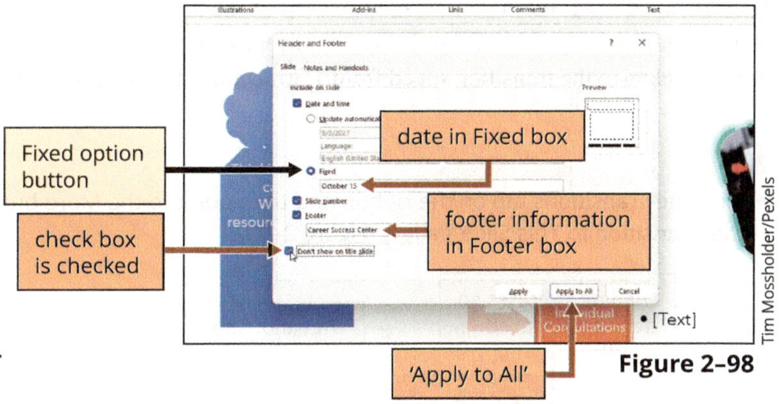

Figure 2–98

Q&A Can the footer information also appear on all the slides?
Yes. If the 'Don't show on title slide' check box is not selected, the footer will appear on all slides.

What if I want the current date and time to appear?
Click Update automatically in the 'Date and time' section.

3

- Click the 'Apply to All' button to display the date, footer text, and slide number on all slides except the title slide (Slide 1).

Q&A When would I click the Apply button instead of the 'Apply to All' button?
Click the Apply button when you want the header and footer information to appear only on the slide currently selected.

Other Ways

1. Click Insert Slide Number button (Insert tab | Text group), click Slide number check box (Header and Footer dialog box)
2. Click 'Date & Time' button (Insert tab | Text group), click 'Date and time' check box (Header and Footer dialog box)

To Edit a Footer The PowerPoint theme determines where the slide numbers, date, and footer text display on a slide. It also determines the font and font size. You can format the footer text in the same manner that you format slide text, such as changing the font, font size, and font color. In addition, you can change the slide numbering. By default, the starting slide number is 1. You can, however, change this footer character. To start your slide numbering with a specific number, you would follow these steps.

1. Display the Design tab and then click the Slide Size button (Design tab | Customize group).
2. Click Custom Slide Size to display the Slide Size dialog box.
3. Click the 'Number slides from' up or down arrow to change the slide number.
4. Click OK.

BTW
Displaying Slides
The slides in this presentation have important information about the Career Success Center. Your audience needs time to read and contemplate the advice you are providing in the content placeholders, so you must display the slides for a sufficient amount of time. Some public speaking experts recommend each slide in a presentation should display for at least one minute so that audience members can look at the material, focus on the speaker, and then refer to the slide again.

Adding a Transition

PowerPoint includes a wide variety of visual and sound effects that can be applied to text or content. A **slide transition** is a special effect used to progress from one slide to the next in a slide show. Most transitions have default rotations, but you can change the direction. You also can control the speed of the transition effect and add a sound.

To Add a Transition between Slides

Why? Transitions add interest when you advance the slides in a presentation and make a slide show presentation look professional. In this presentation, you apply the Pan transition in the Dynamic Content category to all slides. The default rotation is From Bottom, so the current slide moves to the top of the screen and a new slide appears from the bottom of the screen. When you change the Pan rotation to From Left, the current slide moves to the right of the screen and the new slide appears from the left. You also change the transition speed from 1.30 seconds to 3 seconds. The following steps apply this transition to the presentation.

1

- Click the Transitions tab on the ribbon and then point to the More button (Transitions tab | Transition to This Slide group) in the 'Transition to This Slide' gallery (Figure 2–99).

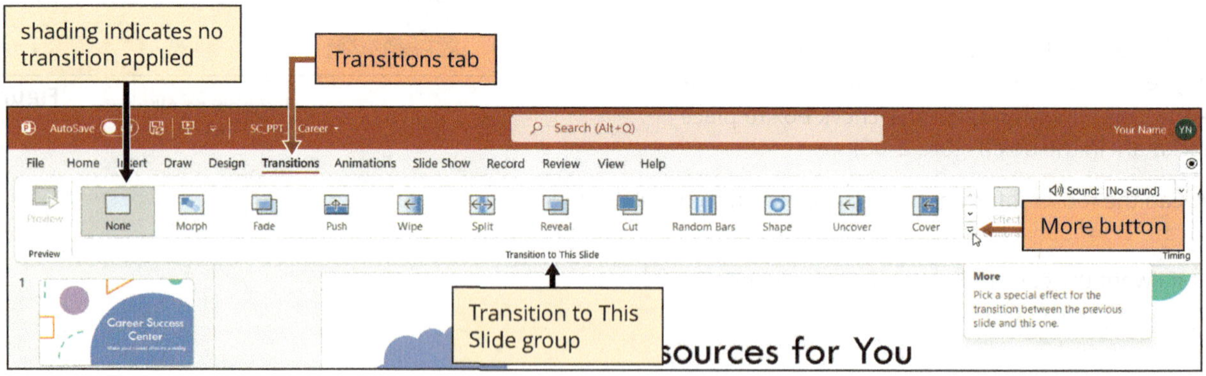

Figure 2–99

2

- Click the More button to expand the Transitions gallery.
- Point to the Pan transition in the Dynamic Content category in the Transitions gallery (Figure 2–100).

3

- Click Pan to view a preview of this transition and to apply this transition to the slide.

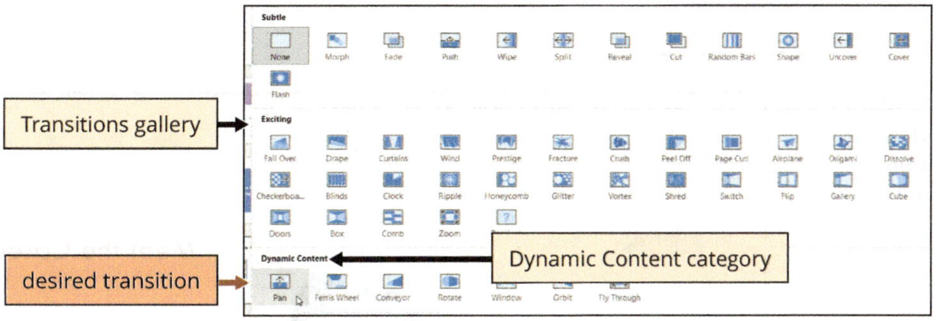

Figure 2–100

4

- Click the Effect Options button (Transitions tab | Transition to This Slide group) to display the Effect Options gallery (Figure 2–101).

Q&A Are the same four effects available for all transitions?
No. The transition effects vary depending upon the particular transition applied.

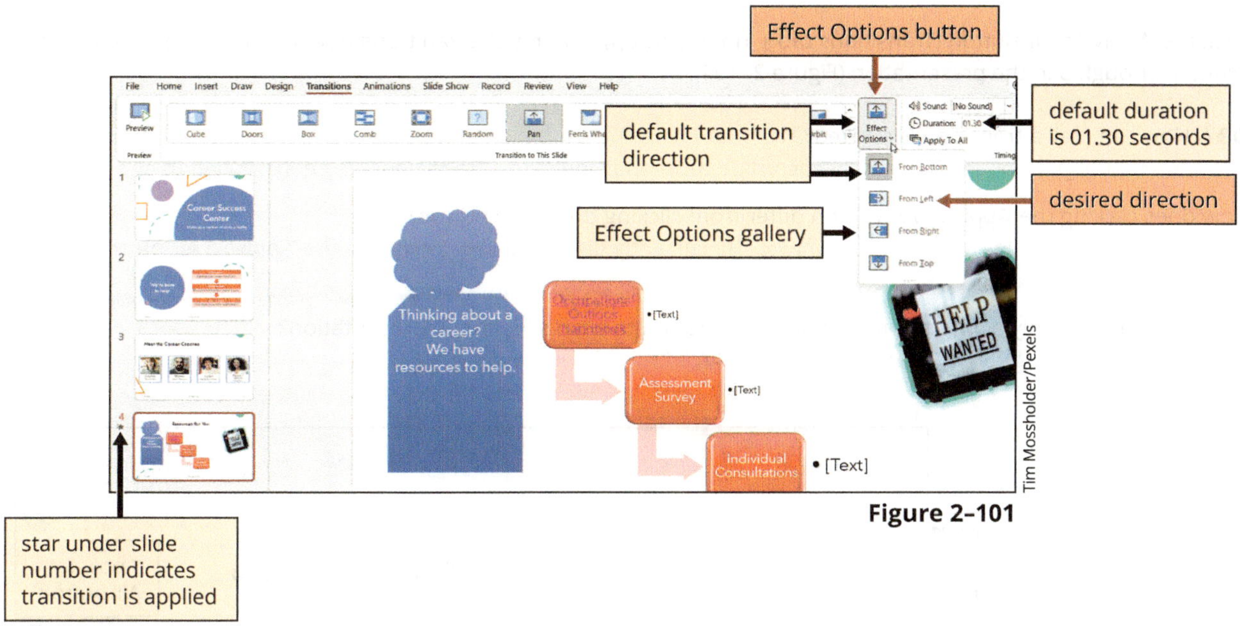

Figure 2–101

5

- Click the From Left effect to change the direction and preview the change.
- Click the Duration up arrow (Transitions tab | Timing group) several times to change the transition speed from 01.30 seconds to 03.00 seconds (Figure 2–102).

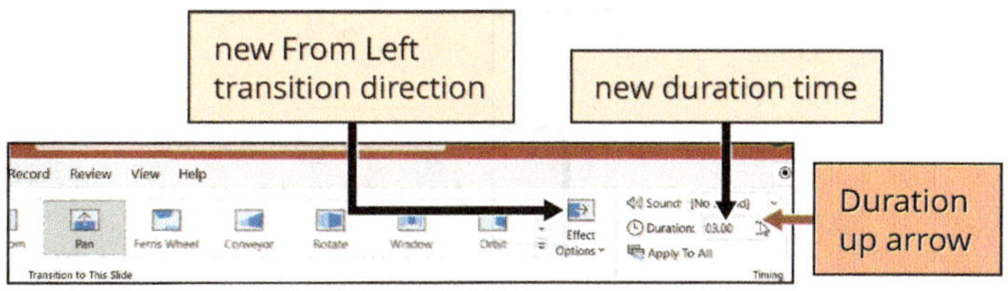

Figure 2–102

Q&A Does every transition have a default duration time of 01.00 seconds?
No. Each transition has its own default duration time.

6

- Click the Preview button (Transitions tab | Preview area) to view the transition and the new transition time (Figure 2–103).

Q&A Can I adjust the duration time I just set?
Yes. Click the Duration up or down arrows or type a speed in the Duration box and preview the transition until you find the time that best fits your presentation.

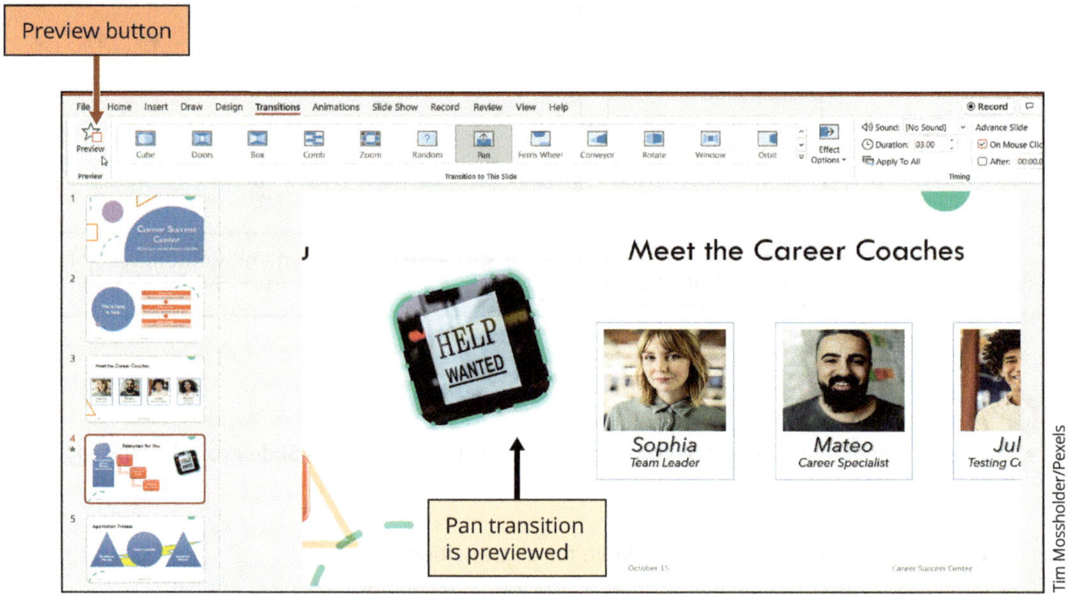

Figure 2–103

7

- Click the 'Apply To All' button (Transitions tab | Timing group) to apply the Pan transition and the increased transition time to Slides 1 through 5 in the presentation (Figure 2–104).

Q&A How can I tell a transition is applied?
The stars that appear on the left side of each slide thumbnail indicate a transition has been applied to all slides.

How does clicking the 'Apply to All' button differ from clicking the Apply button?
The Apply button applies the transition only to the currently displayed slide, whereas the 'Apply to All' button applies the transition to all slides.

What if I want to apply a different transition and duration to each slide in the presentation?
Repeat Steps 2 through 5 for each slide individually.

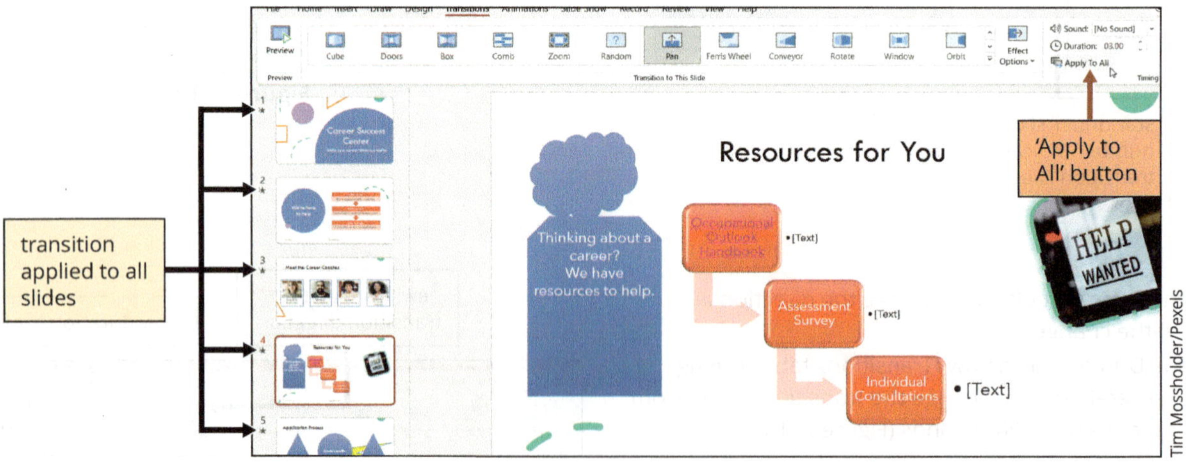

Figure 2–104

To Save and Print the Presentation

It is a good practice to save a presentation before printing it, in the event you experience difficulties printing. The following steps save and print the presentation.

1. Save the presentation again in the same storage location with the same file name.

2. Print the slides as a handout with two slides per page.

   Q&A Do I have to wait until my presentation is complete to print it?
   No, you can follow these steps to print a presentation at any time while you are creating it.

3. sam Because the project now is complete, you can close the presentation and exit PowerPoint.

BTW
Conserving Ink and Toner
If you want to conserve ink or toner, you can instruct PowerPoint to print draft quality documents by clicking File on the ribbon to open Backstage view, clicking Options in Backstage view to display the PowerPoint Options dialog box, clicking Advanced in the left pane (PowerPoint Options dialog box), scrolling to the Print area in the right pane, verifying there is no check mark in the High quality check box, and then clicking OK. Then, use Backstage view to print the document as usual.

BTW
Printing Document Properties
PowerPoint does not allow you to print document properties. This feature, however, is available in Word.

Summary

In this module, you learned how to use PowerPoint to enhance a presentation with SmartArt and formatted shapes. You searched for and downloaded an online theme; inserted a symbol and hyperlink; inserted, edited, and formatted SmartArt; resized and formatted shapes; moved objects using guides, gridlines, and the ruler; modified a footer; and added a transition.

Consider This: Plan Ahead

What decisions will you need to make when creating your next presentation?

Use these guidelines as you complete the assignments in this module and create your own slide show decks outside of this class.

1. Determine if an online theme can help you design and develop the presentation efficiently and effectively.
2. Identify symbols, shapes, and pictures that would create interest and promote the message being presented.
3. Develop SmartArt that emphasizes major presentation messages.
   a) Format text.
   b) Add styles.
   c) Add effects.
4. Locate shapes that supplement the verbal and written message.
   a) Size and position them aesthetically on slides.
   b) Add styles.
   c) Add and format outlines.
   d) Add a picture fill.
5. Use the guides, gridlines, and ruler to position slide elements.
6. Add a footer.
7. Add a transition.

Student Assignments

Apply Your Knowledge

Reinforce the skills and apply the concepts you learned in this module.

Adding Shapes and SmartArt

Note: To complete this assignment, you will be required to use the Data Files. Please contact your instructor for information about accessing the Data Files.

Instructions: Start PowerPoint. Open the presentation called SC_PPT_2-1.pptx, which is located in the Data Files. The presentation you open contains four unformatted slides. You work as a customer service representative at your local automotive repair facility, and many customers have been asking how they can improve their vehicles' fuel efficiency. You have decided to create a presentation with helpful answers to their questions and display it on monitors in the waiting area. You begin by modifying the unformatted slides by adding a theme, adding shapes and SmartArt, modifying a footer, and applying a transition so the slides look like Figure 2–105.

Perform the following tasks:

1. Add the Savon theme to the presentation. Apply the green color variant. If the Design Ideas pane opens, close it.
2. On the title slide, bold the subtitle text and then apply a text shadow.
3. With Slide 1 still displayed, insert the Rectangle: Top Corners Snipped shape located in the Rectangles area (fourth shape) and then resize it to a height of 2.2" and a width of 2". Insert the picture named Support_PPT_2_Fuel.png as a fill for this shape. Display the ruler, gridlines, and guides, and then align this shape so that the right edge is 1 inch right of the center and the top edge is at the top of the slide, as shown in Figure 2–105a.
4. On Slide 2 (Ways to Increase Gas Mileage), convert the numbered list into the Chevron List SmartArt graphic located in the Process category (first graphic in the sixth row). Change the SmartArt style to Metallic Scene (seventh style in the first 3-D row).
5. On Slide 2, insert a check mark symbol (symbol and character code 97) from the Webdings font before the words, Check, Reduce, and Avoid, in the first first-level paragraphs, as shown in Figure 2–105b.
6. Hide the ruler, gridlines, and guides.
7. On Slide 3 (Choose the Best Tire Type), change the fill color of the left circle (All Season) to Orange, the middle circle (All Terrain) to Dark Blue, and the right circle (Winter) to Light Blue. Resize each circle to a height of 3" and a width of 3" and then apply the 'Glow: 18 point; Green, Accent color 1' Glow Variation effect (first variation in last Glow Variations row) to the three shapes. Change the font of the text in these three circles to Rockwell and the font size to 40 point. Align these three circles to the slide and then distribute them horizontally.
8. Group the three circles.
9. With Slide 3 still displayed, insert the Arrow: Curved Right shape (first shape in the second Block Arrows row). Change the fill color to Dark Red and the outline weight to 3 point. Then add the 'Inside: Top Right' Shadow effect (last shadow in the first Inner row).
10. Resize the arrow shape to a height of 8" and a width of 3.3". Flip the shape vertical. Rotate this shape right 90 degrees. Use the smart guides to center the shape vertically at the top edge of the slide.
11. Send the arrow shape to the back (Figure 2–105c).
12. Delete Slide 4.
13. Add slide numbers and the fixed date of **October 21** to all slides except the title slide. Then use your name in place of Student Name as the footer text.

    If requested by your instructor, change your first name to your mother's first name in the footer text.

14. Apply the Peel Off transition in the Exciting category to all slides. Change the effect option to Right. Change the duration to 02.00 seconds.
15. Save the file with the file name, **SC_PPT_2_Fuel**, and submit the revised presentation in the format specified by your instructor. Slide Sorter view is shown in Figure 2–105d. Exit PowerPoint.
16. **Consider This:** In Steps 7 and 9 you applied many formatting styles to the circle and arrow shapes. How did these styles enhance the graphics?

Figure 2–105(a): Slide 1

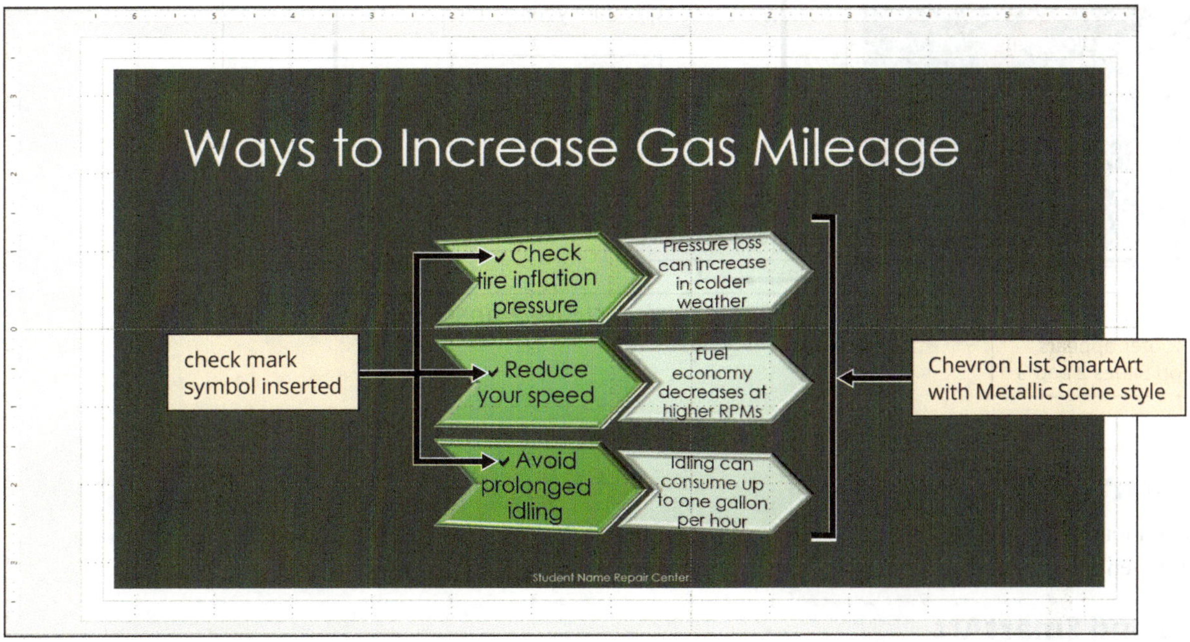

Figure 2–105(b): Slide 2

Continued on next page

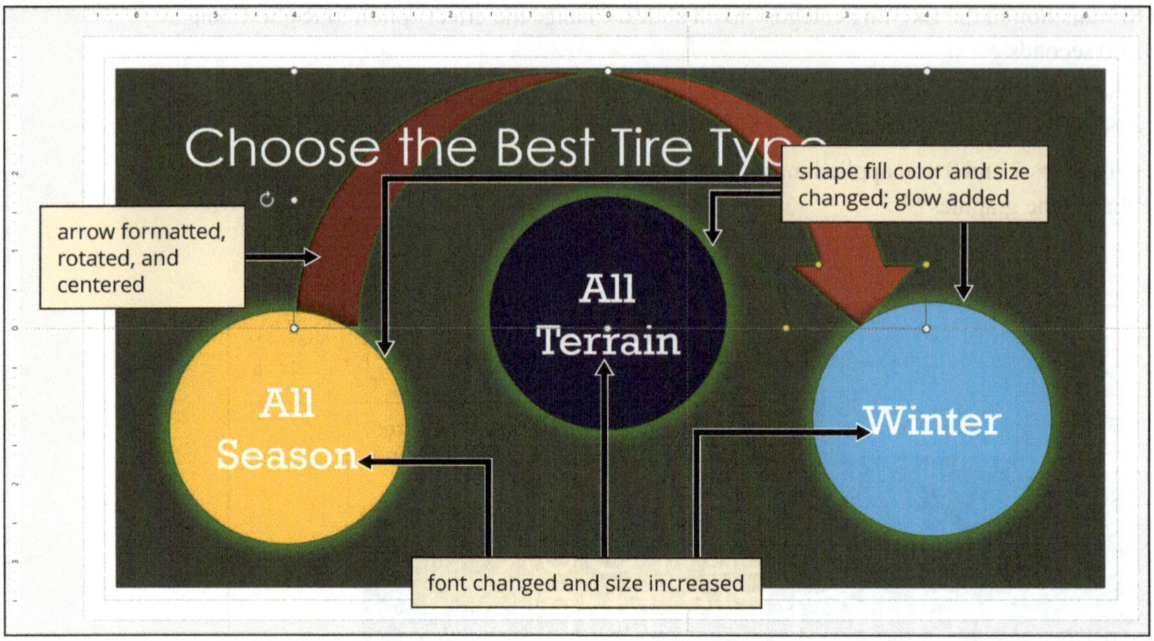

Figure 2–105(c): Slide 3

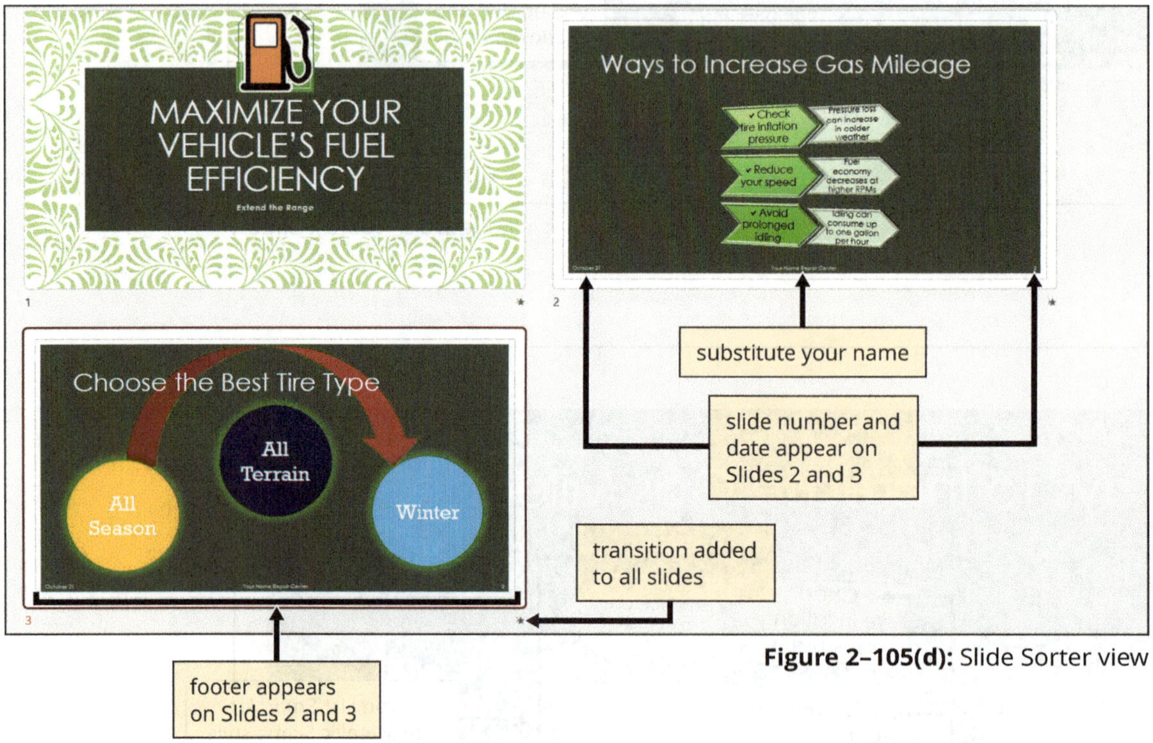

Figure 2–105(d): Slide Sorter view

OpenClipart-Vectors/Pixabay

Extend Your Knowledge

Extend the skills you learned in this module and experiment with new skills. You may need to use Help to complete the assignment.

Adding Icons and SmartArt

Note: To complete this assignment, you will be required to use the Data Files. Please contact your instructor for information about accessing the Data Files.

Instructions: Start PowerPoint. Open the presentation, SC_PPT_2-2.pptx, which is located in the Data Files. You will insert icons, apply a SmartArt Style and effect, and align the graphic to create the presentation.

Perform the following tasks:

1. On the title slide, insert the icon shown in Figure 2–106a in the hexagon shape. Inserting an icon is similar to inserting a picture from a file: you select the shape, click the Shape Fill button, and then click Picture in the Fill menu. When the Insert Pictures dialog box is displayed, click From Icons to display a dialog box with many categories of icons. Type **phone** in the search box to locate several icons with that description. Select the smartphone icon with a black border and then click Insert.
2. Center the title and subtitle paragraphs. Increase the subtitle paragraphs font size to 28 point.

   If requested by your instructor, add your current or previous pet's name in the Slide 1 subtitle text placeholder in place of Student Name.
3. On Slide 2, insert the Ascending Picture Accent Process SmartArt in the Picture category (second graphic in the sixth row). Type **Weather alerts** in the upper text placeholder and then type **Pedometer** in the lower text placeholder.
4. Add a third picture and caption by right-clicking the lower text placeholder, pointing to Add Shape in the shortcut menu, and then clicking 'Add Shape After'. Type **Document scanner** in the new text placeholder.
5. In the upper picture placeholder, insert a thunderstorm icon. In the middle picture placeholder, insert a scanner icon category. In the lower placeholder, insert a running icon, as shown in Figure 2–106b.
6. Change the SmartArt layout by clicking the More button in the Layouts group and then selecting 'Vertical Picture Accent List' in the Picture category (first graphic in the last row). Apply the Metallic Scene 3-D style.
7. Reverse each picture and text placeholder by clicking the 'Right to Left' button (SmartArt Design tab | Create Graphic category).
8. Align the SmartArt graphic in the middle of the slide.
9. On both slides, insert a footer with the text, **Available for iOS and Android** in the placeholder.
10. Apply an appropriate transition to all slides.
11. Save the presentation using the file name, **SC_PPT_2_Smartphone**, and submit the revised presentation in the format specified by your instructor.
12. **Consider This:** In this assignment, you used icons instead of shapes. How useful were these graphical elements in promoting the presentation's message? Did the new SmartArt layout and design in Step 6 enhance the presentation? Why or why not? Did reversing the picture and text placeholders in Step 7 add value to the design? Why or why not?

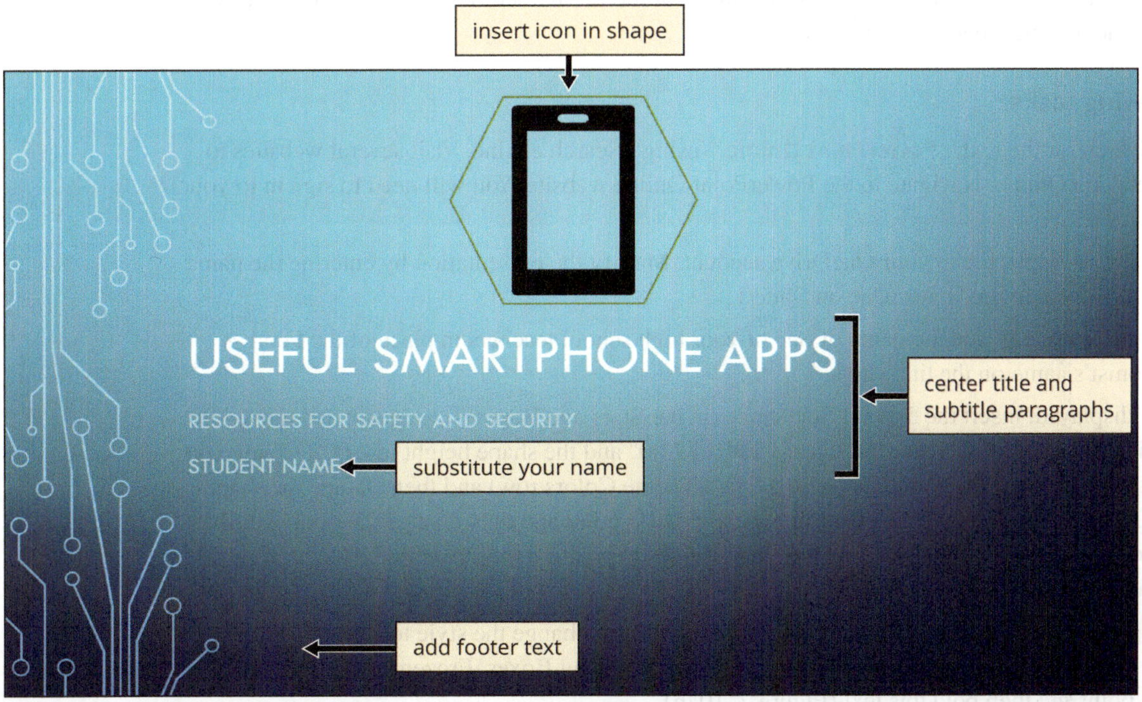

Figure 2–106(a): Slide 1

Continued on next page

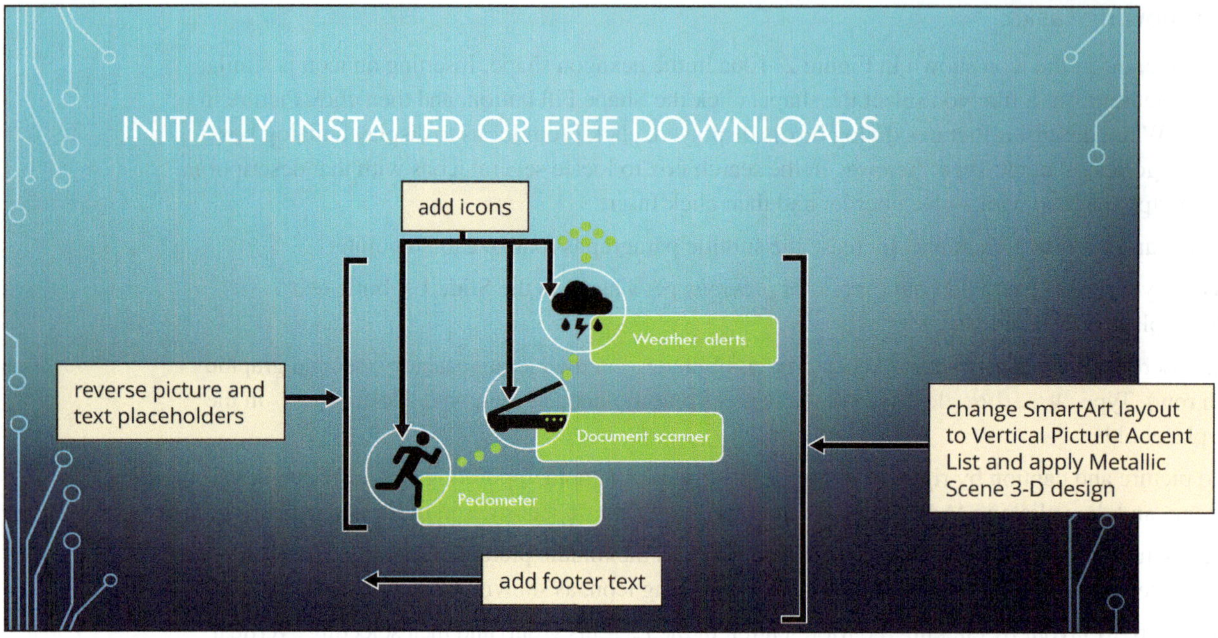

Figure 2–106(b): Slide 2

Expand Your World

Create a solution that uses cloud or web technologies by learning and investigating on your own from general guidance.

Modifying a Presentation Using PowerPoint Online

Note: To complete this assignment, you will be required to use the Data Files. Please contact your instructor for information about accessing the Data Files.

Instructions: As a receptionist in the food services department at your school, you are assisting the manager by developing slides for an upcoming presentation on recycling paper products. The presentation shows the paper products that can be recycled. You have created the slides in the file named SC_PPT_2-3.pptx, and you want to view and edit them using PowerPoint Online.

Perform the following tasks:

1. Run a browser. Search for the text, **PowerPoint Online**, using a search engine. Visit several websites to learn about PowerPoint Online. Navigate to the PowerPoint Online website. You will need to sign in to your OneDrive account.
2. Upload the SC_PPT_2-3.pptx file to your OneDrive account. Modify the presentation by entering the name and address of your school in the Notes pane on Slide 1.

   If requested by your instructor, add the name of one of your high school teachers in place of the Food Services Receptionist's name on the title slide.
3. With Slide 1 still displayed, insert the 5-Point Star shape (in the Stars and Banners category) and move it to the upper-right side of the slide. Increase the shape width to 2.00" and the shape height to 2.00". Change the shape fill color to Orange, Accent 5 (ninth color in the first Theme Colors row) and then change the shape outline color to Dark Red. Change the shape outline weight to 4½ point and then change the outline dashes to Round Dot. Rotate the shape 90° Right. Use the smart guides to position the shape in the location shown in Figure 2–107a.
4. On Slide 2, change the SmartArt layout to Vertical Box List and then change the style to Brick Scene. Increase the font size of the three paper products (Pizza boxes, Shipping Boxes, Frozen food and takeout containers) to 28 point and then bold this text (Figure 2–107b).

5. Add the Uncover transition and then change the effect option to From Top Right. Increase the duration to 2 seconds and then apply the transition to both slides.
6. Play the presentation from the beginning.
7. Rename the presentation using the file name, **SC_PPT_2_Paper**, and submit the presentation in the format requested by your instructor.
8. **Consider This:** How does modifying presentations using PowerPoint Online differ from modifying other presentations you have created in Module 2? Which tabs are not available when the simplified ribbon is used in PowerPoint Online? View the Home, Design, and Transitions tabs. Do you think the formatting functions, themes, and transitions are adequate to develop effective presentations? Why or why not?

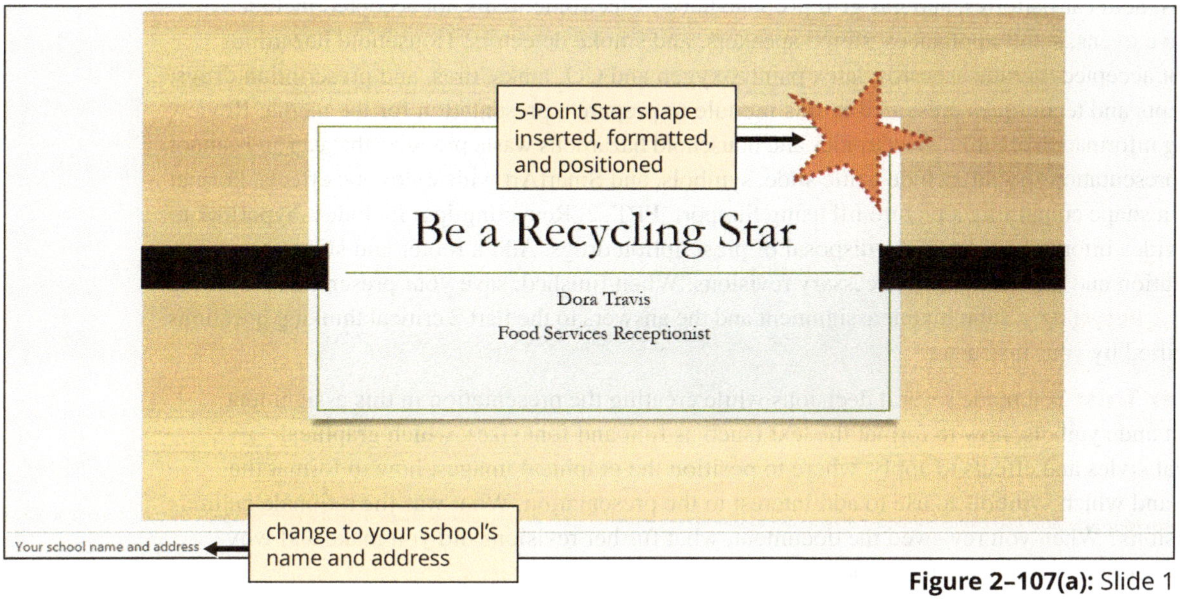

Figure 2–107(a): Slide 1

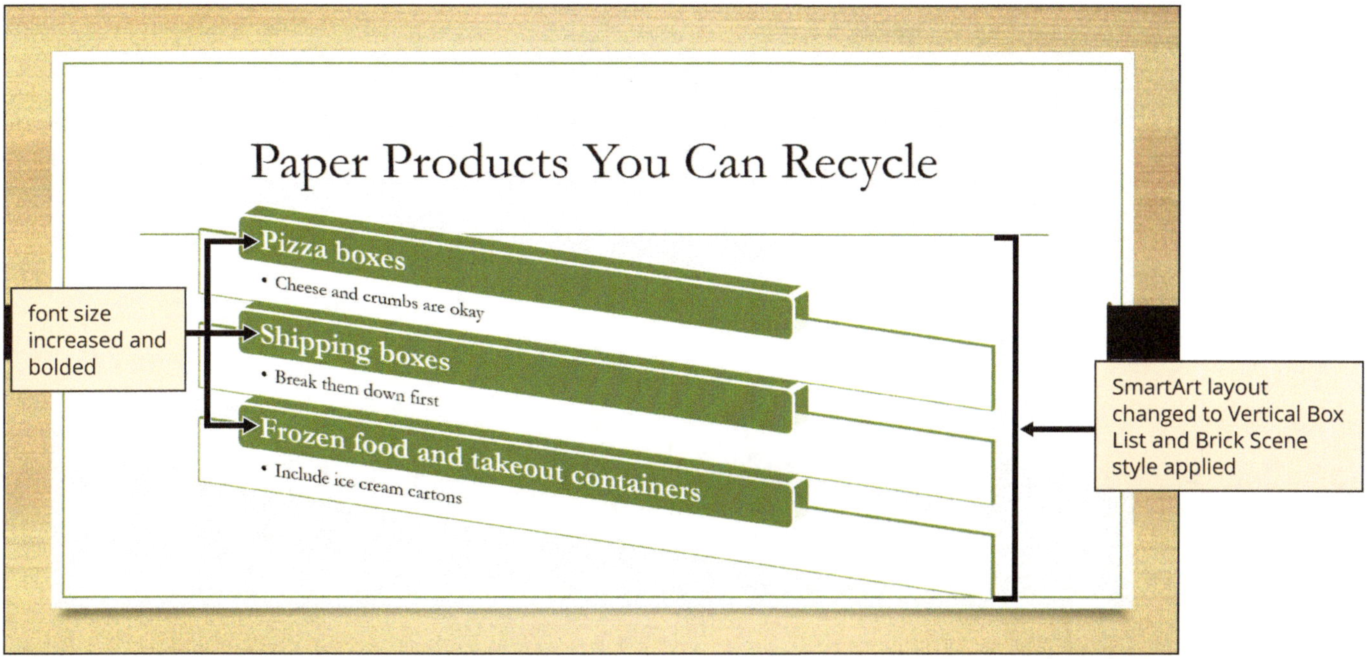

Figure 2–107(b): Slide 2

In the Lab

Apply your creative thinking and problem-solving skills to design and implement a solution.

Design and Create a Presentation about Your Town's Recycling Event

Part 1: Officials in the Public Works department in your town have scheduled a free electronics and household hazardous waste recycling event for the first Saturday of next month. They would like you to help prepare a presentation for the local media. Your town has been holding this event twice a year for the past five years and has collected thousands of pounds of waste. Residents who have participated in this program are helping to keep their neighborhood clean, which, in turn, helps improve the quality of life and protects the environment for future generations. Electronic items accepted include computers, monitors, printers, televisions, phones, and rechargeable batteries. Household hazardous waste materials include fire extinguishers, oil-based paints, household batteries, acid car batteries, and gas grill propane tanks. Electronic items not accepted include software, microwave ovens, small appliances, stereo speakers, and smoke detectors. Household hazardous waste materials not accepted include asbestos, latex paint, oxygen and CO_2 tanks, tires, and prescription drugs.

Use the concepts and techniques presented in this module to prepare a presentation for the media. Review websites containing information regarding electronics and household hazardous waste products that can and cannot be recycled. Your presentation should include a title slide, symbols, and SmartArt with styles and effects. Format the title slide with a shape containing a picture fill using Support_PPT_2_Recycling.jpg. Include a hyperlink to a website that provides information about the disposal of prescription drugs. Add a footer and slide transitions. View your presentation and then make any necessary revisions. When finished, save your presentation with the file name **SC_PPT_2_Recycling**. Submit your assignment and the answers to the Part 2 critical thinking questions in the format specified by your instructor.

Part 2: **Consider This:** You made several decisions while creating the presentation in this assignment: where to place text and symbols, how to format the text (such as font and font size), which graphical images to use, what styles and effects to apply, where to position the graphical images, how to format the graphical images, and which symbols to use to add interest to the presentation. What was the rationale behind each of these decisions? When you reviewed the document, what further revisions did you make and why? Where would you recommend showing this slide show?

Inserting WordArt, Charts, and Tables

Objectives

After completing this module, you will be able to:

- Insert a chart and enter data
- Change a chart style
- Insert a table and enter data
- Apply a table style
- Insert a text box
- Change text box defaults and apply preset effects
- Reuse slides from another presentation
- Insert a picture without using a content placeholder
- Crop a picture
- Change a picture color tone and softness
- Convert text to WordArt
- Change WordArt style, fill, and outline
- Animate text and change options
- Insert a video

Introduction

Audiences generally focus first on the visual elements displayed on a slide. Graphical elements increase **visual literacy**, which is the ability to examine and assess these images. Visual elements can be divided into two categories: images and information graphics. Images are the pictures you have used in Modules 1 and 2, and information graphics are tables, charts, graphs, and diagrams. Both sets of visuals help audience members interpret and retain material, so they should be designed and presented with care.

Project—Presentation with WordArt, a Chart, and a Table

In this module's project, you will follow proper design guidelines and learn to use PowerPoint to create the slides shown in Figures 3–1a through 3–1d. The objective is to produce a presentation for the Shelly Nature Center's annual tree sale. The Nature Center offers hundreds of carefully chosen resilient trees that are native to your area. These trees are resistant to disease and are customer favorites. Nature Center employees and volunteers will be present at the sale to help residents select the proper trees to enhance their landscapes and provide advice on tree growth rates and maximum heights. After community residents select their trees, they can enjoy the Nature Center's 1,500 acres of woodlands and hiking trails. The trees in this environment can boost mental and physical well-being and lift spirits with their beauty.

The PowerPoint presentation uses several visual elements to help audience members understand the benefits that trees provide and the species of trees that thrive in their climate. The title slide is enhanced with a WordArt graphic and formatted picture. The health and happiness benefits listed

BTW
Increasing Audience Retention
When audience members view graphics and listen to a speaker, they become engaged in the presentation. They tune out distractions and recall more material during a presentation when clear graphics, including WordArt, charts, and tables, are displayed visually and then explained verbally.

on Slide 2 are reinforced with a video clip. The three-dimensional pie chart on Slide 3 depicts the five popular trees in the region, and the three-column table on Slide 4 lists the tree names, their mature height, and the purchase price.

Figure 3–1(a): Slide 1 (Title Slide with WordArt and Enhanced Photo)

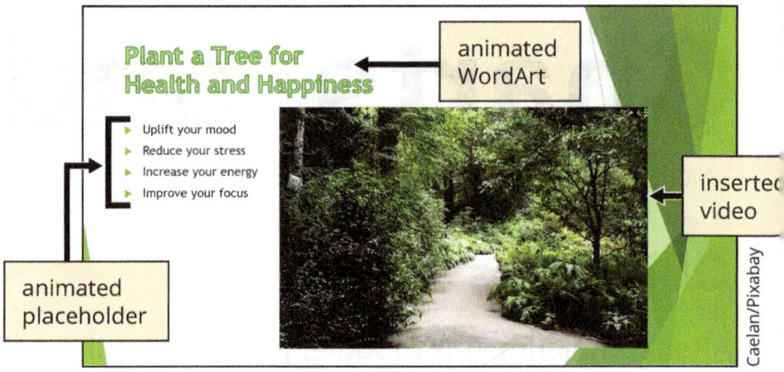

Figure 3–1(b): Slide 2 (WordArt and Video Clip)

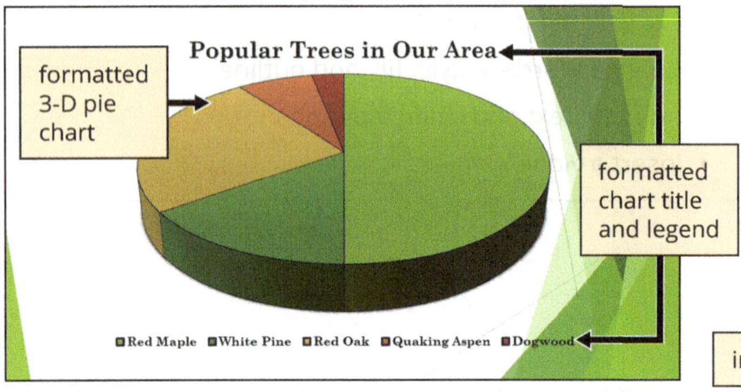

Figure 3–1(c): Slide 3 (3-D Chart)

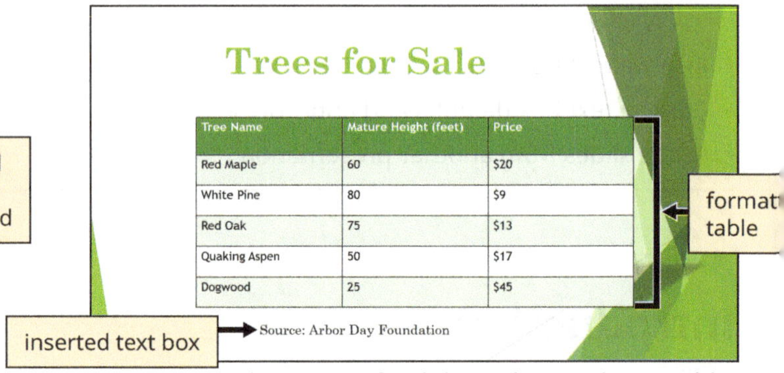

Figure 3–1(d): Slide 4 (Three-column Table)

BTW

Preparation Time

Be certain to begin developing a presentation well in advance of assignment deadlines when incorporating information graphics. Create a schedule so that you have adequate time to prepare clear visuals. Developing a presentation incorporating charts and tables generally requires extra preparation time because you need to gather data from reputable and current sources to incorporate into these visual elements.

In this module, you will learn how to create the slides shown in Figure 3–1. You will perform the following general tasks as you progress through this module:

1. Create a chart to show proportions.
2. Format a chart by changing the chart style.
3. Create a table to compare and contrast data.
4. Change table format and content style.
5. Insert a text box.
6. Insert slides from another presentation.
7. Crop a picture and apply picture effects.
8. Insert and modify WordArt.
9. Add WordArt styles and effects.
10. Animate text.
11. Insert a video.

Adding a Chart to a Slide and Formatting

Many of the outstanding trees in your town thrive because the soil conditions and climate are optimal for their growth and health. Shade trees, such as maples, oaks, and aspens help conserve energy by providing summer shade. Ornamental trees, including dogwoods, provide interest during the growing season. Attractive evergreens, such as the white pine, provide color throughout the year and are ideal for most landscapes. The chart on Slide 3, shown earlier in Figure 3–1c, shows the proportion of the popular trees in your area.

When a slide contains a content placeholder, you can click the placeholder's Insert Chart button to start creating a chart. Alternatively, you can click the Chart button (Insert tab | Illustrations group) to add a chart to any slide. A sample **Clustered Column chart** displays in the Insert Chart dialog box. This default chart type is appropriate when comparing two or more items in specified intervals, such as comparing how inflation has risen during the past 10 years. Other popular chart types are line, bar, and pie. You will use a pie chart in Slide 3.

When you select a chart type and then click OK, the sample chart is inserted in the current slide and an associated Excel **worksheet** with sample data is displayed in a separate window. You enter data for the chart in this worksheet, which is a rectangular grid containing vertical columns and horizontal rows. Column letters display above the grid to identify each vertical **column**, and row numbers display on the left side of the grid to identify each horizontal **row**. A **cell** is the intersection of a row and a column. For example, cell A1 is the intersection of column A and row 1. Cells are the locations for chart data and text labels. Numeric and text data are entered in the **active cell**, which is the currently selected cell surrounded by a heavy border. You will replace the sample data in the worksheet by typing entries in the cells, but you also can import data from a text file, import an Excel worksheet or chart, or paste data obtained from another program. Once you have entered the data, you can modify the appearance of the chart using menus and commands.

In the following pages, you will perform these tasks:

1. Insert a chart and then replace the sample data.
2. Change the line and shape outline weights.
3. Resize the chart and then change the title and legend font size.

BTW
PowerPoint Help
At any time while using PowerPoint, you can find answers to questions and display information about various topics through PowerPoint Help. Used properly, this form of assistance can increase your productivity and reduce your frustrations by minimizing the time you spend learning how to use PowerPoint.

BTW
Screen Resolution
If you are using a computer to step through the project in this module and you want your screens to match the figures in this book, you should change your screen's resolution to 1920 × 1080.

To Run PowerPoint, Apply a Theme, and Save the Presentation

You can keep track of the changes you make as you progress through this module. The following steps open PowerPoint, apply a theme and a slide layout, and save the file as a PowerPoint presentation.

1. sam ⬇ Run PowerPoint. Create a blank presentation. If necessary, maximize the PowerPoint window.
2. Apply the Facet theme.
3. Apply the Title and Content layout. Close the Design Ideas pane if it opens (Figure 3–2).
4. Save the presentation using **SC_PPT_3_Trees** as the file name.

BTW
Organizing Files and Folders
You should organize and store files in folders so that you easily can find the files later. For example, if you are taking an introductory technology class called CIS 101, a good practice would be to save all PowerPoint files in a PowerPoint folder in a CIS 101 folder.

BTW
Ribbon and Screen Resolution
PowerPoint may change how the groups and buttons within the groups appear on the ribbon, depending on the screen resolution of your computer. Thus, your ribbon may look different from the ones in this book if you are using a screen resolution other than 1920 × 1080.

Figure 3–2

To Delete a Placeholder

When you run a slide show, empty placeholders do not display. You may desire to delete unused placeholders from a slide. **Why?** Empty placeholders can be a distraction when you are designing slide content because they cover an area of the slide that can display other slide content. The title text placeholder on Slide 1 is not required for this presentation, so you can remove it. The following steps remove the Slide 1 title text placeholder.

1

- Click a border of the title text placeholder so that it appears as a solid or finely dotted line (Figure 3–3). The words, Click to add title, still will be displayed.

2

- Press DELETE to remove the title text placeholder.

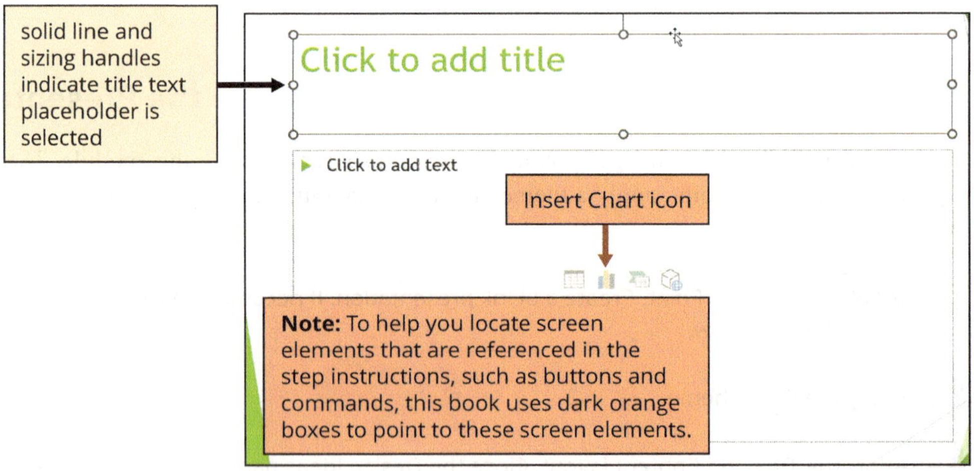

Figure 3–3

Q&A Can I also click the Cut button (Home tab | Clipboard group) to delete the placeholder?
Yes. Generally, however, Cut is used when you desire to remove a selected slide element, place it on the Clipboard, and then paste it in another area. DELETE is used when you do not want to reuse that particular slide element.

If I am using a touch screen, how do I delete the placeholder?
Press and hold on a border of the title text placeholder and then tap DELETE on the shortcut menu to remove the placeholder.

Other Ways

1. Select placeholder, press BACKSPACE

Consider This

How can I choose an appropriate chart type?

General adult audiences are familiar with bar and pie charts, so those chart types are good choices. Specialized audiences, such as engineers and architects, are comfortable reading scatter and bubble charts. Common chart types and their purposes are as follows:

- Column—Vertical bars compare values over a period of time.
- Bar—Horizontal bars compare two or more values to show how the proportions relate to each other.
- Line—A line or lines show trends, increases and decreases, levels, and costs during a continuous period of time.
- Pie—A pie chart divides a single total into parts to illustrate how the segments differ from each other and the whole.
- Scatter—A scatterplot displays the effect on one variable when another variable changes.

In general, three-dimensional charts are more difficult to comprehend than two-dimensional charts. The added design elements in a three-dimensional chart add clutter and take up space. A chart may include a **legend**, which is information that identifies parts of the chart and coordinates with the colors assigned to the chart categories. A legend may help to unclutter the chart, so consider using one prominently on the slide.

To Insert a Chart

The first step in developing slide content for this presentation is to insert a pie chart. **Why?** The pie chart is a useful tool to show proportional amounts. In this presentation, you want to show the proportion of popular trees in your region. The following steps insert a chart with sample data into a content placeholder on Slide 1.

1

- Click the Insert Chart icon in the content placeholder to display the Insert Chart dialog box.
- Click Pie in the left pane to display the Pie gallery and then click the 3-D Pie button (second chart) to select that chart type (Figure 3–4).
- **Experiment:** Point to the 3-D Pie chart to see a large preview of this type.

Q&A Can I change the chart type after I have inserted a chart?
Yes. Click the 'Change Chart Type' button in the Type group on the Chart Design tab to display the Change Chart Type dialog box and then make another selection.

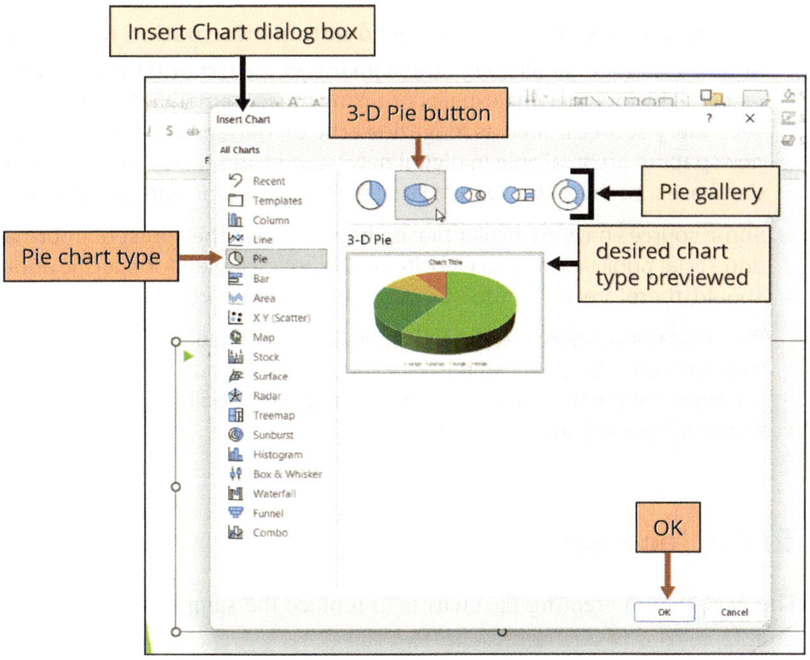

Figure 3–4

2

- Click OK (Insert Chart dialog box) to start the Excel program and open a worksheet on the top of the Trees presentation (Figure 3–5).

Q&A What do the numbers in the worksheet and the chart represent?
Excel places sample data in the worksheet and charts the sample data in the default chart type.

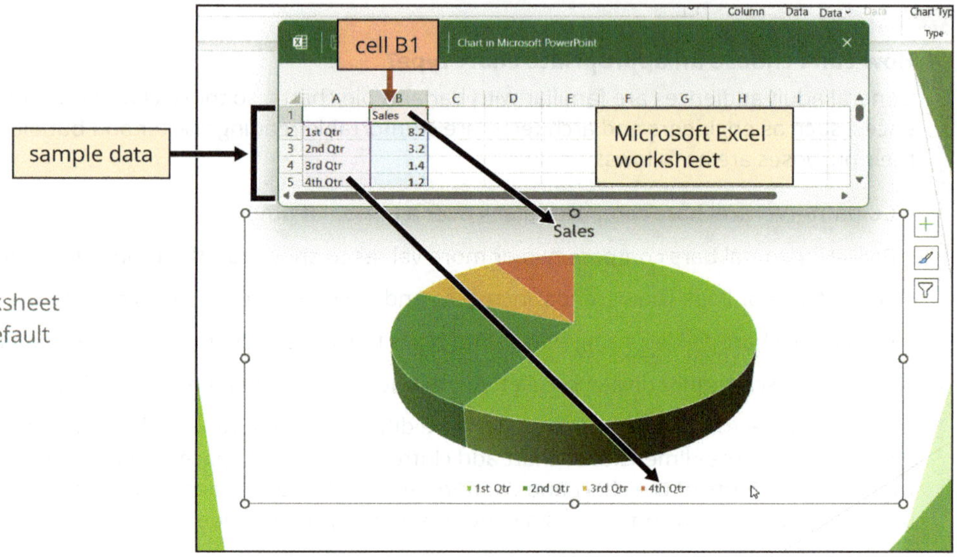

Figure 3–5

Other Ways

1. Click Chart (Insert tab | Illustrations group)

Consider This

How do I locate credible sources to obtain information for the graphic?

At times, you are familiar with the data for your chart or table because you have conducted in-the-field, or primary, research by interviewing experts or taking measurements. Other times, however, you must gather the data from secondary sources, such as magazine articles, newspaper articles, or websites. Digital and print magazines and newspapers are available in digital newsstands and have features that provide in-depth information. Also, online databases, such as EBSCOhost, FirstSearch, Nexis Uni, and NewsBank contain articles from credible sources.

Some sources have particular biases, however, and they present information that supports their causes. Political, religious, and social publications and websites often are designed for specific audiences who share a common point of view. You should, therefore, recognize that data from these sources can be skewed.

If you did not conduct the research yourself, you should give credit to the source of your information. You are acknowledging that someone else provided the data and giving your audience the opportunity to obtain the same materials you used. Type the source at the bottom of your chart or table, especially if you are distributing handouts of your slides. At the very least, state the source during the body of your speech.

To Replace Sample Data

The next step in creating the chart is to replace the sample data, which will redraw the chart. **Why?** The worksheet displays sample data in two columns and five rows, but you want to change this data to show the specific trees and the numbers of each tree in your area. The first row and left column contain text labels and will be used to create the chart title and legend. The other cells contain numbers that are used to determine the size of the pie slices. The following steps replace the sample data in the worksheet.

1

- If necessary, click cell B1, which is the intersection of column B and row 1, to select it.
- Type **Popular Trees in Our Area** in cell B1 (Figure 3–6).

Q&A Why did my pointer change shape?
The pointer changes to a block plus sign to indicate a cell is selected.

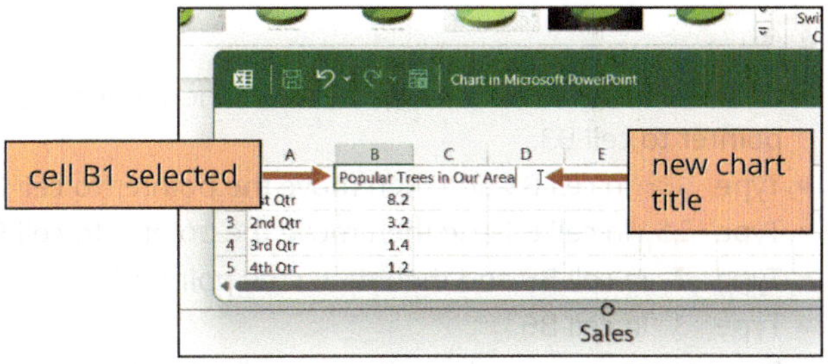

Figure 3–6

2

- Click cell A2 to select that cell and to replace the sample chart title.
- Type **Red Maple** in cell A2 (Figure 3–7).

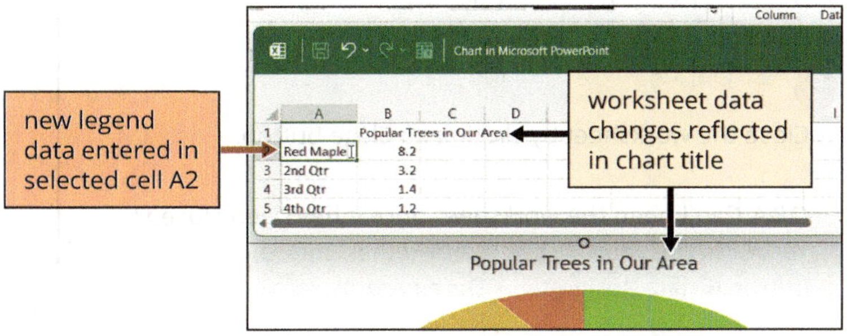

Figure 3–7

3

- Move the pointer to cell A3.
- Type **White Pine** in cell A3 and then move the pointer to cell A4.
- Type **Red Oak** in cell A4 and then move the pointer to cell A5.
- Type **Quaking Aspen** in cell A5 and then press ENTER to move the pointer to cell A6.
- Type **Dogwood** in cell A6 (Figure 3–8).

Q&A Dogwood is displayed in cell A6 but not in the chart legend. Why?
Dogwood will appear in the chart legend once the cell pointer moves away from cell A6.

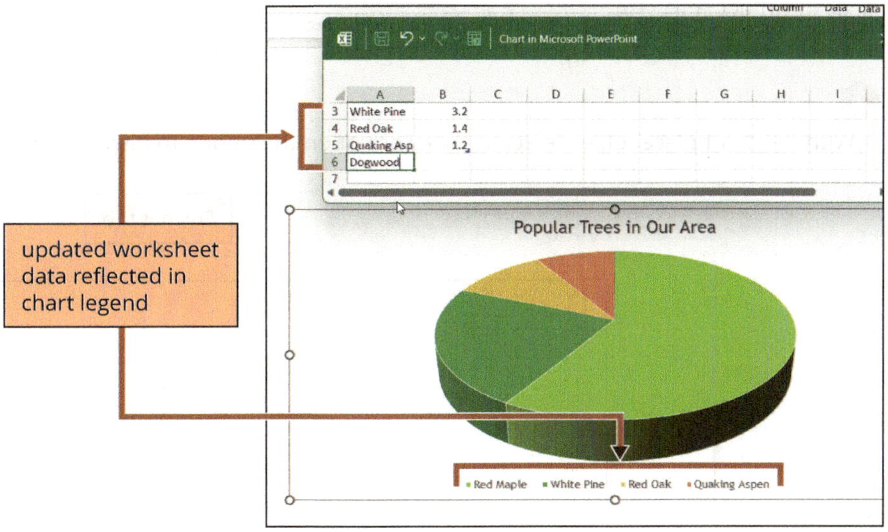

Figure 3–8

4

- Click cell B2, type **50** in that cell, and then move the pointer to cell B3.
- Type **15** in cell B3 and then move the pointer to cell B4.
- Type **25** in cell B4 and then move the pointer to cell B5.
- Type **7** in cell B5 and then move the pointer to cell B6.
- Type **3** in cell B6.
- Press ENTER to move the pointer to cell B7 (Figure 3–9).

Q&A Why do the slices in the PowerPoint pie chart change locations?
As you enter data in the worksheet, the chart slices rotate to reflect these new figures.

5

- Close the worksheet by clicking its Close button.

Q&A Can I open the worksheet once it has been closed?
Yes. Click the chart to select it and then click the Edit Data button (Chart Design tab | Data group).

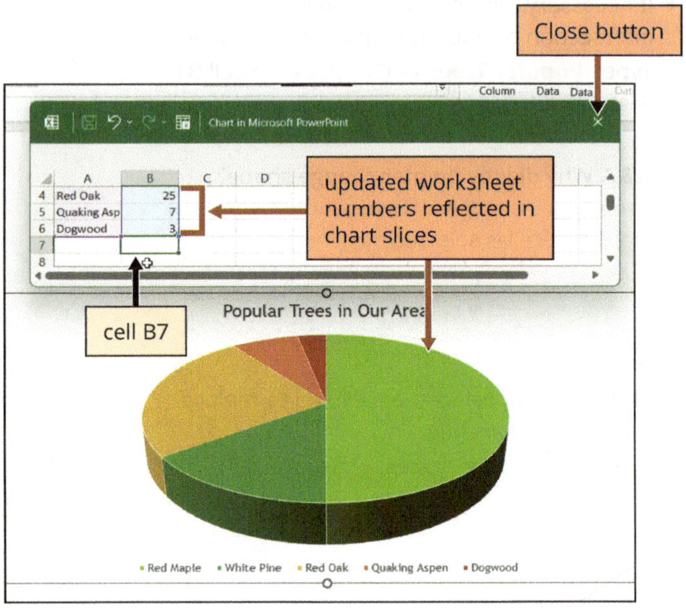

Figure 3–9

To Resize a Chart

You resize a chart the same way you resize a SmartArt graphic or any other graphical object. The following steps resize the chart to fill the slide. **Why?** The slide has a large area of white space, so you are able to enlarge the chart to aid readability. In addition, the chart layout displays a title that provides sufficient information to describe the chart's purpose.

1

- With the chart placeholder selected, click Format on the ribbon to display the Format tab (Figure 3–10).

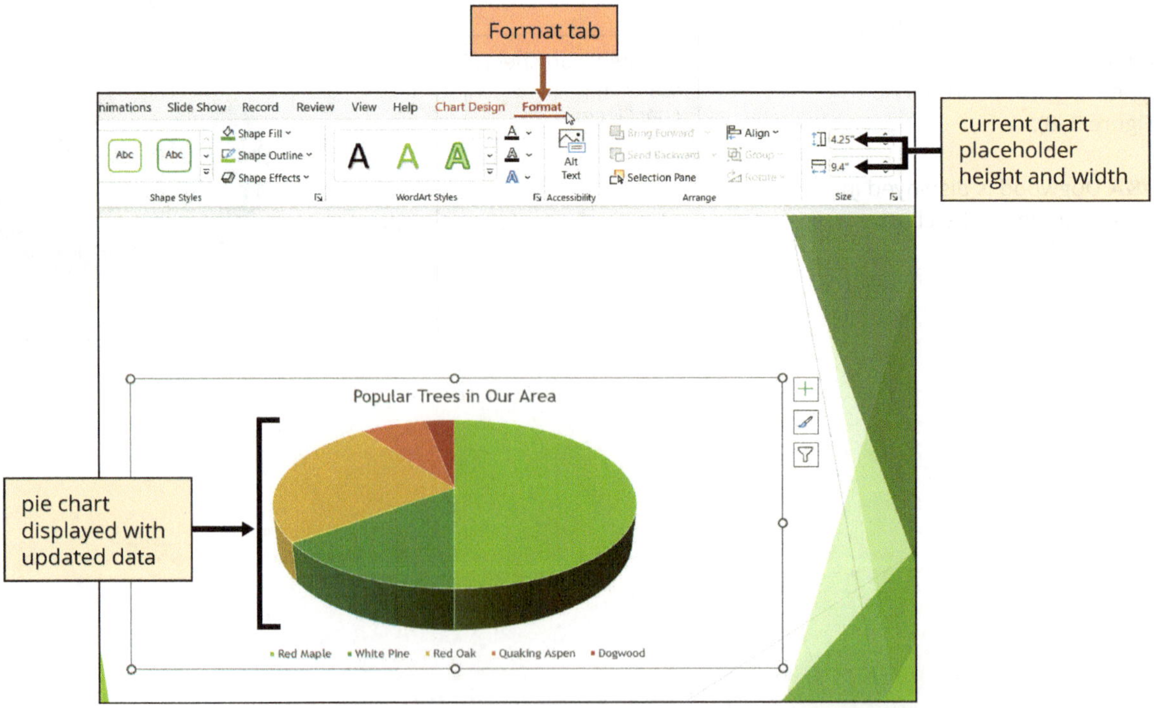

Figure 3–10

2

- Click the Shape Height up arrow repeatedly until 6.5" is displayed in the box.
- Click the Shape Width up arrow repeatedly until 10.5" is displayed in the box (Figure 3–11).

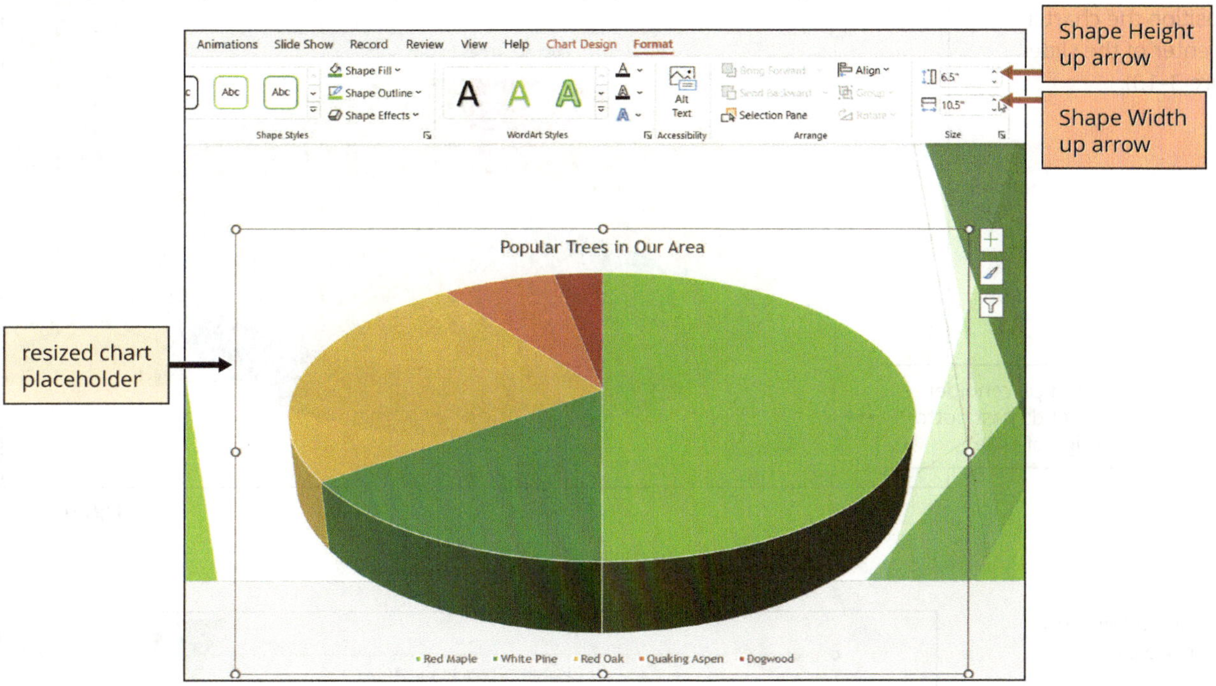

Figure 3–11

To Align a Chart

Part of the resized chart placeholder is located below the slide, so you need to reposition it. **Why?** You can move the placeholder to the center and middle of the slide so that the entire chart and legend can be seen. The following steps align the chart.

1

- With the chart selected and the Format tab displayed, click the Align button (Format tab | Arrange group) to display the Align Objects menu (Figure 3–12).

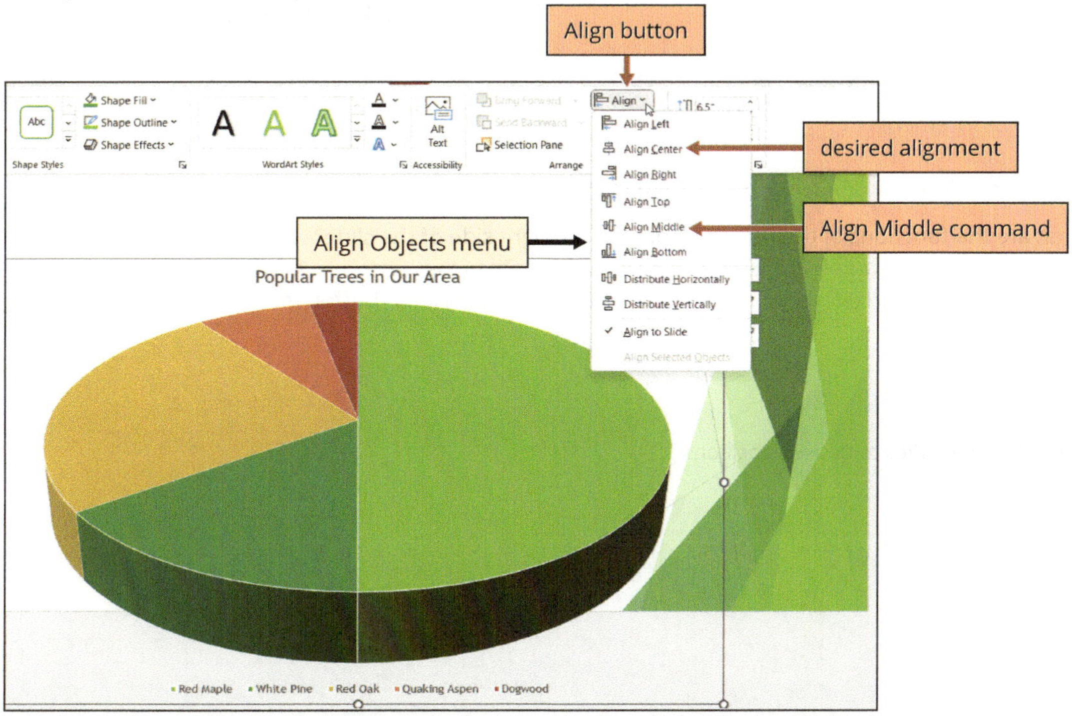

Figure 3–12

2

- Click Align Center on the Align Objects menu to position the chart in the center of the slide (Figure 3–13).

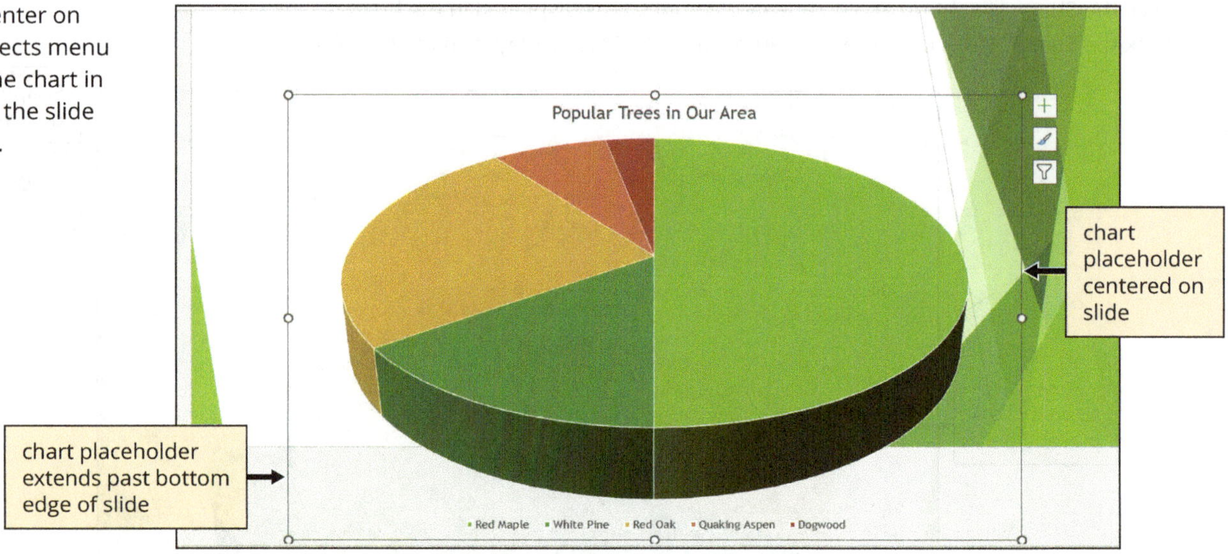

Figure 3–13

3

- Click Align again and then click Align Middle (shown in Figure 3–12) to position the chart in the middle of the slide (Figure 3–14).

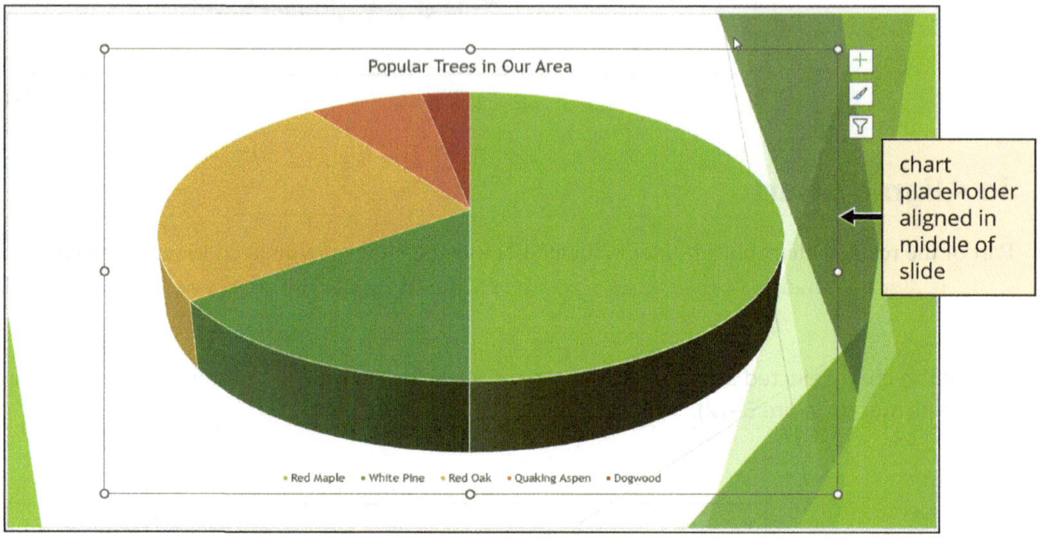

Figure 3–14

Q&A Can I specify a precise position where the chart will display on the slide?

Yes. Right-click the edge of the chart, click 'Format Chart Area' on the shortcut menu, click 'Size & Properties' in the Format Chart Area pane, enter measurements in the Position section, and then specify from the Top Left Corner or the Center of the slide.

What are the functions of the three buttons on the right side of the slide?

The Chart Elements button (plus sign) allows you to display the chart title, data labels, and legends; the Chart Styles button (paintbrush) shows chart styles and color options; the Chart Filters button (funnel) allows you to show, hide, edit, or rearrange data.

Other Ways

1. Drag sizing handles to desired positions

To Change a Chart Style

Once you have selected a chart type, you can modify the look of the chart elements by changing its style. The various layouts move the legend above or below the chart, or they move some or all of the legend data directly onto the individual chart pieces. For example, in the pie chart type, seven different layouts display various combinations of percentages and identifying information on the chart, and they show or do not show the chart title. The following steps apply a chart style with a title and legend that displays below the pie slices. **Why?** Your data consists of tree names and percentages, so you need a layout that shows the proportion of each category along with a corresponding legend.

1

- With the chart still selected, click the Chart Styles button (paintbrush icon) on the right side of the chart area to display the Chart Styles gallery with the Style tab displayed.
- Scroll down until the fifth style (Style 5) in the Chart Styles gallery is displayed and then point to this style to see a live preview on the slide (Figure 3–15).
- **Experiment:** Point to various chart styles and watch the layouts on the chart change.

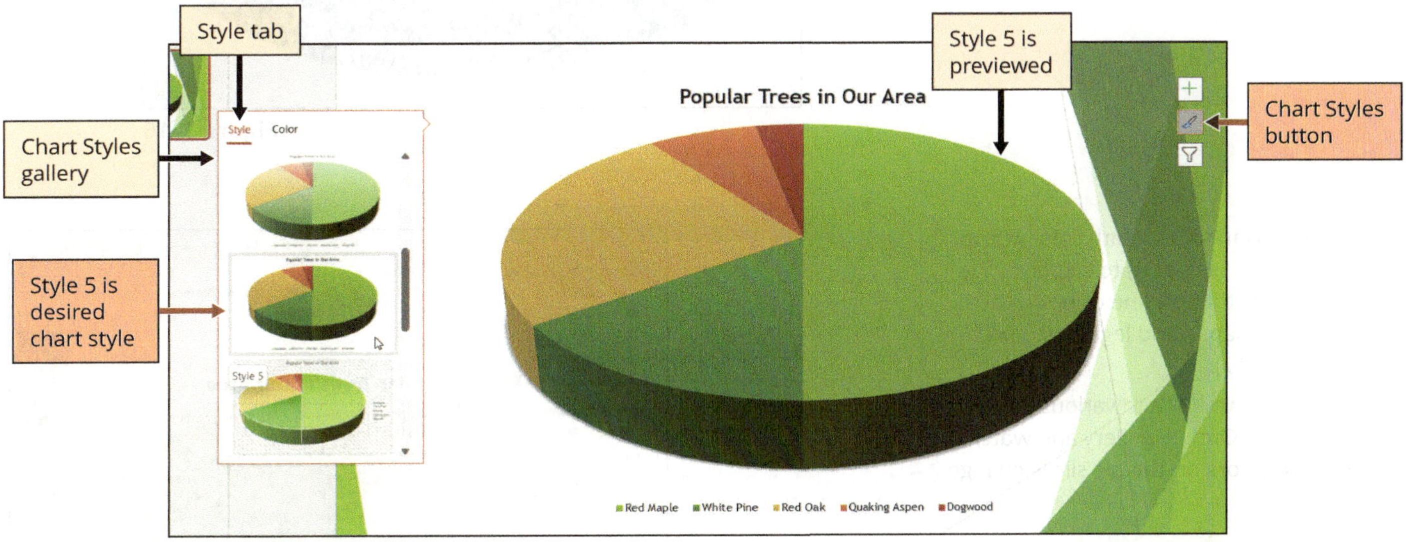

Figure 3–15

2

- Click Style 5 in the Chart Styles gallery to apply the selected chart style to the chart.

3

- Click the Chart Styles button to hide the Chart Styles gallery.

To Change the Shape Outline Color

You can change the outline color to add contrast to each slice and legend color square. The following steps change the shape outline color to Dark Blue. **Why?** At this point, it is difficult to see the borders around the legend squares and around each pie slice. The chart colors resemble colors found in nature, and the color blue also is seen in natural settings such as in the sky or lakes.

1

- Click the center of the pie chart to select it and to display the sizing handles around each slice.

2

- Click the Shape Outline arrow (Format tab | Shape Styles group) to display the Shape Outline gallery (Figure 3–16).

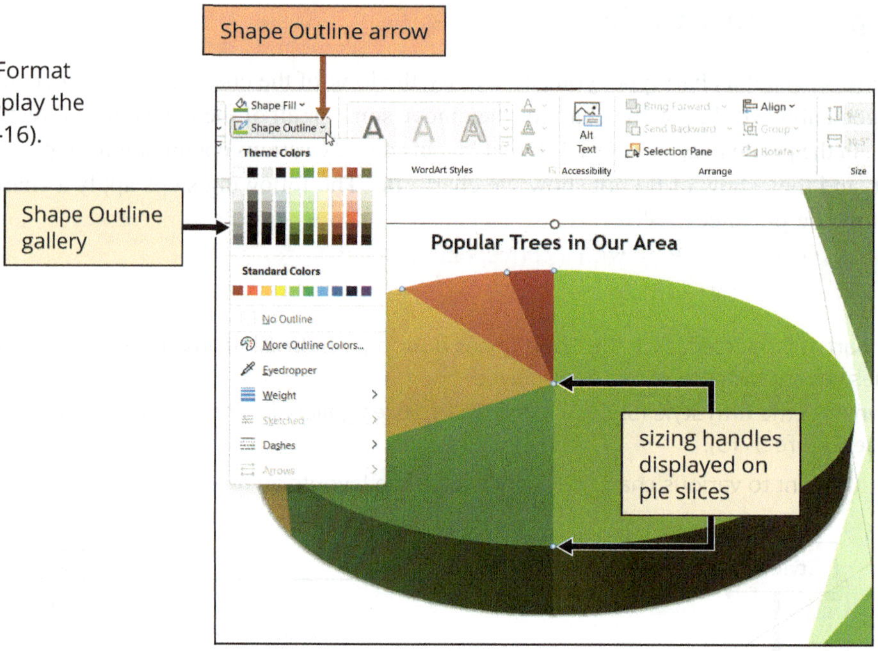

Figure 3–16

3

- Point to Dark Blue (ninth color in the Standard Colors row) to display a live preview of that outline color on the pie slice shapes and legend squares (Figure 3–17).
- **Experiment:** Point to various colors in the Shape Outline gallery and watch the outline colors on the pie slices change.

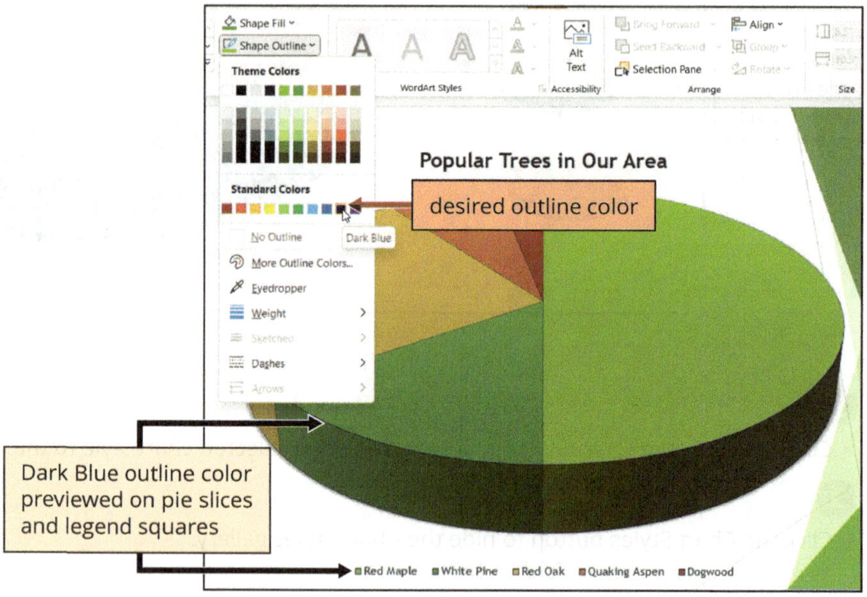

Figure 3–17

4

- Click Dark Blue to add dark blue outlines around each slice and also around the color squares in the legend.

Other Ways

1. Right-click chart, Outline, click desired color

To Change the Shape Outline Weight

The chart has a thin outline around each pie slice and around each color square in the legend. You can change the weight of these lines. **Why?** A thicker line can accentuate each slice and add another strong visual element to the slide. The following steps change the outline weight.

1

- If necessary, click the center of the pie chart to select it and to display the sizing handles around each slice.
- Click the Shape Outline arrow (Format tab | Shape Styles group) again to display the Shape Outline gallery.
- Point to Weight in the Shape Outline gallery to display the Weight gallery.
- Point to 3 pt to display a live preview of this outline line weight (Figure 3–18).

- **Experiment:** Point to various weights on the submenu and watch the border weights on the pie slices change.

2

- Click 3 pt to increase the border around each slice to that width.

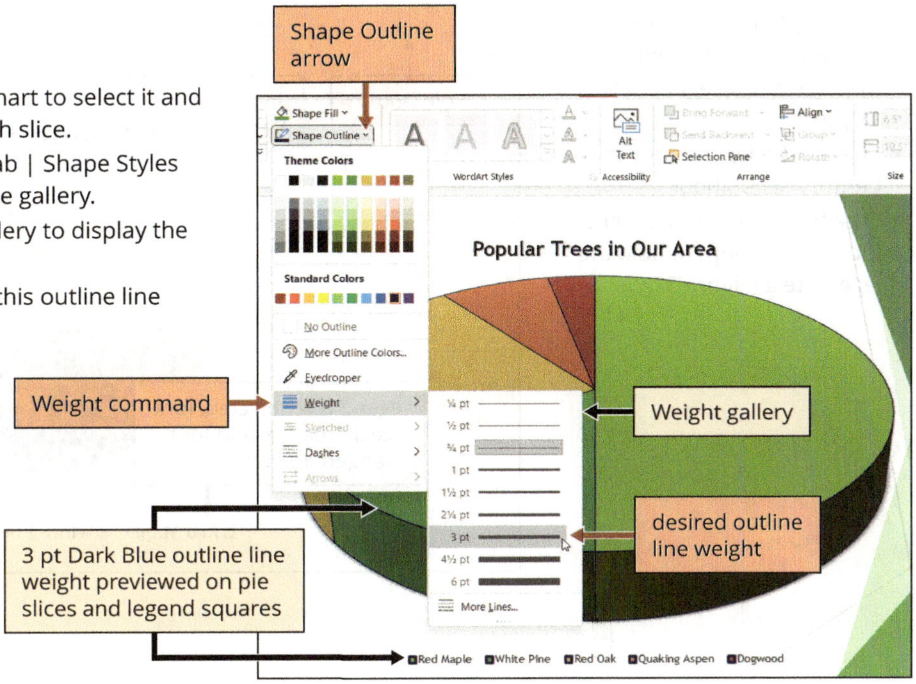

Figure 3–18

Other Ways

1. Right-click chart, click Outline button, click Weight

To Change the Title and Legend Font and Font Size

Depending upon the complexity of the chart and the overall slide, you may want to increase the font size of the chart title and legend. **Why?** The larger font size increases readability. The following steps change the font size of both of these chart elements.

1

- Click the chart title, Popular Trees in Our Area, to select the text box.
- Display the Home tab and then click the 'Increase Font Size' button (Home tab | Font group) repeatedly until the font size is 32 point.
- Change the font of the chart title to Century Schoolbook (Figure 3–19).

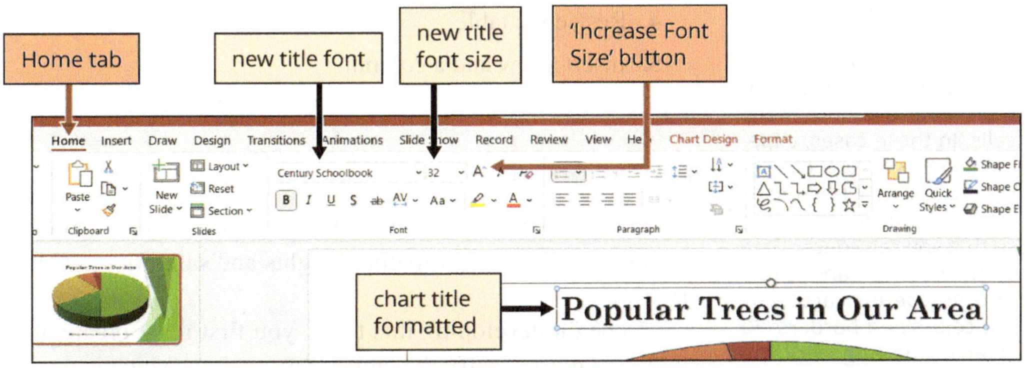

Figure 3–19

2

- Click one of the legends to select the legends text box.
- Click the 'Increase Font Size' button (Home tab | Font group) repeatedly until the font size of the legend text is 18 point.
- Change the legend font to Century Schoolbook.
- Click the Bold button (Home tab | Font group) to bold the legend text (Figure 3–20).

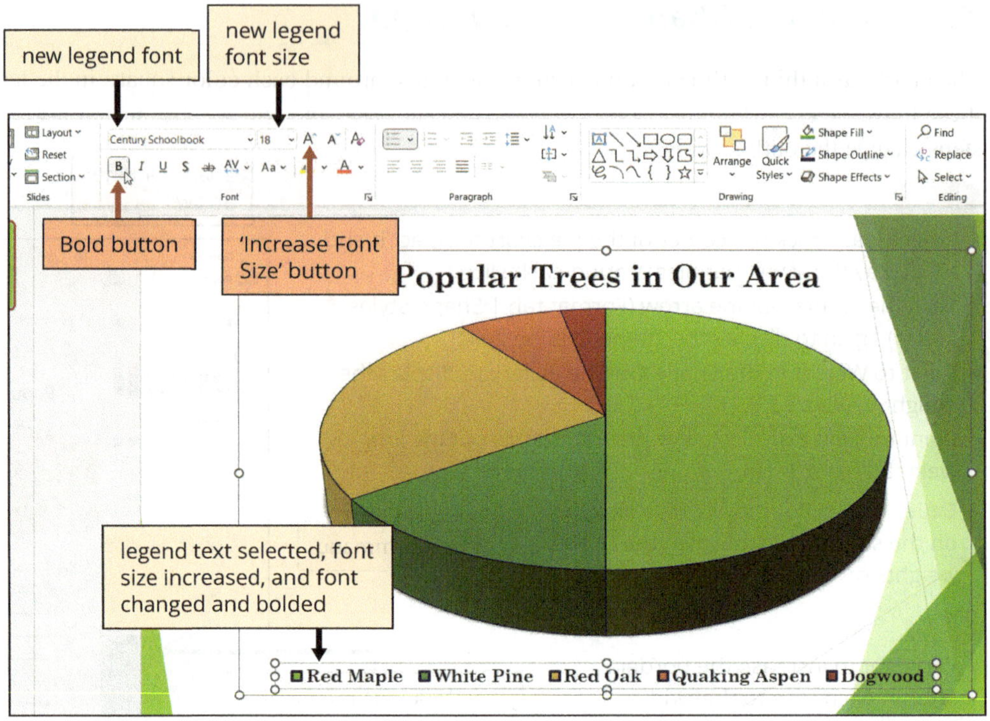

Figure 3–20

Adding a Table to a Slide and Formatting

One effective method of organizing information on a slide is to use a **table**, which is a grid consisting of rows and columns that can contain text and graphics. You can enhance a table with formatting, including adding colors, lines, and backgrounds, and changing fonts.

In the following pages, you will perform these tasks:

1. Insert a table and then enter data.
2. Apply a table style.
3. Add table borders and an effect.
4. Resize the table.
5. Insert a row and a column.

BTW
Clearing Table Formatting
Many times you may need to create large tables and then enter data into many cells. In these cases, experienced PowerPoint designers recommend clearing all formatting from the table so that you can concentrate on the numbers and letters and not be distracted by the colors and borders. To clear formatting, click the Clear Table command at the bottom of the Table Styles gallery (Table Design tab | Table Styles group). Then, add a table style once you have verified that all table data is correct.

Tables

The table on Slide 2 (shown earlier in Figure 3–1d) contains information about specific trees for sale, including their mature heights and sale prices. This data is listed in two columns and six rows.

To begin developing this table, you first must create an empty table and insert it into the slide. You must specify the table's **dimension**, which is the total number of rows and columns. This table will have a 2 × 5 dimension: the first number indicates the number of columns and the second specifies the number of rows. You will fill the cells with data pertaining to each tree and its maximum height. Later in this module you will add a column to show the sale price for each tree. Then you will format the table using a table style. You will also add a table row to display information about dogwood trees.

To Insert an Empty Table

The following steps create a new slide and insert an empty table with two columns and five rows into a content placeholder on the slide. **Why?** The first row will contain the column headings, and the additional rows will have information about four trees. The two columns will contain tree names and the mature heights.

1

- Click the New Slide button to add a new slide to the presentation with the Title and Content layout (Figure 3–21).

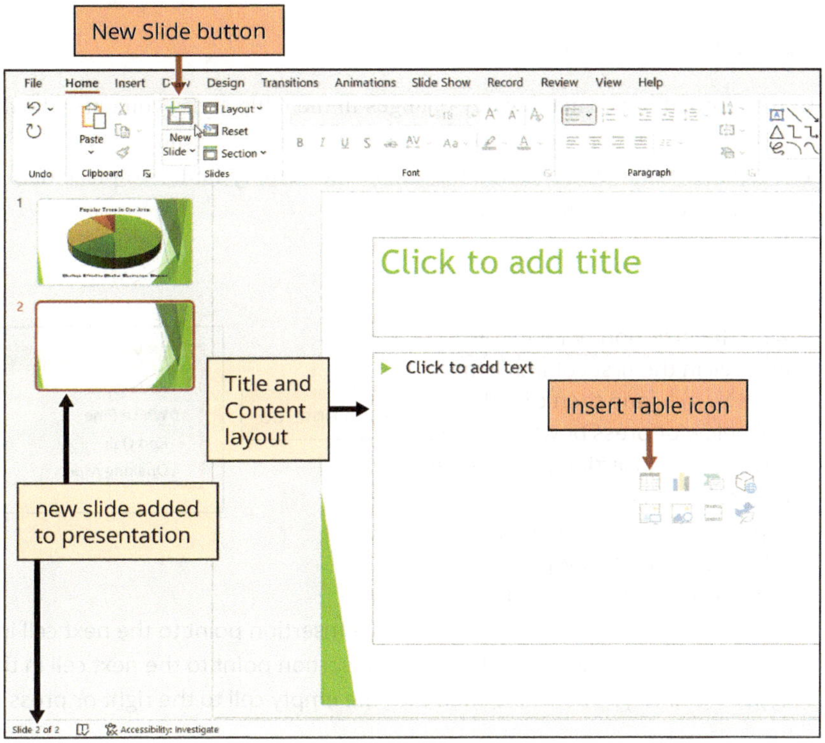

Figure 3–21

2

- Click the Insert Table icon in the content placeholder to display the Insert Table dialog box.
- Click the down arrow to the right of the 'Number of columns' box three times so that the number 2 appears in the box.
- Click the up arrow to the right of the 'Number of rows' box three times so that the number 5 appears in the box (Figure 3–22).

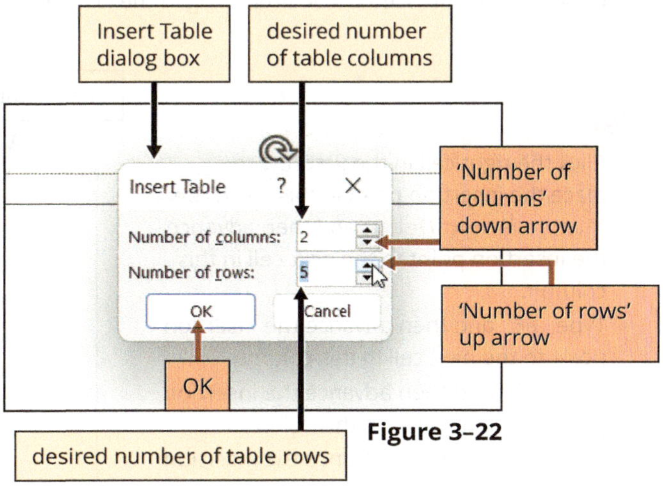

Figure 3–22

3

- Click OK (Insert Table dialog box) to insert the table into Slide 2 (Figure 3–23).

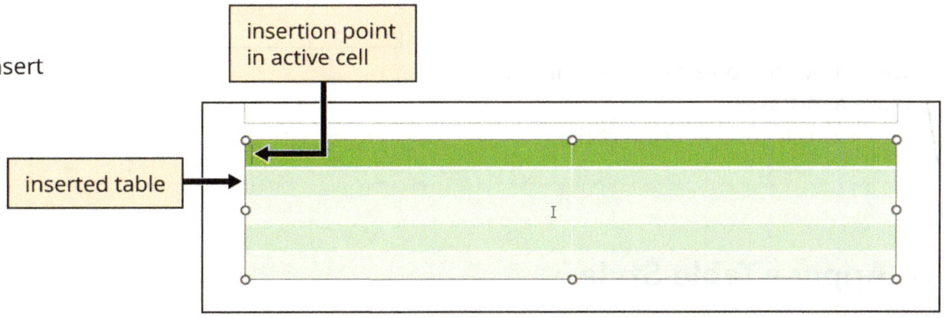

Figure 3–23

Other Ways

1. Click Table (Insert tab | Tables group), drag to select columns and rows, click or press ENTER

To Enter Data in a Table

Before formatting or making any changes in the table style, you enter the data in the table. **Why?** It is easier to see formatting and style changes applied to existing data. The second column will have the mature height for each tree listed in the first column. The next step is to enter data in the cells of the empty table. To place data in a cell, you click the cell and then type text. The following steps enter the data in the table.

1

- With the insertion point in the first cell in the first column, type **Tree Name** and then click the cell below or press DOWN ARROW to advance the insertion point to the next cell in this column.
- Type **Red Maple** and then advance the insertion point to the next cell in this column.
- Type **White Pine** and then advance the insertion point to the next cell in this column.
- Type **Red Oak** and then advance the insertion point to the next cell in this column.
- Type **Quaking Aspen** and then click the empty cell to the right or press TAB (Figure 3–24).

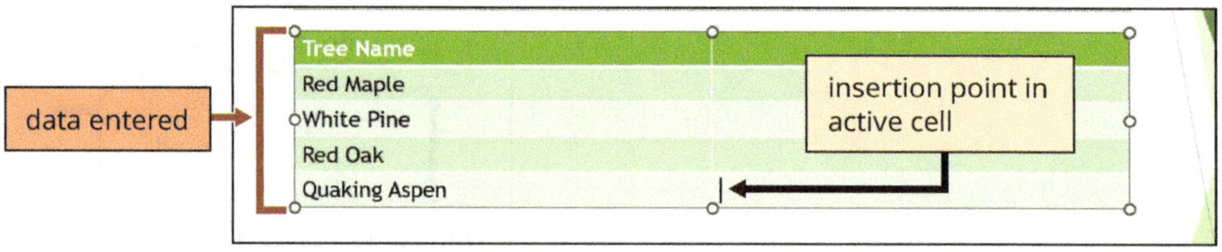

Figure 3–24

Q&A What if I pressed ENTER after filling in the last cell?
Press BACKSPACE.

2

- Click the right cell in the first row to place the insertion point in this cell. Type **Mature Height (feet)** and then advance the insertion point to the next cell in this column.
- Type **60** and then advance the insertion point to the next cell in this column.
- Type **80** and then advance the insertion point to the next cell in this column.
- Type **75** and then advance the insertion point to the next cell in this column.
- Type **50** as the cell content (Figure 3–25).

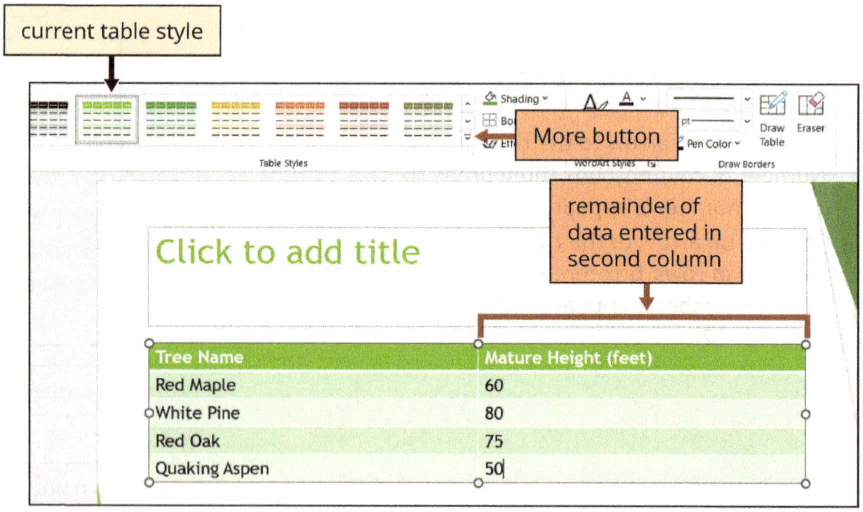

Figure 3–25

Q&A How do I correct cell contents if I make a mistake?
Click the cell and then correct the text.

To Apply a Table Style

When you inserted the table, PowerPoint automatically applied a style. Thumbnails of this style and others are displayed in the Table Styles gallery. These styles use a variety of colors and shading and are grouped in the categories of Best Match for

Document, Light, Medium, and Dark. The following steps apply a table style in the Medium area to the Slide 2 table. **Why?** The green styles in the Medium area use the colors appearing on the slide, so they coordinate nicely with the Facet theme colors in this presentation.

1

- With the insertion point in the table and the Table Design tab displayed, click the More button in the Table Styles gallery (Table Design tab | Tables Styles group) (shown in Figure 3–25) to expand the Table Styles gallery.
- Point to 'Medium Style 1 – Accent 2' in the Medium area (third style in the first Medium row) to display a live preview of that style applied to the table (Figure 3–26).

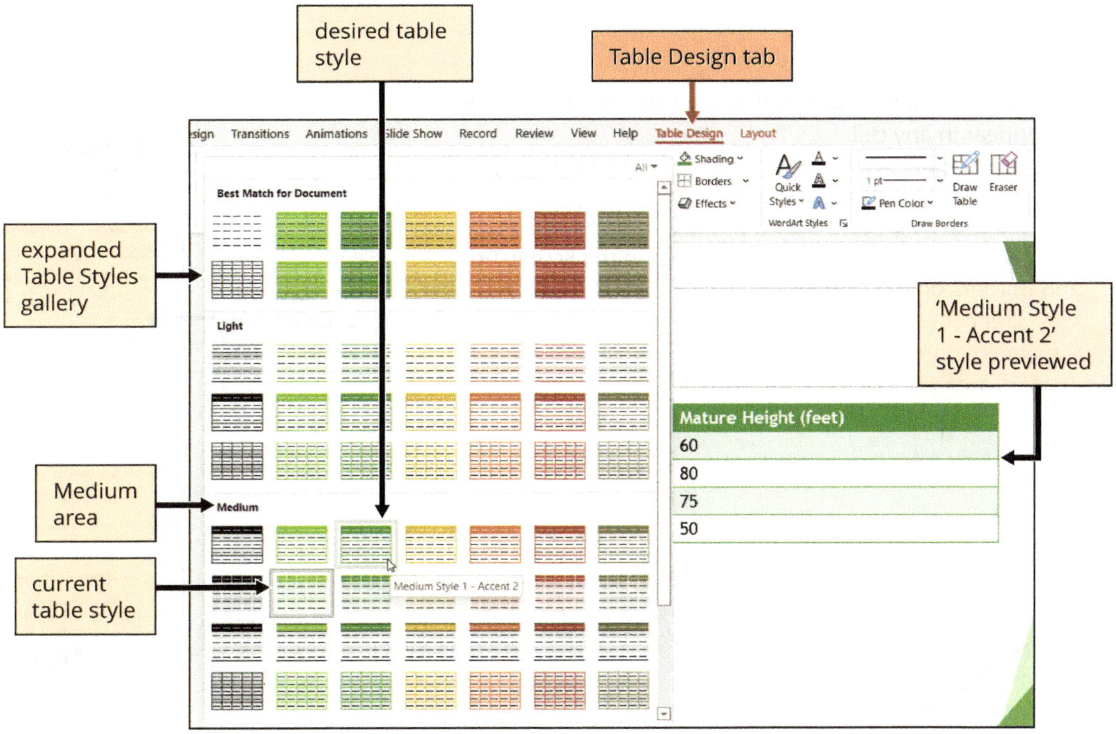

Figure 3–26

- **Experiment:** Point to various styles in the Table Styles gallery and watch the colors and format change on the table.

2

- Click 'Medium Style 1 – Accent 2' in the Table Styles gallery to apply the selected style to the table (Figure 3–27).

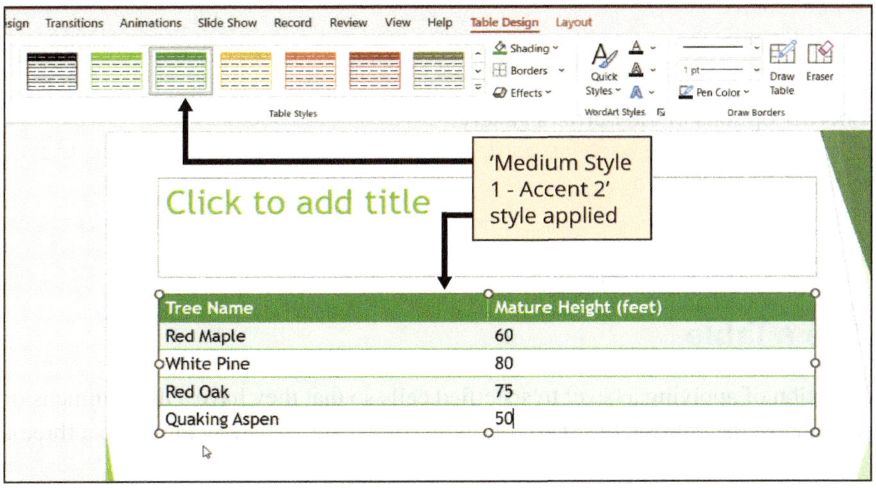

Figure 3–27

Q&A Can I resize the columns and rows or the entire table?
Yes. To resize columns or rows, drag a **column boundary** (the border to the right of a column) or the **row boundary** (the border at the bottom of a row) until the column or row is the desired width or height. To resize the entire table, drag a **table sizing handle**, the small circle that appears when you point to any corner of a table.

To Add Borders to a Table

The Slide 2 table does not have borders around the entire table or between the cells. The following steps add borders to the entire table. **Why?** These details will give the chart some dimension and add to its visual appeal.

1

- Click the edge of the table so that the insertion point does not appear in any cell.
- Click the Borders arrow (Table Design tab | Table Styles group) to display the Borders gallery (Figure 3–28).

Q&A Why is the button called No Border in the ScreenTip and Borders on the ribbon?
The ScreenTip name for the button will change based on the type of border, if any, present in the table. Currently, no borders are applied.

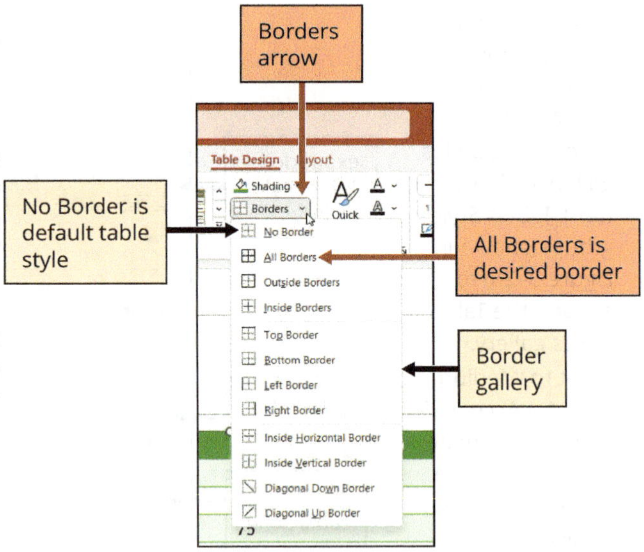

Figure 3–28

2

- Click All Borders in the Borders gallery to add borders around the entire table and to each table cell (Figure 3–29).

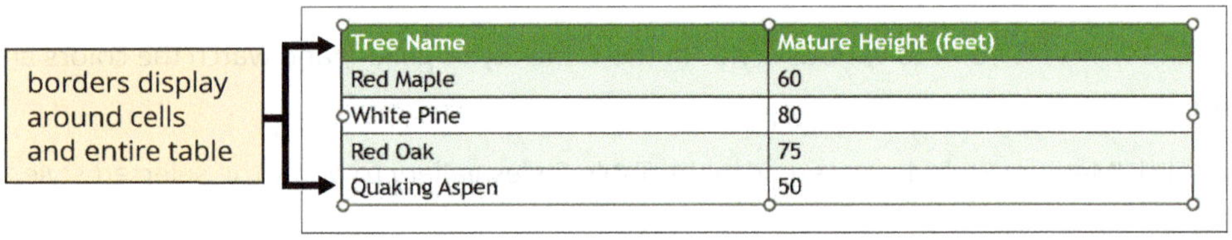

Tree Name	Mature Height (feet)
Red Maple	60
White Pine	80
Red Oak	75
Quaking Aspen	50

Figure 3–29

Q&A Why is the border color black?
PowerPoint's default border color is black. This color is displayed on the Pen Color button (Table Design tab | Draw Borders group).

Can I apply any of the border options in the Borders gallery?
Yes. You can vary the look of your table by applying borders only to the cells, around the table, to the top, bottom, left, or right edges, or a combination of these areas.

To Add an Effect to a Table

PowerPoint gives you the option of applying a bevel to specified cells so that they have a three-dimensional appearance. You also can add a shadow or reflection to the entire table. The following steps add a shadow and give a three-dimensional appearance to the entire table. **Why?** Adding an effect will enhance the table design.

1

- With the table selected, click the Effects button (Table Design tab | Table Styles group) to display the Effects menu.

Q&A What is the difference between a shadow and a reflection?
A shadow gives the appearance that light is falling on the table, which causes a shadow behind the graphic. A reflection gives the appearance that the table is shiny, so a mirror image appears below the actual graphic.

2

- Point to Shadow to display the Shadow gallery (Figure 3–30).

Q&A How do the shadows differ in the Outer, Inner, and Perspective categories?
The Outer shadows are displayed on the outside of the table, whereas the Inner shadows are displayed in the interior cells. The Perspective shadows give the illusion that a light is shining from the right or left side of the table or from above, and the table is casting a shadow.

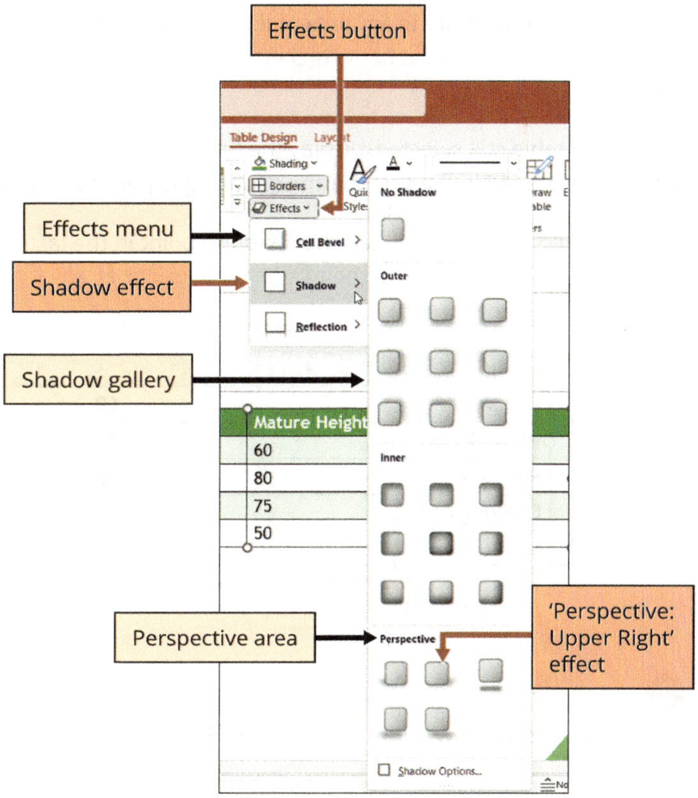

Figure 3–30

3

- Point to 'Perspective: Upper Right' in the Perspective category (second shadow in the first row) to display a live preview of this shadow (Figure 3–31).
- **Experiment:** Point to the various shadows in the Shadow gallery and watch the shadows change in the table.

4

- Click 'Perspective: Upper Right' to apply this shadow to the table.

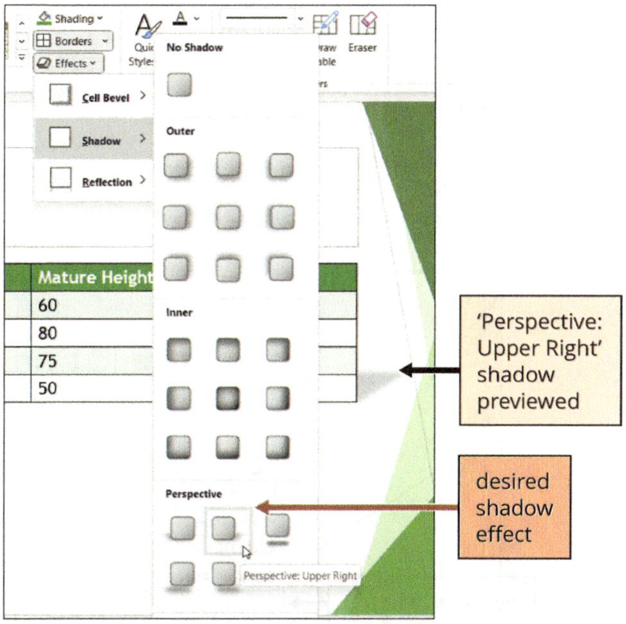

Figure 3–31

To Insert a Table Row

You can add a row easily in any area of the table. The following steps insert a row in the table. **Why?** You want to add information pertaining to the dogwood trees for sale.

1

- With the table still selected, display the Layout tab.
- Click the last cell in the first column (Quaking Aspen) to place the insertion point in this cell (Figure 3–32).

Q&A Could I also have placed the insertion point in the last cell in the second column (50)?
Yes. You are going to insert the row below these cells, so either location would work.

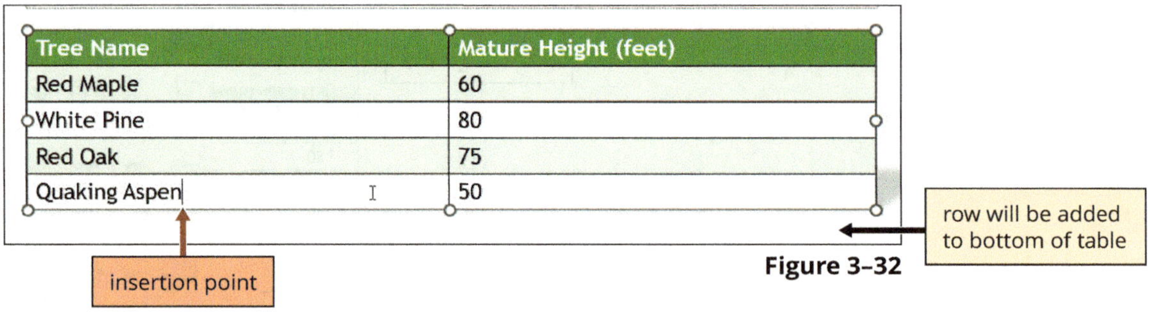

Figure 3–32

2

- Click the Insert Below button (Layout tab | Rows & Columns group) to insert a new row at the bottom of the table (Figure 3–33).

Q&A Can I insert a row anywhere in the table?
Yes. You can insert the row either below or above the cell where the insertion point is positioned.

If I am using a touch screen, how do I add rows to the table?
Press and hold the bottom-right cell, tap Insert on the shortcut menu, and then tap Insert Rows Below.

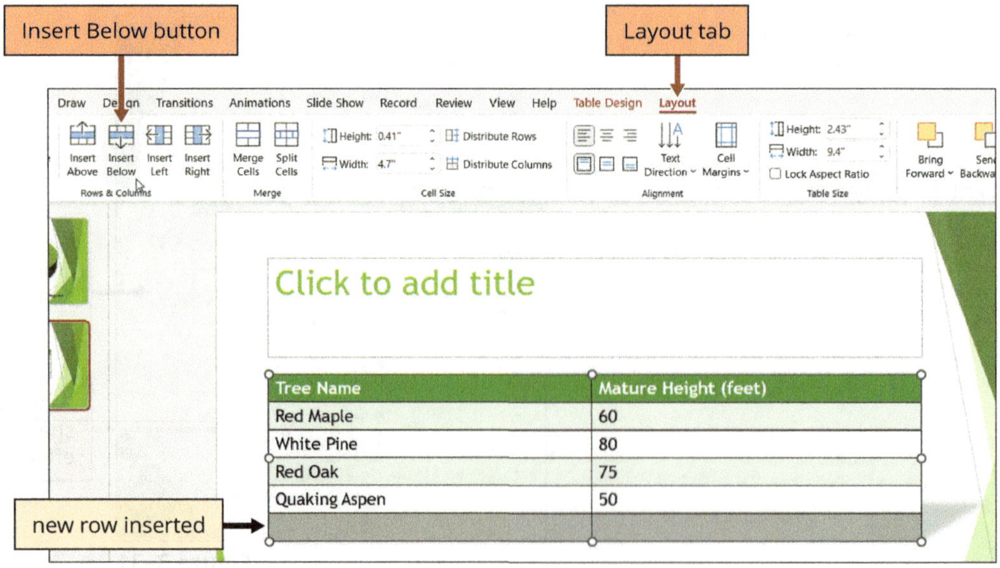

Figure 3–33

BTW
Touch Mode Differences
The Microsoft 365 and Windows interfaces may vary if you are using a touch screen. For this reason, you might notice that the function or appearance of your touch screen differs slightly from this module's presentation.

3

- Click the new cell in the Tree Name column and then type **Dogwood** in the cell.
- Type **25** in the new Mature Height column cell (Figure 3–34).

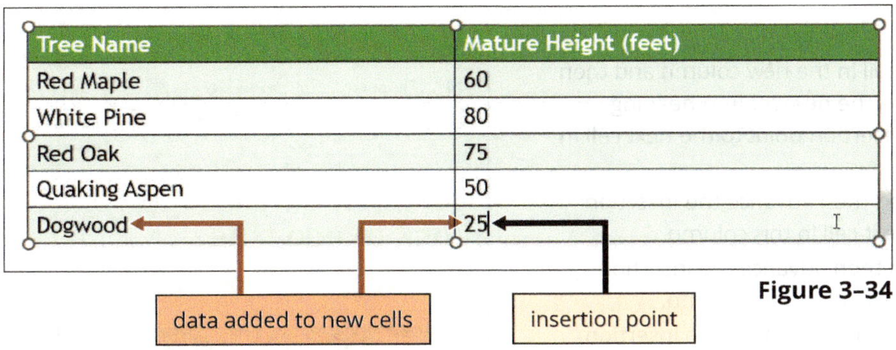

Figure 3–34

Other Ways

1. Position insertion point in bottom-right cell, press TAB

To Insert a Table Column

You add a column in a similar manner that you added a row to the table. The following steps insert a column in the table. **Why?** The right table column lists each tree's maximum height. A third column can list the selling price.

1

- With the insertion point still in the lower-right cell (25), click the Insert Right button (Layout tab | Rows & Columns group) to insert a column to the right of the Mature Height column (Figure 3–35).

Q&A Could I have placed the insertion anywhere in the Mature Height column?

Yes. You are going to insert the row to the right of these cells, so any location in the column would work.

Can I insert a column anywhere in the table?

Yes. You can insert the column to the left or the right of any cell where the insertion point is positioned.

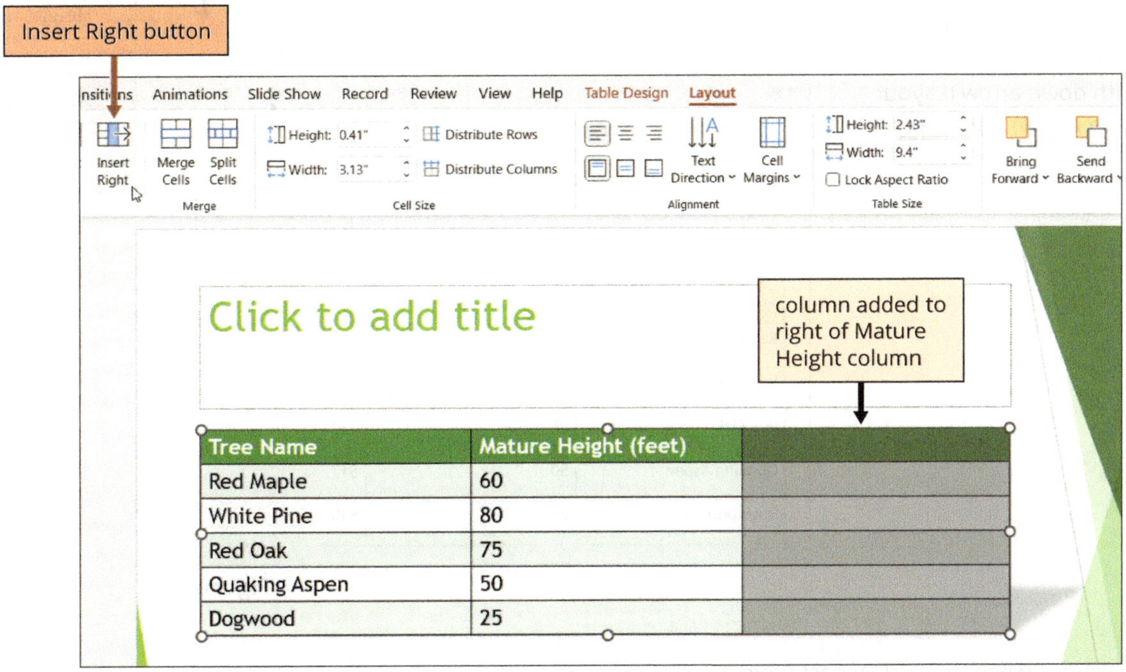

Figure 3–35

2

- Click the first cell in the new column and then type **Price** as the new column heading. Advance the insertion point to the next cell in this column.
- Type **$20** and then advance the insertion point to the next cell in this column.
- Type **$9** and then advance the insertion point to the next cell in this column.
- Type **$13** and then advance the insertion point to the next cell in this column.
- Type **$17** and then advance the insertion point to the next cell in this column.
- Type **$45** as the cell content (Figure 3-36).

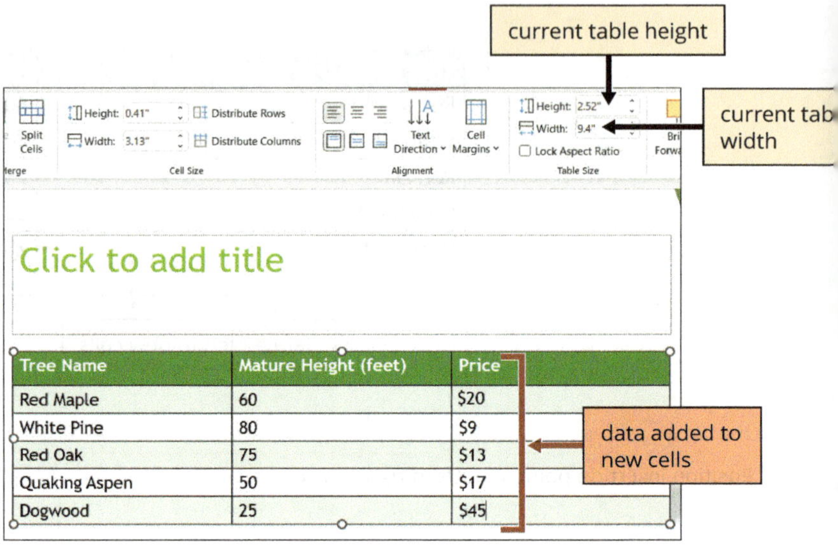

Figure 3-36

To Resize a Table

You resize a table the same way you resize a chart, a SmartArt graphic, or any other graphical object. The following steps resize the table on Slide 2. **Why?** Slide 2 has much white space below the chart. If you resize the table to fill this white space, it will be more readable.

1

- With the table still selected and the Layout tab displayed, click the Height up arrow (Layout tab | Table Size group) repeatedly until 4" is displayed in the box.
- Click the Width down arrow (Layout tab | Table Size group) repeatedly until 9" is displayed in the box (Figure 3-37).

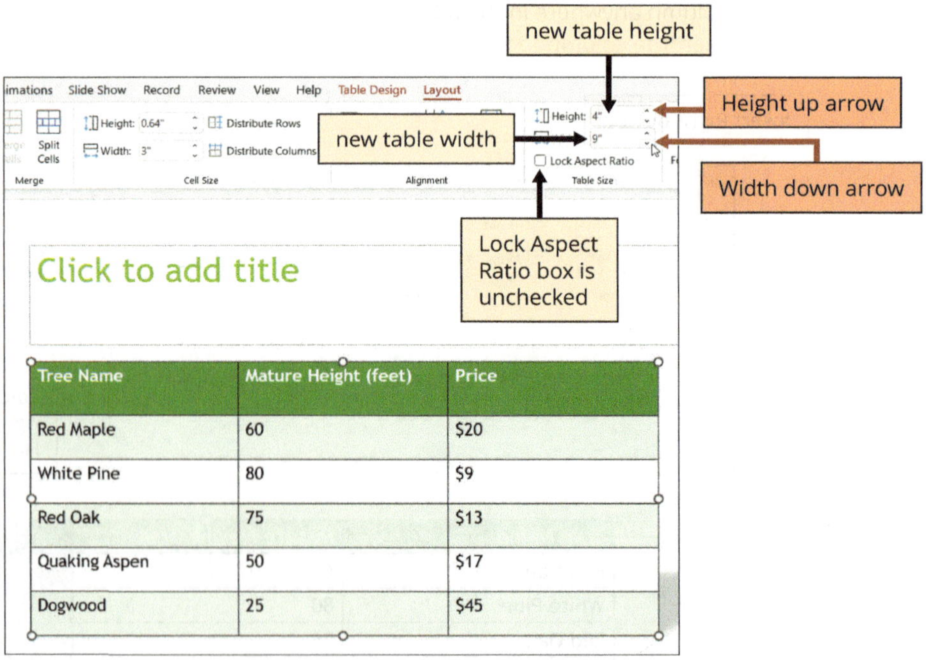

Figure 3-37

Q&A What happens when the Lock Aspect Ratio box (Layout tab | Table Size group) is checked?

The same ratio between the table height and width is maintained when the table is resized.

To Align a Table

The resized table can be positioned directly in the center of the slide. **Why?** Your slide content looks balanced when it is aligned between the left and right slide edges. The following steps align the table.

1

- With the table selected and the Layout tab displayed, click the Align button (Layout tab | Arrange group) to display the Align Objects menu (Figure 3–38).

Q&A What is the difference between the commands on the Layout tab | Arrange group and the commands on the Layout tab | Alignment group?
The items in the Arrange group align objects, such as tables, charts, and images, on the slide, while the Alignment buttons align text within an object or placeholder.

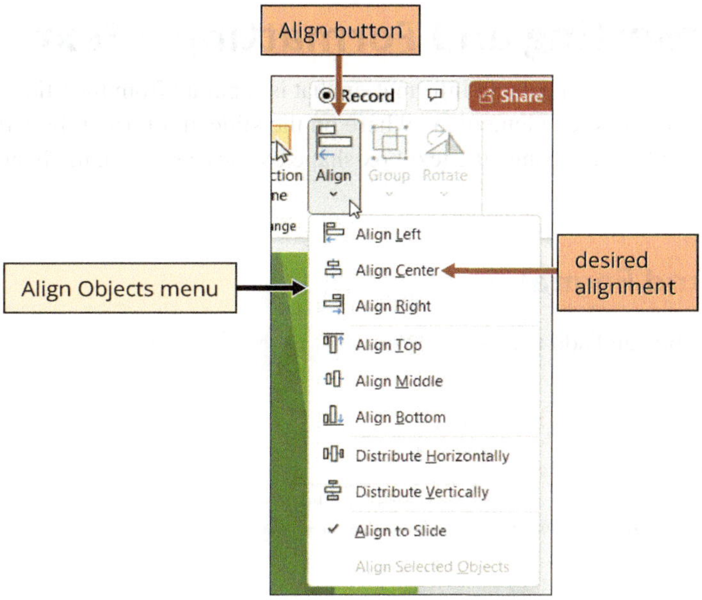

Figure 3–38

2

- Click Align Center on the Align Objects menu to position the table in the center of the slide (Figure 3–39).

Q&A Can I use the smart guides to align the table?
Yes.

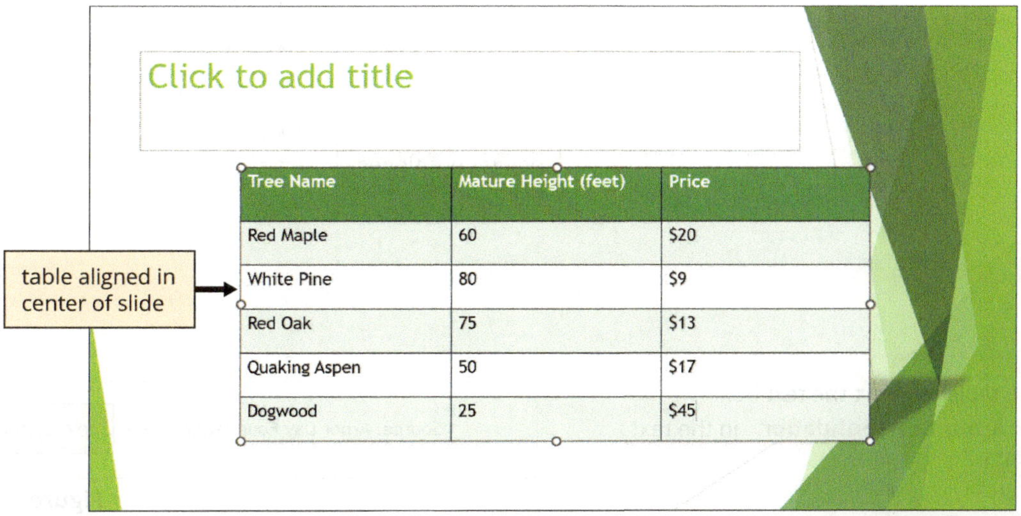

Tree Name	Mature Height (feet)	Price
Red Maple	60	$20
White Pine	80	$9
Red Oak	75	$13
Quaking Aspen	50	$17
Dogwood	25	$45

Figure 3–39

To Add a Slide Title

The slide needs a title to inform your audience about the table content. The following steps add a title to Slide 2.

1. With Slide 2 displayed, type **Trees for Sale** in the title text placeholder.
2. Change the title text font to Century Schoolbook.
3. Bold this title text, increase the font size to 54 point, and then center it in the title text placeholder.

Inserting and Formatting a Text Box

A text box can contain information that is separate from the title or content placeholders. You can place this slide element anywhere on the slide and format the letters using any style and effect. You also can change the text box shape by moving the sizing handles.

To Insert a Text Box and Format Text

The following steps insert a text box and add text. **Why?** You want to reference the source of the table data.

1

- Display the Insert tab, click the Text Box button (Insert tab | Text group), and then position the pointer below the table (Figure 3–40).

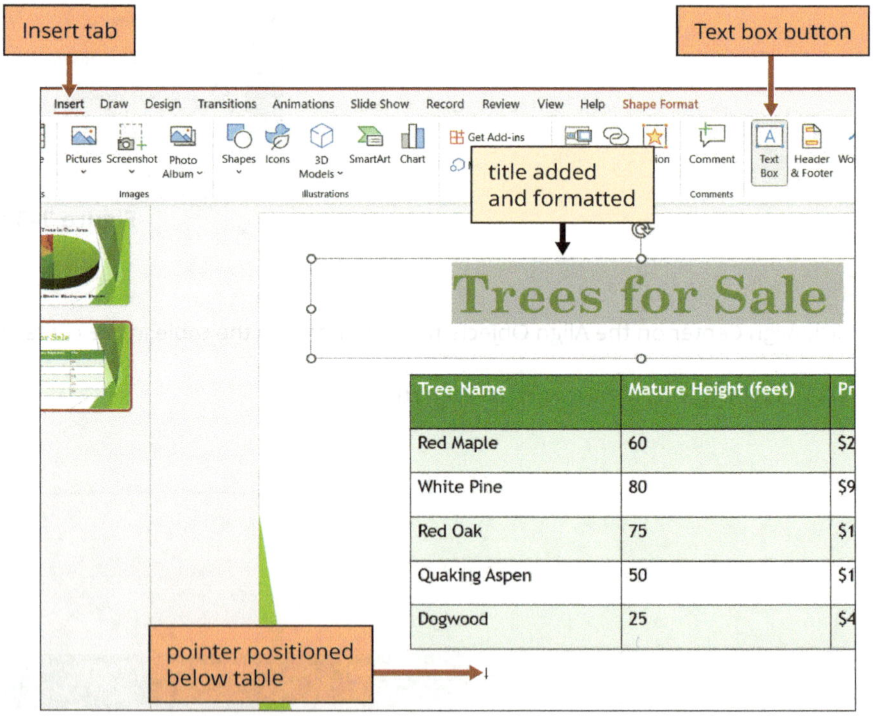

Figure 3–40

2

- Click below the table to insert the text box.
- Type **Source: Arbor Day Foundation** in the text box (Figure 3–41).

Figure 3–41

To Format Text Box Characters

The following steps format the text box characters to coordinate the font with the title text font.

1. Select the text in the text box, increase the font size to 20 point, and then change the font to Century Schoolbook.

2. Use the smart guides to align the text box, as shown in Figure 3–42.

Q&A Can I change the shape of the text box?
Yes. Drag the sizing handles to the desired dimensions.

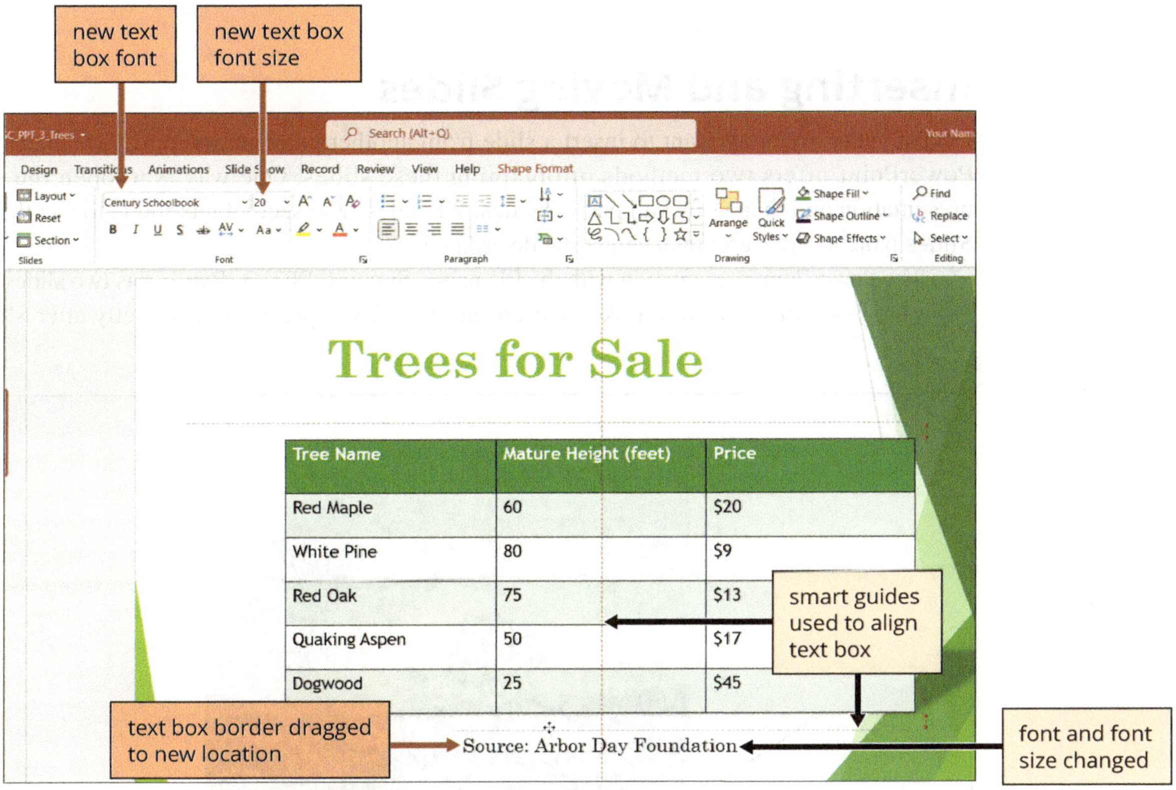

Figure 3–42

3. Click outside the text box to deselect this object.

To Apply a Preset Shape Effect

Once you have inserted a text box, you can format it in a variety of ways to draw attention to slide content. You can, for example, add a fill to change the inside color of the text box. A **fill** is a color, pattern, texture, picture, or gradient applied to the interior of a shape or slide background. You also can combine multiple individual effects to create a custom design. To apply a preset shape effect to the text box, you would perform the following steps.

1. Select the text box.
2. Display the Shape Format tab and then click the Shape Effects button (Shape Format tab | Shape Styles group) to display the Shape Effects menu.
3. Select the desired effect (Shadow, Reflection, Glow, Soft Edges, Bevel, or 3-D Rotation).

To Change Text Box Defaults

You can set the formatting of the text box you inserted as the default for all other text boxes you insert into the presentation so that the text boxes have a consistent look. To change the text box defaults, you would perform the following steps.

1. Right-click the text box outline to display the shortcut menu.
2. Click 'Set as Default Text Box' on the shortcut menu.

Break Point: If you wish to take a break, this is a good place to do so. Be sure the Trees file is saved and then you can exit PowerPoint. To resume later, start PowerPoint, open the file called SC_PPT_3_Trees, and continue following the steps from this location forward.

Inserting and Moving Slides

Occasionally you may want to insert a slide from another presentation into your presentation. PowerPoint offers two methods of obtaining these slides. One way is to open the second presentation and then copy and paste the desired slides. The second method is to use the Reuse Slides pane to view and then select the desired slides.

The PowerPoint presentation with the file name, Support_PPT_3_Reuse, has two slides, shown in Figure 3–43, that you would like to insert into your Trees presentation directly after Slide 3.

Figure 3–43(a): Slide 1 (Insert and Use as Title Slide)

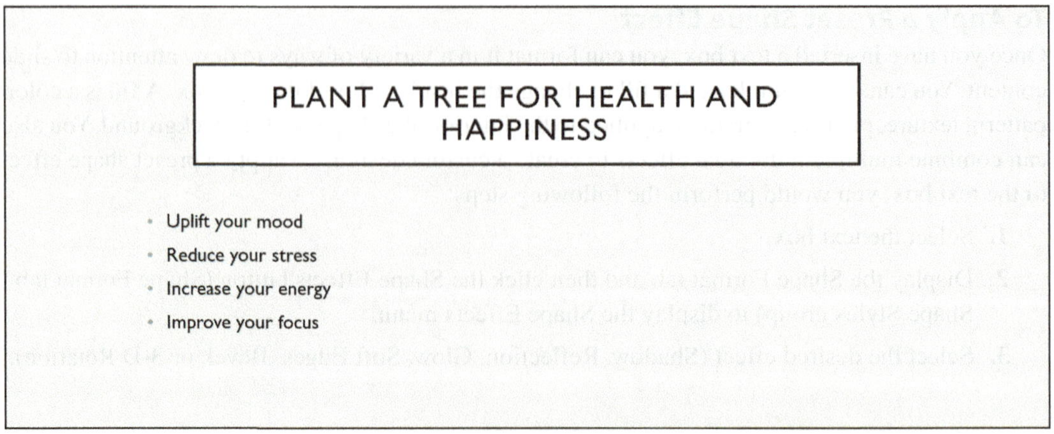

Figure 3–43(b): Slide 1 (Insert and Move to Slide 2)

To Reuse Slides from an Existing Presentation

PowerPoint converts inserted slides to the theme and styles of the current presentation, so the inserted slides will inherit the styles of the current Facet theme. The Support_PPT_3_Reuse.pptx presentation is in your Data Files. The following steps add these two slides to your presentation and specify that you want to change the design to the Facet formatting. **Why?** One slide has a picture you can change, and the second has useful information about the mental and physical health benefits that trees provide.

1

- If necessary, display the Home tab and then click the New Slide arrow (Home tab | Slides group) to display the Facet layout gallery (Figure 3–44).

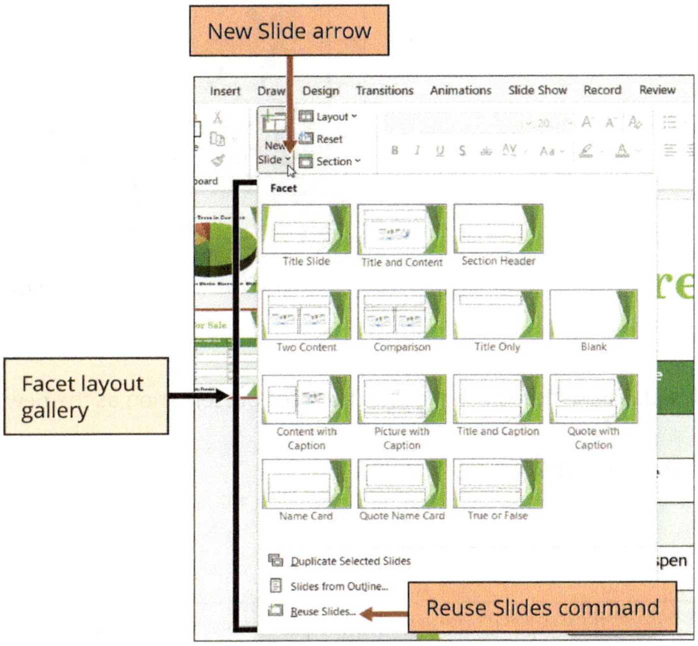

Figure 3–44

2

- Click Reuse Slides in the Facet layout gallery to display the Reuse Slides pane.
- Click the Browse button (Reuse Slides pane) to display the Browse dialog box.
- If necessary, navigate to the location of your Data Files and then click Support_PPT_3_Reuse.pptx to select the file.
- Click the Open button (Browse dialog box) to display thumbnails of the two slides in the Reuse Slides pane (Figure 3–45).

Q&A Could I have clicked the 'Open a PowerPoint File' link to display the Browse dialog box?
Yes. Either method will display the dialog box.

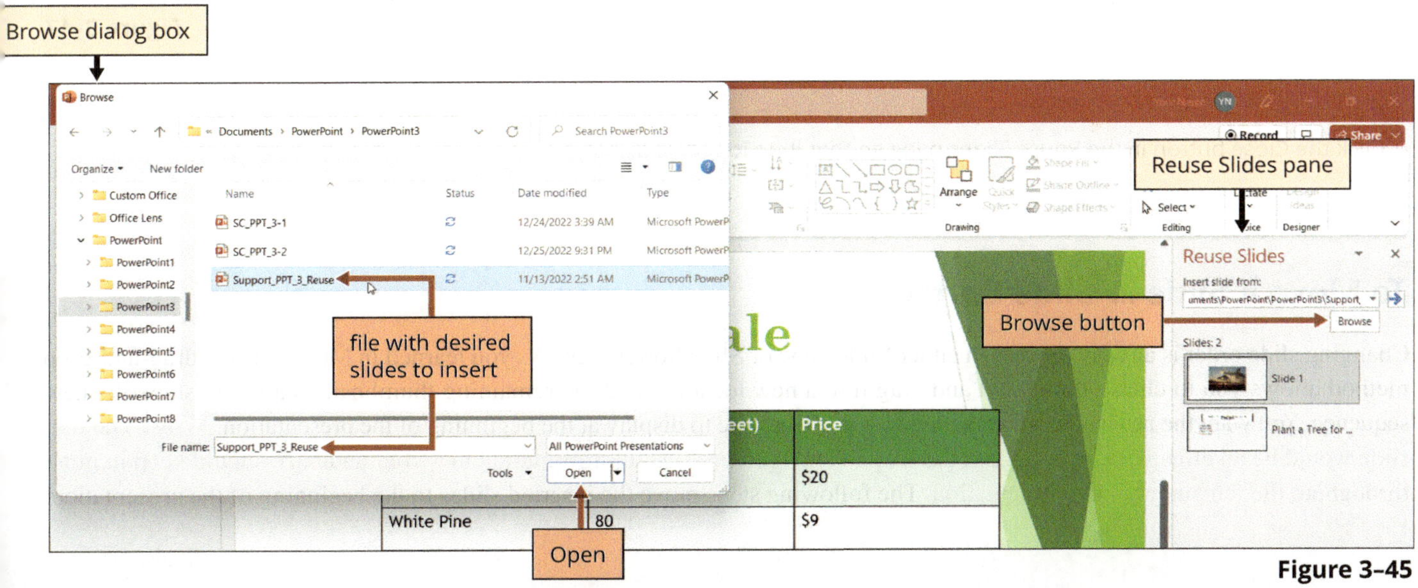

Figure 3–45

3

- Right-click either slide thumbnail to display the Reuse Slides menu (Figure 3–46).

Q&A What would happen if I click the 'Keep source formatting' check box at the bottom of the Reuse Slides pane?
PowerPoint would preserve the formatting characteristics found in the Reuse file's Mesh theme for the slides that you insert.

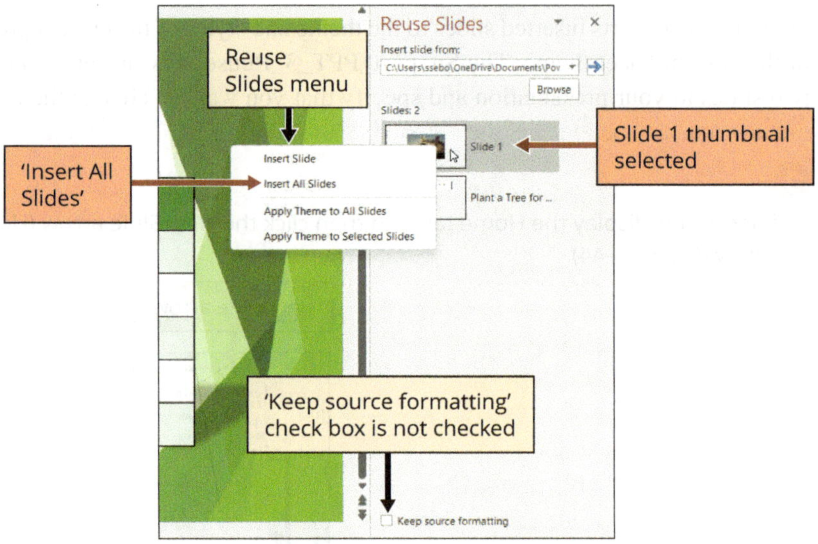

Figure 3–46

4

- Click 'Insert All Slides' to insert both slides from the Reuse file into the Trees presentation as the new slides 3 and 4 (Figure 3–47).

Q&A Can I insert only one slide in the Insert file?
Yes. Click the thumbnail of the slide you wish to insert and then click 'Insert Slide.'

Figure 3–47

5

- Click the Close button in the Reuse Slides pane so that it no longer is displayed.

To Move a Slide in Slide Sorter View

Changing slide order is an easy process in either Slide view or Slide Sorter view. As you learned in Module 1, the drag-and-drop method allows you to click a thumbnail and drag it to a new location, and the remaining thumbnails realign to show the new sequence. You want the new slides you inserted into the Trees file to display at the beginning of the presentation. **Why?** The first slide would be an effective title slide, and the second slide presents useful information that your audience should keep in mind throughout the remainder of the presentation. The following steps move the inserted slides to the beginning of the presentation.

1

- Click the Slide Sorter view button on the right side of the status bar to display the presentation in Slide Sorter view. Click the Slide 3 thumbnail to select it (Figure 3–48).

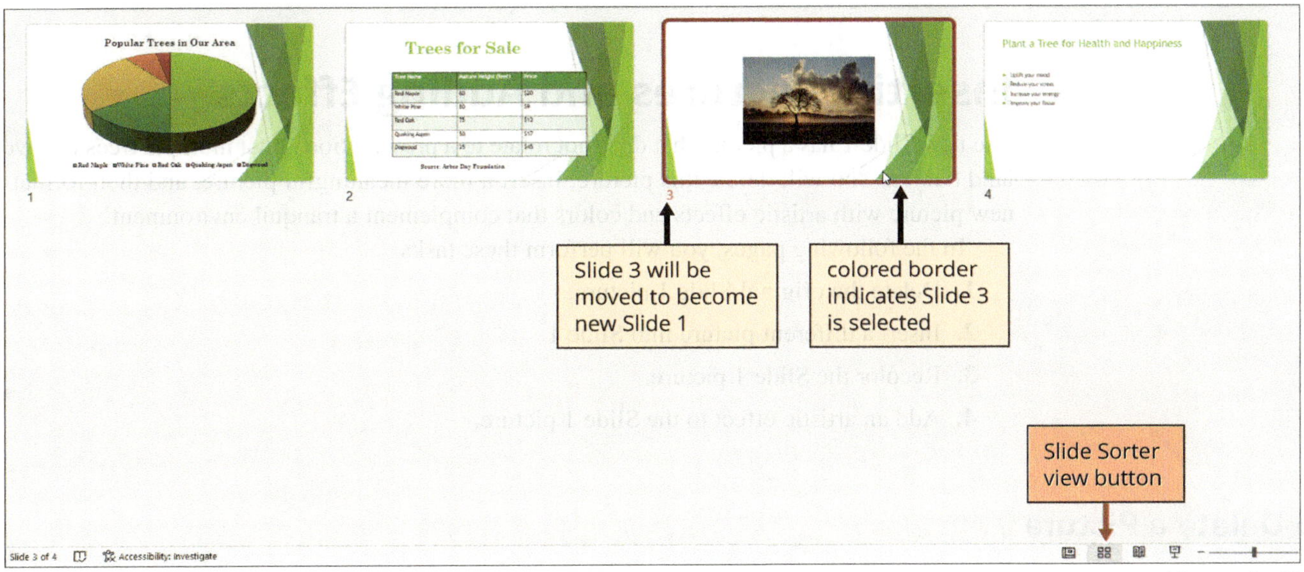

Mbll/Pixabay

Figure 3–48

2

- Drag the Slide 3 thumbnail to the left of the current Slide 1, as shown in Figure 3–48, so that it becomes the new Slide 1 (Figure 3–49).

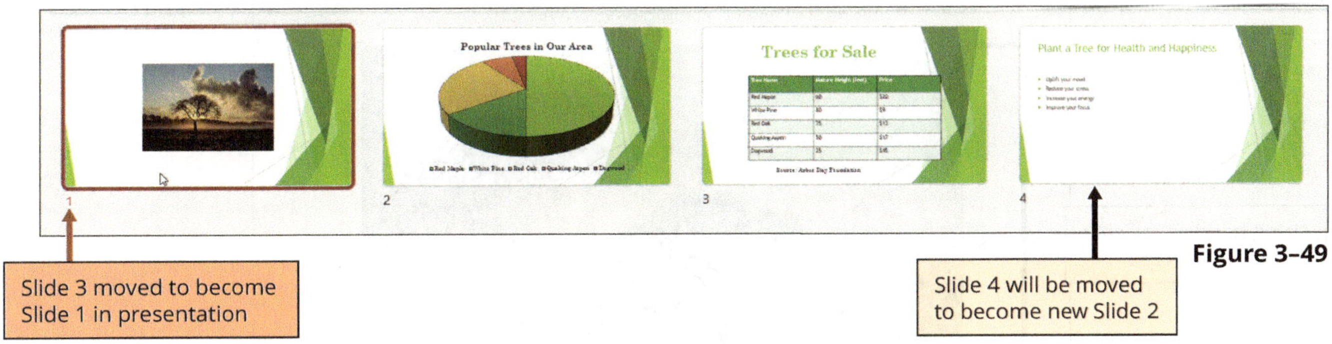

Mbll/Pixabay

Figure 3–49

3

- Click the Slide 4 thumbnail and then drag it to the right of the new Slide 1 so that it becomes the new Slide 2 (Figure 3–50).

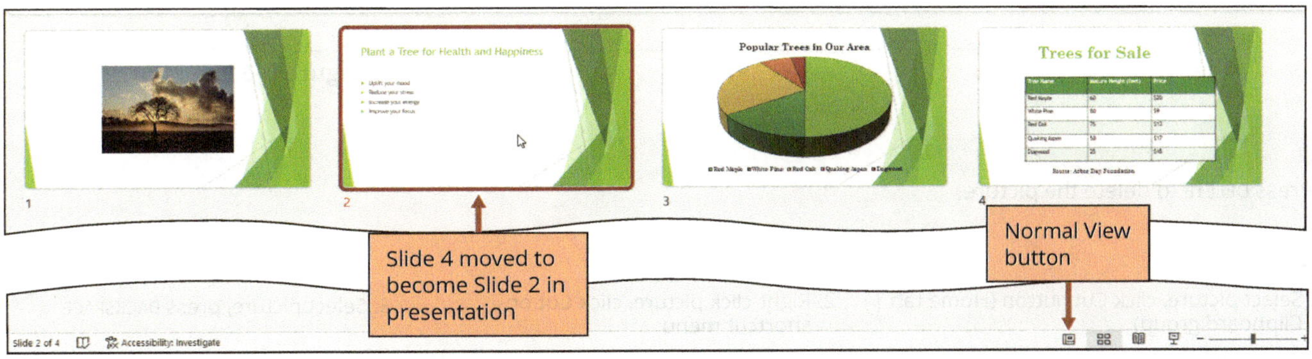

Mbll/Pixabay

Figure 3–50

4

- Click the Normal view button to display the presentation in Normal view.

Inserting Pictures and Adding Effects

The new Slide 1 has a picture that does not relate to a presentation about multiple trees in a woodland habitat. You will delete this picture, insert a more meaningful picture, and then format this new picture with artistic effects and colors that complement a tranquil environment.

In the following pages, you will perform these tasks:

1. Delete the original Slide 1 picture.
2. Insert a different picture into Slide 1.
3. Recolor the Slide 1 picture.
4. Add an artistic effect to the Slide 1 picture.

To Delete a Picture

1

- Display Slide 1 and then click the picture to select it (Figure 3–51).

Figure 3–51

2

- Press DELETE to delete the picture.

Other Ways

1. Select picture, click Cut button (Home tab | Clipboard group)
2. Right-click picture, click Cut on shortcut menu
3. Select picture, press BACKSPACE

To Insert and Resize a Picture into a Slide without Content Placeholders

The next step in developing the title slide is to insert a different picture. The slide layout is Blank and does not have a content placeholder, so the picture will display in the center of the slide when you insert it. The picture is available in the Data Files. The following steps insert a picture into Slide 1.

1. With Slide 1 displayed, click Insert on the ribbon to display the Insert tab, click the Pictures button (Insert tab | Images group) to display the Insert Picture From menu, and then click This Device to display the Insert Picture dialog box.
2. If necessary, navigate to the picture location and then click Support_PPT_3_Landscape.jpg to select the file.
3. Click the Insert button (Insert Picture dialog box) to insert the picture into Slide 1. Close the Design Ideas pane if it opens.
4. Click the Size Dialog Box Launcher in the Picture Format | Size group and make sure the Lock aspect ratio box is unchecked in the Format Picture pane.
5. Resize the picture to an approximate height of 6.6" and width of 12". Use the smart guides to move the picture to the center of the slide, as shown in Figure 3-52.

Figure 3-52

To Crop a Picture

You can remove the unnecessary elements of the picture and crop it. **Why?** The left side of the picture contains a grove of trees, and you want to focus on this particular area. When you crop a picture, you trim the vertical or horizontal sides so that the most important area of the picture is displayed. Any picture file type except animated GIF can be cropped. The following steps crop the title slide picture.

1

- With the picture selected and the Picture Format tab displayed, click the Crop button (Picture Format tab | Size group) to display the cropping handles on the picture.
- Position the pointer over the center cropping handle on the right edge of the picture (Figure 3–53).

Q&A Why did my pointer change shape?
The pointer changed to indicate you are about to crop a picture.

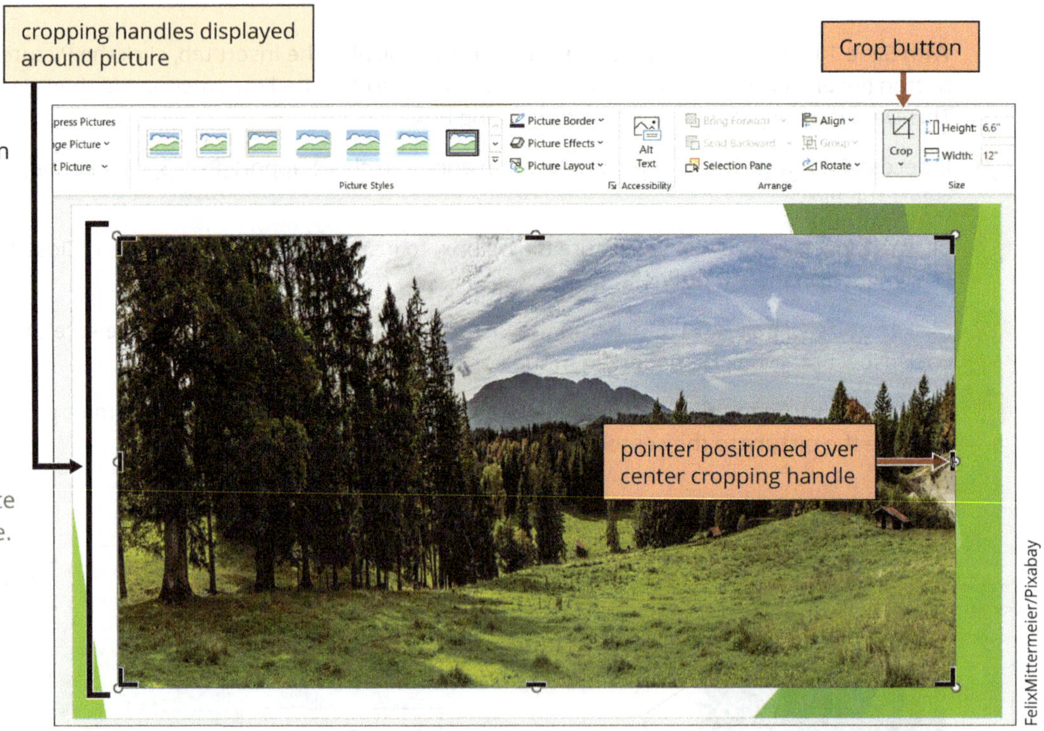

Figure 3–53

2

- Drag the center cropping handle on the right edge of the picture inward so that the right edge of the marquee is along the right edge of the grove of trees.
- Drag the center cropping handle on the bottom edge of the picture inward toward the trunk of the left tree (Figure 3–54).

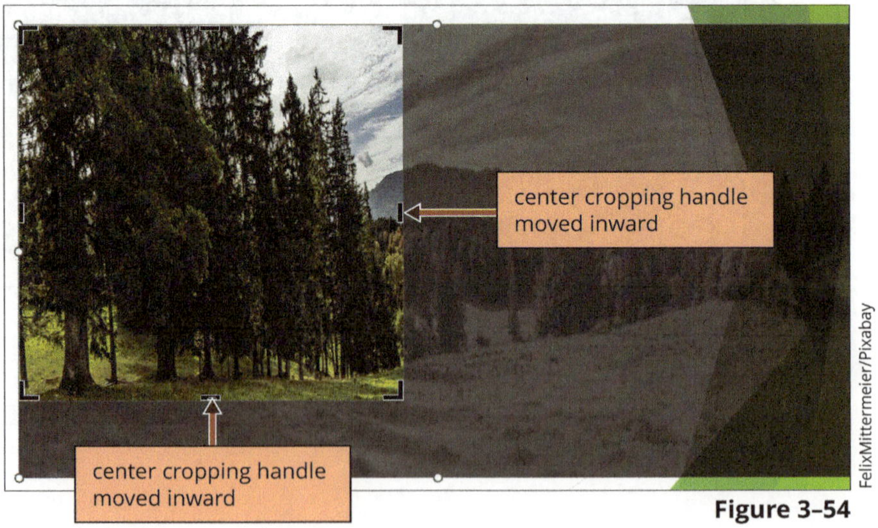

Figure 3–54

Q&A Does cropping actually cut the picture's edges?
No. Although you cannot see the cropped edges, they exist until you save the file.

Can I crop a picture to exact dimensions?
Yes. Right-click the picture and then click Format Picture to open the Format Picture pane. Click the Picture icon, then Crop. Under Picture position, enter the measurements in the Width and Height boxes.

3

- Click the Crop button again to crop the edges (Figure 3–55).

Q&A Can I press ESC to crop the edges?
Yes.

Can I change the crop lines?
If you have not saved the file, you can undo your crops by clicking Undo on the Quick Access Toolbar, clicking the Reset Picture button (Picture Format tab | Adjust group), or pressing CTRL+Z. If you have saved the file, you cannot undo the crop.

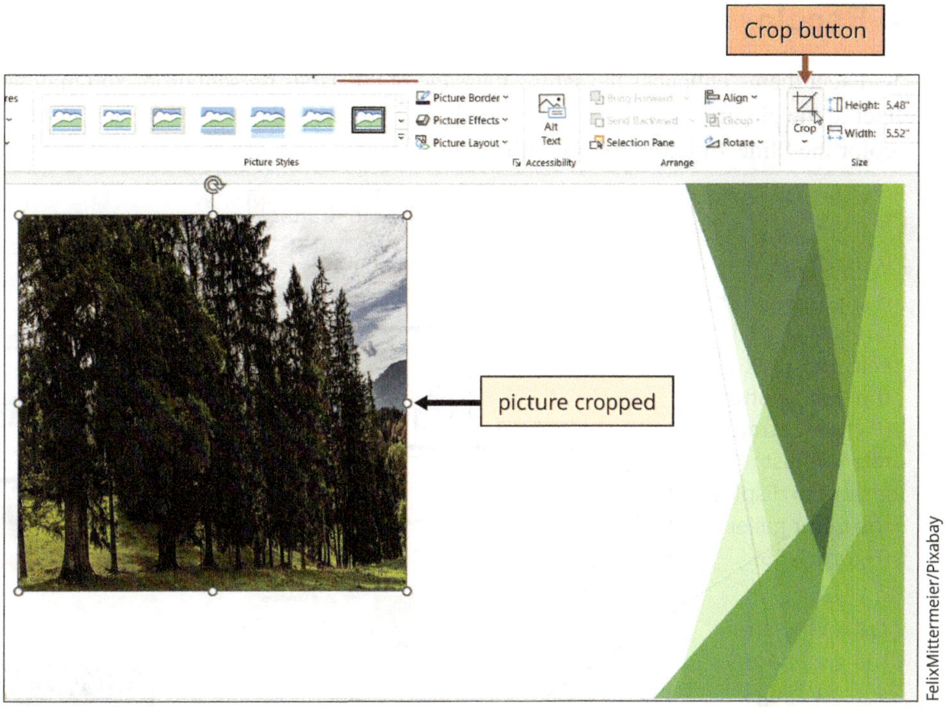

Figure 3–55

Other Ways

1. Right-click picture, click Crop on Mini toolbar

To Crop a Picture to a Shape

In addition to cropping a picture, you can change the shape of a picture by cropping it to a specific shape. The picture's proportions are maintained, and it automatically is trimmed to fill the shape's geometry. To crop to a specific shape, you would perform the following steps.

1. Select the picture you want to crop.
2. Display the Picture Format tab and then click the Crop arrow (Picture Format tab | Size group) to display the Crop menu.
3. Point to 'Crop to Shape' and then click the desired shape in the Shape gallery.

BTW
Simultaneous Cropping on Two or Four Sides
To crop equally on two sides simultaneously, press CTRL while dragging the center cropping handle on either side inward. To crop all four sides equally, press CTRL while dragging a corner cropping handle inward.

Adjusting Picture Colors

PowerPoint allows you to adjust picture colors. The Color gallery has a wide variety of preset formatting combinations. The thumbnails in the gallery display the more common color saturation, color tone, and recolor adjustments. **Color saturation** changes the intensity of colors. High saturation produces vivid colors; low saturation produces gray tones. **Color tone** affects the coolness, called blue, or the warmness, called orange, of pictures. Color tones are denoted by temperature in degrees Kelvin (K), with lower numbers having coolness and higher numbers having warmness. When a digital camera does not measure the tone correctly, a **color cast** occurs, and, as a result, one color dominates the picture. **Recolor** effects convert the picture into a wide variety of hues. The more common recolor effects are **grayscale**, which changes a color picture into black, white, and shades of gray, and **sepia**, which changes picture colors into brown, gold, and yellow, reminiscent of a faded picture. You also can fine-tune the color adjustments by clicking the Picture Color Options and More Variations commands in the Color gallery.

To Recolor a Picture

The Facet theme enhances the serene message of the Trees presentation. You may want to supplement this theme by adding an effect to the picture. **Why?** An effect adds variety to the presentation and helps enhance ordinary pictures. The following steps recolor the Slide 1 picture to soften the trees.

1

- With Slide 1 displayed and the landscape picture selected, click the Color button (Picture Format tab | Adjust group) to display the Color gallery (Figure 3–56).

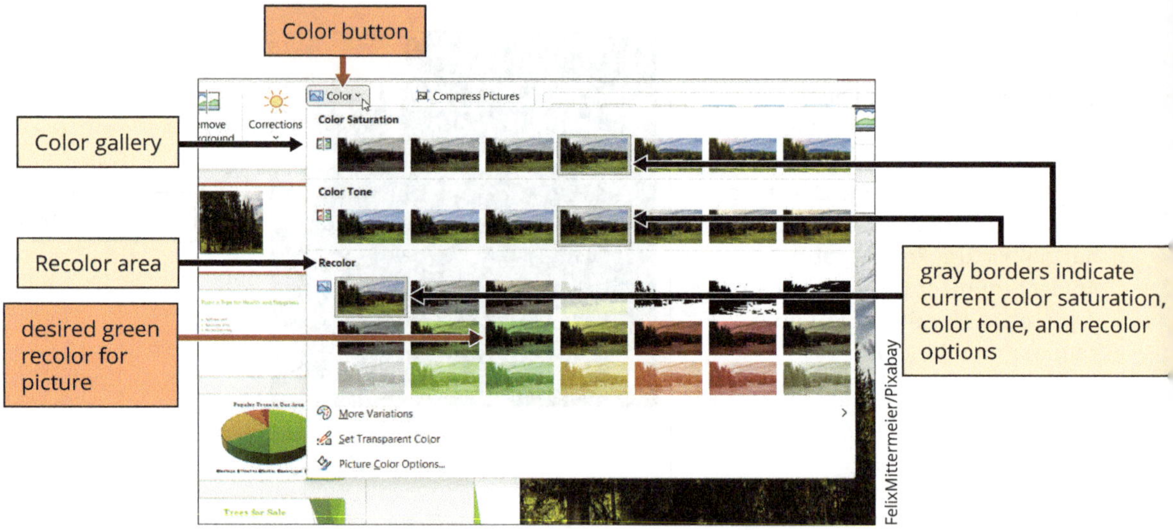

Figure 3–56

Q&A Why are the gray borders surrounding the thumbnails in the Color Saturation, Color Tone, and Recolor areas in the gallery?
The gray borders show the color saturation, tone, and recolor settings currently in effect for the image on Slide 1.

2

- Point to 'Dark Green, Accent color 2 Dark' (third thumbnail in the second Recolor row) to display a live preview of this adjustment on the picture (Figure 3–57).
- **Experiment:** Point to various thumbnails in the Recolor area and watch the colors change on the picture in Slide 1.

3

- Click 'Dark Green, Accent color 2 Dark' to apply this setting to the landscape picture.

Figure 3–57

Q&A Could I have applied this recoloring to the picture if it had been a background instead of a file inserted into the slide?
No. Artistic effects and recoloring cannot be applied to backgrounds.

Other Ways

1. Click Format Picture on shortcut menu, click Picture icon (Format Picture pane), click Picture Color, click Recolor

To Add an Artistic Effect to a Picture

Artists use a variety of techniques to create effects in their paintings. They can vary the amount of paint on their brushstroke, use fine bristles to add details, mix colors to increase or decrease intensity, and smooth their paints together to blend the colors. You, likewise, can add similar effects to your pictures using PowerPoint's built-in artistic effects. **Why?** The completed Slide 1 will have both a picture and WordArt, so applying an artistic effect to the picture will provide a contrast between the two images. The following steps add an artistic effect to the Slide 1 picture.

1

- With the landscape picture still selected, click the Artistic Effects button (Picture Format tab | Adjust group) to display the Artistic Effects gallery (Figure 3–58).

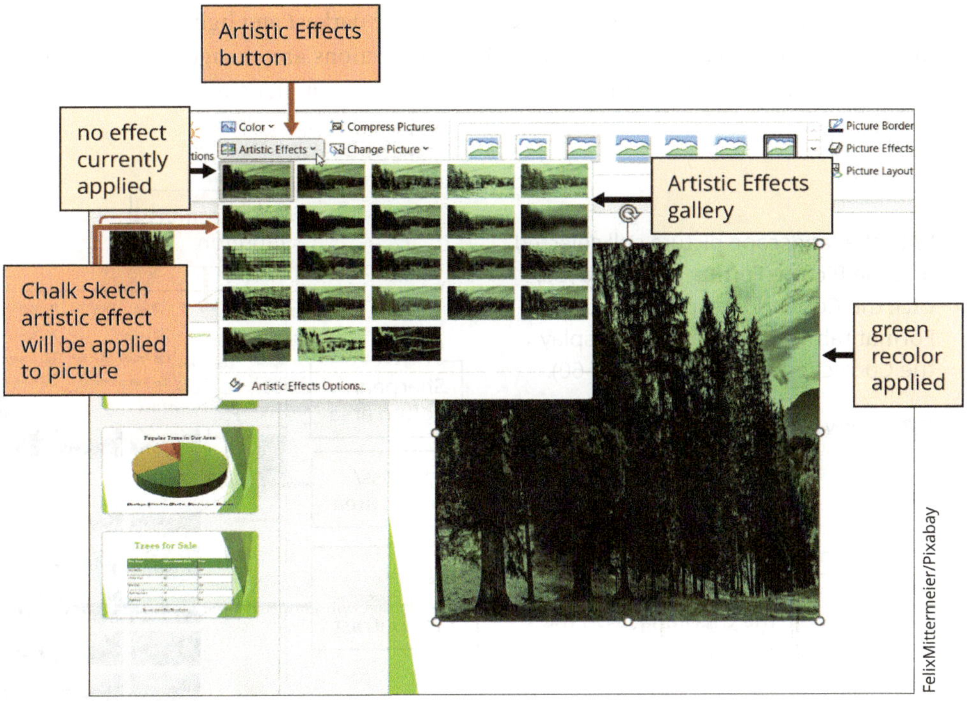

Figure 3–58

2

- Point to Chalk Sketch (first thumbnail in the second row) to display a live preview of this effect on the picture (Figure 3–59).
- **Experiment:** Point to various artistic effects and watch the hues change on the picture in Slide 1.

3

- Click Chalk Sketch to apply this artistic effect to the picture.

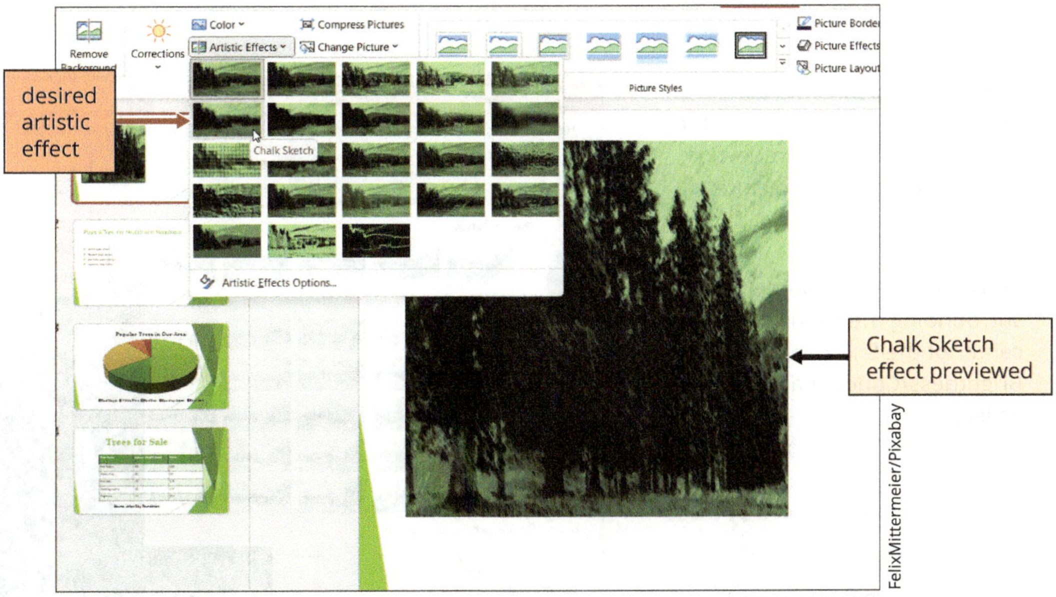

Figure 3–59

Q&A Can I adjust a picture by recoloring and applying an artistic effect?

Yes. You can apply both a color and an effect. You may prefer at times to mix these adjustments to create a unique image.

Other Ways

1. Click Format Picture on shortcut menu, click Effects icon, click Artistic Effects

To Change the Picture Softness

The Corrections tools allow you to change a picture's brightness, contrast, sharpness, and softness. A picture's color intensity can be modified by changing the brightness and contrast. **Brightness** determines the overall lightness or darkness of the entire image, whereas **contrast** is the difference between the darkest and lightest areas of the image. **Sharpness** increases (sharpens) or decreases (softens) a picture's clarity. These corrections are changed in predefined percentage increments. The following steps increase the picture's softness. **Why?** The softness complements the calm theme and allows the audience to focus on the overall message.

1

- With the landscape picture still selected and the Picture Format tab displayed, click the Corrections button (Picture Format tab | Adjust group) to display the Corrections gallery (Figure 3–60).

Q&A How are the thumbnails arranged?
The thumbnails on the left of the Sharpen/Softness area show more softness, and those on the right show more sharpness. In the Brightness/Contrast area, the thumbnails on the left are less bright than those on the right, and the thumbnails on the top have less contrast than those on the bottom.

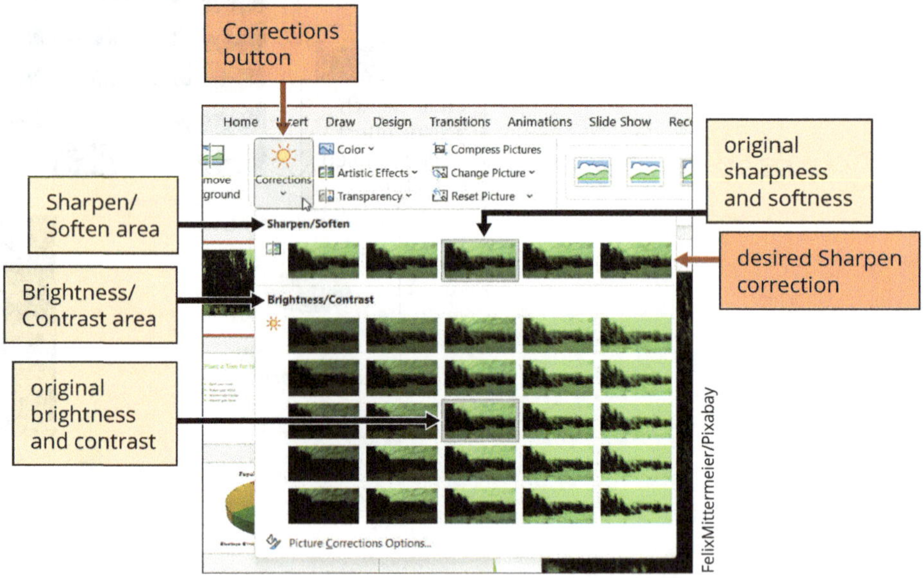

Figure 3–60

2

- Point to Sharpen: 50% (last thumbnail in the Sharpen/Soften row) to display a live preview of this correction on the picture (Figure 3–61).

Q&A Why is a gray border surrounding the pictures in the center of the Sharpen/Soften and Brightness/Contrast areas of the gallery?
The image currently has normal sharpness, brightness, and contrast (0%), which is represented by these center images in the gallery.

- **Experiment:** Point to various pictures in the Sharpen/Soften area and watch the sharpness change on the picture in Slide 1.

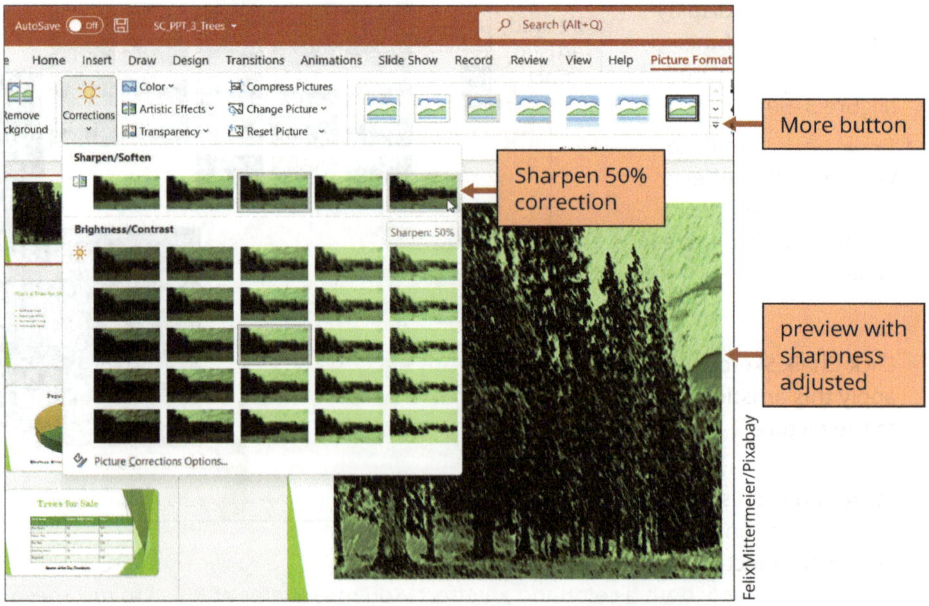

Figure 3–61

3

- Click Sharpen: 50% to apply this correction to the landscape picture.

Q&A How can I remove all effects from the picture?
Click the Reset Picture button (Picture Format tab | Adjust group).

Can I fine-tune any correction?
Yes. Click Picture Corrections Options and then move the slider for Sharpness, Brightness, or Contrast.

Other Ways

1. Click Picture Corrections Options (Corrections gallery), move Sharpness slider, or enter number in box next to slider (Format Picture pane)

To Apply a Picture Style

A **style** is a named collection of formats that can be applied to text or objects. The picture on Slide 1 emphasizes the health benefits of walking among trees, and you can increase its visual appeal by applying a picture style. **Why?** PowerPoint provides more than 25 picture styles that enable you to change a picture's look to a more visually appealing style, including a variety of shapes, angles, borders, and reflections. You want to use a style that applies a shadow to the landscape picture. The following steps apply a picture style to the Slide 1 picture.

1

- With the Slide 1 picture selected and the Picture Format tab displayed, click the More button in the Picture Styles gallery (Picture Format tab | Picture Styles group) (shown in Figure 3–61) to expand the gallery.
- Point to 'Soft Edge Oval' in the Picture Styles gallery (sixth style in the third row) to display a live preview of that style applied to the picture in the document (Figure 3–62).
- **Experiment:** Point to various picture styles in the Picture Styles gallery and watch the style of the picture change in the document window.

2

- Click 'Soft Edge Oval' in the Picture Styles gallery to apply the style to the selected picture.

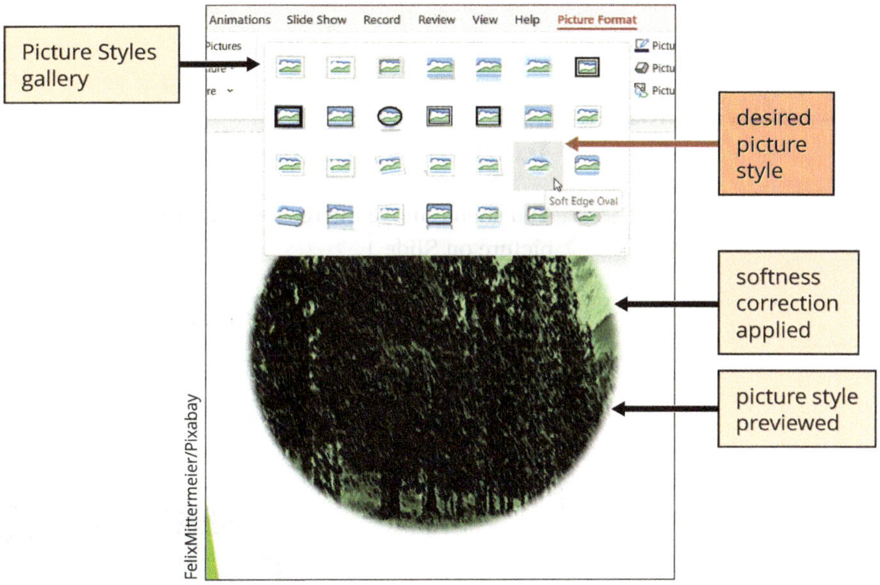

Figure 3–62

To Size a Picture

The formatted picture is too small for Slide 1, so you need to resize it. You can resize this slide element by dragging the sizing handles or by specifying exact measurements for the height and width. The following step resizes the picture by entering an exact measurement.

1 With the picture selected and the Picture Format tab displayed, move the sizing handles so that the Height measurement is approximately 6" and the Width measurement is approximately 8.5" (Figure 3–63).

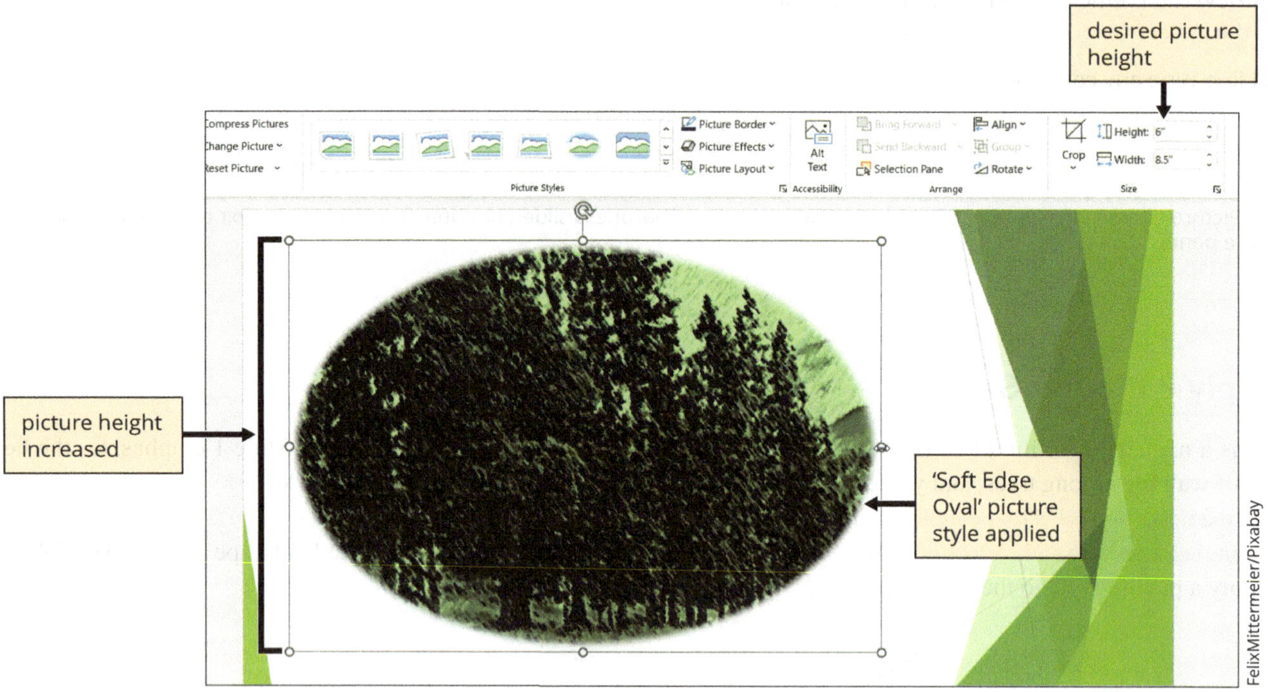

Figure 3–63

To Move a Picture

You should move the resized picture to allow space for a slide title. The following step moves the picture on Slide 1.

1 With the picture selected, use the smart guides to position the picture as shown in Figure 3–64.

Figure 3–64

To Align Pictures

You should move the picture to the top of Slide 1. **Why?** You want to add a slide title at the bottom of the slide, so you need to make room for this graphical element. The following steps align the picture at the top of the slide.

1

- With the picture selected and the Picture Format tab displayed, click the Align button (Picture Format tab | Arrange group) to display the Align Objects menu (Figure 3-65).

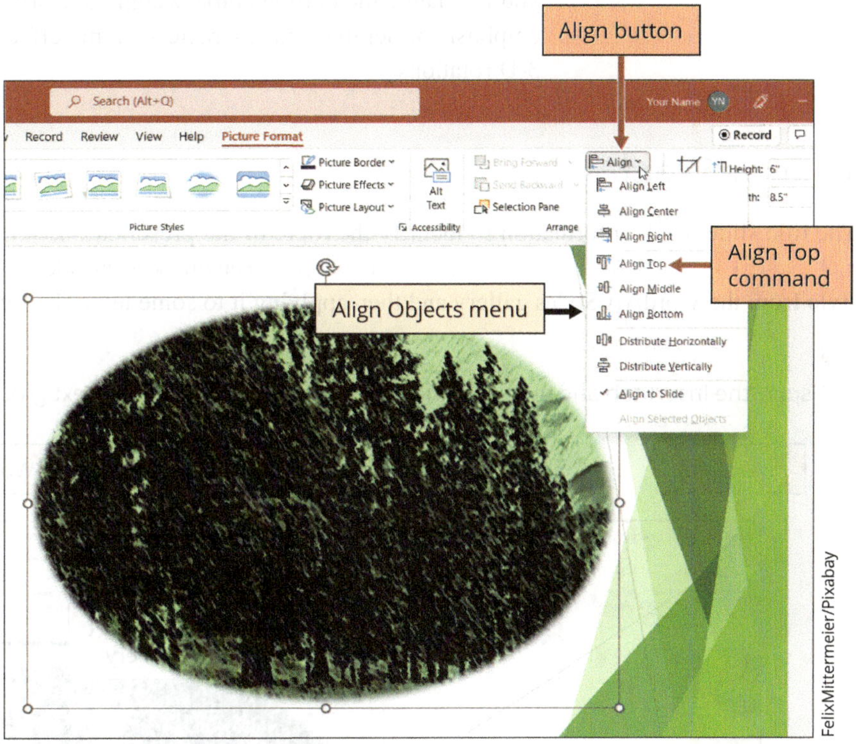

Figure 3-65

2

- Click Align Top to move the picture to the top edge of the slide (Figure 3-66).

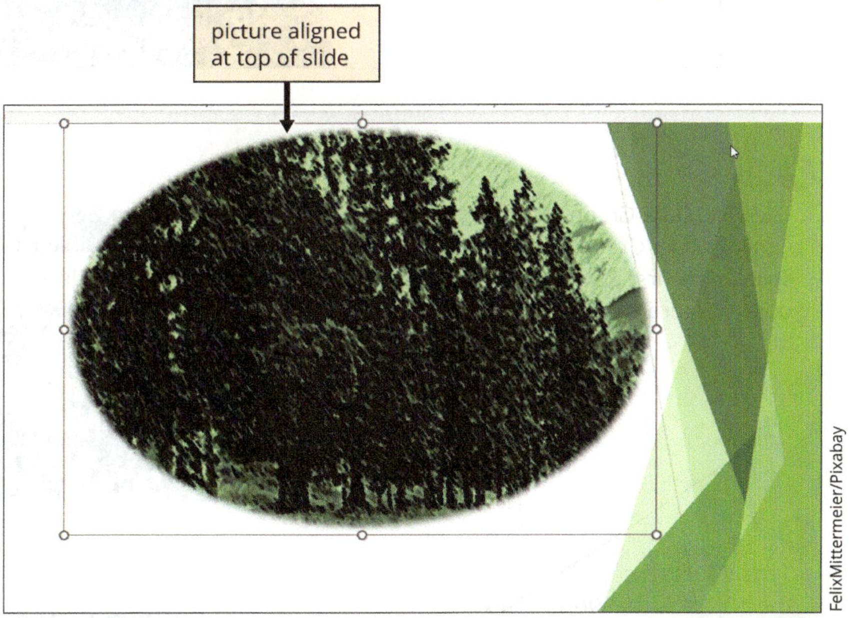

Figure 3-66

Creating and Formatting WordArt

One method of adding appealing visual elements to a presentation is by using **WordArt**, formatted decorative text. This feature is found in other Microsoft 365 applications, including Word and Excel.

This gallery of decorative effects allows you to type new text or convert existing text to WordArt. You then can add elements such as fills, outlines, and effects.

WordArt fill in the interior of a letter can consist of a solid color, texture, picture, or gradient. The WordArt **outline** is the exterior border surrounding each letter or symbol. PowerPoint allows you to change the outline color, weight, and style. You also can add an **effect**, which helps add emphasis or depth to the characters. Some effects are shadows, reflections, glows, bevels, and 3-D rotations.

To Insert WordArt

The title slide needs information to identify the topic of the presentation. **Why?** Audience members will see the woodlands picture, and the text will reinforce the presentation topic. You quickly can add a visual element to the slide by selecting a WordArt style from the WordArt Styles gallery and then applying it to some text. The following steps insert WordArt.

1

- Display the Insert tab and then click the WordArt button (Insert tab | Text group) to display the WordArt gallery (Figure 3–67).

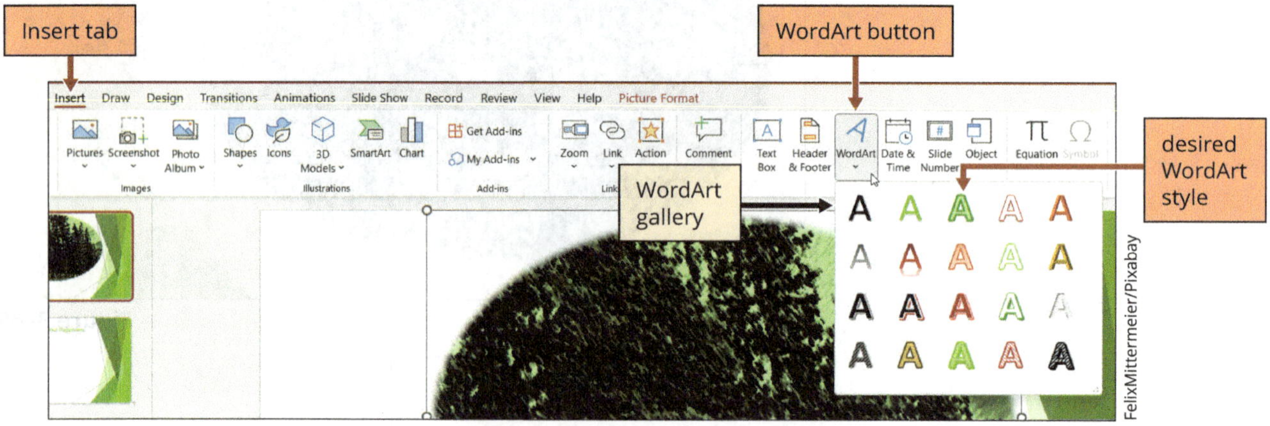

Figure 3–67

2

- Click 'Fill: Dark Green, Accent color 2; Outline: Dark Green, Accent color 2' (third style in the first row) to insert the WordArt object (Figure 3–68).

Figure 3–68

3

- Type **Wellness in the Woods** in the object as the WordArt text (Figure 3–69).

Q&A Why did the Shape Format tab appear automatically in the ribbon?
It appears when you select text to which you could add a WordArt style or other effect.

Figure 3–69

To Change the WordArt Shape

PowerPoint provides a variety of graphical shapes that add interest to WordArt text. The following steps change the Transform effect of the WordArt shape to 'Double Wave: Down-Up'. **Why?** The text provides the presentation's subject, and you want to emphasize the serene topic further by changing the WordArt shape.

1

- With the WordArt object still selected, click the Text Effects button (Shape Format tab | WordArt Styles group) to display the Text Effects menu (Figure 3–70).

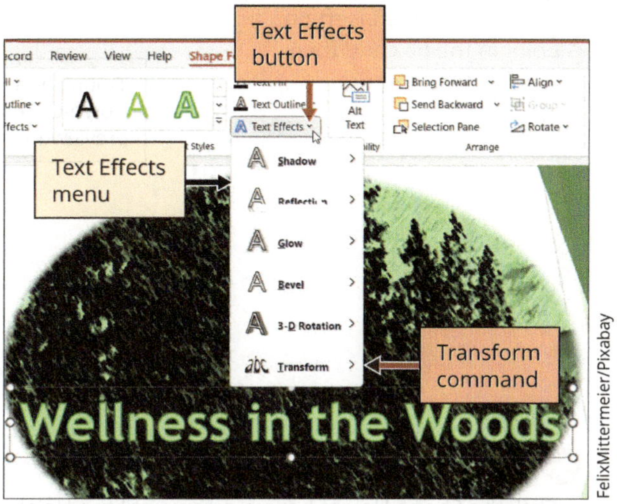

Figure 3–70

2

- Point to Transform in the Text Effects menu to display the WordArt Transform gallery (Figure 3–71).

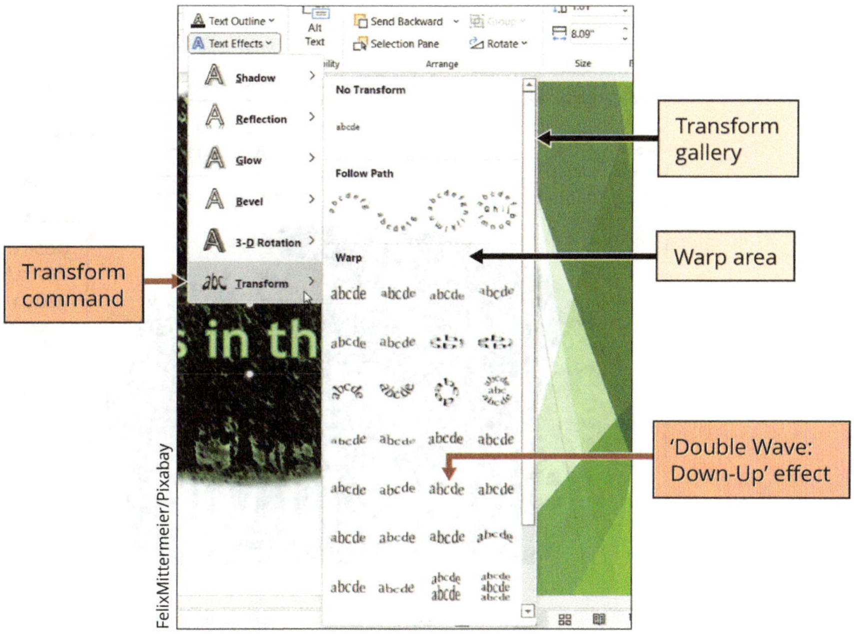

Figure 3–71

3

- Point to the 'Double Wave: Down-Up' effect in the Warp area (third effect in the fifth row in the Warp area) to display a live preview of that text effect applied to the WordArt object (Figure 3–72).
- **Experiment:** Point to various effects in the Transform gallery and watch the format of the text and borders change.

Q&A How can I see the preview of a Transform effect if the gallery overlays the WordArt letters?
Move the WordArt box to the left or right side of the slide and then repeat Steps 1 and 2.

4

- Click the 'Double Wave: Down-Up' effect to apply this text effect to the WordArt object.

Q&A Can I change the effect I applied to the WordArt?
Yes. Position the insertion point in the box and then repeat Steps 1 and 2.

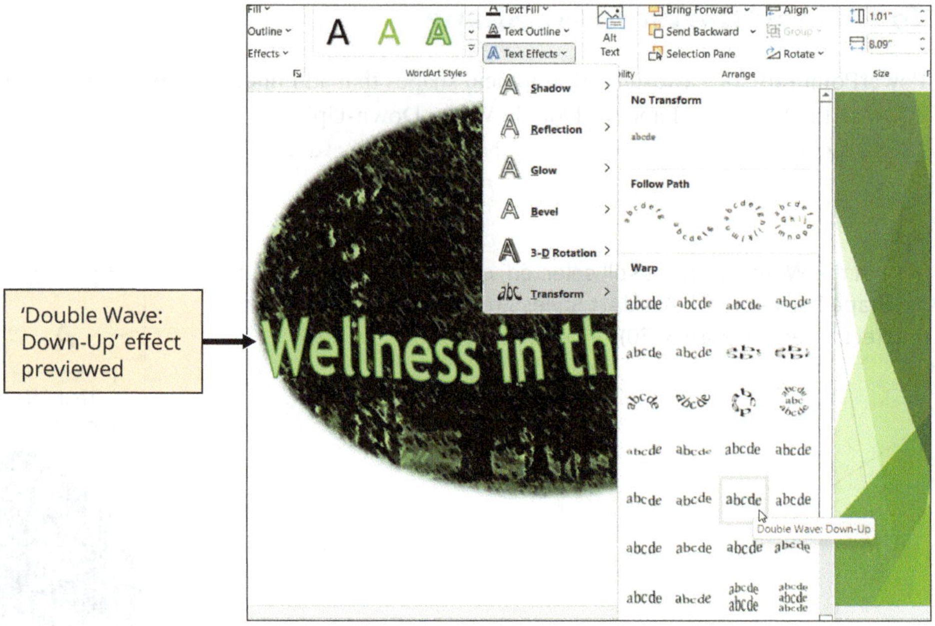

FelixMittermeier/Pixabay

Figure 3–72

5

- Click the Shape Height box up arrow until the Height measurement is 1.5".
- Click the Shape Width box up arrow until the Width measurement is 10" (Figure 3–73).

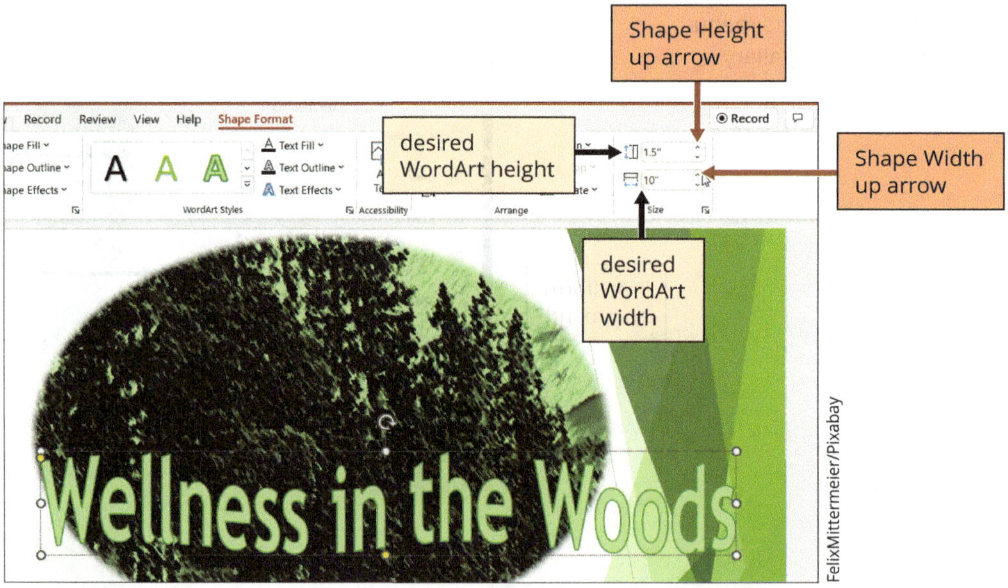

FelixMittermeier/Pixabay

Figure 3–73

6

- Use the smart guides to position the WordArt as shown in Figure 3–74.

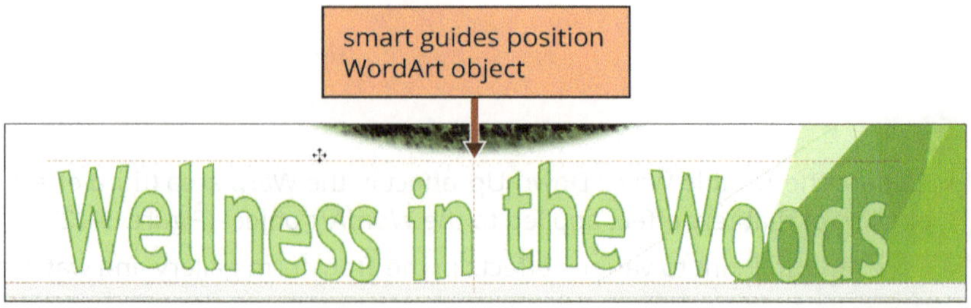

FelixMittermeier/Pixabay

Figure 3–74

To Change the WordArt 3-D Rotation Effect

The following steps change the WordArt 3-D rotation effect. **Why?** The 3-D effect is a subtle visual element that enhances the slide feature.

1

- With the WordArt object still selected, display the Text Effects menu.
- Point to 3-D Rotation to display the 3-D Rotation gallery.
- Point to 'Perspective: Relaxed Moderately' (second rotation in the second Perspective row) to display a live preview of this effect (Figure 3–75).

◦ **Experiment:** Point to various rotations in the gallery and watch the WordArt change.

2

- Click 'Perspective: Relaxed Moderately' to apply this rotation to the WordArt.

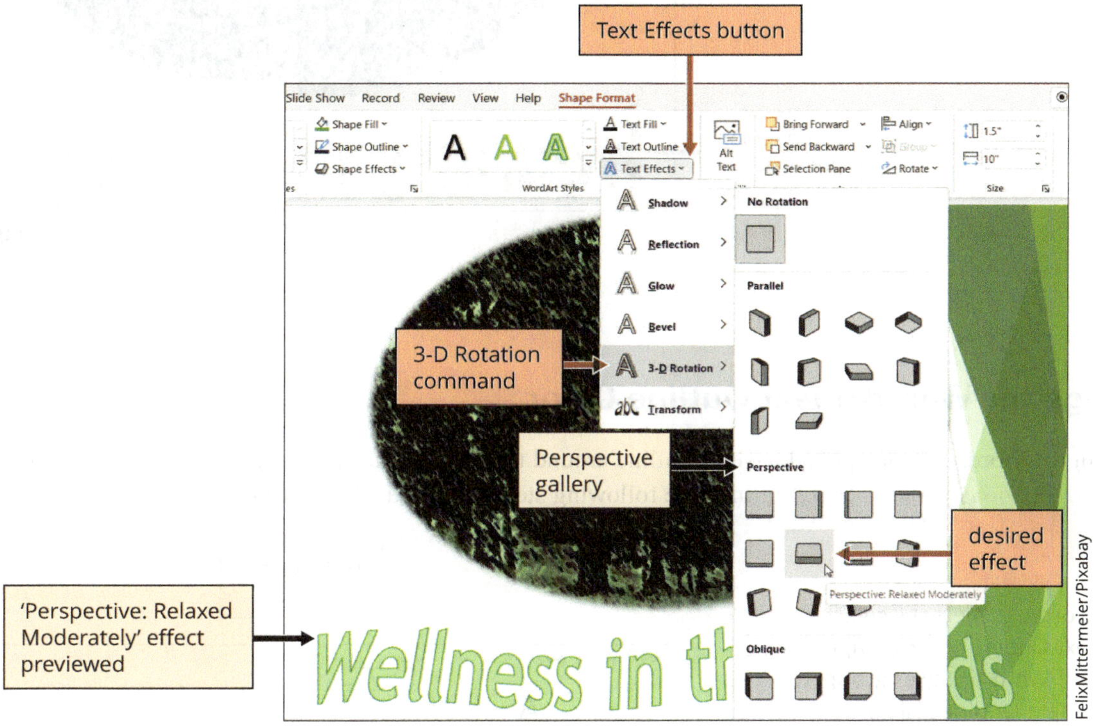

Figure 3–75

To Change the WordArt Text Fill Color

The Facet theme determines the available WordArt fill colors. You can change the default WordArt colors to give the characters a unique look. **Why?** The green fill coordinates well with the Facet background colors. The following steps change the WordArt text fill color.

1

- With the WordArt object selected, click the Text Fill arrow (Shape Format tab | WordArt Styles group) to display the Text Fill gallery.
- Point to 'Brown, Accent 6' (last color in the first Theme Colors row) to display a live preview of that color applied to the WordArt object (Figure 3–76).
- **Experiment:** Point to various colors and watch the fill color change.

2

- Click 'Brown, Accent 6' to apply this color as the fill for the WordArt object.

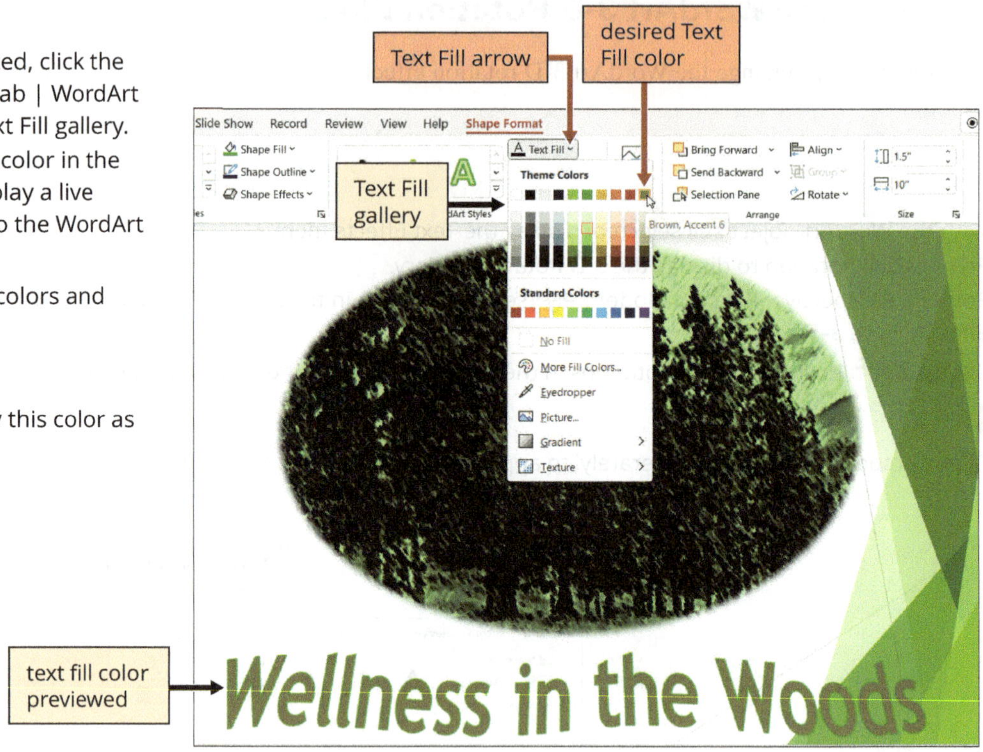

Figure 3–76

To Change the WordArt Text Outline Color

The letters in the WordArt style applied have an outline around the edges. You can change the color of the outline. **Why?** You used this color previously for the chart outline. The following steps change the WordArt outline color.

1

- With the WordArt object still selected, click the Text Outline arrow (Shape Format tab | WordArt Styles group) to display the Text Outline gallery.
- Point to Dark Blue (ninth color in the Standard Colors row) to display a live preview of that color applied to the WordArt outline (Figure 3–77).
- **Experiment:** Point to various colors and watch the outline color change.

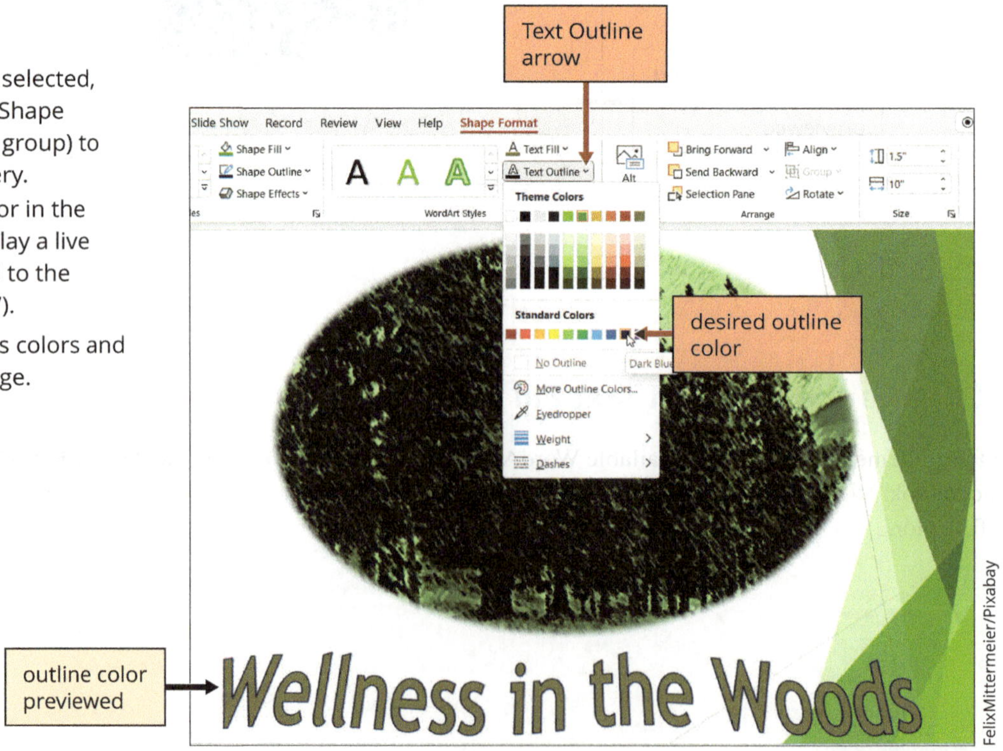

Figure 3–77

2

- Click Dark Blue to apply this color to the WordArt outline.

Q&A Can I change the outline line width?
Yes. Click the Text Outline button, point to Weight, and then click the desired line weight.

Must my text have an outline?
No. To remove the outline, click No Outline in the Text Outline gallery.

To Convert Text to WordArt

You wish to convert the title text letters on Slide 2 to WordArt. **Why?** WordArt can enhance the visual appeal of the slide. The following steps convert the title text of Slide 2 to WordArt.

1

- Display Slide 2 and then select the title text (Plant a Tree for Health and Happiness) (Figure 3–78).

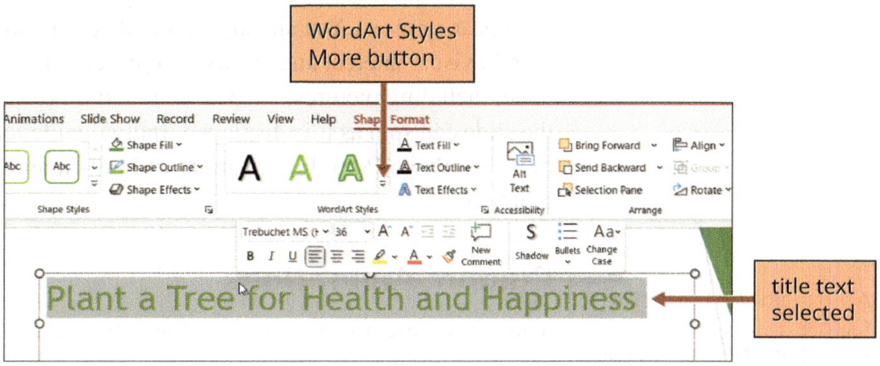

Figure 3–78

2

- If necessary, display the Shape Format tab and then click the WordArt Styles More button (Shape Format tab | WordArt Styles group) (shown in Figure 3–78) to display the WordArt Styles gallery.
- Point to 'Fill: Dark Green, Accent color 2; Outline: Dark Green, Accent color 2' (third color in the first row) to display a live preview of that style applied to the title text (Figure 3–79).

- **Experiment:** Point to various styles and watch the text change.

Figure 3–79

3

- Click 'Fill: Dark Green, Accent color 2; Outline: Dark Green, Accent color 2' to apply this style to the title text.

To Resize WordArt Proportionally

The WordArt object can be stretched, shrunk, or resized in two ways: using the sizing handles or changing the Size options on the Shape Format tab. To maintain the height and width proportions, press and hold SHIFT when dragging a sizing handle. Similarly, if you want to keep the proportions and also keep the center in the same location, press and hold both CTRL and SHIFT while dragging the sizing handle. On Slide 2, you want to resize the WordArt object proportionally. **Why?** Moving the WordArt above the bulleted list allows extra space on the slide for the video you insert later in this module. The following step resizes the WordArt proportionally.

1

- With the WordArt object still selected, press and hold SHIFT and then drag the middle sizing handle on the right side of the box inward, as shown in Figure 3–80.

Q&A Does resizing change the WordArt font size?
No. Resizing a WordArt object only resizes the box the WordArt is in. If you want to resize the WordArt characters, you would select the text and then change the font size on the Home tab of the ribbon.

Figure 3–80

Animating Slide Content

Animation includes special effects applied to text or other objects that make the object appear, disappear, or move. You already are familiar with one form of animation: transitions between slides. To add visual interest and clarity to a presentation, you can animate various parts of an individual slide, including pictures, shapes, text, and other slide elements. For example, each paragraph on the slide can spin as it is displayed. Individual letters and shapes also can spin or move in various motions. PowerPoint has a variety of built-in animations that will fade, wipe, or fly-in text and graphics.

BTW
Animation Effect Icon Colors
Animation effects allow you to control how objects enter, move on, and exit slides. Using a traffic signal analogy may help you remember the sequence of events. Green icons indicate when the animation effect starts on the slide. Yellow icons represent the object's motion; use them with caution so they do not distract from the message you are conveying to your audience. Red icons indicate when the object stops appearing on a slide.

Custom Animations

You can create a **custom animation** to meet your unique needs. Custom animation effects are grouped into categories: entrance, exit, emphasis, and motion paths. An **entrance effect**, as the name implies, determines how slide elements first appear on a slide. An **exit effect** works in the opposite manner: It determines how slide elements disappear. An **emphasis effect** modifies text and objects displayed on the screen. For example, letters may darken or increase in font size. The entrance, exit, and emphasis animations are grouped into categories: Basic, Subtle, Moderate, and Exciting. You can set the animation speed to Very Fast, Fast, Medium, Slow, or Very Slow.

Slide 2 has two elements with text: the WordArt title and the content placeholder with four bulleted paragraphs. When the slide is displayed, the audience will see the WordArt enter from the top of the slide. Then, the four paragraphs will display simultaneously. In the following steps, you will perform these tasks:

1. Apply an entrance effect to the WordArt.
2. Change the WordArt direction.
3. Change the animation start option.
4. Preview the animation sequence.
5. Modify the entrance timing.
6. Animate text paragraphs.
7. Change the animation sequence.

To Animate an Object Using an Entrance Effect

The WordArt will enter the slide from the top when you display this slide. **Why?** The graphic is positioned above the bulleted paragraphs, so you want it to enter and then move into this location. Entrance effects are colored green in the Animation gallery. The following step applies an entrance effect to the WordArt in Slide 2.

1

- With the WordArt on Slide 2 still selected, click Animations on the ribbon to display the Animations tab.
- Click the Float In animation in the Animation gallery (Animations tab | Animation group) to display a live preview of this animation and to apply this entrance animation to the WordArt object (Figure 3–81).

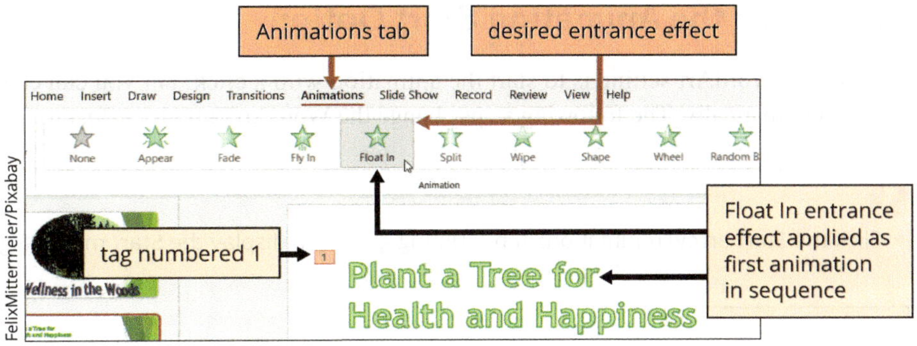

Figure 3–81

Q&A Are more entrance animations available?

Yes. Click More in the Animation gallery to see additional animations. You can select one of the entrance animations that are displayed, or you can click the 'More Entrance Effects' command to expand the selection. You can click any animation to see a preview of the effect.

Why does the number 1 appear in a box on the left side of the WordArt?

The 1 is a sequence number and indicates Float In is the first animation that will appear on the slide when you click the slide.

To Change Animation Direction

You can modify an animation's direction and specify that it enters from another side or from a corner. The following steps change the WordArt entrance animation to enter from the top. **Why?** By default, the WordArt appears on the slide by entering from the bottom edge, and you want it to enter from the top.

1

- Click the Effect Options button (Animations tab | Animation group) to display the Direction gallery (Figure 3–82).

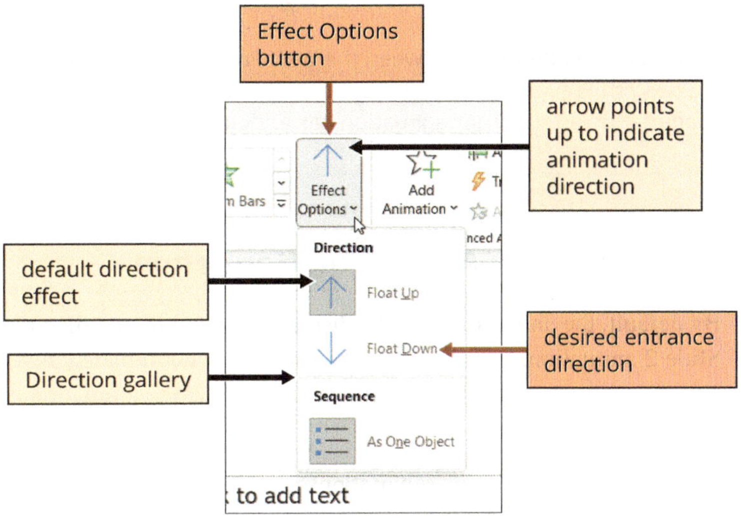

Figure 3–82

Q&A Why does a box appear around the Float Up arrow?

Float Up is the default entrance direction applied to the animation.

2

- Click the Float Down arrow to see a preview of this animation and apply this direction to the entrance animation (Figure 3–83).

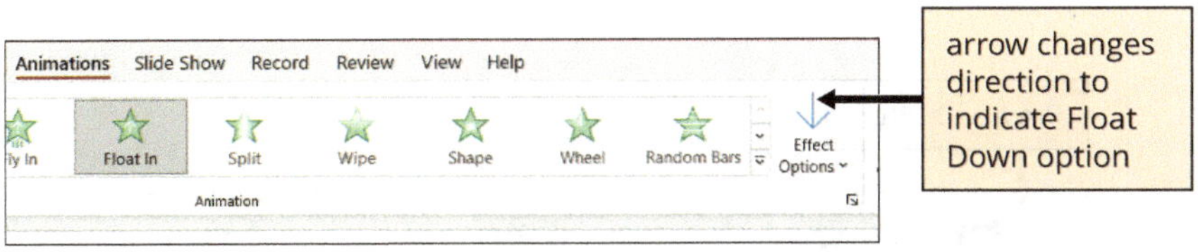

Figure 3–83

Q&A Can I change an entrance effect?

Yes. Repeat Step 1 to select another direction if several effects are available.

How can I delete an animation effect?

Click the number associated with the animation you wish to delete and then press DELETE.

To Change the Animation Start Option

The default WordArt setting is to start the animation with a click, but you can change this setting so that the entrance effect occurs automatically. The following steps change the WordArt entrance effect to automatic. **Why?** You want the slide title text animation to display when the slide is displayed.

1

- Click the Start arrow (Animations tab | Timing group) to display the Start menu (Figure 3–84).

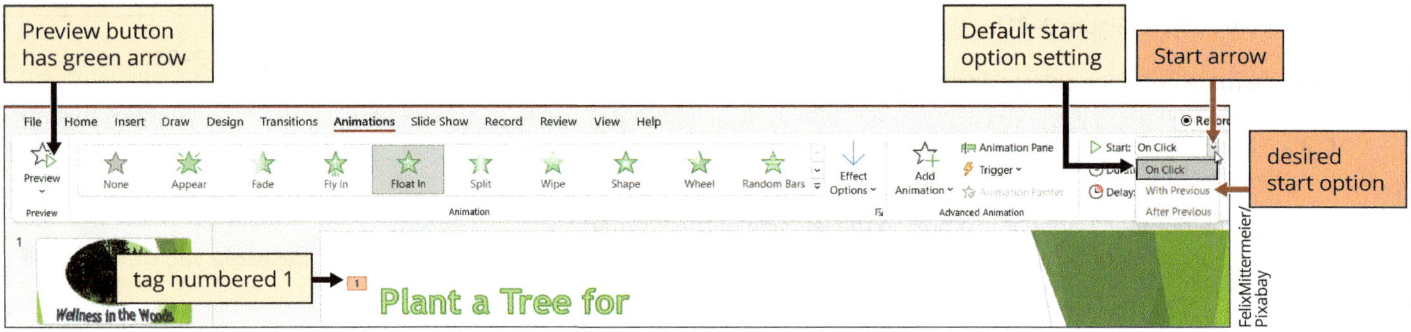

Figure 3–84

2

- Click With Previous to change the start option.

Q&A Why did the numbered tag change from 1 to 0?
The animation now occurs automatically without a click.

What is the difference between the With Previous and After Previous settings?
The With Previous setting starts the effect simultaneously with any prior animation; the After Previous setting starts the animation after a prior animation has ended.

To Preview an Animation Sequence

By default, the animations will be displayed when you run the presentation and click the slide. The following step previews the Slide 2 animation. **Why?** Although you have not completed developing the presentation, you should view the animation you have added to check for continuity and verify that the animation is displaying as you expected.

1

- Click the Preview button (Animations tab | Preview group) to view the Slide 2 animation (Figure 3–85).

Q&A Why does a red square appear in the middle of the Preview button when I click that button?
The red square indicates the animation sequence is in progress. Ordinarily, a green arrow is displayed in the button.

Figure 3–85

To Change the Animation Duration

The entrance animation effect is displayed quickly. To create a dramatic effect, you can change this setting so that the entrance effect occurs slowly during a specified number of seconds. The following step modifies the duration setting for the entrance animation. **Why?** You want the slide title text to move down from the top of the slide slowly.

1

- Click the Duration up arrow (Animations tab | Timing group) several times to increase the time from 01.00 second to 02.00 seconds (Figure 3-86).
- Click the Preview button to view the animation.

Figure 3-86

Q&A What is the difference between the duration time and the delay time?
The duration time is the length of time in which the animation occurs; the delay time is the length of time that passes before the animation begins.

Can I type the speed in the Duration box instead of clicking the arrow to adjust the speed?
Yes. Typing the numbers allows you to set precise timing.

To Animate Text

You can animate the four bulleted paragraphs in the left Slide 2 content placeholder. **Why?** For a special effect, you can display each paragraph individually during a presentation rather than have all four paragraphs appear together. The following steps animate the bulleted list paragraphs.

1

- Click any bulleted list text in the Slide 2 left content placeholder to select the placeholder (Figure 3-87).

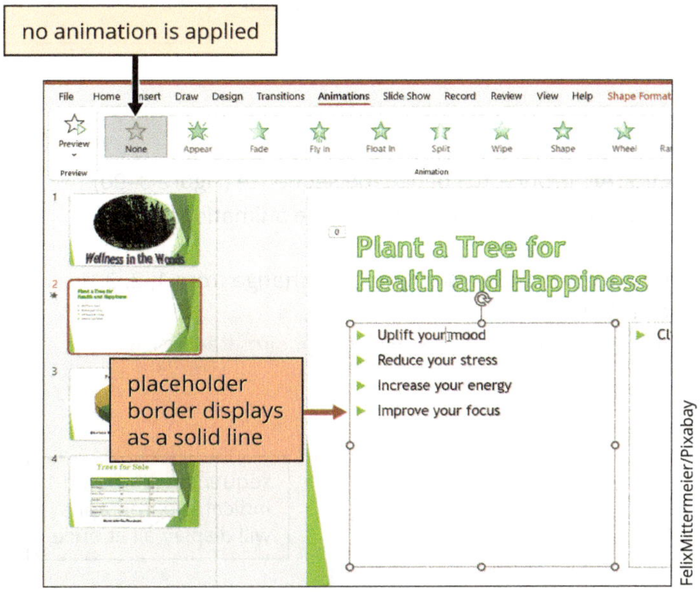

Figure 3-87

2

- Click the Fade entrance effect in the Animation gallery to add and preview this animation.
- Change the Duration time to 02.00 seconds (Figure 3–88).
- Click the Preview button to view the animations.

Figure 3–88

To Change the Animation Sequence Effect Option

By default, each paragraph in the content placeholder enters one at a time in response to a click when you present in Slide Show view. You can modify this entrance sequence setting. **Why?** You want all the paragraphs to enter the slide simultaneously. The following steps change the sequence for the paragraphs to appear all at once.

1

- Click the Effect Options button to display the Effect Options menu (Figure 3–89).

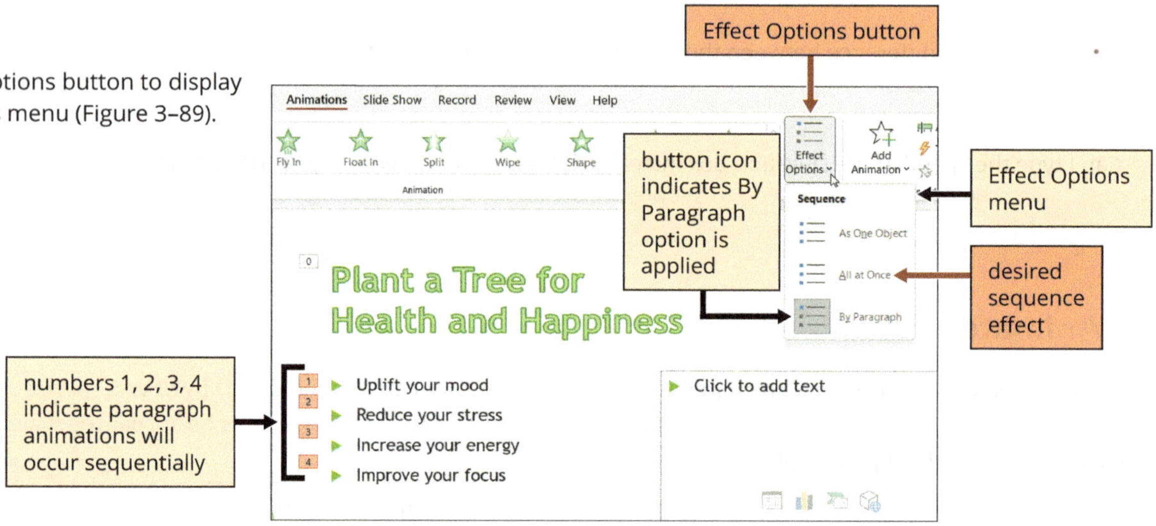

Figure 3–89

2

- Click 'All at Once' to change the sequence (Figure 3–90).
- Click the Preview button to view the animations.

Q&A Why did the numbered tags change from 1, 2, 3, 4 to 1, 1, 1, 1?

All four paragraphs now will appear simultaneously.

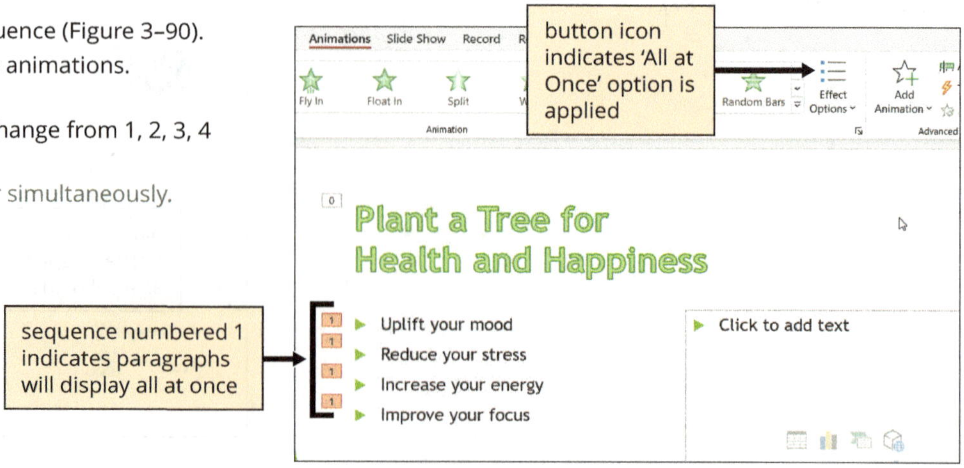

Figure 3–90

Adding Media to Slides

Media files can enrich a presentation if they are used correctly. Video files can be downloaded from the Internet or produced with a camera and editing software. Sound files also can come from the Internet, be stored on your computer, or be an audio track on other media. If you did not create the media files you use in a PowerPoint presentation, ensure you have permission to use them and give the original creators credit for their work.

Once an audio or video clip is inserted into a slide, you can specify options that affect how the file is displayed and played. For example, you can have the video play automatically when the slide is displayed, or you can click the video frame when you are ready to start the playback. You also can have the video fill the entire slide, which is referred to as **full screen**. If you decide to play the slide show automatically and have it display full screen, you can drag the video frame to the gray area off the slide so that it does not display briefly before going to full screen. You can select the 'Loop until Stopped' option to have the video repeat until you click the next slide, or you can choose not to have the video frame display on the slide until you click the slide.

If your video clip has recorded sounds, the volume controls give you the option to set how loudly this audio will play. They also allow you to mute the sound so that your audience will hear no background noise or music.

In the following steps, you will perform these tasks:

1. Insert a video file into Slide 2.
2. Resize and move the clip.
3. Change the clip contrast.
4. Play the video automatically.

BTW

Using Codecs

Video and audio content developers use a codec (compressor/decompressor) to reduce the file size of digital media. The reduced file size helps transfer files across the Internet quickly and smoothly and helps save space on storage media. Your computer can play any compressed file if the specific codec used to compress the file is available on your computer. If the codec is not installed or is not recognized, your computer attempts to download this file from the Internet. Many codec files are available to download from the Internet at no cost.

To Insert a Video File

When you run your slide show, you want to show a video clip in the Slide 2 content placeholder of trees along a path in a forest. **Why?** This clip emphasizes the tranquil experience of walking along the Nature Center's trails. PowerPoint allows you to insert this clip into your slide in the same manner that you insert a picture in a content placeholder. The following steps insert this video clip into Slide 2.

1

- With Slide 2 still displayed, click the Insert Video icon in the right content placeholder to display the Insert Video dialog box.
- Navigate to the location where your Data Files are located.
- Click Support_PPT_3_Forest.mp4 to select the file (Figure 3–91).

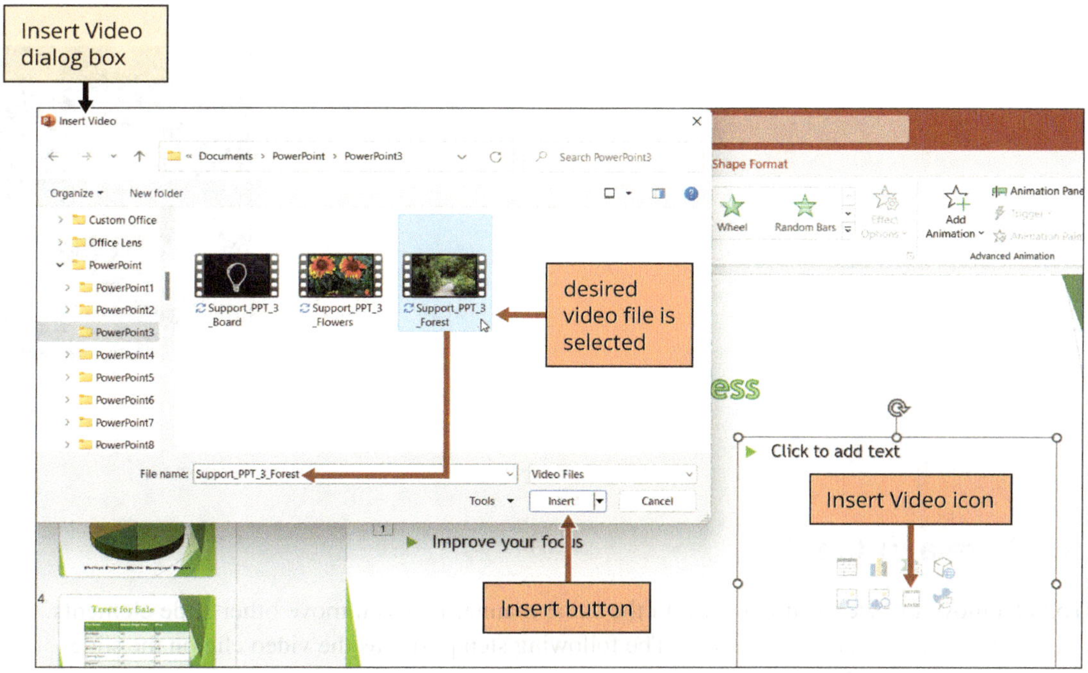

Figure 3–91

2

- Click the Insert button (Insert Video dialog box) to insert the video clip into Slide 2 (Figure 3–92).
- If the Design Ideas pane opens, close it.

Q&A Can I adjust the color of a video clip?
Yes. You can correct the brightness and contrast, and you also can recolor a video clip using the same methods you learned in this module to color a picture. You will adjust the contrast and brightness later in this module.

3

- Click the Play/Pause button to review the video clip.

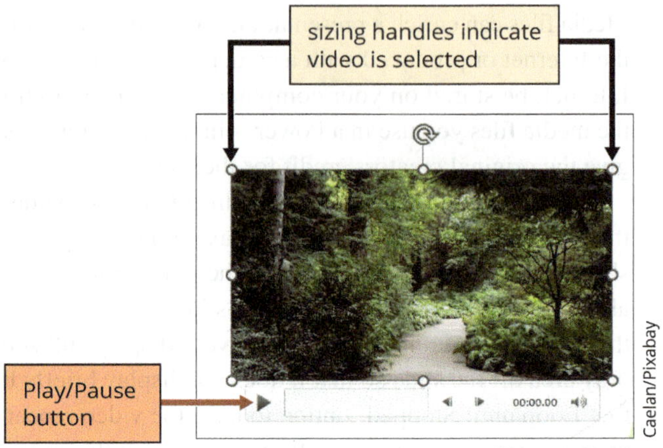

Figure 3–92

To Resize a Video Clip

You can change the dimensions of the video clip in the same manner that you adjust the size of a picture. **Why?** You have sufficient space on the slide to resize the video clip. The following step adjusts the video clip size.

1

- With the Video Format tab displayed, click the Size Dialog Box Launcher in the Video Format | Size group and make sure the Lock aspect ratio box is unchecked in the Format Video pane.
- Click the Video Height up arrow several times until the height is approximately 5".
- Click the Video Width down arrow several times until the width is approximately 7.5" (Figure 3–93).

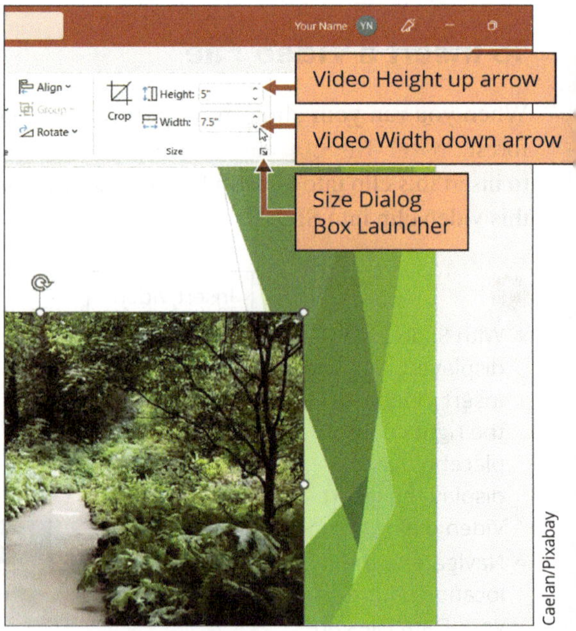

Figure 3–93

To Move a Video Clip

You can move the video clip upward in the same manner that you move other slide elements. **Why?** The video clip size is balanced with the content placeholder. The following step positions the video clip on the slide.

1 Use the smart guides to position the video clip, as shown in Figure 3–94.

Figure 3–94

To Change Video Contrast

PowerPoint provides the ability to correct a video by changing the brightness and contrast. The following steps increase the video clip brightness and contrast. **Why?** The video clip you inserted is dark, so you want to apply these corrections to help viewers see the clip clearly.

1

- With the video clip selected, click the Corrections button (Video Format tab | Adjust group) to display the Brightness/Contrast gallery (Figure 3–95).

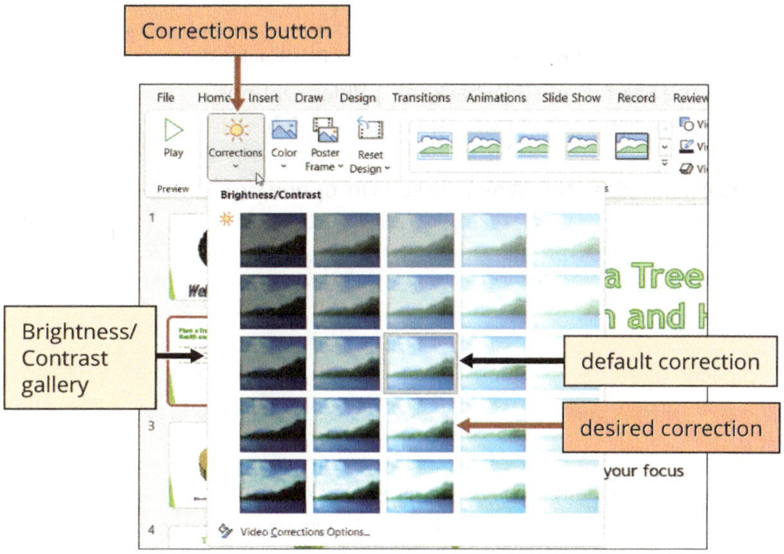

Figure 3–95

2

- Point to 'Brightness: 0% (Normal) Contrast: +20%' (third thumbnail in the fourth row) to display a preview of this correction on the clip (Figure 3–96).

Q&A Why does the gray box display in the center of the gallery?
That setting is the default brightness/contrast setting of 'Brightness: 0% (Normal) Contrast: 0% (Normal).'

- **Experiment:** Point to various pictures in the Brightness/Contrast area and watch the brightness and contrast change on the video clip.

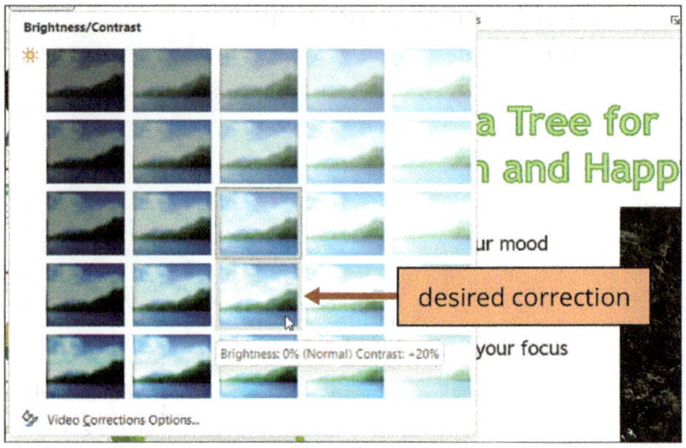

Figure 3–96

3

- Click 'Brightness: 0% (Normal) Contrast: +20%' (third thumbnail in the fourth row) to apply this correction to the video clip.

To Play a Video File Automatically

Once the video clip is inserted, you can specify that the video plays automatically when the slide is displayed. **Why?** When you are giving your presentation, you do not want to click the mouse to start the video. The following steps play the video file automatically.

1

- With the video clip selected, display the Playback tab.
- Click the Start arrow (Playback tab | Video Options group) to display the Start menu (Figure 3–97).

Q&A What does the 'When Clicked On' option do?
The video clip would begin playing when the presenter clicks the video frame during the slide show.

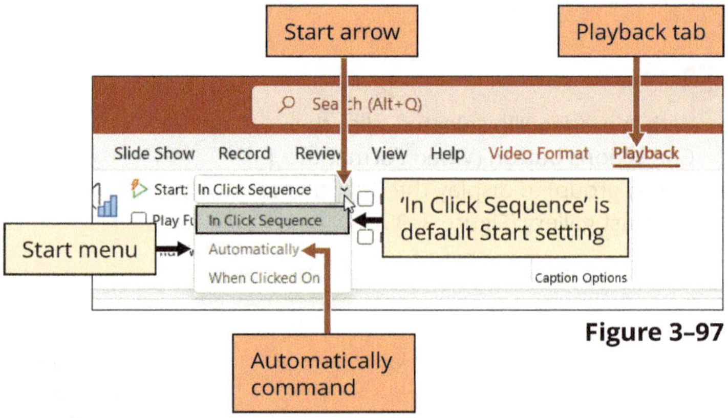

Figure 3–97

2

- Click Automatically to have the video clip play automatically when the slide is displayed.
- Click the Play button (Playback tab | Preview group) to preview the video (Figure 3–98).

Q&A Why did the Play button change to Pause when the video was playing?
The button changes to allow you to stop the preview if desired.

BTW
Restricting Permissions
You can allow PowerPoint users to see your presentation but not allow them to change the slide content, copy the slides, or print the presentation. To protect your presentation, click File on the ribbon to open Backstage view, display the Info tab, click Protect Presentation, and then click Always Open Read-Only.

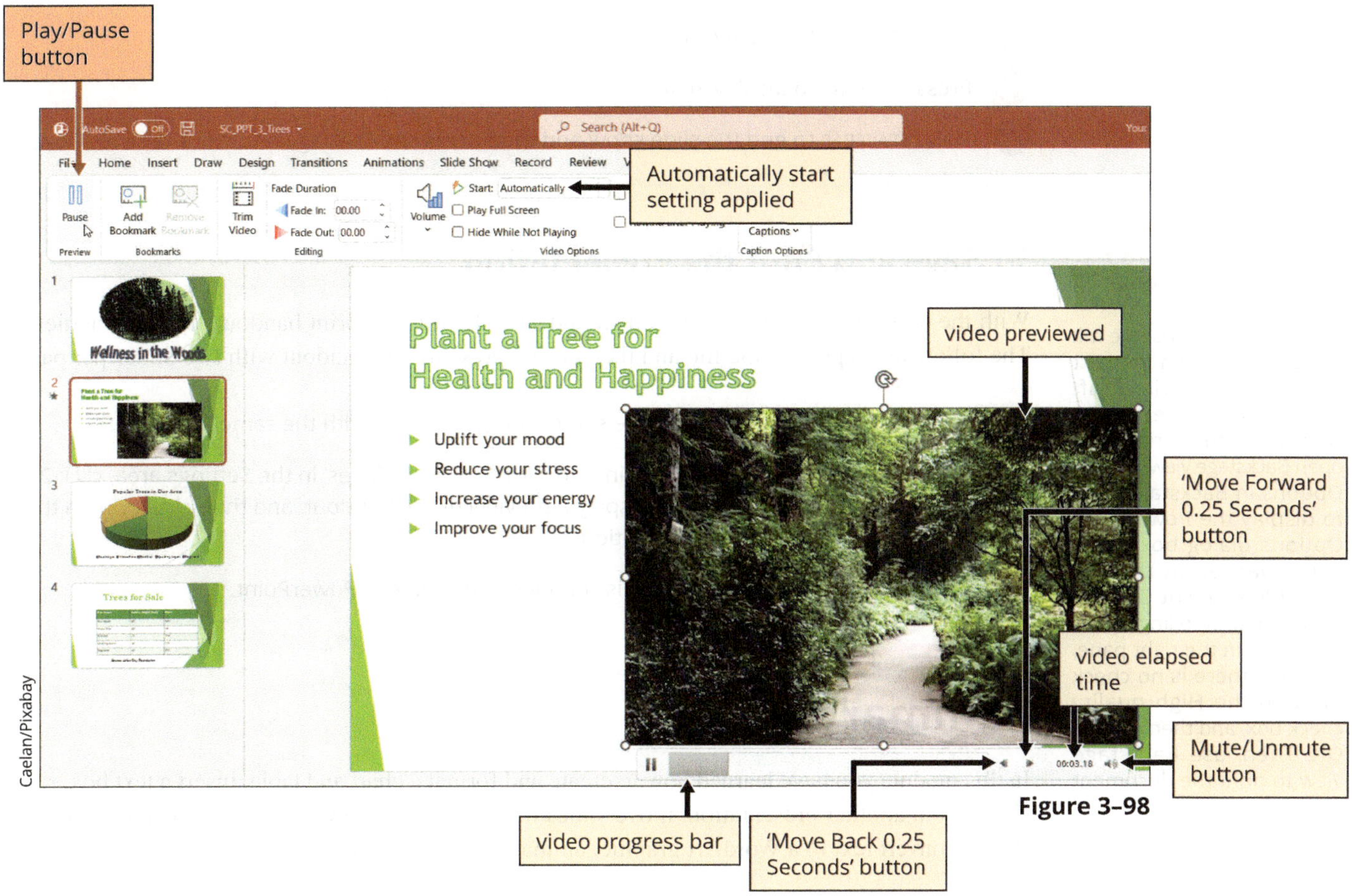

Figure 3–98

To Add a Transition between Slides

A final enhancement you will make in this presentation is to apply the Wind transition in the Exciting category to all slides and change the transition duration to 3.00. The following steps apply this transition to the presentation.

1. Apply the Wind transition in the Exciting category (Transitions tab | Transition to This Slide group) to all four slides in the presentation.
2. Change the transition duration from 02.00 to 03.00 for all slides.

To Run a Slide Show with Animations and Video

All changes are complete, so you now can view the Trees presentation. The following steps start Slide Show view.

1. Display Slide 1 and then click the Slide Show button on the status bar to begin the presentation.
2. Press SPACEBAR to display Slide 2. Watch the WordArt appear. Press SPACEBAR to view the four bulleted paragraphs and watch the video clip.

BTW
Printing Document Properties
PowerPoint does not allow you to print document properties. This feature, however, is available in Microsoft 365 Word.

BTW
Distributing a Document
Instead of printing and distributing a hard copy of PowerPoint slides, you can distribute the slides electronically. Options include sending the slides via email; posting it on cloud storage (such as OneDrive) and sharing the link with others; posting it on social media, a blog, or other website; and sharing a link associated with an online location of the slides. You also can create and share a PDF or XPS image of the slides, so that users can view the file in Acrobat Reader or XPS Viewer instead of in PowerPoint.

3. Press SPACEBAR to display Slide 3.
4. Press SPACEBAR to display Slide 4.
5. Press SPACEBAR to end the slide show and then press SPACEBAR again to exit the slide show.

BTW
Conserving Ink and Toner
If you want to conserve ink or toner, you can instruct PowerPoint to print draft quality documents by clicking File on the ribbon to open Backstage view, clicking Options in Backstage view to display the PowerPoint Options dialog box, clicking Advanced in the left pane (PowerPoint Options dialog box), scrolling to the Print area in the right pane, verifying there is no check mark in the High quality check box, and then clicking OK. Then, use Backstage view to print the document as usual.

To Save and Print the Presentation

With the presentation completed, you should save the file and print handouts for your audience. The following steps save the file and then print a presentation handout with two slides per page.

1. Save the presentation again in the same storage location with the same file name.
2. Open Backstage view, click the Print tab, click 'Full Page Slides' in the Settings area, click 2 Slides in the Handouts area to display a preview of the handout, and then click Print in the Print gallery to print the presentation.
3. sam↑ Because the project now is complete, you can exit PowerPoint.

Summary

In this module you have learned how to create and format a chart and table, insert a text box, reuse slides from another presentation, move slides in Slide Sorter view, crop a picture and then apply styles, convert text to a WordArt graphic, animate an object and text, and insert a video.

Consider This: Plan Ahead

What decisions will you need to make when creating your next presentation?

Use these guidelines as you complete the assignments in this module and create your own slide show decks outside of this class.

1. Audiences recall visual concepts more quickly and accurately than text alone, so consider using graphics in your presentation.
    a) Decide the precise message you want to convey to your audience.
    b) Determine if a chart or table is the better method of presenting the information.
2. Choose an appropriate chart or table.
    a) Charts are excellent visuals to show relationships between groups of data, especially numbers.
    b) Tables are effective for organizing information in a grid.
    c) Decide which chart or table type best conveys the points you are attempting to make in your presentation. PowerPoint provides a wide variety of styles within each category, so determine which one is most effective in showing the relationships.
3. Obtain information for the graphic from credible sources.
    a) Text or numbers should be current and correct.
    b) Verify the sources of the information.
    c) Be certain you have typed the data correctly.
    d) Acknowledge the source of the information on the slide or during your presentation.
4. Choose an appropriate WordArt style.
    a) Determine which style best represents the concept you are attempting to present.
5. Test your visual elements.
    a) Show your slides to several friends or colleagues and ask them to interpret what they see.
    b) Have your test audience summarize the information they perceive on the tables and charts and compare their analyses to what you are attempting to convey.

Student Assignments

Apply Your Knowledge

Reinforce the skills and apply the concepts you learned in this module.

Creating and Formatting a Chart, Table, and WordArt

Note: To complete this assignment, you will be required to use the Data Files. Please contact your instructor for information about accessing the Data Files.

Instructions: Start PowerPoint. Garden club members have scheduled a variety of programs for the next year. They want to encourage community members to attend the events and have asked you to develop slides to publicize the schedule. The annual meeting in January covers budgetary concerns, including sources of revenue. Open the presentation called SC_PPT_3-1.pptx, which is located in the Data Files. You will create a chart and table, format WordArt and a picture, and insert a video to create the presentation shown in Figure 3–99.

Perform the following tasks:

1. On Slide 1 (Figure 3–99a), convert the title text, Garden Club Annual Meeting, to WordArt by applying the 'Pattern Fill: Dark Red, Accent color 1, 50%; Hard Shadow: Dark Red, Accent color 1' WordArt style (third style in the last row). Change the WordArt outline weight to 2¼ pt and the outline color to 'Olive Green, Accent 4' (eighth color in the Theme Colors row). Apply the Square transform text effect (first effect in the first Warp row). Increase the WordArt height to 4".
2. Insert the video with the file name Support_PPT_3_Flowers.mp4 in the Slide 1 content placeholder. Start the video Automatically. Unlock the aspect ratio and then increase the video height to 4.5". Use the smart guides to position the video as shown in Figure 3–99a.
3. Insert a text box under the WordArt and video and then type **Join us at the Fieldhouse on January 15** as the text box text. Change the font to Papyrus and increase the font size to 40 point. Use the smart guides to center the text box near the bottom of the slide, as shown in Figure 3–99a.

   If requested by your instructor, insert a text box on Slide 1 in the lower-right area of the slide and add the name of the first school you attended.
4. On Slide 2 (Figure 3–99b), insert two table rows and then enter the data shown in Table 3–1. Apply the 'Medium Style 2 – Accent 1' table style (second style in the second Medium row). Change the table height to 4" and the width to 9". Align the table in the center of the slide.

   Table 3–1

Date	Topic
February 6	Native Plants
April 2	Woodland Flowers
June 4	Garden Walk
August 6	Beneficial Insects
October 8	Garden Design

5. Convert the title text, Upcoming Programs, to WordArt and then apply the 'Fill: Olive Green, Accent color 5; Outline: White, Background color 1; Hard Shadow: Olive Green, Accent color 5' (third style in the third row) style. Change the WordArt outline weight to 1½ pt and the outline color to Dark Red (first color in the Standard Colors row).
6. Apply the Wave: Down transform text effect (first effect in the fifth Warp row) to the title text and then decrease the width to 7.5".

Continued on next page

7. On Slide 3 (Figure 3–99c), delete the title text placeholder. Insert a Pie chart and change the layout to Doughnut (last layout in the Pie gallery). Insert the data shown in Table 3–2.

Table 3–2: Garden Club YTD Revenue

	YTD Revenue
Membership	$2,700
Donations	$2,200
Rentals	$1,100
Grants	$500

8. Increase the chart height to 7" and the width to 11.5". Increase the chart title text to 40 point and change the font to Papyrus. Increase the legend to 20 point and change the font to Papyrus. Align the chart in the middle and the center of the slide.
9. Insert the picture Support_PPT_3_Dahlias.png. Crop the picture as shown in Figure 3–99c. Make sure the Lock aspect ratio box is checked, change the height to 4", and then use the smart guides to align the picture in the center of the slide.
10. Apply the 'Center Shadow Rectangle' picture style (sixth style in the second row) to the picture and then change the color tone to 'Temperature: 11200 K' (last thumbnail).
11. Apply the Fall Over transition in the Exciting category to all slides and then change the duration to 3.00 seconds.
12. View the presentation and then save the file using the file name, **SC_PPT_3_Garden** and submit the revised presentation in the format specified by your instructor.
13. **Consider This:** In this assignment, you formatted WordArt and a picture. You also changed the table style and formatted the chart. How did these edits enhance the presentation? Does the video clip add interest to the presentation? Why or why not?

Figure 3–99(a): Slide 1

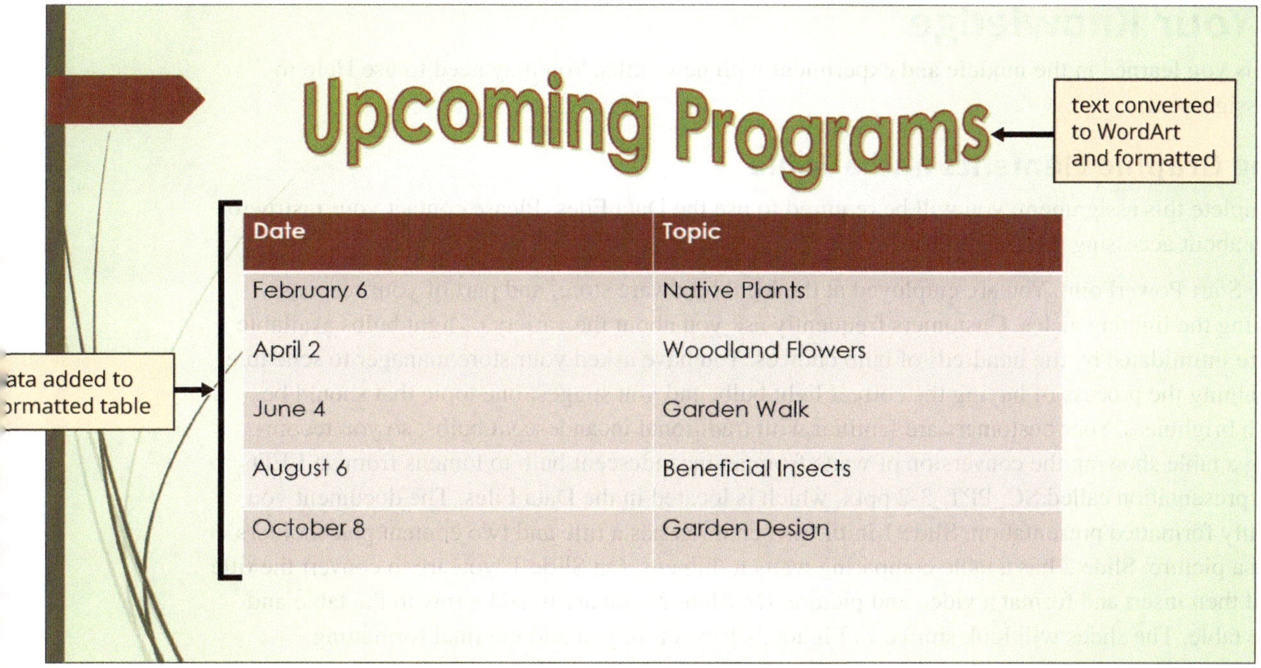

Figure 3–99(b): Slide 2

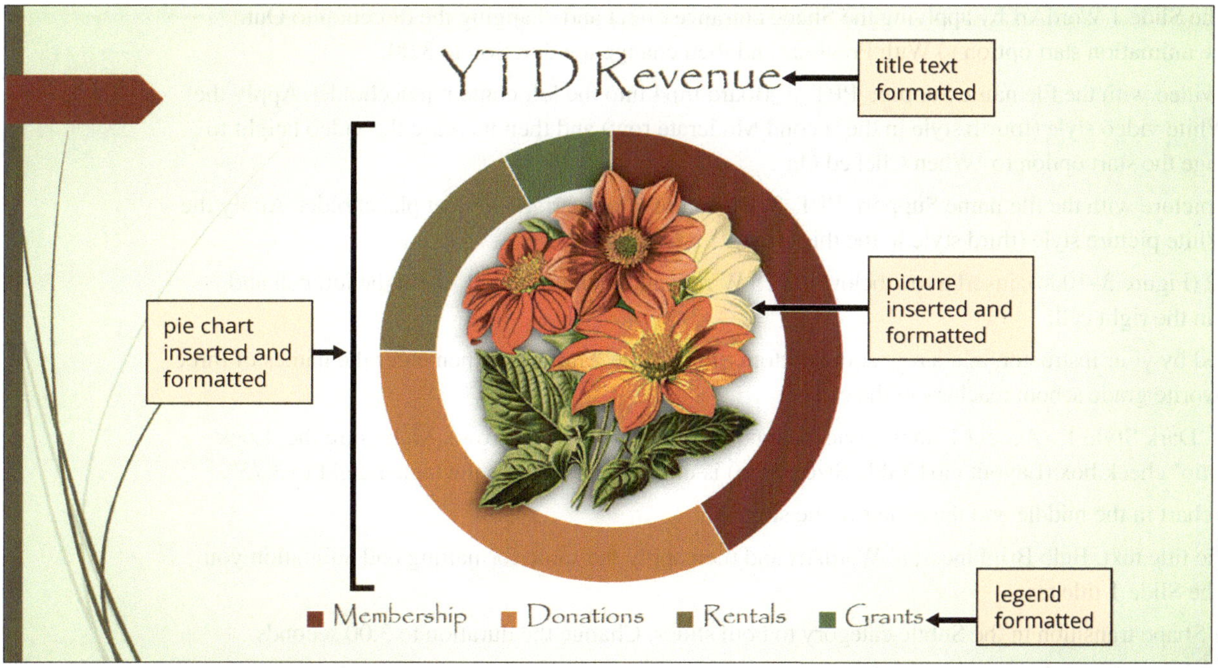

Darkmoon_Art/Pixabay

Figure 3–99(c): Slide 3

Extend Your Knowledge

Extend the skills you learned in the module and experiment with new skills. You may need to use Help to complete the assignment.

Formatting Graphic Elements and a Table

Note: To complete this assignment, you will be required to use the Data Files. Please contact your instructor for information about accessing the Data Files.

Instructions: Start PowerPoint. You are employed at the local hardware store, and part of your responsibilities is stocking the lighting aisles. Customers frequently ask you about the variety of light bulbs available because they are intimidated by the hundreds of bulb choices. You have asked your store manager to schedule a seminar explaining the process of buying the correct light bulb, and you suggest one topic that should be included is bulb brightness. Your customers are familiar with traditional incandescent bulbs, so you recommend including a table showing the conversion of watts from an incandescent bulb to lumens from an LED bulb. Open the presentation called SC_PPT_3-2.pptx, which is located in the Data Files. The document you open is a partially formatted presentation. Slide 1 in the presentation has a title and two content placeholders for a video and a picture. Slide 2 has a table comparing watts to lumens. On Slide 1, you are to convert the title to WordArt and then insert and format a video and picture. On Slide 2, you are to add a row to the table and then format the table. The slides will look similar to Figure 3–100 before you add the final formatting.

Perform the following tasks:

1. On Slide 1 (Figure 3–100a), convert the title text, Buying the Right Light Bulb, to WordArt style 'Fill: White; Outline: Gold, Accent color 1; Glow: Gold, Accent color 1' (fourth style in the second row). Change the text fill color to 'Black, Text 1' (second color in the first Theme Colors row) and then add the 'Glow: 11 point; Gold, Accent color 1' glow text effect (first variation in the third Glow Variations row). Increase the font size to 60 point.
2. Animate the Slide 1 WordArt by applying the Shape entrance effect and changing the direction to Out. Change the animation start option to With Previous and then change the duration to 3.00.
3. Insert the video with the file name Support_PPT_3_Board.mp4 into the left content placeholder. Apply the Rotated White video style (fourth style in the second Moderate row) and then increase the video height to 3.5". Change the start option to 'When Clicked On'.
4. Insert the picture with the file name Support_PPT_3_Bulbs.jpg into the right content placeholder. Apply the Rotated White picture style (third style in the third row).
5. On Slide 2 (Figure 3–100b), insert a row below the 75 W row and then type **100 W** in the left cell and **1500 lm** in the right cell.

   If requested by your instructor, add a row at the bottom of the Slide 2 table and then enter the names of three of your favorite grade school teachers in the cells.
6. Apply the 'Dark Style 1 – Accent 1' table style (second style in the first Dark row). Make sure the 'Lock Aspect Ratio' check box (Layout tab | Table Size group) is unchecked. Change the table height to 3.75".
7. Align the chart in the middle and the center of the slide.
8. Convert the title text, Bulb Brightness, to WordArt and then apply the same formatting and animation you added to the Slide 1 title text.
9. Apply the Shape transition in the Subtle category to both slides. Change the duration to 3.00 seconds.
10. View the presentation and then save the file using the file name, **SC_PPT_3_Bulb** and submit the revised presentation in the format specified by your instructor.
11. **Consider This:** You applied the same formatting and animation to the title text on both slides. You also applied the same style to the picture and video. Does this consistency help or hinder the presentation? Why? In Step 6, you chose a table style in the Dark category. Was this style effective? How did this style improve the slide and increase the audience's attention to the table content?

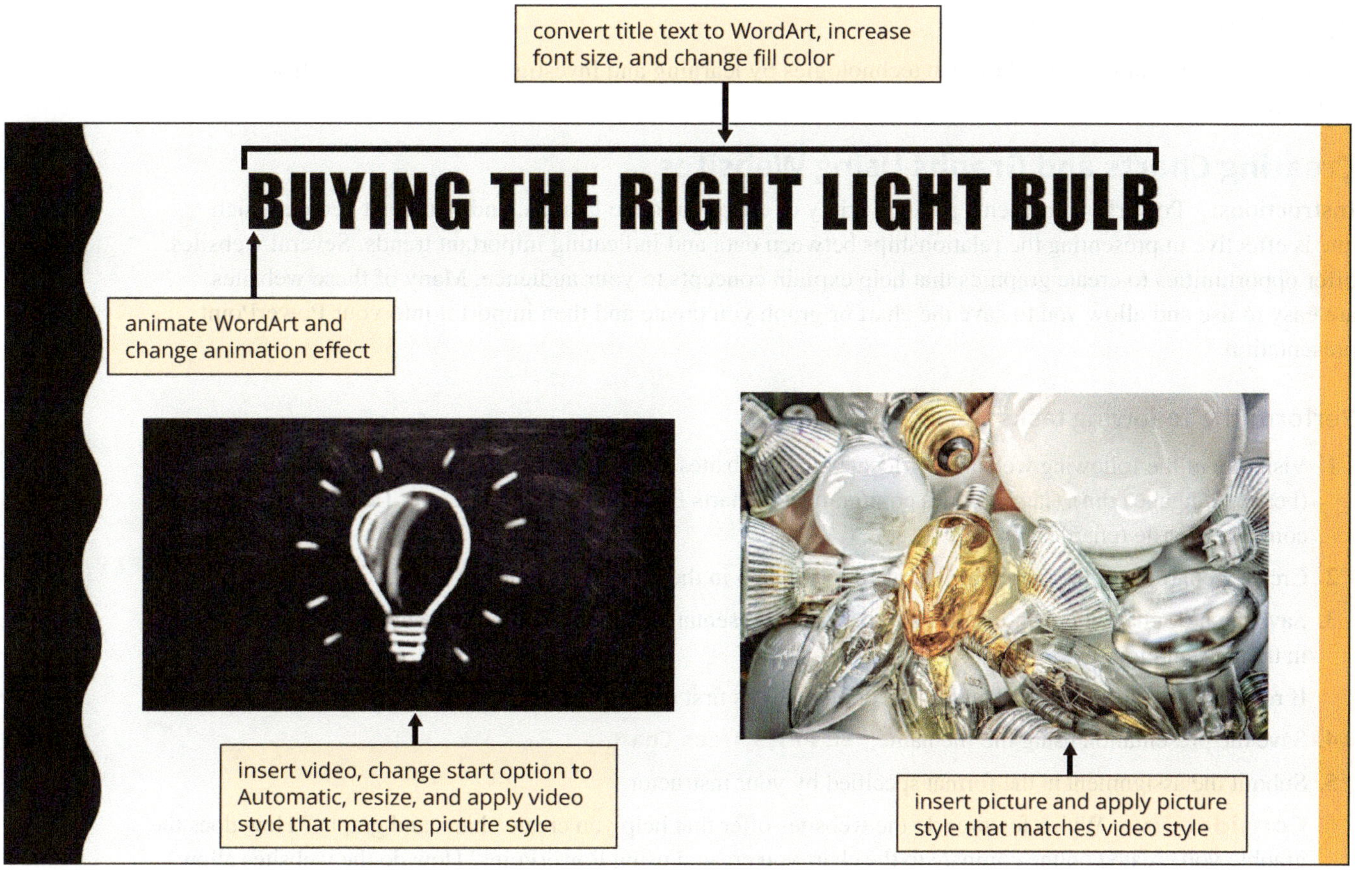

Athree23/Pixabay; Analogicus/Pixabay

Figure 3–100(a): Slide 1

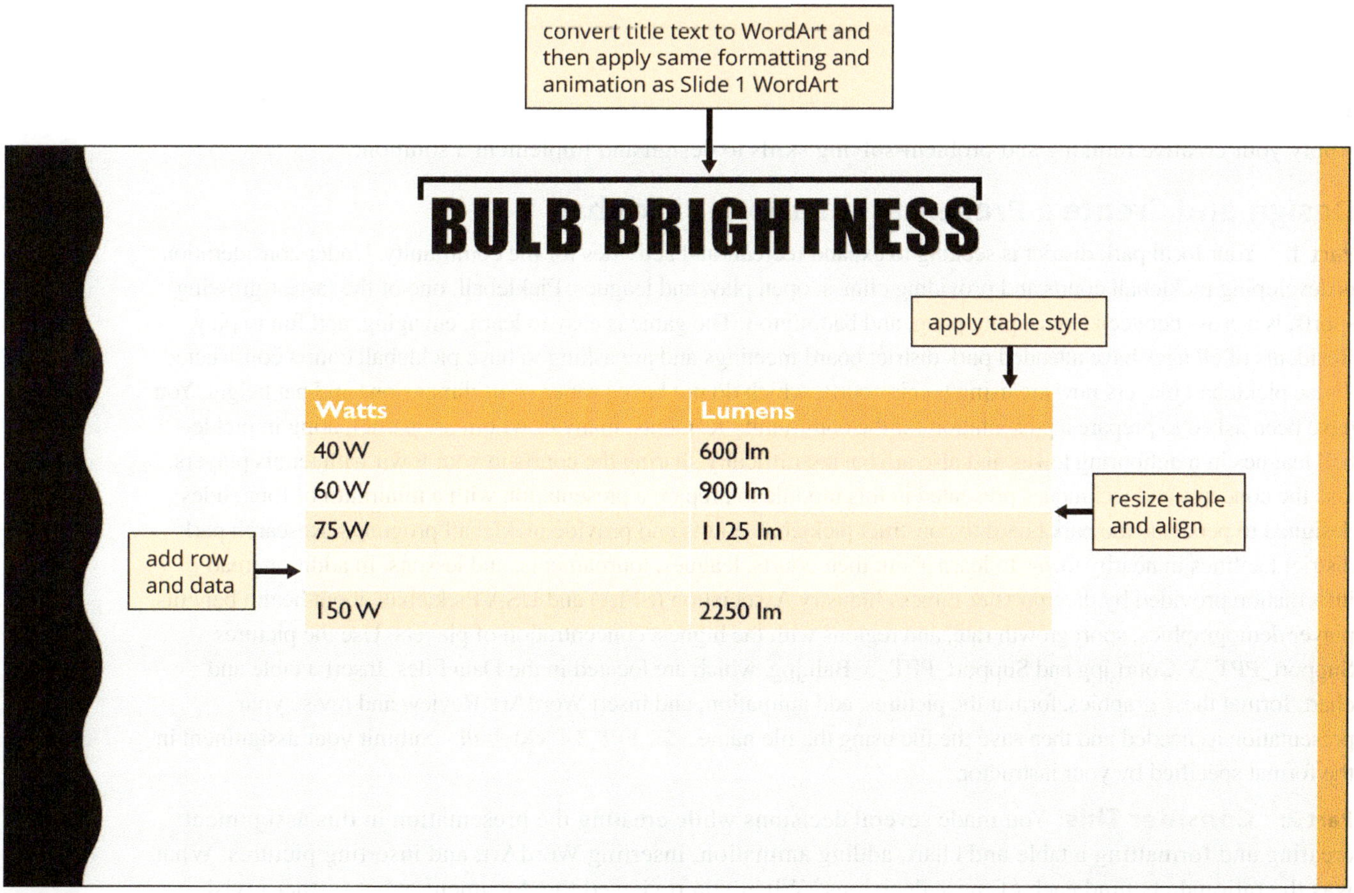

Figure 3–100(b): Slide 2

Expand Your World

Create a solution that uses cloud or web technologies by learning and investigating on your own from general guidance.

Creating Charts and Graphs Using Websites

Instructions: PowerPoint presents a wide variety of chart and table layouts, and you must decide which one is effective in presenting the relationships between data and indicating important trends. Several websites offer opportunities to create graphics that help explain concepts to your audience. Many of these websites are easy to use and allow you to save the chart or graph you create and then import it into your PowerPoint presentation.

Perform the following tasks:

1. Visit one of the following websites, or locate other websites that help you create a chart or graph: Beam (beam.venngage.com), Canva (canva.com/graphs/), Charts Builder (charts.hohli.com), Lucidchart (lucidchart.com), or Chartle (chartle.com).
2. Create a chart using the same data supplied for Slide 3 in the Trees presentation.
3. Save the new chart and then insert it into the Trees presentation as a new Slide 3. Delete the original Slide 3 in the presentation.

   If requested by your instructor, add your grandparent's first name to the chart title.
4. Save the presentation using the file name, **SC_PPT_3_Trees_Chart**.
5. Submit the assignment in the format specified by your instructor.
6. **Consider This:** Which features do the websites offer that help you create charts and graphs? How does the graphic you created online compare to the chart you created using PowerPoint? How do the websites allow you to share your graphics using social networks?

In the Lab

Apply your creative thinking and problem-solving skills to design and implement a solution.

Design and Create a Presentation about Pickleball

Part 1: Your local park district is seeking to expand recreational activities for the community. Under consideration is developing pickleball courts and providing clinics, open play, and leagues. Pickleball, one of the fastest-growing sports, is a cross between tennis, ping pong, and badminton. The game is easy to learn, engaging, and fun to play. Residents of all ages have attended park district board meetings and are asking to have pickleball courts constructed. These pickleball players now are using tennis courts, which do not have proper court dimensions and net height. You have been asked to prepare a presentation for the community residents, many of whom are participating in pickleball leagues in neighboring towns and also are having difficulty sharing the courts in your town with tennis players. Use the concepts and techniques presented in this module to prepare a presentation with a minimum of four slides designed to persuade the park board to construct pickleball courts and provide pickleball programs. Research park district facilities in nearby towns to learn about their courts, leagues, tournaments, and lessons. In addition, read information provided by the Sports & Fitness Industry Association (SFIA) and USA Pickleball about health benefits, player demographics, sport growth rate, and regions with the highest concentration of players. Use the pictures Support_PPT_3_Court.jpg and Support_PPT_3_Ball.jpg, which are located in the Data Files. Insert a table and chart, format these graphics, format the pictures, add animation, and insert WordArt. Review and revise your presentation as needed and then save the file using the file name, **SC_PPT_3_Pickleball**. Submit your assignment in the format specified by your instructor.

Part 2: **Consider This:** You made several decisions while creating the presentation in this assignment: creating and formatting a table and chart, adding animation, inserting WordArt, and inserting pictures. What was the rationale behind each of these decisions? When you reviewed the document, what further revisions did you make and why? Where would you recommend showing this slide show?

Customizing Slide Masters and Presentations

Objectives

After completing this module, you will be able to:

- Apply slide and font themes and effects to a slide master
- Add a placeholder into a slide layout
- Change a slide master background
- Add a background style and graphic to a slide master
- Crop a picture to a shape
- Save a presentation as a template
- Use the Thesaurus
- Change the theme variant
- Change an individual slide background to a pattern, texture, or gradient fill
- Inspect a presentation
- Protect a presentation
- Annotate slides with highlights and a pen and pointer during a slide show
- Rehearse slide timings

Introduction

PowerPoint provides a variety of designs and layouts to meet most presenters' needs. At times, however, you may want a different set of colors, fonts, placeholders, or graphics to display throughout a presentation. PowerPoint allows you to customize the master layouts for slides, handouts, and speaker notes. These masters specify the precise locations and styles of placeholders, pictures, text boxes, and other slide and handout elements.

Once you determine your custom specifications in these masters, you can save the file as a template so that you can reuse these key elements as a starting point for multiple presentations. This unique **template** is a predesigned, preformatted Microsoft 365 file that contains default text formats, themes, placeholder text, headers and footers, and graphics that you can replace with your own information for hundreds of purposes, including budgets, flyers, and resumes; the PowerPoint template files have a slightly different file extension (.potx) than standard application files (.pptx). You use this set of special slides to create and then use similar presentations. A template consists of a general master slide layout that has elements common to all the slide layouts. One efficient way to create similar presentations is to create a template, save the template, open the template, and then save the slides as a different PowerPoint presentation each time a new presentation is required.

Templates help speed and simplify the process of creating a presentation, so many PowerPoint designers create a template for common presentations they develop frequently. Templates can have a variable number of slide layouts depending upon the complexity of the presentation. A simple presentation can have a few slide layouts; for example, the emergency preparedness presentation will have three slide layouts. A more complex template can have many slide masters and layouts.

Project: Presentation with Customized Slides

BTW

Masters Assure Universal Style

Masters are convenient because they allow you to make unique and uniform style changes to every slide in your presentation, including ones added later. Using slide masters saves time because you do not need to format every slide or type the same information repeatedly. You can customize the presentation theme and slide layouts, including the background, color, fonts, effects, and placeholder sizes and location.

In this module's project, you will follow proper design guidelines and learn to use PowerPoint to create the slides shown in Figures 4–1a through 4–1i. The objective is to produce a presentation for customers of the local credit union to inform them of strategies to save money, such as when they are shopping online or at the grocery store, dining out, and using electricity at home. All five slides are created by starting with an overall template, called the **slide master** (Figure 4–1a), that is formatted with a theme, customized title and text fonts, and other objects that appear on all slides in the presentation. The Title Slide Layout (Figure 4–1b) is used to create Slide 1 (Figure 4–1c), which introduces audiences to methods of reducing expenses. Similarly, the Master Comparison Layout (Figure 4–1d) is used for Slide 2 (Figure 4–1e), which describes strategies for saving money when shopping online, and Slide 5 (Figure 4–1f), which gives tips when shopping for groceries or dining at restaurants. The Master Title and Content Layout (Figure 4–1g) is used to develop the Slide 3 text (Figure 4–1h) describing money management techniques and reducing electricity on Slide 4 (Figure 4–1i).

In this module, you will learn how to create the slides shown in Figure 4–1. You will perform the following general tasks as you progress through this module:

1. Customize slide masters by changing theme fonts and colors.
2. Format and arrange slide master placeholders.
3. Rename and delete slide layouts.
4. Save a presentation as a template.
5. Change slide backgrounds.
6. Use presentation tools.
7. Inspect and protect a presentation.
8. Rehearse slide timings.

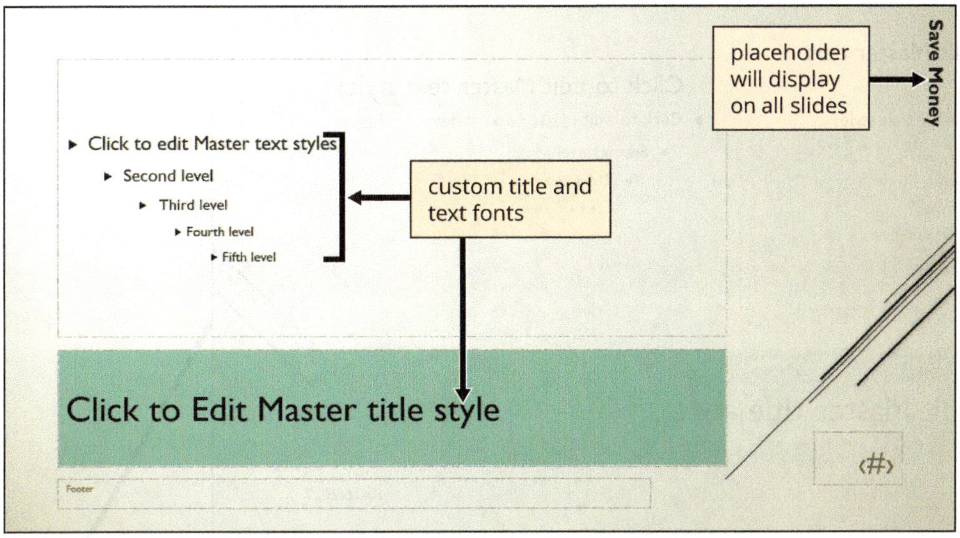

Figure 4–1(a): Slide Master

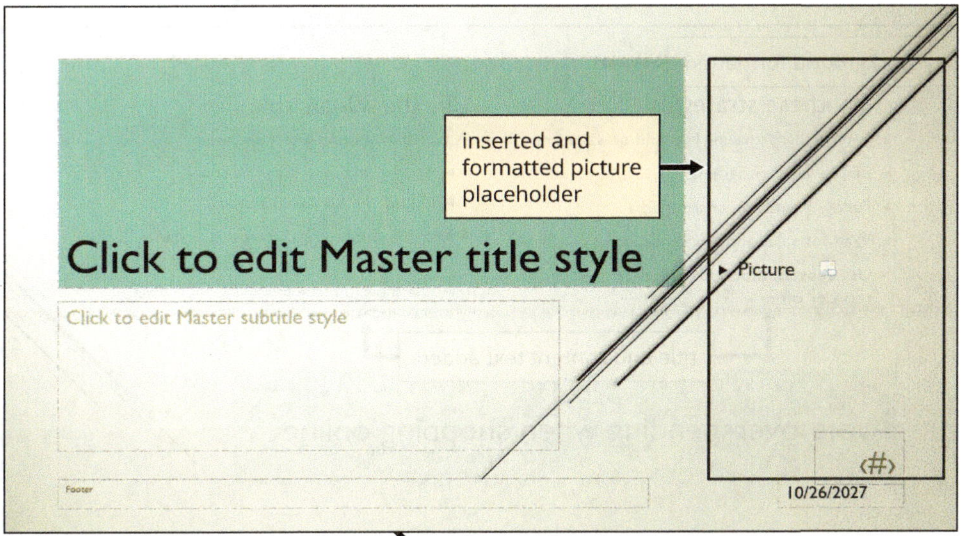

Figure 4–1(b): Master Title Slide Layout

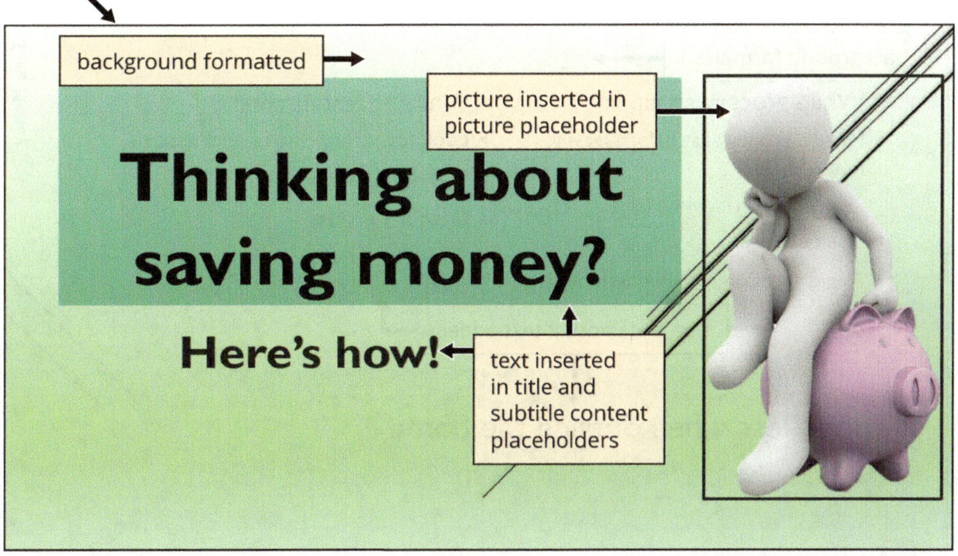

Peggy_Marco/Pixabay

Figure 4–1(c): Slide 1

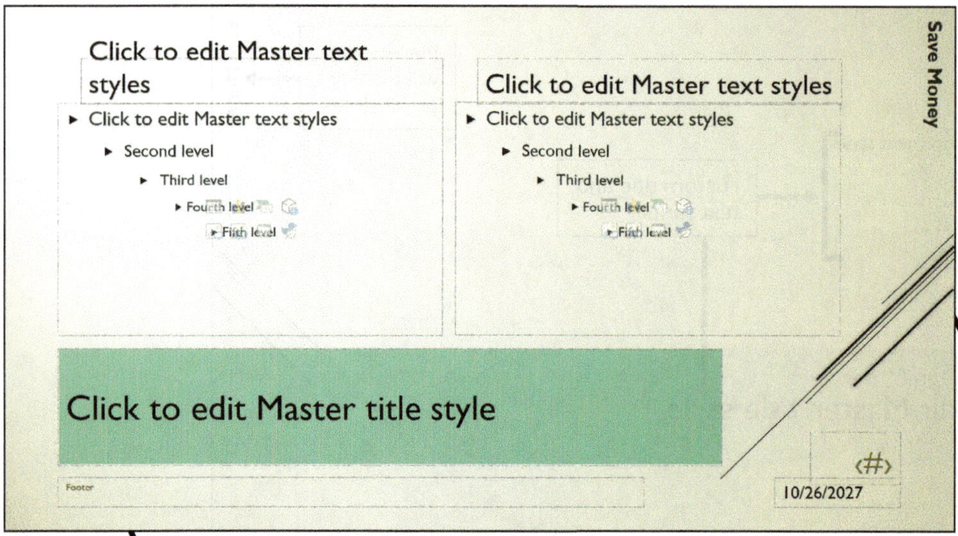

Figure 4–1(d): Master Comparison Layout

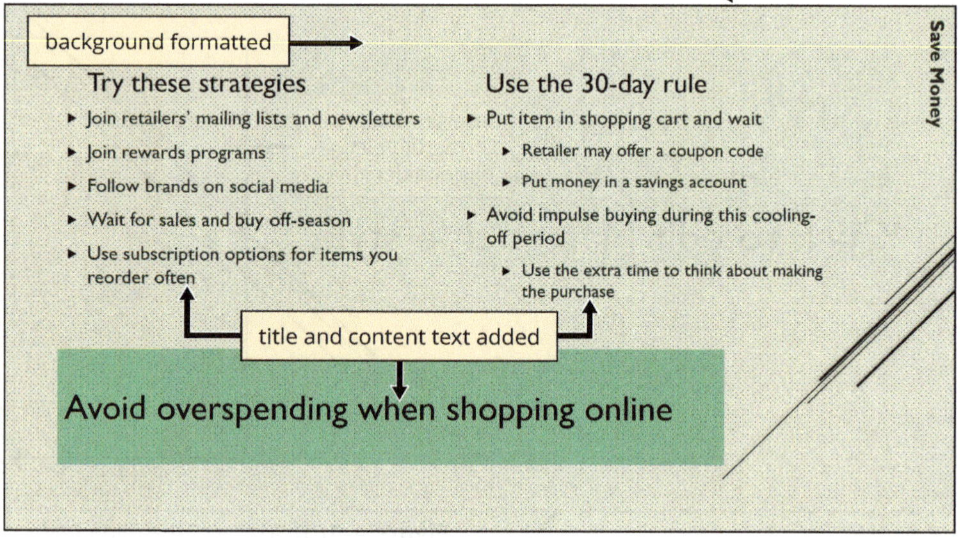

Figure 4–1(e): Slide 2

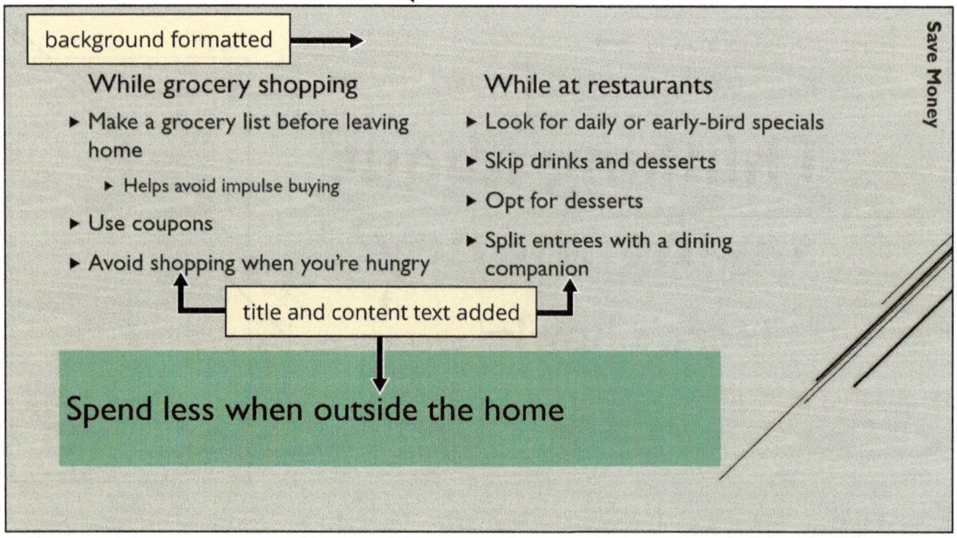

Figure 4–1(f): Slide 5

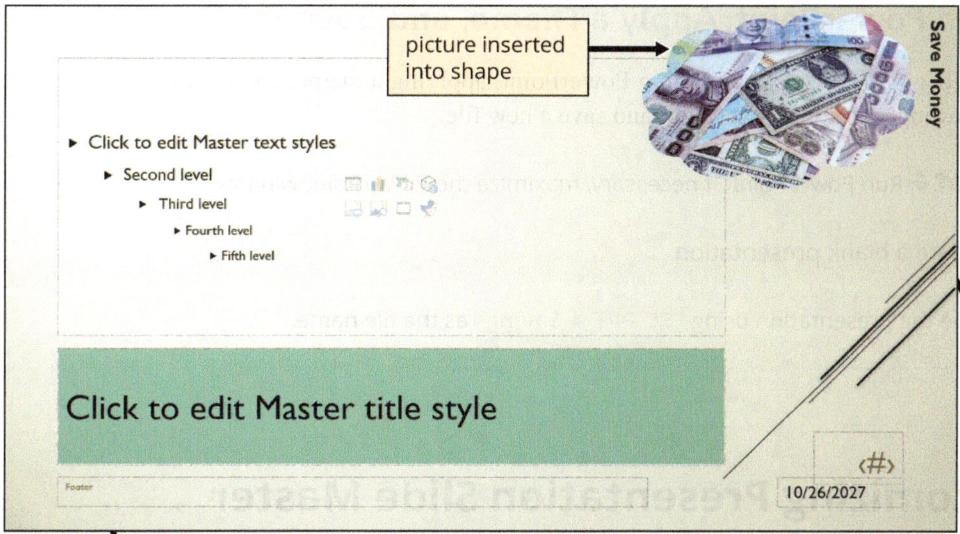

TheDigitalWay/Pixabay

Figure 4–1(g): Master Title and Content Layout

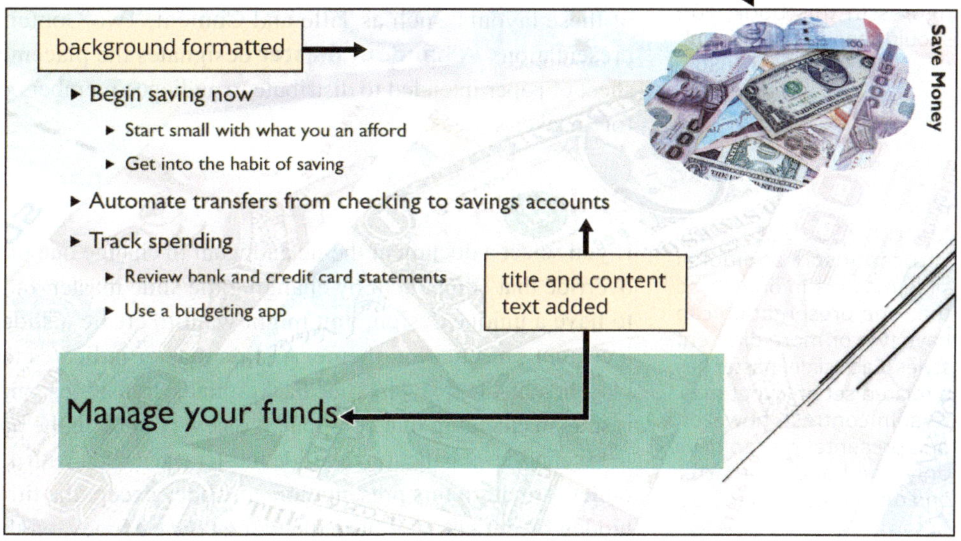

TheDigitalWay/Pixabay

Figure 4–1(h): Slide 3

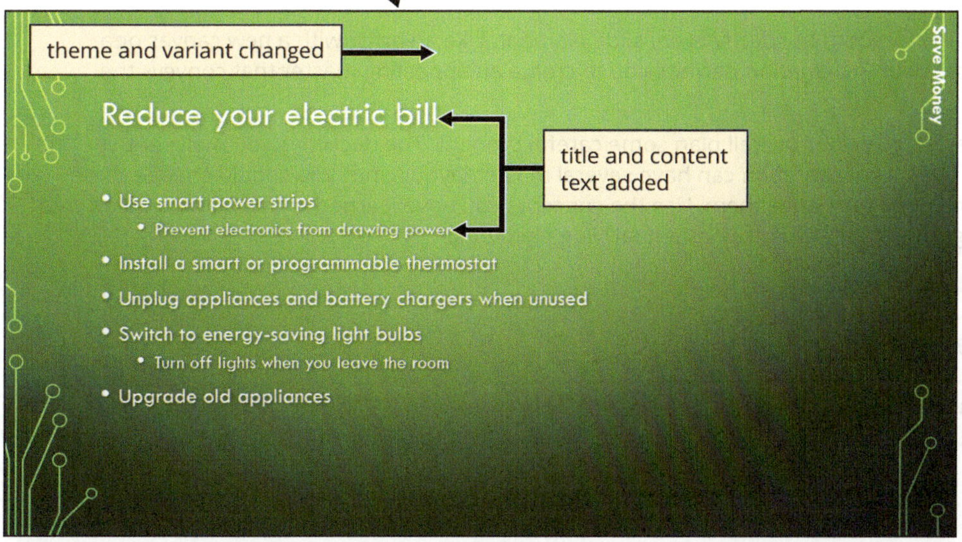

Figure 4–1(i): Slide 4

To Run PowerPoint, Apply a Theme, and Save the Presentation

You can begin the project by running PowerPoint, applying a theme, and then saving the slide. The following steps run PowerPoint and save a new file.

1. sam Run PowerPoint. If necessary, maximize the PowerPoint window.
2. Create a blank presentation.
3. Save the presentation using **SC_PPT_4_Saving** as the file name.

BTW
Screen Resolution
If you are using a computer to step through the project in this module and you want your screens to match the figures in this book, you should change your screen's resolution to 1920 × 1080.

Customizing Presentation Slide Master Backgrounds and Fonts

PowerPoint has many template files with the file extension .potx. Each template file has three masters: slide, handout, and notes. A slide master has at least one layout; you have used many of these layouts, such as Title and Content, Two Content, and Picture with Caption, to create presentations. A **handout master** designates the placement of text, such as page numbers, on a sheet of paper intended to distribute to audience members. A **notes master** defines the formatting for speaker's notes.

BTW
Multiple Slide Masters
You can insert additional slide masters in one file so that one presentation can have two or more different styles. Each slide master has a related set of layout masters. In contrast, however, one presentation can have only one handout master and one notes master.

Slide Master

If you select a document theme and want to change one of its components on every slide, you can override that component by changing the slide master. In addition, if you want your presentation to have a unique design, you might want to create a slide master rather than attempt to modify a current presentation theme. A slide master indicates the size and position of text and object placeholders, font styles, slide backgrounds, transitions, and effects. Any change to the slide master results in changing that component on every slide in the presentation. For example, if you change the second-level bullet on the slide master, each slide with a second-level bullet will display this new bullet format. In this presentation, all slides except the title slide, which has background graphics hidden by default, will have the words, Save Money, on the slide master.

Consider This

Plan the slide master.

Using a new slide master gives you the freedom to specify every slide element. Like an artist with a new canvas or a musician with a blank sheet of music, your imagination permits you to create an appealing master that conveys the overall look of your presentation.

Before you start developing the master, give your overall plan some careful thought. The decisions you make at this point should be reflected on every slide. A presentation can have several master layouts, but you should change these layouts only if you have a compelling need to change them. Use the concepts you have learned in this book to guide your decisions about fonts, colors, backgrounds, art, and other essential slide elements.

To Switch to Slide Master View

To begin developing the saving money slides, you need to display the slide master. **Why?** The slide master allows you to customize the slide components and create a unique design. The following steps switch to Slide Master view and display the slide master.

1

- Click View on the ribbon to display the View tab (Figure 4–2).

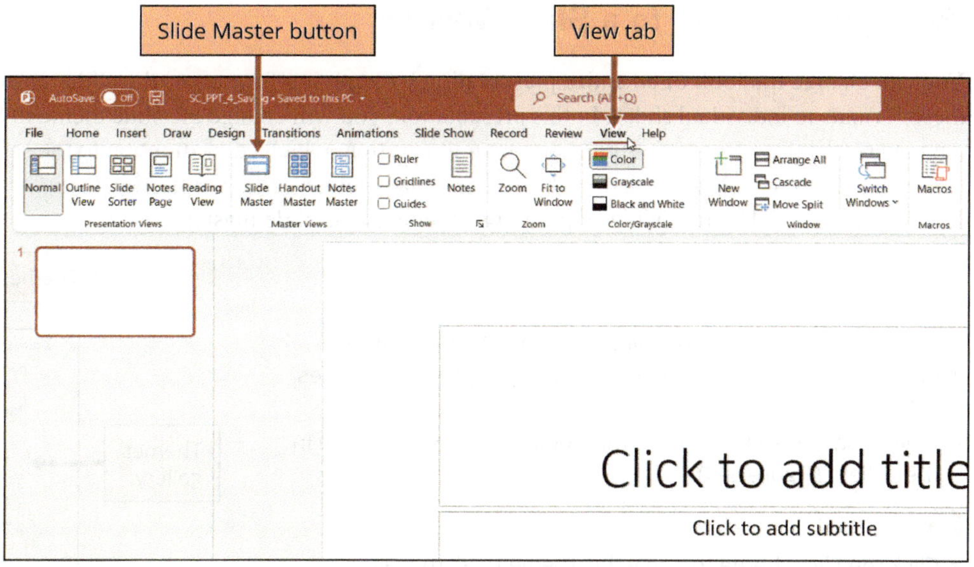

Figure 4–2

2

- Click the Slide Master button (View tab | Master Views group) to display the Slide Master tab and the slide thumbnails in the Slides tab.
- Scroll up and then click the Office Theme Slide Master layout (Figure 4–3).

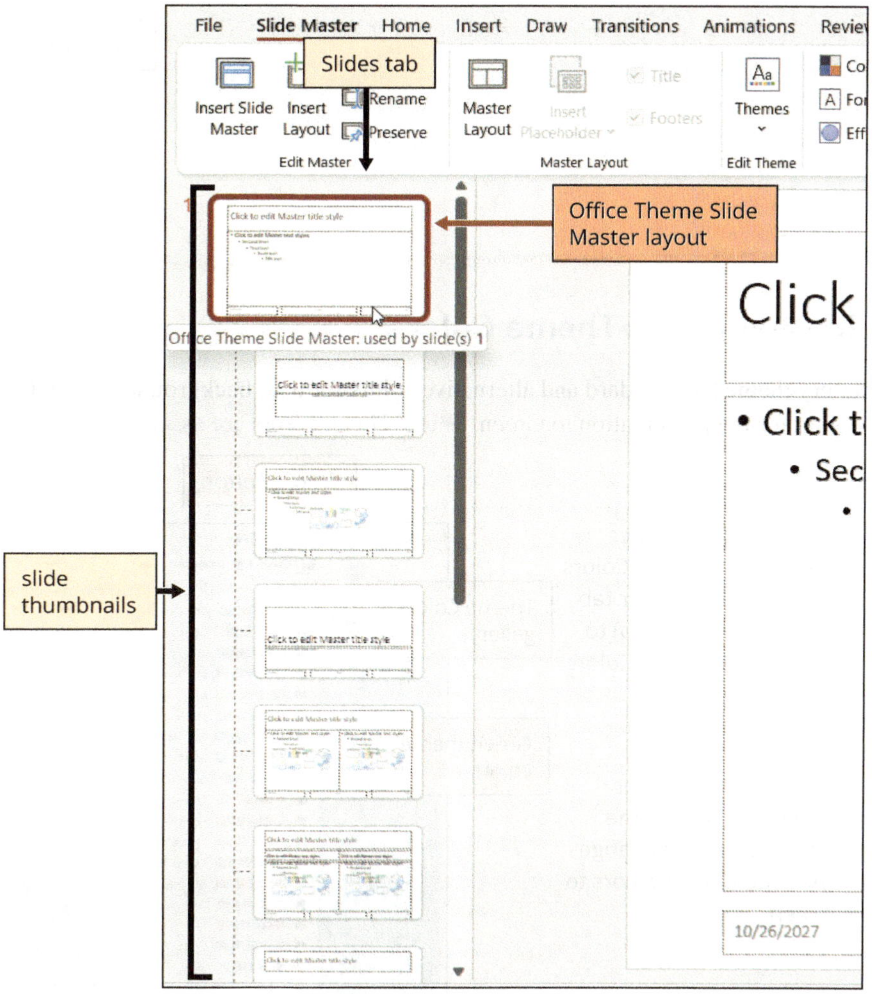

Figure 4–3

Q&A What are all the other thumbnails below the slide master?

They are all the slide layouts associated with this slide master. You have used many of these layouts in the presentations you have developed in the exercises in this book.

Why is the layout given this name?

The slide layout names begin with the theme applied to the slides. In this case, the default Office Theme is applied. The first slide layout in the list is called the master because it controls the colors, fonts, and objects that are displayed on all the other slides in the presentation.

To Apply a Theme to a Slide Master

You can change the look of an entire presentation by applying formats to the slide master in the same manner that you apply these formats to individual slides. In this presentation, you will change the slide theme to Slice. **Why?** The Slice theme features a large area on the right side of the slide for an illustration, which calls attention to the subject matter of people wondering how they can save money. It also features the title text placeholder under the subtitle text placeholder, which is a departure from the usual slide layout. The following steps apply a theme to the slide master.

1

- With the slide master displayed, click the Themes button (Slide Master tab | Edit Theme group) to display the Themes gallery.
- If necessary, scroll down and then point to the Slice theme in the gallery (Figure 4–4).

2

- Click the Slice theme to apply this theme to all the layouts associated with the slide master.

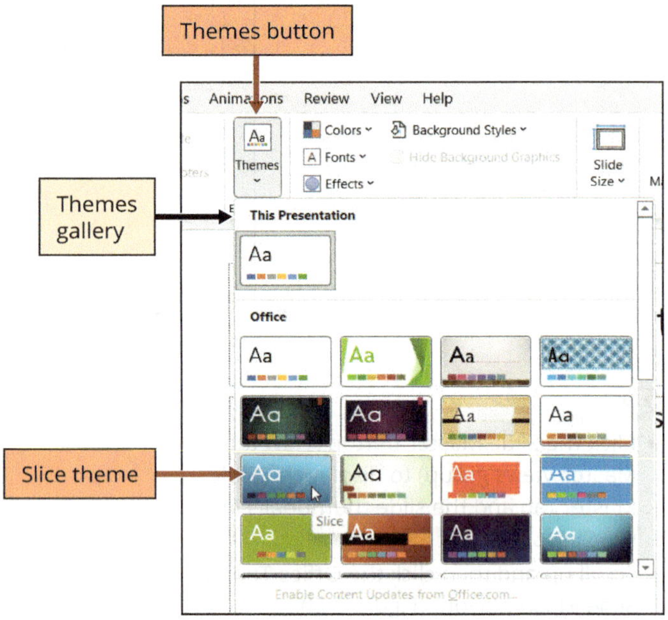

Figure 4–4

To Change the Theme Colors

Every theme has standard and alternative colors for text, backgrounds, accents, and hyperlinks. The following steps change the colors for the presentation to Green. **Why?** Green colors are associated with banking, money, and finances.

1

- With the slide master displayed, click the Colors button (Slide Master tab | Background group) to display the Theme Colors gallery (Figure 4–5).

2

- Click the Green color scheme in the Theme Colors gallery to change the slide master colors to Green.

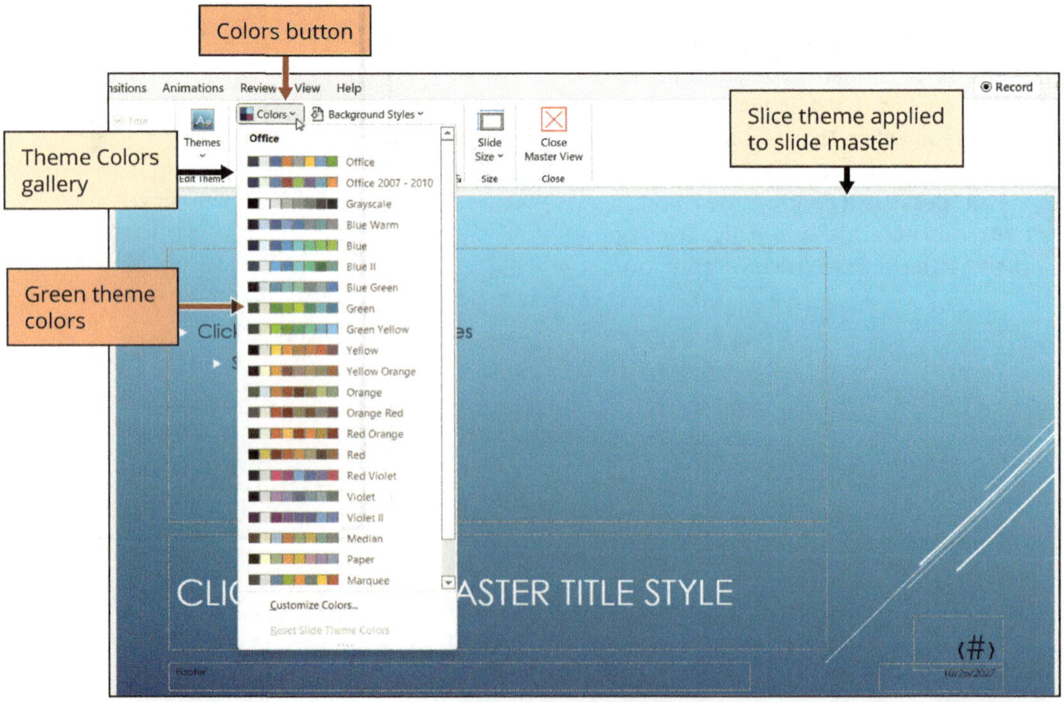

Figure 4–5

To Create Custom Theme Colors

You can modify the colors associated with a particular theme by selecting specific colors and then see samples in the 'Create New Theme Colors' dialog box. Once you determine the specific colors you desire, you can save this combination in the Colors menu. **Why?** You can use this color scheme in other presentations. The following steps customize the colors for the Slice theme.

1

- Click Colors again to display the Theme Colors gallery (Figure 4–6).

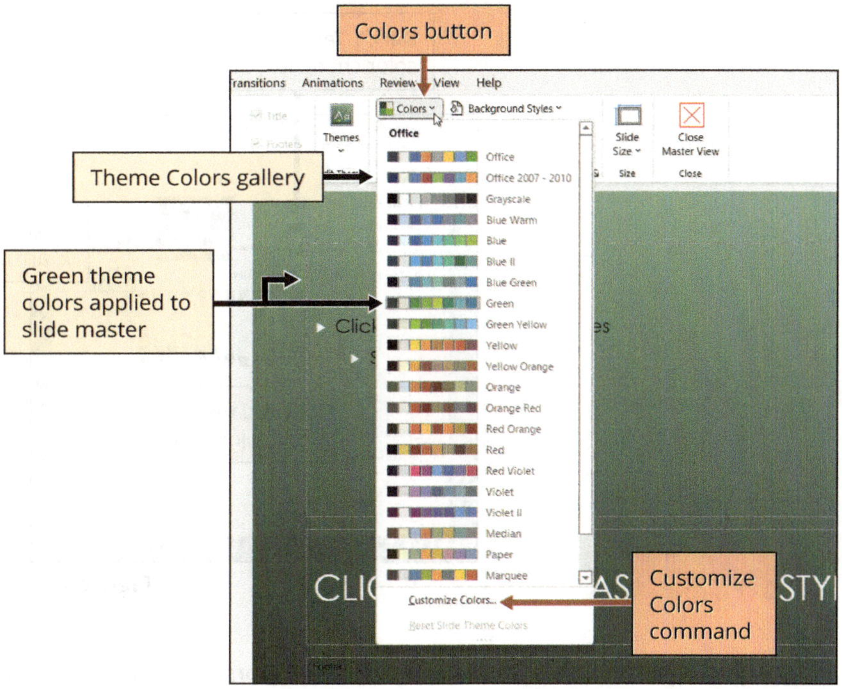

Figure 4–6

2

- Click Customize Colors in the Theme Colors gallery to display the Create New Theme Colors dialog box.
- Click the 'Text/Background-Light 1' arrow to display the Colors gallery (Figure 4–7).

Q&A Can I preview the colors to see how they are displayed on the slide master?
No preview is available when using the Create New Theme Colors dialog box. Once you select the color, however, PowerPoint will display text in the Sample box.

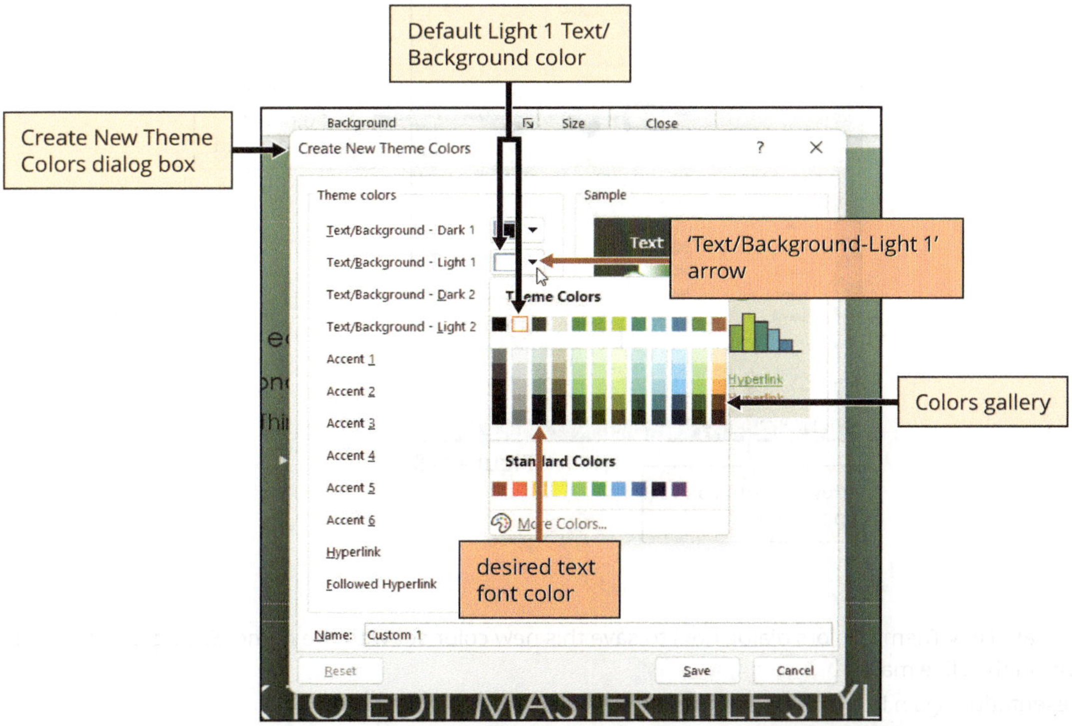

Figure 4–7

3

- Click 'Dark Green, Background 2, Darker 50%' (last color in the third Theme Colors column) to apply that color as the title text font color.
- Click the 'Text/Background-Dark 2' arrow to display the Colors gallery again (Figure 4–8).

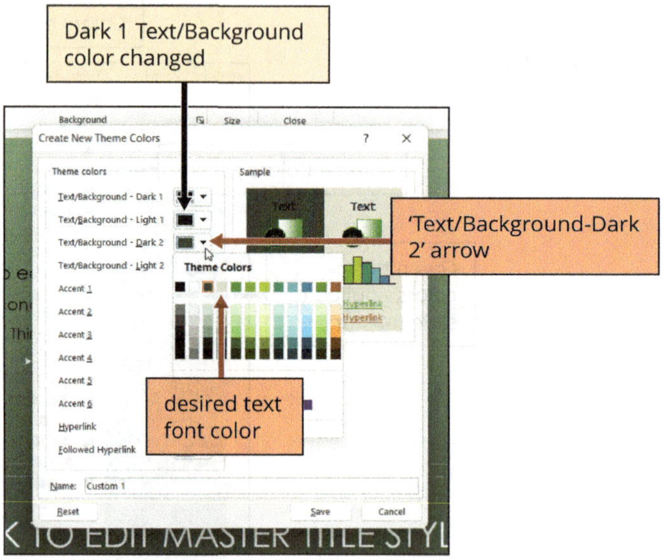

Figure 4–8

4

- Click 'Tan, Text 2' (fourth color in the first Theme Colors row) to apply that color as the background color.
- Select the text, Custom 1, in the Name text box (Create New Theme Colors dialog box) and then type **Saving** as the name of the new custom theme colors palette (Figure 4–9).

Q&A Must I name this custom color scheme I just created?
No. If you name the set, however, you easily will recognize this combination in your color set if you want to use it in new presentations. It will display in the Custom area of the Colors gallery.

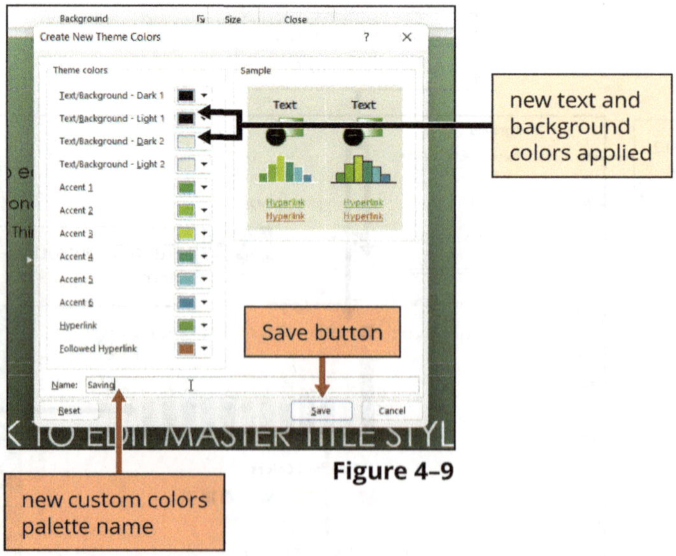

Figure 4–9

5

- Click Save (Create New Theme Colors dialog box) to save this new color set with the name, Saving, and to display the font color changes in the slide master.
- Save the presentation again in the same storage location with the same file name.

To Edit Master Text Styles

You can modify the text styles associated with a particular theme, such as changing from uppercase to sentence case. **Why?** You want to change from UPPERCASE (all caps) to Sentence case (initial cap only) because Sentence case is considered easier to read. The following steps edit the master title text style for the Slice theme.

1

- With the slide master displayed, click the label, 'CLICK TO EDIT MASTER TITLE STYLE' to select the title text placeholder.
- Display the Home tab and then click the Change Case button (Home tab | Font group) to display the Change Case gallery (Figure 4-10).
- **Experiment:** Point to various options in the Sentence case gallery and watch the words in the placeholder change case.

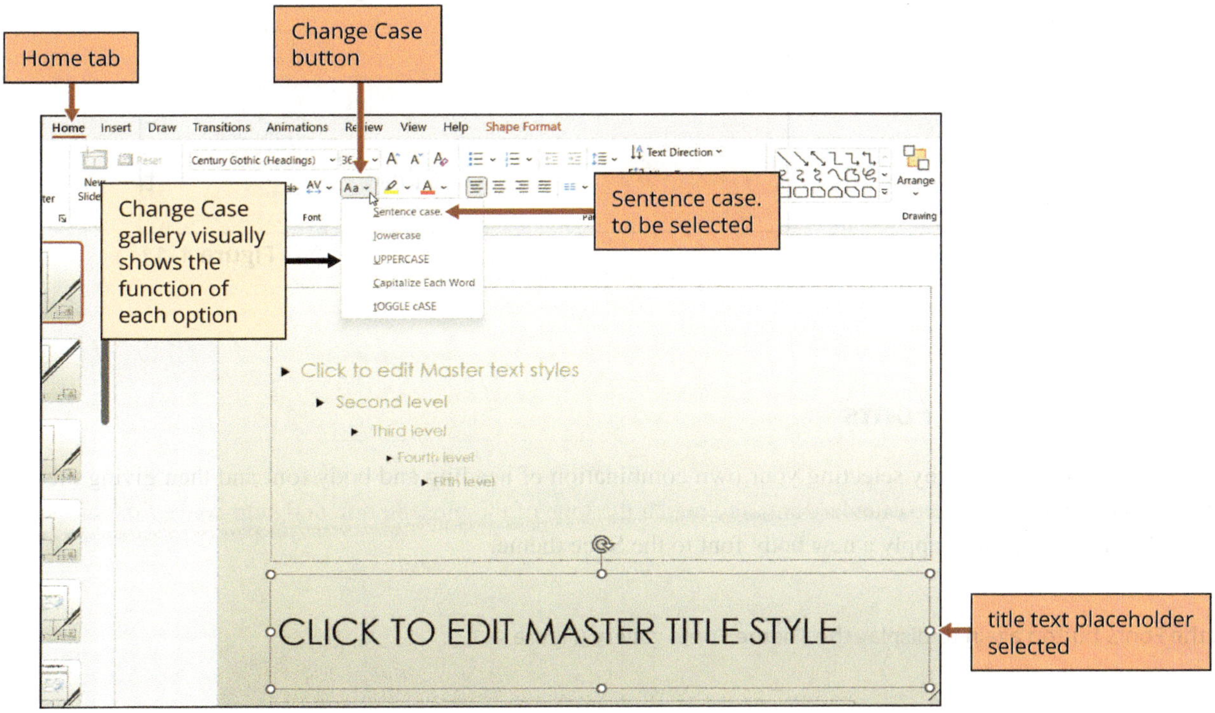

Figure 4-10

2

- Click Sentence case. in the Change Case gallery to change the case of the title text from UPPERCASE to Sentence case.

Other Ways

1. Press SHIFT+F3 repeatedly until text is desired case

To Change the Theme Fonts

Each theme has a heading font and a body font applied to it. At times both fonts are the same, and at other times, the heading font differs from the body font, but both fonts coordinate with each other. You can change the text in your slides by selecting one of the font sets. **Why?** This is a quick and easy method of changing all the text simultaneously. The following steps apply a new heading font and body font to the Slice theme.

1

- Display the Slide Master tab.
- With the slide master displayed, click the Fonts button (Slide Master tab | Background group) to display the Theme Fonts gallery.

- Scroll down and then point to the Calibri-Cambria font set (Figure 4–11).

Q&A How are the font sets arranged in the Theme Fonts gallery?
Calibri is the heading font, and Cambria is the body font. The fonts are previewed in the boxes on the left side of the gallery and in the text displaying their names.

2

- Click Calibri-Cambria to apply the two fonts to the Slice theme.

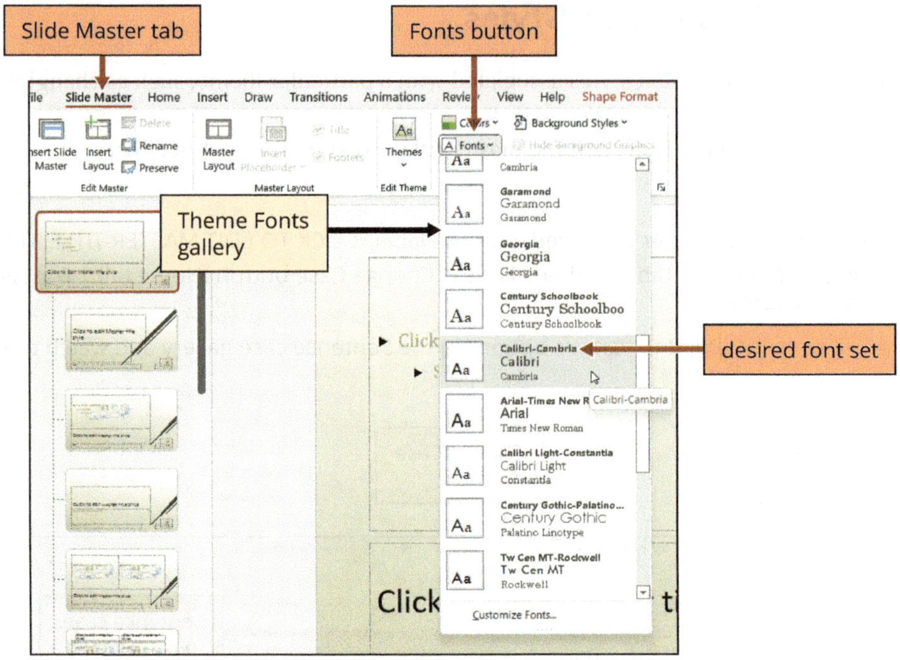

Figure 4–11

To Customize Theme Fonts

You can customize theme fonts by selecting your own combination of heading and body font and then giving the new theme font set a unique name. **Why?** A particular font may match the tone of the presentation and help convey the message you are presenting. The following steps apply a new body font to the Slice theme.

1

- Click the Fonts button again to display the Theme Fonts gallery (Figure 4–12).

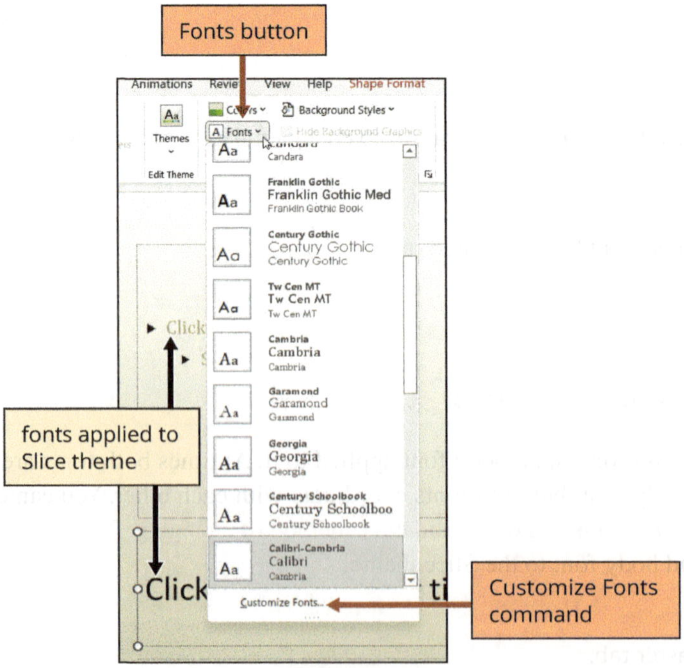

Figure 4–12

2

- Click Customize Fonts in the Theme Fonts gallery to display the Create New Theme Fonts dialog box.
- Click the Body font arrow and then scroll down and point to Gill Sans MT in the list (Figure 4–13).

Q&A Can I preview the fonts to see how they are displayed on the slide master?
No preview is available when using the Create New Theme Fonts dialog box. Once you select the font, however, PowerPoint will apply the font to the text in the Sample box.

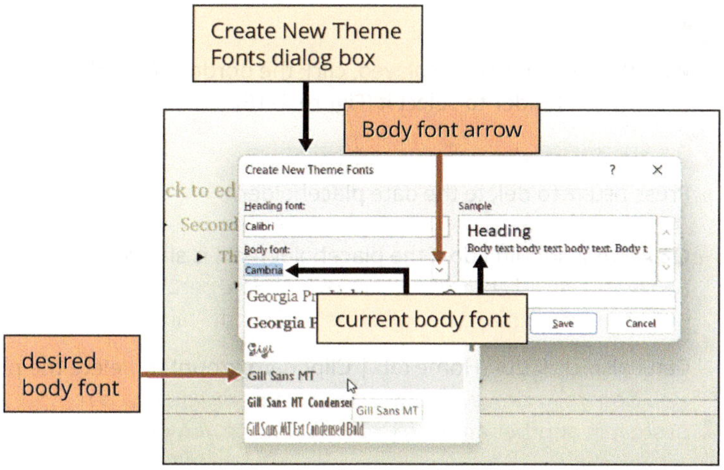

Figure 4–13

3

- Click Gill Sans MT to apply that font as the new body text font (Figure 4–14).

Q&A What if the Gill Sans MT font is not in my list of fonts?
Select a font that resembles the font shown in Figure 4–14.

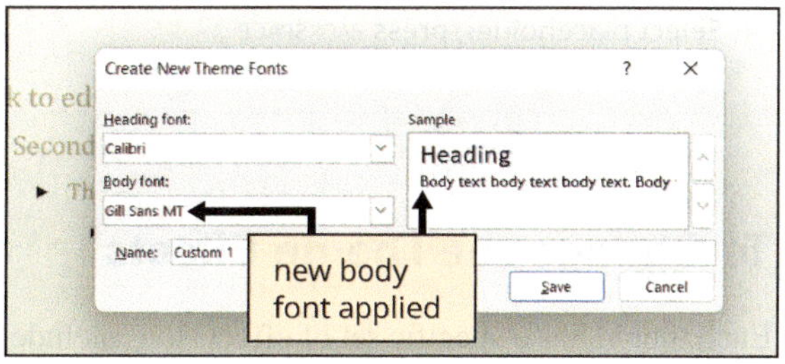

Figure 4–14

4

- Select the text, Custom 1, in the Name text box and then type **Saving** to name the new font set (Figure 4–15).

Q&A Must I name this font set I just created?
No. If you name the set, however, you easily will recognize this combination in your font set if you want to use it in new presentations. It will display in the Custom area of the Fonts gallery.

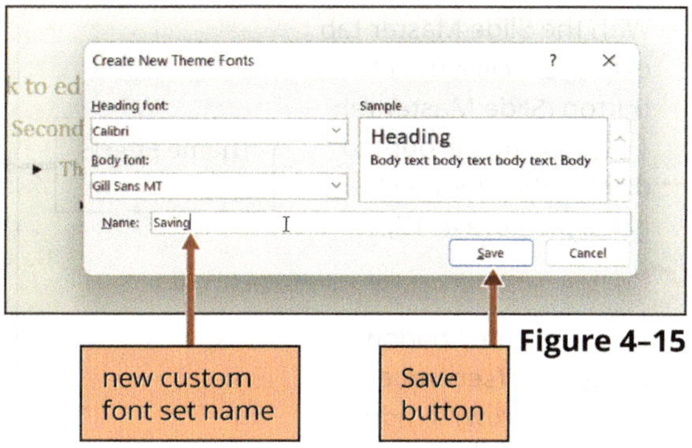

Figure 4–15

5

- Click Save (Create New Theme Fonts dialog box) to save this new font set with the name, Saving, and to display the font changes in the slide master.
- Save the presentation again in the same storage location with the same file name.

To Delete a Content Placeholder

When you run a slide show, empty placeholders do not display. At times, you may desire to delete these unused elements, such as a slide number, date and time, and footer placeholder, from a slide. **Why?** Empty placeholders can be a distraction when you are designing slide content because they interfere with other slide content or they use an area of the slide that can display other slide content. Or, you might not want to display information, such as a page number. The following steps delete the date placeholder on the slide master.

1

- With the slide master displayed, click the border of the date footer placeholder to select it (Figure 4–16).

2

- Press DELETE to delete the date placeholder.

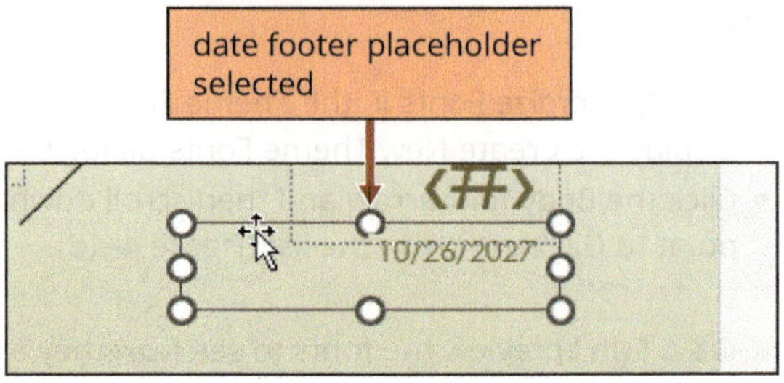

Figure 4–16

Q&A What should I do if the placeholder still is showing on the slide?
Be certain you clicked the placeholder border and not just the text. The border must display as a solid line before you can delete it.

Can I also click Cut (Home tab | Clipboard group) to delete the placeholder?
Yes. Generally, however, Cut is used when you desire to remove a selected slide element, place it on the Clipboard, and then paste it in another area. DELETE is used when you do not want to reuse that particular slide element.

If I am using a touch screen, how do I delete the placeholder?
Press and hold on a border of the title text placeholder and then tap DELETE on the shortcut menu to remove the placeholder.

Other Ways

1. Select placeholder, press BACKSPACE

To Change the Theme Effects

Each theme has a specific set of effects that include such elements as shadows, reflections, lines, and fills. You cannot customize a set of theme effects, but you can change the effects associated with a particular theme. **Why?** A set of effects may fit the message you are giving in the presentation. The following steps change the theme effects.

1

- With the Slide Master tab displayed, click the Effects button (Slide Master tab | Background group) to display the Theme Effects gallery (Figure 4–17).

2

- Click Extreme Shadow in the gallery (second effect in the last row) to add this effect.

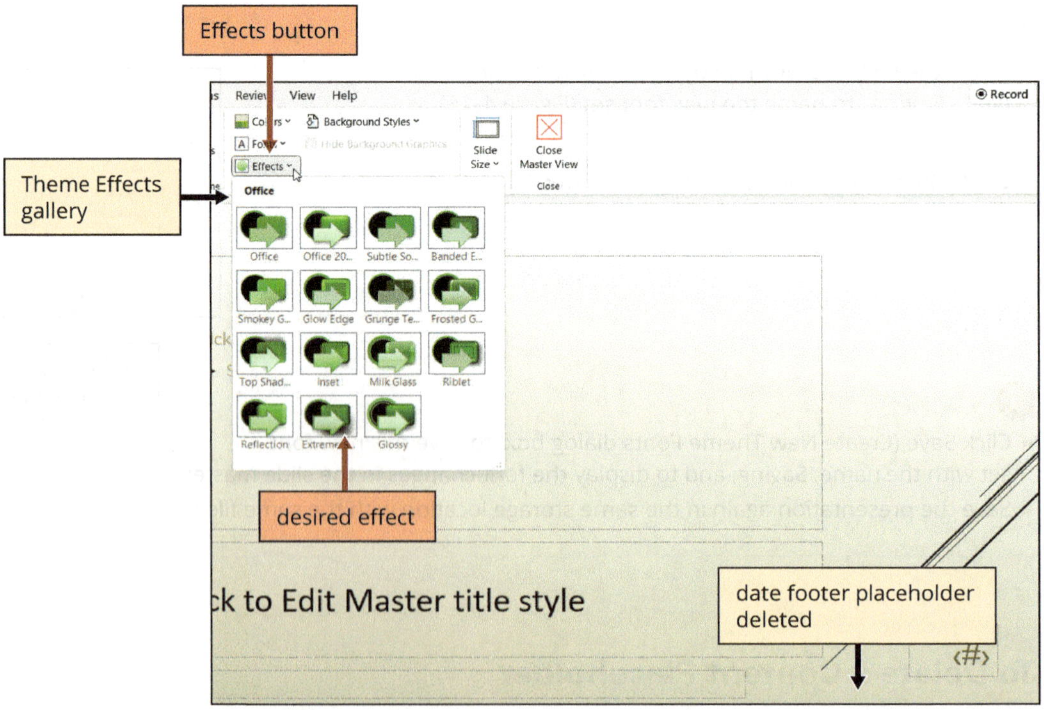

Figure 4–17

Adding and Formatting Placeholders

Each design theme determines where placeholders appear on individual layouts. The slide master has placeholders for bulleted lists, title text, pictures, and other graphical elements. At times, you may find that you need a specific placeholder for a design element not found on any of the slide master layouts. You can add a placeholder in Slide Master view for text, SmartArt, charts, tables, and other graphical elements.

To Insert a Placeholder into a Blank Layout

The words, Save Money, will appear in the title text on the title slide, but you may desire to add these words to every text slide. **Why?** Displaying this text in the same location on all slides helps emphasize the goal of the presentation and provides a consistent, uniform look. One efficient method of adding this text is to insert a placeholder, type the words, and, if necessary, format the characters. The following steps insert a text placeholder into the Blank Layout.

1

- In the Slides tab, scroll down and then click the Blank Layout to display this layout.
- Click the Insert Placeholder arrow (Slide Master tab | Master Layout group) to display the Insert Placeholder gallery (Figure 4–18).

Q&A Why does the Insert Placeholder button on my screen differ from the button shown in Figure 4–18?
The image on the button changes based on the type of placeholder content that was last inserted. A placeholder can hold any content, including text, pictures, and tables. If the last type of placeholder inserted was for a picture, for example, the Insert Placeholder button would display the Picture icon.

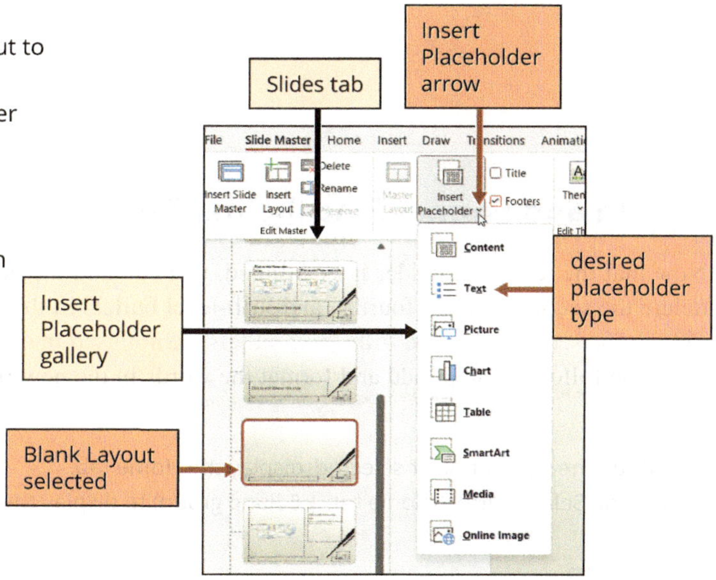

Figure 4–18

2

- Click Text in the gallery.

Q&A Could I have inserted a Content placeholder rather than a Text placeholder?
Yes. The Content placeholder is used for any of the seven types of slide content: text, table, chart, SmartArt, picture, clip art, or media. In this project, you will insert text in the placeholder. If you know the specific kind of content you want to place in the placeholder, it is best to select that placeholder type.

3

- Position the pointer, which is a crosshair, near the upper-right corner of the slide layout (Figure 4–19).

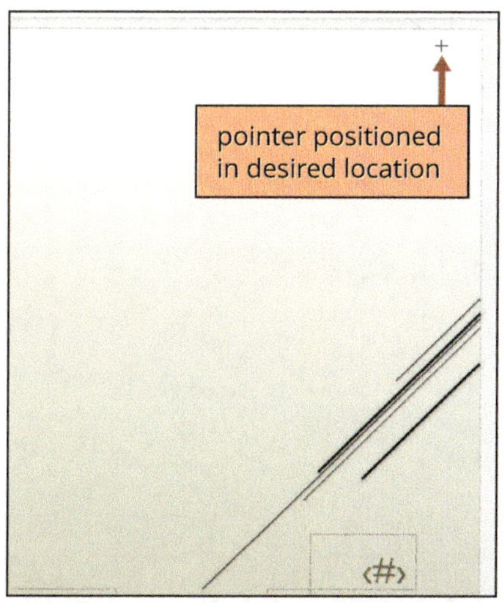

Figure 4–19

4

- Click to insert the new placeholder into the layout. Click inside the new placeholder (Figure 4–20).

Q&A Could I have inserted the Text placeholder anywhere on the slide rather than in the upper-right corner?
Yes. Because you are going to display that placeholder on every slide, however, it is best to make the necessary formatting changes and see how it is going to appear on your final product.

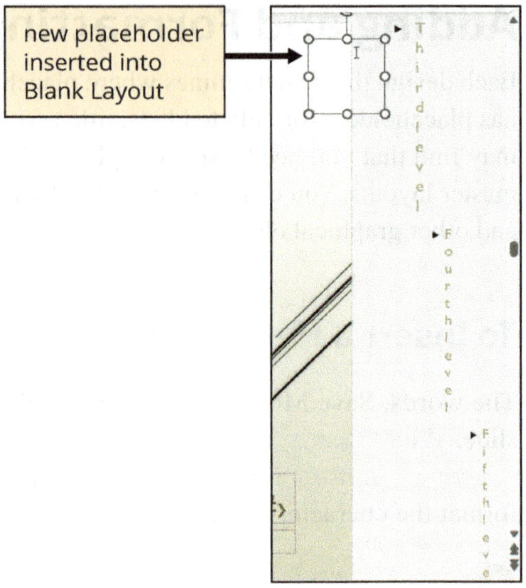

Figure 4–20

To Add and Format Placeholder Text

Now that the text placeholder is positioned, you can add the desired text and then format the characters. You will need to delete the second-, third-, fourth-, and fifth-level bullets in this placeholder and remove the bullet from the first-level text. **Why?** The second- through fifth-level bullets are not used in this presentation, and you do not want a bullet on your primary text. The following steps add and format the words in the new Blank Layout placeholder.

1

- With the new placeholder selected, display the Home tab.
- Click the Select button (Home tab | Editing group) to display the Select menu (Figure 4–21).

Figure 4–21

2

- Click Select All in the Select menu to select all the text in the placeholder (Figure 4–22).

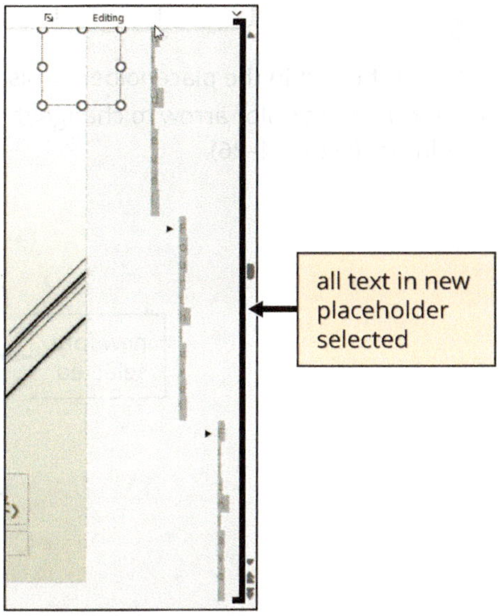

Figure 4–22

3

- Press DELETE to delete all the selected text in the placeholder.
- Click the Bullets button (Home tab | Paragraph group) to remove the bullet from the placeholder.
- Type **Save Money** in the placeholder (Figure 4–23).

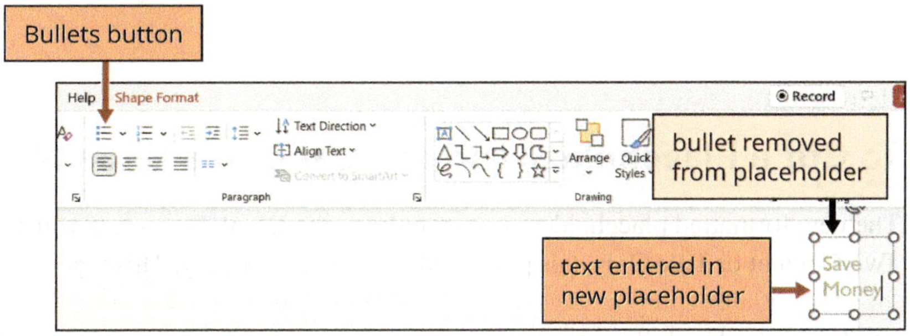

Figure 4–23

4

- Click the Shape Format tab and then change the height of the placeholder to 2" and the width to 0.5" (Figure 4–24).

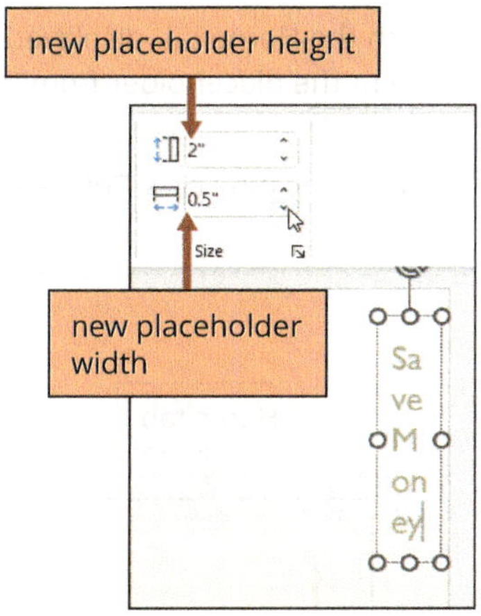

Figure 4–24

5

- Display the Home tab, select the new placeholder, and then click the Text Direction button (Home tab | Paragraph group) to display the Text Direction gallery (Figure 4–25).
- **Experiment:** Point to various directions in the Text Direction gallery and watch the words in the placeholder change direction on the layout.

6

- Click 'Rotate all text 90°' to turn the text so that it faces inward.

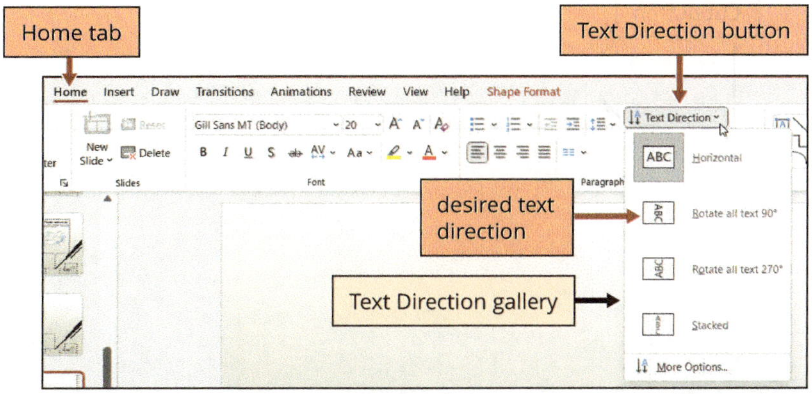

Figure 4–25

7

- Select the text in the placeholder to display the Mini toolbar and then click the Bold button to bold the text.
- Click the Font Color arrow to change the color to 'Dark Green, Text 1, Lighter 10%' (last color in the second Theme Colors column) (Figure 4–26).

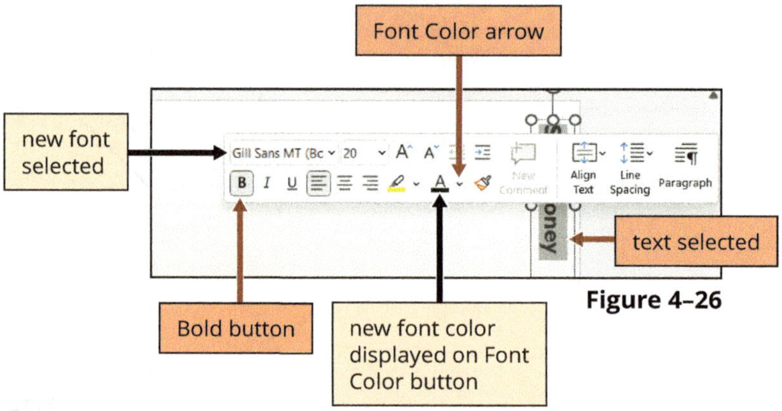

Figure 4–26

To Cut a Placeholder and Paste It into a Slide Master

The new formatted placeholder appears only on the Blank Layout. If you selected any other layout in your presentation, such as Two Content or Title Only, this placeholder would not display. This placeholder should appear on all text slides. **Why?** Repeating this placeholder will provide consistency throughout the presentation. You can paste a placeholder that you copied or cut from another slide. The following steps cut the new placeholder from the Blank Layout and paste it into the slide master.

1

- With the Home tab displayed, click the new placeholder border, and then click the Cut button (Home tab | Clipboard group) to cut the placeholder from the layout and copy it to the Clipboard (Figure 4–27).

Q&A Why did I click Cut instead of Copy?
Tapping or clicking Cut deletes the placeholder. Tapping or clicking Copy keeps the original placeholder on the slide, so if you paste the placeholder on the slide master, a second, identical placeholder would display on the Blank Layout.

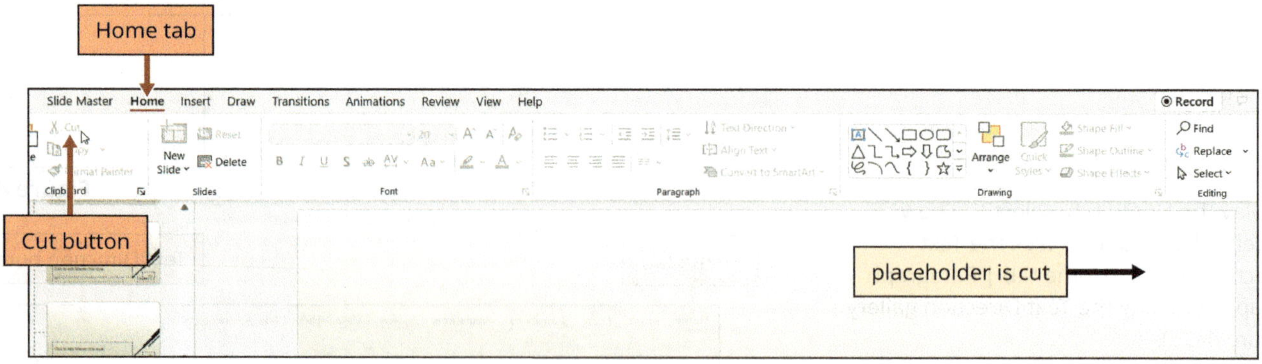

Figure 4–27

2

- Scroll up and then click the Slice Slide Master thumbnail in the Slides tab to display the slide master.
- Click the Paste button (Home tab | Clipboard group) to copy the placeholder from the Clipboard to the slide master.
- Use the smart guides to position the placeholder in the location shown in Figure 4–28.

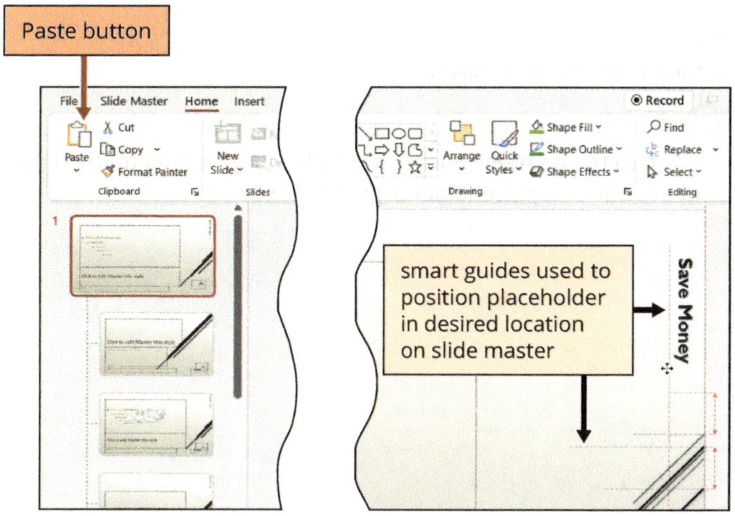

Figure 4–28

To Insert a Picture Placeholder

The right side of the Title Slide Layout contains a large area to the right of the title text placeholder. You can add a picture placeholder to this area of the slide in the slide master. **Why?** You can draw attention to your presentation's purpose if you add a picture to this slide layout. You add a picture placeholder in the same manner as you add a text placeholder. You then can size and format this placeholder by adding an outline, effect, or other enhancements. The following steps insert a picture placeholder into the Title Slide Layout.

1

- In the Slides tab, click the Title Slide Layout to display this layout.
- Display the Slide Master tab and then click the Insert Placeholder arrow (Slide Master tab | Master Layout group) to display the Insert Placeholder gallery (Figure 4–29).

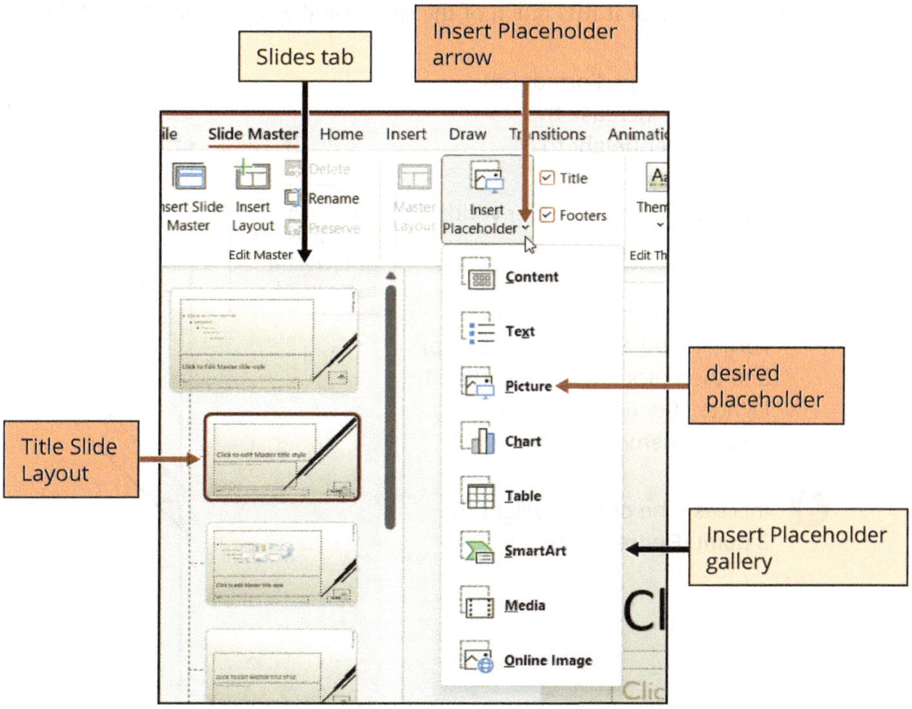

Figure 4–29

2

- Click Picture in the gallery.

3

- Position the pointer, which is a crosshair, in the area to the right of the title text placeholder (Figure 4–30).

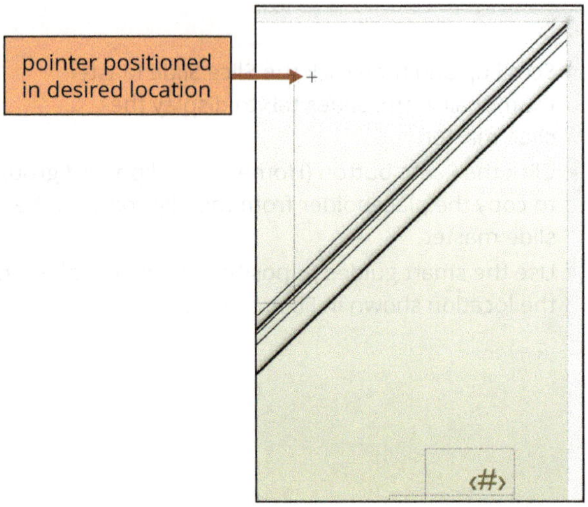

Figure 4–30

4

- Click to insert the new placeholder into the Title Slide Layout (Figure 4–31).

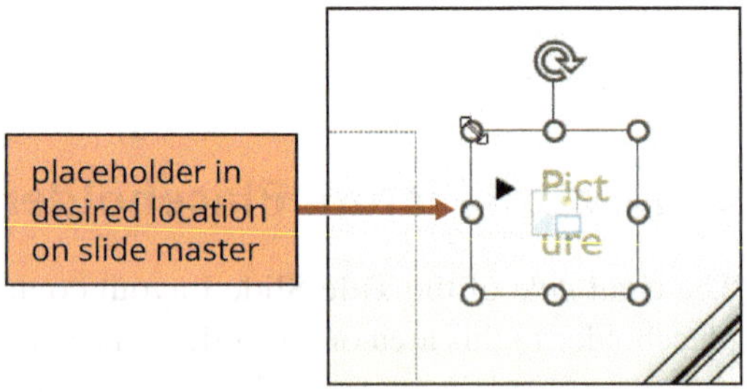

Figure 4–31

To Size and Format the Picture Content Layout

You can size the picture placeholder on the right side of the title slide. You also can add an outline to enhance the visual appeal of this element. The following steps increase the size of the picture placeholder so that it fills much of the space on the right side of the slide and then add an outline.

1. With the Shape Format tab displayed, increase the placeholder height to 6".
2. Increase the placeholder width to 3.3".
3. Click Shape Outline (Shape Format tab | Shape Styles group) and then click 'Dark Green, Text 1, Lighter 10%' (last color in the second Theme Colors column).
4. Increase the outline weight to 3 point (Figure 4–32).

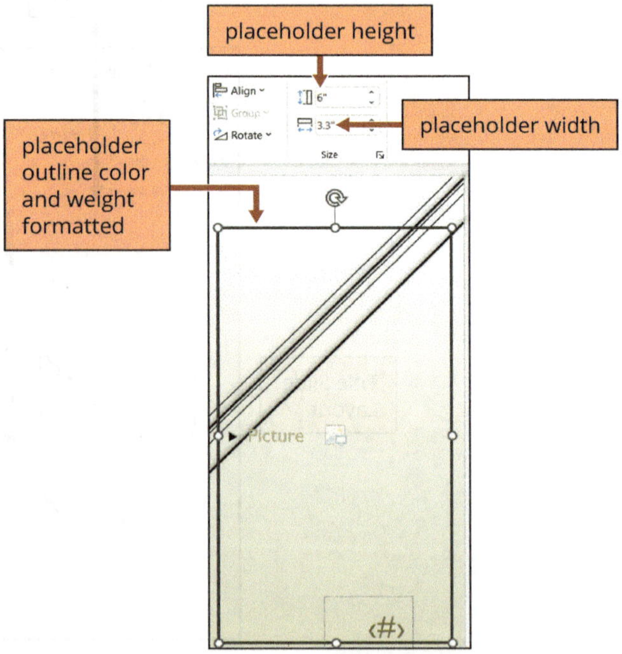

Figure 4–32

To Copy a Content Placeholder

At times you may want the same slide content to appear in another area of the slide or on another slide. To perform this action, you would copy the element, such as a placeholder, and then paste it. When you copy this element, it is stored on the **Clipboard**. You can copy a maximum of 24 items from Office documents and then paste them in the same or other documents. To copy a placeholder to another slide master, you would perform the following steps.

1. Select the item you want to copy.
2. Display the Home tab and then click Copy (Home tab | Clipboard group).
3. Place the insertion point where you want the item to display and then click Paste (Home tab | Clipboard group).

To Format a Slide Master Background, Apply a Quick Style, and Format Text

Once you have applied a theme to the slide master and determined the fonts for the presentation, you can further customize the slide master. **Why?** Adding a unique background and customizing the colors can give your presentation a unique look that matches the message you are conveying. The following steps format the slide master background, apply a Quick Style, and format the subtitle text.

1

- Display the Slice Slide Master and then, if necessary, display the Slide Master tab.
- Click the Background Styles button (Slide Master tab | Background group) to display the Background Styles gallery (Figure 4–33).

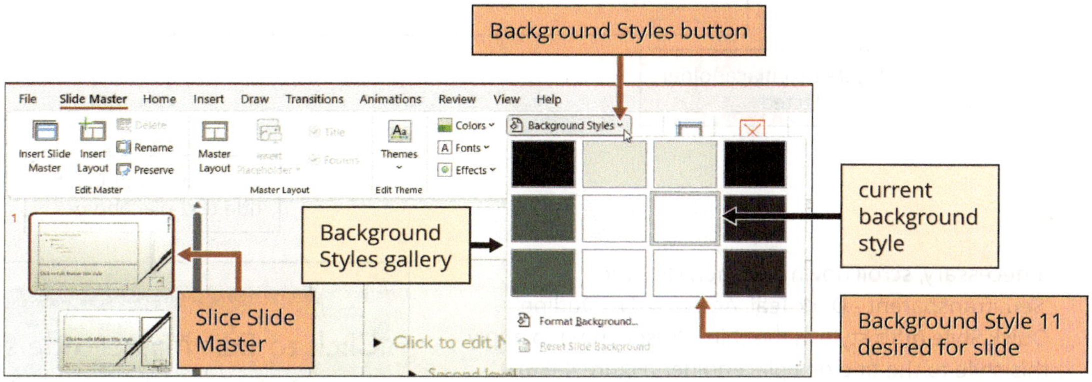

Figure 4–33

- **Experiment:** Point to various styles in the Background Styles gallery and watch the backgrounds change on the slide master.

2

- Click Style 11 (third style in the third row) to apply this background to the slide master (Figure 4–34).

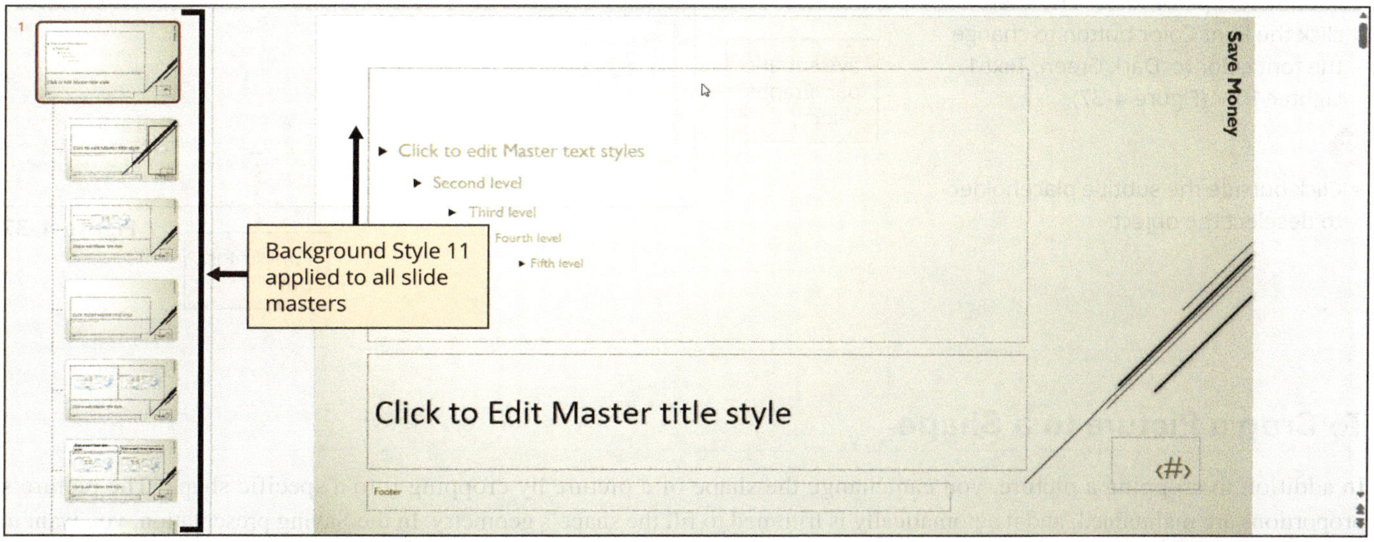

Figure 4–34

3

- Click the outer edge of the slide master title text placeholder to select it.
- Display the Home tab and then click the Quick Styles button (Home tab | Drawing group) to display the Shape Quick Styles gallery (Figure 4–35).
- **Experiment:** Point to various styles in the Quick Styles gallery and watch the background and borders change on the slide master title text placeholder.

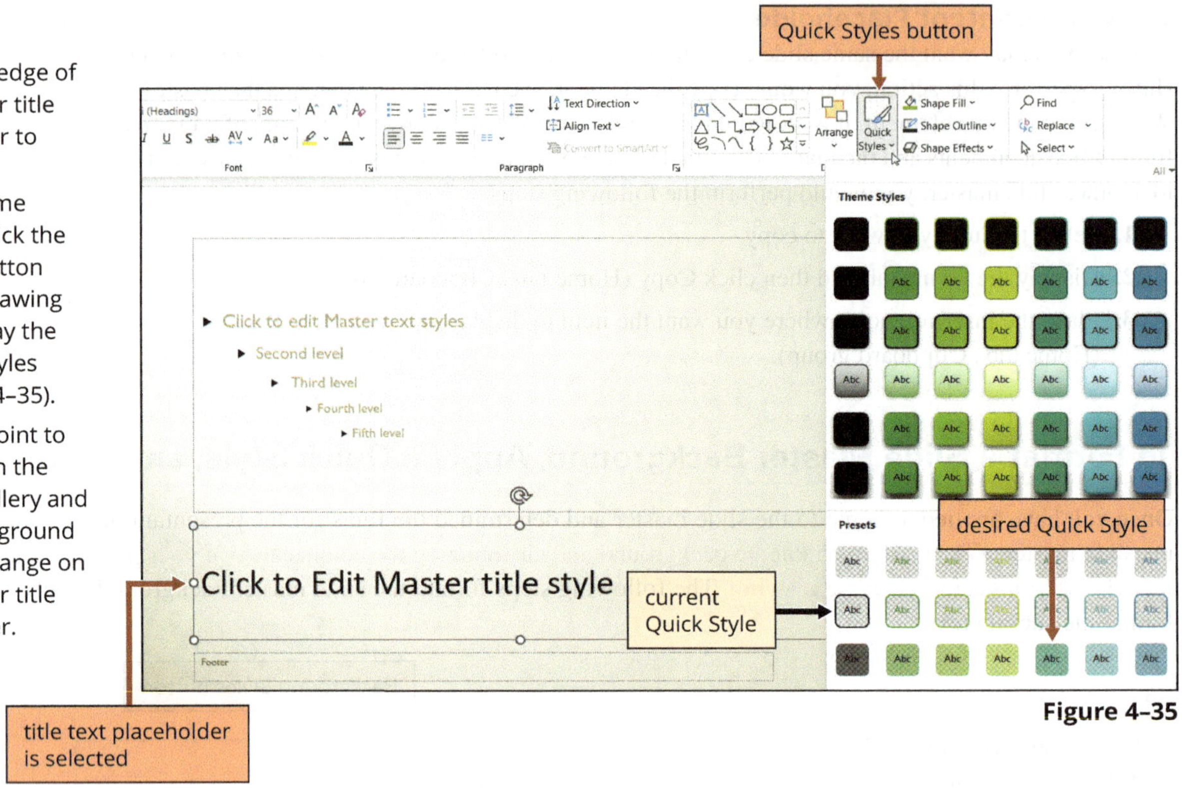

Figure 4–35

4

- If necessary, scroll down and then click the 'Semitransparent - Dark Teal, Accent 4, No Outline' Quick Style (fifth style in the third Presets row) to apply this style to the title text placeholder (Figure 4–36).

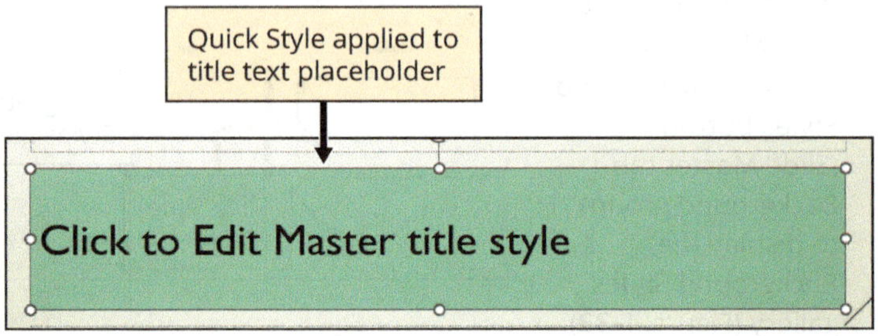

Figure 4–36

5

- Select all five-paragraphs in the subtitle text placeholder and then click the Font Color button to change the font color to 'Dark Green, Text 1, Lighter 10%' (Figure 4–37).

6

- Click outside the subtitle placeholder to deselect the object.

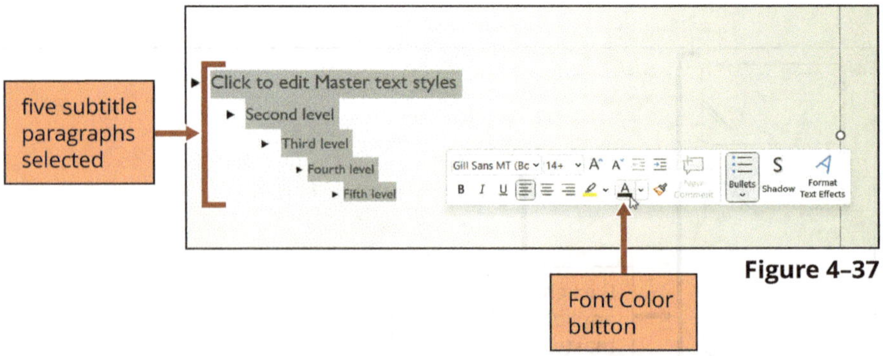

Figure 4–37

To Crop a Picture to a Shape

In addition to cropping a picture, you can change the shape of a picture by cropping it to a specific shape. The picture's proportions are maintained, and it automatically is trimmed to fill the shape's geometry. In the Saving presentation, you want to insert a picture of money cropped in a cloud shape on the Title and Content Layout. You will use the same picture as the Slide 3 background. **Why?** Displaying the same picture repeats the money topic, and the cloud shape reinforces the idea of thinking about money on the title slide. The following steps crop the money picture to a cloud shape.

1

- Display the Title and Content Layout and then display the Insert tab.
- Click the Pictures button, click This Device, and then insert the Support_PPT_4_Money.jpg file, which is located in the Data Files.

2

- Select the money picture and then click the Crop arrow (Picture Format Tab | Size group) to display the Crop menu.
- Point to 'Crop to Shape' to display the Shapes gallery (Figure 4–38).

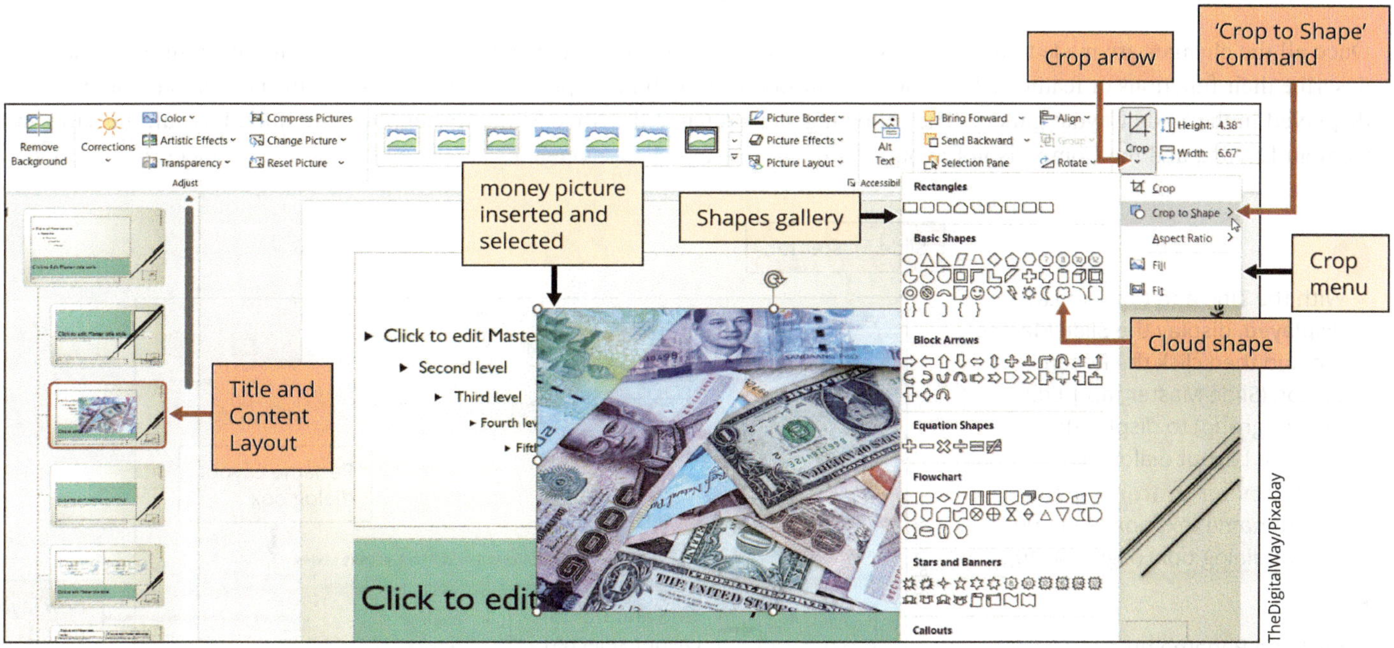

Figure 4–38

3

- Click the Cloud shape (tenth shape in the third Basic Shapes row) to crop the picture.
- Change the shape height to 2.5".
- Use the smart guides to move the picture to the upper-right area of the slide, as shown in Figure 4–39.

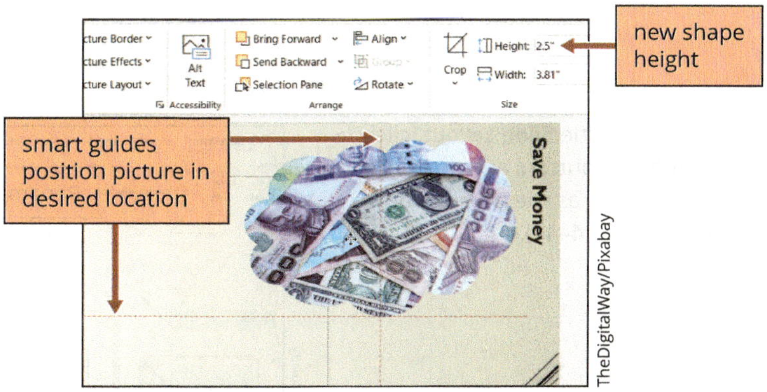

Figure 4–39

To Hide and Unhide Background Graphics

The placeholder, text box, pictures, and other graphical elements are displayed on some slide master layouts and are hidden on others. You have the ability to change the default setting by choosing to hide or unhide the background graphics. The Hide Background Graphics check box is a toggle that displays and conceals the graphics. To hide background graphics on a layout, you would perform the following steps.

1. Display the Slide Master tab, select the desired layout, and then click the Hide Background Graphics check box (Slide Master tab | Background group) to insert a check mark in it.
2. To unhide the graphics, click the same check box to make them appear.

To Rename a Slide Master and a Slide Layout

Once all the changes are made to a slide master and a slide layout, you may want to rename them with meaningful names that describe their functions or features. The new slide master name will be displayed on the status bar; the new layout name will be displayed in the Slide Layout gallery. The following steps rename the Slice Slide Master, the Title Slide Layout, the Title and Content Layout, and the Comparison Layout. **Why?** Renaming the layouts gives meaningful names that reflect the purpose of the design.

1

- With the Title and Content Layout displayed, display the Slide Master tab and then click the Rename button (Slide Master tab | Edit Master group) to display the Rename Layout dialog box.
- Type **Saving Content** in the Layout name text box (Rename Layout dialog box) (Figure 4–40).

2

- Click the Rename button (Rename Layout dialog box) to give the Title and Content Layout the new name, Saving Content Layout.

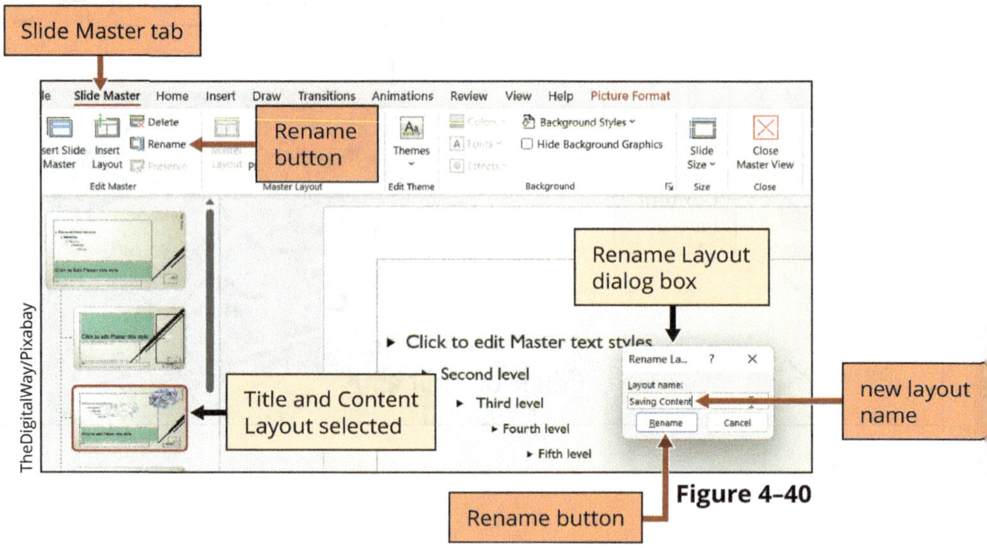

Figure 4–40

3

- Display the Title Slide Layout, click the Rename button, and then type **Saving Title** as the new layout name (Figure 4–41).

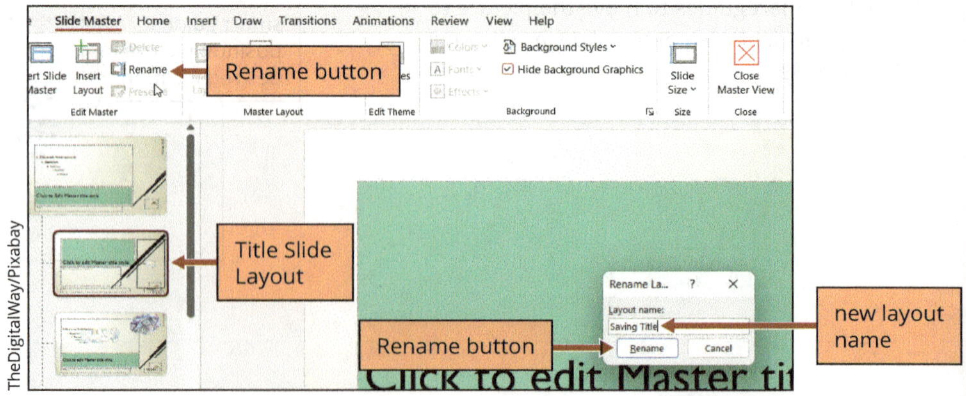

Figure 4–41

4

- Click the Rename button (Rename Layout dialog box) to rename the Title Slide Layout.
- Click the Slice Slide Master layout to display it, click the Rename button, and then type **Saving Master** as the new layout name (Figure 4–42).

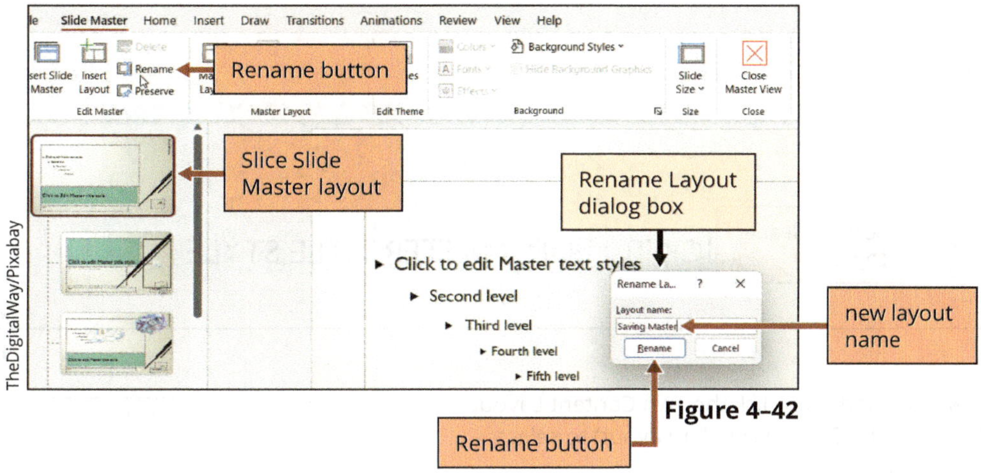

Figure 4–42

5

- Click the Rename button (Rename Layout dialog box).
- Scroll down and display the Comparison Layout, click the Rename button, and then type **Saving Compare** as the new layout name (Figure 4–43).
- Click the Rename button.

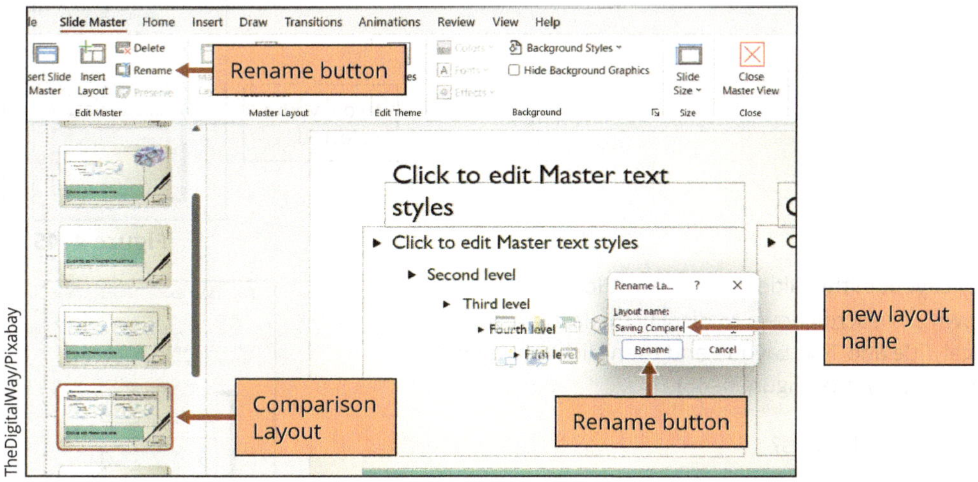

Figure 4–43

To Delete a Slide Layout

You have made many changes to the slide master and three slide layouts. You will use these layouts when you close Master view and then add text to the presentation in Normal view. You can delete the other layouts in the Slides tab. **Why?** You will not use them in this presentation. The following steps delete slide layouts that will not be used to create the presentation.

1

- Scroll up and then click the Section Header Layout in the Slides tab to select it (Figure 4–44).

Figure 4–44

2

- Press and hold down CTRL and then click the Two Content Layout (the layout directly below the Section Header Layout) to select both layouts (Figure 4–45).

3

- Click the Delete button (Slide Master tab | Edit Master group) to delete the two layouts.

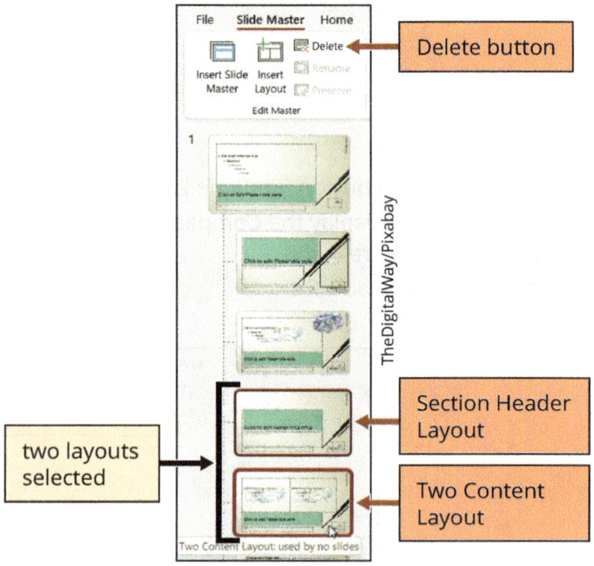

Figure 4–45

4

- Click the Title Only Layout in the Slides tab to select it.
- Press and hold down SHIFT, scroll down to display the last layout, which is the Vertical Title and Text Layout, and then click this layout to select 12 consecutive layouts (Figure 4–46).

Q&A Why did I select these layouts?
You will not use any of these layouts in your presentation.

Why did I hold down SHIFT instead of CTRL to select these layouts?
You press SHIFT to select a range of consecutive slides whereas you press CTRL to select specific slides that may or may not be consecutive.

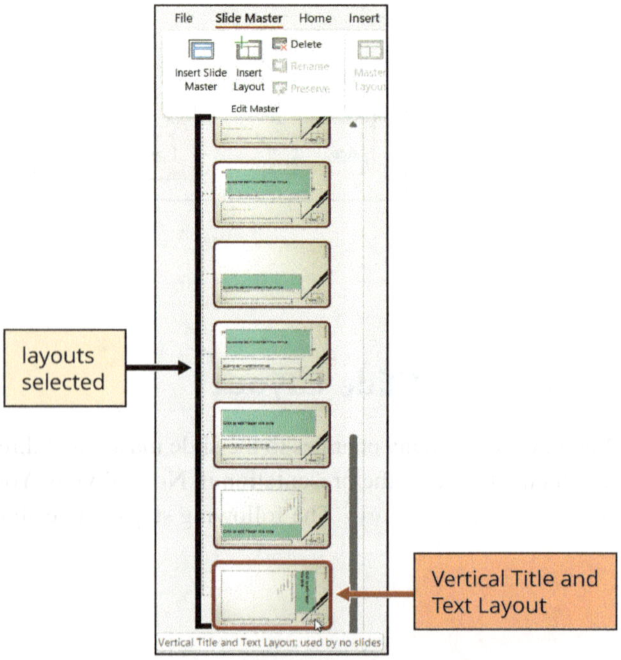

Figure 4–46

5

- Click the Delete button (Slide Master tab | Edit Master group) to delete the 12 layouts (Figure 4–47).

Q&A Now that I have created this slide master, can I ensure that it will not be changed when I create future presentations?
Yes. Normally a slide master is deleted when a new design template is selected. To keep the original master as part of your presentation, you can preserve it by selecting the thumbnail and then clicking Preserve in the Edit Master group. An icon in the shape of a pushpin is displayed below the slide number to indicate the master is preserved. If you decide to unpreserve a slide master, select this thumbnail and then click Preserve.

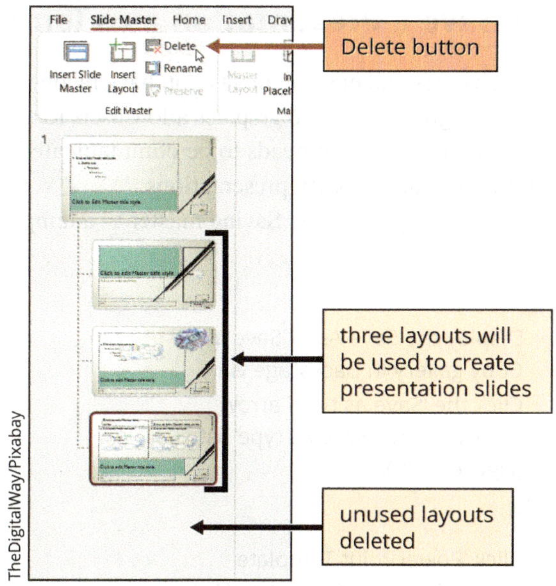

Figure 4–47

Other Ways

1. Click Delete (Home tab | Slides group)
2. Right-click selected slide, click Delete Layout on shortcut menu
3. Press DELETE on keyboard

To Add a New Slide Master Layout

The slide layouts included within each slide master are practical and varied. At times, however, you may desire to create a layout from scratch, especially if your design requires many placeholders and unique design elements. To add a new slide layout, you would perform the following steps.

1. Display the Slide Master tab and then click between the layout thumbnails in the Slides tab to place the pointer where you desire the new slide layout to appear.
2. Click Insert Layout to insert a new slide layout with the name, Custom Layout.
3. Click the Rename button (Slide Master tab | Edit Master group) and type a meaningful name for the new layout.

To Close Master View

You now can exit Master view and return to Normal view. **Why?** All the changes to the slide master are complete. The following steps close Master view.

1

- If necessary, display the Slide Master tab (Figure 4–48).

2

- Click the 'Close Master View' button (Slide Master tab | Close group) to exit Master view and return to Normal view.

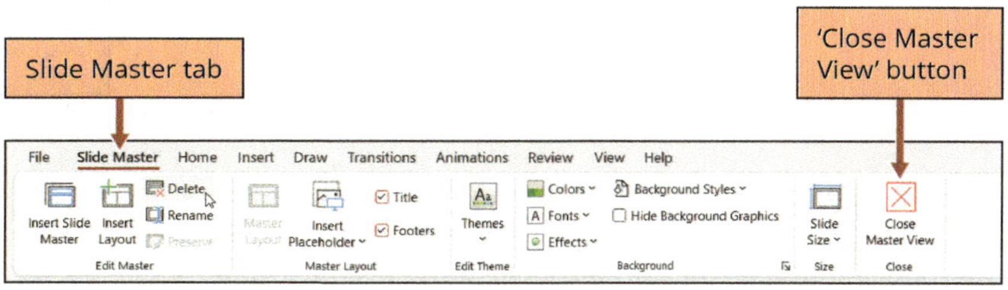

Figure 4–48

To Save a Presentation as a Template

The changes and enhancements you have made to the Saving slide master are excellent starting points for future presentations. The background text and graphics allow users to add text boxes, pictures, SmartArt, tables, and other elements depending upon the specific message that needs to be communicated to an audience. Saving a slide master as a template is convenient when you often reuse and modify presentations. **Why?** You can save your slide layouts as a template to use for a new presentation. The following steps save the Saving master as a template.

1

- Display the Save As or Save a Copy gallery in Backstage view.
- Click the 'Save as type' arrow to display the 'Save as type' list (Figure 4–49).

2

- Click 'PowerPoint Template (*.potx)' in the 'Save as type' list to change the save as type.

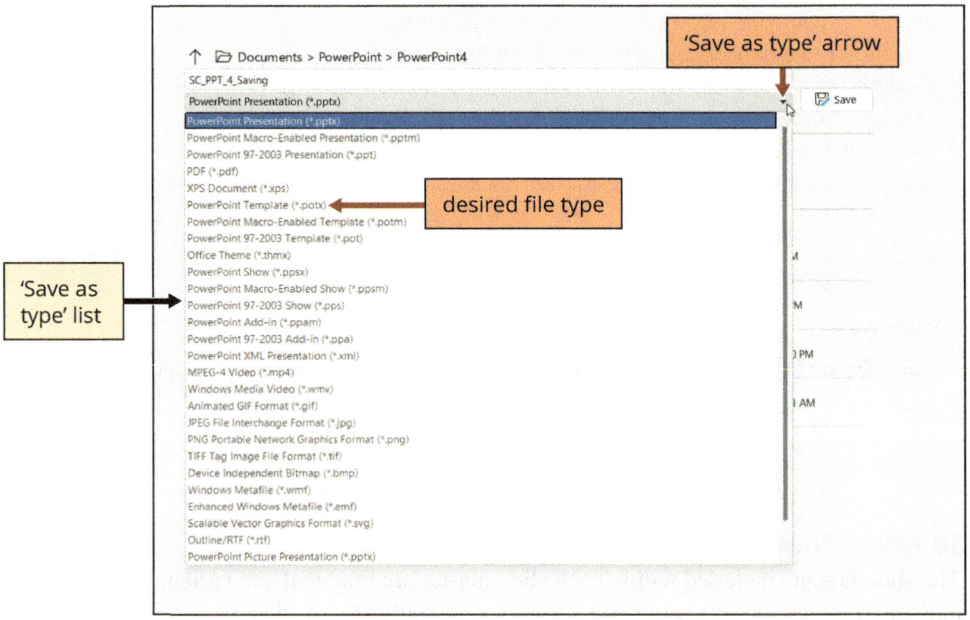

Figure 4–49

Q&A Why do the file name extensions, such as (*.potx), display after the file type in my 'Save as type' list?
These letters identify the file format or type. You can configure Windows to show or hide all common file extensions by opening File Explorer, displaying the View tab, clicking Options, clicking the View tab in the Folder Options dialog box, and then either checking or unchecking 'Hide extensions for known file types' in the Advanced settings area.

- Type **SC_PPT_4_Saving_Template** in the File name box and then navigate to the desired save location (Figure 4–50).

3

- Click Save (Save As or Save a Copy gallery) to save the Saving presentation as a template.

4

- Close the Saving Template file.

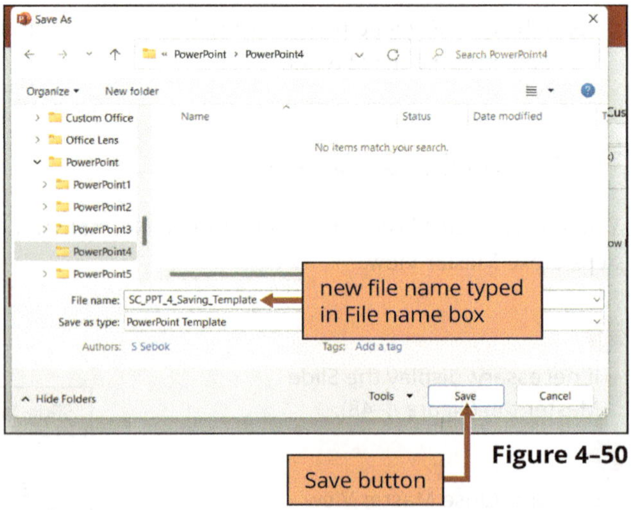

Figure 4–50

Break Point: If you wish to take a break, this is a good place to do so. Be sure the SC_PPT_4_Saving_Template file is saved and then you can exit PowerPoint. To resume later, start PowerPoint and continue following the steps from this location forward.

To Open a Template and Save a Presentation

The Saving Template file you created is a convenient start to a new presentation. The graphical elements and essential slide content are in place; you then can customize the layouts for a specific need, such as a new event or special program. Unless users specify a different location, PowerPoint saves templates they create in a folder called 'Custom Office Templates' in the Documents folder. The following steps open the Saving Template file and save the presentation with the Saving name.

1

- In Backstage view, click the Open tab to display the Open pane.
- If necessary, navigate to the save location, click the file name, SC_PPT_4_Saving_Template.potx, and then click Open (Open dialog box) to open the Saving Template file (Figure 4–51).

Q&A If I did not change the default save location, can I select SC_PPT_4_Saving_Template.potx from the list of Recent Presentations or by opening the Custom Office Templates folder?
Yes. Either technique will locate the desired template.

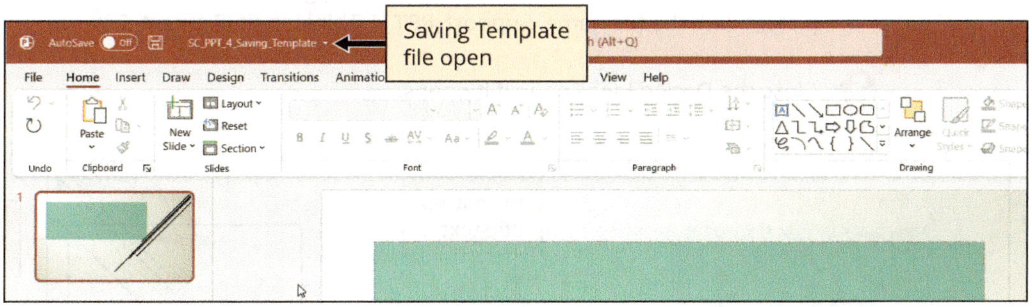

Figure 4–51

2

- In Backstage view, click the Save As or Save a Copy tab to display the Save As or Save a Copy pane.

Q&A Why do I see 'Save a Copy' instead of Save As?
PowerPoint automatically defaults to AutoSave when opening documents.

- Navigate to the location where your files are saved.
- Click the 'Save as type' arrow to display the 'Save as type' list, and then click PowerPoint Presentation (*.pptx) in the 'Save as type' list to change the save as type.
- Click SC_PPT_4_Saving in the Save As dialog box to select the file (Figure 4–52).

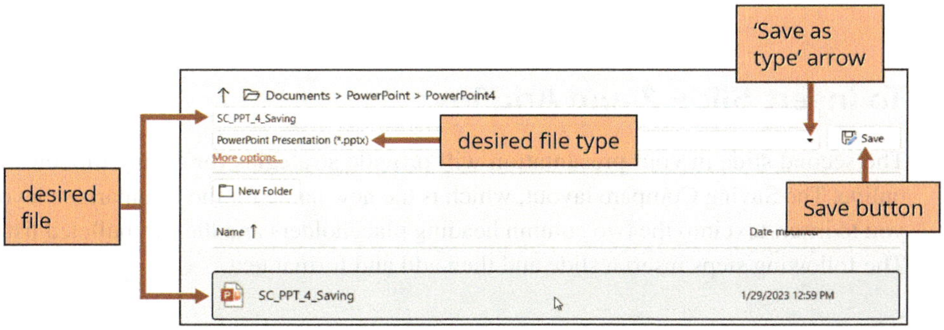

Figure 4–52

3

- Click Save (Save As dialog box) to display the Confirm Save As dialog box.
- Click OK to replace the file.

To Add Text to the Title Slide Layout

The Saving Title layout needs to be applied so that the picture placeholder is displayed on Slide 1. The following steps apply the Saving Title layout and then add text and a picture to the Slide 1 Saving Title layout.

1. Apply the Saving Title layout (Home tab | Slides group), type **Thinking about saving money?** as the title text, and then type **Here's how!** as the subtitle text.
2. Increase the title text font to 72 point and then center and bold this text.
3. Increase the subtitle text font to 48 point, bold and center this text, and then click the Font Color button to change the font color to 'Dark Green, Text 1, Lighter 10%' (last item in the second Theme Colors column).
4. Click the Pictures content placeholder on the right side of the slide and then insert the picture with the file name, Support_PPT_4_Thinking.tif (Figure 4–53).
5. Close the Design Ideas pane if it opens.

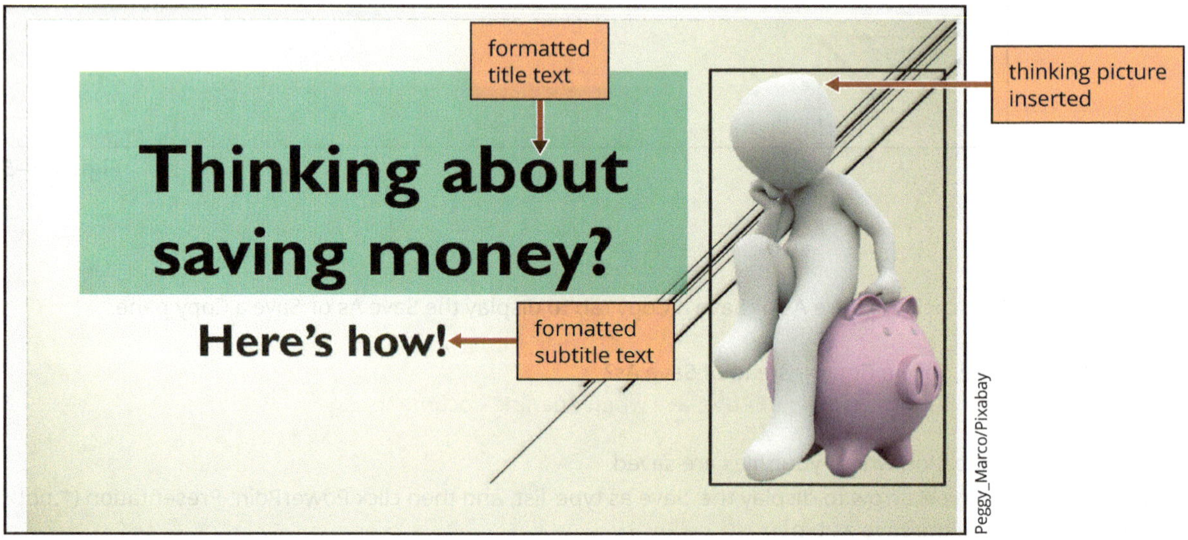

Figure 4–53

To Insert Slide 2 and Add Text

The second slide in your presentation will provide strategies for saving money when shopping online. The Saving Compare layout, which is the new name for the Comparison layout, will allow you to insert text into the two column heading placeholders and the two bulleted list placeholders. The following steps insert a slide and then add and format text.

1. Click the Home tab, insert a slide with the Saving Compare layout, and then type the column headings, bulleted paragraphs, and title text shown in Figure 4–54.

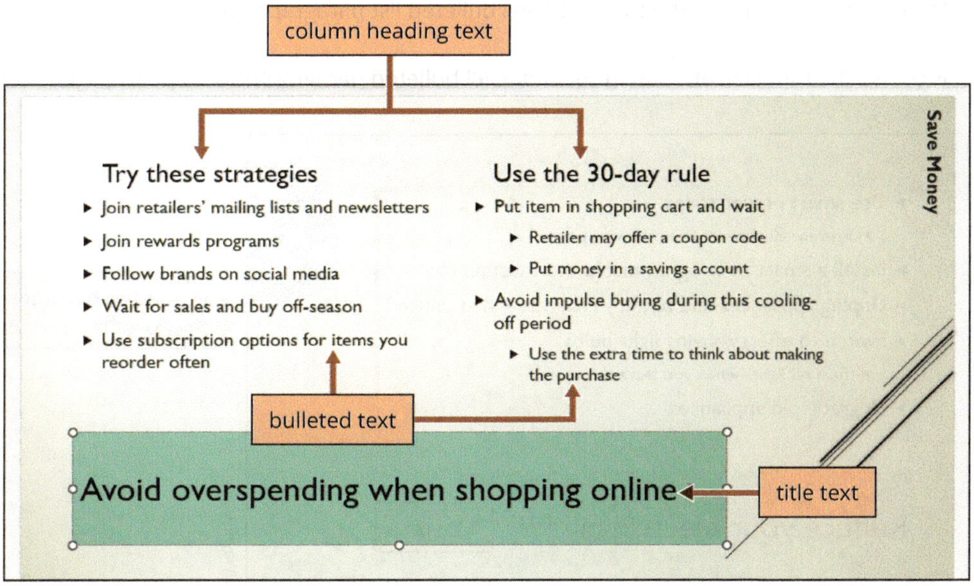

Figure 4–54

To Insert Slide 3 and Add Text

The third slide in your presentation will list details about handling funds and reviewing your spending. The Saving Content layout, which is the new name for the Title and Content Layout, is designed so that you can add variable slide content in the placeholder located next to the picture. The following steps insert a slide and then add and format text.

1. Insert a slide with the Saving Content layout and then type the text shown in Figure 4–55.

2. Increase the font size of the three first-level bulleted paragraphs to 24 point.

3. Increase the font size of the four second-level bulleted paragraphs to 20 point (Figure 4–55).

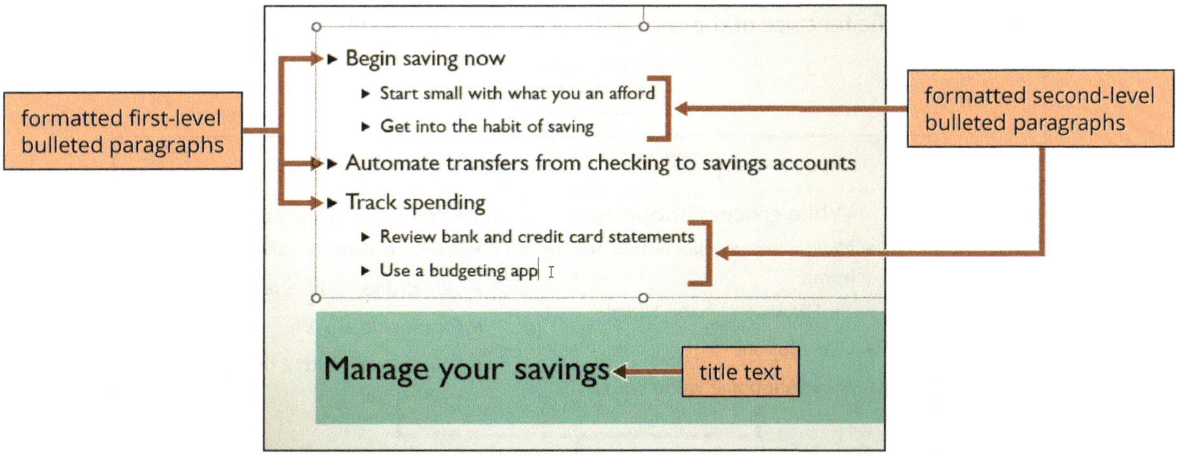

Figure 4–55

To Insert Slide 4 and Add Text

The fourth slide in your presentation will list steps to conserve electricity. This slide uses the Saving Content layout, which you used to create Slide 3. The following steps insert a slide and then add and format text.

1. Insert a slide with the Saving Content layout and then type the text shown in Figure 4–56.
2. Increase the font size of the five first-level bulleted list paragraphs to 24 point.
3. Increase the font size of the two second-level bulleted paragraphs to 20 point (Figure 4–56).

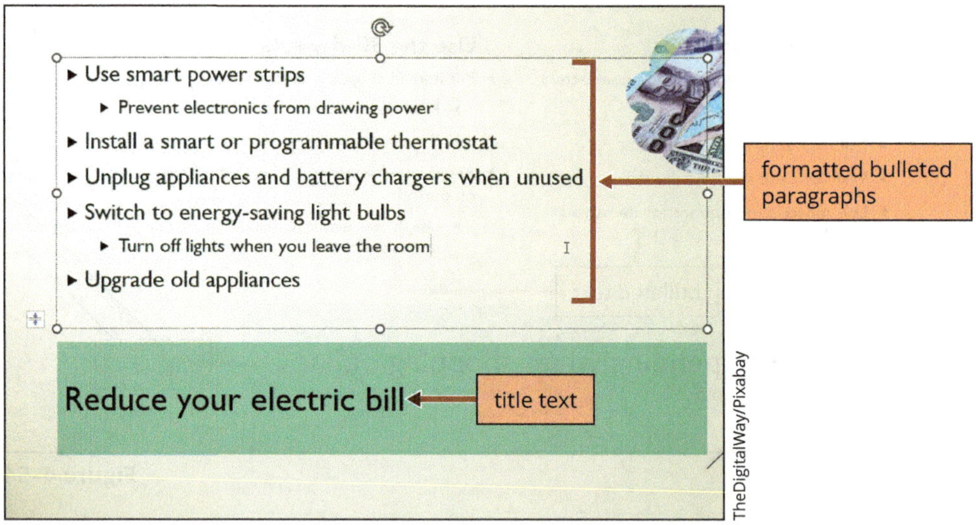

Figure 4–56

To Insert Slide 5 and Add Text

The last slide in your presentation gives advice on saving money when grocery shopping and dining at restaurants. It uses the Saving Compare layout, which is the layout you used for Slide 2. The following steps insert a slide and then add and format text.

1. Insert a slide with the Saving Compare layout and then type the text shown in Figure 4–57.
2. Increase the font size of the seven first-level bulleted paragraphs to 24 point.
3. Increase the font size of the second-level bulleted paragraph to 20 point (Figure 4–57).

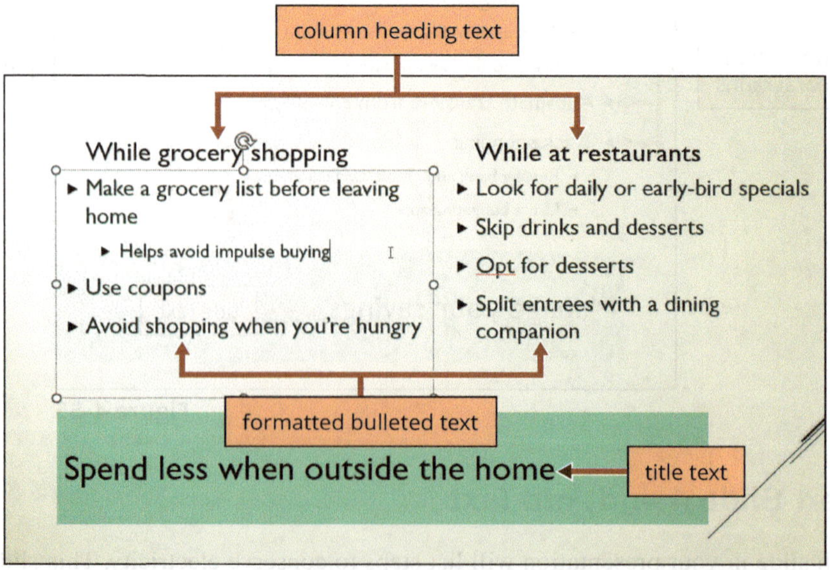

Figure 4–57

To Use the Thesaurus

Why? When reviewing your slide show, you may decide that a particular word does not express the exact usage you intended or that you used the same word on multiple slides. In these cases, you could find a **synonym**, or word similar in meaning, to replace the inappropriate or duplicate word. PowerPoint provides a **thesaurus**, which is a list of synonyms, to help you find a replacement word.

In this project, you want to find a synonym to replace the word, savings, on Slide 3 with the word, funds. The following steps locate an appropriate synonym and replace the word.

1

- Display Slide 3 and then place the insertion point in the word, savings, in the title text placeholder.

2

- Display the Review tab and then click the Thesaurus button (Review tab | Proofing group) to display the Thesaurus pane with synonyms for the word, savings (Figure 4–58).

BTW
Touch Mode Differences
The Microsoft 365 and Windows interfaces may vary if you are using a touch screen. For this reason, you might notice that the function or appearance of your touch screen differs slightly from this module's presentation.

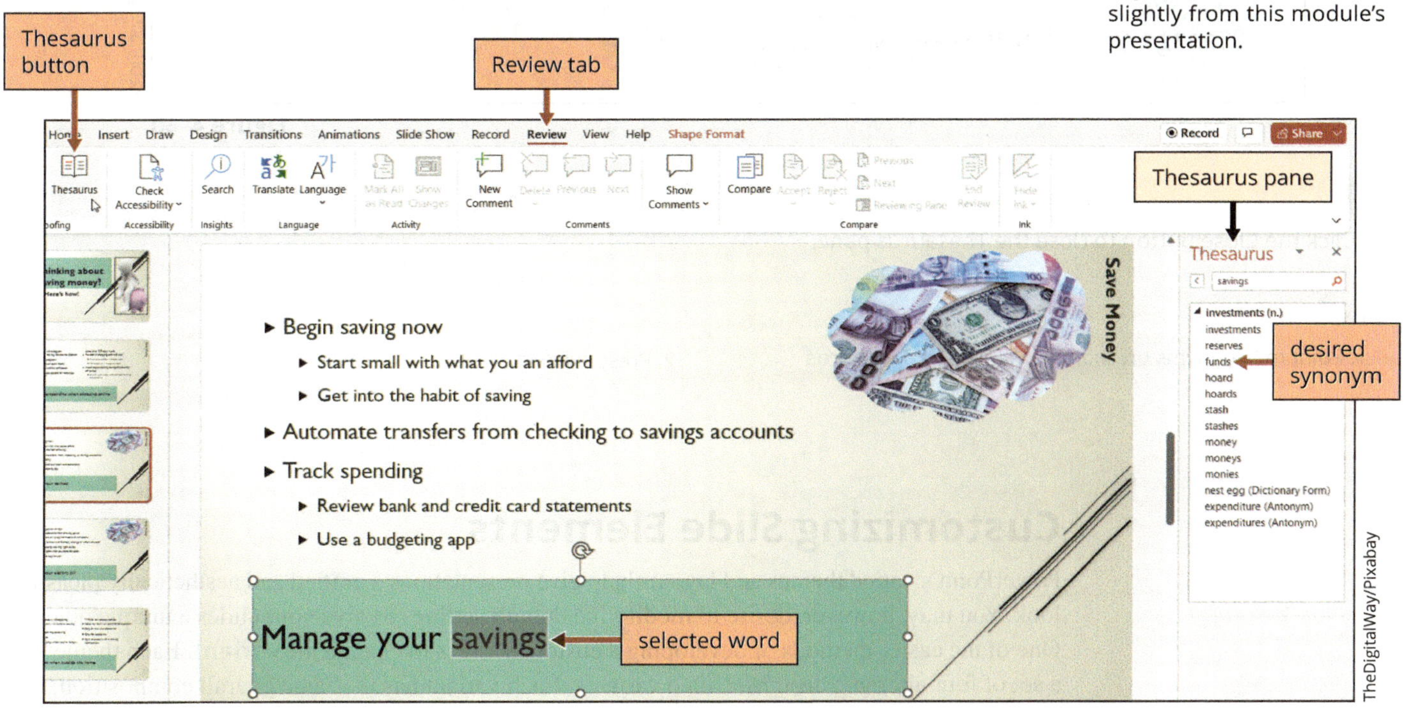

Figure 4–58

3

- Point to the synonym you want (funds) in the synonyms list and then click the arrow on the right side of that word to display the synonym menu (Figure 4–59).

Q&A How do I locate a synonym for multiple words?
You need to select all the words and then right-click to display the shortcut menu.

If I am using a touch screen, how do I find a synonym?
Tap Thesaurus (Review tab | Proofing group) to display the Thesaurus pane for the selected word. Then, in the pane, tap the arrow next to the word to display a shortcut menu.

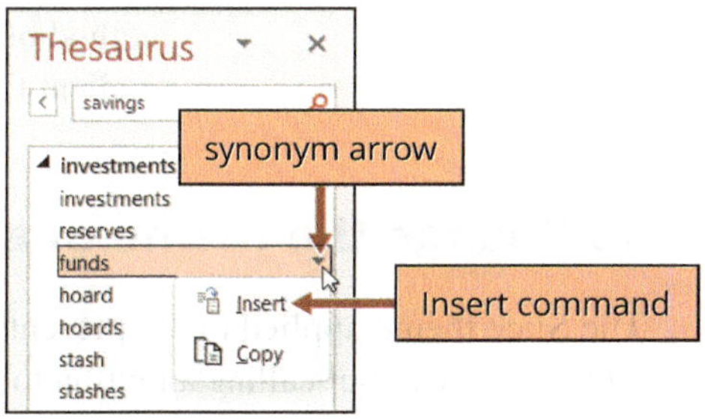

Figure 4–59

4

- Click Insert to replace the word, savings, with the word, funds (Figure 4–60).

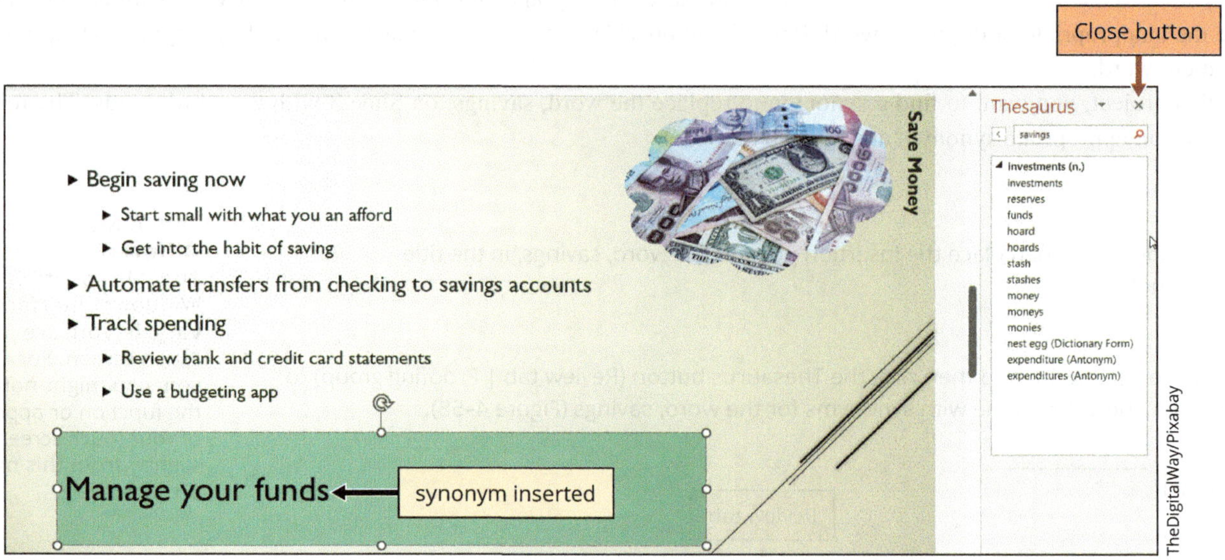

Figure 4–60

5

- Click the Close button to close the Thesaurus pane.

Other Ways

1. Point to Synonyms on shortcut menu, click Thesaurus
2. Press SHIFT+F7

Customizing Slide Elements

PowerPoint's varied themes and layouts help give presentations a unified and aesthetically pleasing look. You may, however, desire to modify the default settings to give your slides a unique quality. One of the easier methods of developing a custom show is to change the **variant**. Each theme has a set of four alternate designs, called variants. Each variant has the same overall composition, but the colors, fonts, and design elements differ. You can select a variant that best fits your overall design needs. If you later decide that another variant would better fit the presentation's general theme, you can change this element while you are developing slides.

You also can change the theme for one or more slides, not an entire presentation. One other method of altering your slides slightly is to change the backgrounds, including adding a picture, gradient fill, pattern, or texture.

To Change the Theme of a Single Slide

The Slice theme applied to the presentation is appropriate for this topic. The font and placeholder locations are simple and add variety without calling attention to the design elements. The following steps change the theme for Slide 5. **Why?** To call attention to the electricity content in the bulleted list on Slide 5, you can apply an equally effective theme that has a design element resembling a circuit board. You then can modify this new theme by changing the variant on one slide.

1

- Display Slide 4, click the Design tab, click the Themes More button, and then point to the Circuit theme to see a preview of that theme on Slide 4 (Figure 4–61).
- **Experiment:** Point to various document themes in the Themes gallery and watch the colors and fonts change on Slide 4.

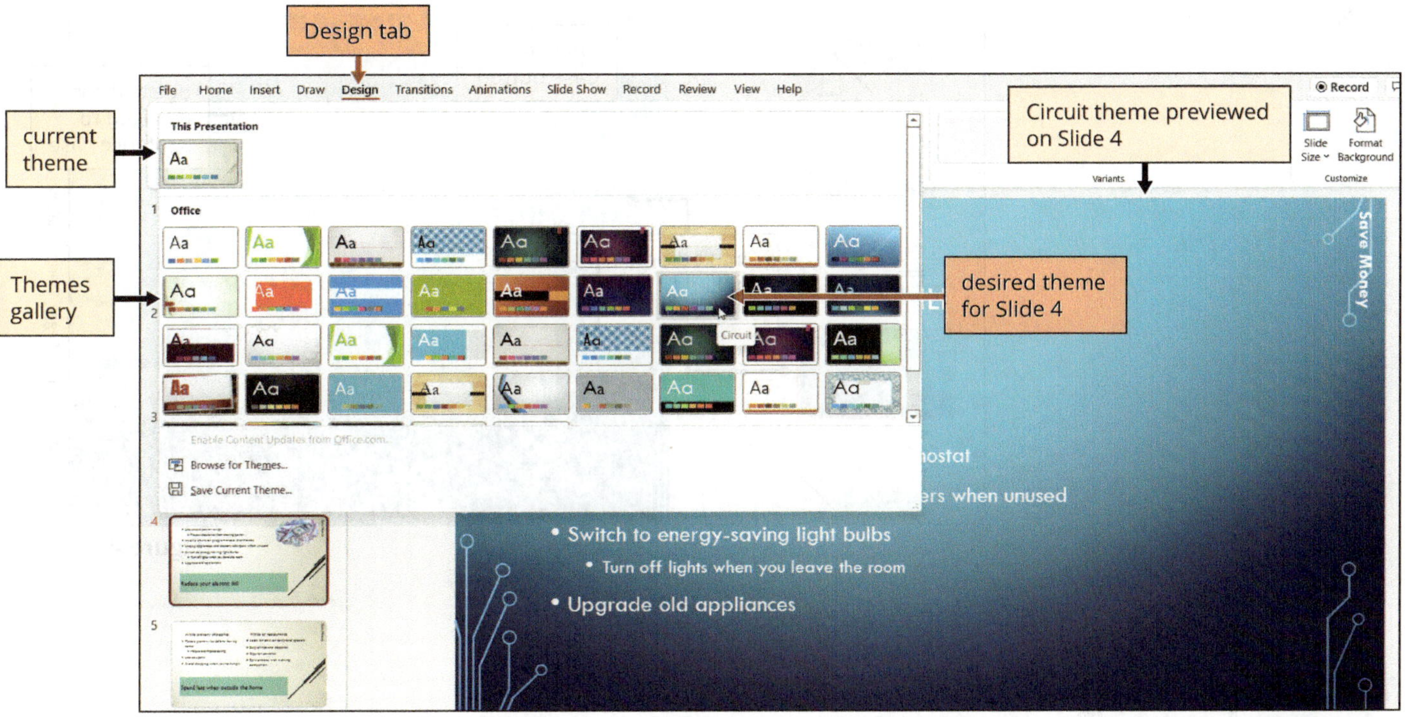

Figure 4–61

2

- Right-click the Circuit theme to display a shortcut menu (Figure 4–62).

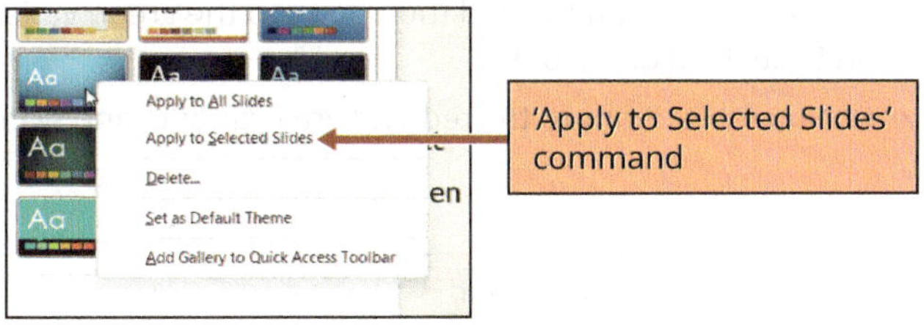

Figure 4–62

3

- Click 'Apply to Selected Slides' to apply the Circuit theme to Slide 4 only.

4

- Select the title text (REDUCE YOUR ELECTRIC BILL), display the Home tab, and then click the Change Case button.
- Click Sentence case. in the Change Case gallery to change the case of the title text.

5

- Click outside of the title text placeholder to deselect the object (Figure 4-63).
- If the Design Ideas pane is displayed, close it.

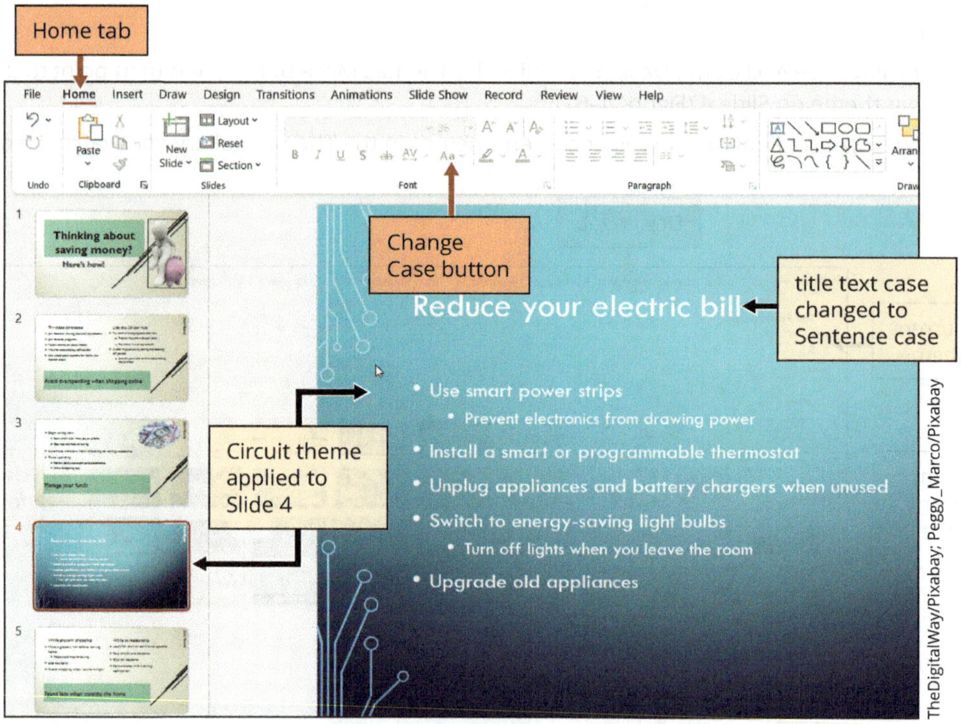

Figure 4–63

To Change the Theme Variant

The Circuit theme on Slide 4 has a default blue variant. You can change the color variant for this slide at any time for any theme, and you want to change the color to green **Why?** The theme colors are green, so this color on Slide 4 complements the presentation's color scheme. The following steps change the variant from blue to green.

1

- Display the Design tab and then point to the green variant (Design tab | Variants group) to see a preview of the green variant on Slide 4 (Figure 4–64).
- **Experiment:** Point to the red and gray variants and watch the colors change on the slide.

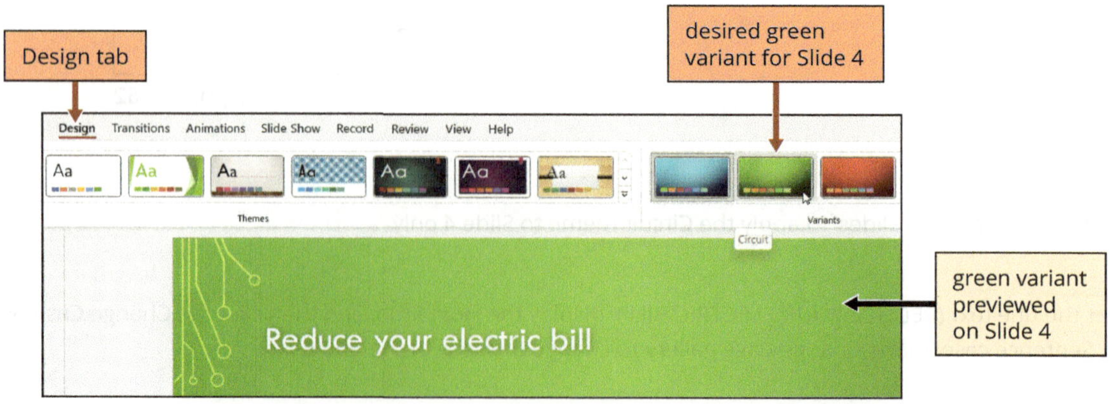

Figure 4–64

2

- Click the green variant to apply this color to Slide 4 (Figure 4–65).

Q&A If I decide at some future time that this color variation does not fit the theme of my presentation, can I apply a different variant?
Yes. You can repeat these steps at any time.

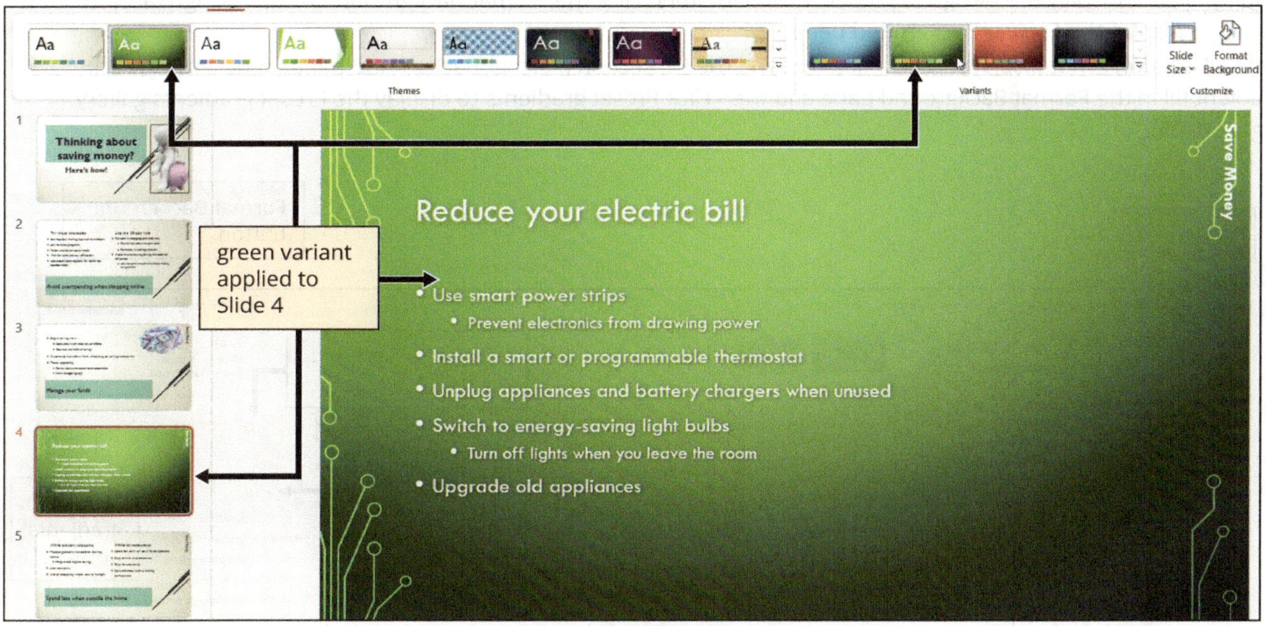

TheDigitalWay/Pixabay; Peggy_Marco/Pixabay

Figure 4–65

3

- If the Design Ideas pane is displayed, close it.

Formatting Slide Backgrounds

A slide's background is an integral part of a presentation because it can generate audience interest. Every slide can have the same background, or different backgrounds can be used in a presentation. This background is considered **fill**, which is the content that makes up the interior of a shape, line, or character. Four fills are available: solid, gradient, picture or texture, and pattern. **Solid fill** is one color used throughout the entire slide. **Gradient fill** is one color shade gradually progressing to another shade of the same color or one color progressing to another color. **Picture fill** uses a specific file or image to fill the background or shape. **Texture fill** uses a specific file or an image that simulates a material, such as cork, granite, marble, or canvas. **Pattern fill** adds designs, such as dots or dashes, which repeat in rows across the slide.

Once you add a fill, you can adjust its appearance. For example, you can adjust its **transparency**, or the opacity of an object, which allows you to see through the background, so that any text on the slide is visible. You also can select a color that is part of the theme or a custom color. You can use an **offset**, another background feature, to move the background away from the slide borders in varying distances by percentage. A **tiling option** repeats the background image many times vertically and horizontally on the slide; the smaller the tiling percentage, the greater the number of times the image is repeated.

To Change the Slide Background to a Gradient Fill

For each theme, PowerPoint provides 30 preset gradient fills with five designs for each of the six major theme colors. Each fill has one dark color shade that gradually lightens to either another shade of the same color or another color. You decide that a gradient fill would be suitable for Slide 1. **Why?** The current background is plain, so you want to add a minimal design element to enhance the overall slide. The following steps replace the background on Slide 1 to a preset gradient fill.

1

- Display Slide 1, display the Design tab if necessary, and then click the Format Background button (Design tab | Customize group) to display the Format Background pane.
- If the Fill section is not displayed, click Fill to expand the Fill section (Format Background pane). If necessary, click Gradient fill in the Format Background pane and then click Preset gradients to display the Preset gradients gallery (Figure 4–66).

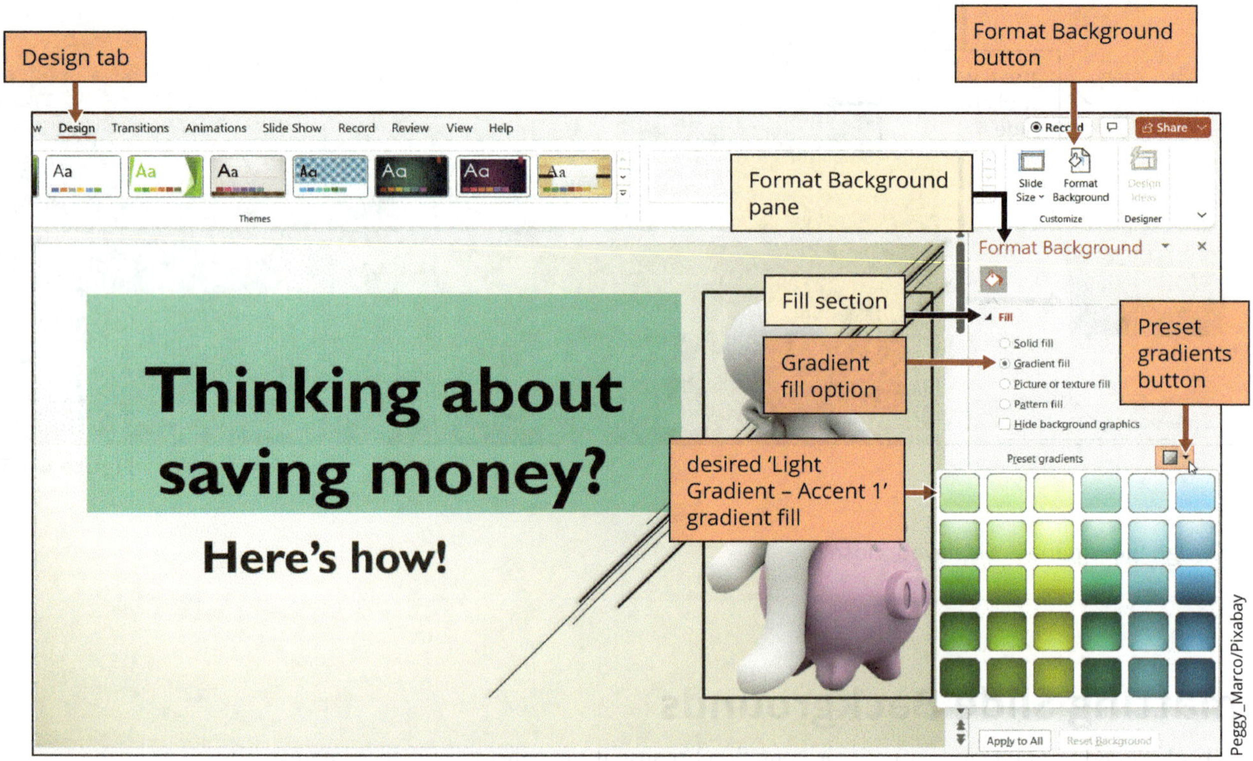

Figure 4–66

Q&A Are the backgrounds displayed in a specific order?

Yes. The first row has light colors at the top of the background; the middle rows have darker fills at the bottom; the bottom row has overall dark fills on all edges.

Is a live preview available to see the various gradients on this slide?

No. Live preview is not an option with the background textures and fills.

2

- Click 'Light Gradient – Accent 1' (first fill in the first row) to apply that style to Slide 1 (Figure 4–67).

Q&A If I decide later that this background gradient does not fit the theme of my presentation, can I apply a different background?

Yes. You can repeat these steps at any time while creating your presentation.

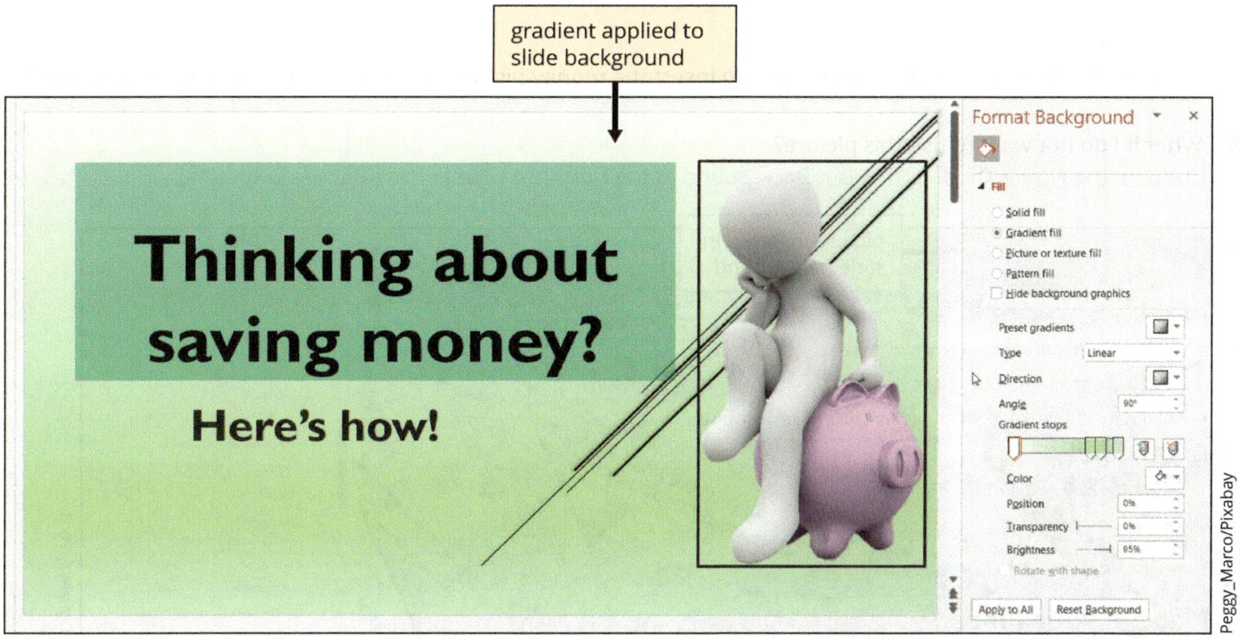

Figure 4–67

Other Ways

1. Click Design tab, click Format Background (Customize group), select desired options (Format Background pane)
2. Right-click background, click Format Background on shortcut menu, select desired options (Format Background pane)

To Change the Slide Background to a Picture

Why? For variety and interest, you want to use a picture as the Slide 3 background. The picture can be the same picture inserted in the Saving Content slide master. PowerPoint will stretch the height and width of this picture to fill the slide area. The following steps insert the money picture as a background on Slide 3 only.

1

- Display Slide 3. With the Fill section displayed (Format Background pane), click 'Picture or texture fill', click Insert (Format Background pane), and then click From a File to display the Insert Picture dialog box. If necessary, navigate to the location where your Data Files are located.
- Click Support_PPT_4_Money to select the .jpg file (Figure 4–68).

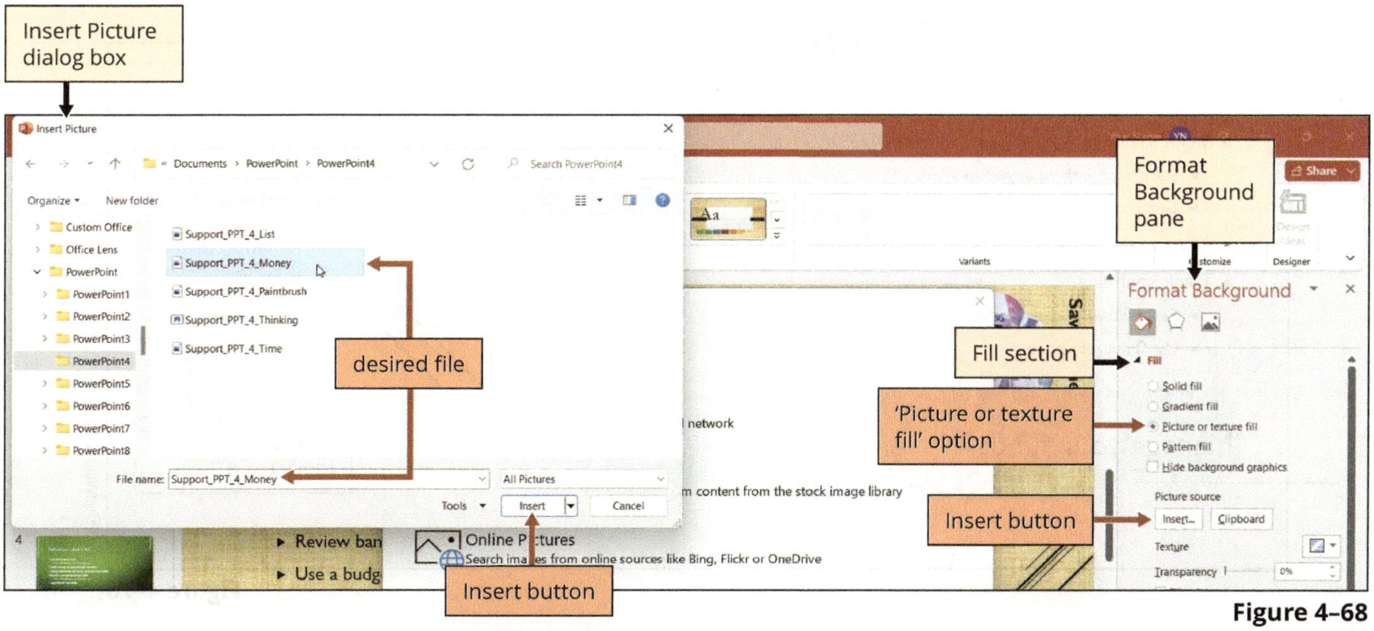

Figure 4–68

2

- Click the Insert button (Insert Picture dialog box) to insert the money picture as the Slide 2 background (Figure 4–69).

Q&A What if I do not want to use this picture?
Click Undo on the Home tab or click Reset Background at the bottom of the Format Background pane.

Figure 4–69

To Change the Transparency of a Slide Background

The **Transparency slider** lets you indicate the degree of an object's opaqueness. The default setting is 0, which is fully opaque. The opposite extreme is 100%, which is fully transparent. To change the transparency, you can move the Transparency slider or enter a number in the box next to the slider. The following step increases the Slide 3 background transparency to 85%. **Why?** The colorful money picture is obscuring the slide text.

1

- Click the Transparency slider in the Fill section (Format Background pane) and drag it to the right until 85% is displayed in the Transparency box (Figure 4–70).

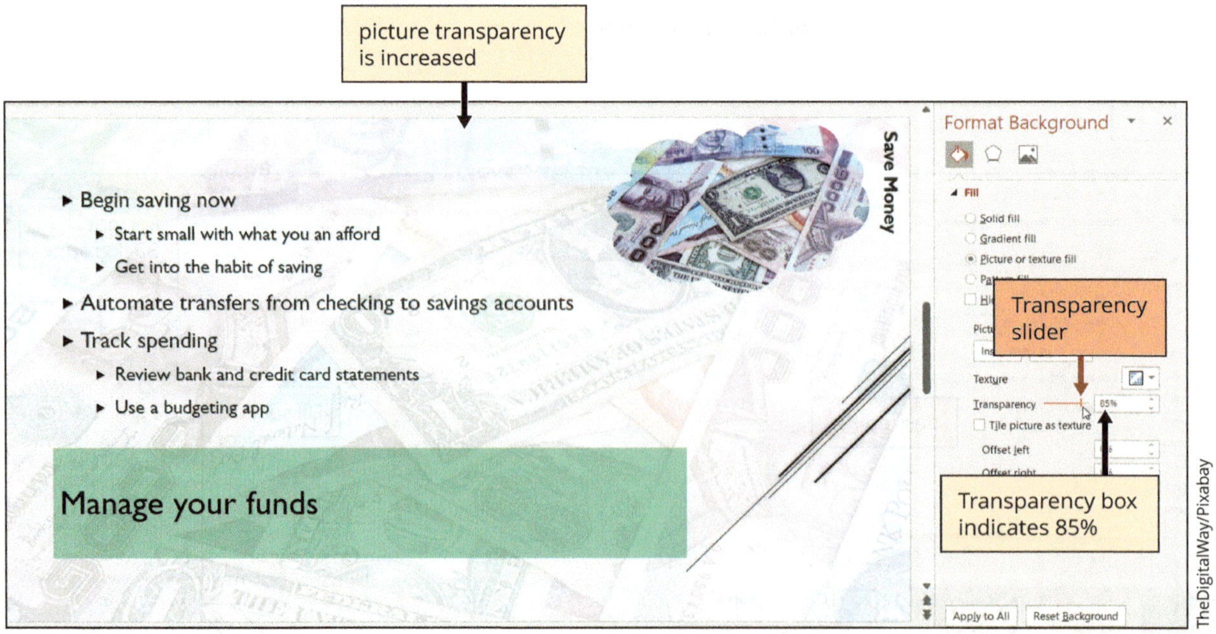

Figure 4–70

- **Experiment:** Drag the Transparency slider to the left and right and watch the text box background change.

Q&A Can I move the slider in small increments so that I can get a precise percentage easily?
Yes. Click the up or down arrows in the Transparency box to move the slider in 1% increments.

Other Ways

1. Enter percentage in Transparency text box
2. Click Transparency up or down arrow

To Change the Slide Background to a Pattern

You add variety to a slide by making a pattern fill. This design of repeating horizontal or vertical lines, dots, dashes, or stripes can enhance the visual appeal of one or more slides in the presentation. If you desire to change the colors in the pattern, PowerPoint allows you to select the fill foreground and background colors by clicking Color and then choosing the desired colors. The following steps apply a pattern to Slide 2. **Why?** The dots in this pattern are a subtle contrast to the Slice theme slide elements.

1

- Display Slide 2. With the Fill section displayed (Format Background pane), click Pattern fill to display the Pattern gallery and the Dotted: 5% pattern on Slide 2 (Figure 4–71).
- **Experiment:** Click various patterns in the Pattern gallery and watch the Slide 3 background change.

Q&A How can I delete a pattern if I decide not to apply one to my slide?
If the Format Background pane is displayed, click Reset Background. If you already have applied the pattern, you must click Undo on the Quick Access Toolbar.

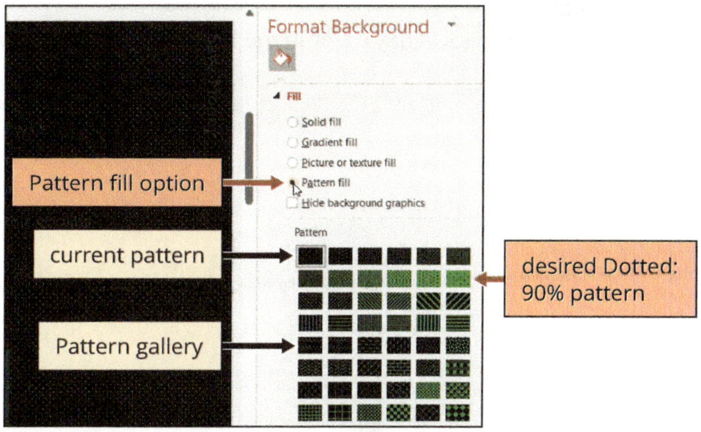

Figure 4–71

2

- Click Dotted: 90% (last pattern in the second row) to apply this pattern to the Slide 2 background (Figure 4–72).

Q&A Can I apply this pattern to all the slides in the presentation?
Yes. You would click 'Apply to All' in the Format Background pane.

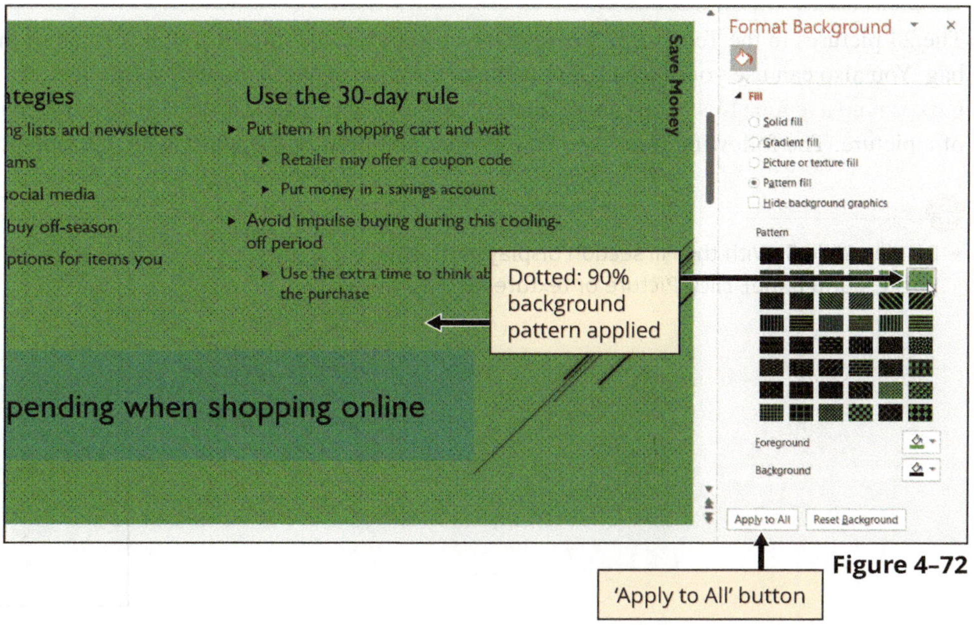

Figure 4–72

3

- Click the Foreground button (Format Background pane) to display the Colors gallery (Figure 4–73).

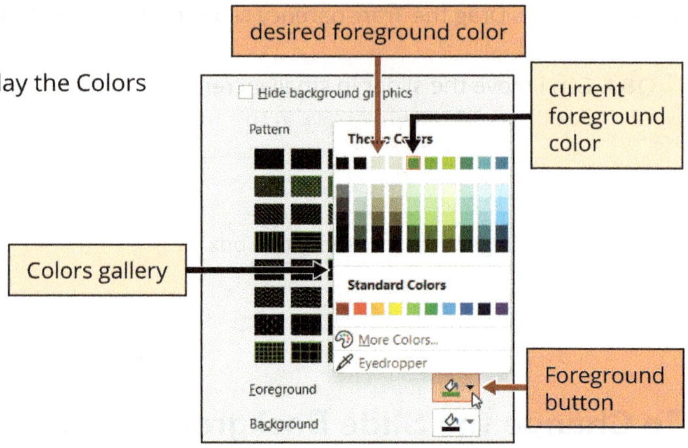

Figure 4–73

4

- Click 'Tan, Background 2' (third color in the first Theme Colors row) to change the foreground color (Figure 4–74).

Q&A Can I apply this pattern and color to all the slides in the presentation?
Yes. You would click 'Apply to All' in the Format Background pane.

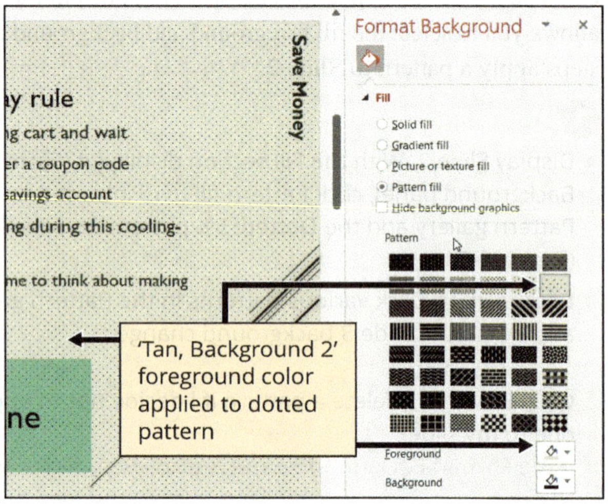

Figure 4–74

To Change the Slide Background to a Texture

The 24 pictures in the Texture gallery give the appearance of a physical object, such as marble, sand, tissue paper, and a paper bag. You also can use your own texture pictures for custom backgrounds. **Why?** Various texture fills are available to give your background a unique look. You can adjust the transparency of a slide texture in the same manner that you change the transparency of a picture. The following steps insert the Walnut texture fill on Slide 5 in the presentation and then change the transparency.

1

- Display Slide 5. With the Fill section displayed (Format Background pane), click 'Picture or texture fill' (Figure 4–75).

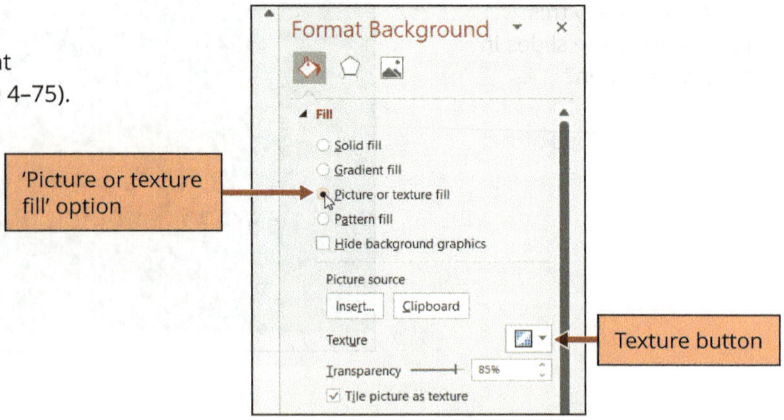

Figure 4–75

2

- Click the Texture button to display the Texture gallery (Figure 4–76).

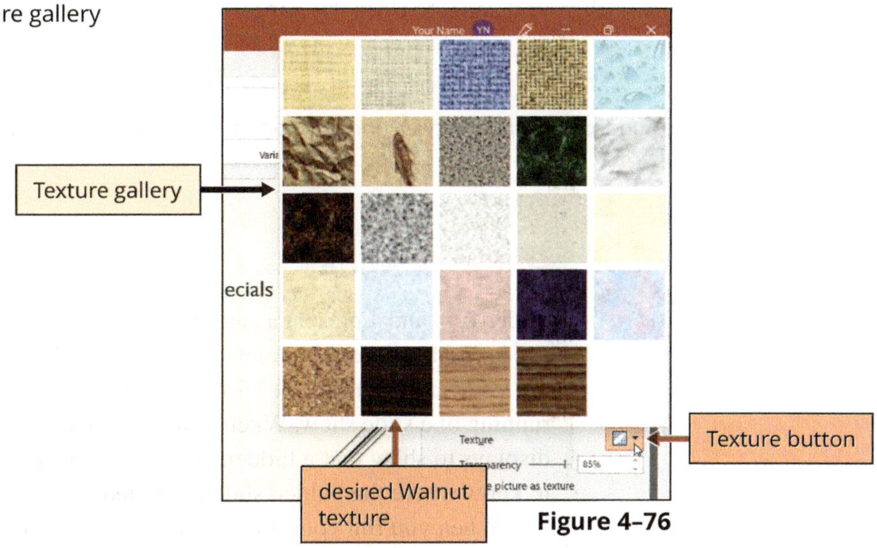

Figure 4–76

3

- Click the Walnut texture (second texture in the last row) to insert this texture fill as the background on Slide 5 (Figure 4–77).

Q&A Is a live preview available to see the various textures on this slide?

No. Live preview is not an option with the background textures and fills.

Why doesn't the Walnut texture appear dark brown as shown in the Texture gallery?

Because the transparency still is set to 85%.

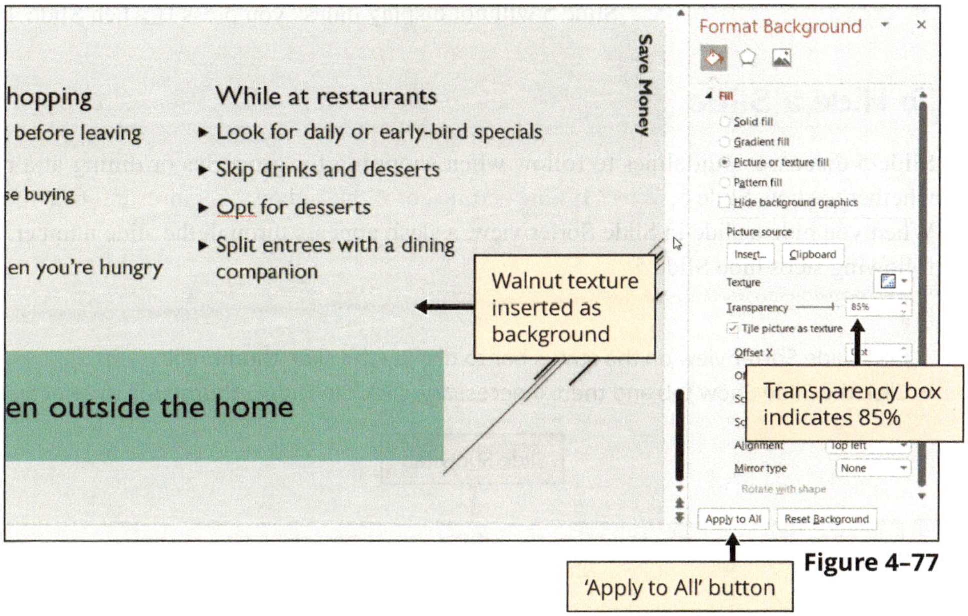

Figure 4–77

4

- Click the Transparency slider and drag it to the left until 75% is displayed in the Transparency box (Figure 4–78).
- **Experiment:** Drag the Transparency slider to the left and right and watch the slide background change.

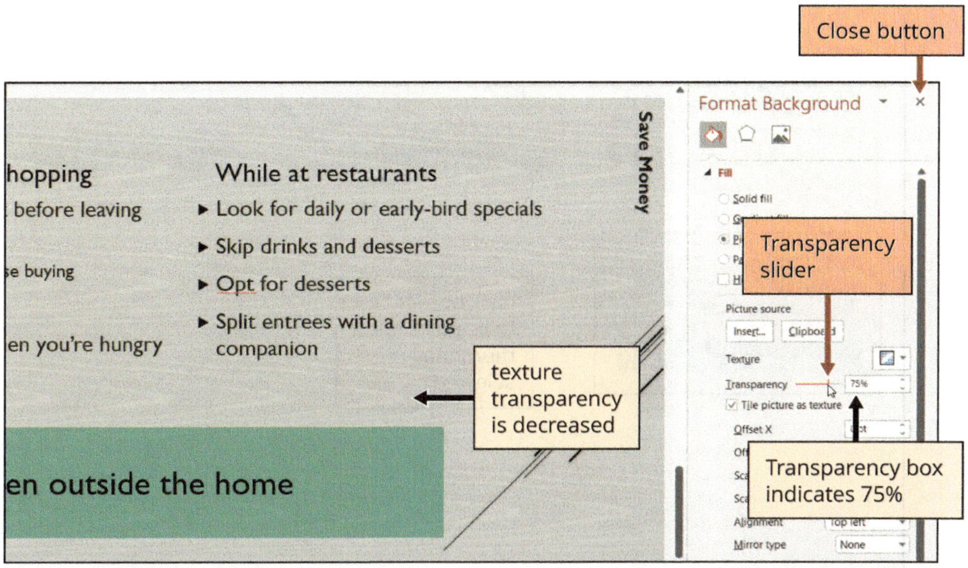

Figure 4–78

5

- Click Close (Format Background pane) to close the pane.

Other Ways

1. Right-click background, click Format Background on shortcut menu, select desired options (Format Background pane)

Hiding a Slide

Slides 2, 3, and 4 present a variety of emergency preparation advice. Depending on the audience's needs and the time constraints, you may decide not to display one or more of these slides. If need be, you can use the **Hide Slide** command to hide a slide from the audience during the normal running of a slide show. When you want to display the hidden slide, press H. No visible indicator displays to show that a hidden slide exists. You must be aware of the content of the presentation to know where the hidden slide is located.

When you run your presentation, the hidden slide does not display unless you press H when the slide preceding the hidden slide is displayed. For example, if you choose to hide Slide 5, then Slide 5 will not display unless you press H when Slide 4 displays in Slide Show view.

To Hide a Slide

Slide 5 discusses guidelines to follow when shopping for groceries or dining at a restaurant. As the presenter, you decide whether to show Slide 5. **Why?** If time permits, or if the audience requires information on this subject, you can display Slide 5. When you hide a slide in Slide Sorter view, a slash appears through the slide number, which indicates the slide is hidden. The following steps hide Slide 5.

1

- Click Slide Sorter view on the status bar to display the slide thumbnails.
- Click the Slide Show tab and then, if necessary, click the Slide 5 thumbnail to select it (Figure 4–79).

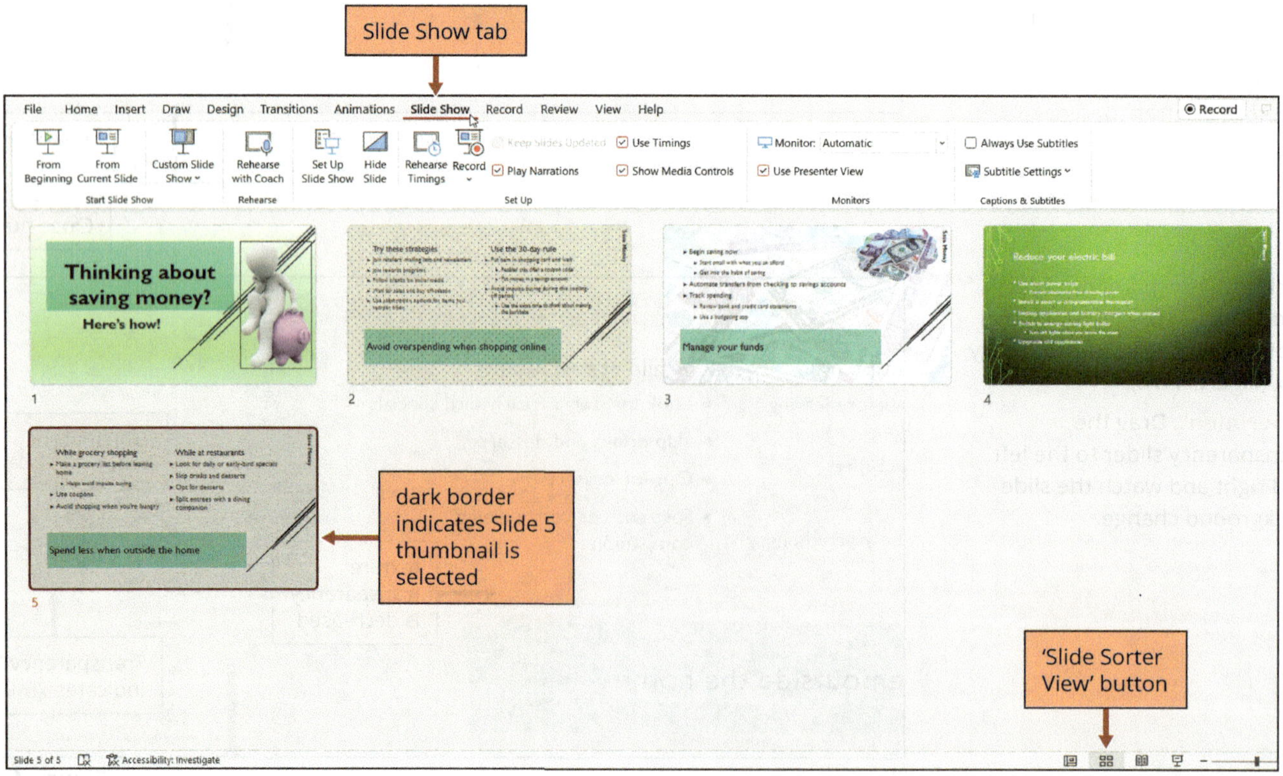

TheDigitalWay/Pixabay; Peggy_Marco/Pixabay

Figure 4–79

2

- Click the Hide Slide button (Slide Show tab | Set Up group) to hide Slide 5 (Figure 4–80).

Q&A How do I know that Slide 5 is hidden?
The slide number has a slash through it and the slide thumbnail is shaded to indicate Slide 5 is a hidden slide.

What if I decide I no longer want to hide a slide?
Repeat Step 2. The Hide Slide button is a toggle; it either hides or displays a slide.

3

- Click the Normal view button to display Slide 5.

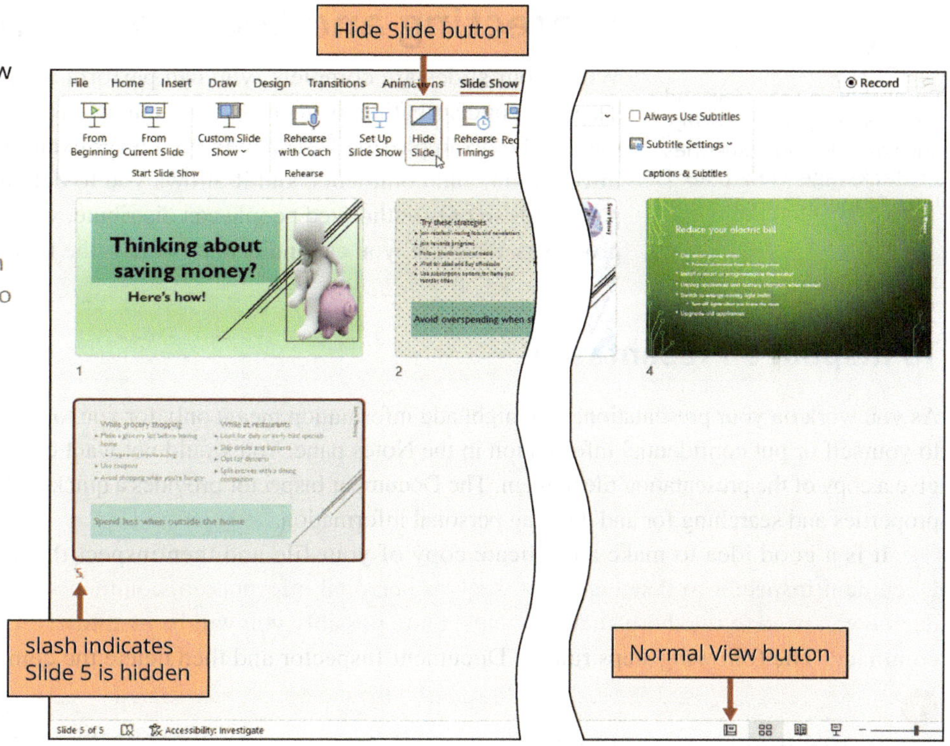

TheDigitalWay/Pixabay; Peggy_Marco/Pixabay

Figure 4–80

Other Ways

1. Right-click desired slide in Slide Sorter view or Normal view on Slides tab, click Hide Slide on shortcut menu

To Add a Slide Transition

A final enhancement you will make in this presentation is to apply the Cube transition to all slides and then change the transition speed and effect option. The following steps apply a transition and effect to the presentation.

1 Display the Transitions tab and then apply the Cube transition in the Exciting category.

2 Change the duration to 03.00 to all five slides in the presentation (Figure 4–81).

Figure 4–81

BTW
Editing Document Properties
Recall that you can view and edit document properties such as Title and Categories in Backstage view (File | Info, Properties area).

Protecting and Securing a Presentation

When your slides are complete, you can perform additional functions to finalize the file and prepare it for distributing to other users or running on a computer other than the one used to develop the file. For example, the **Document Inspector** examines a file for hidden properties, personal information, and comments, and it allows you to delete these slide elements. You also can set passwords so only authorized people can distribute, view, or modify your slides. When the review process is complete, you can indicate this file is the final version.

To Inspect a Presentation

As you work on your presentation, you might add information meant only for you to see. For example, you might write comments to yourself or put confidential information in the Notes pane. You would not want other people to access this information if you give a copy of the presentation file to them. The Document Inspector provides a quick and efficient method of viewing all document properties and searching for and deleting personal information.

It is a good idea to make a duplicate copy of your file and then inspect this new second copy. **Why?** If you tell the Document Inspector to delete content, such as personal information, comments, invisible slide content, or notes, and then decide you need to see those slide elements, quite possibly you will be unable to retrieve the information by using the Undo command. The following steps run the Document Inspector and then delete the comments.

1

- Open Backstage view, click the Info tab, and then click 'Check for Issues' to display the 'Check for Issues' menu (Figure 4–82).

2

- Click Inspect Document. If the Microsoft PowerPoint dialog box is displayed asking if you want to save your presentation, click Yes to save the file.
- Click Inspect to check the document and display the inspection results.

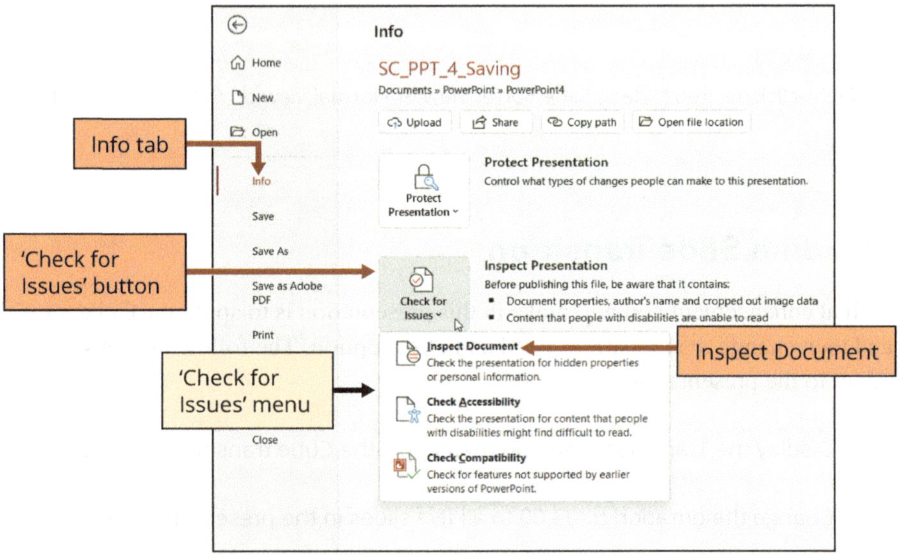

Figure 4–82

Q&A What information does the Document Inspector check?
This information includes text in the Info pane, such as your name and company. Other information includes details of when the file was last saved, objects formatted as invisible, graphics and text you dragged off a slide, presentation notes, and email headers.

3

- View the inspection results to see information that possibly could be removed (Figure 4–83).

Q&A What would happen if I click Remove All in the 'Document Properties and Personal Information' section of the inspection results?
You would delete all identifying information, such as your name, that is saved.

4

- Click the Close button (Document Inspector dialog box) to close the dialog box without removing any information.

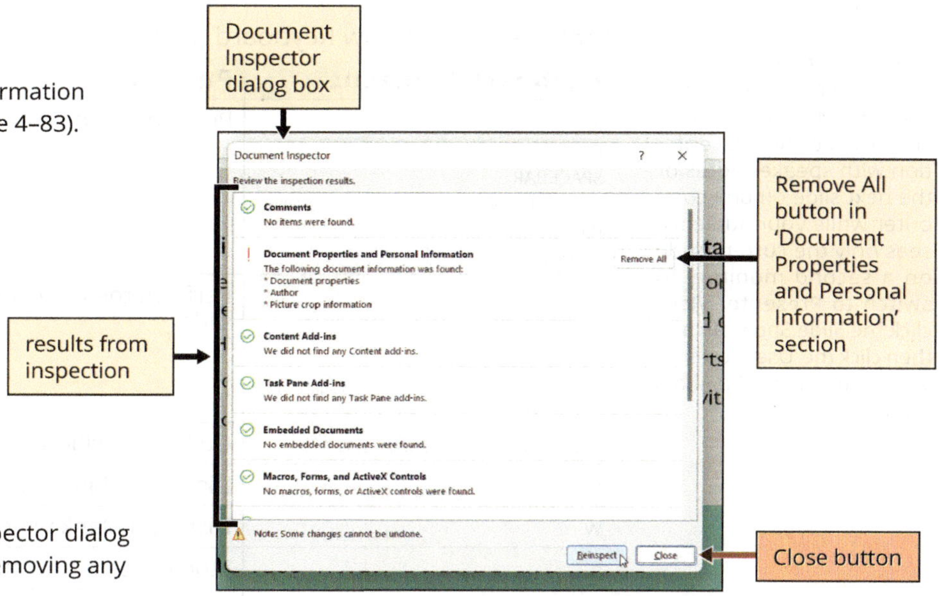

Figure 4–83

To Mark a Presentation as Final

When your slides are completed, you may want to prevent others or yourself from accidentally changing the slide content or features. If you use the **Mark as Final** command, the presentation becomes a read-only document. To mark the presentation as a final (read-only) document you would perform the following steps.

1. With Backstage view open and the Info tab displayed for the Saving file, click Protect Presentation to display the Protect Presentation menu.
2. Click 'Mark as Final' to display the Microsoft PowerPoint dialog box indicating that the presentation will be saved as a final document.
3. Click OK (Microsoft PowerPoint dialog box) to save the file and to display another Microsoft PowerPoint dialog box with information about a final version of a document and indicating that the presentation is final.

   Q&A Can I turn off this read-only status so that I can edit the file?
   Yes. Click Mark as Final in the Protect Presentation menu to toggle off the read-only status.

4. Click OK (Microsoft PowerPoint dialog box). If an Information bar is displayed above the slide, click Edit Anyway to allow changes to be made to the presentation.

BTW
Printing Document Properties
PowerPoint does not allow you to print document properties. This feature, however, is available in Microsoft 365 Word.

Navigating to a Slide During a Slide Show

When you display a particular slide and view the information, you may want to return to one of the other slides in the presentation. You **navigate** when you jump to other slides in a presentation. A set of keyboard shortcuts can help you navigate to various slides during the slide show. When running a slide show, you can press F1 to see a list of these keyboard controls. These navigational features are listed in Table 4–1.

BTW
Using Presenter View
If you have two monitors, you can switch to Presenter view to see the presentation with speaker notes or the next slide on one computer while your audience sees only the current slide on a second monitor. To switch to Presenter view, click the Slide Show tab and then click the 'Use Presenter View' button in the Monitors group.

Table 4–1: Slide Show Keyboard Shortcuts

Keyboard Shortcut	Purpose
N ENTER SPACEBAR PAGE DOWN RIGHT ARROW DOWN ARROW	Perform the next animation or advance to the next slide
P BACKSPACE LEFT ARROW UP ARROW PAGE UP	Perform the previous animation or return to the previous slide
NUMBER FOLLOWED BY ENTER	Go to a specific slide number
B	Display a blank black slide
W	Display a blank white slide
S	Stop or restart an automatic presentation
ESC	End a presentation
E	Erase on-screen annotations
H	Go to the next slide if the next slide is hidden
T	Set new timings while rehearsing
R	Rerecord slide narration and timing
CTRL+P	Change the pointer to a pen
CTRL+A	Change the pointer to an arrow
CTRL+E	Change the pointer to an eraser
CTRL+M	Show or hide ink markup

Navigating to a Slide Using the Control Bar

When you begin running a presentation and move the pointer, a control bar is displayed with buttons that allow you to navigate to the next slide or previous slide, mark up the current slide, display slide thumbnails, zoom, or change the current display. When you move the mouse, the control bar is displayed in the lower-left corner of the slide; it disappears after the mouse has not been moved for three seconds. Table 4–2 describes the buttons on the control bar.

Table 4–2: Slide Show Control Bar Buttons

Description	Image	Function
Previous		Go to previous slide or previous animated element on the slide
Next		Go to next slide or next animated element on the slide
Pen and laser pointer tools		Shortcut menu for laser pointer, pen, highlighter, and eraser
See all slides		View thumbnails of all slides in presentation
Zoom into the slide		Zoom in on specific slide area
Toggle Subtitles		Use the Subtitles feature to have PowerPoint transcribe your words as you present and display them on-screen as captions; also turns off the Subtitles feature.
Options		Shortcut menu for slide navigation and screen displays; also displays Presenter View on a single monitor

To Highlight Text

You click the arrows on the left side of the control bar to navigate backward or forward through the slide show. The 'Pen and laser pointer tools' button has a variety of functions, most often to emphasize aspects of slides or to make handwritten notes. The following steps highlight an item on a slide in Slide Show view. **Why?** You want to call attention to the presentation's emphasis on developing a plan.

1

- Display Slide 1 and then run the slide show.
- If the control bar is not visible in the lower-left corner of the slide, move the pointer on the slide.
- Click the 'Pen and laser pointer tools' icon on the control bar to display a menu (Figure 4–84).

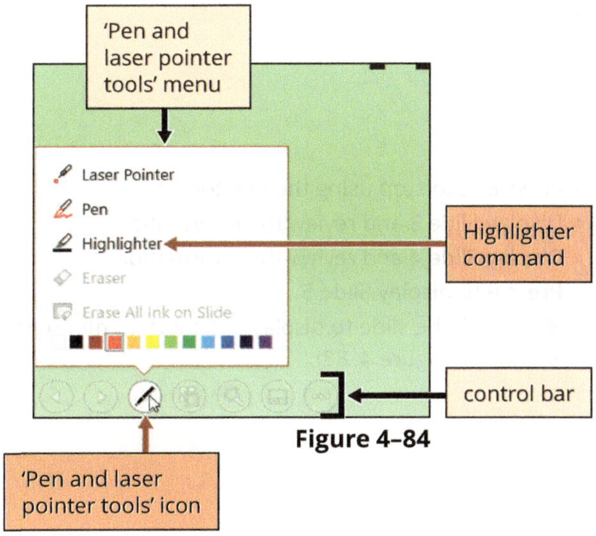

Figure 4–84

2

- Click the Highlighter icon on the control bar and then drag over the words, Here's how!, several times until all the letters are highlighted (Figure 4–85).

Figure 4–85

To Use Pen and Pointer Options During a Slide Show

Instead of Highlighter, you also can click Pen to draw or write notes on the slides. **Why?** The Pen tool is much thinner than the Highlighter, so you can write words or draw fine lines on the slides. When the presentation ends, PowerPoint will prompt you to keep or discard the ink annotations. The following steps change the pointer to a pen and then change the color of the ink during the presentation.

1

- Click Next on the control bar to display Slide 2. Click the 'Pen and laser pointer tools' icon on the control bar and then click Pen on the menu.
- Click 'Pen and laser pointer tools' on the control bar and then point to the color Dark Blue (Figure 4–86).

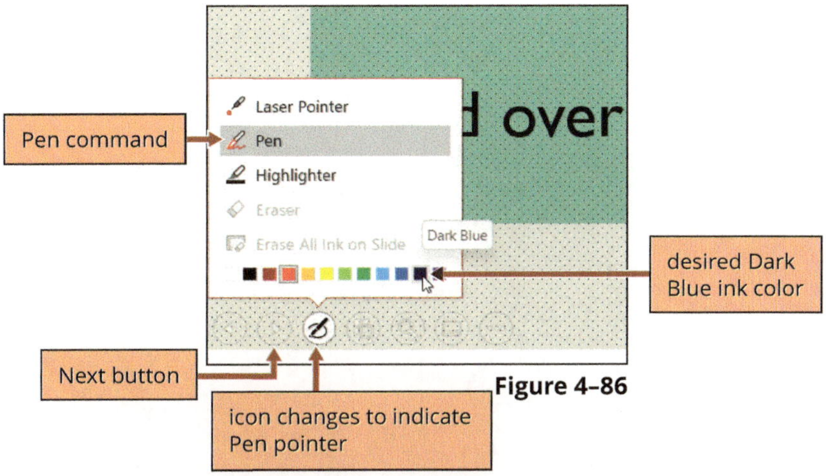

Figure 4–86

2

- Click the color Dark Blue.
- Drag the pointer around the title text words, Avoid overspending, to draw a circle around them (Figure 4–87).

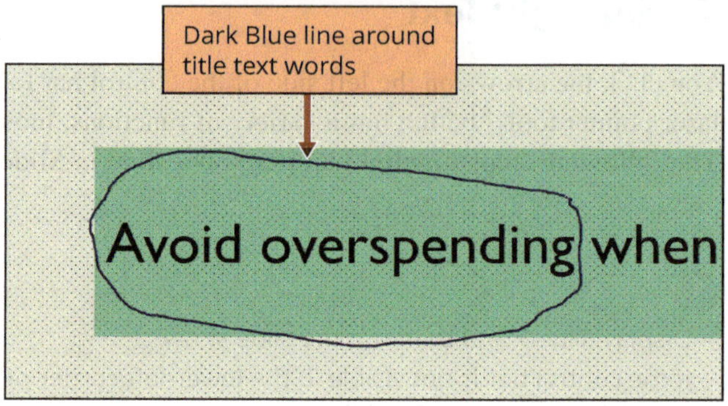

Figure 4–87

3

- Press ESC to stop using the Pen tool.
- Display Slide 3 and review the information.
- Display Slide 4 and review the information.
- Press H to display Slide 5.
- Right-click the slide to display the shortcut menu and then point to End Show (Figure 4–88).

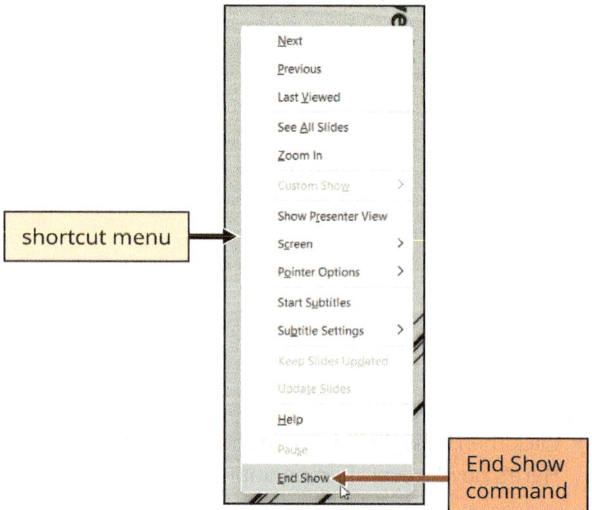

Figure 4–88

4

- Click End Show to display the Microsoft PowerPoint dialog box (Figure 4–89).

5

- Click the Discard button (Microsoft PowerPoint dialog box) to end the presentation without saving the ink annotations.

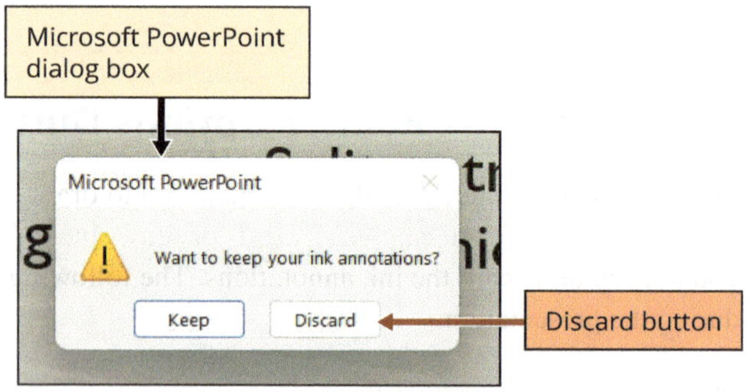

Figure 4–89

To Hide the Pointer and Slide Show Control Bar

To hide the pointer and the control bar during the slide show, you would perform the following step.

1. Click Options on the control bar, click Arrow Options, and then click Hidden.

To Constantly Display the Pointer and Slide Show Control Bar

By default, the pointer and control bar are set at Automatic, which means they are hidden after three seconds of no movement. After you hide the pointer and control bar, they remain hidden until you choose one of the other commands on the Options menu. They are displayed again when you move the mouse.

To keep the pointer and control bar displayed at all times during a slide show, you would perform the following step.

1. Click Options on the control bar, click Arrow Options, and then click Visible.

Rehearsing Slide Timings

In previous slide shows, you clicked to advance from one slide to the next. You also can set the time each slide is displayed on the screen. You can set these times in one of two ways. The first method is to specify each slide's display time manually. The second method is to use PowerPoint's **rehearsal feature**, which allows you to advance through the slides at your own pace, and the amount of time you view each slide is recorded. You will use the second technique in this module and then adjust the fourth slide's timing manually.

When you begin rehearsing a presentation, the Rehearsal toolbar is displayed. The **Rehearsal toolbar** contains buttons that allow you to start, pause, and repeat viewing the slides in the slide show and to view the times for each slide as well as the elapsed time. Table 4–3 describes the buttons on the Rehearsal toolbar.

BTW

Turn Off Slide Timings

PowerPoint gives you the option to turn slide timings off and then turn them back on without having to recreate them. Click the 'Set Up Slide Show' button (Slide Show tab | Set Up group) and then click Manually in the Advance slides area (Set Up Show dialog box). To turn the slide timings back on, click 'Using timings, if present' in the Advance slides area (Set Up Show dialog box).

Table 4–3: Rehearsal Toolbar Buttons

Button Name	Image	Description
Next	→	Displays the next slide or next animated element on the slide.
Pause Recording	❚❚	Stops the timer. Tap or click Next or Pause Recording to resume timing.
Slide Time	0:00:00	Indicates the length of time a slide has been displayed. You can enter a slide time directly in the Slide Time box.
Repeat	↺	Clears the Slide Time box and resets the timer to 0:00:00.
Elapsed Time	0:00:00	Indicates slide show total time.

Consider This

Give your audience sufficient time to view a slide.

The presentation in this module is designed to run continuously at a kiosk without a speaker's physical presence. Your audience, therefore, must read or view each slide and absorb the information without your help as a narrator. Be certain to give them time to read each slide and grasp the concept you are presenting. They will become frustrated if the slide changes before they have finished viewing and assimilating the material. As you set the slide timings, read each slide aloud and note the amount of time that elapses. Add a few seconds to this time and use this amount for the total time the slide is displayed.

To Rehearse Slide Timings

You need to determine the length of time each slide should be displayed. **Why?** Audience members need sufficient time to read the text and watch the animations. Table 4–4 indicates the desired timings for the five slides in the Saving presentation. Slide 1 is displayed and then the text appears for 10 seconds. Slides 2, 3, and 4 are displayed for 15 seconds. Slide 5 is displayed for 20 seconds.

Table 4–4: Slide Rehearsal Timings

Slide Number	Display Time	Elapsed Time
1	0:00	0:10
2	0:15	0:25
3	0:15	0:40
4	0:15	0:55
5	0:20	1:15

The following steps add slide timings to the slide show.

1

- Display Slide 1 and then click Slide Show on the ribbon to display the Slide Show tab (Figure 4–90).

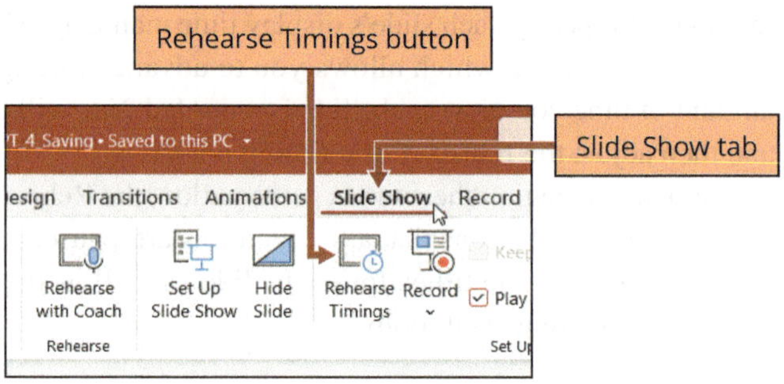

Figure 4–90

2

- Click the Rehearse Timings button (Slide Show tab | Set Up group) to start the slide show and the counter (Figure 4–91).
- If the 'Always Use Subtitles' pane is displayed, close it.

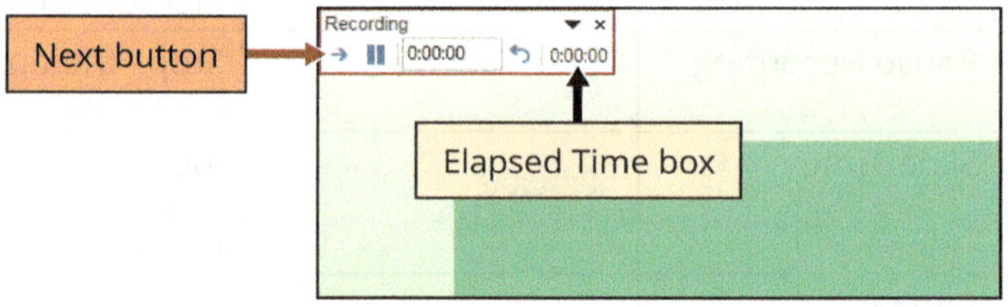

Figure 4–91

3

- When the Elapsed Time displays 00:10, click Next to display Slide 2.
- When the Elapsed Time displays 00:25, click Next to display Slide 3.
- When the Elapsed Time displays 00:40, click Next to display Slide 4.
- When the Elapsed Time displays 00:55, type H to display the hidden Slide 5.
- When the Elapsed Time displays 01:15, click Next to display the Microsoft PowerPoint dialog box (Figure 4–92).

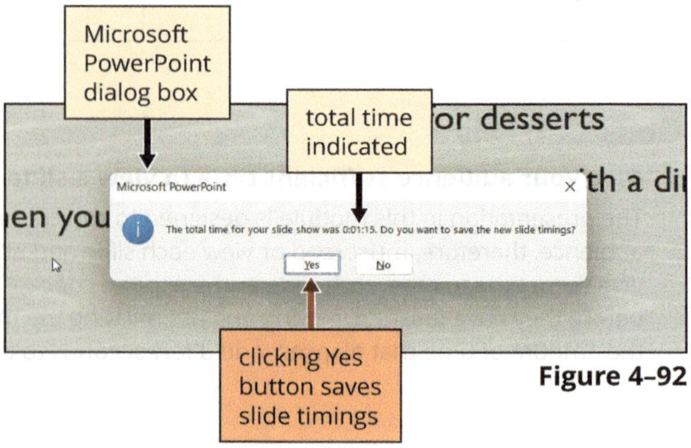

Figure 4–92

4

- Click Yes to keep the new slide timings with an elapsed time of 01:15.
- Click Slide Sorter view and then, if necessary, zoom the view to display all five thumbnails. Review the timings displayed in the lower-right corner of each slide (Figure 4–93).
- If the Always Use Subtitles pane opens, click Close to close it.

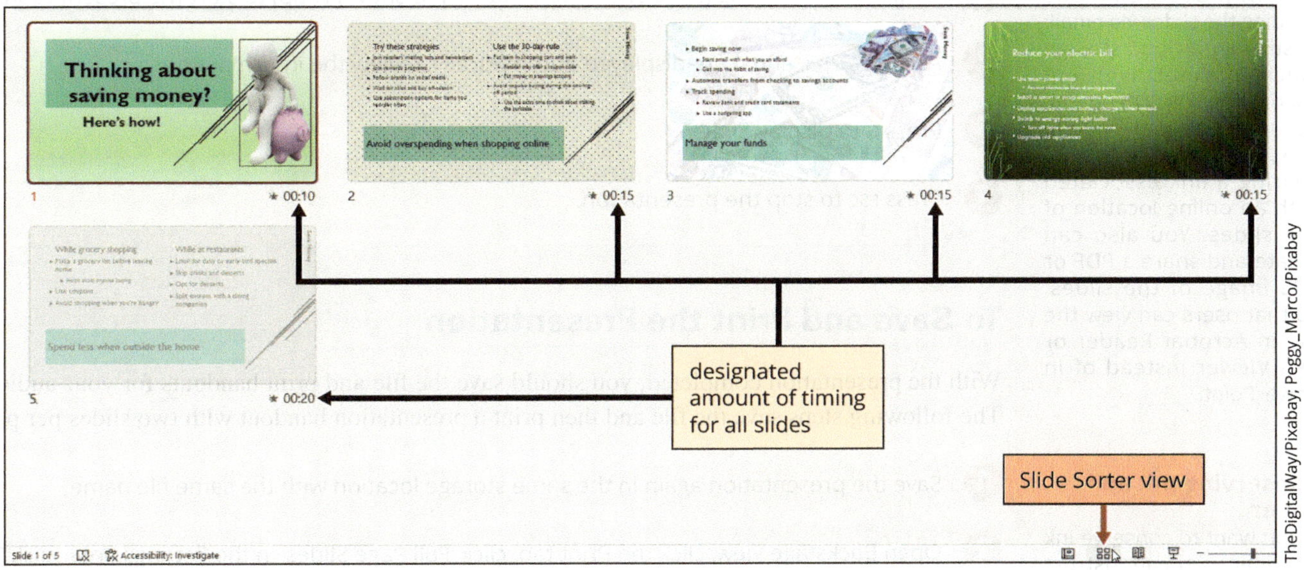

Figure 4–93

To Advance a Slide After a Specified Number of Seconds

Why? If the slide timings need adjustment, you manually can change the length of time each slide is displayed. In this presentation, you decide to display Slide 4 for 20 seconds instead of 15 seconds. The following step increases the Slide 4 timing.

1

- In Slide Sorter view, display the Transitions tab and then select Slide 4.
- Change the 'Advance Slide After' setting (Transitions tab | Timing group) to 00:20.00 (Figure 4–94).

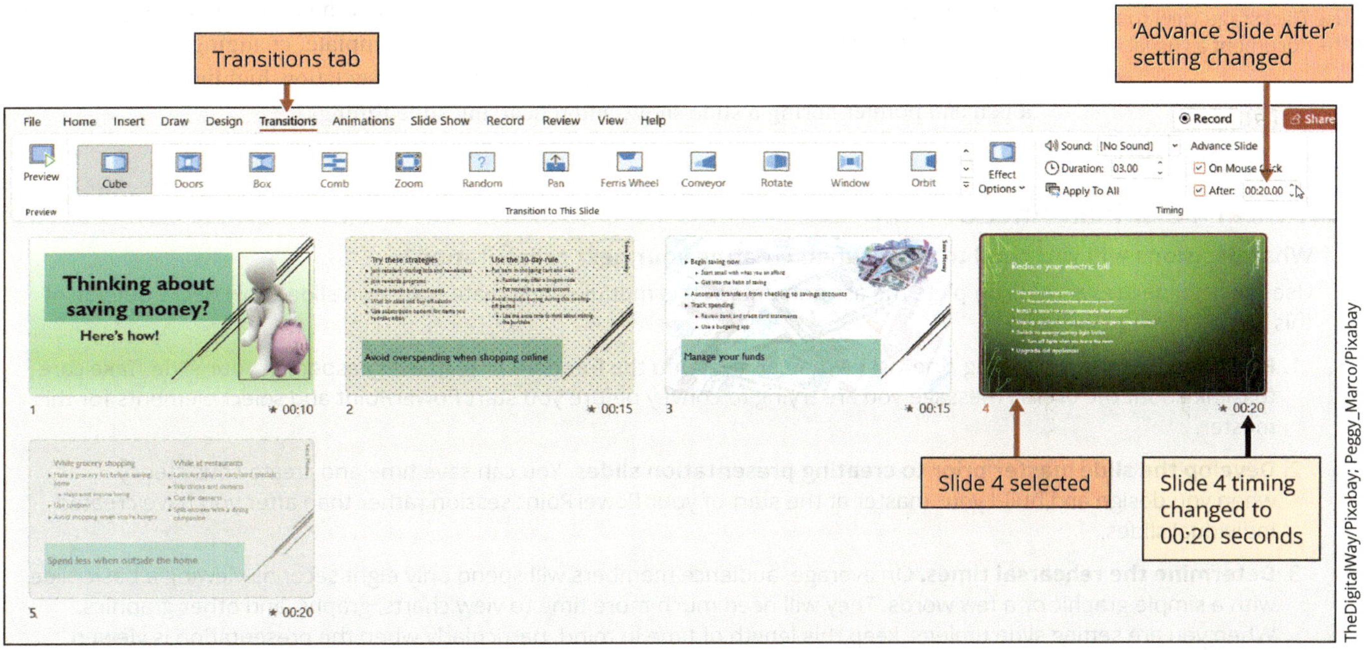

Figure 4–94

BTW
Distributing a Document
Instead of printing and distributing a hard copy of PowerPoint slides, you can distribute the slides electronically. Options include sending the slides via email; posting it on cloud storage (such as OneDrive) and sharing the link with others; posting it on social media, a blog, or other website; and sharing a link associated with an online location of the slides. You also can create and share a PDF or XPS image of the slides, so that users can view the file in Acrobat Reader or XPS Viewer instead of in PowerPoint.

BTW
Conserving Ink and Toner
If you want to conserve ink or toner, you can instruct PowerPoint to print draft quality documents by clicking File on the ribbon to open Backstage view, clicking Options in Backstage view to display the PowerPoint Options dialog box, clicking Advanced in the left pane (PowerPoint Options dialog box), scrolling to the Print area in the right pane, verifying there is no check mark in the High quality check box, and then clicking OK. Then, use Backstage view to print the document as usual.

To Run a Slide Show with Timings

All changes are complete. You now can view the presentation with timings. The following steps run the slide show.

1. Click From Beginning (Slide Show tab | Start Slide Show group) to start the presentation.
2. As Slides 2, 3, and 4 are displayed automatically, review the information.
3. Press H to display Slide 5.
4. Press ESC to stop the presentation.

To Save and Print the Presentation

With the presentation completed, you should save the file and print handouts for your audience. The following steps save the file and then print a presentation handout with two slides per page.

1. Save the presentation again in the same storage location with the same file name.
2. Open Backstage view, click the Print tab, click 'Full Page Slides' in the Settings area, click 2 Slides in the Handouts area to display a preview of the handout, and then click Print in the Print gallery to print the presentation.
3. sam Because the project now is complete, you can exit PowerPoint.

Summary

In this module, you learned how to customize slide masters and presentations. Topics covered included applying slide and font themes to a slide master, adding and formatting placeholders, cropping a picture to a shape, saving a presentation as a template, changing the theme variant, formatting slide backgrounds, inspecting and protecting a presentation, highlighting text and using a pen and pointer during a slide show, and rehearsing slide timings.

Consider This: Plan Ahead

What decisions will you need to make when creating your next presentation?

Use these guidelines as you complete the assignments in this module and create your own slide show decks outside of this class.

1. **Plan the slide master.** Using a new slide master gives you the freedom to plan every aspect of your slide. Take care to think about the overall message you are trying to convey before you start PowerPoint and select elements for this master.
2. **Develop the slide master prior to creating presentation slides.** You can save time and create consistency when you design and build your master at the start of your PowerPoint session rather than after you have created individual slides.
3. **Determine the rehearsal times.** On average, audience members will spend only eight seconds viewing a basic slide with a simple graphic or a few words. They will need much more time to view charts, graphs, and other graphics. When you are setting slide timings, keep this length of time in mind, particularly when the presentation is viewed without a speaker's physical presence.

Student Assignments

Apply Your Knowledge

Reinforce the skills and apply the concepts you learned in this module.

Creating and Formatting Slide Masters and a Template

Note: To complete this assignment, you will be required to use the Data Files. Please contact your instructor for information about accessing the Data Files.

Instructions: Start PowerPoint. Your school is promoting noncredit art classes for adults and teens, and the marketing department has asked you to help with the campaign. You decide to design a template that can be customized for sessions held throughout the year. Open the presentation called SC_PPT_4-1.pptx, which is located in the Data Files. You will delete and rename slide layouts, change slide backgrounds, save a slide master as a template, and then create the presentation shown in Figure 4–95.

Perform the following tasks:

1. Display Slide Master view. Delete all layouts except the Title Slide Layout and the Comparison Layout.
2. Display the Banded Slide Master. Delete the date footer placeholder. Change the title text case to Sentence case. Change the theme colors to Blue Warm. Customize the theme fonts by changing the heading font to Verdana and the body font to Times New Roman. Save the new font set with the name, **Art**.
3. On the Banded Slide Master, insert the picture Support_PPT_4_Paintbrush.jpg and then crop it to the Flowchart: Data shape (fourth shape in the first Flowchart area row). Click the More button in the Picture Format | Size group and uncheck the Lock aspect ratio box. Resize the paintbrush picture to a height of 2" and a width of 13" and then align it in the center and the top of the slide. Rename the Banded Slide Master as **Art**.
4. Display the Title Slide Layout, format the background texture fill to Purple mesh (fourth background in the fourth row), and then change the transparency to 15%. Close the Format Background pane.
5. To display the paintbrush picture on the Title Slide Layout (Figure 4–95a), click the 'Hide Background Graphics' check box (Slide Master tab | Background group) so that it no longer is checked. Rename this layout **Art Title**.
6. On the Art Title Layout, delete the date footer placeholder, insert a Text placeholder, and then change the height to 0.5" and the width to 4". Delete the default text and the bullet in the new placeholder and then type **Learn a new creative skill!** in the placeholder. Bold this text, increase the font size to 24 point, and then center it in the placeholder. Cut this placeholder from the layout and then paste it on the Art Slide Master layout. Position this placeholder by aligning it in the center and the bottom of the slide.
7. Display the Comparison Layout and then delete the title text placeholder. Change the slide background fill to the 'Radial Gradient – Accent 1' style (first fill in the last row), as shown in Figure 4–95b. Close the Format Background pane. Rename this layout **Art Comparison**.
8. Close Master view. Save the file as a template using the file name, **SC_PPT_4_Art_Template**.
9. On Slide 1, type **Programs for all ability levels** in the subtitle placeholder and then increase the font size to 48 point (Figure 4–95c).

   If requested by your instructor, replace the word, Spring, with the name of the first school you attended.
10. Insert a new slide as Slide 2 with the Art Comparison layout. Type the text shown in Figure 4–95d. Increase the font size of the two column headings to 32 point.
11. Apply the Page Curl transition in the Exciting category to both slides and then change the duration to 2.00 seconds.
12. View the presentation and then save the file as a PowerPoint presentation using the file name, **SC_PPT_4_Art**, and submit the revised presentation in the format specified by your instructor.

Continued on next page

13. **Consider This:** In this assignment, you created a new theme font in the Slide Master and named it Art. Are the fonts appropriate for this presentation? You also changed the theme colors to Blue Warm. Was this a good choice? Would another set of colors be a better complement for this topic? Why or why not?

Figure 4–95(a): Formatted Art Title Slide Master

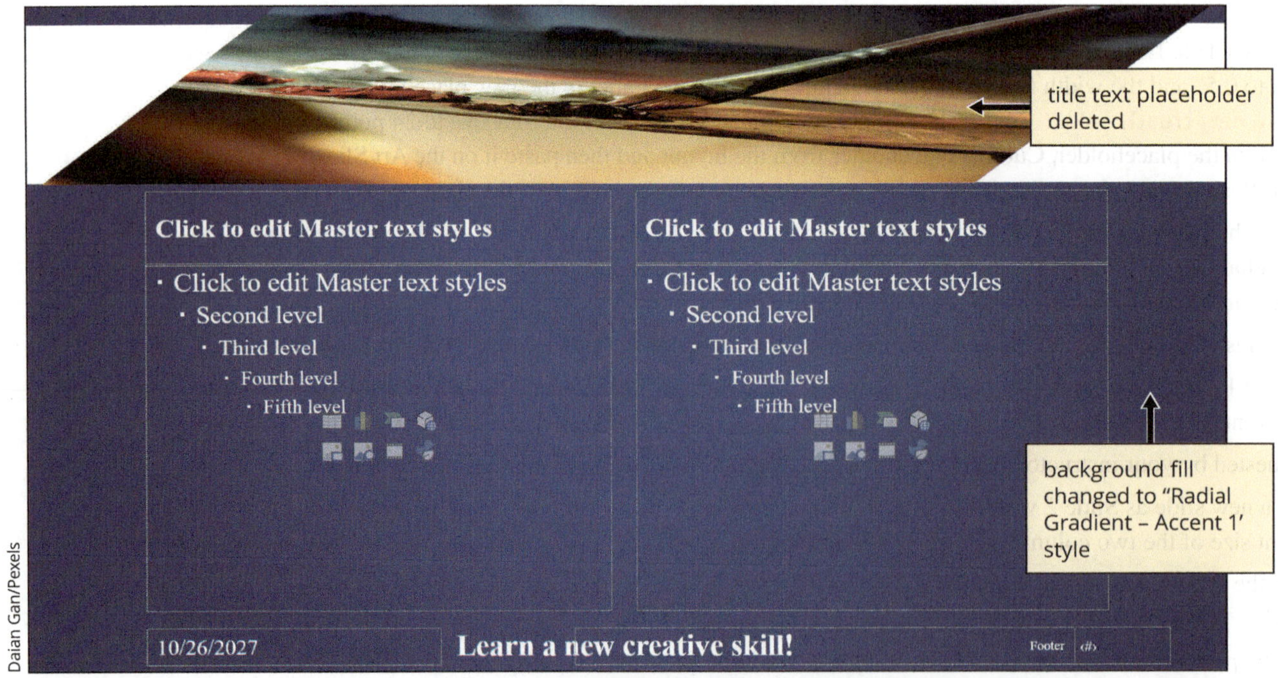

Figure 4–95(b): Formatted Art Comparison Slide Master

Figure 4–95(c): Slide 1

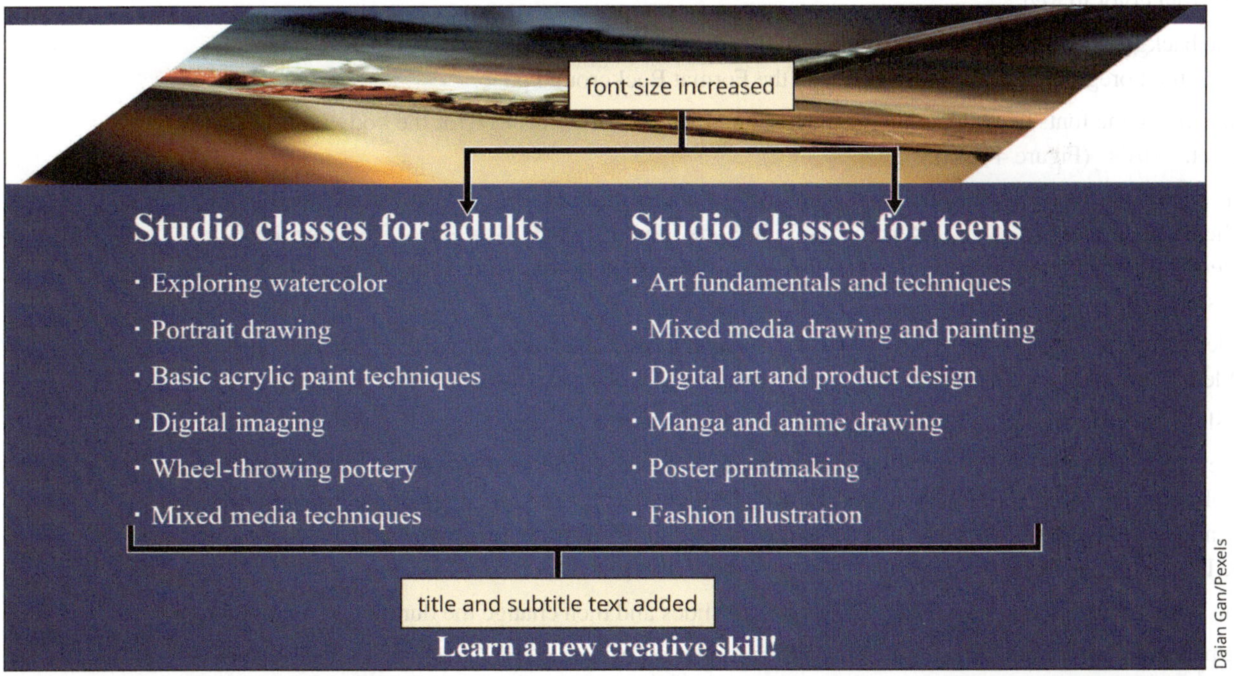

Figure 4–95(d): Slide 2

Extend Your Knowledge

Extend the skills you learned in the module and experiment with new skills. You may need to use Help to complete the assignment.

Using Design Ideas and Adjusting Footer Content

Note: To complete this assignment, you will be required to use the Data Files. Please contact your instructor for information about accessing the Data Files.

Instructions: Start PowerPoint. This semester you are interning at the Swallow Meadow Nature Center and are helping the naturalists develop fun and educational events and programs. One upcoming session will help area residents learn the basics about winter bird feeding, protecting birds in flight, and growing native plants. The naturalists have asked you to prepare slides to show at the Nature Center. They want you to create a PowerPoint template so they can change photographs for each program they have scheduled. Open the presentation called SC_PPT_4-2.pptx, which is located in the Data Files. You will use the Design Ideas pane to develop the title slide, adjust the footer content, and insert and rename a layout. The document you open is a partially formatted presentation. Slide 1 in the presentation has a title and three pictures. Slide 2 has a list of actions residents can take to help protect the birds. You will create the slide master layouts in Figure 4–96 and then add the slide content.

Perform the following tasks:

1. Display Slide Master view and then select the Office Theme Slide Master. Type the text, **Swallow Meadow Nature Center**, in the Footer text box and then apply the footer text box to all slides.

   If requested by your instructor, replace the word, Swallow, with the name of your high school mascot.
2. Align the Footer placeholder in the center and top of the slide and then increase font size to 20 point and change the font color to Red.
3. Format the background by adding the Divot pattern fill (first pattern in the seventh row) to all layouts and then change the Foreground color to Green. Close the Format Background pane.
4. Customize the theme fonts using Georgia for the heading font and Gill Sans MT for the body font. Name the new font set, **Birds** (Figure 4–96a).
5. Select the Section Header Layout and then delete this layout and all other layouts below it. Rename the Office Theme Slide Master, **Birds**. Rename the Title Slide Layout, **Birds Title Slide**. Rename the Title and Content Layout, **Birds Content**. Insert a layout and rename it, **Birds Final Slide** (Figure 4–96b). Close Master view.
6. With Slide 1 displayed (Figure 4–96c), click Design Ideas (Design tab | Designer group) to display the Design Ideas pane. Click the first design in the pane to apply that design to the title slide.
7. Display Slide 2 (Figure 4–96d). Click the first design in the pane to apply that design to the slide.
8. Insert a new slide with the Birds Final Slide layout. Type **Use binoculars and share your sightings** in the title text placeholder. Insert the picture, Support_PPT_4_Binoculars.jpg, and then select the first design in the Design Ideas pane. If, however, the first design in the Design Ideas pane does not match the other slides, scroll the Design Ideas to find the best match.
9. Apply the Wind transition in the Exciting category to all slides and then change the duration to 3.00 seconds.
10. View the presentation, save the file as a PowerPoint presentation using **SC_PPT_4_Birds** as the file name, and then submit the revised presentation in the format specified by your instructor.
11. **Consider This:** In this assignment, you created a new theme font in the Slide Master and named it Birds. Are the fonts appropriate for this presentation? Why or why not? How did the design ideas enhance the three slides?

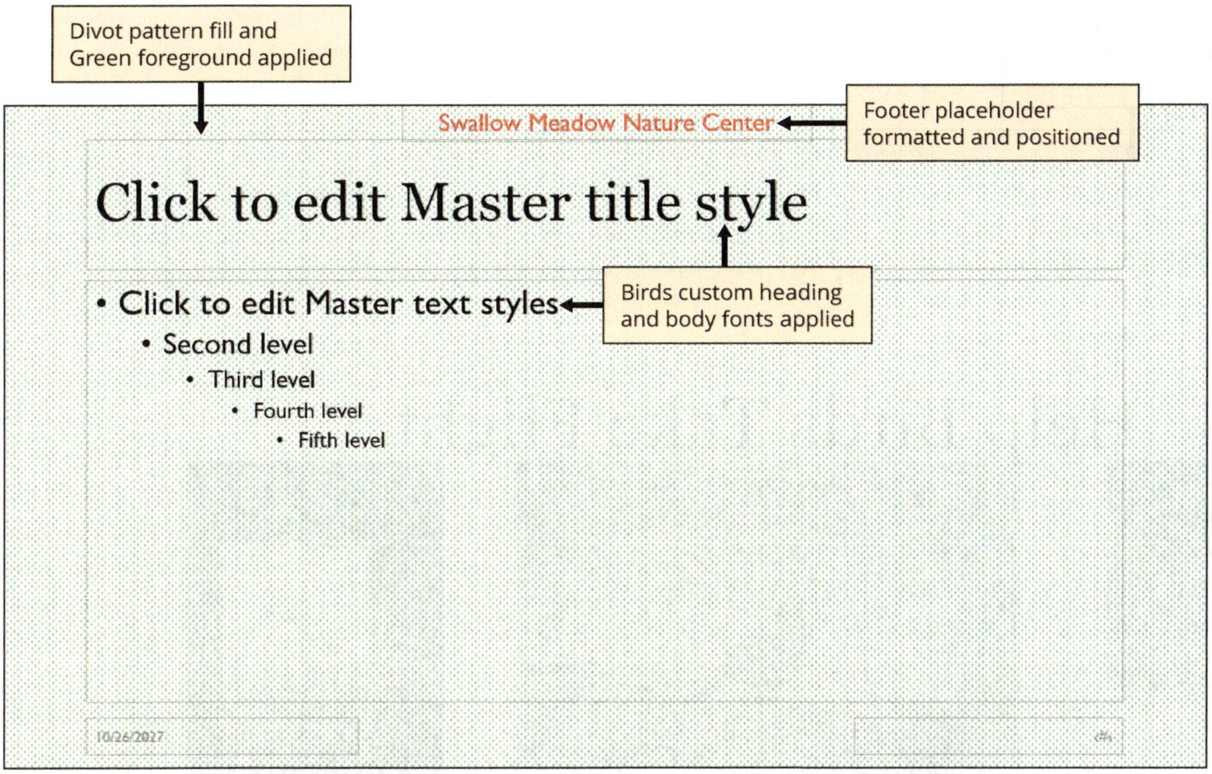

Figure 4–96(a): Birds Slide Master

Figure 4–96(b): Birds Final Slide Layout

Continued on next page

Rajesh S Balouria/Pexels; Büşranur Aydın/Pexels; Harrison Haines/Pexels

Figure 4–96(c): Slide 1

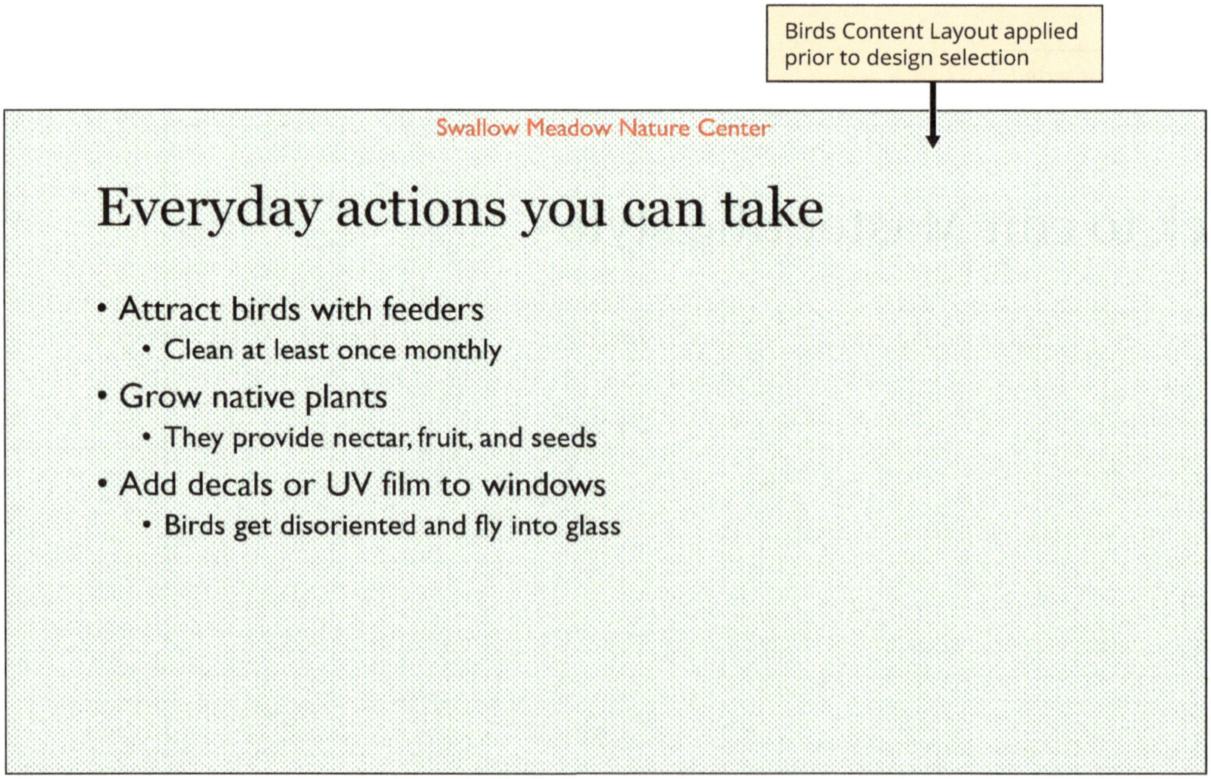

Figure 4–96(d): Slide 2

Expand Your World

Create a solution that uses cloud or web technologies by learning and investigating on your own from general guidance.

Exploring Add-ins

Instructions: You use apps on your phone and tablet to access information on the web. Similarly, when you are working with PowerPoint and other Microsoft 365 apps, you can use add-ins, which essentially are apps designed to increase your productivity. When you download an add-in from a reliable source, you enable it by clicking Enable Content on the Message Bar. You would like to investigate some of the add-ins available for PowerPoint to determine which ones would be helpful for you to use.

Note: You will be required to use your Microsoft account to complete this assignment. If you do not have a Microsoft account and do not want to create one, read this assignment without performing the instructions.

Perform the following tasks:

1. Use Help to learn about Office add-ins. If necessary, sign in to your Windows account and your Microsoft account in PowerPoint.
2. Display the Insert tab and then click Get Add-ins (Insert tab | Add-ins group) to display the Office Add-ins dialog box. (If a menu is displayed, click the 'See My Add-ins' link to display the Office Add-ins dialog box.) If necessary, click the STORE tab to visit the online Office Store (Figure 4–97).
3. Scroll through the add-ins in the various categories. Locate a free add-in that you feel would be helpful to you while you use PowerPoint, click this desired add-in, and then follow the instructions to add the add-in to PowerPoint.
4. In PowerPoint, click Get Add-ins to display the Office Add-ins dialog box. Click the MY ADD-INS tab to display the add-in you added, click this add-in, and then click Add (Office Add-ins dialog box) to use the add-in.
5. Practice using the add-in.
6. **Consider This:** Which add-in did you download and why? Does the add-in work as you intended? Would you recommend this add-in to others? Which add-ins, if any, were already on your computer?

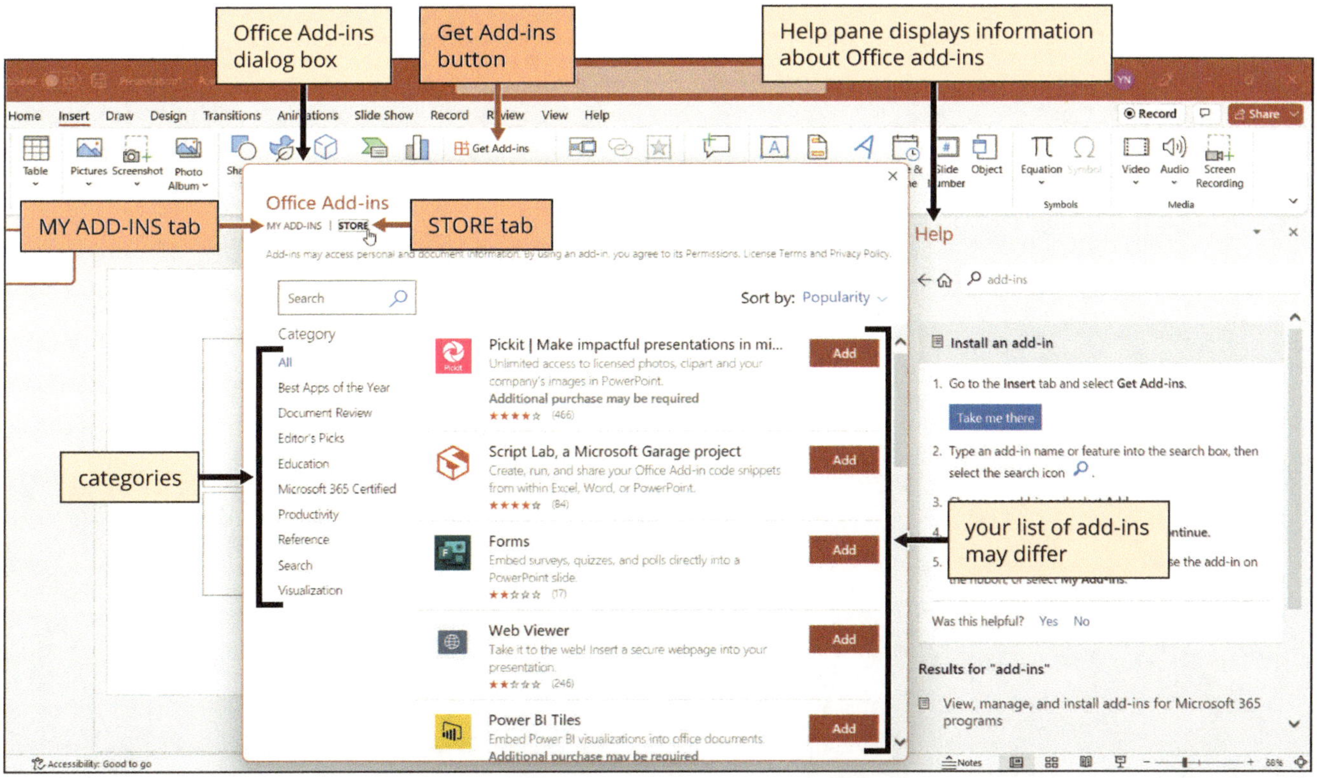

Figure 4–97

In the Lab

Apply your creative thinking and problem-solving skills to design and implement a solution.

Design and Create a Presentation about Increasing Productivity

Part 1: It may seem there are not enough hours in the day to complete all the items on your to-do list. One method of coping with the tasks at-hand is increasing productivity. You can implement several time-saving strategies to become more effective. For example, create a schedule with blocks of time for specific tasks. Eliminate visual distractions and social media notifications. Eat healthy snacks and get adequate sleep. You work in the counseling department at school and are helping to prepare a presentation for incoming students with advice on increasing productivity. Use the concepts and techniques presented in this module to prepare a presentation with a minimum of three slides with productivity tips. Review some websites to learn realistic methods of enhancing productivity at school. Use the pictures, Support_PPT_4_List.jpg and Support_PPT_4_Time.jpg, which are located in the Data Files. Develop at least two slide master layouts that include a picture and then rename these layouts. Delete the layouts you do not use. Change the theme colors. Customize the theme fonts. Modify a slide background. Add slide transitions. Rehearse the slide timings. Review and revise your presentation as needed and then save the file using the file name, **SC_PPT_4_Productive**. Submit your assignment in the format specified by your instructor.

Part 2: **Consider This:** You made several decisions while creating the presentation in this assignment: creating and formatting slide masters, changing theme colors and fonts, modifying a slide background, and rehearsing slide timings. What was the rationale behind each of these decisions? When you reviewed the document, what further revisions did you make and why? Where would you recommend showing this slide show?

Collaborating and Adding Animation

Objectives

After completing this module, you will be able to:

- Compare and merge presentations
- Accept and reject a reviewer's proposed changes
- Delete, reply to, and insert comments
- Change line and paragraph spacing
- Apply an artistic effect to a picture
- Change bullets to pictures and symbols
- Animate slide content
- Duplicate animations with the Animation Painter
- Apply the same formatting to objects with the Format Painter
- Add motion paths for animations
- Align content placeholders
- Control animation timing
- Create and manage sections

Introduction

Often presentations are enhanced when you collaborate with others to fine-tune text, visuals, and design elements on your slides. A **review cycle** occurs when a slide show designer shares a file with multiple reviewers so they can make comments and changes to their copies of the slides and then return the file to the designer. A **comment** is a note that an author or a reviewer adds to a document that normally does not display as part of the slide show. It can be used to clarify information that may be difficult to understand, to pose questions, or to communicate suggestions. The designer then can display the comments, add replies, ask the reviewers to again review the presentation, and continue this process until the slides are satisfactory. In addition, a presenter can use PowerPoint's variety of tools to run the show effectively and modify the presentation if needed.

BTW
Review Cycle Value
The review cycle plays an important role in developing an effective PowerPoint presentation. Your reviewers may raise issues and make comments about your material, and their concerns may help enhance your final slides. Terms and graphics that seem clear to you may raise questions among people viewing your material. Audience members may have diverse technical skills and educational levels, so it is important to understand how they may interpret your slides.

Project: Presentation with Comments and Animation

In this module's project, you will follow proper design guidelines and learn to use PowerPoint to create the slides shown in Figure 5–1a through 5–1e. The objective is to produce a presentation for a seminar at a car dealership in your town regarding strategies for driving safely. A variety of topics will be covered, including caring for tires, learning about available driver-assistance safety features, determining which vehicle has the right-of-way at a four-way intersection, and packing an emergency kit.

BTW
Pixels
Screen resolution specifies the amount of pixels displayed on your screen. The word, pixel, combines pix (for "pictures") and el (for "element").

All slides in the presentation were developed using an older version of PowerPoint. In the older version, the slides used a 4:3 width-to-height ratio, which was the standard proportion of computer monitors at that time. Today, however, most people use PowerPoint's default 16:9 ratio, which is the proportion of most widescreen monitors today. You will change the slide size in your presentation after all the slides are created.

When you are developing a presentation, it often is advantageous to ask a variety of people to review your work in progress. These individuals can evaluate the wording, art, and design, and experts in the subject can check the slides for accuracy. They can add comments to the slides in specific areas, such as a paragraph, a graphic, or a table. You then can review their comments and use them to modify and enhance your work. You also can insert slides from other presentations into your presentation.

In this module, you will learn how to create the slides shown in Figure 5–1. You will perform the following general tasks as you progress through this module:

1. Collaborate on a presentation by using comments.
2. Format and manage text spacing and bullets.
3. Format pictures with effects.
4. Modify bullets.
5. Animate paragraphs and objects.
6. Create and manage sections.
7. Use zoom links.

BTW
Reviewers' Technology Limitations
People who receive copies of your presentation to review may not be able to open a PowerPoint file saved in the default .pptx format because they have a previous version of this software or may not have Internet access available readily. For these reasons, you need to know their software and hardware limitations and distribute your file or handouts accordingly.

Collaborating on a Presentation

PowerPoint provides several methods to collaborate with friends or coworkers who can view your slide show and then provide feedback. When you **collaborate**, you work together on a presentation with other PowerPoint users who are cooperating jointly and assisting willingly with the endeavor. You can distribute your slide show physically to others by exchanging a flash drive or other portable storage media. You also can share your presentation through the Internet by sending the file as an email attachment or saving the file to a storage location, such as Microsoft OneDrive.

Consider This

What are some tips for collaborating successfully?

Working with others can yield numerous benefits. Your peers can assist in brainstorming, developing key ideas, revising your project, and keeping you on track so that your presentation meets the assignment goals.

The first step when collaborating with peers is to define success. What, ultimately, is the goal? For example, are you developing a persuasive presentation to school administrators in an effort to fund a new club? Next, you can set short-term and long-term goals that help lead you to completing the project successfully. These goals can be weekly tasks to accomplish, such as interviewing content experts, conducting online research, or compiling an annotated bibliography. After that, you can develop a plan to finish the project by outlining subtasks that each member must accomplish. Each collaborator should inform the group members when the task is complete or if problems are delaying progress. When collaborators meet, whether in person or online, they should establish an agenda and have one member keep notes of topics discussed.

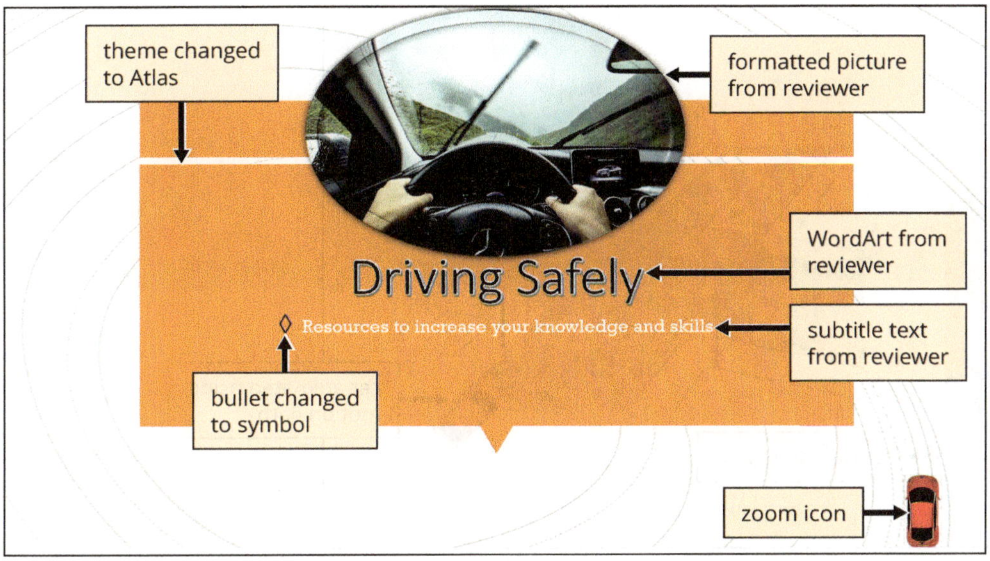

StockSnap/27551 images/Pixabay; OpenClipart-Vectors/27376 images/Pixabay

Figure 5–1(a): Slide 1 (Title Slide Enhanced from Reviewer)

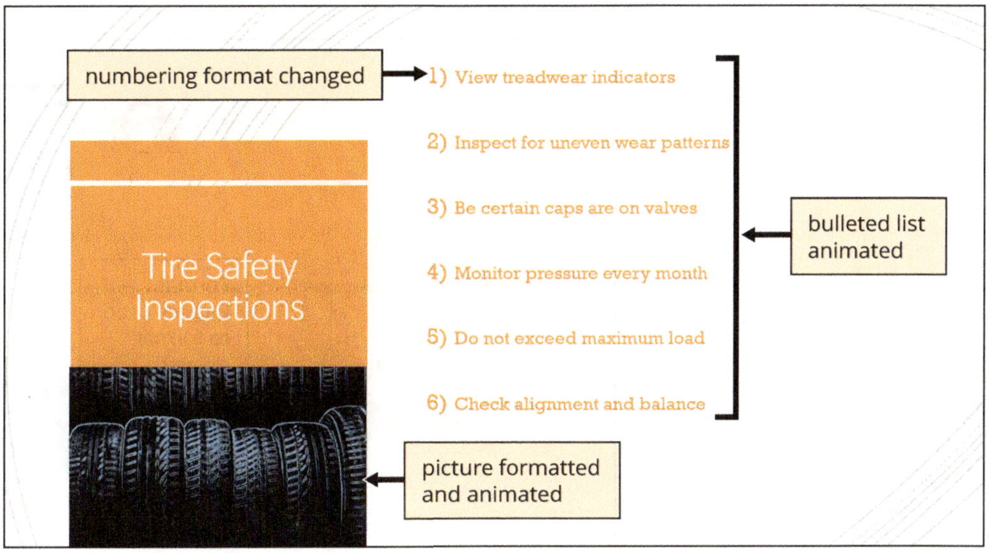

FlenderFunways/4 images/Pixabay

Figure 5–1(b): Slide 2 (Redesigned from Reviewer)

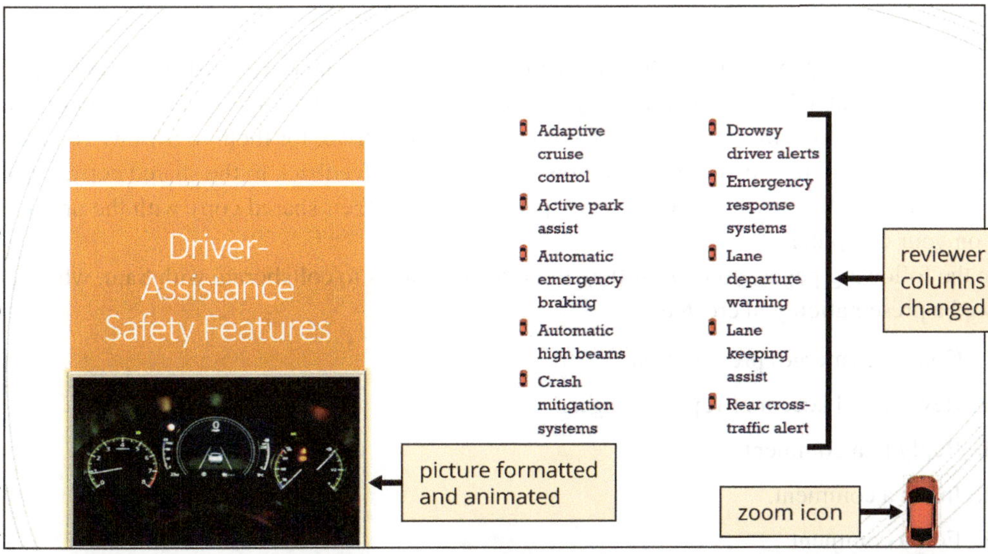

Nick Fewings/Unsplash.com; OpenClipart-Vectors/27376 images/Pixabay

Figure 5–1(c): Slide 3 (Enhanced from Reviewer)

Figure 5–1(d): Slide 4 (Animation Added to Reviewer's Slide)

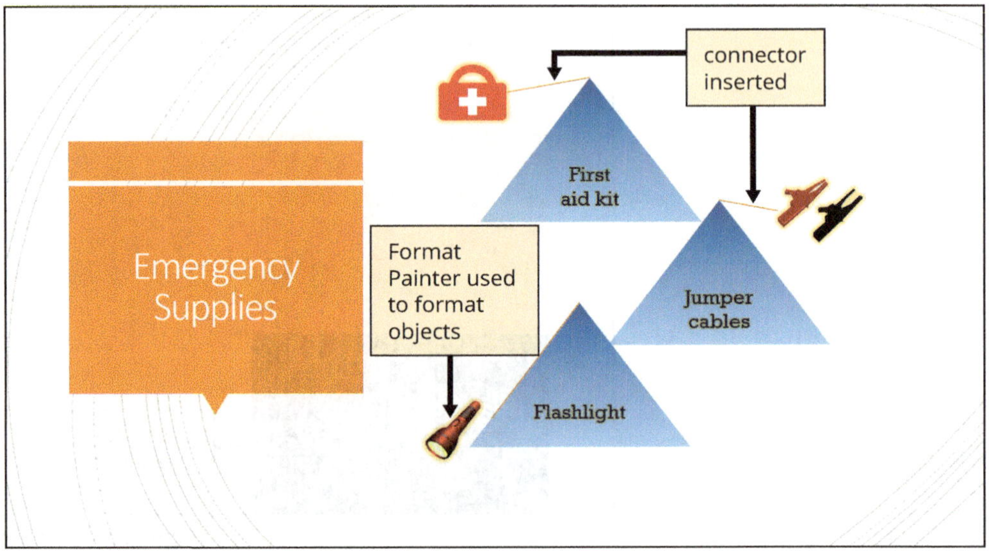

Figure 5–1(e): Slide 5 (Enhanced from Reviewer)

BTW
Screen Resolution
If you are using a computer to step through the project in this module and you want your screens to match the figures in this book, you should change your screen's resolution to 1920 × 1080.

BTW
Touch Mode Differences
The Microsoft 365 and Windows interfaces may vary if you are using a touch screen. For this reason, you might notice that the function or appearance of your touch screen differs slightly from this module's presentation.

PowerPoint does not have a track changes feature like the one found in Word. You can receive comments and feedback from reviewers by first saving your presentation to your computer and then posting a second copy to a shared location, such as OneDrive, for them to review. You then can ask the reviewers to add comments to your slides and add feedback to the shared copy. Once they have finished their reviews, you can compare and merge their shared copy with the original saved on your computer.

In the following pages, you will follow these general steps to collaborate with Sam, who has reviewed a presentation you created:

1. Combine (merge) presentations.
2. Review and accept or reject changes.
3. Reply to a comment.
4. Insert a comment.
5. Edit a comment.
6. Delete a comment.

To Merge a Presentation

Sam's changes to the initial presentation include adding a subtitle, converting the Slide 1 title text to WordArt, and changing the Slide 3 bulleted list into columns. A transition is added to all slides, the theme is changed, and a slide is added. **Why?** Sam reviewed your Driving presentation and made several comments, so you want to combine (merge) his changes with your file to see if they improve the original design and slide content. The following steps merge this reviewer's file with your Driving Final presentation.

1

- **sam** Run PowerPoint. If necessary, maximize the PowerPoint window.
- Open the presentation, SC_PPT_5_Driving, from the Data Files. If a yellow Protected View message is displayed above Slide 1, click the Enable Editing button in the message.
- Save the presentation using **SC_PPT_5_Driving_Final** as the file name.
- Display the Review tab (Figure 5–2).

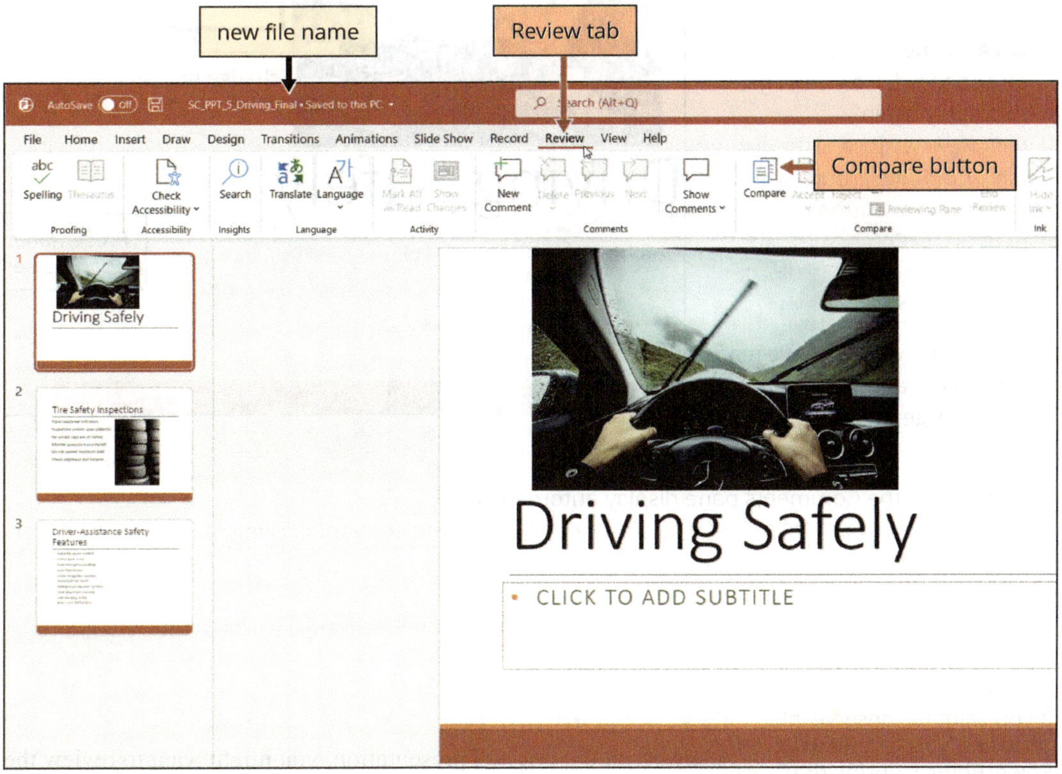

StockSnap/27551 images/Pixabay

Figure 5–2

Q&A Why do the slides have a different size than the slides I have seen in previous presentations? The slides in the Driving presentation use a 4:3 ratio, which was the default setting in PowerPoint versions prior to PowerPoint 2013.

2

- Click the Compare button (Review tab | Compare group) to display the 'Choose File to Merge with Current Presentation' dialog box.
- With the list of your Data Files displayed, click SC_PPT_5_Driving - Sam to select the PowerPoint file (Figure 5–3).

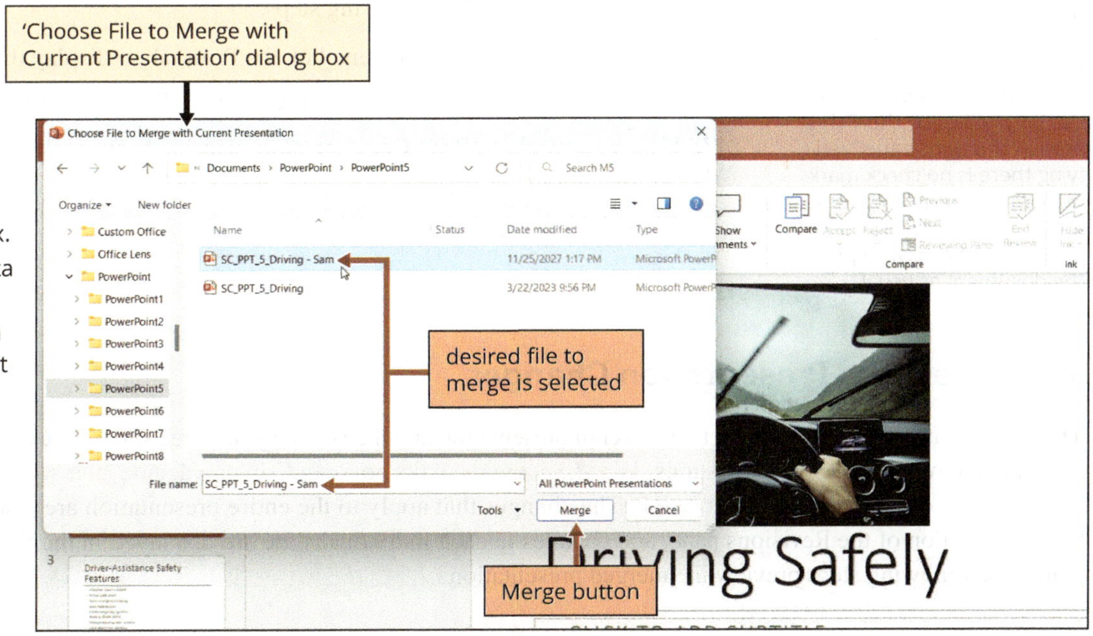

StockSnap/27551 images/Pixabay

Figure 5–3

3

- Click the Merge button (Choose File to Merge with Current Presentation dialog box) to merge Sam's presentation with the Driving_Final presentation and to display the Revisions pane (Figure 5–4).

Q&A My Revisions pane disappeared. How can I get it to display again?
Click Reviewing Pane (Review tab | Compare group) or click the Revisions button to the right of the Comments pane to display the Revisions pane instead of the Comments pane.

If several reviewers have made comments and suggestions, can I merge their files, too?
Yes. Repeat Steps 1, 2, and 3.

When does the Comments pane display automatically?
It displays if it was left open during a previous PowerPoint session. Clicking Show Comments or Comments on the ribbon displays or hides the Comments pane.

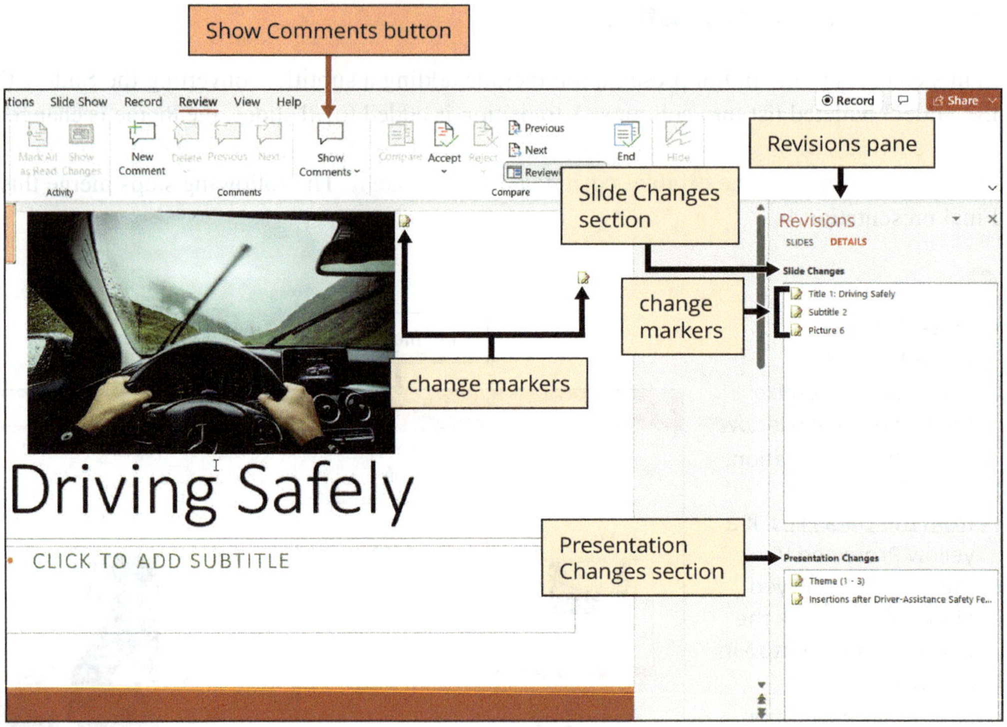

StockSnap/27551 images/Pixabay

Figure 5–4

BTW
Conserving Ink and Toner
If you want to conserve ink or toner, you can instruct PowerPoint to print draft quality documents by clicking File on the ribbon to open Backstage view, clicking Options in Backstage view to display the PowerPoint Options dialog box, clicking Advanced in the left pane (PowerPoint Options dialog box), scrolling to the Print area in the right pane, verifying there is no check mark in the High quality check box, and then clicking OK. Then, use Backstage view to print the document as usual.

To Print Comments

As owner of the original presentation, you might want to review the comments and modifications on a hard copy before making decisions about whether to accept these suggestions. You can print each slide and the comments a reviewer has made before you begin to accept and reject each suggestion. PowerPoint can print these slides and comments on individual pages. To perform this action, you would perform the following steps.

1. Open Backstage view and then click the Print tab to display the Print gallery.
2. Click 'Full Page Slides' in the Print gallery to display print layouts.
3. If necessary, click 'Print Comments' to place a check mark by this option and turn on printing comment pages.
4. Click the Print button to print the pages.

To Preview the Presentation Changes

The reviewer made several changes to the overall presentation and then edited your three slides. You can preview the modifications to obtain an overview of the suggestions. **Why?** Seeing the edits now can help you decide later whether to accept or reject each change as you step through each revision. The changes that apply to the entire presentation are displayed in the Presentation Changes section of the Revisions pane, and changes to each individual slide are displayed in the Slide Changes section of this pane. The following steps preview the merged presentation.

1

- With the Review tab and Slide 1 displayed, click the SLIDES tab in the Revisions pane to display a thumbnail of merged Slide 1.
- Click the Sam check box above the Slide 1 thumbnail (Revisions pane) to view the proposed changes in the main slide pane (Figure 5–5).

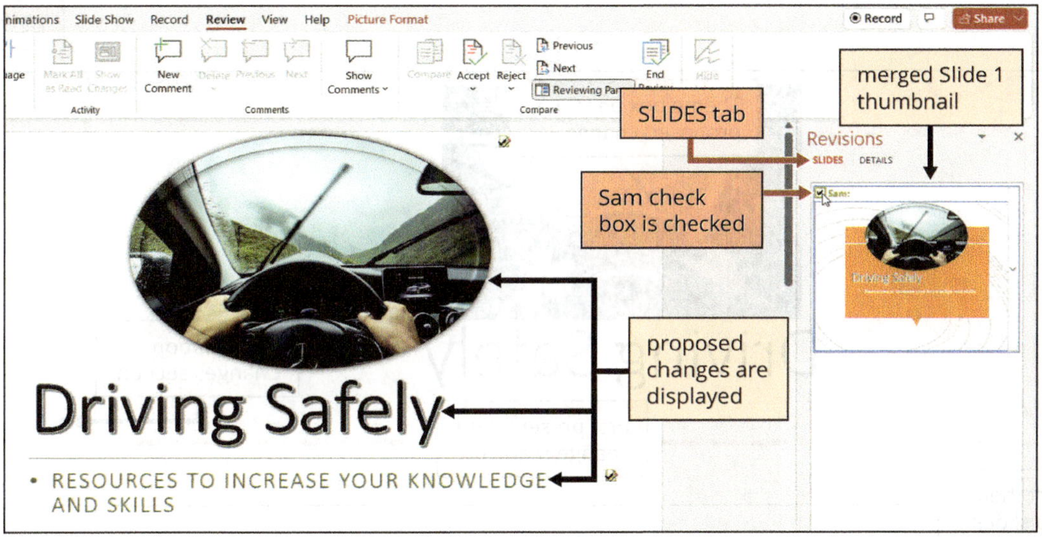

StockSnap/27551 images/Pixabay

Figure 5–5

2

- Click the Sam check box again to remove the check mark and undo the changes.

Q&A Can I make some, but not all, of the reviewer's changes on Slide 1?
Yes. PowerPoint allows you to view each proposed change individually and then either accept or reject the modification.

Consider This

How do I accept and evaluate criticism positively?

Receiving feedback from others ultimately should enhance your presentation. If several of your reviewers make similar comments, such as too much text appears on one slide or that a chart would help present your concept, then you should heed their criticism and modify your slides. Criticism from a variety of people, particularly if they are from different cultures or vary in age, gives a wide range of viewpoints. Some reviewers might focus on the font size, some on color and design choices, while others might single out the overall message. These individuals should evaluate and comment on your work, such as saying that the overall presentation is good or that a particular paragraph is confusing, and then give specific information about what elements are effective or how you can edit the paragraph.

When you receive these comments, do not get defensive. Ask yourself why your reviewers would have made these comments. Perhaps they lack a background in the subject matter. Or they may have a particular interest in this topic and can add their expertise.

To Review, Accept, and Reject Presentation Changes

Changes that affect the entire presentation are indicated in the Presentation Changes section of the Revisions pane. These changes can include transitions, color schemes, fonts, and backgrounds. They also can include slide insertions. Sam added three slides in his review, so you can insert these slides in your presentation and then accept or reject each one. The following steps display and accept the reviewer's three slides and then delete one of the inserted slides. **Why?** You want to see all the slides and then evaluate how they add value to the presentation. One of the slides has a topic you want to use in another presentation, so you want to delete that slide.

1

- Click the DETAILS tab in the Revisions pane.
- In the Presentation Changes section of the Revisions pane, click the first presentation change marker, Theme (1 - 3) to display the Theme box with an explanation of the proposed change for all slides in the presentation (Figure 5–6).

StockSnap/27551 images/Pixabay; FlenderFunways/4 images/Pixabay

Figure 5–6

2

- Click the Theme check box to view the new Atlas theme on all slides (Figure 5–7).

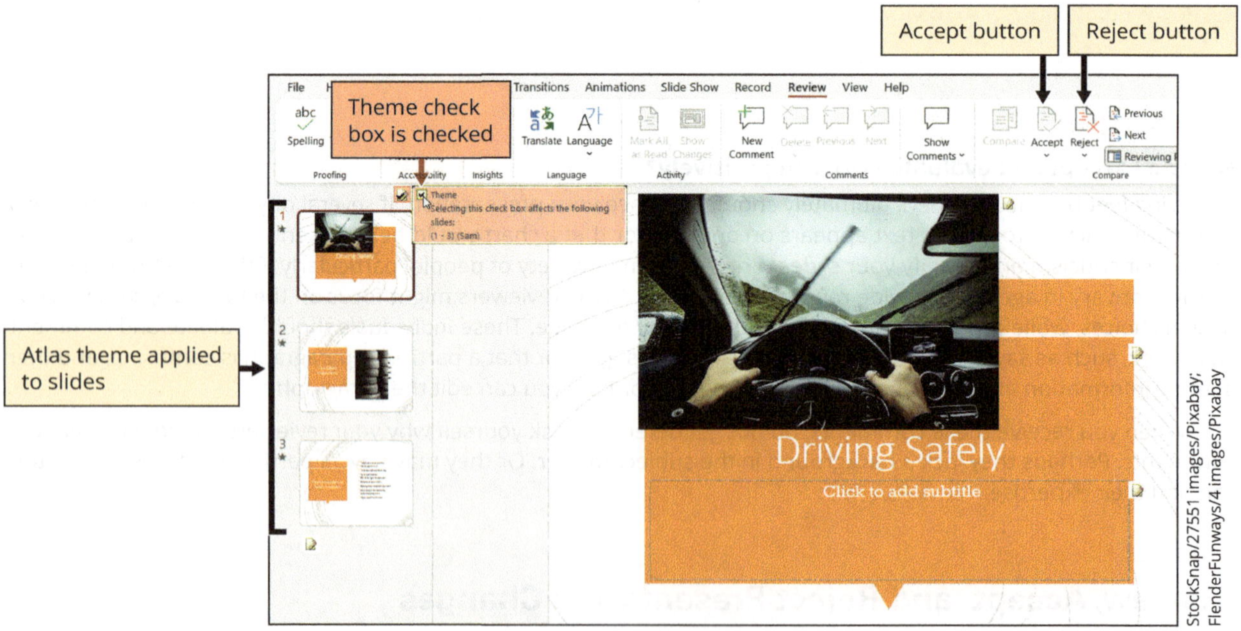

StockSnap/27551 images/Pixabay; FlenderFunways/4 images/Pixabay

Figure 5–7

Q&A Can I also apply the change by tapping or clicking the Accept button (Review tab | Compare group)?
Yes. Either method applies the Atlas theme.

If I decide not to apply the new theme, can I reverse this change?
Yes. Click Reject (Review tab | Compare group) or click the check box to remove the check and reject the reviewer's theme modification.

3

- Click the second presentation change marker, 'Insertions after Driver-Assistance Safety Fe...' in the Presentation Changes section to display an insertion box with a list of the three proposed new slides to insert into the presentation (Intersection Right-of-Way, Distracted Driving, and Emergency Supplies) (Figure 5–8).

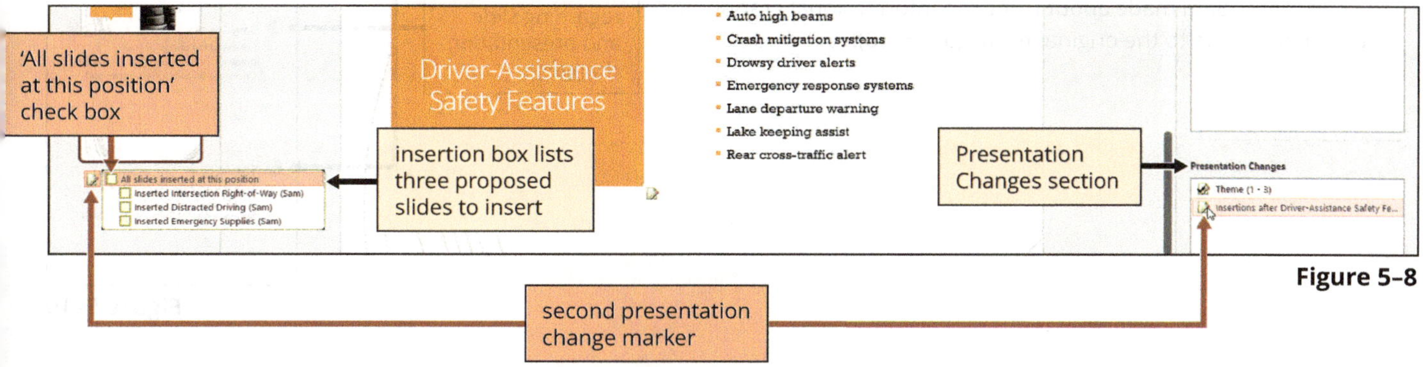

Figure 5–8

Q&A What is the significance of the check boxes in the insertion box?
You can click the first check box to insert all three slides in your presentation. You can elect to insert one or two slides by clicking the check mark to the left of each slide title.

4

- Click the 'All slides inserted at this position' check box to insert the three new slides (Figure 5–9).

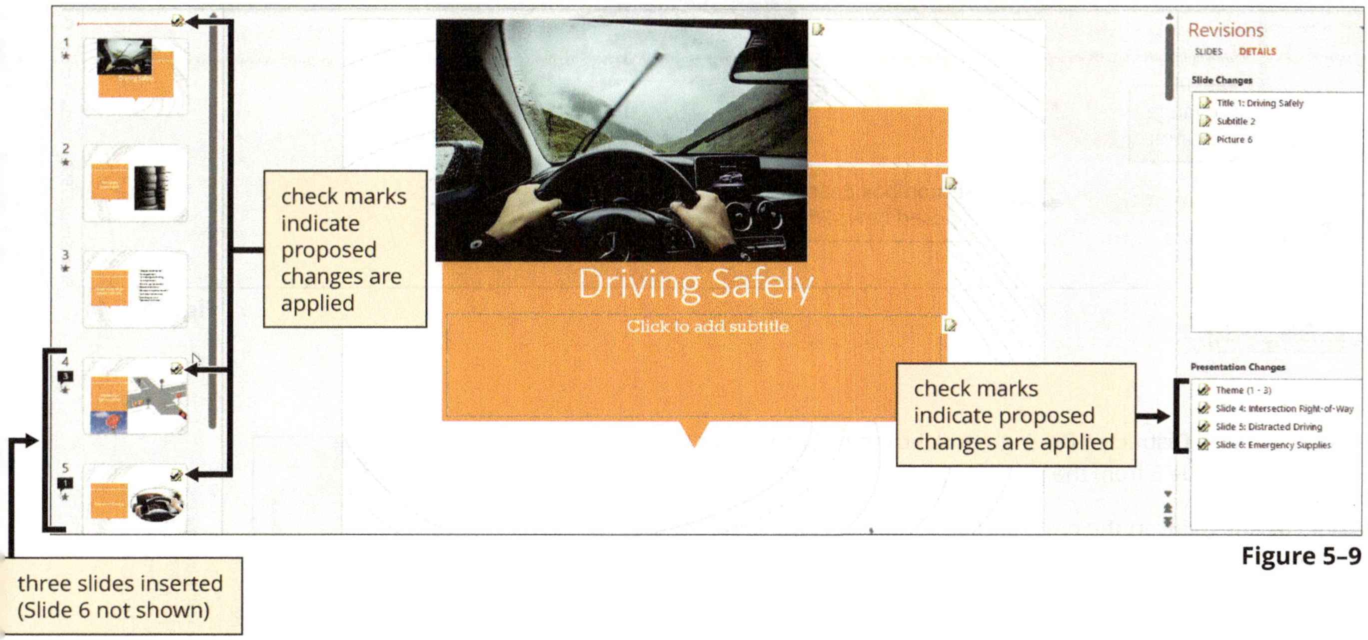

Figure 5–9

StockSnap/27551 images/Pixabay; OpenClipart-Vectors/27376 images/Pixabay; ElasticComputeFarm/39 images/Pixabay; Clker-Free-Vector-Images/29538 images/Pixabay; FlenderFunways/4 images/Pixabay

Q&A Why do check marks appear in the Slides 4, 5, and 6 thumbnails in the Slides tab and in the Presentation Changes section?
The check marks indicate you have applied the proposed changes.

5

- Display Slide 4 and review the slide contents. Then, display Slide 5 and review the information.
- Display Slide 4 again. If necessary, click the Show Comments button (Review tab | Comments group) to display comments, and then read the comments Sam made about using the informational graphic and the changes made to the original file (Figure 5–10).

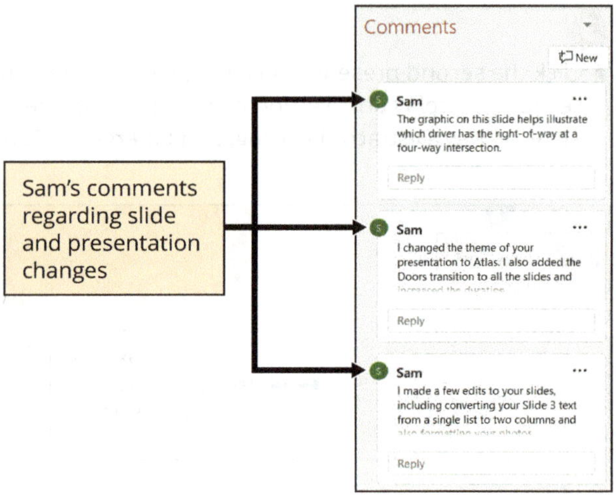

Figure 5–10

6

- Display Slide 5, read Sam's comment, and then click the change marker on the Slide 5 thumbnail to display the insertion box (Figure 5–11).

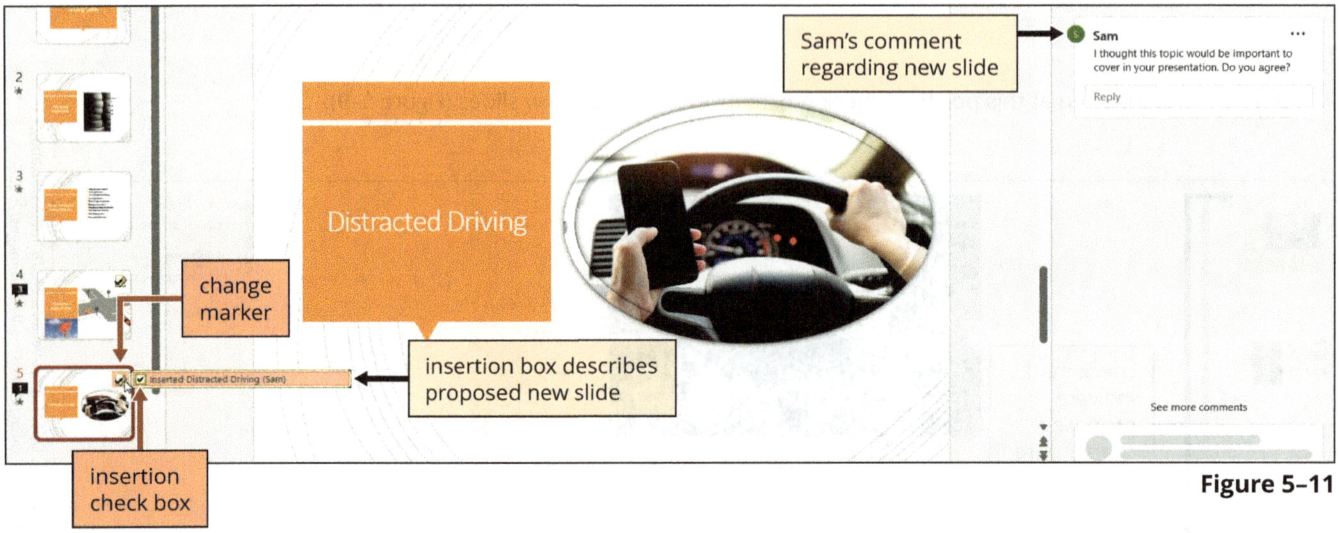

Figure 5–11

StockSnap/27551 images/Pixabay; OpenClipart-Vectors/27376 images/Pixabay; ElasticComputeFarm/39 images/Pixabay; Clker-Free-Vector-Images/29538 images/Pixabay;

7

- Click the 'Inserted Distracted Driving' check box to clear this check box and delete Slide 5 from the presentation (Figure 5–12).

Q&A If I decide to insert the original Slide 5, how can I perform this task?
Click the change marker above the current Slide 5 to insert the slide you deleted.

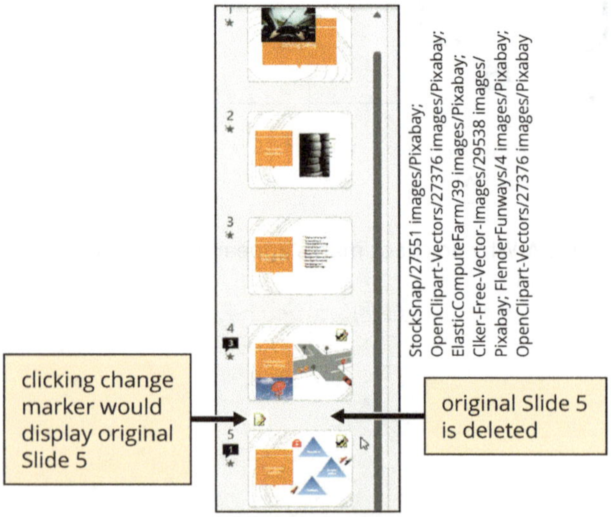

StockSnap/27551 images/Pixabay; OpenClipart-Vectors/27376 images/Pixabay; ElasticComputeFarm/39 images/Pixabay; Clker-Free-Vector-Images/29538 images/Pixabay; FlenderFunways/4 images/Pixabay; OpenClipart-Vectors/27376 images/Pixabay

Figure 5–12

Other Ways

1. Click Next or Previous (Review tab | Compare group), click Accept or Reject button
2. Right-click proposed change, click Accept Change or Reject Change on shortcut menu

To Review, Accept, and Reject Slide Changes

Changes that affect only the displayed slide are indicated in the Slide Changes section of the DETAILS tab on the Revisions pane. A reviewer can modify many aspects of the slide, such as adding and deleting pictures and clips, editing text, and moving placeholders. The following steps display and accept the reviewer's revisions to Slide 1. **Why?** You agree with most of the changes Sam suggested because they enhance your slides.

1

- Display Slide 1, if necessary display the Revisions pane, and then click the slide change 'Title 1: Driving Safely' in the Slide Changes section of the Revisions pane to display the Title 1 box with Sam's two proposed changes for the Driving Safely text in the rectangle (Figure 5–13).

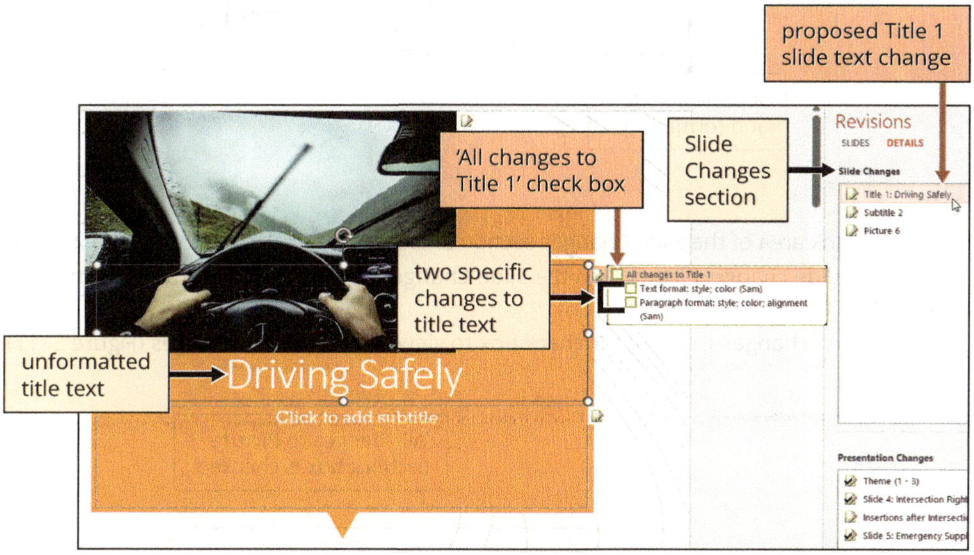

StockSnap/27551 images/Pixabay

Figure 5–13

2

- Click the 'All changes to Title 1' check box to preview all proposed changes to the Driving Safely text (Figure 5–14).

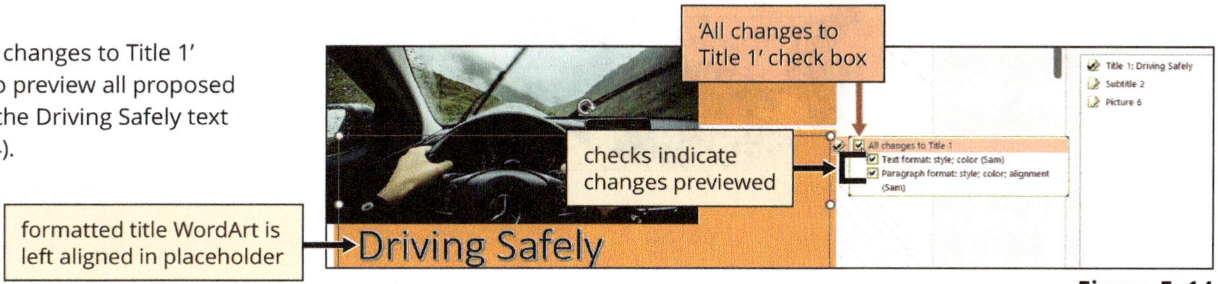

StockSnap/27551 images/Pixabay

Figure 5–14

3

- Click the Paragraph format check box to uncheck it and preview only the other change to the title text, not the alignment of the title WordArt paragraph (Figure 5–15).

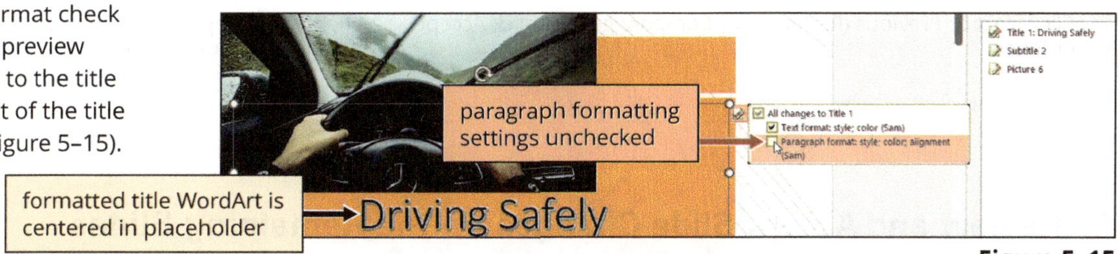

StockSnap/27551 images/Pixabay

Figure 5–15

Q&A Can I select any combination of the check boxes to modify the text in the rectangle?
Yes. You can click the individual check boxes to preview the reviewer's modifications.

4

- Click a blank area of the Slide Changes section to close the 'All changes to Title 1' insertion box.
- Click the slide change, Subtitle 2, in the Slide Changes section to display the insertion box showing the changes to the Slide 1 subtitle.
- Click the 'All changes to Subtitle 2' check box to view the proposed changes (Figure 5–16).

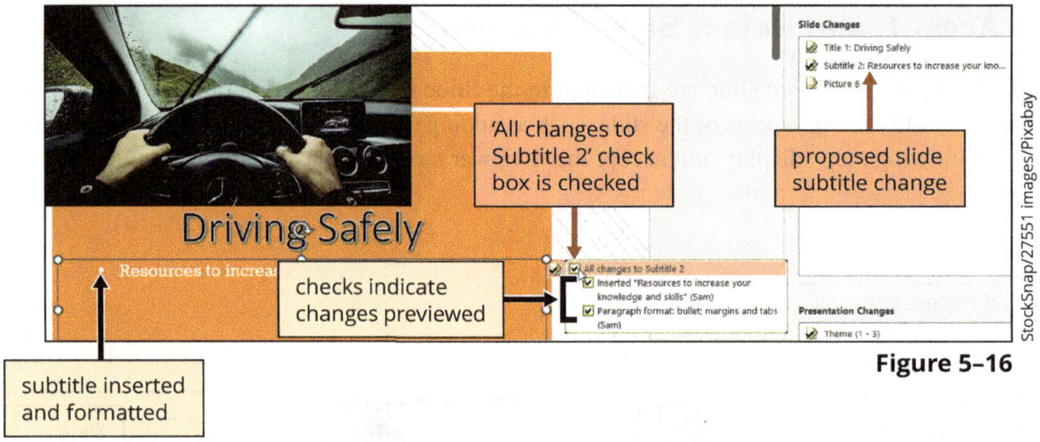

Figure 5–16

5

- Click a blank area of the Slide Changes section to close the 'All changes to Subtitle 2' insertion box.
- Click the slide change, Picture 6, in the Slide Changes section to display the insertion box showing the changes to the Slide 1 picture.
- Click the 'All changes to Picture 6' check box to view the proposed changes (Figure 5–17).

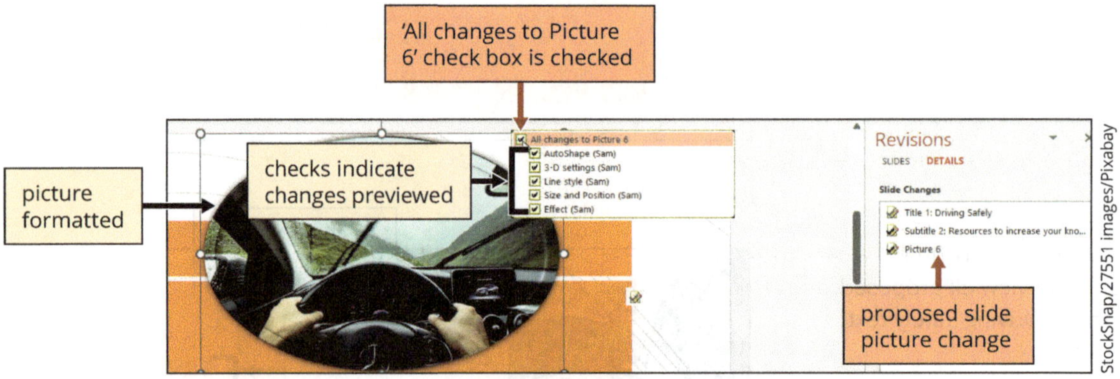

Figure 5–17

6

- Click a blank area of the Slide Changes section to close the 'All changes to Picture 6' insertion box.

Other Ways

1. Click Next or Previous (Review tab | Compare group), click Accept or Reject
2. Right-click proposed change, click Accept Change or Reject Change on shortcut menu

To Review and Accept Slide Changes on the Remaining Slides

You have accepted most of Sam's presentation and Slide 1 changes. He also made changes to slides 2 and 3. The following steps accept his modifications.

1

- Display Slide 2 and then click the SLIDES tab in the Revisions pane to show a thumbnail of Slide 2.

2

- Click the Sam check box above the Slide 2 thumbnail (Revisions pane) to display a preview of and accept the Slide 2 revisions (Figure 5–18).

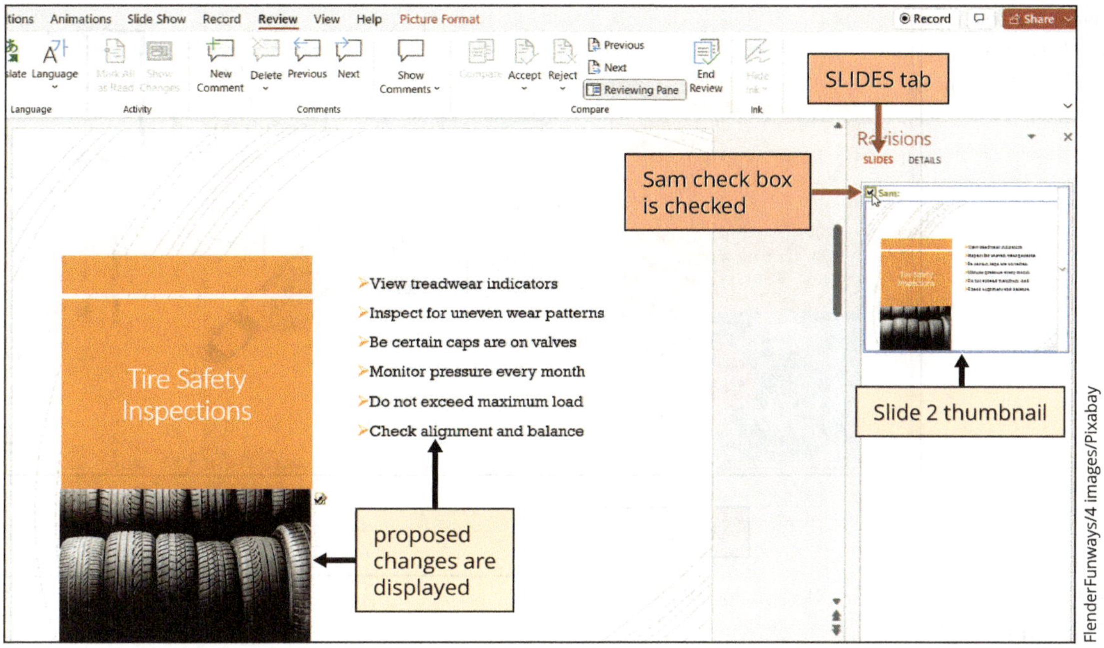

Figure 5–18

3

- Display Slide 3 and then click the Sam check box above the Slide 3 thumbnail (Revisions pane) to display a preview of and accept the Slide 3 revisions (Figure 5–19).

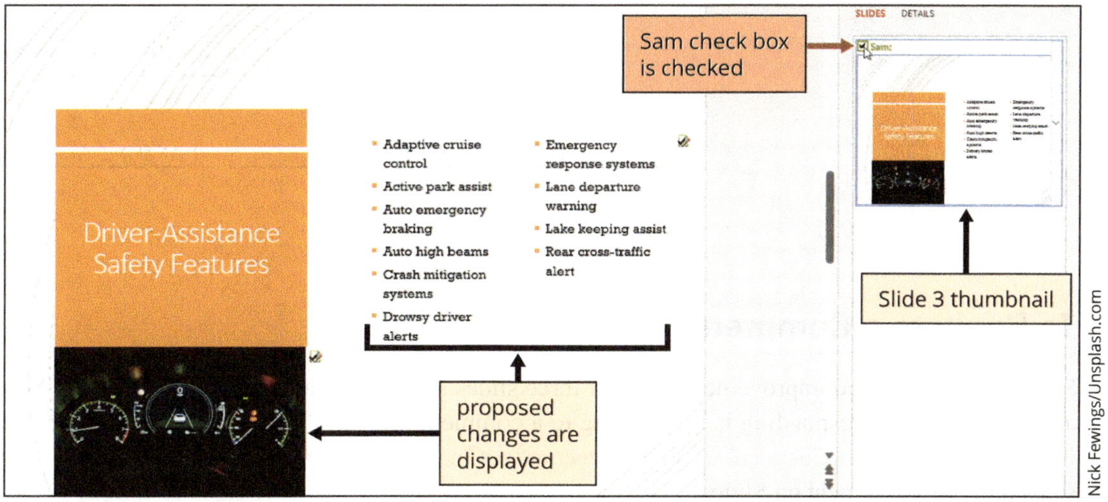

Figure 5–19

To Review Comments

The Comments pane displays the reviewer's name above each comment, and an associated comment marker is displayed on the slide. The following steps review comments for Slide 4. **Why?** You want to look at each comment before deciding to accept or reject the changes.

1

- Display Slide 4 and then click the Next button (Review tab | Comments group) to read Sam's first comment.
- Click the Next button to view Sam's second comment (Figure 5–20).

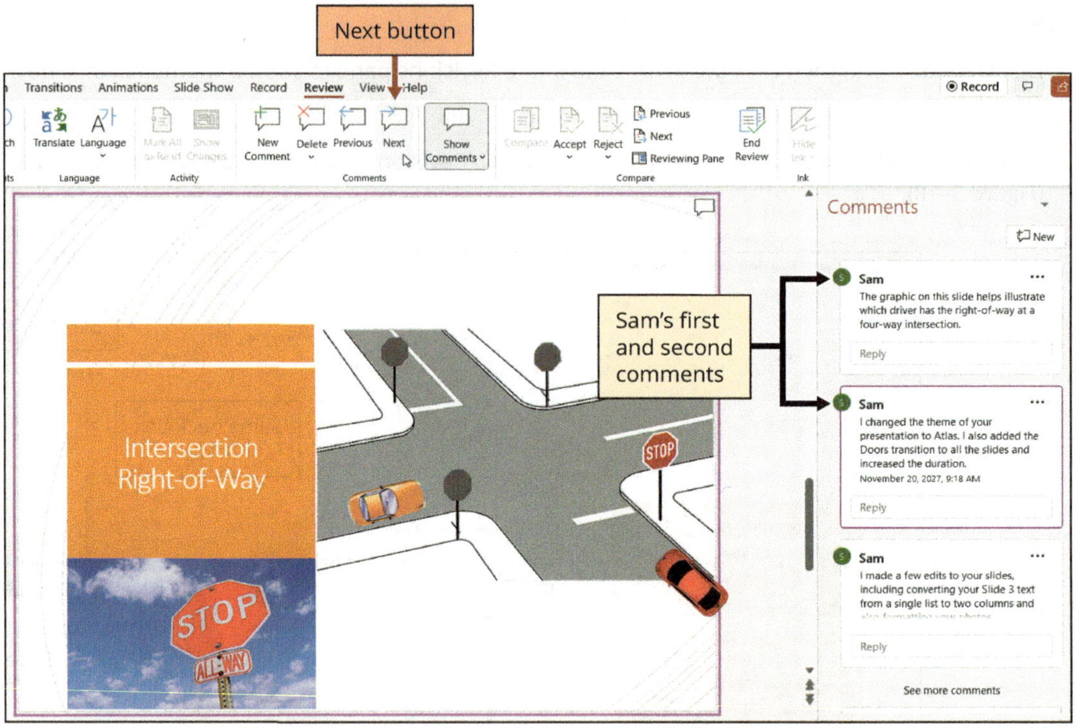

Figure 5–20

2

- Click the Next button to view Sam's third comment.
- Display Slide 5 and then read Sam's comment (Figure 5–21).

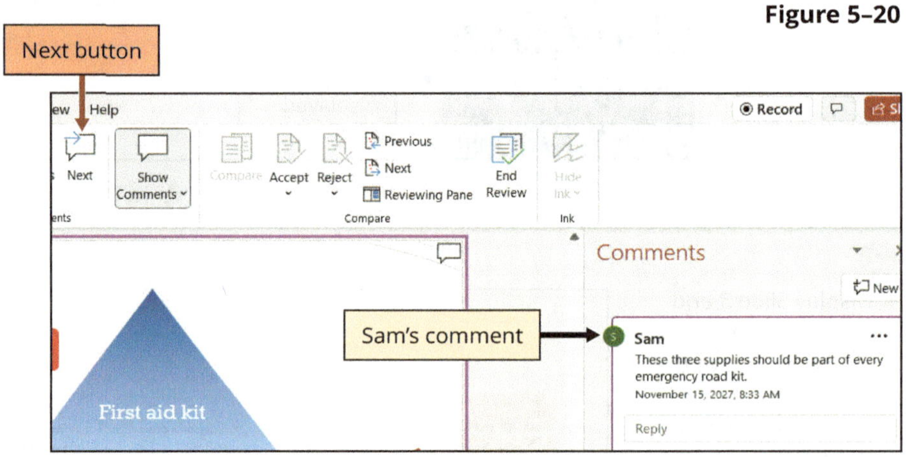

Figure 5–21

To Reply to a Comment

Sam made many good improvements to your three slides and also created some useful slides. You want to provide feedback, and one method of responding is by replying to a comment. **Why?** Giving feedback helps reviewers realize their efforts in improving the presentation were useful and encourages them to continue to participate in collaboration efforts. The following steps reply to a comment on Slide 4.

1

- Display Slide 4 and then select the first comment.
- Click the Reply box to place the insertion point in that box (Figure 5–22).

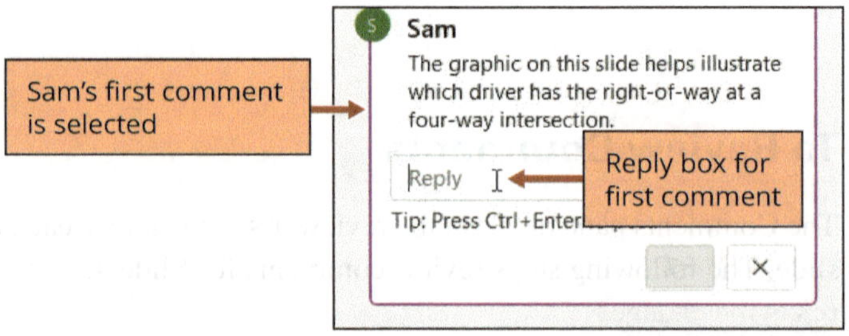

Figure 5–22

2

- Type **This graphic is great!** in the Reply box (Figure 5–23).

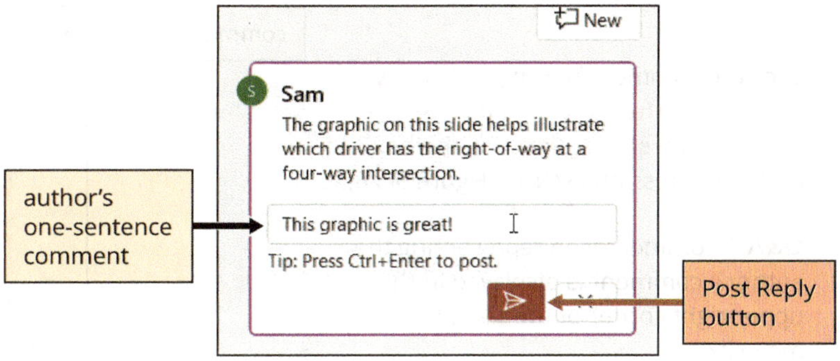

Figure 5–23

3

- Click the Post Reply button to post the comment (Figure 5–24).

Q&A Why does my name differ from that shown in the figure, which is Your Name?
The name reflects the information that was entered when Microsoft 365 was installed on your computer.

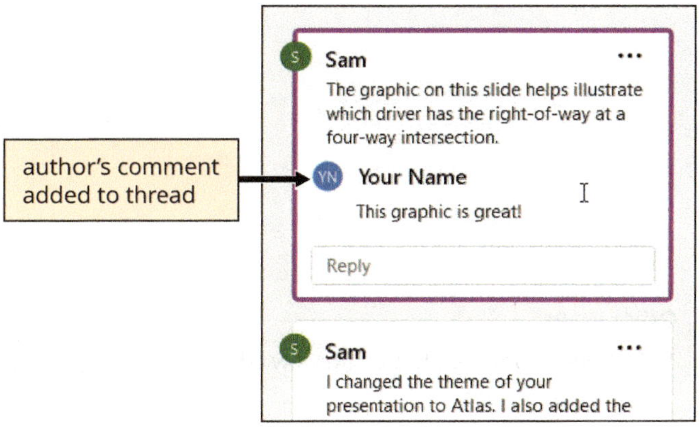

Figure 5–24

Other Ways

1. Press CTRL+ENTER

To Insert a Comment

Sam's comments and changes greatly enhanced your slide show, and you would like to thank him for taking the time to review your original slides. **Why?** He will be able to see what modifications you accepted. The following steps insert a comment on Slide 5.

1

- Display Slide 5 and then click the New button (Comments pane) to open a comment box in the Comments pane (Figure 5–25).

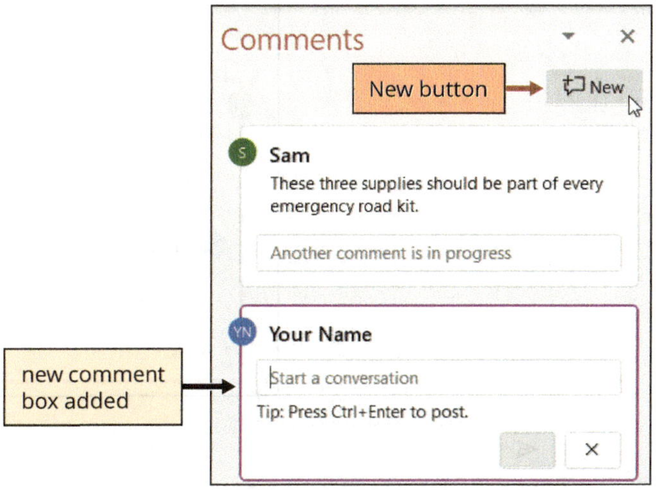

Figure 5–25

2

- Click the comment box, type **I really appreciate the work you did to improve my slides, Sam.** in the box, and then press CTRL+ENTER (Figure 5–26).

Q&A A comment icon representing the author's comment is displayed in the upper-right corner of the slide. Can I move it?
Yes. Select the comment icon on the slide and then drag it to another location on the slide.

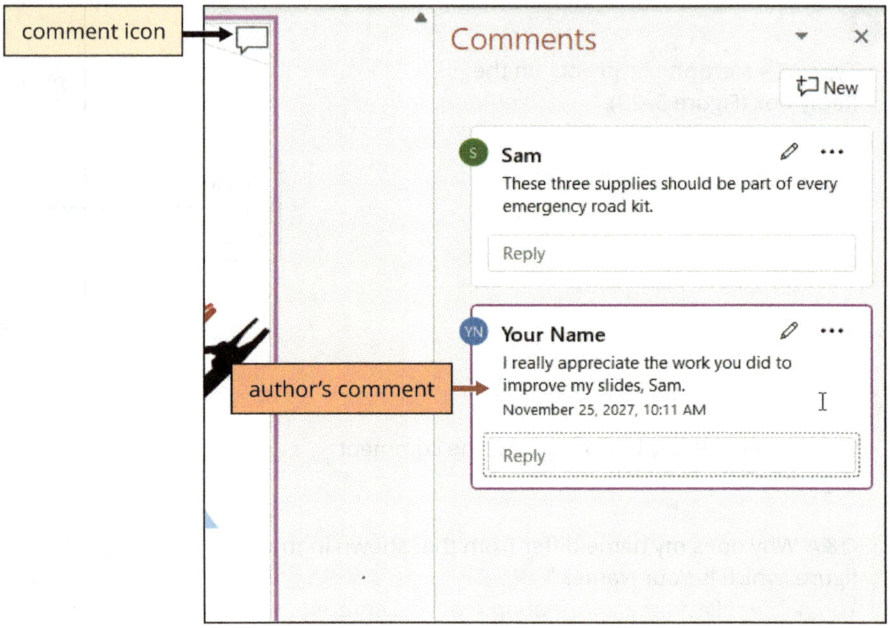

Figure 5–26

Other Ways

1. Click New Comment button (Review tab | Comments group)

To Edit a Comment

Once you have reviewed comments, you may decide to change a comment you made to a reviewer. The following steps edit your comment to add another sentence. **Why?** You want to give Sam additional information about how you are going to modify one of the slides.

1

- Display Slide 4, click the first comment in the Comments pane to select it, and then point to your comment to display the Edit comment and 'More comment actions' buttons (Figure 5–27).

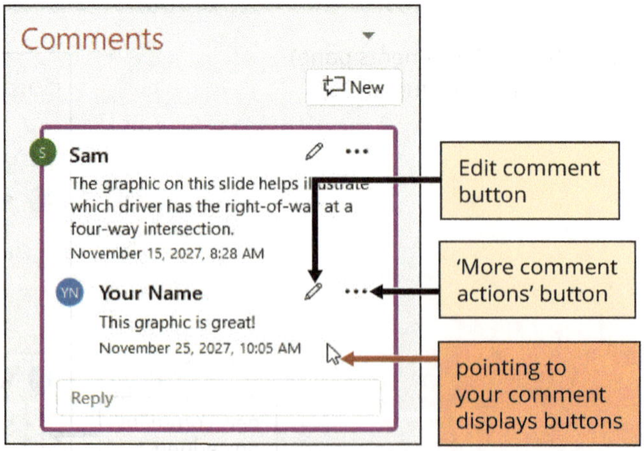

Figure 5–27

- Click the Edit comment button, place the insertion point after the exclamation point in your sentence, press SPACEBAR, type **I'm going to add some animation to illustrate which driver has the right-of-way in this intersection.** in the box, and then press CTRL+ENTER (Figure 5–28).

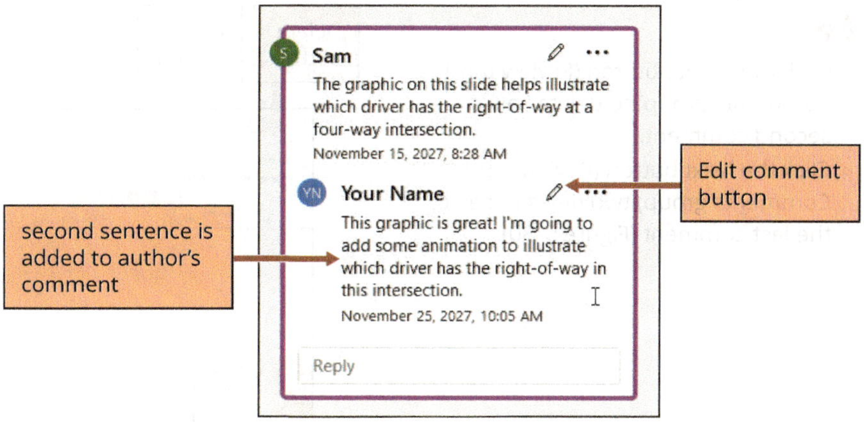

Figure 5–28

To Delete a Comment

Once you have reviewed comments, you may no longer want them to be a part of your slides. You can delete comments that you have read and considered as you are preparing your slides. The following steps delete three of Sam's comments. **Why?** They are not necessary now because you have incorporated the changes into your initial presentation.

1

- With Slide 4 displayed, click Sam's second comment in the Comments pane to select it (Figure 5–29).

Figure 5–29

2

- Click the Delete button (Review tab | Comments group) to delete Sam's second comment.
- Click the Next button (Review tab | Comments group) two times to select the last comment (Figure 5–30).

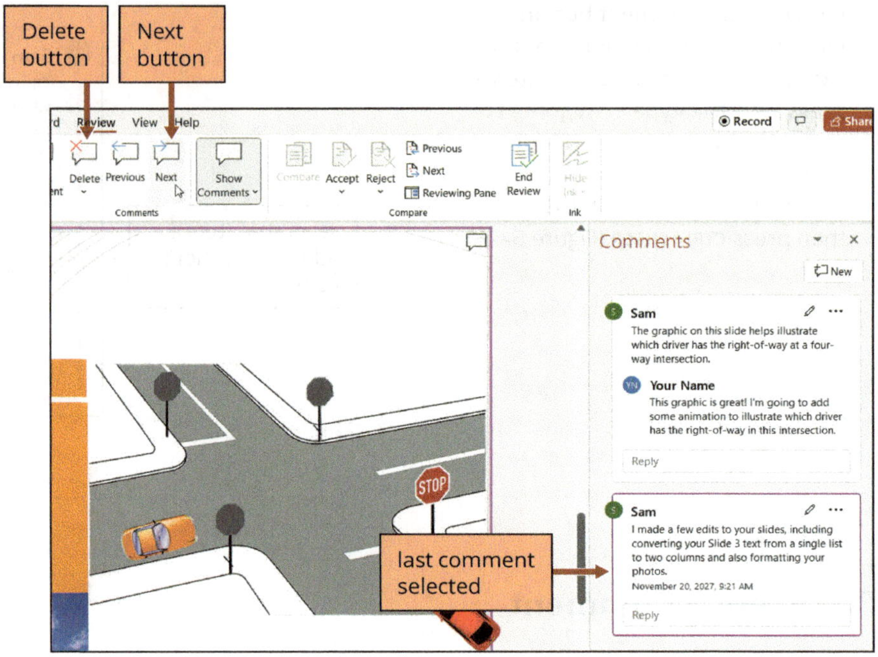

Figure 5–30

3

- Delete the selected comment and then click the Next button two times to select the first comment on Slide 5 (Figure 5–31).

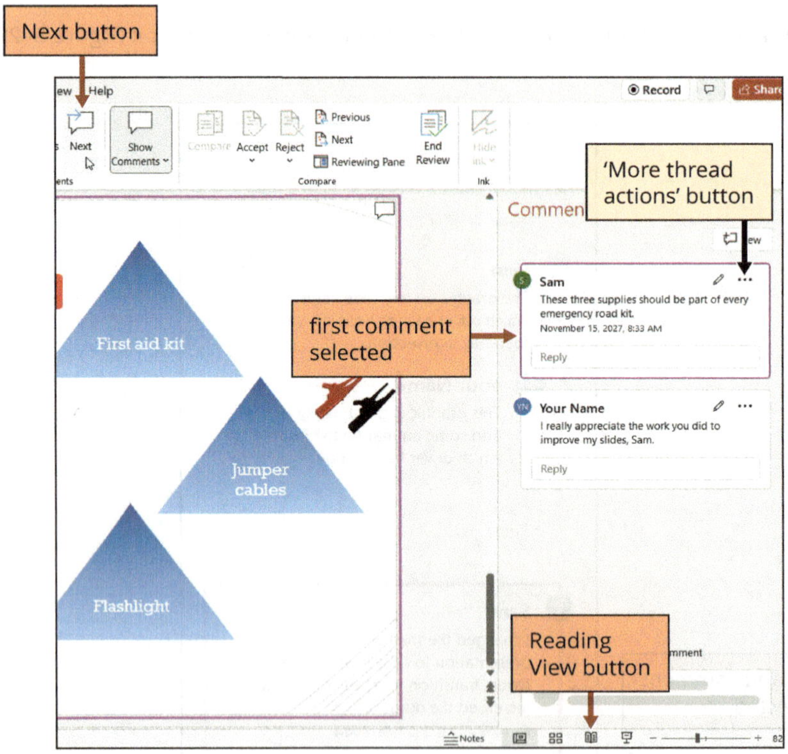

Figure 5–31

4

- Delete the selected comment.
- Skip the last comment.

Other Ways

1. Click 'More thread actions' button (Comments pane), click Delete thread

To Run the Revised Presentation in Reading View

Sam's changes modified the original presentation substantially, so it is a good idea to review the new presentation. The following steps review the slides in Reading view. **Why?** This view helps you see large images of the slides so you can evaluate their content without needing to start Slide Show view.

1

- Display Slide 1 and then click the Reading View button on the status bar (shown in Figure 5–31) to display Slide 1 in this view (Figure 5–32).

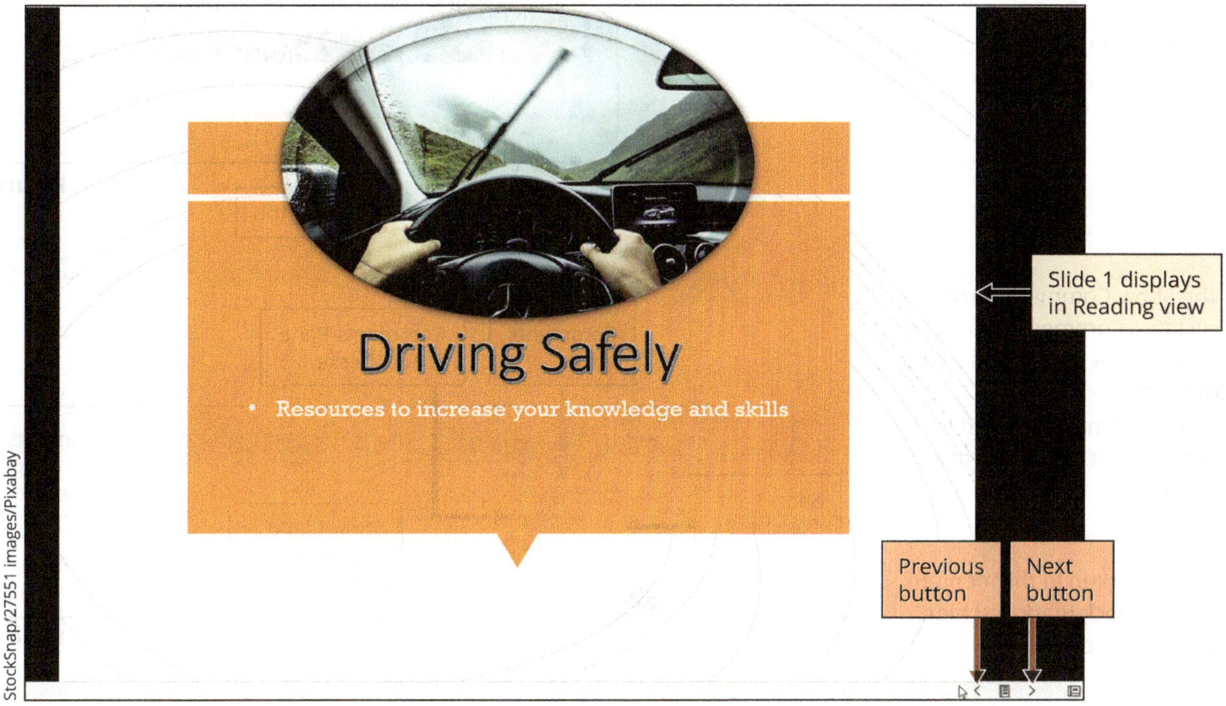

Figure 5–32

2

- Click the Next and Previous buttons to advance the slides and review the changes on each slide.
- Click the black 'End of slide show' screen to end the slide show and return to Normal view.

Other Ways

1. Click Reading View button (View tab | Presentation Views group)

Consider This

How should I give constructive criticism when I am reviewing a presentation?

If you are asked to critique a presentation, begin and end with positive comments. Give specific details about a few key areas that can be improved. Be honest, but be tactful. Avoid using the word, you. For example, instead of writing, "You need to give some statistics to support your viewpoint," write "I had difficulty understanding which departments' sales have increased in the past six months. Perhaps a chart with specific figures would help depict how dramatically revenues have improved."

To End the Review and Hide Markup

You have analyzed all of the reviewer's proposed changes, so your review of the merged presentation is complete. You now can accept and apply all the changes and hide the comments that are present on slides 4 and 5. **Why?** You do not need to see the comments when you are developing the remainder of the presentation, so you can hide them. The following steps end the review of the merged slides.

BTW
Removing Comments
If you want to remove comments on slides before saving your presentation, inspect your presentation. To perform this action, open Backstage view, click the 'Check for issues' button in the Info tab, click Inspect Document, and then click the Inspect button.

1

- With the Review tab displayed, click the End Review button (Review tab | Compare group) to display the Microsoft PowerPoint dialog box (Figure 5–33).

2

- Click Yes (Microsoft PowerPoint dialog box) to apply the changes you accepted and discard the changes you rejected.

Q&A Which changes are discarded?
You did not apply the aligned WordArt on Slide 1 and did not insert Sam's proposed Slide 5.

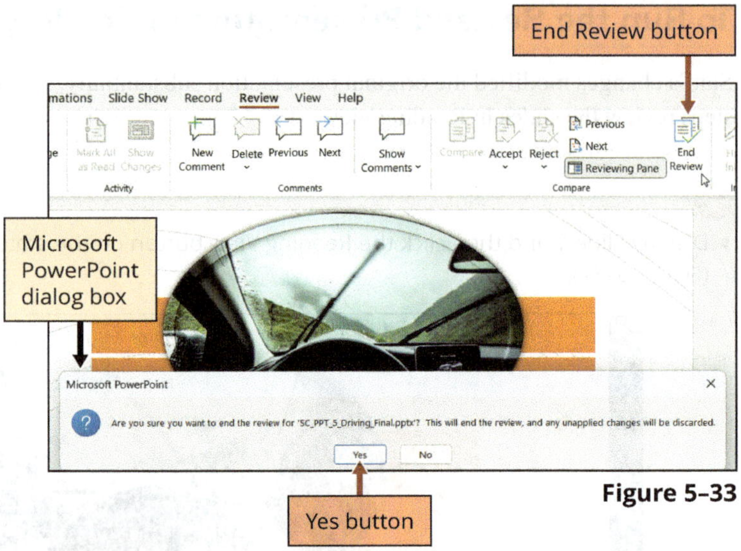

StockSnap/27551 images/Pixabay

Figure 5–33

- Click the Show Comments arrow (Review tab | Comments group) to display the Show Comments menu (Figure 5–34).
- If Comments Pane is checked in the menu, click it to remove the check mark.

3

- Click Show Markup in the menu to remove the check mark and hide comments on the slide.

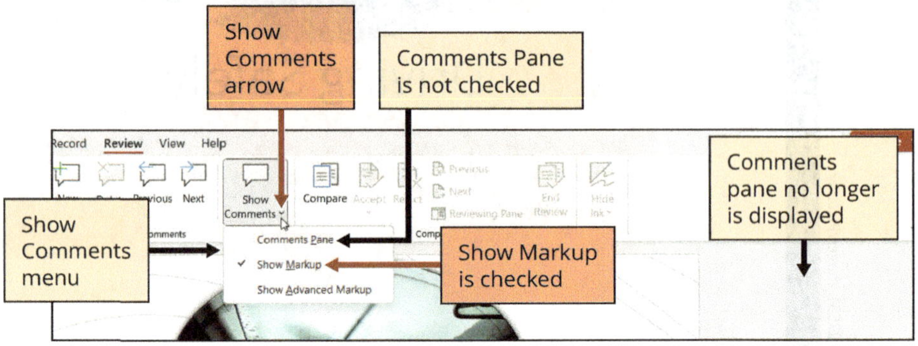

StockSnap/27551 images/Pixabay

Figure 5–34

To Resize Slides

Prior to PowerPoint 2013, PowerPoint set slides in a 4:3 aspect ratio, commonly known as the fullscreen or widescreen aspect ratio. This format was the first standard for monitors and televisions. Many videos were recorded in this configuration, which is the ratio between the width and height of the display. The higher the first number compared to the second number, the wider the screen will be compared to the height. If you know your presentation will be viewed on a widescreen display, you can change the slide size to optimize the proportions. The following steps change the default setting to 16:9. **Why?** This 16:9 dimension is the proportion of most widescreen displays.

1

- Display the Design tab and then click the Slide Size button (Design tab | Customize group) to display the Slide Size gallery (Figure 5–35).

StockSnap/27551 images/Pixabay

Figure 5–35

2

- Click Widescreen (16:9) to change the slide size setting.

To Align Pictures

You have accepted most of Sam's presentation and Slide 1 changes. He also made changes to other slides. The following steps change the picture sizes and alignments to better correspond to the Widescreen slide size.

1. Display Slide 2, change the tires picture width to 2.5", and then center the picture under the Tire Safety Inspections placeholder. If necessary, change the font size of the title text to 40 point, the font size of the six content paragraphs to 18 point, and the title text placeholder width to 3.83".
2. Display Slide 3, change the dashboard picture width to 4", and then center the picture under the Driver-Assistance Safety Features placeholder. If necessary, change the font size of the title text to 40 point, the font size of the content paragraphs in the two columns to 16 point, and the title text placeholder width to 3.83".
3. Display Slide 4, change the stop sign photo width to 4", and then center the picture under the Intersection Right-of-Way placeholder (Figure 5–36). If necessary, change the font size of the title text to 40 point and the title text placeholder width to 3.83".
4. Display Slide 5 and, if necessary, change the font size of the title text to 40 point.
5. Display Slide 1 and, if necessary, change the font size of the title text to 54 point.
6. If the Comments pane is displayed, close it.

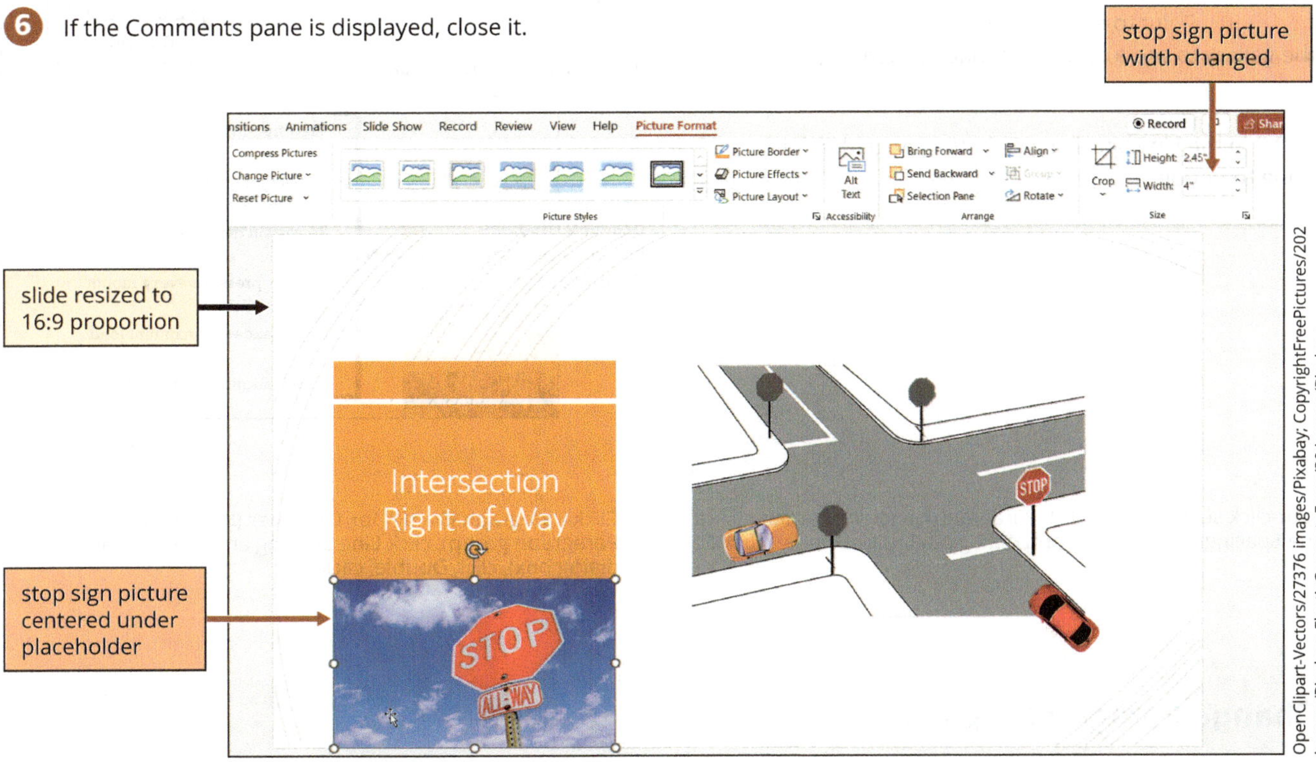

OpenClipart-Vectors/27376 images/Pixabay; CopyrightFreePictures/202 images/Pixabay; ElasticComputeFarm/39 images/Pixabay; Clker-Free-Vector-Images/29538 images/Pixabay

Figure 5–36

Break Point: If you wish to take a break, this is a good place to do so. Be sure the Driving Final file is saved and then you can exit PowerPoint. To resume later, start PowerPoint, open the file called SC_PPT_5_Driving_Final, and continue following the steps from this location forward.

Formatting and Managing Text

Design templates determine formatting characteristics, such as fonts, font styles, effects, colors, paragraph alignment, indentation, and spacing. The design theme also determines the amount of spacing around the sides of the placeholder and between the lines of text. An internal **margin** provides a cushion of space between text and the top, bottom, left, and right sides of the placeholder. **Line spacing** is the amount of vertical space between the lines of text in a paragraph, and **paragraph spacing** is the amount of space above and below a paragraph.

To Change Line Spacing

PowerPoint adjusts the amount of line spacing based on font size. Default line spacing is 1.0, which is considered single spacing. Other preset options are 1.5, 2.0 (double spacing), 2.5, and 3.0 (triple spacing). You can specify precise line spacing intervals between, before, and after paragraphs in the Indents and Spacing tab of the Paragraph dialog box. The following steps increase the line spacing of the content paragraphs from single (1.0) to double (2.0) on Slide 2. **Why?** The additional space helps fill some of the area on the slide and helps your audience read the paragraph text more easily.

1

- Display Slide 2 and then, if necessary, display the Home tab. Select the six content paragraphs.
- Click the Line Spacing button (Home tab | Paragraph group) to display the Line Spacing gallery.
- Point to 2.0 in the Line Spacing gallery to display a live preview of this line spacing (Figure 5-37).
- **Experiment:** Point to each of the line spacing options in the gallery to see a preview of that line spacing.

2

- Click 2.0 in the Line Spacing gallery to change the line spacing to double.

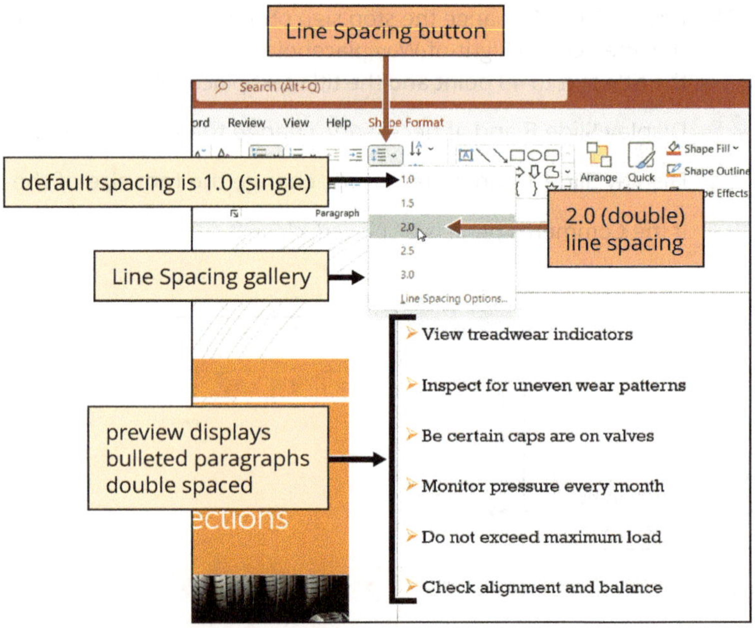

FlenderFunways/4 images/Pixabay

Figure 5-37

Other Ways

1. Right-click selected text, click Paragraph on shortcut menu, click Line Spacing arrow (Paragraph dialog box), click Double, click OK
2. Click Paragraph Dialog Box Launcher (Home tab | Paragraph group), click Line Spacing arrow (Paragraph dialog box), click Double, click OK

To Change Paragraph Spacing

PowerPoint adjusts the paragraph spacing above and below a paragraph automatically to accommodate various font sizes within the placeholder. The following steps change the paragraph spacing to add more space after each paragraph on Slide 2. **Why?** The additional space helps fill some of the area on the slide and also helps your audience read the paragraph text more easily.

1

- With the six content paragraphs selected, click the Line Spacing button (Home tab | Paragraph group) to display the Line Spacing gallery again (Figure 5–38).

2

- Click 'Line Spacing Options' to display the Paragraph dialog box.

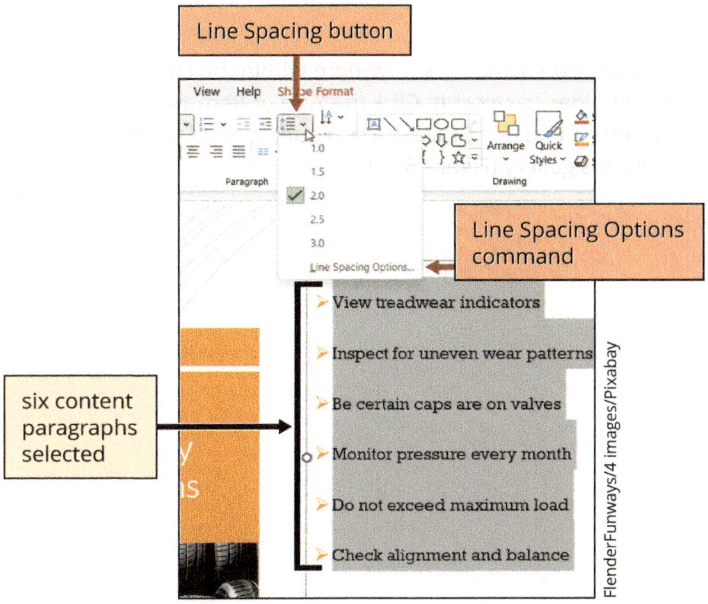

Figure 5–38

3

- Click the Spacing After up arrow twice to increase the spacing to 12 pt (Figure 5–39).

4

- Click OK to close the Paragraph dialog box and apply the new paragraph spacing setting.

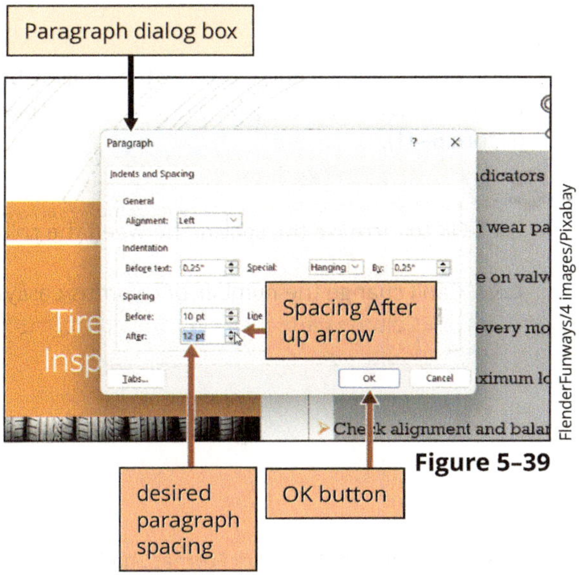

Figure 5–39

Other Ways

1. Right-click selected text, click Paragraph on shortcut menu, click Before or After Spacing arrows (Paragraph dialog box), click OK
2. Click Paragraph Dialog Box Launcher (Home tab | Paragraph group), click Before or After Spacing arrows (Paragraph dialog box), click OK

To Change Column Spacing

The following steps increase the spacing between the columns on Slide 3. **Why?** You wish to increase the space between the columns in the placeholder to fill the width of the placeholder.

1

- Display Slide 3 and click anywhere within the column placeholder to select it. Click the 'Add or Remove Columns' button (Home tab | Paragraph group) to display the Columns gallery (Figure 5–40).

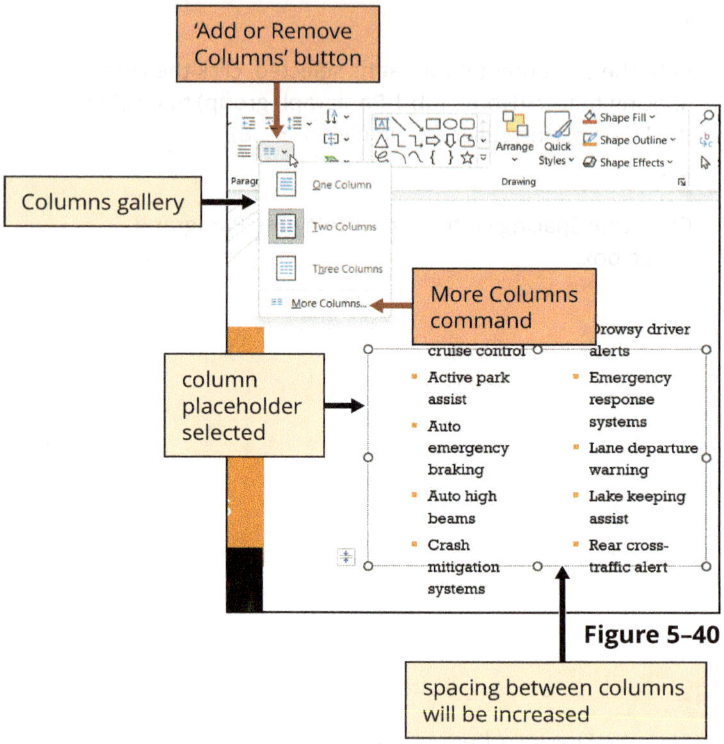

Figure 5–40

2

- Click More Columns and then click the Spacing box up arrow (Columns dialog box) until 0.5" is displayed (Figure 5–41).

3

- Click OK to increase the spacing between the columns.

Q&A Can I change the number of columns easily?
Yes. Click Columns and then click the number of columns you desire.

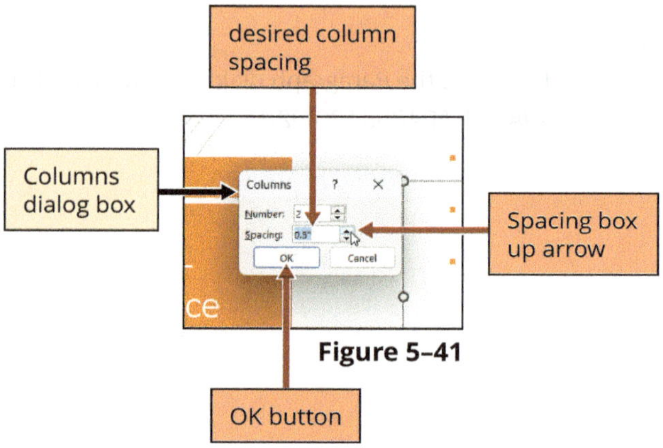

Figure 5–41

Other Ways

1. Right-click placeholder, click Format Shape, click Text Options (Format Shape pane), click Textbox, click Columns button, enter space between columns in Spacing box

To Format Text in Columns

You can add formatting characteristics to the column text to add interest. The following steps change the font color of the column text.

1 Select the text in the Slide 3 placeholder and then change the font color to Dark Blue (ninth color in the Standard Colors row).

2 Click a blank area of the slide to deselect the column text (Figure 5–42).

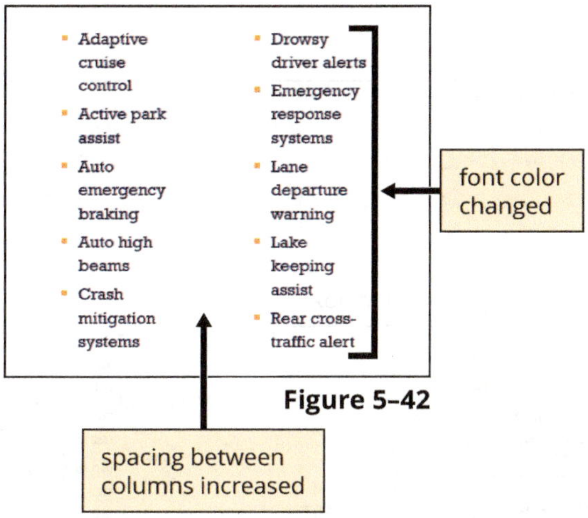

Figure 5–42

To Find Text

You can have PowerPoint locate specific text on any slide in your presentation and in the Notes pane. **Why?** This feature allows you to find particular text quickly and efficiently. It is especially useful when your presentation has many slides. The following steps find the word, Safety, which is found on two slides.

1

- With the Home tab selected, click the Find button (Home tab | Editing group) to display the Find dialog box.
- Type **Safety** in the Find what box (Figure 5–43).

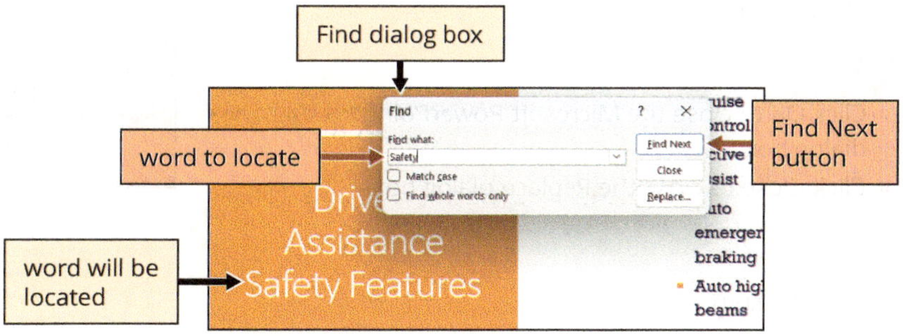

Figure 5–43

2

- Click the Find Next button to display the word, Safety, highlighted on Slide 3.
- Click the Find Next button to display the next occurrence of the word, Safety, on Slide 2 (Figure 5–44).

3

- Click Close to close the Find dialog box.

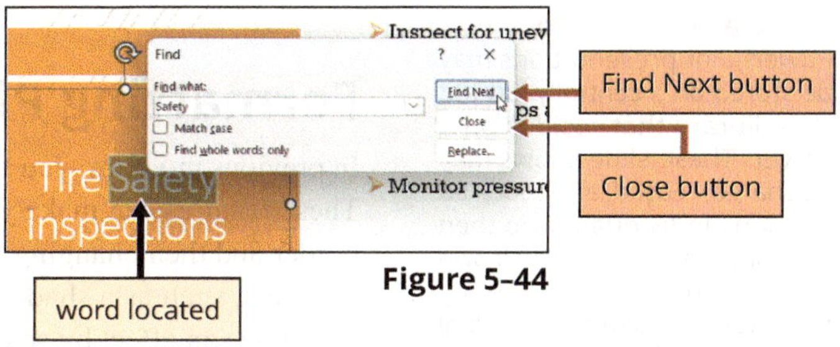

Figure 5–44

Other Ways

1. Press CTRL+F

To Find and Replace Text

If your presentation has many slides and you need to replace a word or phrase, use Find and Replace to efficiently modify the text. You can search for a word or phrase and then replace it with another word or phrase. To change the highlighted text, click the Replace button. To change wherever this text is found in your slides, click the Replace All button. To cancel a search in progress, press ESC. The following steps search for the word, Auto, and replace it with the word, Automatic. **Why?** You want to use the full word instead of a shortened form.

1

- With the Home tab displayed, click the Replace button (Home tab | Editing group) to display the Replace dialog box.
- Type **Auto** in the Find what box.
- Type **Automatic** in the Replace with box.
- Click the Find Next button to display the first occurrence of the word, Auto, on Slide 3 (Figure 5–45).

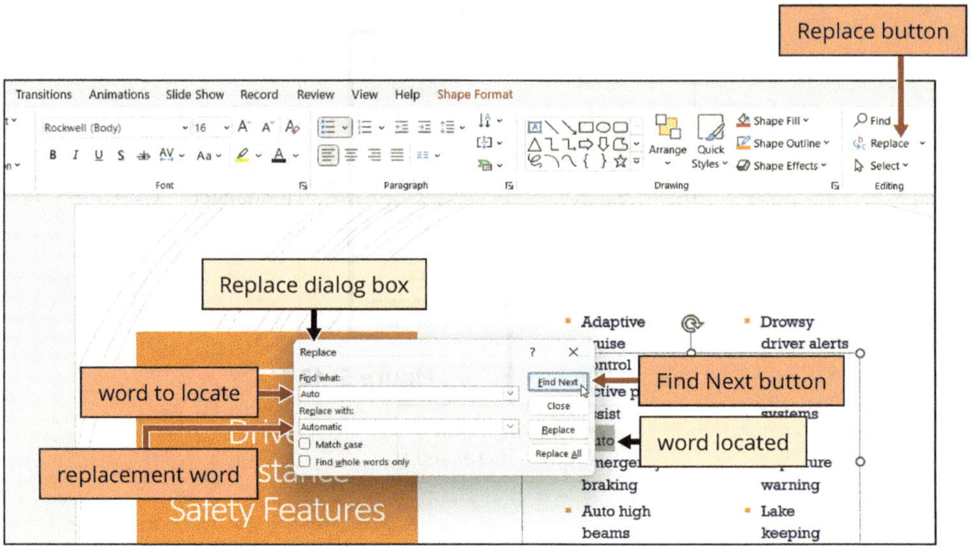

Figure 5–45

2

- Click the Replace button to change the highlighted word, Auto, to Automatic.
- Click the Replace button to change the second occurrence of the word, Auto, to Automatic (Figure 5–46).

3

- Click OK to close the Microsoft PowerPoint dialog box.
- Click Close to close the Replace dialog box.

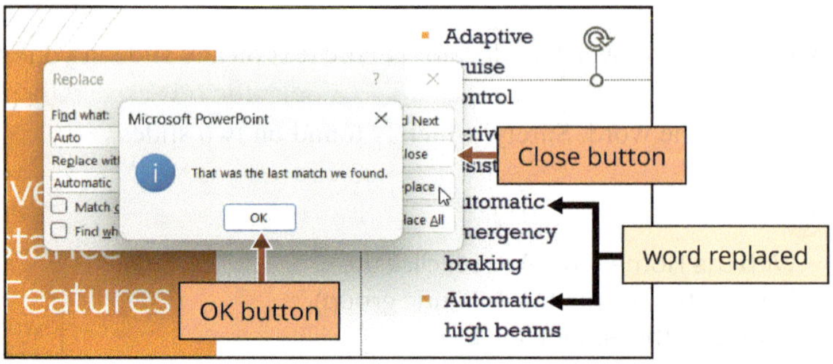

Figure 5–46

Other Ways

1. Press CTRL+H

BTW
Using a Slide Library
PowerPoint presentations may be stored on a centrally located slide library that resides on a server. These slide shows may be shared, reused, and accessed by many individuals who then can copy materials into their own presentations. The slide library time stamps when an individual has borrowed a particular slide or presentation and then time stamps the slide or presentation when it is returned. If a particular slide in the library has been updated, anyone who has borrowed that slide is notified that the content has changed. In this way, people creating PowerPoint presentations can track changes to presentations, locate the latest versions of slides, and check for slide updates.

Formatting Pictures

In previous modules, you formatted pictures by adding artistic effects and adjusting colors. These features can make your slides expressive and unique. One enhancement is adding a border and then changing the color, width, and line style of the shape. Another is creating an effect, such as a shadow, glow, reflection, soft edges, bevels, or 3-D rotation. You can customize an effect by selecting variations in the Format Picture pane.

PowerPoint includes accessibility features, including **alternative text**, also called **alt text**, which is descriptive text added to an object such as a picture, shape, text box, SmartArt graphic, or chart. Alt text helps people understand the content of graphics. When a screen reader is used to view a slide, alt text is displayed or read aloud when you move the pointer over an object. Alt text is a primary element of good design. The biggest advantage of having accurate and comprehensive alt text is that it makes digital assets more accessible. When giving a presentation, whether you are presenting it in person or sharing it on the web, having alt text is key to enhancing your information.

To Add an Artistic Effect to a Picture

In Module 3 you added an artistic effect to the Slide 1 picture. You similarly want to add an artistic effect to the Slide 2 picture in this presentation. The following steps add the Glow Edges artistic effect to the tires picture.

1. Display Slide 2 and then select the tires picture.
2. Click the Picture Format tab and then click the Artistic Effects button (Picture Format tab | Adjust group) to display the Artistic Effects gallery.
3. Point to Glow Edges (last thumbnail in the last row) to display a live preview of this effect on the picture.
4. Click Glow Edges to apply this artistic effect to the picture (Figure 5–47).

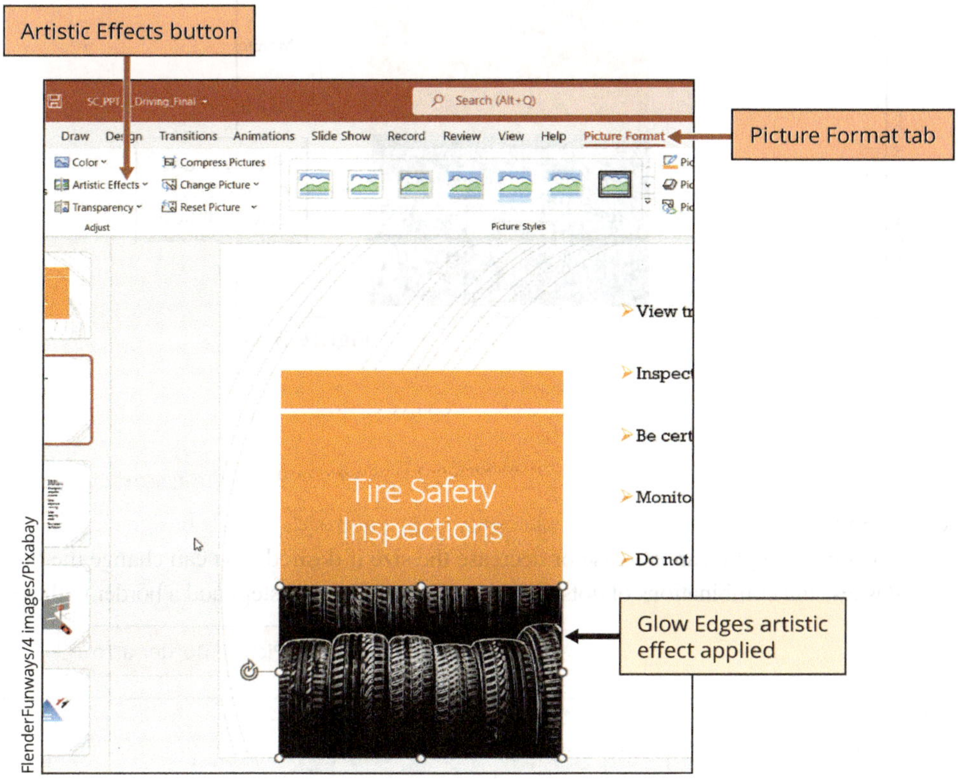

Figure 5–47

To Recolor a Picture

The Atlas theme is appropriate for this presentation on the subject of driving safely, and you have enhanced a slide with dark blue text. The following steps recolor the Slide 2 picture to further coordinate with the blue hues found in the presentation.

1. With the tires picture still selected, click the Color button (Picture Format tab | Adjust group) to display the Color gallery.
2. Point to 'Blue, Accent color 4 Dark' (fifth thumbnail in the second Recolor row) to display a live preview of this adjustment on the picture.

3. Click 'Blue, Accent color 4 Dark' to apply this recolor to the tires picture (Figure 5–48).

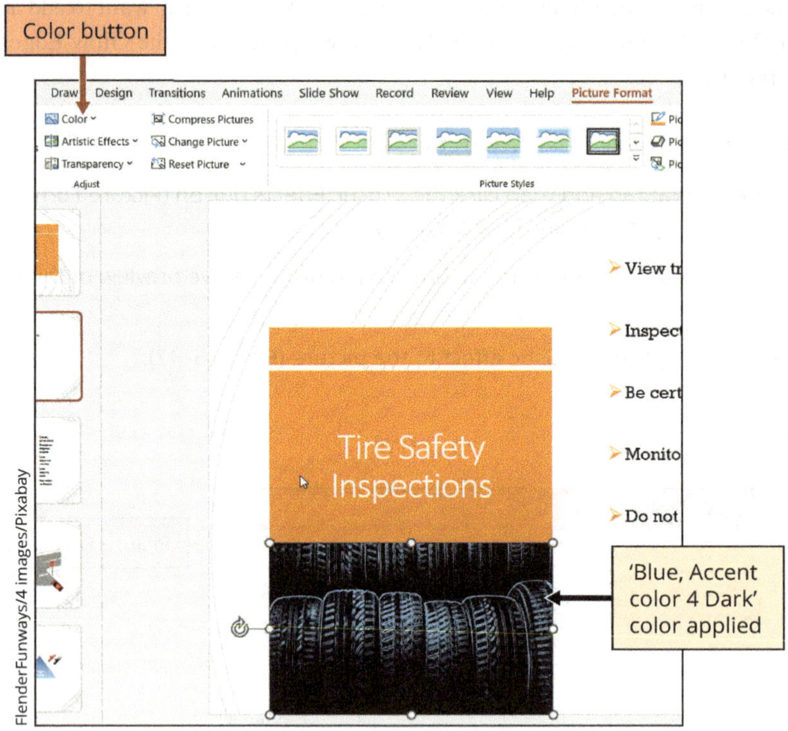

Figure 5–48

To Add a Picture Border

The next step is to add a border to the Slide 3 picture. **Why?** A border completes the picture and adds a subtle design element. Default borders range from a width of ¼ point to 6 point, and you can increase or decrease the size if desired. You can change the line style from a solid line to round or square dots, dashes, and combinations of dots and dashes. The following steps add a border to the picture.

1.
- Display Slide 3 and select the picture.
- With the Picture Format tab displayed, click the Picture Border arrow (Picture Format tab | Picture Styles group) to display the Picture Border gallery.

2.
- Point to Weight on the Picture Border gallery to display the Weight gallery.
- Point to 6 pt to display a live preview of this line weight on the picture (Figure 5–49).

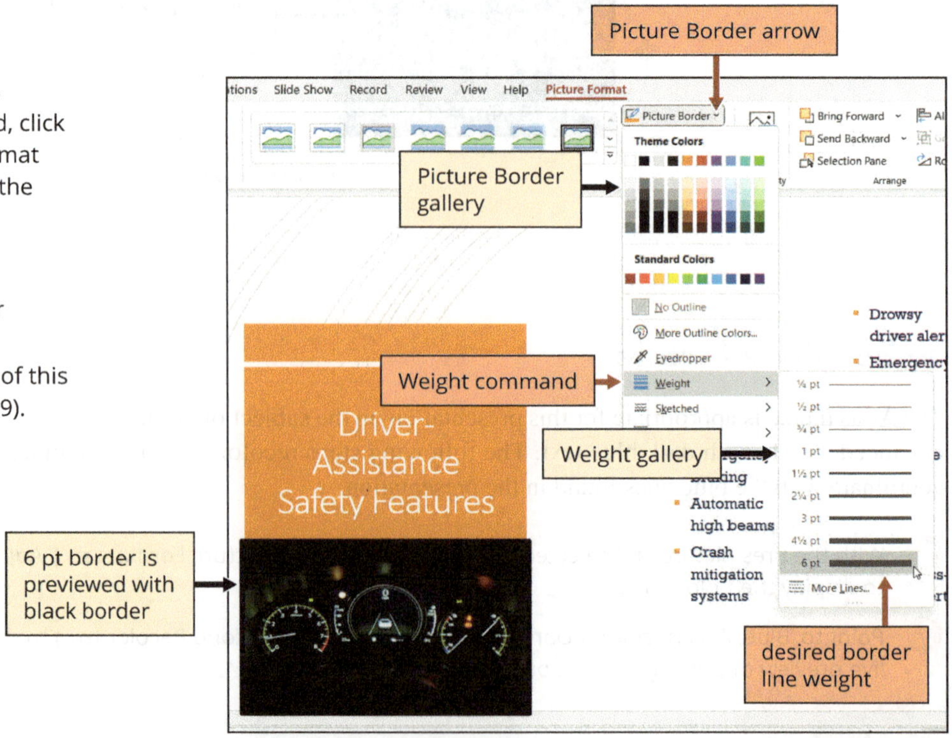

Nick Fewings/Unsplash.com

Figure 5–49

Q&A How can I make the line width more than 6 pt?
Click More Lines, click Solid line in the Line section of the Format Picture pane, and then increase the amount in the Width box.

- **Experiment:** Point to various line weights in the Weight gallery and watch the line thickness change.

3

- Click 6 pt to add this line weight to the picture.

To Change a Picture Border Color

The default color for the border you added to the Slide 3 picture is black, but you will change the border color to orange. **Why?** This color coordinates with the orange elements on the slide. The following steps change the Slide 3 picture border color.

1

- With the Slide 3 picture still selected, click the Picture Border arrow (Picture Format tab | Picture Styles group) to display the Picture Border gallery again.

2

- Point to 'Orange, Accent 1, Lighter 80%' (fifth color in the second Theme Colors row) in the Picture Border gallery to display a live preview of that border color on the picture (Figure 5–50).
- **Experiment:** Point to various colors in the Picture Border gallery and watch the border on the picture change on the slide.

3

- Click 'Orange, Accent 1, Lighter 80%' in the Picture Border gallery to change the picture border color.

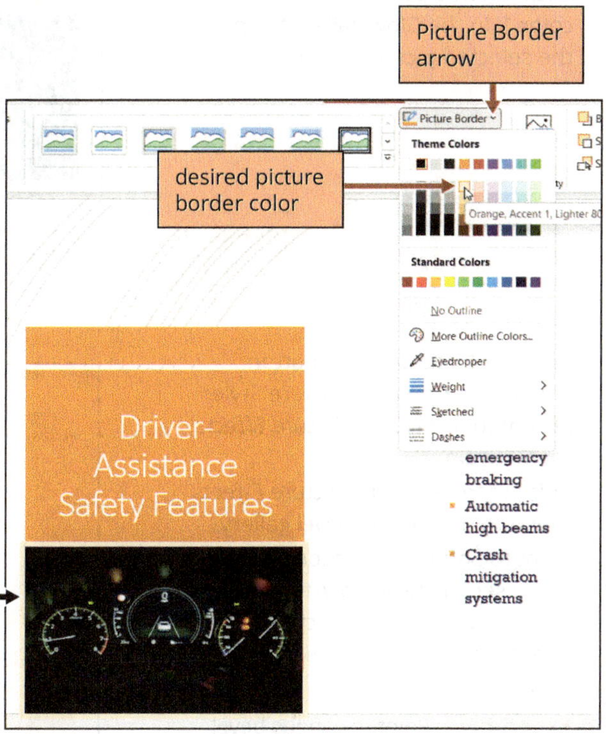

Nick Fewings/Unsplash.com

Figure 5–50

To Apply a Picture Effect

PowerPoint provides a variety of picture effects, including shadows, reflections, glow, soft edges, bevel, and 3-D rotation. **Why?** Picture effects allow you to further customize a picture. The difference between the effects and the styles is that each effect has several options, providing you with more control over the exact look of the image.

In this presentation, the picture on Slide 3 has an orange glow effect and a bevel applied to its edges. The following steps apply picture effects to the selected picture.

BTW
Compressing Pictures
Click the Compress Pictures button (Picture Format tab | Adjust group) to reduce the presentation file size. Determine the optimum resolution by selecting where or how you will show the slides, such as on the web or via printed handouts.

1

- With the Slide 3 picture still selected, click Picture Effects (Picture Format tab | Picture Styles group) to display the Picture Effects menu.

Q&A What if the Picture Format tab no longer is displayed on my ribbon?
Click the picture to display the Picture Format tab.

- Point to Glow on the Picture Effects menu to display the Glow gallery.
- Point to 'Glow: 8 point; Orange, Accent color 1' in the Glow Variations area (first glow in the second row) to display a live preview of the selected glow effect applied to the picture in the document window (Figure 5–51).

Experiment: Point to various glow effects in the Glow gallery and watch the picture change in the document window.

2

- Click 'Glow: 8 point; Orange, Accent color 1' in the Glow gallery to apply the selected picture effect.

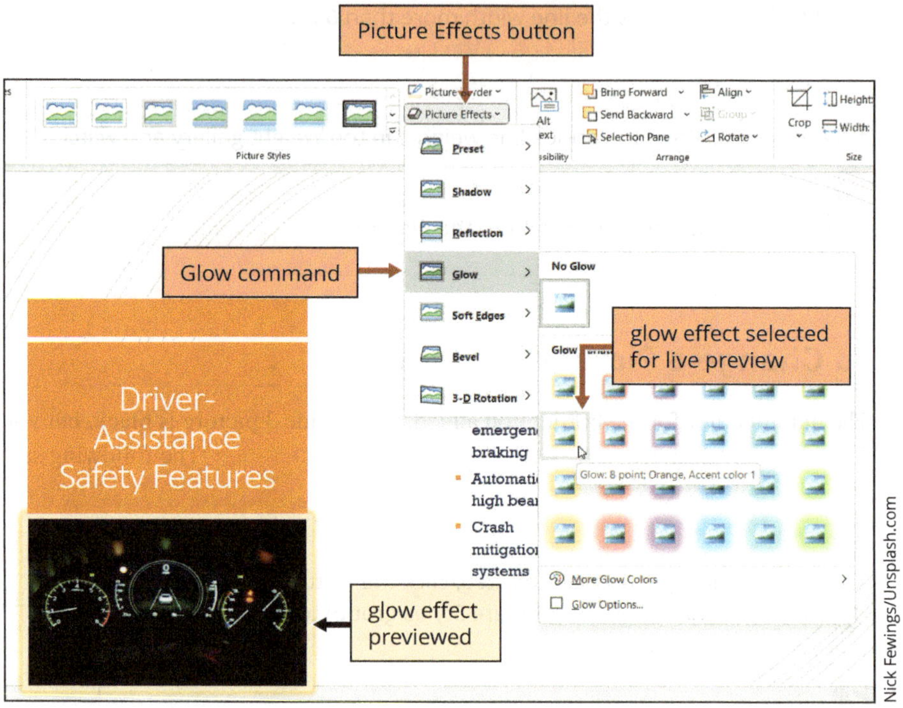

Figure 5–51

3

- Click the Picture Effects button (Picture Format tab | Picture Styles group) to display the Picture Effects menu again.
- Point to Bevel on the Picture Effects menu to display the Bevel gallery.
- Point to Soft Round (second bevel in the second Bevel row) to display a live preview of the selected bevel effect applied to the Slide 3 picture (Figure 5–52).

Experiment: Point to various bevel effects in the Bevel gallery and watch the picture change on the slide.

4

- Click Soft Round in the Bevel gallery to apply the selected picture effect.

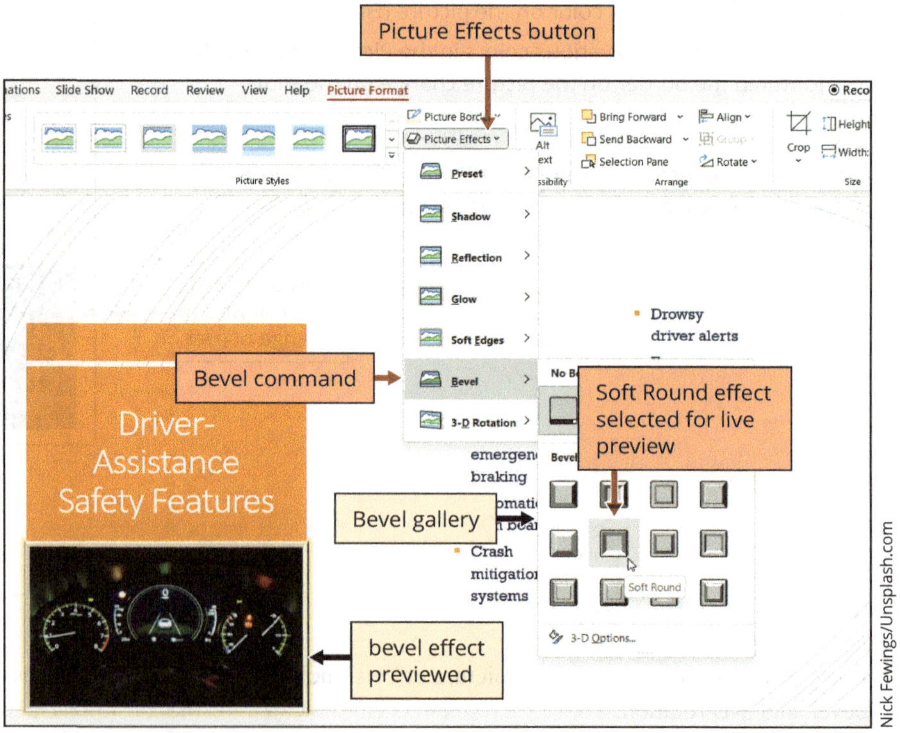

Figure 5–52

Other Ways

1. Right-click picture, click Format Picture on shortcut menu, select desired options (Format Picture pane), click Close
2. Click Format Picture dialog box launcher (Picture Format tab | Picture Styles group), select desired options (Format Picture pane), click Close

To Add Alt Text

The Slide 3 picture alt text has a general description of the dashboard. The following steps modify this text. **Why?** You want to add detail to the Alt text picture description.

1

- With the Slide 3 picture selected, click the Alt Text button (Picture Format tab | Accessibility group) to display the Alt Text pane.

2

- Click the Alt Text text box, delete any text in the box, and then type **Vehicle dashboard showing the tachometer, speedometer, and safety features** as the descriptive text (Figure 5–53).

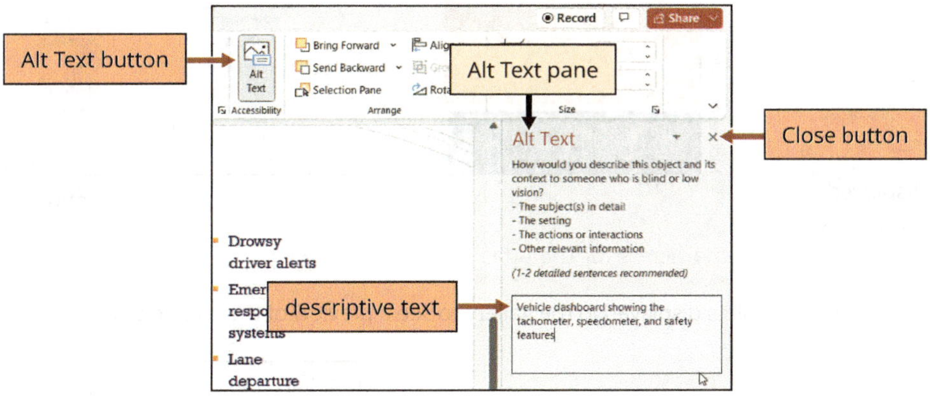

Figure 5–53

3

- Close the Alt Text pane.

Modifying Bullets and Adding Effects

PowerPoint allows you to change the default appearance of bullets in a slide show. The document themes determine the bullet character. A **bullet character** is a small graphic symbol, traditionally a closed circle, that sets off items in a list. It can be a predefined style, a variety of fonts and characters displayed in the Symbol gallery, or a picture from a file, from Online Pictures, or from the Microsoft icon collection. You may want to change a bullet character to add visual interest and variety. Once you change the bullet character, you also can change its size and color.

If desired, you can change every bullet in a presentation to a unique character. If your presentation has many bulleted slides, however, you can create a consistent look on all slides by making the bullets a similar color and size.

To customize your presentation, you can change the default slide layout bullets to numbers by changing the bulleted list to a numbered list. PowerPoint provides a variety of numbering options, including Arabic and Roman numerals. These numbers can be sized and recolored, and the starting number can be something other than 1 or I. In addition, PowerPoint's numbering options include uppercase and lowercase letters.

To Change a Bullet Character to a Picture

One method of modifying these bullets is to use a relevant picture. The following steps change the first paragraph bullet character to the red car picture, which is located in the Data Files. **Why?** The plain bullet characters for the Atlas document theme do not add much visual interest and do not relate to the topic of driving.

1

- With Slide 3 displayed, select all 10 paragraphs in the two columns.
- Click the Bullets arrow (Home tab | Paragraph group) to display the Bullets gallery (Figure 5–54).

Q&A What should I do if I clicked the Bullets button instead of the Bullets arrow?
If the paragraphs are bulleted, clicking the Bullets button removes the bullets. Click the Bullets button again to display the bullets.

Why is a gray box displayed around the three characters?
They are the default first-level bullet characters for the Atlas document theme.

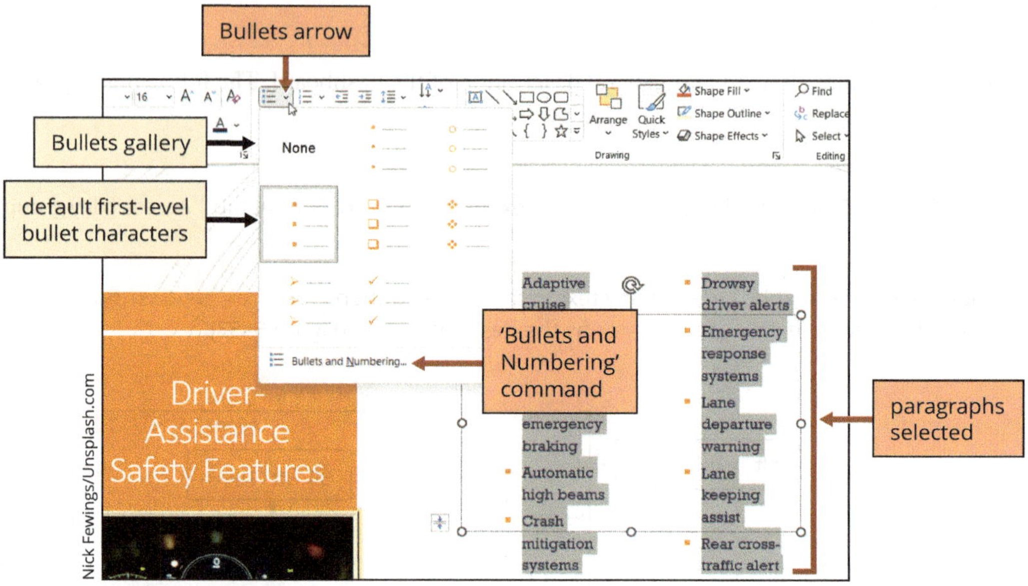

Figure 5–54

- **Experiment:** Point to each of the bullets displayed in the gallery to see a preview of the characters.

2

- Click 'Bullets and Numbering' to display the Bullets and Numbering dialog box (Figure 5–55).

Q&A Why are my bullets different from those displayed in Figure 5–55?
The bullets most recently inserted are displayed as the first items in the dialog box.

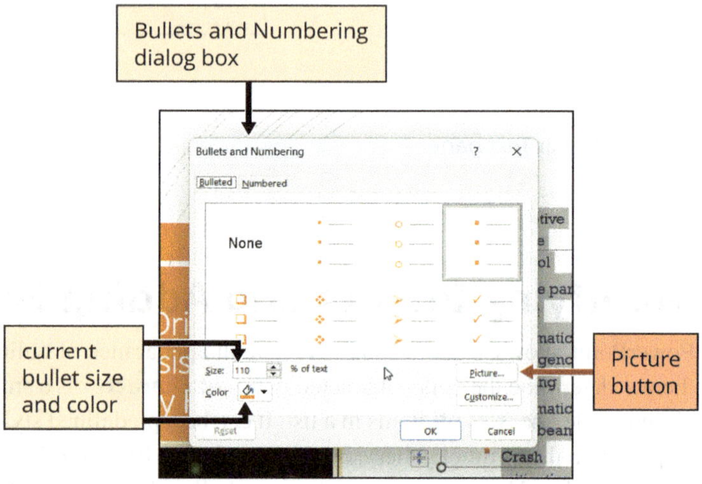

Figure 5–55

3

- Click the Picture button (Bullets and Numbering dialog box) to display the Insert Pictures dialog box (Figure 5–56).

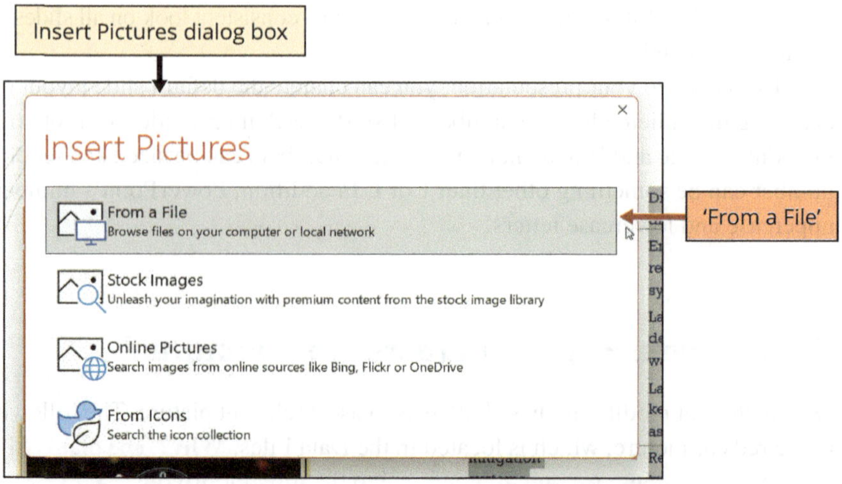

Figure 5–56

4

- Click 'From a File' (Insert Pictures dialog box) to display the Insert Picture dialog box.
- If necessary, navigate to the location of the Data Files.
- Click **Support_PPT_5_Red_Car** to select the .png file (Figure 5–57).

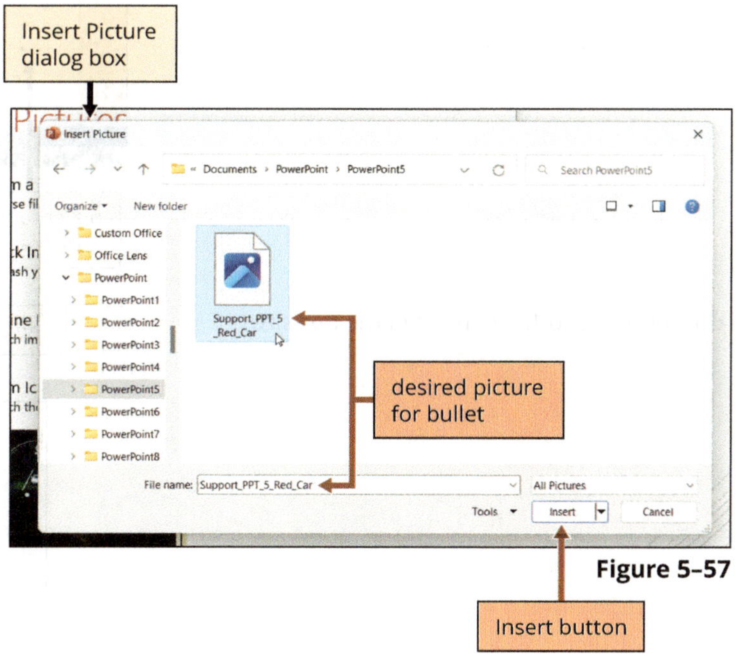

Figure 5–57

5

- Click the Insert button (Insert Picture dialog box) to insert the red car picture as the paragraph bullet character (Figure 5–58).

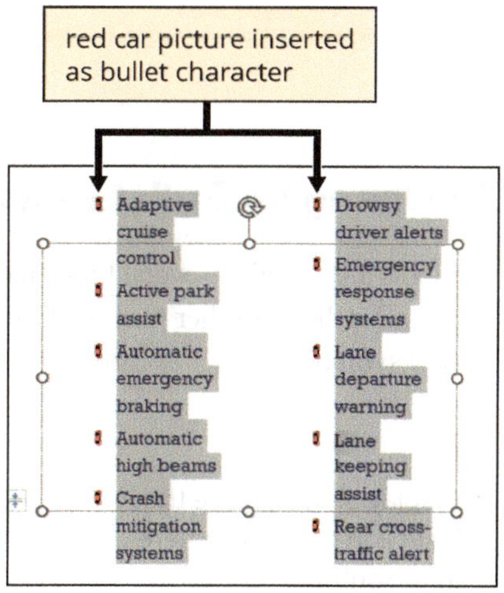

Figure 5–58

Other Ways

1. Right-click paragraph, point to Bullets on shortcut menu, click 'Bullets and Numbering'

To Change Bullet Size

Bullets have a default size determined by the document theme. **Bullet size** is measured as a percentage of the text size and can range from 25 to 400 percent. The following steps change the red car picture size. **Why?** It is difficult to see the picture, so increasing its size draws attention to the visual element and increases readability.

1

- With the Slide 3 paragraphs still selected, click the Bullets arrow (Home tab | Paragraph group) and then click 'Bullets and Numbering' in the Bullets gallery to display the Bullets and Numbering dialog box.
- Click the Size up arrow until 150 is displayed in the '% of text' Size box (Figure 5–59).

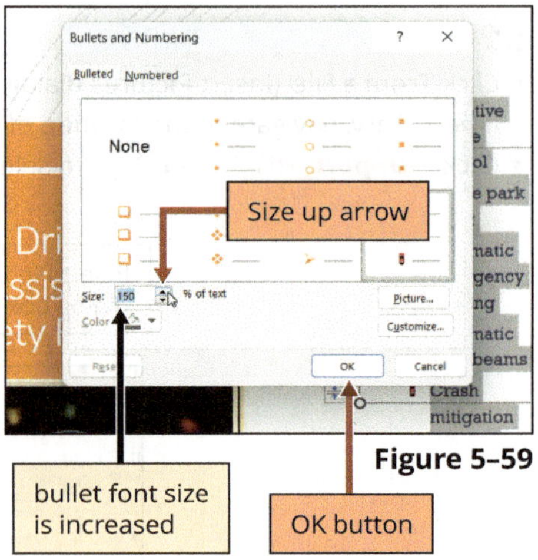

Figure 5–59

2

- Click OK to increase the red car bullet size to 150 percent of the text size (Figure 5–60).

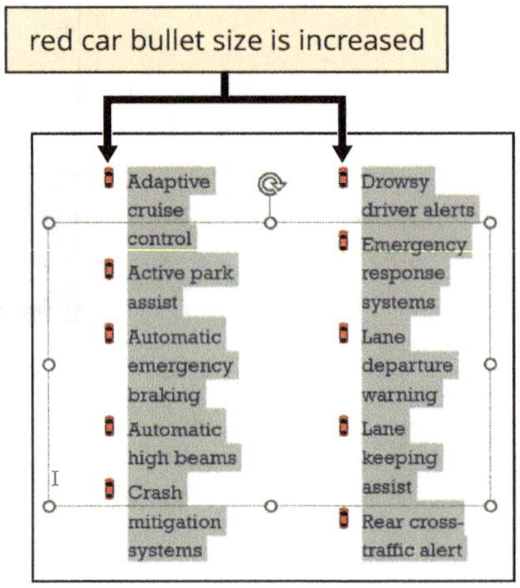

Figure 5–60

To Change a Bullet to a Symbol

Symbols are found in several fonts, including Webdings, Wingdings, Wingdings 2, and Wingdings 3. These fonts are available when slides have themes other than the Office theme. The following steps change the bullet character on Slide 1 to a Lozenge (diamond shape) symbol. **Why?** For variety and to add a unique characteristic to the presentation, you can insert a symbol as the character.

1

- Display Slide 1, place the insertion point anywhere in the subtitle text, click the Bullets arrow (Home tab | Paragraph group), and then click 'Bullets and Numbering' to display the Bullets and Numbering dialog box (Figure 5–61).

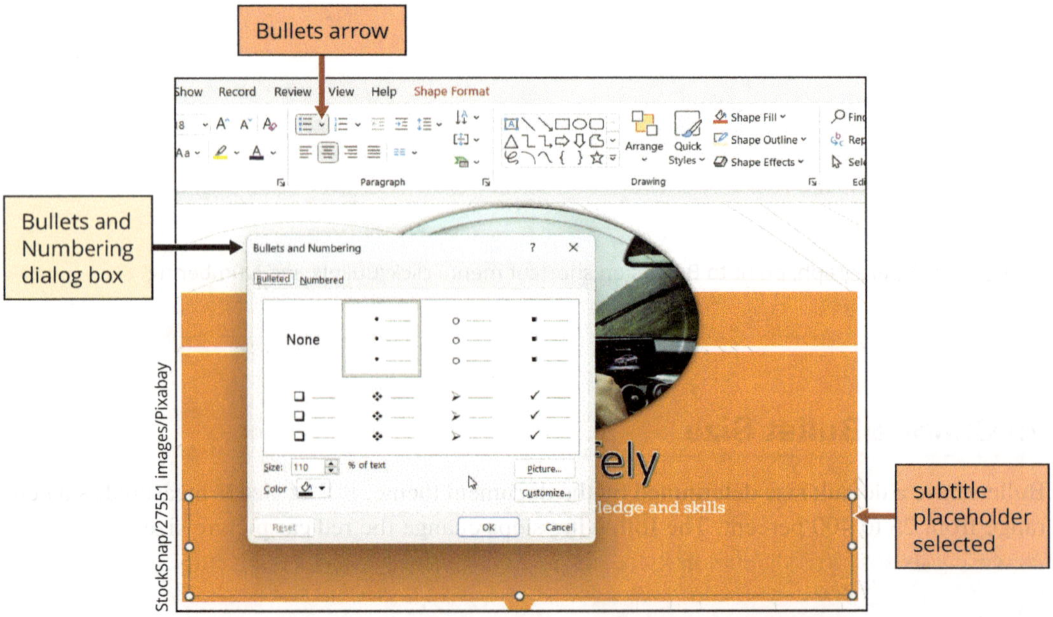

Figure 5–61

2

- Click the Customize button (Bullets and Numbering dialog box) to display the Symbol dialog box (Figure 5–62).

Q&A Why is a symbol selected?
That symbol is the default bullet for the first-level paragraphs in the Atlas document theme.

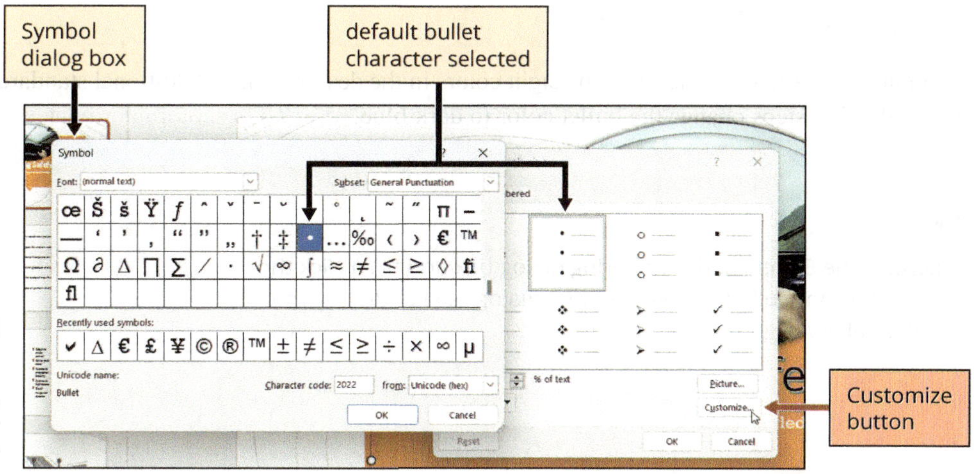

Figure 5–62

3

- Locate the Lozenge symbol (◊); scroll if necessary to find it.
- Click the Lozenge symbol to select it. The Unicode name and character code (25CA) appear at the bottom of the dialog box (Figure 5–63).

Q&A Why does my dialog box have more rows of symbols and different fonts from which to choose?
The rows and fonts displayed depend upon how PowerPoint was installed on your system and the screen you are viewing.

What is the character code that is displayed in the Symbol dialog box?
Each character in each font has a unique code. If you know the character code, you can type the number in the Character code box to display that symbol. The character code for the Lozenge symbol is 25CA.

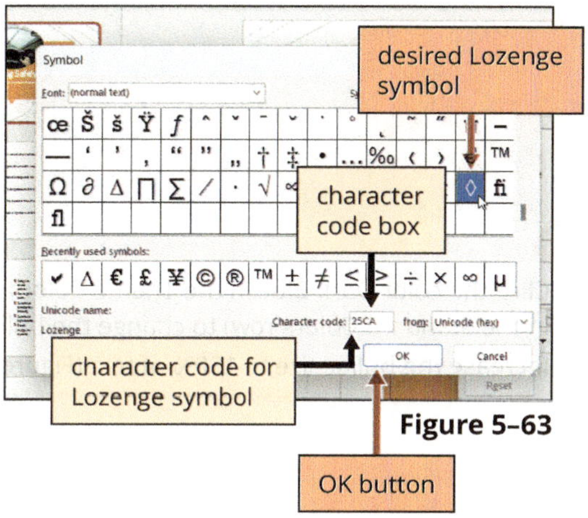

Figure 5–63

4

- Click OK (Symbol dialog box) to display the Lozenge bullet in the Bullets and Numbering dialog box (Figure 5–64).

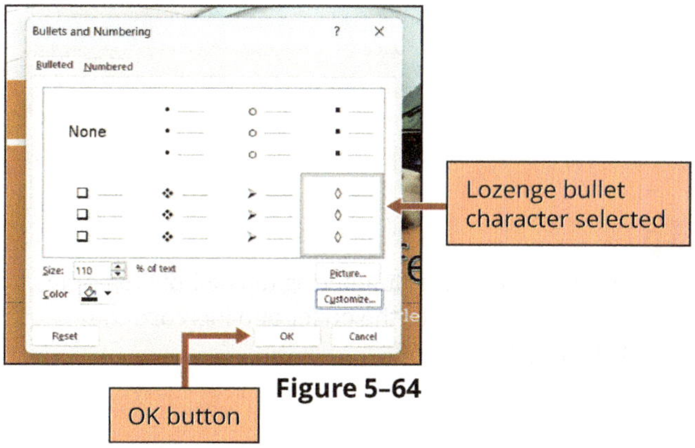

Figure 5–64

5

- Click OK (Bullets and Numbering dialog box) to insert the Lozenge symbol as the paragraph bullet (Figure 5–65).

Figure 5–65

To Format Bullet Color

A default **bullet color** is based on the eight colors in the design theme. Additional standard and custom colors also are available. The following steps change the bullet color to dark blue. **Why?** This color coordinates with other dark blue colors used in the presentation.

1

- Display the Bullets and Numbering dialog box and then click the Color button (Bullets and Numbering dialog box) to display the Color gallery (Figure 5-66).

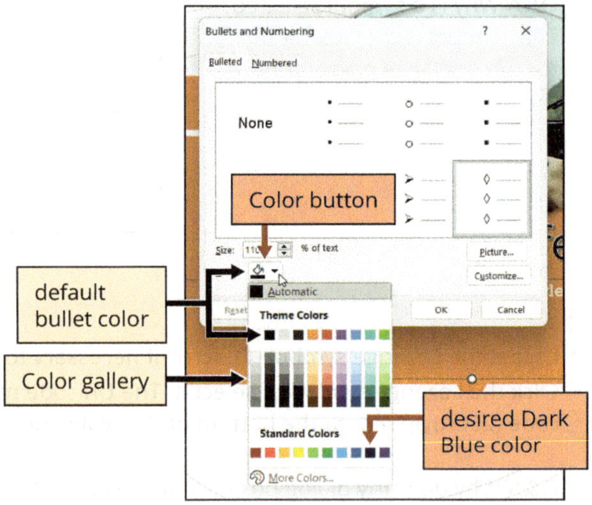

Figure 5-66

2

- Click the color Dark Blue in the Theme Colors area (ninth color in the Standard Colors row) to change the bullet color.
- Increase the bullet size to 150% of text (Figure 5-67).

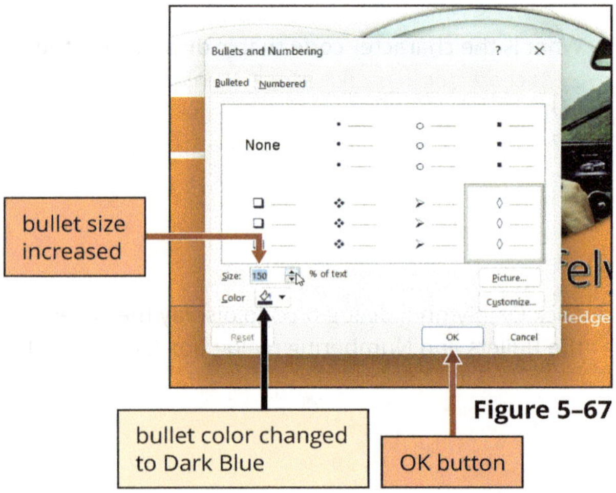

Figure 5-67

3

- Click OK (Bullets and Numbering dialog box) to apply the color Dark Blue to the bullet and increase the bullet size (Figure 5-68).

Figure 5-68

Other Ways

1. Right-click paragraph, point to Bullets on shortcut menu, click Bullets and Numbering, select color

To Change a Bullet Character to a Number

PowerPoint allows you to change the default bullets to numbers. The following steps change the first-level paragraph bullet characters on Slide 2 to numbers. **Why?** Numbers help to show steps in a sequence and also help guide a speaker during the presentation when referring to specific information in the paragraphs.

1

- Display Slide 2 and then select all six paragraphs in the content placeholder.
- With the Home tab displayed, click the Numbering arrow (Home tab | Paragraph group) to display the Numbering gallery.
- Point to the 1) 2) 3) numbering option in the Numbering gallery to display a live preview of these numbers (Figure 5–69).
- **Experiment:** Point to each of the numbers in the Numbering gallery to watch the numbers change on Slide 2.

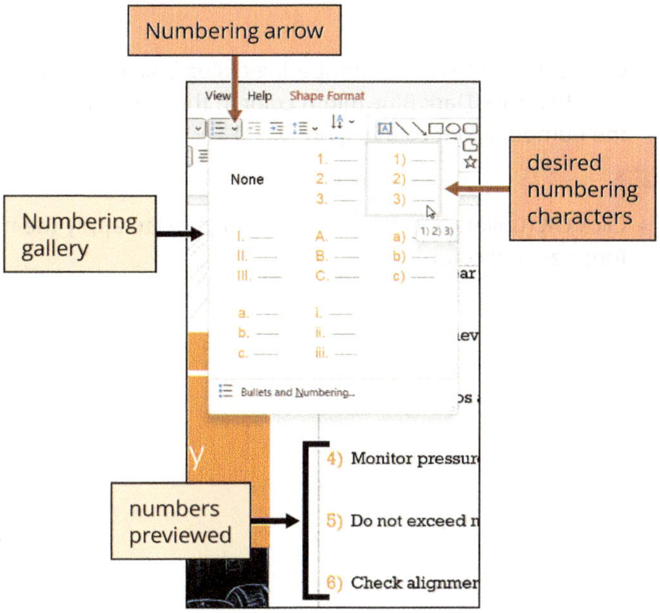

Figure 5–69

2

- Click the 1) 2) 3) numbering option to insert these numbers as the first-level paragraph characters (Figure 5–70).

Q&A How do I change the first number in the list?
Click 'Bullets and Numbering' at the bottom of the Numbering gallery and then click the up or down arrow in the Start at box to change the number.

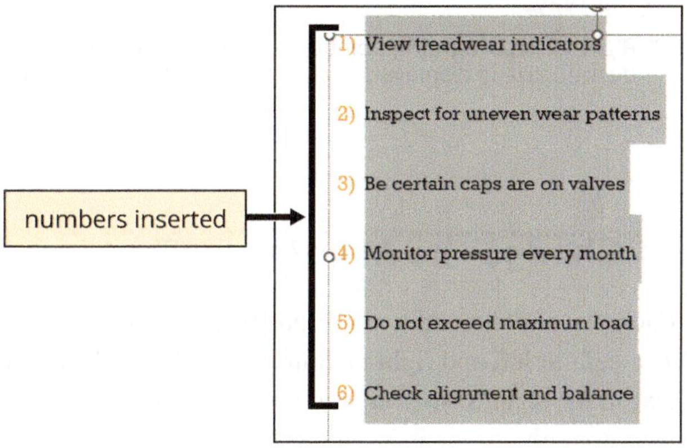

Figure 5–70

Other Ways

1. Right-click paragraph, point to Numbering on shortcut menu, select numbering characters

To Change the List Numbering Style

As with bullets, numbering characters are measured as a percentage of the text size and can range from 25 to 400 percent. The color of these numbers also can change. The following steps change the numbering color to dark blue and the size to 125 percent. **Why?** To add emphasis, you choose to increase the size of the new numbers inserted in Slide 2, and the color coordinates with other dark blue elements in the presentation.

1

- With the Slide 2 content placeholder paragraphs still selected, click the Numbering arrow (Home tab | Paragraph group) to display the Numbering gallery and then click 'Bullets and Numbering' to display the Bullets and Numbering dialog box again.
- Click the Size up arrow until 125 is displayed in the '% of text' Size text box.

2

- Click Color (Bullets and Numbering dialog box) to display the Color gallery and then click Dark Blue (ninth color in the Standard Colors row) to change the numbers' font color (Figure 5–71).

3

- Click OK (Bullets and Numbering dialog box) to apply the new numbers' font size and color.

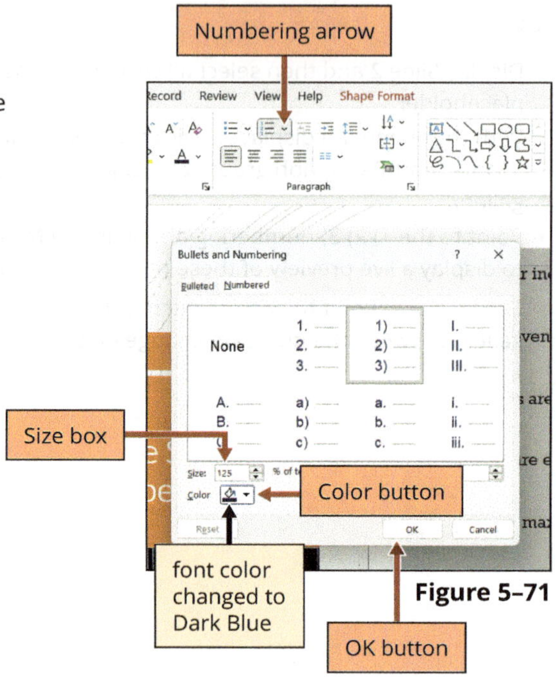

Figure 5–71

Other Ways

1. Right-click paragraph, point to Numbering on shortcut menu, click 'Bullets and Numbering', click up or down Size arrow until desired size is displayed, click Color, select color, click OK

To Change the Margins for Text in a Shape

Each placeholder and text box has preset internal margins, which are the spaces between the border and the contents of the box. The default left and right margins are 0.1", and the default top and bottom margins are 0.05". In this project, you will format the text in the shapes, so you need to increase the left and right margins and then decrease the top and bottom margins. **Why?** You want to allow room and sufficient white space for these design elements. The following steps change all three shape margins.

1

- Display Slide 5 and then right-click the First aid kit shape to display the shortcut menu (Figure 5–72).

2

- Click Format Shape to display the Format Shape pane and then click the 'Size & Properties' Shape Options button.

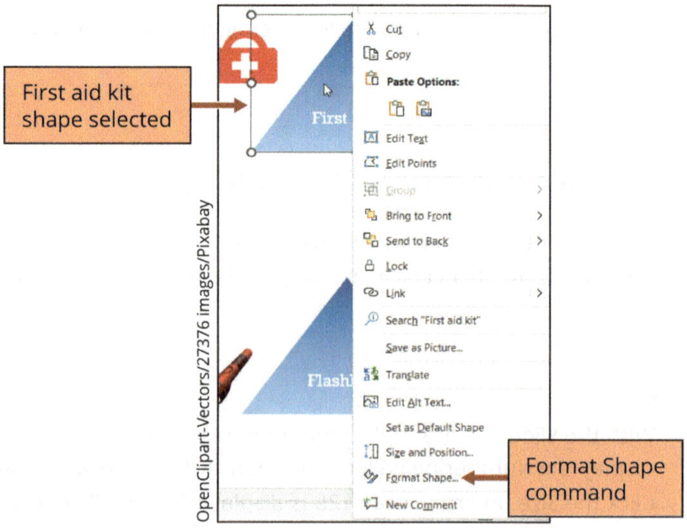

Figure 5–72

- If necessary, click Text Box to display the Text Box section (Figure 5–73).

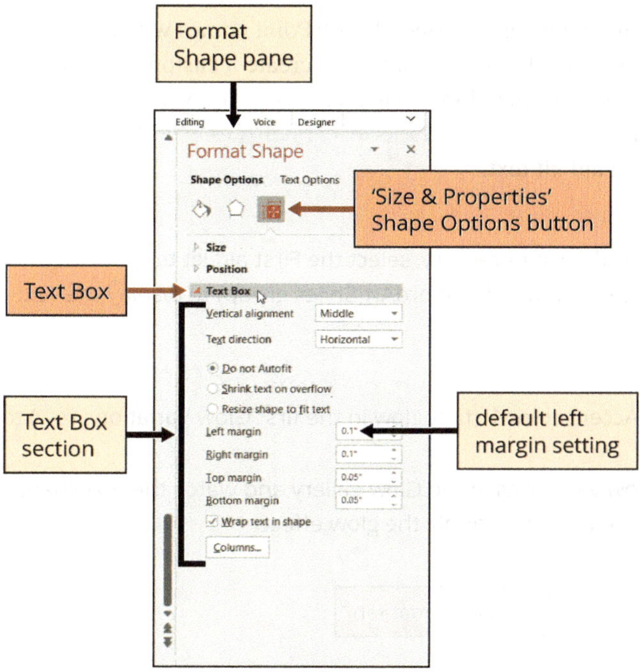

Figure 5–73

3

- If necessary, scroll down to display the entire Text box section and then increase the Left margin setting to 0.3".
- Increase the Right margin setting to 0.3".
- Decrease the Top margin setting to 0".
- Decrease the Bottom margin setting to 0" (Figure 5–74).

Q&A Must I change all the margins?

No. You can change one, two, three, or all four internal margins depending upon the placeholder shape and the amount of text entered.

4

- Click the Close button (Format Shape pane).

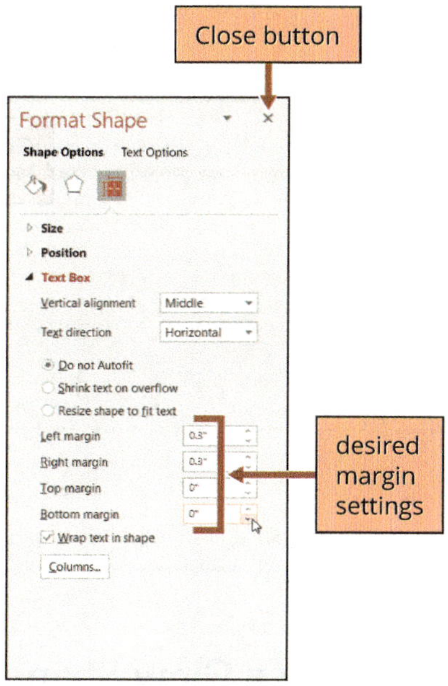

Figure 5–74

To Format Shape Text

Sufficient space exists in the shape to increase the font size. In addition, changing the font color adds a custom design element to the final slide in the presentation. The following steps format the First aid kit shape text.

1. Change the font size to 20 point.
2. Change the font color to Dark Blue (ninth color in the Standard Colors row).

To Apply a Glow Text Effect

You can add dimension to text by applying a glow effect. PowerPoint comes with a number of common preset glow variations. Once you have added this effect, you can choose a variation to create a custom style, color, and size. You also can change the transparency, which specifies how much of the glow is visible. **Why?** You want to emphasize items that drivers should have in their vehicles to deal with problems on the road, and this effect helps to call attention to the text in the shape. The following steps apply a glow effect to the First aid kit text.

1

- Display the Shape Format tab and then, if necessary, select the First aid kit text.
- Click the Text Effects button (Shape Format tab | WordArt Styles group) to display the Text Effects menu and then point to Glow to display the Glow gallery.

2

- Point to 'Glow: 5 point; Orange, Accent color 1' (first glow in the first Glow Variations row) to display a live preview of the glow effect (Figure 5–75).
- **Experiment:** Point to various glow variations in the Glow gallery and watch the text change in the shape.
- Click 'Glow: 5 point; Orange, Accent color 1' to apply the glow effect.

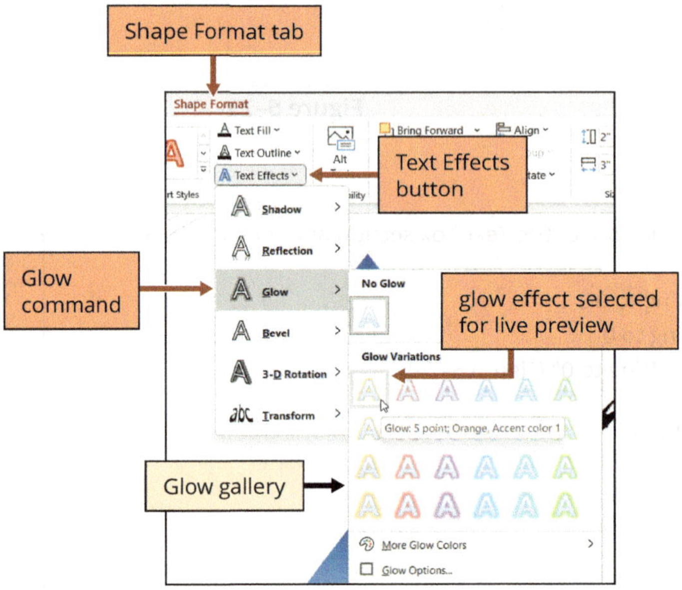

Figure 5–75

To Apply a Glow Shape Effect

You can apply glow effects to shapes and other objects. As with the glow text effect, the glow shape effect has several preset variations. The color, size, and transparency also can be changed. **Why?** You want to coordinate the text and icon design elements. The following steps apply a glow effect to the First aid kit icon.

1

- Select the First aid kit icon and then display the Picture Format tab.
- Click the Picture Effects button (Picture Format tab | Picture Styles group) to display the Picture Effects menu and then point to Glow to display the Glow gallery.

2

- Point to 'Glow: 5 point; Orange, Accent color 1' (first glow in the first Glow Variations row) to display a live preview of the glow effect (Figure 5–76).
- **Experiment:** Point to various glow variations in the Glow gallery and watch the image change in the shape.
- Click 'Glow: 5 point; Orange, Accent color 1' to apply the glow effect.

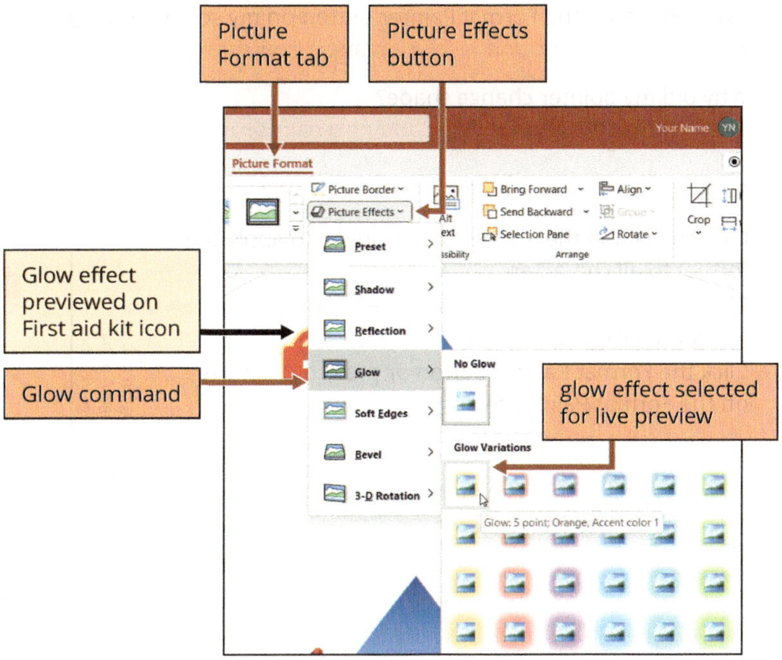

Figure 5–76

Format Painter

To save time and avoid formatting errors, you can use the **Format Painter** to copy custom formatting to other places in your presentation quickly and easily. You can use this feature in three ways:

- To copy only character attributes, such as font and font effects, select text that has these qualities.
- To copy both character attributes and paragraph attributes, such as alignment and indentation, select the entire paragraph.
- To apply the same formatting to multiple words, phrases, or paragraphs, double-click the Format Painter button and then select each item you want to format. You then can press ESC or click the Format Painter button to turn off this feature.

To Use the Format Painter with Text

The following steps use the Format Painter to copy formatting features. **Why?** To save time and duplicated effort, you quickly can use the Format Painter to copy formatting attributes from the First aid kit shape text and apply them to the two other shapes.

1

- Display the Home tab, select the First aid kit text, and then double-click the Format Painter button (Home tab | Clipboard group).
- Move the pointer off the ribbon (Figure 5–77).

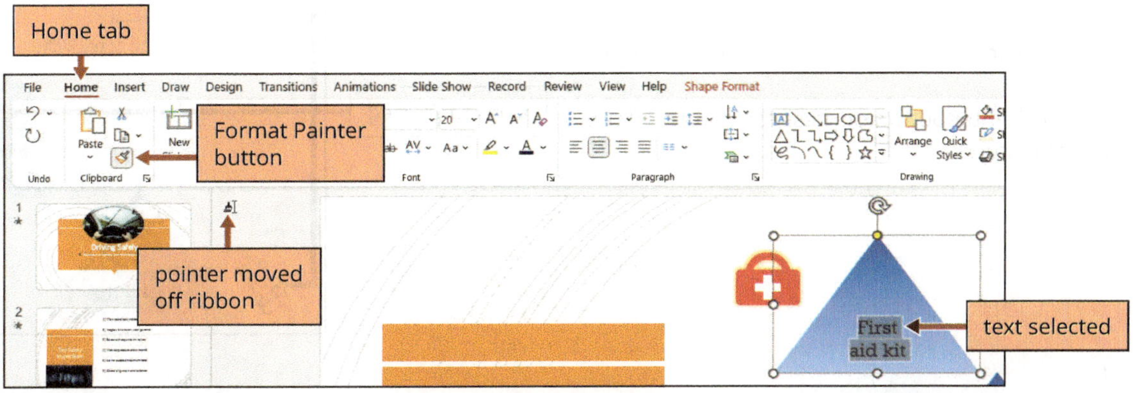

OpenClipart-Vectors/27376 images/Pixabay/StockSnap/27551 images/Pixabay; FlenderFunways/4 images/Pixabay

Figure 5–77

Q&A Why does the Format Painter button on my screen display only a paintbrush and not the words, Format Painter?
Monitor dimensions and resolution affect how buttons display on the ribbon.

Why did my pointer change shape?
The pointer changed shape by adding a paintbrush to indicate that the Format Painter function is active.

2

- Click the text in the Jumper cables shape to apply the format to all characters.
- Click the text in the Flashlight shape to apply the format to all characters (Figure 5–78).
- Click the Format Painter button or press ESC to turn off the Format Painter feature.

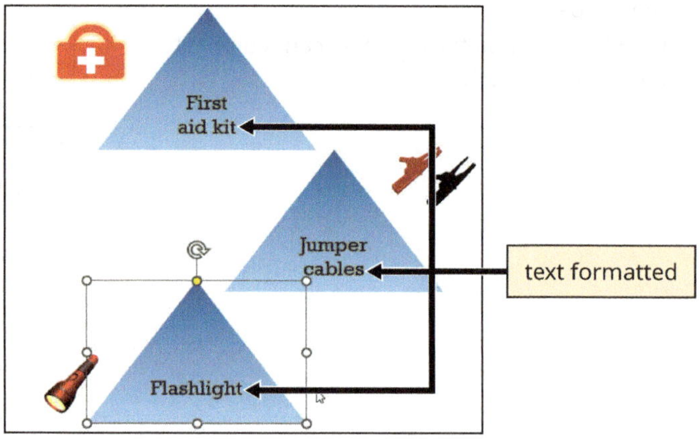

Figure 5–78

Other Ways

1. Select text, double-click Format Painter button on Mini toolbar

To Use the Format Painter with Objects

The following steps use the Format Painter to copy an object's formatting features. **Why?** To save time and duplicated effort, you quickly can use the Format Painter to copy formatting attributes from the First aid kit icon and apply them to Jumper cables and Flashlight icons.

1

- Select the First aid kit icon and then double-click the Format Painter button (Home tab | Clipboard group).
- Move the pointer off the ribbon (Figure 5–79).

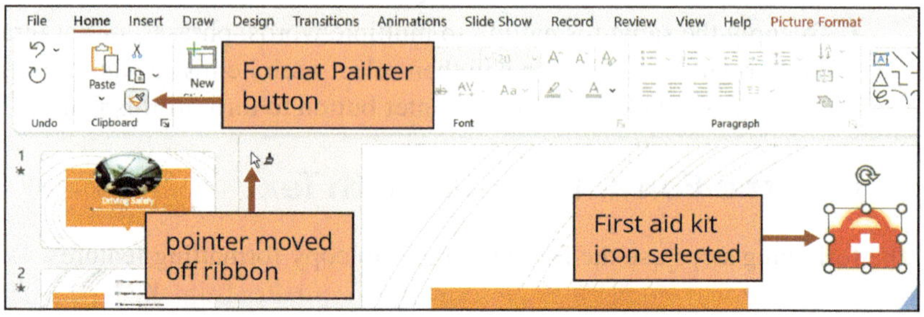

Figure 5–79

2

- Click the Jumper cables icon to apply the format to the graphic.
- Click the Flashlight icon to apply the format to the graphic (Figure 5–80).
- Click the Format Painter button or press ESC to turn off the Format Painter feature.

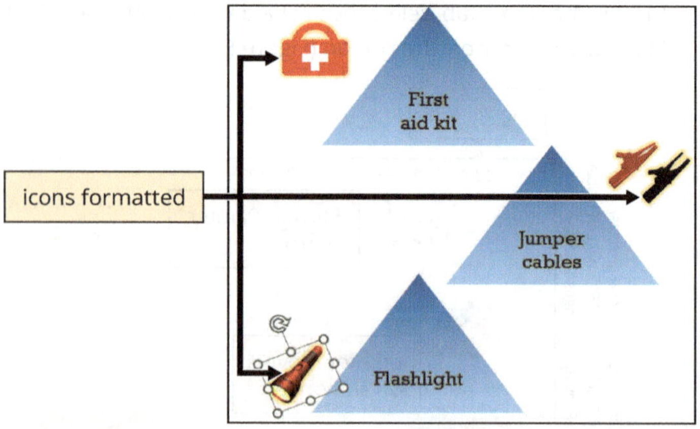

Figure 5–80

Break Point: If you wish to take a break, this is a good place to do so. Be sure the Driving Final file is saved and then you can exit PowerPoint. To resume later, start PowerPoint, open the file called SC_PPT_5_Driving_Final, and continue following the steps from this location forward.

Animating Slide Content

If you need to move objects on a slide once they are displayed, you can define a **motion path**. This predefined movement determines where an object will be displayed and then travel. Motion paths are grouped into the Basic, Lines & Curves, and Special categories. You can draw a custom path if none of the predefined paths meets your needs.

Slide 2 contains several animation effects. When this slide is displayed, the tires automatically will float up under the title text after a brief delay. Next, the first content paragraph will display and then fade as the second paragraph displays. This animation sequence will continue until the sixth paragraph is displayed. Finally, the tires picture will pulse slightly. To create this animation on the slide, you will use entrance and emphasis effects.

BTW

Adding a Sound to an Animation

Once you have added an animation effect to text or an object, you then can add a sound. To do so, display the Animation Pane and then click the down arrow to the right of the effect. Click Effect Options in the menu, click the Sound arrow in the Enhancements area to display the Sound list, and then choose a sound. If none of the default sounds seems appropriate to accompany an animation, you can add your own. Click the Sound arrow to display the sound list, scroll down, click Other Sound, and then locate the sound you want to use from your storage medium.

To Animate a Picture Using an Entrance Effect

In Module 3 you animated a WordArt object using an entrance effect, changed its direction, and then changed the start option so that it displayed automatically. Similarly, you can animate a picture and change the animation effects. The tires picture you modified in Slide 2 will enter the slide from the lower edge and then continue moving upward until it is under the title text. The following steps apply an entrance effect to the tires picture.

1. Display Slide 2 and then click the tires picture to select it.
2. Display the Animations tab and then click the Float In animation in the Animation gallery (Animation group) to apply and preview this entrance animation for the tires picture.
3. Change the Start animation timing option to With Previous (Figure 5–81).

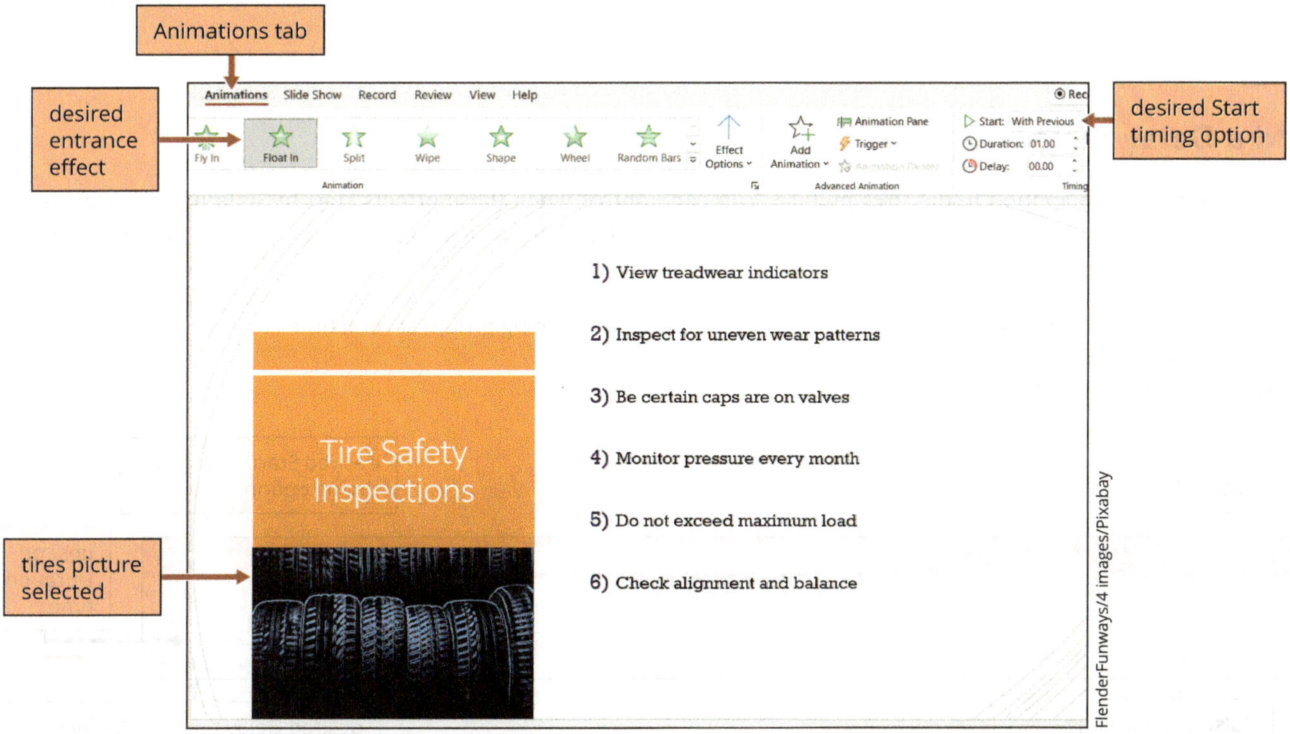

Figure 5–81

To Add an Emphasis Effect Animation

Once the tires picture has entered the slide, you want it to fade out and in, or pulse, slightly. PowerPoint provides several effects that you can apply to a picture once it appears on a slide. These movements are categorized as emphasis effects, and they are colored yellow in the Animation gallery. You already have applied an entrance effect to the tires picture, so you want to add another animation to this picture. **Why?** You want to call attention to this object as a subtle reminder of the need to inspect tires periodically. The following steps apply an emphasis effect to the tires picture after the entrance effect.

1

- Select the tires picture again and then click the Add Animation button (Animations tab | Advanced Animation group) to expand the Animation gallery (Figure 5–82).

2

- Click Pulse in the Emphasis section (first animation in the first row) to apply this effect to the tires picture.
- Change the Start animation timing option to With Previous.
- Change the Duration time to 02.00 seconds.

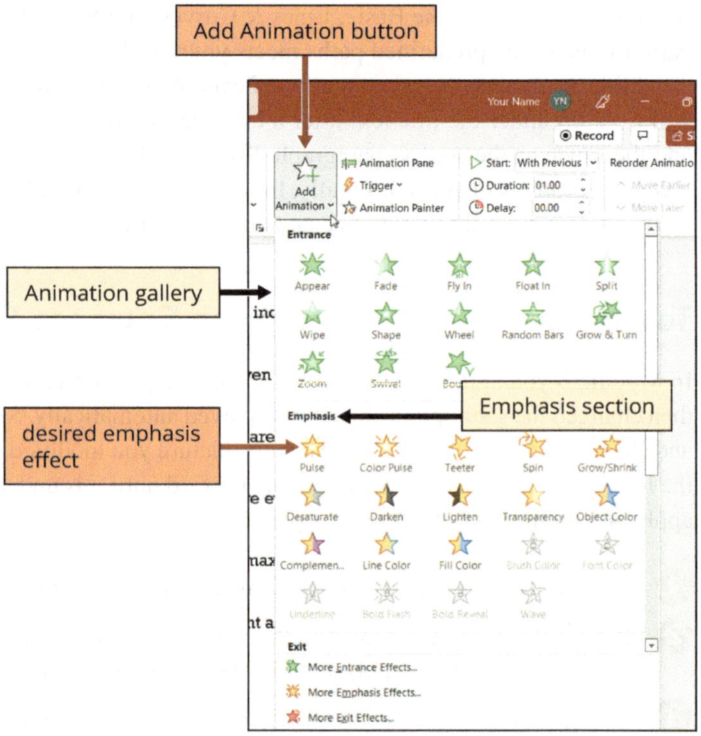

Figure 5–82

To Add a Delay to an Animation

All animations have been applied to the tires picture. You can control when these effects start by delaying the start time. **Why?** You want several seconds to pass before the animation runs. The following step adds a delay to the tires animations.

1

- Select the tires picture again, click the Delay up arrow (Animations tab | Timing group) several times to increase the delay time from 00.00 seconds to 03.00 seconds (Figure 5–83).
- Click the Preview button to view the animations.

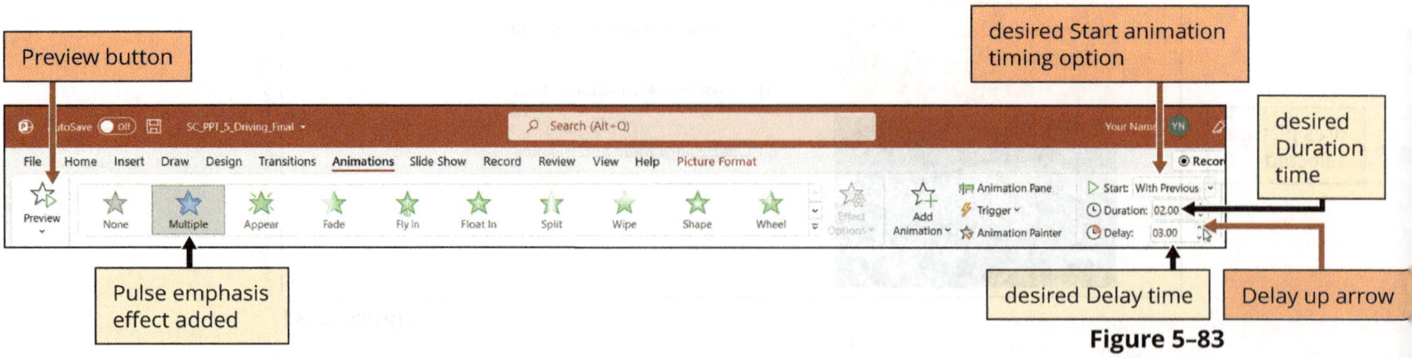

Figure 5–83

Q&A Can I type the time in the Delay box instead of click the arrow to adjust the time?
Yes. Typing the numbers allows you to set a precise timing.

Can I adjust the delay time I just set?
Yes. Click the Delay up or down arrows and run the slide show to display Slide 2 until you find the time that best fits your presentation.

To Animate Text

You can animate the six numbered paragraphs in the Slide 2 content placeholder. The following steps animate the numbered list paragraphs.

1. Click any numbered list paragraph in the Slide 2 content placeholder to select the placeholder and then click a placeholder border so that it displays as a solid line.
2. Click the Fade entrance effect in the Animation gallery to add and preview this animation.
3. Change the Start animation timing option to After Previous.
4. Change the Duration time to 02.00 seconds (Figure 5–84).
5. Click the Preview button to view the animations.

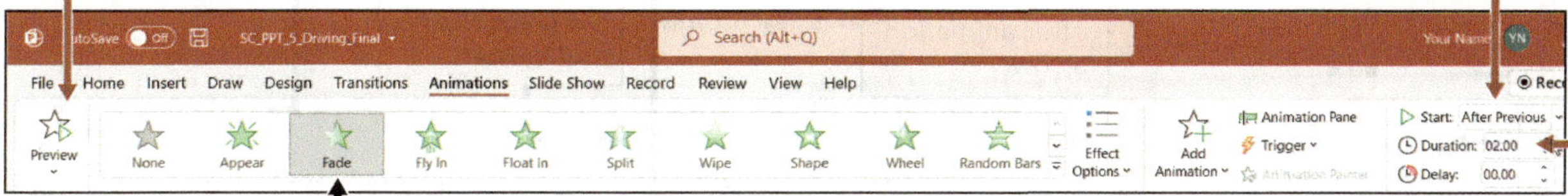

Figure 5–84

Consider This

Select colors for dimming text.

After paragraphs of text are displayed, you can change the color, or dim the text, to direct the audience's attention to another area of the slide. Choose the dimming colors carefully. Be certain the color you choose can be seen against the background. In addition, use a maximum of three colors unless you have a compelling need to present more variety.

To Dim Text after Animation

As each item in the list is displayed, you may desire to have the previous item removed from the screen or to have the font color change or **dim**. PowerPoint provides several options for you to alter this text by specifying an After Animation effect. The following steps dim each paragraph in the content placeholder by changing the font color to orange. **Why?** That color is found in many of the design elements throughout the presentation.

1

- With Slide 2 displayed, click the Animation Pane button (Animation tab | Advanced Animation group) to display the Animation Pane. Click the double arrow in the gray bar below the content placeholder to expand the contents showing the six placeholder paragraphs.

BTW
Turning Off Animations
You cannot remove all animations from an entire presentation in one step, but you can disable all animations in your presentation. To do this, click the 'Set Up Slide Show' button (Slide Show tab | Set Up group) to display the 'Set Up Show' dialog box and then click 'Show without animation' in the Show options area.

- Right-click the first paragraph in the list (View treadw...) to display the Animation Order menu (Figure 5–85).

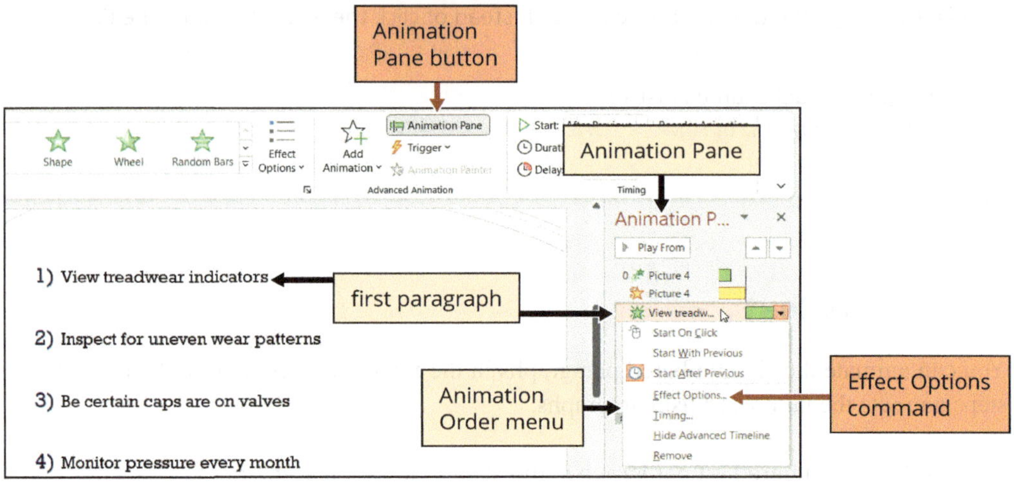

Figure 5–85

2

- Click Effect Options in the Animation Order menu to display the Fade dialog box.
- Click the After animation arrow to display the After animation menu (Figure 5–86).

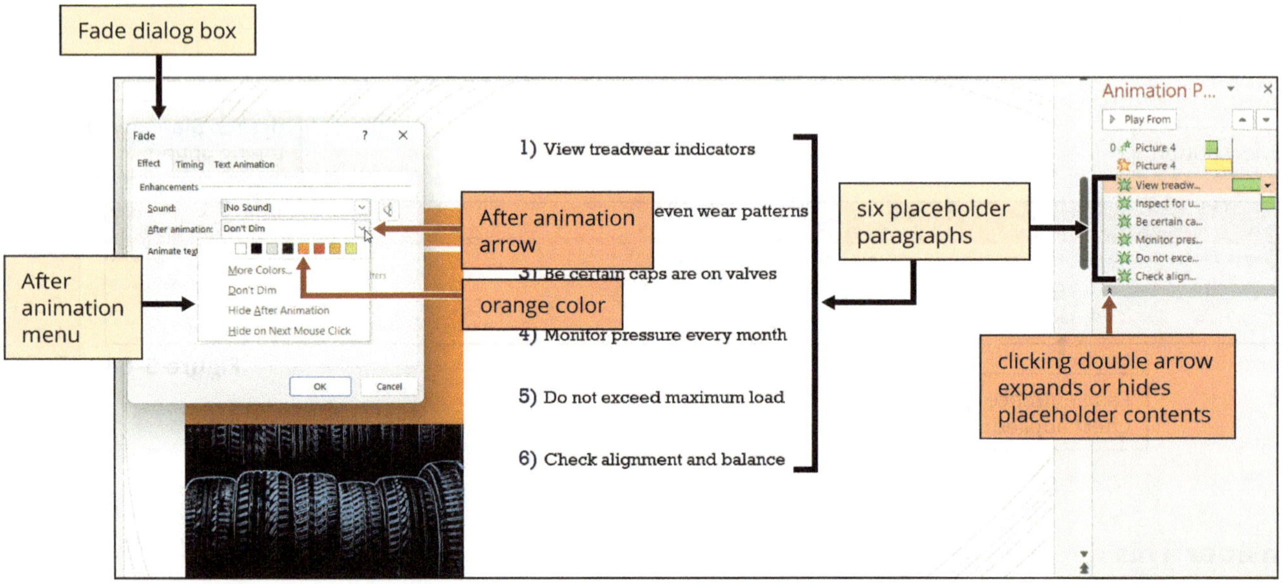

FlenderFunways/4 images/Pixabay

Figure 5–86

3

- Click the orange color (fifth color in the row of colors) to select this color for the dim effect (Figure 5–87).

4

- Click OK (Fade dialog box) to apply the dim effect to the first item in the content placeholder on Slide 2 and preview the animations.

5

- Repeat Steps 1 to 4 for each of the remaining five paragraphs in the list to apply and preview the dim After animation effect.

Q&A Could I select all six paragraphs and then apply the dim effect to them simultaneously?

Yes. This method is efficient and ensures consistency if you are applying the same effect to all the paragraphs.

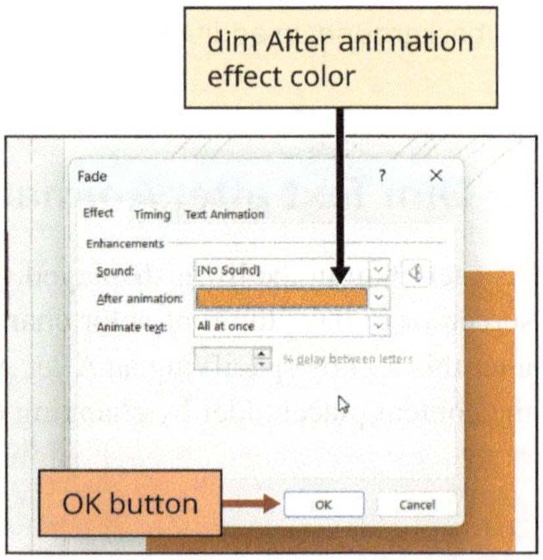

Figure 5–87

To Reorder Animations on a Slide

By default, the tires picture's entrance and emphasis effects occur sequentially. You can modify this order by moving each animation earlier or later in the animation list. The following steps change the sequence for the Slide 2 animations so the tires picture is displayed when Slide 2 is shown, but the Pulse animation effect will occur after the six bulleted paragraphs are displayed. **Why?** You will direct the audience's attention to the picture after they have learned about factors to consider when inspecting tires.

1

- Click the Picture 4 Pulse Emphasis animation (with the yellow star) in the Animation Pane to select it (Figure 5–88).

2

- Click the Move Later button (Animations tab | Timing group) six times to move the Pulse animation after all the content paragraphs.

Q&A Can I click the Move Later button in the Animation Pane instead of the button on the Animations tab to reorder the animation?
Yes. Either button performs the same action.

Would I click the Move Earlier button on the Animations tab if I wanted the animation to occur earlier in the sequence?
Yes. You also could click the Move Earlier button in the Animation Pane.

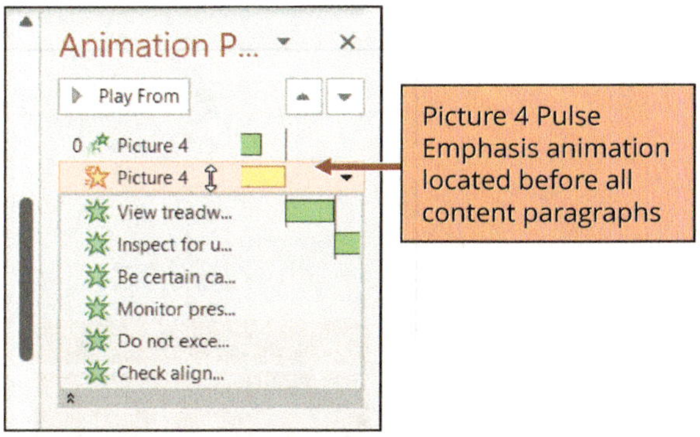

Figure 5–88

- Change the Start animation timing option to After Previous.
- Change the Delay time to 02.00 seconds (Figure 5–89).

3

- Preview the animations.

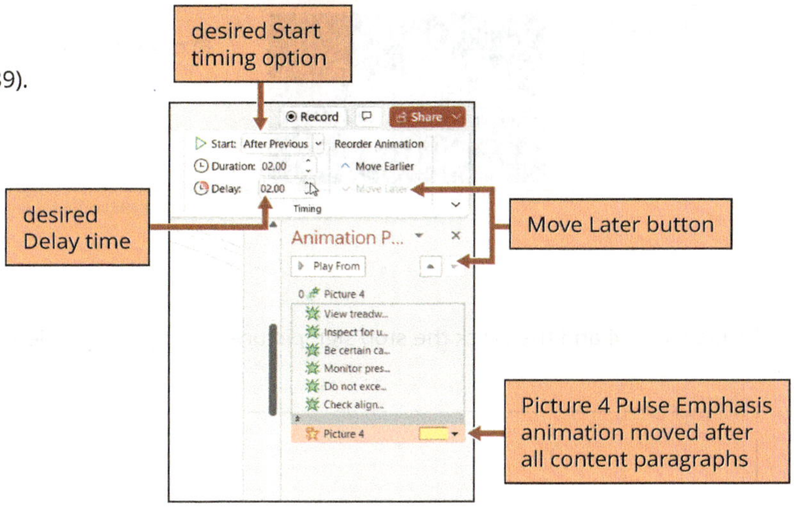

Figure 5–89

To Remove an Animation

You can remove an animation effect that has been applied to text or an object. To remove an animation, you would perform the following steps.

1. Display the Animations tab and then click the Animation Pane button.
2. Click the animated object that has the effect you want to remove.
3. In the Animation Pane, click the effect to remove, click the down arrow, and then click Remove.

BTW
Removing Multiple Animation Effects
To remove more than one animation effect from text or an object, in the Animation Pane, press CTRL, click each animation effect that you want to remove, and then press DELETE. To remove all animation effects from text or an object, click the object that you want to stop animating and then click None in the gallery of animation effects (Animations tab | Animation group).

To Use the Animation Painter

At times, you may desire to apply the same animation effects to several objects in a presentation. On Slide 4, for example, you want to animate the stop sign picture with the identical entrance and emphasis effects you applied to the Slide 2 tires picture. As with the Format Painter that is used to duplicate formatting attributes, the **Animation Painter** copies animations from one object to another. Using the Animation Painter can save time. **Why?** It duplicates numerous animation effects and characteristics uniformly to other objects with one click. The following steps use the Animation Painter to copy the animations from Slide 2 to Slide 4.

1

- Click the tires picture to select it.
- Click the Animation Painter button (Animations tab | Advanced Animation group).
- Move the pointer off the ribbon (Figure 5–90).

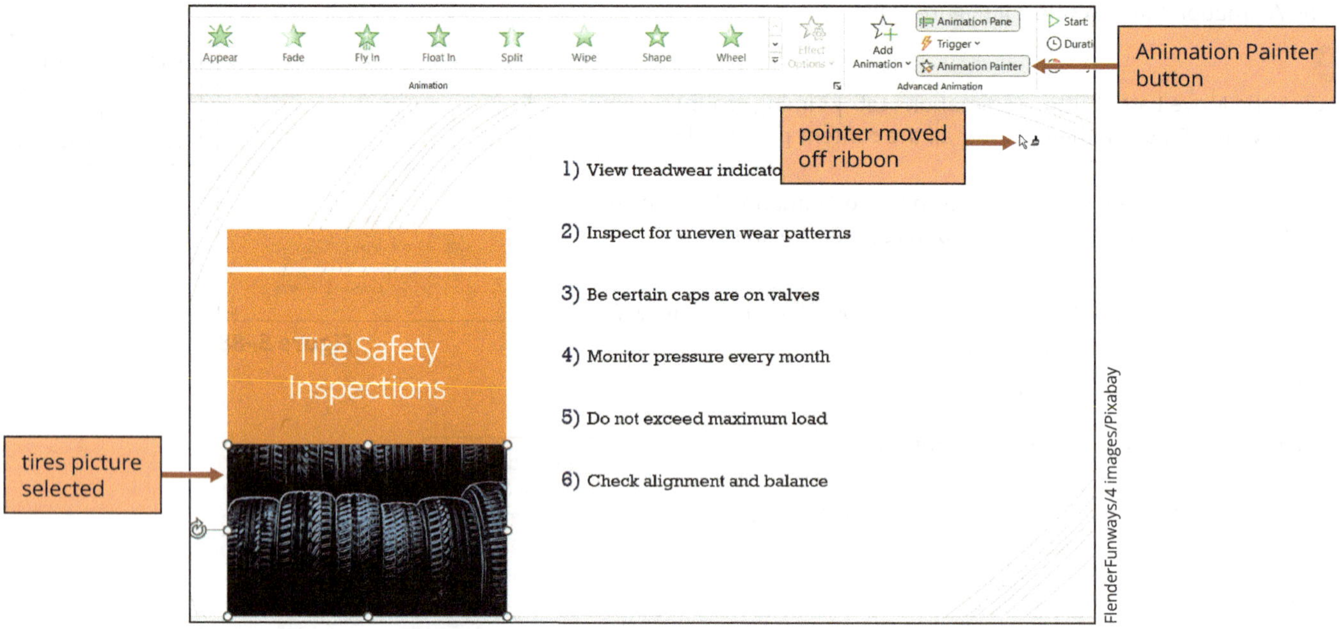

FlenderFunways/4 images/Pixabay

Figure 5–90

2

- Display Slide 4 and then click the stop sign picture to copy and preview the animations from Slide 2 (Figure 5–91).

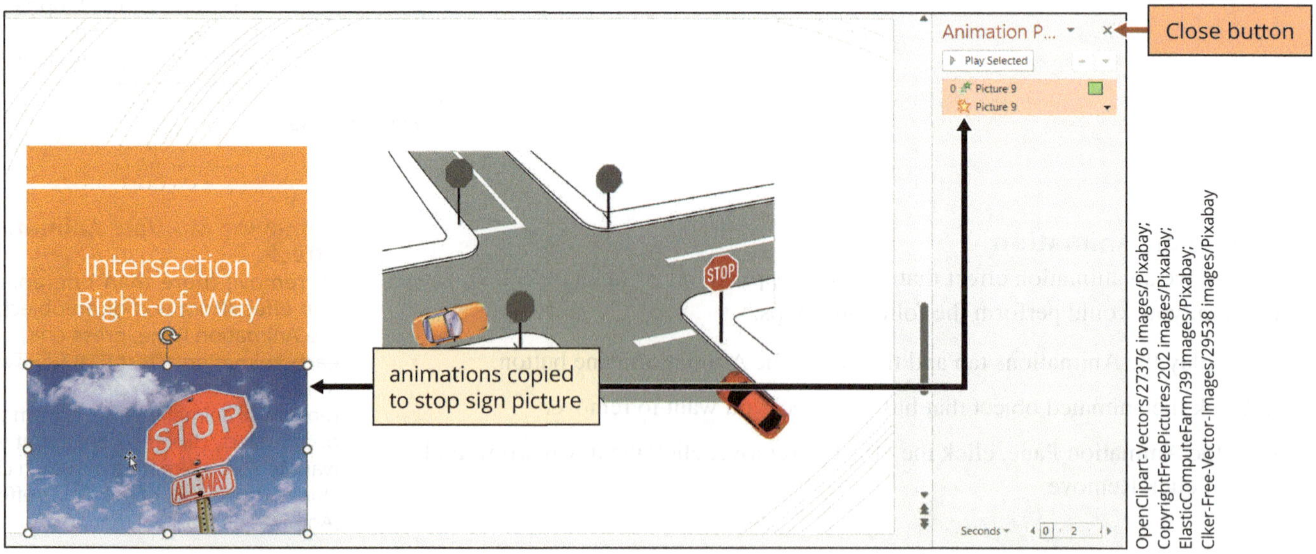

OpenClipart-Vectors/27376 images/Pixabay; CopyrightFreePictures/202 images/Pixabay; ElasticComputeFarm/39 images/Pixabay; Clker-Free-Vector-Images/29538 images/Pixabay

Figure 5–91

3

- If the Comments pane is displayed, close it. Close the Animation Pane.

Q&A My Animation Pane is not displayed. What should I do?
Click the Animation Pane icon to open it, and then you will be able to close it.

Other Ways

1. Press ALT+SHIFT+C

To Animate an Object Using a Preset Motion Path

Slide 3 has a picture you want to animate using a motion path. You will add the Loops motion path, which is one of the six options displayed in the Motion Paths section of the Animation gallery. **Why?** Most newer vehicles have driver-assistance safety features, and icons for many of them are displayed on the dashboard. You want to call attention to viewing them on a dashboard. In addition, many additional motion paths are available when you click More Motion Paths in the lower area of the Animation gallery. The following steps animate the picture using the Loops motion path.

1

- Display Slide 3 and select the dashboard picture.
- With the Animations tab selected, click the Add Animation button (Animations tab | Advanced Animation group) to display the Animation gallery.
- Scroll down until the Motion Paths section is visible (Figure 5–92).

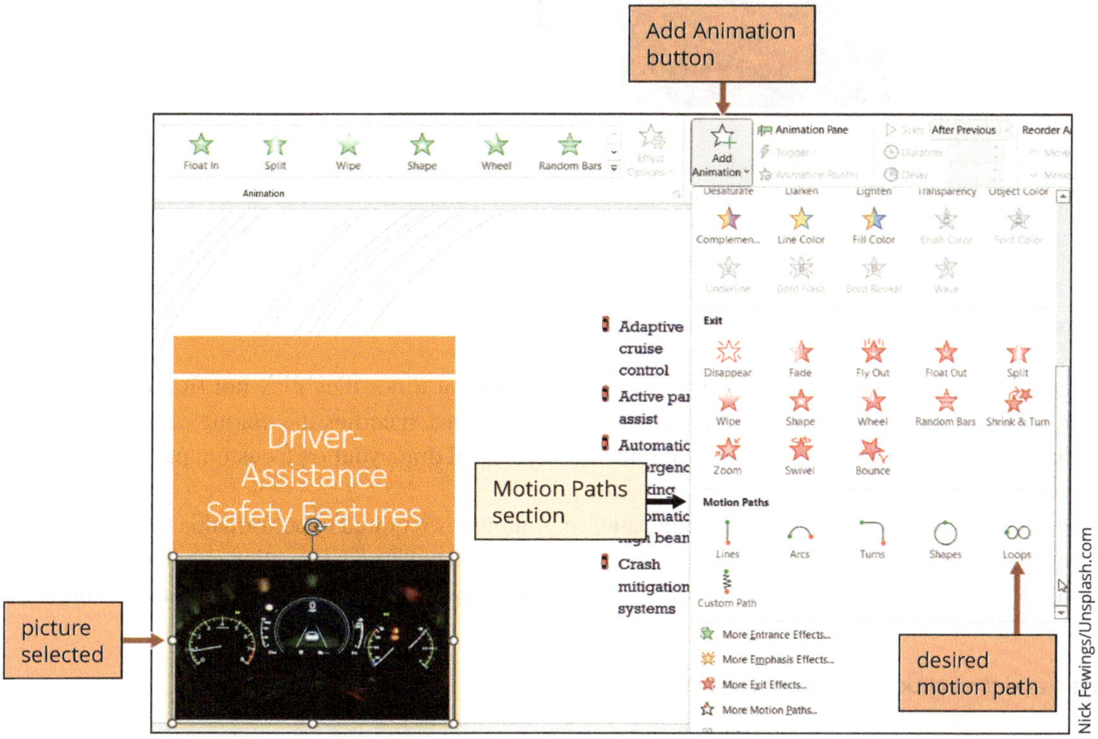

Figure 5–92

2

- Click the Loops motion path to apply the animation to the picture and preview the animation.
- Change the Duration to 05.00 seconds (Figure 5–93) and then preview the animation.

Q&A Are more motion paths available in addition to those shown in the Animation gallery?
Yes. To see additional motion paths, click More Motion Paths in the lower portion of the Animation gallery. The motion paths are arranged in the Basic, Lines & Curves, and Special categories.

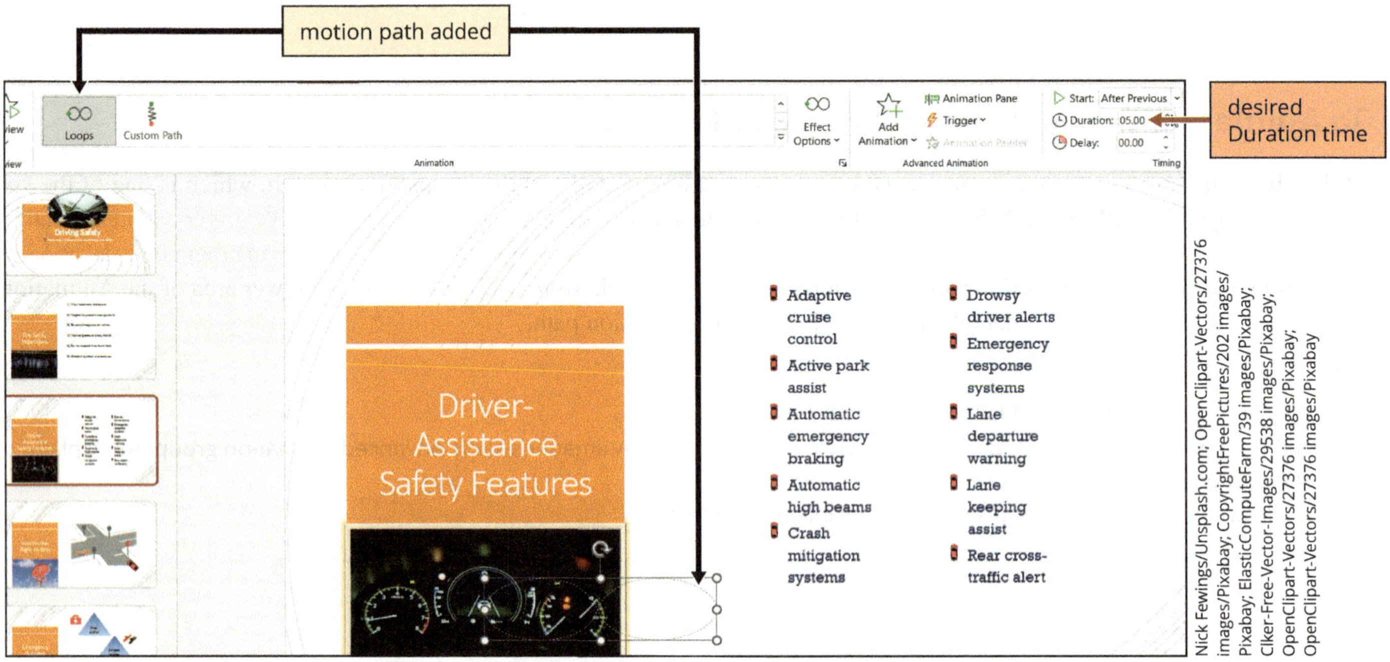

Nick Fewings/Unsplash.com; OpenClipart-Vectors/27376 images/Pixabay; CopyrightFreePictures/202 images/Pixabay; ElasticComputeFarm/39 images/Pixabay; Clker-Free-Vector-Images/29538 images/Pixabay; OpenClipart-Vectors/27376 images/Pixabay; OpenClipart-Vectors/27376 images/Pixabay

Figure 5–93

To Animate an Object Using a Custom Motion Path

Although PowerPoint supplies a wide variety of preset motion paths, at times they may not fit the precise animations your presentation requires. In that situation, you can draw a **custom path** that specifies the unique movement your slide element should make. None of the predefined paths meets your needs, so you will draw your own custom path. **Why?** You want to show a vehicle entering and traveling through an intersection.

Drawing a custom path requires some practice and patience. A mouse is required to perform this task, and you click the mouse to begin drawing the line. If you want the line to change direction, such as to curve, you click again. When you have completed drawing the path, you double-click to end the line. The following steps draw a custom motion path to animate the red car on Slide 4.

1

- Display Slide 4 and then click the red car to select it.

- With the Animations tab selected, click the Add Animation button and then scroll down until the entire Motion Paths section is visible (Figure 5–94).

Q&A Can I draw a custom motion path when using a touch screen?
No. You must use a mouse to perform this task.

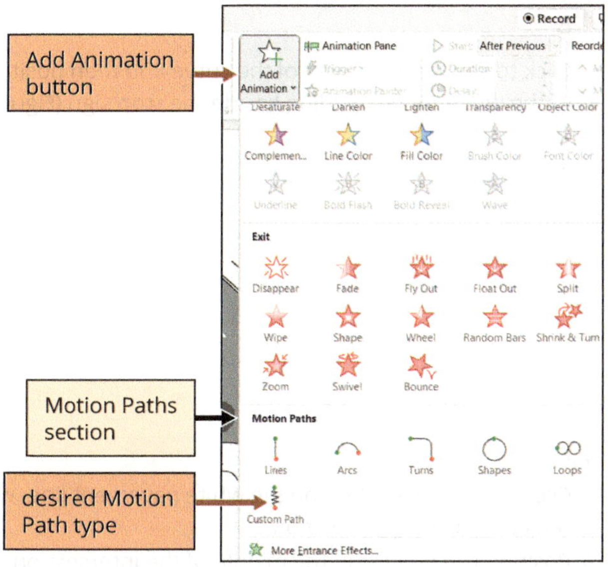

Figure 5–94

2

- Click Custom Path in the Motion Paths section to add this animation.
- Click the Effect Options button (Animations tab | Animation group) to display the Type gallery (Figure 5–95).

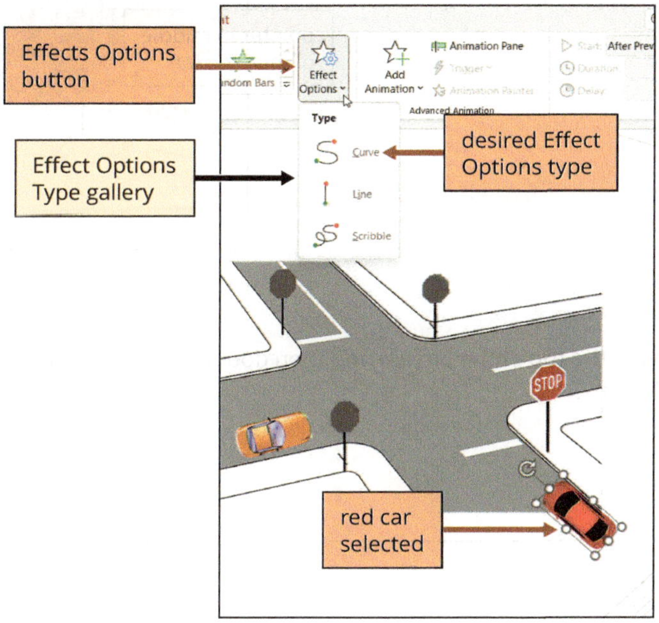

OpenClipart-Vectors/27376 images/Pixabay; CopyrightFreePictures/202 images/Pixabay; ElasticComputeFarm/39 images/Pixabay; Clker-Free-Vector-Images/29538 images/Pixabay

Figure 5–95

3

- Click Curve in the Type gallery and then position the pointer on the sizing handle in the middle of the red car's front bumper (Figure 5–96).

Q&A Why did I need to select Curve rather than Scribble or Line?
Your custom motion path will select particular locations on the slide, and the Curve type will create rounded edges to connect the lines you draw. The Scribble and Line options would draw only straight lines, so the arrow would not have smooth turns as it moves through the intersection.

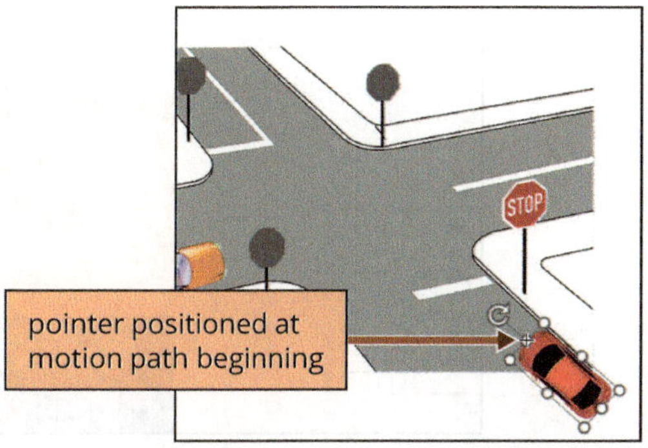

OpenClipart-Vectors/27376 images/Pixabay; CopyrightFreePictures/202 images/Pixabay; ElasticComputeFarm/39 images/Pixabay; Clker-Free-Vector-Images/29538 images/Pixabay

Figure 5–96

4

- Click to set the beginning of the curve and then position the pointer on the center of the white pavement line beside the stop sign (Figure 5–97).

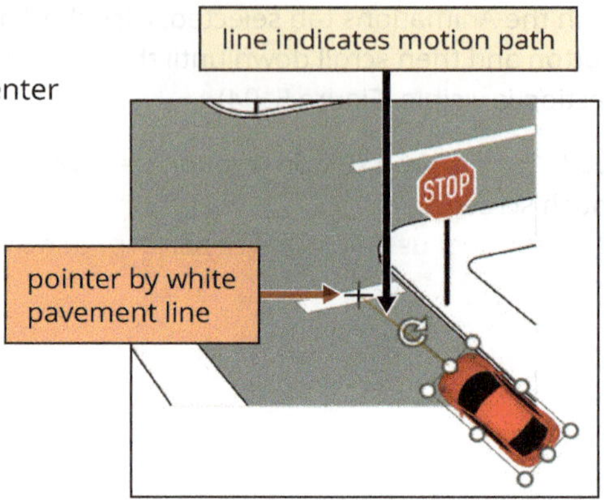

OpenClipart-Vectors/27376 images/Pixabay; CopyrightFreePictures/202 images/Pixabay; ElasticComputeFarm/39 images/Pixabay

Figure 5–97

5

- Click to set the location on the white pavement line, which is where the red car will change direction.
- Position the pointer in the middle of the intersection, as shown in Figure 5–98, and then click to set the top of the curve in this direction of travel.

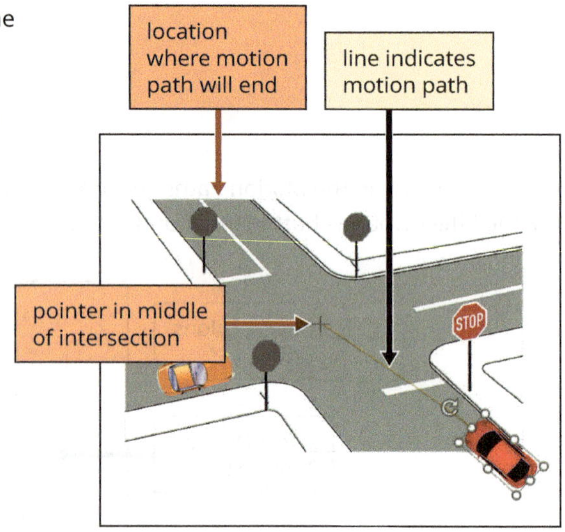

OpenClipart-Vectors/27376 images/Pixabay; CopyrightFreePictures/202 images/Pixabay; ElasticComputeFarm/39 images/Pixabay; Clker-Free-Vector-Images/29538 images/Pixabay

Figure 5–98

6

- Position the pointer at the end of the road at the top of the picture and then double-click to indicate the end of the motion path and preview this animation (Figure 5–99).

OpenClipart-Vectors/27376 images/Pixabay; CopyrightFreePictures/202 images/Pixabay; ElasticComputeFarm/39 images/Pixabay; Clker-Free-Vector-Images/29538 images/Pixabay

Figure 5–99

- Change the Duration setting to 07.00 seconds (Figure 5–100).

Q&A If my curve is not correct, can I delete it?
Yes. Select the motion path, press DELETE, and then repeat the previous steps.

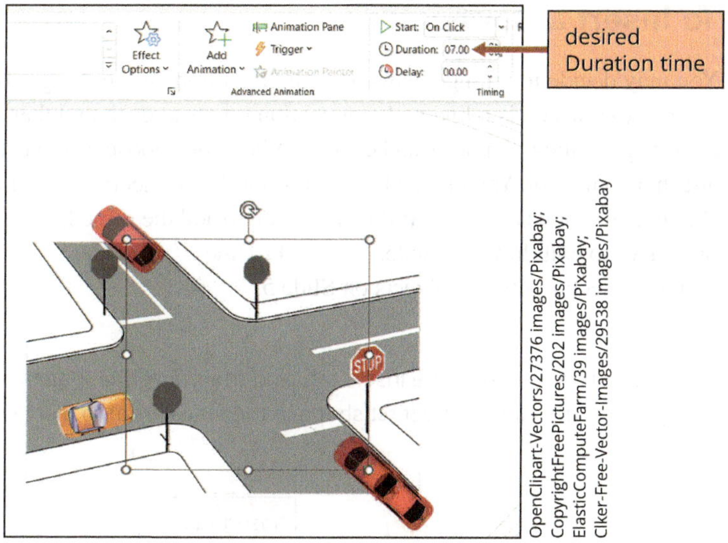

Figure 5–100

OpenClipart-Vectors/27376 images/Pixabay; CopyrightFreePictures/202 images/Pixabay; ElasticComputeFarm/39 images/Pixabay; Clker-Free-Vector-Images/29538 images/Pixabay

To Trigger an Animation Effect

If you select the On Click Start animation timing option and run the slide show, PowerPoint starts the animation when you click any part of the slide or press SPACEBAR. You may, however, want the option to play an animation in a particular circumstance. **Why?** You may have an animated sequence ready to show if time permits or if you believe your audience needs time to understand a process and would understand the concept more readily if you revealed one part of a slide element at a time. A **trigger** specifies when an animation or other action should occur. It is linked to a particular component of a slide so that the action occurs only when you click this slide element. For example, you can trigger an animation effect to start when you click a shape or other object that has the animation applied, or you can trigger an animation effect to begin playing at the start of, or sometime during, an audio or video clip. If you click any other part of the slide, PowerPoint will display the next slide in the presentation. The following steps set clicking the red car on Slide 4 as the trigger to move that vehicle.

1

- Click the red car, click the Trigger button (Animations tab | Advanced Animation group) to display the Trigger menu, and then point to 'On Click of' to display the list of Slide 4 elements (Figure 5–101).

2

- Click Picture 5, which is the red car, as the object that will trigger the animation when clicked.

Q&A How do I know the trigger animation has been added to the red car?
The Animation Pane displays 'Trigger: Picture 5'.

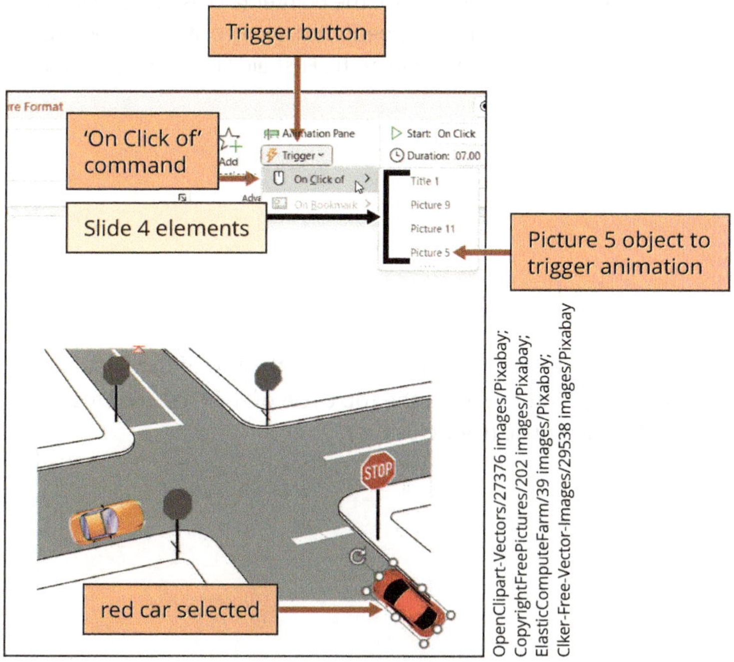

Figure 5–101

OpenClipart-Vectors/27376 images/Pixabay; CopyrightFreePictures/202 images/Pixabay; ElasticComputeFarm/39 images/Pixabay; Clker-Free-Vector-Images/29538 images/Pixabay

To Insert a Connector

You may decide to arrange items on a slide to improve the design. If some slide elements are related to each other, you can use a **connector**, which is a line with connection points at each end that stay attached to related shapes. The three types of connectors are straight, elbow (angled), and curved. When you choose a connector, dots appear on the shape outline to indicate where you can attach a connector. You click where you want the connector to start and then drag the pointer to the location where the connector should end. **Lock Drawing Mode** allows you to add the same line repeatedly. When you have completed adding the connector, you press ESC to exit drawing mode. **Why?** On Slide 5, you want to connect each icon to its related shape. The following steps insert a line connector between objects on Slide 5.

1

- Display Slide 5, display the Insert tab, and then click the Shapes button to display the Shapes gallery.
- Right-click the Line shape (first shape in the Lines area) to display the Drawing Mode menu (Figure 5–102).

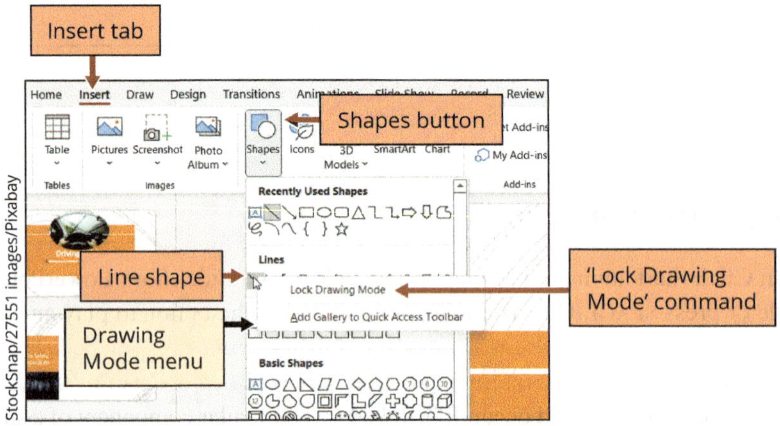

Figure 5–102

2

- Click 'Lock Drawing Mode', move the pointer (a crosshair) over the First aid kit icon until gray circles appear, and then position the pointer over the gray circle on the right side of the First aid kit icon (Figure 5–103).

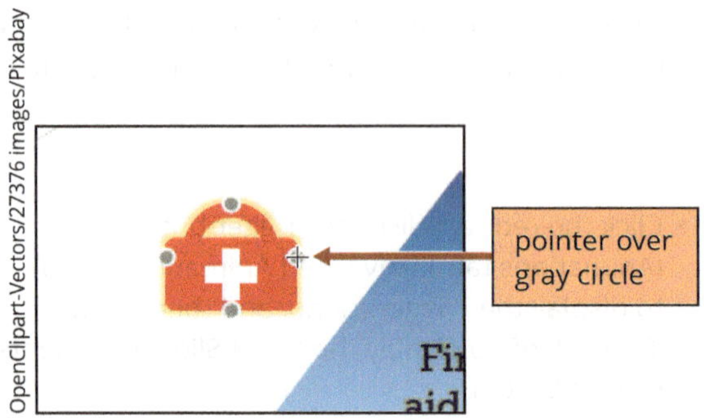

Figure 5–103

3

- Click and then drag the pointer toward the top of the First aid kit shape.
- When the pointer reaches the top circle of the First aid kit shape, release the mouse (Figure 5–104).

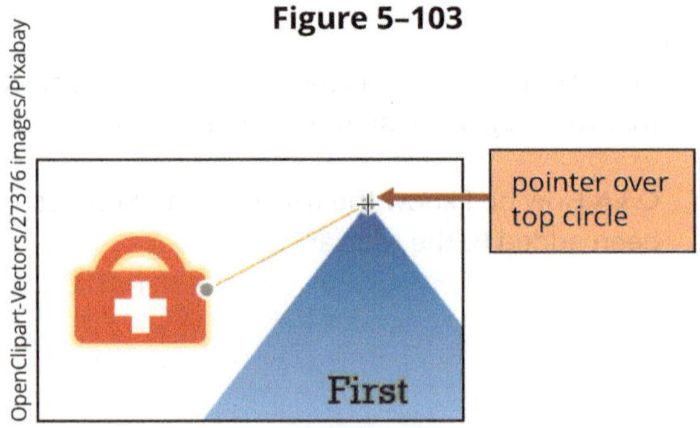

Figure 5–104

4

- Position the pointer over the gray circle on left side of the Jumper cables icon and then click and drag the pointer to the top circle of the Jumper cables shape.
- Position the pointer over the top gray circle on the right side of the Flashlight icon and then click and drag the pointer to the top circle of the Flashlight shape (Figure 5–105).

5

- Press ESC to exit Drawing Mode.

Q&A How do I know I have exited Drawing Mode?
The gray dots no longer are displayed.

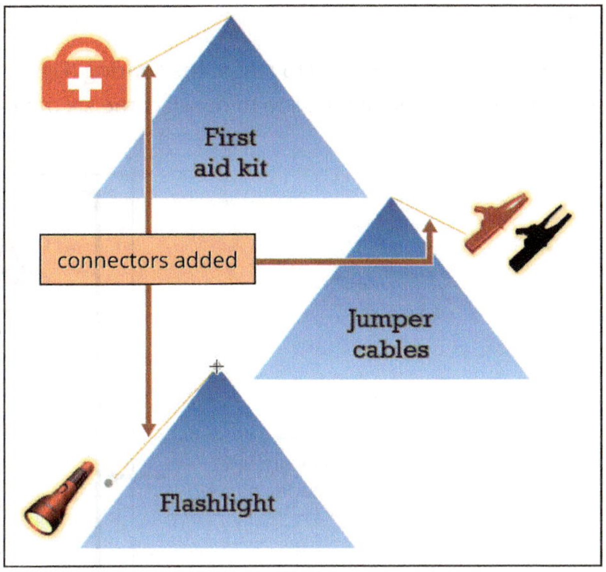

OpenClipart-Vectors/27376 images/Pixabay; OpenClipart-Vectors/27376 images/Pixabay; OpenClipart-Vectors/27376 images/Pixabay

Figure 5–105

To Align Content Placeholders

You can have PowerPoint place the same amount of space between the three sets of icons and shapes on Slide 5. You have two distribution options: 'Align to Slide' spaces all the selected objects evenly across the entire width of the slide; 'Align Selected Objects' spaces the objects between the fixed right and left objects. The following steps use the 'Align Selected Objects' option. **Why?** This option will distribute the Slide 5 pictures and shapes vertically to evenly fill space in the middle of the slide.

1

- Select the six Slide 5 icons and shapes, display the Shape Format tab, and then click the Align button (Shape Format tab | Arrange group) to display the Align Objects menu.

2

- If necessary, click 'Align Selected Objects' so that PowerPoint will adjust the spacing of the pictures evenly and then click the Align button to display the Align menu again (Figure 5–106).

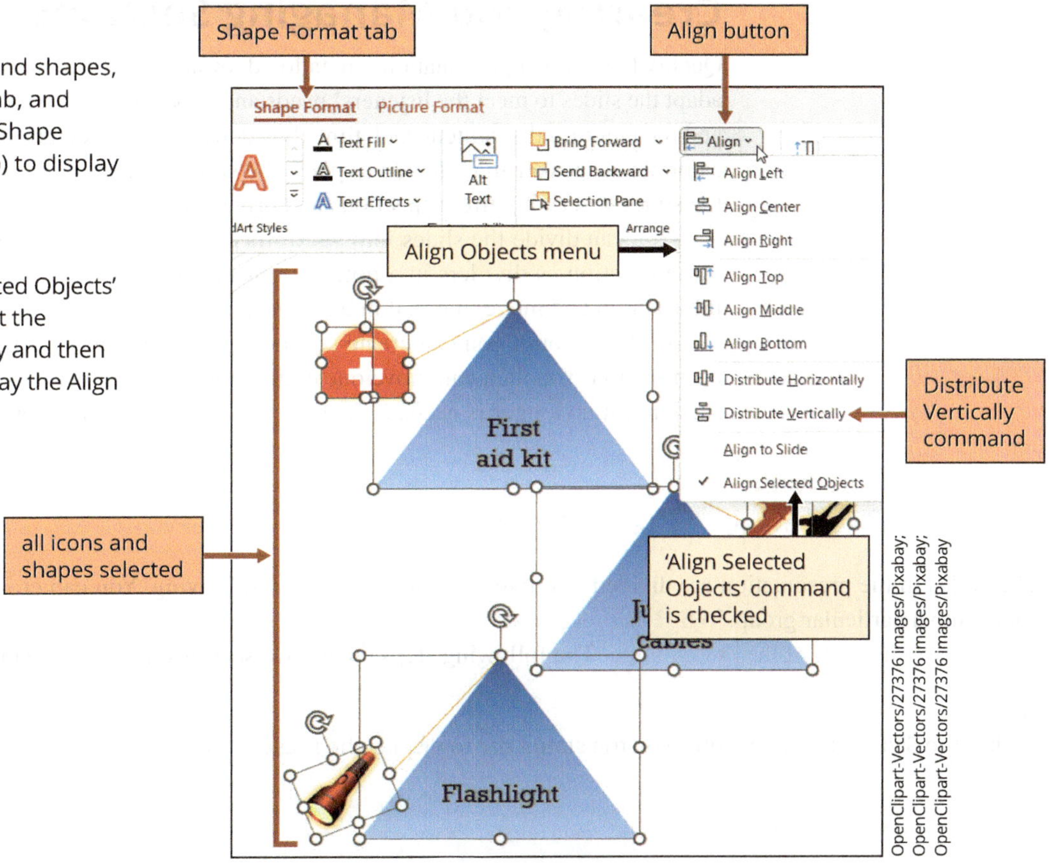

OpenClipart-Vectors/27376 images/Pixabay; OpenClipart-Vectors/27376 images/Pixabay; OpenClipart-Vectors/27376 images/Pixabay

Figure 5–106

3

- Click Distribute Vertically to adjust the spacing (Figure 5–107).
- Click a white area of the slide to deselect the six objects.

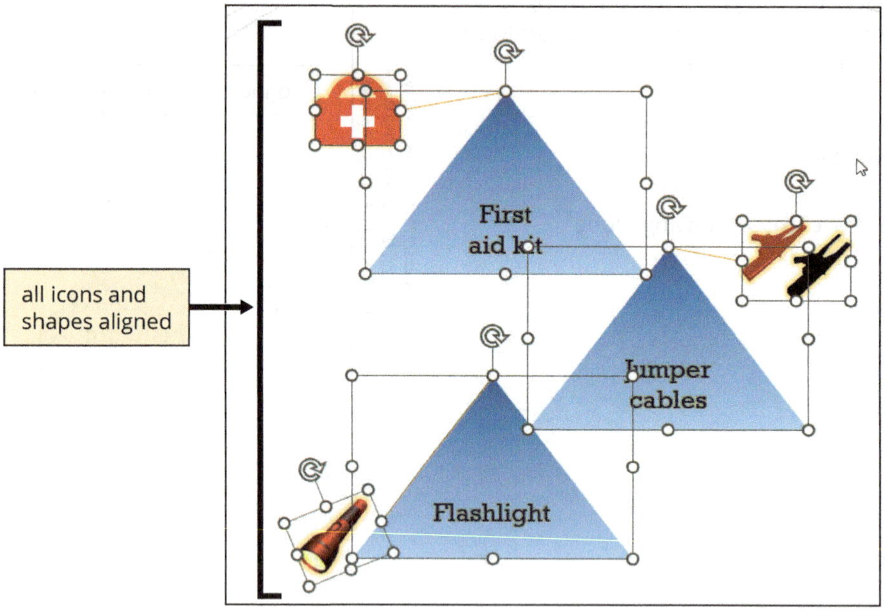

OpenClipart-Vectors/27376 images/Pixabay; OpenClipart-Vectors/27376 images/Pixabay; OpenClipart-Vectors/27376 images/Pixabay

Figure 5–107

Creating and Managing Sections

Quality PowerPoint presentations are tailored toward specific audiences, and experienced presenters adapt the slides to meet the listeners' needs and expectations. Speakers can develop one slide show and then modify the content each time they deliver the presentation. In the Driving slide show, for example, a speaker may decide to place the slides that showcase safe driving techniques before the slides describing tire inspections and driver-assistance features.

You can divide the slides into **sections** to help organize the slides. These sections serve the same function as dividers in a notebook or tabs in a manual: They help the user find required information and move material in a new sequence.

In PowerPoint, you can create sections, give them unique names, and then move slides into each section. You then can move one entire section to another part of the slide show or delete the section if it no longer is needed. Each section can be displayed or printed individually.

To Add a Section to a Presentation

The slides in the presentation are divided into two categories: Safety and Driving. You can create a section break to organize slides into a particular group. **Why?** At times, you may want to display slides from one particular category or move a section of slides to another part of the presentation. The following steps create two sections in the presentation.

1

- Click the Slide Sorter view button on the status bar to display the presentation in Slide Sorter view.

- Position the pointer between Slide 3 and Slide 4 and then click once to display the vertical bar (Figure 5–108).

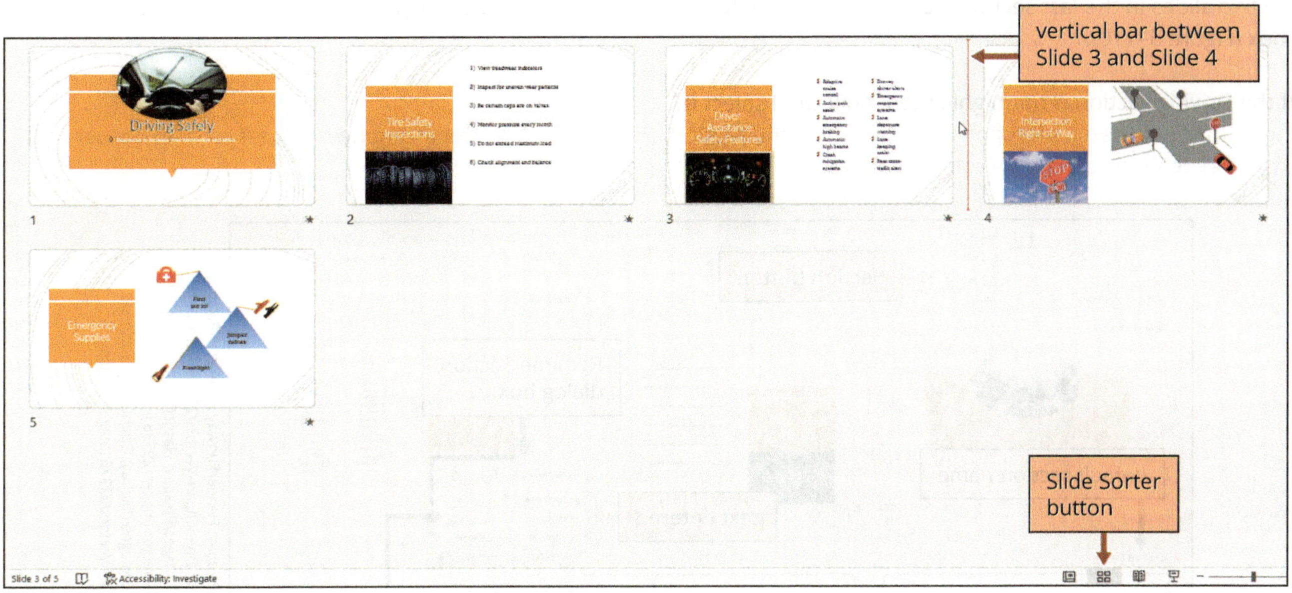

StockSnap/27551 images/Pixabay; FlenderFunways/4 images/Pixabay; Nick Fewings/Unsplash.com; OpenClipart-Vectors/27376 images/Pixabay; CopyrightFreePictures/202 images/Pixabay; ElasticComputeFarm/39 images/Pixabay; Clker-Free-Vector-Images/29538 images/Pixabay; OpenClipart-Vectors/27376 images/Pixabay; OpenClipart-Vectors/27376 images/Pixabay; OpenClipart-Vectors/27376 images/Pixabay

Figure 5–108

Q&A I am using a touch screen. When I tap between the slides to display the vertical bar, a shortcut menu also displays with an Add Section button. Can I just tap that button instead of using the Home tab Section button?
Yes.

2

- With the Home tab displayed, click the Section button (Home tab | Slides group) to display the Section menu (Figure 5–109).

3

- Click Add Section in the menu to create a section with the name, Untitled Section.

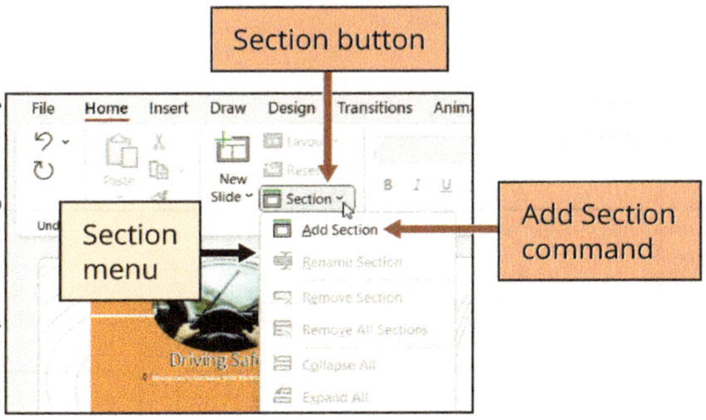

StockSnap/27551 images/Pixabay

Figure 5–109

To Rename a Section

The default section names, Default and Untitled, do not identify the content of the slides in the group. The following steps rename each of the two sections in the presentation. **Why?** Giving each section a unique name helps to categorize the slides easily.

1

- With the two slides in the last section highlighted and the Rename Section dialog box displayed, type **Driving** in the Section name box (Figure 5–110).

Q&A If the Driving section is not highlighted, how can I select it?
Click the divider between the sections. You will know the section is selected when the thumbnails have a colored border and the text and slide numbers have a colored font color.

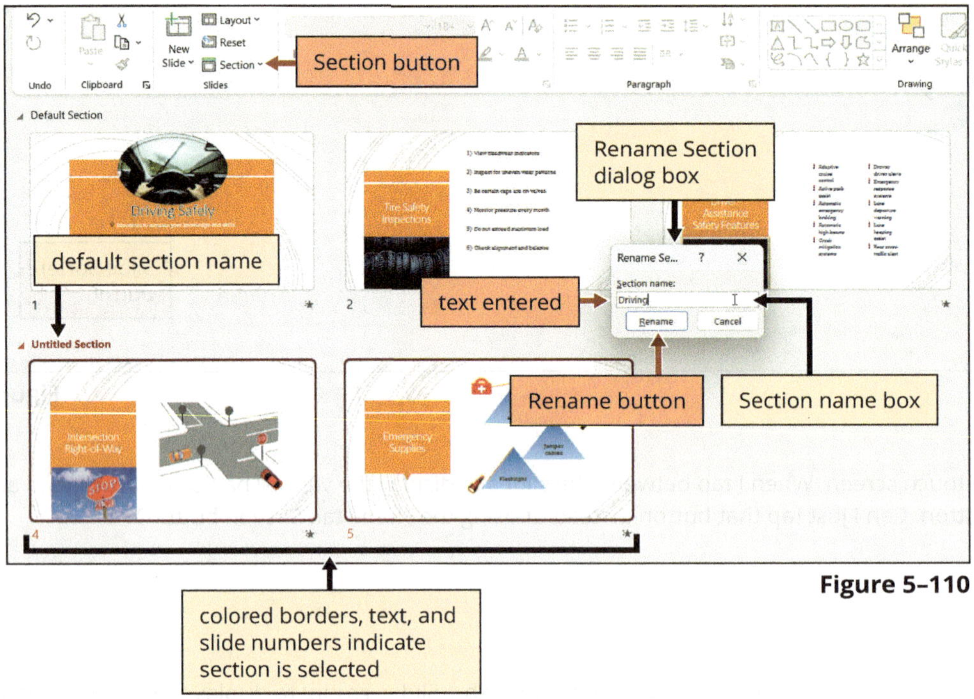

Figure 5–110

StockSnap/27551 images/Pixabay; FlenderFunways/4 images/Pixabay; Nick Fewings/Unsplash.com; OpenClipart-Vectors/27376 images/Pixabay; CopyrightFreePictures/202 images/Pixabay; ElasticComputeFarm/39 images/Pixabay; Clker-Free-Vector-Images/29538 images/Pixabay; OpenClipart-Vectors/27376 images/Pixabay; OpenClipart-Vectors/27376 images/Pixabay; OpenClipart-Vectors/27376 images/Pixabay

2

- Click the Rename button (Rename Section dialog box) to change the section name to Driving.
- Click the Default Section divider for Slides 1, 2, and 3 to select it and then click the Section button to display the Section menu (Figure 5–111).

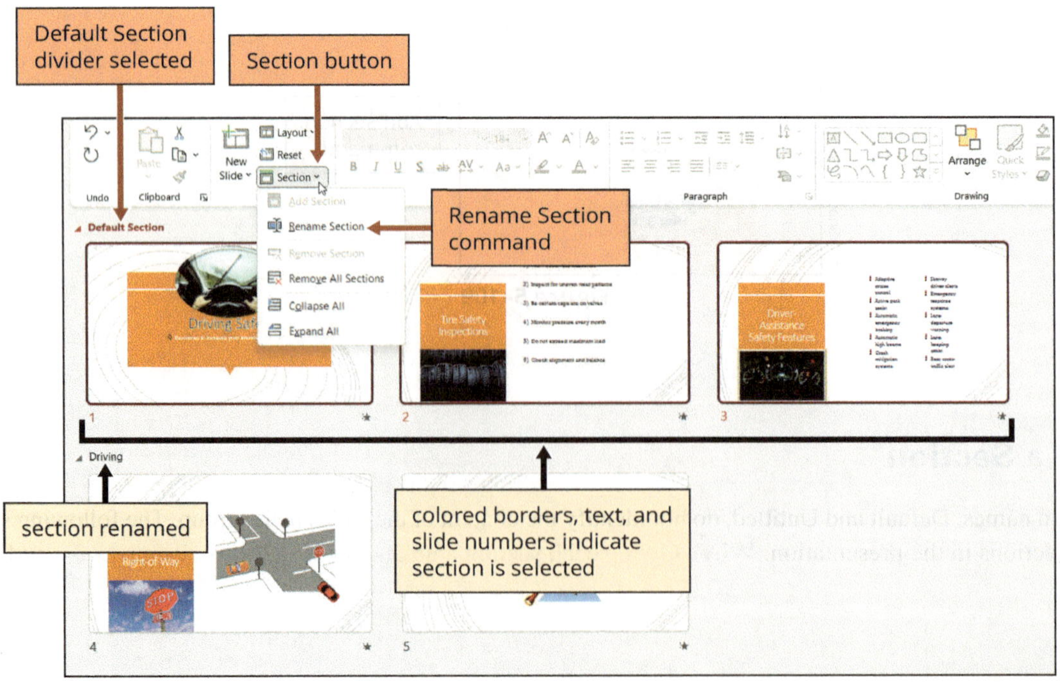

Figure 5–111

StockSnap/27551 images/Pixabay; FlenderFunways/4 images/Pixabay; Nick Fewings/Unsplash.com; OpenClipart-Vectors/27376 images/Pixabay; CopyrightFreePictures/202 images/Pixabay; ElasticComputeFarm/39 images/Pixabay; Clker-Free-Vector-Images/29538 images/Pixabay; OpenClipart-Vectors/27376 images/Pixabay; OpenClipart-Vectors/27376 images/Pixabay; OpenClipart-Vectors/27376 images/Pixabay

3

- Click Rename Section to display the Rename Section dialog box, type **Safety** in the Section name box, and then click the Rename button to change the section name (Figure 5–112).

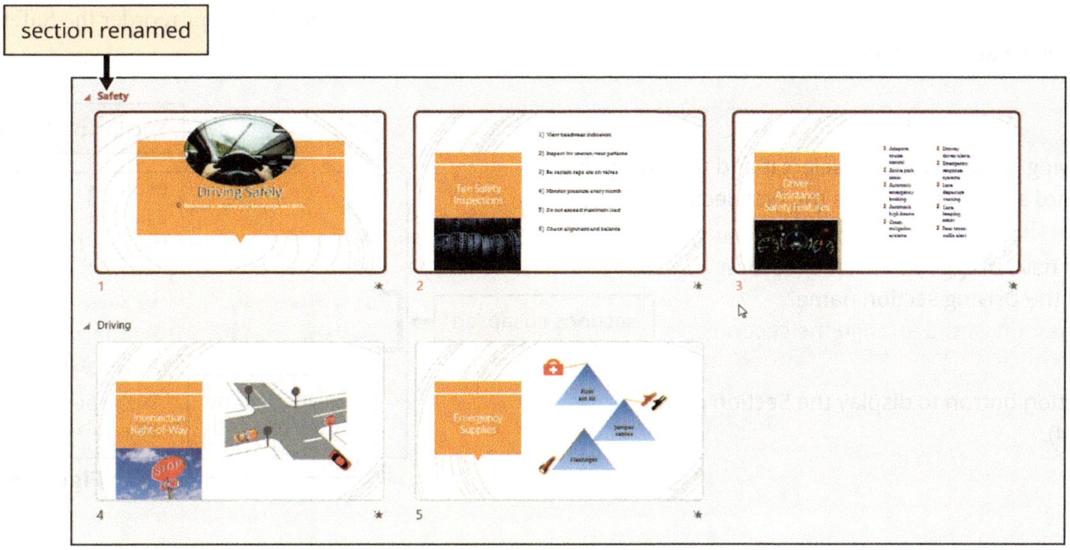

Figure 5–112

Other Ways

1. Right-click section divider, click Rename Section on shortcut menu

To Collapse Sections

You can collapse the sections so that only the two section titles are displayed. **Why?** *It is convenient to view the names when the sections are displayed in a list.* The following steps collapse the sections.

1

- With the first section, Safety, selected and the Home tab displayed, click the Section button (Figure 5–113).

Q&A Can I remove a section?

Yes. To delete one section, select the section title and then click Remove Section in the Section menu. To remove all sections, display the Section menu and then click 'Remove All Sections'.

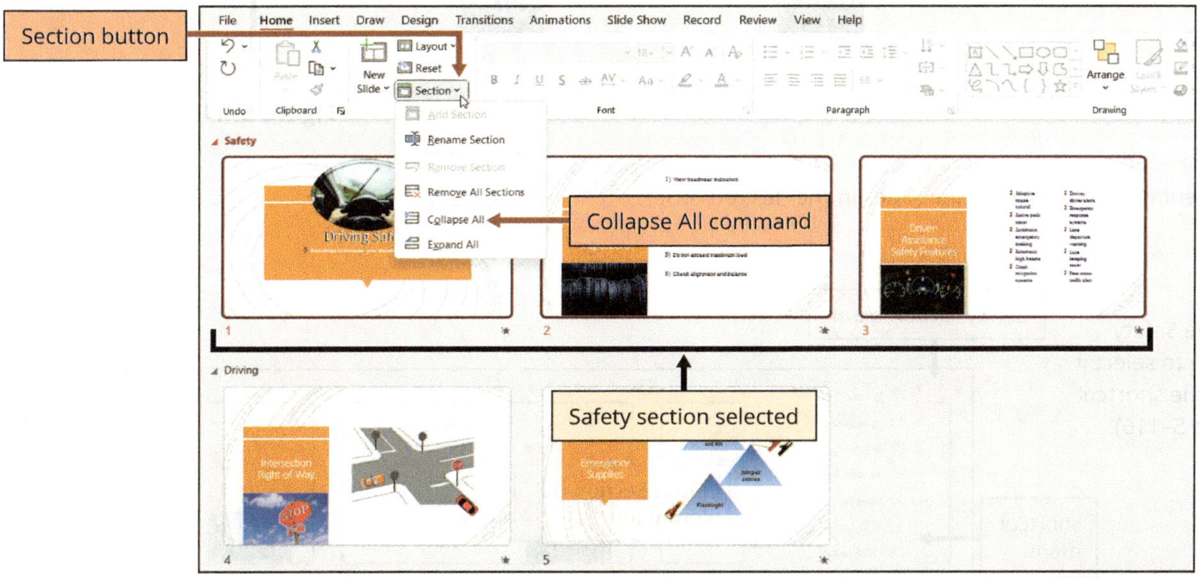

Figure 5–113

2

- Click Collapse All in the Section menu to display only the section names.

To Reorder Sections

When the slide sections are collapsed, it is easy to change the order in which the sections display. **Why?** You want to emphasize safe driving techniques before describing tires and driver safety features, so you want to present this information at the beginning of your talk and change the order of the two sets of slides in your presentation. The following steps reorder the Safety and Driving sections and then expand the sections.

1

- Click the Driving section name to select it and then drag the section upward so that it becomes the first section.

Q&A Could I have dragged the Safety section name below the Driving section name?
Yes. Either method would arrange the sections.

- Click the Section button to display the Section menu (Figure 5–114).

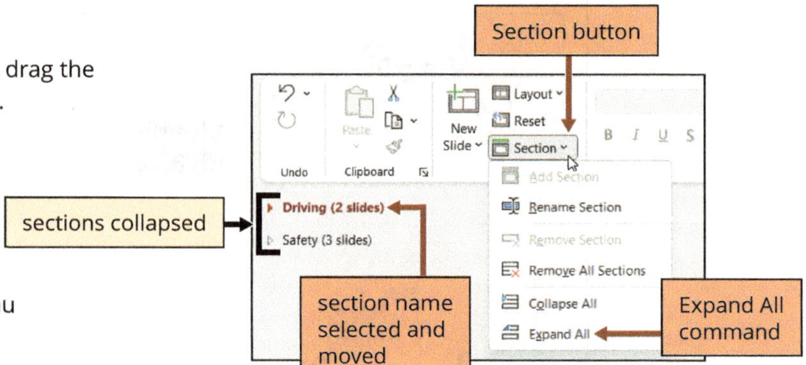

Figure 5–114

2

- Click Expand All to display all the slides in their corresponding sections (Figure 5–115).

StockSnap/27551 images/Pixabay; FlenderFunways/4 images/Pixabay; Nick Fewings/Unsplash.com; OpenClipart-Vectors/27376 images/Pixabay; CopyrightFreePictures/202 images/Pixabay; ElasticComputeFarm/39 images/Pixabay; Clker-Free-Vector-Images/29538 images/Pixabay; OpenClipart-Vectors/27376 images/Pixabay; OpenClipart-Vectors/27376 images/Pixabay; OpenClipart-Vectors/27376 images/Pixabay

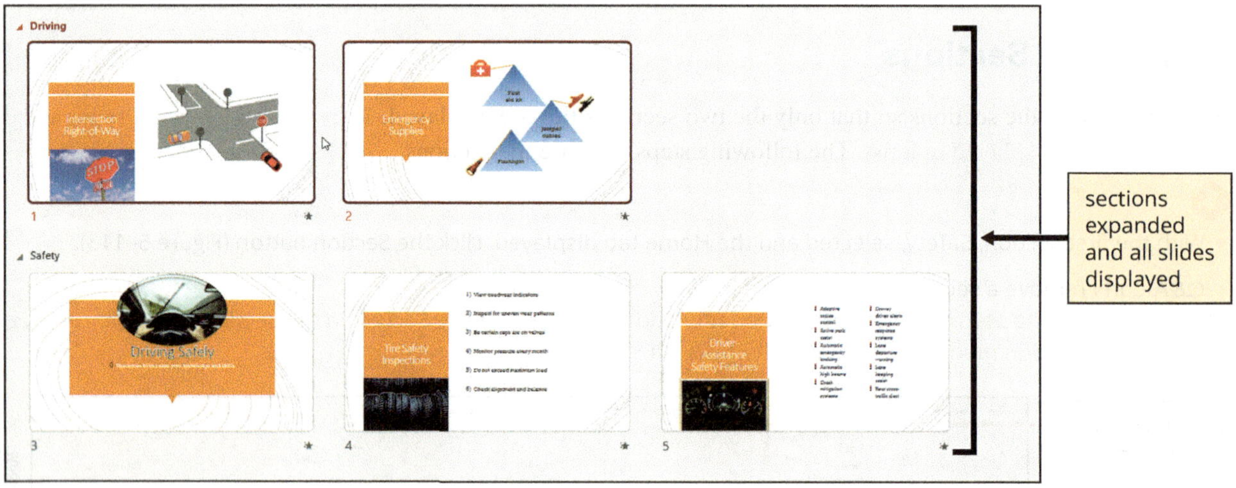

Figure 5–115

3

- Run the presentation to display all the slides in the desired order.

4

- Right-click the Safety section name to select it and display the shortcut menu (Figure 5–116).

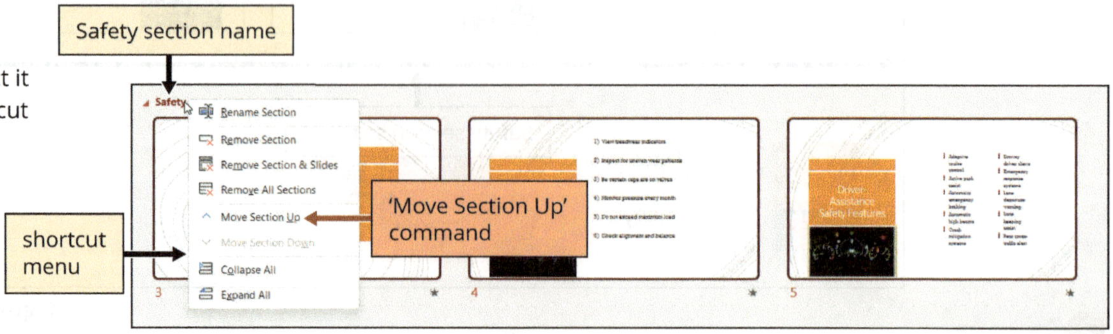

Nick Fewings/Unsplash.com

Figure 5–116

5

- Click 'Move Section Up' to position the Safety section as the first section in the presentation.

Other Ways

1. Right-click section name, click Move Section Up, Move Section Down, Collapse All, or Expand All on shortcut menu

Zoom Links

A **zoom link** is a dynamic feature that allows you to present your content creatively in a nonlinear way. When you create a zoom link, you can jump to and from specific slides, sections, and portions of your presentation in an order you decide when you are presenting. You can jump to specific slides and sections with slide zoom and section zoom. If your presentation has several sections, you can use a **section zoom** to return to sections you want to emphasize or highlight. To show only selected slides, you can use **slide zoom** to show a small version of a slide on another slide that you can click to display the slide in Slide Show view, which is useful when a shorter presentation does not have many sections. In addition, you can create an interactive table of contents with **summary zoom**, which is a slide that contains section zooms, usually for all of the sections in the presentation. When you are presenting your slide show, you click the section zoom or slide zoom to jump to the linked section. If you use the section zoom, PowerPoint will display the slides in a section and then automatically return to the original slide.

To Insert Section Zoom Links and Slide Zoom Links

The zoom link feature can be useful when presenting your Safe Driving slides if your audience expresses interest in a particular section or you need to jump to a particular slide to review or display information. When you are displaying the title slide, for example, you can click a section zoom link and then jump to the Driving section, starting with Slide 4. After Slide 5 is displayed, PowerPoint returns to Slide 1. In another example, you can click the slide zoom link on Slide 3 to skip to Slide 5. Once Slide 5 is displayed, the presentation ends. **Why?** *You may decide to modify the slide order while you are speaking based on the audience's interest and background knowledge.* The following steps insert section and slide zoom links.

1

- Click the Normal view button on the status toolbar.
- With Slide 1 displayed, click the Insert tab and then click the Zoom button (Insert tab | Links group) to display the Zoom menu (Figure 5–117).

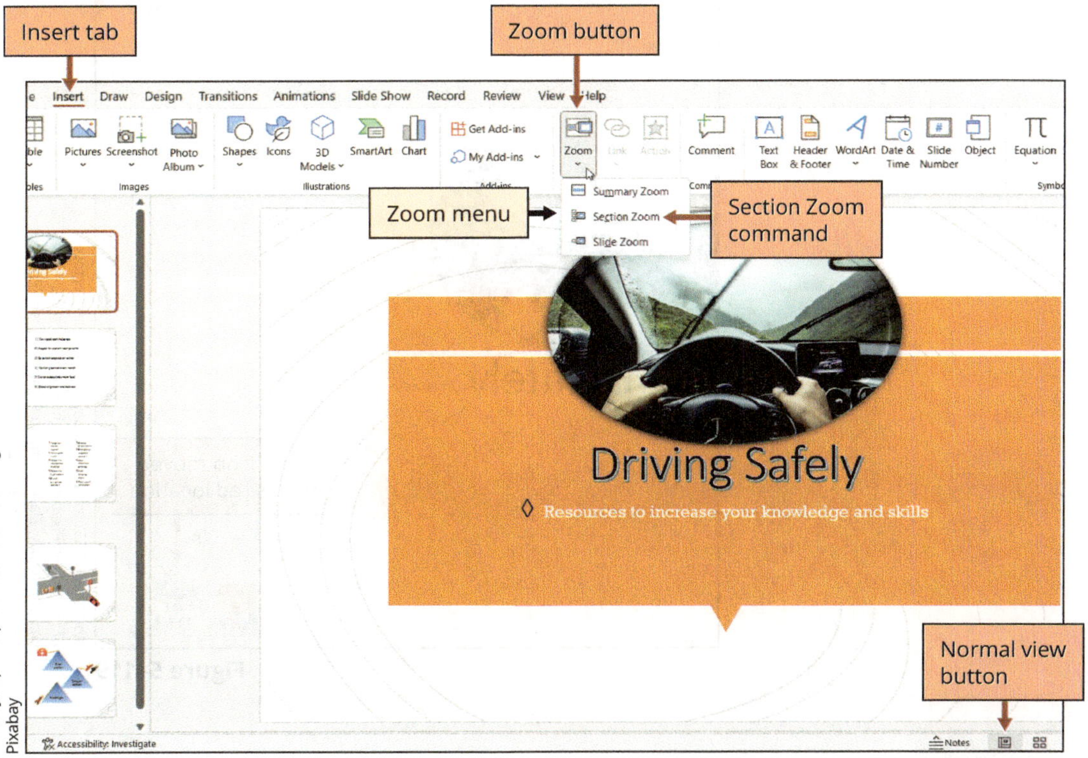

Figure 5–117

2

- Click Section Zoom and then click the 'Section 2: Driving' box to select that section (Figure 5–118).

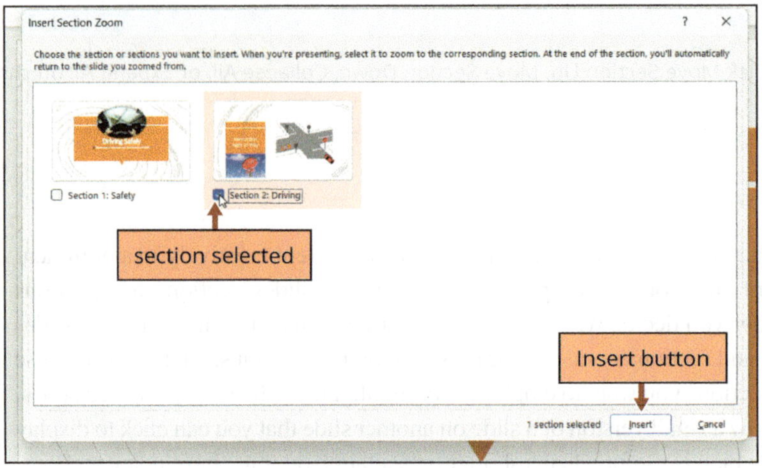

StockSnap/27551 images/Pixabay; OpenClipart-Vectors/27376 images/Pixabay; CopyrightFreePictures/202 images/Pixabay; ElasticComputeFarm/39 images/Pixabay; Clker-Free-Vector-Images/29538 images/Pixabay

Figure 5–118

3

- Click the Insert button ('Insert Section Zoom' dialog box) to create the Section Zoom.
- If a Round Trip box is displayed, click the Got it button to close the box.

4

- Click the Zoom tab and then resize the Section Zoom icon height to 1".
- Move the icon to the lower-right corner of the slide (Figure 5–119).

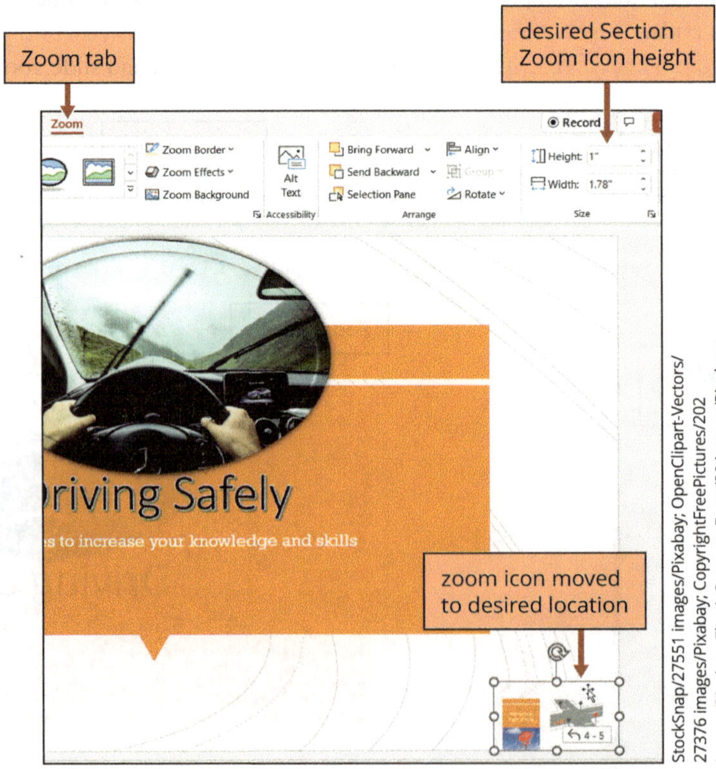

StockSnap/27551 images/Pixabay; OpenClipart-Vectors/27376 images/Pixabay; CopyrightFreePictures/202 images/Pixabay; ElasticComputeFarm/39 images/Pixabay; Clker-Free-Vector-Images/29538 images/Pixabay

Figure 5–119

5

- Display Slide 3. Click the Insert tab and then click the Zoom button to display the Zoom menu.
- Click Slide Zoom and then click the '5. Emergency Supplies' box to select this slide (Figure 5–120).

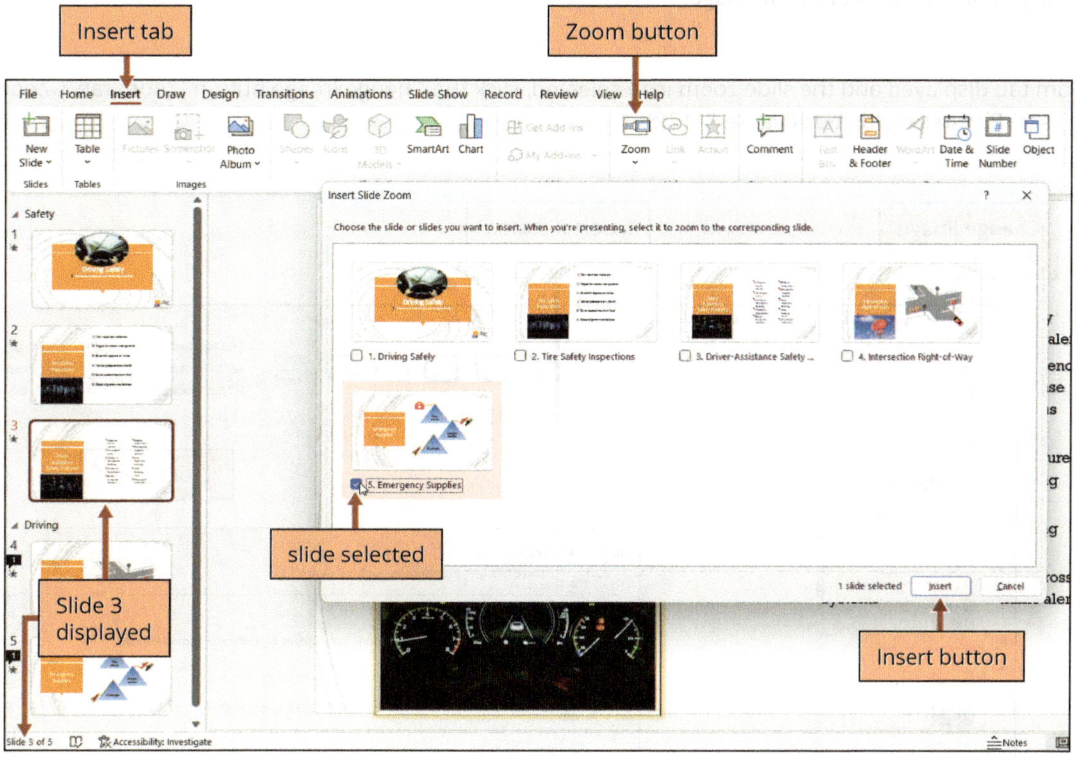

Figure 5–120

6

- Click the Insert button to create the Slide Zoom.
- If a 'Transitions with zip' box is displayed, click the Got it button to close the box.
- Click the Zoom tab and then resize the Slide Zoom icon height to 1".
- Move the icon to the lower-right corner of the slide (Figure 5–121).

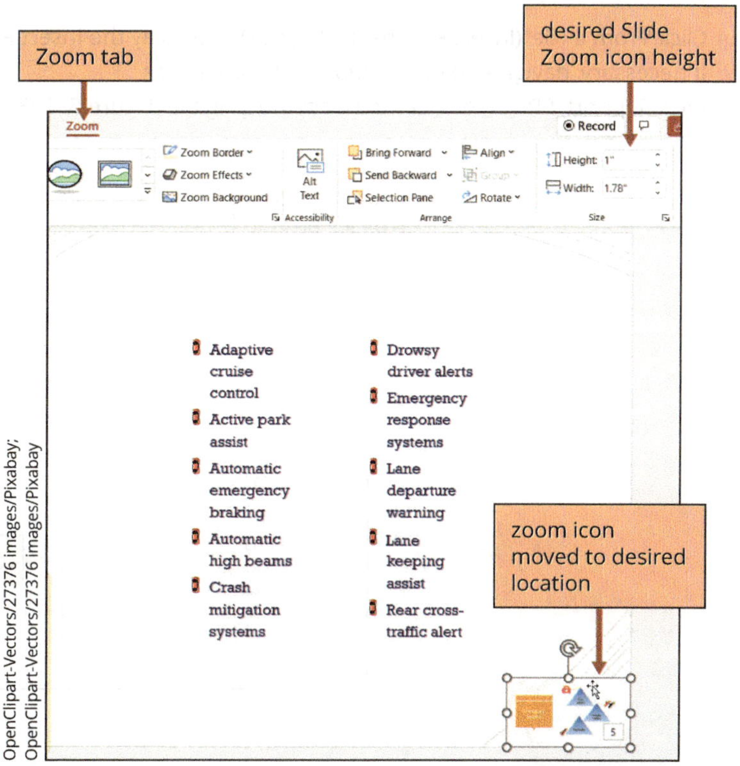

Figure 5–121

To Change the Zoom Icon Image

As a default, PowerPoint uses a miniature copy of the slide as the zoom image. You can change this image and add styles, a border, effects, and a background. **Why?** The red car picture is the Slide 3 bullet, so the image is repeated throughout the slides. The following steps change the zoom icon image.

1

- With the Zoom tab displayed and the slide zoom icon selected, click the Change Image button (Zoom tab | Zoom Options) to display the Insert Pictures dialog box (Figure 5–122).

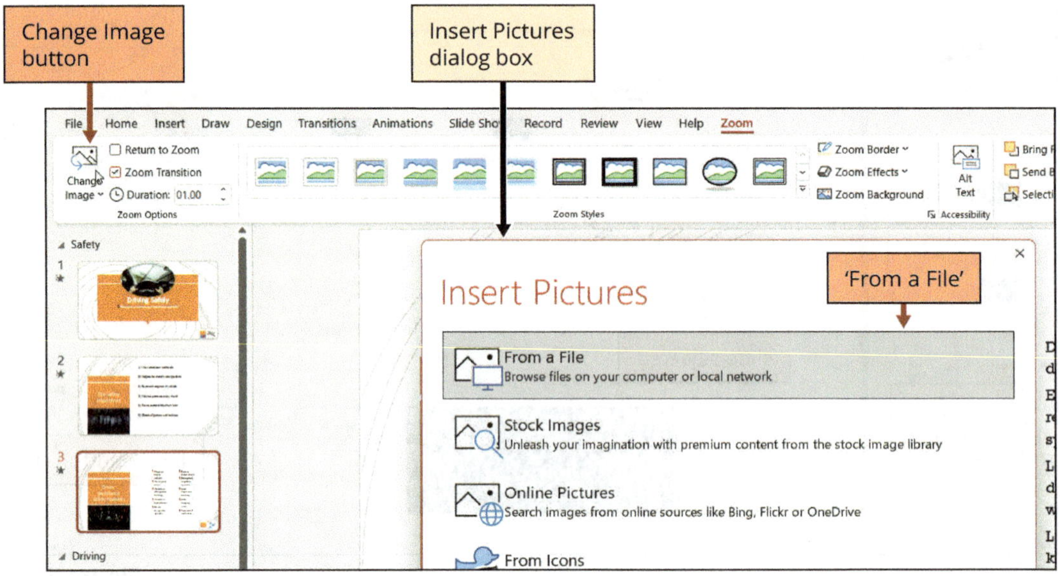

Figure 5–122

2

- Click 'From a File' (Insert Pictures dialog box) to display the Insert Picture dialog box.
- If necessary, navigate to the location of the Data Files.
- Click Support_PPT_5_Red_Car to select the .png file (Figure 5–123).

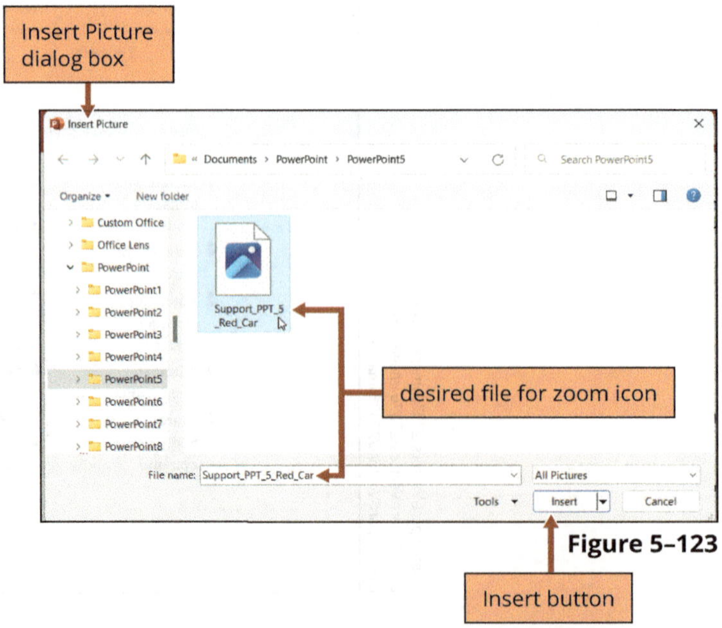

Figure 5–123

3

- Click the Insert button (Insert Picture dialog box) to insert the red car picture as the zoom icon.
- Display Slide 1 and then repeat Steps 1 and 2 above to change the section zoom icon to the red car picture (Figure 5–124).

StockSnap/27551 images/Pixabay; OpenClipart-Vectors/27376 images/Pixabay

Figure 5–124

To Run a Presentation with Section Zoom Links and Slide Zoom Links

All changes are complete. You now can view the presentation with animations and zoom links. The following steps run the slide show.

1. Display Slide 1 and then run the presentation.
2. Click the red car icon on Slide 1 to zoom to the 'Intersection Right-of-Way' Slide 4 and then click the red car to trigger the animation.
3. Click to display Slide 5 and then click to display Slides 1, 2, and 3.
4. When Slide 3 is displayed, click the red car zoom icon to zoom to the 'Emergency Supplies' slide.
5. Click twice to end the presentation.

BTW
Printing Document Properties
PowerPoint does not allow you to print document properties. This feature, however, is available in Microsoft 365 Word.

To Save and Print the Presentation

With the presentation completed, you should save the file and print handouts for your audience. The following steps save the file and then print a presentation handout.

1. Save the presentation again in the same storage location with the same file name.
2. Open Backstage view, click the Print tab, click 'Full Page Slides' in the Settings area, click '6 Slides Horizontal' in the Handouts area to display a preview of the handout, and then click Print in the Print gallery to print the presentation.
3. sam Because the project now is complete, you can exit PowerPoint.

BTW
Distributing a Document
Instead of printing and distributing a hard copy of PowerPoint slides, you can distribute the slides electronically. Options include sending the slides via email; posting it on cloud storage (such as OneDrive) and sharing the link with others; posting it on social media, a blog, or other website; and sharing a link associated with an online location of the slides. You also can create and share a PDF or XPS image of the slides, so that users can view the file in Acrobat Reader or XPS Viewer instead of in PowerPoint.

Summary

In this module, you learned how to merge presentations, evaluate a reviewer's comments, and then review, accept, and reject proposed changes, as well as reply to and insert comments. You managed text in columns and shapes, formatted a picture by adding a border and glow effect, changed bullets to a picture and a symbol, added animation, created and managed sections, and added zoom links.

Consider This: Plan Ahead

What decisions will you need to make when creating your next presentation?

Use these guidelines as you complete the assignments in this module and create your own slide show decks outside of this class.

1. Develop a collaboration plan for group members to follow.
   a) Set an overall group goal.
   b) Set long-term and short-term goals.
   c) Identify subtasks that must be completed.
   d) Set a schedule.
2. Accept both positive and negative feedback.
   a) Realize that this criticism helps you to improve yourself and your work.
   b) Oral and written comments from others can help reinforce positive aspects and identify flaws.
   c) Seek comments from a variety of people who genuinely want to help you develop an effective presentation.
3. Give constructive criticism when asked to critique a presentation.
   a) Begin and end with positive comments.
   b) Give specific details about a few areas that can be improved.
   c) Be honest, but be tactful.

Student Assignments

Apply Your Knowledge

Reinforce the skills and apply the concepts you learned in this module.

Inserting and Deleting Comments, Changing Bullets, and Adding Animations

Note: To complete this assignment, you will be required to use the Data Files. Please contact your instructor for information about accessing the Data Files.

Instructions: Start PowerPoint. Open the presentation called SC_PPT_5-1.pptx, which is located in the Data Files.

The slides in the presentation present information about a seminar for first-time home buyers. The document you open is a partially formatted presentation. You are to change the slide size, insert and reply to comments, add animations, change bullets, and change line spacing. Your presentation should look like Figure 5–125.

Perform the following tasks:

1. Change the slide size to Widescreen (16:9).
2. On Slide 1 (Figure 5–125a), insert a comment and then type **How about adding the word, "Free", to the title?** as the text. In the Reply box, type **That's a great idea! I'll change the title text.** as a reply to the comment.
3. Change the title text to **Free seminar for first-time home buyers** and then change the font size to 44 point.
4. On Slide 2 (Figure 5–125b), select the bulleted list, insert a new comment, and then type **Perhaps you can change the bullets to an image that's related to the presentation.** as the text. In the Reply box, type **I agree. I'll insert a picture of a key.** as a reply to the comment.
5. Edit the house picture's Alt Text to use **A picture of a small red and white house, a key, and a key ring** as the new description.
6. On Slide 2, change the bulleted paragraphs' line spacing to 1.5.
7. Change the bullets to the Support_PPT_5_Key.png picture. Increase the size to 125% of text.
8. Animate the bulleted paragraphs using the Fly In entrance effect. Use the After Previous Start option and change the Duration time to 03.00 seconds. Have each paragraph dim after it is displayed to the color red (the seventh color).
9. On Slide 2, add the Lines motion path to the picture of the house. Add a trigger to this picture (On Click of Picture 5).

   If requested by your instructor, add your current or previous pet's name in the Alt Text text box.
10. Save the presentation using the file name, **SC_PPT_5_House**.
11. Submit the presentation in the format specified by your instructor.
12. **Consider This:** In Step 7, you changed the bullets, and in Step 8 you animated the bulleted paragraphs. Did these changes improve the presentation? Why or why not?

Continued on next page

Figure 5–125(a): Slide 1

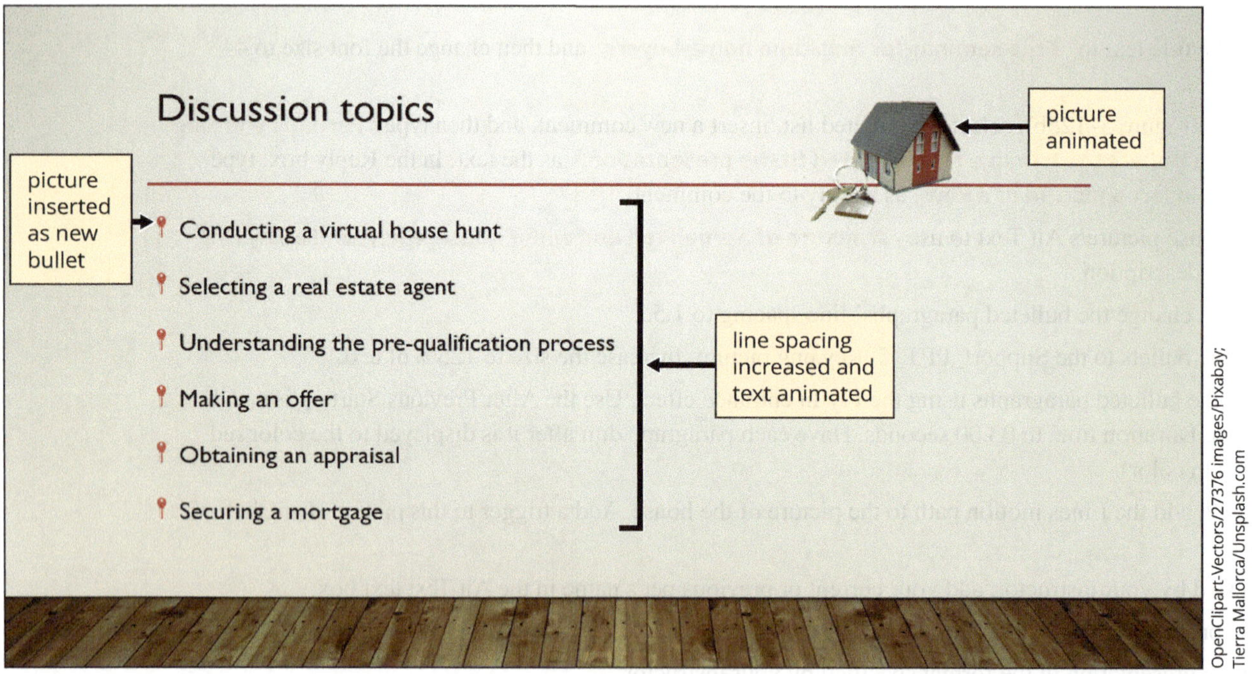

Figure 5–125(b): Slide 2

Extend Your Knowledge

Extend the skills you learned in this module and experiment with new skills. You may need to use Help to complete the assignment.

Creating Credits and Adding a Sound

Note: To complete this assignment, you will be required to use the Data Files. Please contact your instructor for information about accessing the Data Files.

Instructions: Start PowerPoint. Open the presentation called SC_PPT_5-2.pptx, which is located in the Data Files. You will display text as ascending credits on the slide. You then will add a sound to the animation (Figure 5–126).

Perform the following tasks:

1. Click the placeholder with the five paragraphs to select it.
2. Display the Animation gallery and then click 'More Entrance Effects' to display the Change Entrance Effect dialog box.
3. Scroll down to display the Exciting section.
4. Click the Credits entrance animation effect in the Exciting section to see a preview of the animation effect.
5. Click OK ('Change Entrance Effect' dialog box) to apply the effect.
6. Click the Effect Options button (Animations tab | Animation group) and then click By Paragraph to see a preview of the new animation effect.

   If requested by your instructor, replace the word, Naomi, in the footer with your high school mascot's name.
7. Change the Start animation timing option to After Previous and the Duration to 10.00 seconds.
8. To add a sound to the animation, display the Animation Pane and then click the down arrow to the right of the TextBox 3 animation. Click Effect Options in the menu to display the Credits dialog box. In the Enhancements area, click the Sound arrow to display the Sound list and then click Click.
9. Run the presentation and then save it using the file name, **SC_PPT_5_Ads**.
10. Submit the revised document in the format specified by your instructor.
11. **Consider This:** In this assignment, you added credits and a sound. Did these changes enhance the slide? Why or why not? Which sound other than Click could be used?

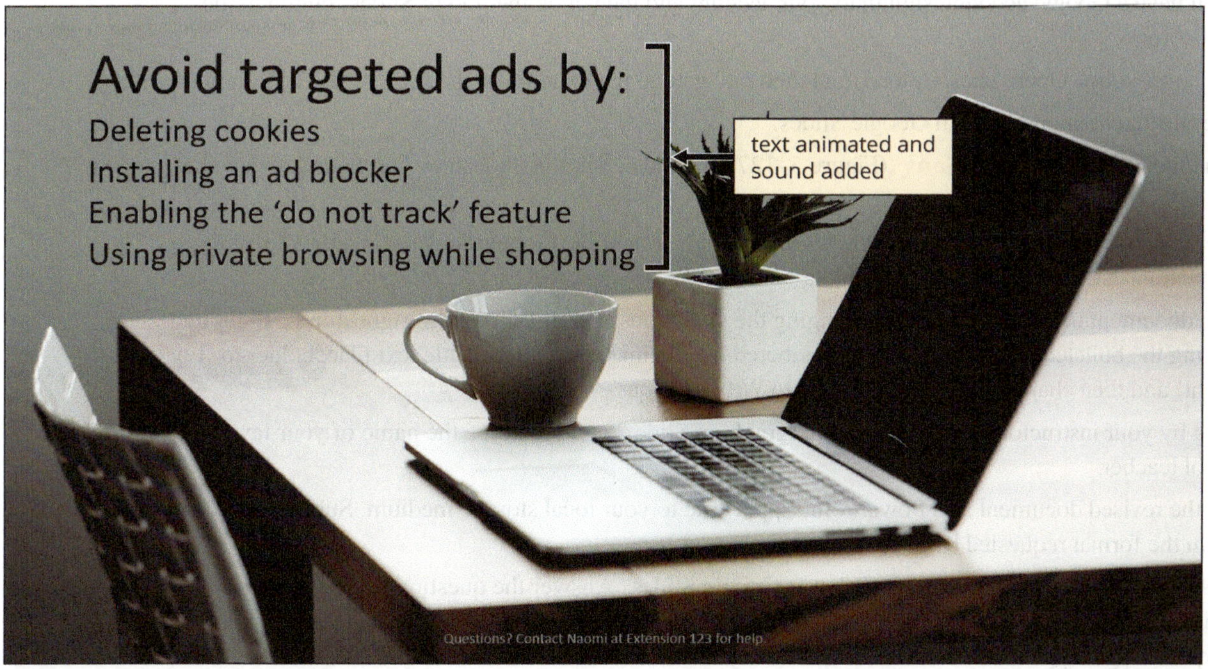

Life Of Pix/Pexels

Figure 5–126

Expand Your World

Create a solution that uses cloud or web technologies by learning and investigating on your own from general guidance.

Using Google Slides to Upload and Edit a File

Instructions: The project manager of the insurance company where you work has asked you to create a presentation to inform your clients about methods of driving in difficult conditions, including rain and snow. You began working on the slides at the office but did not have time to finish the slides there and need to complete the slide deck at home. Although you do not have PowerPoint on your home computer, you have an Internet connection and a Google account. You uploaded your PowerPoint presentation to Google Drive so you can view and edit it later from home.

Note: You will use a Google account, which you can create at no cost, to complete this assignment. If you do not have a Google account and do not want to create one, read this assignment without performing the instructions.

To complete this assignment, you will be required to use the Data Files. Please contact your instructor for information about accessing the Data Files.

Perform the following tasks:

1. Start PowerPoint. Open the presentation called SC_PPT_5-3.pptx, which is located in the Data Files. Review the slides so that you are familiar with their contents and formats. If desired, print the slides so that you easily can compare them to the Google Slides converted file. Close the presentation.
2. Run a browser. Search for the text, Google Slides, using a search engine. Visit several websites to learn about Google Slides and Google Drive. Navigate to the Google Slides website. If you do not have a Google account and you want to create one, click the 'Sign up for free' link and follow the instructions. If you do not have a Google account and do not want to create one, read the remaining instructions without performing them. If you have a Google account, sign in to your account and then click the 'Go to Slides' button in the upper-right corner.
3. Click the File tab, click Open, click Upload, and then navigate to the location of the file, SC_PPT_5-3.pptx.
4. Upload the file and then open it with Google Slides.
5. Rename the file **SC_PPT_5_Conditions** (Figure 5–127) and then click the Slideshow button and review the slides.
6. What differences do you see between the PowerPoint document and the Google Slides converted document? Which animations are shown? How do you add a comment?
7. Modify the document in Google Slides by changing the slide transition to 'Slide from right' for all slides and then changing the bulleted list on Slide 3 to a numbered list. Animate the Slide 1 title text placeholder to 'Fly in from right' and then change the Start condition to With previous.

   If requested by your instructor, add a bulleted paragraph on Slide 2 and then type the name of your favorite grade school teacher.
8. Download the revised document as a PowerPoint (.pptx) file to your local storage medium. Submit the document in the format requested by your instructor.
9. **Consider This:** What is Google Drive? What is Google Slides? Answer the questions posed in Step 6. If you have an Android smartphone, download the Google Slides app and edit the SC_PPT_5_Conditions file. Do you prefer using Google Slides or PowerPoint? Why?

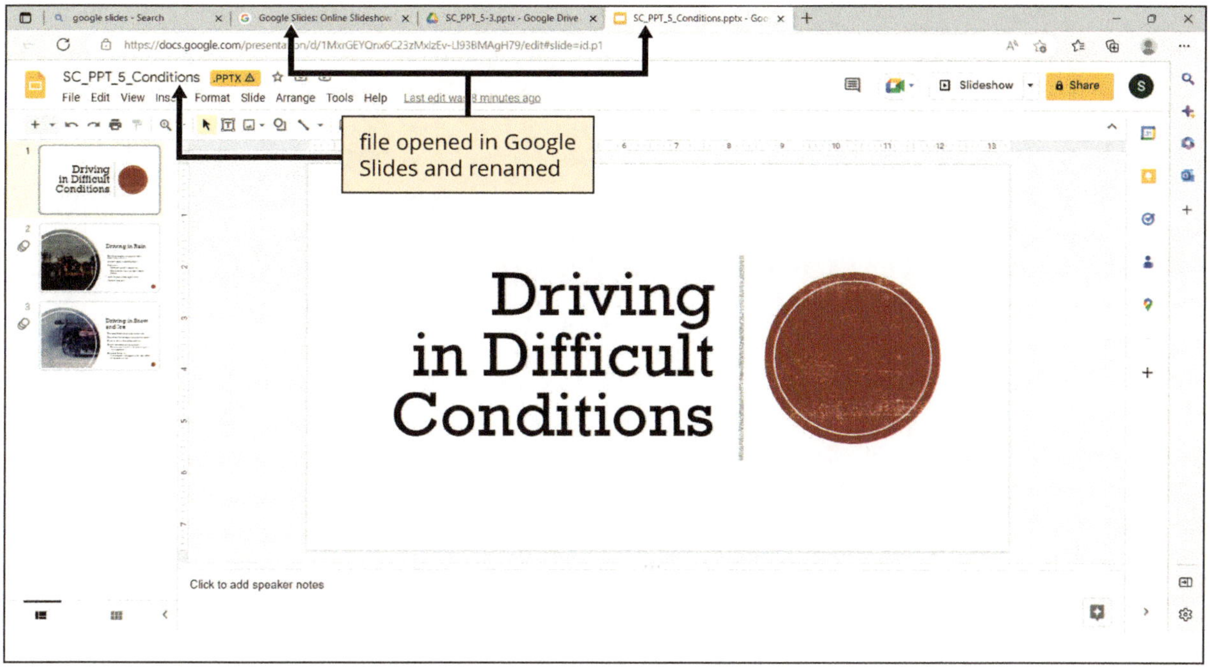

Valeriia Miller/Pexels; Geni Hoka/Pexels

Figure 5–127

In the Lab

Apply your creative thinking and problem-solving skills to design and implement a solution.

Design and Create a Presentation about Getting a Car Loan

Part 1: The credit union near your school is planning a seminar for recent college graduates on the topic of car loans. The branch managers have begun developing content for PowerPoint slides and have located some pictures they would like to use in the presentation. They want to provide information about how graduates should prepare to obtain a loan and some of the terms they will encounter during the application process. Part of the loan process involves preparation, including budgeting, checking their credit report, securing required documents, and determining the best interest rates. Applicants will encounter many financial terms in the loan agreement, such as the annual percentage rate, the required down payment, and how much they will pay over the course of the loan. You agree to help them complete the project by developing slides. Perform some research about the process of obtaining a car loan and then create slides with animation. At least two of the slides should have bulleted lists with customized bullets and animation. Create the animation for one slide and then use the Animation Painter to copy these effects to another slide. Provide alt text when necessary. Change the line spacing for the bulleted lists. The Data Files folder contains pictures you could use. Add a comment asking for the branch managers' approval of your work. Review and revise your presentation as needed and then save the file using the file name, **SC_PPT_5_Loan**. Submit your assignment in the format specified by your instructor.

Part 2: **Consider This:** You made several decisions while creating the presentation in this assignment: what content to include, how to format the bulleted list, what text or pictures to animate, and which styles and effects to apply. What was the rationale behind each of these decisions? Where would you recommend showing this slide show? When you reviewed the document, what changes did you make?

Formatting Tables and Charts

Objectives

After completing this module, you will be able to:

- Insert slides from an outline
- Edit an embedded file
- Insert an object from a file
- Draw a table
- Format a table
- Resize, split, and distribute table columns and rows
- Insert and edit a linked Excel worksheet
- Switch chart rows and columns
- Change a chart type and layout
- Apply effects to chart elements
- Edit chart data
- Update linked objects
- Add a link to a file
- Navigate between slides in Reading and Outline views

Introduction

Adding visuals to a presentation can help audience members remember the important facts you want to share. Researchers have found that adding graphics such as tables, charts, graphs, and maps increases retention by more than 50 percent. Audiences also believe that speakers who include visuals in their presentations are more qualified and believable than speakers who do not have accompanying visuals. In addition, studies have shown that meeting times are reduced and decisions are reached more quickly when group members have seen visuals that help them reach a consensus.

PowerPoint has many features that allow you to insert visuals and then modify them directly on the slide. For example, you can embed a Word document and then edit its text or replace its graphics. You can link an Excel worksheet with a PowerPoint slide so that when numbers are modified in the slide, the corresponding numbers on the worksheet also are updated. These tools help you work productively and generate slides with graphics that help your audience comprehend and remember your message.

BTW
Using Tables and Charts
Charts and tables help audiences understand abstract concepts and the relationships between sets of data. These tools can give meaning to the figures and facts you want to emphasize in your presentation. Present only one main idea in a chart or table. Overloading your slides with data may confuse your audience and defeat the purpose of these graphical elements.

Project: Presentation with Embedded and Linked Files and Formatted Table and Chart

Fun runs are popular in many communities because they are enjoyable, stress-free events that bring families, friends, and co-workers together. The goal is for participants of all fitness levels to have fun while getting some exercise. The course distance often varies so that beginners easily can cross the finish line while experienced runners can challenge their times and speeds. Prizes can be awarded for first-place finishers, and people share a sense of accomplishment to cross

BTW
Checking for Accessibility Issues
As you develop tables and other slide elements, you may want to check the presentation for content that people with disabilities may be unable to read. To identify possible accessibility problems, display the Info tab in Backstage view and notice if the message, 'Content that people with disabilities are unable to read', is displayed next to the 'Check for Issues' button. If so, click the 'Check for Issues' button and then click Check Accessibility in the menu. The Accessibility Checker pane will display issues you can address.

the finish line and join the festivities awaiting them. Many fun runs are organized by charitable organizations, and the small entry fee and merchandise sales help raise funds for worthy causes.

In this module's project, you will follow proper design guidelines and learn to use PowerPoint to create the slides shown in Figure 6–1a through 6–1h. The objective is to produce a presentation that will be shown at fitness centers and sporting equipment stores in the city and suburbs to promote the Fun Run scheduled for June 21. You begin by importing a Word outline with the slide titles. On Slide 1 (Figure 6–1a), you insert and edit a flyer with graphics and text (Figure 6–1b) created in Word. You decide that the word, Fun, should be changed from multiple font colors to one color, so you edit this word directly on the slide.

The Fun Run promoters have used Excel to record data on the number of t-shirts and sweatshirts people have ordered. Slide 2 (Figure 6–1c) shows this Excel chart (Figure 6–1d), which you copy and then format. You obtain updated sales data, so you update the worksheet data that generated the chart, which, in turn, modifies the chart automatically.

The third slide (Figure 6–1e) includes a table that you draw and enhance using PowerPoint's tools and graphical features. The table shows the five course distances, start times, and prizes for the first-place finishers. If you click the title text when running the presentation, a linked Adobe PDF file displays showing the certificate all participants will receive (Figure 6–1f).

People have been registering for the past five months. The event promoters have tracked each month whether the participants are living in the city or the suburbs in a chart shown on Slide 4 (Figure 6–1g). This chart is inserted from an Excel worksheet (Figure 6–1h). Projected registrations also are included in the spreadsheet, and you will update these figures based on inquiries made via text and social media. The spreadsheet is linked to Slide 4, so once the numbers change in the spreadsheet, the updated numbers change on the slide.

Figure 6–1(a): Slide 1 (Title Slide)

Figure 6–1(b): Original Word Document

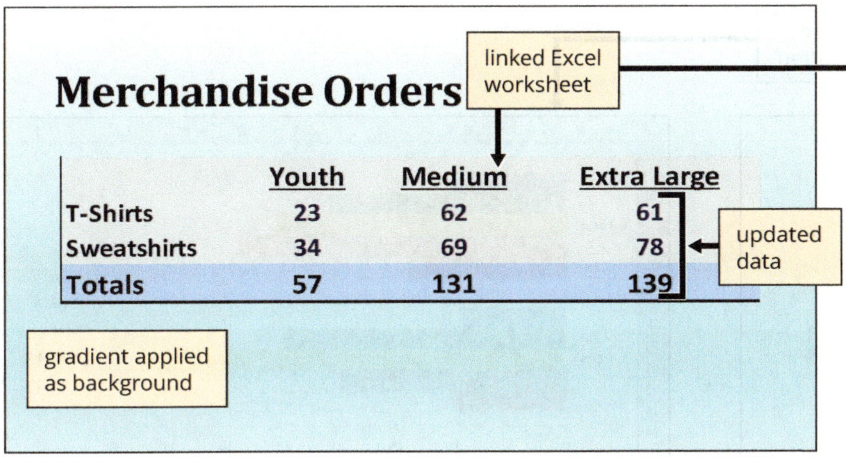

Figure 6–1(c): Slide 2

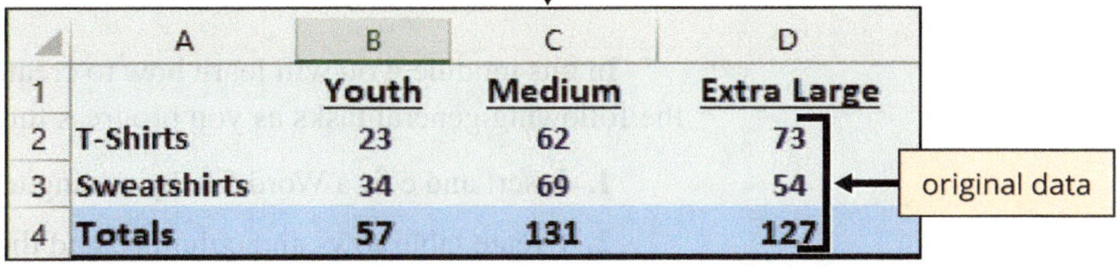

Figure 6–1(d): Original Excel Worksheet

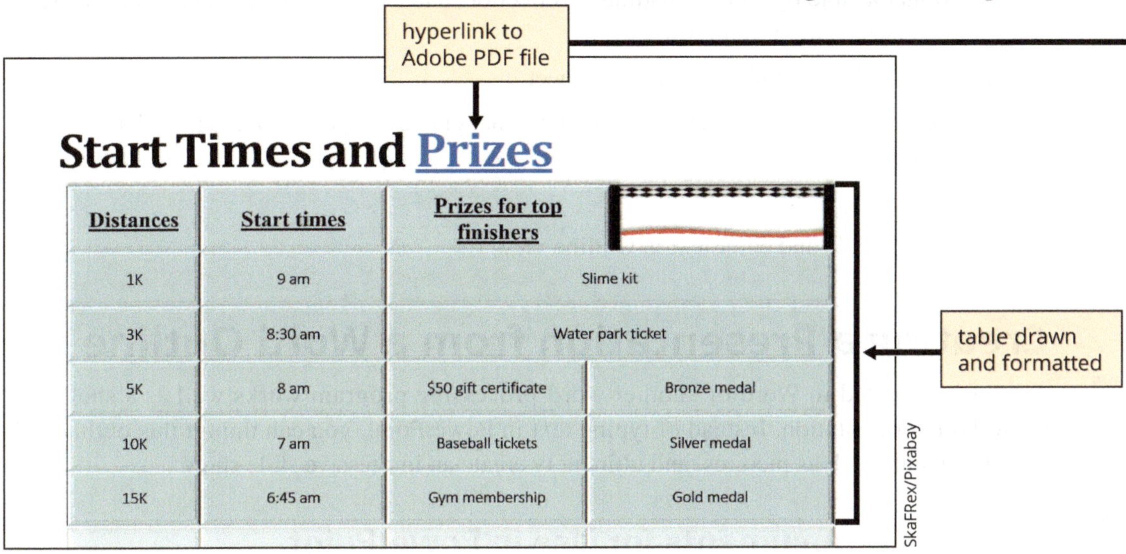

Figure 6–1(e): Slide 3

Figure 6–1(f): Hyperlinked Adobe PDF File

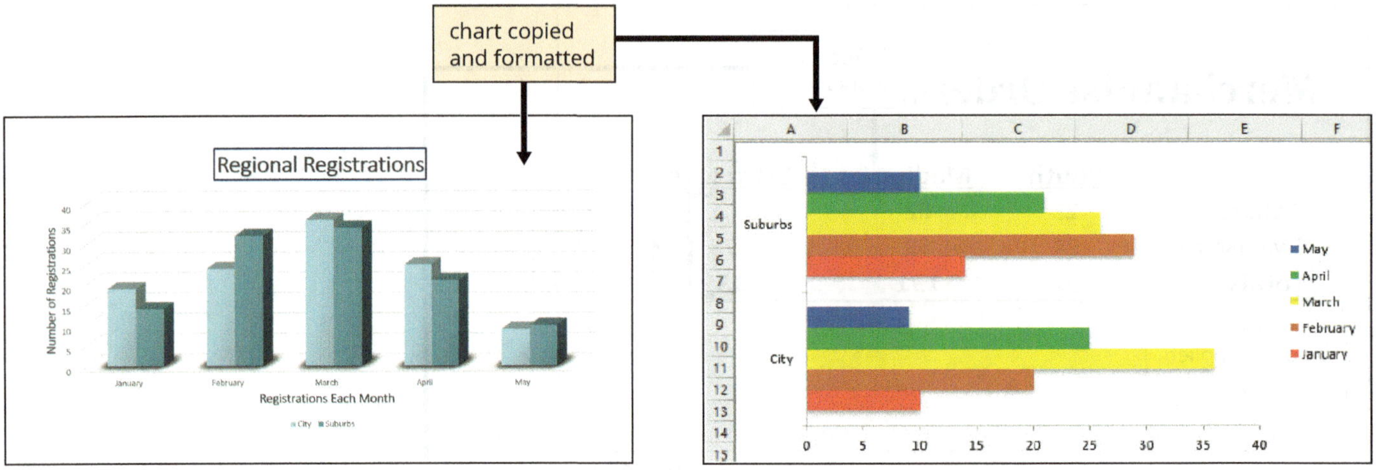

Figure 6–1(g): Slide 4

Figure 6–1(h): Original Excel Chart

In this module, you will learn how to create the slides shown in Figure 6–1. You will perform the following general tasks as you progress through this module:

1. Insert and edit a Word file by adding text.
2. Create table rows and columns, and then erase lines and split columns and rows.
3. Format a table by adding shading, a reflection, and a cell bevel, and then distribute rows and resize columns and rows.
4. Insert and edit a linked Excel worksheet.
5. Copy, format, and edit an Excel chart by changing the type, colors, legend, labels, and data.
6. Add a link to text.
7. Move a slide and enter text in Outline view.

Creating a Presentation from a Word Outline

An outline created in Word or another word-processing program works well as a shell for a PowerPoint presentation. Instead of typing text in PowerPoint, you can import this outline, add visual elements such as pictures, and ultimately create an impressive slide show.

Converting Documents for Use in PowerPoint

PowerPoint can produce slides based on an outline created in Word, another word-processing program, or a webpage if the text was saved in a format that PowerPoint can recognize. Word files use the **.docx** file extension in their file names. Text originating in other word-processing programs for later use with PowerPoint should be saved in Rich Text Format (.rtf) or plain text (.txt). Webpage documents that use an HTML extension (.htm or .html) also can be imported.

PowerPoint automatically opens Microsoft 365 files, and many other types of files, in the PowerPoint format. When you insert a Word document into a presentation, PowerPoint creates an outline structure based on heading styles in the document. A Heading 1 in a source document becomes a slide title in PowerPoint, a Heading 2 becomes the first level of content text on the slide, a Heading 3 becomes the second level of text on the slide, and so on.

If the original document contains no heading styles, PowerPoint creates an outline based on paragraphs. For example, in a .docx or .rtf file, for several lines of text styled as Normal and broken into paragraphs, PowerPoint turns each paragraph into a slide title.

BTW

Defining Outline Levels

Imported outlines can have a maximum of nine outline levels, whereas PowerPoint outlines are limited to six levels (one for the title text and five for body paragraph text). When you import an outline, all text in outline levels six through nine is treated as a fifth-level paragraph.

BTW

Ribbon and Screen Resolution

PowerPoint may change how the groups and buttons within the groups appear on the ribbon, depending on the screen resolution of your computer. Thus, your ribbon may look different from the ones in this book if you are using a screen resolution other than 1920 × 1080.

To Insert Slides from an Outline

The title text for the Run presentation is contained in a Word file. The following steps open this Word outline located in the Data Files as a presentation in PowerPoint. **Why?** Instead of typing text for each of the four PowerPoint slides, you can open a Word outline and have PowerPoint create the slides automatically.

1

- sam Run PowerPoint, create a blank presentation, and then apply the Metropolitan theme. If necessary, maximize the PowerPoint window. If the Design Ideas pane opens, close it.
- Save the presentation using the file name, **SC_PPT_6_Run**.

2

- Display the Home tab and then click the New Slide arrow (Home tab | Slides group) to display the New Slide gallery (Figure 6–2).

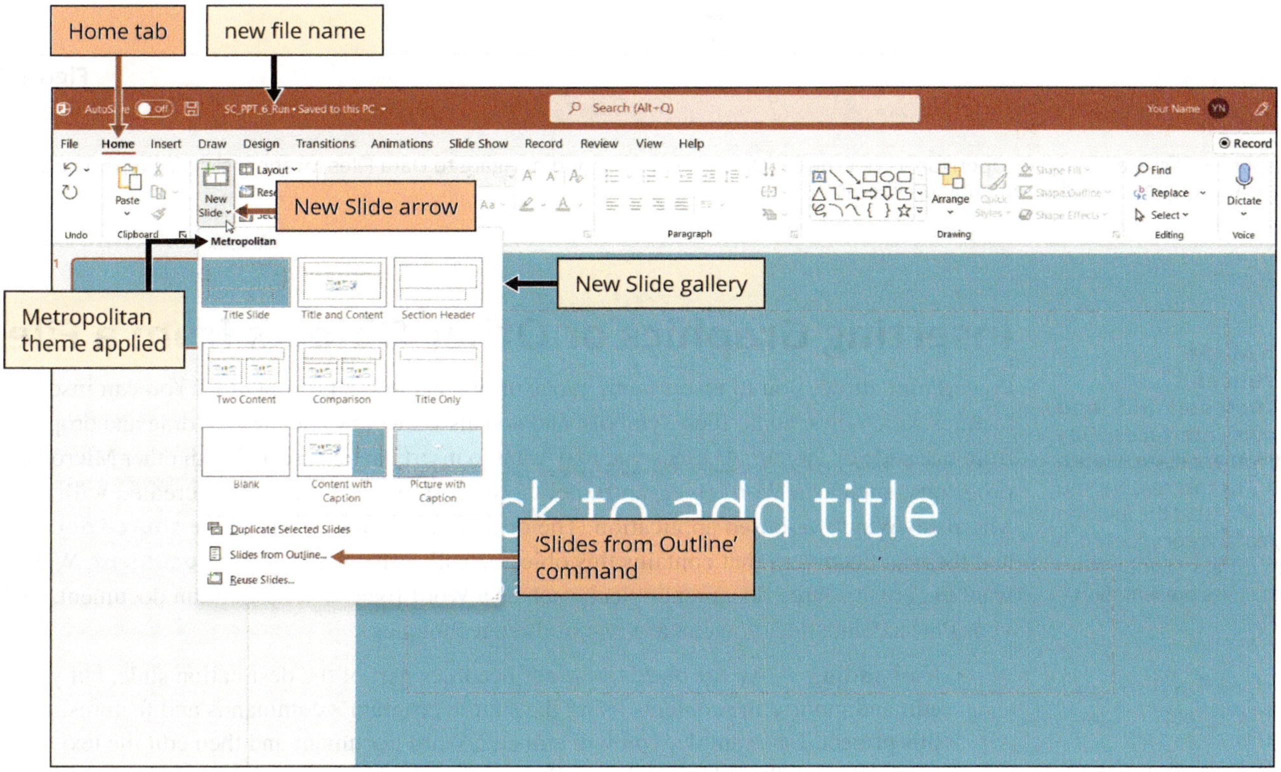

Figure 6–2

3

- Click 'Slides from Outline' to display the Insert Outline dialog box.
- Navigate to the location of the Data Files and then click Support_PPT_6_Run_Outline.docx to select the file (Figure 6–3).

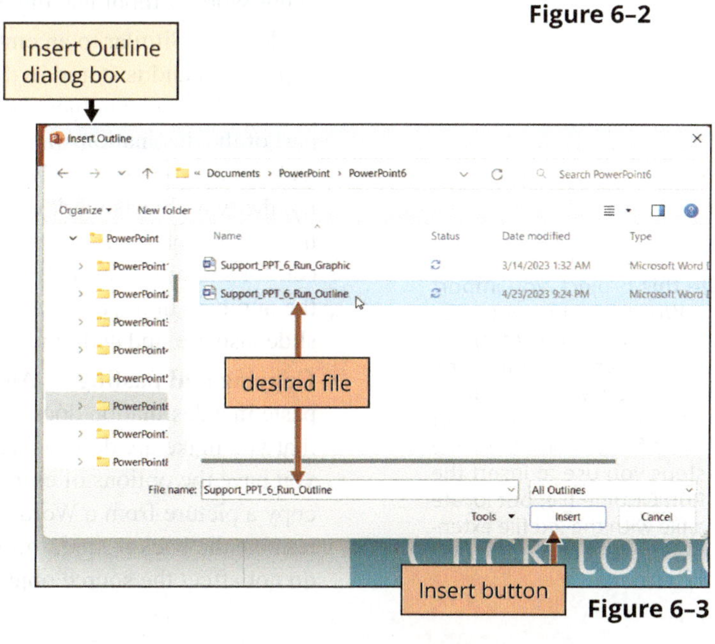

Figure 6–3

4

- Click the Insert button (Insert Outline dialog box) to add three slides based on your outline to your presentation (Figure 6–4).

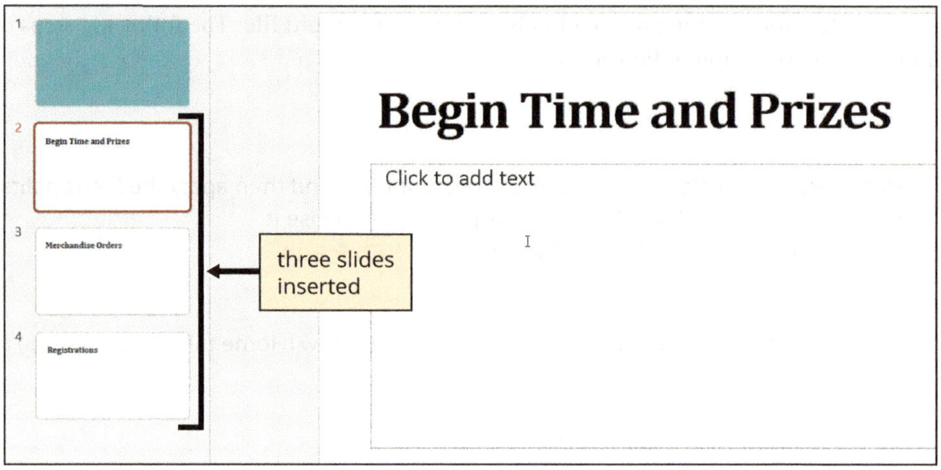

Figure 6–4

Other Ways

1. Display Backstage view, click Open tab, click Browse (Open dialog box) and navigate to Data Files location, click file type arrow, click All Outlines, click desired outline, click Insert

BTW
Touch Mode Differences
The Microsoft 365 and Windows interfaces may vary if you are using a touch screen. For this reason, you might notice that the function or appearance of your touch screen differs slightly from this module's presentation.

Inserting Graphics or Other Objects from a File

PowerPoint allows you to insert many types of objects into a presentation. You can insert clips, pictures, video files, audio files, symbols, and you also can copy and paste or drag and drop objects from one slide to another. At times you may want to insert content created with other Microsoft 365 programs, such as a Word flyer, an Excel table or graph, or a document created with another Microsoft Windows-based application. The original document is called the **source document**, and the new document that contains this object is called the **destination document**. When you want to copy a source document object, such as a Word flyer, to a destination document, such as your PowerPoint slide, you can use one of three techniques.

- **Embedding** — An **embedded object** becomes part of the destination slide, but you edit and modify the contents using the source program's commands and features. In this project, for example, you will embed a Word document and then edit the text using Word without leaving PowerPoint.
- **Linking** — Similar to an embedded object, a **linked object** also is created in another application and is stored in the **source file**, the original file in which the object was created. The linked object maintains a connection to its source and does not become part of the destination slide. Instead, a connection, or link, made between the source and destination objects gives the appearance that the objects are independent. In reality, the two objects work together so that when one is edited, the other is updated. If the original object is changed, the linked object on the slide also changes. In this project, for example, you will link an Excel table and then edit the data using Excel. As the numbers in the table change, the numbers in the linked table on the PowerPoint slide also are updated to reflect those changes.
- **Copying and pasting** — An object that you copy from a source document and then paste in a destination document becomes part of the destination program. Any edits that you make are done using the destination software. When you paste the object, you have the options of embedding or linking the document. For example, if you copy a picture from a Word document, embed it into your slide, and then recolor or remove the background, those changes are made using PowerPoint's commands and do not affect the source object.

BTW
Importing Text Files
In this project, you import a Word file, but you also can import a text (.txt) file, which has alphanumeric characters with little or no visual formatting. To import a text file, perform the same steps you use to insert the Run Outline file, but locate a file with the .txt file extension instead of the .docx file extension.

The first two techniques described above are termed **object linking and embedding** (**OLE**, pronounced o-lay). This means of sharing material developed in various sources and then updating the files within a destination program is useful when you deliver presentations frequently that display current data that changes constantly. For example, your PowerPoint presentation may contain a chart reflecting current registration statistics, or you may include a table with merchandise ordered totals for the event.

The first object you will add to your presentation is a graphical flyer created in Word. This flyer contains artwork and text developed as part of a promotion for the Fun Run. You desire to use this document in your slide show because the image and text fit the topic of your presentation.

To Delete a Placeholder

When you run a slide show, empty placeholders do not display. You may desire to delete unused placeholders from a slide. **Why?** By deleting them, they will not be a distraction when you are designing slide content. The title and subtitle text placeholders on Slide 1 are not required for this presentation, so you can remove them. The following steps remove the Slide 1 title and subtitle text placeholders.

1

- Display Slide 1 and then click a border of the title text placeholder so that it displays as a solid or finely dotted line (Figure 6–5).

title text placeholder border displays as solid line

Figure 6–5

2

- Press DELETE to remove the title text placeholder.

Q&A Can I also click the Cut button to delete the placeholder?
Yes. Generally, however, the Cut button is used when you desire to remove a selected slide element, place it on the Clipboard, and then paste it in another area. The DELETE key is used when you do not want to reuse that particular slide element.

3

- Click a border of the subtitle text placeholder to select it (Figure 6–6).

4

- Press DELETE to remove the subtitle placeholder.

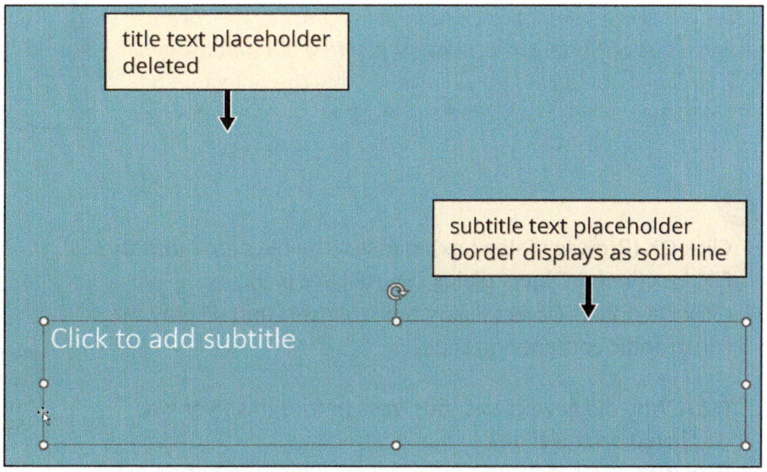

Figure 6–6

Other Ways

1. Select placeholder, press BACKSPACE
2. Right-click placeholder border, click Cut on shortcut menu

To Embed an Object from Another App

The first object you will add to your presentation is the artwork that was created for a graphical flyer being created in Word. This flyer eventually will be completed by promotions committee volunteers, and it contains a colorful graphic and text that should generate interest in the Fun Run. You desire to use this document in your slide show. **Why?** The flyer will be distributed to community members when they arrive at fitness centers and shop at sporting equipment stores. It will contain pertinent information about the Fun Run date, times, distances, and prizes. The following steps insert a Word file with a graphic and text.

1

- Display the Insert tab and then click the Object button (Insert tab | Text group) to display the Insert Object dialog box (Figure 6–7).

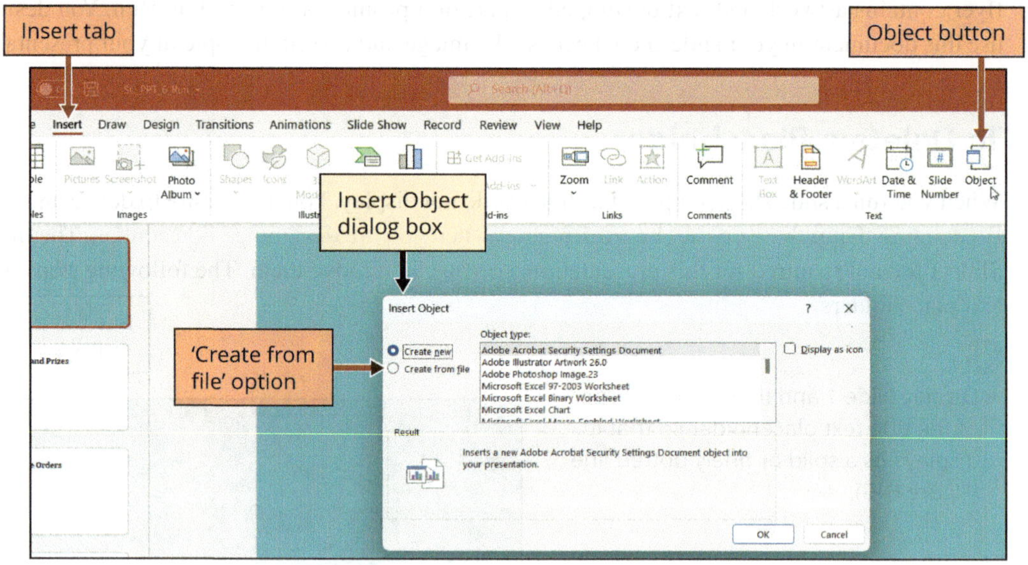

Figure 6–7

2

- Click 'Create from file' (Insert Object dialog box) to display the File box.
- Click the Browse button and then navigate to the location of the Data Files.
- Click Support_PPT_6_Run_Graphic.docx to select the Word file (Figure 6–8).

Q&A What is the difference between the 'Create new' and the 'Create from file' options?
The 'Create new' option opens an application and allows you to develop an original object. In contrast, the 'Create from file' option prompts you to locate a file that already is created and saved so you can modify the object using the program that was used to create it.

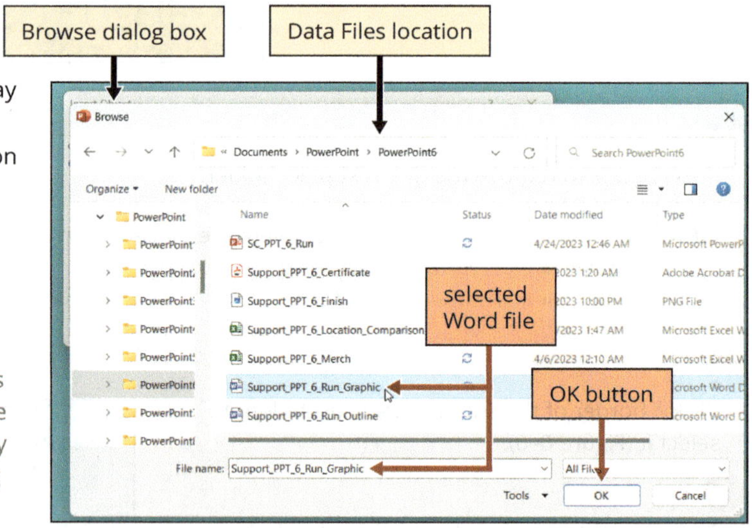

Figure 6–8

3

- Click OK (Browse dialog box) to insert the file name into the File box (Insert Object dialog box) (Figure 6–9).
- Click OK (Insert Object dialog box) to insert and display the run graphic contents on Slide 1.

Q&A Why did several seconds pass before this flyer was displayed on the slide?
PowerPoint takes more time to insert embedded and linked inserted objects than it takes to perform an ordinary cut-and-paste or copy-and-paste action. You must be patient while PowerPoint is inserting the object.

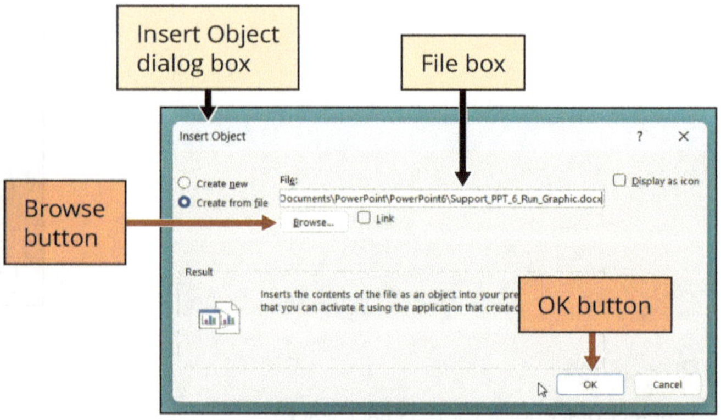

Figure 6–9

4

- Display the Shape Format tab and then click the Height up arrow to increase the height of the run graphic to 6".
- Click the Align button (Shape Format tab | Arrange group) to display the Align menu (Figure 6–10).

5

- Click Align Center to position the run graphic in the center of the slide.
- Click the Align button again and then click Align Middle to position the run graphic in the middle of the slide.

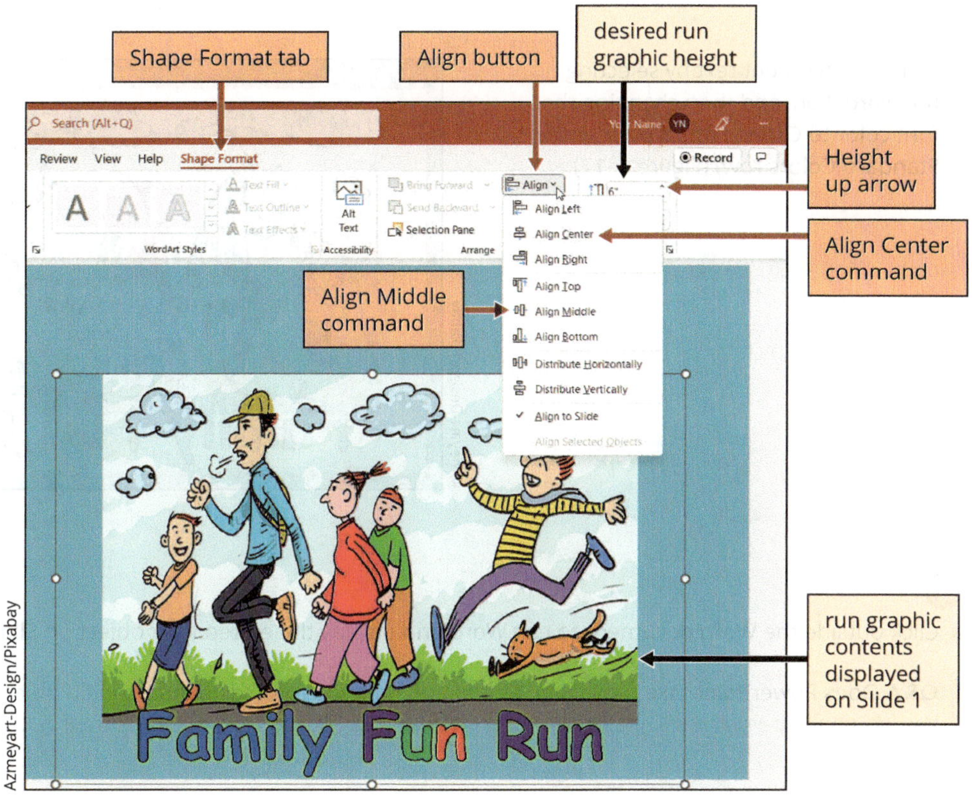

Figure 6–10

To Edit an Embedded File

The run graphic provides an excellent image and text to use on Slide 1, but you want to edit the text by changing the multiple colors in the word, Fun, to one color, orange. **Why?** You want to call attention to the fun aspect of the event, and the orange color is bright and vibrant. PowerPoint allows you to edit an embedded file easily by opening the source program, which in this case is Word. The following steps edit the Word text.

1

- Double-click the embedded run graphic to run Word and open the document on Slide 1 (Figure 6–11).

Figure 6–11

2

- Edit the document text by selecting the word, Fun, and then changing the font color to Orange (third color in the Standard Colors row) (Figure 6–12).

Figure 6–12

3

- Click outside the Word document to exit Word and display the edited flyer object on Slide 1.

Q&A Does PowerPoint take more time to position embedded objects than copied objects?
Yes, you must be patient while PowerPoint responds to your touch, mouse, or arrow key movements.

Other Ways

1. Right-click Word object, click Document Object on shortcut menu, click Edit

Drawing and Formatting a Table

Tables are useful graphical elements to present data organized in descriptive rows and columns. Each cell created from the intersection of a row and column has a unique location name and contains numeric or textual data that you can edit.

In the following steps, you will perform these tasks on Slide 2:

1. Draw a table.
2. Draw table rows and columns.
3. Erase a table border and enter text in a table.
4. Split a table cell.
5. Add bevel and shadow effects.
6. Distribute table rows.
7. Align data in cells.
8. Center the table and format table data.

Consider This

Develop tables that are clear and meaningful.

Use a table to present complex material, but be certain the information makes useful comparisons. Tables generally are used to show relationships between sets of data. For example, they may show prices for grades of gasoline in three states, the number of in-state and out-of-state students who have applied for admission to various college programs, or the rushing and passing records among quarterbacks in a particular league. The units of measurement, such as dollars, specific majors, or yards, should be expressed clearly on the slides. The data in the rows and columns should be aligned uniformly. Also, the table labels should be meaningful and easily read.

To Draw a Table

PowerPoint allows you to insert a table in several ways. You can click the Table button on the Insert tab (Tables group) and click the Insert Table command. You also can click the Insert Table button in a content placeholder. Another method that allows flexibility is to draw the entire table. However, you must use a mouse or other pointing device to use the Draw Table command. The following steps draw a table on Slide 2. **Why?** This method allows flexibility to draw the outer edges and then add the columns and rows.

1

- Display Slide 2, click a border of the content placeholder, and then press DELETE to remove this placeholder.

2

- Display the View tab and then, if necessary, select the Ruler check box (View tab | Show group) to display the horizontal and vertical rulers (Figure 6–13).

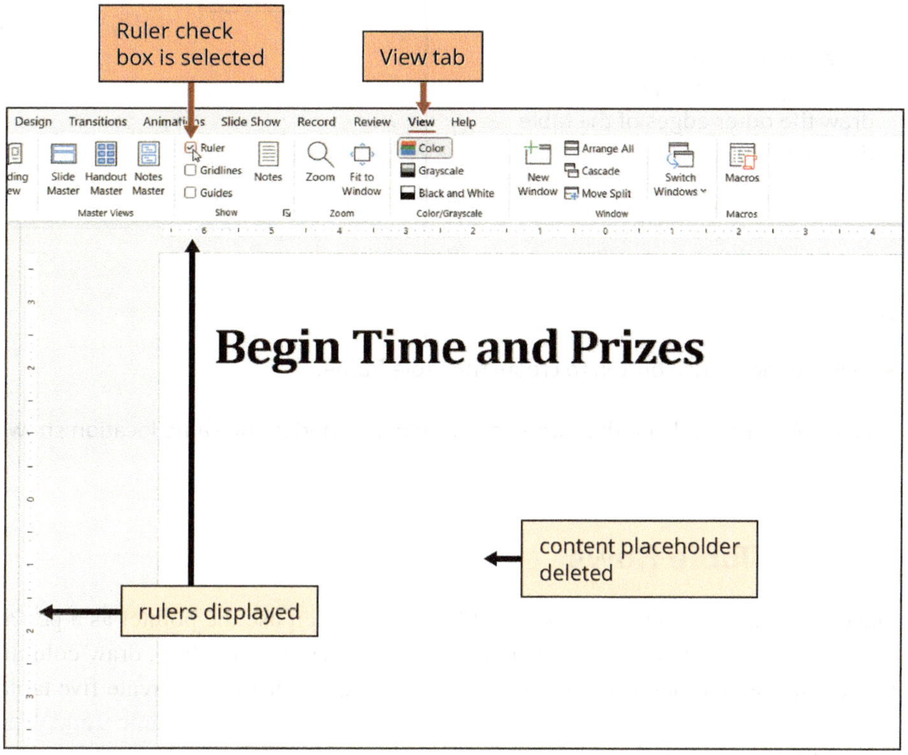

Figure 6–13

3

- Display the Insert tab and then click the Table button (Insert tab | Tables group) to display the Insert Table gallery (Figure 6–14).

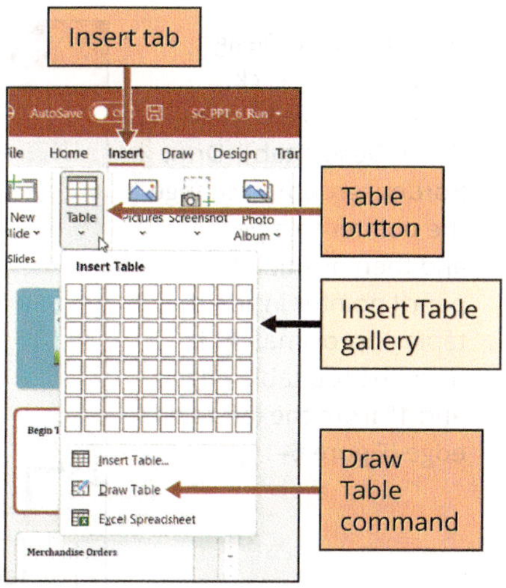

Figure 6–14

4

- Click Draw Table and then position the pointer, which has the shape of a pencil, under the word, Begin, in the upper-left area of the slide.

Q&A If I decide I do not want to draw a table, how can I change the pointer to the block arrow?
Press ESC.

- Drag the pencil pointer to the lower-right corner of the slide to draw the outer edges of the table (Figure 6–15).

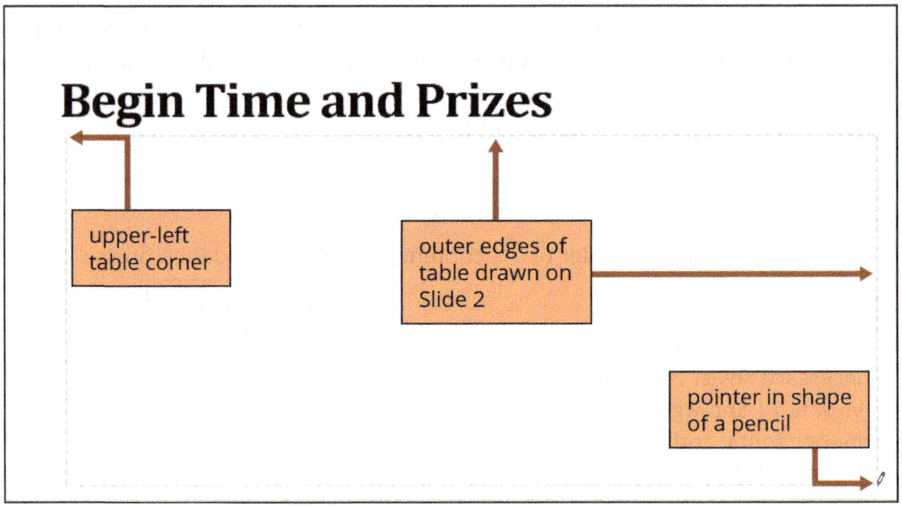

Figure 6–15

5

- Release the mouse button to create the table frame.

Q&A Must my table be the same size or be positioned in the same location shown in the figure?
No. You will resize and reposition the table later in this project.

To Draw Table Rows

Once you draw the four sides of the table, you then can use the pointer as a pencil to draw lines for the columns and rows in the positions where you desire them to display. You could, therefore, draw columns having different widths and rows that are spaced in irregular heights. The following steps draw four lines to create five table rows. **Why?** The first row will contain the table title, and the remaining rows will list specific distances, start times, and prizes. You must use a mouse or other pointing device to draw table rows.

1

- With the Table Design tab displayed, click the Draw Table button (Table Design tab | Draw Borders group) to change the pointer to a pencil and then position the pencil pointer inside the table approximately 1" from the top table edge and 1" from the left table edge (Figure 6–16).

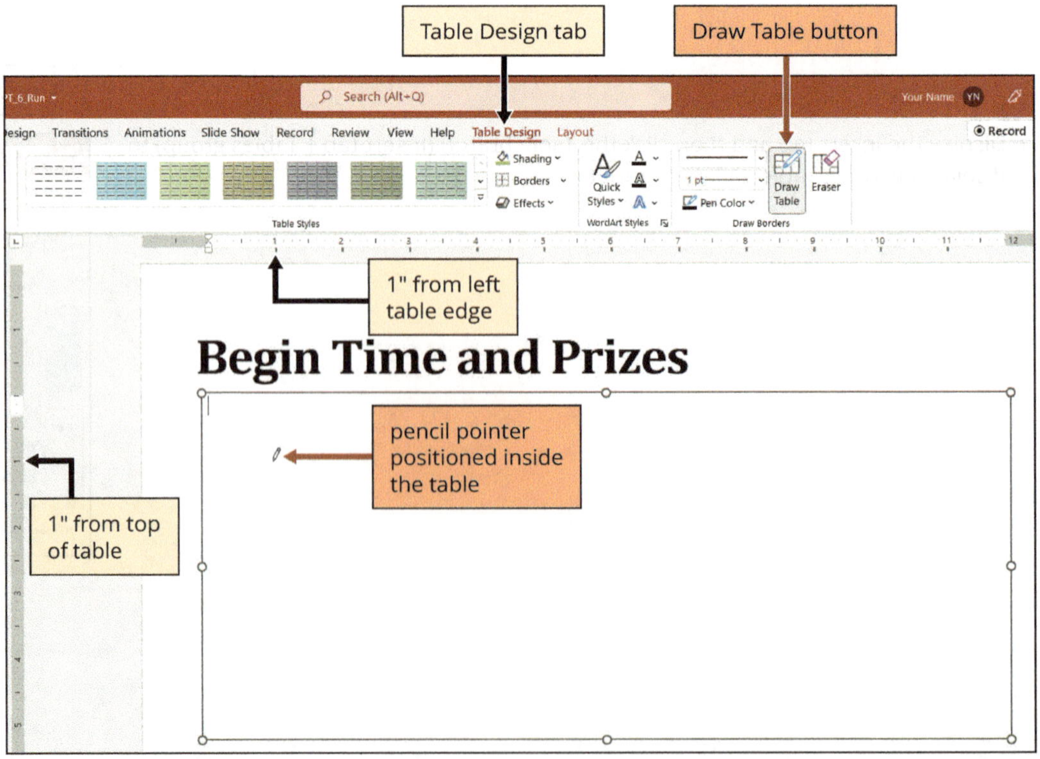

Figure 6–16

2

- Drag the pencil pointer to the right to draw a horizontal line across the entire table and divide it into two cells (Figure 6–17).

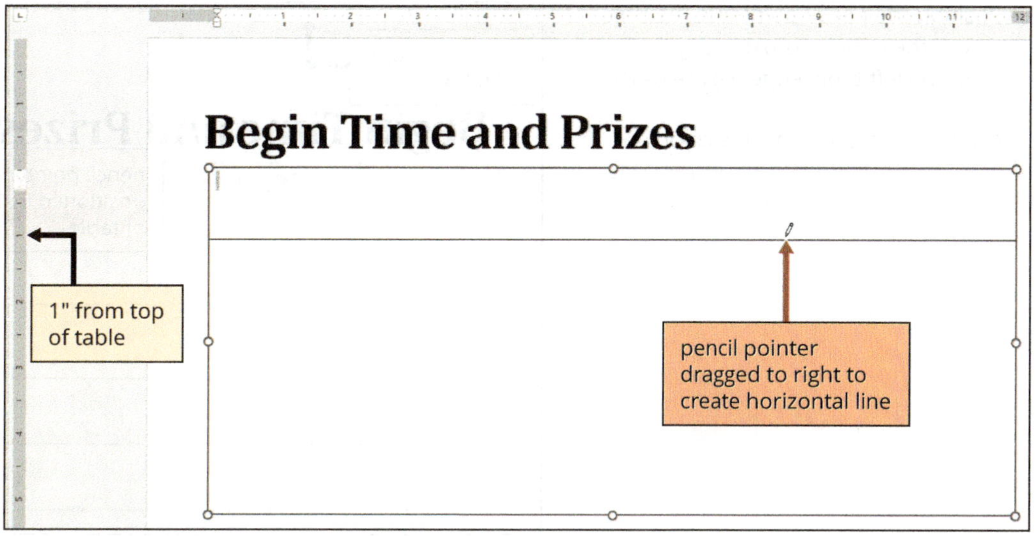

Figure 6–17

Q&A Should I drag the pencil pointer to the right edge of the table?
No. PowerPoint will draw a complete line when you begin to move the pencil pointer in one direction.

If I drew the line in an incorrect location, how can I erase it?
Press CTRL+Z, click the Undo button on the Quick Access Toolbar, or click the Eraser button (Table Design tab | Draw Borders group) and then click the line.

3

- Draw three additional horizontal lines, as shown in Figure 6–18. When you start drawing the lines, place your pencil pointer at a location away from the table border, not at a border, to prevent creating a new table.

Figure 6–18

Q&A How can I get my pencil pointer to reappear if it no longer is displayed?
Click the Draw Table button again.

Do I need to align the lines in the precise positions shown?
No. You will create evenly spaced rows later in this project.

To Draw Table Columns

The pencil pointer is useful to draw table columns with varying widths. Each distance row has one start time and either one or two prizes. The title row will be subdivided. **Why?** You want to add interest to the slide, so you will insert a picture in the upper-right table cell. The following steps draw three vertical lines to create columns. You must use a mouse or other pointing device to draw table columns.

1

- Position the pencil pointer in the first row of the table approximately 2.5" from the left table edge (Figure 6–19).

Q&A Can I change the line color?
Yes. Click the Pen Color button (Table Design tab | Draw Borders group) and then select a different color.

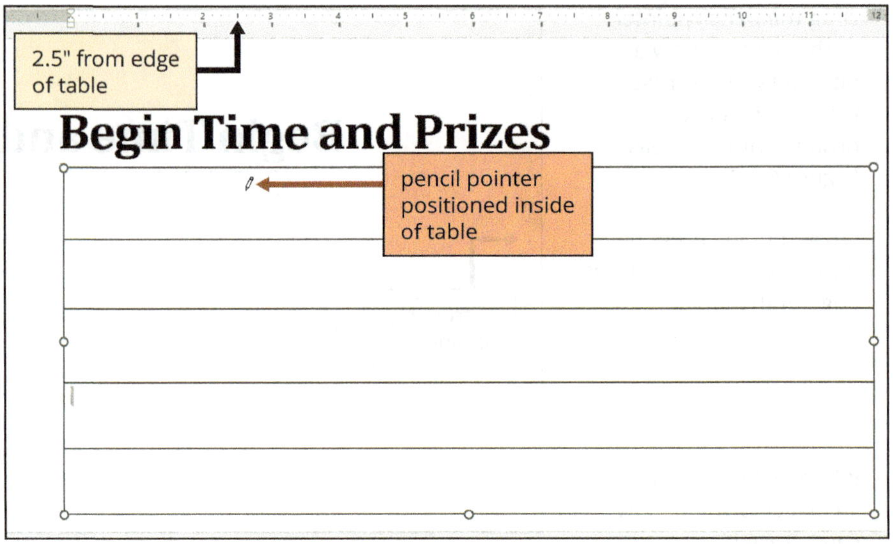

Figure 6–19

2

- Drag the pencil pointer down through all the horizontal lines to draw a vertical line that divides the table into 10 cells.
- Position the pencil pointer in the first row of the table approximately 5" from the left table edge (Figure 6–20).

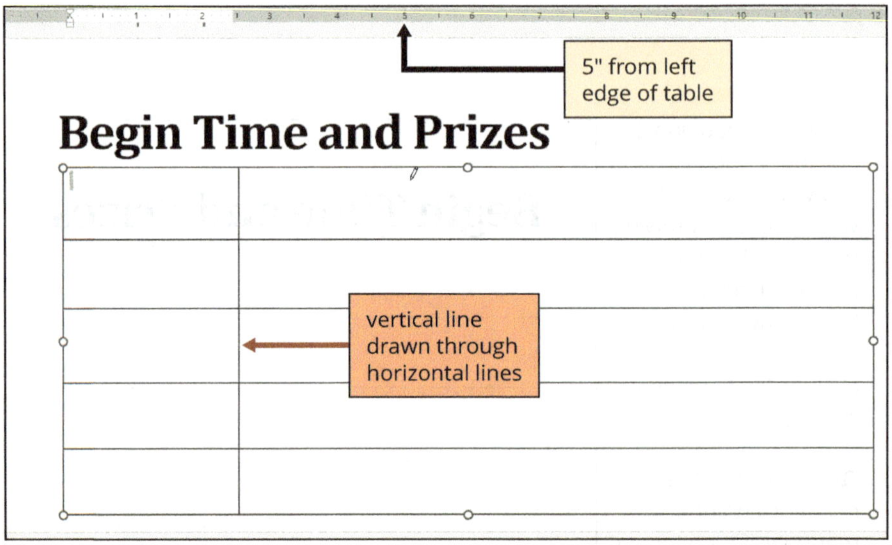

Figure 6–20

3

- Drag the pencil pointer down through all the horizontal lines to draw a vertical line that divides the table now into 15 cells.
- Position the pencil pointer in the middle of the right (last) cell in the second row and then drag down to the bottom edge of the table to draw a vertical line in second, third, fourth, and fifth rows (Figure 6–21).

Q&A Are vertical and horizontal lines the only types of lines I can draw?
No. You also can draw a diagonal line from one corner of a cell to another corner.

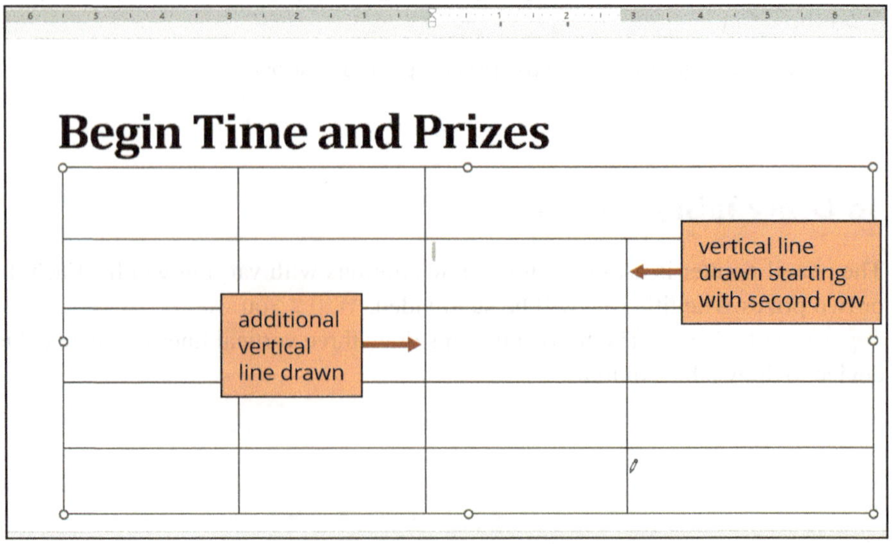

Figure 6–21

To Erase a Table Border

PowerPoint supplies an eraser tool that allows you to delete vertical and horizontal lines in a table. This eraser is useful to delete unnecessary column lines. You must use a mouse or other pointing device to use this tool. The following steps use the eraser to delete one vertical line in the second row. **Why?** You want to erase the vertical line because you need only three columns in this row, not four.

1

- Click the Eraser button (Table Design tab | Draw Borders group).
- Position the pointer, which has the shape of an eraser, over the rightmost vertical line in the second row (Figure 6–22).

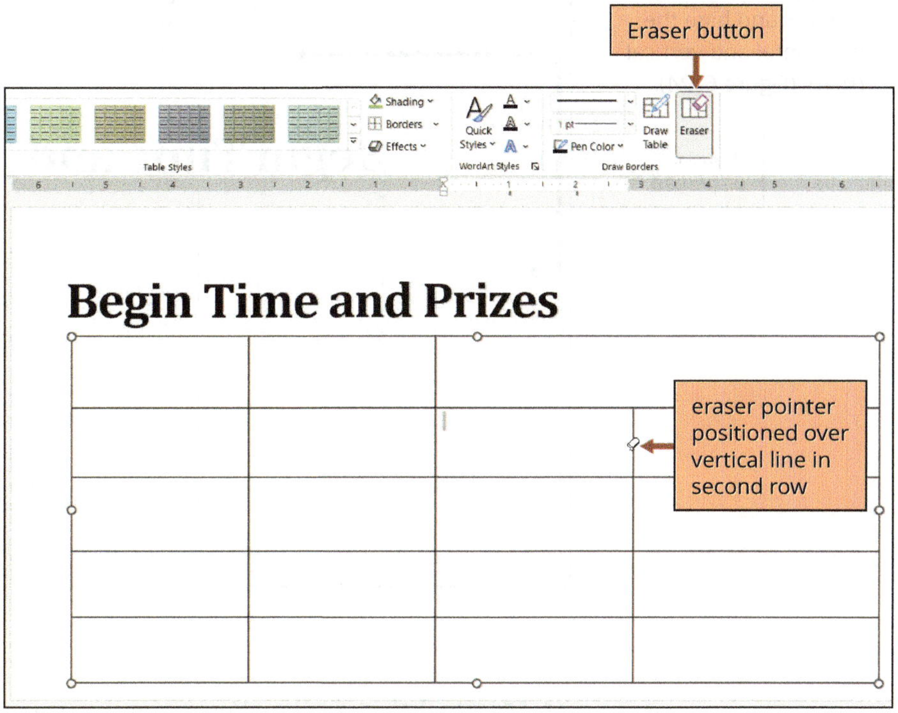

Figure 6–22

2

- Click the vertical line to erase it.
- Press ESC and then click inside the cell to change the pointer to the I-beam and display the insertion point (Figure 6–23).

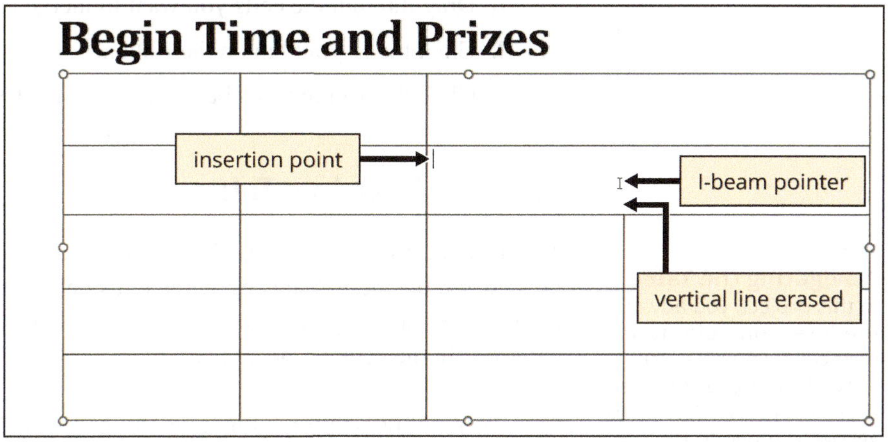

Figure 6–23

3

- Display the View tab and then click the Ruler check box (View tab | Show group) to uncheck the box and hide the horizontal and vertical rulers (Figure 6–24).

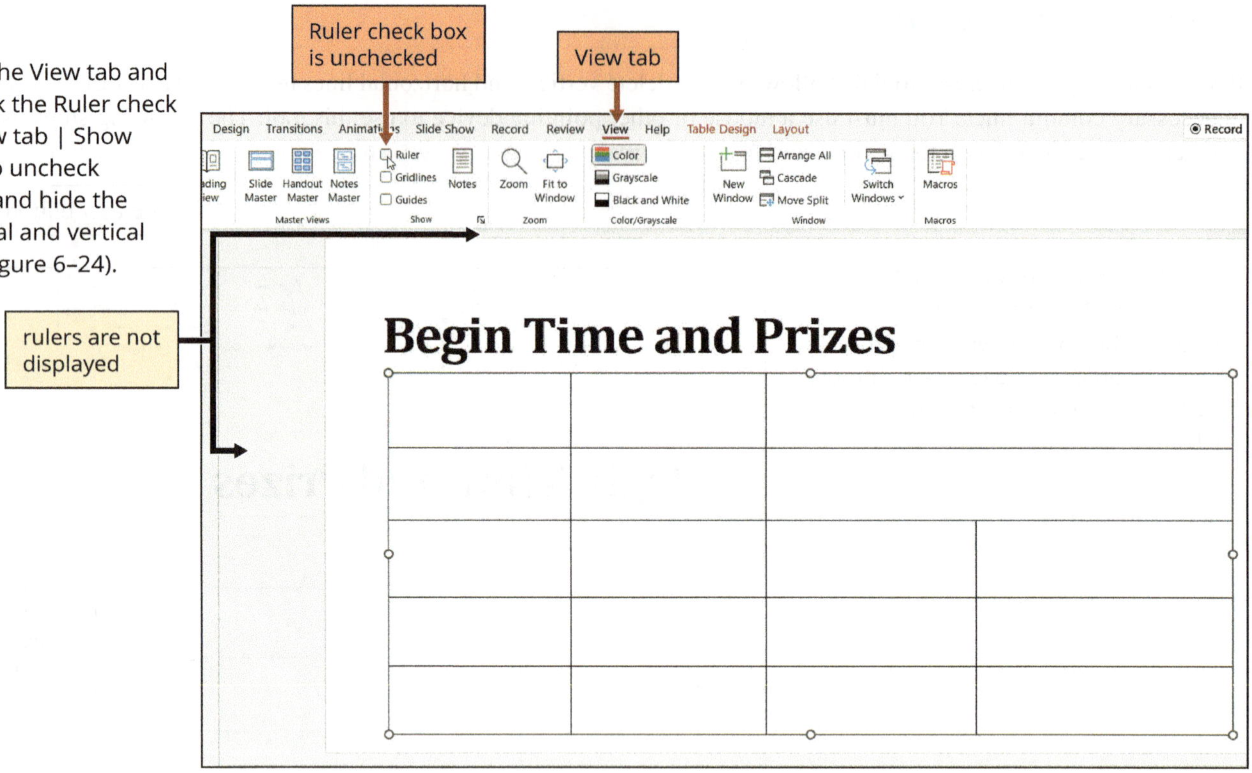

Figure 6–24

To Merge Table Cells You can merge two or more cells to create one large cell, making room for text or graphics. If you wanted to merge two or more cells in a table row or column into a single cell, you would perform the following steps. You may see a warning about an accessibility issue when you merge the table cells.

1. Drag through the cells you want to merge to select them.
2. Click the Layout tab on the ribbon.
3. Click the Merge Cells button (Layout tab | Merge group) to merge the cells into one cell.

To Enter Text in a Table

At this point, four distances will be featured in your table: 1K, 5K, 10K, and 15K. The table you created will list these distances on the left side of each row and give specific start times and prizes on the right side. To place data in a cell, you click the cell and then type text. The following steps enter text in the cells of the empty table.

BTW
Navigating the Table
In this project, you advance the insertion point to the next cell by pressing TAB. To move to the previous cell, press SHIFT+TAB. Press DOWN ARROW to move to the next row and UP ARROW to move up one row.

1. Position the pointer in the leftmost cell in the first row, click, and then type **Distances** in the cell. Press TAB to advance the insertion point to the second cell in the first row, type **Start times**, and then press TAB. Type **Prizes for top finishers** in the rightmost cell and then press TAB to advance the insertion point to the second row.

2. In the second row, type **1K** in the first cell, **9 am** in the second cell, and **Slime kit** in the third cell. Press TAB to advance the insertion point to the first cell in the third row.

3. In the third row, type **5K** in the first cell, **8 am** in the second cell, **$50 gift certificate** in the third cell, and **Bronze medal** in the last cell. Advance the insertion point to the first column of the fourth row.

4. In the fourth row, type **10K** in the first cell, **7 am** in the second cell, **Baseball tickets** in the third cell, and **Silver medal** in the last cell. Advance the insertion point to the first column of the last row.

5 In the last row, type **15K** in the first cell, **6:45 am** in the second cell, **Gym membership** in the third cell, and **Gold medal** in the last cell (Figure 6–25).

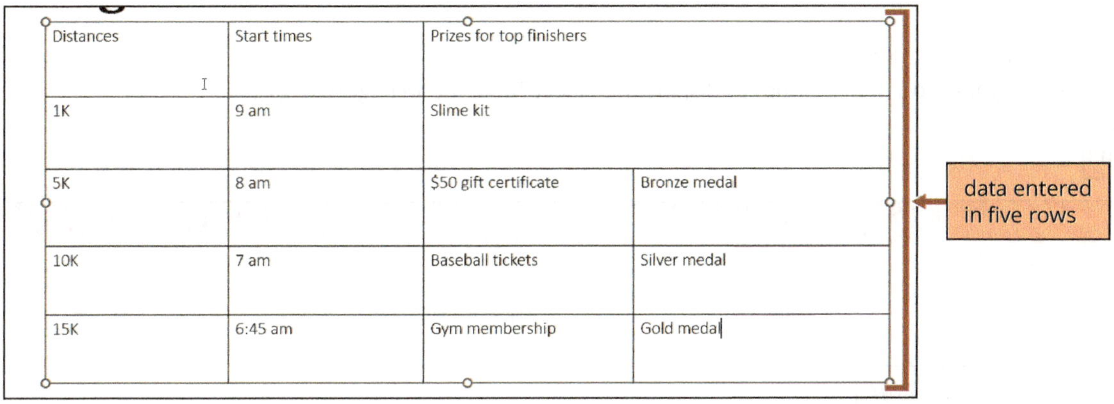

Figure 6–25

To Change the Direction of Text in a Table Cell By default, the text in a cell displays horizontally. You can, however, change the direction to rotate the text 90 degrees or 270 degrees, or you can stack the letters vertically. If you wanted to change the direction, you would perform the following steps.

1. Select the text you want to change and then click the Text Direction button (Layout tab | Alignment group) to display the Text Direction gallery.
2. Click the desired direction ('Rotate all text 90', 'Rotate all text 270', or Stacked) in the Text Direction gallery.

To Split Table Cells

You easily can create additional table columns and rows by dividing current cells and rows. The following steps use the Split Cells feature to divide a cell into two columns and to add a row. *Why? You want to add a cell for a picture in the first row and add another distance category below the 1K row.* You may see a warning about an accessibility issue when you split the table cells.

1

- Position the insertion point in the Prizes for top finishers cell.
- Click Layout on the ribbon to display the Layout tab and then click the Split Cells button (Layout tab | Merge group) to display the Split Cells dialog box (Figure 6–26).

Q&A Are the default numbers in the dialog box always 2 columns and 1 row?
Yes, but you can increase the numbers if you need to divide the cell into more than two halves or need to create two or more rows within one cell.

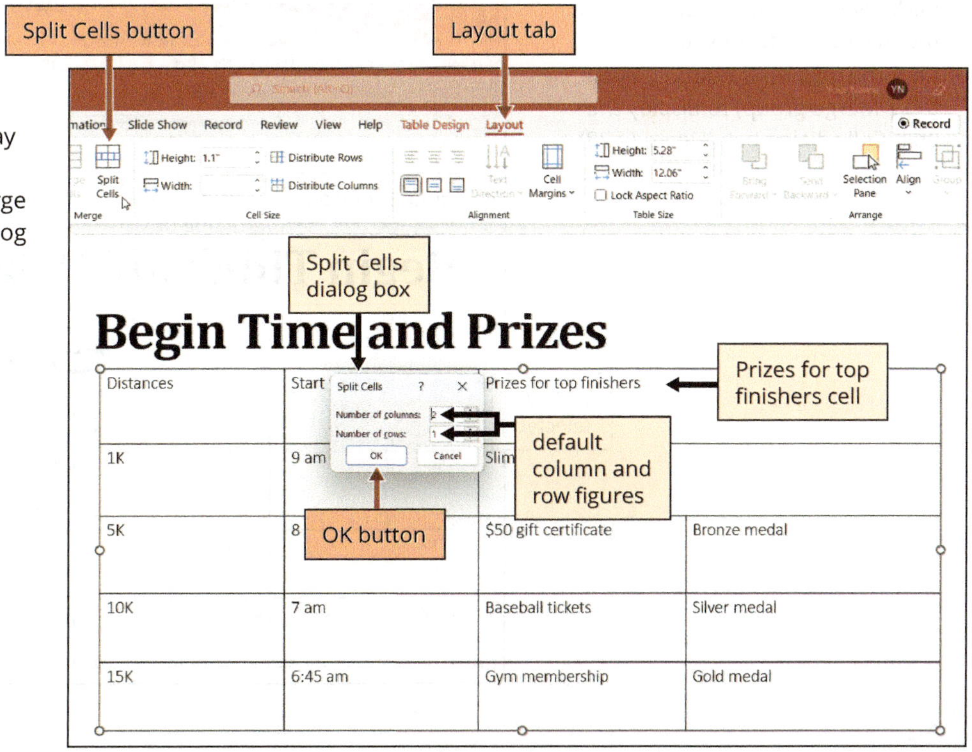

Figure 6–26

2

- Click OK (Split Cells dialog box) to create a fourth cell in the first row.

3

- Position the insertion point in the 1K cell.
- Click the Select button (Layout tab | Table group) to display the Select Table menu (Figure 6–27).

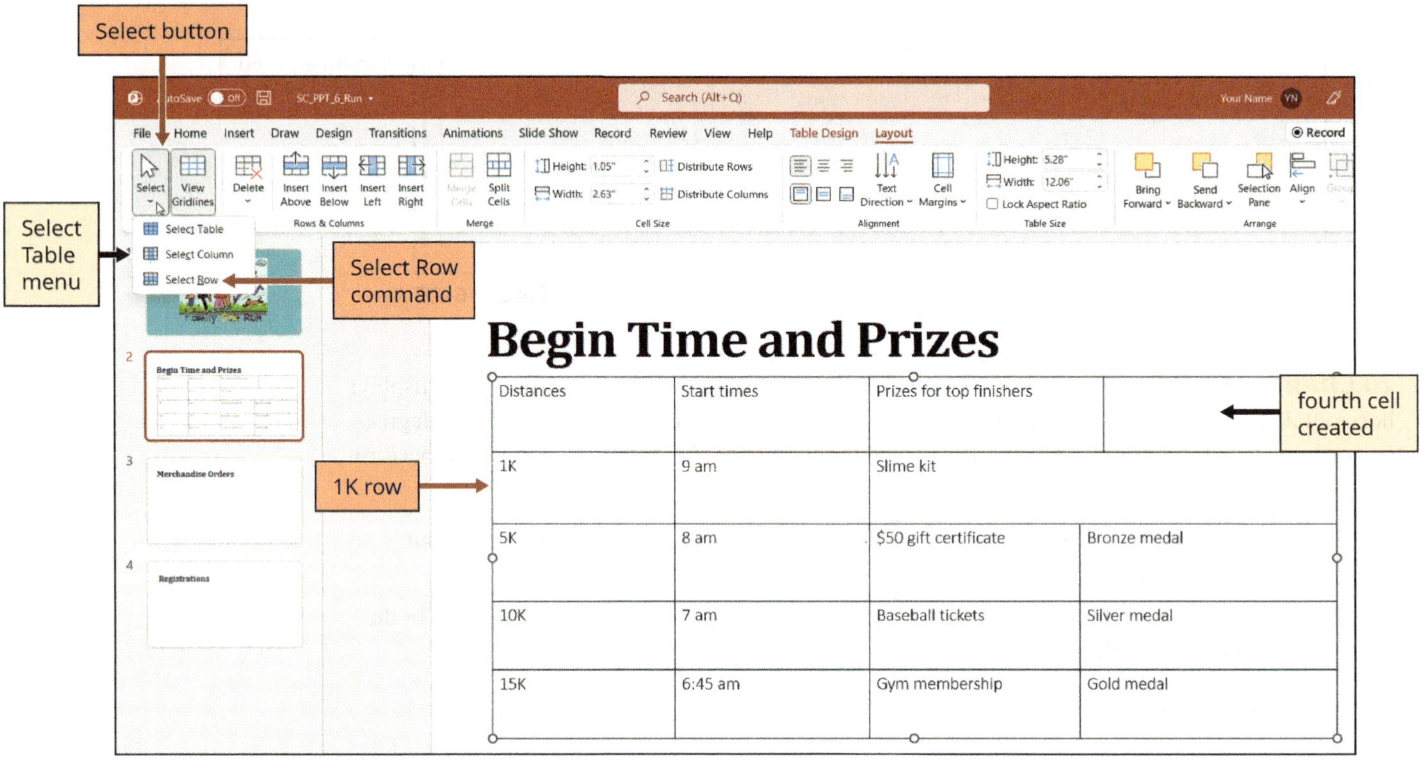

Figure 6–27

4

- Click Select Row in the Select Table menu to select the 1K row.
- Click the Split Cells button (Layout tab | Merge group) to display the Split Cells dialog box (Figure 6–28).

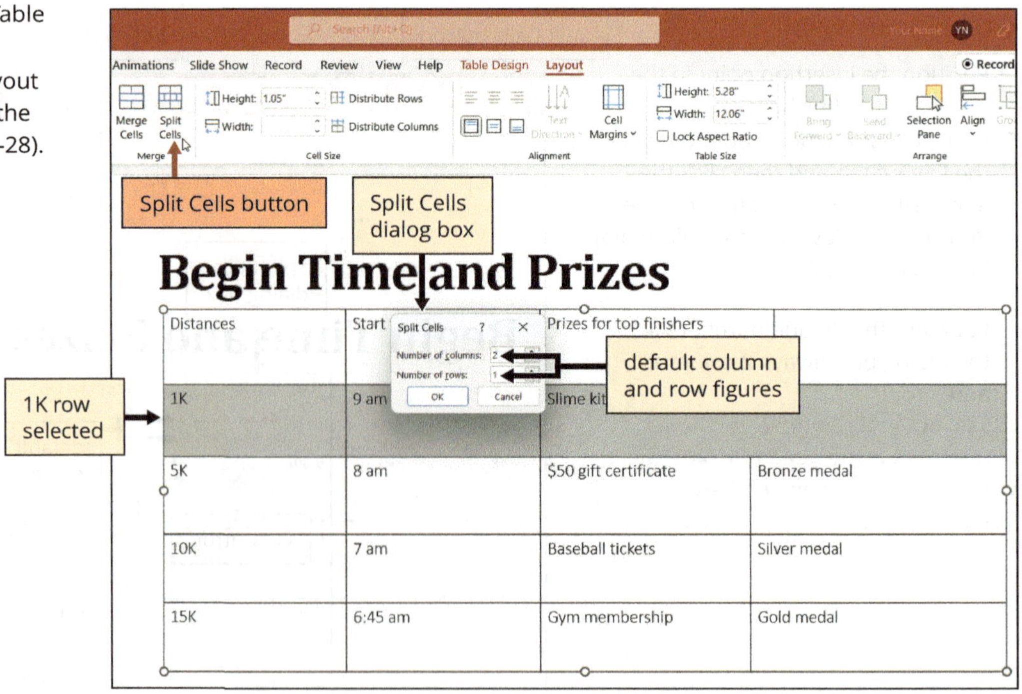

Figure 6–28

5

- Click the 'Number of columns' down arrow once to decrease the number of columns from 2 to 1.
- Click the 'Number of rows' up arrow once to increase the number of rows from 1 to 2 (Figure 6–29).

Q&A How many rows and columns can I create by splitting the cells?
The maximum number varies depending upon the width and height of the selected cell.

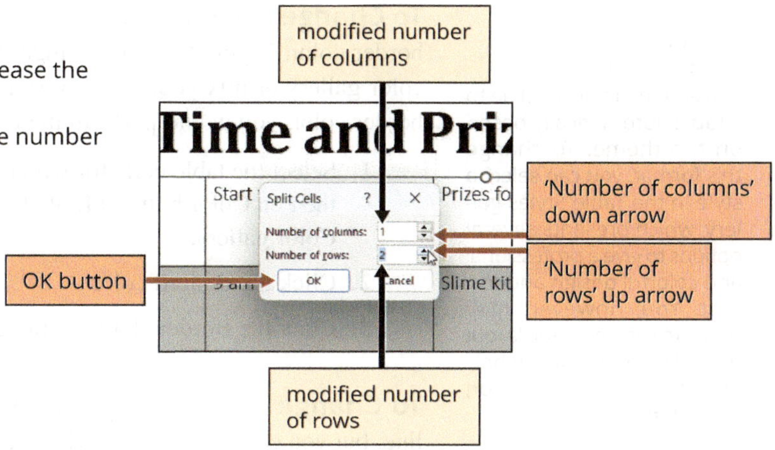

Figure 6–29

6

- Click OK (Split Cells dialog box) to create a row below the 1K row.

Other Ways

1. Right-click table, click Split Cells on shortcut menu, enter number of columns and rows, click OK

To Enter Additional Text in a Table

With the additional row added to the table, you now can add the 3K information in the inserted row. The following steps enter text in the new cells.

1 Position the insertion point in the first cell of the new row and then type **3K** in the cell. Advance the insertion point to the adjacent right column cell and then type **8:30 am** in the second cell and **Water park ticket** in the last cell in this row (Figure 6–30).

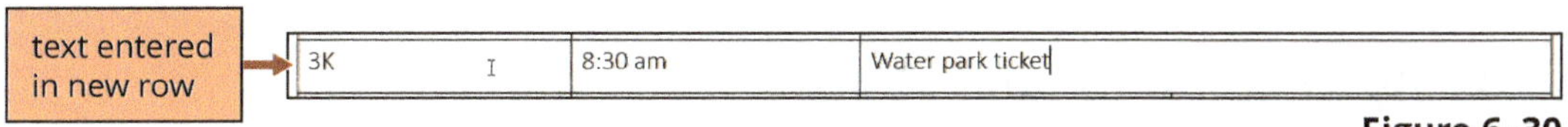

Figure 6–30

Consider This

Use appropriate colors when formatting graphics you want people to remember.

Studies have shown that men and women differ slightly in their recall of graphics formatted with various colors. Men remembered objects colored with shades of violet, dark blue, olive green, and yellow. Women recalled objects they had seen with dark blue, olive green, yellow, and red hues.

To Add a Table Border You can give your table some dimension and add to its visual appeal by adding borders. These lines can be applied around the entire table; between the cells; to the top, bottom, left, or right edges; or a combination of these areas. To add a table border, you would perform the following steps.

1. Select the table cells that you want to have a border and then click the Borders arrow (Table Design tab | Table Styles group) to display the Borders gallery.
2. Click the desired border in the Borders gallery.

BTW
Customizing Table Formatting
PowerPoint applies a style to a table automatically based on the theme. To change this format, you can select a style in the Table Styles gallery, which presents several options to give a professional and colorful design and format. You, however, may desire to customize the layout by adding or modifying borders, the background color, or the font.

To Change the Color of a Table Border The design theme determines the default table border color. If you desire to change this color, you can select a theme or standard color in the color gallery or mix your own color in the Custom tab (Colors dialog box). To change the table border color, you would perform the following steps.

1. Select the table cells for which you want to change the border color and then click the Pen Color button (Table Design tab | Draw Borders group) to display the Pen Color gallery.
2. Click the desired color.
3. Click the Borders button (Table Design tab | Table Styles group).

To Change the Line Style of a Table Border The default border line style is a solid line, but you can change this style to add a custom design element to this element. To change the table border line style, you would perform the following steps.

1. Select the table cells for which you want to change the border line style and then click the Pen Style button (Table Design tab | Draw Borders group) to display the Pen Style gallery.
2. Click the desired line style.
3. Click the Borders button (Table Design tab | Table Styles group).

To Change the Weight of a Table Border You can change the default 1 point border weight to a width ranging from ¼ point to 6 point. To change the table border weight, you would perform the following steps.

1. Select the table cells for which you want to change the weight and then click the Pen Weight arrow (Table Design tab | Draw Borders group) to display the Pen Weight gallery.
2. Click the desired line weight.
3. Click the Borders button (Table Design tab | Table Styles group).

To Select a Table and Apply Shading to Table Cells

You can format the table in several ways, including adding shading to color the background. The following steps add shading to the table. **Why?** Shading makes the table more visually appealing and helps distinguish each cell.

1

- With the Layout tab displayed, click the Select button to display the Select Table menu (Figure 6–31).

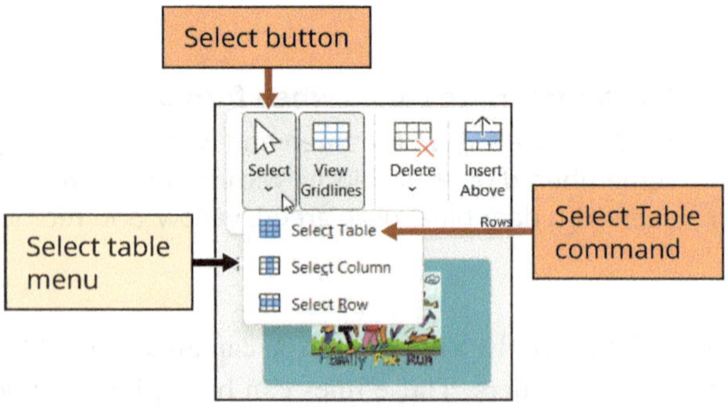

Figure 6–31

2

- Click Select Table in the Select Table menu to select the entire table.
- Click the Table Design tab and then click the Shading arrow (Table Design tab | Table Styles group) to display the Shading gallery.
- Point to 'Aqua, Accent 1, Lighter 80%' (fifth color in the second Theme Colors row) in the Shading gallery to display a live preview of that color applied to the table in the slide (Figure 6–32).
- **Experiment:** Point to various colors in the Shading gallery and watch the background of the table change.

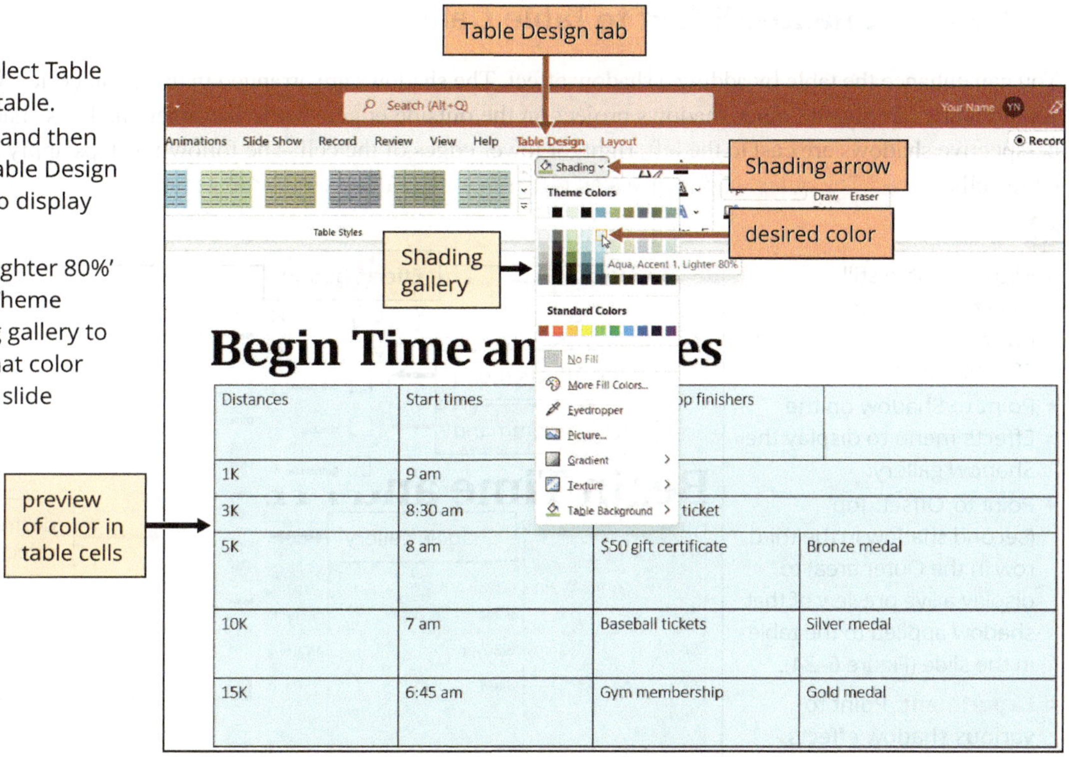

Figure 6–32

3

- Click 'Aqua, Accent 1, Lighter 80%' in the Shading gallery to apply the selected color to the table.

To Apply a Bevel Effect to Table Cells

Bevels modify the cell edges to give a 3-D effect. Some bevels give the appearance that the cell is protruding from the table, while others give the effect that the cell is depressed into the table. The following steps apply a bevel effect to the table cells. **Why?** You desire to make the individual table cells stand out.

1

- With the table still selected, click the Effects button (Table Design tab | Table Styles group) to display the Effects menu.
- Point to Cell Bevel on the Effects menu to display the Cell Bevel gallery.
- Point to Divot (first bevel in the third Bevel row) to display a live preview of that bevel applied to the table in the slide (Figure 6–33).
- **Experiment:** Point to various bevel effects in the Bevel gallery and watch the table cells change.

2

- Click Divot in the Bevel gallery to apply the selected bevel effect to the table.

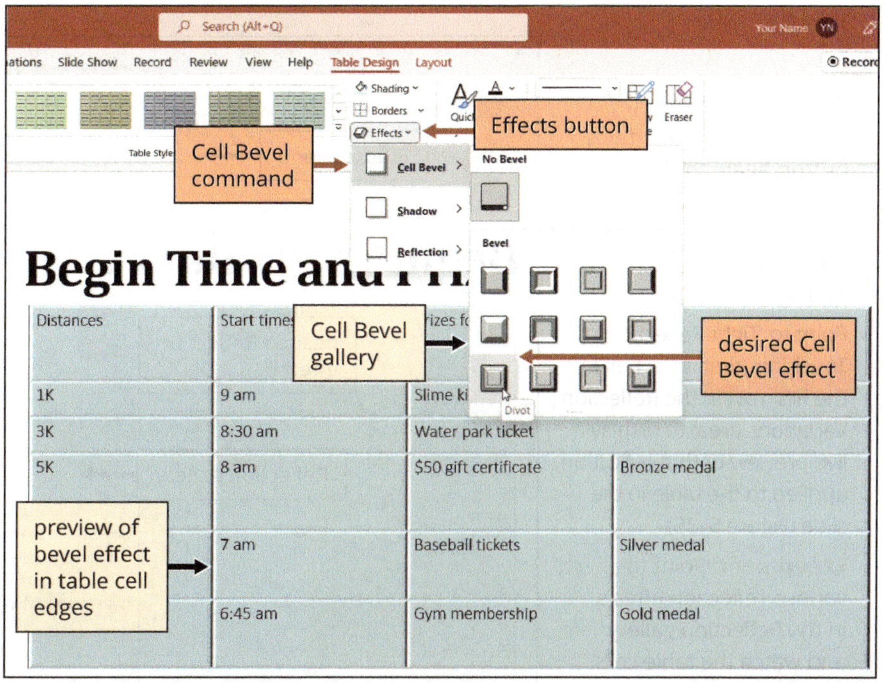

Figure 6–33

To Apply a Shadow Effect to Table Cells

You can enhance the table by adding a shadow effect. The shadows are arranged in three categories: Outer, Inner, and Perspective. As the names imply, the outer shadows project on the outside edges, while the inner shadows shade the inside edges. The five perspective shadows are cast to the left, right, or lower edges of the cell. The following steps apply an outer shadow effect to the table cells. **Why?** The outer shadow gives an effect that a light source is present on the lower edge of the slide.

1

- With the table still selected, click the Effects button again to display the Effects menu.
- Point to Shadow on the Effects menu to display the Shadow gallery.
- Point to 'Offset: Top' (second shadow in the third row in the Outer area) to display a live preview of that shadow applied to the table in the slide (Figure 6–34).
- **Experiment:** Point to various shadow effects in the Shadow gallery and watch the table cells change.

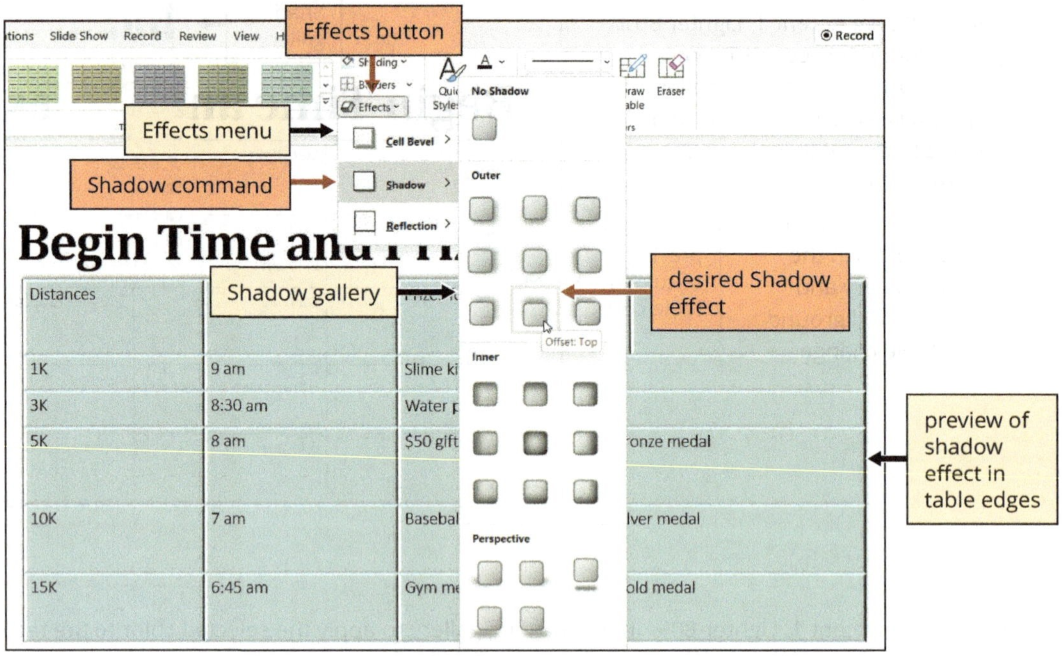

Figure 6–34

2

- Click 'Offset: Top' in the Shadow gallery to apply the selected shadow effect to the table.

To Apply a Reflection Effect to Table Cells

Reflections add a subtle effect by repeating the image beneath the slide. The various options in the Reflection gallery modify the distance and transparency. **Why?** Adding a reflection repeats the last table row. The following steps apply a reflection effect to the table cells.

1

- With the table still selected, click the Effects button again to display the Effects menu.
- Point to Reflection on the Effects menu to display the Reflection gallery.
- Point to 'Tight Reflection: Touching' (first reflection in the first row in the Reflection Variations area) to display a live preview of that reflection applied to the table in the slide (Figure 6–35).
- **Experiment:** Point to various reflection effects in the Reflection gallery and watch the table cells change.

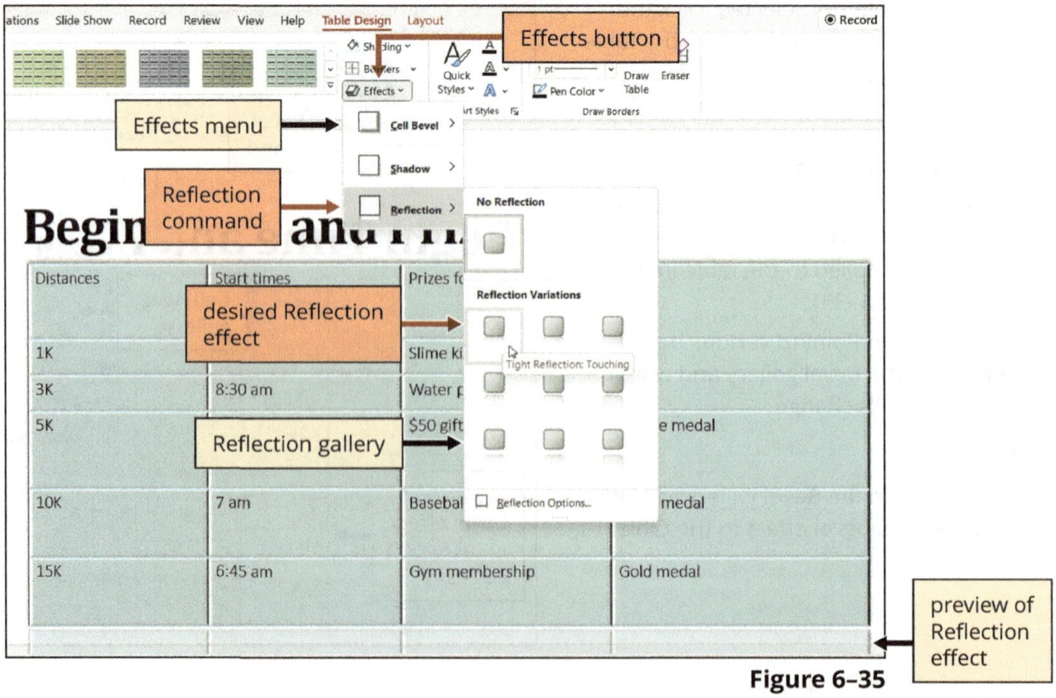

Figure 6–35

2

- Click 'Tight Reflection: Touching' in the Reflection gallery to apply the selected reflection effect to the table.

To Include a Total Row in a Table Many PowerPoint table styles emphasize particular rows by shading them a darker color. In many cases, the first row, called the header row, is highlighted. If you want to emphasize the last row, called the total row, in a table, you can apply a table style to this row. To include a total row, you would perform the following step.

1. Display the Table Design tab and then click the Total Row box (Table Design tab | Table Style Options) to select it and style the total row in the table.

To Add an Image to a Table Cell

A table enhancement you can make is to add a photo or illustration to a table cell. The following steps add a picture of a finish line to the upper-right table cell. **Why?** This illustration is another graphical element that reinforces the purpose of the table.

1

- Right-click the last cell in the first row to display the shortcut menu and Mini toolbar (Figure 6–36).

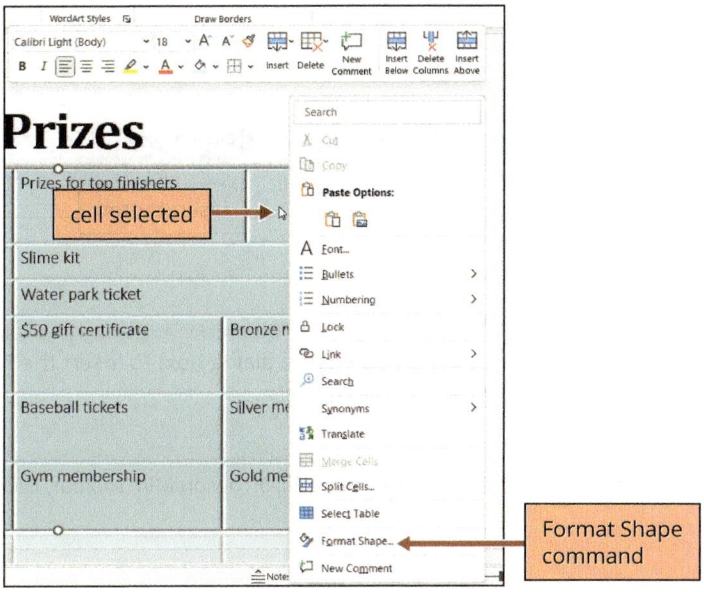

Figure 6–36

2

- Click Format Shape to display the Format Shape pane and then, if necessary, click Fill to expand the Fill section.
- Click 'Picture or texture fill' to select this option (Figure 6–37).

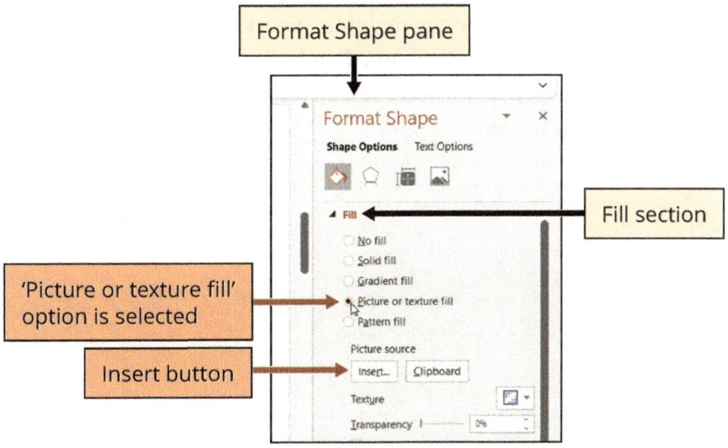

Figure 6–37

3

- Click the Insert button to display the Insert Pictures dialog box.
- Click From a File to display the Insert Picture dialog box.
- Navigate to the location of your Data Files and then click the Support_PPT_6_Finish picture to select this picture (Figure 6–38).

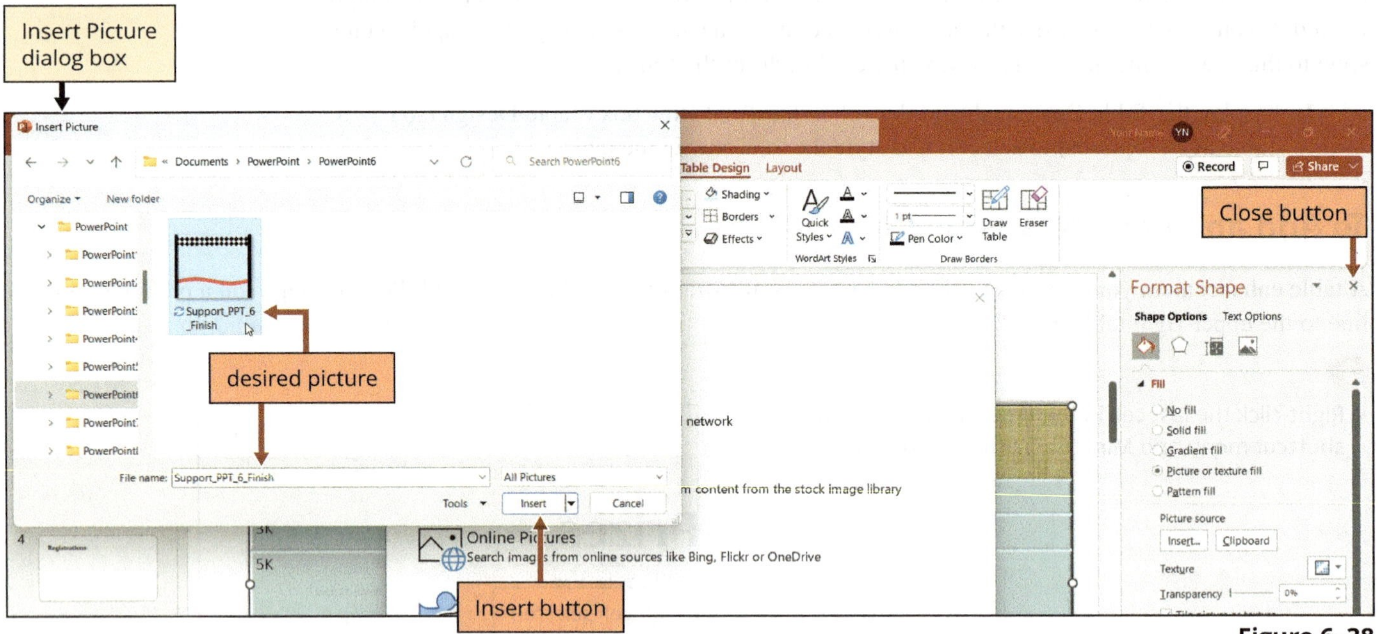

SkaFRex/Pixabay

Figure 6–38

4

- Click the Insert button (Insert Picture dialog box) to insert the Finish picture into the table cell.
- Click Close (Format Shape pane).

Other Ways

1. Right-click selected cell, click Shape Fill arrow on Mini toolbar, click Picture

To Distribute Table Rows

At times you may desire the row heights to vary. In the Slide 2 table, however, you desire the heights of the rows to be uniform. To make each selected row the same height, you distribute the desired rows. The following steps distribute table rows. **Why?** The horizontal lines you drew are not spaced equidistant from each other, and distributing the rows is an efficient manner of creating rows with the same height.

1

- With the table still selected, display the Layout tab and then select the cells in the second, third, fourth, fifth, and sixth rows (all rows except the first row) (Figure 6–39).

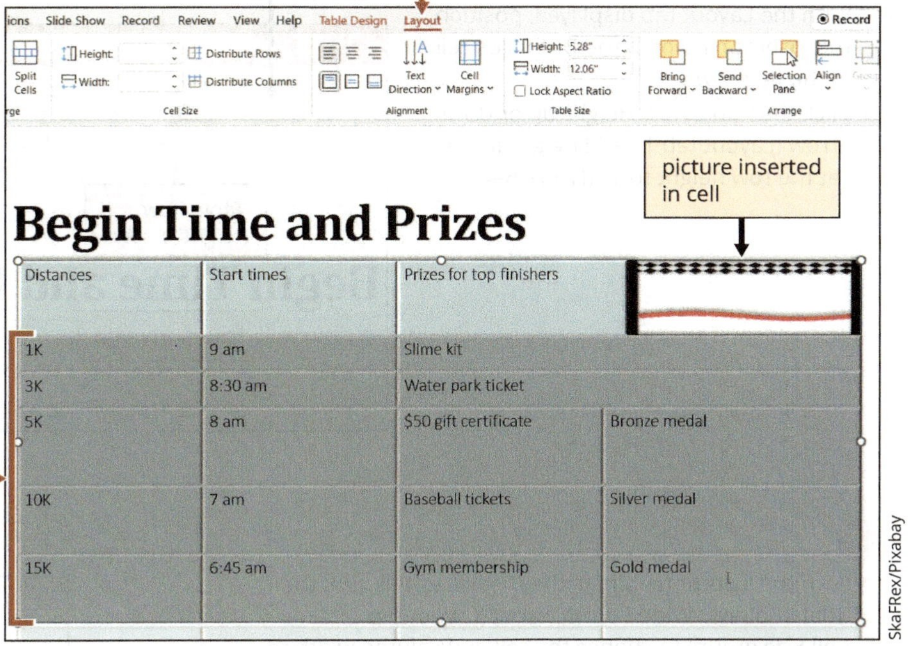

Figure 6–39

2

- Click the Distribute Rows button (Layout tab | Cell Size group) to equally space these five rows vertically (Figure 6–40).

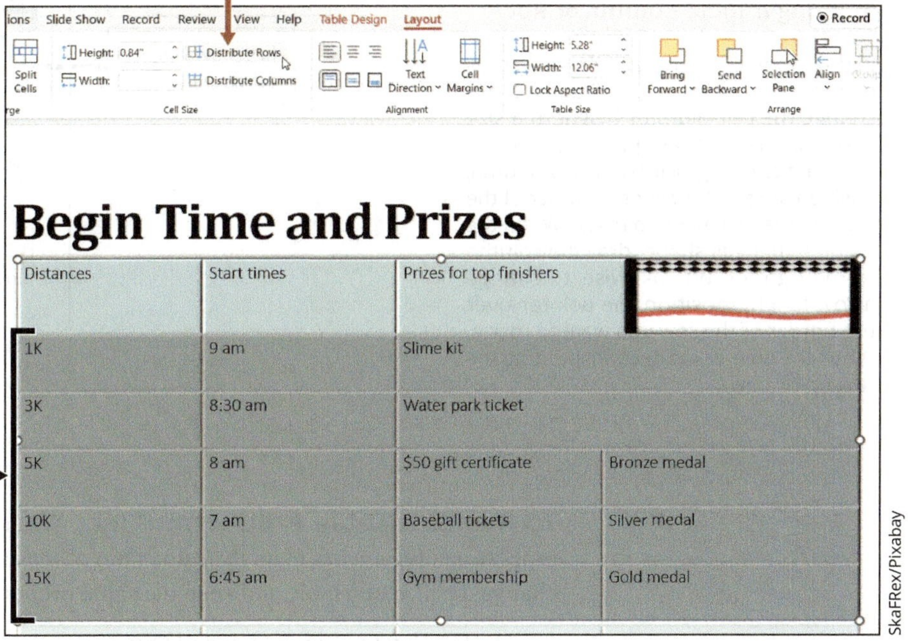

Figure 6–40

To Resize a Table Column and Row

The first table row should have a height taller than the rows beneath it. In addition, the cell width can be changed. **Why?** You can eliminate the extra space in the cells and allow sufficient room for all letters. The following steps resize the table columns and rows.

1

- With the Layout tab displayed, position the insertion point in the Distances cell in the first row.
- Click the 'Table Row Height' up or down arrow (Layout tab | Cell Size group) to set the row height to 1" (Figure 6–41).

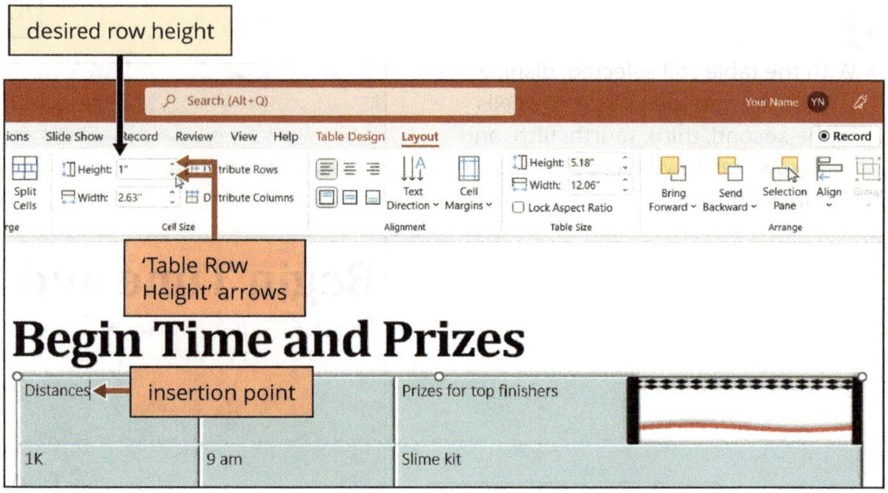

SkaFRex/Pixabay

Figure 6–41

2

- With the insertion point in the Distances cell, click the 'Table Column Width' down arrow (Layout tab | Cell Size group) to change the cell and column width to 2" (Figure 6–42).

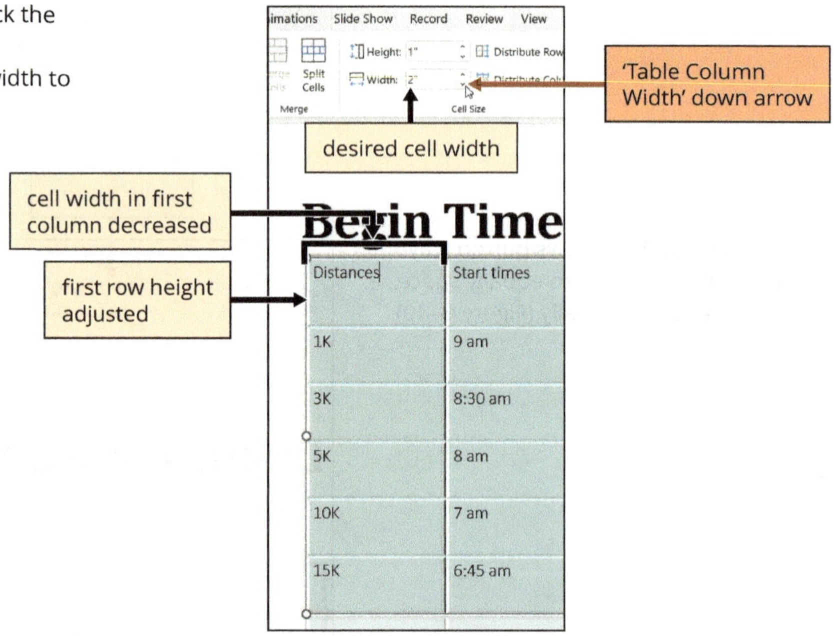

Figure 6–42

BTW

Resizing a Table Column or Row to an Approximate Value

In this module, you resized the table cells by entering a specific size. You also can change the cell width or height to a size that looks aesthetically pleasing to you. If you want to change the width of a column, position the pointer over the border of the column that you want to resize. When the pointer changes shape, drag the column to the right or left. Likewise, to change a row height, position the pointer over the border of the row you want to resize. When the pointer changes shape, drag the row up or down.

To Resize a Table Proportionally When you change the height and width of a table proportionally, you maintain the same ratio of these dimensions. If you want to enlarge, reduce, or change the size of a table and keep the same proportions, you would perform the following steps.

1. Display the Layout tab and then select the 'Lock Aspect Ratio' check box (Layout tab | Table Size group) to check the box.
2. Click the Height or Width up or down arrow to change the table dimensions.

To Align Data in a Table Cell

The data in each cell can be aligned horizontally and vertically. You change the horizontal alignment of each cell in a similar manner as you center, left-align, or right-align text in a placeholder. You also can change the vertical alignment so that the data displays at the top, middle, or bottom of each cell. The following steps center the text both horizontally and vertically in each table cell. **Why?** Having the text centered vertically and horizontally helps balance the cells by distributing the empty space evenly around the cell contents.

1

- Click the Select button to display the Select menu and then click Select Table to select the entire table.
- Click the Center button (Layout tab | Alignment group) to center the text between the left and right borders of each cell in the table (Figure 6–43).

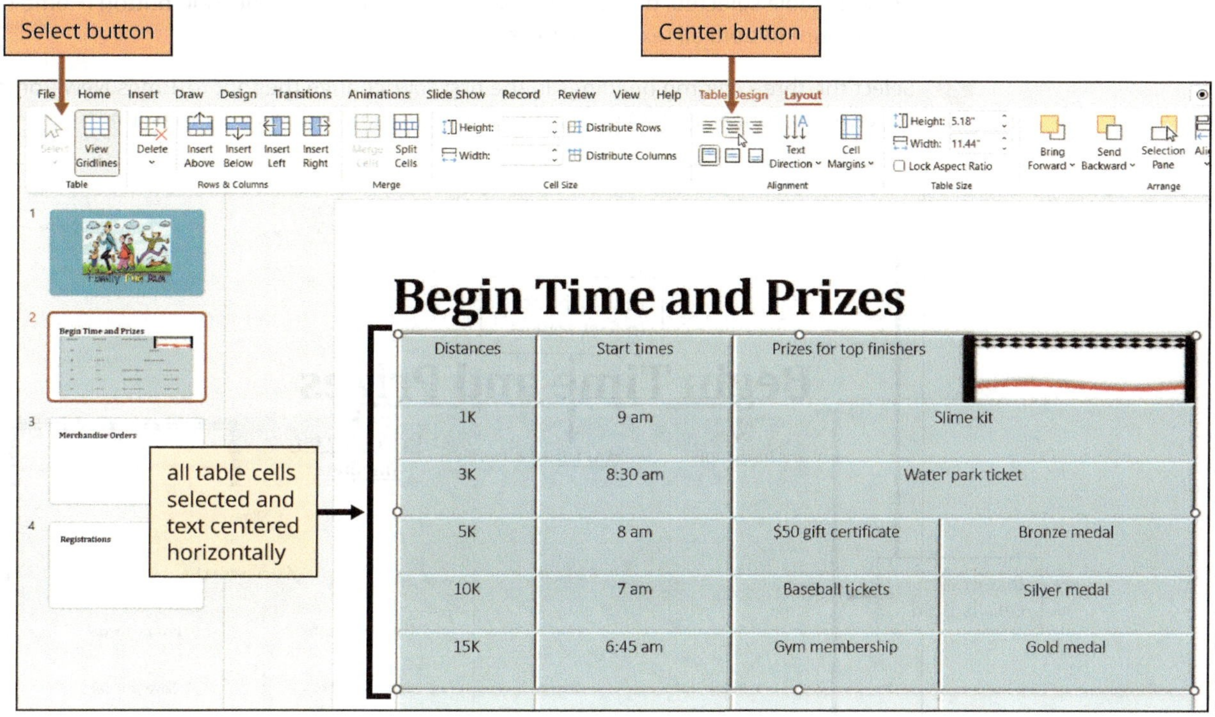

SkaFRex/Pixabay; Azmeyart-Design/Pixabay

Figure 6–43

2

- Click the Center Vertically button (Layout tab | Alignment group) to center the text between the top and bottom borders of each cell in the table (Figure 6–44).

Q&A Must I center all the table cells, or can I center only specific cells?

You can center as many cells as you desire at one time by selecting one or more cells.

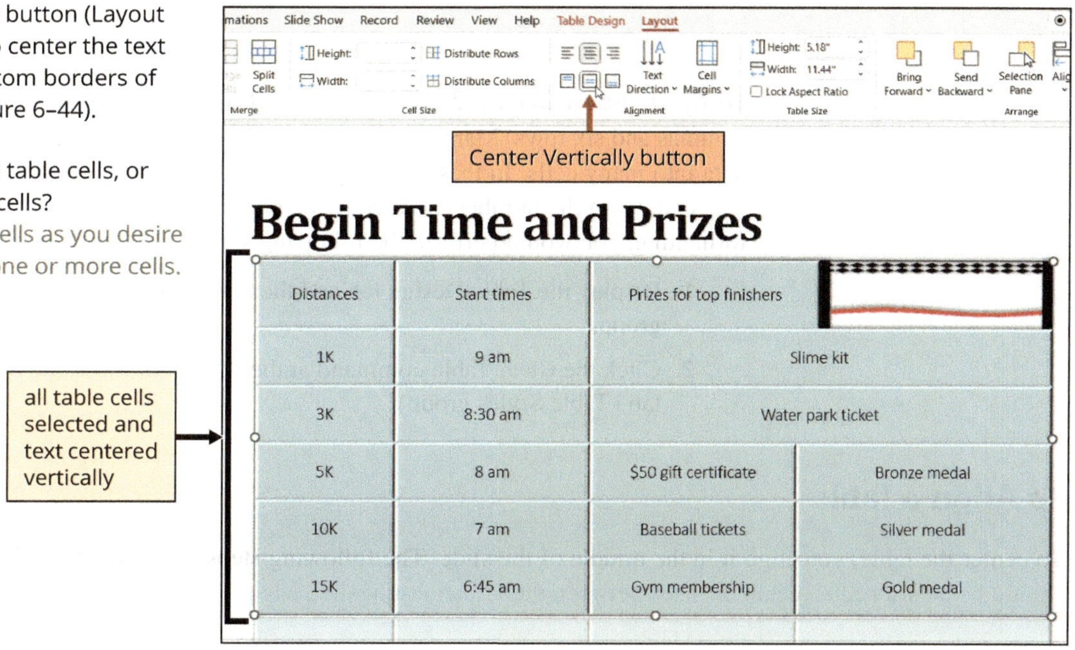

SkaFRex/Pixabay

Figure 6–44

Other Ways

1. Right-click selected cells, click Format Shape on shortcut menu, click Text Options tab, click Textbox icon, click Vertical alignment arrow

To Format Table Data

The final table enhancement is to bold the text in all cells and format the column headings. The entire table is selected, so you can bold all text simultaneously. The following steps format the data.

1. With the table selected, display the Home tab and then click the Bold button (Home tab | Font group) to bold all text in the table.

2. Select the three column headings in the first row, change the font to Times New Roman, increase the font size to 24 point, and then underline this text (Figure 6–45).

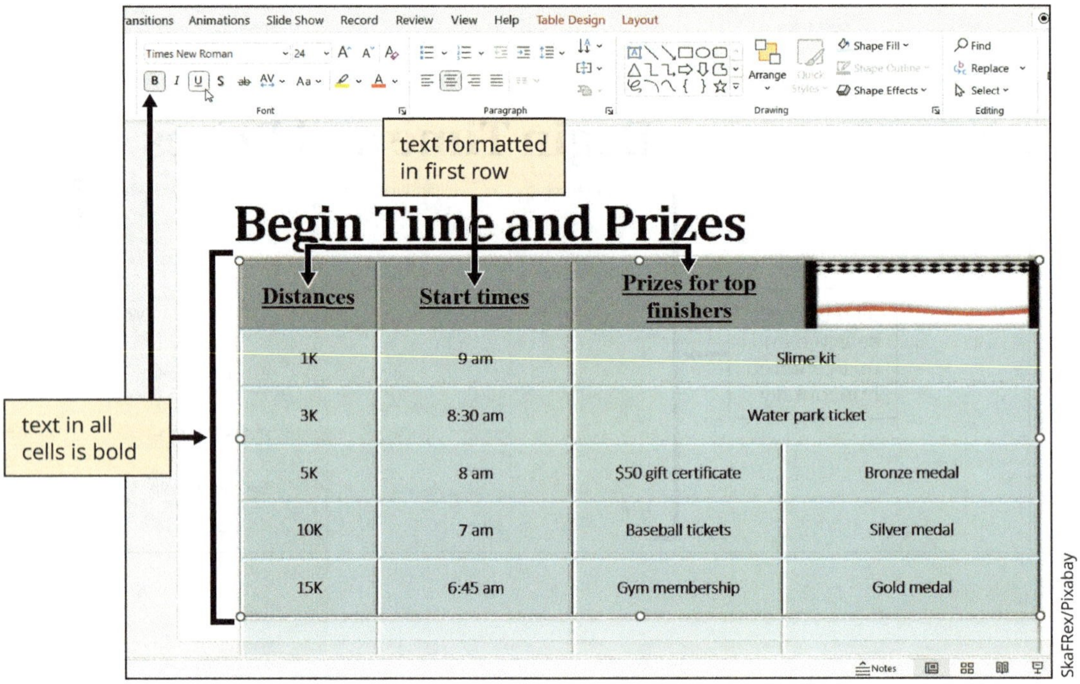

Figure 6–45

To Clear Formatting from a Table The table you created on the current Slide 2 has four columns and six rows. Many times, however, you may need to create larger tables and then enter data into many cells. In these cases, you can clear all formatting from the table so that you can concentrate on the numbers and letters and not be distracted by the colors and borders. To clear formatting, you would perform the following steps.

1. Display the Table Design tab and then click the More button in the Table Styles group.
2. Click the Clear Table command at the bottom of the Table Styles gallery (Table Design tab | Table Styles group).

To Align a Table

To center the table, you align it in the middle of the slide. The following steps center the table horizontally. **Why?** The table should be positioned an equal distance between the left and right slide edges to balance this object in the slide.

1

- With the table selected, display the Layout tab and then click the Align button (Layout tab | Arrange group) to display the Align Objects menu (Figure 6–46).

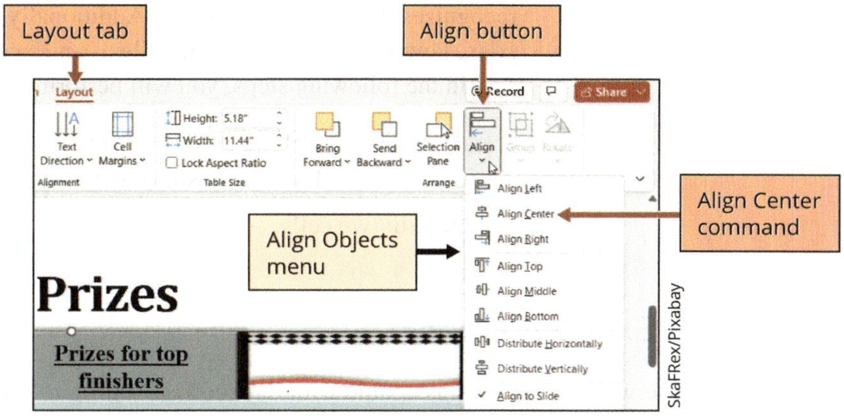

Figure 6–46

2

- Click Align Center on the Align Objects menu, so PowerPoint adjusts the position of the table evenly between the left and right sides of the slide (Figure 6–47).

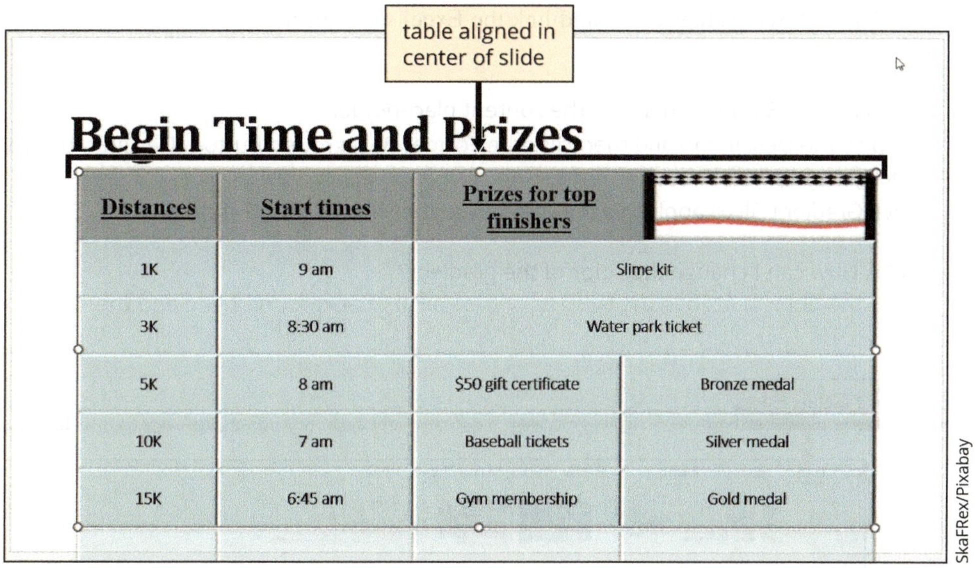

Figure 6–47

Break Point: If you wish to take a break, this is a good place to do so. Be sure the Run file is saved and then you can exit PowerPoint. To resume later, start PowerPoint, open the file called SC_PPT_6_Run, and continue following the steps from this location forward. Note: PowerPoint will prompt you to update any files you modified.

Inserting a Linked Excel Worksheet

Linked files maintain a connection between the source file and the destination file. When you select the **Link check box** in the Insert Object dialog box, the object is inserted as a linked object instead of an embedded object. Your PowerPoint presentation stores a representation of the original file and information about its location. If you later move or delete the source file, the link is broken, and the object will not be available. Consequently, if you make a presentation on a computer other than the one on which the presentation was created, and the presentation contains linked objects, be certain to include a copy of the source files. The source files must be stored in the exact location as originally specified when you linked them to your presentation.

PowerPoint associates a linked file with a specific application, which PowerPoint bases on the file extension. For example, if you select a source file with the file extension .docx, PowerPoint

BTW
File Sizes
Files with embedded objects typically have larger file sizes than those with linked objects because the source data is stored in the presentation. To keep file sizes manageable, Microsoft recommends inserting a linked object rather than an embedded object when the source file is large or complex.

recognizes the file as a Word file. Additionally, if you select a source file with the file extension .xlsx, PowerPoint recognizes the file as an Excel file.

In the following steps, you will perform these tasks on Slide 3:

1. Insert a linked Excel worksheet.
2. Align the Excel worksheet on the slide.
3. Edit two cells.

To Link an Excel Worksheet

The merchandise worksheet contains a table with data corresponding to t-shirt and sweatshirt sales for three sizes and total sales for each of these items. You will update this table by editing the number of extra-large t-shirt and sweatshirt orders. These figures will update the original Excel worksheet. When you insert the merchandise table, you can specify that it is linked from the PowerPoint slide to the Excel worksheet. **Why?** Any edits made to specific cells are reflected in both the source and destination files. The following steps insert and link the Excel worksheet.

1

- Display Slide 3 and then delete the content placeholder.
- Display the Design tab and then click the Format Background button (Design tab | Customize group) to display the Format Background pane.
- Click Gradient fill to apply this background to the slide (Figure 6–48).

Q&A How can I change the color of the gradient?
Click the Color button in the Fill area of the Format Background pane and then choose the desired color.

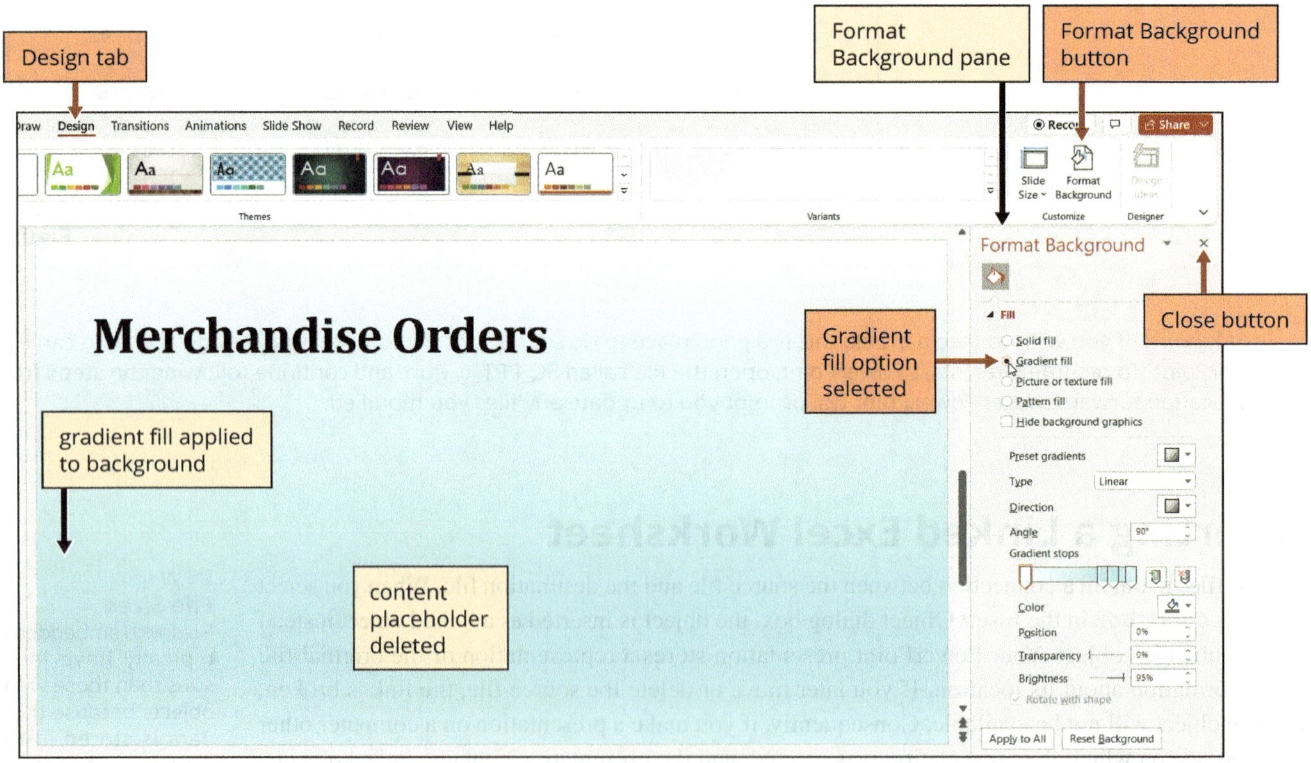

Figure 6–48

2

- Close the Format Background pane.
- Display the Insert tab and then click the Object button (Insert tab | Text group) to display the Insert Object dialog box.
- Click 'Create from file' (Insert Object dialog box) to display the File box (Figure 6–49).

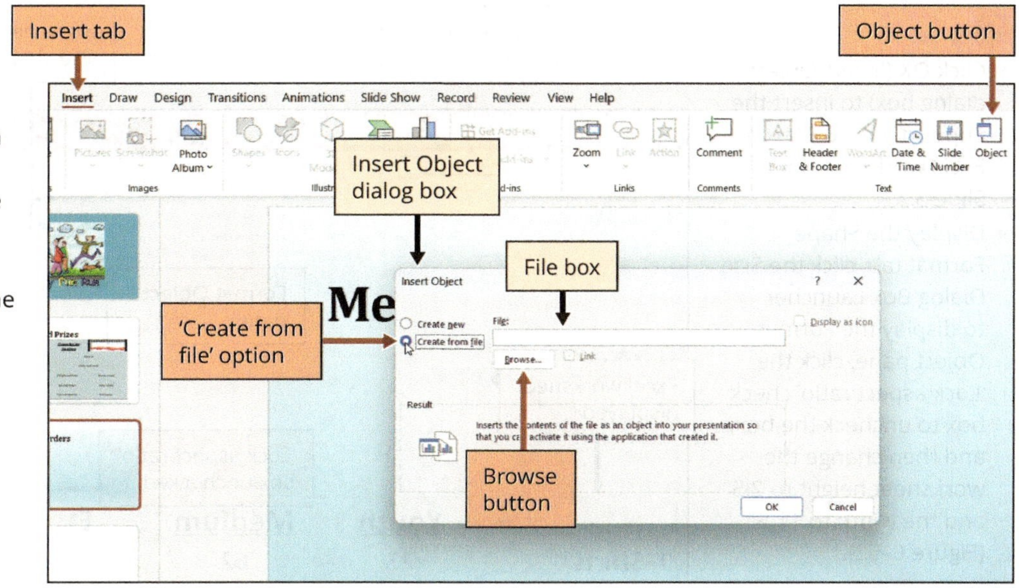

SkaFRex/Pixabay; Azmeyart-Design/Pixabay

Figure 6–49

3

- Click the Browse button to display the Browse dialog box, navigate to the location of your Data Files, and then click Support_PPT_6_Merch to select the Excel file name (Figure 6–50).

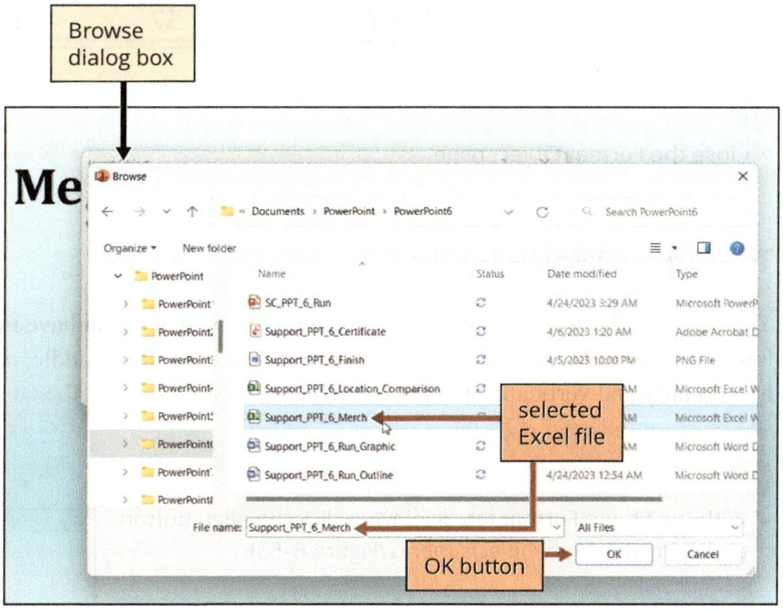

Figure 6–50

4

- Click OK (Browse dialog box) to insert the file name into the File box (Insert Object dialog box).
- Click the Link check box (Insert Object dialog box) to select the check box (Figure 6–51).

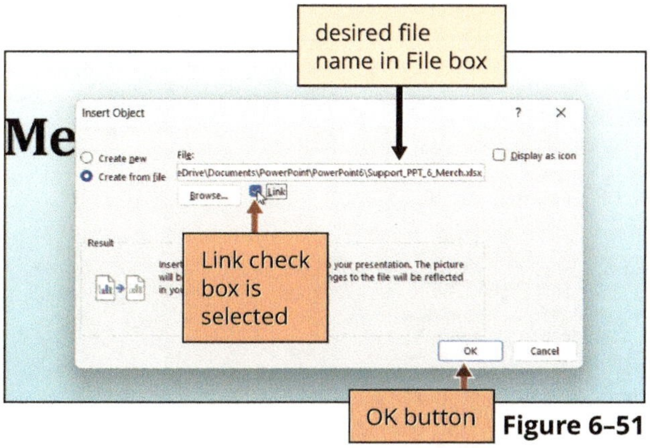

Figure 6–51

5

- Click OK (Insert Object dialog box) to insert the Support_PPT_6_Merch Excel worksheet into Slide 3.
- Display the Shape Format tab, click the Size Dialog Box Launcher to display the Format Object pane, click the 'Lock aspect ratio' check box to uncheck the box, and then change the worksheet height to 2.5" and the width to 11.5" (Figure 6–52).

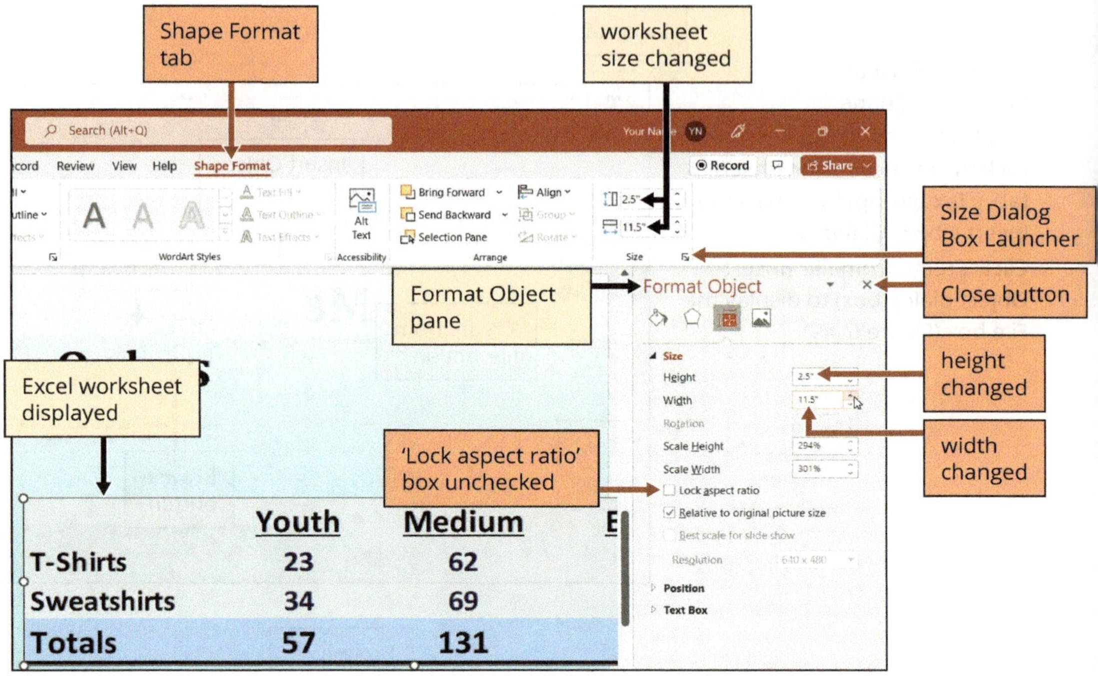

Figure 6–52

6

- Close the Format Object pane.

To Align a Worksheet

You can drag the worksheet table to a location, but you also can have PowerPoint precisely align the object horizontally in the left, center, or right areas of the slide, and vertically in the top, middle, or bottom of the slide. The following steps align the table horizontally and vertically on Slide 3. **Why?** PowerPoint inserts the table on Slide 3 in a location that is not visually appealing, so you want to center it on the slide.

1

- With the Shape Format tab displayed, click the Align button to display the Align Objects menu (Figure 6–53).

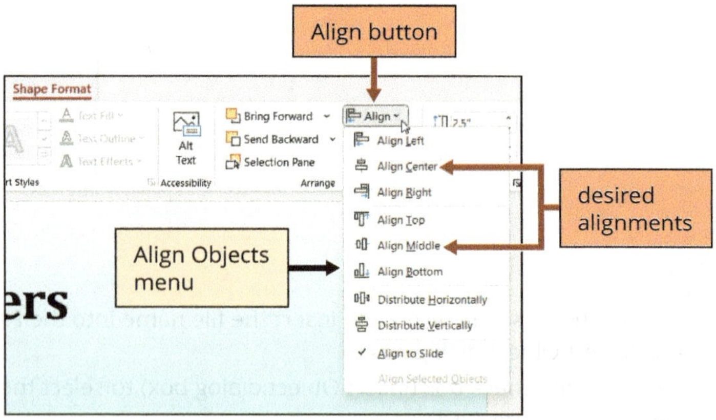

Figure 6–53

2

- Click Align Center on the Align Objects menu to position the worksheet evenly between the left and right edges of the slide.
- Click the Align button again to display the Align Objects menu and then click Align Middle to position the worksheet in the center of the slide (Figure 6–54).

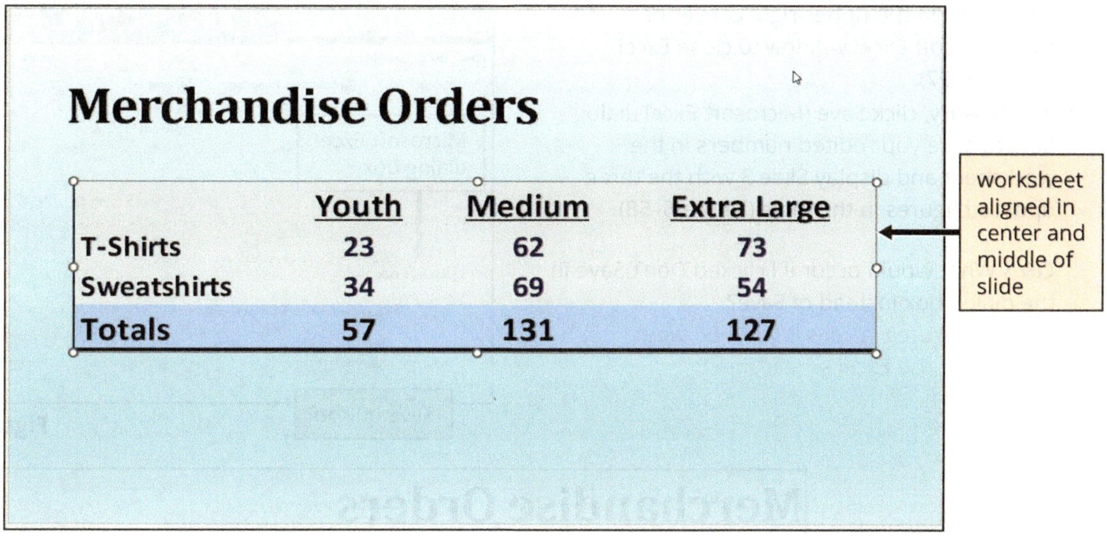

Figure 6–54

To Update a Linked Worksheet

Each table or worksheet cell is identified by a unique address, or **cell reference**, representing the intersection of a column and row. The column letter is first and is followed by the row number. For example, cell D2 is located at the intersection of the fourth column, D, and the second row. Two cells need updating. **Why?** You have received orders today for extra-large t-shirts and sweatshirts. The following steps edit cells in the linked table.

1

- Double-click the worksheet to run Excel and display the worksheet.
- Click the number 73 underneath the Extra Large column heading to make cell D2 the active cell (Figure 6–55).

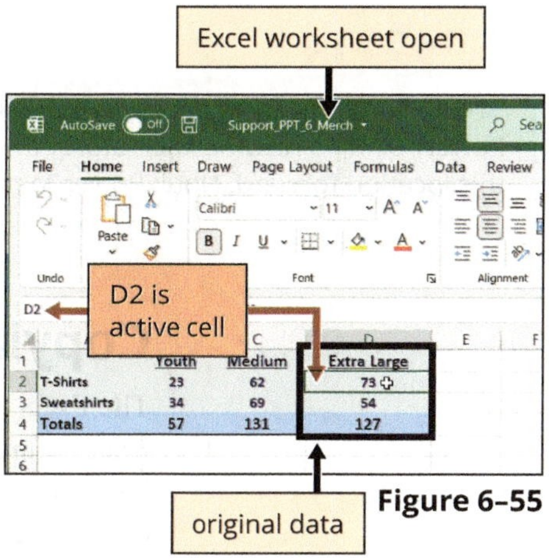

Figure 6–55

2

- Type **61** as the new Extra Large t-shirts number and then press ENTER to complete the entry and make cell D3 the active cell.
- Type **78** as the new Extra Large sweatshirts number and then press ENTER to complete the entry and make cell D4 the active cell (Figure 6–56).

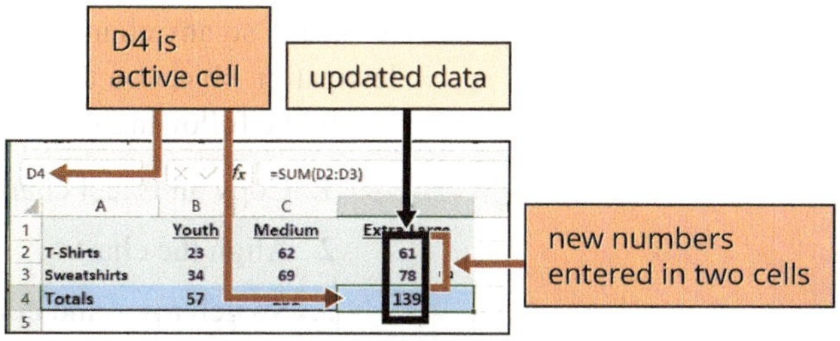

Figure 6–56

3

- Click Close in the upper-right corner of the Microsoft Excel window to close Excel (Figure 6–57).
- If necessary, click Save (Microsoft Excel dialog box) to save your edited numbers in the worksheet and display Slide 3 with the three updated figures in the table (Figure 6–58).

Q&A What would occur if I clicked Don't Save in the dialog box instead of Save?
The new figures in cells B3 and B4 would not be updated in the Excel spreadsheet.

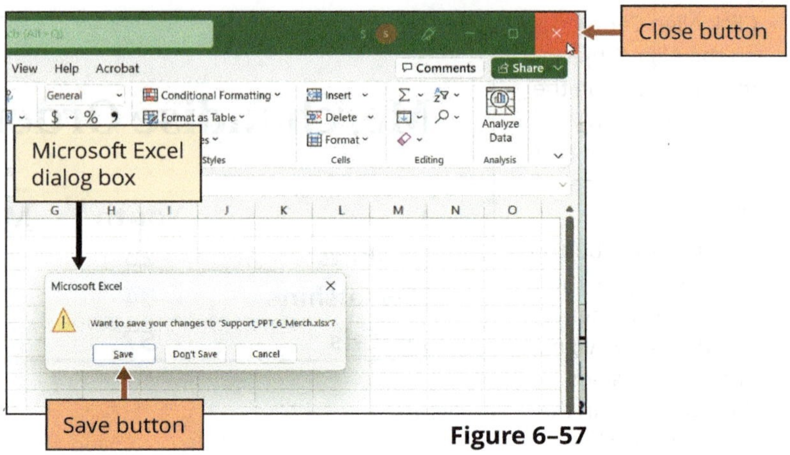

Figure 6–57

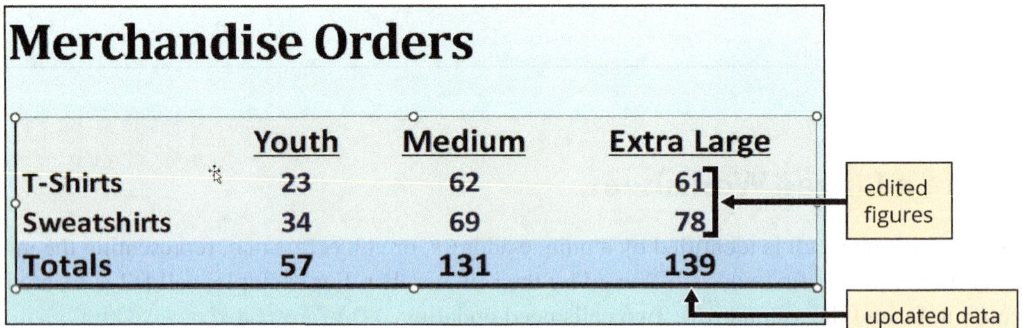

Figure 6–58

Break Point: If you wish to take a break, this is a good place to do so. Be sure the Run file is saved and then you can exit PowerPoint. To resume later, start PowerPoint, open the file called SC_PPT_6_Run, and continue following the steps from this location forward. Note: PowerPoint will prompt you to update any files you modified.

Copying and Modifying a Linked Excel Chart

The Excel table you inserted into Slide 3 is a linked object. You added data to the table using the Excel source program, and that change is reflected on the PowerPoint slide and in the original Excel document. Now you will insert and then modify an Excel chart on Slide 4. The registration committee members tracked the number of people living in the city and suburbs who have registered during the past five months and have used this data to develop this chart. This object will be linked, so any changes you make to the layout, legend, or background will be reflected in the destination object on the slide and in the original Excel worksheet.

In the following steps, you will perform these tasks on Slide 4:

1. Copy an Excel chart.
2. Align the chart.
3. Switch rows and columns.
4. Change the chart type.
5. Apply a style.
6. Add and format axis titles.
7. Add a chart title.
8. Edit data.

To Copy an Excel Chart

The chart you want to insert into your slide show was created in Excel. The file consists of two sheets: one for the chart and another for the numbers used to create the chart. The chart is on the sheet labeled Chart. One method of placing this chart into a PowerPoint presentation is to copy this object from the Excel worksheet and then paste it into a slide. The following steps copy and link a chart from the Chart sheet of the Excel file using the source formatting. **Why?** Copying and linking allows you to modify the chart content easily. You want to use the source formatting so that the chart uses the Office 2007-2010 theme colors and styles.

1

- Display Slide 4, delete the title text (Registrations), and then delete the title and content placeholders.

2

- Click the File Explorer app button (folder icon) on the taskbar to make the File Explorer window the active window. Navigate to the location where your Data Files are stored and then point to the Support_PPT_6_Location_Comparison Excel file in the Name list (Figure 6–59).

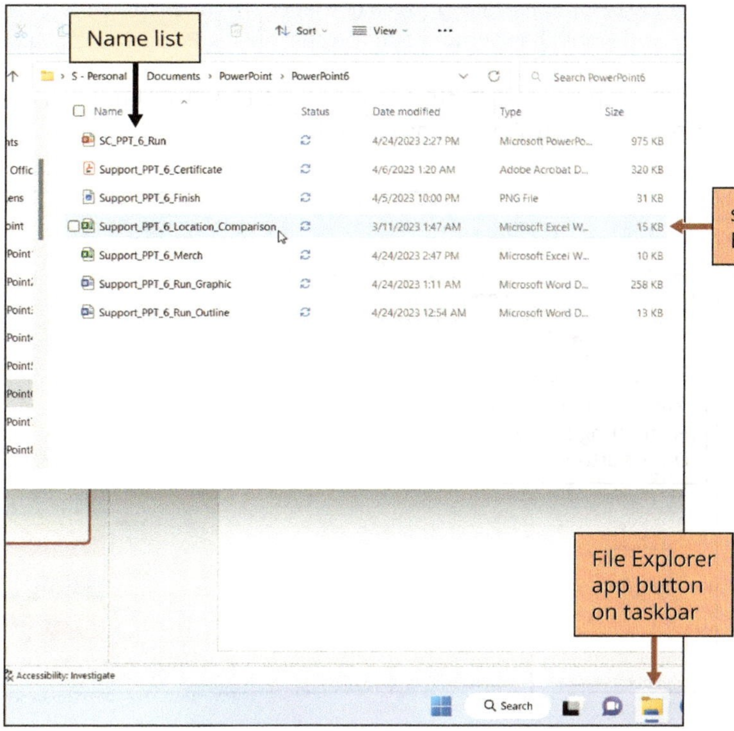

Figure 6–59

3

- Double-click the Support_PPT_6_Location_Comparison file to run Excel. If necessary, display the chart on the Chart sheet.
- Click a blank area above the chart legend in the Chart Area to select the entire chart.
- Click the Copy button (Home tab | Clipboard group) to copy the chart to the Office Clipboard (Figure 6–60).

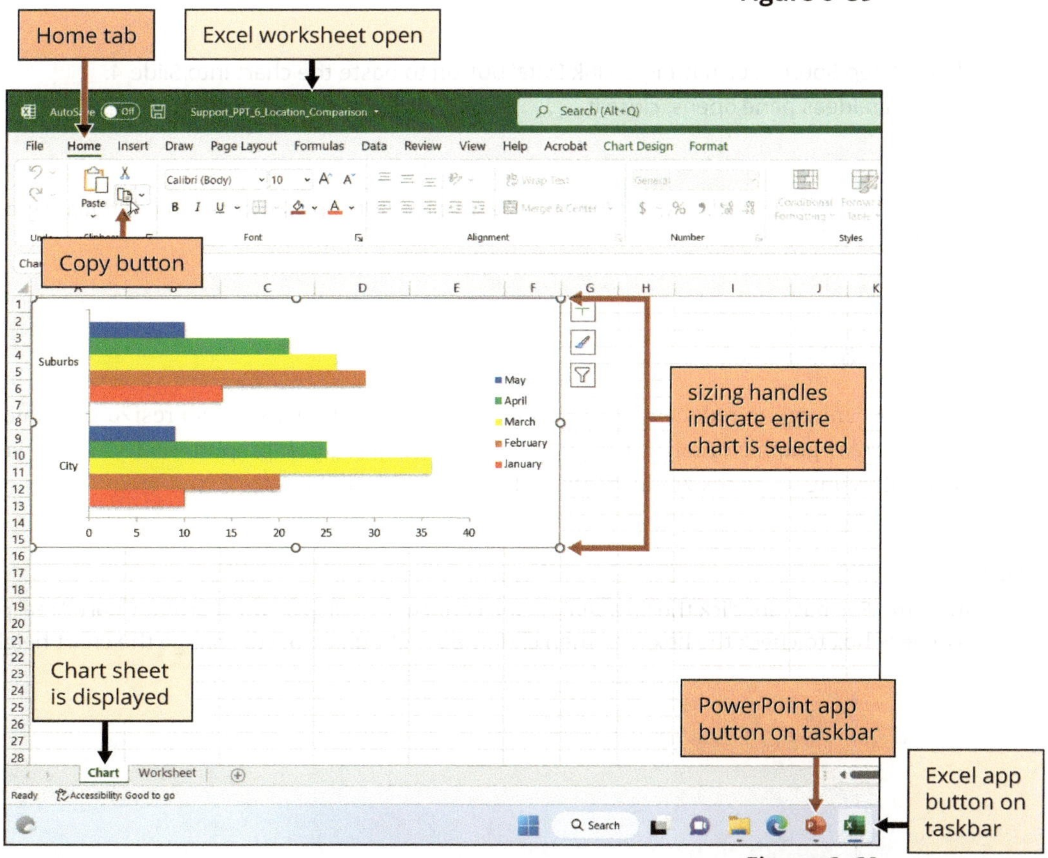

Figure 6–60

4

- Click the PowerPoint app button on the taskbar to make the PowerPoint window the active window. With Slide 4 and the Home tab displayed, click the Paste arrow (Home tab | Clipboard group) to display the Paste Options gallery.
- Point to the 'Keep Source Formatting & Link Data' button to display a live preview of the chart in the slide (Figure 6–61).

Q&A Why did I click the Paste arrow instead of the Paste button?
You want to use the colors and style of the chart on the Chart sheet of the Excel workbook (the source theme), so you need to display the Paste Options gallery to make that choice and to link the chart to the original Excel file. If you had clicked the Paste button, you would have embedded the chart using PowerPoint's Metropolitan theme (the destination theme).

- **Experiment:** Point to the 'Use Destination Theme & Link Data' button in the Paste Options gallery to display a live preview of the chart with the Metropolitan theme applied.

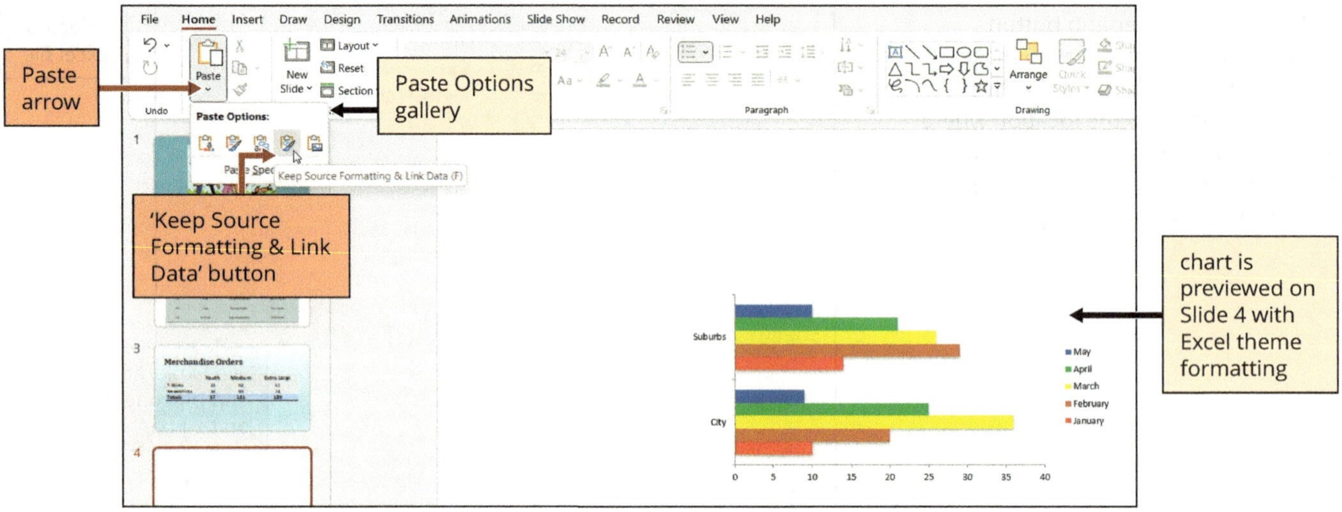

Figure 6–61

5

- Click the 'Keep Source Formatting & Link Data' button to paste the chart into Slide 4.
- If the Design Ideas pane opens, close it.

Other Ways

1. Right-click Excel chart, click Copy, exit Microsoft Excel, click Paste arrow (Home tab | Clipboard group), click 'Keep Source Formatting & Link Data'

To Resize a Chart Proportionally

If you want to enlarge or reduce a chart, or change its proportions, you can resize this object in the same manner that you resize a SmartArt graphic or any other graphical object. When you proportionally resize, you select the Lock Aspect Ratio box. The following steps resize the Slide 4 chart proportionally. **Why?** You want to maintain the same ratio between the height and width.

1

- Display the Format tab, click the Size Dialog Box Launcher to display the 'Format Chart Area' pane, select the 'Lock aspect ratio' check box to check the box, and then click the Height up arrow to change the chart height to 5.5" (Figure 6–62).

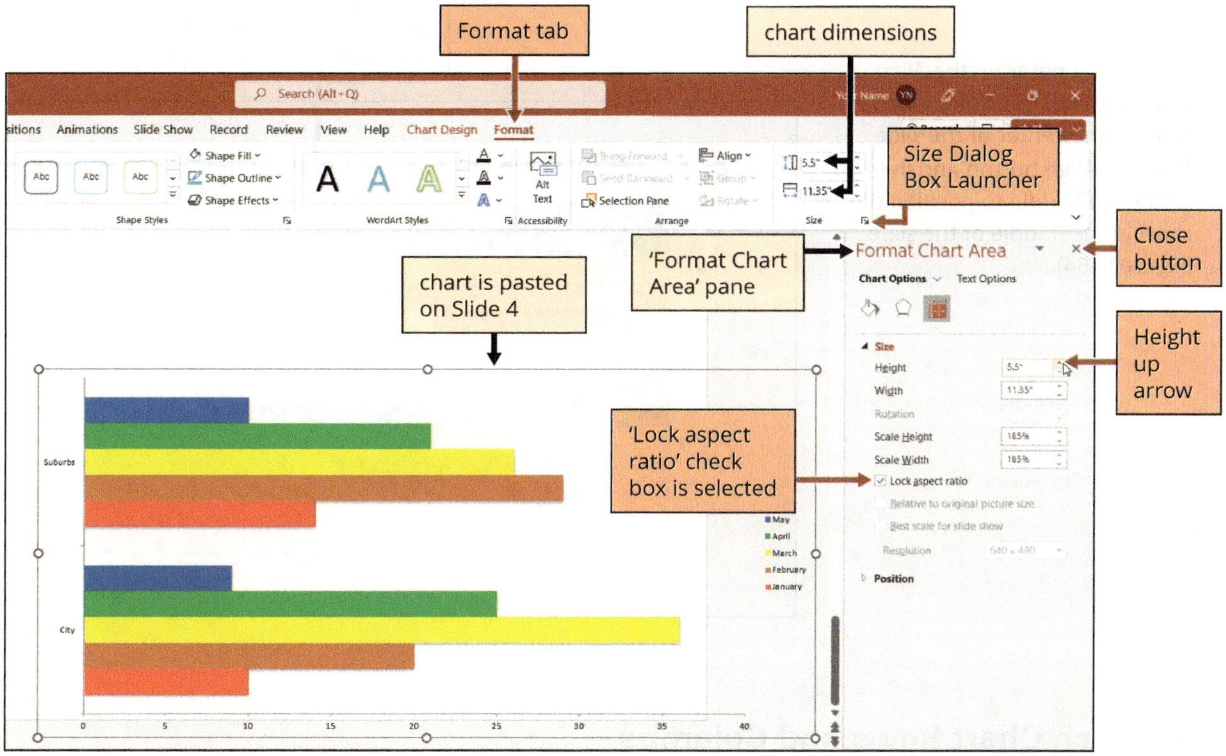

Figure 6–62

2

- Close the Format Chart Area pane.

To Align a Chart

Although you can drag the chart on the slide to realign it manually, you also can use PowerPoint commands to align the object horizontally in the left, center, or right areas of the slide, and vertically in the top, middle, or bottom of the slide. The following steps align the chart horizontally and vertically on Slide 4. **Why?** You aligned the table on Slide 3 horizontally and vertically. Likewise, you want to align the chart on Slide 4 so that it is displayed in an appropriate location on the slide.

1

- With the chart selected and the Format tab displayed, click the Align button to display the Align Objects menu (Figure 6–63).

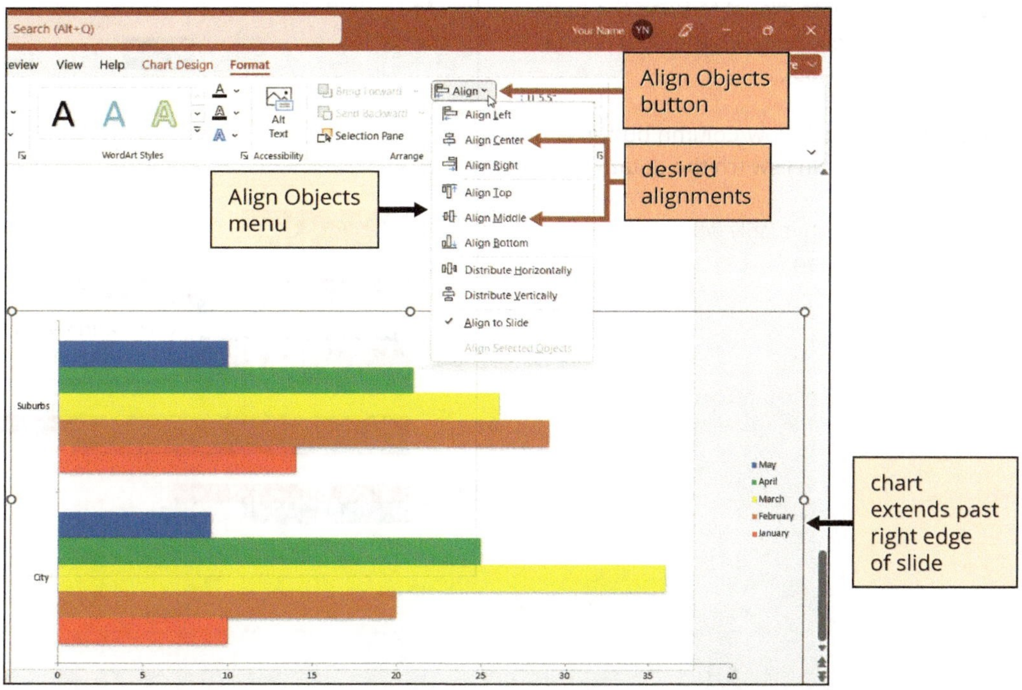

Figure 6–63

2

- Click Align Center on the Align Objects menu to position the chart in the center of the slide.
- Click the Align button and then click Align Middle to position the chart in the middle of the slide (Figure 6–64).

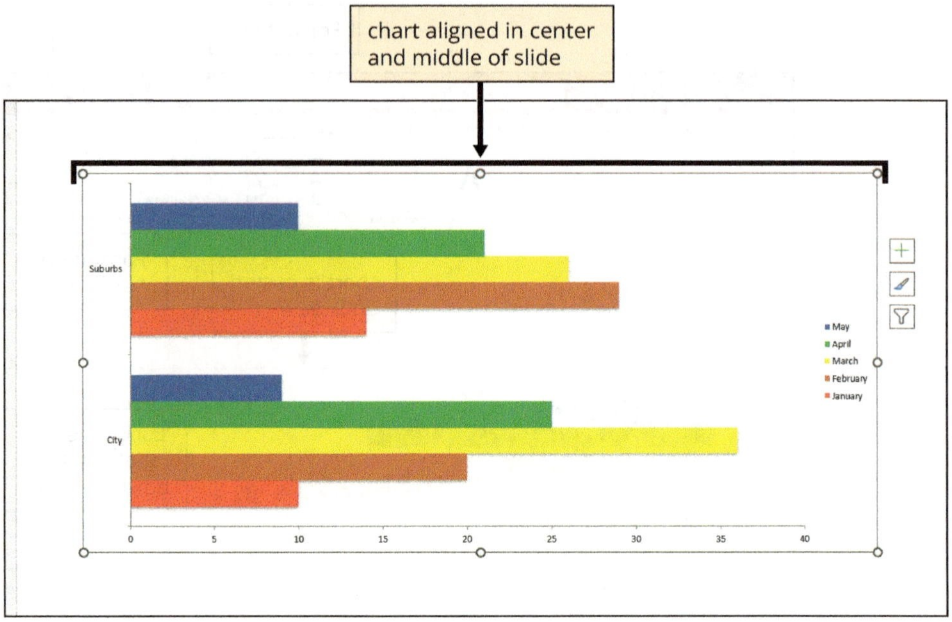

Figure 6–64

To Switch Chart Rows and Columns

Excel created the chart on Slide 4 (the Chart sheet in the Excel file) based on the values in the worksheet on the Worksheet sheet of the Excel file. The scale is based on the values in the **y-axis**, which also is called the **vertical axis** or **value axis**. The titles along the **x-axis**, also referred to as the **horizontal axis** or **category axis**, are derived from the top row of the Worksheet sheet and are displayed along the left edge of the chart. Each bar in the chart has a specific color to represent one of the five months—January, February, March, April, and May—grouped by city and suburbs. You can switch the data in the chart so that the city and suburbs totals display together in each month. **Why?** Audience members may be interested in comparing variations between the city and suburbs registrations during each month. The following step switches the rows and columns in the chart.

1

- Display the Chart Design tab on the ribbon.
- Click the Switch Row/Column button (Chart Design tab | Data group) to swap the data charted on the x-axis with the data on the y-axis (Figure 6–65).

Q&A If the Switch Row/Column button is dimmed, how can I switch the data?
Be certain the Excel worksheet is open. The button is active only when the worksheet is open.

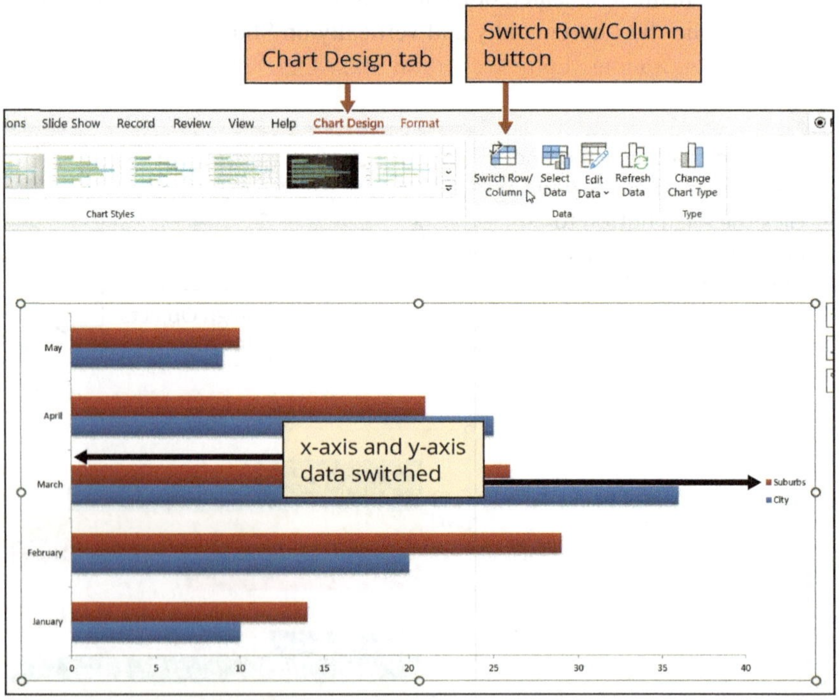

Figure 6–65

To Change the Chart Type

The bar chart represents data horizontally for each of five months. You can change the chart appearance by selecting another type in the Change Chart Type dialog box. The sample charts are divided into a variety of categories, including column, line, pie, and bar. The clustered column type that you want to use in the presentation is located in the Column area, which has seven layouts. The following steps change the chart to a 3-D Clustered Column chart type. **Why?** The vertical bars show the registrations during each month, and the 3-D effect adds an interesting visual element.

1

- Click the 'Change Chart Type' button (Chart Design tab | Type group) to display the 'Change Chart Type' dialog box.
- Click Column in the left pane ('Change Chart Type' dialog box) to display a Clustered Column thumbnail (Figure 6–66).

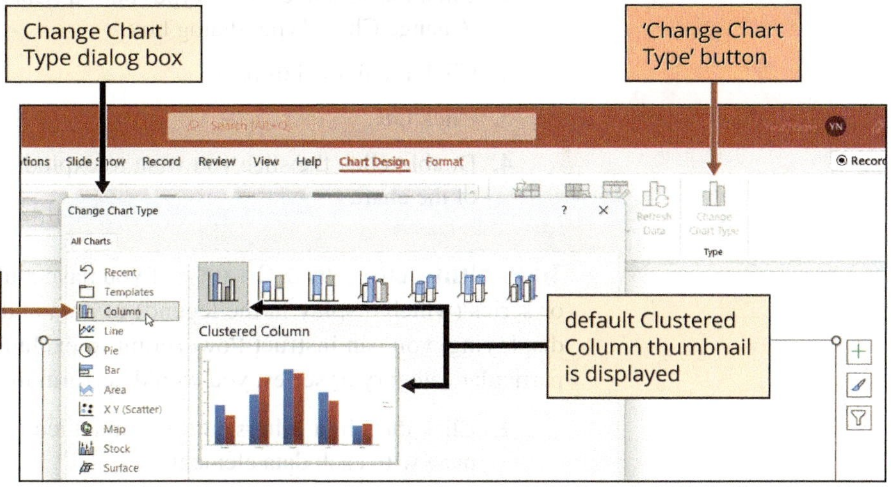

Figure 6–66

2

- Click the '3-D Clustered Column' chart (fourth chart) to select this chart type and display a thumbnail with a 3-D effect (Figure 6–67).

Q&A Can I see a larger preview of the chart?
Yes. You can point to the chart to enlarge the preview.

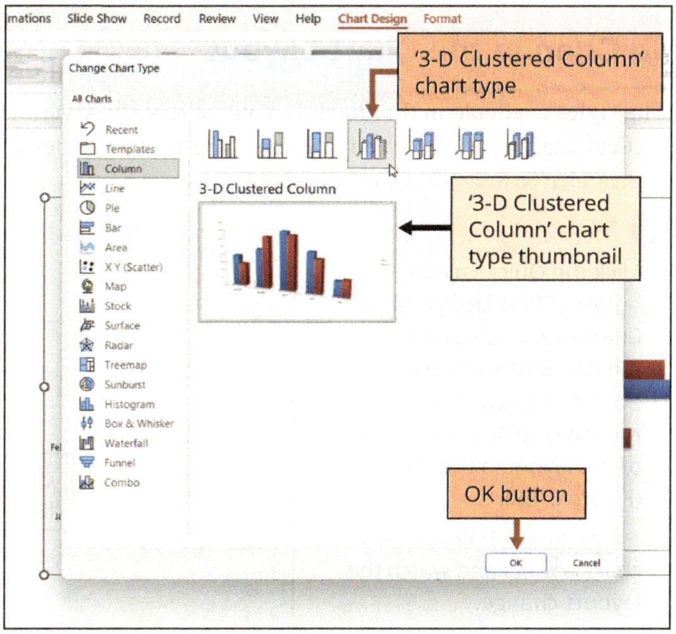

Figure 6–67

3

- Click OK ('Change Chart Type' dialog box) to change the chart type to 3-D Clustered Column.

BTW
Displaying Gridlines
Gridlines can help you align charts, shapes, and other objects on slides. To show the gridlines, display the View tab and then select the Gridlines check box (View tab | Show group).

To Change the Chart Type to Pie and Explode a Pie Chart Slice Pie charts are a popular method of showing how individual amounts contribute to a total amount. Each pie slice represents the size or percentage of that slice relative to the entire pie. You can emphasize an individual slice of the pie by moving, or exploding, it outward. If you wanted to change the 3-D Clustered Column chart on your slide to a pie chart and then explode a particular slice, you would perform the following steps.

1. Click the 'Change Chart Type' button (Chart Design tab | Type group) to display the 'Change Chart Type' dialog box.
2. Click Pie in the left pane.
3. Click OK.
4. Double-click the slice you want to explode and then drag that slice away from the center of the chart.

To Exclude Data in a Chart If you have multiple categories (which display in the x-axis) or series (which display in the legend) of data and want to exclude one or more of them from displaying, you can instruct PowerPoint to exclude data elements. If you wanted to exclude a particular category or series, you would perform the following steps.

1. Click the Chart Filters button (funnel icon) on the right side of the chart to display a pane with each data element.
2. Clear the check boxes of the elements you want to exclude in the chart.
3. To display an excluded data element, select the check box.

To Change the Chart Layout

The styles available in the Quick Layout gallery show various chart elements, including the chart title, legend, horizontal and vertical axes, data labels, and gridlines. The following steps change the layout of the chart. **Why?** You can modify the chart's appearance easily by selecting a predefined layout.

1

- Click the Quick Layout button (Chart Design tab | Chart Layout group) to display the Quick Layout gallery.
- Point to Layout 10 (in the last row) to display a live preview of the layout in the slide (Figure 6–68).
- **Experiment:** Point to various chart layouts and watch the layouts change.

2

- Click Layout 10 in the Quick Layout gallery to apply the layout to the chart.

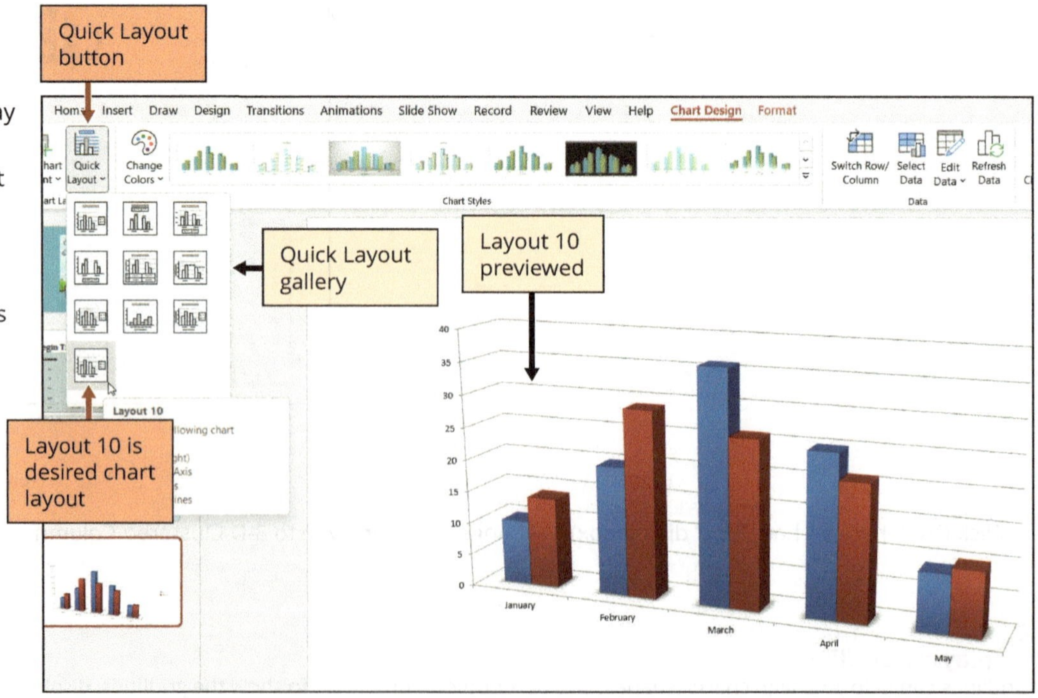

Figure 6–68

To Apply a Style to a Chart

The styles available in the Chart Styles gallery have a variety of colors and backgrounds and display in both 2-D and 3-D. The following steps apply a style to the chart. **Why?** You can modify the chart's appearance easily by selecting a predefined style.

1

- Click the Chart Styles button (paintbrush icon) on the right side of the chart area to display the Chart Styles gallery with the Style tab displayed.
- Scroll down until Style 11 (last style) is displayed in the Chart Styles gallery and then point to this style to see a live preview on Slide 4 (Figure 6–69).
- **Experiment:** Point to various chart styles and watch the layouts change.

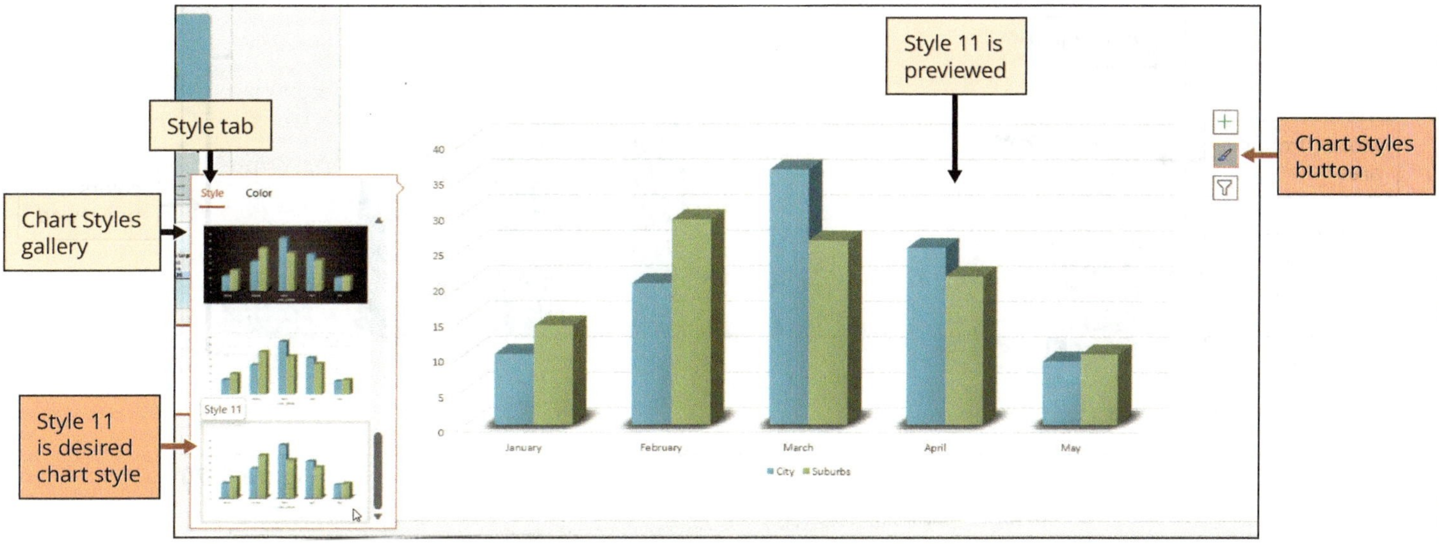

Figure 6–69

2

- Click Style 11 in the Chart Styles gallery to apply the chart style to the chart.

To Change Chart Colors

You can modify a chart's colors easily by selecting one of the color groups available in the Chart Color gallery. These colors are grouped into two categories: Colorful and Monochromatic. For a unique look, PowerPoint also allows you to create a custom color combination. The following steps change the chart colors. **Why?** The two columns' blue colors will coordinate with the blue hues displayed on the other slides in the presentation.

1

- With the Chart Styles gallery still displayed, click the Color tab at the top of the pane to display the Chart Color gallery.
- Scroll down and then point to 'Monochromatic Palette 8' (eighth row in the Monochromatic area) to display a live preview of the layout in the slide (Figure 6–70).
- **Experiment:** Point to various color groups and watch the chart colors change.

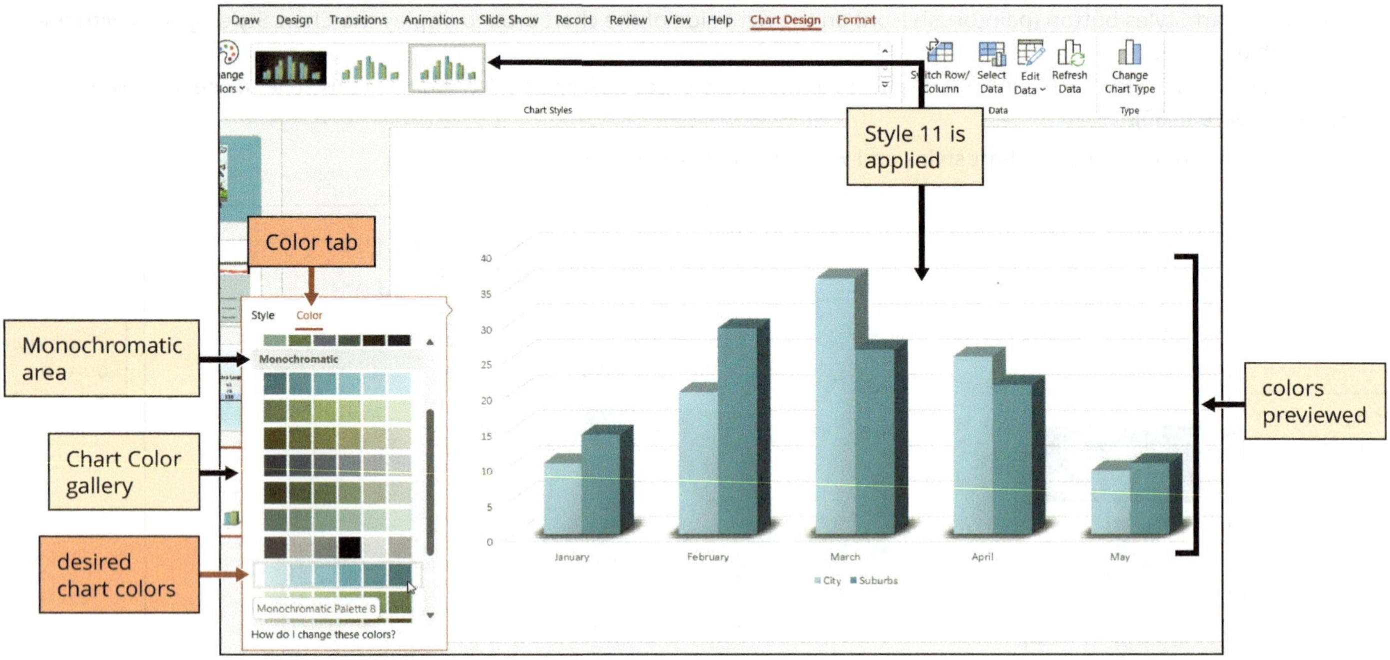

Figure 6–70

2

- Click 'Monochromatic Palette 8' to apply these colors to the chart.

Other Ways

1. Click Change Colors button (Chart Design tab | Chart Styles group)

To Add an Axis to a Chart

The legend below the chart identifies the colors assigned to each of the bars. You can modify the default legend in a variety of ways, including moving its location, changing the fill and outline, adding an effect, and changing the font. The Chart Elements button on the right side of the chart area allows you to display or hide a chart element. When you click this button, the Chart Elements pane is displayed. A check mark appears in the check box for each chart element that is displayed. You can check and uncheck each chart element to display or hide axes, the chart title, labels, gridlines, and the legend. The following steps display the axis titles and then format the text. **Why?** You want your audience to recognize that the y-axis represents the number of registrations and the x-axis represents each month.

1

- Click the Chart Elements button (plus sign icon) on the right side of the chart area to display the Chart Elements pane.
- Select the Axis Titles check box to display the two default titles for the x and y axes (Figure 6–71).

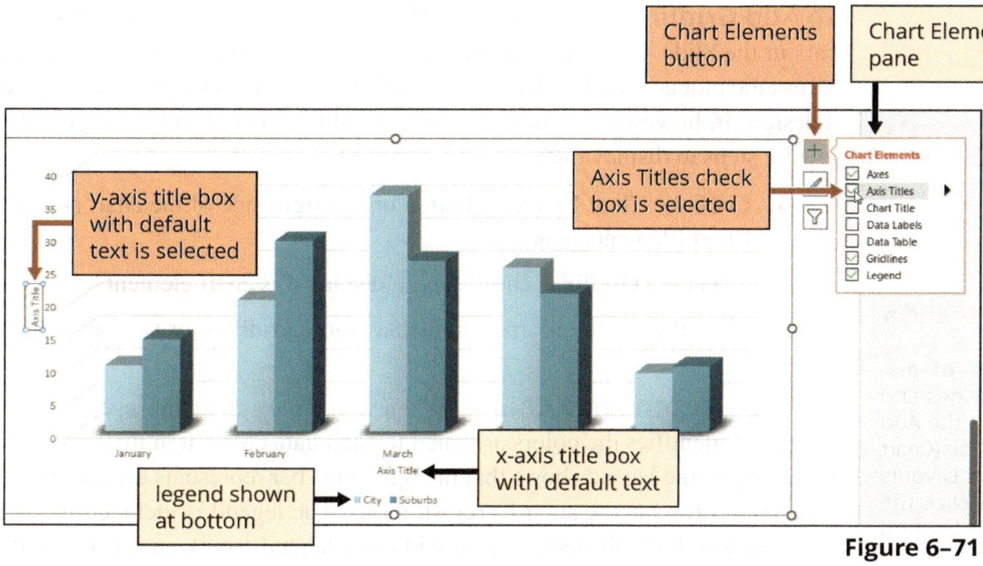

Figure 6–71

2

- With the default y-axis title box selected, type **Number of Registrations** in the text box.
- Select the text and then increase the font size to 18 point and bold the text.

3

- Click the x-axis title to select it and then type **Registrations Each Month** as the replacement text.
- Select the text and then increase the font size to 18 point and bold the text (Figure 6–72).

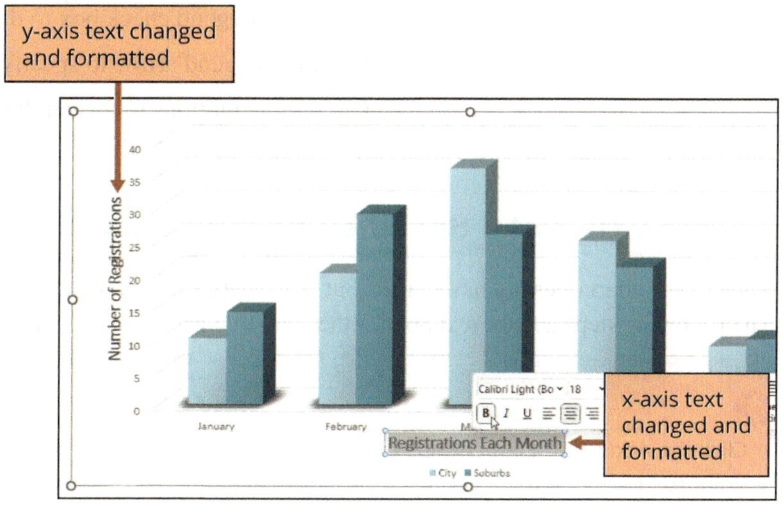

Figure 6–72

Other Ways

1. Click Add Chart Element button (Chart Design tab | Chart Layouts group), click Axis Titles

To Add Data Labels to a Chart

The figures at the top of each bar in the Slide 4 chart are called **data labels**. They show the exact amount of average minutes the groups have exerted in each exercise Location. Data labels help audience members understand a chart's content by showing details about the data series. The data labels are included in the Layout 4 design. If, however, you had selected a layout without data labels, you would perform the following steps to display them.

1. Click the Chart Elements button on the right side of the chart area to display the Chart Elements pane.
2. Select the Data Labels check box to display the labels.
3. Click the Data Labels arrow to display more details or to format the labels.

Other Ways

1. Click Add Chart Element button (Chart Design tab | Chart Layouts group), click Data Labels

BTW

Embedding Fonts

If you plan to show your presentation using a computer other than yours, consider embedding the fonts to ensure that the fonts on your slides will be available. To embed the fonts, display the Save As dialog box, click the Tools button, click Save Options, select the 'Embed fonts in the file' check box in the 'Preserve fidelity when sharing this presentation' area (PowerPoint Options dialog box), and then click the OK and Save buttons.

To Add Gridlines to a Chart The eight horizontal lines along the left side and behind the bars in the Slide 4 chart are called **gridlines**. They extend from the horizontal and vertical axes across the plot area of the chart and provide visual cues. The gridlines are included in the Layout 4 design. If, however, you had selected a layout without data labels, you would perform the following steps to display them.

1. Click the Chart Elements button on the right side of the chart area to display the Chart Elements pane.
2. Select the Gridlines check box to display this chart element.
3. Click the Gridlines arrow to display more gridlines or to format the lines.

BTW
Adding Gridlines and a Legend
Another method of displaying chart gridlines and a legend is to click the Add Chart Element button (Chart Design tab | Chart Layouts group) and then click the Gridlines or the Legend button.

To Add a Legend to a Chart When you create a chart, the legend is displayed automatically. A **legend** identifies the colors assigned to each data element in the chart. In the chart on Slide 4, for example, the legend shows that the light aqua bar represents the city registrations and the dark aqua bar represents the suburbs registrations. The legend is included in the Layout 4 design. If, however, you had selected a layout without a legend, you would perform the following steps to display this chart element.

1. Click the Chart Elements button on the right side of the chart area to display the Chart Elements pane.
2. Select the Legend check box to display this chart element.
3. Click the Legend arrow to specify where the legend should appear.
4. Click More Options to format the legend by adding borders; a fill; and effects such as a shadow, glow, or soft edges.

To Add a Title at a Specified Position in a Chart

The default chart does not have a title, but you easily can add this element and specify where you want it to appear on the slide. The following steps add the text box for the chart title and display centered above the March registrations. **Why?** A title on Slide 4 would help audience members recognize the purpose of presenting this information.

1

- Click the Add Chart Element button (Chart Design tab | Chart Layouts group) to display the Add Chart Element menu.
- Point to Chart Title to display the Chart Title gallery and then point to Above Chart in the gallery (Figure 6–73).

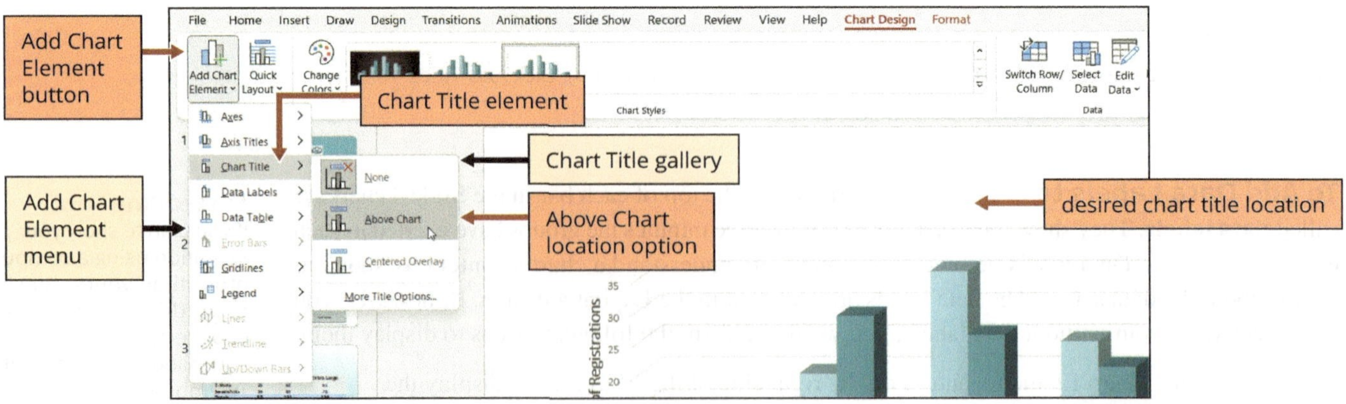

Figure 6–73

2

- Click Above Chart to display the default chart title.
- Type **Regional Registrations** as the chart title replacement text.
- Select the text and then increase the font size to 32 point (Figure 6–74).

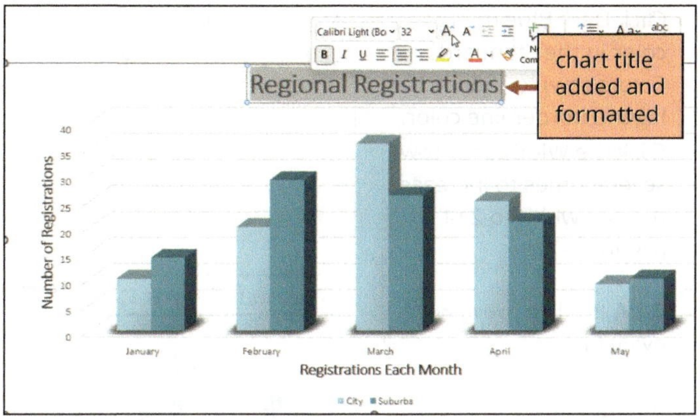

Figure 6–74

Other Ways

1. Click Chart Elements button on right side of chart, click Chart Title check box to select it, click Chart Title arrow

To Add a Border to a Chart Element

You can modify chart elements in a variety of ways, including adding borders and changing the border color. The following steps add a border to the chart title and then change the color and width. **Why?** Adding a border will call attention to the title text and help audience members understand the chart's purpose.

1

- With the chart title still selected, right-click to display the shortcut menu (Figure 6–75).

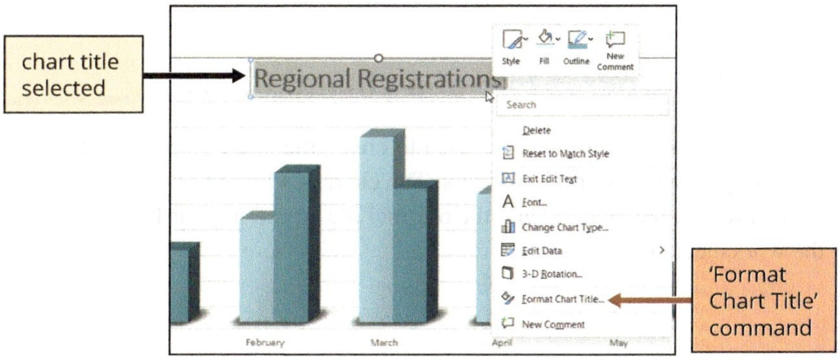

Figure 6–75

2

- Click 'Format Chart Title' to display the 'Format Chart Title' pane. If necessary, click the 'Fill & Line' button and then, if necessary, click Border to display the Border area. Scroll down to display the entire Border area.
- Click Solid line and then click the Color button to display the Color gallery (Figure 6–76).

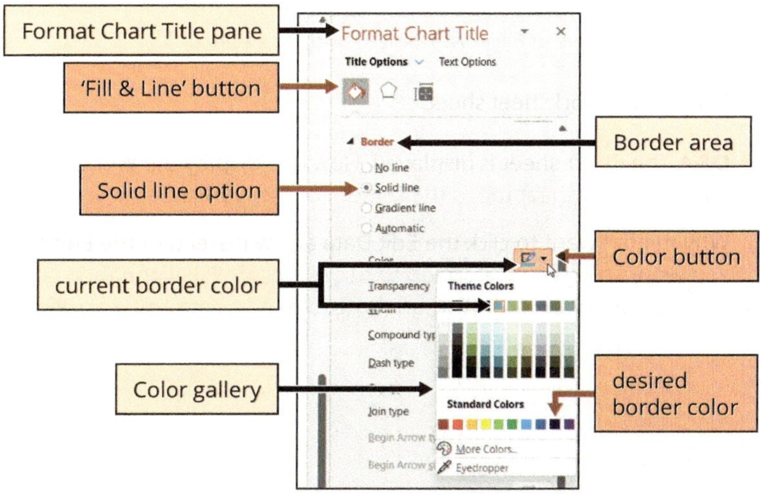

Figure 6–76

3

- Click Dark Blue (ninth color in the Standard Colors row) to change the legend border line color.
- Click the Width up arrow several times to increase the line width to 2 pt (Figure 6–77).

Q&A Is a live preview available?
No, this feature is not offered.

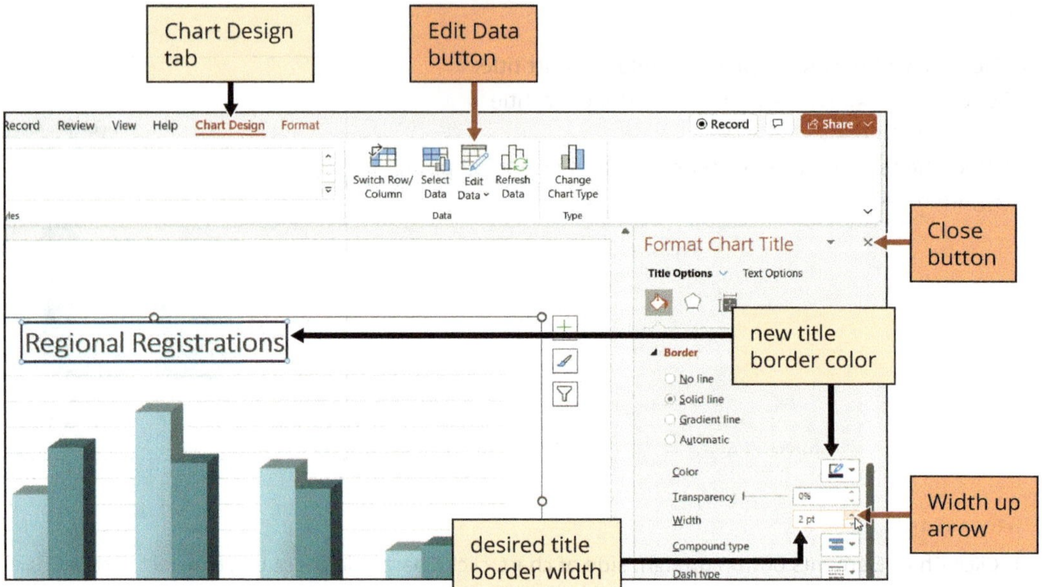

Figure 6–77

4

- Click Close ('Format Chart Title' pane).

Other Ways

1. Click Chart Elements button on right side of chart, click Chart Title, click Chart Title arrow, click More Options, click Solid Line, choose color

To Edit the Source File of a Linked Chart

The data in the Worksheet sheet is used to create the chart on Slide 4. If you edit this data, the corresponding bars in the chart change height to reflect new numbers. The chart is a linked object, so when you modify the data and close the worksheet, the chart will reflect the changes and the original file stored in your Data Files also will change. The following steps edit three cells in the worksheet. **Why?** Fun Run registrations have increased since the last time the worksheet was saved, so you need to update your chart and the Excel worksheet with this information.

1

- With the Chart Design tab displayed, click the Edit Data button (Chart Design tab | Data group) (shown in Figure 6–77) to display Excel.

Q&A I see a message that the data wasn't available because the worksheet was open in another application. What should I do?
Save and close the Excel worksheet and try again.

- Display the Worksheet sheet.

Q&A The Chart sheet is displayed. How do I display the Worksheet sheet?
Click the Worksheet tab at the bottom of the worksheet.

Why might I want to click the Edit Data arrow instead of the Edit Data button?
You would be given the option to run Microsoft Excel and then edit the worksheet using that app. More options would be available using Excel. If you simply need to edit data, you can perform that task easily using PowerPoint.

2

- Click cell B2 (city registrations in January) to make cell B2 the active cell (Figure 6–78).

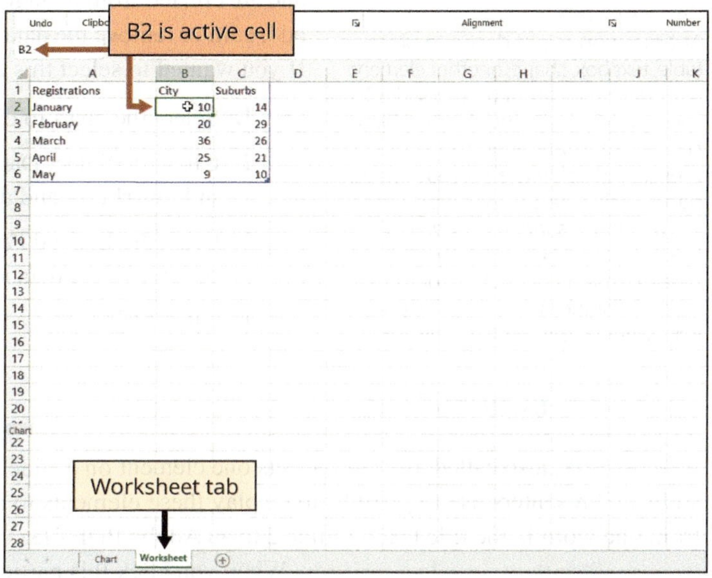

Figure 6–78

3

- Type **19** as the replacement number and then press DOWN ARROW to make cell B3 (city registrations in February) the active cell.
- Type **24** as the replacement number and then press RIGHT ARROW to make cell C3 (suburbs registrations in February) the active cell.
- Type **32** as the replacement number and then press DOWN ARROW to make cell C4 (suburbs registrations in March) the active cell.
- Type **34** as the replacement number and then press ENTER (Figure 6–79).

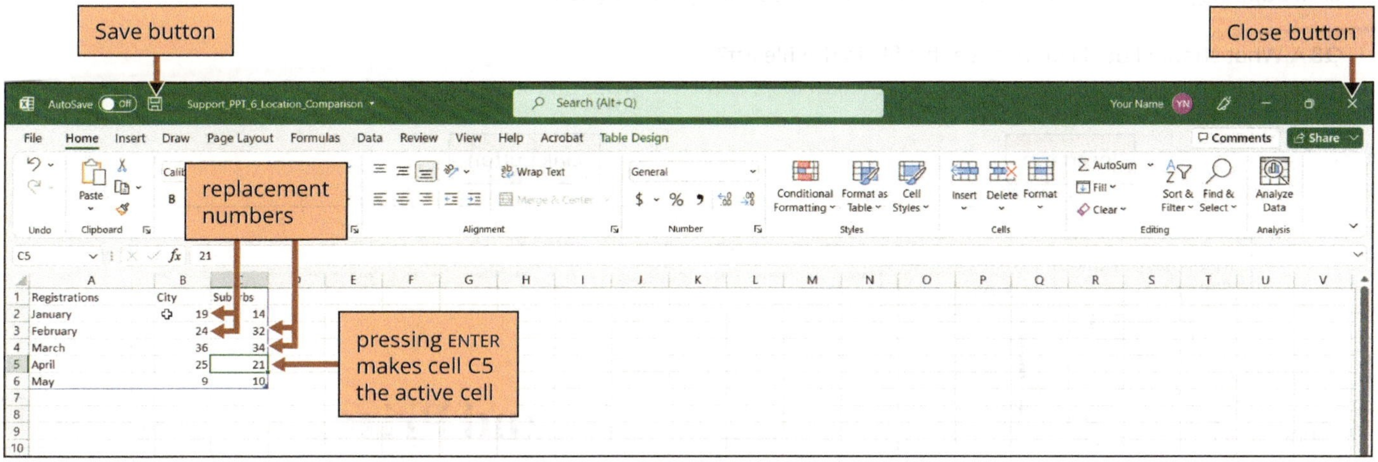

Figure 6–79

4

- If necessary, click Save on the spreadsheet toolbar to save the data to the Excel spreadsheet.
- Click Close on the spreadsheet to close the window and view the updated PowerPoint chart (Figure 6–80).

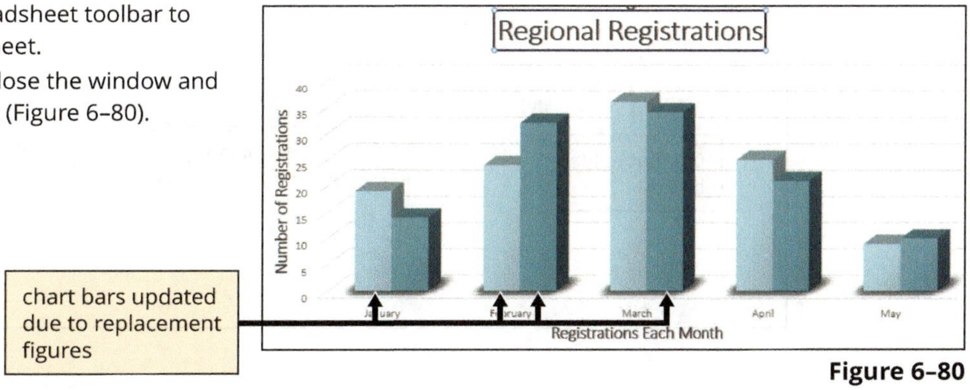

Figure 6–80

BTW

Positioning a Chart or Other Slide Object

At times you might desire to place a table, text box, shape, or other element in a precise location on the slide. To specify a position, right-click the object, click Format Shape on the shortcut menu to display the Format Shape pane, click 'Size & Properties' in the Shape Options tab, if necessary click Position, and then enter the precise measurements of the horizontal and vertical distances from either the top-left corner or the center of the slide.

To Select Chart Data Charts always are associated with an Excel-based worksheet and are created from a range of data in a row or column, called a data series. If you want to add, edit, or remove the data used to develop the chart, you need to select a new data series. If you wanted to select this chart data, you would perform the following steps.

1. Select the chart to display the Chart Design tab.
2. Click the Select Data button (Chart Design tab | Data group) to display the chart in PowerPoint and display the 'Select Data Source' dialog box.
3. Click the Legend Entries or the Horizontal Axis Labels check boxes to add, edit, or remove the data series in the chart.
4. Click OK.

To Add a Link to Text

A **hyperlink**, also called a **link**, connects one element on a slide to another slide, presentation, picture, file, webpage, or email address. Presenters use hyperlinks to display these elements to an audience. In this presentation, you will create a hyperlink from one word in the title text on Slide 2 to an Adobe PDF file. **Why?** You want to show your audience the certificate they will receive when they complete their run. When you click this particular word during a slide show, Adobe Acrobat starts and then opens this PDF file. The following steps hyperlink title text to a PDF file.

1

- Display Slide 2 and then select the word, Prizes, in the title.
- Display the Insert tab and then click the Link button (Insert tab | Links group) to display the Insert Hyperlink dialog box.
- If necessary, click the 'Existing File or Web Page' button in the Link to area.
- If necessary, click the Current Folder button in the Look in area and navigate to the location where your Data Files are stored.
- Click Support_PPT_6_Certificate.pdf to select this file as the hyperlink (Figure 6–81).

Q&A What should I do if I do not see this file in the file list?

Click the file type arrow ('Link to File' dialog box) to display the file types and then click 'All Files (*.*)' in the list.

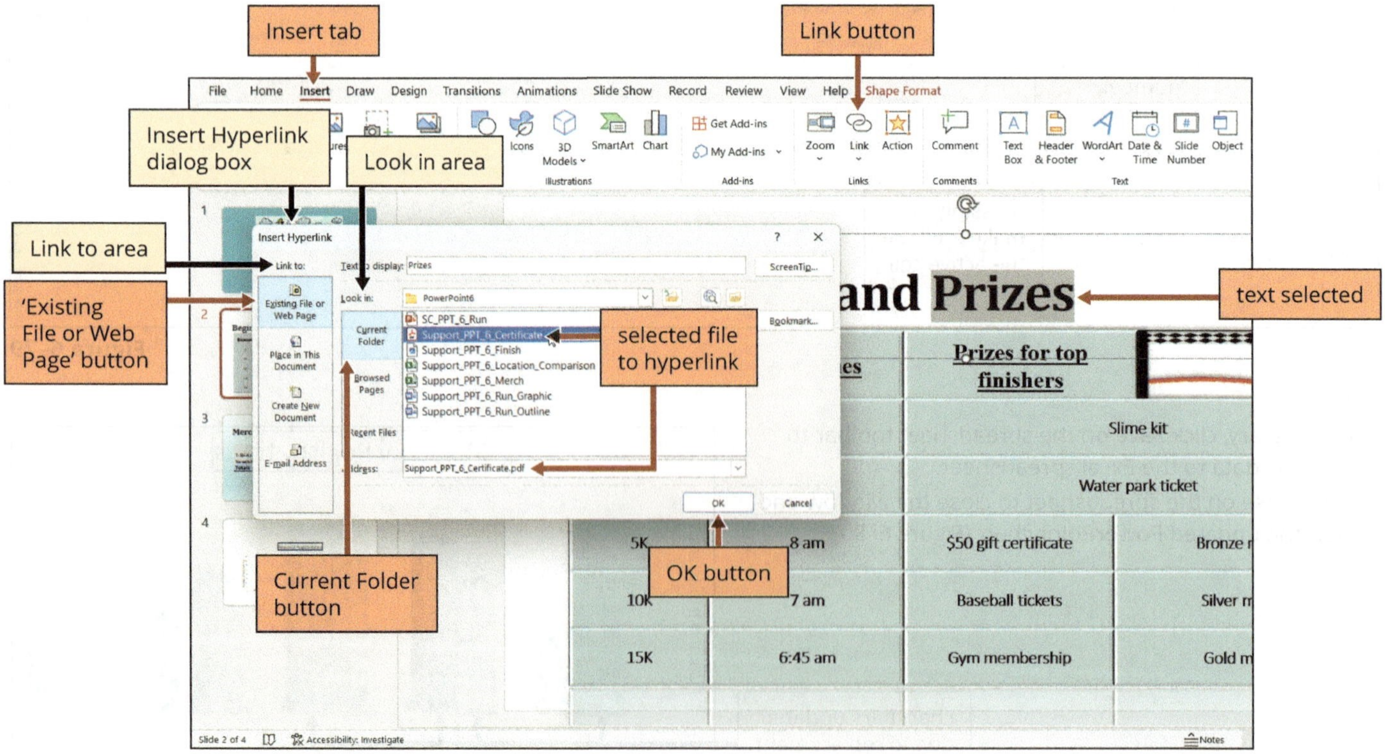

Figure 6–81

2

- Click OK (Insert Hyperlink dialog box) to insert the hyperlink.

Q&A How do I remove a hyperlink?
Select the text, click the Hyperlink button (Insert tab | Links group), and then click Remove Link (Edit Hyperlink dialog box).

Changing Views

You have been using Normal view to create and edit your slides. Once you completed your slides in projects for previous modules, you reviewed the final products by displaying each slide in Slide Show view, which occupies the full computer screen. You were able to view how the transitions, graphics, and effects will display in an actual presentation before an audience.

PowerPoint has other views to help review a presentation for content, organization, and overall appearance. **Reading view** is similar to Slide Show view because each slide displays individually, but the slides do not fill the entire screen. Using this view, you easily can progress through the slides forward or backward with simple controls at the bottom of the window. Switching between Slide Sorter, Reading, and Normal views helps you review your presentation, assess whether the slides have an attractive design and adequate content, and make sure they are organized for the most impact. After reviewing the slides, you can change the view to Normal so that you may continue working on the presentation.

You also can display your presentation in **Outline view** to show the titles and main text from each slide. Each title is displayed on the left side of the pane along with a slide icon and slide number. A slide without a title has no text displayed on the right side of the slide number. You can create a presentation in Outline view by typing or copying text.

To Navigate between Slides in Reading View

The following steps change the view from Normal view to Reading view and back to Normal view. **Why?** You want to use Reading view to display all the slides in the presentation in a full screen.

1

- Display Slide 1 and then click the Reading View button on the status bar to display Slide 1 of the presentation in Reading view (Figure 6–82).

Azmeyart-Design/Pixabay

Figure 6–82

2

- Click the Next button three times to advance through the presentation.
- Click the Previous button three times to display Slide 3, Slide 2, and then Slide 1.
- Click the Menu button to display commonly used commands (Figure 6–83).

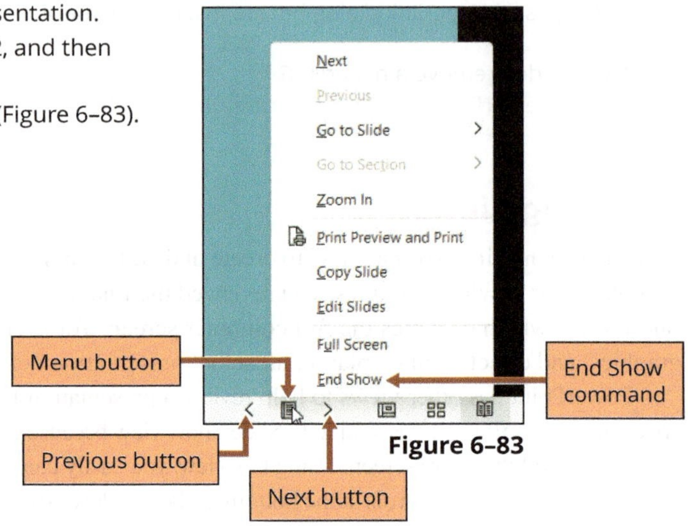

Figure 6–83

3

- Click End Show to return to Normal view, which is the view you were using before Reading view.

To Switch to Outline View

The following step changes the view from Normal view to Outline view. **Why?** You can review the text on your slides without seeing any graphical items.

1

- With Slide 1 displayed, click the View tab and then click the Outline View button (View tab | Presentation Views group) (Figure 6–84).
- If you see a Microsoft PowerPoint dialog box stating, 'Real-time editing is not supported in outline view', click OK to close the dialog box.

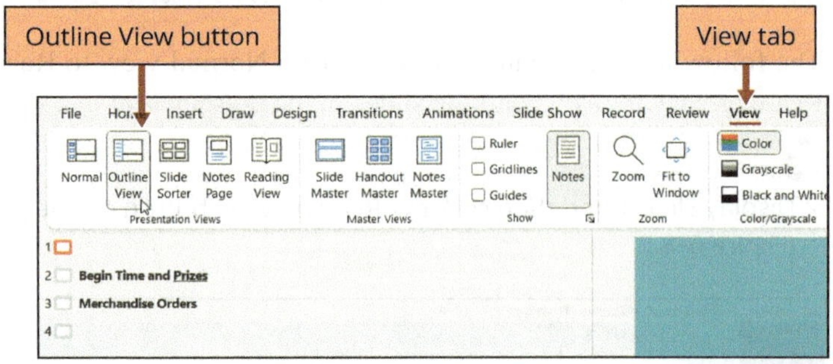

Figure 6–84

To Navigate between Slides in Outline View

The following steps display all four slides in Outline view. **Why?** Using Outline view, you can click a slide icon to display any slide.

1

- Click the Slide 2 icon to select that slide (Figure 6–85).

2

- Press DOWN ARROW to navigate to Slide 3.
- Press DOWN ARROW again to navigate to Slide 4.

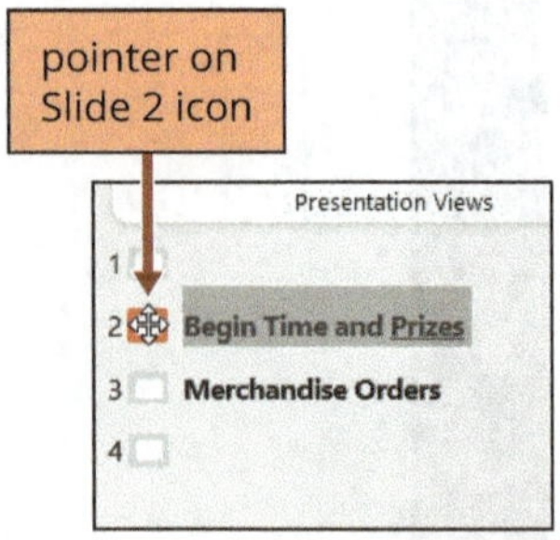

Figure 6–85

To Move a Slide in Outline View

The following steps reverse the order of Slides 2 and 3. **Why?** You desire to change the slide order, which you can do easily in Outline view by dragging the slide icon to the desired location.

1

- Click the Slide 2 icon and then drag the pointer downward between the Slides 3 and 4 icons (Figure 6–86).

2

- Release the mouse to move Slide 2 so that it becomes the new Slide 3.

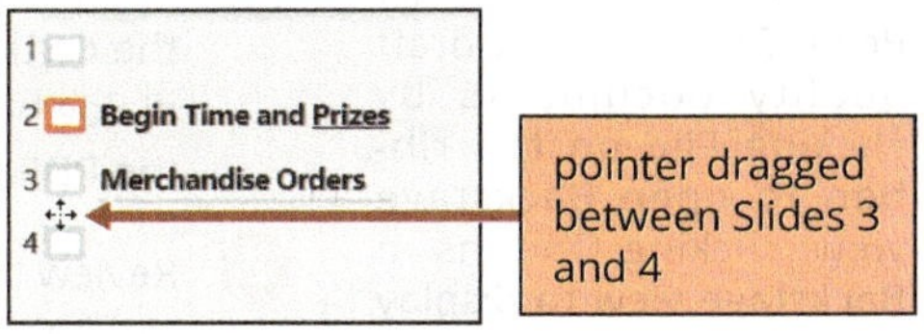

Figure 6–86

To Enter Text in Outline View

The following steps edit the Slide 3 title text in Outline view. **Why?** You decide that the words, Start Times, rather than Begin Time should match the second column title text in the table.

1

- With Slide 3 displayed in Outline view, select the words, Begin Time, and then type **Start Times** as the replacement text (Figure 6–87).

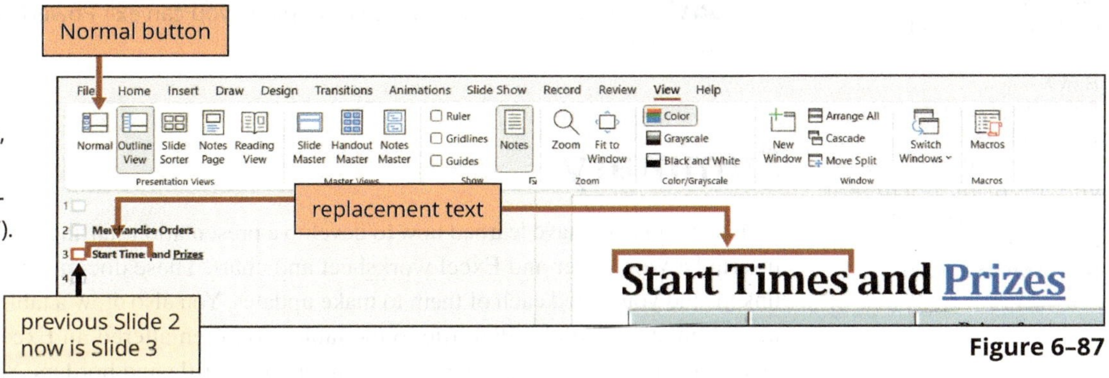

Figure 6–87

2

- Click the Normal button (View tab | Presentation Views group) (shown in Figure 6–87) to display the slides in Normal view.

Other Ways

1. Click Normal view button on status bar

To Add a Transition between Slides

The final enhancements you will make in this presentation are to apply a transition, change the transition effect option, and change the transition speed. The following steps apply these transition effects to the presentation.

1. Apply the Clock transition in the Exciting category to all slides.
2. Change the effect option to Wedge.
3. Change the transition duration to 03.00 seconds.

BTW
Distributing a Document
Instead of printing and distributing a hard copy of PowerPoint slides, you can distribute the slides electronically. Options include sending the slides via email; posting it on cloud storage (such as OneDrive) and sharing the link with others; posting it on social media, a blog, or other website; and sharing a link associated with an online location of the slides. You also can create and share a PDF or XPS image of the slides, so that users can view the file in Acrobat Reader or XPS Viewer instead of in PowerPoint.

To Run, Print, Save, and Exit PowerPoint

BTW
Conserving Ink and Toner
If you want to conserve ink or toner, you can instruct PowerPoint to print draft quality documents by clicking File on the ribbon to open Backstage view, clicking Options in Backstage view to display the PowerPoint Options dialog box, clicking Advanced in the left pane (PowerPoint Options dialog box), scrolling to the Print area in the right pane, verifying there is no check mark in the High quality check box, and then clicking OK. Then, use Backstage view to print the document as usual.

BTW
Printing Document Properties
PowerPoint does not allow you to print document properties. This feature, however, is available in Microsoft 365 Word.

The presentation now is complete. You should run the presentation, view the hyperlinked file, print the slides, save the presentation, and then exit PowerPoint.

1. Run the Run presentation. When Slide 3 is displayed, click Prizes in the title text to display the certificate document as the hyperlinked file. If the Microsoft PowerPoint Security Notice dialog box is displayed, click Yes, then click OK in the Microsoft Office dialog box, to open the PDF file.
2. Review the contents of the certificate document. Point to the PowerPoint app button on the taskbar to see the PowerPoint window and a live preview of Slide 3.
3. Click the thumbnail of Slide 3 to display that slide and then display Slide 4.
4. End the slide show. Close the certificate document.
5. Print the Run presentation as a handout with two slides per page.
6. Save the Run presentation again with the same file name.
7. sam Because the project now is complete, you can exit PowerPoint, closing all open documents.

Summary

In this module you have learned how to develop a presentation starting with a Word outline. You then inserted a Word flyer and Excel worksheet and chart. These documents were either embedded or linked, and you edited each of them to make updates. You also drew a table, enhanced and formatted it, and linked an Adobe PDF file to the table. You then altered an Excel object by changing the chart type and layout, applying a style, and adding a title and borders. You reviewed the slides by changing views and then moved a slide and edited text in Outline view.

Consider This: Plan Ahead

What decisions will you need to make when creating your next presentation?

Use these guidelines as you complete the assignments in this module and create your own slide show decks outside of this class.

1. **Use powerful words to accompany the text on your slides.** The slides are meant to enhance your talk by clarifying main points and calling attention to key ideas. Your speech should use words that explain and substantiate your visuals.
2. **Develop tables that are clear and meaningful.** Tables are extremely useful vehicles for presenting complex relationships. Their design plays an important part in successfully conveying the information to the audience.
3. **Use appropriate colors when formatting graphics you want people to remember.** Numerous studies have shown that appropriate graphics help audiences comprehend and remember the information presented during a speech. Color has been shown to increase retention by as much as 80 percent. When choosing colors for your graphics, use hues that fit the tone and objective of your message.

Student Assignments

Apply Your Knowledge

Reinforce the skills and apply the concepts you learned in this module.

Inserting Slides from an Outline, Adding a Link, and Inserting and Formatting a Table and Chart

Note: To complete this assignment, you will be required to use the Data Files. Please contact your instructor for information about accessing the Data Files.

Instructions: Start PowerPoint and create a blank presentation.

The nature center in your town has a birding club with more than 100 members. The club promotes birding through many activities, including nature walks, bird counts, and various contests. Community residents often contact club members to ask about which feeders are appropriate to attract particular types of birds, so the club president is preparing a presentation to describe various types of feeders and also to display the results of a recent bird count event. In addition, the club wants to promote its birdhouse building event. The president has given you a Word document with topics to cover in the presentation and has supplied an Excel file that includes a chart showing the number of four common birds that visited feeders during a recent weekend. You also have a PDF file promoting the Birdhouse Building Challenge event. You will create the three slides shown in Figure 6–88.

Perform the following tasks:

1. Apply the Frame theme and then use the Slides from Outline feature to insert slides from the Word outline, Support_PPT_6_Feeder_Outline.docx, which is located in the Data Files. Delete Slide 1.
2. Change the new Slide 1 layout to Title Slide and then increase the title text font size to 72 point and the subtitle text font size to 40 point.
3. Add a link from the subtitle text to the file named Support_PPT_6_Challenge.pdf, which is located in the Data Files. Change the subtitle text color to Purple (last color in the Standard Colors row).
4. Insert the picture Support_PPT_6_Birdhouse.png, change the height to 7.5", and then move the photo to the right side of the slide, as shown in Figure 6–88a.

   If requested by your instructor, change the words, Your Yard, in the title text placeholder to the city where you were born.
5. Display Slide 2, delete the content placeholder, and then draw the table shown in Figure 6–88b. Size the table with a height of 6" and a width of 9" and then move it to the right of the title text placeholder. Merge or split cells as necessary and add the table text as shown in Figure 6–88b.
6. Apply the 'Medium Style 4 – Accent 1' table style (second style in the fourth Medium row). Apply the 'Linear Diagonal – Bottom Right to Top Left' shading gradient (last gradient in the third Variations row). Apply the 'Perspective: Lower Left' shadow effect (first shadow in the last Perspective row). Add borders to all table cells.
7. Increase the font size of the table column headings (Bird and Type of Feeder) to 32 point and then, if necessary, bold this text and change the font color to Purple. Increase the font size of the four bird rows to 28 point.
8. Align all the table text in the center of the table cells. Distribute the table rows. Align the table to the right and the middle of the slide.
9. Display Slide 3 and then delete the content placeholder. Open the Excel file called Support_PPT_6_Feeder_Counts.xlsx, which is located in the Data Files, and then copy the bar chart located on the Chart sheet. Paste the chart onto Slide 3 with the 'Use Destination Theme & Link Data' option and then resize the chart height to 6" and the width to 9.5". Align the chart in the right and the middle of the slide.
10. Close Excel.

Continued on next page

11. Change the chart style to Style 16.
12. Click the Edit Data button (Chart Design tab | Data group) to display Excel and then, if necessary, click the Worksheet tab to display the worksheet. Change the House Finch figure in cell B2 from 38 to 67, as shown in Figure 6–88c. Save and close the worksheet.
13. Save the presentation using the file name, **SC_PPT_6_Birding**.
14. Submit the presentation in the format specified by your instructor.
15. **Consider This:** Did the formatting and effects enhance the Slide 2 table? What other enhancements could you have made to improve the table? In Step 11, you changed the chart style to Style 16. Was this style a good choice? Why or why not?

Figure 6–88(a): Slide 1

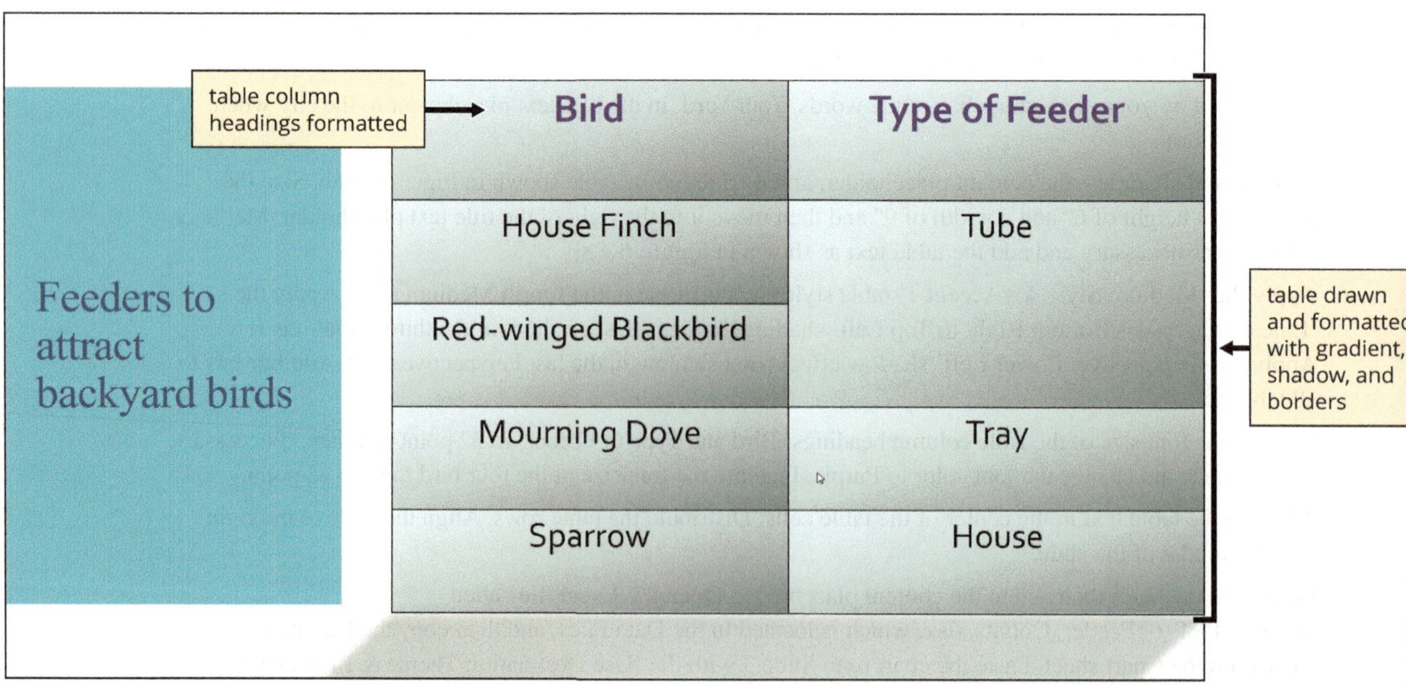

Figure 6–88(b): Slide 2

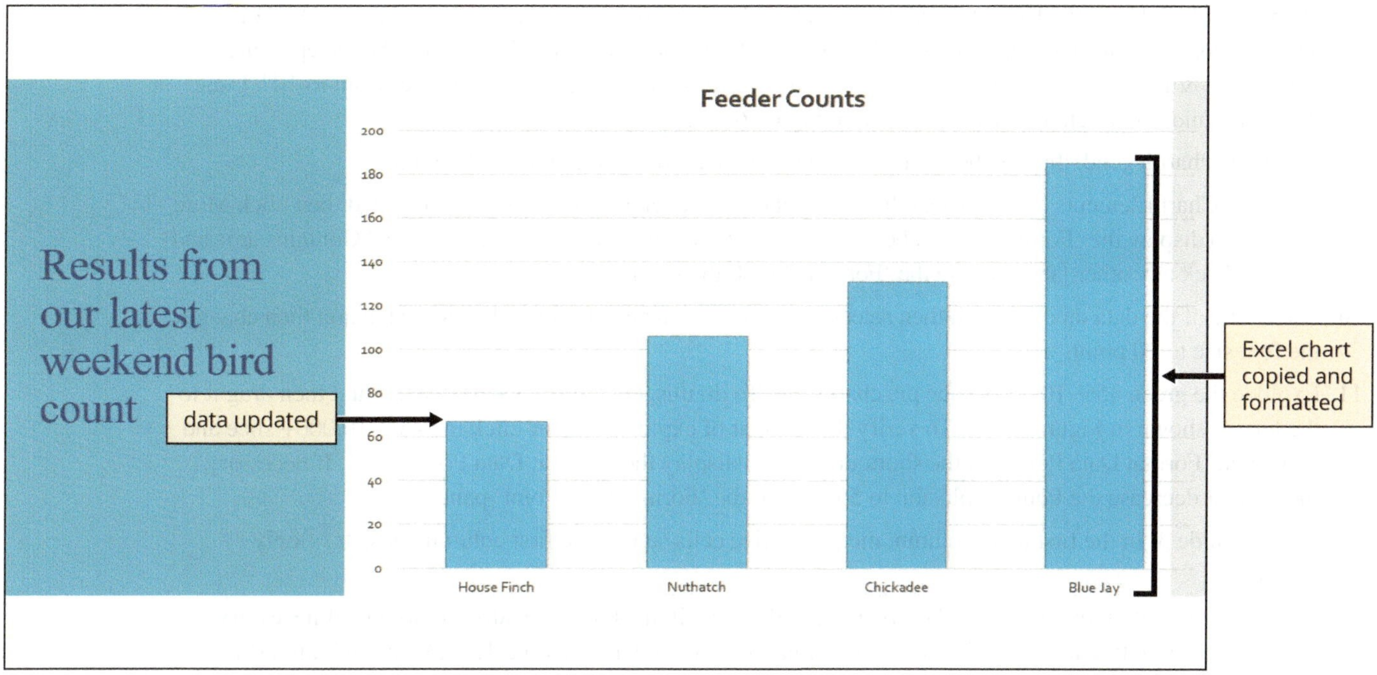

Figure 6–88(c): Slide 3

Extend Your Knowledge

Extend the skills you learned in this module and experiment with new skills. You may need to use Help to complete the assignment.

Modifying a Word Document, Excel Pie Chart, and Table

Note: To complete this assignment, you will be required to use the Data Files. Please contact your instructor for information about accessing the Data Files.

Instructions: Start PowerPoint. Open the presentation called SC_PPT_6-1.pptx, which is located in the Data Files.

Going for a walk is one of the most beneficial activities people can take. This form of exercise improves fitness and well-being, and its many health benefits include working arm, leg, and shoulder muscles, easing stress, and strengthening the heart and lungs. Studies indicate that walking in nature is particularly effective. Students at your school participate in a walking group, and they encourage members to log their steps, often exceeding 10,000 steps per outing. These facts are applied in the slides you will create in this assignment. You will insert and format a Word object, copy and modify an Excel pie chart, and format a table.

Perform the following tasks:

1. On Slide 1, display the Design tab and then click the Format Background button (Design tab | Customize group) to display the Format Background pane.
2. Click Gradient fill and then click the Color button in the Fill area to display the Color gallery. Click Light Blue (seventh color in Standard Colors row) to change the gradient color.
3. In the Position box, located below the Color button, change the Position setting to 30%. Close the Format Background pane.
4. Insert the Word object, Support_PPT_6_Walk.docx, which is located in the Data Files. Display the Shape Format tab and then click the Size Dialog Box Launcher to display the Format Object pane. Click the 'Lock aspect ratio' check box to uncheck it and then increase the Word object size height to 6" and the width to 13".
5. Change the text, Let's Walk, to Let's Take a Walk in the title. (You may need to scroll up in the Word object to display the title text.)
6. Click outside the Word object and then close the Format Object pane. Align the object in the center and middle of the slide (Figure 6–89a).

Continued on next page

7. Display Slide 2. Open the Excel file called Support_PPT_6_Steps.xlsx, which is located in the Data Files, and then copy the pie chart located on the Chart sheet. Paste the chart onto Slide 2 with the 'Keep Source Formatting & Embed Workbook' option and then resize the chart height to 5.5" and the width to 10". Use the smart guides to align the chart, as shown in Figure 6–89b.
8. Select the chart legend, display the Home tab, and then increase the font size to 24 point.
9. Click the Chart Elements button, select the Data Label box, click the Data Labels arrow, and then click More Options to display the 'Format Data Labels' pane. Check the Percentage label in the Label Contains area and then uncheck any other labels. Close the 'Format Data Labels' pane.
10. Select one of the data labels, which then selects the other two labels. Display the Home tab and then change the font size to 20 point.
11. Explode the green 45% 10,000+ slice pie chart slice. To do this, click this slice to select it and then drag it to the left, as shown in Figure 6–89c. To verify the amount of explosion, right-click the 45% 10,000+ slice and then click 'Format Data Point' on the shortcut menu to display the 'Format Data Point' pane. If necessary, increase or decrease the Point Explosion to 5%. Close the 'Format Data Point' pane.
12. Display Slide 3. In the first table column, merge the five cells so that the first column consists of only one cell.
13. Change the direction of the data in the first table cell so that it displays vertically. To do this, if necessary, select the column title text (Walking Works), display the Layout tab, click the Text Direction button (Layout tab | Alignment group) to display the Text Direction gallery, and then click 'Rotate all text 270°' to rotate the text in the cell. Change the font size to 28 point and then center this text.
14. Change the first column cell size width to 1.5" and the second column cell size width to 2". Change the table height to 4" and the table width to 10.5" and then align the table in the center and middle of the slide (Figure 6–89d).

    If requested by your instructor, add the name of your high school mascot in the first column.
15. Save the presentation using the file name, **SC_PPT_6_Walk**.
16. Submit the revised document in the format specified by your instructor.
17. **Consider This:** In this assignment, you modified the gradient and edited a Word document. You also exploded a pie chart slice. Did these changes enhance the slides and increase the audience's understanding of the benefits of walking? Why or why not?

Figure 6–89(a): Slide 1

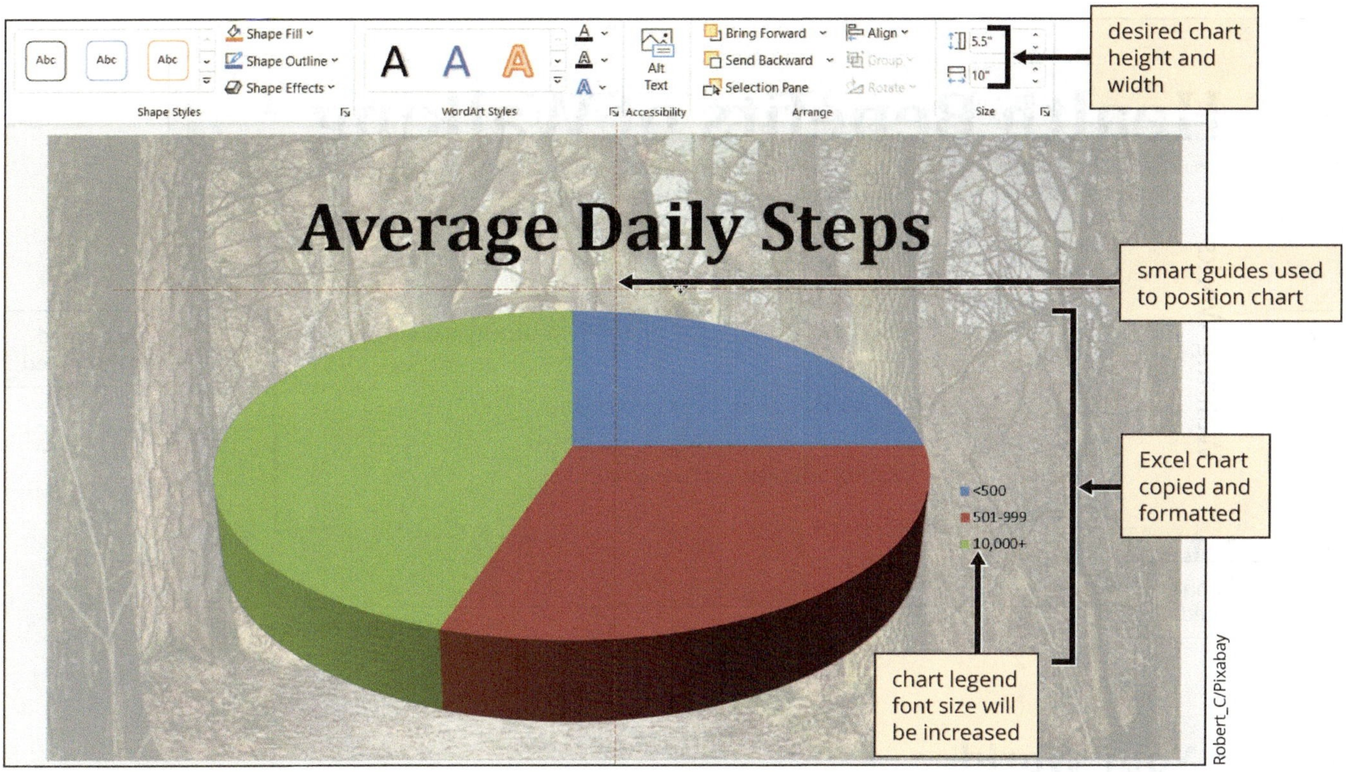

Figure 6–89(b): Slide 2 Chart Positioned with Smart Guides

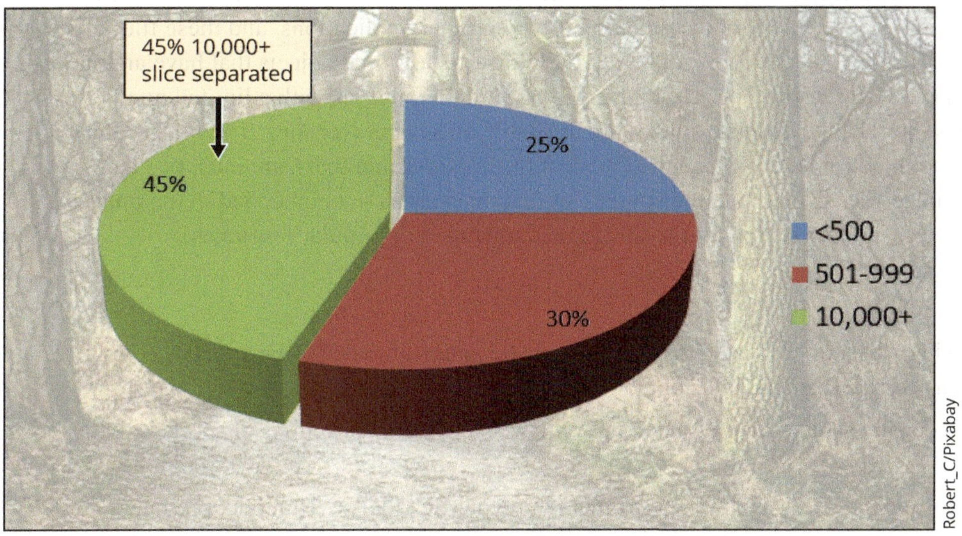

Figure 6–89(c): Slide 2 Pie Slice Exploded

Continued on next page

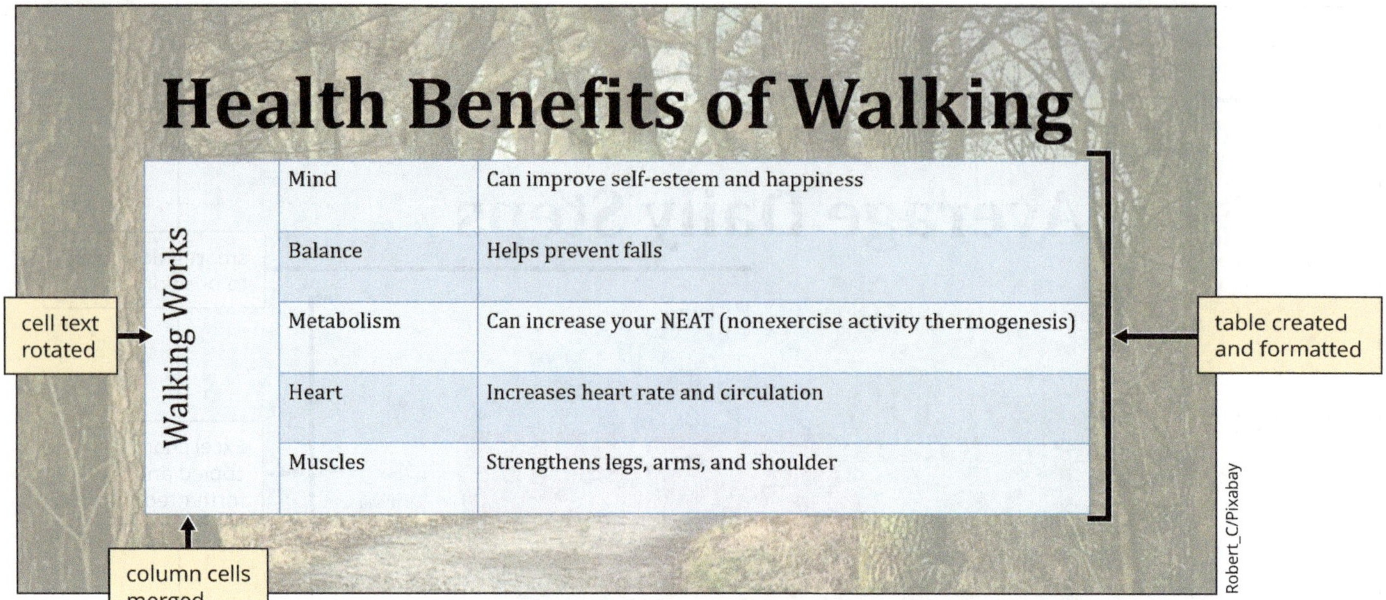

Figure 6-89(d): Slide 3

Expand Your World

Create a solution that uses cloud or web technologies by learning and investigating on your own from general guidance.

Locating and Inserting Animated GIF Files

Instructions: In this module, you created a presentation for the fun run promoters to encourage people to register for the event. You embedded, linked, and edited objects from other applications, and these files greatly enhanced the presentation. The promoters now would like you to insert additional objects that have animation. You decide to locate animated GIF files because they generally are simple pictures with a limited number of colors. GIF, or Graphics Interchange Format, images are available on several websites. The images may or may not be animated, and they can be downloaded at no cost or for a minimal fee. Care must be taken, however, to visit and download files from reputable sources so that malware is not embedded in the images. You can use a search engine or another search tool to locate recommended or popular resources.

Perform the following tasks:

1. Visit one of the following websites or locate other websites that contain animated GIFs: pixabay.com/gifs, gifs.cc, BestAnimations.com, GIFanimations.com, or Giphy.com.
2. Locate files that could enhance your Run presentation. Some websites have collections of sports activities that could be useful.
3. Download at least two animated GIFs and then insert them into your SC_PPT_6_Run.pptx presentation.

   If requested to do so by your instructor, change the word, Water, in the Slide 3 table to the town where you were born.
4. Save the presentation using the file name, **SC_PPT_6_Run_GIF**.
5. Submit the assignment in the format specified by your instructor.
6. **Consider This:** Why did you select these particular images for your slides? Do the animated GIF images enhance or detract from your presentation? Where might you use GIF files other than in PowerPoint slides?

In the Lab

Apply your creative thinking and problem-solving skills to design and implement a solution.

Design and Create a Presentation about Gardening

Part 1: Students at your school have established a community garden in a one-acre plot on campus. While the vegetables and fruit provide nutritious produce, the garden also provides health benefits for the students who tend to the area. When these gardeners pull weeds, haul buckets of water, and rake the soil, they are stretching, bending, and twisting, which adds to their flexibility and strength. They are connecting with nature, increasing their exposure to Vitamin D, improving their self-esteem, and reducing their stress levels.

The students also have planted flowers and shrubs to support monarch butterflies and hummingbirds. The monarchs depend on milkweed and also favor purple coneflowers, asters, meadow blazing stars, and prairie phlox. The hummingbirds are attracted to columbine, milkweed, wild bergamot, spotted jewelweed, and cardinal flower. The students want to promote interest in their community garden, and you have been tasked with creating a PowerPoint presentation to accompany a webinar on this topic.

Perform some research about the benefits of gardening and the plants that attract butterflies and hummingbirds. Begin by creating a Word outline with the information for each slide and then insert the slides from this outline. Also create a Word document flyer promoting the community garden and showing the plants community members can purchase to provide a feeding station for butterflies and hummingbirds. Link this document to one of your PowerPoint slides. The Data Files folder contains pictures you could use. Review and revise your presentation as needed and then save the file using the file name, **SC_PPT_6_Garden**. Submit your assignment in the format specified by your instructor.

Part 2: **Consider This:** You made several decisions while creating the presentation in this assignment: what content to include, how to format the Word documents, where to insert the link to the Word flyer, and which styles and effects to apply. What was the rationale behind each of these decisions? Where would you recommend showing this slide show? When you reviewed the document, what changes did you make?

Adding Media and Enhancing SmartArt

Objectives

After completing this module, you will be able to:

- Insert a SmartArt graphic
- Convert a picture to SmartArt
- Add pictures into a SmartArt shape
- Change the SmartArt color
- Rearrange SmartArt shape locations
- Promote and demote SmartArt shapes
- Remove a picture background
- Change picture brightness, contrast, and color saturation
- Insert and edit a video clip
- Insert and edit an audio clip
- Compress a video
- Insert a hyperlink
- Add a hyperlink action
- Insert an action button

Introduction

Well-produced slides are enhanced with a variety of visual content. PowerPoint's themes determine the default characteristics of slide objects, but colors, fills, effects, and other formatting options can give the slides a unique character. Graphics, such as SmartArt, have individual layouts, styles, and color schemes. If a SmartArt design does not meet the specific needs of your slide content, you can modify it by adding shapes, reordering the current shapes, and changing the color and effects.

Audio and video clips can emphasize slide content and focus the audience's attention on the material, particularly when they present a concept that a picture or graphic cannot depict. A simple, uncluttered picture can help audience members comprehend and retain important facts, and removing a picture's background can direct the audience's attention to the material being presented. You can save your presentation as a PDF (Portable Document Format) file, which is an electronic image file format by Adobe® that mirrors the appearance of the original document and allows you to present and exchange your presentation independent of software, hardware, or operating system.

BTW
PDF Option Settings
Your PDF file can include comments, ink notations, handouts, outlines, and non-printing information such as document properties. You can choose the number of slides to include and specify whether the order is horizontal or vertical.

Project: Presentation with Audio and Video Clips, SmartArt, and Hyperlinks

People begin a fitness program for many reasons. Some may train to look better, manage stress, or simply feel better. Whatever the goal, total body fitness should become part of an overall lifetime health habit. Elements include cardio and strength exercises, recovery activities such as yoga, and proper nutrition. To reduce injury and promote recovery, warmup and cooldown exercises provide benefits well beyond the actual exercise session.

In this module's project, you will follow proper design guidelines and learn to use PowerPoint to create the slides shown in Figure 7–1a through 7–1f. You also will create a PDF file of the presentation, shown in Figure 7–1g. The objective is to produce a presentation for health professionals to use during their seminars held for individuals considering beginning a fitness program. You begin by opening a file and then changing the image on Slide 1 (Figure 7–1a). You will insert a screen clipping from another PowerPoint presentation and then later edit a video and an audio clip.

The second slide (Figure 7–1b) includes SmartArt that you will create and enhance. The slide shows a picture of various fitness elements and four aspects of a complete healthy regimen.

On Slide 3 (Figure 7–1c), you will add a video poster frame that covers the first frame of a video that you will insert on that slide. When the slide is displayed, the poster frame uncovers the video that plays full screen (Figure 7–1d).

The final slide (Figure 7–1e) shows three steps people can take to begin a fitness program. The slide contains another SmartArt graphic that you will format by moving the shapes. The picture on this slide has a background that you will remove, and then you will change the contrast and color saturation and flip the image. The slide contains a hyperlink from the words, Getting Started, to a slide in another PowerPoint presentation showing warmup benefits and exercises (Figure 7–1f). That slide contains an action button that will return the presenter to Slide 4 in the original presentation.

The final steps in the project create and save a PDF file (Figure 7–1g) from the presentation.

In this module, you will learn how to create the slides shown in Figure 7–1. You will perform the following general tasks as you progress through this module:

1. Change a picture.
2. Create, format, and modify a SmartArt graphic by inserting pictures, changing colors and effects, and moving shapes.
3. Format a picture by removing the background, changing the contrast and color saturation, and flipping the image.
4. Insert and trim a video and an audio clip.
5. Add a video poster frame.
6. Insert a link to a second PowerPoint presentation.
7. Save the presentation as a PDF.

BTW
Ribbon and Screen Resolution
PowerPoint may change how the groups and buttons within the groups appear on the ribbon, depending on the screen resolution of your computer. Thus, your ribbon may look different from the ones in this book if you are using a screen resolution other than 1920 × 1080.

BTW
Distributing a Document
Instead of printing and distributing a hard copy of PowerPoint slides, you can distribute the slides electronically. Options include sending the slides via email; posting it on cloud storage (such as OneDrive) and sharing the link with others; posting it on social media, a blog, or other website; and sharing a link associated with an online location of the slides. You also can create and share a PDF or XPS image of the slides, so that users can view the file in Acrobat Reader or XPS Viewer instead of in PowerPoint.

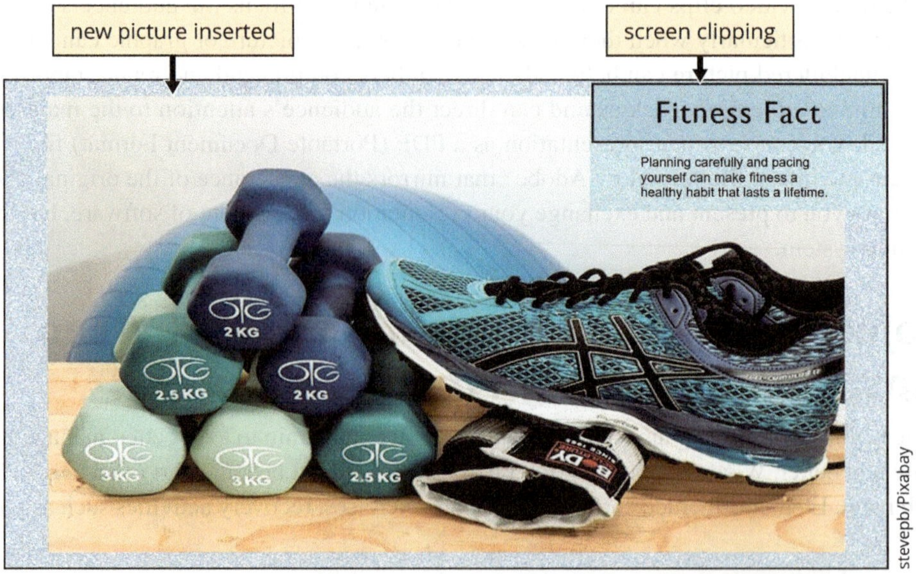

Figure 7–1(a): Slide 1

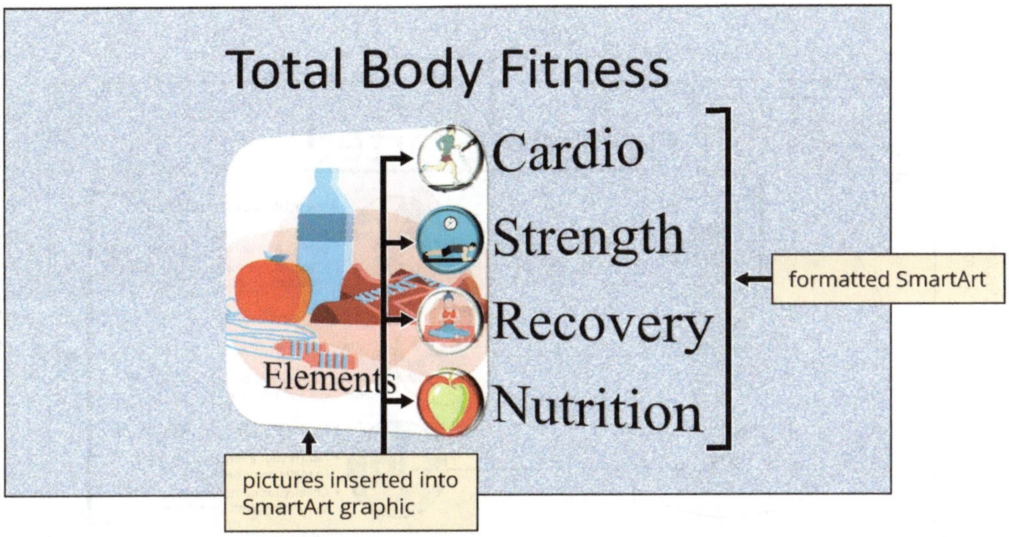

TotalShape/Pixabay; Bill_Bowler/Pixabay; Mohamed_hassan/Pixabay; TotalShape/Pixabay; Merio/Pixabay

Figure 7–1(b): Slide 2 (SmartArt Enhanced with Pictures)

Greg Rosenke/Unsplash.com

Figure 7–1(c): Slide 3 (Video Poster Frame)

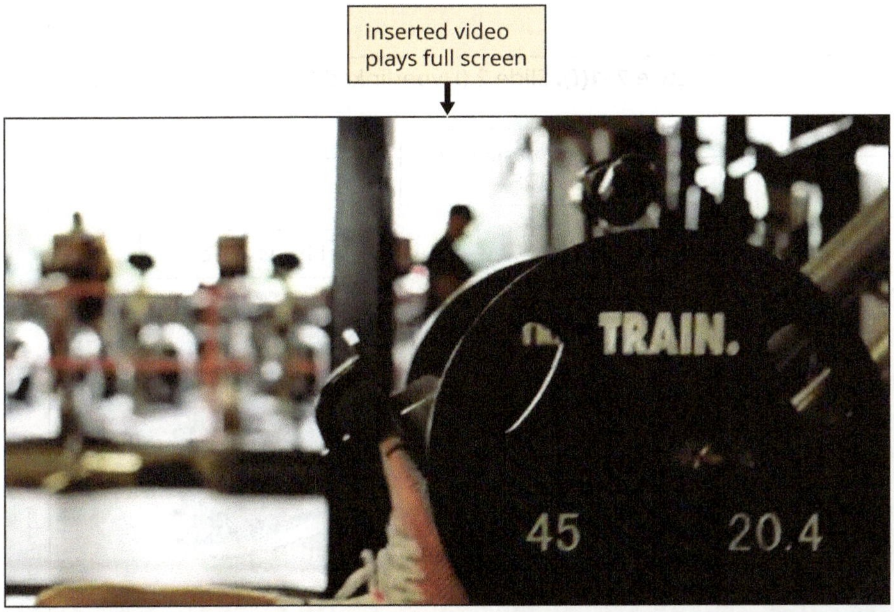

freefitnessmedia/Pixabay

Figure 7–1(d): Slide 3 (Video Clip)

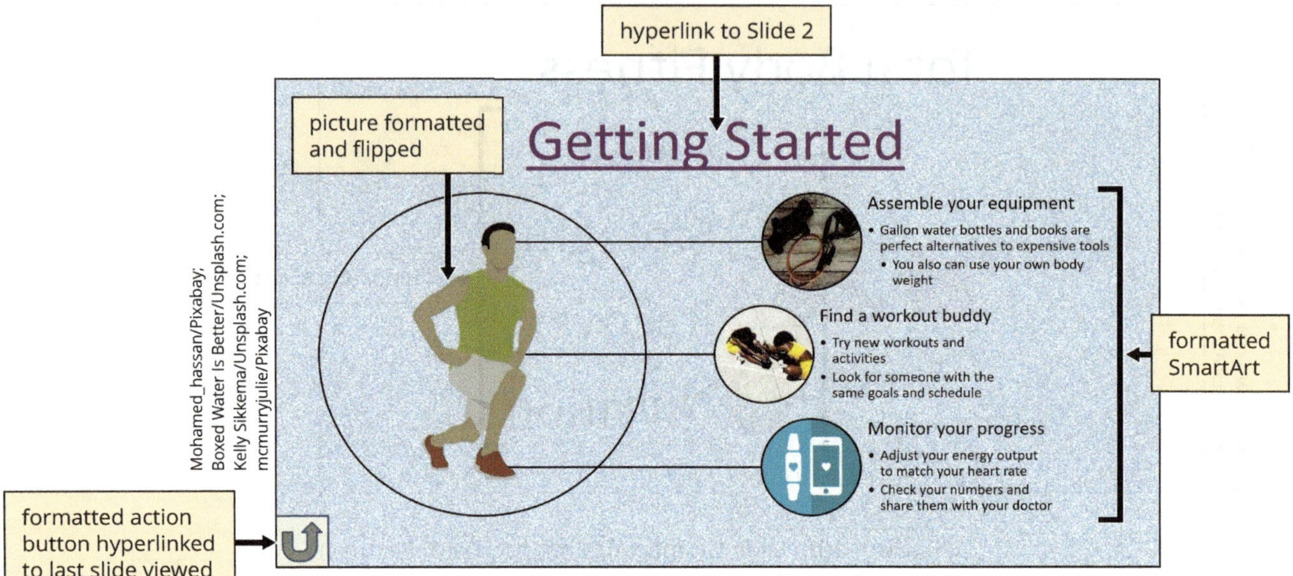

Mohamed_hassan/Pixabay; Boxed Water Is Better/Unsplash.com; Kelly Sikkema/Unsplash.com; mcmurryjulie/Pixabay

Figure 7–1(e): Slide 4 (SmartArt with Formatted Picture)

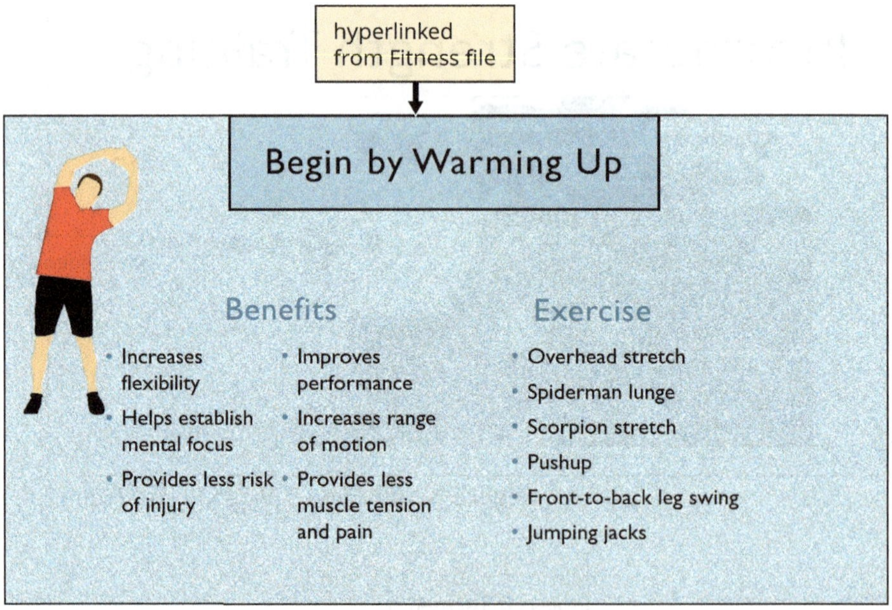

Mohamed_hassan/Pixabay

Figure 7–1(f): Slide 2 (Hyperlinked from First Presentation)

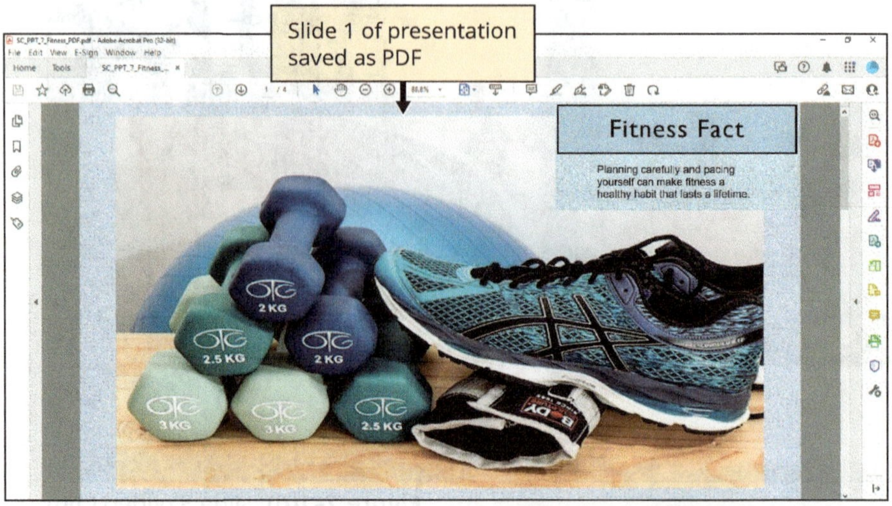

stevepb/Pixabay

Figure 7–1(g): Slide 1 of PDF file

Modifying a Slide by Changing a Picture and Inserting a Screen Clipping

You begin this module by opening a file containing four partially completed slides. You then change, resize, and align the picture on the first slide, open a second file, and insert a screen clipping from the last slide in the second presentation.

In the following pages, you will perform these tasks:

1. Change and resize the picture on Slide 1.
2. Insert a screen clipping.

BTW

Touch Mode Differences

The Microsoft 365 and Windows interfaces may vary if you are using a touch screen. For this reason, you might notice that the function or appearance of your touch screen differs slightly from this module's presentation.

To Open and Save a Presentation

The following steps open the starting file and then save it with a new file name.

1. sam Run PowerPoint. If necessary, maximize the PowerPoint window.
2. Open the presentation, SC_PPT_7_Starting.pptx, from the Data Files.
3. Save the presentation using **SC_PPT_7_Fitness** as the file name.

To Change a Picture

The starting file has a picture on Slide 1 of a person running on a treadmill. You want to change that picture to one of the pictures in the Data Files showing a variety of fitness equipment. **Why?** The health professionals who will present this slide show want to introduce audience members to the overall theme of the presentation instead of focusing on the cardio aspect of total body fitness. The following steps change the Slide 1 picture to the Equipment picture, which is located in the Data Files folder.

1.

- Click the Slide 1 picture to select it and then display the Picture Format tab.
- Click the Change Picture button (Picture Format tab | Adjust group) to display the Change Picture menu (Figure 7–2).

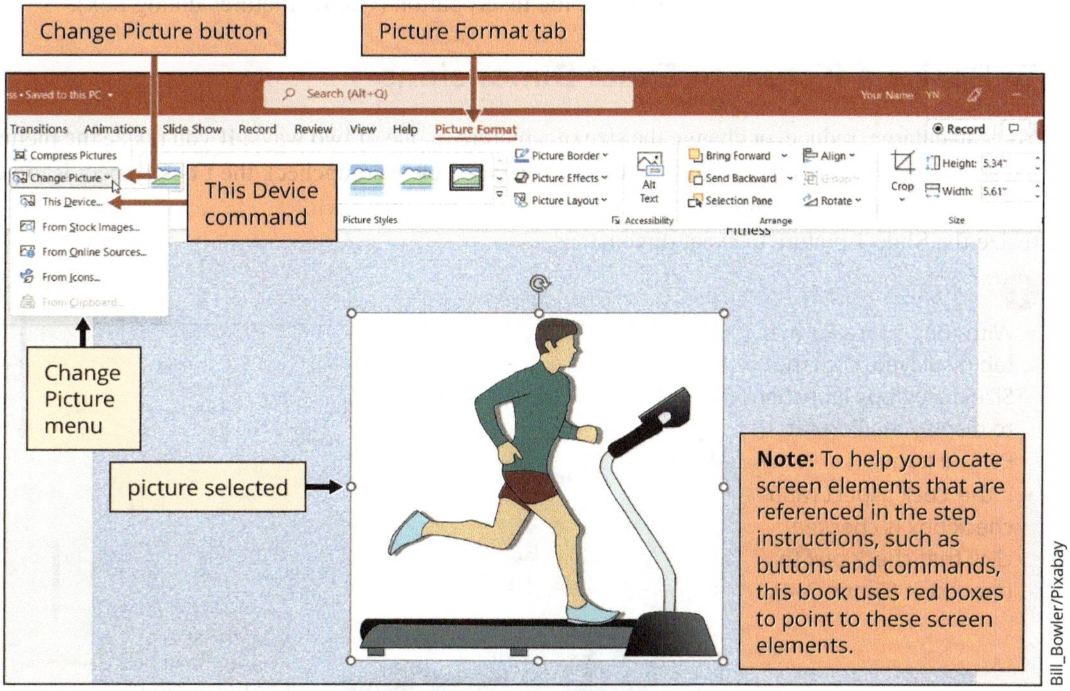

Figure 7–2

2

- Click 'This Device' or 'From a File' to display the Insert Picture dialog box.
- If necessary, navigate to the location where the Data Files are located and then click Support_PPT_7_Equipment to select the .jpg file (Figure 7–3).

3

- Click the Insert button (Insert Picture dialog box) to insert the picture into Slide 1 and change the original picture.
- If the Design Ideas pane is displayed, close it.

stevepb/Pixabay; TotalShape/Pixabay; Bill_Bowler/Pixabay; Greg Rosenke/Unsplash.com; Mohamed_hassan/Pixabay; Merio/Pixabay; TotalShape/Pixabay

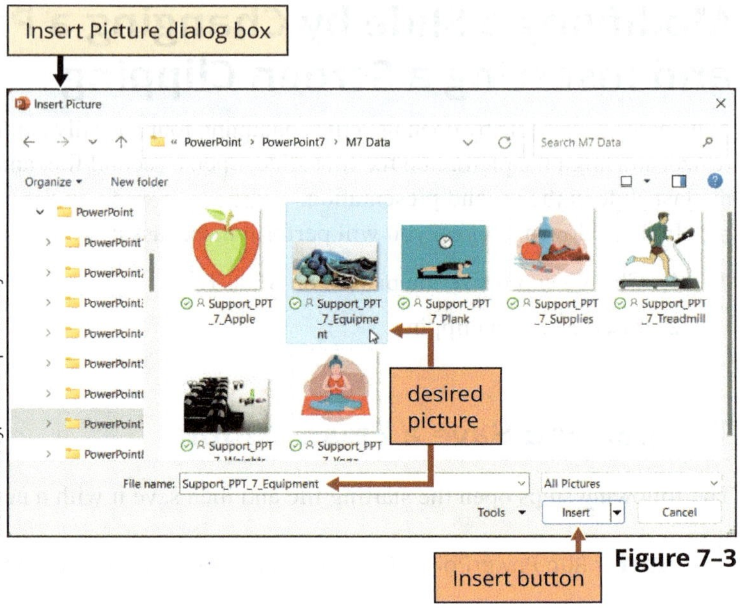

Figure 7–3

Other Ways

1. Right-click picture, click Change Picture on shortcut menu, click 'From a File'

To Insert an Online Picture without Using a Content Placeholder If you wanted to change or insert an online picture into a slide that does not have a content placeholder, you would perform the following steps.

1. Display the Insert tab, click the Pictures button (Insert tab | Images group), and then click Online Pictures to display the Online Pictures dialog box.
2. Select a category and then select the desired picture.
3. Click the Insert button (Online Pictures dialog box).

To Resize a Picture to Exact Dimensions

You can enlarge, reduce, or change the size of a picture in one of two ways. If you resize the picture proportionally, you maintain the same ratio between the height and width. You can, however, uncheck the Lock Aspect Ratio check box and then change the dimensions to a precise number. **Why?** You want the height or width to fit a particular area of the slide. The following steps resize the Slide 1 picture to exact dimensions.

1

- With the Picture Format tab displayed, click the Size dialog box launcher to display the Format Picture pane.
- If the 'Lock aspect ratio' check box is checked, click that check box to uncheck it (Figure 7–4).

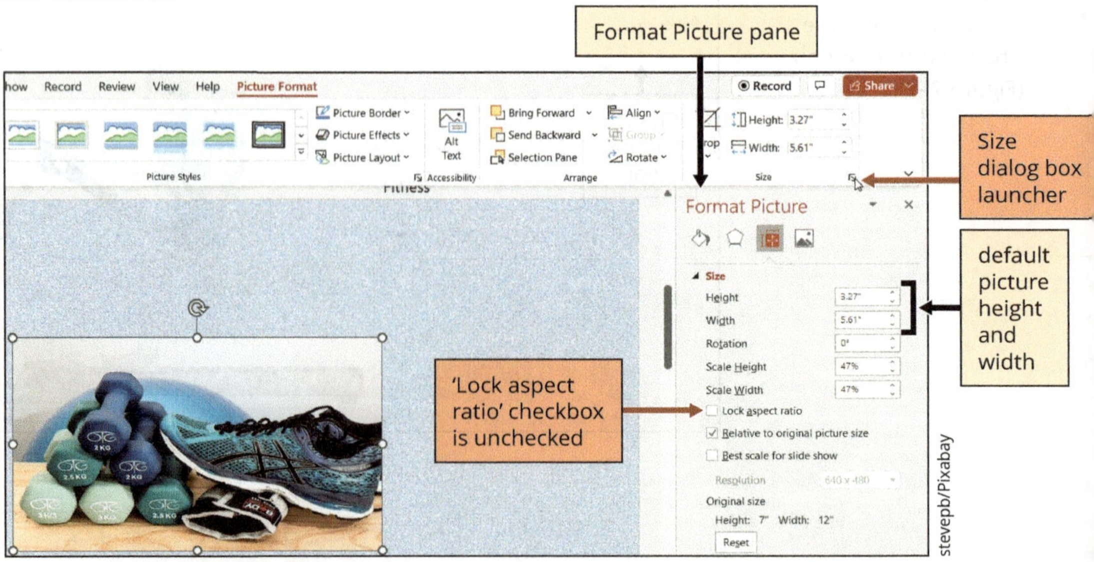

Figure 7–4

2

- Click the Height up arrow several times to change the picture height to 7".
- Click the Width up arrow several times to change the picture width to 12" (Figure 7–5).

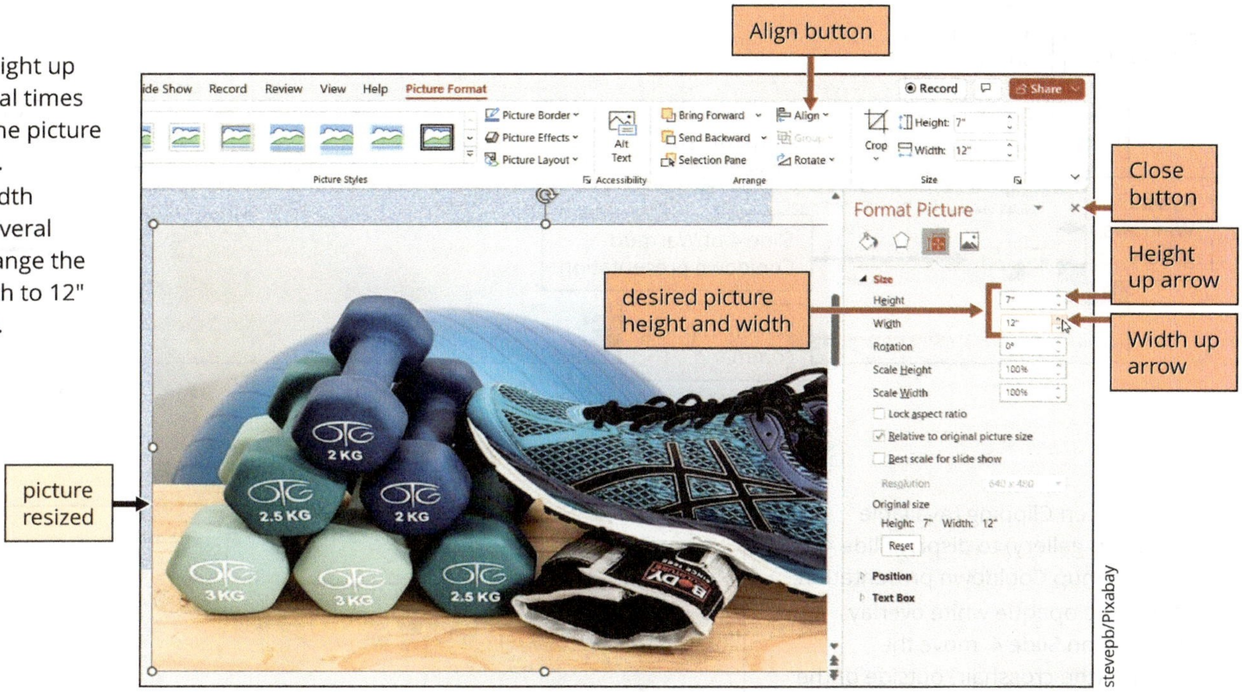

Figure 7–5

3

- Close the Format Picture pane.
- Click the Align button (Picture Format tab | Arrange group) and then click the Align Center button.
- Click the Align button again and then click the Align Middle button.
- Click an area outside the picture so that it no longer is selected.

To Insert a Screen Clipping

At times you may be developing a presentation and need a portion of a clip or picture from another presentation. You can capture all or part of a slide in another presentation that is open. PowerPoint refers to this presentation as being open or available. Open program windows are displayed as thumbnails in the Available Windows gallery. A **screenshot** is a snapshot of a program or window that is open. A **screen clipping** is a screen capture of part of an open window. When you click the Screen Clipping tool, your window becomes opaque. After you select the part of the window that you desire to capture, your selection is displayed through this opaqueness. The following steps clip part of an image on Slide 4 of another presentation that is available in the Data Files and then paste this selection on Slide 1 of your Fitness presentation. **Why?** On the first slide, you want to focus on how proper planning and execution can lead to a lifetime of healthy habits.

1

- Open the Support_PPT_7_Warmup.pptx file from your Data Files and then save it in the same location as your Fitness file using **SC_PPT_7_Warmup_Cooldown** as the file name.
- Display Slide 4 of that presentation.
- Display Slide 1 of the Fitness presentation.
- Display the Insert tab and then click the Screenshot button (Insert tab | Images group) to display the Available Windows gallery (Figure 7–6).

Q&A What if more than one available window is displayed?
Select the window showing Slide 4 of the Warmup Cooldown presentation and then continue with the steps.

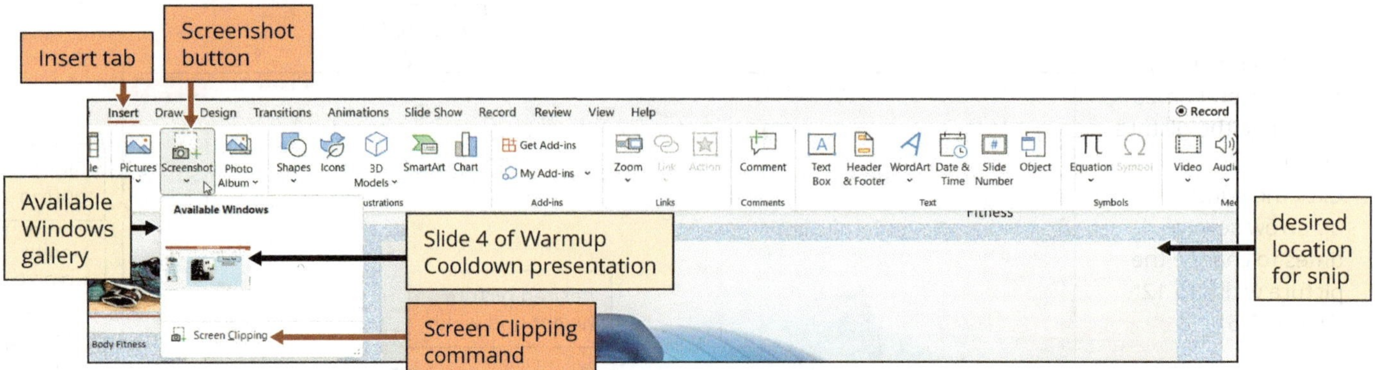

stevepb/Pixabay

Figure 7–6

2

- Click Screen Clipping (Available Windows gallery) to display Slide 4 of the Warmup Cooldown presentation.
- When the opaque white overlay displays on Slide 4, move the pointer (the crosshair) outside of the upper-left corner of the Fitness Fact text box, as shown in Figure 7–7.
- Press and hold the left mouse button and drag diagonally downward to the right to select the text box and the entire text paragraph. Do not release the mouse button (Figure 7–8).

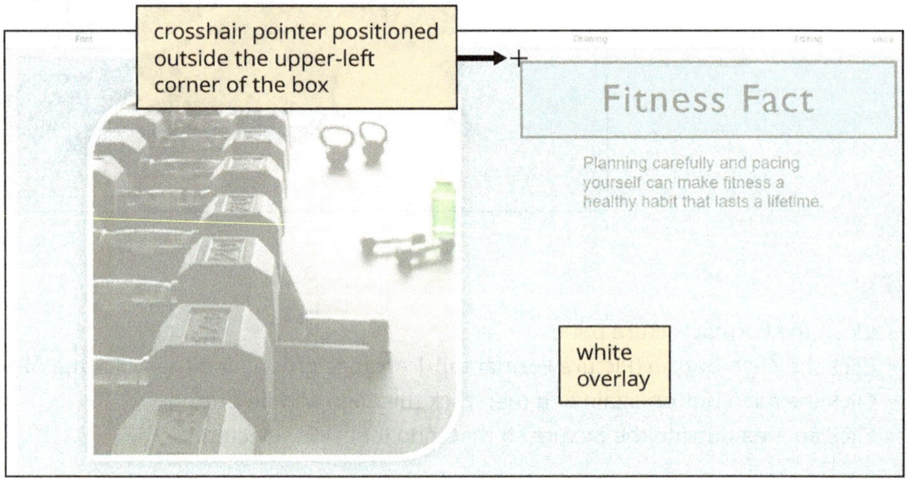

Greg Rosenke/Unsplash.com

Figure 7–7

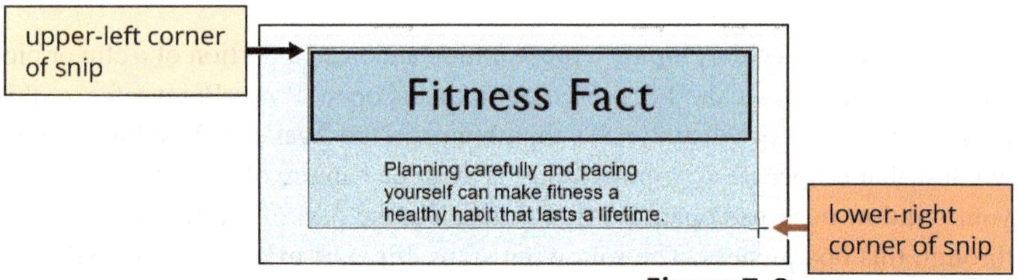

Figure 7–8

3

- Release the mouse button.
- When the clip displays on Slide 1 of the Fitness presentation, resize it to a height of 2".
- Drag the clip to the upper-right corner of the slide (Figure 7–9).

4

- Close the Warmup Cooldown presentation.

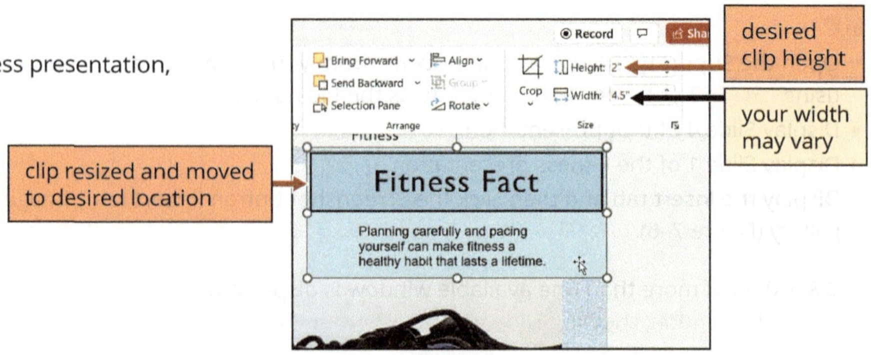

Figure 7–9

To Insert a Screenshot To insert a screenshot, you would perform the following steps.

1. Click the slide where you want to insert the screenshot.
2. Display the Insert tab and then click the Screenshot button (Insert tab | Images group).
3. Click the thumbnail of the desired window in the Available Windows gallery.

To Insert an Equation The Microsoft 365 apps have built-in equations for common calculations, such as the area of a circle and the Pythagorean Theorem. You can include one of these equations in your slide. If you need a different equation, you can edit, change the existing equation, or insert math symbols to develop your own equation. If you wanted to insert a built-in equation in a slide, you would perform the following steps.

1. Display the Insert tab and then click the Equation button (Insert tab | Symbols group) to display the Equation tab.
2. Choose the equation you want from the gallery.
3. If needed, add symbols and structures available on the Equation tab.

BTW
Creating Equations with Touch Screens
If you are using a touch screen, use your finger or stylus to write the numbers and symbols, being certain the Math Input Control box understands your handwriting.

Creating and Formatting a SmartArt Graphic

The predefined SmartArt graphics are visual representations of information to help convey information to your audience. The variety of shapes, arrows, and lines correspond to the major points you want your audience to remember. You can create a SmartArt graphic and then customize the content and design.

In the following pages, you will perform these tasks:

1. Insert a SmartArt graphic.
2. Enter and format text.
3. Add pictures.
4. Add and move SmartArt shapes.
5. Promote and demote SmartArt shapes.

To Insert SmartArt Using a Content Placeholder

Several SmartArt layouts have placeholders for one or more pictures, and they are grouped in the Picture category. The Accented Picture graphic is appropriate for this presentation. **Why?** It has one large area for a picture and three other areas for smaller pictures. These images help generate an understanding that total body fitness involves more than just exercising or eating healthy foods. The following steps insert the Accented Picture SmartArt graphic on Slide 2.

1

- Display Slide 2 and then point to the 'Insert a SmartArt Graphic' icon in the content placeholder (Figure 7–10).

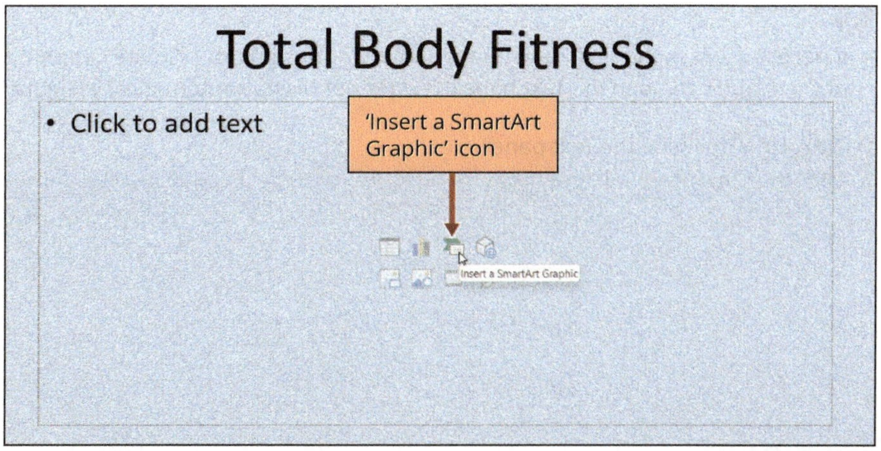

Figure 7–10

2

- Click the 'Insert a SmartArt Graphic' icon to display the 'Choose a SmartArt Graphic' dialog box.
- Click Picture in the left pane to display the Picture gallery.
- Click the Accented Picture graphic (first graphic in the first row) to display a preview of this layout in the right pane (Figure 7–11).
- **Experiment:** Click various categories and graphics in the SmartArt Styles gallery and view the various layouts.

3

- Click OK to insert this SmartArt layout into Slide 2.

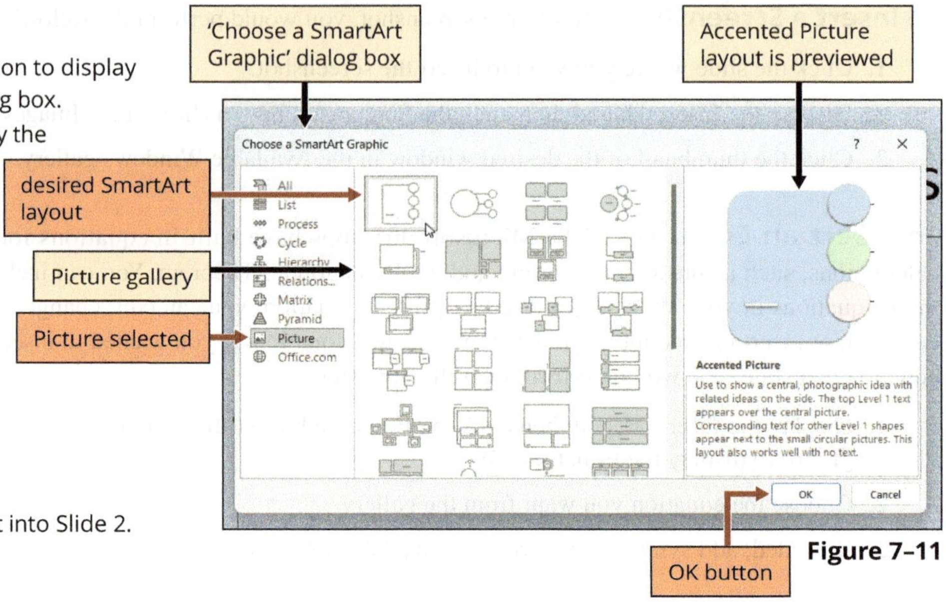

Figure 7–11

Other Ways

1. Click SmartArt button (Insert tab | Illustrations group)

To Convert a Picture to SmartArt You quickly can convert a picture on your slide into a SmartArt graphic. PowerPoint automatically places the picture into a shape and arranges it based on the layout you choose. If you wanted to convert a picture to SmartArt, you would perform the following steps.

1. Select the picture you want to convert and then display the Picture Format tab.
2. Click the Picture Layout button (Picture Format tab | Picture Styles group) to display the Picture Layout gallery.
3. Click the desired layout.

To Show or Hide the SmartArt Text Pane

You can show the Text pane to add or edit text in the SmartArt graphic, or you can hide it to see more of your slide when you are developing the graphic. If you are entering a large amount of text, consider showing the Text pane. **Why?** The bullets in the top portion of the pane function as an outline. You can create new lines of bulleted text and then indent and demote these lines. You also can check spelling. The following step shows the Text pane on Slide 2.

1

- If necessary, click the Text Pane button (SmartArt Design tab | Create Graphic group) or the arrow icon in the center-left edge of the graphic to open the Text pane if it does not display automatically (Figure 7–12).

Q&A How do I hide the Text pane?
Click the Close button in the upper-right corner of the Text pane or click the Text Pane button again.

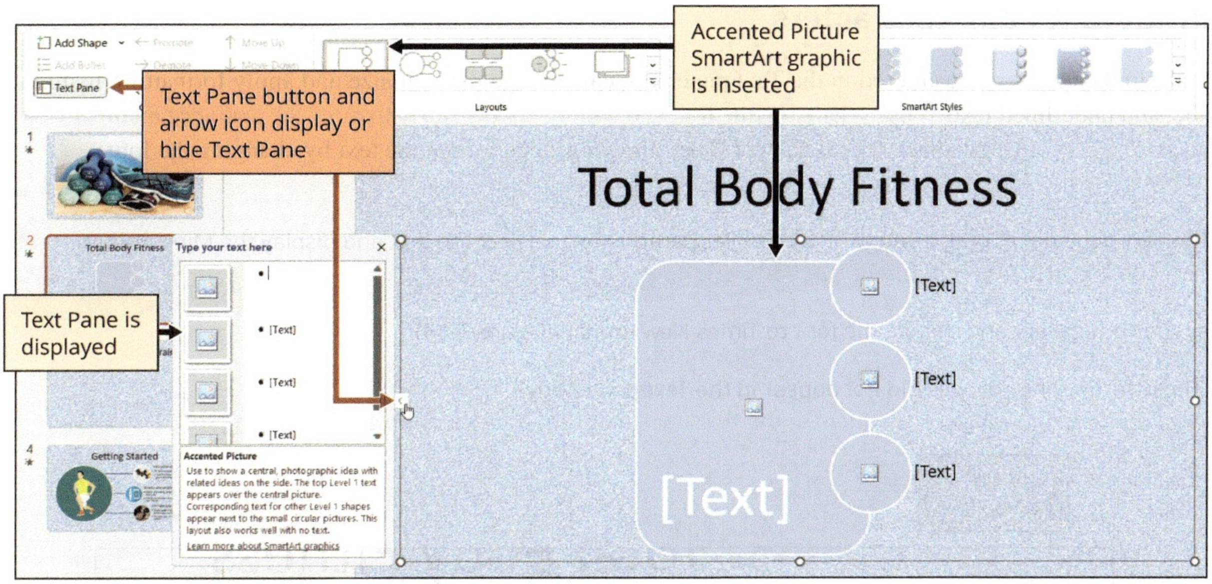

stevepb/Pixabay; Mohamed_hassan/Pixabay; Boxed Water Is Better/Unsplash.com; mcmurryjulie/Pixabay; Kelly Sikkema/Unsplash.com

Figure 7–12

To Enter Text in SmartArt

The Accented Picture graphic has placeholders for text that can supplement the visuals. The following steps insert four lines of text in the Text pane and in the corresponding SmartArt shapes on Slide 2.

1. If necessary, position the insertion point beside the first bullet in the Text pane. Type **Elements** in the first bullet paragraph and then click the second bullet line or press DOWN ARROW to move the insertion point to the second bullet paragraph.

2. Type **Cardio** in the second bullet paragraph and then click the third bullet line or press DOWN ARROW to move the insertion point to the third bullet paragraph.

3. Type **Strength** in the third bullet paragraph and then click the fourth bullet line or press DOWN ARROW to move the insertion point to the fourth bullet paragraph.

4. Type **Nutrition** in the fourth bullet paragraph. Do not press DOWN ARROW or ENTER (Figure 7–13).

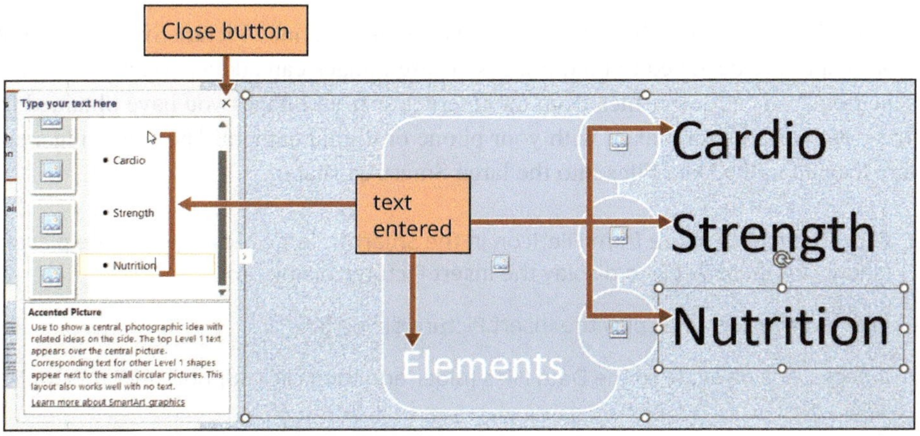

Figure 7–13

Other Ways

1. Enter text directly in SmartArt text boxes

To Format Text Pane Characters

Once the desired characters are entered in the Text pane, you can change the font size and apply formatting features, such as bold, italic, and underlined text. **Why?** Changing the font and adding effects can help draw the audience members to the varied slide content and coordinate with the visual content. The following steps format the text by changing the font.

1

- With the Text pane open, drag through all four bullet paragraphs to select the text and display the Mini toolbar.

2

- Display the Font gallery and change the font to Times New Roman (Figure 7–14).

Q&A These formatting changes did not appear in the Text pane. Why?
Not all the formatting changes are evident in the Text pane, but they appear in the corresponding shape.

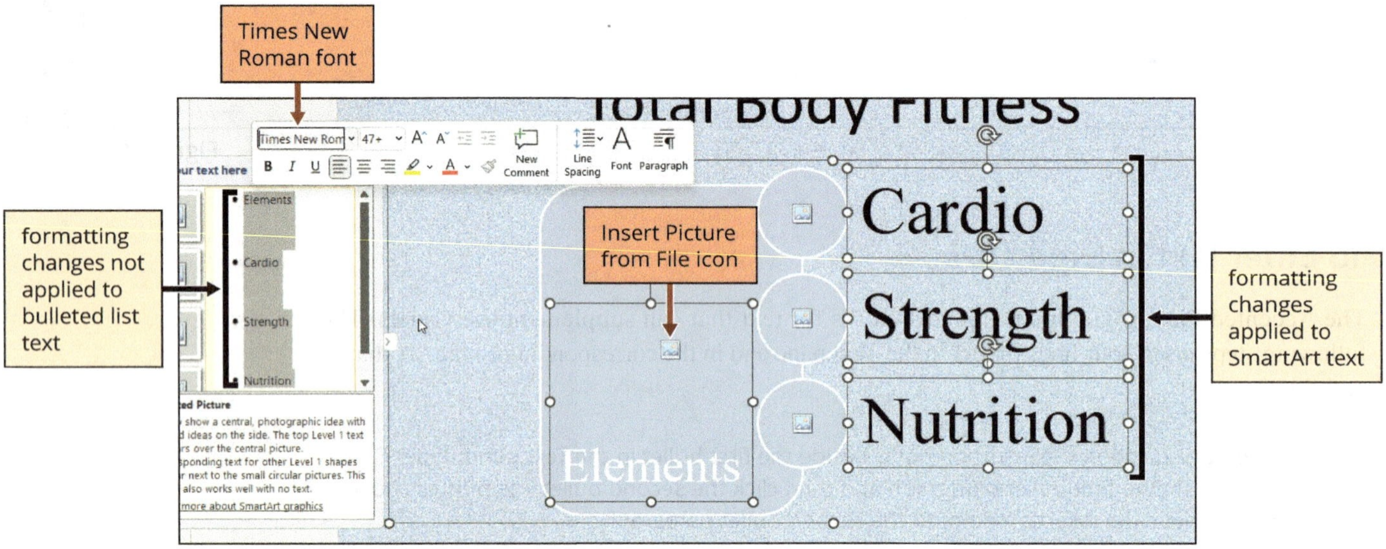

Figure 7–14

3

- Click the SmartArt Text pane Close button (shown in Figure 7–13) so that the pane no longer is displayed.

To Add a Picture to SmartArt

The picture icons in the middle of the four shapes in the Accented Picture SmartArt layout indicate that the shapes are designed to hold images. These images can add a personalized touch to your presentation. You can select files from the Internet or from images you have obtained from other sources, such as a picture taken with your phone or digital camera. The following steps insert a picture located in the Data Files into the large SmartArt shape.

1. Click the 'Insert Picture from File' icon in the SmartArt large rectangle picture placeholder (shown in Figure 7–15) to display the Insert Pictures dialog box.
2. Click 'From a File' to display the Insert Picture dialog box.
3. If necessary, navigate to the Data Files folder and then click Support_PPT_7_Supplies.png to select the file.
4. Click the Insert button (Insert Picture dialog box) to insert the Supplies picture into the SmartArt large rectangle picture placeholder.

Figure 7–15

To Insert a Picture into a SmartArt Shape

The Supplies picture fills the left shape in the SmartArt graphic, and you want to insert additional fitness pictures in the three circles in the right portion of the graphic. These images are located in the Data Files. The following steps insert pictures into the three smaller SmartArt graphic circles.

1. Click the 'Insert Picture from File' icon in the top circle to the left of the word, Cardio, to display the Insert Pictures dialog box.
2. Click 'From a File', click Support_PPT_7_Treadmill.png in the list of picture files, and then click the Insert button (Insert Picture dialog box) to insert the picture into the top-right SmartArt circle picture placeholder.
3. Click the center 'Insert Picture from File' icon to the left of the word, Strength, click 'From a File', and then insert the picture with the file name, Support_PPT_7_Plank.png, into the placeholder.
4. Click the bottom 'Insert Picture from File' icon to the left of the word, Nutrition, and then insert the picture with the file name, Support_PPT_7_Apple.jpg, into the placeholder (Figure 7–16).

Figure 7–16

To Add a SmartArt Shape

You can add a new SmartArt shape to the layout if you need to display additional information. PowerPoint gives you the option of adding this shape above or below a selected shape or to the left or the right side of the shape. **Why?** You want to display another element of providing total body fitness. The following steps add a SmartArt shape.

1

- With the Apple picture shape selected and the SmartArt Design tab displayed, click the Add Shape arrow (SmartArt Design tab | Create Graphic group) to display the Add Shape menu (Figure 7–17).

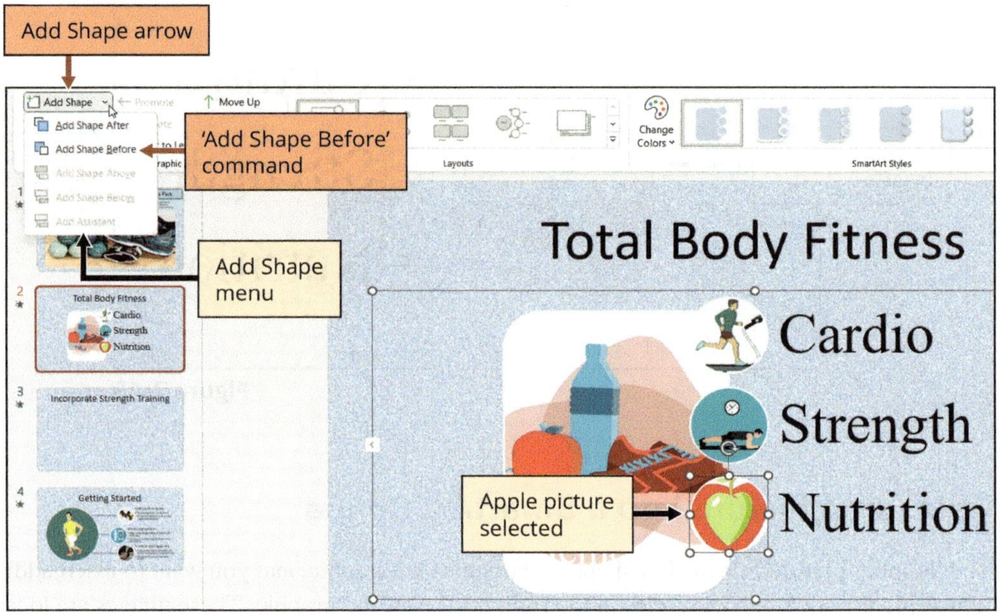

TotalShape/Pixabay; Merio/Pixabay; Bill_Bowler/Pixabay; Mohamed_hassan/Pixabay

Figure 7–17

2

- Click 'Add Shape Before' to create a new shape above the Nutrition shape.
- Type **Recovery** as the new shape text and then change the font to Times New Roman.
- Insert the Support_PPT_7_Yoga.jpg file into the placeholder (Figure 7–18).

Q&A What happens if I click the Add Shape button instead of the Add Shape arrow?
A shape would be added below the selected shape by default.

TotalShape/Pixabay; Merio/Pixabay; Bill_Bowler/Pixabay; Mohamed_hassan/Pixabay

Figure 7–18

To Apply 3-D Effects to SmartArt

You can change the look of your SmartArt graphic easily by applying a SmartArt style. **Why?** These professionally designed effects customize the appearance of your presentation with a variety of shape fills, edges, shadows, line styles, gradients, and dimensions. The following steps add the Metallic Scene 3-D effect to the SmartArt.

1

- Select the entire SmartArt graphic by clicking an outer edge of the graphic and then, if necessary, display the SmartArt Design tab (Figure 7–19).

Q&A How will I know the entire graphic is selected?
You will see the Text pane control and sizing handles around the outer edge of the SmartArt.

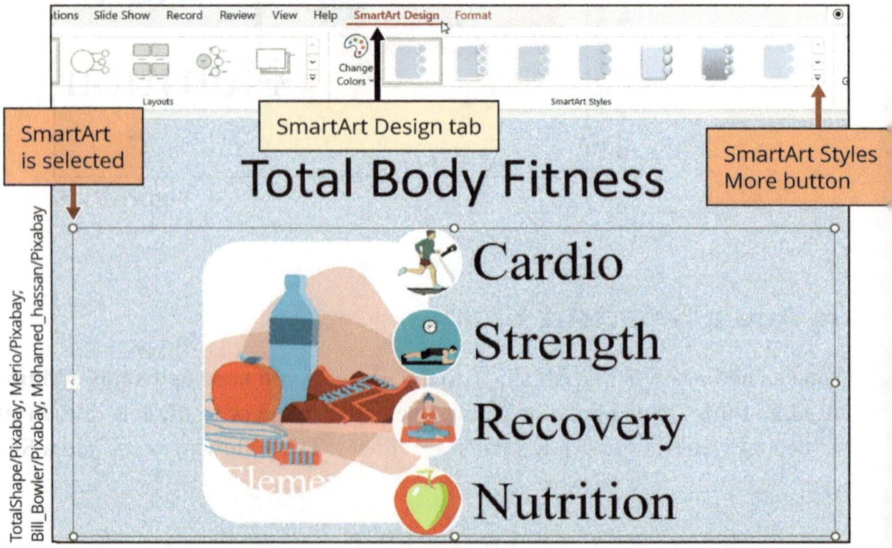

TotalShape/Pixabay; Merio/Pixabay; Bill_Bowler/Pixabay; Mohamed_hassan/Pixabay

Figure 7–19

2

- Click the SmartArt Styles More button (SmartArt Design tab | SmartArt Styles group) (shown in Figure 7–19) to expand the SmartArt Styles gallery (Figure 7–20).

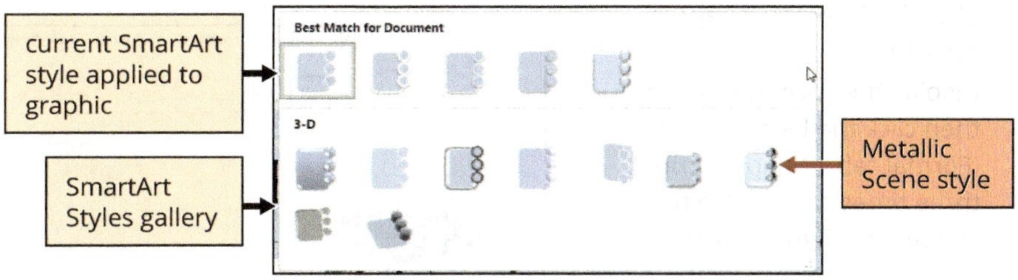

Figure 7–20

3

- Point to the Metallic Scene style in the 3-D area (seventh style in the first 3-D row) in the SmartArt Styles gallery to display a live preview of this style (Figure 7–21).
- **Experiment:** Point to various styles in the SmartArt Styles gallery and watch the Accented Picture graphic change styles.

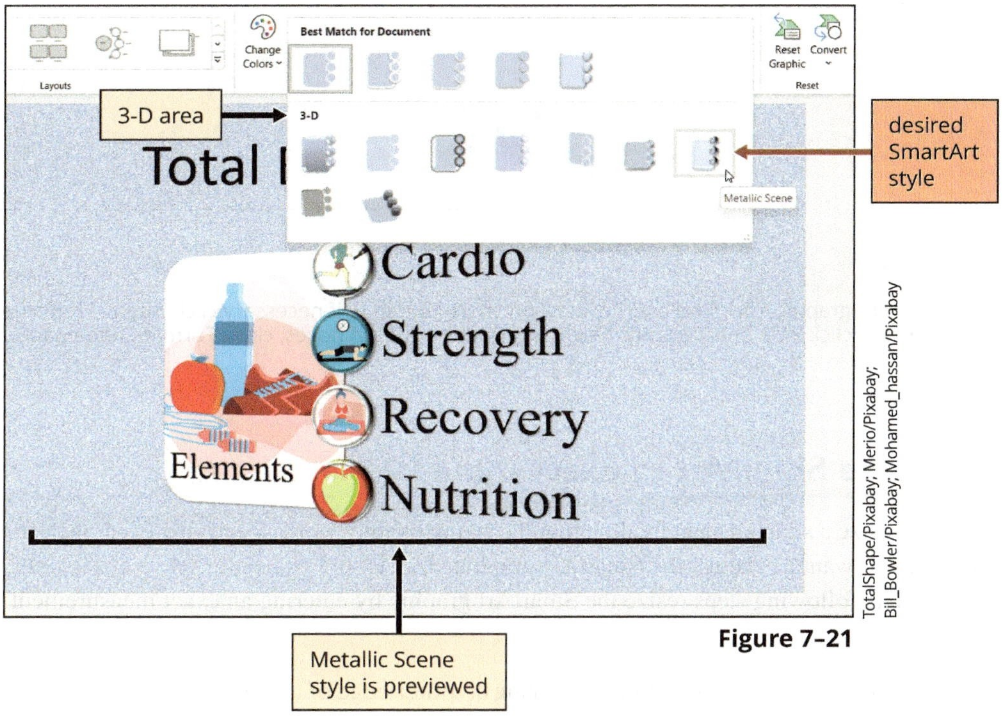

TotalShape/Pixabay; Merio/Pixabay; Bill_Bowler/Pixabay; Mohamed_hassan/Pixabay

Figure 7–21

4

- Click Metallic Scene to apply this style to the graphic.

Other Ways

1. Right-click SmartArt graphic in an area other than a picture, click Style button

To Increase the Size of a SmartArt Shape

When you view the completed graphic, you may decide that individual shapes or the entire piece of art needs to be enlarged or reduced. All the shapes will enlarge proportionally when you adjust the graphic's height and width to maintain proportions. Likewise, the font size may change in all the shapes if you increase or decrease the font size of one shape. On Slide 2, you want to change the SmartArt graphic size. **Why?** A larger graphic size will fill the empty space on the slide and add readability. The following step resizes one SmartArt graphic shape.

1

- Click the Elements shape to select it.
- Display the Format tab and then click the Larger button (Format tab | Shapes group) three times to increase the shape size (Figure 7–22).

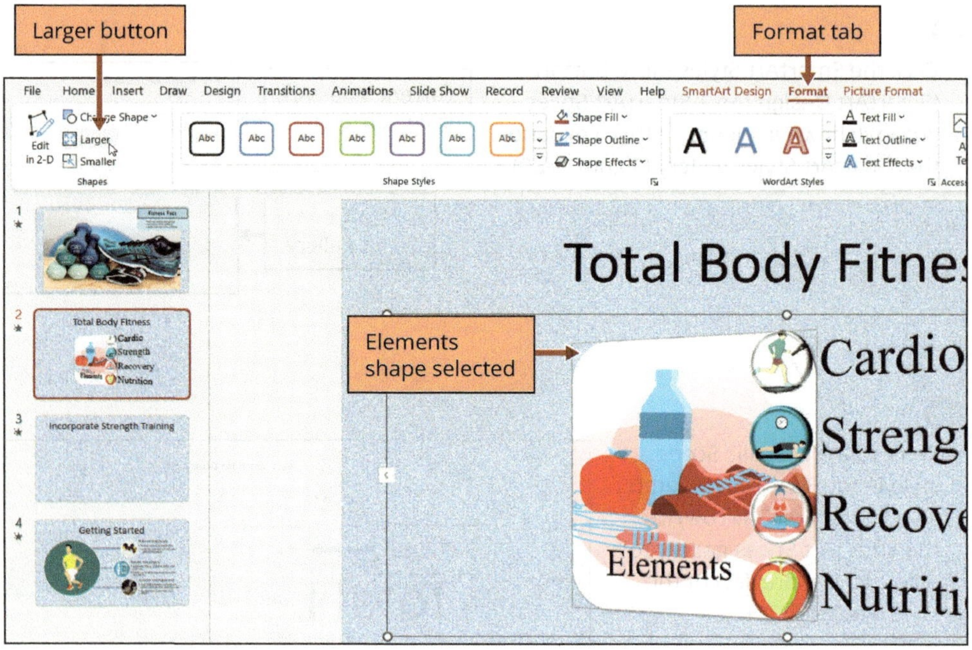

TotalShape/Pixabay; Merio/Pixabay; Bill_Bowler/Pixabay; Mohamed_hassan/Pixabay; stevepb/Pixabay

Figure 7–22

Other Ways

1. Right-click graphic, click 'Size and Position' on shortcut menu, if necessary click 'Size & Properties' icon (Format Shape pane), if necessary click Size, enter graphic height and width values in boxes, close Format Shape pane

To Resize SmartArt to Exact Dimensions

You can resize a slide element by dragging the sizing handles or by specifying exact measurements for the height and width. On Slide 2, you want to change the SmartArt graphic size. **Why?** Adequate space exists on the slide to increase all the SmartArt shapes. The following steps resize the SmartArt graphic by entering an exact measurement.

1

- Select the entire SmartArt graphic by clicking an outer edge of the graphic.
- With the Format tab displayed, change the Height measurement to 5.3" and the Width measurement to 13" (Figure 7–23).

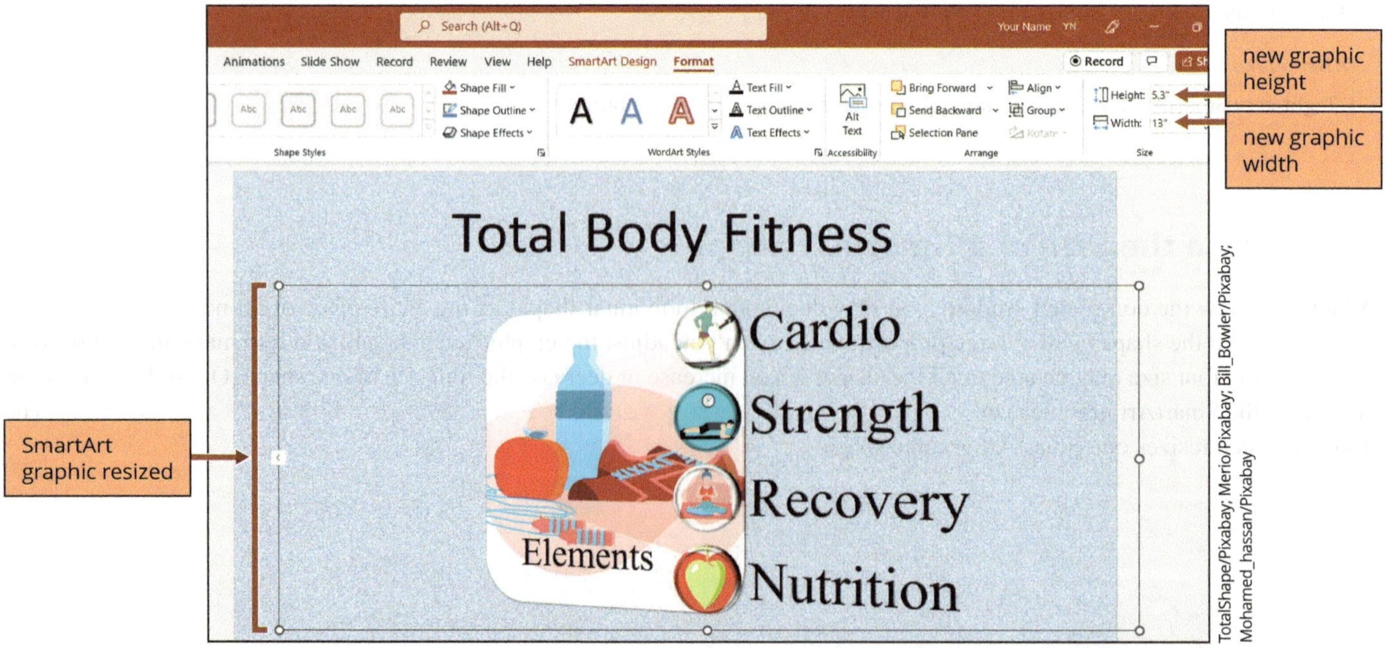

TotalShape/Pixabay; Merio/Pixabay; Bill_Bowler/Pixabay; Mohamed_hassan/Pixabay

Figure 7–23

3

- Use the smart guides to align the SmartArt object, as shown in Figure 7–24.

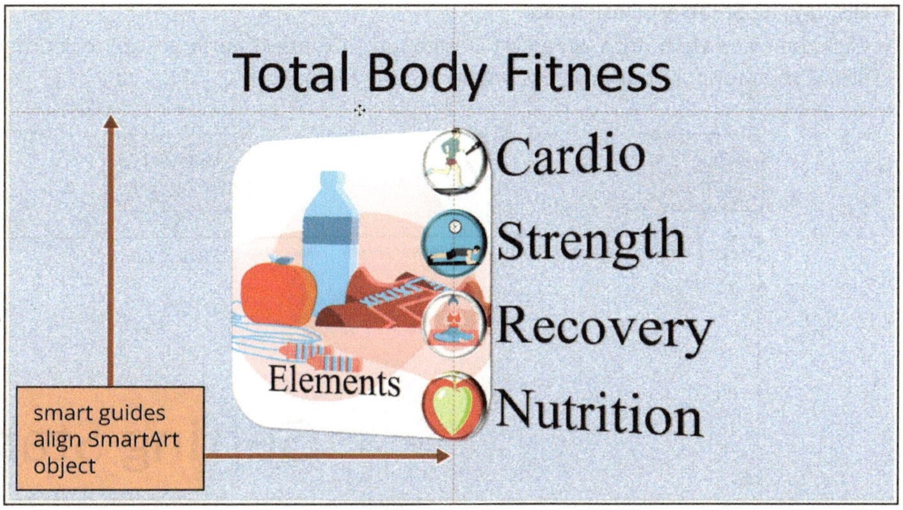

TotalShape/Pixabay; Merio/Pixabay; Bill_Bowler/Pixabay; Mohamed_hassan/Pixabay

Figure 7–24

Other Ways

1. Right-click graphic, click 'Size and Position' on shortcut menu, if necessary click 'Size & Properties' icon (Format Shape pane), if necessary click Size, enter graphic height and width values in boxes, close Format Shape pane

To Move a SmartArt Shape Up

One modification that you can make to a SmartArt layout is to change the order of the shapes. Slide 4 contains SmartArt with information about beginning a fitness program. You decide that two items in the graphic should be displayed in a different order. **Why?** Audience members may be concerned about the equipment they will need to obtain when beginning their fitness routines, so you want to display this information more prominently in the graphic. A workout buddy helps with accountability and motivation, and you want to emphasize that fact, too. PowerPoint provides tools to move shapes and paragraphs in a vertical layout up or down. The following steps move the Assemble your equipment shape up in the graphic.

1

- Display Slide 4.
- Position the pointer in the words, Assemble your equipment, and then click to select it and the bulleted paragraphs (Figure 7–25).

Q&A Is all the text selected in the Assemble your equipment shape?

Yes. The words, Assemble your equipment, are in a first-level paragraph, and the bulleted second-level paragraphs are associated with it. When a shape is selected, all related paragraphs are selected with it.

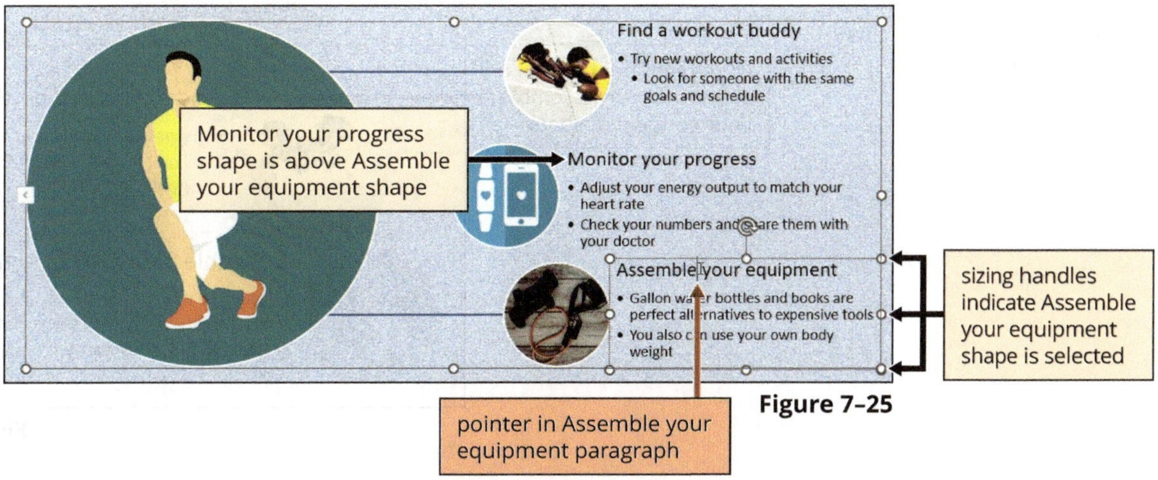

Mohamed_hassan/Pixabay; Boxed Water Is Better/Unsplash.com; mcmurryjulie/Pixabay; Kelly Sikkema/Unsplash.com

Figure 7–25

2

- Display the SmartArt Design tab.
- Click the Move Up button (SmartArt Design tab | Create Graphic group) to reorder the Assemble your equipment shape above the Monitor your progress shape (Figure 7–26).

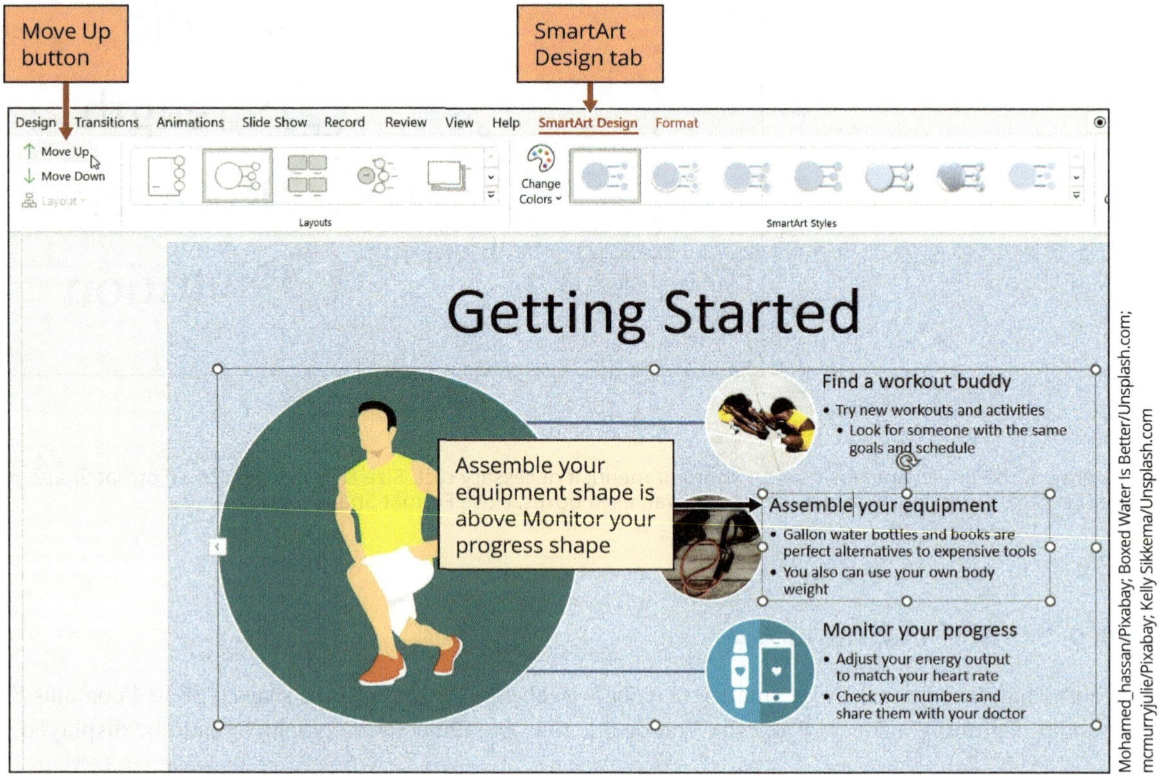

Figure 7–26

To Move a SmartArt Shape Down

You can move shapes down in a SmartArt graphic in a similar manner that you move a shape up. You desire to move the Find a workout buddy shape down. **Why?** While a workout partner and a fitness monitor are important aspects of a successful fitness program, having proper equipment is key to achieving goals and preventing injuries. The Assemble your equipment shape, therefore, should be at the top of the graphic so that your audience members remember this information. The following steps move the Find a workout buddy shape down in the graphic.

1

- Position the pointer in the words, Find a workout buddy, and then click to select the shape (Figure 7–27).

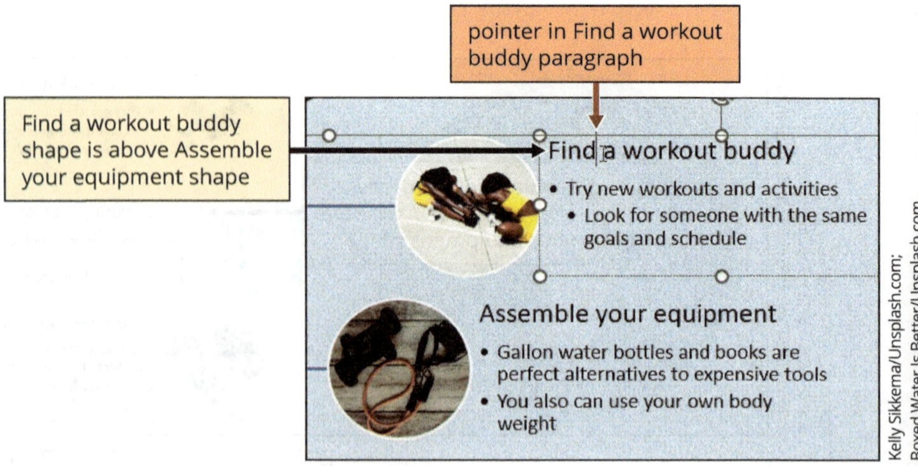

Figure 7–27

2

- Click the Move Down button (SmartArt Design tab | Create Graphic group) to reorder the Find a workout buddy shape below the Assemble your equipment shape (Figure 7–28).

Mohamed_hassan/Pixabay; Boxed Water Is Better/Unsplash.com; mcmurryjulie/Pixabay; Kelly Sikkema/Unsplash.com

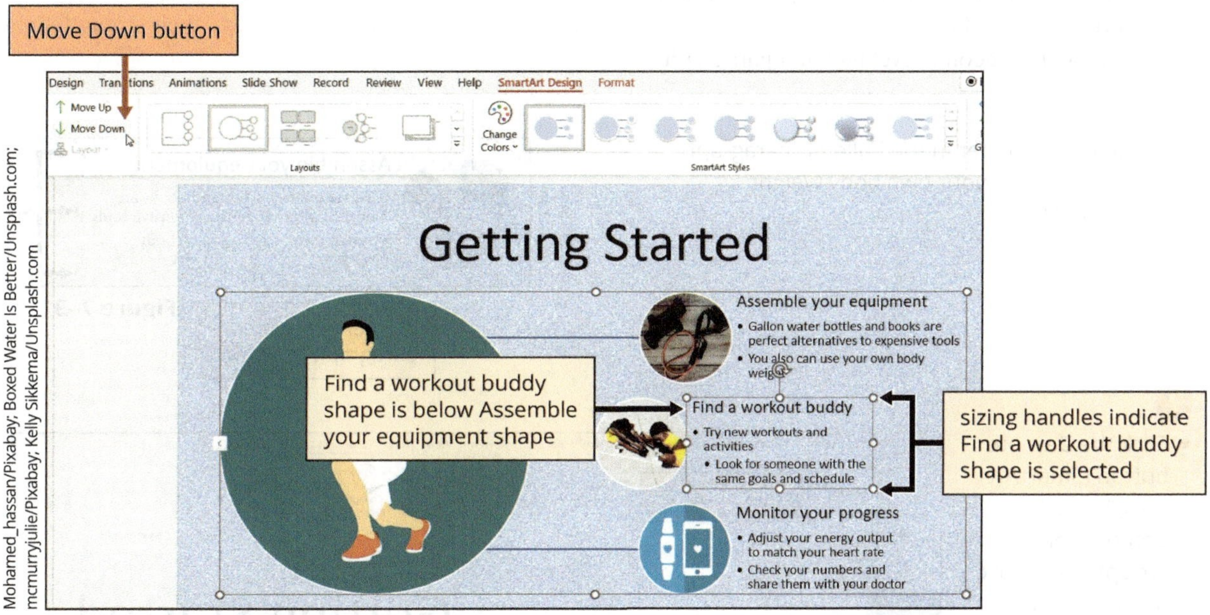

Figure 7–28

To Promote SmartArt Text

PowerPoint provides tools that allow you to promote and demote bulleted text to change the indents for these elements. In the Find a workout buddy shape, you want to promote the bulleted paragraph, Look for someone with the same goals and schedule, to the same level as the bullet above it. **Why?** Both these elements are equally important in encouraging people to find a suitable workout partner. The following steps promote the second bullet in the Find a workout buddy shape.

1

- Position the pointer in the bulleted paragraph, Look for someone with the same goals and schedule (Figure 7–29).

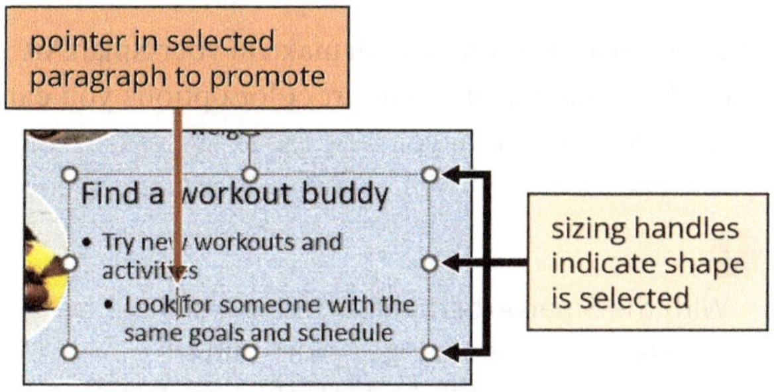

Figure 7–29

2

- Click the Promote button (SmartArt Design tab | Create Graphic group) to decrease the indent of the bulleted paragraph (Figure 7–30).

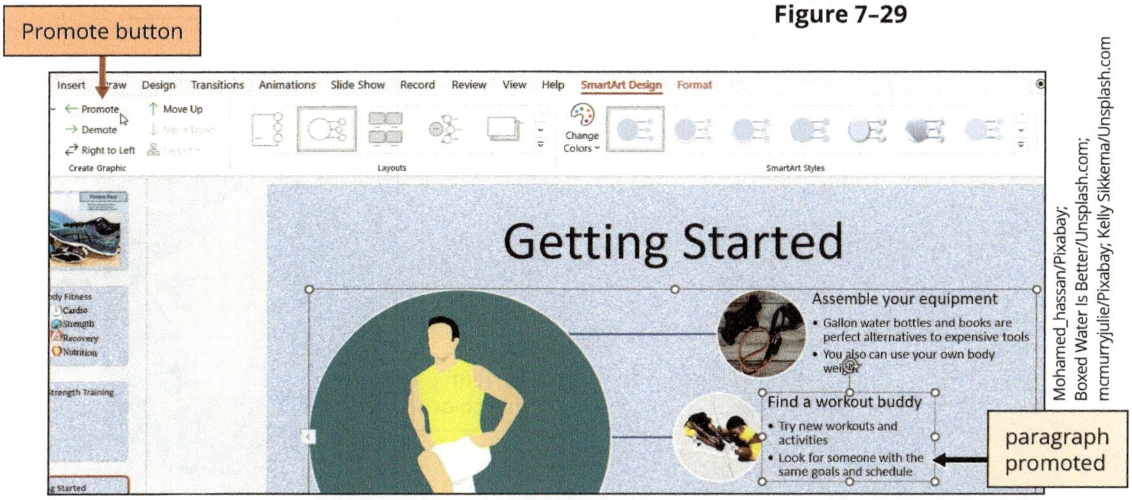

Mohamed_hassan/Pixabay; Boxed Water Is Better/Unsplash.com; mcmurryjulie/Pixabay; Kelly Sikkema/Unsplash.com

Figure 7–30

To Demote SmartArt Text

Another change you want to make on Slide 4 is to demote a paragraph in the Assemble your equipment shape. The bulleted items in this shape are second-level paragraphs, but you decide to demote the second paragraph, You also can use your own body weight. **Why?** People can realize that they do not need to purchase weights to achieve their strength goals. The following steps demote the second-level bulleted paragraph.

1

- Position the pointer in the bulleted paragraph, You also can use your own body weight (Figure 7–31).

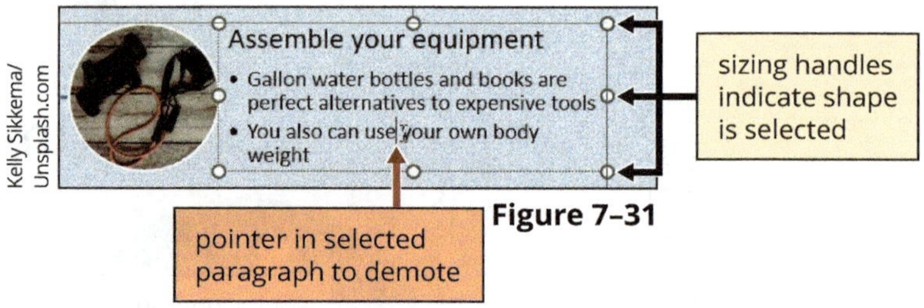

Figure 7–31

2

- Click the Demote button (SmartArt Design tab | Create Graphic group) to increase the indent of the bulleted paragraph (Figure 7–32).

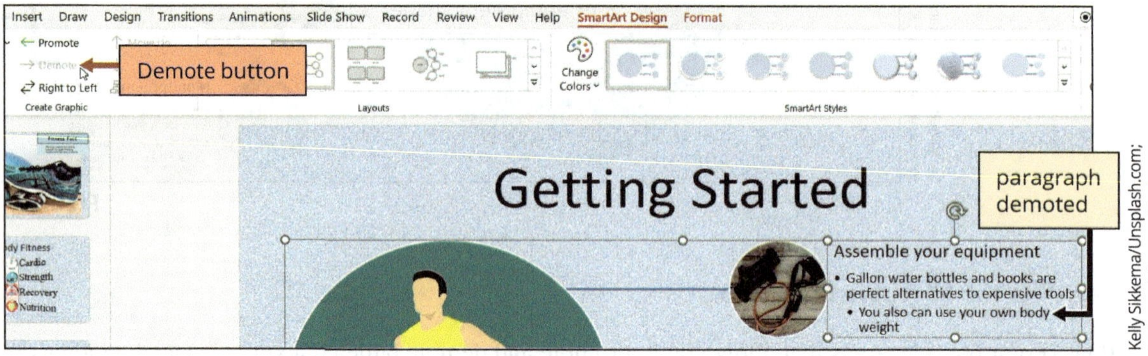

Figure 7–32

To Change the Color of SmartArt

Another modification you can make to your SmartArt graphic is to change its color. As with the WordArt Style gallery, PowerPoint provides a gallery of SmartArt color options you can preview and evaluate. The following steps change the SmartArt graphic color to a Colorful range. **Why?** The slide background and the line colors are blue. Also, the lines around the circles are white. You want these SmartArt line elements to change to black so they are more visible against the blue background.

1

- With the SmartArt graphic on Slide 4 still selected, click the Change Colors button (SmartArt Design tab | SmartArt Styles group) to display the Change Colors gallery (Figure 7–33).

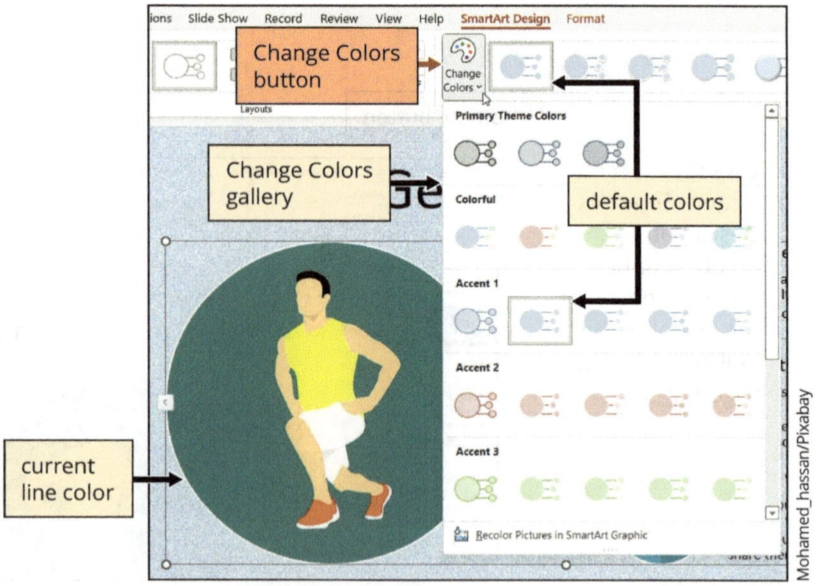

Figure 7–33

2

- Point to 'Dark 1 Outline' (first theme) in the Primary Theme Colors area to display a live preview of these colors (Figure 7–34).
- **Experiment:** Point to various colors in the Change Colors gallery and watch the shapes change colors.

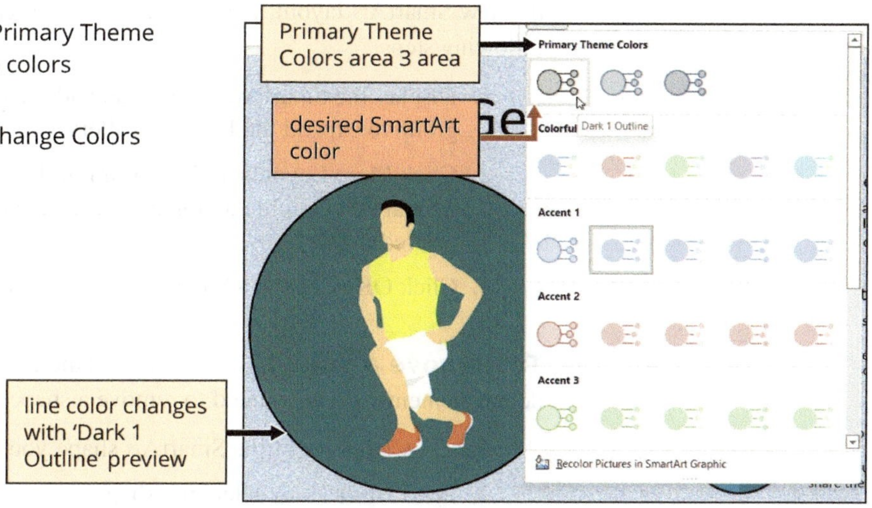

Mohamed_hassan/Pixabay

Figure 7–34

3

- Click 'Dark 1 Outline' to apply this color variation to the graphic (Figure 7–35).

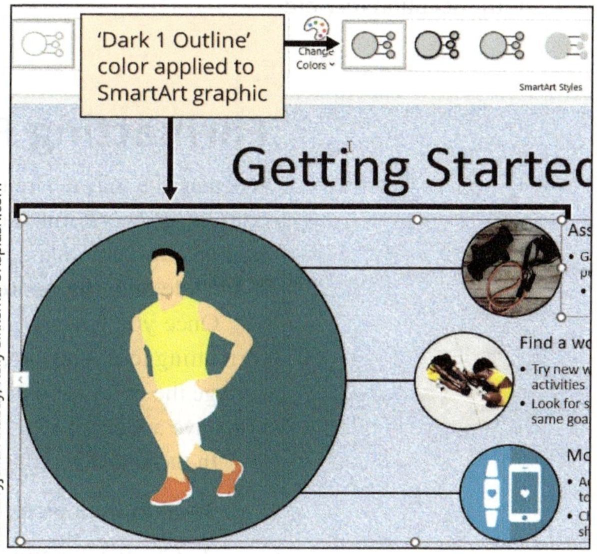

Mohamed_hassan/Pixabay; Boxed Water Is Better/Unsplash.com; mcmurryjulie/Pixabay; Kelly Sikkema/Unsplash.com

Figure 7–35

Other Ways

1. Right-click SmartArt graphic in an area other than a picture, click Color button

To Add a Bullet to a SmartArt Shape If you need to add information to a SmartArt shape, you can create a new bulleted paragraph. This text would display below the last bulleted paragraph in the shape. If you wanted to add a SmartArt bullet, you would perform the following steps.

1. Select the SmartArt graphic shape where you want to insert the bulleted paragraph.
2. Click the Add Bullet button (SmartArt Design tab | Create Graphic group) to insert a new bulleted paragraph below any bulleted text.

To Change the SmartArt Layout Once you begin formatting a SmartArt shape, you may decide that another layout better conveys the message you are communicating to an audience. PowerPoint allows you to change the layout easily. Any graphical changes that were made to the original SmartArt, such as moving shapes or promoting and demoting paragraphs, are applied to the new SmartArt layout. If you wanted to change the SmartArt layout, you would perform the following steps.

1. Display the SmartArt Design tab and then click the More button in the Layouts group to expand the Layouts gallery.
2. Click More Layouts at the bottom of the Layouts gallery to display the Choose a SmartArt Graphic dialog box, click the desired category, and then click the desired layout.
3. Click OK (Choose a SmartArt Graphic dialog box).

To Remove a SmartArt Shape One change you can make to a SmartArt graphic is to delete elements. If you wanted to remove a shape, you would perform the following steps.

1. Click a border of the SmartArt shape you wish to delete to select the entire shape.
2. Press DELETE to delete the shape.

Break Point: If you wish to take a break, this is a good place to do so. Be sure the Fitness file is saved and then you can quit PowerPoint. To resume at a later time, start PowerPoint, open the file called Fitness, and continue following the steps from this location forward.

Formatting Pictures

At times you may desire to emphasize one section of a picture and eliminate distracting background content. PowerPoint includes formatting tools that allow you to edit pictures. The **Remove Background** command isolates the foreground from the background. Once you format the picture to include only the desired content, you can **compress** the image to reduce the file size.

Once you have removed the background, you may want to enhance the image with another formatting tool. You can, for example, improve the picture's brightness and contrast. You also can change the color to match other content on the slide based on the design theme or other elements you have added.

In the following pages, you will perform these tasks:

1. Remove a picture's background.
2. Change a picture's contrast and brightness.
3. Compress pictures.

To Remove a Picture Background

Slide 4 in the Fitness presentation has a picture of a person on the left side of the SmartArt graphic. You want to eliminate the green background from the image. **Why?** The green circle is a large element on the slide and detracts from the message being presented. The person can display prominently if it is the only element within the circle border. The PowerPoint Background Removal feature makes it easy to eliminate unwanted background aspects. When you click the Remove Background button, PowerPoint attempts to select the foreground of the picture and overlay a magenta marquee selection on this area. You then can adjust the marquee shape and size to contain all foreground picture components you want to keep. The following steps remove the background from the picture.

1

- With Slide 4 displayed, click the large circle picture with the green background to select it and then click the Picture Format tab (Figure 7–36).

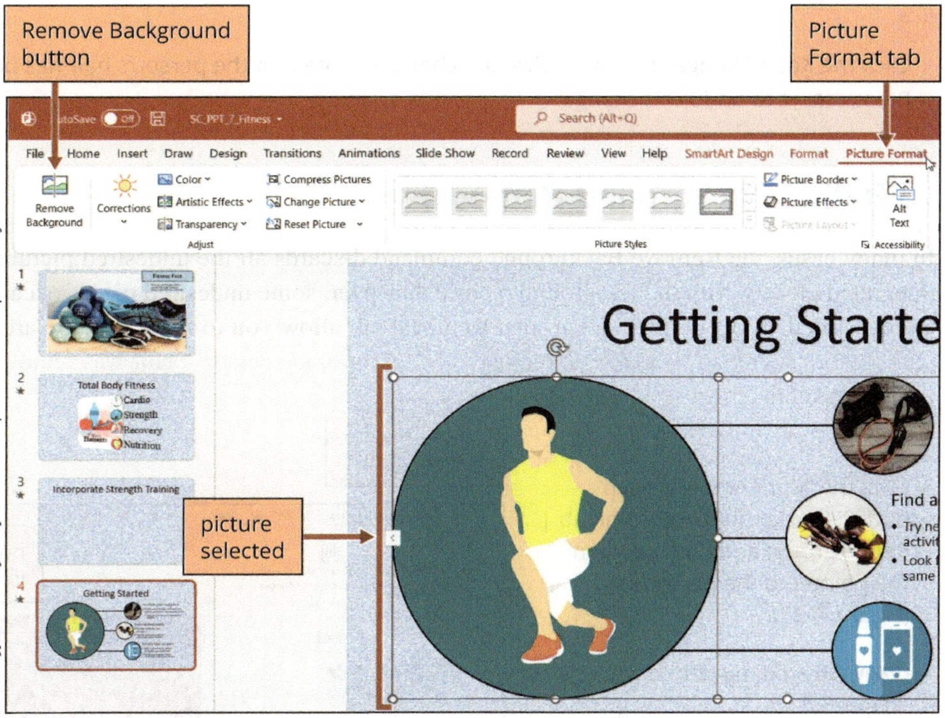

Mohamed_hassan/Pixabay; Boxed Water Is Better/Unsplash.com; mcmurryjulie/Pixabay; Kelly Sikkema/Unsplash.com; stevepb/Pixabay

Figure 7–36

2

- Zoom the slide to 140%. If necessary, use the vertical and horizontal scroll bars to adjust the slide so the entire picture of the person is visible.
- Click the Remove Background button (Picture Format tab | Adjust group) to display the Background Removal tab and a marquee selection area (Figure 7–37).

Q&A How does PowerPoint determine the area to display within the marquee?
Microsoft Research software engineers developed the algorithms that determine the portions of the picture in the foreground.

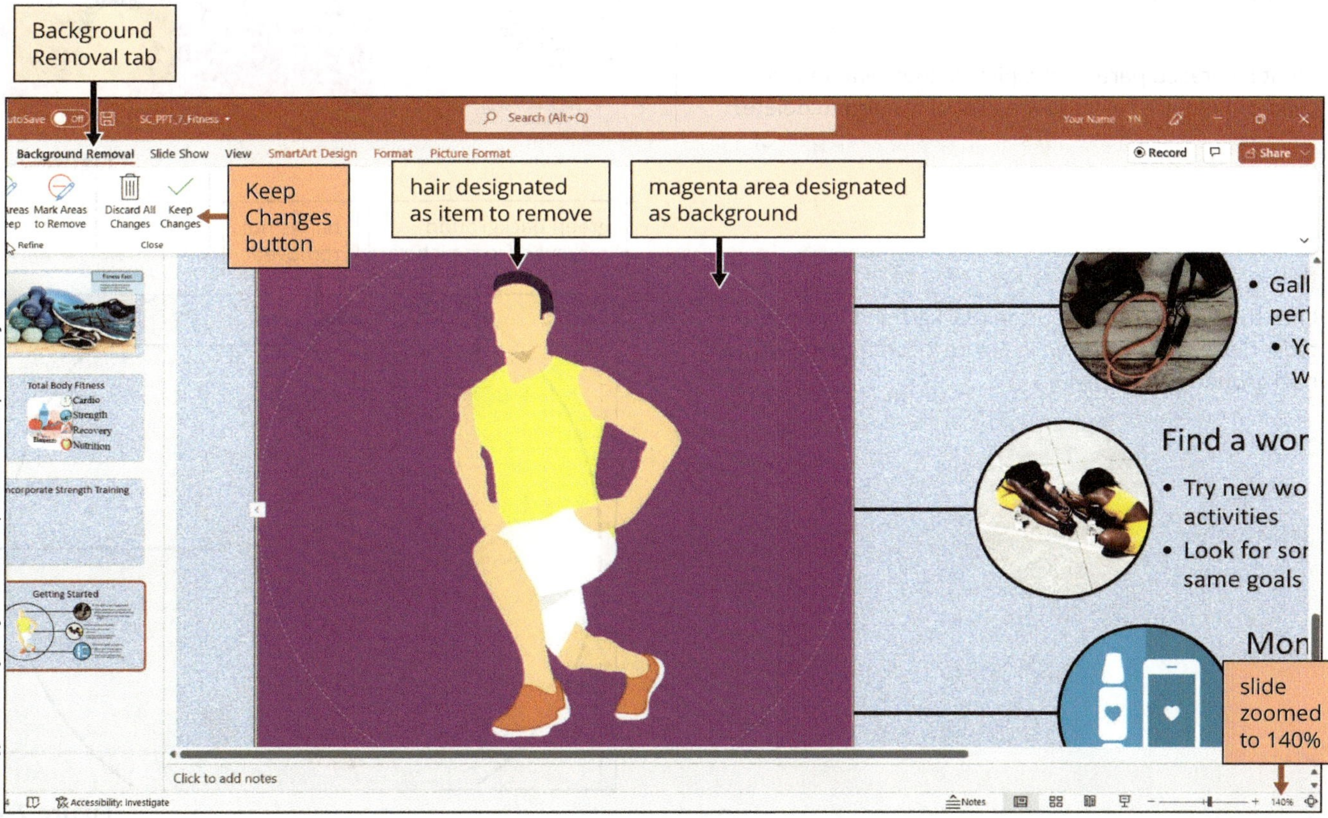

Mohamed_hassan/Pixabay; Boxed Water Is Better/Unsplash.com; mcmurryjulie/Pixabay; Kelly Sikkema/Unsplash.com; stevepb/Pixabay

Figure 7–37

3

- Click the Keep Changes button to view the changes. Note that the person's hair has been removed.
- Press CTRL+Z to undo this change.

To Refine Background Removal

In many cases, the Remove Background command discards all the undesired picture components. When the background is integrated closely with the foreground picture, however, some undesired pieces occasionally remain and other desired pieces are discarded. Tools on the Background Removal tab allow you to mark specific areas to remove and to keep. **Why?** In the picture, the green background was removed. In addition, the person's hair was removed. The following steps mark the hair as an area to keep.

1

- Click the 'Mark Areas to Keep' button (Background Removal tab | Refine group) and then position the pointer in the person's hair (Figure 7–38).

Q&A Why did my pointer change shape?
The pointer changed to a pencil to indicate you are about to draw on a precise area of the picture.

Figure 7–38

2

- Click and then drag the pointer in the person's hair to indicate the portion of the picture to keep (Figure 7–39).

Q&A If I marked an area that I want to delete, can I reverse my action?
Yes. Press CTRL+Z immediately after you click the area.

What if I erased parts of the picture that I wanted to keep or I did not select all the areas I wanted to delete?
You may need to make several passes to keep part of the picture.

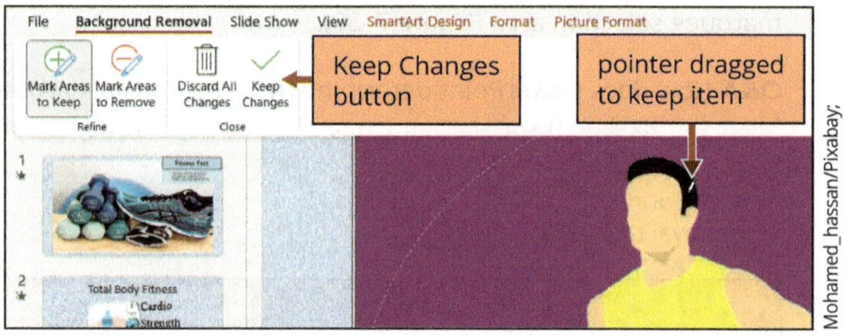

Figure 7–39

3

- Click the Keep Changes button (Background Removal tab | Close group) (shown in Figure 7–39) to remove the background (Figure 7–40).

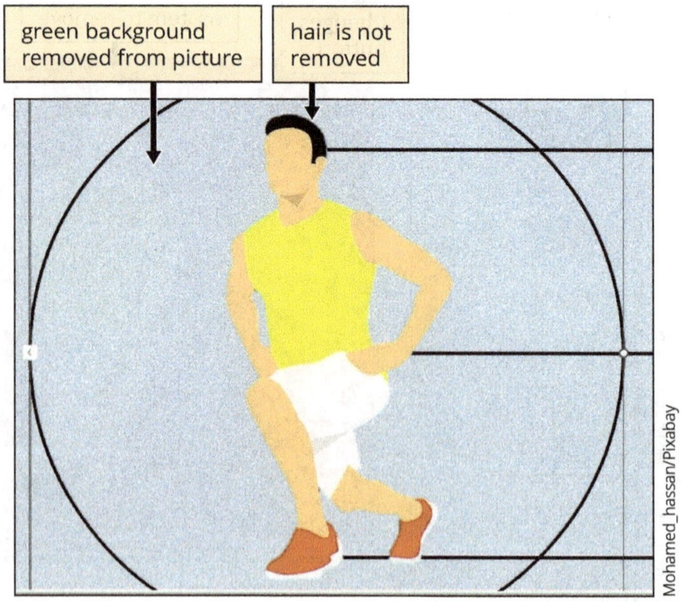

Figure 7–40

To Mark Areas to Remove If you wanted to remove areas of a picture, you would perform the following steps.

1. Click the 'Mark Areas to Remove button (Background Removal tab | Refine group) and then position the pointer in the desired area.
2. Click and then drag the pointer across the area to remove.
3. Click the Keep Changes button (Background Removal tab | Close group).

To Flip a Picture

You can flip the picture so that the person is pointed in the opposite direction. **Why?** The person's knees will point inward toward the graphic's content and help direct the audience's attention to the three getting started measures. The following steps flip the picture horizontally.

1

- With the picture selected and the Picture Format tab displayed, click the Rotate button (Picture Format tab | Arrange group) to display the Rotate Objects menu.
- Point to Flip Horizontal in the list to see a preview of the flipped picture (Figure 7–41).

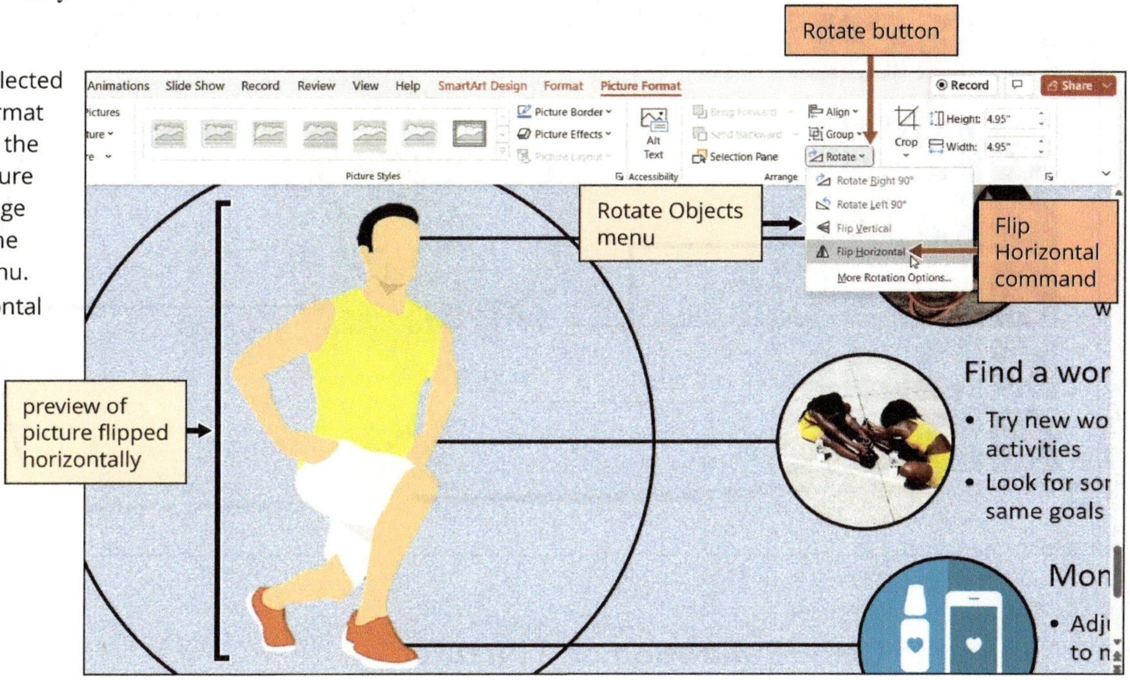

Figure 7–41

2

- Click Flip Horizontal in the Rotate Objects menu to flip the picture.

To Change the Brightness and Contrast of a Picture

A picture's brightness and contrast can be altered in predefined percentage increments. The overall lightness or darkness of the entire image is determined by the brightness setting, and the difference between the darkest and lightest areas of the image is determined by the contrast setting. **Why?** The person's bright yellow shirt displays prominently on the slide. Decreasing the contrast will help direct the audience's attention to the other slide elements. The following step decreases the contrast and brightness.

1

- Zoom the slide to 200%.

2

- With the picture still selected, click the Corrections button (Picture Format tab | Adjust group) to display the Corrections gallery.
- Point to 'Brightness: -20% Contrast: -20%' (second picture in the second Brightness/Contrast row) to display a live preview of this correction on the picture (Figure 7–42).
- **Experiment:** Point to various brightness and contrast variations in the gallery and watch the colors change in the picture.
- Click 'Brightness: -20% Contrast: -20%' to apply this correction.

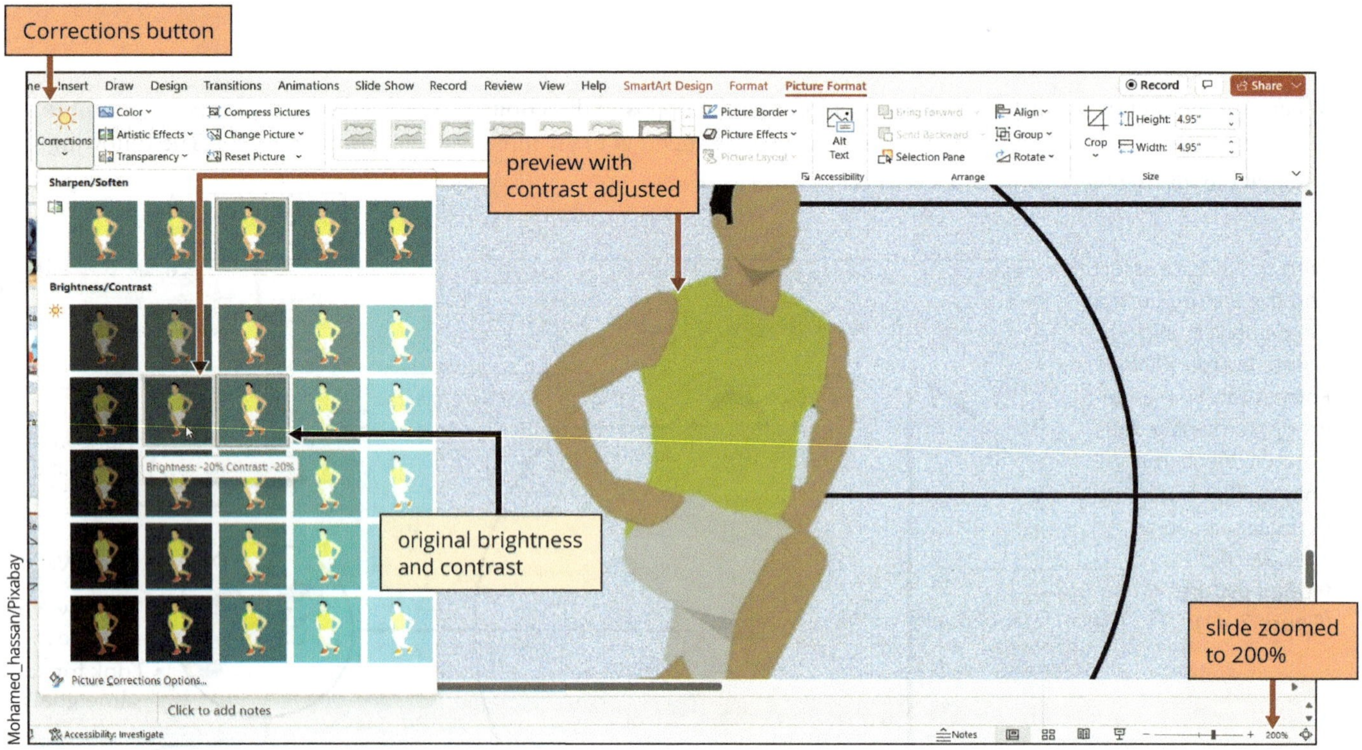

Figure 7–42

To Change the Color Saturation of a Picture

The Color gallery has a wide variety of preset formatting combinations that allow you to match or add contrast to slide elements. High color saturation produces vivid colors, and low saturation produces gray tones. The following steps change the color saturation of the Slide 4 picture. **Why?** You want to make the shirt's yellow color less vivid.

1

- With the picture still selected, click the Color button (Picture Format tab | Adjust group) to display the Color gallery (Figure 7–43).

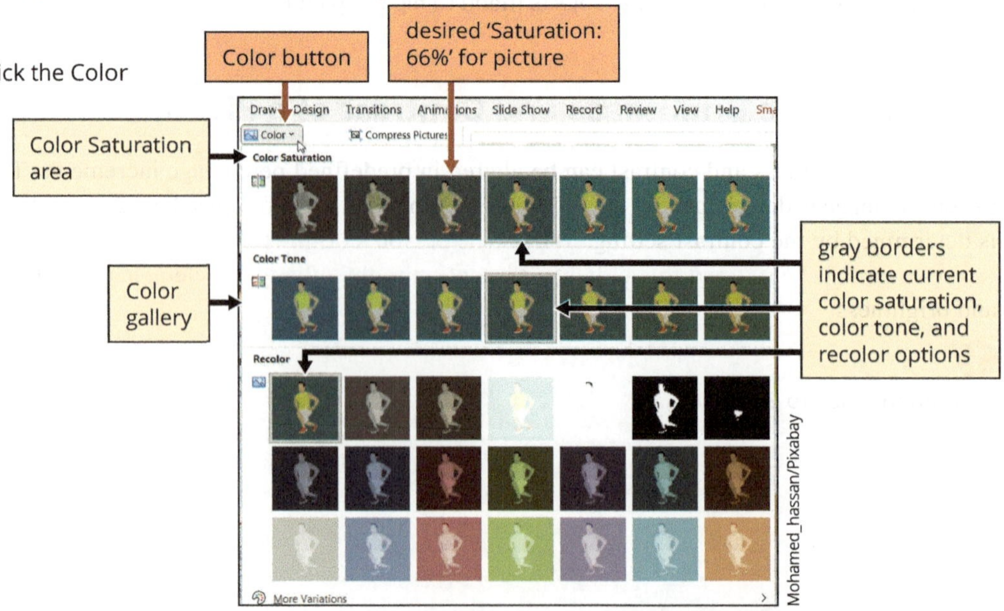

Figure 7–43

2

- Point to 'Saturation: 66%' (third thumbnail in the Color Saturation row) to display a live preview of this adjustment on the picture (Figure 7–44).
- **Experiment:** Point to various saturation variations in the gallery and watch the colors change in the picture.
- Click 'Saturation: 66%' to apply this saturation to the picture.

3

- Zoom the slide to 80%.

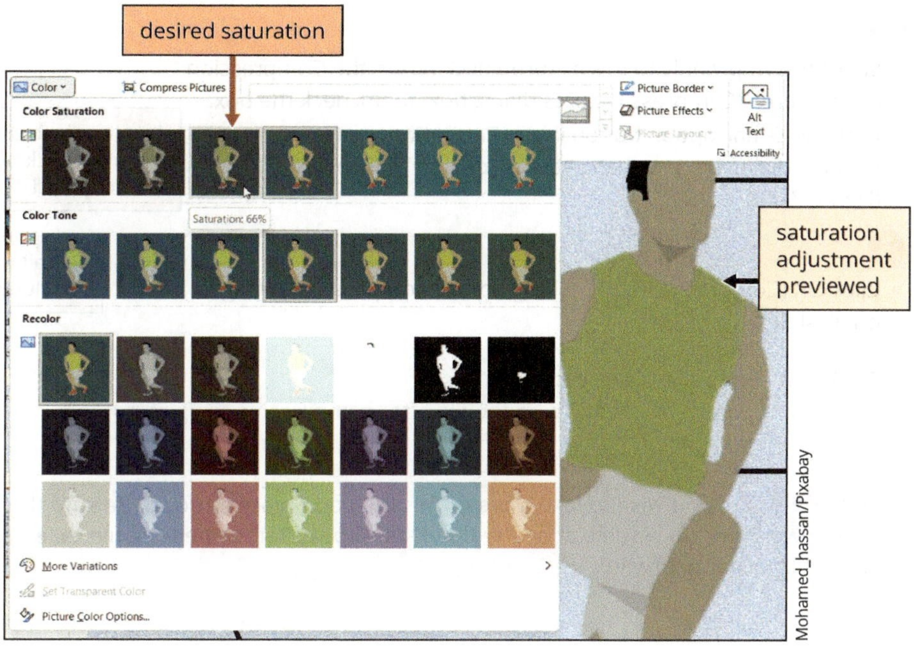

Figure 7–44

To Reset a Picture To remove all effects from a picture, you would perform the following step.

1. Click the Reset Picture button (Picture Format tab | Adjust group).

To Compress a Picture

Photos inserted into slides greatly increase the total PowerPoint file size. PowerPoint automatically compresses picture files inserted into slides by eliminating details, generally with no visible loss of quality. You can increase the compression and, in turn, decrease the file size if you instruct PowerPoint to compress a picture you have modified or cropped so you can save space on a storage medium such as a solid-state drive, memory card, or USB flash drive. Although these storage devices generally have a large storage capacity, you might want to reduce the file size. **Why?** A smaller size reduces the download time from a server or website. Also, some Internet service providers restrict an attachment's file size.

The background of the picture on Slide 4 has been removed. You will not need any of the invisible portions of the picture, so you can delete them permanently and reduce the picture file size. The following steps compress the size of the Slide 4 picture.

1

- With the picture selected, click the Compress Pictures button (Picture Format tab | Adjust group) to display the Compress Pictures dialog box (Figure 7–45).

Q&A If I want to add an artistic effect, should I apply the effect prior to or after compressing a picture?
Compress a picture and then apply the artistic effect.

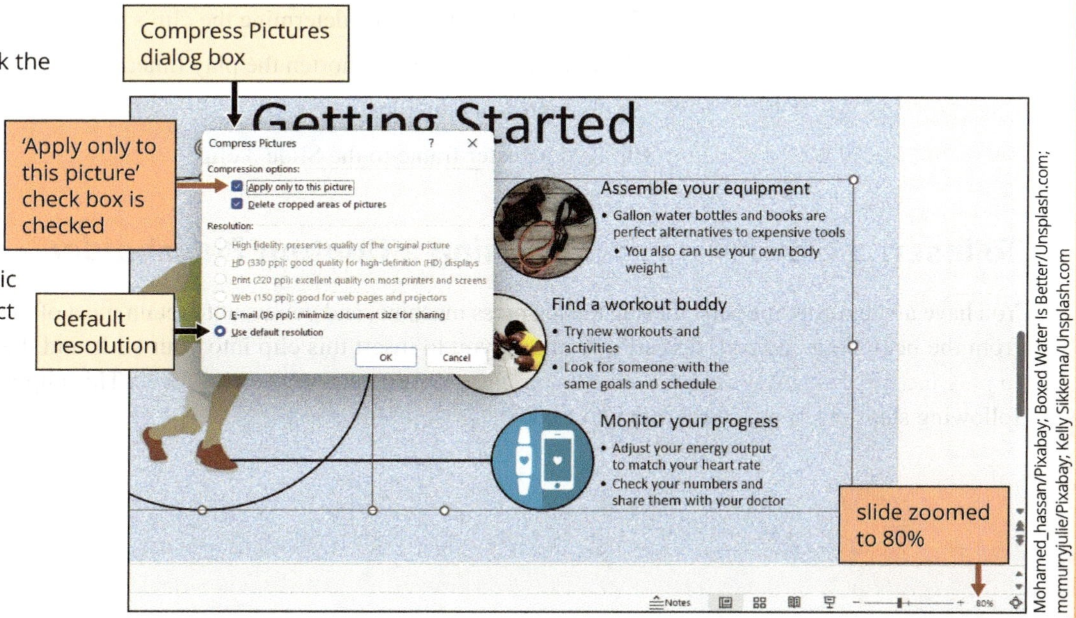

Figure 7–45

2

- Select the 'Apply only to this picture' check box in the Compression options area (Compress Pictures dialog box) to uncheck the box.
- Click the E-mail option button in the Resolution area (Compress Pictures dialog box) to change the resolution to 96 ppi (Figure 7–46).

3

- Click OK (Compress Pictures dialog box) to compress the images on all slides.

Q&A Can I undo the compression?
Yes, as long as you have not saved the file after compressing the pictures.

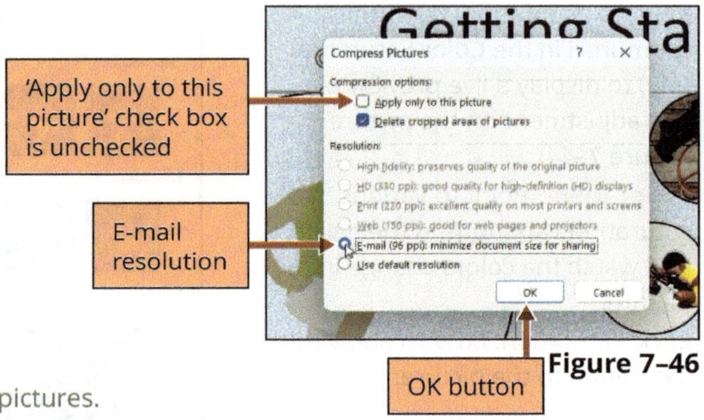

Figure 7–46

Break Point: If you wish to take a break, this is a good place to do so. Be sure the Fitness file is saved and then you can quit PowerPoint. To resume at a later time, start PowerPoint, open the file called Fitness, and continue following the steps from this location forward.

BTW
Play Options for Online Videos
Play options are not available for online videos, such as YouTube videos. They are available only for videos inserted from your computer, network, or OneDrive.

Inserting a Video and an Audio Clip

Strength is an important element of total body fitness, as shown by the SmartArt on Slide 2. On Slide 3 you want to emphasize that regular strength exercises can help develop strong bones, increase metabolism, contribute to better balance, and protect joints from injury. You can enhance this presentation's content by adding a video clip on Slide 3 demonstrating one strength training technique: leg presses. The clip does not have audio, so you will add an audio clip of upbeat music.

In the following pages, you will perform these tasks:

1. Insert a video file into Slide 3.
2. Trim the video file to shorten the play time.
3. Add video options that determine the clip's appearance and playback.
4. Resize the Slide 3 video clip.
5. Add a video style to the Slide 3 clip.
6. Insert an audio file into Slide 3.
7. Add audio options that determine the clip's appearance and playback.
8. Trim the audio file to shorten the play time.
9. Compress media files.
10. Add a poster frame to the Slide 3 clip.

To Insert a Video File without Using a Content Placeholder

You have a video clip of a person using the leg press machine, and you want to retain most of the clip but eliminate a few seconds from the beginning and end. PowerPoint allows you to insert this clip into your slide and then trim the file. Why? You want to play just a portion of the video when you preview the clip or run the slide show. This clip is available in the Data Files. The following steps insert this video clip into Slide 3.

1

- Display Slide 3 and then display the Insert tab.
- Click the Video button (Insert tab | Media group) to display the Insert Video menu (Figure 7–47).

stevepb/Pixabay

Figure 7–47

2

- Click This Device on the Insert Video From menu to display the Insert Video dialog box.
- If necessary, navigate to the location where the Data Files are located and then click Support_PPT_7_Leg_Press to select the .mp4 file (Figure 7–48).

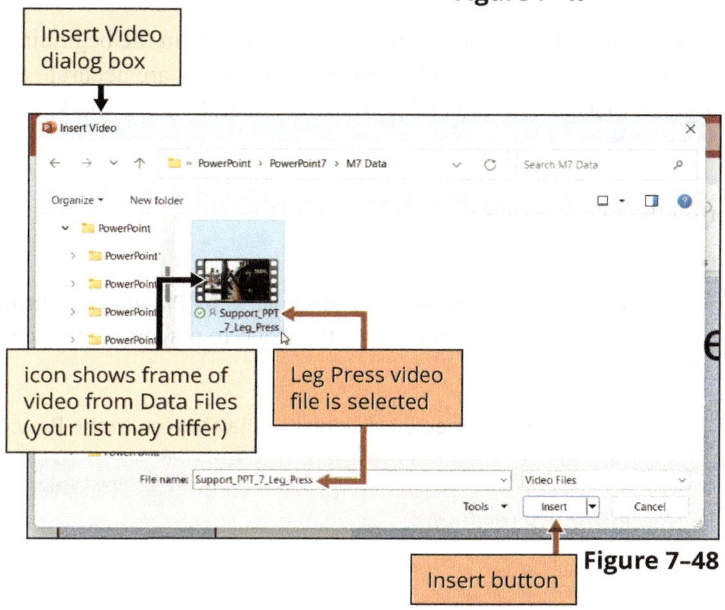

freefitnessmedia/Pixabay

Figure 7–48

3

- Click the Insert button (Insert Video dialog box) to insert the Leg Press video clip into Slide 3 (Figure 7–49).
- If the Design Ideas pane opens, close it.

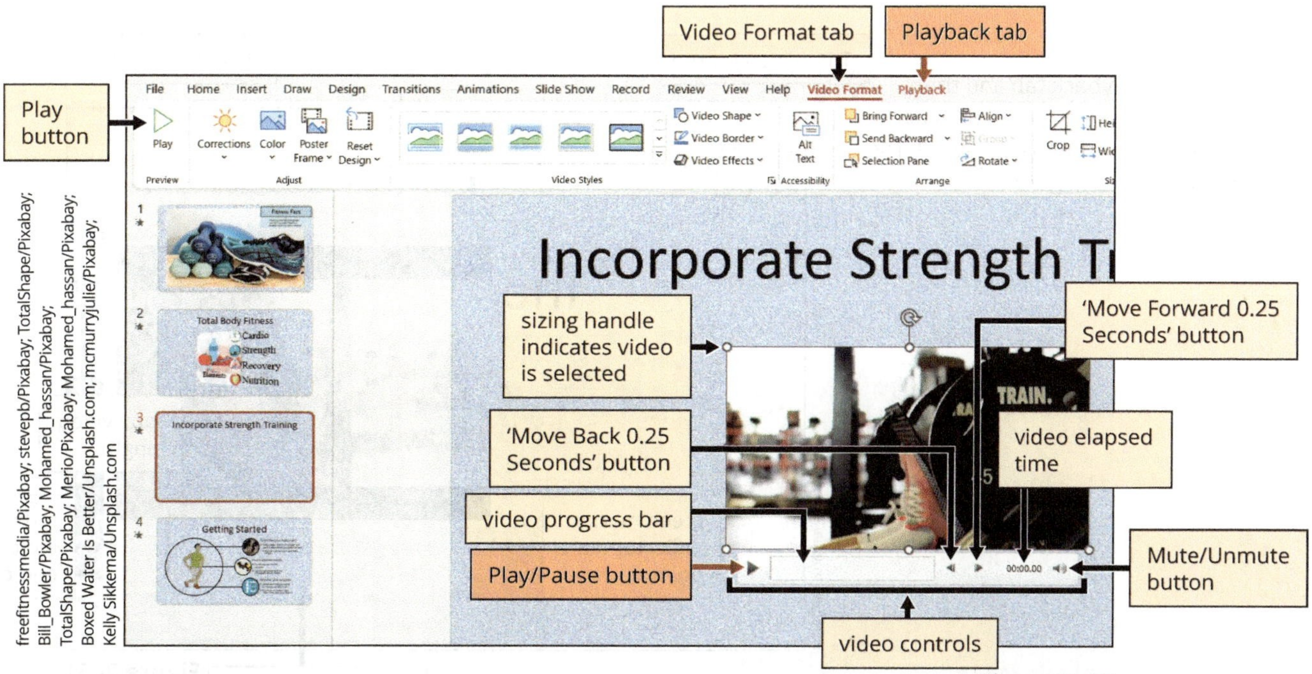

freefitnessmedia/Pixabay; stevepb/Pixabay; TotalShape/Pixabay; Bill_Bowler/Pixabay; Mohamed_hassan/Pixabay; TotalShape/Pixabay; Merio/Pixabay; Mohamed_hassan/Pixabay; Boxed Water Is Better/Unsplash.com; mcmurryjulie/Pixabay; Kelly Sikkema/Unsplash.com

Figure 7–49

To Insert an Online Video PowerPoint allows you to insert or link to an online video, such as those found on YouTube, and then play this file during your presentation. These videos are stored on and played from the website, so you must be connected to the Internet when you play these files. To insert an online video, you would perform the following steps.

1. Display the Insert tab and then click the Video button (Insert tab | Media group) to display the Video menu.
2. Click Online Video to display the Insert Video dialog box.
3. In the search box, enter the web address of a video from a supported video provider to insert a video from a website.
4. Click the Insert button to insert the video clip into the slide.

To Trim a Video File

PowerPoint's Trim Video feature allows you to trim the beginning and end of your clip by designating your desired Start Time and End Time. These precise time measurements are accurate to one-thousandth of a second. The start point is indicated by a green marker, and the end point is indicated by a red marker. You want to shorten the duration of the Leg Press video clip. **Why?** The Leg Press video file has a running time of almost 12 seconds. Much of the video is the same view of the person exercising, so you decide to delete a few seconds from the beginning and the end to shorten the duration. The following steps trim the Leg Press clip.

1

- With the video clip selected on Slide 3, click the Play/Pause button in the video controls underneath the video to play the entire video (Figure 7-50).

Q&A Can I play the video by clicking the Play button in the Preview group?
Yes. This Play button plays the entire clip. You may prefer to click the Play/Pause button displayed in the video controls to stop the video and examine one of the frames.

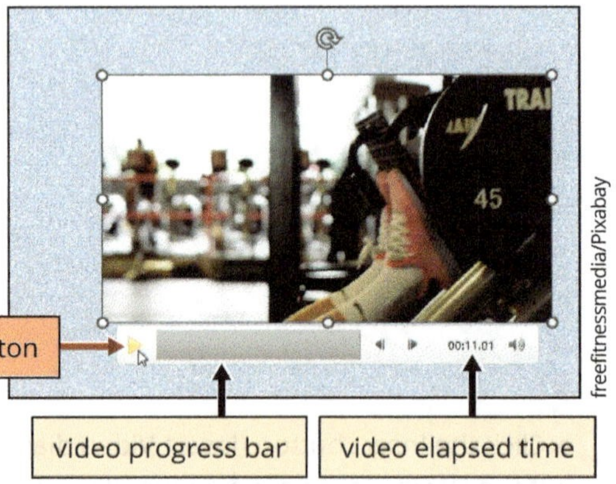

Figure 7-50

2

- Display the Playback tab and then click the Trim Video button (Playback tab | Editing group) to display the Trim Video dialog box (Figure 7-51).

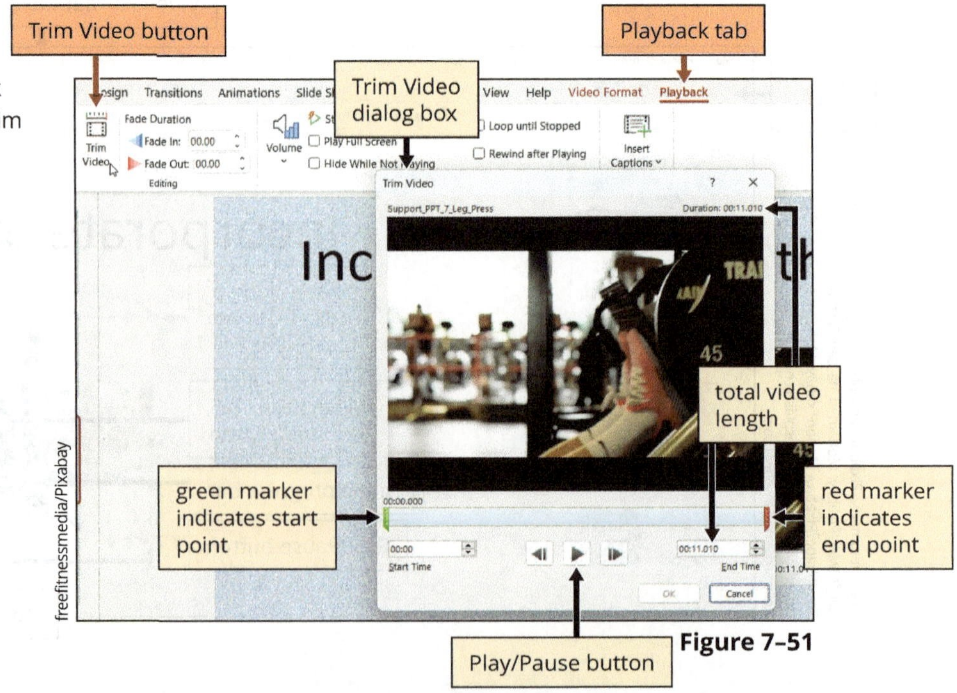

Figure 7-51

3

- Click the Start Time up arrow several times until 00:01.353 is displayed (Figure 7–52).

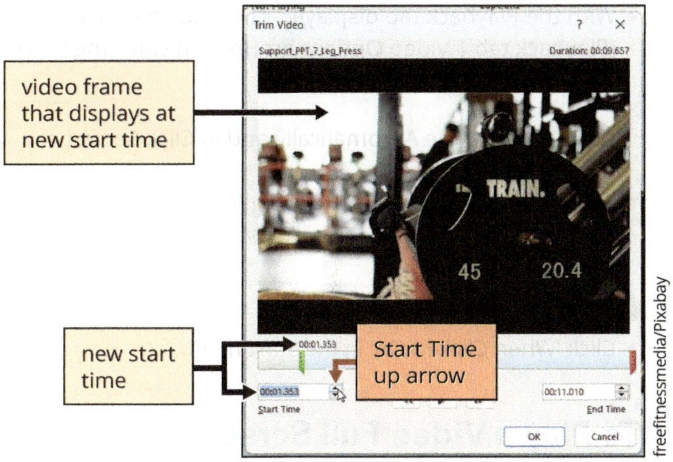

Figure 7–52

4

- Click the End Time down arrow several times until 00:10.263 is displayed (Figure 7–53).

Q&A Can I specify the start or end times by dragging the markers?
Yes. You can drag the green marker to determine the start time and the red marker to determine the end time. You also can click the Next Frame and Previous Frame buttons or enter the time in the Start Time or End Time boxes (Trim Video dialog box).

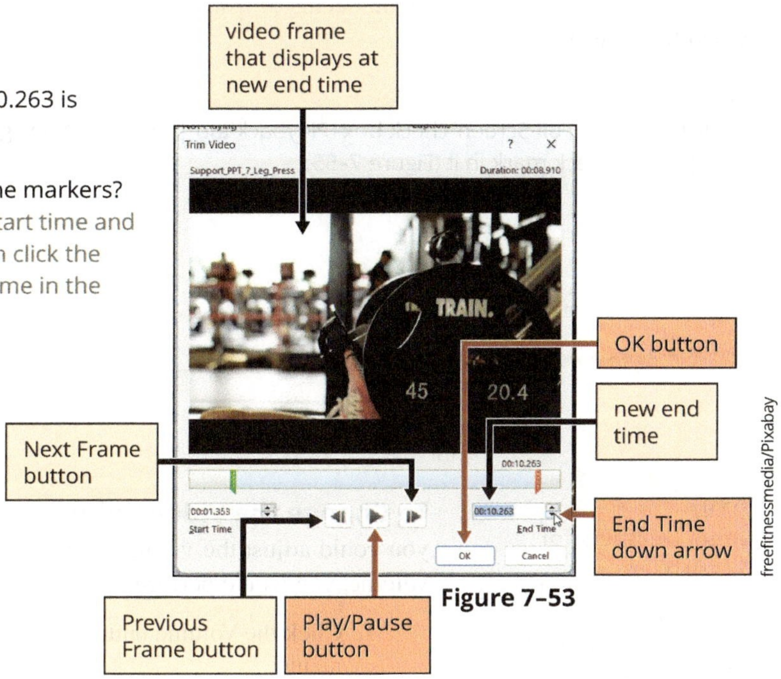

Figure 7–53

5

- Click the Play/Pause button (Trim Video dialog box) to review the shortened video clip.
- Click OK (Trim Video dialog box) to set the Start Time and End Time and to close the Trim Video dialog box.

Other Ways

1. Right-click clip, click Trim on Mini toolbar
2. In Trim Video dialog box, press ALT+S and ALT+E

To Change the Video Start Option

Once the video clip is inserted into Slide 3, you can specify that the video plays when the presenter clicks the area of the slide with the video after the slide is displayed. Other options are to run the video immediately when the slide is displayed or in a click sequence. **Why?** When you are giving your presentation, you want to discuss the slide topic and then click the mouse to start the video. The following steps add the option of playing the video when a frame is clicked.

1

- With the Playback tab displayed, click the Start arrow (Playback tab | Video Options group) to display the Start menu (Figure 7–54).

Q&A What do the Automatically and In Click Sequence options do?
The video clip would begin playing immediately when a slide is displayed during the slide show.

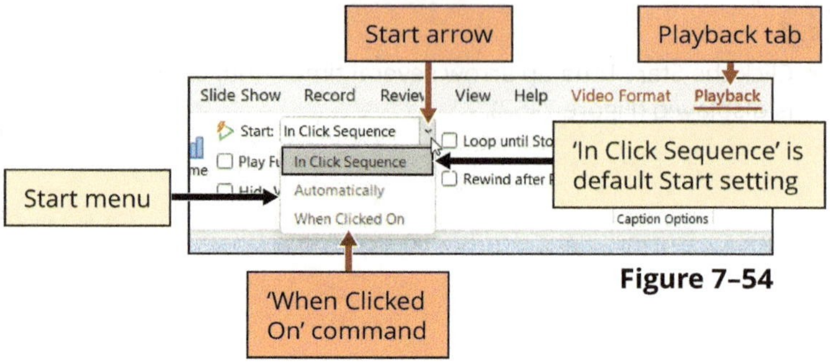

Figure 7–54

2

- Click 'When Clicked On' in the Start menu.

To Play a Video Full Screen

Once the video clip is inserted into Slide 3, you can specify that the video fills the entire screen when the video plays. **Why?** You want your audience to see the details of using the leg press machine. The following step adds the option of playing the video full screen.

1

- Click the 'Play Full Screen' check box (Playback tab | Video Options group) to place a check mark in it (Figure 7–55).

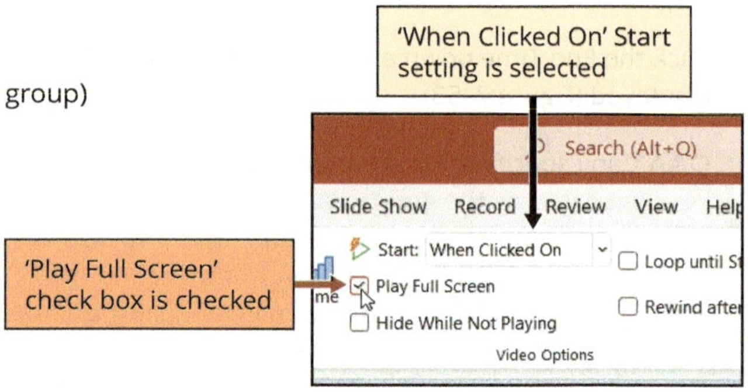

Figure 7–55

BTW
Ideal Decibels for Creativity
When you need to be creative, move to an environment filled with moderate background noise, such as a coffee shop. Researchers at the University of British Columbia state that a noise level of approximately 70 decibels, which is the sound of a quiet conversation or highway noise from afar, fosters original ideas. Anything louder than this ambient noise level decreases the thought process.

To Change the Video Volume The Leg Press video does not have audio. If it did, however, you could adjust the volume of the sound. The default video volume is High. To decrease the volume, you would perform the following steps.

1. Click the Volume button (Playback tab | Video Options group) to display the Volume menu.
2. Click Medium or Low on the Volume menu to set the audio volume or click Mute if you do not want your audience to hear any recorded sounds.

To Rewind a Video after Playing To rewind your video clip after playing during your presentation, you would perform the following step.

1. Click the 'Rewind after Playing' check box (Playback tab | Video Options group) to place a check mark in it.

To Resize a Video Proportionally

The default Leg Press video frame size can be changed. You resize a video clip in the same manner that you resize pictures. The following steps increase the Leg Press video frame using a sizing handle. **Why?** You want to fit the video near the center of the slide.

1

- With the video still selected, click Video Format on the ribbon to display the Video Format tab (Figure 7–56).

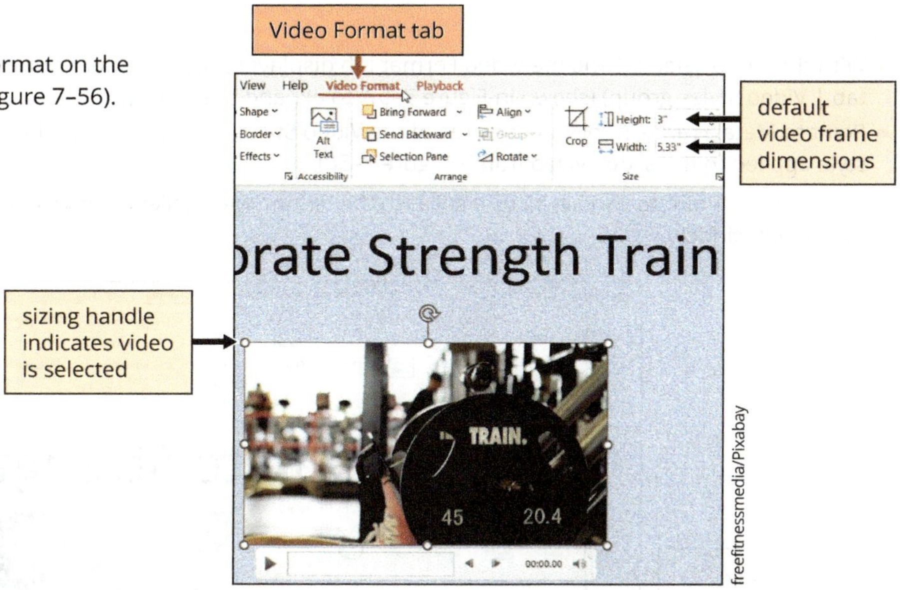

Figure 7–56

2

- Drag any corner sizing handle diagonally outward until the frame is resized to approximately 5.6" × 9.96".
- Use the smart guides to position the clip, as shown in Figure 7–57.

Figure 7–57

To Apply a Video Style

The video styles are similar to the picture styles you applied in previous modules and include various shapes, angles, borders, and reflections. The following steps apply a video style to the Leg Press video clip on Slide 3. **Why?** The Leg Press video clip on Slide 3 displays full screen when it is playing, but you decide to increase the visual appeal of the clip when it is not playing by applying a video style.

1

- With the video selected and the Video Format tab displayed, click the More button in the Video Styles gallery (Video Format tab | Video Styles group) (shown in Figure 7–57) to expand the gallery.
- Point to Metal Frame in the Intense area of the Video Styles gallery (last style in the last row) to display a live preview of that style applied to the slide's video frame (Figure 7–58).
- **Experiment:** Point to various picture styles in the Video Styles gallery and watch the style of the video frame change in the document window.

Figure 7–58

2

- Click Metal Frame in the Video Styles gallery to apply the style to the selected video (Figure 7–59).

Figure 7–59

To Add a Video Poster Frame

A **poster frame** is the frame that appears on a video object when the video is not playing. This preview image of your video helps an audience anticipate the content of the video. This frame can be a picture or one frame from the video you are going to play. In this module, you will use a picture from the Data Files. **Why?** You used this Weights picture as part of the SmartArt graphic on Slide 2, so your audience will be familiar with this image. The following steps apply a poster frame to the Leg Press video clip.

1

- With the video clip selected, click the Poster Frame button (Video Format tab | Adjust group) to display the Poster Frame menu (Figure 7–60).

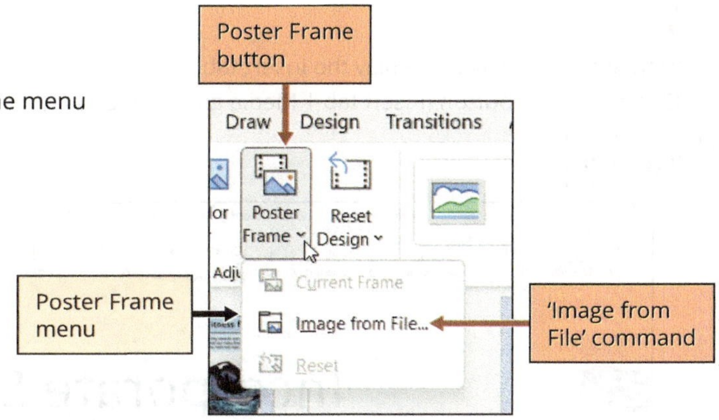

Figure 7–60

stevepb/Pixabay

2

- Click 'Image from File' to display the Insert Pictures dialog box.
- Click 'From a File' to display the Insert Picture dialog box.
- If necessary, navigate to the location where the Data Files are located and then click Support_PPT_7_Weights.png to select the file (Figure 7–61).

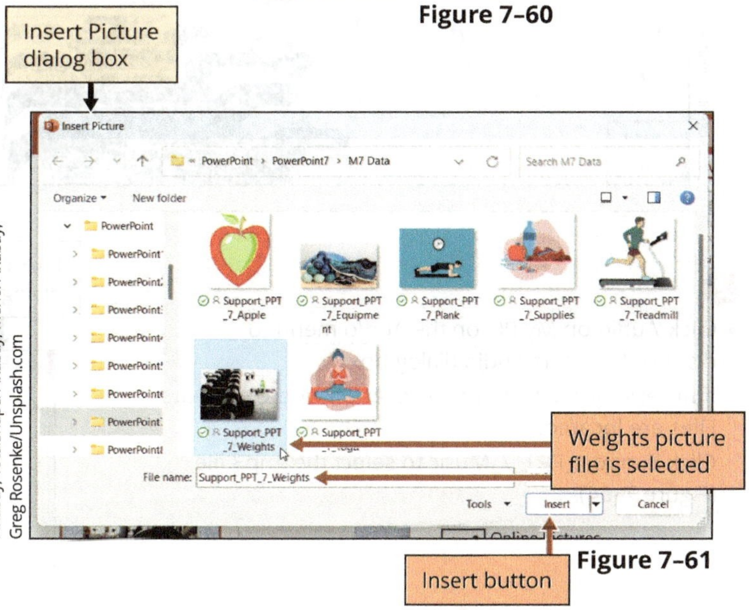

Figure 7–61

stevepb/Pixabay; TotalShape/Pixabay; Bill_Bowler/Pixabay; Mohamed_hassan/ Pixabay; TotalShape/Pixabay; Merio/Pixabay; Greg Rosenke/Unsplash.com

3

- Click the Insert button (Insert Picture dialog box) to insert this picture into Slide 3 as a poster frame (Figure 7–62).

Figure 7–62

Greg Rosenke/Unsplash.com

To Insert an Audio Clip from a File

If your computer has a microphone, you can enable it and record audio for your presentation. In addition, if you have an app on your smartphone or mobile device or a digital audio recorder, you can record sounds to insert into your presentation. You also can locate audio files on a variety of websites. The following steps insert an audio clip into Slide 3. **Why?** The video clip does not have any sound, so you want to add an audio clip of upbeat music to add interest when Slide 3 is displayed.

1

- With Slide 3 displayed, display the Insert tab.
- Click the Audio button (Insert tab | Media group) to display the Audio menu (Figure 7–63).

Greg Rosenke/Unsplash.com

Figure 7–63

2

- Click 'Audio on My PC' on the Audio menu to display the Insert Audio dialog box.
- If necessary, navigate to the location where the Data Files are located.
- Click Support_PPT_7_Music to select the .mp3 file (Figure 7–64).

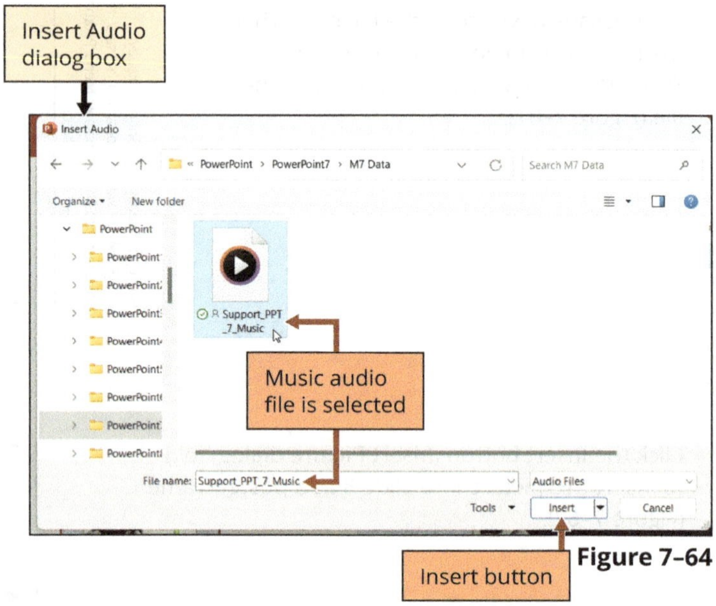

Figure 7–64

3

- Click the Insert button (Insert Audio dialog box) to insert the audio clip into Slide 3 (Figure 7–65).

Q&A Why does a sound icon display on the slide?

The icon indicates an audio file is inserted.

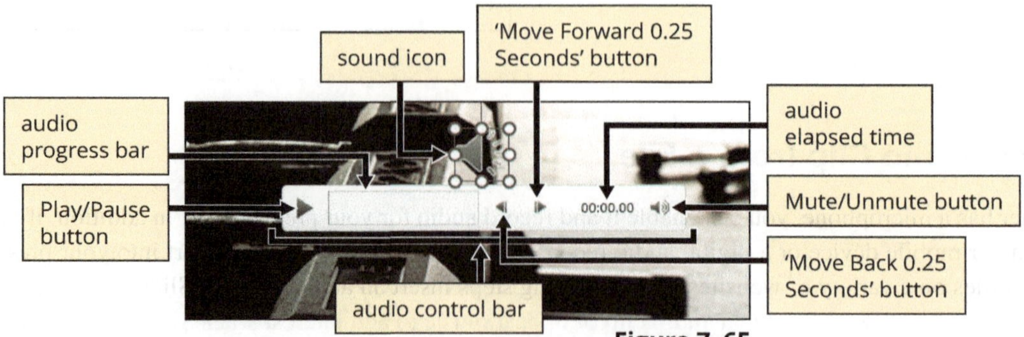

Greg Rosenke/Unsplash.com

Figure 7–65

4

- Drag the sound icon and the audio control bar near the lower-left corner of the slide (Figure 7–66).

Q&A Must I move the icon on the slide?
No. Although your audience will not see the icon when you run the slide show, it is easier for you to see the audio controls in this area of this slide.

Can I preview the audio clip?
Yes. Click the Play button on the ribbon (Preview group) or the Play/Pause button on the audio controls.

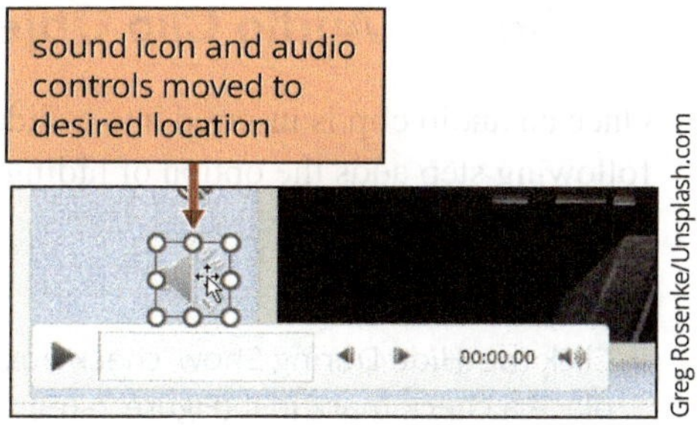

Figure 7–66

To Change the Audio Clip Start Option

Once an audio clip is inserted into a slide, you can specify options that control playback and appearance. The audio clip can play either automatically or when clicked. The following steps add the option of starting automatically. **Why?** You do not want to click the screen to start the sound.

1

- With the Playback tab displayed, click the Start arrow (Playback tab | Audio Options group) to display the Start menu (Figure 7–67).

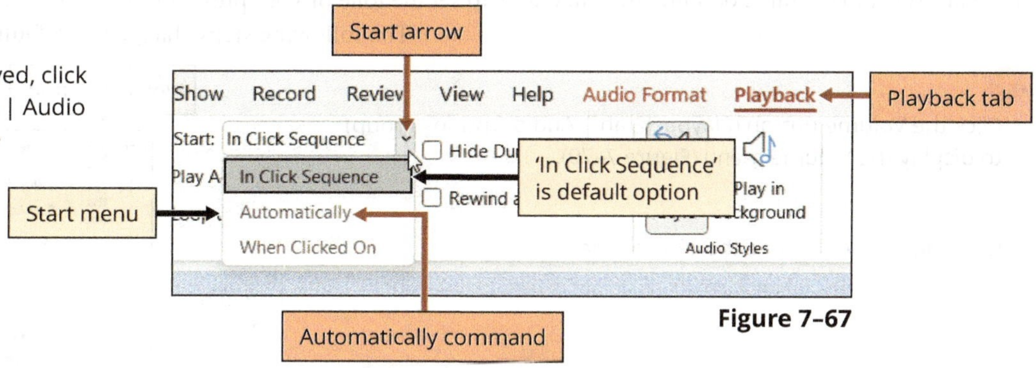

Figure 7–67

2

- Click Automatically in the Start menu.

Q&A How do the 'In Click Sequence' and the 'When Clicked On' options function?
If you were to select either of these options, the sound would begin playing only after the presenter clicks Slide 3 during a presentation.

To Loop an Audio Clip

Once an audio clip is inserted into a slide, you can specify that it can repeat while a particular slide is displayed. The following step adds the option of playing until the slide no longer is displayed. **Why?** You want the music to repeat while the slide is displayed to coordinate with the picture prominently shown and to keep the audience's attention focused on the video.

1

- Click the 'Loop until Stopped' check box (Playback tab | Audio Options group) to place a check mark in it (Figure 7–68).

Q&A What is the difference between the 'Loop until Stopped' option and the 'Play Across Slides' option?
The audio clip in the 'Loop until Stopped' option repeats for as long as one slide is displayed. In contrast, the 'Play Across Slides' option would play the clip only once, but it would continue to play while other slides in the presentation are displayed. Once the end of the clip is reached, the sound would end and not repeat.

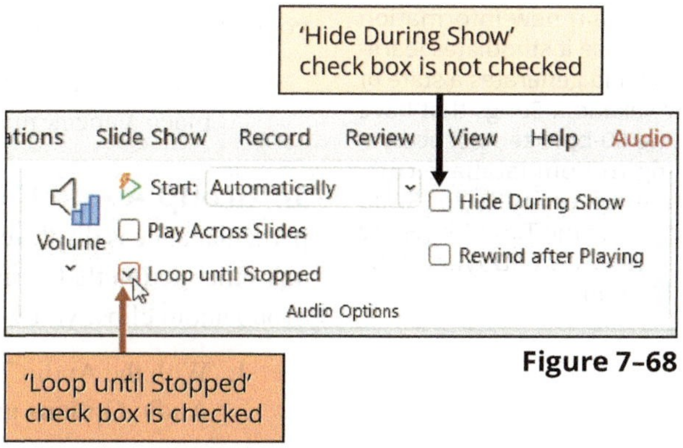

Figure 7–68

To Hide an Audio Clip Object during a Slide Show

Once an audio clip is inserted into a slide, you can specify that the icon does not display when the presentation is running. The following step adds the option of hiding the sound icon on the slide. **Why?** You will not click the screen to start the sound, so you do not need to see the icon.

1

- Click the 'Hide During Show' check box (Playback tab | Audio Options group) to place a check mark in it (Figure 7-69).

Q&A Why would I want the icon to display during the show?
If you had selected the On Click option, you would need to find this icon on the slide and click it to start playing the clip.

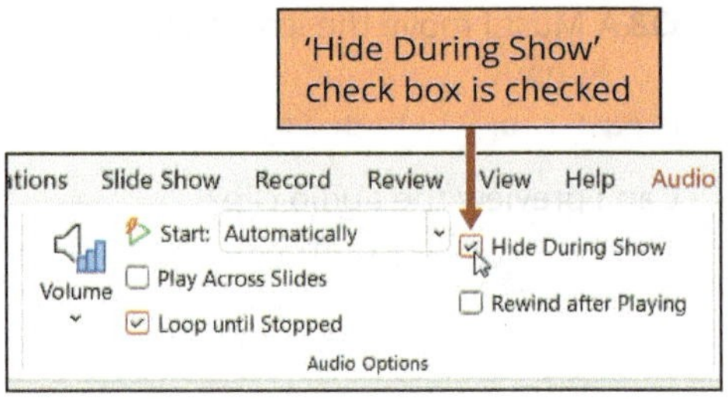

Figure 7-69

To Change the Volume of an Audio Clip

You can adjust the volume or mute the sound to help set the tone of your presentation. **Why?** The default High sound level may be too loud and distract from the content being presented. The following steps change the default volume from High to Medium.

1

- Click the Volume button (Playback tab | Audio Options group) to display the Volume menu (Figure 7-70).

2

- Click Medium to change the clip volume.

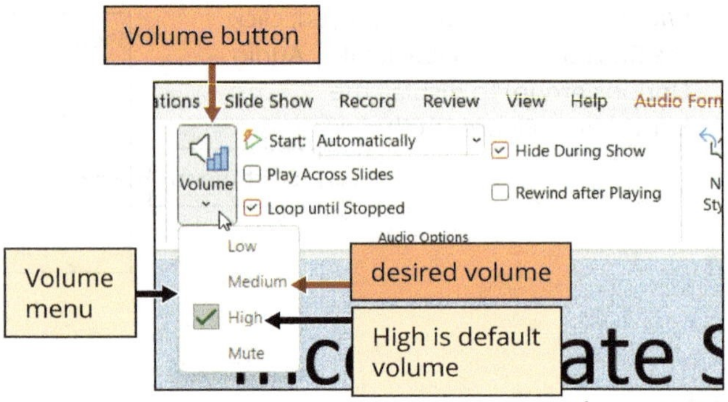

Figure 7-70

Other Ways

1. Click Mute/Unmute button on Media Controls bar, adjust volume slider

BTW
Ideal Beats Per Minute
Keep your mind alert, but calm, by listening to music that has 60 beats per minute (bpm). According to brain-research.us, this rate allows you to keep focused and to retain new information because it stimulates learning and generates a state of relaxation. Songs that have the 60-bpm tempo, according to bpmdatabase.com, are "Lover" by Taylor Swift, "Sign of the Times" by Harry Styles, and "Daylight" by Maroon 5.

To Play an Audio Clip across Slides If you wanted the audio clip to play during the entire presentation, you would perform the following step.

1. Click the 'Play Across Slides' check box (Playback tab | Audio Options group) to place a check mark in it.

To Rewind an Audio Clip after Playing To rewind your audio clip after playing during your presentation, you would perform the following step.

1. Click the 'Rewind after Playing' check box (Playback tab | Audio Options group) to place a check mark in it.

To Group Audio Clips You may desire to play several audio clips in sequence while a particular slide is displayed. If so, you can specify that they begin by clicking the slide or performing any other action that activates the next action on the slide, such as pressing the RIGHT ARROW. To group audio clips, you would perform the following steps.

1. With the Audio Tools Playback tab displayed, click the Start arrow (Playback tab | Audio Options group) to display the Start menu.
2. Click 'In Click Sequence' in the Start menu.

To Trim an Audio Clip

The audio control buttons have the same functions as the video control buttons that were displayed when you inserted the Leg Press video clip. They include playing and pausing the sound, moving back or forward 0.25 seconds, audio progress, elapsed time, and muting or unmuting the sound.

As with the video clip you inserted on this slide, PowerPoint's Trim Audio feature allows you to set the beginning and end of a clip. You select the desired sound to play by designating a Start Time and End Time, which are accurate to one-thousandth of a second. The Start Time is indicated by a green marker and the End Time is indicated by a red marker. The following steps trim the music file. **Why?** The audio clip is too long and you want a shorter clip.

1

- Click the Play/Pause button in the audio controls to play the entire clip.

Q&A Can I play the clip by clicking the Play button in the Preview group?
Yes. This Play button plays the entire clip. You may prefer to click the Play/Pause button displayed in the audio controls to pause and play the audio.

- With the Playback tab displayed, click the Trim Audio button (Playback tab | Editing group) to display the Trim Audio dialog box.
- Click and hold the Start Time up arrow or drag the green marker to the right until 00:08.000 is displayed (Figure 7–71).

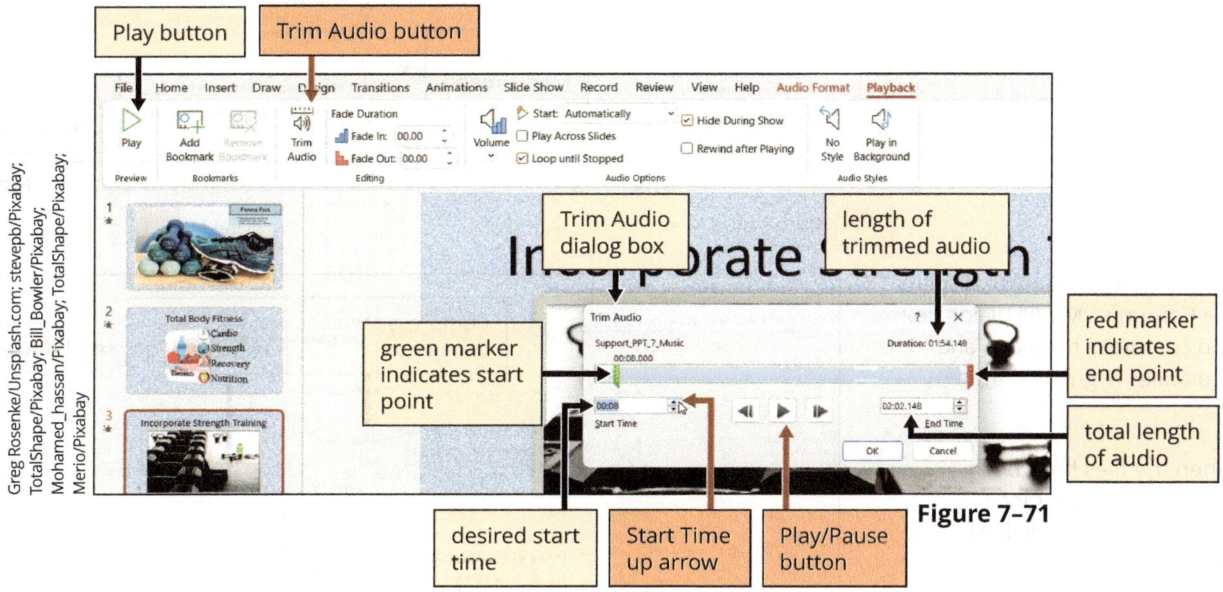

Figure 7–71

2

- Click and hold the End Time down arrow or drag the red marker to the left until 00:15.500 is displayed.
- Click the Play/Pause button (Trim Audio dialog box) to review the shortened audio clip (Figure 7–72).

Q&A Can I specify the start or end times by entering the time in the Start Time and End Time boxes (Trim Audio dialog box)?
Yes. You also can click the Next Frame and Previous Frame buttons.

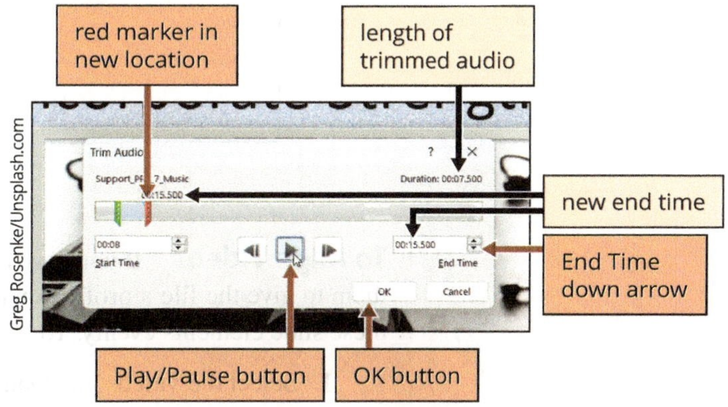

Figure 7–72

3

- Click OK to set the Start Time and End Time and to close the Trim Audio dialog box.

Other Ways

1. Right-click clip, click Trim on Mini toolbar
2. In Trim Audio dialog box, press ALT+S and ALT+E

To Compress a Video and an Audio File

PowerPoint includes a feature that will compress your audio and video files to reduce their size. Media files can be quite large, which can pose a problem if you want to email a presentation or if the space on your storage device is small. You can specify one of three compression qualities: Full HD, HD, or Standard. **Why?** You want to decrease the file size of the audio and video files you have inserted so you can email the presentation if desired. The following steps compress the media files.

1

- With the audio clip selected on Slide 3, click the File tab to display Backstage view and then click the Info tab.
- Click the Compress Media button (Info tab | Media Size and Performance section) to display the Compress Media menu (Figure 7–73).

Q&A Why am I seeing an error message stating that the media could not be compressed?
Graphics cards have acceleration capabilities that allow video, animation, transitions, and other graphics to display smoothly. Your PowerPoint file may have too many graphics that are consuming the resources of your graphics card. If so, you may need to disable hardware graphics acceleration. These settings are found in the Display section of the PowerPoint Options Advanced tab.

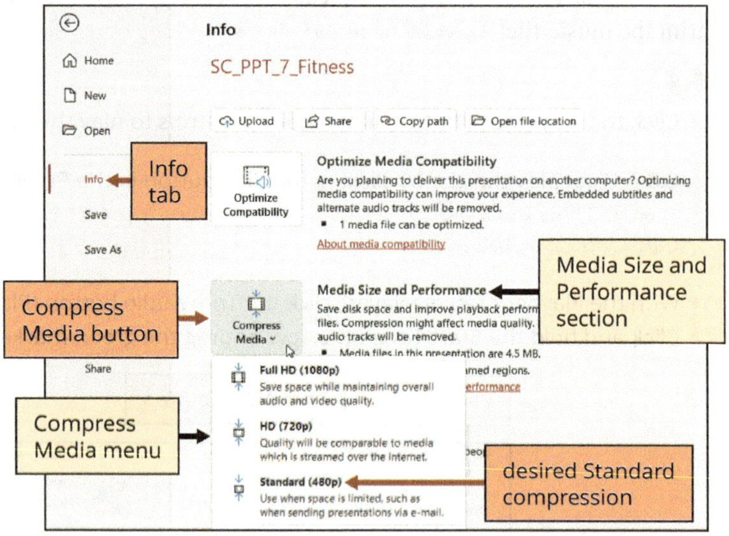

Figure 7–73

2

- Click Standard (480p) to display the Compress Media dialog box and compress the video and audio files (Figure 7–74).

3

- When the files have been compressed, click Close (Compress Media dialog box) to return to Backstage view.
- Click the Back button (Info tab) to return to Slide 3.

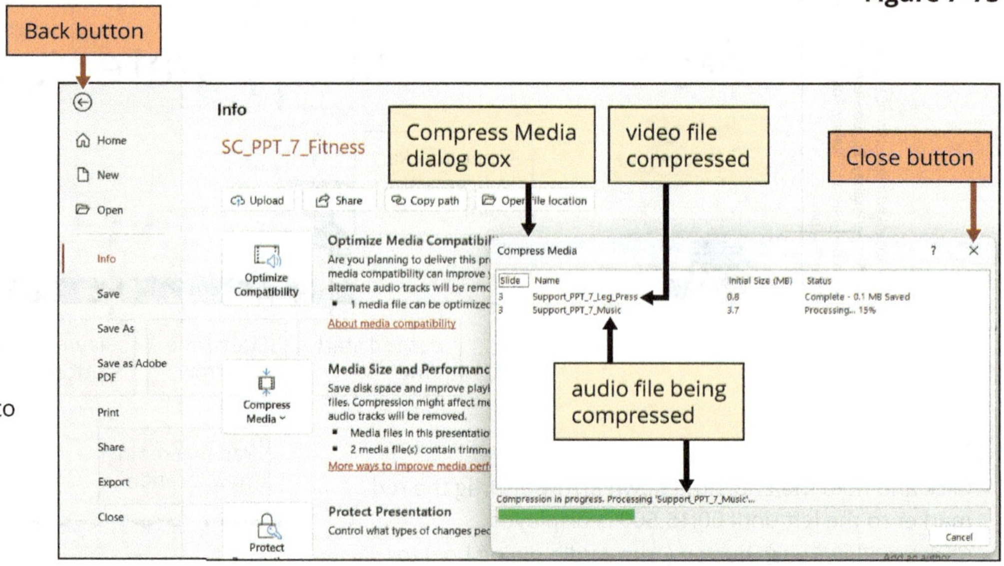

Figure 7–74

To Align Videos If you have multiple videos displayed on one slide, you may desire to arrange them to give the file a professional appearance. PowerPoint includes a feature to help you space these slide elements evenly. To align videos, you would perform the following steps.

1. Select the videos you want to align by pressing SHIFT and clicking each object.
2. Display the Video Format tab, click the Align button (Arrange group), and then click one of the align or distribute options in the Align menu.

Break Point: If you wish to take a break, this is a good place to do so. Be sure the Fitness file is saved and then you can quit PowerPoint. To resume at a later time, start PowerPoint, open the file called Fitness, and continue following the steps from this location forward.

Consider This

Choose outstanding hyperlink images or text.

Good speakers are aware of their audiences and know their speech material well. They have rehearsed their presentations and know where the hypertext is displayed on the slides. During a presentation, however, they sometimes need to divert from their planned material. Audience members may interrupt with questions, the room may not have optimal acoustics or lighting, or the timing may be short or long. It is helpful, therefore, to make the slide hyperlinks as large and noticeable to speakers as possible. The presenters can glance at the slide and receive a visual cue that it contains a hyperlink. They then can decide whether to click the hyperlink to display a webpage or other link.

Adding Hyperlinks and Action Buttons

When presenting the Fitness slide show, you may want to jump nonsequentially to omit some material or to display one or more slides in another presentation in response to audience needs or timing issues. To skip to particular slides, you can click a hyperlink or an action button on a slide. The hyperlink, or link, can be any element of a slide, such as a single letter, a word, a paragraph, or any graphical image such as a picture, shape, or graph. The link connects one slide to another slide, another PowerPoint presentation, a webpage, an email address, or a file.

To Insert a Hyperlink to a Place in the Current Presentation

When you point to a hyperlink, the pointer becomes the shape of a hand to indicate the text or object contains a hyperlink. When you click this hyperlink, PowerPoint connects to the specified slide or other designated area. **Why?** In the Fitness presentation, the Equipment picture on Slide 1 will link to the next slide in the same presentation. The following steps create the first hyperlink for the Equipment picture on Slide 1.

1

- Display Slide 1, select the Equipment picture, and then display the Insert tab.
- Click the Link button (Insert tab | Links group) to display the Insert Hyperlink dialog box.
- Click the 'Place in This Document' button in the Link to area.
- Click '2. Total Body Fitness' in the 'Select a place in this document' area (Insert Hyperlink dialog box) to select and display a preview of this slide (Figure 7–75).

Q&A Could I also have selected the Next Slide link in the 'Select a place in this document' area?
Yes. Either action would create the hyperlink to Slide 2.

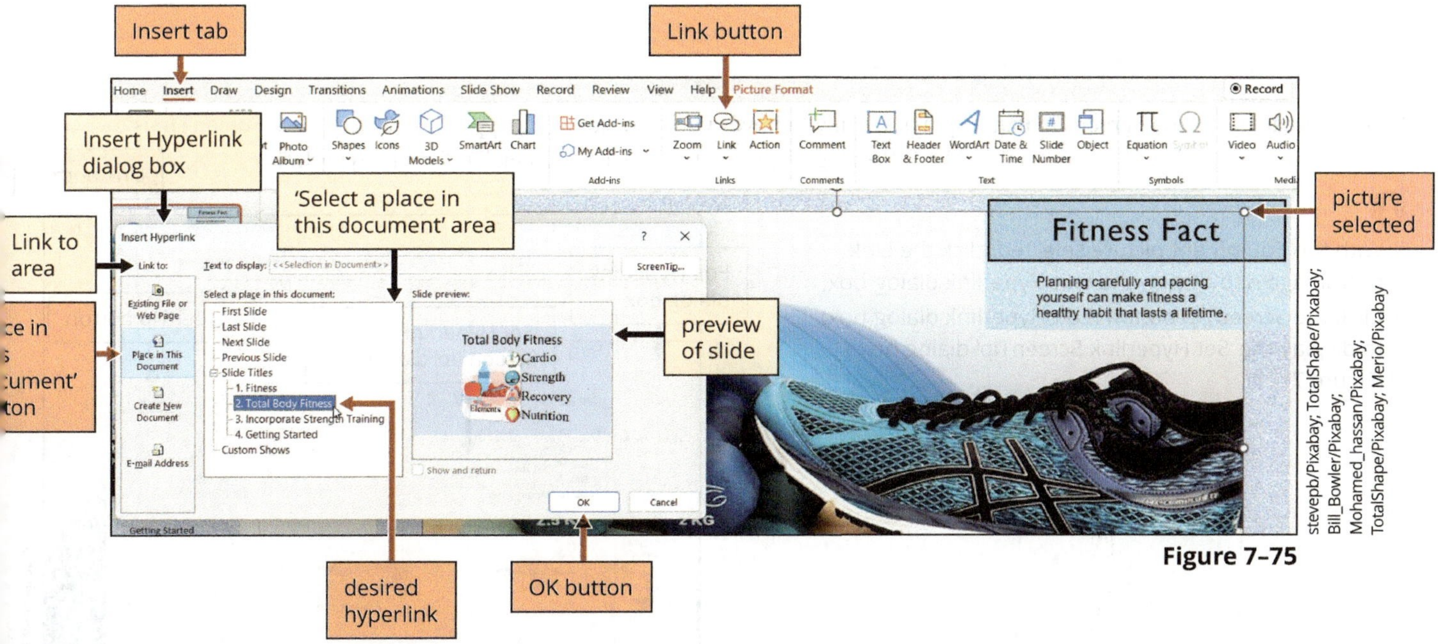

Figure 7–75

stevepb/Pixabay; TotalShape/Pixabay; Bill_Bowler/Pixabay; Mohamed_hassan/Pixabay; TotalShape/Pixabay; Merio/Pixabay

2

- Click OK (Insert Hyperlink dialog box) to insert the hyperlink.

Q&A I clicked the Equipment picture, but Slide 2 did not display. Why?
Hyperlinks are active only when you run the presentation or are in Reading view, not when you are creating a presentation in Normal or Slide Sorter view.

Other Ways

1. Right-click text or object, click Link, select slide, click OK
2. Select text or object, press CTRL+K, select slide, press ENTER

To Edit a Hyperlink

Once you have created the hyperlink, you may decide to change the specified action. In the Fitness presentation, you want to hyperlink to Slide 4 instead of Slide 2. **Why?** You decide that audience members may be eager to begin their healthy programs rather than learn about the components of total body fitness. The following steps edit the hyperlink on Slide 1.

1

- With the Equipment picture still selected, click the Link button again to display the Edit Hyperlink dialog box.
- Click '4. Getting Started' in the 'Select a place in this document' area to select and display a preview of this slide (Figure 7–76).

Q&A Could I also have selected the Last Slide link in the 'Select a place in this document' area?
Yes. Either action would create the hyperlink to Slide 4.

2

- Click OK (Edit Hyperlink dialog box) to change the hyperlink.

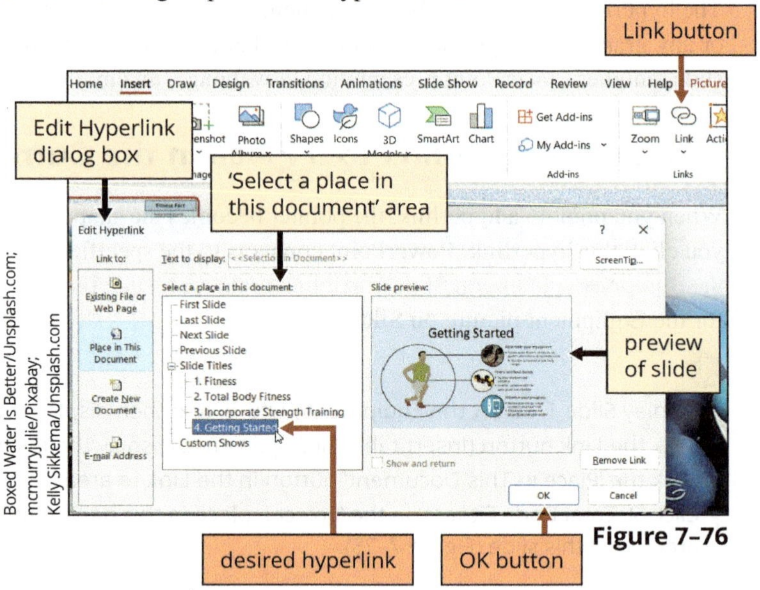

stevepb/Pixabay; Mohamed_hassan/Pixabay; Boxed Water Is Better/Unsplash.com; mcmurryjulie/Pixabay; Kelly Sikkema/Unsplash.com

Figure 7–76

Other Ways

1. Right-click text or object, click Edit Link, select slide, click OK
2. Select text or object, press CTRL+K, select slide, press ENTER

To Add a ScreenTip to a Hyperlink

You can create a custom ScreenTip that displays when you hover your mouse over a hyperlink. **Why?** This ScreenTip is a visual cue of the action the hyperlink will take. The following steps create a custom ScreenTip for the hyperlink.

1

- With the Equipment picture selected, click the Link button again to display the Edit Hyperlink dialog box.
- Click the ScreenTip button (Edit Hyperlink dialog box) to display the 'Set Hyperlink ScreenTip' dialog box (Figure 7–77).

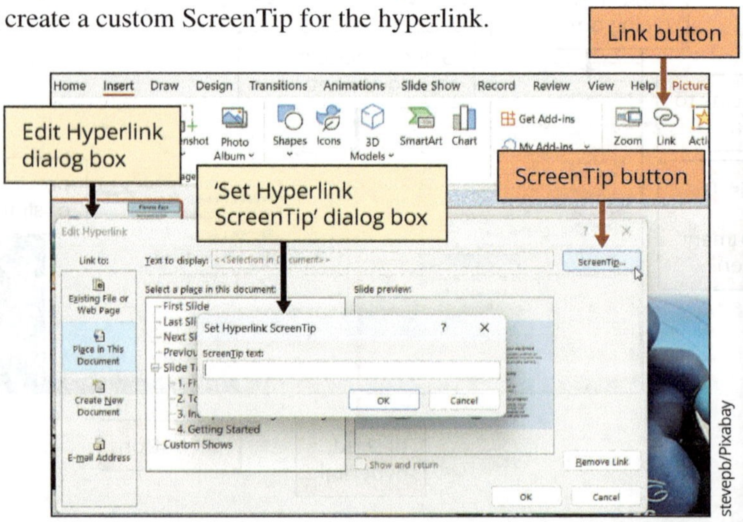

stevepb/Pixabay

Figure 7–77

2

- Type **Getting Started** in the 'ScreenTip text' box (Figure 7–78).

3

- Click OK ('Set Hyperlink ScreenTip' dialog box).
- Click OK (Edit Hyperlink dialog box).

4

- Click outside the image to deselect it.
- Hover the mouse over the image until the ScreenTip and 'Ctrl+Click to follow link' are displayed.
- Press CTRL+CLICK to test the link.

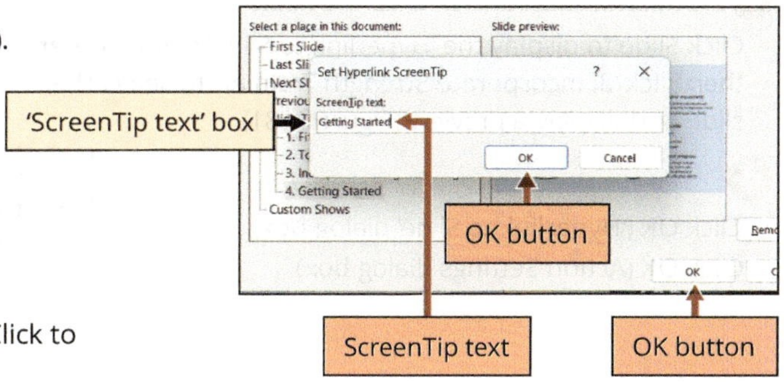

Figure 7–78

To Add a Hyperlink Action Setting to a Picture

You also can use an Action to create a link to another slide or object. In the Fitness presentation, you used the Plank picture in the SmartArt and the Weights picture as the poster frame. You can create a hyperlink between these two elements. **Why?** When you are discussing the four components of total body fitness shown in the Slide 2 SmartArt graphic, you can mention the importance of strength training and then quickly jump to the leg press video. The following steps create a hyperlink from the Plank picture in the Slide 2 SmartArt to Slide 3.

1

- Display Slide 2 and then click the Plank picture to select it.
- Click the Action button (Insert tab | Links group) to display the Action Settings dialog box (Figure 7–79).

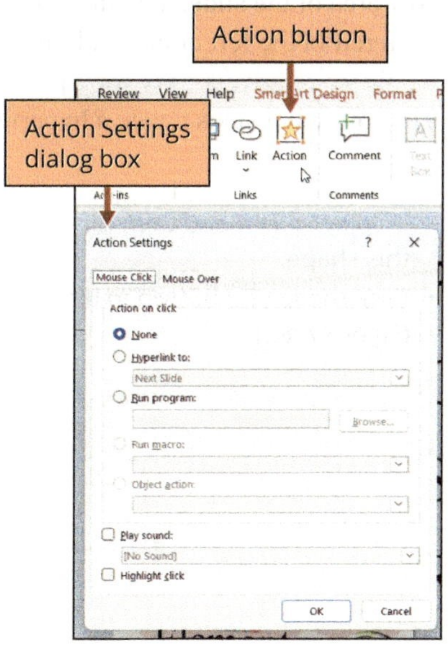

Figure 7–79

2

- Click Hyperlink to, click the Hyperlink to arrow in the 'Action on click' area to display the Hyperlink to menu, and then point to Slide (Figure 7–80).

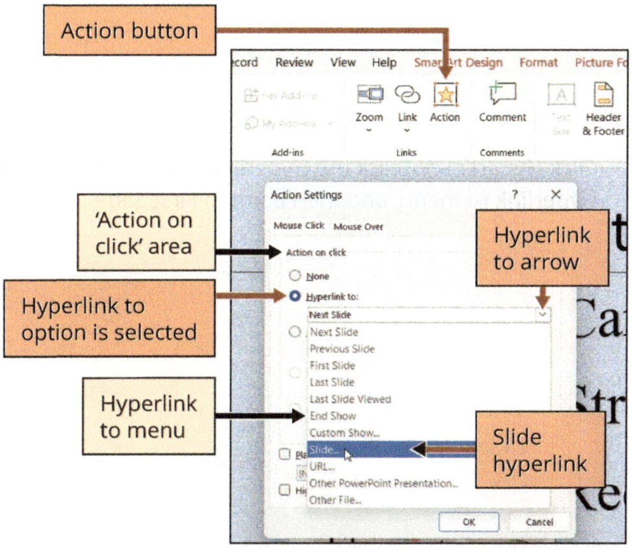

Figure 7–80

3

- Click Slide to display the 'Hyperlink to Slide' dialog box and then click '3. Incorporate Strength Training' to select this slide and display a preview (Figure 7–81).

4

- Click OK ('Hyperlink to Slide' dialog box).
- Click OK (Action Settings dialog box).

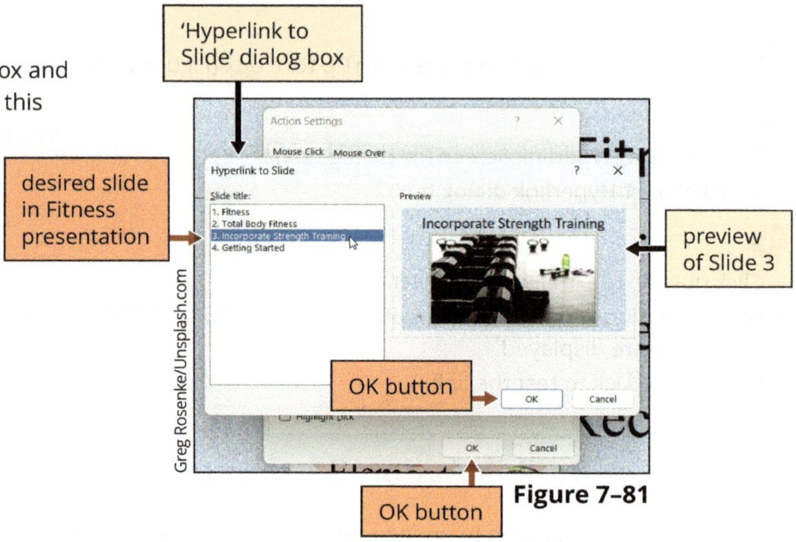

Figure 7–81

To Add a Hyperlink Action Setting to a Shape

Any area of the slide, including shapes, can be designated as a hyperlink element. The SmartArt graphic on Slide 4 has a person centered in the left circle, and this person can serve as the hyperlink. **Why?** The person is a large component of the slide, so it would be relatively easy for a presenter to locate this graphic and then click to jump to another slide or presentation element. The following steps create a hyperlink for the person in the SmartArt shape.

1

- Display Slide 4 and then click the person in the left circle to select this shape.
- Click the Action button to display the Action Settings dialog box (Figure 7–82).

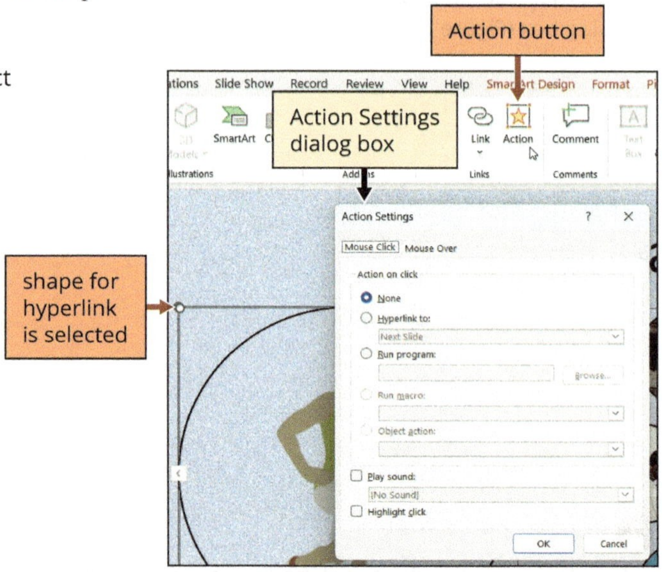

Figure 7–82

2

- Click Hyperlink to, click the Hyperlink to arrow to display the Hyperlink to menu, and then point to First Slide (Figure 7–83).

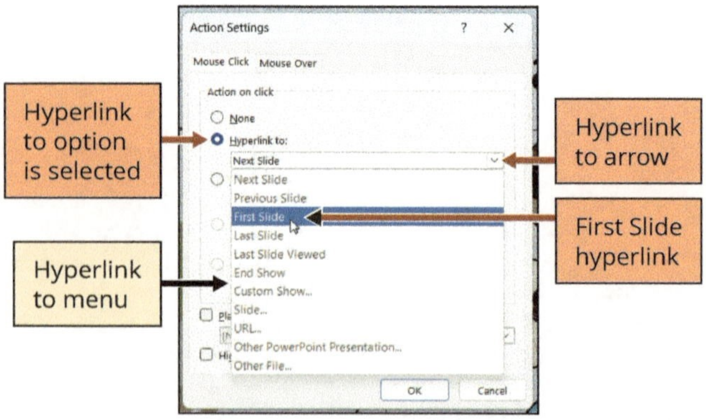

Figure 7–83

3

- Click First Slide to select this slide as the hyperlink (Figure 7–84).

4

- Click OK (Action Settings dialog box).

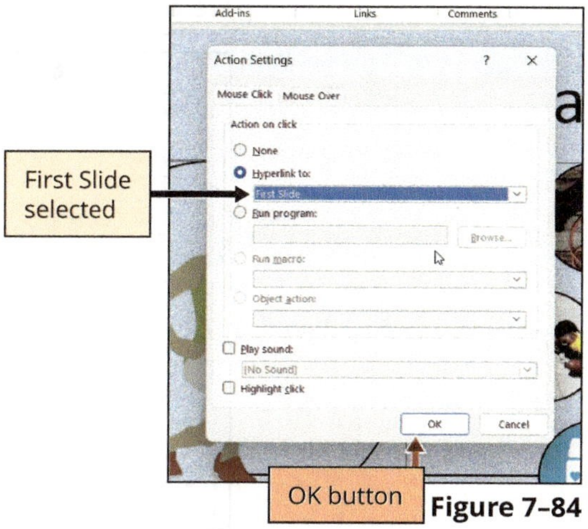

Figure 7–84

To Insert a Hyperlink to a Slide in Another Presentation

While hyperlinks are convenient tools to navigate through the current PowerPoint presentation, they also allow you to open a second PowerPoint presentation and display a particular slide in that file. A hyperlink offers a convenient method of moving from one presentation to another. A speaker has the discretion to use the hyperlink depending on the audience's interest in the topic and time considerations. The following steps hyperlink the words, Getting Started, on Slide 4 to the second slide in the Warmup Cooldown presentation. **Why?** You want to emphasize that the warmup phase is important to prepare your muscles and joints for the exercise session and to reduce the likelihood of injuries.

1

- With Slide 4 displayed, select the words, Getting Started, in the title text placeholder.
- Click the Action button, click Hyperlink to, and then click the Hyperlink to arrow to display the Hyperlink to menu (Figure 7–85).

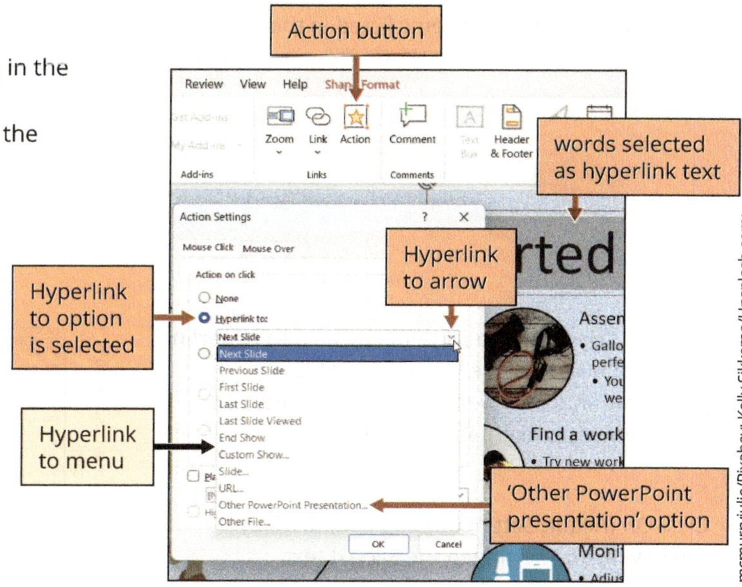

Figure 7–85

mcmurryjulie/Pixabay; Kelly Sikkema/Unsplash.com; Boxed Water Is Better/Unsplash.com

2

- Scroll down and then click 'Other PowerPoint Presentation' to display the 'Hyperlink to Other PowerPoint Presentation' dialog box.
- If necessary, navigate to the location where you saved the Warmup Cooldown file.
- Click SC_PPT_7_Warmup_Cooldown to select this .pptx file as the hyperlinked presentation (Figure 7–86).

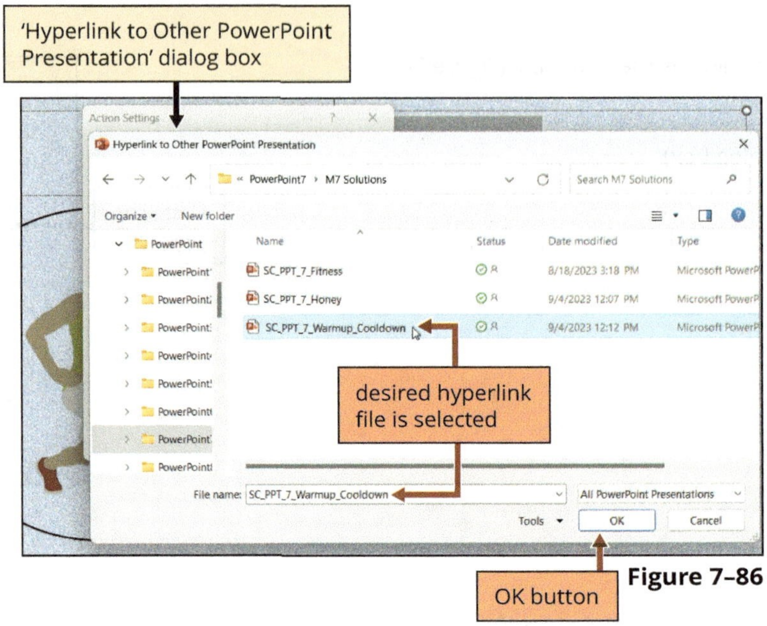

Figure 7–86

3

- Click OK ('Hyperlink to Other PowerPoint Presentation' dialog box) to display the 'Hyperlink to Slide' dialog box.
- Click '2. Begin by Warming Up' ('Hyperlink to Slide' dialog box) to hyperlink the second slide in the Warmup Cooldown presentation to the words, Getting Started, in the Fitness presentation (Figure 7–87).

Q&A What are the four items listed in the Slide title area?
They are the title text of the four slides in the Warmup Cooldown presentation.

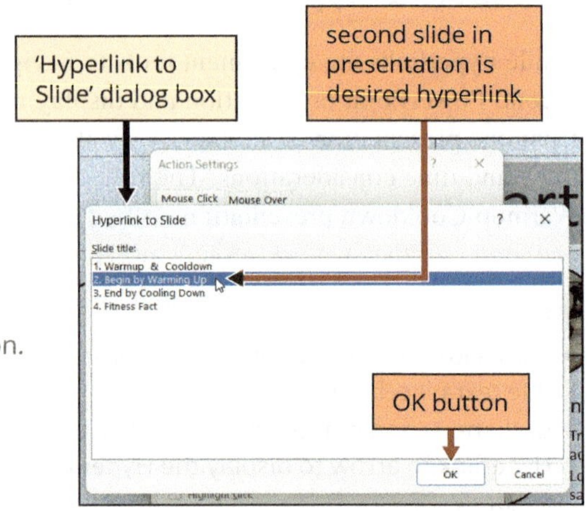

Figure 7–87

4

- Click OK ('Hyperlink to Slide' dialog box) to hyperlink the second slide in the Warmup Cooldown presentation to the words, Getting Started, in the Fitness presentation (Figure 7–88).

5

- Click OK (Action Settings dialog box) to apply the new action setting to the Slide 4 text.

mcmurryjulie/Pixabay; Kelly Sikkema/Unsplash.com; Boxed Water Is Better/Unsplash.com

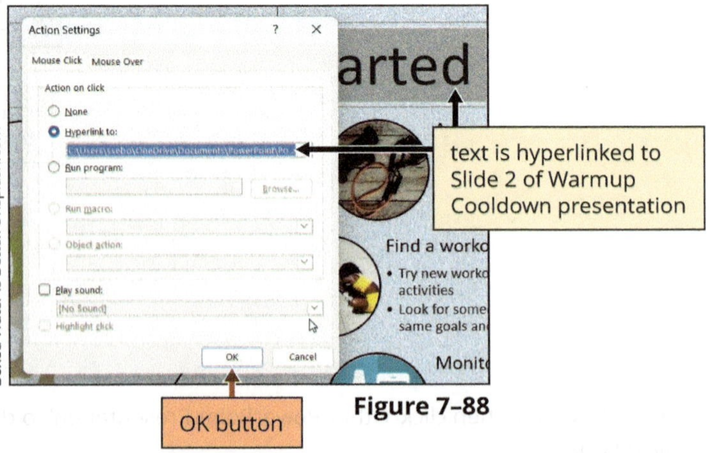

Figure 7–88

Other Ways

1. Select picture, click Hyperlink button (Insert menu | Links group), click 'Existing File or Web Page' (Link to: area), browse to and select desired file, click OK
2. Right-click picture, click Hyperlink on shortcut menu, click 'Existing File or Web Page' (Link to: area), browse to and select desired file, click OK

To Remove a Hyperlink If you wanted to remove a hyperlink, you would perform the following steps.

1. Select the text or object from which you want to remove the hyperlink.
2. Display the Insert tab and then click the Hyperlink button (Insert tab | Links group) to display the Edit Hyperlink dialog box.
3. Click the Remove Link button (Edit Hyperlink dialog box).

Action Buttons

PowerPoint provides 12 built-in action buttons. An **action button** is an interactive button you click in Slide Show view to perform an activity, such as advancing to the next slide. This particular type of hyperlink can activate a hyperlink that allows users to jump to a specific slide in the presentation. The picture on the action button indicates the type of function it performs. For example, the button with the house icon represents the home slide, or Slide 1. To achieve a personalized look, you can customize an action button with a picture, graph, piece of clip art, logo, text, or any graphic you desire. Table 7–1 describes each of the built-in action buttons.

BTW

Using Action Buttons

The action buttons have images representing their functions, such as a right-pointing arrow representing moving forward to the next slide. These buttons are useful when using a touch screen or when a keyboard is not present, such as when a presentation is run at a kiosk. Slide designers also type specific years or descriptive words, such as True or False, on action buttons that link to slides with corresponding information. Be imaginative when developing your own presentations and creating buttons that have a specific meaning for your intended audience.

Table 7–1: Built-In Action Buttons

Button Name	Image	Description
Back or Previous		Returns to the previous slide displayed in the same presentation.
Forward or Next		Jumps to the next slide in the presentation.
Beginning		Jumps to Slide 1. This button performs the same function as the Home button.
End		Jumps to the last slide in the presentation.
Home		Jumps to Slide 1. This button performs the same function as the Beginning button.
Information		Does not have any predefined function. Use it to direct a user to a slide with details or facts.
Return		Returns to the previous slide displayed in any presentation. For example, you can place it on a hidden slide or on a slide in a custom slide show and then return to the previous slide.
Movie		Does not have any predefined function. You generally would use this button to jump to a slide with an inserted video clip.
Document		Opens a program other than PowerPoint. For example, you can open Word or Excel and display a page or worksheet.
Sound		Does not have any predefined function. You generally would use this button to jump to a slide with an inserted audio clip.
Help		Does not have any predefined function. Use it to direct a user to a slide with instructions or contact information.
Custom		Does not have any predefined function. You can add a clip, picture, graphic, or text and then specify a unique purpose.

Consider This

Customize action buttons for a unique look.

PowerPoint's built-in action buttons have icons that give the presenter an indication of their function. Designers frequently customize these buttons with images related to the presentation. For example, in a grocery store presentation, the action buttons may have images of a coupon, dollar sign, and question mark to indicate links to in-store coupons, sale items, and the customer service counter. Be creative when you develop your own presentations and attempt to develop buttons that have specific meanings for your intended audience.

To Insert an Action Button

In the Fitness slide show, you will insert an action button shape in Slide 4 and then create a link to the previous slide displayed. **Why?** After your audience members learn how to begin their exercise program, you may want to emphasize that when they incorporate a variety of exercises and eat well, they can establish a lifetime of healthy habits. The following steps insert an action button on Slide 4 of the Warmup Cooldown presentation and link it to the previous slide displayed.

1

- With Slide 4 and the Insert tab displayed, click the Shapes button (Insert tab | Illustrations group) to display the Shapes gallery.
- Scroll down and then point to the 'Action Button: Return' shape in the Action Buttons area (seventh image) (Figure 7–89).

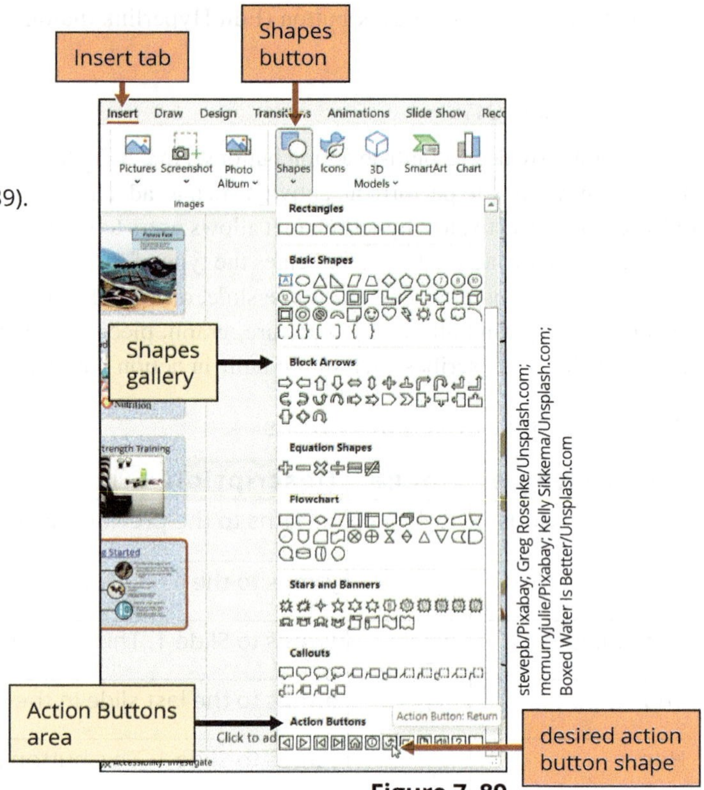

stevepb/Pixabay; Greg Rosenke/Unsplash.com; mcmurryjulie/Pixabay; Kelly Sikkema/Unsplash.com; Boxed Water Is Better/Unsplash.com

Figure 7–89

2

- Click the 'Action Button: Return' shape.
- Click the lower-left corner of the slide to insert the action button and to display the Action Settings dialog box.
- If necessary, click the Mouse Click tab (Action Settings dialog box) (Figure 7–90).

Q&A Why is 'Last Slide Viewed' the default hyperlink setting?
The 'Action Button: Return' shape establishes a hyperlink to the previous slide displayed in any presentation.

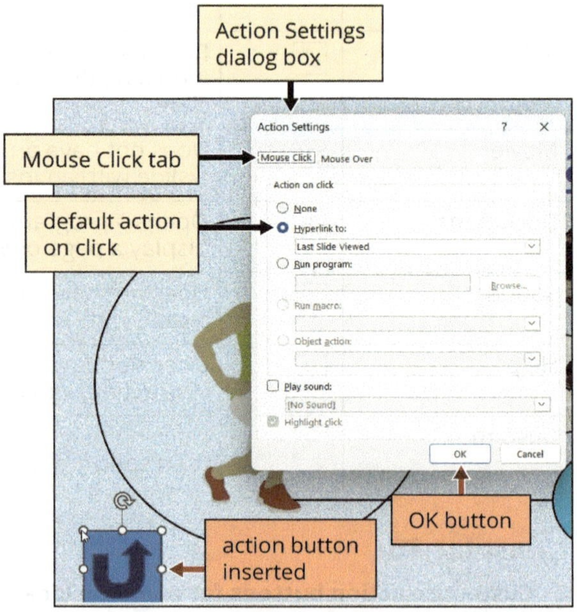

Figure 7–90

3

- Click OK (Action Settings dialog box) to apply the hyperlink setting.

To Size an Action Button

The Return action button size can be decreased to make it less obvious on the slide. The following step resizes the selected action button.

1 With the action button still selected and the Shape Format tab displayed, size the action button so that the height and width are 0.8". If necessary, move the action button to the lower-left corner of the slide (Figure 7–91).

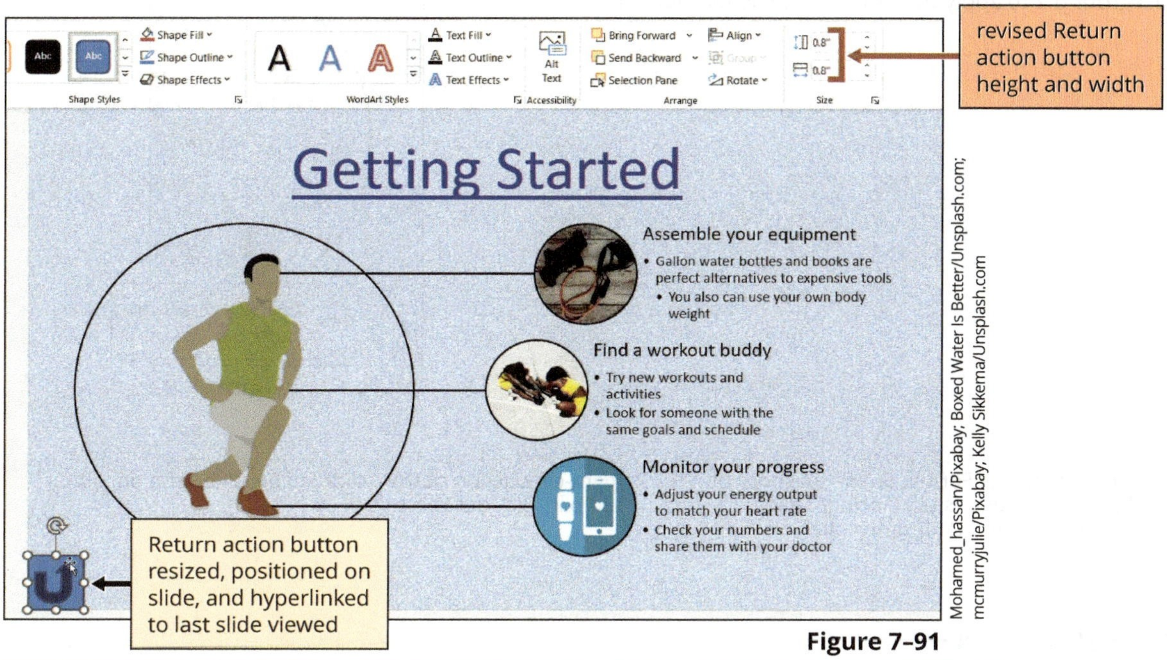

Mohamed_hassan/Pixabay; Boxed Water Is Better/Unsplash.com; mcmurryjulie/Pixabay; Kelly Sikkema/Unsplash.com

Figure 7–91

To Change an Action Button Fill Color

You can select a new action button fill color to coordinate with slide elements. The following steps change the fill color to tan. **Why?** The action button's blue color is prominent and the tan color would be more subtle.

1

- With the action button still selected, click the Shape Fill arrow (Shape Format tab | Shape Styles gallery) to display the Shape Fill gallery (Figure 7–92).

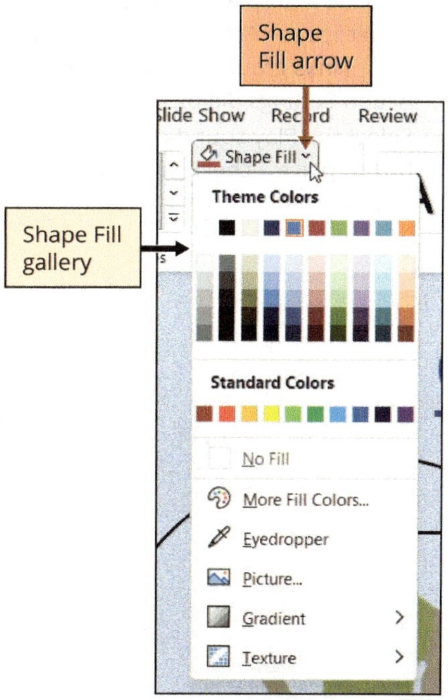

Figure 7–92

2

- Point to Tan, Background 2 (third color in the first Theme Colors row) to display a live preview of that fill color on the action button (Figure 7–93).
- **Experiment:** Point to various colors in the Shape Fill gallery and watch the fill color change in the action button.

3

- Click Tan, Background 2 to apply this color to the action button.

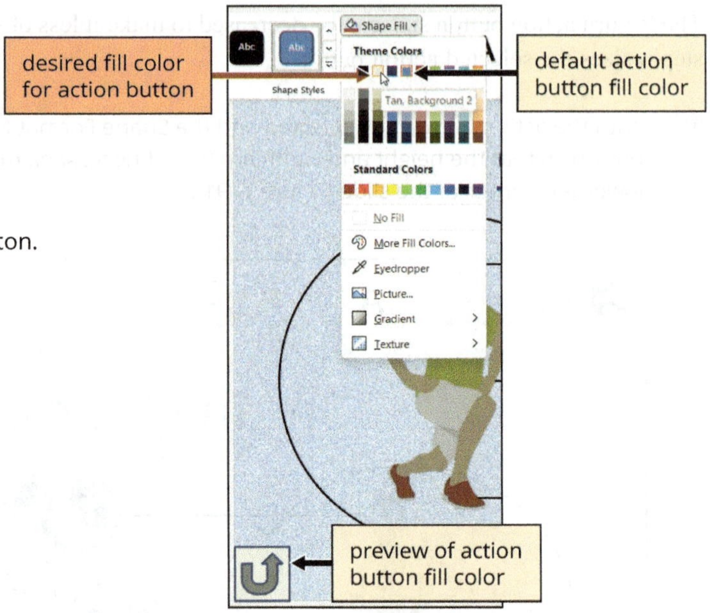

Figure 7–93

Other Ways

1. Right-click action button, click Format Shape on shortcut menu, click Fill on Shape Options tab (Format Shape pane), click Fill Color button, click desired color
2. Right-click action button, click Shape Fill button on Mini toolbar, click desired color

To Add Sound to an Action

To emphasize a hyperlink, you can add a sound. PowerPoint includes a variety of sounds that you can use. The following steps edit the Slide 4 hyperlink by adding a sound. **Why?** For variety, you want a sound to play when the action button is clicked.

1

- With the action button still selected on Slide 4, display the Insert tab and then click the Action button (Insert tab | Links group) to display the Action Settings dialog box.
- Select the Play sound check box to place a check in that box (Figure 7–94).

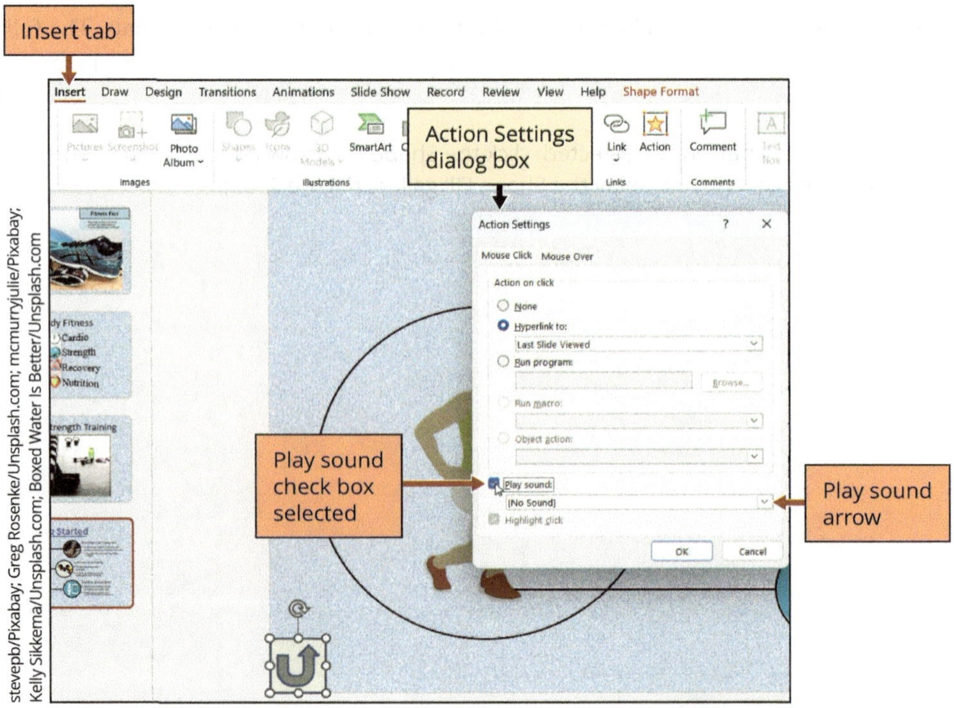

stevepb/Pixabay; Greg Rosenke/Unsplash.com; mcmurryjulie/Pixabay; Kelly Sikkema/Unsplash.com; Boxed Water Is Better/Unsplash.com

Figure 7–94

2

- Click the Play sound arrow to display the Play sound list (Figure 7–95).

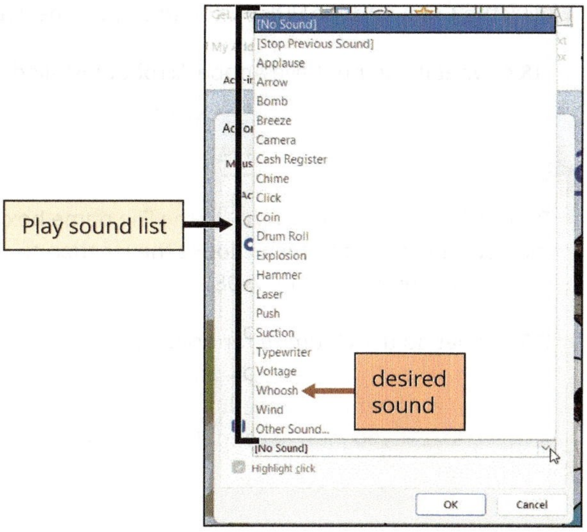

Figure 7–95

3

- Click Whoosh in the Play sound list to select that sound to play when the action button is clicked (Figure 7–96).

Q&A I did not hear the sound when I selected it. Why not?
The Whoosh sound will play when you run the slide show and click the action button.

4

- Click OK to apply the sound to the action button and to close the Action Settings dialog box.
- If necessary, save the Fitness presentation using the same file name.

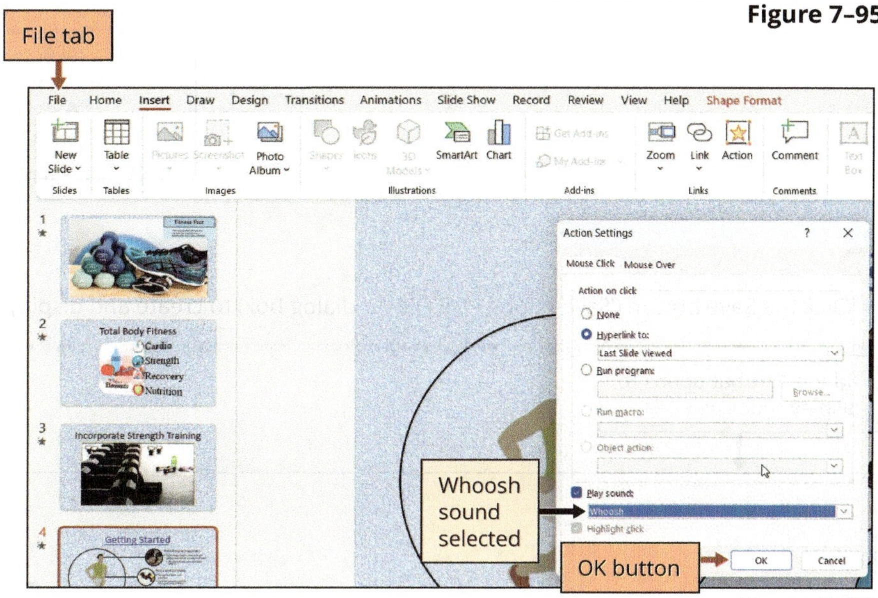

Figure 7–96

stevepb/Pixabay; Greg Rosenke/Unsplash.com; mcmurryjulie/Pixabay; Kelly Sikkema/Unsplash.com; Boxed Water Is Better/Unsplash.com

To Save the Presentation as a PDF

When you save your presentation as a PDF file, the formatting and layouts cannot be changed. This file format is convenient when you want to distribute your document online. **Why?** People who do not have PowerPoint can view the slides, but they cannot make changes to the file. The following steps save the Fitness presentation as a PDF.

1

- With the Fitness presentation displayed, click the File tab (shown in Figure 7–96) and then click the Export tab to open the Export panel (Figure 7–97).

Q&A Could I select the 'Save as Adobe PDF' tab instead of the Export tab?
Yes, if you see that option.

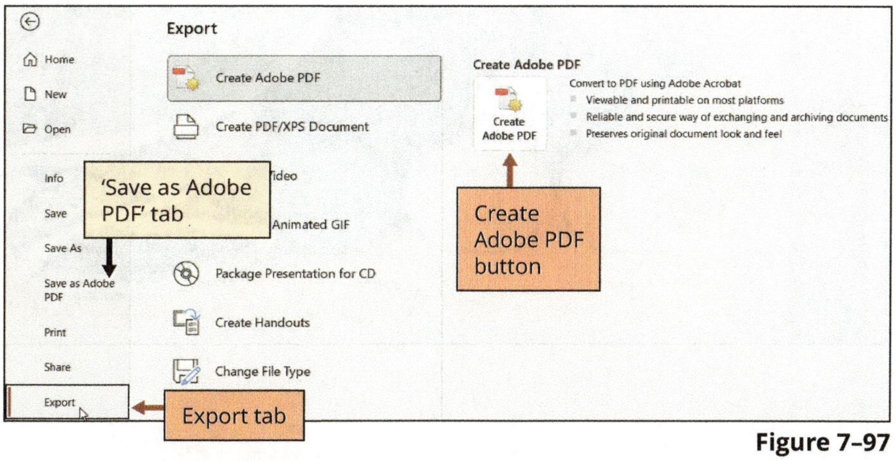

Figure 7–97

2

- Click the Create Adobe PDF button to display the 'Save Adobe PDF File As' dialog box.

Q&A What if I do not have Adobe Acrobat installed on my computer?
You can choose Create PDF/XPS Document instead.

3

- Type **SC_PPT_7_Fitness_PDF** in the File name box as the new file name and then choose the location to save the document (Figure 7–98).

Q&A What do the Optimize for options do?
Standard saves the file in high quality, which is good for printing. Minimum size reduces the file size and is preferable if you plan to send the file as an email attachment.

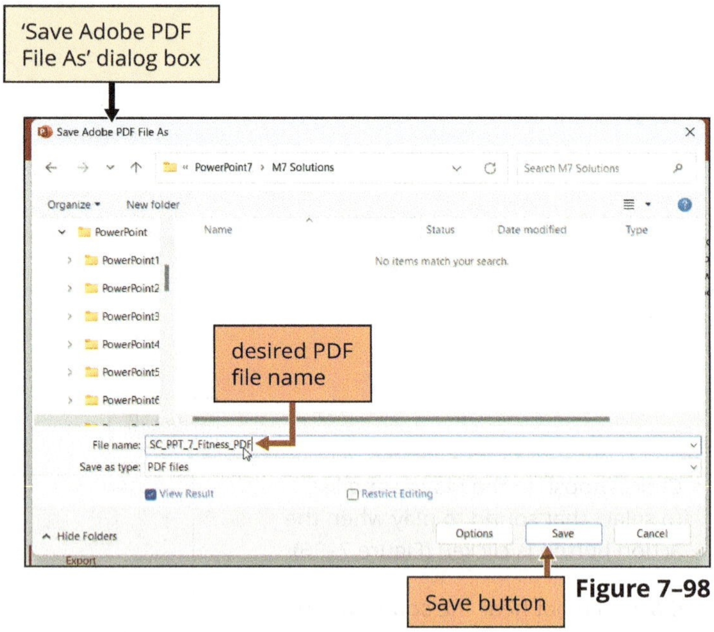

Figure 7–98

4

- Click the Save button ('Save Adobe PDF File As' dialog box) to create and display the PDF (Figure 7–99).

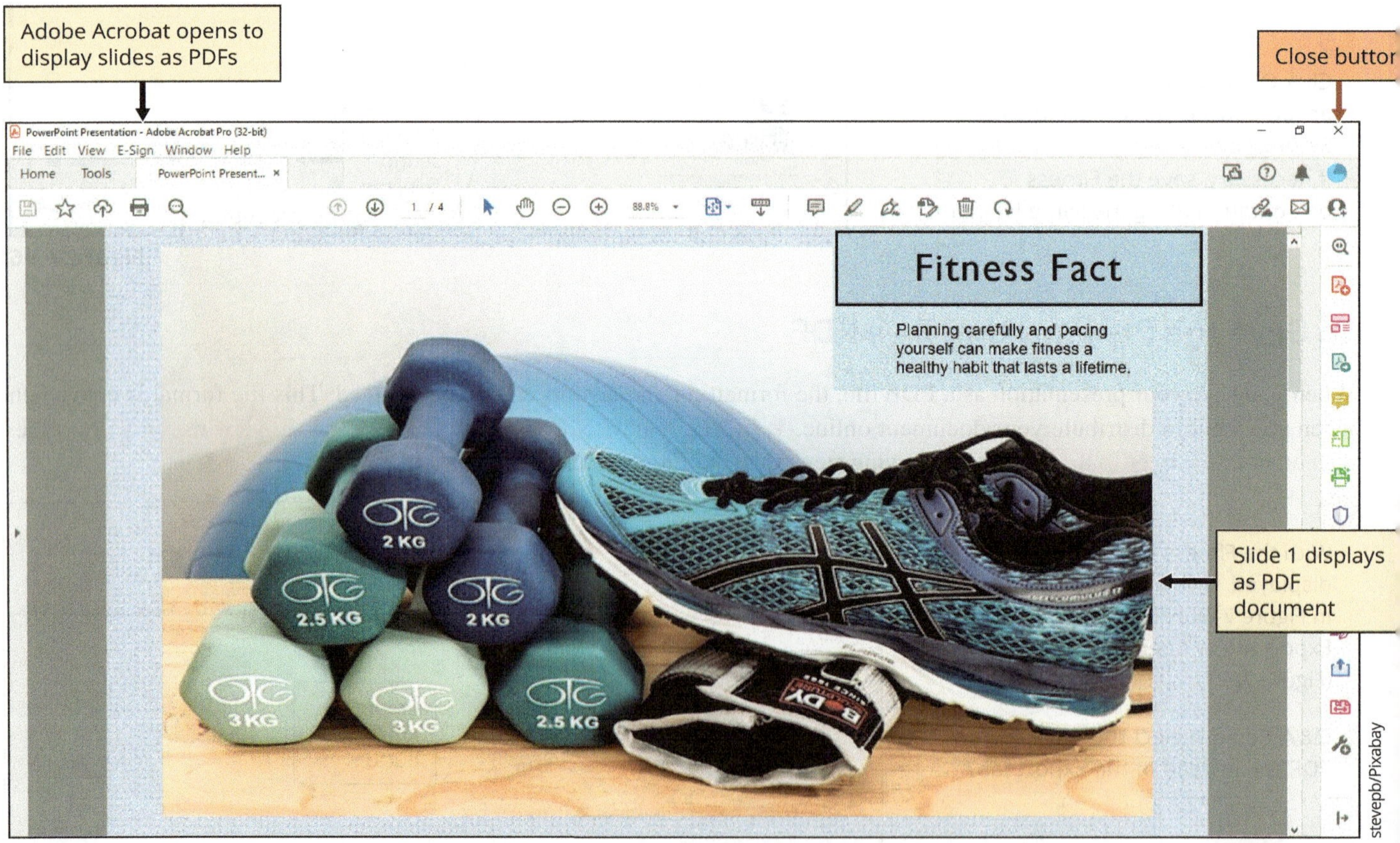

Figure 7–99

5
- Click Close ('PowerPoint Presentation – Adobe Acrobat' dialog box).

Q&A What if my PDF displays in a different program?
Depending on your computer settings and available software, the PDF may display in Adobe Acrobat, Word, OneDrive, or a different program.

Other Ways

1. Click File tab, click Save As, click Save as type arrow, click PDF (*.pdf), click Save

To Run, Save, and Exit PowerPoint

The presentation now is complete. You should run the presentation, view the hyperlinks, save the presentation, and then exit PowerPoint.

1. Run the Fitness presentation. Click the Equipment picture on Slide 1 to display Slide 4.
2. Click the Return button on Slide 4 to hear the Whoosh sound and return to Slide 1.
3. Display Slide 2 and then click the Plank picture on Slide 2 to display Slide 3. When the audio begins to play, click the Weights picture to view the video.
4. When the video is complete, display Slide 4.
5. Click the words, Getting Started, in the Slide 4 title text to open the Warmup Cooldown file and display its Slide 2. If the Microsoft PowerPoint Security Notice is displayed, click the Yes button to proceed.
6. View the Slide 2 contents and then display Slide 3 and Slide 4.
7. End the Warmup Cooldown slide show.
8. End the Fitness slide show.
9. sam ↑ Because the project now is complete, you can exit PowerPoint, closing all open documents.

BTW
Conserving Ink and Toner
If you want to conserve ink or toner, you can instruct PowerPoint to print draft quality documents by clicking File on the ribbon to open Backstage view, clicking Options in Backstage view to display the PowerPoint Options dialog box, clicking Advanced in the left pane (PowerPoint Options dialog box), scrolling to the Print area in the right pane, verifying there is no check mark in the High quality check box, and then clicking OK. Then, use Backstage view to print the document as usual.

BTW
Printing Document Properties
PowerPoint does not allow you to print document properties. This feature, however, is available in Microsoft 365 Word.

Summary

In this module, you have learned how to develop a presentation with SmartArt, digital media, and hyperlinks. You started by changing a picture and inserting a screen clip. You then inserted, edited, and enhanced a SmartArt graphic. You also removed a picture background and enhanced a picture by changing the contrast and color saturation. You inserted and edited video and audio clips and then compressed media to reduce the overall PowerPoint file size. Next, you inserted hyperlinks and an action button. Finally, you saved a presentation as a PDF file.

Consider This: Plan Ahead

What decisions will you need to make when creating your next presentation?

Use these guidelines as you complete the assignments in this module and create your own slide show decks outside of this class.

1. **Choose outstanding hyperlink images or text.** Format hypertext graphics or words that are easy to find on the slide. Make the hypertext graphics or letters large so a speaker is prompted to click them easily during a speaking engagement.
2. **Customize action buttons.** Create a unique look for your action buttons by adding pictures and other graphical elements to add interest or to make the buttons less obvious to your viewers.

Student Assignments

Apply Your Knowledge

Reinforce the skills and apply the concepts you learned in this module.

Adding Media and Enhancing SmartArt

Note: To complete this assignment, you will be required to use the Data Files. Please contact your instructor for information about accessing the Data Files.

Instructions: Start PowerPoint. Open the presentation called SC_PPT_7-1.pptx, which is located in the Data Files.

Vendors at the farmers' market in your town offer a variety of items, including local produce, flowers, and honey. You talked to the apiarists, who are the people caring for and raising bees and then extracting honey from the hives. They are planning a presentation at the local library about bees and the practice of beekeeping, and they have asked you to help develop slide content. You have received a PowerPoint presentation, video and audio files, and a picture, and you need to format the slides. You will create the three slides shown in Figure 7–100.

Perform the following tasks:

1. On Slide 1, change the color saturation to 33% (second Color Saturation picture) and then change the brightness and contrast setting to 'Brightness: +20% Contrast: -20' (fourth picture in the second Brightness/Contrast row) (Figure 7–100a).
2. On Slide 2, insert the video file named Support_PPT_7_Hive.mp4, which is located in the Data Files. Start the video clip to play automatically and to play full screen. Trim the video clip to a Start Time at 00:06 seconds and an End Time at 00.27 seconds. Resize the video height to 6" and then align the video in the center and the middle of the slide.
3. Add a poster video frame using the picture named Support_PPT_7_Apiary.jpg, which is located in the Data Files. Apply the 'Snip Diagonal Corner, White' video style (last style in the first Moderate row) (Figure 7–100b).
4. On Slide 3, delete the blue background from the bee picture in the upper-left corner of the slide. Flip the picture horizontally. Delete the dark blue background from the beekeeper picture in the upper-right corner of the slide. You may want to zoom the slide to simplify the background removal process. Resize the height of the bee picture to 3" and the beekeeper picture to 3" and then move them to the upper-left and upper-right corners of the slide.
5. Convert the bulleted list to a SmartArt graphic by right-clicking anywhere in the content placeholder, pointing to 'Convert to SmartArt' in the shortcut menu, and then clicking 'More SmartArt Graphics'. Display the List gallery and then select the 'Varying Width List' graphic (last graphic in the second row).
6. Move the Average hive shape up so that it is the first shape in the SmartArt graphic.
7. Insert the equation shown in Figure 7–100c. To insert the equation, position the pointer after the word, tall, in the last paragraph and then press ENTER. Display the Insert tab and then click the Equation button (Insert tab | Symbols group). Type **Beehive volume** in the 'Type equation here' box, click the Equal symbol (Equation tab | Symbols group) to insert that symbol, type **Length,** click the Multiplication Sign symbol, type **Width** in the box, click the Multiplication Sign, and then type **Height,** as shown in Figure 7–100c. Click an area other than the equation to close the 'Type equation here' box.
8. Select the entire SmartArt graphic, resize the height to 4" and width to 11", and then align it in the center and middle of the slide.
9. Change the SmartArt colors to 'Colored Outline – Accent 2' (first color in the Accent 2 area).

   If requested by your instructor, insert your grandmother's first name after the word, queen, in the first SmartArt shape.

10. Insert the audio file named Support_PPT_7_Buzzing.mp3, which is located in the Data Files. Start the audio clip to play Automatically and then change the volume to Medium. Hide the sound icon during the show. Trim the audio clip to a Start Time at 00:07 seconds and an End Time at 00:30 seconds (Figure 7–100d).
11. Insert a hyperlink from the Slide 3 title text (Busy Beekeepers) to Slide 2.
12. Compress the media in the presentation using the Standard setting.
13. Run the presentation and then save it using the file name, **SC_PPT_7_Honey**.
14. Submit the presentation in the format specified by your instructor.
15. **Consider This:** Did the color and corrections formatting changes enhance the Slide 1 picture? Why would you click the Slide 3 hyperlink? Were the revised lengths of the video and audio clips sufficient? In Step 5 you converted the bulleted list to the 'Varying Width List' SmartArt graphic. Was this layout a good choice? Why or why not? In Step 9, you changed the SmartArt colors. Was the Colored Outline a good choice? Why or why not?

picture color saturation, brightness, and contrast changed

Figure 7–100(a): Slide 1

poster video frame picture inserted and video style applied

Figure 7–100(b): Slide 2 (Video Poster Frame)

Continued on next page

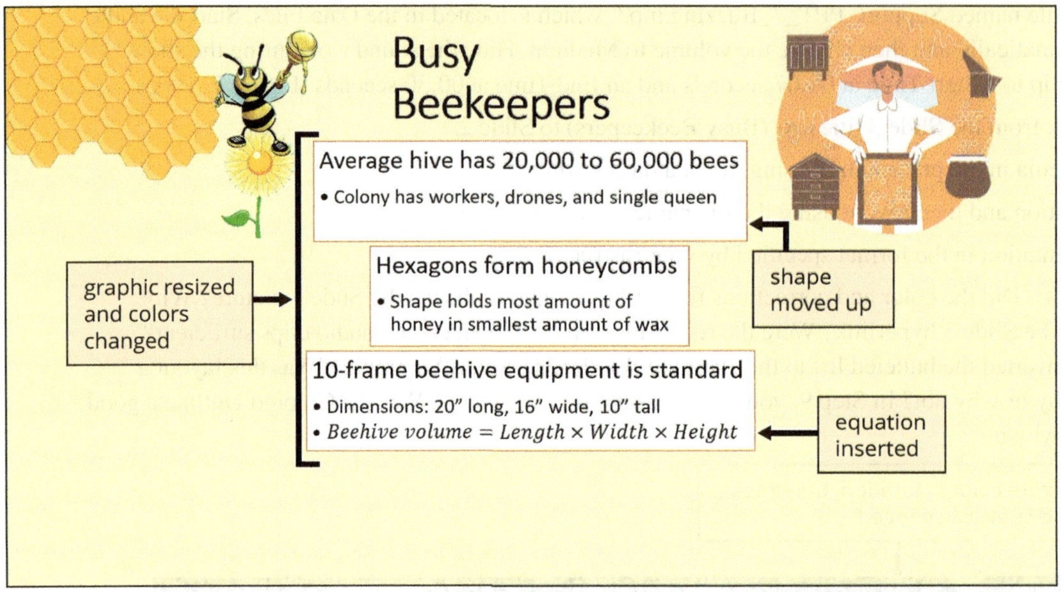

Elf-Moondance/Pixabay; Mohamed_hassan/Pixabay

Figure 7–100(c): Slide 3

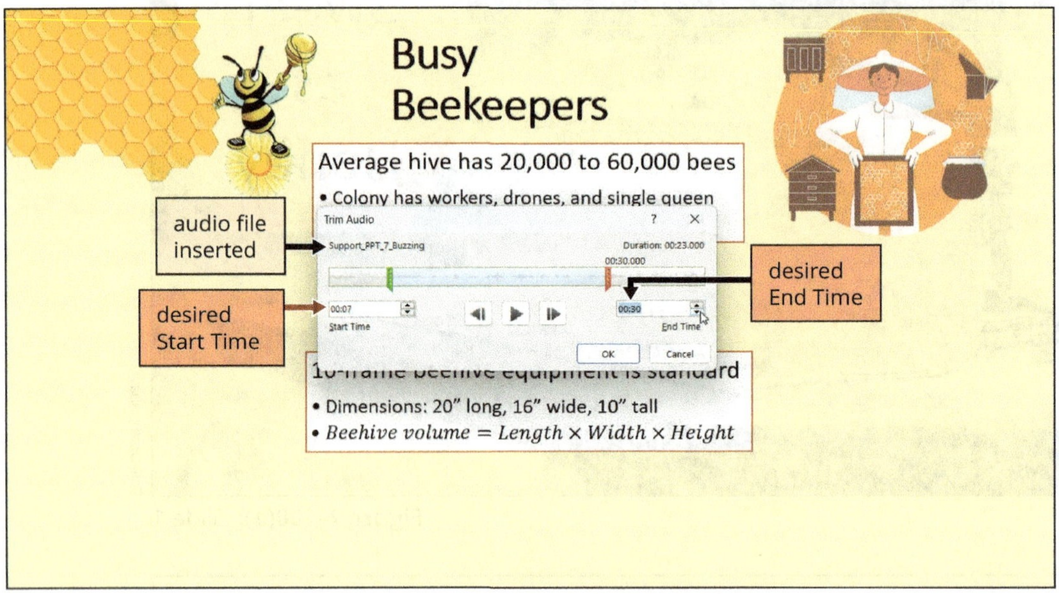

Elf-Moondance/Pixabay; Mohamed_hassan/Pixabay

Figure 7–100(d): Slide 3 (Trim Audio Dialog Box)

Extend Your Knowledge

Extend the skills you learned in this module and experiment with new skills. You may need to use Help to complete the assignment.

Creating and Modifying SmartArt

Note: To complete this assignment, you will be required to use the Data Files. Please contact your instructor for information about accessing the Data Files.

Instructions: Start PowerPoint. Open the presentation called SC_PPT_7-2.pptx, which is located in the Data Files.

Social media sites offer convenient methods of purchasing items, but influencers sometimes urge users to buy quickly, which can lead to overspending and sometimes fraudulent sites. To make wise purchases, check online reviews, use a VPN when shopping, and use browser extensions to compare prices. This information is listed in the slides you will create for this assignment. On Slide 1, you will convert WordArt to a SmartArt graphic. You then will duplicate Slide 2 and convert the SmartArt graphic on Slide 2 to text and the SmartArt graphic on Slide 3 to a shape. Finally, you will copy the Slide 3 graphic to Slide 4 and delete Slide 3.

Perform the following tasks:

1. On Slide 1, right-click anywhere in the WordArt bulleted list paragraphs to display the shortcut menu.
2. Point to 'Convert to SmartArt' to display the SmartArt gallery.
3. Click 'More SmartArt Graphics' to display the 'Choose a SmartArt Graphic' dialog box.
4. Click List in the list of graphic categories and then click 'Vertical Bullet List' (first graphic in the second row). Click OK to convert the SmartArt.
5. With the entire SmartArt graphic selected, resize the graphic height to 5" and width to 10" and then align the graphic in the center and bottom of the slide (Figure 7–101a).
6. Display Slide 2 and then duplicate this slide. On Slide 2, select the entire SmartArt graphic. Click the Convert button (SmartArt Design tab | Reset group) and then click 'Convert to Text' to display the four bulleted list paragraphs.
7. Change the font size of the bulleted list paragraphs to 44 point. Increase the list level of the second paragraph, Open another browser to check, to a second-level paragraph. Align the content placeholder in the center and bottom of the slide (Figure 7–101b).
8. Display Slide 3. Select the entire SmartArt graphic and then click the Convert button. Click 'Convert to Shapes' to change the graphic to a shape.
9. Copy the SmartArt shape to Slide 4. Resize the shape height to 5" and the width to 10". Align the shape in the center and the bottom of the slide (Figure 7–101c).
10. Delete Slide 3.

    If requested by your instructor, change the words, a public area, on Slide 1 to the city where you attended first grade.
11. Run the presentation and then save it using the file name, **SC_PPT_7_Shopper.**
12. Submit the revised document in the format specified by your instructor.
13. **Consider This:** In this assignment, you changed WordArt to SmartArt and then changed a SmartArt graphic to text and a shape. Was the original Slide 1 with WordArt easier or more difficult to comprehend than the revised Slide 1 with SmartArt? Was the Vertical Bullet List a good layout choice? Is Slide 2 or Slide 3 the better choice to display the 'Resist the urge to purchase instantly' information? What are the advantages and disadvantages of converting a SmartArt graphic to a shape?

Figure 7–101(a): Slide 1 (WordArt Converted to SmartArt)

Continued on next page

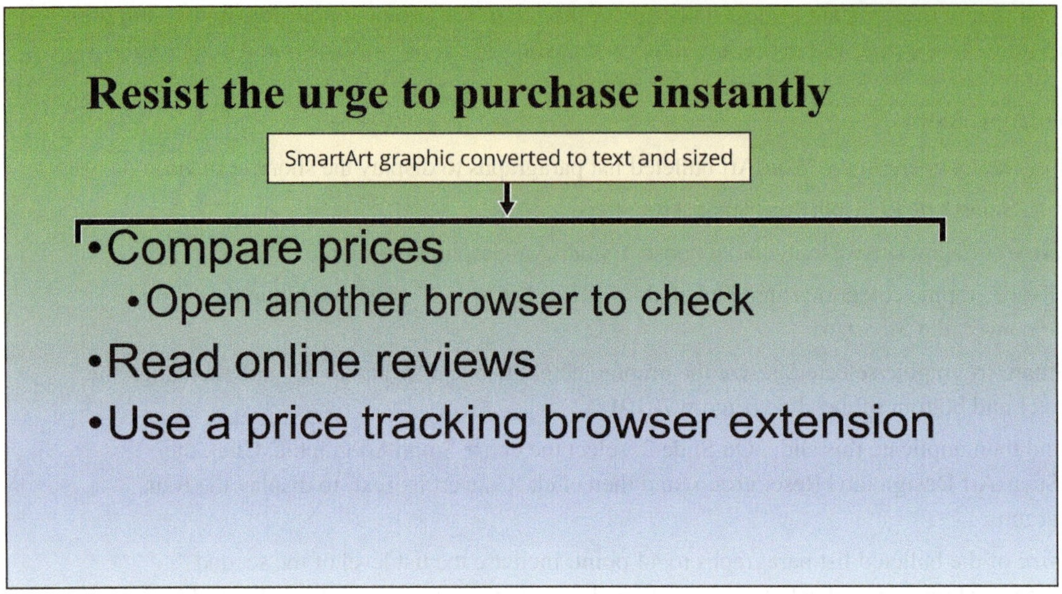

Figure 7–101(b): Slide 2 (Smart Art Converted to Text)

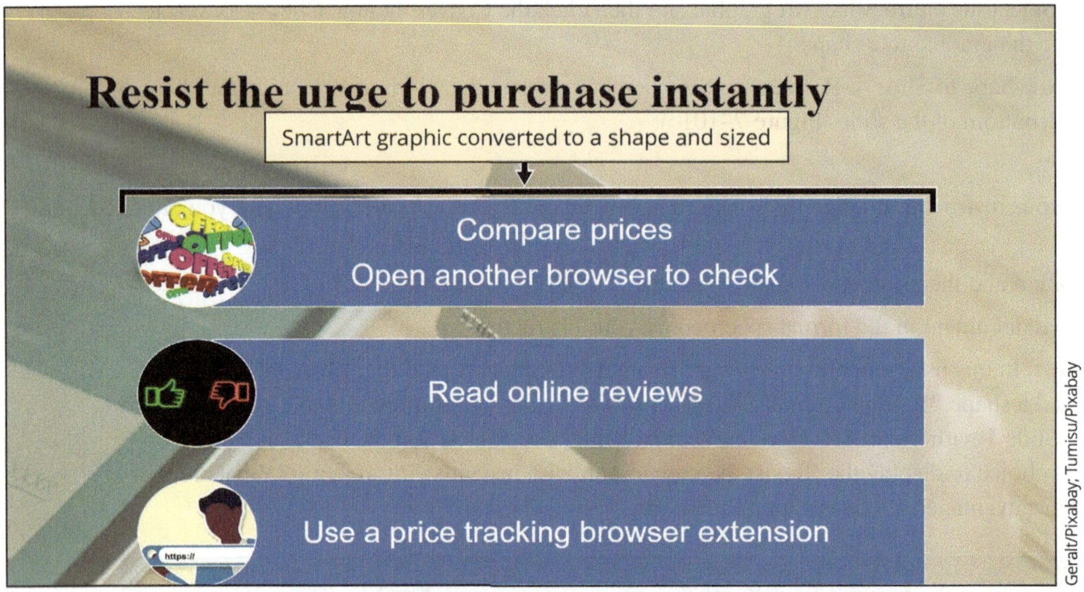

Figure 7–101(c): Slide 3 (SmartArt Converted to a Shape)

Expand Your World

Create a solution that uses cloud or web technologies by learning and investigating on your own from general guidance.

Reviewing Google Images SmartArt

Note: To complete this assignment, you will be required to use the Data Files. Please contact your instructor for information about accessing the Data Files.

Instructions: You want to add SmartArt to a presentation you have created to accompany the Fitness presentation you developed in this module. The counselors at your school have added meditation sessions at the Wellness Center to help students find methods to reduce stress and anxiety. The counselors want a second presentation to use at their seminars to promote the sessions. You have developed four slides, but you want to add graphical interest and decide to browse Google Images for SmartArt ideas.

Perform the following tasks:

1. Start PowerPoint. Open the presentation called SC_PPT_7-3.pptx, which is located in the Data Files.
2. Open your browser and navigate to Google.com. Click Images at the top of the screen to display the Google Images webpage. Click the Google Images search box, type **creative smartart design** as the search text, and then click the Search button (the magnifying glass) or press ENTER.
3. View several SmartArt images with designs that would be appropriate for the material on all slides and then use these design ideas as inspiration to convert the SmartArt on these slides. Do not click or download any files; simply use them as suggestions for design concepts. Recall that to change the SmartArt design you would select the SmartArt, click the More button (SmartArt Design tab | Layouts gallery), click More Layouts, and then select the desired category and layout.
4. If desired, you can change the SmartArt styles and colors and also arrange the slide elements.

   If requested to do so by your instructor, change the word, Wellness, on the title slide to the make of your first car.
5. Save the presentation using the file name, **SC_PPT_7_Meditation_SmartArt**.
6. Submit the assignment in the format specified by your instructor.
7. **Consider This:** Which SmartArt images on the Google Images webpage did you use for your presentation? Why did you select these particular examples? Did you change any SmartArt styles and colors or arrange the slide elements? Why or why not?

In the Lab

Apply your creative thinking and problem-solving skills to design and implement a solution.

Design and Create a Presentation about Teaching Children to Use Debit and Credit Cards

Part 1: One of the best methods of teaching children how to use financial products, including debit and credit cards, is to talk to them at an early age. Even preschoolers can learn skills that will give them a foundation for becoming financially responsible adults. Parents can introduce tweens and teens to debit cards and prepaid credit cards and opening a checking account. The New Account managers at the bank where you work are developing materials to distribute to parents of tweens and teens at a financial literacy program they are planning. They have asked you to create a PowerPoint presentation giving advice on teaching children to use debit and credit cards responsibly.

Your bank has a debit card specifically for children, and it has parental controls for setting spending limits. In addition, your bank allows children to open a secured credit card that is backed by a cash deposit used as collateral. When children use this card, they will be building a credit history because your bank reports payments and other account activity to the three major credit bureaus. Parents should give their children the freedom to spend, but rules should be established limiting where the card can be used. Parents also should monitor due dates and monthly balances, explaining that penalties and interest will be incurred for late and partial payments.

Perform some research to learn additional methods of educating children about sensibly using debit and credit cards. Then create slides with this information. The Data Files folder contains pictures you could use, and change the color saturation, brightness, or contrast on at least one of these images. Create at least one slide with SmartArt. Review and revise your presentation as needed and then save the file using the file name, **SC_PPT_7_Credit**. Submit your assignment in the format specified by your instructor.

Part 2: **Consider This:** You made several decisions while creating the presentation in this assignment: what content to include, how to format the slides and pictures, and which styles and effects to apply. What was the rationale behind each of these decisions? Where would you recommend showing this slide show? When you reviewed the document, what changes did you make?

Creating Photo Albums and Delivering Presentations

Objectives

After completing this module, you will be able to:

- Create a custom slide show
- Save a slide as a picture
- Create handouts by exporting to Word
- Record slide timings and narration
- Save a presentation as a PowerPoint show
- Use the Accessibility Checker to inspect design, colors, contrast, and fonts
- Encrypt a presentation with a password
- Print handouts and notes
- Customize the Notes Master
- Change slide orientation and resolution
- Insert a summary zoom slide

Introduction

Sharing pictures has become a part of our everyday lives. We use smartphones, digital cameras, and mobile devices, and we visit social media websites to share our adventures, special occasions, and business activities. PowerPoint has the ability to create custom slide shows with these pictures so you can show particular slides to specific audiences. For example, one large presentation created for students interested in enrolling in classes internationally can be separated into custom shows describing particular cities where study abroad programs are offered.

In addition, the PowerPoint photo album feature allows you to organize and enhance your pictures. These photo albums can be shared with people who do not have PowerPoint installed on their devices. You can create custom handouts to distribute to audience members and develop notes to help you deliver your presentation effectively.

BTW
Using Photographs
A carefully selected image can convey an engaging message that your audience will remember long after the presentation has ended. One picture can evoke emotions and create a connection between the speaker and the listeners. The adage, "A picture is worth a thousand words," is relevant when audience members view PowerPoint slides.

Project: Presentation with a Custom Slide Show and Photo Album

In this module's project, you will follow proper design guidelines and learn to use PowerPoint to create the slides and printouts shown in Figure 8–1a through 8–1g. The objective is to produce a presentation for a seminar on campus for students considering studying abroad. You will create a custom slide show highlighting two cities: Paris and London. You will save one slide as a picture, create handouts to distribute to audience members, and save the presentation as a PowerPoint show. You then will create a photo album with all the slides in the presentation.

rockyscotty20/Unsplash.com; geralt/Pixabay

Figure 8–1(a): Custom Slide Show Title Slide

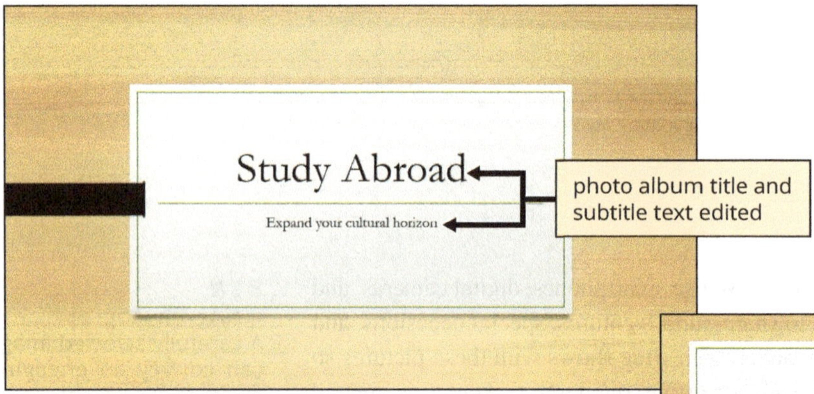

Figure 8–1(b): Photo Album Title Slide

Gonzalo Kenny/Unsplash.com

Figure 8–1(c): Photo Album Slide

Figure 8–1(d): Summary Zoom Slide

iankelsall1/Pixabay; Alexas_Fotos/Pixabay; Andrea De Santis/Unsplash; cmmellow/Pixabay; Gonzalo Kenny/unsplash; matcuz/Pixabay; DUCTINH91/Pixabay; scharfsascha/Pixabay; Pharaoh_EZYPT/Pixabay; Ledoc/Pixabay; acheemete/Pixabay

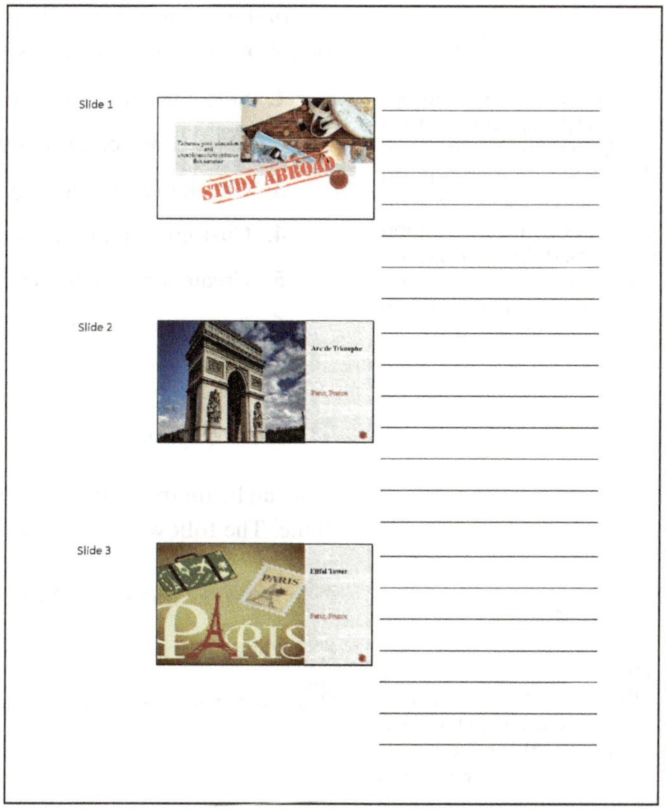

Figure 8–1(e): Microsoft Word Handout

geralt/Pixabay; Rocky Scotty/Unsplash; iankelsall1/Pixabay; Alexas_Fotos/Pixabay

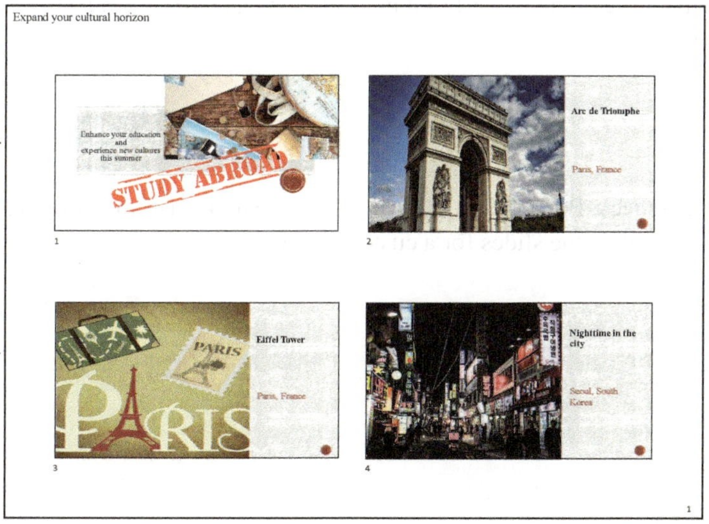

Figure 8–1(f): Handout in Landscape Orientation

geralt/Pixabay; Rocky Scotty/Unsplash; Andrea De Santis/Unsplash; Andrea De Santis/Unsplash

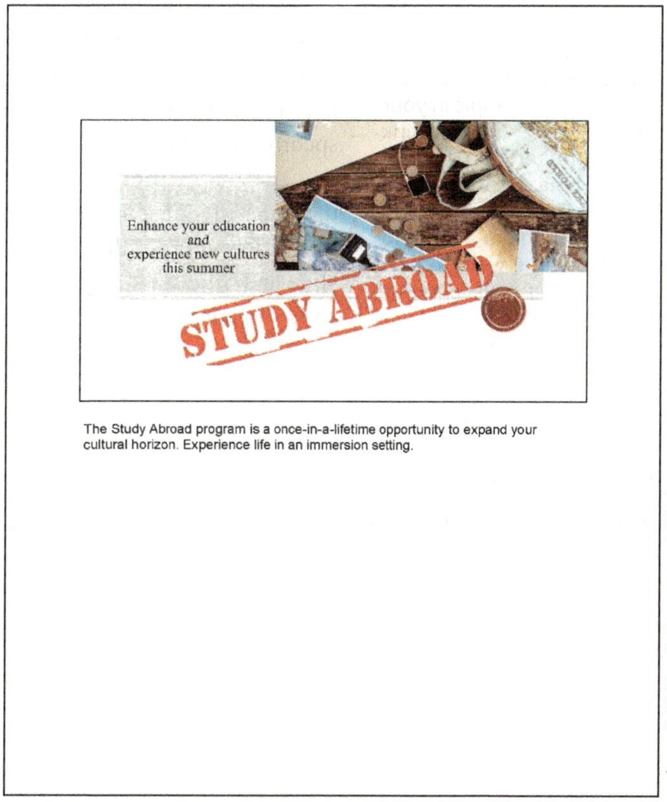

Figure 8–1(g): Speaker Notes in Portrait Orientation

rockyscotty20/Unsplash.com; geralt/Pixabay

BTW
Ribbon and Screen Resolution
PowerPoint may change how the groups and buttons within the groups appear on the ribbon, depending on the screen resolution of your computer. Thus, your ribbon may look different from the ones in this book if you are using a screen resolution other than 1920 × 1080.

In this module, you will learn how to create the slides shown in Figure 8–1. You will perform the following general tasks as you progress through this module:

1. Select specific slides to create a custom slide show.
2. Share a presentation by saving the presentation as a PowerPoint show.
3. Check presentation compatibility and accessibility.
4. Customize handout and notes pages.
5. Create a photo album.
6. Insert a summary zoom slide.

To Start PowerPoint and Save a File

You can begin the project by starting PowerPoint and then saving the presentation with a new file name. The following steps start PowerPoint and then save a file.

1. sam Start PowerPoint. If necessary, maximize the PowerPoint window.
2. Open the presentation, SC_PPT_8_International, from the Data Files.
3. Save the presentation using **SC_PPT_8_Study_Abroad** as the file name.

BTW
Touch Mode Differences
The Microsoft 365 and Windows interfaces may vary if you are using a touch screen. For this reason, you might notice that the function or appearance of your touch screen differs slightly from this module's presentation.

Creating a Custom Slide Show

Quality PowerPoint presentations are tailored toward specific audiences, and experienced presenters adapt the slides to meet the listeners' needs and expectations. Speakers can develop one slide show and then modify the content each time they deliver the presentation. For example, the director of human resources may present one set of slides for new employees, another set for potential retirees, and a third for managers concerned with new regulations and legislation. Slides for all these files may be contained in one file, and the presenter can elect to show particular slides to accompany specific speeches.

A **custom show** is a subset of slides in a presentation that can be reordered without affecting the order of slides in the original presentation. This can be useful when you want to show slides in a different order than in the original presentation. For example, you may desire to show a title slide and Slides 2, 4, 8, and 9, in that order. One PowerPoint presentation can have several custom shows to adapt to specific audiences.

BTW
Hyperlinking Custom Shows
You can hyperlink to a custom show with slides relating to a specific topic in your presentation. Click the Link button (Insert tab | Links group), if necessary click the 'Place in This Document' button in the Link to area, and then select the custom show in the 'Select a place in this document' area.

To Select Slides for a Slide Show

Many presenters deliver their speeches in front of targeted audiences. PowerPoint allows you to create a custom show that displays only selected slides for these people. The following steps select the slides for a custom show. **Why?** You decide to use the slides that showcase two cities: Paris and London.

1

- Click the Slide Show tab and then click the 'Custom Slide Show' button (Slide Show tab | Start Slide Show group) to display the 'Custom Slide Show' menu (Figure 8–2).

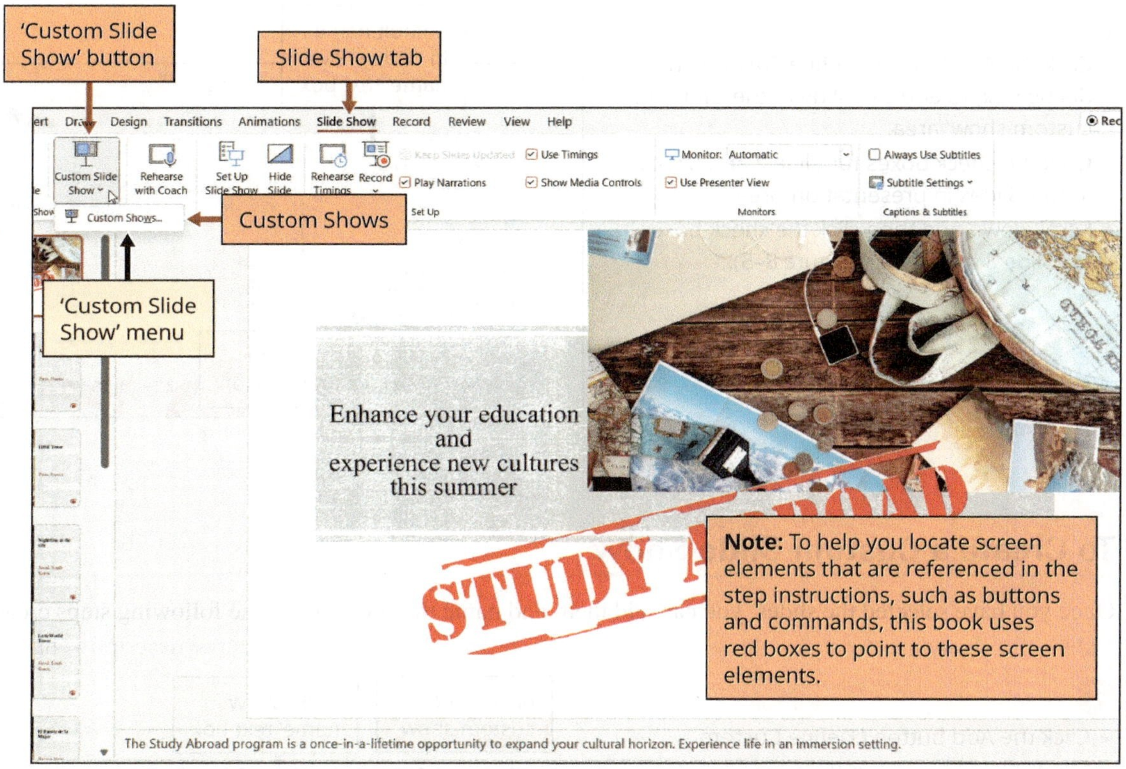

geralt/Pixabay; Rocky Scotty/Unsplash

Figure 8–2

2

- Click Custom Shows to open the Custom Shows dialog box (Figure 8–3).

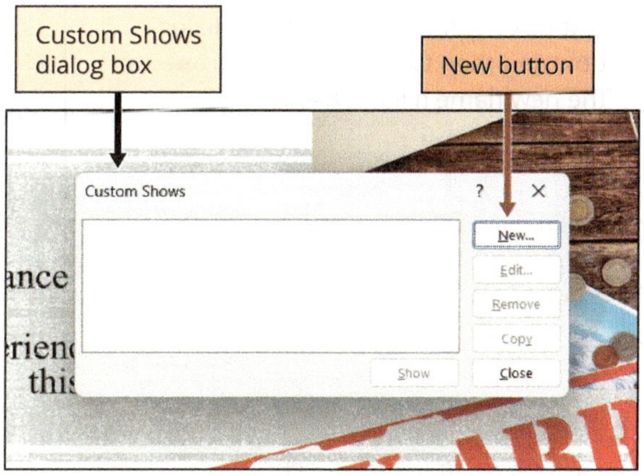

geralt/Pixabay; Rocky Scotty/Unsplash

Figure 8–3

3

- Click the New button (Custom Shows dialog box) to display the 'Define Custom Show' dialog box.
- Click '1. Enhance your education and experience' in the 'Slides in presentation' area to place a check mark in the check box and select this slide (Figure 8–4).

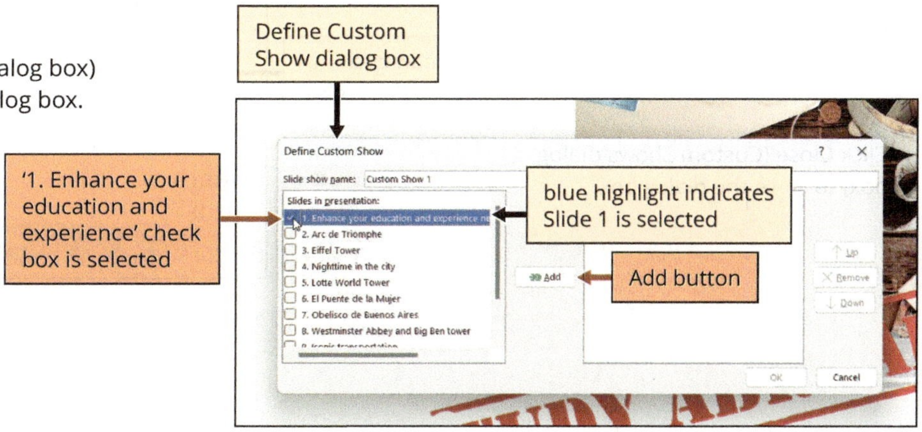

geralt/Pixabay; Rocky Scotty/Unsplash

Figure 8–4

4

- Click the Add button ('Define Custom Show' dialog box) to add this slide to the 'Slides in custom show' area.
- Click the check boxes for Slide 2 and Slide 3 in the 'Slides in presentation' area.
- Scroll down and then click the check boxes for Slide 8 and Slide 9 (Figure 8–5).

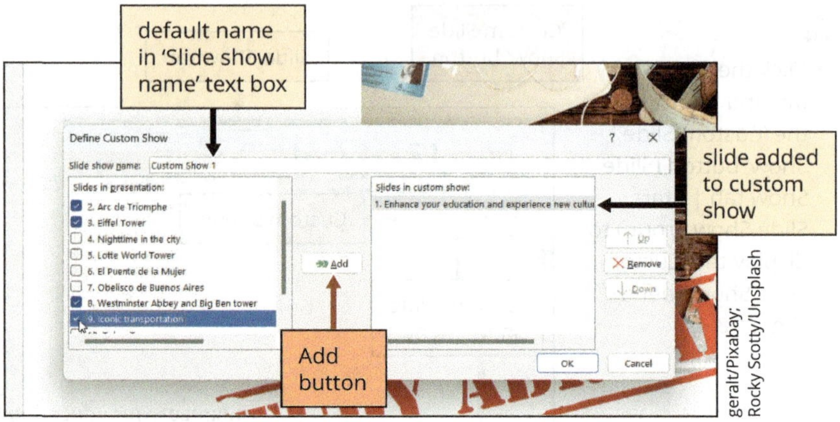

geralt/Pixabay; Rocky Scotty/Unsplash

Figure 8–5

To Create a Custom Slide Show

Once you have selected the slides, you can add them and name the slide show. The following steps create this show. **Why?** You want to finish adding the slides you wish to use and then give the presentation a more descriptive name.

1

- Click the Add button ('Define Custom Show' dialog box) to add these slides to the 'Slides in custom show' area.
- Select the text in the 'Slide show name' text box ('Define Custom Show' dialog box) and then type **Study in Europe** as the new name (Figure 8–6).

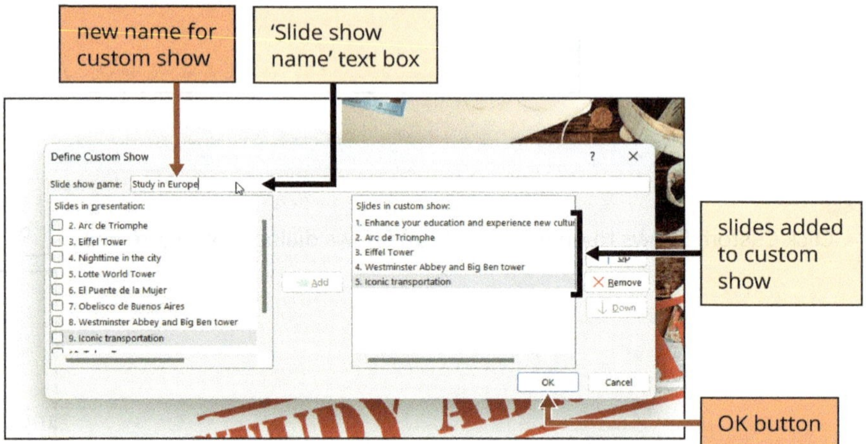

Figure 8–6

geralt/Pixabay; Rocky Scotty/Unsplash

2

- Click OK ('Define Custom Show' dialog box) to create the new Study in Europe custom show and display the Custom Shows dialog box (Figure 8–7).

3

- Click Close (Custom Shows dialog box) to close the dialog box.

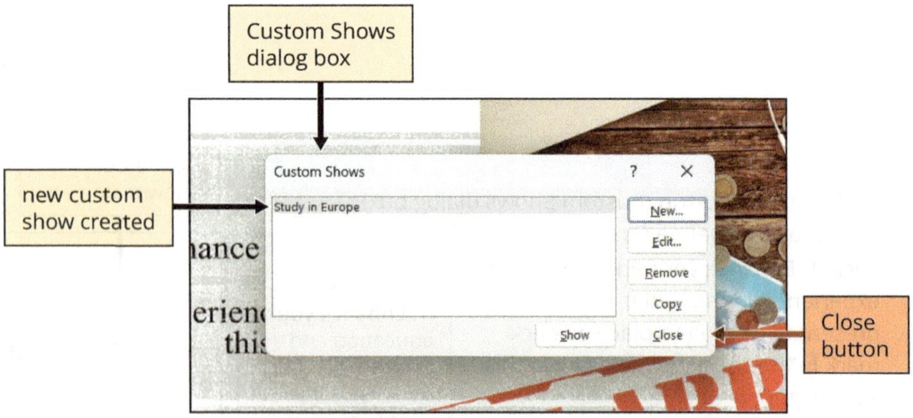

Figure 8–7

geralt/Pixabay; Rocky Scotty/Unsplash

To Open and Edit a Custom Slide Show

A PowerPoint file can have several custom slide shows. You can elect to display one of them at any time. **Why?** If you need to reorder the slides based on the particular needs of your audience, you can change the sequence easily. The following steps open a custom show and edit the slide sequence.

1

- With the Slide Show tab displayed, click the 'Custom Slide Show' button (Slide Show tab | Start Slide Show group) to display the 'Custom Slide Show' menu (Figure 8–8).

Q&A Why does 'Study in Europe' display in the 'Custom Slide Show' menu?
The names of any custom shows will display in the menu. If desired, you could click this custom show name to run the slide show and display the selected slides.

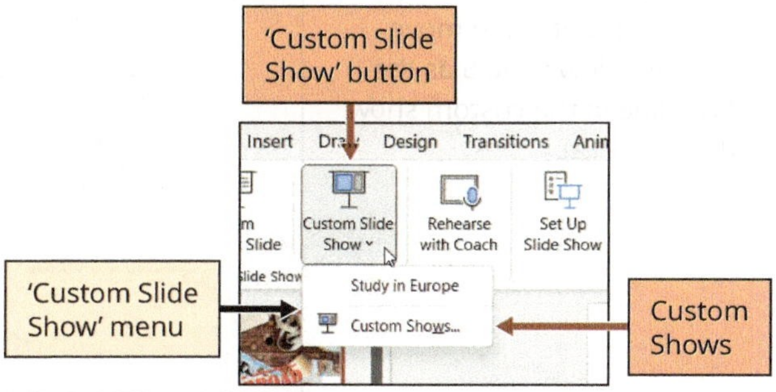

Figure 8–8

2

- Click Custom Shows to display the Custom Shows dialog box (Figure 8–9).

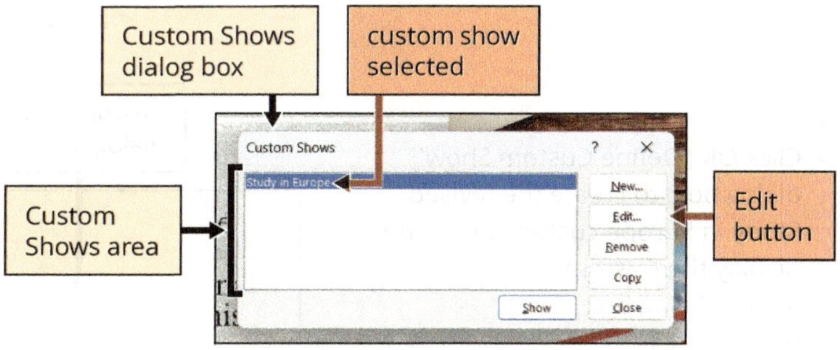

Figure 8–9

3

- With the Study in Europe custom show name displayed in the Custom Shows area, click the Edit button (Custom Shows dialog box) to display the 'Define Custom Show' dialog box.
- Click '3. Eiffel Tower' in the 'Slides in custom show' area to select it (Figure 8–10).

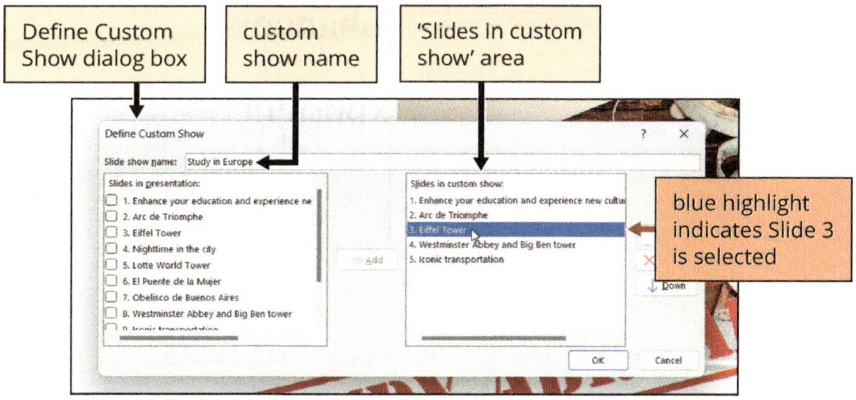

Figure 8–10

geralt/Pixabay; Rocky Scotty/Unsplash

4

- Click the Up button to move Slide 3 below Slide 1 as the second slide in the custom show (Figure 8–11).

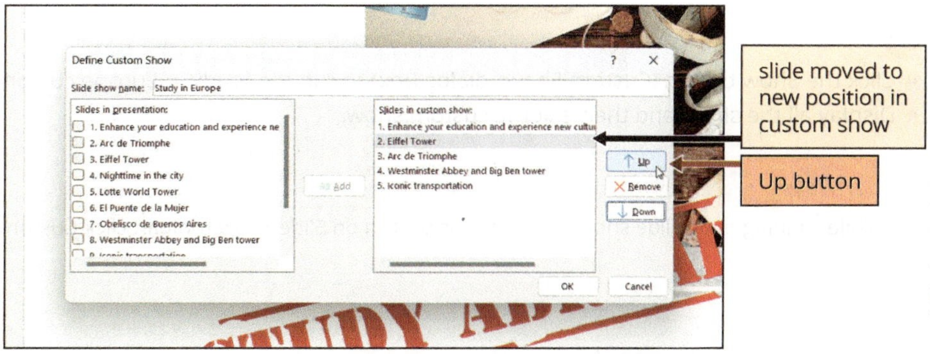

Figure 8–11

geralt/Pixabay; Rocky Scotty/Unsplash

5

- Click '4. Westminster Abbey and Big Ben tower' in the 'Slides in custom show' area to select it and then click the Down button to move Slide 4 below Slide 5 as the last slide in the custom show (Figure 8–12).

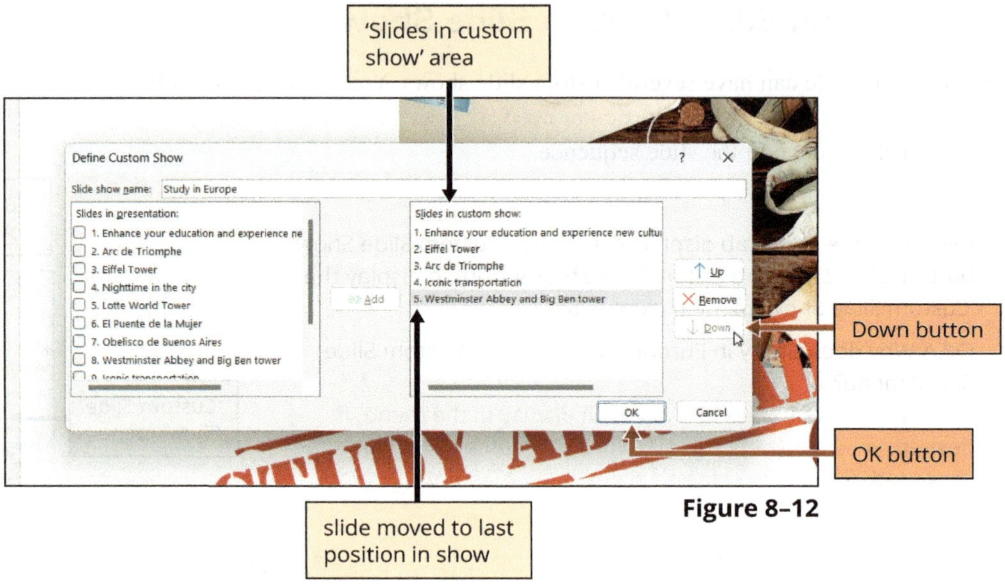

Figure 8–12

geralt/Pixabay; Rocky Scotty/Unsplash

6

- Click OK ('Define Custom Show' dialog box) to create the revised Study in Europe custom show and display the Custom Shows dialog box (Figure 8–13).

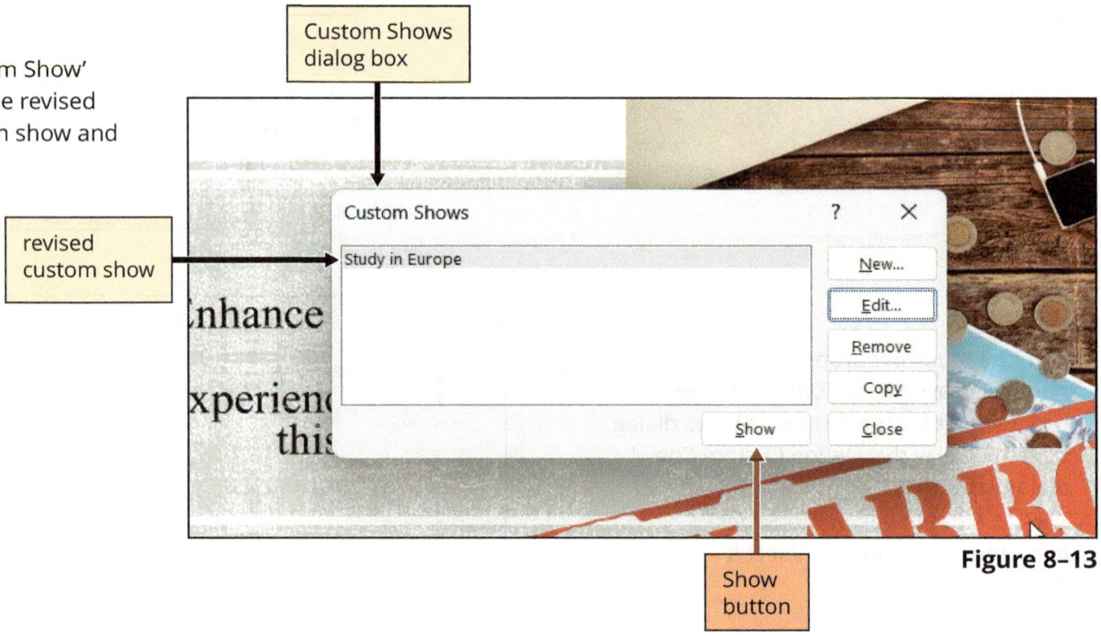

Figure 8–13

geralt/Pixabay; Rocky Scotty/Unsplash

To Run a Custom Slide Show

Once the custom show is created, you can run the show from within the Custom Shows dialog box. **Why?** You want to review the slides to ensure they are in the desired order. The following step runs the custom slide show.

1

- Click the Show button (Custom Shows dialog box) to run the Study in Europe custom show.
- Display all the slides and then exit the custom show.

Other Ways

1. While running main slide show, click Options button on Slide Show toolbar, click Custom Shows, select desired custom show

3D Models

If you have a Microsoft 365 subscription, you can enhance your creativity and productivity by embedding 3D models in your presentations. A **3D model** is an illustration created using 3D animation techniques, which you can rotate in three dimensions. The Online 3D Models gallery of stock 3D models contains hundreds of free 3D models in a wide variety of categories, many of them animated. Once you have inserted a 3D model into your slide, you can rotate and tilt the image. If an image isn't already animated, you can add animation with PowerPoint's animation features. The 3D objects can be matched with 2D content to illustrate your points.

To Insert a 3D Model You insert 3D images into your slide in the same manner that you insert pictures or other content. To insert a 3D model, you would perform the following steps.

1. Click the Insert tab and then click the 3D Models arrow (Insert tab | Illustrations Group) to display the 3D Models menu. If you have a model already created, click This Device. Otherwise, click 'Stock 3D Models' to display the 'Online 3D Models' dialog box.
2. Select a category and then click a picture to place a check mark in that model.
3. Click the Insert button to insert the model into your slide.

BTW
Embedding Animated 3D Graphics
Microsoft 365 subscribers can embed an animated 3D graphic in Word or PowerPoint for Windows. Each one has preset animations, or scenes. When you display the 'Online 3D Models' dialog box, look for the categories that have a runner badge, which indicates the graphics in it are animated. Each graphic has multiple scenes, or animations, from which to choose.

To Modify a 3D Model PowerPoint's controls help you manipulate a 3D model to focus on an area you want to highlight. These controls are available on the contextual tab that is displayed when you insert the image. The 3D Model Views gallery has a collection of views you can use, such as head-on or top-down. The Align tool helps you position the image in a precise area of the slide, in the same manner that you position pictures and other slide objects. The Pan & Zoom control allows you to click and drag the object within the frame, and the Zoom icon that displays on the right side of the frame when you click the Pan & Zoom button makes the object larger or smaller within the frame. To modify a 3D model, you would perform the following steps.

1. With the model selected, click a view (3D Model tab | 3D Model Views group) to change the view.
2. Click the 'Pan & Zoom' button (3D Model tab | Size group) and then click the Pan & Zoom 3D control in the middle of the image to rotate and tilt the model in any direction.
3. Click the Zoom icon on the right side of the image to increase or decrease the size of the image.

To Animate a 3D Model You can add animation effects to your 3D model. Along with the effects available to animate 2D content, 3D options include Arrive, Turntable, Swing, Jump & Turn, and Leave. All the animations have options to adjust the direction, intensity, or movement. For example, the Turntable animation allows you to showcase the object slowly and smoothly. You also can have two animations play simultaneously. To animate a 3D model, you would perform the following steps.

1. Display the Animations tab and then click one of the animation effects (Animations tab | Animation group) to see a preview of that animation and apply the animation to the model.
2. Click the Effect Options button to view the Effect Options menu and then choose a property related to the movement direction, amount, or rotation axis.
3. Click the Preview button (Animations tab | Preview group) to view the effect.

Saving and Sharing a Presentation

Many people design PowerPoint presentations to accompany a speech given in front of an audience, and they also develop slide shows to share with family, work associates, and friends in a variety of ways. PowerPoint saves files by default as a PowerPoint Presentation with a .pptx file extension. You can, however, select other file types that allow other users to view your slides if they do not have one of the newer PowerPoint versions installed. You also can save the file as a PowerPoint show so that it runs automatically when opened and does not require the user to have the PowerPoint program. Another option is to save one slide as an image that can be inserted into another program, such as Word, or emailed.

To Save a Slide as a Picture

To create visually interesting slides, you insert pictures, clips, and video files into your presentation. Conversely, you may want to insert a PowerPoint slide into another document, such as a file you created in Word. **Why?** A slide may have information that you want to share with an audience and include with other material that is not part of the PowerPoint presentation. You can save one slide as an image and then insert this file into another document. The following steps save Slide 1 as a JPEG File Interchange Format (.jpg) image.

1

- With Slide 1 of the SC_PPT_8_Study_Abroad presentation displayed, open Backstage view, display the Export tab, and then click 'Change File Type' in the Export section to display the 'Change File Type' section.
- Click 'JPEG File Interchange Format (*.jpg)' in the 'Image File Types' section (Figure 8–14).

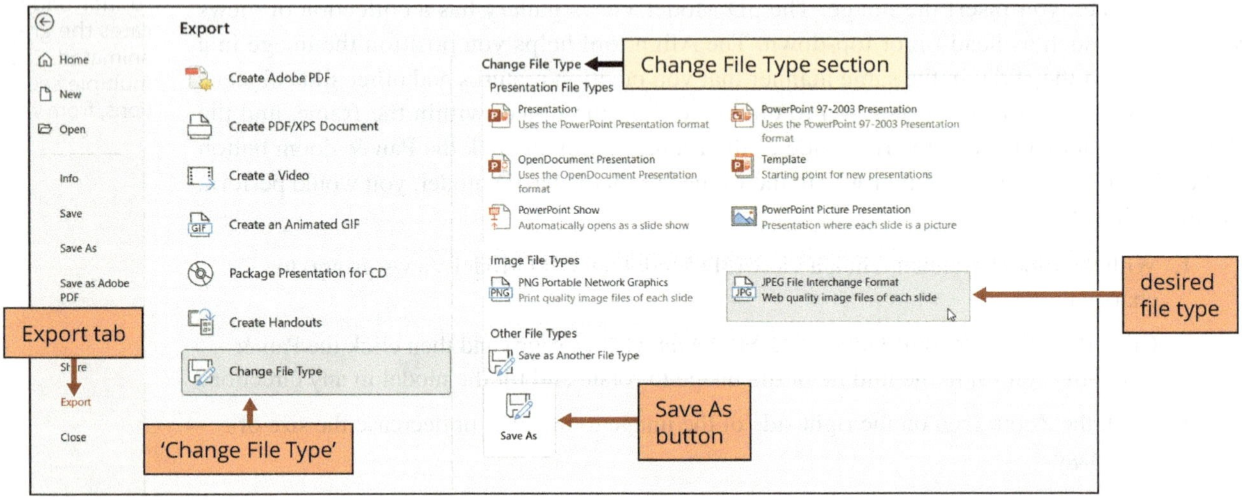

Figure 8–14

2

- Click the Save As button to display the Save As dialog box.
- Change the file name to **SC_PPT_8_Study_Abroad_Slide** in the File name box (Figure 8–15).

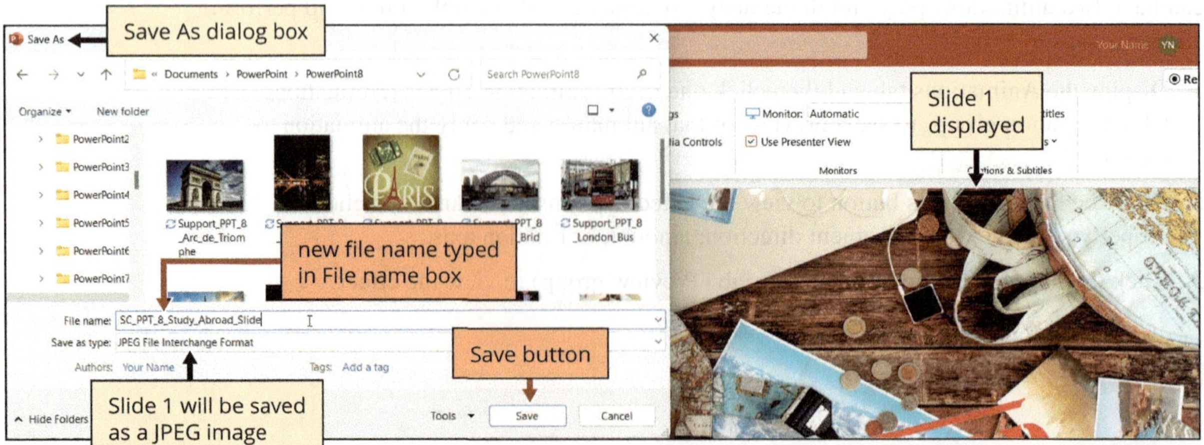

Figure 8–15

3

- Click the Save button (Save As dialog box) to display the Microsoft PowerPoint dialog box (Figure 8–16).

4

- Click the 'Just This One' button to save only Slide 1 as a file in JPEG (.jpg) format.

Q&A What would happen if I clicked All Slides?
PowerPoint would save each slide as a separate file in a folder with the file name you specified.

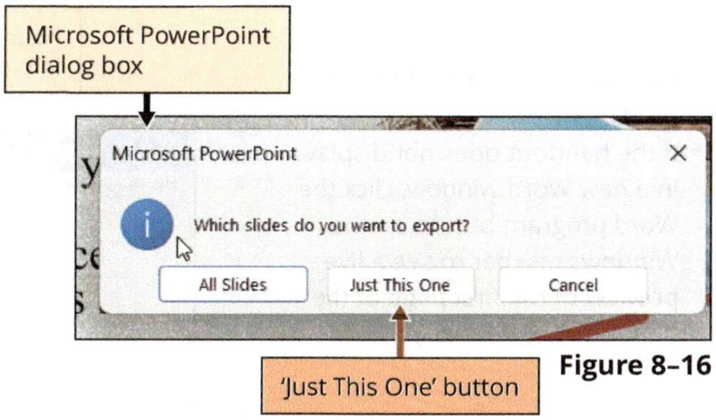

Figure 8–16

Other Ways

1. Click File on ribbon, click Save As in Backstage view, click Browse button to locate save location, click 'Save as type' arrow, select 'JPEG File Interchange Format (*.jpg)', click Save button

To Create Handouts by Exporting to Word

The handouts you create using PowerPoint are useful to distribute to audiences. Each time you need to create these handouts, however, you need to open the file in PowerPoint and then print from Backstage view. As an alternative, it might be convenient to save, or export, the file as a Word document if you are going to be using Word to type a script or lecture notes. **Why?** The handout can have a variety of layouts; for example, the notes you type in the Notes pane can display to the right of or beneath the slide thumbnails, blank lines can display to the right of or beneath the slide thumbnails, or just an outline can display. The following steps export the presentation to Word and then create a handout.

1

- Open Backstage view, display the Export tab, and then click Create Handouts in the Export section to display the 'Create Handouts in Microsoft Word' section (Figure 8–17).

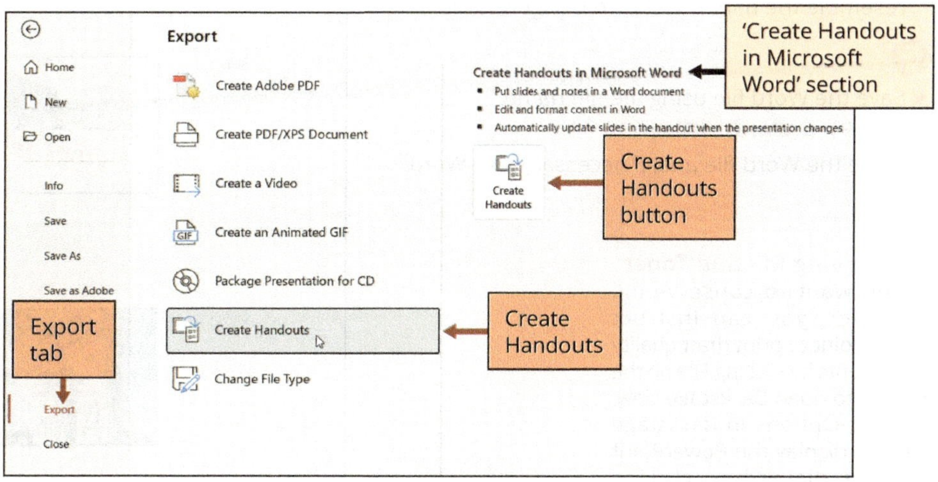

Figure 8–17

2

- Click the Create Handouts button to display the 'Send to Microsoft Word' dialog box.
- Click 'Blank lines next to slides' to add blank lines next to the slides when the handout is printed (Figure 8–18).

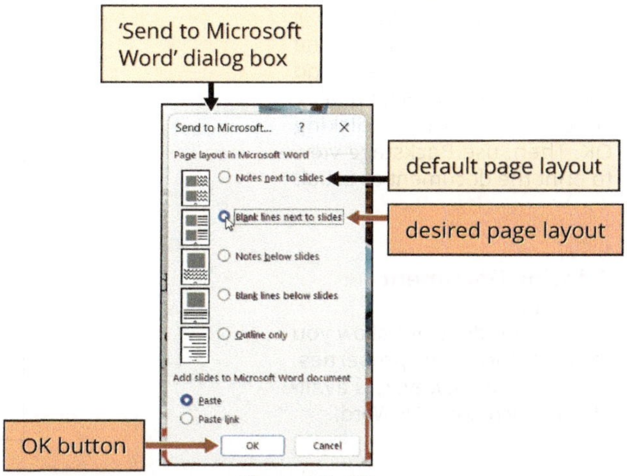

Figure 8–18

3

- Click OK to create the file with this layout.
- If the handout does not display in a new Word window, click the Word program button on the Windows taskbar to see a live preview of the first page of the handout (Figure 8–19).

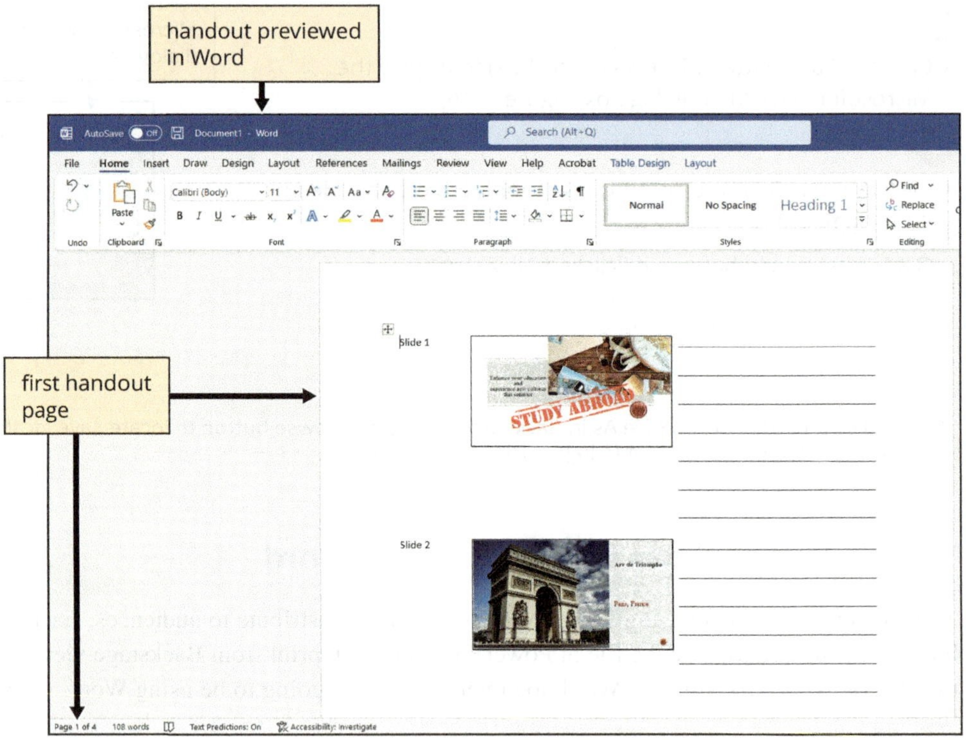

geralt/Pixabay; Rocky Scotty/Unsplash; iankelsall1/Pixabay

Figure 8–19

4

- If you print the handouts, the first page will resemble the handout shown in Figure 8–20.

5

- Save the Word file using the file name, **SC_PPT_8_Word**.
- Close the Word file and, if necessary, exit Word.

iankelsall1/Pixabay; Alexas_Fotos/Pixabay; geralt/Pixabay; Rocky Scotty/Unsplash

Figure 8–20

BTW
Conserving Ink and Toner

If you want to conserve ink or toner, you can instruct PowerPoint to print draft quality documents by clicking File on the ribbon to open Backstage view, clicking Options in Backstage view to display the PowerPoint Options dialog box, clicking Advanced in the left pane (PowerPoint Options dialog box), scrolling to the Print area in the right pane, verifying there is no check mark in the High quality check box, and then clicking OK. Then, use Backstage view to print the document as usual.

BTW
Printing Document Properties

PowerPoint does not allow you to print document properties. This feature, however, is available in Microsoft 365 Word.

To Record Slide Timings and Narration In some situations, you may want your viewers to hear recorded narration that accompanies slides. You can record narration separately and then add this file to the slide. You also can record narration while the slide show is running. To record this narration, you would perform the following steps.

1. Display the Record tab and then click From Beginning (Record tab | Record group) if you want to begin with the first slide or click 'From Current Slide' (Record tab | Record group) if you want to begin with the slide that is displayed on your screen.
2. Click the red Start recording button.
3. When you have finished speaking, click the red Stop recording button.

Other Ways

1. Display Slide Show tab, click Record arrow (Slide Show tab | Set Up group), click 'From Beginning' or 'From Current Slide', click Start recording, right-click slide, click End Show on shortcut menu

BTW
Digital Inking
Digital inking allows you to draw and write anywhere on your slides, even during a presentation. The pens in the Drawing Tools group on Draw tab can have a variety of thicknesses, colors, and textures. Once you write on your slide, you can use the Lasso tool to convert the ink to an equation, shape, or formatted text. The Ink Replay button allows you to play back your animated drawing.

To Preview Narration Once you have recorded some narration, you can play the audio to review the sound. To preview this narration, you would perform the following steps.

1. In Normal view, click the sound icon on the slide.
2. Display the Playback tab and then click the Play button (Playback tab | Preview group).

To Show a Presentation with or without Narration If you have recorded narration to accompany your slides, you can choose whether to include this narration when you run your slide show. To run the slide show either with or without narration, you would perform the following steps.

1. Display the Slide Show tab and then click the Play Narrations check box (Slide Show tab | Set Up group) to remove the check from the box.
2. If you have chosen to show the presentation without narration and then desire to allow audience members to hear this recording, click the Play Narrations check box (Slide Show tab | Set Up group) to check this option.

To Save a Presentation as a PowerPoint Show

Why? To simplify giving a presentation in front of an audience, you may want to start your slide show without having to start PowerPoint, open a file, and then click the Slide Show button. When you save a presentation as a **PowerPoint Show (.ppsx)**, it automatically begins running when opened. The following steps save the SC_PPT_8_Study_Abroad presentation as a PowerPoint show.

1

- Open Backstage view, display the Export tab, and then click 'Change File Type' to display the 'Change File Type' section.
- Click PowerPoint Show in the Presentation File Types section (Figure 8–21).

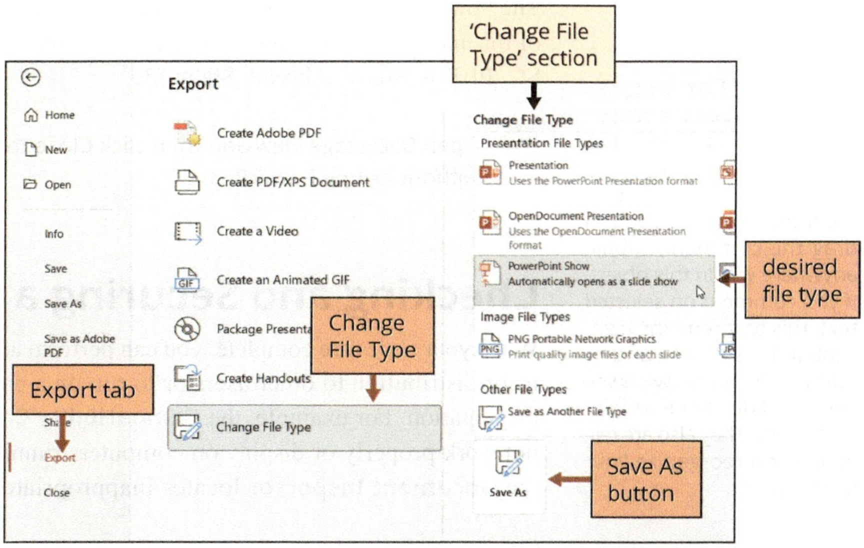

Figure 8–21

2

- Click the Save As button to display the Save As dialog box.
- Change the file name to **SC_PPT_8_Study_Abroad_Show** in the File name box (Figure 8–22).

3

- Click the Save button to close the Save As dialog box.

4

- Close the file and then reopen it to see it as a PowerPoint show.

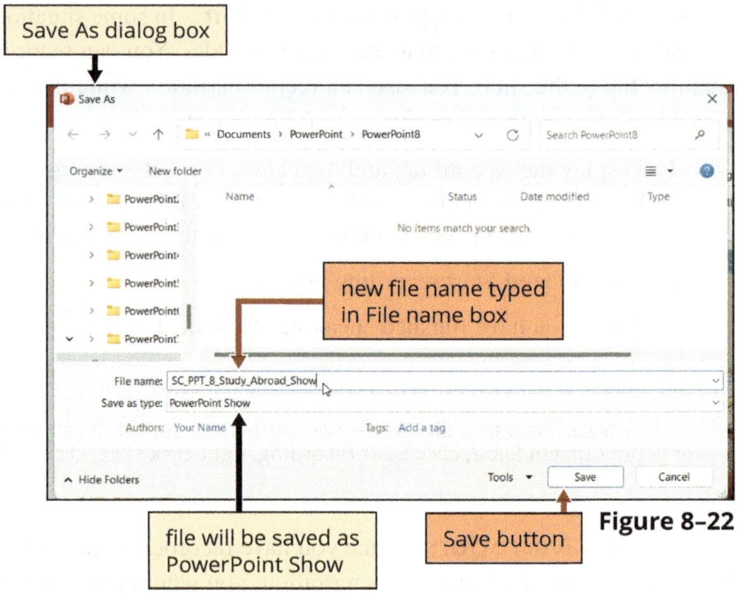

Figure 8–22

Other Ways

1. Click Save As, click Browse, click 'Save as type' arrow, select PowerPoint Show, click Save

To Share a Presentation on OneDrive You can save a presentation in your OneDrive account and then share this file with specific individuals. To share a presentation, you first upload it to your OneDrive account and then determine the individuals who can access this file. To share a presentation, you would perform the following steps.

1. Display Backstage view, click the Share tab, and then click 'Share with People' in the Share area.
2. If necessary, select your OneDrive account, choose a permission level, and then click Apply.
3. Click the 'Share with People' button in the Share with People area, enter the names of the individuals with whom you want to share the file, and then add a message.
4. Click Send.

To Close a Presentation

The PowerPoint show is complete. You will use the SC_PPT_8_Study_Abroad file for the remainder of this module, so you can close the PowerPoint show presentation. The following step closes the SC_PPT_8_Study_Abroad_Show file.

1 Open Backstage view and then click Close to close the SC_PPT_8_Study_Abroad_Show file without exiting PowerPoint.

BTW
Anchoring Comments
Once you post a comment on a slide element, it becomes anchored to an object or range of text. If you comment on an object, you can drag the comment bubble anywhere within this object. If you comment on selected text, this text remains highlighted. These useful anchor features help reviewers see specific slide elements with comments. They also are reliable if you reorganize your slide content.

Checking and Securing a Presentation

When your slides are complete, you can perform additional functions to finalize the file and prepare it for distribution to other users or to run on a computer other than the one used to develop the presentation. For example, the **Compatibility Checker** reviews the file for any feature that will not work properly or display on computers running a previous PowerPoint version. In addition, the **Document Inspector** locates inappropriate information, such as comments, in a file and allows you to delete these slide elements. You also can set passwords so only authorized people can distribute, view, or modify your slides. When the review process is complete, you can indicate this file is the final version.

To Check Presentation Compatibility

This version of PowerPoint has many new features not found in some previous versions, especially versions older than PowerPoint 2007. If you give your file to people who have a previous PowerPoint version installed on their computers, they will be able to open the file but may not be able to see or edit some special features and effects. The following steps run the Compatibility Checker. **Why?** You can use the Compatibility Checker to see if any presentation elements will not function in earlier versions of PowerPoint and display a summary of any elements in your presentation that will be lost if your file is opened in some earlier PowerPoint versions.

1

- Open the SC_PPT_8_Study_Abroad presentation.
- Open Backstage view, if necessary click the Info tab, and then click the 'Check for Issues' button to display the 'Check for Issues' menu (Figure 8–23).

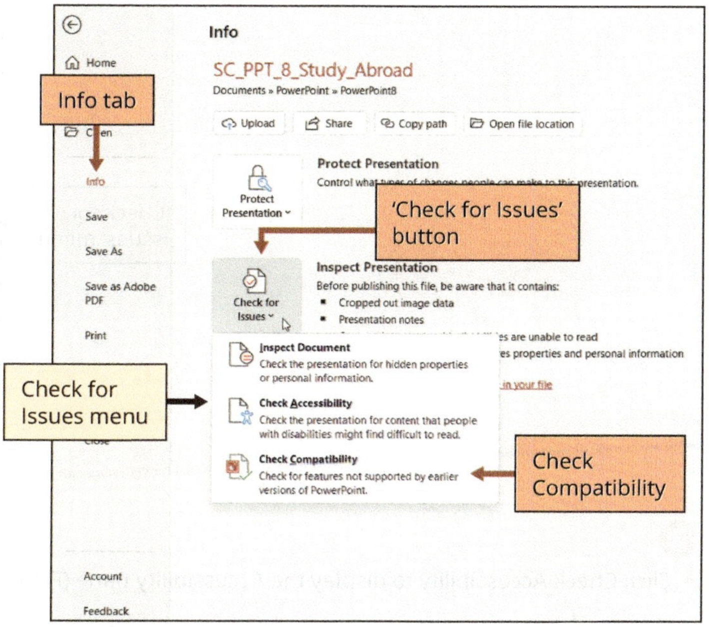

Figure 8–23

2

- Click Check Compatibility to display the 'Microsoft PowerPoint Compatibility Checker' dialog box.
- If any features are not supported by earlier versions of PowerPoint, they are displayed in the Summary box (Figure 8–24).

3

- Click OK ('Microsoft PowerPoint Compatibility Checker' dialog box) to close the dialog box and return to the presentation.

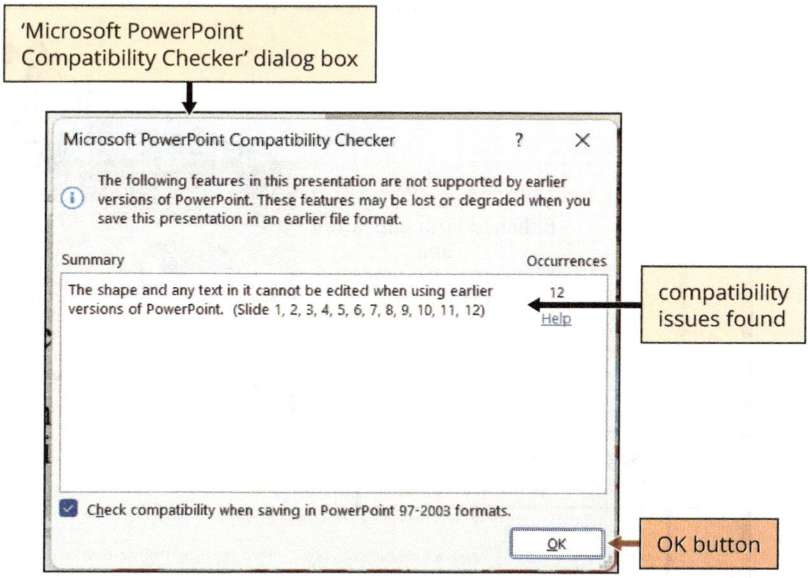

Figure 8–24

To Check Presentation Accessibility

An effective PowerPoint presentation is highly visual, so a good designer creates slides that people with disabilities such as those who are visually impaired can understand easily. PowerPoint includes an **Accessibility Checker** to identify potential issues. This feature scans the slides and finds missing alternative text, possible problems with the reading order, insufficient color contrast, slides without titles, and complex tables. The following steps run the Accessibility Checker. **Why?** This feature can identify slide elements that may not be accessible and provide advice on how to fix these issues.

1

- Open Backstage view, click the Info tab, and then click the 'Check for Issues' button to display the Check for Issues menu (Figure 8–25).

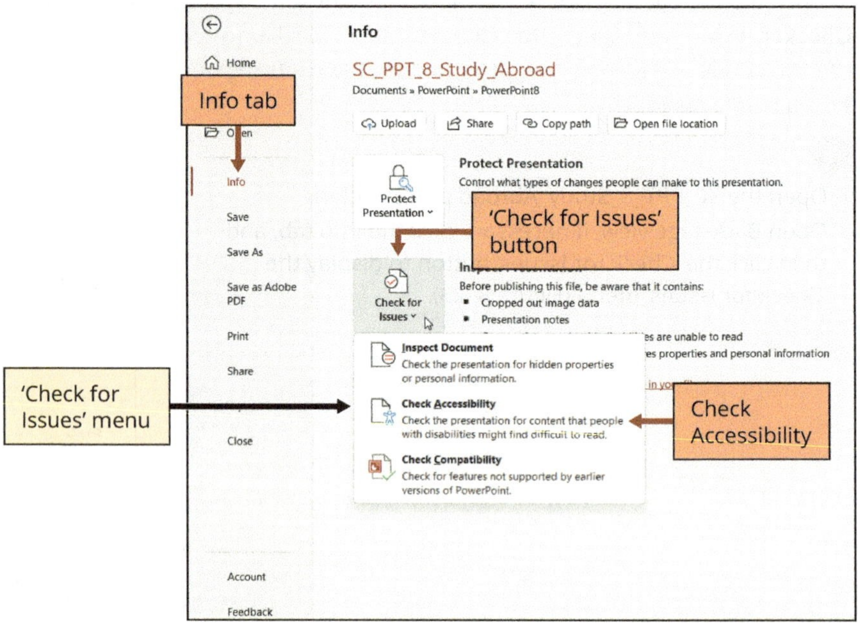

Figure 8–25

2

- Click Check Accessibility to display the Accessibility pane (Figure 8–26).

geralt/Pixabay; Rocky Scotty/Unsplash

Figure 8–26

3

- Click the 'Missing alternative text (1)' error and then click the Picture 6 (Slide 1) arrow (Figure 8–27).

Q&A Can PowerPoint generate sample alternative text?
Yes. Click the 'Suggest a description for me' link to obtain possible wording. You can verify or modify this text if necessary.

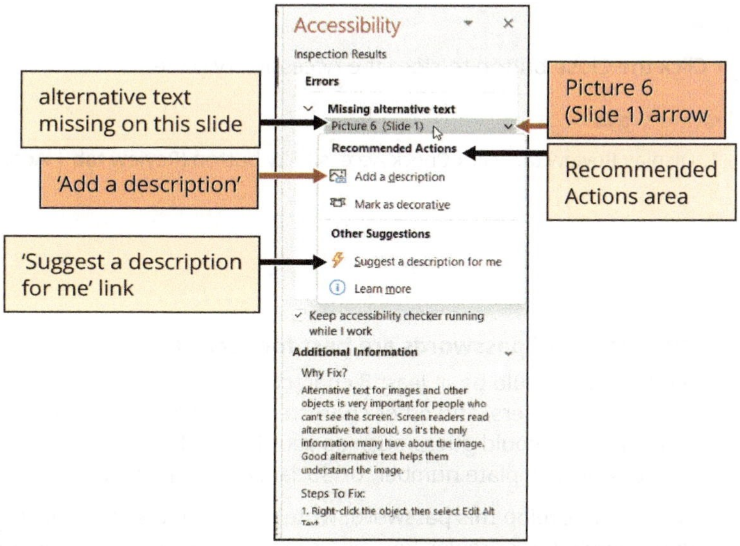

Figure 8–27

4

- Click 'Add a description' in the Recommended Actions area and then type **Computer, camera, coins, tote bag, photos, and an ID on a table** as the alt text description (Figure 8–28).

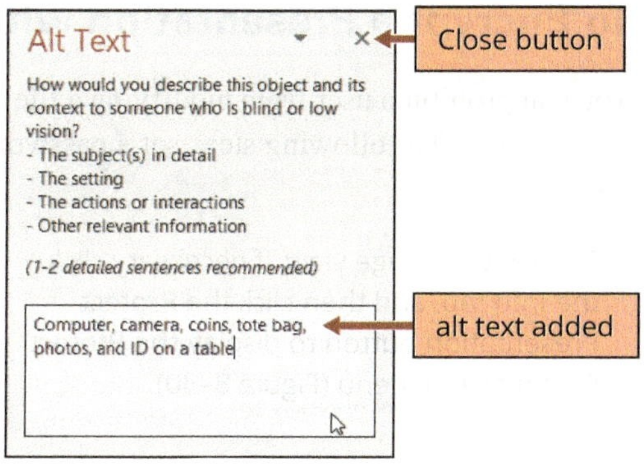

Figure 8–28

5

- Click the Close button to close the Alt Text pane and display the Accessibility Pane (Figure 8–29). Note that there are now no Accessibility issues.

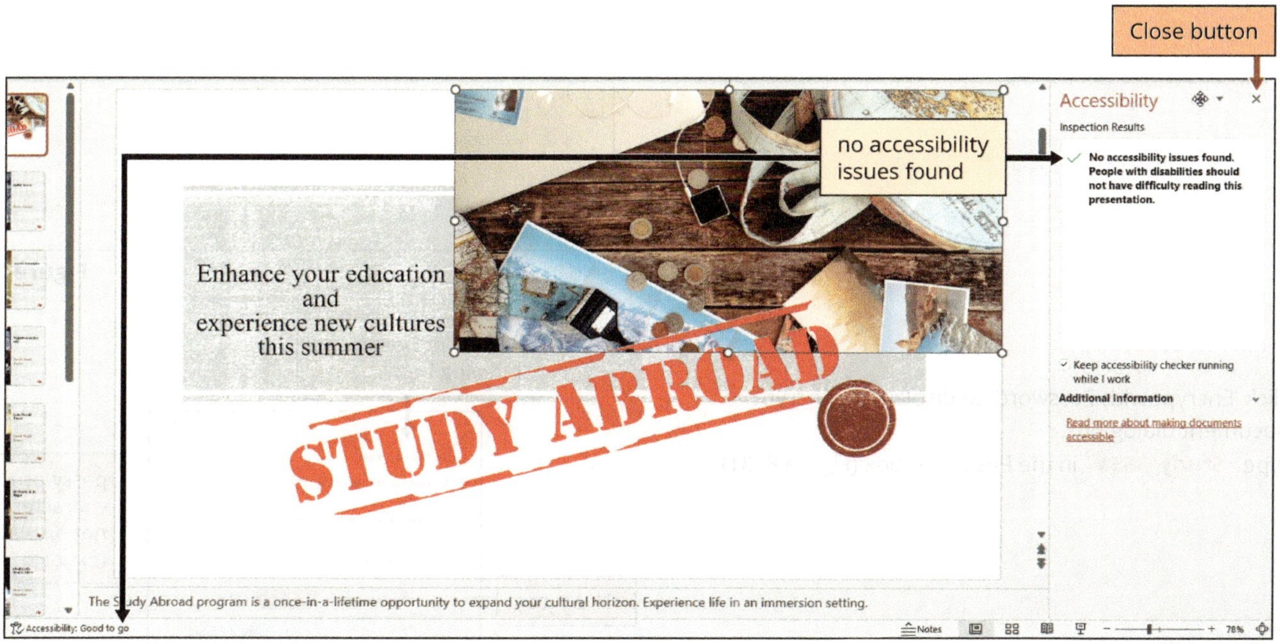

geralt/Pixabay; Rocky Scotty/Unsplash

Figure 8–29

6

- Click the Close button to close the Accessibility pane.

Other Ways

1. Display Review tab, click Check Accessibility button (Review tab | Accessibility group)

BTW

Finding a Definition

If you need the definition of a word or phrase, select the Microsoft Search box (or press ALT+Q), type it in the Microsoft Search box and then click 'More search results' for that term. The right pane will display articles, files, and other media.

Consider This

What types of passwords are best for security?

A password should be at least 8 characters (some experts recommend at least 20 characters) and contain a combination of letters, numbers, and other characters. Using both uppercase and lowercase letters is advised. Do not use a password that someone could guess, such as your first or last name, spouse's or child's name, telephone number, birth date, street address, license plate number, or Social Security number.

Once you develop this password, write it down in a secure place. Underneath your keyboard is not a secure place, nor is your middle desk drawer. You also can use a password manager program for added security.

To Encrypt a Presentation with a Password

You can prohibit a user from modifying a file without entering the password. **Why?** You can protect your slide content by using a password. The following steps set a password for the SC_PPT_8_Study_Abroad file.

1

- Display Backstage view, if necessary click the Info tab, and then click the Protect Presentation button to display the Protect Presentation menu (Figure 8–30).

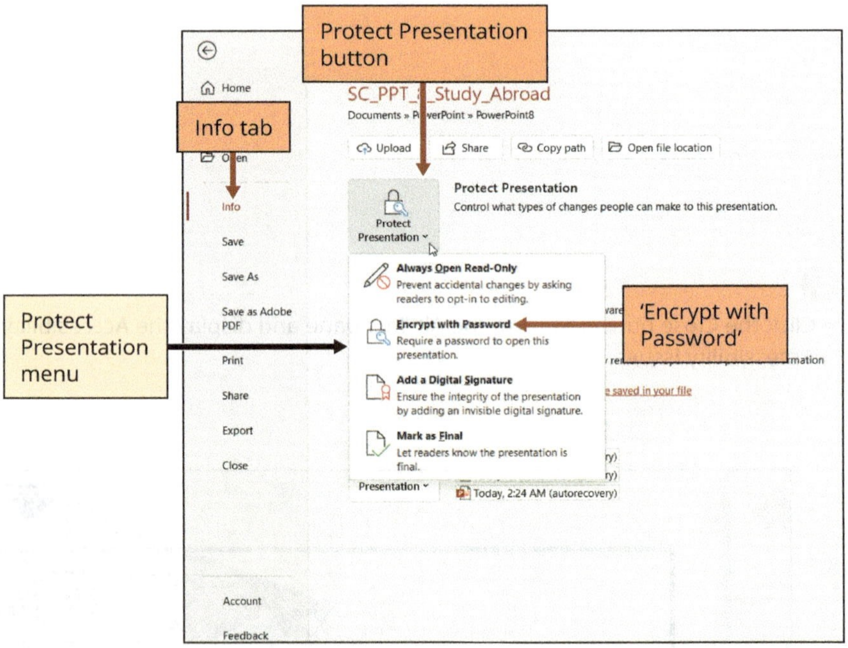

Figure 8–30

2

- Click 'Encrypt with Password' to display the Encrypt Document dialog box.
- Type **Study_365#** in the Password box (Figure 8–31).

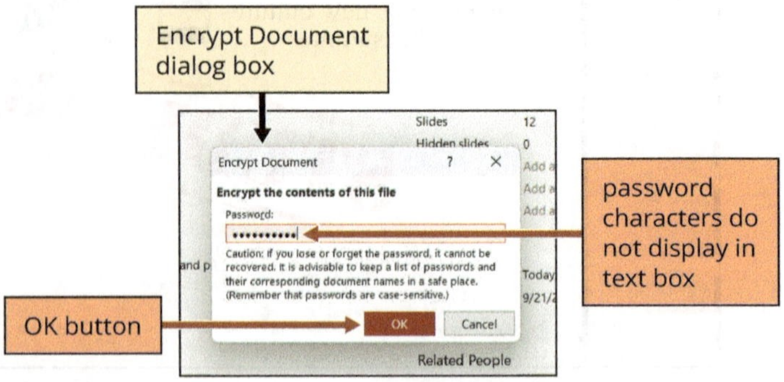

Figure 8–31

3

- Click OK to display the Confirm Password dialog box.
- Type **Study_365#** in the Reenter password box (Figure 8–32).

Q&A What if I forget my password?
You will not be able to open your file. For security reasons, Microsoft or other companies cannot retrieve a lost password.

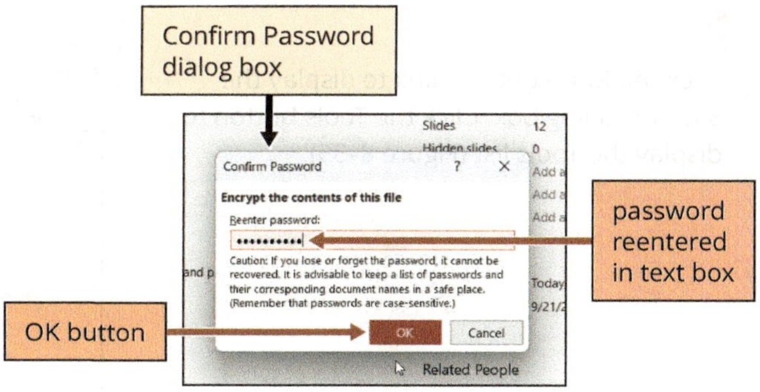

Figure 8–32

4

- Click OK in the Confirm Password dialog box to encrypt the file with a password and display a message that the file is protected (Figure 8–33).

Q&A When does the password take effect?
You will need to enter your password the next time you open your presentation.

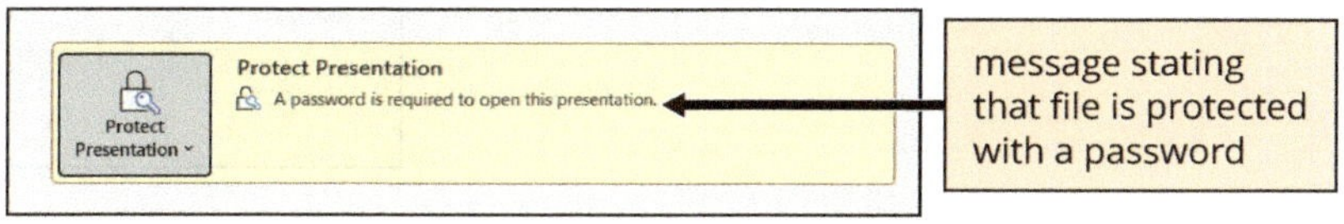

Figure 8–33

To Open a Presentation with a Password To open a file that has been protected with a password, you would perform the following steps.

1. Display the Open dialog box, locate the desired file, and then click the Open button to display the Password dialog box.
2. When the Password dialog box appears, type the password in the Password box and then click OK to display the presentation.

BTW
Searching for Help
Microsoft Search can provide help with performing a particular task. Type your question in the Microsoft Search box. Then view Microsoft Support articles in the Get Help section or click 'More search results' for that particular question and review additional support articles displayed in the right pane.

To Change or Remove Password Protection

You can change a password that you added to a file or remove all password protection from the file. **Why?** Another password may be more secure or password protection may be unnecessary. The following steps remove the password from the SC_PPT_8_Study_Abroad file.

1

- With Backstage view open, click Save As to display the Save As gallery (Figure 8–34).

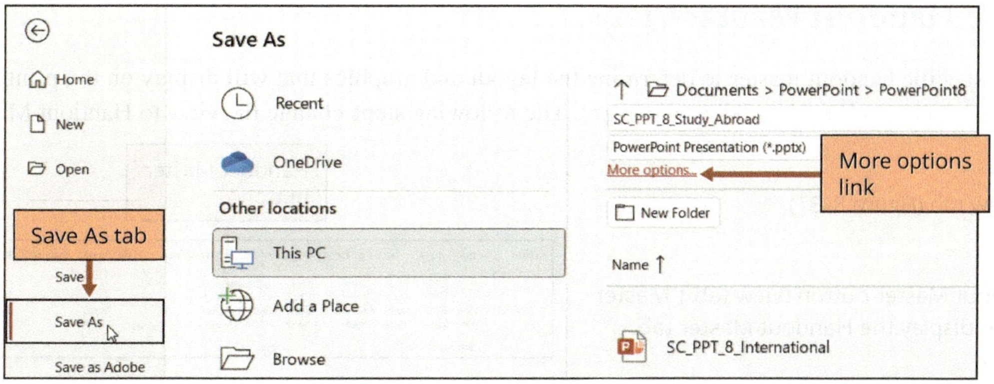

Figure 8–34

2

- Click the More options link to display the Save As dialog box. Click the Tools button to display the Tools list (Figure 8–35).

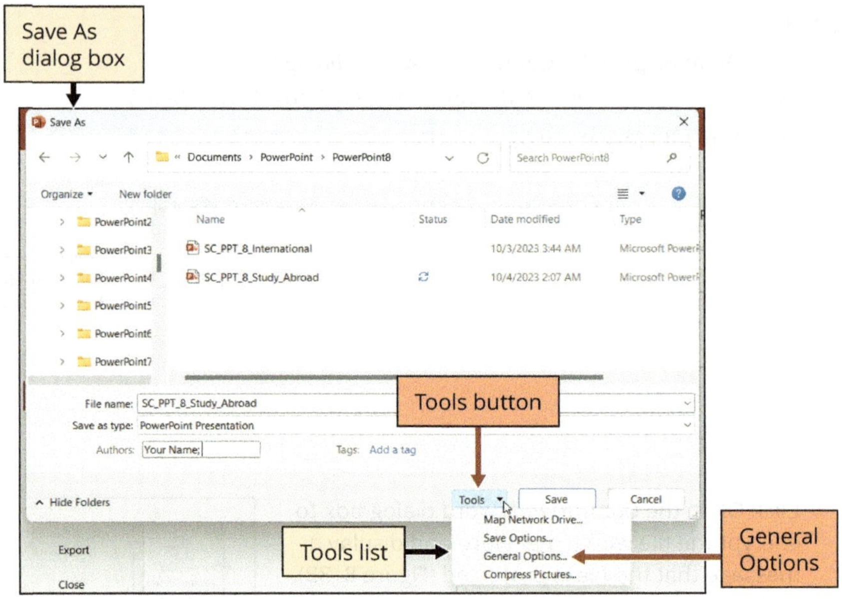

Figure 8–35

3

- Click General Options in the Tools list to display the General Options dialog box.
- Delete the contents of the 'Password to open' box (Figure 8–36).

4

- Click OK (General Options dialog box), click the Save button (Save As dialog box), and then click Yes ('Confirm Save As' dialog box) to resave the presentation.

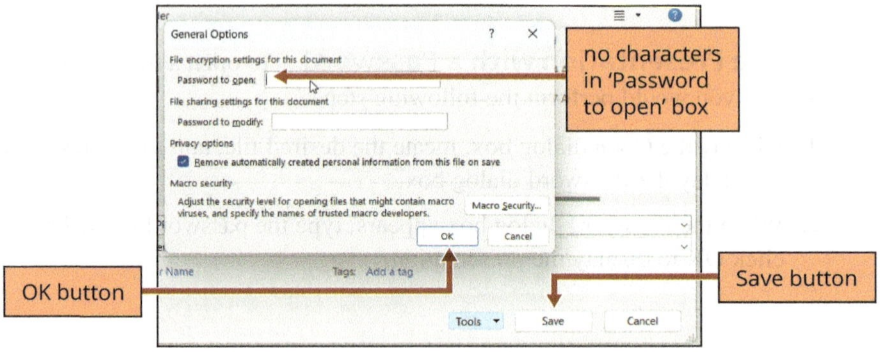

Figure 8–36

Customizing Handout and Notes Masters

PowerPoint has master template files to create handouts and notes. If you are going to distribute handouts to your audience, you can customize the handout master so that it coordinates visually with the presentation slides and reinforces your message. In addition, if you are going to use speaker notes to guide you through a presentation, you can tailor the notes master to fit your needs.

To Switch to Handout Master View

You can create a specific handout master to determine the layout and graphics that will display on the printed handout. **Why?** *You can customize handouts for your audience's needs.* The following steps change the view to Handout Master.

1

- Display the View tab (Figure 8–37).

2

- Click the Handout Master button (View tab | Master Views group) to display the Handout Master tab.

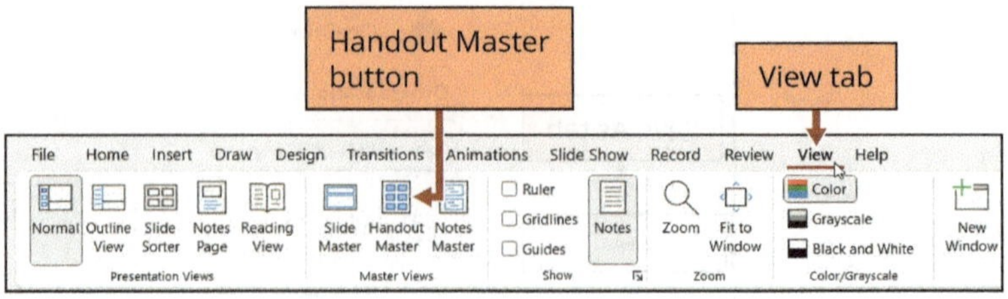

Figure 8–37

To Customize the Handout Master

The Handout Master tab has buttons and controls that allow you to design a custom handout master. **Why?** You can format the header and footer placeholders, set the page number orientation, add graphics, and specify the number of slides to print on each page. The following steps customize the handout master to create a custom handout.

1

- With the Handout Master tab displayed, click the 'Slides Per Page' button (Handout Master tab | Page Setup group) to display the 'Slides Per Page' gallery (Figure 8–38).

Q&A Is 6 Slides the default layout for all themes?

Yes. If you have fewer than six slides in your presentation or want to display slide details, then choose a handout layout with 1, 2, 3, or 4 slides per sheet of paper.

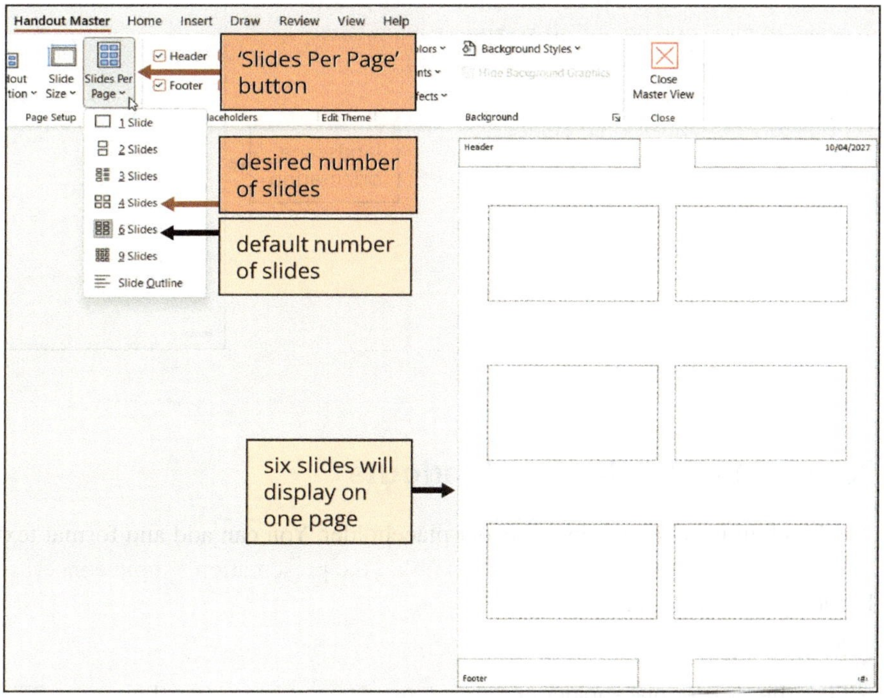

Figure 8–38

2

- Click 4 Slides in the list to change the layout from six slides to four slides.
- Click the Handout Orientation button (Handout Master tab | Page Setup group) to display the Handout Orientation gallery (Figure 8–39).

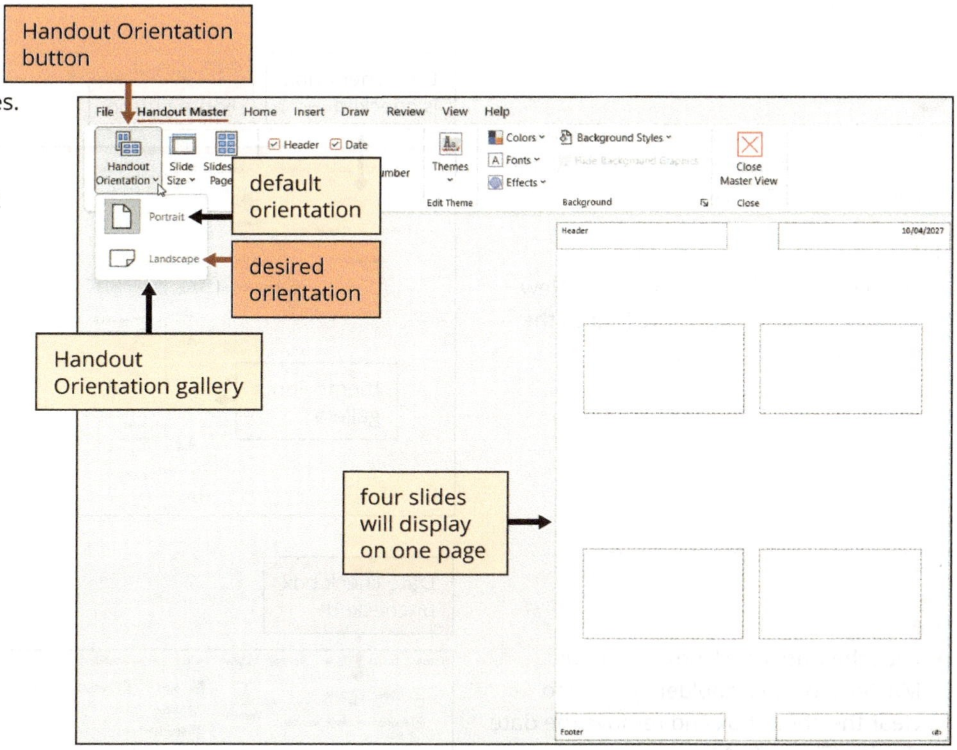

Figure 8–39

3

- Click Landscape in the gallery to display the page layout in landscape orientation (Figure 8–40).

Q&A How do I decide between portrait and landscape orientation?
If your slide content is predominantly vertical, such as an athlete running or a skyscraper in a major city, consider using the default portrait orientation. If, however, your slide content has long lines of text or pictures of four-legged animals, landscape orientation may be more appropriate.

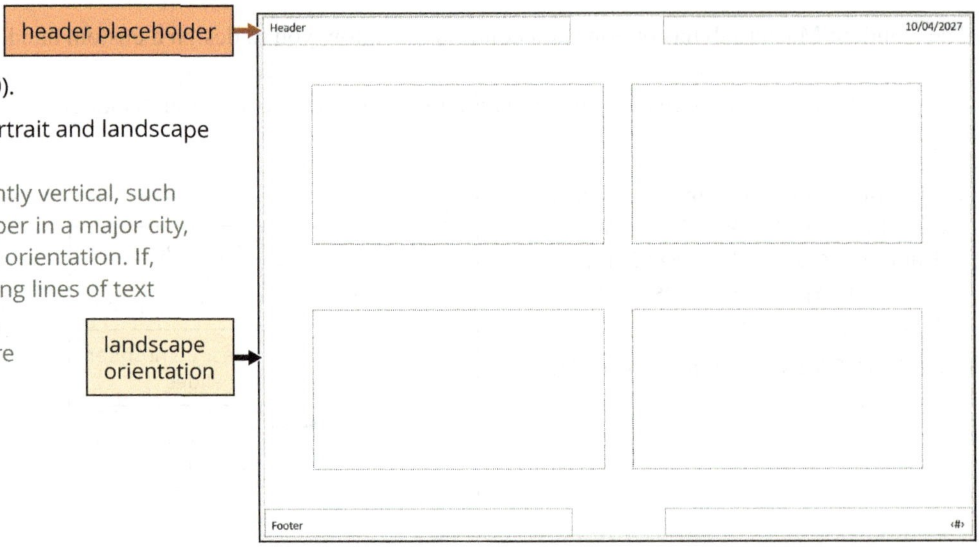

Figure 8–40

To Insert a Header for Handouts

The handout master contains a header placeholder. You can add and format text in that box and also position it on the slide. **Why?** The header informs your audience that the presentation's topic concerns studying abroad. The following steps insert a header for the custom handout.

1

- Click the Header placeholder and then type **Study Abroad** as the header text (Figure 8–41).

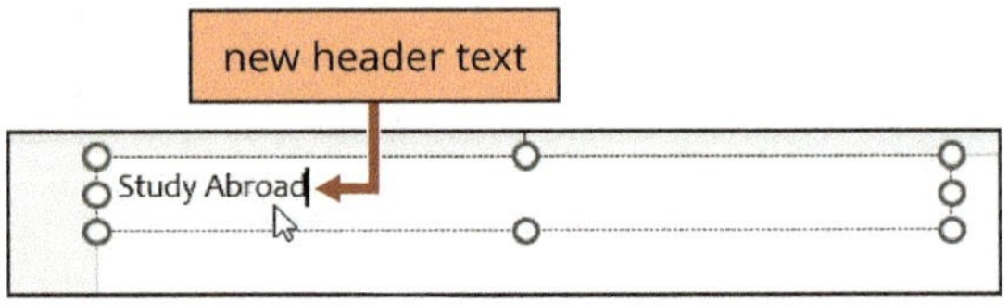

Figure 8–41

2

- Click the Fonts button (Handout Master tab | Background group) to display the Fonts gallery (Figure 8–42).

3

- Scroll down and then click 'Times New Roman – Arial' to apply the font to the text in the placeholders.

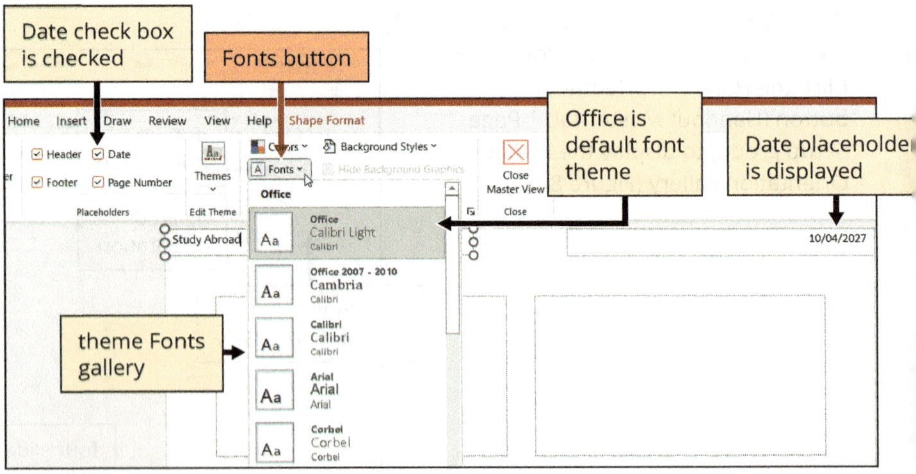

Figure 8–42

4

- Click the Date check box (Handout Master tab | Placeholders group) to clear the check box and remove the date display (Figure 8–43).

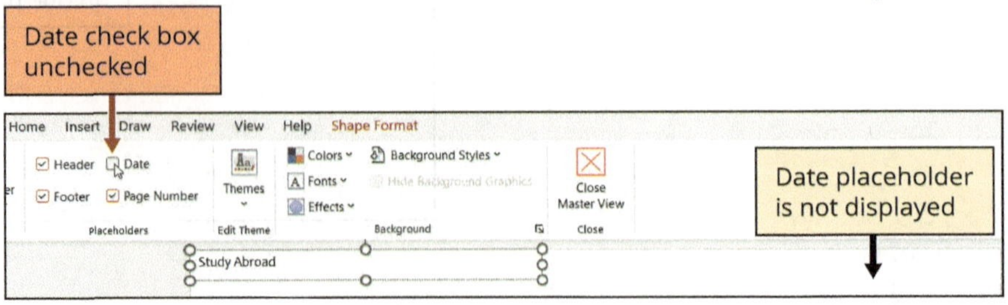

Figure 8–43

To Switch to Notes Page View

If you type notes in the Notes pane, you can print them for yourself or your audience. The basic format found in Backstage view generally suffices for handouts. **Why?** This format includes placeholders for the header, date, slide image, footer, body, and page number. The following steps change the view to Notes Page.

1

- Display the View tab (Figure 8–44).

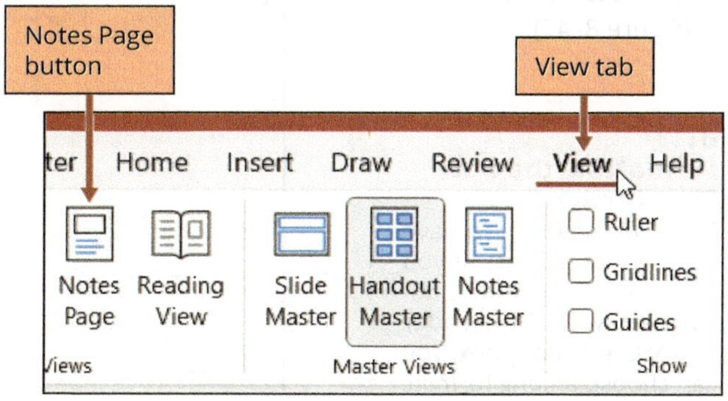

Figure 8–44

2

- Click the Notes Page button (View tab | Presentation Views group) to display Notes Page view.
- Press RIGHT ARROW repeatedly to view all 12 notes pages (Figure 8–45).

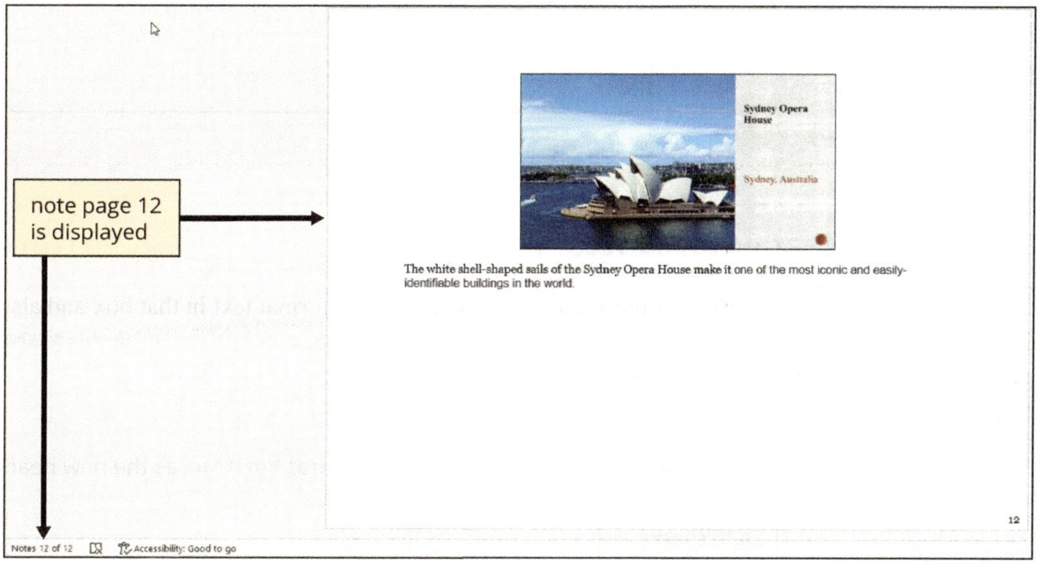

Taschengeld/Pixabay

Figure 8–45

To Switch to Notes Master View

You may desire to alter the layout using the notes master. **Why?** You can add graphics and rearrange and format the header, footer, and page number placeholders. The following steps use the notes master to create a custom handout.

1

- Display the View tab (Figure 8–46).

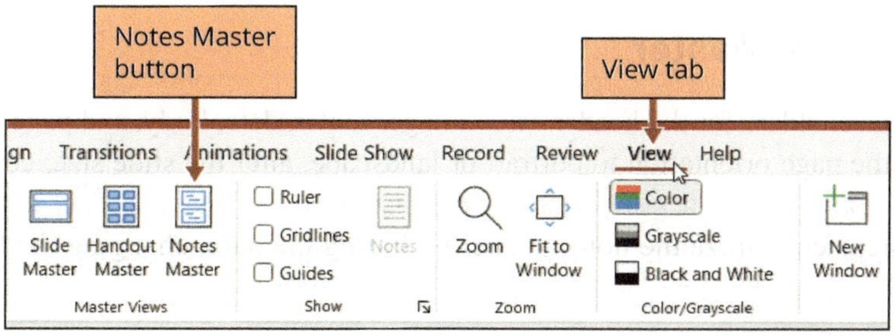

Figure 8–46

2

- Click the Notes Master button (View tab | Master Views group) to display the Notes Master tab (Figure 8–47).

BTW
Formatting the Date Placeholder
The Date header can have a variety of formats. If you click the Update automatically arrow in the 'Header and Footer' dialog box, you can choose among formats that display the date in a variety of combinations.

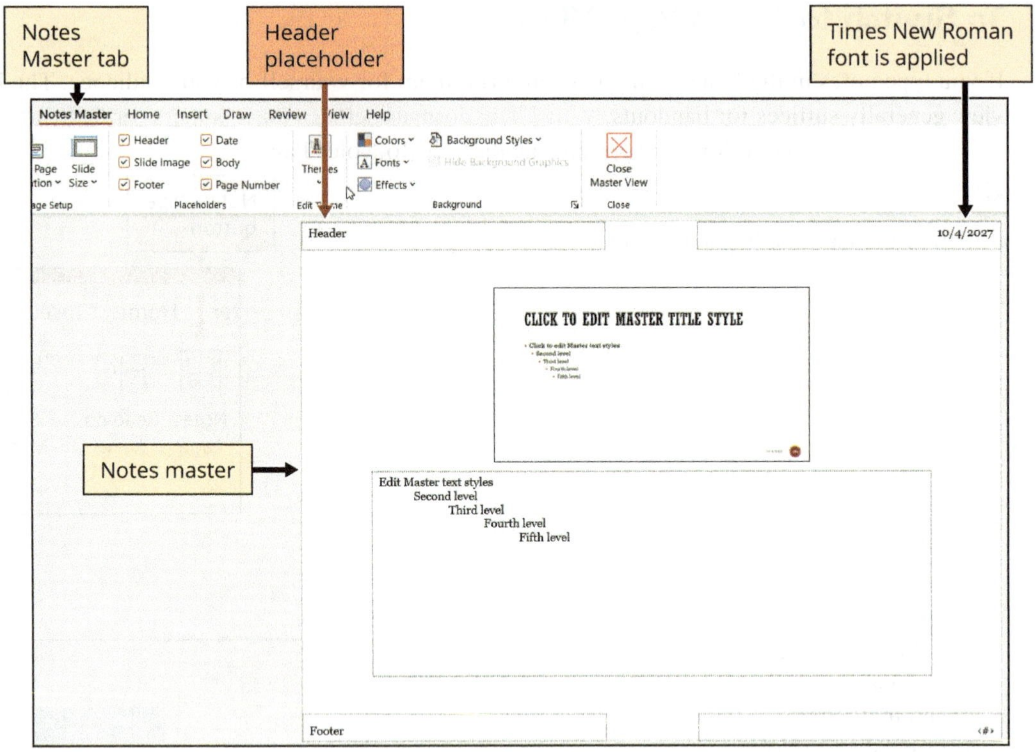

Figure 8–47

To Insert a Header for Notes

The notes master contains a header placeholder. You can add and format text in that box and also position it on the slide. **Why?** You can view the header and quickly see your presentation's topic or other information that you added to this box. The following step inserts a header for the custom handout.

1

- Click the Header placeholder and then type **Expand your cultural horizon** as the new header text (Figure 8–48).

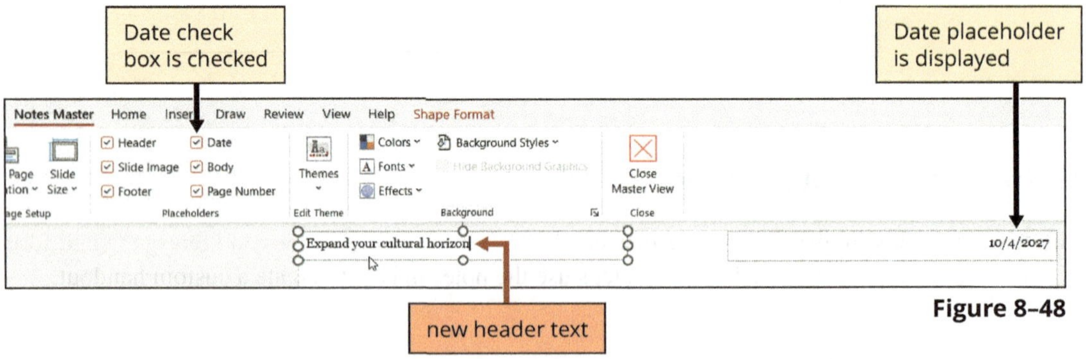

Figure 8–48

To Customize the Notes Master

The notes master contains placeholders for the header, slide image, footer, date, body, and page number. You can hide any of these placeholders, change the page orientation to portrait or landscape, alter the slide size, edit the theme, and change the fonts and colors. **Why?** It is not important to view the date. You also want to change the font and change the page orientation to portrait. The following steps customize the notes master by hiding the date, changing the font, and changing the page orientation to portrait.

1

- Click the Date check box to remove the check mark.
- Click the Fonts button to display the Fonts gallery (Figure 8–49).

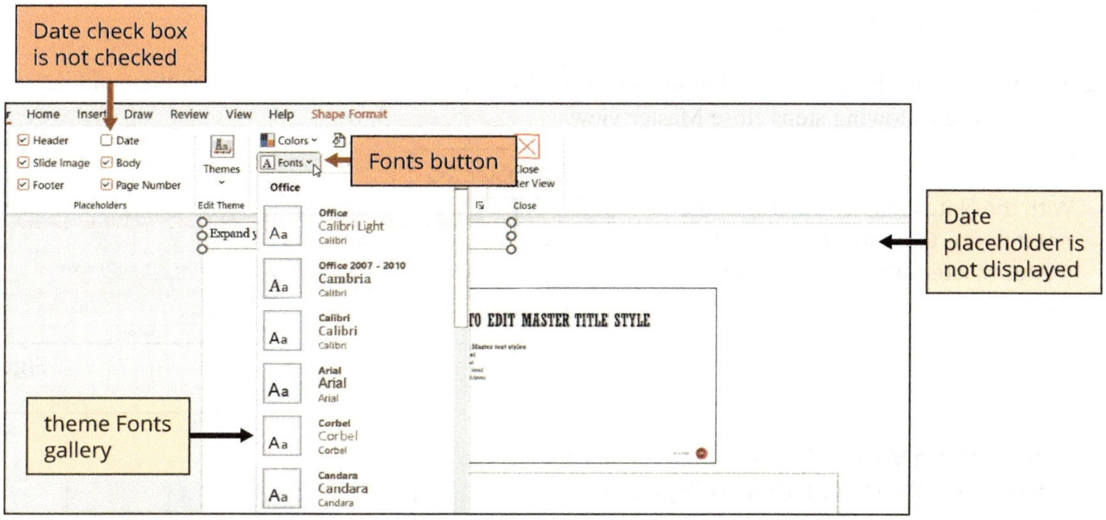

Figure 8–49

2

- Scroll down and then click 'Times New Roman – Arial' in the Fonts gallery to apply that font to the text in the header and page number placeholders.
- Click the 'Notes Page Orientation' button (Notes Master tab | Page Setup group) to display the 'Notes Page Orientation' gallery (Figure 8–50).

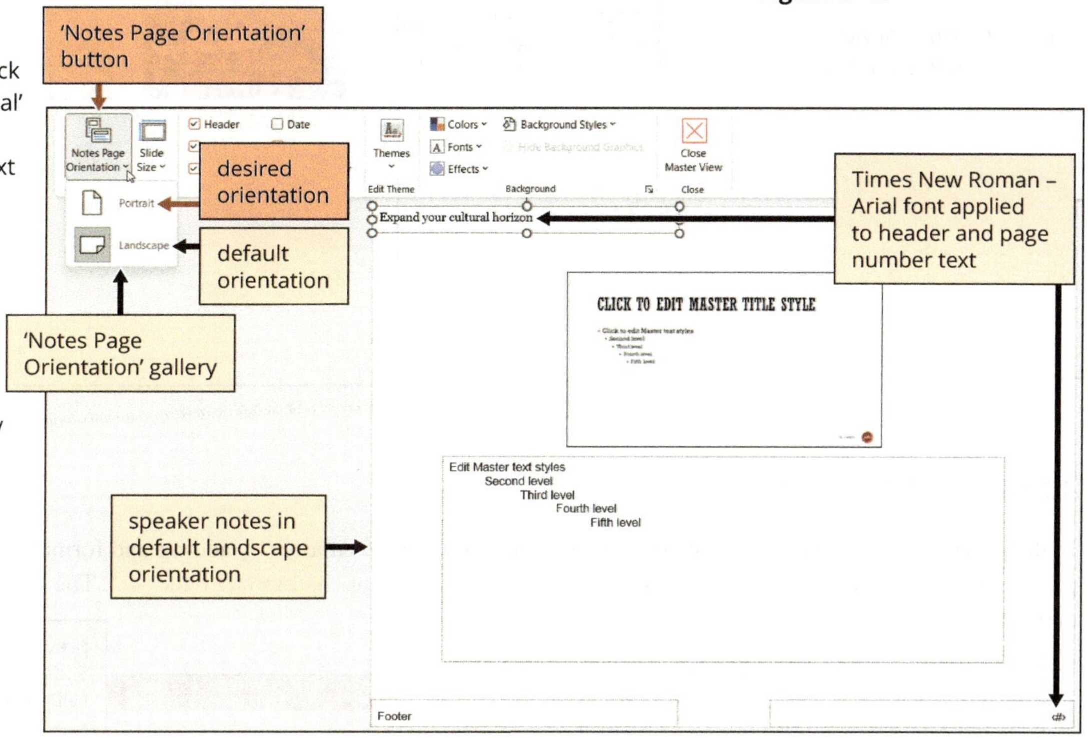

Figure 8–50

3

- Click Portrait in the gallery to display the page layout in portrait orientation (Figure 8–51).

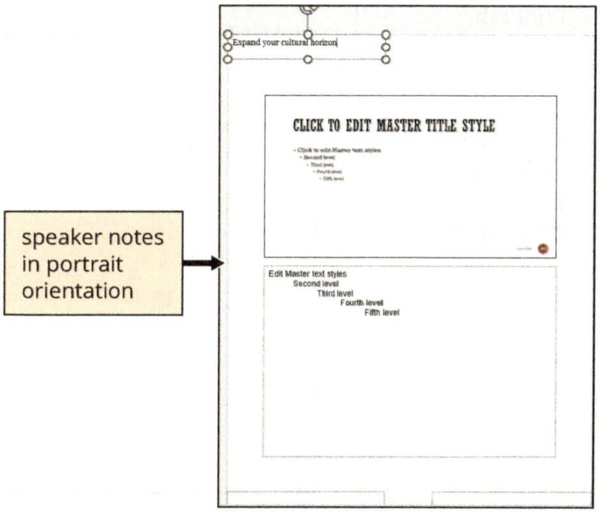

Figure 8–51

To Close Master View

You now can exit Master view and return to Normal view. **Why?** All the changes to the handout master and notes master are complete. The following steps close Master view.

1

- With the Notes Master tab displayed, point to the 'Close Master View' button (Notes Master tab | Close group) (Figure 8–52).

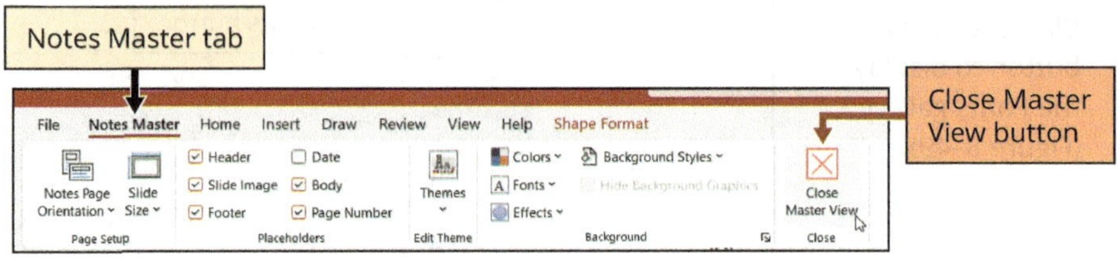

Figure 8–52

2

- Click the 'Close Master View' button to exit Master view and return to the Notes Page view (Figure 8–53).

3

- Click the Normal view button on the status bar.

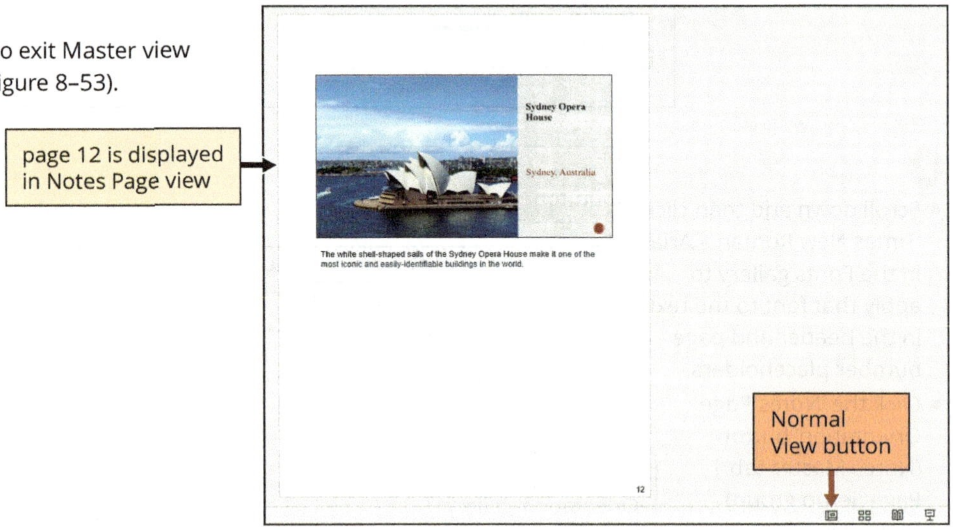

Taschengeld/Pixabay

Figure 8–53

To Print Handouts

In the previous steps, you customized the handout master and notes master by adding and formatting header text. You now can print handouts easily using these masters. **Why?** You want to print customized handouts. The following steps print handouts and speaker notes pages.

1

- Open Backstage view and then click the Print tab.

2

- Click 'Full Page Slides' in the Settings area to display the Print gallery (Figure 8–54).

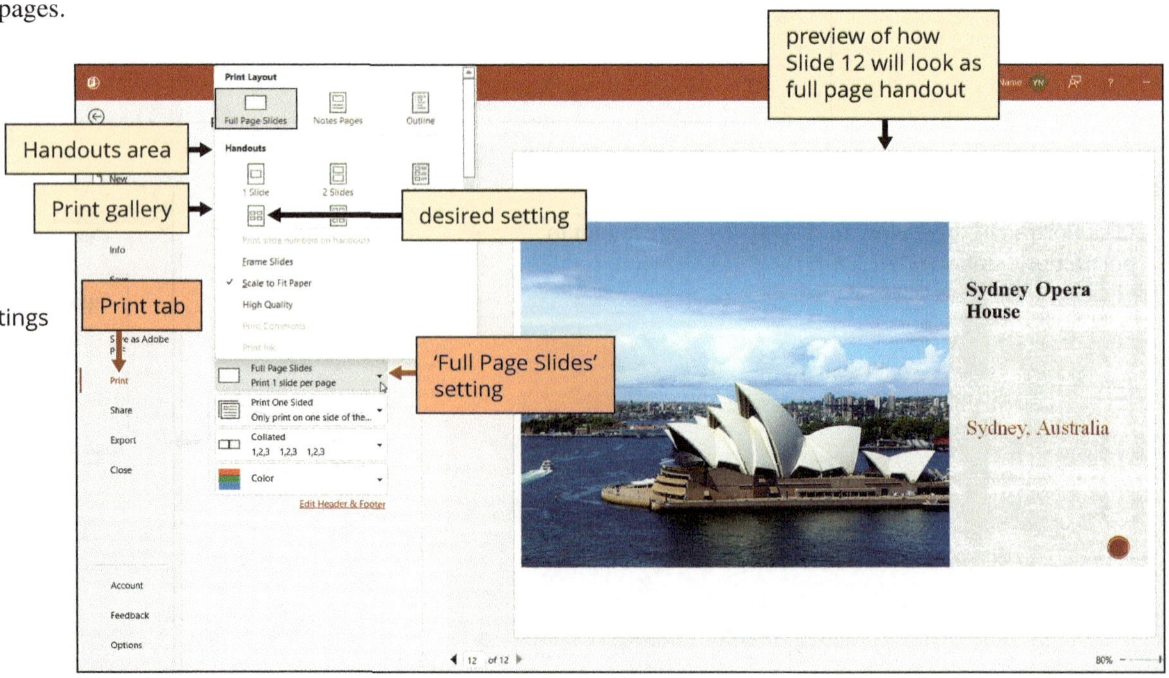

Taschengeld/Pixabay

Figure 8–54

3

- Scroll down and then click '4 Slides Horizontal' in the Handouts area.
- Click Portrait Orientation in the Settings area to display the Orientation gallery (Figure 8–55).

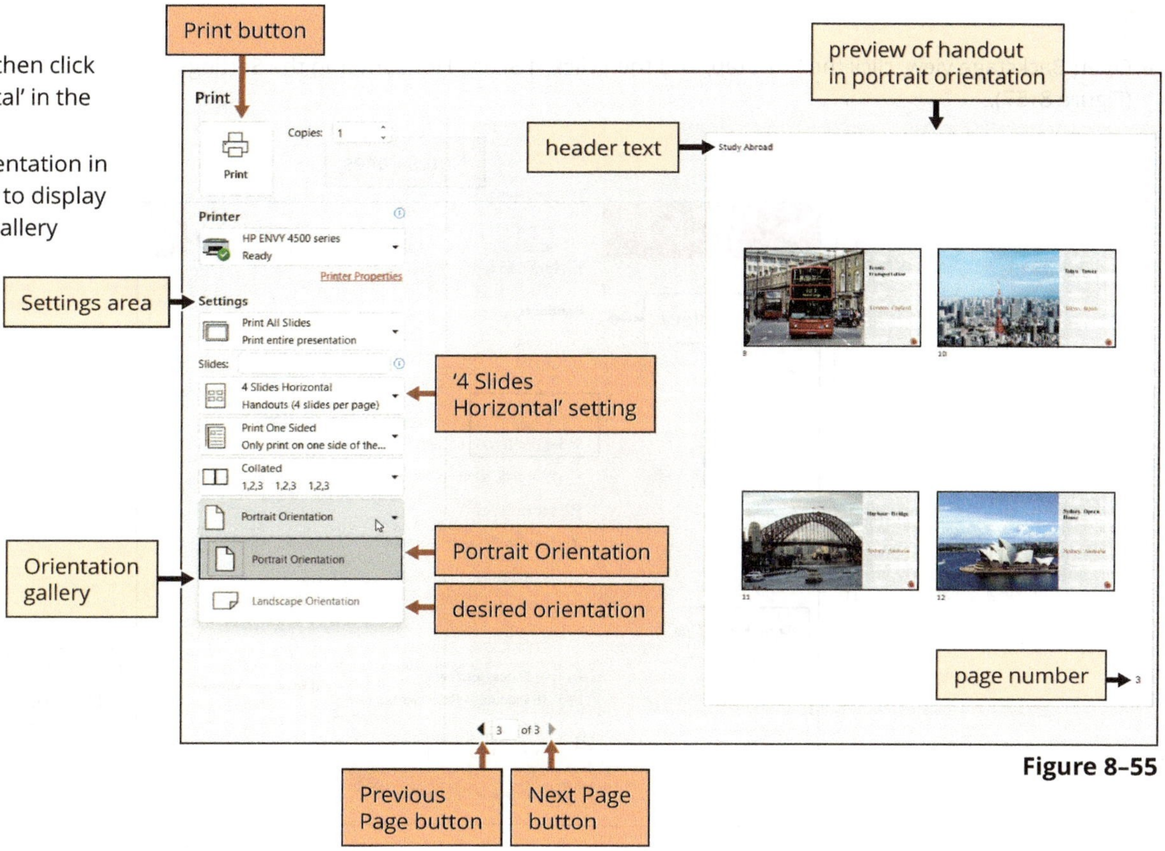

acheemete/Pixabay; scharfsascha/Pixabay; Ledoc/Pixabay; cmmellow/Pixabay

Figure 8–55

4

- Click Landscape Orientation to change the setting.
- Verify that '4 Slides Horizontal' is selected as the option in the Settings area and that the preview shows the header text, page number, and four slides in landscape orientation.
- Click the Previous Page and Next Page buttons to display previews of the other pages and then display Page 1.
- Click the Print button in the Print gallery to print the handout.

Figure 8–56 shows the first page of the printout.

geralt/Pixabay; Rocky Scotty/Unsplash; iankelsall1/Pixabay; Alexas_Fotos/Pixabay; Andrea De Santis/Unsplash

Figure 8–56: Handout in Landscape Orientation – Page 1

BTW
Printing Selections
When you are developing slides or creating handouts for a particular audience, you may not want to print every slide in your presentation. To print specific slides, select the desired slides in the Slide pane. Then, open Backstage view, display the Print tab, click the first button in the Settings area, click Print Selection in the list to specify you want to print the slides you have selected, and then click the Print button in the Print gallery to print these slides.

5

- Open Backstage view, click the Print tab, and then click '4 Slides Horizontal' in the Settings area to display the Print gallery (Figure 8–57).

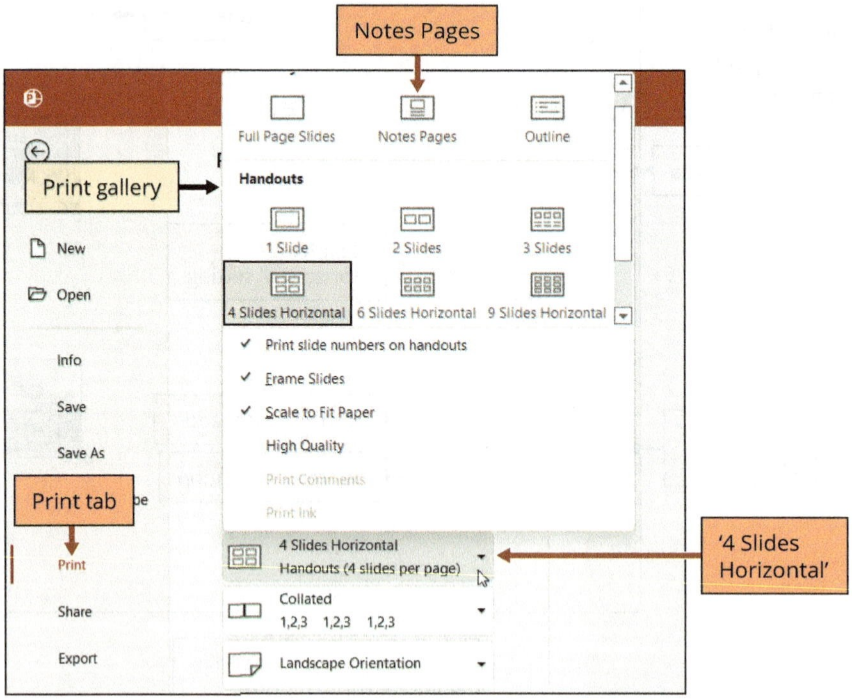

Figure 8–57

6

- Click Notes Pages in the Print Layout area.
- Click Landscape Orientation in the Settings area (Figure 8–58).

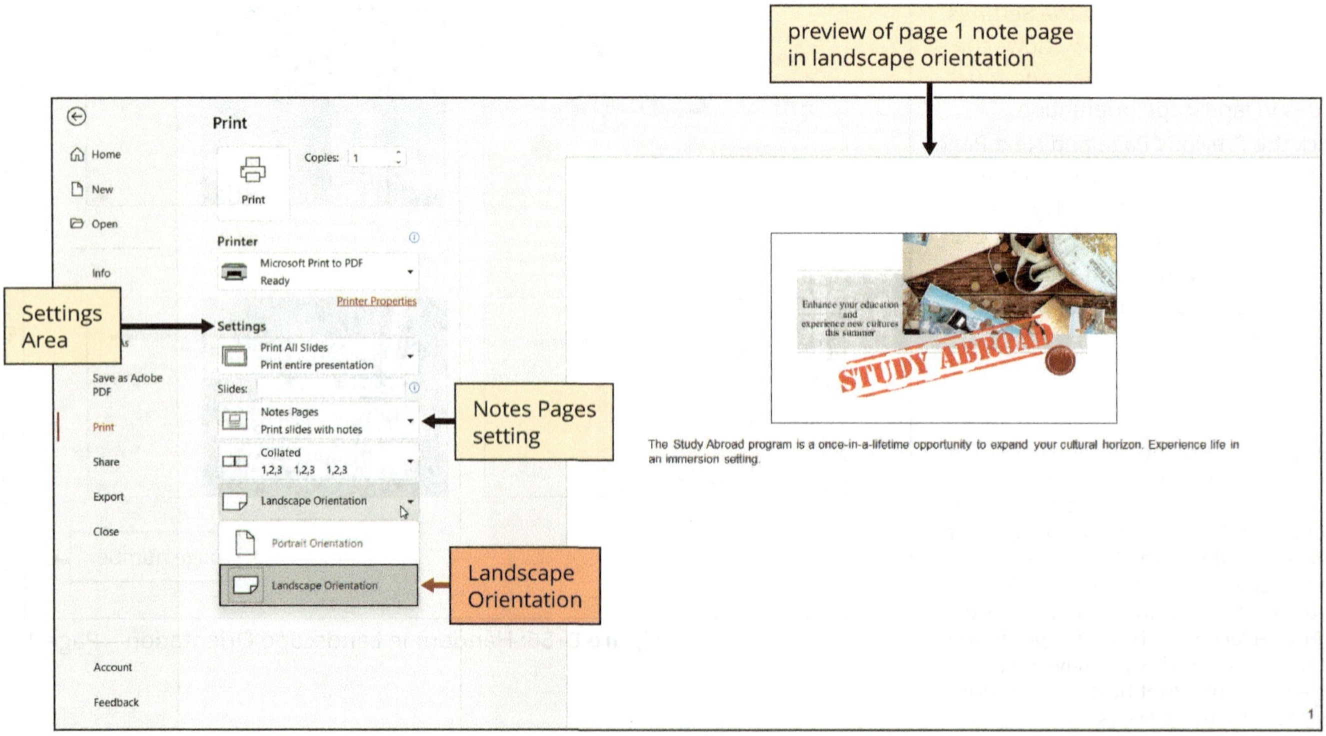

geralt/Pixabay; Rocky Scotty/Unsplash

Figure 8–58

7

- Click Portrait Orientation in the gallery to change the setting.
- Verify that the page preview shows the speaker notes and page number in portrait orientation (Figure 8–59).

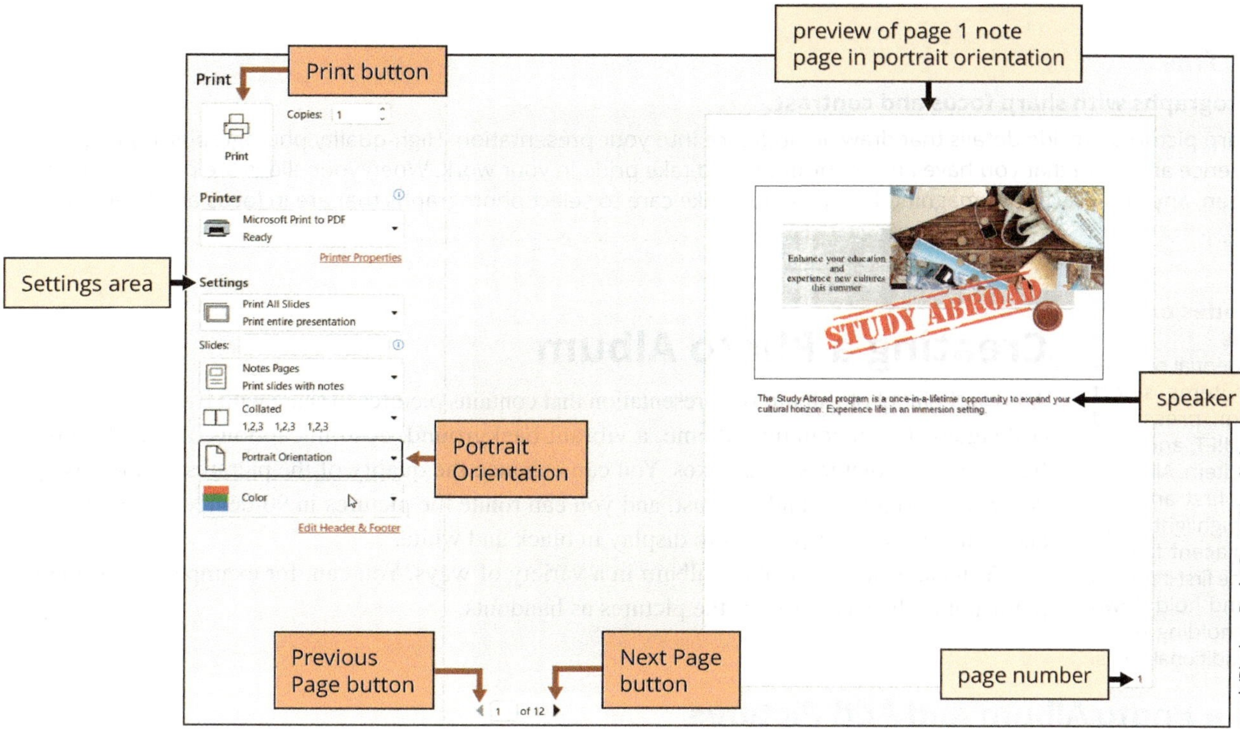

geralt/Pixabay; Rocky Scotty/Unsplash

Figure 8–59

8

- Click the Previous Page and Next Page buttons to display previews of the other pages.
- Click the Print button to print the notes. Figure 8–60 shows the first page of the printout.

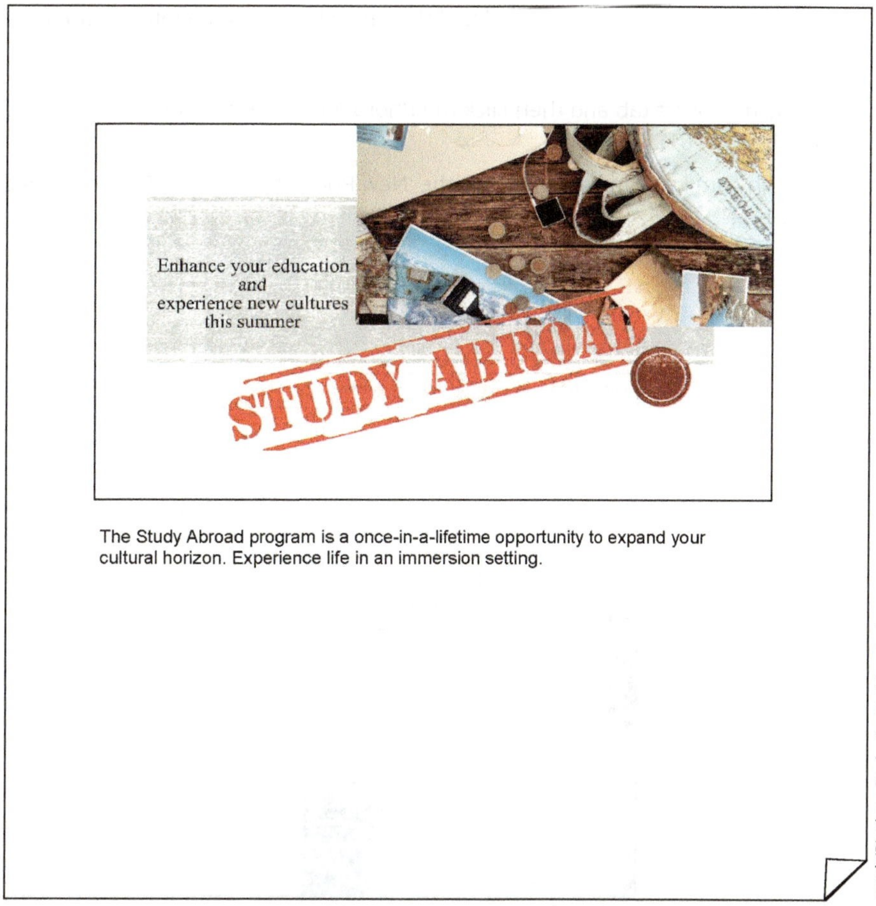

geralt/Pixabay; Rocky Scotty/Unsplash

Figure 8–60: Speaker Notes in Portrait Orientation – Page 1

BTW

Printing in Grayscale

If you desire to keep your images in color but do not have a color printer or do not require a color printout, choosing Grayscale will print all the slide objects in shades of gray. In grayscale, some objects on the slides will appear crisper and cleaner than if you choose the Color option on a non-color printer. Open Backstage view, click the Print tab to display the Print pane, click the Color button in the Settings area, click Grayscale, and then click Print. If you then want to print in color, click the Grayscale button and then click Color.

Break Point: If you wish to take a break, this is a good place to do so. Be sure the Study Abroad file is saved and then you can exit PowerPoint. To resume later, start PowerPoint, open the file called SC_PPT_8_Study_Abroad.pptx, and continue following the steps from this location forward.

Consider This

Use photographs with sharp focus and contrast.

Clear, sharp pictures provide details that draw an audience into your presentation. High-quality photographs impress your audience and state that you have an eye for detail and take pride in your work. When your slides are projected on a large screen, any imperfection is magnified, so you must take care to select photographs that are in focus and have high contrast.

BTW

Selecting Slides or Other Items

To select sequential or adjacent files or items, select the first item, press and hold down SHIFT, and then select the last item. All items between the first and last item will be highlighted. To select nonadjacent files or items, select the first item and then press and hold down CTRL. While holding down CTRL, select additional items.

Creating a Photo Album

A PowerPoint photo album is a presentation that contains pictures to share with friends and business colleagues. It can contain a theme, a vibrant background, custom captions, a specific layout, frames around pictures, and boxes. You can enhance the quality of the pictures by increasing or decreasing brightness and contrast, and you can rotate the pictures in 90-degree increments. You also can change color pictures to display in black and white.

You can share your photo album in a variety of ways. You can, for example, email the file, publish it to the web, or print the pictures as handouts.

To Start a Photo Album and Add Pictures

You initially create the album and then later enhance its appearance. **Why?** Once you have gathered files of digital pictures, you can begin building a photo album. The following steps start a photo album and add pictures.

1

- Display the Insert tab and then click the Photo Album button (Insert tab | Images group) to display the Photo Album dialog box (Figure 8–61).

Q&A Why am I viewing a menu with the 'New Photo Album' and 'Edit Photo Album' commands instead of the Photo Album dialog box?

You mistakenly clicked the 'New Photo Album' arrow instead of the 'New Photo Album' button.

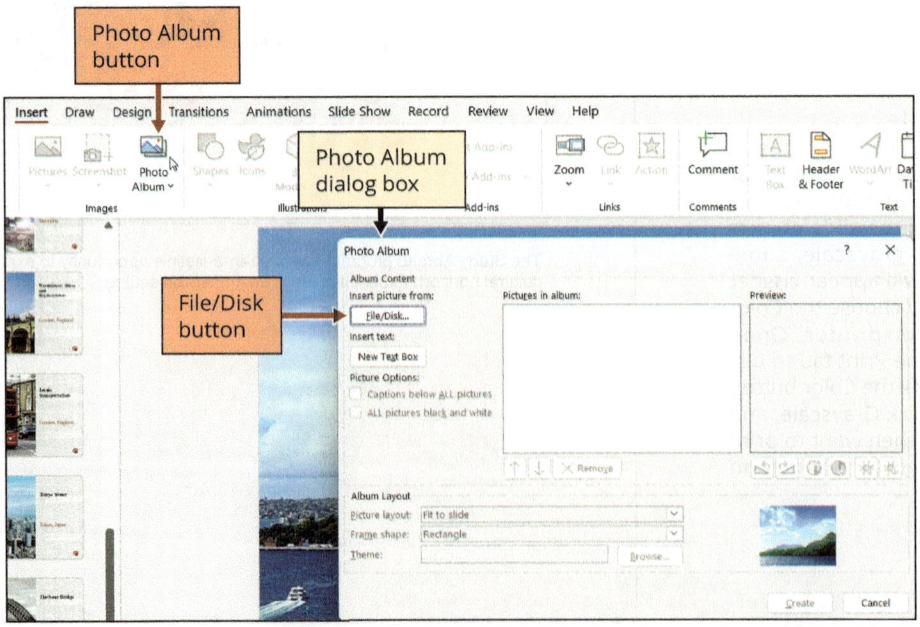

Figure 8–61

2

- Click the File/Disk button to display the 'Insert New Pictures' dialog box.
- If necessary, navigate to the location where your Data Files are stored (Figure 8–62).

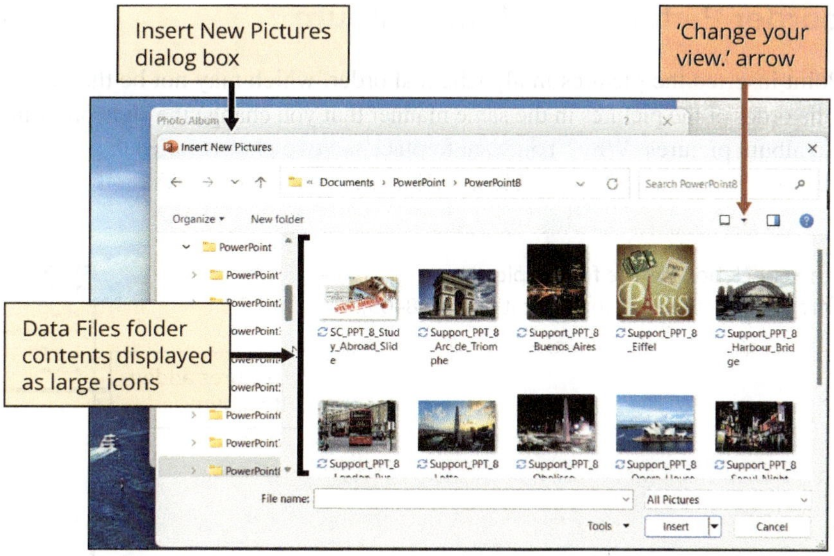

Figure 8–62

iankelsall1/Pixabay; Alexas_Fotos/Pixabay; Andrea De Santis/Unsplash; cmmellow/Pixabay; Gonzalo Kenny/unsplash; matcuz/Pixabay; DUCTINH91/Pixabay; scharfsascha/Pixabay; Pharaoh_EZYPT/Pixabay; Ledoc/Pixabay; acheemete/Pixabay

3

- If necessary, display only the picture file names by clicking the 'Change your view.' arrow (shown in Figure 8–62), on the toolbar ('Insert New Pictures' dialog box) to display the view settings (Figure 8–63).
- Click List in the view settings to change the view setting and display only the picture file names.

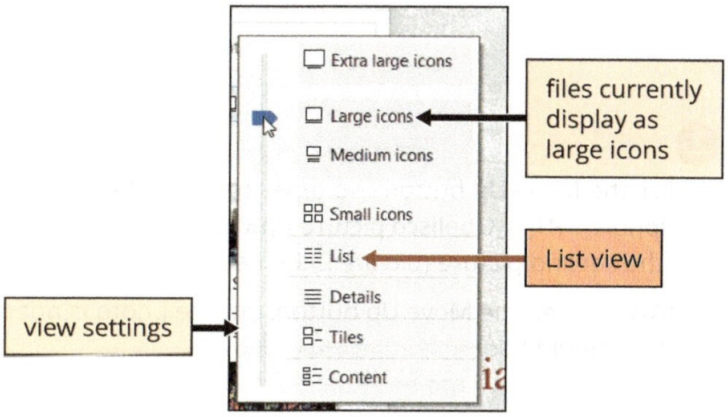

Figure 8–63

4

- Click Support_PPT_8_Buenos_Aires to select the file name. Press and hold down CTRL and then select the file names Support_PPT_8_Harbour_Bridge, Support_PPT_8_Lotte, Support_PPT_8_Obelisco, Support_PPT_8_Opera_House, and Support_PPT_8_Seoul_Night as additional files to insert (Figure 8–64).

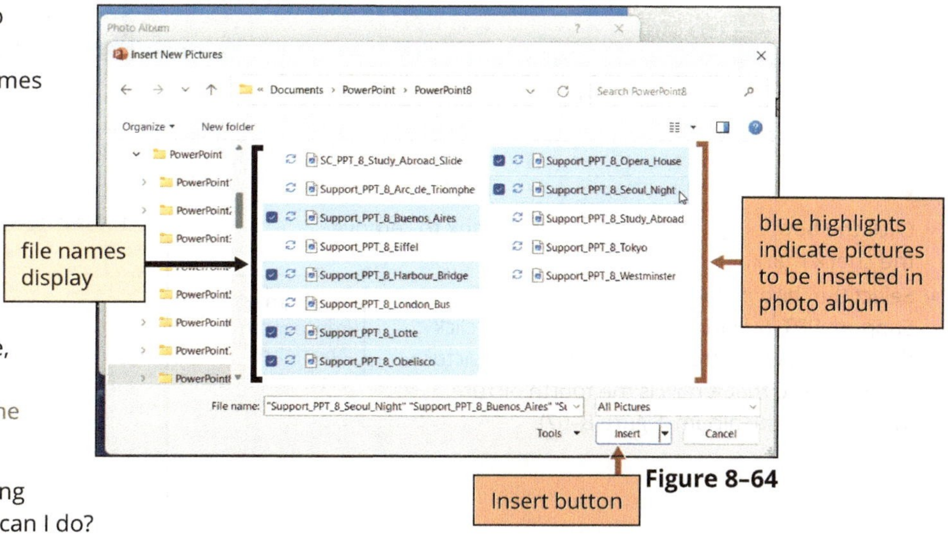

Figure 8–64

Q&A If I mistakenly select a file name, how can I remove the selection?
Click the file name again to remove the check mark.

I'm using a touch screen and am having trouble selecting multiple files. What can I do?
You may need to use a mouse in combination with the onscreen keyboard CTRL, or you can select and insert each file individually.

5

- Click Insert ('Insert New Pictures' dialog box) to add the pictures to the album and display the Photo Album dialog box showing the inserted pictures.

To Reorder Pictures in a Photo Album

PowerPoint inserted the pictures in alphabetical order, which may not be the desired sequence for your album. You easily can change the order of the pictures in the same manner that you change the slide order in a custom show. The following steps reorder the photo album pictures. **Why?** You want to place the two photos for each destination together. For example, you want the two Australia photos (Harbour Bridge and Opera House) to appear adjacent to each other in the middle of the album.

1

- Click the check box for the fourth picture, Support_PPT_8_Obelisco, to select it (Figure 8–65).

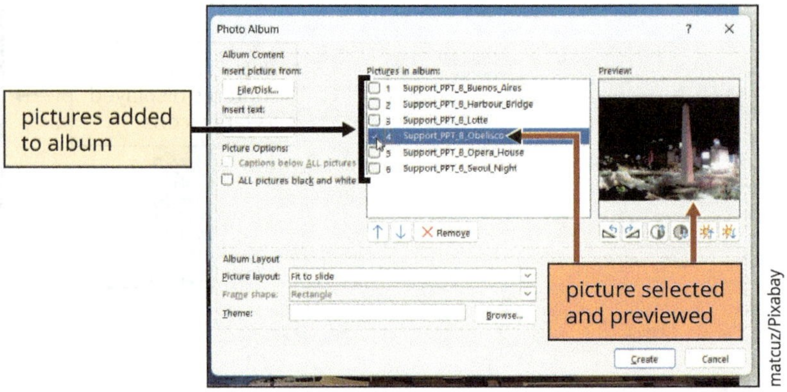

Figure 8–65

2

- Click the Move Up button two times to move the Support_PPT_8_Obelisco picture upward so that it now is the second picture (picture 2) in the album (Figure 8–66).

Q&A I clicked the Move Up button, but the photo is not moving. What should I do?

Be patient. The photo eventually will move.

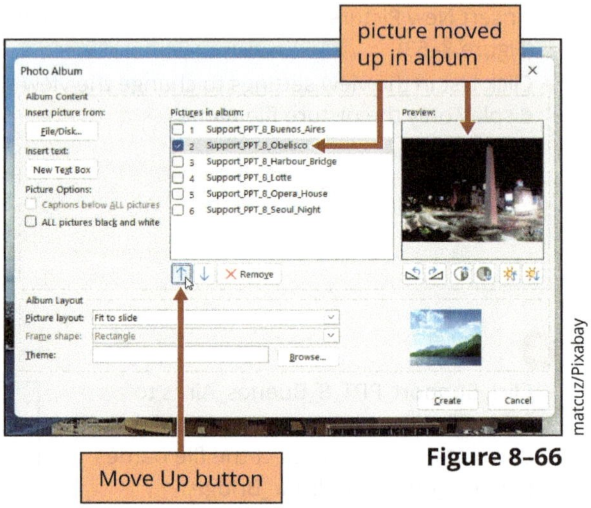

Figure 8–66

3

- Click the Support_PPT_8_Obelisco check box to remove the check mark.
- Select the third picture, Support_PPT_8_Harbour_Bridge, and then click the Move Down button once to move this picture downward so that it now is the fourth picture (picture 4) in the album (Figure 8–67).

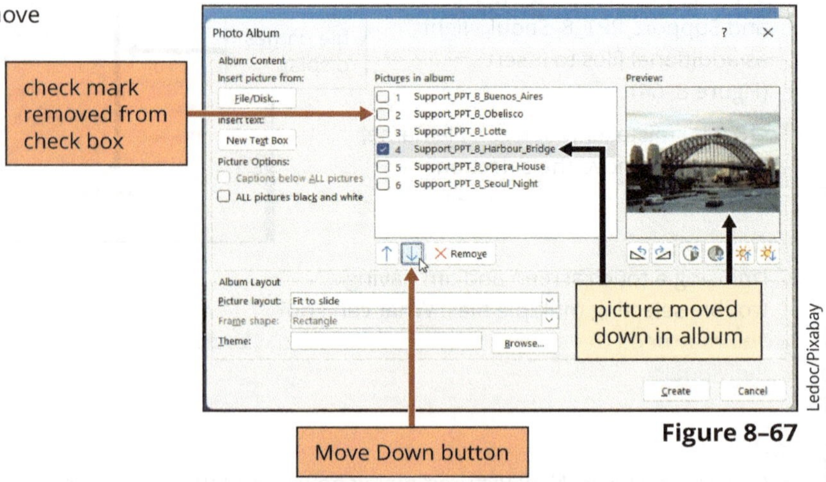

Figure 8–67

4

- Click the Support_PPT_8_Harbour_Bridge check box to remove the check mark.
- Select the third picture, Support_PPT_8_Lotte, and then click the Move Down button three times to move this picture downward so that it now is the last picture (picture 6) in the album.
- Click the Support_PPT_8_Lotte check box to remove the check mark (Figure 8–68).

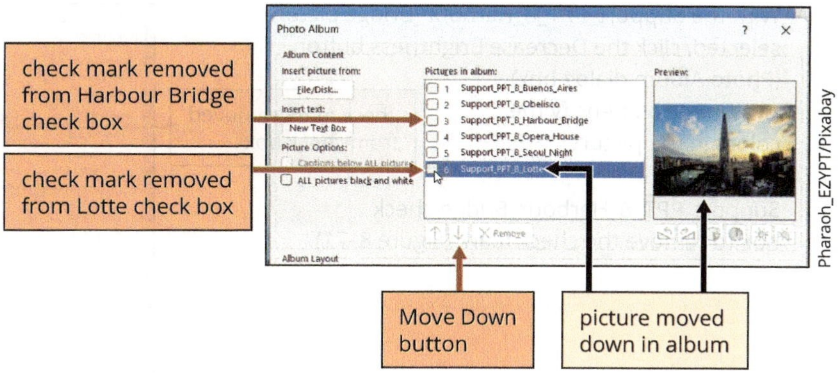

Figure 8–68

To Format Photos in an Album

A picture you insert may need correcting to enhance its visual appeal. You can adjust the difference between the darkest and lightest areas of the picture by increasing or decreasing the contrast. If a picture in the photo album is too light or too dark, you can adjust its brightness to enhance its appearance. The following steps adjust the brightness and contrast of a photo album picture. **Why?** The Harbour Bridge picture is somewhat dark, so increasing the brightness would help the colors stand out on the slide and give more depth to the image. In addition, it lacks contrast and would be more dramatic if it had a wide variety of dark and light regions.

1

- Click the check box for the third picture, Support_PPT_8_Harbour_Bridge, to select it and display a preview (Figure 8–69).

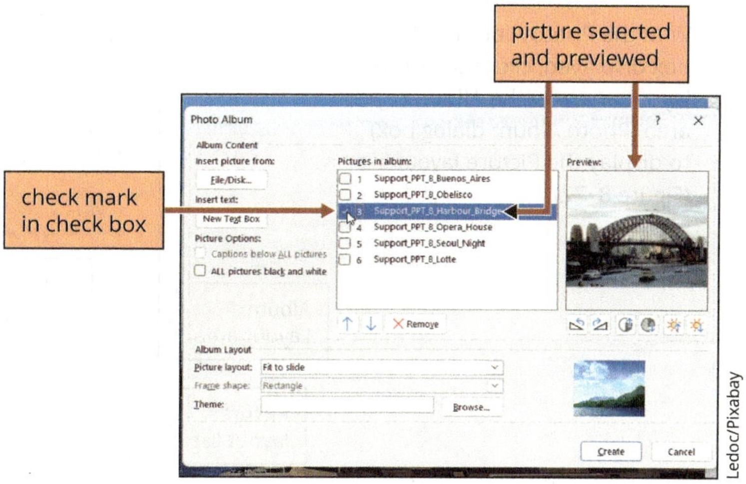

Figure 8–69

2

- Click the Increase Contrast button (Photo Album dialog box) four times to increase the contrast of this picture (Figure 8– 70).

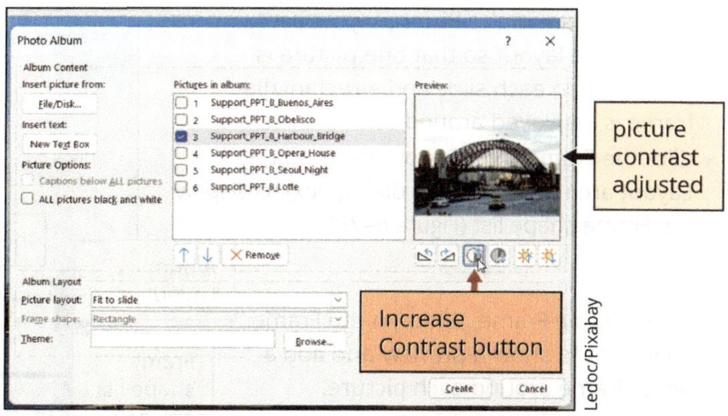

Figure 8–70

3

- With the Support_PPT_8_Harbour_Bridge picture selected, click the Decrease Brightness button (Photo Album dialog box) two times to intensify the colors in the picture.
- Click the Support_PPT_8_Harbour_Bridge check box to remove the check mark (Figure 8–71).

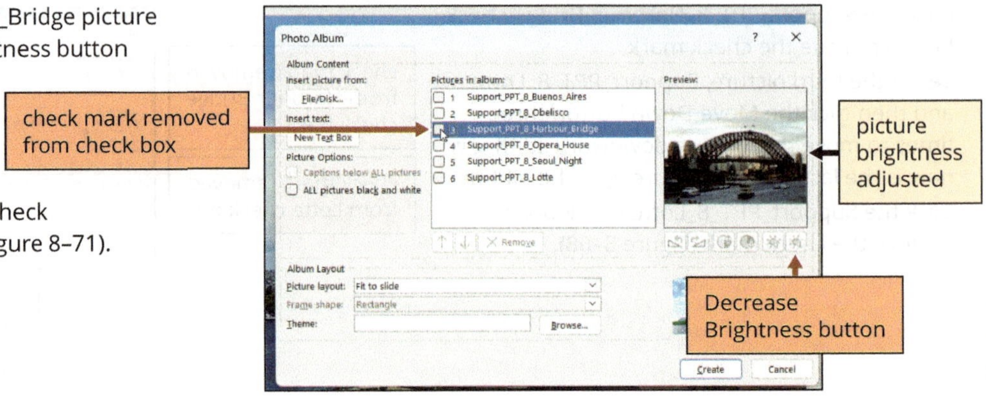

Ledoc/Pixabay

Figure 8–71

To Change a Photo Album Layout

PowerPoint inserts each photo album picture so that it fills, or fits, one entire slide. You can modify this layout to display two or four pictures on a slide, display a title, or add white space between the image and the slide edges. You also can add a white or black frame around the perimeter of each picture. The following steps change an album layout. **Why?** You want to display only one picture on each slide so that you can discuss each destination thoroughly during your presentation. Adding a frame provides contrast between the photos and the background.

1

- With the Photo Album dialog box displayed, click the Picture layout arrow in the Album Layout area (Photo Album dialog box) to display the Picture layout list (Figure 8–72).

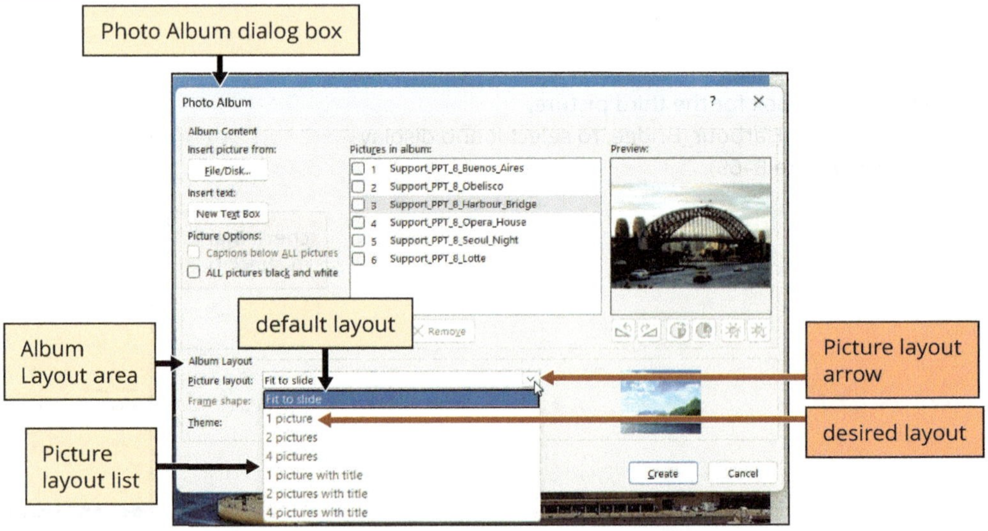

Ledoc/Pixabay

Figure 8–72

2

- Click 1 picture in the Picture layout list to change the layout so that one picture is displayed on each slide and a rectangular frame is displayed around each picture.
- Click the Frame shape arrow in the Album Layout area (Photo Album dialog box) to display the Frame shape list (Figure 8–73).

3

- Click 'Simple Frame, White' in the Frame shape list to show a preview and add a white frame around each picture.

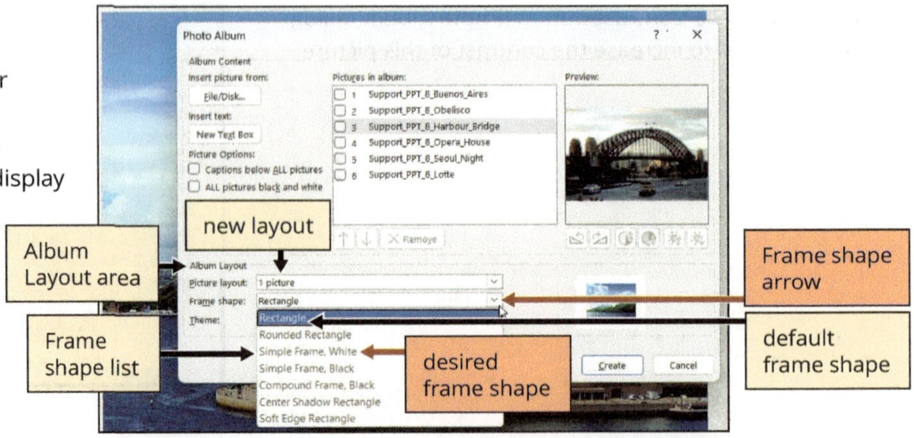

Ledoc/Pixabay

Figure 8–73

To Add a Photo Album Theme

The themes that are used to design a presentation also are available to add to a photo album. These themes determine the colors and fonts that complement each other and increase the visual appeal of the slides. The following steps add a theme to the photo album. **Why?** You want to select a simple theme that has an uncluttered layout and font that will complement the pictures.

1

- Click the Browse button in the Album Layout area (Photo Album dialog box) to display the Choose Theme dialog box.
- Click Organic in the theme list to select this theme (Figure 8–74).

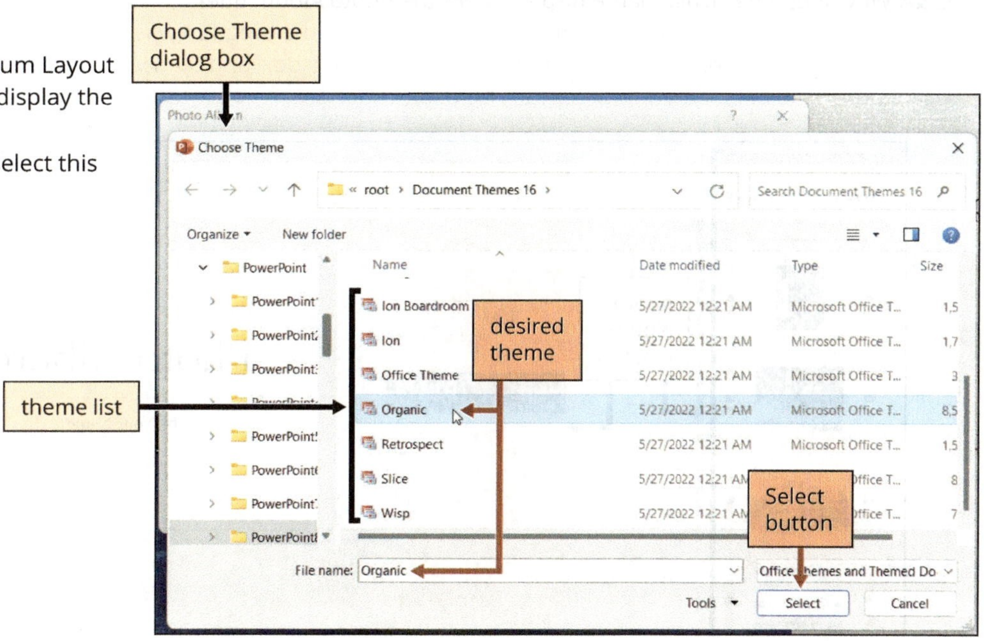

Figure 8–74

2

- Click the Select button (Choose Theme dialog box) to apply this theme to the presentation (Figure 8–75).

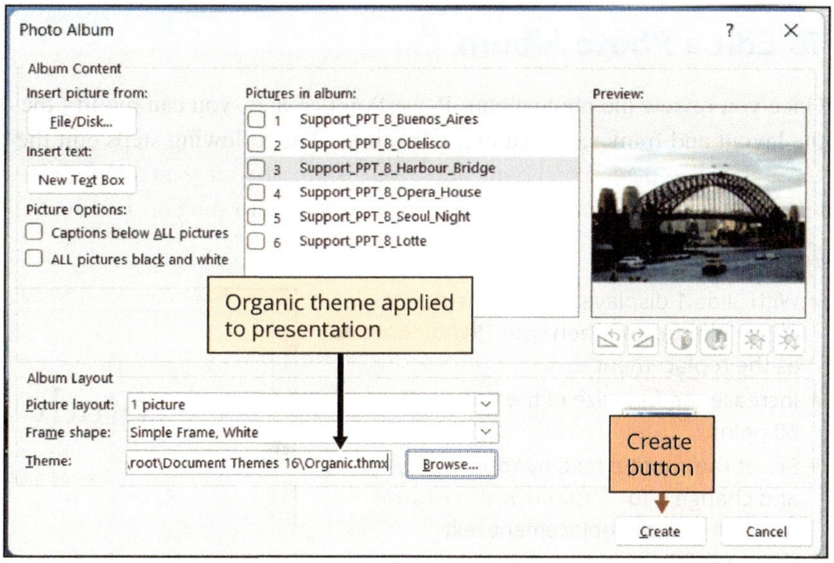

Ledoc/Pixabay

Figure 8–75

To Create a Photo Album

Once you have inserted the pictures and determined the picture sequence, layout, frame shape, and theme, you are ready to make the photo album. **Why?** You have specified all the information PowerPoint needs to create this album. The following step creates the photo album.

1

- Click the Create button (Photo Album dialog box) to close the dialog box and create a photo album with a title slide and six pictures (Figure 8–76).
- If the Design Ideas pane is displayed, close it.

Q&A Why does a particular name display below the Photo Album title?
PowerPoint displays the user name that was entered when the program was installed. To see this name, display Backstage view, click Options to display the 'PowerPoint Options' dialog box, and then view or change the name entered in the User name box in the Personalize your copy of Microsoft Office area.

Figure 8–76

To Edit a Photo Album

Once you review the photo album PowerPoint creates, you can modify the contents by adding and deleting pictures, changing the layout and frames, and adding transitions. The following steps edit the photo album. **Why?** The Organic theme has black accent lines on the left and right sides of the slide, so you want a black picture frame to coordinate with this slide element. You also want to add the Page Curl transition that relates to students turning pages in a book.

1

- With Slide 1 displayed, select the title text, Photo Album, and then type **Study Abroad** as the replacement text.
- Increase the font size of the title text to 60 point.
- Select the subtitle text, by Your Name, and change it to **Expand your cultural horizon** as the replacement text (Figure 8–77).

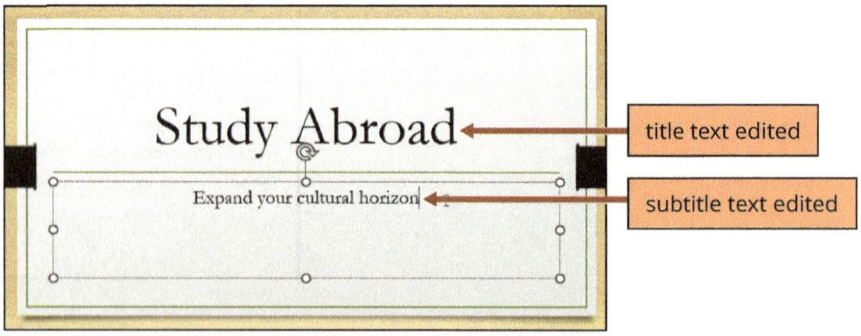

Figure 8–77

2

- Display the Insert tab and then click the Photo Album arrow (Insert tab | Images group) to display the Photo Album menu (Figure 8–78).

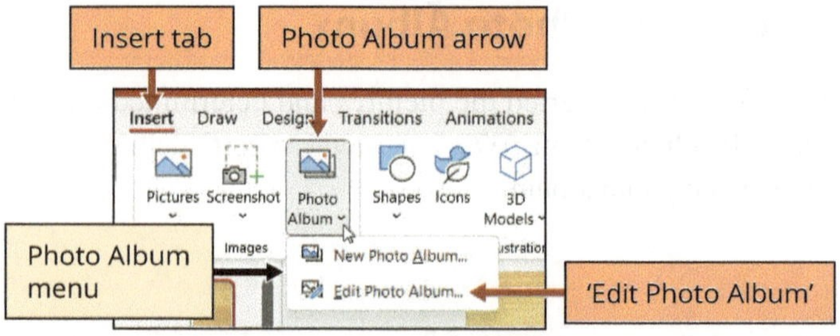

Figure 8–78

3

- Click 'Edit Photo Album' in the menu to display the 'Edit Photo Album' dialog box.
- Click the Frame shape arrow to display the Frame shape list and then click 'Compound Frame, Black' in the list to change the frame from a single white border to a double black border (Figure 8–79).

4

- Click the Update button (Edit Photo Album dialog box) to make the frame change to the photo album.
- If the Design Ideas pane displays, close it.
- Apply the Page Curl transition and then change the duration to 03.00 seconds for all slides.
- Save the file using **SC_PPT_8_Photo_Album** as the file name.
- Close the SC_PPT_8_Photo_Album presentation to return to the open Study Abroad presentation.

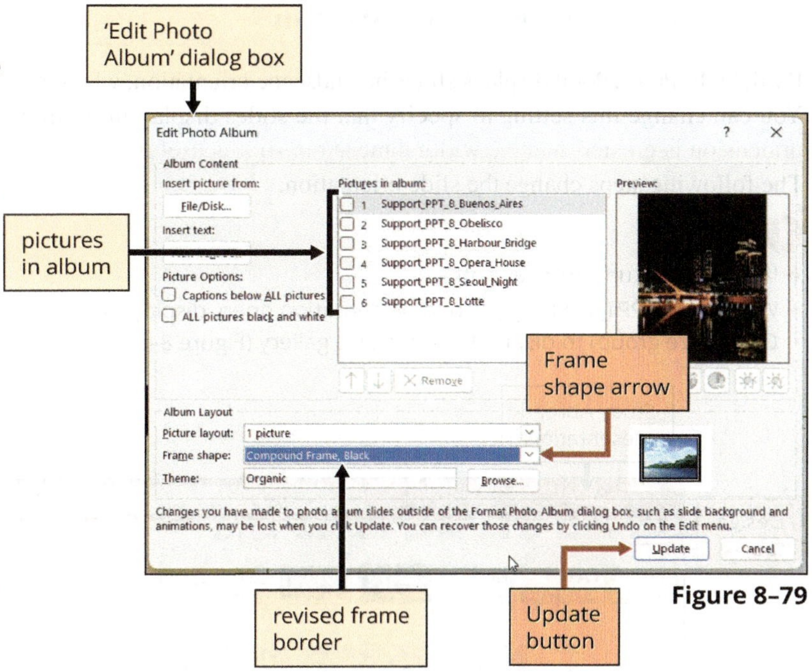

Gonzalo Kenny/unsplash

Figure 8–79

Modifying and Presenting Slides

PowerPoint's default settings generally suffice for most presentations. At times, however, the slide content can be presented more effectively in a different perspective or resolution. You easily can modify these settings to tailor the slides to your specific needs. In addition, many designers create one comprehensive slide deck and then elect to display particular parts of that file when presenting to varied audiences. They create a **summary zoom** slide as the first slide in their presentation, which allows them to jump to a specific slide or section and then return to this initial slide.

Speakers often deliver a presentation using two monitors: one to display their speaker notes privately, and a second to display the slides and project them on a large screen for the audience to view. PowerPoint's **Presenter view** supports the use of two monitors connected to one computer so presenters can view the slide currently being projected while viewing the slide thumbnails, seeing a preview of the next slide or animation, reading their speaker notes, viewing the elapsed time, lightening or darkening the audience's screen, or customizing the presentation by skipping the next slide or reviewing a slide previously displayed. A computer must support the use of multiple monitors and must be configured to use this feature.

BTW
Zoom Availability
Zoom for PowerPoint is available only in Microsoft 365 and PowerPoint 2019 and later. Summary zoom also is supported for Microsoft 365 for Mac.

BTW
Speaker Coach
PowerPoint Speaker Coach (called Presenter Coach in some earlier versions of PowerPoint) can help you become a more confident presenter. It uses AI to give feedback about a speaker's body language, including eye contact and distance from the camera. Also, it identifies repeated words and phrases and provides a list of synonyms. Another feature detects perceived mispronounced words. This feedback is detailed in a Summary Report provided at the end of each rehearsal, and it includes statistics and suggested recommendations. To rehearse your presentation with Speaker Coach, click the Slide Show tab, click the 'Rehearse with Coach' button (Slide Show tab | Rehearse group), and then click Get Started.

Consider This

Use hyperlinks to show slides with landscape and portrait orientations.

When you are creating your presentation, you have the option to display all your slides in either the default landscape orientation or portrait orientation. You may, however, desire to have slides with both orientations during a single presentation. Using hyperlinks is one solution to mixing the orientations. Apply a hyperlink to an object on the last slide in one orientation and then hyperlink to another presentation with slides in the other orientation. If you desire to hyperlink to one particular slide in a second presentation, click the Bookmark button in the Insert Hyperlink dialog box and then select the title of the slide you want to use as your link. Once you have displayed the desired slides in the second presentation, create another hyperlink from that presentation back to a slide in your original presentation.

To Change the Slide Orientation

By default, PowerPoint displays slides in landscape orientation, where the width dimension is greater than the height dimension. You can change this setting to specify that the slides display in portrait orientation. **Why?** In portrait orientation, the height dimension is greater than the width dimension, so it is useful to display tall objects, people who are standing, or monuments. The following steps change the slide orientation.

1

- If necessary, turn AutoSave off.
- With the SC_PPT_8_Study_Abroad presentation open, display the Design tab and then click the Slide Size button (Design tab | Customize group) to display the Slide Size gallery (Figure 8–80).

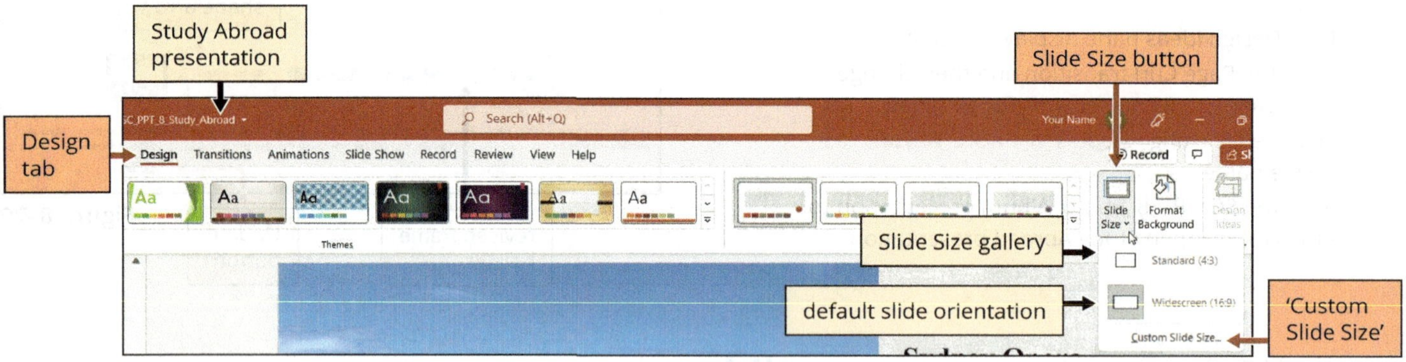

Figure 8–80

2

- Click 'Custom Slide Size' to display the Slide Size dialog box and then click Portrait in the Slides area of the Orientation section to change the slide orientation from Landscape to Portrait (Figure 8–81).

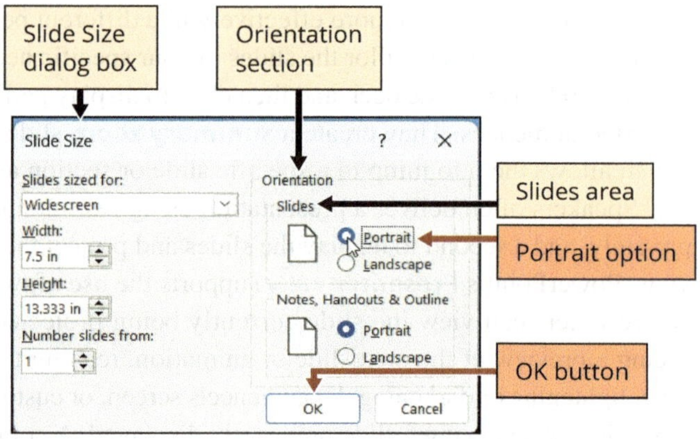

Figure 8–81

3

- Click OK to display the Microsoft PowerPoint dialog box (Figure 8–82).

4

- Click Ensure Fit to scale the slide content to fit on each slide.

Q&A I see an Ensure Fit icon and an Ensure Fit button. Can I click either one to scale the slide content?
Yes.

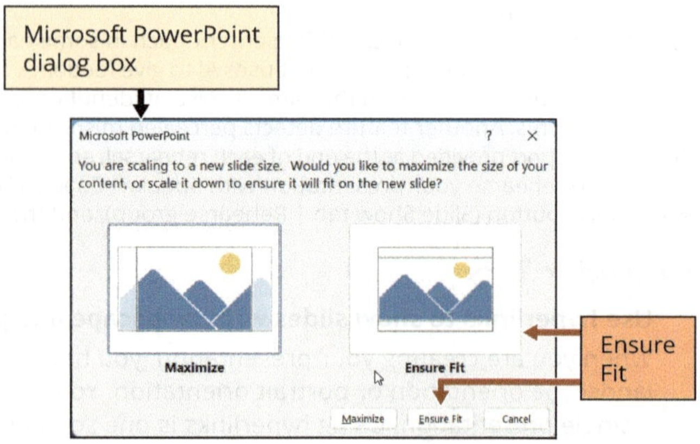

Figure 8–82

To Change the Slide Show Resolution

Screen resolution affects the number of pixels that are displayed on your screen. When screen resolution is increased, more information is displayed, but it is decreased in size. Conversely, when screen resolution is decreased, less information is displayed, but that information is increased in size. You can change the resolution you want to use to display your presentation. This feature is valuable when your computer is connected to two different monitors, when you are delivering your presentation using a computer other than the one used to create the slides, or when the projector does not support the resolution you specified when you saved the presentation. Throughout this book, the screen resolution has been set to 1920 × 1080. The following steps change the presentation resolution to 1360 × 768. **Why?** You may need to run your presentation on a monitor that has a different resolution.

1

- Display the Slide Show tab and then click the 'Set Up Slide Show' button (Slide Show tab | Set Up group) to display the 'Set Up Show' dialog box.

2

- If necessary, click the 'Slide show monitor' arrow in the Multiple monitors section and then choose Primary Monitor.
- Click the Resolution arrow in the Multiple monitors section to display the Resolution list (Figure 8–83).

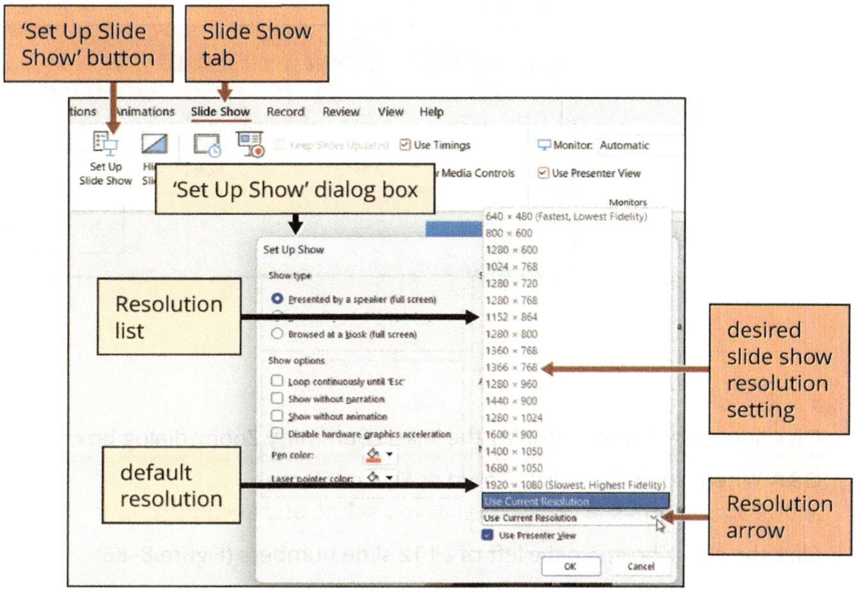

Figure 8–83

3

- Click 1360 × 768 (or a similar resolution) to change the slide show resolution setting.
- If necessary, click the 'Use Presenter View' check box to clear the check box (Figure 8–84).

Q&A What is Presenter view?
When you use Presenter view, you control the slide show using one screen only you can see, but your audience views the slides on another main screen.

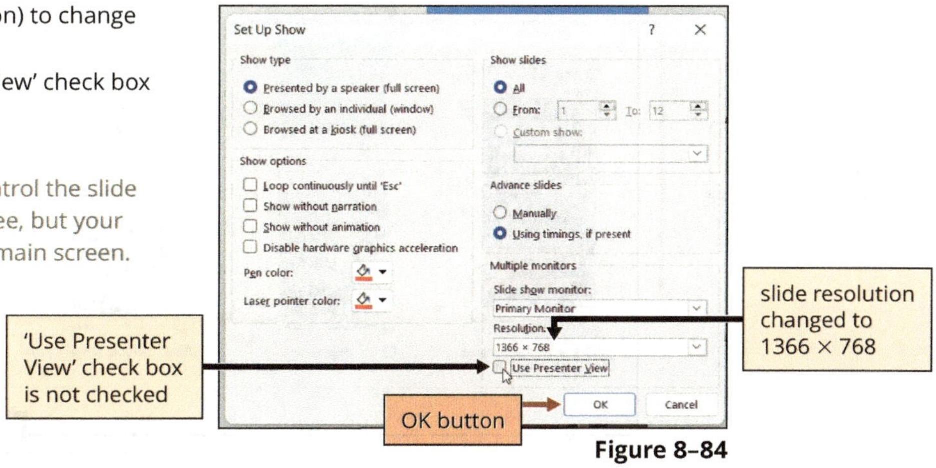

Figure 8–84

4

- Click OK to close the 'Set Up Show' dialog box and apply the new resolution to the slides.
- Save the presentation using **SC_PPT_8_Study_Abroad_Portrait** as the file name.

To Insert a Summary Zoom Slide

Speakers often use their PowerPoint files in many venues for different types of audiences. They may, for example, need to condense the presentation and display only a few slides when time is short. Or, in another situation, the audience may be familiar with the topic and need to know only specific information located on slides near the end of the slide deck. When a Zoom is created in PowerPoint, a speaker can decide which slides, sections, and portions of a presentation to display in a nonlinear way depending upon the audience's needs. The following steps insert a summary zoom slide in the SC_PPT_8_Study_Abroad_Portrait file. **Why?** When this slide is displayed during the presentation, you will see thumbnails of all the slides on one slide and then interactively can decide which slide to display next in any order.

1

- Display the Insert tab and then click the Zoom button (Insert tab | Links group) to display the Zoom menu (Figure 8–85).

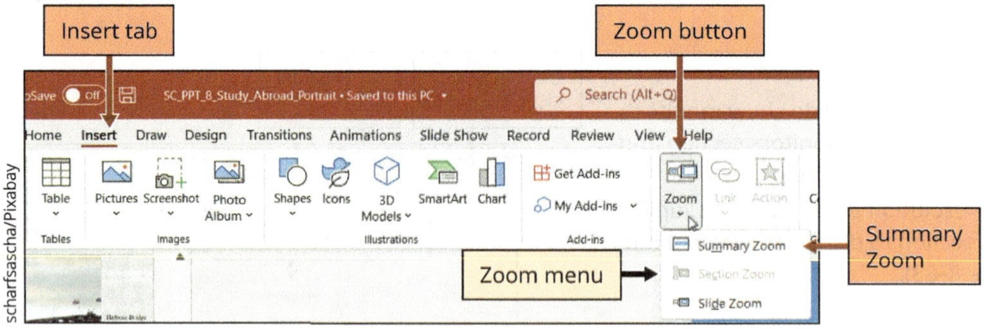

Figure 8–85

2

- Click Summary Zoom to display the 'Insert Summary Zoom' dialog box.

Q&A When would I use Slide Zoom or Section Zoom?
Slide Zoom shows specific slides that you select, and Section Zoom shows slides contained in a single section.

- Click the check boxes to the left of all 12 slide numbers (Figure 8–86).

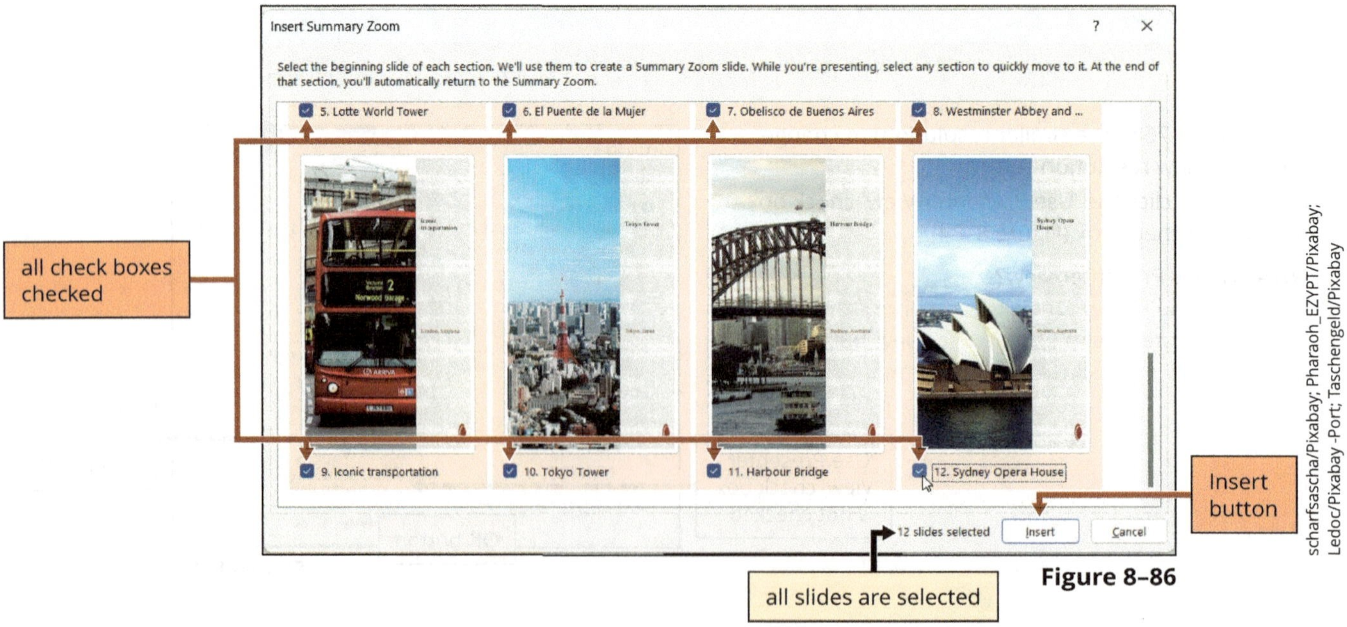

Figure 8–86

BTW
Updating Summary Zoom
If you make changes to your presentation after you have created the summary zoom, you can update the summary zoom by clicking the Edit Summary button (Zoom tab | Zoom Options), selecting the sections you want to include in your summary zoom, and then clicking the Update button.

3

- Click the Insert button ('Insert Summary Zoom' dialog box) to create the summary zoom slide and insert it as a new Slide 1 in the slide deck.
- Click the text box at the top of the summary zoom slide and then type **Study Abroad** as the slide title.
- Change the font to Times New Roman, increase the font size to 48 point, and then center the title (Figure 8–87).

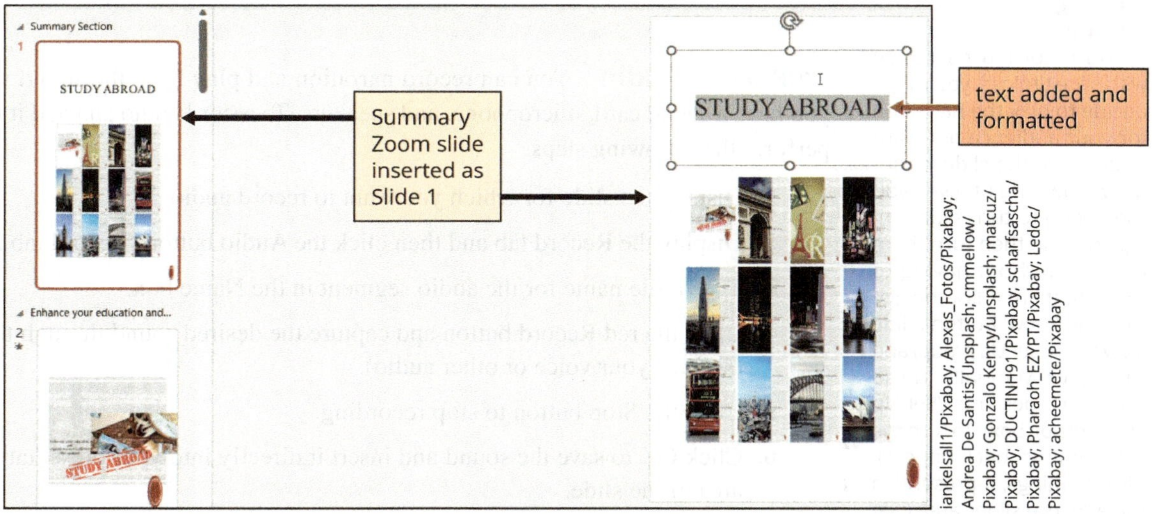

iankelsall1/Pixabay; Alexas_Fotos/Pixabay; Andrea De Santis/Unsplash; cmmellow/ Pixabay; Gonzalo Kenny/unsplash; matcuz/ Pixabay; DUCTINH91/Pixabay; scharfsascha/ Pixabay; Pharaoh_EZYPT/Pixabay; Ledoc/ Pixabay; acheemete/Pixabay

Figure 8–87

4

- Save the presentation again.

Consider This

Rehearse, rehearse, rehearse.

Speakers should spend as much time practicing their presentations as they do preparing their PowerPoint slides. Frequently, however, they use the majority of their preparation time designing and tweaking the slides. Audience members expect to see a presenter who is prepared, confident, and enthusiastic. Practicing the presentation helps convey this image. As you rehearse, focus on a strong introduction that grasps the audience's attention and previews the main points of your talk. You have only one chance to make a good first impression, so begin the speech by establishing eye contact with audience members in various parts of the room. Resist the urge to stare at the slides projected on the screen. Consider rehearsing using PowerPoint's Speaker Coach to help you deliver a high-quality talk that exceeds your audience's expectations.

To Create and Insert Screen Recordings You can create screen recordings in your PowerPoint presentations if you have a sound card, microphone, and speakers. To create and insert a screen recording in your presentation, you would perform the following steps.

1. Display the slide you would like to record at the beginning of the presentation.
2. Display the Record tab and then click the Screen Recording button (Record tab | Record group).
3. Select an area of your screen to record and then click the Record button.
4. Capture the desired information, including voice narrations, slide timings, and pointer gestures.

5. When you have finished recording, click the Stop button and save the presentation.
6. The recording is directly inserted into your presentation in the desired area of the slide

Other Ways

1. Display Insert tab, click Screen Recording button (Insert tab | Media group), select area to record, click Record button, capture information, click Stop

BTW
Turning Off Slide Timings
If you recorded narration with slide timings, you might decide to play the narration for your audience but want to advance the slides manually. PowerPoint gives you the option to turn slide timings off and then turn them back on without having to recreate them. Click the 'Set Up Slide Show' button (Slide Show tab | Set Up group) and then click Manually in the Advance slides area ('Set Up Show' dialog box). To turn the slide timings back on, click 'Using timings, if present' in the Advance slides area ('Set Up Show' dialog box).

BTW
Using Reading View
Most people reviewing a PowerPoint presentation without a presenter will want to use Reading view. It displays the presentation in a full screen like Slide Show view, and it includes a few simple controls to make it easy to flip through the slides.

BTW
Using Your Mouse as a Laser Pointer
When you are presenting, you can emphasize an important point in your slide by using your mouse as a laser pointer. In Slide Show view, click either the From Beginning or the 'From Current Slide' button (Slide Show tab | Start Slide Show group), press and hold CTRL, and then click and drag the left mouse button to point to specific slide contents. To change the laser pointer color, click the 'Set Up Slide Show' button (Slide Show tab | Set Up group) to display the 'Set Up Show' dialog box. Then, in the Show options area, click the 'Laser pointer color' button, select the desired color in the gallery, and then click OK.

To Record Audio You can record narration and play back the sound within PowerPoint if you have a sound card, microphone, and speakers. To record audio and add it to a slide, you would perform the following steps.

1. Display the slide for which you want to record audio.
2. Display the Record tab and then click the Audio button (Record tab | Record group).
3. Type a file name for the audio segment in the Name box.
4. Click the red Record button and capture the desired sound through the microphone (such as your voice or other audio).
5. Click the Stop button to stop recording.
6. Click OK to save the sound and insert it directly into your presentation in the desired area of the slide.
7. Drag the audio icon to the desired location on the slide.

Other Ways

1. Display Insert tab, click Audio button (Insert tab | Media group), click Record Audio (Insert tab | Media group), type file name, click Record button, capture sound, click Stop

To Display All Slides in Presenter View Presenter view allows a speaker to use dual monitors: one that displays what the audience is seeing, and another with controls to aid the presenter. You can rehearse using Presenter view with one monitor so that you are comfortable using the features. You will not be able to edit the slides while using Presenter view. To use Presenter view, you would perform the following steps.

1. Display the Slide Show tab and then if necessary click the 'Use Presenter View' check box to place a check in the box (Slide Show tab | Monitors group).
2. Press ALT+F5.

To Zoom Using the Magnifying Glass in Presenter View While using Presenter view, you can magnify part of the slide on the screen. When you click the magnifying glass icon, a bright rectangle is displayed on the slide and the mouse pointer changes to a hand. To zoom using this magnifying glass, you would perform the following steps.

1. In Slide Show view, click the magnifying glass icon in the Control bar on the lower edge of Presenter view.
2. Position your mouse pointer over the area of the slide that you want to magnify and then click to zoom in on that location.
3. Press ESC or click the magnifying glass icon again to turn off the zoom effect.

To Run a Presentation with Slide Zoom Links

All changes are complete. You now can view the Study Abroad Portrait presentation with zoom links. The following steps run the slide show.

1. Display Slide 1 and then run the presentation.
2. Click the Eiffel Tower slide to display it and then click the slide to return to Slide 1.
3. Click the title slide and then click this slide to return to Slide 1.
4. Continue displaying the slides in the presentation using the summary zoom slide. When the last slide (Sydney Opera House) is displayed, press ESC to end the presentation.

To Save the Presentation

With the presentation completed, you should save the file. The following steps save the Study Abroad Portrait file and then exit PowerPoint.

1. Save the presentation again in the same storage location with the same file name.
2. Because the project now is complete, you can exit PowerPoint.

BTW

Using a Laser Pointer on a Smartphone

You can use your smartphone as a laser pointer. Open the file in Presenter view on your mobile device and then emphasize content with the laser pointer. This feature requires that your smartphone has a gyroscope. If you do not have a Microsoft 365 subscription or your phone does not have a gyroscope, you still can use the laser pointer by pressing and holding on the slide area and moving your finger around the slide.

Summary

In this module, you learned how to create a custom slide show by selecting specific slides and then reordering their sequence. You also saved a slide as a .jpg file and saved a presentation as a PowerPoint show. You created handouts by exporting the file to Word and customized handouts and notes pages. You checked the presentation for compatibility and accessibility and then protected it with a password. Next, you created a photo album, formatted a photo, and changed the album theme and slide borders. Finally, you modified the slide show orientation and resolution and inserted a summary zoom slide.

Consider This: Plan Ahead

What decisions will you need to make when creating your next presentation?

Use these guidelines as you complete the assignments in this module and create your own slide show decks outside of this class.

1. **Use secure passwords.** A password should be at least 8 characters and contain a combination of letters, numbers, and other characters. Using both uppercase and lowercase letters is advised. Do not use a password that someone could guess, such as your first or last name, spouse's or child's name, telephone number, birth date, street address, license plate number, or Social Security number. Once you develop this password, write it down in a secure place. Underneath your keyboard is not a secure place, nor is your middle desk drawer. You also can use a password manager program for added security.
2. **Use photographs with sharp focus and contrast.** The adage, "A picture is worth a thousand words," is relevant in a PowerPoint presentation. When your audience can see a visual representation of the concept you are describing during your talk, they are apt to understand and comprehend your message. Be certain your pictures are sharp and clear.
3. **Use hyperlinks to show slides with landscape and portrait orientations.** All slides in one presentation must display in either landscape or portrait orientation. If you want to have variety in your slide show or have pictures or graphics that display best in one orientation, consider using hyperlinks to mix the two orientations during your presentation.
4. **Rehearse, rehearse, rehearse.** Outstanding slides lose their value when the presenter is unprepared to speak. Always keep in mind that the visual aspects are meant to supplement a speaker's verbal message. Practice your presentation before different types of audiences to solicit feedback and use their comments to improve your speaking style. You also can use PowerPoint's Speaker Coach to obtain a critique and suggested recommendations.

Student Assignments

Apply Your Knowledge

Reinforce the skills and apply the concepts you learned in this module.

Creating a Custom Show and Notes

Note: To complete this assignment, you will be required to use the Data Files. Please contact your instructor for information about accessing the Data Files.

Instructions: Start PowerPoint. Open the presentation called SC_PPT_8-1.pptx, which is located in the Data Files.

Nature centers rely upon and value volunteers to help care for their valuable resources. These people give back to their communities by offering their time and skills while enjoying the mental and physical benefits of being outdoors. They can help in many ways, such as removing invasive species, planting and mulching trees, or leading a family-friendly seminar. Your local nature center's naturalists want to inform the community about the programs available for all ages. You have received a PowerPoint presentation with 10 slides, and you need to develop two custom shows and the notes shown in Figure 8–88.

Perform the following tasks:

1. Create a custom slide show with slides 1, 2, 4, 6, 7, and 8.
2. Type **Restore the forest** as the new custom show name.
3. Edit the custom show by moving the last slide (6. Prune a tree) up below the third slide (3. Restore the forest) and the second slide (2. Volunteers make a difference) down to the end of the custom show.
4. Create a second custom show with slides 1, 3, 5, 11, and 12.
5. Type **Share your knowledge** as the new custom show name (Figure 8–88a).
6. Edit the custom show by moving Slide 3 (3. Help our feathered friends) down to the end of the custom show.
7. Display the notes master. Change the font to Arial Black-Arial and do not display the date.
8. Display the notes page in Landscape orientation and then print the notes pages (Figure 8–88b).
9. Create a handout in Word with notes below the slides. Save the Word file using the file name, **SC_PPT_8_Volunteer_Word** (Figure 8–88c).
10. Save Slide 2 as a .jpg picture using the file name, **SC_PPT_8_Volunteer_Slide** (Figure 8–88d). If requested by your instructor, insert the day of the week you were born after the word, swim, in the title text placeholder on the last slide.
11. Insert a summary zoom slide with all 12 slides in the presentation. Type **Become a Volunteer** as the title text for the new slide and then center this text in the placeholder (Figure 8–88e).
12. Check the presentation accessibility and compatibility.
13. Run the presentation using the summary zoom slide to display various slides.
14. Run the presentation showing the two custom slide shows.
15. Save the presentation using the file name, **SC_PPT_8_Volunteer**.
16. Submit the presentation in the format specified by your instructor.
17. **Consider This:** Where would a presenter use the two custom shows? What were the Accessibility Checker's inspection results? Did the Compatibility Checker summary display any features not supported by earlier versions of PowerPoint? If so, what were they?

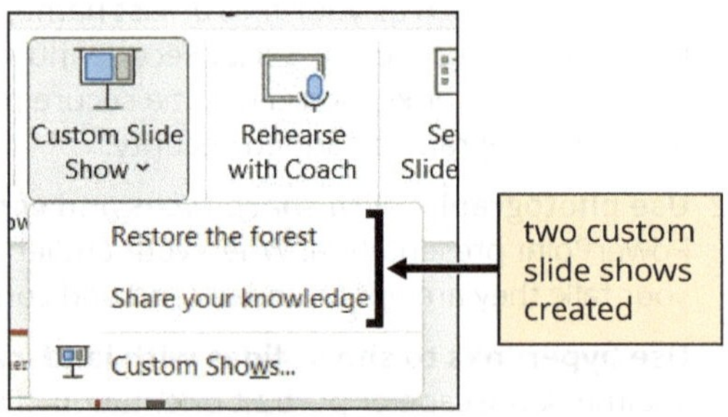

Figure 8-88(a): Custom Slide Shows

geralt/Pixabay

Figure 8–88(b): Speaker Notes in Landscape Orientation

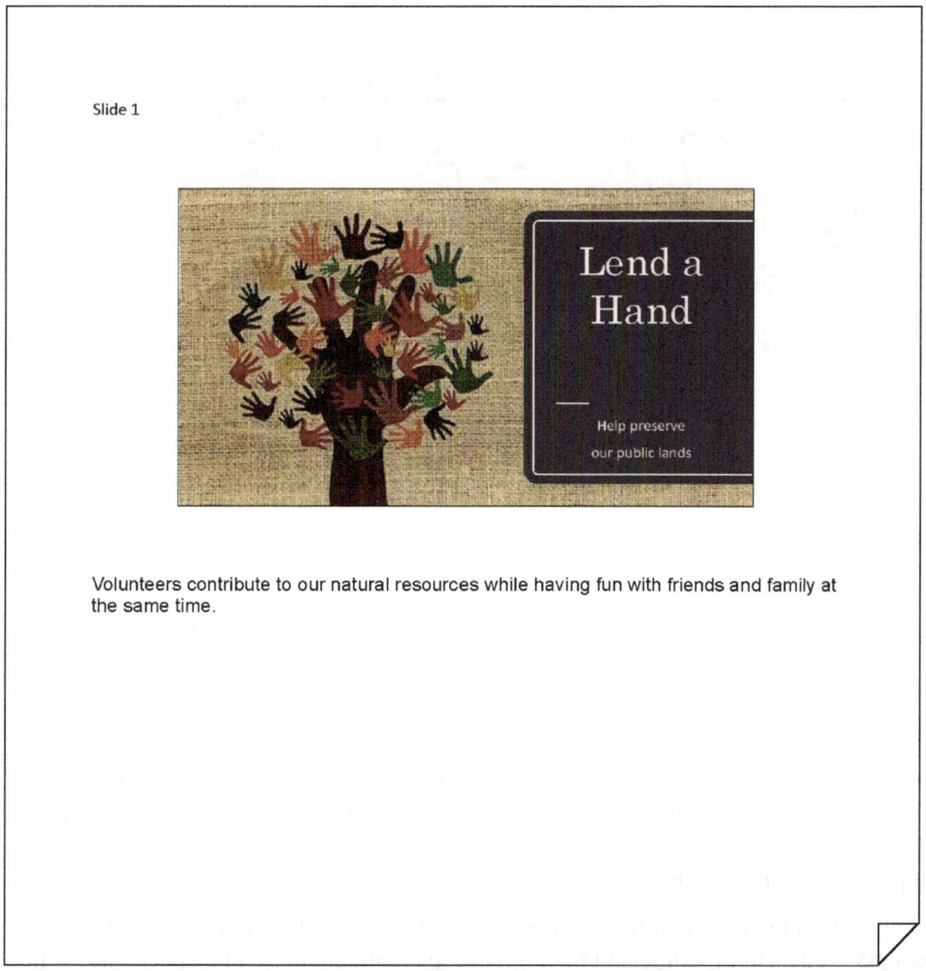

geralt/Pixabay

Figure 8–88(c): Word Handout

Continued on next page

Matheus Bertelli/Pexels

Figure 8–88(d): Slide Saved as a Picture

geralt/Pixabay; Matheus Bertelli/Pexels; Ray_Shrewsberry/Pixabay; Thirdman/Pexels; Alfo Medeiros/Pexels; ajcespedes/Pixabay; antoinetteforwine/Pixabay; MaBraS/Pixabay; Bessi/Pixabay; ignartonosbg/Pixabay

Figure 8–88(e): Summary Zoom Slide

Extend Your Knowledge

Extend the skills you learned in this module and experiment with new skills. You may need to use Help to complete the assignment.

Inserting, Modifying, and Animating 3D Models

Note: To complete this assignment, you will be required to use the Data Files. Please contact your instructor for information about accessing the Data Files. You will need Internet access and a Microsoft 365 subscription to obtain the 3D models and complete this assignment. If you do not have Internet access and a subscription, read this assignment without performing the instructions.

Instructions: Start PowerPoint. Open the presentation called SC_PPT_8-2.pptx, which is located in the Data Files. You will insert two 3D models in this slide and then modify and animate these objects, as shown in Figure 8–89.

Perform the following tasks:

1. Display the Insert tab and then click the 3D Models arrow (Insert tab | Illustrations group) to display the 3D Models menu. Click 'Stock 3D Models' to display a window with galleries of 3D models.
2. Click the Animated Animals gallery to view the models and then click the five fish (or similar fish) to place a check mark in that model.
3. Click the Insert button on the search results page to insert the selected fish model on the slide. Resize the fish height to approximately 7" and the width to approximately 11", and then align it on the right and in the middle of the slide.
4. With the fish selected, click the Right 3D model view (fifth model in the first row) to turn the fish and have them swim around the slide.
5. Display the Insert tab, click the 3D Models button, click the Animated Animals gallery, type **shark** after the words, Animated Animals, in the search box, and then press ENTER to display shark models. Click the shark that looks like the one in Figure 8-89 to place a check mark in that model and then click the Insert button.
6. Resize the shark's height to approximately 6". Click the 'Above Front Right' 3D model view (fifth view in the second row) and then position the shark in the upper-right corner of the slide.
7. With the shark selected, display the Animations tab and then click the Swing animation (Animations tab | Animation group). Click the Effect Options button (Animations tab | Animation group) and then click Subtle in the Intensity area and Continuous in the Amount area.
8. Click Preview (Animations tab | Preview group) to view the animations.

   If requested by your instructor, add the city in which you were born to the Notes pane.
9. Save the presentation using the file name, **SC_PPT_8_Fish_3D**.
10. Submit the revised document in the format specified by your instructor.
11. **Consider This:** In this assignment, you searched for and selected two 3D models. Were these models appropriate for this presentation? Which other models would be suitable? Does the animation add interest to the slide, or is the shark animation a distraction and should be eliminated? What are the advantages and disadvantages of adding 3D models to a slide?

Figure 8-89

Expand Your World

Create a solution that uses cloud or web technologies by learning and investigating on your own from general guidance.

Linking to an Online Video

Note: You will need Internet access to complete this assignment. If you do not have Internet access, read this assignment without performing the actions specified in the instructions.

Instructions: You have created a presentation and want to play a video from an online website, such as YouTube, SlideShare, Vimeo, Stream, or Flip, as part of your slide show. Some websites encourage users to share video clips, while others restrict users from performing this process. The videos are not downloaded and inserted, or embedded, in the file; instead, they are linked to the presentation so that when the slide show is running and an Internet connection is present, the user can click the Play button to begin watching the video. PowerPoint includes instructions to insert a video clip from video providers.

Perform the following tasks:

1. Start PowerPoint and then open the SC_PPT_8_Study_Abroad presentation you created in this module. At the end of the presentation, insert one slide using the Title and Content layout and then type the title text, **Studying Abroad Advice** on Slide 13. Change the font to Times New Roman
2. Display the Insert tab and then click the Video button (Insert tab | Media group) to display the Video menu. Click Online Videos in the menu to display a dialog box with an Address bar where you can enter a Web address.
3. Locate a video in your web browser, copy the web address of the webpage from the browser's Address bar, switch back to PowerPoint, and then paste the web address of the online video in the Address bar.
4. Click the Insert button to display the selected clip on Slide 13. Increase the clip size and then align it in the center and the bottom of the slide. Add a border and an effect.

   If requested by your instructor, change the word, Napoleon, in the Notes pane on Slide 2 to your grandmother's or guardian's first name.
5. Run the presentation. If you see a yellow security warning at the top of the presentation, click Enable Content and then click Yes on the Security Warning dialog to make the file a trusted document and view the video.
6. Save the file with the new file name, **SC_PPT_8_Study_Abroad_Video**.
7. **Consider This:** Do videos add to the audience's ability to retain information presented during a presentation? Do they increase interest in the topic? Why did you select this specific video to display on Slide 13?

In the Lab

Apply your creative thinking and problem-solving skills to design and implement a solution.

Design and Create a Presentation about Nature Programs

Part 1: Public lands are a vital component of the overall ecosystem. They clean our air, purify our water, and provide food and habitat for wildlife. In addition, they help us reduce stress, stimulate the imagination, and promote a sense of community. The naturalists and programming teams at the nature center in your community are creating a new campaign directed toward residents of all ages, and they have asked you to create a PowerPoint photo album highlighting the variety of events offered.

Perform some research to learn about events and sessions at your local park district, woodlands, or forest. These programs could include disc golf, ziplining, guided hikes, and bird walks. Perhaps seminars are offered on the topics of seed collecting, invasive plant species, therapy walks, and owl prowls. Possible pictures to use for your slides are available in your Data Files folder. Use these files and other pictures to create a photo album. Format at least two pictures in the album by changing the contrast and brightness. Add a frame and a theme. Save the photo album file using the file name, **SC_PPT_8_Nature_Photo_Album**. Review and revise your presentation as needed and then save the file as a PowerPoint show using the file name, **SC_PPT_8_Nature_Show**. Submit your assignment in the format specified by your instructor.

Part 2: **Consider This:** You made several decisions while creating the presentation in this assignment: what content to include, how to format the album with a frame and theme, and which pictures to format. What was the rationale behind each of these decisions? Where would you recommend distributing this album? When you reviewed the document, what changes did you make?

Index

Note: Page numbers in **bold** indicate key terms.

A

Accessibility Checker, **PPT 8-16**
action button, **PPT 7-47**
  adding sound, PPT 7-50 – PPT 7-51
  changing fill color, PPT 7-49 – PPT 7-50
  inserting, PPT 7-48
  sizing, PPT 7-49
  using, PPT 7-47
active cell, **PPT 3-3**
active tab, **PPT 1-7**
adding
  artistic effect to picture, PPT 3-35
  bullet to SmartArt shape, PPT 7-21
  footer, PPT 2-48 – PPT 2-49
  hyperlinks, PPT 7-41 – PPT 7-53
  hyperlinks action setting to picture, PPT 7-43 – PPT 7-44
  hyperlinks action setting to shape, PPT 7-44 – PPT 7-45
  media to slides, PPT 3-51 – PPT 3-56
  new slide master layout, PPT 4-27
  photo album theme, PPT 8-35
  placeholder, PPT 4-15 – PPT 4-37
  placeholder text, PPT 4-16 – PPT 4-18
  ScreenTip to hyperlinks, PPT 7-42 – PPT 7-43
  shape to SmartArt, PPT 7-13 – PPT 7-14
  slide title, PPT 2-40
  slide transition, PPT 4-45
  sound, PPT 7-50 – PPT 7-51
  table to a slide and formatting, PPT 3-14 – PPT 3-24
  transition, PPT 2-50 – PPT 2-52
  transition between slides, PPT 3-55
  video poster frame, PPT 7-34 – PPT 7-35
Adobe Acrobat, PPT 1-7
album, formatting photos in, PPT 8-33 – PPT 8-34
aligning
  chart, PPT 6-37 – PPT 6-38
  data in table cells, PPT 6-26 – PPT 6-27
  Excel worksheet in PowerPoint, PPT 6-32 – PPT 6-33
  objects, **PPT 2-32**
  table, PPT 6-28 – PPT 6-29
  videos, PPT 7-40
alignment options, PPT 2-32
alternative text. *See* Alt Text
Alt Text, **PPT 5-26**
  adding to pictures, PPT 5-31
animated 3D graphics, embedding, PPT 8-9
animating 3D model, PPT 8-9
animation(s), **PPT 3-46**
  adding delay, PPT 5-44 – PPT 5-45
  adding sound from a file, PPT 5-43
  changing direction, PPT 3-47
  changing duration, PPT 3-49
  changing start option, PPT 3-48
  custom, **PPT 3-46**
  effects, icon colors, PPT 3-46
  emphasis effect, PPT 5-44
  entrance effect, PPT 5-43
  object using an entrance effect, PPT 3-46 – PPT 3-47
  presentation, PPT 5-1 – PPT 5-21
  previewing sequence, PPT 3-48
  removing multiple effects, PPT 5-47
  removing, PPT 5-47
  reordering, on slide, PPT 5-47
  running slide show with, PPT 3-55 – PPT 3-56
  slide content, PPT 5-43 – PPT 5-56
  text, PPT 3-49 – PPT 3-50, PPT 5-45 – PPT 5-46
  triggering, PPT 5-53
  turning off, PPT 5-45
Animation Painter
  defined, **PPT 5-47 – PPT 5-48**
  using, PPT 5-47 – PPT 5-49
animation sequence effect option, PPT 3-50
applying
  bevel effects to table cells, PPT 6-21
  reflection effects to table cells, PPT 6-22 – PPT 6-23
  shading to table cells, PPT 6-20 – PPT 6-21
  shadow effects to table cells, PPT 6-22
  style to chart, PPT 6-41
  3D effects to SmartArt, PPT 7-14 – PPT 7-15
Apply to All button *vs.* Apply button, PPT 2-49, PPT 2-52
audio clip(s)
  changing picture and inserting, PPT 7-1 – PPT 7-4
  changing volume, PPT 7-38
  compressing, PPT 7-40 – PPT 7-41
  grouping, PPT 7-38
  hiding object during slide show, PPT 7-38
  inserting from file, PPT 7-35 – PPT 7-37
  inserting, PPT 7-28 – PPT 7-41
  looping, PPT 7-37
  playing across slides, PPT 7-38
  presentation with, PPT 7-1 – PPT 7-4
  rewinding after playing, PPT 7-38
  start option, changing, PPT 7-37
  trimming, PPT 7-39
audio recording, PPT 8-42
automatic spelling correction, PPT 1-49
automatically updated properties, **PPT 1-52**
axis, adding to charts, PPT 6-42 – PPT 6-44

B

background, removing, PPT 7-24 – PPT 7-25
Background Graphics
  hiding, PPT 4-23 – PPT 4-24
  unhiding, PPT 4-23 – PPT 4-24
background images, printing, PPT 1-58
Backstage view, **PPT 1-20**
  closing a file using, PPT 1-45
  opening a recent file using, PPT 1-45 – PPT 1-46
bar chart, PPT 3-5, PPT 6-38
black and white setting, PPT 1-60
black slide, PPT 1-56
Blank Layout
  inserting placeholder into, PPT 4-15 – PPT 4-16
bold text, **PPT 1-27**
border color of pictures, PPT 5-29
brightness, **PPT 3-36**

Bring Forward command, **PPT 2-38**
Bring to Front command, **PPT 2-38**
bullet(s)
  button, PPT 5-32
  changing size, PPT 5-33 – PPT 5-34
  changing to symbol, PPT 5-34 – PPT 5-35
  color, **PPT 5-36**
  modifying, PPT 5-31 – PPT 5-43
  size, **PPT 5-33**
bullet character
  changing to number, PPT 5-36 – PPT 5-37
  changing to picture, PPT 5-31 – PPT 5-33
  defined, **PPT 5-31**
bulleted list, **PPT 1-23**
  adding new text slide with, PPT 1-22 – PPT 1-23
  creating text slide with multilevel, PPT 1-23
  multilevel, PPT 1-23
  presentation with pictures, PPT 1-2 – PPT 1-3
  removing extra, PPT 1-26

C

category axis, **PPT 6-38**
cell(s), **PPT 3-3**
  active, PPT 3-3
cell reference, **PPT 6-33**
centered text, **PPT 2-7**
changing
  password protection, PPT 8-19 – PPT 8-20
  photo album layout, PPT 8-34
  slide orientation, PPT 8-38
  slide show resolution, PPT 8-39
characters, formatting in presentation, PPT 1-16 – PPT 1-22
characters, inserting special, PPT 2-9 – PPT 2-10
chart(s)
  adding axis, PPT 6-42 – PPT 6-44
  adding border to chart elements, PPT 6-45 – PPT 6-46
  adding data labels, PPT 6-43
  adding title at specified position, PPT 6-44 – PPT 6-45
  adding to slide and formatting, PPT 3-3 – PPT 3-14
  aligning, PPT 3-9 – PPT 3-10, PPT 6-37 – PPT 6-38
  applying style to, PPT 6-41
  bar, PPT 3-5
  changing chart type to pie and exploding pie chart slice, PPT 6-40
  changing colors, PPT 6-41 – PPT 6-42
  changing layout, PPT 6-40
  changing shape outline color, PPT 3-11 – PPT 3-12
  changing shape outline weight, PPT 3-13
  changing style, PPT 3-11
  changing title and legend font and font size, PPT 3-13 – PPT 3-14
  changing types, PPT 6-39 – PPT 6-40
  column, PPT 3-5
  inserting, PPT 3-5 – PPT 3-6
  legend, PPT 3-5
  line, PPT 3-5
  pie, PPT 3-5
  presentation with, PPT 3-1 – PPT 3-3
  replacing sample data, PPT 3-6 – PPT 3-8
  resizing proportionally, PPT 6-36 – PPT 6-37
  resizing, PPT 3-8 – PPT 3-9
  scatterplots, PPT 3-5
  selecting data, PPT 6-48
  switching rows and columns, PPT 6-38
  types of, PPT 3-5
chart style, changing, PPT 3-11
check boxes, PPT 5-8 – PPT 5-10
checking
  presentation accessibility, PPT 8-16 – PPT 8-18
  presentation compatibility, PPT 8-15
  presentation, PPT 8-14 – PPT 8-15
closing
  Master view, PPT 8-26
  presentation, PPT 1-66
Clustered Column chart, **PPT 3-3**
codecs, PPT 3-51
collaboration
  defined, **PPT 5-2**
  on presentation, PPT 5-2 – PPT 5-21
  tips for successful, PPT 5-2
color(s)
  changing a shape fill, PPT 2-30 – PPT 2-31
  changing shape outline, PPT 2-45
  changing table border, PPT 6-20
  changing text, PPT 1-18 – PPT 1-19
color cast, **PPT 3-33**
color saturation, **PPT 3-33**
color tone, **PPT 3-33**
columns, **PPT 3-3**
  chart, PPT 3-5
  drawing table, PPT 6-13 – PPT 6-14
  formatting text, PPT 5-24 – PPT 5-25
  resizing table, PPT 6-25 – PPT 6-26
  spacing, changing, PPT 5-23 – PPT 5-24
  switching chart, PPT 6-38
comment(s)
  anchoring, PPT 8-14
  defined, **PPT 5-1**
  deleting, PPT 5-17 – PPT 5-18
  editing, PPT 5-16 – PPT 5-17
  hiding, PPT 5-19 – PPT 5-20
  inserting, PPT 5-15 – PPT 5-16
  presentation, PPT 5-1 – PPT 5-2
  printing, PPT 5-6
  removing, PPT 5-19
  replying, PPT 5-14 – PPT 5-15
  reviewing, PPT 5-13 – PPT 5-14
Comments pane, PPT 5-6
Compatibility Checker, **PPT 8-14**
compressing
  audio clip, PPT 7-40 – PPT 7-41
  picture, PPT 7-27 – PPT 7-28
  video file, PPT 7-40 – PPT 7-41
connector
  defined, **PPT 5-54**
  inserting, PPT 5-54 – PPT 5-55
conserving ink and toner, PPT 1-57
content placeholder, PPT 4-15
  aligning, PPT 5-55 – PPT 5-56
  copying, PPT 4-21
  deleting, PPT 4-13 – PPT 4-14
  inserting online picture without using, PPT 7-6
  inserting SmartArt using, PPT 7-9 – PPT 7-10
contextual tabs, **PPT 1-7**
contrast, **PPT 3-36**
converting
  documents for use in PowerPoint, PPT 6-4 – PPT 6-6
  picture to SmartArt, PPT 7-10
copying
  Excel chart, PPT 6-35 – PPT 6-36
  linked Excel chart, PPT 6-34 – PPT 6-52
copying and pasting, PPT 6-6
creating
  custom slide show, PPT 8-4 – PPT 8-9
  equations with touchscreen, PPT 7-9
  handouts by exporting to Word, PPT 8-11 – PPT 8-13
  photo album, PPT 8-30 – PPT 8-37
  presentation from Microsoft Word outline, PPT 6-4 – PPT 6-6
  screen recordings, PPT 8-41 – PPT 8-42
  sections, PPT 5-56 – PPT 5-65

SmartArt graphics, PPT 7-9 – PPT 7-22
creativity, decibels for, PPT 7-32
criticism, accepting and evaluating, PPT 5-7
cropping
pictures, PPT 3-32 – PPT 3-33, PPT 4-22 – PPT 4-24
pictures, simultaneously on two or four sides, PPT 3-33
picture to a shape, PPT 3-33
custom animations, **PPT 3-46,** PPT 3-46 – PPT 3-50
emphasis effects, PPT 3-46
entrance effects, PPT 3-46
exit effects, PPT 3-46
customized slides
presentation with, PPT 4-2 – PPT 4-6
customizing
handout, PPT 8-20 – PPT 8-30
handout master, PPT 8-21 – PPT 8-22
table formatting, PPT 6-20
theme colors, PPT 4-9 – PPT 4-10
theme fonts, PPT 4-12 – PPT 4-13
custom layout, **PPT 1-28**
custom path, PPT 5-43, **PPT 5-50**
animating an object using, PPT 5-50 – PPT 5-53
defined, **PPT 5-50**
custom slide show
creating, PPT 8-4 – PPT 8-9
defined, **PPT 8-4**
opening and editing, PPT 8-7 – PPT 8-8
presentation with, PPT 8-2 – PPT 8-4
running, PPT 8-8
selecting slides for, PPT 8-4 – PPT 8-6
3D models, PPT 8-9

D

data
adding labels to chart, PPT 6-43
aligning in table cells, PPT 6-26 – PPT 6-27
entering in tables, PPT 3-16
excluding in chart, PPT 6-40
formatting in table, PPT 6-28
labels, **PPT 6-43**
selecting in chart, PPT 6-48
Date placeholder
formatting, PPT 8-24
decibels for creativity, PPT 7-32
deck, **PPT 1-1**
Delay box, PPT 5-45
deleting
button, PPT 5-18
comment(s), PPT 5-17 – PPT 5-18
content placeholder, PPT 4-13 – PPT 4-14
placeholders, PPT 6-7
slide layout, PPT 4-25 – PPT 4-27
demoting text, **PPT 1-24**
destination document, **PPT 6-6**
Dialog Box Launcher, **PPT 1-9**
digital inking, **PPT 8-13**
dimension, table, **PPT 3-14**
dimming text, **PPT 5-45** – PPT 5-46
distributing
slides, PPT 4-54
table rows, PPT 6-24 – PPT 6-25
distributing a document, PPT 1-59
distributing objects, **PPT 2-32**
document(s)
converting for use in PowerPoint, PPT 6-4 – PPT 6-6
distributing, PPT 1-59
distributing electronically, PPT 2-48, PPT 3-55
printing document properties, PPT 1-52
Document Inspector, **PPT 4-46** – PPT 4-47, **PPT 8-14**
document properties, **PPT 1-52**
automatically updated properties, PPT 1-52
changing, PPT 1-52
editing, PPT 4-46
printing, PPT 1-52
standard properties, PPT 1-52
.docx file extension, **PPT 6-4**
drag and drop, **PPT 1-44**
drawing
table columns, PPT 6-13 – PPT 6-14
table rows, PPT 6-12 – PPT 6-13
tables, PPT 6-10 – PPT 6-16
drawing guides, **PPT 2-31**
displaying, PPT 2-32 – PPT 2-33
Drawing Tools Format tab, PPT 2-22, PPT 2-24, PPT 2-25 – PPT 2-26

E

edit/editing
comment(s), PPT 5-16 – PPT 5-17
custom slide show, PPT 8-7 – PPT 8-8
embedded file, PPT 6-9 – PPT 6-10
hyperlinks, PPT 7-42
photo album, PPT 8-36 – PPT 8-37
source file of linked chart, PPT 6-46 – PPT 6-48
effects
emphasis, PPT 3-46
entrance, PPT 3-46
exit, PPT 3-46
WordArt, **PPT 3-40**
embedded object, **PPT 6-6**
embedding, PPT 6-6
animated 3D graphics, PPT 8-9
editing embedded file, PPT 6-9 – PPT 6-10
object from another app, PPT 6-8 – PPT 6-9
emphasis effect animations, PPT 5-44
emphasis effects, **PPT 3-46**
encrypting presentation with password, PPT 8-18 – PPT 8-19
entrance effects, **PPT 3-46,** PPT 5-43
equation
creating with touchscreen, PPT 7-9
inserting, PPT 7-9
erasing table border, PPT 6-15 – PPT 6-16
Excel chart, copying, PPT 6-35 – PPT 6-36
Excel worksheet
aligning, PPT 6-32 – PPT 6-33
inserting linked, PPT 6-29 – PPT 6-34
linking, PPT 6-30 – PPT 6-32
excluding data in a chart, PPT 6-40
exit effects, **PPT 3-46**

F

feedback
presentation, PPT 5-7
file(s), **PPT 1-20**
closing using Backstage view, PPT 1-45
inserting audio clip, PPT 7-35 – PPT 7-37
opening a recent file using Backstage view, PPT 1-45 – PPT 1-46
organizing, PPT 1-20, PPT 2-5, PPT 3-3
saving and printing, PPT 1-57 – PPT 1-62
starting PowerPoint and saving, PPT 8-4
file name, **PPT 1-20**
extensions, PPT 4-28
saving file with a different, PPT 1-57
fill, **PPT 3-25, PPT 4-37**
fill color
changing action button, PPT 7-49 – PPT 7-50
flipping picture, PPT 7-25
folder(s)
organizing, PPT 1-20

font, **PPT 1-16**
and font styles, PPT 1-16
changing, PPT 1-29 – PPT 1-30, PPT 2-27, PPT 2-50
increasing size, PPT 1-17 – PPT 1-18, PPT 1-27
legend, PPT 3-13 – PPT 3-14
point size, PPT 1-16
font color, **PPT 1-16**
font size, **PPT 1-16**
changing, PPT 3-13 – PPT 3-14
font style, **PPT 1-16**
footer, **PPT 2-48**
adding, PPT 2-48 – PPT 2-49
adding with fixed information, PPT 2-49
Format Painter
defined, **PPT 5-41**
using with objects, PPT 5-42 – PPT 5-43
using with text, PPT 5-41 – PPT 5-42
formatting, **PPT 1-16**
adding chart to slide, PPT 3-3 – PPT 3-14
characters in presentation, PPT 1-16 – PPT 1-22
customizing table, PPT 6-20
Date placeholder, PPT 8-24
photos in album, PPT 8-33 – PPT 8-34
picture placeholder, PPT 4-20 – PPT 4-21
pictures, PPT 5-26 – PPT 5-31, PPT 7-22 – PPT 7-28
placeholder, PPT 4-15 – PPT 4-37
placeholder text, PPT 4-16 – PPT 4-18
shape(s), PPT 2-22 – PPT 2-31
slide backgrounds, PPT 4-37 – PPT 4-45
slide master background, PPT 4-21 – PPT 4-22
SmartArt graphics, PPT 2-11 – PPT 2-22
table, PPT 3-14 – PPT 3-24
table data, PPT 6-28
text, PPT 5-22 – PPT 5-26
Text Pane characters, PPT 2-15 – PPT 2-16, PPT 7-12
full screen, **PPT 3-51**

G

gallery, **PPT 1-8**
Live Preview, PPT 1-8
glow shape effect, PPT 5-40 – PPT 5-41
glow text effect, PPT 5-40
gradient fill
changing slide backgrounds to, PPT 4-38 – PPT 4-39
defined, **PPT 4-37**
graphics
audience retention, PPT 3-1
inserting from file, PPT 6-6 – PPT 6-10
sources to obtain information for, PPT 3-6
grayscale, **PPT 1-61, PPT 3-33**
printing in, PPT 8-29
grid, hiding, PPT 2-47
gridlines, **PPT 2-32, PPT 6-44**
adding, PPT 6-44
adding to chart, PPT 6-44
displaying, PPT 2-34
positioning shape using, PPT 2-34 – PPT 2-35
grid measurements, changing, PPT 2-36
group, **PPT 1-7**
group objects, **PPT 2-39** – PPT 2-40
grouping, audio clips, PPT 7-38
guides
displaying drawing, PPT 2-32 – PPT 2-33
hiding, PPT 2-47
positioning shape using, PPT 2-34 – PPT 2-35

H

handout(s)
creating by exporting to Word, PPT 8-11 – PPT 8-13
customizing, PPT 8-20 – PPT 8-30
inserting header for, PPT 8-22
presentation, PPT 2-48
previewing and printing, PPT 1-59 – PPT 1-60
printing, PPT 8-26 – PPT 8-30
handout master, **PPT 4-6**
handout master view, PPT 8-20
header, **PPT 2-48**
inserting for handouts, PPT 8-22
Hide Slide, **PPT 4-44**
hiding markups, PPT 5-19 – PPT 5-20
hiding slides, PPT 4-44 – PPT 4-45
highlighting text, PPT 4-49
Home tab, **PPT 1-7**
horizontal axis, **PPT 6-38**
hyperlink, **PPT 2-21, PPT 6-48**
adding, PPT 7-41 – PPT 7-53
adding action setting to picture, PPT 7-43 – PPT 7-44
adding action setting to shape, PPT 7-44 – PPT 7-45
adding to paragraphs, PPT 2-21 – PPT 2-22
adding ScreenTip, PPT 7-42 – PPT 7-43
editing, PPT 7-42
inserting to place in current presentation, PPT 7-41 – PPT 7-42
inserting to slide, PPT 7-45 – PPT 7-47
presentation with, PPT 7-1 – PPT 7-4
removing, PPT 7-47
using to show slides with landscape and portrait orientations, PPT 8-37
hyperlinking custom shows, PPT 8-4

I

illustration, resizing, PPT 1-38 – PPT 1-46
image
adding to table cells, PPT 6-23 – PPT 6-24
ink, conserving, PPT 1-57
insert/inserting
action button, PPT 7-48
audio clips from file, PPT 7-35 – PPT 7-37
comment(s), PPT 5-15 – PPT 5-16
connector, PPT 5-54 – PPT 5-55
equation, PPT 7-9
graphics or other objects from file, PPT 6-6 – PPT 6-10
header for handouts, PPT 8-22
header for notes, PPT 8-24
hyperlinks to place in current presentation, PPT 7-41 – PPT 7-42
hyperlinks to slide, PPT 7-45 – PPT 7-47
linked Excel worksheet, PPT 6-29 – PPT 6-34
online picture without using content placeholder, PPT 7-6
online video, PPT 7-30
picture into SmartArt shape, PPT 7-13
screen clipping, PPT 7-7 – PPT 7-9
screen recordings, PPT 8-41 – PPT 8-42
section zoom links, PPT 5-61 – PPT 5-63
slide zoom links, PPT 5-61 – PPT 5-63
slides from outline, PPT 6-5 – PPT 6-6
SmartArt using content placeholder, PPT 7-9 – PPT 7-10

summary zoom slide, PPT 8-40 – PPT 8-42
3D model, PPT 8-9
Insert Picture dialog box, **PPT 1-34**
insertion box, PPT 5-9
insertion point, **PPT 1-6**
italic text, **PPT 1-17**

J

justified text, **PPT 2-8**

K

KeyTips, **PPT 1-10**

L

landscape orientation, **PPT 1-12**
laser pointer
using mouse as, PPT 8-42
using on smartphone, PPT 8-43
layout gallery, **PPT 1-28**
layout, slide, **PPT 1-28**
left-aligned text, **PPT 2-7**
legend, **PPT 3-5, PPT 6-44**
adding to chart, PPT 6-44
legend font, changing, PPT 3-13 – PPT 3-14
level, paragraph, **PPT 1-14**
library, slide, PPT 5-26
line chart, PPT 3-5
line spacing
changing, PPT 5-22
defined, **PPT 5-22**
line style
changing table border, PPT 6-20
link, **PPT 2-21, PPT 6-48**
adding to text, PPT 6-48 – PPT 6-49
Excel worksheet, PPT 6-30 – PPT 6-32
Link check box, **PPT 6-29**
linked chart
editing source file, PPT 6-46 – PPT 6-48
linked Excel chart
copying and modifying, PPT 6-34 – PPT 6-52
linked Excel worksheet
inserting, PPT 6-29 – PPT 6-34
updating, PPT 6-33 – PPT 6-34
linked object, **PPT 6-6**
linking, PPT 6-6
list numbering style, PPT 5-37 – PPT 5-38
live preview, PPT 4-38, PPT 4-43
Lock Drawing Mode, **PPT 5-54**
looping audio clip, PPT 7-37

M

margin
changing for text in a shape, PPT 5-38 – PPT 5-39
defined, **PPT 5-22**
Mark as Final command, **PPT 4-47**
markups, hiding, PPT 5-19 – PPT 5-20
Master Comparison Layout, PPT 4-2, PPT 4-4
Masters for universal style, PPT 4-2
master text styles
editing, PPT 4-11
Master Title and Content Layout, PPT 4-2, PPT 4-5
Master view, PPT 4-27
closing, PPT 8-26
measurement unit, changing, PPT 2-32
media
adding to slides, PPT 3-51 – PPT 3-56
changing video contrast, PPT 3-53 – PPT 3-54
moving video clip, PPT 3-52 – PPT 3-53
playing video file automatically, PPT 3-54 – PPT 3-55
resizing video clip, PPT 3-52
video file, PPT 3-51 – PPT 3-52
merge/merging
presentation, PPT 5-5 – PPT 5-6
table cells, PPT 6-16
Microsoft 365 Suite, PPT 1-1
Microsoft account area, **PPT 1-10**
Microsoft Clip Organizer, PPT 1-34
Microsoft Search box, PPT 8-18 – PPT 8-19
Mini toolbar, **PPT 1-10**
modify/modifying
bullets, PPT 5-31 – PPT 5-43
linked Excel chart, PPT 6-34 – PPT 6-52
3D model, PPT 8-9
motion path, **PPT 5-43**
animating an object using custom, PPT 5-50 – PPT 5-53
animating an object using preset, PPT 5-49 – PPT 5-50
mouse
using as laser pointer, PPT 8-42
multilevel bulleted list, **PPT 1-23**, PPT 1-24 – PPT 1-25

N

narration
previewing, PPT 8-13
recording, PPT 8-13
showing presentation with or without, PPT 8-13
navigating
between slides in Outline view, PPT 6-50
between slides in Reading view, PPT 6-49 – PPT 6-50
defined, **PPT 4-47**
to a slide using the control bar, PPT 4-48
nonadjacent text, selecting, PPT 1-26
Normal view, **PPT 1-33,** PPT 6-49
moving to another slide in, PPT 1-33 – PPT 1-34, PPT 1-44
notes
adding, PPT 1-48 – PPT 1-49
button, **PPT 1-33**
inserting header for, PPT 8-24
pages, **PPT 1-48**
pane, **PPT 1-33**
notes master view
switching to, PPT 8-23 – PPT 8-24
notes masters, **PPT 4-6**
customizing, PPT 8-20 – PPT 8-30
Notes Page view
switching to, PPT 8-23
Notes pane
formatting text in, PPT 1-48
number
changing bullet character to, PPT 5-36 – PPT 5-37

O

object linking and embedding (OLE), **PPT 6-7**
objects
aligning, PPT 2-32 – PPT 2-53
animating, using custom motion path, PPT 5-50 – PPT 5-53
distributing, PPT 2-32 – PPT 2-53
Format Painter, using with, PPT 5-42 – PPT 5-43
grouping, PPT 2-39 – PPT 2-40
replacing words with, PPT 2-40
Office Clipboard, **PPT 4-21**
offset, **PPT 4-37**
OLE (object linking and embedding), **PPT 6-7**
OneDrive
sharing presentation on, PPT 8-14
online theme, downloading, PPT 2-3 – PPT 2-4
online video
inserting, PPT 7-30
play options, PPT 7-20
opening
custom slide show, PPT 8-7 – PPT 8-8
presentation with password, PPT 8-19
opening presentation, PPT 7-5

outline
inserting slides, PPT 6-5 – PPT 6-6
levels, defining, PPT 6-4
WordArt, **PPT 3-40**
Outline view, **PPT 6-49**
entering text, PPT 6-51
moving slide, PPT 6-51
navigating between slides, PPT 6-50
switching to, PPT 6-50

P

pane, **PPT 1-9**
Comments, PPT 5-6
Revisions, PPT 5-6
paragraph(s)
adding hyperlink to, PPT 2-21 – PPT 2-22
aligning, PPT 2-7 – PPT 2-8
entering presentation subtitle, PPT 1-15
left-aligned, PPT 2-7
right-aligned, PPT 2-7
selecting, PPT 1-16 – PPT 1-17
paragraph spacing
changing, PPT 5-22 – PPT 5-23
defined, **PPT 5-22**
password(s)
best for security, PPT 8-18
encrypting presentation with, PPT 8-18 – PPT 8-19
opening presentation with, PPT 8-19
password protection
changing, PPT 8-19 – PPT 8-20
removing, PPT 8-19 – PPT 8-20
pattern
changing slide backgrounds to, PPT 4-41 – PPT 4-42
pattern fill
defined, **PPT 4-37**
PDF file
option settings, PPT 7-1
Pen and laser pointer tools, PPT 4-49 – PPT 4-51
photo album
adding photo album theme, PPT 8-35
changing layout, PPT 8-34
creating, PPT 8-30 – PPT 8-37
editing, PPT 8-36 – PPT 8-37
formatting photos, PPT 8-33 – PPT 8-34
layout, changing, PPT 8-34
presentation with, PPT 8-2 – PPT 8-4
reordering pictures in, PPT 8-32 – PPT 8-33
starting and adding pictures, PPT 8-30 – PPT 8-31
photograph(s)
formatting in an album, PPT 8-33 – PPT 8-34
using, PPT 8-1
using with sharp focus and contrast, PPT 8-30
picture(s)
adding Alt Text, PPT 5-31
adding artistic effect to, PPT 3-35, PPT 5-27
adding border, PPT 5-28 – PPT 5-29
adding hyperlink action setting, PPT 7-43 – PPT 7-44
adding to SmartArt, PPT 7-12 – PPT 7-13
adjusting colors, PPT 3-33 – PPT 3-39
aligning, PPT 3-39, PPT 5-21
animating, using entrance effect, PPT 5-43
border, PPT 5-28 – PPT 5-29
brightness, PPT 3-36
changing, PPT 7-5 – PPT 7-6
changing border color, PPT 5-29
changing brightness and contrast, PPT 7-25 – PPT 7-26
changing bullet character, PPT 5-31 – PPT 5-33
changing color saturation, PPT 7-26 – PPT 7-27
changing slide backgrounds to, PPT 4-39 – PPT 4-40
changing softness, PPT 3-36 – PPT 3-37
compressing, PPT 5-29, PPT 7-27 – PPT 7-28
contrast, PPT 3-36
converting to SmartArt, PPT 7-10
cropping, PPT 3-32 – PPT 3-33
cropping simultaneously on two or four sides, PPT 3-33
cropping to a shape, PPT 3-33
deleting, PPT 3-30
effects, PPT 5-29 – PPT 5-30
flipping, PPT 7-25
formatting, PPT 5-26 – PPT 5-31, PPT 7-22 – PPT 7-28
inserting, PPT 1-34 – PPT 1-38, PPT 3-30 – PPT 3-39
inserting into a slide without content placeholders, PPT 3-31
inserting into SmartArt shape, PPT 7-13
moving, PPT 1-34 – PPT 1-38, PPT 1-40 – PPT 1-41, PPT 3-38
nonproportionally resizing, PPT 1-43
presentation with, PPT 2-1 – PPT 2-3
presentation with bulleted list, PPT 1-2 – PPT 1-3
proportionally resizing, PPT 1-39 – PPT 1-40
recoloring, PPT 3-34, PPT 5-27 – PPT 5-28
refining background removal, PPT 7-24 – PPT 7-25
removing background, PPT 7-22 – PPT 7-24
reordering in photo album, PPT 8-32 – PPT 8-33
resetting, PPT 7-27
resizing, PPT 1-34 – PPT 1-38, PPT 1-40, PPT 7-6 – PPT 7-7
resizing into a slide without content placeholders, PPT 3-31
rotating, PPT 1-42 – PPT 1-43
saving slide as, PPT 8-10 – PPT 8-11
sharpness, PPT 3-36
sizing, PPT 3-37 – PPT 3-38
starting photo album and adding, PPT 8-30 – PPT 8-31
wrapping text around, PPT 1-36
picture content layout
sizing and formatting, PPT 4-20 – PPT 4-21
picture fill, PPT 2-43 – PPT 2-44
defined, **PPT 4-37**
Picture Format tab, PPT 1-7 – PPT 1-8
picture placeholder, PPT 4-19 – PPT 4-20
Picture Tools Format tab, PPT 5-29 – PPT 5-30
pie chart, PPT 3-5, PPT 6-40
pixels, PPT 5-2
placeholders, **PPT 1-12**
adding, PPT 4-15 – PPT 4-37
aligning content, PPT 5-55 – PPT 5-56
cutting and pasting into slide master, PPT 4-18 – PPT 4-19
deleting, PPT 3-4, PPT 6-7
deleting content, PPT 4-13 – PPT 4-14
deleting text in, PPT 1-47
formatting, PPT 4-15 – PPT 4-37
inserting and resizing a picture into slide without content, PPT 3-31
inserting into Blank Layout, PPT 4-15 – PPT 4-16
inserting picture into content, PPT 1-37 – PPT 1-38
inserting picture without content, PPT 1-35 – PPT 1-37, PPT 1-42
picture, PPT 4-19 – PPT 4-20
selecting text, PPT 1-24
placeholder text

adding, PPT 4-16 – PPT 4-18
formatting, PPT 4-16 – PPT 4-18
point, **PPT 1-16**
pointer, **PPT 1-6**
in touch screen, PPT 1-33
portrait and landscape orientation, PPT 8-22
poster frame, **PPT 7-34**
adding video, PPT 7-34 – PPT 7-35
PowerPoint, **PPT 1-1,** PPT 3-3 – PPT 3-4
Help, PPT 2-7, PPT 1-62 – PPT 1-65, PPT 3-3
starting and using, PPT 1-3 – PPT 1-10
PowerPoint Show (.ppsx), **PPT 8-13**
saving a presentation as, PPT 8-13 – PPT 8-14
presentation, **PPT 1-1**
accepting changes, PPT 5-7 – PPT 5-11
adding media to slides, PPT 3-51 – PPT 3-56
adding new slide to, PPT 1-22 – PPT 1-28, PPT 1-28 – PPT 1-34
adding sections, PPT 5-56 – PPT 5-57
adding text to, PPT 4-30 – PPT 4-32
animation(s), PPT 5-1 – PPT 5-2
assigning document properties to, PPT 1-51
with audio and video clips, PPT 7-1 – PPT 7-4
building speaker confidence, PPT 2-1
bulleted list and pictures, PPT 1-2 – PPT 1-3
changing views, PPT 6-49 – PPT 6-51
with chart, PPT 3-1 – PPT 3-3
checking accessibility, PPT 8-16 – PPT 8-18
checking compatibility, PPT 8-15
checking spelling, PPT 1-49 – PPT 1-51
closing, PPT 8-14
collaborating, PPT 5-2 – PPT 5-21
comment(s), PPT 5-1 – PPT 5-2
constructive criticism, PPT 5-19
converting documents for use, PPT 6-4 – PPT 6-6
creating blank, PPT 1-4 – PPT 1-5
creating from Microsoft Word outline, PPT 6-4 – PPT 6-6
creating handouts by exporting to Word, PPT 8-11 – PPT 8-13
with custom slide show and photo album, PPT 8-2 – PPT 8-4
with customized slides, PPT 4-2 – PPT 4-6
Dialog Box Launcher, PPT 1-9
distributing a document, PPT 1-59
document properties, PPT 1-51 – PPT 1-52
with embedded and linked files, PPT 6-1 – PPT 6-4
encrypting with password, PPT 8-18 – PPT 8-19
entering presentation title, PPT 1-14
with formatted table and chart, PPT 6-1 – PPT 6-4
formatting characters in, PPT 1-16 – PPT 1-22
handout(s), PPT 2-48
with hyperlinks, PPT 7-1 – PPT 7-4
inserting and formatting a text box, PPT 3-24 – PPT 3-26
inserting hyperlinks to place in current, PPT 7-41 – PPT 7-42
inserting objects into presentation, PPT 6-6 – PPT 6-7
inserting pictures and adding effects, PPT 3-30 – PPT 3-39
inserting slides in, PPT 4-30 – PPT 4-32
inspecting, PPT 4-46 – PPT 4-47
making changes to slide text content, PPT 1-46 – PPT 1-56
merging, PPT 5-5 – PPT 5-6
opening with password, PPT 8-19
previewing changes, PPT 5-6 – PPT 5-7
printing, PPT 1-57 – PPT 1-62, PPT 2-52 – PPT 2-53, PPT 3-56, PPT 4-54, PPT 5-65, PPT 6-52
protecting, PPT 3-54, PPT 4-46 – PPT 4-47
Quick Access Toolbar, PPT 1-9 – PPT 1-10
rejecting changes, PPT 5-7 – PPT 5-11
reusing slides from an existing, PPT 3-27 – PPT 3-28
reviewing changes, PPT 5-7 – PPT 5-11
running revised, in Reading view, PPT 5-19
running with slide zoom links, PPT 8-43
saving as PDF, PPT 7-51 – PPT 7-53
saving as PowerPoint show, PPT 8-13 – PPT 8-14
saving as template, PPT 4-28
saving, PPT 1-20 – PPT 1-22, PPT 1-44, PPT 1-57, PPT 2-4 – PPT 2-5, PPT 2-52 – PPT 2-53, PPT 3-3 – PPT 3-4, PPT 3-56, PPT 4-6, PPT 5-65, PPT 8-10 – PPT 8-14, PPT 8-43
screen resolution, PPT 1-3
ScreenTip, PPT 1-8
Search box, PPT 1-9
section zoom links, PPT 5-65
securing, PPT 4-46 – PPT 4-47
sharing, PPT 8-10 – PPT 8-14
sharing on OneDrive, PPT 8-14
showing with or without narration, PPT 8-13
slide elements, PPT 4-34 – PPT 4-37
slide master backgrounds and fonts, PPT 4-6 – PPT 4-14
slide show, PPT 4-47 – PPT 4-51
slide zoom links, PPT 5-65
with SmartArt, PPT 7-1 – PPT 7-4
starting PowerPoint and saving file, PPT 8-4
with table, PPT 3-1 – PPT 3-3
templates, PPT 4-1 – PPT 4-2
using thesaurus, PPT 4-33 – PPT 4-34
views, PPT 1-33 – PPT 1-34, PPT 1-52 – PPT 1-56
Welcome back! feature, PPT 1-45
window, PPT 1-2, PPT 1-5 – PPT 1-10
with WordArt, PPT 3-1 – PPT 3-3
Presenter view, PPT 4-48, **PPT 8-37,** PPT 8-39
displaying all slides in, PPT 8-42
using, PPT 4-48
zooming using the magnifying glass in, PPT 8-42
presenting slides, PPT 8-37 – PPT 8-43
previewing narration, PPT 8-13
print color, changing, PPT 1-61 – PPT 1-62
printing
document properties, PPT 3-55
handouts, PPT 8-26 – PPT 8-30
in Grayscale, PPT 8-29
presentation, PPT 3-56
selections, PPT 8-27
promoting text, **PPT 1-24**
protecting a presentation, PPT 3-54

Q

Quick Access Toolbar, **PPT 1-9** – PPT 1-10
Quick Style, PPT 4-21 – PPT 4-22

R

Reading view, **PPT 1-52, PPT 6-49**
navigating between slides, PPT 6-49 – PPT 6-50
running revised presentation, PPT 5-19
using, PPT 8-42
recolor, **PPT 3-33**

recoloring pictures,
PPT 5-27 – PPT 5-28
recording
audio, PPT 8-42
slide timings and narration, PPT 8-13
rehearsal feature, **PPT 4-51**
Rehearsal toolbar, **PPT 4-51**
buttons, PPT 4-51
Remove Background, **PPT 7-22**
removing
background picture,
PPT 7-22 – PPT 7-24
hyperlinks, PPT 7-47
password protection,
PPT 8-19 – PPT 8-20
SmartArt shape, PPT 7-22
reordering pictures in photo album,
PPT 8-32 – PPT 8-33
reordering sections,
PPT 5-60 – PPT 5-61
resetting picture, PPT 7-27
resizing
chart, PPT 3-8 – PPT 3-9
chart proportionally,
PPT 6-36 – PPT 6-37
nonproportionally, PPT 1-43
photos and illustrations,
PPT 1-38 – PPT 1-46
picture, PPT 3-31, PPT 7-6 – PPT 7-7
shape nonproportionally by entering
an exact measurement,
PPT 2-25 – PPT 2-26
shape proportionally,
PPT 2-24 – PPT 2-25
shapes, PPT 2-24 – PPT 2-26
slide(s), PPT 5-20 – PPT 5-21
SmartArt to exact dimensions,
PPT 7-16 – PPT 7-17
table column and row,
PPT 6-25 – PPT 6-26
table proportionally, PPT 6-26
video clip, PPT 3-52
video file, PPT 7-32 – PPT 7-33
WordArt, PPT 3-45 – PPT 3-46
resolution, PPT 1-4
Review and Hide markup, ending,
PPT 5-19 – PPT 5-20
review cycle, **PPT 5-1**
reviewers' technology limitations,
PPT 5-2
reviewing presentation changes,
PPT 5-7 – PPT 5-11
Revisions pane, PPT 5-6, PPT 5-11
rewinding
audio clip after playing, PPT 7-38
video file after playing, PPT 7-32
ribbon, **PPT 1-6** – PPT 1-7
icons, PPT 1-7
and screen resolution, PPT 1-3
right-aligned text, **PPT 2-7** – PPT 2-8
rotate handle, **PPT 1-42**
rows, **PPT 3-3**
ruler(s), **PPT 2-31**
displaying, PPT 2-33
hiding, PPT 2-48
positioning shape using,
PPT 2-34 – PPT 2-35
running
custom slide show, PPT 8-8
presentation with slide zoom links,
PPT 8-43

S

sample data, replacing,
PPT 3-6 – PPT 3-8
saving
presentation, **PPT 1-20,** PPT 3-56,
PPT 7-5, PPT 8-10 – PPT 8-14,
PPT 8-43
presentation as PDF,
PPT 7-51 – PPT 7-53
presentation as PowerPoint show,
PPT 8-13 – PPT 8-14
slide as picture, PPT 8-10 – PPT 8-11
scatterplots, PPT 3-5
screen clipping, **PPT 7-7**
inserting, PPT 7-7 – PPT 7-9
screen recordings
creating, PPT 8-41 – PPT 8-42
inserting, PPT 8-41 – PPT 8-42
screen resolution, PPT 2-3, PPT 3-3,
PPT 4-6
ribbon, PPT 1-3, PPT 2-9, PPT 3-3,
PPT 7-2
screenshot, **PPT 7-7**
ScreenTip, **PPT 1-8**
scroll arrows, **PPT 1-6**
scroll bar, **PPT 1-6**
scroll boxes, **PPT 1-6**
Search box, **PPT 1-9,** PPT 1-65
section(s)
adding to presentation,
PPT 5-56 – PPT 5-57
collapsing, PPT 5-59
creating, PPT 5-56 – PPT 5-65
defined, **PPT 5-56**
managing, PPT 5-56 – PPT 5-65
renaming, PPT 5-57 – PPT 5-59
reordering, PPT 5-60 – PPT 5-61
zoom, **PPT 5-61**
section zoom links,
PPT 5-61 – PPT 5-63
and presentation, PPT 5-65
securing presentation,
PPT 8-14 – PPT 8-20
selecting slides for slide show,
PPT 8-4 – PPT 8-6
selection rectangle, **PPT 1-38**
Send Backward command, **PPT 2-38**
Send to Back command, **PPT 2-38**
sepia, **PPT 3-33**
shape(s)
adding text to, PPT 2-29
aligning, PPT 2-37
applying an effect to, PPT 2-46
applying picture fill to,
PPT 2-43 – PPT 2-44
applying style, PPT 2-27 – PPT 2-28
changing fill color,
PPT 2-30 – PPT 2-31
changing outline color, PPT 2-45
changing outline style, PPT 2-45
changing outline weight, PPT 2-44
copying and pasting,
PPT 2-28 – PPT 2-29
distributing, PPT 2-35 – PPT 2-36
flipping, PPT 2-38
formatting, PPT 2-22 – PPT 2-31
gridlines, positioning using,
PPT 2-34 – PPT 2-35
guides, positioning using,
PPT 2-34 – PPT 2-35
hiding rulers, PPT 2-48
hiding the grid and guides, PPT 2-47
inserting, PPT 2-22 – PPT 2-24
inserting additional,
PPT 2-40 – PPT 2-41
merging, PPT 2-41 – PPT 2-42
positioning, PPT 2-35
presentation with, PPT 2-1 – PPT 2-3
resizing, PPT 2-24 – PPT 2-26,
PPT 5-20 – PPT 5-21
rotating to an exact value,
PPT 2-46 – PPT 2-47
ruler, positioning using,
PPT 2-34 – PPT 2-35
text in, PPT 2-29 – PPT 2-30
shape text, PPT 5-39
sharing
presentation on OneDrive, PPT 8-14
presentation, PPT 8-10 – PPT 8-14
sharpness, **PPT 3-36**
shortcut menu, **PPT 1-10**
showing presentation with or without
narration, PPT 8-13
signing out of a Microsoft account,
PPT 1-65 – PPT 1-66
sizing
action button, PPT 7-49
sizing handles, **PPT 1-38**

slide(s), **PPT 1-5**
adding chart to, PPT 3-3 – PPT 3-14
adding media to, PPT 3-51 – PPT 3-56
adding new, PPT 1-28 – PPT 1-29
adding table to, PPT 3-14 – PPT 3-24
adding title to, PPT 2-40
adding with Title Only layout, PPT 1-31
adding transition between, PPT 2-50 – PPT 2-52, PPT 3-55, PPT 6-51
advancing after specified number of seconds, PPT 4-53
changing orientation, PPT 8-38
copying symbol, PPT 2-11
creating first text, PPT 2-9
creating title, PPT 2-7
deleting, PPT 2-5 – PPT 2-7
deleting text in, PPT 1-46
distributing, PPT 4-54, PPT 5-65
duplicating, PPT 2-18
editing, PPT 2-3 – PPT 2-11
entering a slide title and headings, PPT 1-28 – PPT 1-29
entering title, PPT 1-24, PPT 1-31
inserting, PPT 3-26 – PPT 3-30
inserting hyperlink, PPT 7-45 – PPT 7-47
inserting number, PPT 2-49
inserting symbol, PPT 2-9 – PPT 2-10
layout, changing, PPT 1-28 – PPT 1-34
layout, customizing, PPT 1-12
moving, PPT 3-26 – PPT 3-30
moving in Outline view, PPT 6-51
moving in Slide Sorter view, PPT 3-28 – PPT 3-29
navigating between in Outline view, PPT 6-50
navigating between in Reading view, PPT 6-49 – PPT 6-50
positioning elements, PPT 2-31 – PPT 2-53
presenting, PPT 8-37 – PPT 8-43
printing, PPT 1-57 – PPT 1-62, PPT 2-52 – PPT 2-53, PPT 3-56, PPT 4-54, PPT 5-65, PPT 6-52
printing full page, PPT 1-57 – PPT 1-59
reordering animations, PPT 5-47
replacing text in an existing, PPT 1-46
reusing from an existing presentation, PPT 3-27 – PPT 3-28
saving as picture, PPT 8-10 – PPT 8-11
selecting consecutive, PPT 2-5
selecting slides for slide show, PPT 8-4 – PPT 8-6
selecting slides or other items, PPT 8-30
transitions, PPT 4-45
zooming, PPT 1-15 – PPT 1-16, PPT 1-19, **PPT 5-61**
slide backgrounds
changing to gradient fill, PPT 4-38 – PPT 4-39
changing to pattern, PPT 4-41 – PPT 4-42
changing to picture, PPT 4-39 – PPT 4-40
changing to texture, PPT 4-42 – PPT 4-44
formatting, PPT 4-37 – PPT 4-45
hiding slides, PPT 4-44 – PPT 4-45
slide changes
accepting, PPT 5-11 – PPT 5-13
rejecting, PPT 5-11 – PPT 5-12
reviewing, PPT 5-11 – PPT 5-13
slide content
animation, PPT 5-43 – PPT 5-56
custom animations, PPT 3-46 – PPT 3-50
slide elements
adding a footer, PPT 2-48 – PPT 2-50
adding a transition, PPT 2-50 – PPT 2-52
aligning and distributing objects, PPT 2-32 – PPT 2-53
changing theme of single slide, PPT 4-34 – PPT 4-36
changing theme variant, PPT 4-36 – PPT 4-37
positioning, PPT 2-31 – PPT 2-53
slide indicator, **PPT 1-33**
slide layout, PPT 4-7
adding new, PPT 4-27
deleting, PPT 4-25 – PPT 4-27
renaming, PPT 4-24 – PPT 4-25
slide library
using, PPT 5-26
slide master, **PPT 4-2**
applying theme to, PPT 4-8
backgrounds and fonts, PPT 4-6 – PPT 4-14
changing theme colors, PPT 4-8
cutting and pasting placeholder into, PPT 4-18 – PPT 4-19
formatting background of, PPT 4-21 – PPT 4-22
multiple, PPT 4-6
planning, PPT 4-6
renaming, PPT 4-24 – PPT 4-25
Slide Master view, PPT 4-6 – PPT 4-7
themes colors, customizing, PPT 4-9 – PPT 4-10
Slide Master view, PPT 4-6 – PPT 4-7
slide orientation, changing, PPT 8-38
Slide pane, **PPT 1-33**
slide show, **PPT 1-1,** PPT 4-47 – PPT 4-51. *See also* presentation
advancing a slide after specified number of seconds, PPT 4-53
control bar buttons, PPT 4-48
moving manually through slides in, PPT 1-55 – PPT 1-56
navigating slide during, PPT 4-47 – PPT 4-51
resolution, changing, PPT 8-39
setting up, PPT 4-48 – PPT 4-51
shortcuts, PPT 4-48
slide timings, PPT 4-51 – PPT 4-53
using pen and pointer options during, PPT 4-49 – PPT 4-51
with timings, PPT 4-54
Slide Show view, **PPT 1-52**
moving manually through slides in, PPT 1-55 – PPT 1-56
moving slide in, PPT 3-28 – PPT 3-29
starting, PPT 1-54 – PPT 1-55
Slides tab, **PPT 1-33**
slide timings
recording, PPT 8-13
rehearsing, PPT 4-51 – PPT 4-54
turning off, PPT 4-51, PPT 8-42
slide transition, **PPT 2-50**
slide zoom links
running presentation with, PPT 8-43
slide zoom links, PPT 5-61 – PPT 5-63
presentation, PPT 5-65
SmartArt
adding picture, PPT 7-12 – PPT 7-13
adding shape, PPT 7-13 – PPT 7-14
applying 3D effects, PPT 7-14 – PPT 7-15
changing color, PPT 7-20 – PPT 7-22
changing layout, PPT 7-21 – PPT 7-22
converting picture to, PPT 7-10
entering text, PPT 7-11
increasing size of, PPT 7-16
inserting picture into, PPT 7-13
inserting, using content placeholder, PPT 7-9 – PPT 7-10
presentation with, PPT 7-1 – PPT 7-4
resizing to exact dimensions, PPT 7-16 – PPT 7-17
text pane, showing or hiding, PPT 7-10 – PPT 7-11

SmartArt graphics, **PPT 2-11**
adding text to, PPT 2-19 – PPT 2-20
creating and formatting, PPT 2-11 – PPT 2-22
editing SmartArt shape text, PPT 2-13 – PPT 2-14
inserting, PPT 2-18 – PPT 2-19
layout types and purposes, PPT 2-12
presentation with, PPT 2-1 – PPT 2-3
text conversion, PPT 2-12 – PPT 2-13
SmartArt layout, changing, PPT 2-16 – PPT 2-17
SmartArt shape
adding bullet to, PPT 7-21
demoting, PPT 7-20
moving down, PPT 7-18 – PPT 7-19
moving up, PPT 7-17 – PPT 7-18
promoting, PPT 7-19
removing, PPT 7-22
SmartArt Style, **PPT 2-20**
applying, PPT 2-20
SmartArt Styles gallery, updates, PPT 2-12
SmartArt text, editing, PPT 2-15
smart guides, **PPT 1-40**
displaying, PPT 1-40
smartphone
using laser pointer on, PPT 8-43
snaps, **PPT 2-31**
snap-to options, PPT 2-35
solid fill, **PPT 4-37**
source document, **PPT 6-6**
source file, **PPT 6-6**
sources of information
for graphics, PPT 3-6
spacing
column, PPT 5-23 – PPT 5-24
line, PPT 5-22
paragraph, PPT 5-22 – PPT 5-23
Speaker Coach, PPT 8-37
speaker notes, printing, PPT 1-60 – PPT 1-61
spelling
checking, PPT 1-49 – PPT 1-51, PPT 2-14
errors, detecting, PPT 1-49
Pane buttons and actions, PPT 1-50
splitters in a window, moving, PPT 2-6 – PPT 2-7
splitting, table cells, PPT 6-17 – PPT 6-19
stacking order, changing, PPT 2-38 – PPT 2-39
standard properties, **PPT 1-52**
status bar, **PPT 1-6**
Stock Images and Online Pictures, PPT 1-34
style (picture), **PPT 3-37**
applying, PPT 3-37
summary zoom, **PPT 5-61, PPT 8-37**
updating, PPT 8-40
summary zoom slide
inserting, PPT 8-40 – PPT 8-42
switching
chart rows and columns, PPT 6-38
to Outline view, PPT 6-50
symbol
changing bullet, PPT 5-34 – PPT 5-35
copying, PPT 2-11
delta, PPT 2-9
inserting, PPT 2-9 – PPT 2-10
selecting, PPT 5-35
Symbol dialog box, PPT 5-35
synonym, **PPT 4-33**

T

table(s), **PPT 3-14**
adding borders to, PPT 3-18
adding effect to, PPT 3-18 – PPT 3-19
adding to slide and formatting, PPT 3-14 – PPT 3-24
aligning, PPT 3-23, PPT 6-28 – PPT 6-29
applying style, PPT 3-16 – PPT 3-17
clearing formatting, PPT 3-14, PPT 6-28
dimensions of, PPT 3-14
distributing table rows, PPT 6-24 – PPT 6-25
drawing, PPT 6-10 – PPT 6-16
drawing columns, PPT 6-13 – PPT 6-14
drawing rows, PPT 6-12 – PPT 6-13
entering additional text, PPT 6-19 – PPT 6-20
entering data in, PPT 3-16
entering text, PPT 6-16 – PPT 6-17
erasing border, PPT 6-15 – PPT 6-16
formatting, PPT 3-14 – PPT 3-24, PPT 6-10 – PPT 6-29
formatting data, PPT 6-28
including total row, PPT 6-23
inserting column, PPT 3-21 – PPT 3-22
inserting empty, PPT 3-15 – PPT 3-16
inserting table row, PPT 3-20 – PPT 3-21
merging cells, PPT 6-16
presentation with, PPT 3-1 – PPT 3-3
resizing, PPT 3-22
resizing column and row, PPT 6-25 – PPT 6-26
resizing proportionally, PPT 6-26
table border
adding, PPT 6-19
changing color, PPT 6-20
changing line style, PPT 6-20
changing weight, PPT 6-20
table cells
adding image, PPT 6-23 – PPT 6-24
aligning data, PPT 6-26 – PPT 6-27
applying bevel effects, PPT 6-21
applying reflection effects, PPT 6-22 – PPT 6-23
applying shadow effects, PPT 6-22
changing direction of text, PPT 6-17
merging, PPT 6-16
selecting table and applying shading, PPT 6-20 – PPT 6-21
splitting, PPT 6-17 – PPT 6-19
table column, inserting, PPT 3-21 – PPT 3-22
table row, inserting, PPT 3-20 – PPT 3-21
tabs, **PPT 1-7**
active, PPT 1-7
contextual, **PPT 1-7**
Home, PPT 1-7
templates, **PPT 1-11, PPT 4-1**
Custom Office Templates folder, PPT 4-29
opening, PPT 4-29
presentations, PPT 4-1 – PPT 4-2
saving presentation as, PPT 4-28
text
adding, PPT 4-30
adding link, PPT 6-48 – PPT 6-49
adding to presentation, PPT 4-30 – PPT 4-32
adding to SmartArt graphic, PPT 2-19 – PPT 2-20
animating, PPT 3-49 – PPT 3-50
animations, PPT 5-45 – PPT 5-46
bold, PPT 1-27
centered, PPT 2-7
changing color of, PPT 1-18 – PPT 1-19
changing direction in table cell, PPT 6-17
changing margins, PPT 5-38 – PPT 5-39
converting to SmartArt graphic, PPT 2-12 – PPT 2-13
converting to WordArt, PPT 3-45
deleting, PPT 1-46
dimming text, PPT 5-45 – PPT 5-46
editing SmartArt shape, PPT 2-13 – PPT 2-14
editing title, PPT 2-17

entering additional text in tables, PPT 6-19 – PPT 6-20
entering in tables, PPT 6-16 – PPT 6-17
finding, PPT 5-25
finding and replacing, PPT 5-25 – PPT 5-26
Format Painter, using with, PPT 5-41 – PPT 5-42
formatting, PPT 3-24, PPT 5-22 – PPT 5-26
highlighting, PPT 4-49
italicizing, PPT 1-17
justified, PPT 2-8
layouts for, PPT 1-28
left-aligned, PPT 2-7
managing, PPT 5-22 – PPT 5-26
replacing in an existing slide, PPT 1-46
right-aligned, PPT 2-7 – PPT 2-8
selecting nonadjacent, PPT 1-26
shadowing, PPT 2-29 – PPT 2-30
typing remaining, PPT 1-26
underlining, PPT 1-27 – PPT 1-28
undo text formatting changes, PPT 2-30
text box
applying preset shape effect, PPT 3-25
changing defaults, PPT 3-26
formatting characters, PPT 3-25 – PPT 3-26
inserting, PPT 3-24
Text Pane, **PPT 2-14**
formatting characters, PPT 2-15 – PPT 2-16, PPT 7-12
keyboard shortcuts, PPT 2-14
text styles, master
editing, PPT 4-11
texture
changing slide backgrounds to, PPT 4-42 – PPT 4-44
texture fill
defined, **PPT 4-37**
theme(s), **PPT 1-11,** PPT 4-9, PPT 4-12
applying, PPT 3-3 – PPT 3-4, PPT 4-6
applying to slide master, PPT 4-8
changing, PPT 1-28 – PPT 1-34
changing colors of, PPT 1-47 – PPT 1-48
changing of single slide, PPT 4-34 – PPT 4-36
choosing presentation, PPT 1-12 – PPT 1-14
colors, customizing, PPT 4-9 – PPT 4-10
colors and slide master, PPT 4-8
download online, PPT 2-3 – PPT 2-4
effects, PPT 4-14
fonts, changing, PPT 4-11 – PPT 4-12
fonts, customizing, PPT 4-12 – PPT 4-13
thesaurus, **PPT 4-33**
3D effects
applying to SmartArt, PPT 7-14 – PPT 7-15
3D models, **PPT 8-9**
animating, PPT 8-9
inserting, PPT 8-9
modifying, PPT 8-9
thumbnails, PPT 4-7
tiling option, **PPT 4-37**
title, changing, PPT 3-13 – PPT 3-14
Title and Content slide layout
adding new slide with, PPT 1-22 – PPT 1-23
Title Only layout, PPT 1-31
Title Slide layout, **PPT 1-5,** PPT 4-2 – PPT 4-3
adding text, PPT 4-30
choosing words for, PPT 1-12
creating, PPT 1-11 – PPT 1-14, PPT 2-7
customizing, PPT 1-12
inserting picture into, PPT 1-35 – PPT 1-37
picture placeholder, PPT 4-19 – PPT 4-20
replacing in an existing, PPT 1-46
title text
entering, PPT 2-47
toner, conserving, PPT 1-57
touch mode
differences, PPT 1-14, PPT 2-24
stylus, PPT 1-33
touch screen
creating equations with, PPT 7-9
differences, PPT 1-14, PPT 4-14, PPT 4-33
drawing guides, PPT 2-32
transition
adding between slides, PPT 2-50 – PPT 2-52
transparency
changing slide background, PPT 4-40 – PPT 4-41
defined, **PPT 4-37**
Transparency slider, **PPT 4-40**
trigger
animation effect, PPT 5-53
defined, **PPT 5-53**
trimming
audio clip, PPT 7-39
video file, PPT 7-30 – PPT 7-31
turning off slide timings, PPT 8-42
typing, correcting mistakes when, PPT 1-23

U

updating
summary zoom, PPT 8-40

V

value axis, **PPT 6-38**
variants
changing theme, PPT 4-36 – PPT 4-37
defined, **PPT 4-34**
vertical axis, **PPT 6-38**
vertical ruler, hiding, PPT 2-33
video
clip, resizing, PPT 3-52
contrast, changing, PPT 3-53 – PPT 3-54
inserting, PPT 7-28 – PPT 7-41
inserting without using content placeholder, PPT 7-28 – PPT 7-30
playing full screen, PPT 7-32
running slide show with, PPT 3-55 – PPT 3-56
start option, changing, PPT 7-31 – PPT 7-32
video file
aligning, PPT 7-40
applying video style, PPT 7-33 – PPT 7-34
changing volume, PPT 7-32
compressing, PPT 7-40 – PPT 7-41
inserting, PPT 3-51 – PPT 3-52
playing automatically, PPT 3-54 – PPT 3-55
presentation with, PPT 7-1 – PPT 7-4
resizing, PPT 7-32 – PPT 7-33
rewinding after playing, PPT 7-32
trimming, PPT 7-30 – PPT 7-31
video poster frame, adding, PPT 7-34 – PPT 7-35
views, **PPT 1-33** – PPT 1-34
changing, PPT 1-52 – PPT 1-54
Slide Show view, PPT 1-54 – PPT 1-56
visual literacy, **PPT 3-1**

W

Word
creating handouts by exporting to, PPT 8-11 – PPT 8-13

Word outline
creating presentation from, PPT 6-4 – PPT 6-6
WordArt, **PPT 3-39**
animating object using an entrance effect, PPT 3-46 – PPT 3-47
animating text, PPT 3-49 – PPT 3-50
changing animation direction, PPT 3-47
changing animation duration, PPT 3-49
changing animation sequence effect option, PPT 3-50
changing animation start option, PPT 3-48
changing shape of, PPT 3-41 – PPT 3-42
changing WordArt 3D rotation effect, PPT 3-43
changing WordArt text fill color, PPT 3-43 – PPT 3-44
changing WordArt text outline color, PPT 3-44 – PPT 3-45
creating, PPT 3-39 – PPT 3-46
effect, PPT 3-40
formatting, PPT 3-39 – PPT 3-46
inserting, PPT 3-40
outline, PPT 3-40
presentation with, PPT 3-1 – PPT 3-3
previewing animation sequence, PPT 3-48
resizing proportionally, PPT 3-45 – PPT 3-46
text conversion, PPT 3-45
WordArt text fill color, PPT 3-43 – PPT 3-44
WordArt text outline color, PPT 3-44 – PPT 3-45
WordArt 3D rotation effect, PPT 3-43
words
selecting, PPT 1-18
selecting group of, PPT 1-26
worksheet, **PPT 3-3**

X

x-axis, **PPT 6-38**

Y

y-axis, **PPT 6-38**

Z

zoom, **PPT 1-15, PPT 5-61**
availability, PPT 8-37
changing icon image, PPT 5-64 – PPT 5-65
links, **PPT 5-61** – PPT 5-65
section, PPT 5-61
slide, PPT 1-15 – PPT 1-16, PPT 1-19, PPT 5-61
summary, PPT 5-61
zooming using magnifying glass in Presenter view, PPT 8-42

9 780357 881705